A WEB OF STORIES

AN INTRODUCTION TO SHORT FICTION

JON FORD
College of Alameda

MARJORIE FORD
Stanford University

PRENTICE HALL
Upper Saddle River, New Jersey 07458

Library of Congress Cataloging-in-Publication Data

A web of stories : an introduction to short fiction / [compiled by]
   Jon Ford, Marjorie Ford.
         p.   cm.
      Includes bibliographical references and index.
      ISBN 0-13-455651-8
      1. Short stories. 2. Short story. 3. Fiction--Technique.
4. Creative Writing. 5. College readers. I. Ford, Jon. II. Ford,
Marjorie (Marjorie A.)
PN6120.2.W43 1997
808.3' 1--dc21   97-26235
                                                                    CIP

Editorial/Production Supervision: Julie Sullivan
Interior Design: Melodie Wertelet
Prepress and Manufacturing Buyer: Mary Ann Gloriande
Cover Design: Jayne Conte
Cover Image: Gunta Stolz, *Slit Tapestry*, 1926. Wandbehang 110 x 150 cm.
Cover Photo: Hans-Joachim Bartsoh. Bauhaus-Archiv/Berlin, Germany.

Acknowledgments appear on pages 1180–1186,
which constitute an extension of the copyright page.

Pearson
Education   98 by Prentice-Hall, Inc.
                   n & Schuster/A Viacom Company
                   r Saddle River, New Jersey 07458

Printed in the United States of America
10 9 8 7 6 5 4 3 2 1

ISBN 0-13-455651-8

Prentice-Hall International (UK) Limited, *London*
Prentice-Hall of Australia Pty. Limited, *Sydney*
Prentice-Hall Canada Inc., *Toronto*
Prentice-Hall Hispanoamericana, S.A., *Mexico*
Prentice-Hall of India Private Limited, *New Delhi*
Prentice-Hall of Japan, Inc., *Tokyo*
Simon & Schuster Asia Pte. Ltd., *Singapore*
Editora Prentice-Hall do Brasil, Ltda., *Rio de Janeiro*

Fiction is like a spider's web, attached ever so slightly perhaps, but still attached to life at all four corners.

—Virginia Woolf, *A Room of One's Own*

Children in oral societies grow up within a web of stories. . . . We listen before we can read. . . . From all these scraps of voices . . . we patch together for ourselves an order of events, a plot or subplots; these, then, are the things that happen, these are the people they happen to, this is the forbidden knowledge.

—Margaret Atwood, "Stories and Voices"

For while the tale of how we suffer, and how we are delighted, how we may triumph is never new, it always must be heard. There isn't any other tale to tell, it's the only light we've got in all this darkness.

—James Baldwin, "Sonny's Blues"

Preface
to the Instructor

A Web of Stories is an anthology of short fiction designed for an introduction to the short story course, a second semester composition course, or a creative writing course with an emphasis on the story. We include a range of stories from the 19th century to the present, drawn from a variety of countries and cultures and accompanied by extensive biographical headnotes and thought-provoking study questions. In addition, based on our experience as writing instructors, we have emphasized throughout the text effective strategies for close reading and for writing about short stories using a variety of approaches, from analytical to creative to research-oriented — with student examples of each. To facilitate research, we have treated six writers in-depth — providing multiple stories by each as well as extensive critical and biographical casebook material — and have included materials on library research and samples of documentation formats. Finally, an appendix offers a brief history of the short story from its earliest origins in folk literature.

In putting this anthology together, we have strived for a balance of familiar classics along with outstanding but less well known works, some anthologized here for the first time. With a close eye toward the concerns of instructors teaching stories to undergraduates, we have taken into account the special needs and questions of students approaching the story form in what could be their first college literature course. We focus on the form of the short story; on the personal, social, and political realities reflected in stories; as well as on the different critical approaches possible when interpreting stories.

To encourage students' understanding of each story, we have provided a number of discussion questions and writing prompts that ask students to look closely at the story and think about it in terms of meaning, structure, and interplay of story elements. We ask students to consider the complex relationship of writers' lives, their cultural backgrounds, and their artistic goals. At the same time, our fundamental assumption in shaping this book is that stories touch people first from within. As students or teachers, we value a story because it appeals to our feelings, our sense of humor, our sense of justice, our sense of vulnerability, our need for hope. So we ask students to respond personally and creatively as well, in order to develop their appreciation and understanding of the short story.

We have designed the following features of *A Web of Stories* to work together in order to create a flexible and engaging text for students and instructors alike:

- *A Carefully Chosen Collection of Stories that Emphasizes Both Historical and Thematic Connections*

  We have brought together well-known writers with some notable voices who have seldom been anthologized. We include many modernist, post-modernist, and magic realist stories along with those by more traditional realist writers — in addition to examples of folk literature and fairy tales. We have maintained a balance of male and female writers, and we have selected works that reflect cultural diversity within the United States and across international borders. Our primary arrangement is chronological/historical. At the same time, though, we have tried to include stories that focus on a number of common themes and philosophical issues. These we have highlighted — along with stories that exemplify particular literary genres or techniques — in an alternative table of contents of themes and styles.

- *Special Emphasis on Reading*

  The book begins with a full chapter devoted to reading stories. "Reading Stories" introduces the reader's journal, describes the stages of reading, and explains the elements fiction writers use to create imaginary worlds and embody ideas. The chapter features a close reading of a short story by Jayne Anne Phillips, including eight brief interpretations about the story, each focusing on a particular element. This chapter can help students become closer readers of short fiction and deepen their understanding and appreciation of the short story form.

- *Special Emphasis on Writing*

  Chapter Two explains in detail how to develop insightful written responses to stories. Here we include examples of student reader's journal entries, effective prewriting activities, drafts, and a finished paper. (Examples of student essays also conclude each of the six casebooks.) In addition, this chapter explains a range of written responses to stories: analysis, comparison, reflection, research, and creative responses — each illustrated by one of the student casebook papers.

- *Casebooks on Individual Authors*

  We have provided six thorough casebooks on key authors who have made significant contributions to the modern short story: Edgar Allan Poe, Anton Chekhov, Katherine Mansfield, Eudora Welty, James Baldwin, and Louise Erdrich. These casebooks — which include critical, cultural, and biographical essays as well as selections from the authors' journals and personal statements about their craft — can enhance the students' understanding of stories by the casebook authors as well as by other authors of the same period. The casebooks provide examples of the types of sources, both primary and secondary, frequently used in research papers. Also included are models of student papers about stories, some of which are documented research projects.

- *Appendixes on the History of the Story Form and on Research and Documentation*

  One appendix presents the history of the short story, integrating a world perspective that includes the evolution of the modern story from its folk origins. Here we provide an overview of the major literary movements and their influence on the short story. A second appendix provides detailed information on documenting research papers using MLA format, as well as examples drawn from typical student essays.

- *Support for a Variety of Instructional Approaches*

  The text offers enough material to shape a variety of short story courses, depending on the instructor's emphasis. For instance, an instructor who uses a biographical approach can focus on our extensive biographical headnotes as well as on the entries from author's journals and letters in our six casebooks. For instructors whose approach is oriented toward close reading and writing about stories, we include a number of essays by professional critics and students, as well as extensive advice on reading about, writing about, and doing research on fiction. Our alternate table of contents offers suggestions for instructors who prefer a thematic approach. A historical approach is supported through our extensive appendix on story history, our headnotes that place each author within a historical and cultural tradition, and the historical organization of the table of contents. For instructors who wish to focus on the creative process or ask students to write stories of their own, creative writing prompts are included with each reading. The book also emphasizes the constructive role that personal and creative responses can play in helping readers to develop an insightful analytical or interpretive response. Along with the creative writing prompts and examples of students writing creatively about fiction, information on the craft of fiction, usually included only in creative writing texts, is presented in Chapter One.

- *Instructor's Resource Manual*

  In addition to the book, a helpful instructor's resource manual is provided. This manual includes extensive commentaries on each story in the text; a bibliography of articles, books, and interviews for each story and author; a bibliogaphy of video materials on many of the authors; and a list

of World Wide Web pages containing biographical information, interviews, critical articles, bibliographies, and on-line links to other writings
by and about the authors included in *A Web of Stories*.

A Web of Stories provides students with directions for navigating the
many meanings of the human condition revealed through short stories. We
think that the wide range of stories included, the thorough coverage we provide
of the reading and writing processes, the emphasis on students' own creativity,
the historical and thematic connections we provide, the study questions and
writing prompts, the detailed author biographies, the casebooks, and the appendixes on the history of the story and on research writing will help students read
and write more effectively about stories. We hope that this book will be a pleasure for students to learn from and a joy for instructors to teach with.

Acknowledgments: We would like to thank our editors at Prentice Hall; our
creative and thoughtful developmental editor, Mark Gallaher; our patient project editor, Julie Sullivan; Fred Courtwright, our resourceful permissions editor; and Swift Dickison, who wrote much of the material in the instructor's
manual. We would also like to thank all of the student writers who contributed essays and prewriting materials to the book. Finally, we would like to
thank our critics around the country whose insights helped us to shape the
manuscript in its early stages: Eileen Schwartz, Purdue University at Calamut;
Andrea Holland, Mary Washington College; Marvin Diogenes, University of
Arizona, Tucson; Libby Falk Jones, Berea College; Patricia Morgan, Louisiana
State University; Nancy Barry, Luther College; René Steinke, Queensborough
Community College; Bob Dees, Orange Coast College; and Susan Weinberg,
Appalachian State University.

Contents

Contents by Theme and
Styles and Techniques

STYLES AND TECHNIQUES

INTRODUCTION to SHORT FICTION

CHAPTER ONE

Reading Stories

All good books are alike in that they are truer than if they really happened . . . and afterwards it all belongs to you.
—*Ernest Hemingway*

I want stories to startle and engage me within the first few sentences, and in their middle to widen or deepen or sharpen my knowledge of human activity, and to end by giving me a sensation of a completed statement.
—*John Updike*

No book . . . can do anything decisive if the person concerned is not already prepared . . . for a deeper receptivity and absorption.
—*Rainer Maria Rilke*

Reading fiction is absorbing, pleasurable, and rewarding. Stories like those in this book put you in contact with other minds, other cultures, and ancient human dilemmas, as well as with contemporary issues in their full moral complexity. Reading sophisticated fiction insightfully requires a recognition that published stories involve a mastery of a number of conventions and a sense of craft. You need to read such fiction slowly, listening to the words and savoring the sounds and images they create in order to become absorbed by and appreciate the "voice" of a particular author; only then can you consider more general issues such as style and theme in the text as a whole.

The Reading Journal: Telling the Story of Your Reading Experience

One way to improve your ability to read fiction with insight is to keep a journal that tells the story of your reading experiences. Write in your journal regularly, taking the time to produce full, thoughtful entries that document how you come to understand a story: your initial impressions, your expectations, and any confusion or experiences of "getting lost" in the text. Write down any questions and your deeper responses after a second or even a third reading. Next, write about your struggle for meaning as you read a new text, creatively filling in details of plot or character for stories in which much is left to the imagination, choosing among ambiguous or alternative meanings of words, or decoding sophisticated writing conventions such as metaphor and symbolism. Through repeated reading and thoughtful study you will come to sense the overall pattern, the ironies, and the larger significance of the story. (See Chapter Two for some typical journal entries that lead the readers to a fuller understanding of a story and form the basis for their more finished essay-length responses.)

Getting Your Bearings: Preparing to Read

Here are some questions to think about and to answer in your journal as you approach the stories in this text. Some students like to get their bearings before reading a new story, but you may prefer simply to plunge into story like an explorer of a new territory. You can always return to ask these and questions of your own in later readings.

1. *What is the culture and historical period of the story?* If the story is removed from your own experiences or cultural background (perhaps it was written in another language), consider the influence of the time and place. How does the culture or historical period in which the story is set influence the story's events and the lives of its characters?

2. *Who is the author?* You can learn about an author's interests, techniques, and background from the headnote introducing each story or from other reference materials. You might consider whether the writer is politically oriented or is articulating the views of a particular social class. You might also wish to find out whether he or she generally works in a realistic mode or uses fantasy and dreamlike approaches to storytelling. To learn more about such writing styles as romanticism, realism, and magical realism, see Appendix A on the history of the story form.

3. *Does the title have a special meaning?* Many titles hint at a story's themes or central conflicts. If the title is a single word, such as "Janus" (the title of a story by Ann Beattie included in this book), look up the word in an unabridged dictionary and consider its various meanings or connotations. If the title is a common phrase such as "The Real Thing" (a story by Henry James), try recording in your journal things that you associate with the title words. As one student wrote in her journal, "'The real thing' suggests something that is genuine; at the same time, it is often hard to know what the 'real thing' actually is. Perhaps this title is ironic, suggesting the complex nature of reality." Thinking about the title of a story can help you to begin to anticipate some of its images and ideas.

Regardless of how much information you have about a story, you need to be prepared to accept it on its own terms, to be open to its particular direction and nature in order to discover what is at the core of its imagination and thought.

A First Reading

As noted earlier, with fiction it is often helpful to read slowly, voicing the words of the story under your breath or even reading aloud in places. Write questions in the margins of the story or in your journal if a word or phrase seems important or confusing; underline it for future consideration and reread-ing. Then read again, faster, trying to draw the story together in your mind into a single major effect or point. It might be helpful at this point to write a response in your journal: What is the dominant impression the story leaves you with? Is this a happy story or a tragedy? Did you like the characters?

A Reading Experience: Jayne Anne Phillips's "Cheers"

Here we examine the process of reading and analyzing fiction through a close reading of a one-page story by Jayne Anne Phillips, "Cheers," that appears in her collection *Black Tickets* (1979). We refer to "Cheers" throughout this chapter.

The back cover of *Black Tickets* informs us that Phillips was born in 1952 in West Virginia and attended the University of West Virginia and the University of Iowa, where she earned an M.F.A. in creative writing. Phillips prefaces her collection of stories, some written when she was still a college student, with the comment, "Characters and voices in these stories began in what is real, but became, in fact, dreams." The book jacket further indicates that Phillips is con-sidered a realistic writer who is conscious of her craft; she depicts ordinary experience in a way that gives events a dreamlike, imaginatively charged sig-nificance. Because of the brevity of "Cheers," you might expect a great deal of concentration: every detail, every word is likely to count here. Even the one-word title commands attention and holds several meanings. "Cheers" suggests holidays, happiness, celebration, and cheers from an enthusiastic crowd (as in "cheerleaders"). Phillips is not a cheery writer, however; she often writes about the tragic lives of ordinary, working-class people, and the title of her collection, *Black Tickets*, implies the inevitability of sickness and death. Thus you might reasonably conclude that "cheers" is likely to be an ironic title, and that the story may be about disappointment rather than easy success.

JAYNE ANNE PHILLIPS   (b. 1952)

Cheers   (1979)

The sewing woman lived across the tracks, down past Arey's Feed Store. Row of skinny houses on a mud alley. Her rooms smelled of salted grease and old newspaper. Behind the ironing board she was thin, scooping up papers that shuffled open in her hands. Her eyebrows were arched sharp and painted on.

She made cheerleading suits for ten-year-olds. Threading the machine, she clicked her red nails on the needle and pulled my shirt over my head. In the other room the kids watched *Queen for a Day*. She bent over me. I saw each eyelash painted black and hard and separate. Honey, she said. Turn around this way. And on the wall there was a postcard of orange trees in Florida. A man in a straw hat reached up with his hand all curled. Beautiful Bounty said the card in wavy red letters.

I got part of it made up, she said, fitting the red vest. You girls are bout the same size as mine. All you girls are bout the same. She pursed her red lips and pinched the cloth together. Tell me somethin Honey. How'd I manage all these kids an no man. On television there was loud applause for the queen, whose roses were sharp and real. Her machine buzzed like an animal beside the round clock. She frowned as she pressed the button with her foot, then furled the red cloth out and pulled me to her. Her pointed white face was smudged around the eyes. I watched the pale strand of scalp in her hair. There, she said.

When I left she tucked the money in her sweater. She had pins between her teeth and lipstick gone grainy in the cracks of her mouth. I had a red swing skirt and a bumpy A on my chest. Lord, she said. You do look pretty.

A First Reading. Even slowing down to read "Cheers" aloud, you probably finished it in a few minutes. Not much happens in the story, but there is a narrative of events, beginning as a movement is made "across the tracks" and into the neighborhood and home of the "sewing woman," an impoverished single parent of young girls. The main action (the fitting of the cheerleader uniform on the ten-year-old narrator) is accomplished without substantial conflict. At the end, the action is resolved simply as the narrator leaves wearing her new uniform.

After reading through this story, one student commented in her journal, "What a sad life the sewing woman leads! Nothing but work, work, work for snobbish little rich girls like the narrator who want to be cheerleaders!"

Later Readings. The initial response to "Cheers" raises some questions and contains some clues for closer reading. Why is the sewing woman a single parent? Is there any joy in her life? Why is the young narrator so observant of the sewing woman's makeup and physical appearance? How does the narrator feel about the sewing woman: confused? frightened? contemptuous? How does Phillips use certain key details to make the impoverished world of the sewing woman real to us, although somewhat distorted and intensified, perhaps because seen through a child's eyes? Is the level of diction consistently that of a ten-year-old, or does the sophistication of detail and word choice suggest an older narrator looking back on a childhood memory? While some of these questions can be answered with direct evidence from the story, others are really speculative and require that you fill in the sketchy details

using your own imagination. Before we try to answer these and other preliminary questions you might have about "Cheers," let's examine some of the literary strategies that writers use to create the worlds of their stories and to
explore the significance of characters and events. We will return to "Cheers"
as we examine each story element.

The Elements of Fiction

> The illusion of art is to make one believe that great literature is
> very close to life, but exactly the opposite is true. Life is amor-
> phous, literature is formal.
>
> —*Françoise Sagan*

To fully appreciate the craft and thought that go into good fiction, we
need to study a story in depth. What follows are brief explanations of the
essential elements or strategies that help authors to create and share their
visions in the form of a story. Because it is impossible in any one reading to
focus on all of these elements, your sense of a story's meaning or significance
will vary according to which of the writer's strategies—plot, character, setting,
point of view, symbolism, style, tone, and theme—you choose to consider and
what values and beliefs you bring to the act of reading.

PLOT

> Plots are, indeed, what the story writer sees with, and so do we as
> we read.
>
> —*Eudora Welty*

Most people notice plot first when they read fiction. The plot of a story is
composed of the key incidents and actions in a narrative arranged in a pattern,
often in chronological order. A plot may, however, also use *flashbacks* to suggest that something that happened in the past still affects more recent events
and helps us to understand the present more fully

"Traditional" Plot: Formula and the Modern Story.   Some traditional works
of drama and fiction involve a gradually unfolding plot line that begins with a
preliminary *exposition* or explanation of related events that happened before the
opening sequence of the story. This narrative is followed quickly by an introduction of *conflict*, along with further conflicts or *complications*. These events
build to a series of *crises*, which lead to a *climax* or high point of the action. The
story may close with a *dénouement*, an unraveling of the complexities and
conflicts introduced earlier, and with a brief *resolution* or ending—a wrapping
up of loose ends. This "formula" for plot appears, often in abbreviated form, in
many folk and fairy tales, as well as in classical and contemporary tales of
adventure and romance, and it survives today in mysteries and other popular

fiction genres, such as television situation comedies and dramas. You will find, however, that few of the plots of the stories in this book adhere very strictly to this formula, which fell into disfavor with the realist writers of the later nineteenth century. Some modern stories are so brief that all the action takes place in a single scene; in others, not much seems to happen at all for pages at a time. Some stories, by abandoning smooth transitions and putting elements of the plot out of sequence, seem to invite the reader to fill in the missing parts of the plot. Thus the reader is engaged in asking and answering questions about the missing transitions and misplaced sections of the narrative.

The Scenic Method.   The scenic method, which involves a focus on many realistically observed details and actions in a series of incidents, slows down the plot's movement through time. In such a story, as in an absorbing film, we seem to be moving through time moment by moment. As a scene ends, we may be thrown forward — and sometimes backward — in time into another scene that we experience as related in a meaningful way to previous scenes. James Baldwin's "Sonny's Blues" is such a story. It traces the relationship between two brothers who grow up, grow apart, and reunite over a period of years. Baldwin uses a series of nine scenes of varying length that move back and forth in time.

Some stories may juxtapose seemingly unrelated scenes or, like Anton Chekhov's "The Schoolmistress," may describe the stages of an errand or a journey. Although it may seem that such a story has no plot structure, a closer reading and some imaginative reconstruction of the inner world of the central character often reveal that each scene or encounter is carefully crafted to represent a step toward that character's self-understanding or a movement toward an important decision.

The Oblique Method.   Many contemporary stories present readers with a "slice of life." Such stories may be very compressed in terms of time, perhaps consisting of only a single scene, and they focus on the activities, conversations, and sometimes thoughts of a small number of characters. On a first reading, oblique stories may seem to lack a plot: action and conflict, in the traditional sense, are minimal, and there may be little exposition and no clear resolution. Consequently, readers have to fill in for themselves what the author leaves unspoken: How did these people get to where they are today? What does this brief episode suggest about their future? What is lying beneath the surface, leading the characters to say what they say and do what they do? What, if anything, changes in the course of the story?

Considering Plot in Interpreting Stories.   Interpreting stories poses the same challenges that interpreting life does. It is important also to think about what the plot — or lack of it — implies about the themes and values implicit in the story. Some writers, such as Guy de Maupassant, conclude with a "twist ending" to emphasize the way that fate and circumstances trick us in arbitrary and unexpected ways, dealing fatal blows to our expectations. In Stephen Crane's "naturalist" story "The Open Boat," plot is controlled by the force of the ocean, as the strongest rower in the lifeboat is killed by a large wave after the boat capsizes, while the least fit person, the correspondent, makes it to shore despite his physical limitations — by sheer luck and the pull of the current. An unusual plot line or an absence of action can reinforce meaning, as in William Faulkner's "A Rose for Emily," where the plot drifts backward and forward in time, helping to emphasize the point that the past exerts a powerful pull on those who have given up on living in the present.

Focus on Plot in "Cheers." Most readers would agree that Phillips's story is obliquely plotted, a slice of remembered life that exhibits little overt development of action or conflict. In fact, not much happens at all: a ten-year-old girl visits the home of a seamstress in a poor neighborhood to pick up and pay for a cheerleader uniform being sewn for her. To discover the plot of the story, it is necessary to go beneath its surface.

One aspect of the plot, then, is what we can infer about the life of the nameless sewing woman. How has she come to have "all these kids an no man"? What were her dreams in the past? What does the future hold for her and her girls? Another aspect of the plot is the life of the ten-year-old cheerleader: How is it different from the sewing woman's and her daughters' lives? How is it similar? How different — or how similar — might her future be? We can also look at this plot in terms of the "I" telling the story — not the girl herself but the older person looking back, remembering: Why does she remember this seemingly insignificant moment so vividly? Where do her sympathies lie? Might she perceive a "conflict," a larger story, in this situation?

As we noted earlier, answering such questions is likely to provide us with a variety of ways of defining the story's plot rather than a single interpretation. We will be thinking more about these questions as we consider the other elements of the story.

CHARACTER

> Is it not astounding that one can love so deeply characters . . . especially when one has never seen or touched them, and they exist only in an imprint of curiously bent lines?
> — *Mark Helprin*

The modern story, with its emphasis on the inner world, is more character-oriented than are traditional tales, which were designed primarily to entertain with plot and to teach moral lessons. In traditional tales, however, characters do perform the actions, participating in the story's conflicts and the resolution of the plot. Such traditional characters may represent either desirable or undesirable human qualities — compassion, devotion, loyalty, treachery, greed — and perform heroic or despicable deeds, displaying their strengths or weaknesses through actions. Because little physical action occurs in many of the reflective modern stories influenced by such authors as Anton Chekhov and Henry James, however, the description and gradual unfolding and discovery of the characters' psychological makeup — their thoughts and motivations, conscious as well as unconscious — often are the writer's major purposes and the reader's major source of pleasure.

Understanding Character.   An author may reveal characters to us from *without*, through direct comments, or from *within*, by allowing access to a character's thoughts either directly or indirectly. Frequently in modern fiction, character materializes for the reader through showing rather than telling, using both actions and physical detail such as descriptions of grooming, clothing, home environments, and possessions. We are also shown how the characters think through the way they speak in dialogue with others and in longer monologues, as well as through comments made by minor characters.

Often a character experiences a moment of breakthrough (what James Joyce called an "epiphany") that may be indicated by an unexpected phrase, a significant gesture, a shift in tone of voice, or an angle of vision. For example, a character may stare silently at a particular object at a key moment in a story, as the young woman in Ernest Hemingway's "Hills like White Elephants" gazes from the patio of a bar across a river at a series of white hills that remind her of both her pregnancy and her sense of loss. Thus very slight alterations in appearance of a character — changes in attire, grooming, or facial expression — can help to emphasize internal changes.

Character Types.   Critics of the story have traditionally argued that characters fall into three major types: round (or dynamic), static (or flat), and "typed." Many stories have a complex central character in the midst of change. Such characters, known as "round" or dynamic, frequently discover something about themselves in the course of the story through making a crucial choice. The "roundness" of a central character or protagonist is heightened by contrast to the lesser characters in the story. Minor, "flat" characters may be described in detail and be present throughout a story as close associates of the major character, but they do not change much in the course of the story, and we learn little about their inner worlds.

On the other hand, "typed" characters do not change at all; they are characterized through only one or two details. Most of the characters in traditional tales and allegories are "types," existing only to represent universal human traits, virtues, or passions. In modern stories typed characters often serve a particular function in relation to the main character: a soldier, a hotel clerk, a waiter, or a fellow worker. Typed characters help to create the realistic environment of the story, forming a backdrop against which the protagonists move or measure their growth. Such characters are not given an inner life; the reader does not enter their minds.

While a character may appear real and seem to have an inner life, his or her struggle is often revealed within a context of larger ideas and forces: traumas of war, broken families, poverty, the absurdity or meaninglessness of life within a decaying society. Characters may even be thought of as representing or exemplifying certain positions and lifestyles—the nihilist, the libertine, the puritan, the conservative.

Focus on Character in "Cheers." The length of "Cheers" does not allow for extensive character development, and it is possible to see the sewing woman and the young cheerleader as flat and essentially static. But if we fill in the plot as suggested by the questions we asked earlier, both become more rounded and dynamic.

For example, filling in the plot of the sewing woman's life suggests several things. Looking at her red fingernails and her makeup, we can see back to a naive and flighty young woman with dreams of glamour and wealth. The fact that she continues to make herself up in this way suggests that she still dreams of youth and beauty. She does not seem merely superficial, however. Having lost the father of her children — whether to death or abandonment is not entirely clear—she exhibits considerable strength of character in her effort to raise her children the best she can despite difficult odds. Her resignation and seeming lack of bitterness make her situation all the more poignant. While the sewing woman is essentially a "type," Phillips provides enough detail to allow us to imagine and to sympathize with at least some of her inner life.

Although we do have direct access to the mind of the cheerleader, she doesn't tell us much about her thoughts and feelings directly. At the same time, however, her vivid memory for detail suggests a keenly observant and curious girl, sensitive to the nuances of her environment. And when we broaden this character to include the older "I" recalling the incident, we add to this a mature intelligence struggling to express something important in her interaction with the sewing woman. Again, while little is told to us directly, we can fill in a more complex inner life for the story's narrator.

SETTING

> Location is the ground conductor of all the currents of emotion and belief and moral conviction that charge out from the story in its course.
>
> —*Eudora Welty*

Historical period, cultural environment, time of day or year, place, architecture, and even weather conditions—all of these details can contribute to a story's setting. The setting often makes a powerful contribution to the story's plot, characterization, and theme. In a realistic story, setting is often described extensively and becomes part of the prose's real-world texture. Settings often acquire symbolic overtones through charged language and images, creating a dominant mood that emphasizes the story's concerns. Notice how James Joyce begins "Araby," a story of adolescent awakening set in a drab, pious neighborhood: "The other houses of the street, conscious of decent lives within them, gazed at one another with brown imperturbable faces." Here the houses assume the appearance of the repressed people who inhabit them. In psychological stories of the fantastic such as those of Edgar Allan Poe, setting can contribute to the tale's emotionally heightened, dreamlike atmosphere and can also represent the distorted minds of the characters, as in the decayed mansion of the Usher family Poe describes at the beginning of "The Fall of the House of Usher."

Often a setting can be so powerful, so antagonistic — as is the ocean in Stephen Crane's "The Open Boat" — that it becomes an oppositional character in itself, a force that the characters must reckon with in their quest for physical or psychological survival: "The horizon narrowed and widened, and dipped and rose, and at all times its edge was jagged with waves that seemed thrust up in points like rocks." In James Baldwin's "Sonny's Blues," a story about the destructive impact of the impoverished community of Harlem on the life of its people, the nighttime streets with their drugs and violence assume the form of a malevolent force, a wild and dangerous creature: "the night is creeping up outside, but nobody knows it yet."

Modern writers often make use of settings to help reveal characters' interests, as well as their internal conflicts and inconsistencies. For instance, the rootlessness and purposelessness of Ernest Hemingway's characters are emphasized by the bars they frequent. On the other hand, as in much contemporary American fiction, Bobbie Ann Mason's characters inhabit domestic environments dominated by media-fueled consumerism: "When Jane puts her groceries away, the cereal tumbles to the floor. The milk carton is leaking. She turns on Rock-95 full blast, then rips the cover off the cheesecake and starts eating from the middle. Jane feels strange, quivery" ("Airwaves").

Domestic or wild, natural or artificial, settings can help to characterize, to create an emotional mood or atmosphere, as well as to reflect the themes and meaning of a story.

Focus on Setting in "Cheers." Setting is the most vivid feature of "Cheers." The "row of skinny houses on a mud alley" on the other side of the railroad tracks, the sewing woman's home that smells of "salted grease and old newspaper," the papers she scoops from the floor — with only a few details Phillips establishes a world on the edge of grim poverty, one we assume to stand in contrast to the more middle-class world of the narrator.

Many other details of setting are equally telling. The sound of the television program *Queen for a Day* both locates the story in time (it was popular in the 1950s and the early 1960s) and reinforces its plot. *Queen for a Day* was a game show on which working-class women with hard-luck stories — women much like the seamstress — competed to gain the audience's sympathy for their plights. The winner — the contestant who was judged most worthy based on the audience's applause — won household appliances, a "fashion" wardrobe, and the like. The show ended with the winner seated on a throne, a crown on her head, a long velvet cape over her shoulders, clutching a bouquet of roses — an illusory "queen for a day."

Physical details stand out as well: the "postcard of orange trees in Florida" with a picture of a man reaching for oranges and the words "Beautiful Bounty"; the sewing machine that "buzzed like an animal beside the round clock"; the "red cloth" that the sewing woman furls. Every detail of the setting contributes to the story's overall effect.

POINT OF VIEW

> What the writer must consider . . . is the extent to which point of view, and all that follows from it, comments on the characters, actions, and ideas.
>
> — *John Gardner*

Point of view refers to the narrative perspective in the story, that which answers the question "Who is telling this story?" This sounds rather simple, but as John Gardner suggests, an author's choice of point of view has many consequences in terms of the reality that the story creates, how well we understand characters, what we are allowed to witness, and the language through which the story is told. In analyzing point of view, we consider whether the narrator serves as an "I" in the story and how much knowledge the narrative voice has about the inner lives of the various characters and past events. It is important to note that a narrative point of view may at one extreme provide an objective account of characters and events, whereas at another extreme it can be so subjective as to cast doubt on the truth of every statement and event in the narrative. In the case of subjective, distorted narrative perspectives, it sometimes may seem that the author is calling into question our ability to make sense of reality itself.

Some of the most common points of view from which stories are told include the following.

Omniscient Viewpoint. The omniscient viewpoint uses an all-knowing yet anonymous narrative voice that can look into the minds of the characters in the story — but usually not deeply enough to provide complex, individualized characterizations. The omniscient narrative perspective usually uses the third-person pronoun: "he thought," "she thought," "they both felt." It is a form most common in traditional narratives, such as folk tales and fairy tales, in which the characters are seen as part of a group or class rather than as strong individuals. Modern authors sometimes use the omniscient point of view to emphasize different perspectives on a single event. James Joyce's "The Boarding House," for example, interweaves the perspectives of three major characters: Mrs. Mooney, the manipulative proprietress of a boardinghouse; her daughter Polly; and Polly's lover, Mr. Doran, who boards at Mrs. Mooney's. We are provided with enough access to the minds and feelings of all three characters to understand fully the nature of their relationship and even to predict their sad future.

First-Person Viewpoint.   If you tell a story based on your own experience, you naturally use the first-person pronoun, "I." Many modern stories use a first-person narrative point of view, which allows the author to maintain a consistent narrative perspective from within the story, such as that provided by a minor character who observes the behavior of the protagonists, or else to explore a major character's perceptions in depth while capturing the rhythms of the character's speech and internal reflections. Sometimes an author may enjoy creating an unreliable first-person narrator who tells obvious lies or indulges in exaggerations that the reader is meant to see through. Unreliable narrators may distort reality moderately or so extremely as to seem mentally imbalanced, like the paranoid murderer in Edgar Allan Poe's "The Tell-Tale Heart," who is convinced that he is supremely rational. In stories like Herman Melville's "Bartleby, the Scrivener," the secondary character may provide a "normal" social view to balance the vision of a more disturbed, eccentric character who is the story's real focus.

Third-Person Limited Viewpoint.   The third-person limited point of view combines the advantages of both the omniscient and the first-person narrative. The third-person limited point of view is used in stories like John Steinbeck's "The Chrysanthemums," in which the reader is engaged with the thoughts, perceptions, and decisions of a "viewpoint" character, the isolated farm wife Elisa: "She turned up her coat collar so he could not see that she was crying weakly — like an old woman." In third-person limited narration, the viewpoint character can become a center from which the world is perceived. At the same time, as in the Steinbeck story, we sometimes see the central character from outside, engaging in behavior that seems strange or excessive. Thus the author is able to encourage the reader to be sympathetic while at the same time moving beyond the limits of the main character's outlook on life. The subtlety and control offered by the third-person limited narrative perspective has made it a favorite choice of modern writers.

Dramatic or No-Character Viewpoint.   Yet another point of view, used in some of Ernest Hemingway's stories and most notably in Shirley Jackson's "The Lottery," is the "dramatic" or "no-character" point of view, using a third-person narration. Like the script of a play, these stories rely on dialogue and external description to communicate nuances of character. The dramatic viewpoint creates a strong sense of scene and builds suspense as we work to imagine what the characters are actually thinking and feeling.

Experimental Viewpoints. Innovative authors sometimes try out new or unusual viewpoints. Sandra Cisneros varies the first-person narrative perspective by combining it with a second-person or "you" point of view in her story "Barbie-Q," so that the reader becomes a character in the story: "Yours is the one with mean eyes and a ponytail." Sometimes authors tell the story from the viewpoint of a character who is dreaming, intoxicated, unconscious, or dying, mixing together levels of reality and time in the shifting thought patterns of a "stream-of-consciousness" narrative. Katherine Anne Porter uses this technique in "The Jilting of Granny Weatherall," a story in which the inner world of an old woman on her deathbed provides the exclusive narrative focus. In stories known as "metafictions," the viewpoint may be that of a self-conscious narrator who speaks out reflectively of his or her intentions, successes, and failures as the "creator" of the story's characters, forms, and events. For example, the self-critical narrator in John Barth's "Autobiography: A Self-Recorded Fiction" observes toward the end of his story that "a proper ending wouldn't spin out so."

Focus on Point of View in "Cheers." The point of view in "Cheers" is first person; the entire story is told from the perspective of the girl who has come into an unfamiliar part of town, a run-down neighborhood and dingy home where the sewing woman lives. Interestingly, Phillips does not use the first-person perspective to reveal directly the girl's responses to the sewing woman and her world. Why does the narrator refrain from evaluating this woman whom she might reasonably consider repulsive, perhaps even frightening? This is one of the major questions that the story's point of view poses, and it is not an easy one to answer. Perhaps the narrator is simply too taken aback by the cultural differences between her world and that of the sewing woman to make a coherent response; on the other hand, perhaps as an innocent child on an adventure, she is opening herself up to a new experience and is deliberately refraining from evaluating or rejecting the woman's home environment. On a deeper emotional level, perhaps she is drawn to the sewing woman, who treats her in a motherly fashion, sharing her experiences and philosophy of life in a confidential tone.

SYMBOLISM AND ALLEGORY

> The more you respect and focus on the singular and strange, the
> more you become aware of the universal and the infinite.
> — *Gail Godwin*

Many parables and extended religious texts such as John Bunyan's *Pilgrim's Progress* and Dante's *Divine Comedy* communicate a set of core beliefs and values through the technique of allegory, in which characters represent specific virtues or vices. In an allegorical tale such as Nathaniel Hawthorne's "The Maypole of Merry Mount," every element of the plot — each character, animal, physical object, and color — contributes directly to meaning and moral theme.

In contrast, modern stories are usually concerned more with representing reality than with teaching religious or philosophical lessons. Nevertheless, many modern writers still reflect on values through significant or "symbolic" objects, characters, and situations. A symbol in a modern story can be simple and literal, such as a gun that represents violence and accidental death. On the other hand, a sign or symbol can be complex, signifying an entire life, as the chest does in John Updike's "The Brown Chest." In modern realist fiction, as Flannery O'Connor comments in "The Nature and Aim of Fiction," symbols are not used self-consciously and artificially but are simply "details that, while having their essential place in the literal level of the story, operate in depth as well as on the surface, increasing the story in every direction."

The Central Symbol.   Sometimes the plot of an entire story will focus on a single symbolic object, as is the case in Ann Beattie's story "Janus," where the bowl functions as a kind of combination best friend and good luck charm to the central character, Andrea. Yet unlike an allegory, where the reader encounters universal symbols with traditional meanings, it is not possible to reduce the bowl in "Janus" to a single meaning; it may signify Andrea's aesthetic needs or her obsessiveness, but it also suggests the key concept of "two-facedness" or hypocrisy that is part of her character.

Symbolic Gestures and Environments.   In some stories, symbolism occurs from a repeated gesture or act, such as the narrator's continual ironing in Tillie Olsen's "I Stand Here Ironing." This symbolic ironing leads to the narrator's wish for her daughter's future at the end of the story: "Let her be more than the dress beneath the iron." This is a powerful statement of the narrator's hope that her daughter might attain some level of freedom and accomplishment. In other stories, the symbol is a place or environment, such as the bazaar in James Joyce's "Araby," which changes meaning for the young narrator in the course of the story, moving from its initial significance as a romantic hope to a final significance as a false and tawdry illusion.

Focus on Symbolism in "Cheers."   As the earlier quote from Flannery O'Connor suggests, in modern fiction symbols are simply part of the story being told; but they also have a significance that goes beyond their surface meaning, deepening the impact of the story in the process. The postcard that the cheerleader notices on the wall might have been sent by the sewing woman's departed husband, the last word she heard from him before he disappeared for good; certainly it is something she has made a point of saving — even displaying — so it clearly represents something important to her. On a symbolic level, the man, frozen in time reaching for the oranges "with his hand all curled," and the legend "Beautiful Bounty" suggest everything that is out of the sewing woman's grasp, the dreams that she will never realize. It is interesting that the cheerleader notices the card after responding to the sewing woman's request "Turn around this way," as though the card contains a message she is directing the girl to see.

When the applause begins for the "queen for a day" on television, the narrator notes that the winner's "roses were sharp and real." The roses represent a "dream come true," but they also have sharp thorns, which seem symbolic of the fact that a few prizes — and a few brief moments wearing a crown — are not really going to do much to change the winner's sad life. The winner's lot is one of continual work and worry, similar to that of the sewing woman, whose work world is symbolized by the sewing machine that "buzzed like an animal" (ironically, more alive than its owner) and the "round clock" (with the implication of working "around the clock").

The color red is also important in this brief story: the woman's fingernails, her "red lips," the "wavy red letters" on the postcard, the vest, the material "furled" over the sewing machine, and the "red swing skirt" sewn from that material. In the context of this story, the color suggests a number of symbolic associations. A "red-letter day" is an important day in one's life, perhaps one filled with hope and promise. Red might also represent blood, specifically the menstrual blood that makes "all you girls bout the same." Red is also the color associated with "fallen women," a symbolic association that is reinforced by the "bumpy A" on the girl's cheerleading vest — which will remind readers familiar with Nathaniel Hawthorne's novel *The Scarlet Letter* of the "A" for "adulteress" that Hester Prynne must wear after conceiving a child out of wedlock in her Puritan community.

STYLE

> Even the sparest [story] in style implies a torrent of additional
> details, barely suppressed, bursting through the seams.
> — *Anne Tyler*

Style refers to the techniques of language, at both the word and the sentence level, that convey the feeling, presence, and meaning of a literary work. Style involves the creation of what novelist John Gardner thought of as a kind of "magic" that occurs through "hot spots or pulsations" of language and written expression. Because of a story's brevity, unity, and use of a single point of view, the magic of style is particularly focused and intense.

Style in Diction.   Style is shaped by the diction or word choice of the story. Writers may choose a vocabulary that is common, concrete and monosyllabic, poetic and allusive, multisyllabic and general — or somewhere in between. Some writers prefer to use simple words, combined with many common or even slang or dialectical expressions. Such a style has its roots in spoken language, as in the following example from Toni Cade Bambara's "Raymond's Run," a story told from the perspective of an inner-city youngster: "Now some people like to act like things come easy to them, won't let on they practice. Not me. I'll prance down 34th Street like a rodeo pony to keep my legs strong even if it does get my mother uptight so that she walks ahead like she's not with me, don't know me, is all by herself on a shopping trip, and I am somebody else's crazy child."

In contrast, story writers such as Edith Wharton and Henry James, whose characters are upper-middle class, highly educated, and restrained, use formal diction and abstract, sometimes analytical language to describe even ordinary daily events and conversations, as in this passage from Wharton's story of mental discord, "The Other Two": "He had heard it rumored that a lack of funds had been one of the determining causes of the Varick separation, but it did not occur to him that Varick's words were intentional. It seemed more likely that the desire to keep clear of embarrassing topics had fatally drawn him into one. Waythorn did not wish to be outdone in civility."

Many modern writers, particularly those who use the third-person point of view, prefer a higher style with less common words and more complex syntax when describing characters and creating settings; they usually reserve the conversational style for dialogue, and sometimes for semi-vocalized thoughts, as in this scene from Isaac Bashevis Singer's "The Séance":

> The widow . . . had lost her fortune in the Wall Street crash, but had recently begun to buy securities again on the advice of her Ouija board, planchette, and crystal ball. Mrs. Kopitsky even asked Bhaghavar Krishna for tips on the horses. In a few cases, he divulged in dreams the names of winning horses.
>
> Dr. Kalisher bowed his head and covered his eyes with his hands, muttering to himself as solitary people often do. "Well, I've played the fool enough. Even from kreplach one has enough. . . . Trance-shmance," Dr. Kalisher grumbled to himself. "The ghost is late, that's all. Who does she think she's fooling? Just crazy — meshugga."

Style in the Sentence.   Sentence structure is also an important part of a writer's style, often coinciding with his or her choice of diction. For instance, if a writer is trying to create a conversational style, or a style suitable for showing interaction and actions of characters who avoid abstract thought, he or she will probably use brief or coordinated sentences, as Hemingway does in his story "Hills like White Elephants": "She put the felt pads and the beer glasses on the table and looked at the man and the girl. The girl was looking off at the line of hills. They were white in the sun and the country was brown and dry."

In contrast, long, carefully subordinated or periodic sentences can reveal characters and situations in which subtle nuances of thought and feeling may be more significant than action or physical reality. This passage from Vladimir Nabokov's "Signs and Symbols" portrays the tragic mental deterioration of the once brilliant son of an elderly Russian immigrant couple: "And then came a time in his life, coinciding with a long convalescence after pneumonia, when these little phobias of his which his parents had stubbornly regarded as the eccentricities of a prodigiously gifted child hardened as it were into a dense tangle of logically interacting illusions, making him totally inaccessible to normal minds."

Style in Detail and Figurative Language. Some story writers create their characters' environments using many strong sensory images and abundant detail. Comparisons also clarify perceptions, as in this descriptive passage of a commuter train from John Cheever's "The Five-Forty-Eight": "The coach was old and smelled oddly like a bomb shelter in which whole families had spent the night. The light that spread from the ceilings down onto their heads was dim. The filth on the window glass was streaked with rain."

Other writers provide only the slightest sketches of the physical world in their stories, preferring to focus more on the inner worlds of their characters — their thoughts, their emotions, and the choices they reflect on. Such writers may rely extensively on figurative language (nonliteral comparisons) such as metaphors and similes to create subtle states of emotional response and thought that are too complex for direct, literal expression, as in this extended metaphor exploring the narrator's fears in James Baldwin's "Sonny's Blues": "I was scared, scared for Sonny. . . . A great block of ice got settled in my belly and kept melting all day long. . . . Sometimes it hardened and seemed to expand until I felt my guts were going to come spilling out or that I was going to choke or scream."

Focus on Style in "Cheers." "Cheers" uses a first-person point of view that reflects both the voice of a bright ten-year-old girl and an older voice recollecting the incident. The narrator expresses herself primarily in short, simple sentences, using common words; but she also avoids the kind of slang and juvenile expressions we might expect from a child narrator. She makes use of imaginative, figurative language that starts out in close observation but goes further, as in her simile about the sewing machine juxtaposed with a clock: "Her machine buzzed like an animal beside the round clock." Note also her peculiar, perhaps unconsciously ironic, observation about the roses of the *Queen for a Day* contestant: "On television there was loud applause for the queen, whose roses were sharp and real." Some of the narrator's sentences have the rhythm and cadence of good poetry, as if she were being characterized as a youthful writer: "I saw each eyelash painted black and hard and separate." The style of the story is defined through the contrast between the language of the narrator and that of the sewing woman, who uses emotional, even sentimental colloquial diction that reflects her lack of formal education and sets her in a different social class from the narrator (who uses language more correctly): "Tell me somethin Honey. How'd I manage all these kids an no man."

TONE

> I want stories in which the author shows frank concern, not self-protective, "sensible" detachment.
> —*John Gardner*

Strong fiction usually has an "attitude," just as strong, remarkable people do. The "attitude" that pervades a story is referred to as its "tone"; it is intimately linked to a consideration of the way all the elements of fiction act together to create a kind of unified vision. Labels that describe tone are approximate: the "concerned" tone to which John Gardner refers; the melancholy or tragic tone; the pious tone; the pathetic tone; the comical, cheery, positive, or optimistic tone; the ironic, cynical, farcical, or sarcastic tone. Almost any reader of Herman Melville's "Bartleby, the Scrivener" would experience its deep sadness, pathos, and sense of loss, although readers might disagree about the exact points Melville draws through Bartleby's deterioration and his employer's inability to fire him.

Readers bring so many of their own values to a work of fiction, however, that they are likely to respond to it according to their own emotional needs; thus many stories may be perceived by individual readers as somewhat more or less somber and pessimistic, or optimistic and comical, depending on the reader's individual beliefs and experiences. To complicate matters, many modern writers, like those to whom John Gardner refers (above), prefer a "detached" tone. In such cases, the reader is deliberately invited to bring his or her own feelings and values into the story to construct a tone as a response to the world of the story. To avoid simply projecting your own emotions into a story, read carefully, watching for clues to the tone, such as negatively or positively charged descriptive details, symbols, and characterizations.

Focus on Tone in "Cheers." In reading "Cheers" for tone, our natural tendency is to get involved with the story from the perspective of the girl. It is easy to imagine how frightened and alienated she must feel in the run-down home of the sewing woman, and thus be led to project into the story an extremely negative tone that we might describe as one of terror and despair. Yet because the narrative does not look into the inner world and responses of the girl, preferring to let her use descriptive details rather than evaluative or directly emotive language, the story's tone should probably come across as mixed because the girl herself seems mixed up, unsure of how to respond to this encounter with a life so different from her own.

If we look closely at the use of detail in the story, however, a tone of sympathy and acceptance seems to emerge. For one thing, we notice that all the details that describe the sewing woman work together to emphasize her enduring nature, along with her poverty and approaching age: she is described as "thin" and "shuffling," her home "across the tracks" on a "mud alley." Her last words to the girl are loving ones ("Lord, she said. You do look pretty"). Overall, we might consider "Cheers" to have a serious, even somber tone, yet it is not a pathetic portrait: a sense of strength in resignation seems to dominate through the language, description, and symbolism.

THEME

> It is the story that saves our progeny from blundering like blind beggars into the spikes of the cactus fence.
> — *Chinua Achebe*

A theme is a major idea in a story, usually presented indirectly through the elements or strategies of fiction. A "thematic statement" is something the reader creates after the fact, rather like a thesis statement in an essay: "Hemingway's 'Hills like White Elephants' presents the idea that a relationship that is not capable of evolution into a stage of commitment and responsibility will deteriorate and eventually die." Making such an interpretive statement, however, simplifies the dynamic process of reading and experiencing fiction. As Flannery O'Connor states in "The Nature and Aim of Fiction," theme or meaning statements are no substitute for and are in no way equivalent to the reading experience: "[For] the fiction writer himself the whole story is the meaning, because it is an experience, not an abstraction."

Nevertheless, as we have noted earlier in this chapter, authors do have strong ideas and moral concerns that motivate them to write, so it is not surprising that the themes in literature are as diverse as human life. Yet the theme of a story is seldom a conscious "message" that the writer inserts into the text. In fact, a story often reveals different themes for different readers. For instance, although Grace Paley may have intended to write her story "A Conversation with My Father" to explore the values about literature that different generations in a family have because of their diverse life experiences and reading experiences, many readers see in the story a meditation on the theme of mortality and the need to accept the inevitability of dying. If you read a story, poem, or novel repeatedly over a period of years, you will likely discover different themes in it as your own life changes. Certainly any two readers are likely to focus on different themes, although part of the pleasure of reading stories in a classroom setting derives from a student's realization, through class discussion, that a certain theme he or she didn't consider significant actually can be.

Notice in the following discussion of themes in "Cheers" how we first discuss a negative theme that appears on the "surface level" of the story and then dig down to a less obvious but perhaps more satisfying sense of meaning that emerges after a second or third reading.

Focus on Theme in "Cheers."   On the surface, "Cheers" can be read as a story about unrealized dreams. Although she continues to paint her face and nails, the sewing woman no longer has much left to hope for; she lives through the "successes" of her young customers ("Lord . . . You do look pretty") and those of the town's more well-off women for whom she must also sew. Even being "queen for a day" would not change her life very much. With a more comfortable family and just elected cheerleader, the girl has much to look forward to. But the story seems to imply that dreams can equal illusions; the girl may one day end up with as little to hope for as the sewing woman has.

Yet more is going on in the story. First of all, the focus is exclusively on female experience: the only characters are female (the solitary man appears on a postcard extolling the "Beautiful Bounty" of the far-off paradise of Florida). The only activities mentioned (sewing, cheerleading, being "queen for a day") are associated with females. The sewing woman even says, "All you girls are bout the same," suggesting at some deep level a common bond for all women.

The girl is a new cheerleader, a position usually reserved for "pretty" or "popular" girls. We might expect her to be exuberant and excited, even to look down on the sewing woman and her family. But the narrator's tone is neither exuberant nor arrogant. Rather, she seems reserved and thoughtful, trying to make sense of contradictory images. After hearing the applause (the "cheers") on television, she notes that the queen's "roses were sharp and real" — a seeming realization that such victories for a woman can be bitter as well as sweet.

We end with an image of a ten-year-old girl on the verge of puberty, wearing "a red swing skirt and a bumpy A on my chest." In contrast is the aging sewing woman, "pins between her teeth and lipstick gone grainy." It would seem that in the intimacy of the sewing room the girl has recognized that they are not so different after all.

Moving beyond Study and Analysis: Synthesizing, Evaluating, and Applying

After studying a story in terms of its conventions and meanings, you naturally move toward a more reflective response to the text as a whole. First, try to *synthesize* or put together all you have learned about the work so that you can develop an overall response to it; then try to *evaluate* the story thoughtfully by probing the nature of your responses. You might pose some of the following questions to yourself.

1. How did reading the story make you feel? Why did you feel the way you did?
2. What is *unique* about the story? How does it compare with other works you have read, both fiction and nonfiction?
3. What did you find most effective and impressive about the story? Would you call it a good story? If so, what do you mean by "good" — exciting? morally uplifting? aesthetically pleasing?
4. If you think the story was unsuccessful or even "bad," how would you define its failings? Does it seem unbelievable, stereotypical, offensive in its ideas or character portrayals?

To evaluate a story objectively, you should consider a range of standards or criteria:

1. *Craft.* Is the story well-developed and complete as an action? Is there a strong sense of style, a powerful use of language?
2. *Human interest.* Are the characters memorable? Are they involved with significant issues and decisions? Do they seem accurately to reflect human nature in their emotional portrayal and choices?
3. *Philosophical concerns.* Are the thematic concerns substantial, perhaps even timeless and universal, or does the story seem pointless, obvious, or clichéd in its "message"?

A story might seem to be "good" in terms of many of the strategies we have discussed in this chapter but still disappoint you in some subtle way that you need to probe and define to better understand both the story and yourself. Most readers would agree, for instance, that Herman Melville's "Bartleby, the Scrivener" — a tale of an office worker who simply refuses either to work or to leave and the employer who becomes obsessed with his refusal — is a powerful, even a great story in terms of its dark humor; its use of grotesque minor characters such as Gingernut and Nippers; its powerful theme of the deadening, repetitive nature of office work; and its careful handling of the point of view and gradual transformation of the narrator, the lawyer who employs Bartleby and who learns to care about him. Many critics also consider the ambiguous Bartleby to be a creation of genius, a perfect symbol for the impossibility of escaping unscathed from the soulless modern work world. On the other hand, some readers might find Bartleby's motives too hazy, his refusal to work and his death more pathological than meaningful. Even if these qualities are admitted as flaws, however, few would deny that "Bartleby" is a moving, mysterious, and even unforgettable work of fiction.

As you go beyond the immediate experience of reading a story, you may carry the work around in your mind for several days, a few weeks, or even for years, letting it dwell in you until it becomes a kind of standard for judging other works, for interpreting people or situations, or for understanding your own emotions and decisions. When you do this, you are *applying* the stories you have read, using fiction in the highest and best sense as a guide through your life.

EVALUATING "CHEERS"

To complete our reading of "Cheers," we move to an overall interpretation and evaluation of the story, which leaves an impression far more
powerful than its length might imply. The story's brevity actually helps to
intensify and focus its meaning. Through its artful use of point of view, language, images, and symbolism, the story seems to be saying that some lives,
like that of the sewing woman, become so stunted that they are almost over
before they begin. Such lives can be said to be one-dimensional, like that of
a typed character in a story. Despite their limits, however, people such as
the sewing woman can have strength and dignity; they may also possess a
sense of aesthetics and a need for romance, fantasy, and hope. This story
leaves us thoughtful and disturbed; it makes a forgotten life seem real and
vital, perhaps asking us not to take a certain type of person for granted. It
also suggests that the sewing woman is in some sense universal, elemental,
that her fate can represent everyone's fate. We can say, then, that "Cheers"
is not only a well-written brief story but also one that allows us to see life
in a new and deeper way.

Questions and Activities on the Elements of Fiction

The following questions and activities invite you to apply some of the
ideas and terminology discussed in this chapter to a particular story or a group
of stories from the text.

PLOT

Activity on Plot.   To help you to understand better how plots are structured, read one of the stories in this book and diagram the plot in the form of
a line graph, marking off the spots at which the plot gains extra complications,
where it begins to build to a climax or to resolve its conflicts — if, that is, they
are resolved at all. Then answer some of these questions.

Questions about Plot
1. What is the overall structure or pattern (if any) of the story's plot? Does
   it have a clear rising action of conflict and resolution? Is it composed of
   a series of interrelated scenes? Does it seem to be simply a "slice
   of life"?
2. Does the story contain digressions or "stories-within-stories," and if so,
   what is implied or revealed by such stories?
3. How much of the story is told in summary exposition (fable/tale method)
   and how much is shown (scenic method)? How much is skipped over in
   moving from scene to scene? *Why* are certain scenes told rather than
   shown, and vice versa?

4. Is there a climax or high point of the action? If so, what forces (or characters) are in conflict at that moment, and which force or character (if any) prevails?
5. What is the story's final resolution (if there is one)? Is it positive or negative? Does it follow naturally from earlier events or does it seem arbitrary? What do you infer from the resolution about the future life of the main character(s)? What does the resolution (or lack thereof) suggest about the story's meaning?

CHARACTER

Activity on Character. A good way to experience the complexity of a character in fiction is to create a character of your own. Try writing a one- or two-page character sketch. What problems did you have in maintaining the consistency of the character or projecting his or her inner conflicts and potential for growth?

Questions about Character
1. Which character, if any, do you consider to be the central character, the "protagonist" in this story? What are this character's qualities — his or her strengths and weaknesses? What outside factors contribute to these qualities?
2. Does the protagonist change or grow in the course of the story, becoming stronger or weaker, more mature and sophisticated, or more in touch with basic human values? Does he or she come to some important realization?
3. Is there a strong antagonistic force to the main character: another character, an outer obstacle, or an inner barrier or weakness to be overcome? How successful is the central character in meeting such challenges?
4. What techniques does the writer rely on to reveal character to you — dialogue, inner voice, appearance, objects and surroundings?
5. Does the story contain characters that you consider flat or stereotyped? What does each of these add to the story? Do any of them contrast with the central character or parallel his or her development?
6. Do any of the characters seem to represent certain values or a way of life that the story embraces or criticizes?

SETTING

Activity on Setting. To develop a sense of the relationship of setting to a story's feeling and meaning, try rewriting the initial paragraph of a story so that you can change the setting — a different physical environment, time of year or weather conditions, choice of colors, architecture, and so forth. Then ask yourself how your substitutions have changed your expectation and experience of the story. Do your changes make the story seem potentially happier and more upbeat or more foreboding and bleak?

Questions about Setting
1. What is the main setting of the story? At what points is it described, and in what language?
2. Is there a secondary setting in the story, or does the main character move back and forth between contrasting settings?
3. How does setting help to reveal the characters and their values?
4. How does the setting help to reveal the story's underlying meaning?

POINT OF VIEW

Activity on Point of View. Try writing a key scene of a story you have read from a different point of view. What has to be re-created? What has to be left out? How does your choice of language differ from the scene in the original story? How do you see characters, events, and meaning differently from within the new narrative perspective?

Questions about Point of View
1. How would you describe the point of view used in the story?
2. What are the limits of the narrative perspective and the reliability of the narrator?
3. What would be altered or lost if the point of view was changed?
4. What does the point of view used reveal and conceal about the central character and his or her thoughts, feelings, and underlying motivations?
5. What kind of meaning is implied or embodied in the choice of this particular point of view?

SYMBOLISM

Activity on Symbolism. Write a short sketch using a single character and a central symbol, preferably an ordinary object such as a bowl, a cup, or an article of clothing. By describing the object as the character sees it and having the character interact with the object, see how much you can reveal about the character and his or her values.

Questions about Symbolism
1. What objects in the story seem to signify ideas and values beyond themselves? Are they introduced primarily as part of the concrete world of the story? At what point does their symbolic quality become apparent?
2. Does the story present any universal or elemental symbols, such as fire, water, or circles?
3. Does the symbolism of a particular object seem to extend throughout the story, so that it organizes the story and clarifies characters and meaning?
4. Does the symbolic meaning of any object change over the course of the story?

5. Do the symbolic objects, events, and characters in the story seem so tied to a set pattern of meaning or "moral" that the work can be considered an allegory? If so, what is the allegorical meaning of the symbolism?

STYLE

Activity on Style. To get a feeling for how the intensity of mood is created through style, pick a passage from a story you have read, or any of the passages cited in this chapter, and rewrite it so that you replace figurative language with literal statement and long, subordinated sentences with simple sentences (or vice versa). You might also substitute a colloquial diction for "high" diction or a high style for a low one. How are the passage's meaning and emotional impact changed by your substitutions?

Questions about Style. Pick out several typical sentences from a story to illustrate your responses to the following questions.

1. How would you describe the style of a story you have read? Is it distinctive and consistent? Does the author have a strong sense of "voice"?
2. Is the story written in a "high" or a "low" (colloquial) style? Does the author use short, common words and slang expressions or larger, less common words and a more abstract, generalized diction? How does the level of diction contribute to the story's feeling, sense of "class level," and portrayal of characters?
3. Are the sentences brief and coordinated or longer, with extensive subordination, withheld main points, lengthy dependent elements, and other sophisticated grammatical forms? How do the length and patterning of the sentences contribute to the quality of thought and meaning in the story and the portrayal of the characters?
4. Does the writer use an abundance of imagery and figurative language or only a little? What function does figurative language, particularly repeated images (such as references to a color) or extended or repeated metaphors, play in the story, and how does such language emphasize character and meaning?

TONE

Activity on Tone. With three or four other students, read a particular story and answer the following questions on tone separately. Share your responses as a group. After the discussion, you might read the story again to see whether your first impressions of tone had been changed by sharing your reactions with group members.

Questions about Tone.   Provide examples of specific sentences from a story to focus your responses to the following questions.

1. How would you define the tone of the story you are reading? Be precise.
2. How is the tone of this story different from and similar to other works you have read?
3. What particular elements in the story — plot, setting, character, point of view, and style — best help to create and emphasize its tone?
4. How does the tone help to achieve the overall purpose and significance of the work?

THEME

Activity on Theme.   Answer the following questions on theme in response to a particular story and then get together in small groups to share your answers. How does each student's view of the themes differ? On what do you all agree? Why did each student perceive a particular theme as dominant in the story? After the group discussion, have any member's views of the story's themes and meaning changed?

Questions about Theme
1. List all the themes you find in the story. Which seems to be the major theme, and which ones are minor or secondary?
2. Does the author seem to set the theme up as an issue to be resolved, or does the story seem to raise questions relative to the theme and leave the reader to answer them?
3. How does the main theme play itself out in the story's plot and conflicts?
4. What in the story lets you know that a certain theme is being used? What strategies and conventions are most effective at conveying the theme?

CHAPTER TWO

Writing about Stories

Writers . . . remember where we were, what valley we ran through, what the banks were like, the light that was there and the route back to our original place. It is emotional memory — what the nerves and the skin remember as well as how it appeared. And a rush of imagination is our flooding.

— *Toni Morrison*

Yes! I too would like to hold the magic wand giving that command over laughter and tears which is declared to be the highest achievement of imaginative literature.

—*Joseph Conrad*

Writing about short stories engages both the imagination and the logical mind: it is an adventure into greater self-understanding and a way to become closer to the story itself. Writing about a story is most insightful when the reader brings his or her heart and mind to the emotional and intellectual material presented. Your honest response will be the best guide as you begin to write. At the same time, however, the process of writing about a story — which includes sharing your drafts with others and revising your work — will help you to deepen your own initial insights and understanding.

Developing an Approach That Works for You

Your ability to write in response to fiction will develop through close reading of and about stories, through discussing your ideas about stories in small groups and large groups, through writing about stories in informal and formal ways, and through revising your work in order to communicate better with your readers.

In this chapter you will learn about a range of approaches to interpreting a given text and formulating a response to it. Our experiences as writing teachers have shown us that each student develops his or her ideas into a formal paper in an individual way. You should try to be open to the strategies and techniques that you will encounter here. Let your responses be spontaneous, candid, playful; don't be afraid to be creative or even emotional in your responses, and don't be concerned as you begin about writing the perfect essay — there is always time to revise later on. Your personal responses will not only help you to develop a unique interpretation of the story's meaning, but they may later be useful to support your formal essay about the story.

There are many ways of responding to any story, and no particular way is "the right way." What is so interesting about reading, writing, and sharing ideas and interpretations about stories is the varied, even unpredictable responses that a given story can elicit. As you develop and share your writing about stories with your classmates, you may find that you are creating a "web of stories" in your own classroom — that is, a series of connections among stories, writers, and ideas that can result in a deeper understanding of individual stories and the nature of fiction itself.

In the following sections we trace the development of a paper about a story. We begin by reading E. M. Forster's "The Other Side of the Hedge," a complex allegory that will require you to engage your imagination in interpreting the text's plot, symbols, characters, and style. Before reading the story, think for a few minutes about connotations of the phrase "the other side of the hedge." As you read the story slowly for the first time, take some notes and ask yourself questions; then use your journal to record personal responses to the story's plot, characters, setting, details and symbols, style, and themes.

We begin with a headnote to give you some insight into the author's cultural background, historical period, and major concerns.

E. M. FORSTER   (1879–1970)

This influential British novelist, short-story writer, and social and literary critic is best known for his novels *Howards End* (1910) and *A Passage to India* (1924). His father died when he was an infant, and he was raised by his mother and several aunts from his father's side of the family. From an early age he witnessed conflicts between his generous and spontaneous mother and his aunts, who came from a strictly religious family. Following his repressive education as a day student at Tonbridge School in Kent, Forster attended Cambridge University, where he was allowed to pursue his own interests and develop his own philosophy. He learned to value the individual over the group or institution and became interested in Greek and Italian culture. After graduation, he traveled extensively in Greece and further developed his interest in the "paganism" of these ancient civilizations — their closeness to the earth and reliance on the imagination. His earliest works — including "The Other Side of the Hedge" (1904), a story he wrote on his return from the Continent — explored such themes using allegorical symbolism and fantasy. Forster continued to reflect on these themes in his great realist novels, *A Passage to India* and *Howards End*, which focus on the conflict between earth-bound, agrarian society, individuality, imagination, and the relentless forces of technological progress and commercialism. Although he was aware of the widespread social and political changes occurring in the twentieth century, Forster's sensibility is in many ways that of a nineteenth-century Romantic, particularly in terms of the Romantics' emphasis on the importance of our relationship to nature and the expression of feeling and the imagination.

The Other Side of the Hedge   (1904)

My pedometer told me that I was twenty-five; and, though it is a shocking thing to stop walking, I was so tired that I sat down on a milestone to rest. People outstripped me, jeering as they did so, but I was too apathetic to feel resentful, and even when Miss Eliza Dimbleby, the great educationist, swept past, exhorting me to persevere, I only smiled and raised my hat.

At first I thought I was going to be like my brother, whom I had had to leave by the roadside a year or two round the corner. He had wasted his breath on singing, and his strength on helping others. But I had travelled more wisely, and now it was only the monotony of the highway that oppressed me — dust under foot and brown crackling hedges on either side, ever since I could remember.

And I had already dropped several things — indeed, the road behind was strewn with the things we all had dropped; and the white dust was settling down on them, so that already they looked no better than stones. My muscles were so weary that I could not even bear the weight of those things I still carried. I slid off the milestone into the road, and lay there prostrate, with my face to the great parched hedge, praying that I might give up.

A little puff of air revived me. It seemed to come from the hedge; and, when I opened my eyes, there was a glint of light through the tangle of boughs and dead leaves. The hedge could not be as thick as usual. In my weak, morbid state, I longed to force my way in, and see what was on the other side. No one was in sight, or I should not have dared to try. For we of the road do not admit in conversation that there is another side at all.

I yielded to the temptation, saying to myself that I would come back in a minute. The thorns scratched my face, and I had to use my arms as a shield, depending on my feet alone to push me forward. Halfway through I would have gone back, for in the passage all the things I was carrying were scraped off me, and my clothes were torn. But I was so wedged that return was impossible, and I had to wiggle blindly forward, expecting every moment that my strength would fail me, and that I should perish in the undergrowth.

Suddenly cold water closed round my head, and I seemed sinking down for ever. I had fallen out of the hedge into a deep pool. I rose to the surface at last, crying for help, and I heard someone on the opposite bank laugh and say: "Another!" And then I was twitched out and laid panting on the dry ground.

Even when the water was out of my eyes, I was still dazed, for I had never been in so large a space, nor seen such grass and sunshine. The blue sky was no longer a strip, and beneath it the earth had risen grandly into hills — clean, bare buttresses, with beech trees in their folds, and meadows and clear pools at their feet. But the hills were not high, and there was in the landscape a sense of human occupation — so that one might have called it a park, or garden, if the words did not imply a certain triviality and constraint.

As soon as I got my breath, I turned to my rescuer and said:

"Where does this place lead to?"

"Nowhere, thank the Lord!" said he, and laughed. He was a man of fifty or sixty — just the kind of age we mistrust on the road — but there was no anxiety in his manner, and his voice was that of a boy of eighteen.

"But it must lead somewhere!" I cried, too much surprised at his answer to thank him for saving my life.

"He wants to know where it leads!" he shouted to some men on the hillside, and they laughed back, and waved their caps.

I noticed then that the pool into which I had fallen was really a moat which bent round to the left and to the right, and that the hedge followed it continually. The hedge was green on this side — its roots showed through the clear water, and fish swam about in them — and it was wreathed over with dog-roses and Traveller's Joy. But it was a barrier, and in a moment I lost all pleasure in the grass, the sky, the trees, the happy men and women, and realized that the place was but a prison, for all its beauty and extent.

We moved away from the boundary, and then followed a path almost parallel to it, across the meadows. I found it difficult walking, for I was always trying to out-distance my companion, and there was no advantage in doing this if the place led nowhere. I had never kept step with anyone since I left my brother.

I amused him by stopping suddenly and saying disconsolately, "This is perfectly terrible. One cannot advance: one cannot progress. Now we of the road —"

"Yes. I know."

"I was going to say, we advance continually."

"I know."

"We are always learning, expanding, developing. Why, even in my short life I have seen a great deal of advance — the Transvaal War, the Fiscal Question, Christian Science, Radium. Here for example —"

I took out my pedometer, but it still marked twenty-five, not a degree more.

"Oh, it's stopped! I meant to show you. It should have registered all the time I was walking with you. But it makes me only twenty-five."

"Many things don't work in here," he said. "One day a man brought in a Lee-Metford, and that wouldn't work."

"The laws of science are universal in their application. It must be the water in the moat that has injured the machinery. In normal conditions everything works. Science and the spirit of emulation — those are the forces that have made us what we are."

I had to break off and acknowledge the pleasant greetings of people whom we passed. Some of them were singing, some talking, some engaged in gardening, hay-making, or other rudimentary industries. They all seemed happy; and I might have been happy too, if I could have forgotten that the place led nowhere.

I was startled by a young man who came sprinting across our path, took a little fence in fine style, and went tearing over a ploughed field till he plunged into a lake, across which he began to swim. Here was true energy, and I exclaimed: "A cross-country race! Where are the others?"

"There are no others," my companion replied; and, later on, when we passed some long grass from which came the voice of a girl singing exquisitely to herself, he said again: "There are no others." I was bewildered at the waste in production, and murmured to myself, "What does it all mean?"

He said: "It means nothing but itself" — and he repeated the words slowly, as if I were a child.

"I understand," I said quietly, "but I do not agree. Every achievement is worthless unless it is a link in the chain of development. And I must not trespass on your kindness any longer. I must get back somehow to the road and have my pedometer mended."

"First, you must see the gates," he replied, "for we have gates, though we never use them."

I yielded politely, and before long we reached the moat again, at a point where it was spanned by a bridge. Over the bridge was a big gate, as white as ivory, which was fitted into a gap in the boundary hedge. The gate opened outwards, and I exclaimed in amazement, for from it ran a road — just such a road as I had left — dusty under foot, with brown crackling hedges on either side as far as the eye could reach.

"That's my road!" I cried.

He shut the gate and said: "But not your part of the road. It is through this gate that humanity went out countless ages ago, when it was first seized with the desire to walk."

I denied this, observing that the part of the road I myself had left was not more than two miles off. But with the obstinacy of his years he repeated: "It is the same road. This is the beginning, and though it seems to run straight away from us, it doubles so often, that it is never far from our boundary and sometimes touches it." He stooped down by the moat, and traced on its moist margin an absurd figure like a maze. As we walked back through the meadows, I tried to convince him of his mistake.

"The road sometimes doubles to be sure, but that is part of our discipline. Who can doubt that its general tendency is onward? To what goal we know not — it may be to some mountain where we shall touch the sky, it may be over precipices into the sea. But that it goes forward — who can doubt that? It is the thought of that that makes us strive to excel, each in his own way, and gives us an impetus which is lacking with you. Now that man who passed us — it's true that he ran well, and jumped well, and swam well; but we have men who can run better, and men who can jump better, and who can swim better. Specialization has produced results which would surprise you. Similarly, that girl—"

Here I interrupted myself to exclaim: "Good gracious me! I could have sworn it was Miss Eliza Dimbleby over there, with her feet in the fountain!"

He believed that it was.

"Impossible! I left her on the road, and she is due to lecture this evening at Tunbridge Wells. Why, her train leaves Cannon Street in — of course my watch has stopped like everything else. She is the last person to be here."

"People always are astonished at meeting each other. All kinds come through the hedge, and come at all times — when they are drawing ahead in the race, when they are lagging behind, when they are left for dead. I often stand near the boundary listening to the sounds of the road — you know what they are — and wonder if anyone will turn aside. It is my great happiness to help someone out of the moat, as I helped you. For our country fills up slowly, though it was meant for all mankind."

"Mankind have other aims," I said gently, for I thought him well-meaning; "and I must join them." I bade him good evening, for the sun was declining, and I wished to be on the road by nightfall. To my alarm, he caught hold of me, crying: "You are not to go yet!" I tried to shake him off, for we had no interests in common, and his civility was becoming irksome to me. But for all my struggles the tiresome old man would not let go; and, as wrestling is not my specialty, I was obliged to follow him.

It was true that I could have never found alone the place where I came in, and I hoped that, when I had seen the other sights about which he was worrying, he would take me back to it. But I was determined not to sleep in the country, for I mistrusted it, and the people too, for all their friendliness. Hungry though I was, I would not join them in their evening meals of milk and fruit, and, when they gave me flowers, I flung them away as soon as I could do so unobserved. Already they were lying down for the night like cattle — some out on the bare hillside, others in groups under the beeches. In the light of an orange sunset I hurried on with my unwelcome guide, dead tired, faint from want of food, but murmuring indomitably: "Give me life, with its struggles and victories, with its failures and hatreds, with its deep moral meaning and its unknown goal!"

At last we came to a place where the encircling moat was spanned by another bridge, and where another gate interrupted the line of the boundary hedge. It was different from the first gate; for it was half transparent like horn, and opened inwards. But through it, in the waning light, I saw again just such a road as I had left — monotonous, dusty, with brown crackling hedges on either side, as far as the eye could reach.

I was strangely disquieted at the sight, which seemed to deprive me of all self-control. A man was passing us, returning for the night to the hills, with a scythe over his shoulder and a can of some liquid in his hand. I forgot the destiny of our race. I forgot the road that lay before my eyes, and I sprang at him, wrenched the can out of his hand, and began to drink.

It was nothing stronger than beer, but in my exhausted state it overcame me in a moment. As in a dream, I saw the old man shut the gate, and heard him say: "This is where your road ends, and through this gate humanity — all that is left of it — will come in to us."

Though my senses were sinking into oblivion, they seemed to expand ere they reached it. They perceived the magic song of nightingales, and the odour of invisible hay, and stars piercing the fading sky. The man whose beer I had stolen lowered me down gently to sleep off its effects, and, as he did so, I saw that he was my brother.

Discovering Your Feelings and Thoughts about a Story

JOURNAL KEEPING

Most writers keep journals that they develop according to their interests and goals. While some writers use their journal simply as a way of reflecting on their private feelings and ideas, others use their journal as the place to record ideas for early drafts of essays, stories, and poems. We suggested in Chapter One that you keep a writer's journal and establish a pattern of writing about each story you read in this anthology.

The following journal entry was written after student Liz Scheps, whose essay we will be following through its stages of development, first read "The Other Side of the Hedge."

> While the green world on the other side of the hedge may be tranquil and relaxing, it is not intellectually stimulating. There is no pressure in this world, and while everyone occasionally needs a release from the stresses of life, a whole existence without pressure would be too languid. It would not allow one to explore the world and live life to the fullest. Pressure encourages people to push their limits and test boundaries that are thought to be rigid. Although it is a strange comparison, the story reminded me of the debates about communism earlier in the century. Communism was supposed to be ideal because everyone would share resources, and everyone would have what they needed. Idealists talked of the great utopias that would arise, similar to this beautiful land. But in reality, people are competitive, and naturally fall into the patterns of capitalism, which allow them to set goals and strive for them. I think that the other side of the hedge is a very unrealistic place because people depend on a system of rewards in order to keep them motivated.

The narrator and his brother represent polar opposites in terms of character. The narrator is a goal-oriented person who can't understand doing anything simply for the sake of doing it. He is unable to accept the laid-back lifestyle of the people on the other side, and even more unable to understand the man who is running and swimming without a race to compete in. On the other hand, his brother is someone who couldn't fathom the point of competition. He is the type of person who enjoys what he is doing, cares about learning over grades, art over money. He was left behind because he "had wasted his breath on singing, and his strength on helping others." Yet in the end, the brother is the one who is strong and happy.

I think that the point of this story was to display the interrelation of two extremes in our world. Life is not strictly a competition, but it is also not merely a community-oriented experience. The narrator is fed up with the high-stress life that he leads, and so he steps back, to a world where he may relax, but once there he is unhappy. Perhaps we should all learn from this, and take time from our daily schedules to step over to the other side of the hedge!

If you have already written your first journal response to "The Other Side of the Hedge," you might take the time to contrast your first responses with those of Liz Scheps. What interests you most about the story?

DRAWING AN IMAGE OF THE STORY

Drawing a picture in response to a place, an image, an idea, or a character that you find puzzling, intriguing, or familiar can help you to capture what is important to you about the story and to understand why. Drawing can help to focus your thoughts on the details in a story that may have appealed to your imagination unconsciously. A number of writers have noted the value of drawing as a way of developing ideas or understanding a new text. In "The Nature and Aim of Fiction," Flannery O'Connor maintains that "any discipline can help your writing . . . particularly drawing. Anything that helps you to see, anything that makes you look."

In creating your drawing, you can use crayons, colored pens, or markers, or a computer program if available. You should also try to share your drawings with classmates. In one of our classes we put every student's drawing on the walls of the classroom, and suddenly the imaginative world of "The Other Side of the Hedge" came dramatically to life, the images revealing a rich diversity of unique responses to the story. At the same time, students discovered common patterns of response. For instance, nearly all of the drawings contained curved lines separating contrasting swatches of color. The students tended to use colors such as yellow, beige, brown, or black to symbolize the world of the "road" in Forster's story, while deep, lush greens and blues signified the world of "the other side."

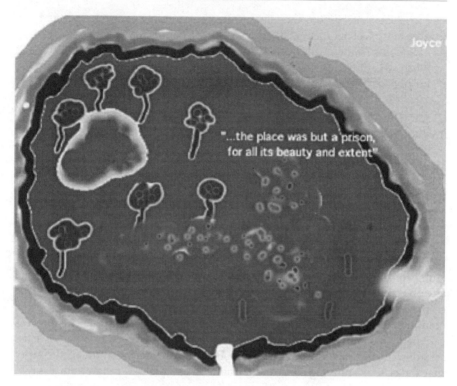

Student Joyce Chang's pictorial interpretation of "The Other Side of the Hedge"

Joyce Chang's computer drawing appears above (reproduced, however, in black and white). The following is her interpretation from her journal of the picture's meaning and the value of the drawing process for her:

> After reading "The Other Side of the Hedge," I thought about the phrase "the place was but a prison, for all its beauty and extent." This phrase caught my attention because I have never thought of a beautiful paradise as being a prison. When I read the story, I had my own image of a road winding in circles and being enclosed by the hedge. I thought of the road as a prison and thought of paradise as extending infinitely outside of the confining hedge.
>
> I decided to draw a picture of an enclosed and prisonlike paradise to see if it would help me have the enclosed prison perspective. I drew a pretty green gardenlike place surrounded by a moat, a hedge, and a dusty yellow expanse on the outside. It turned out that even though paradise was completely enclosed by the moat and the hedge, I could still look at the picture and prefer to be in paradise. It looked like an oasis in the middle of the desert. Drawing the picture helped me to understand the story better because it forced me to look at the story from a perspective different from my own.

I feel that this computer drawing exercise is useful because it prompted me to think about many different ideas in the story without being overly critical of my own thoughts. Usually I am a lot less critical when I am drawing than when I am writing. Thus, drawing allowed me to be more free with exploring my ideas.

CLASS DISCUSSION AND COLLABORATIVE CLASS NOTES AS PREPARATION FOR WRITING

Class discussions about a story are also an excellent way to prepare yourself for writing a formal paper. You can develop your ideas more fully when you talk about them with others. During class discussion it is also important to be a good listener. If you feel that you do not understand what a classmate means, ask for clarification. Often it is worthwhile to restate what a classmate has said to make sure that you understood him or her correctly.

Taking notes about class discussions can enhance your understanding and help you to recall what others have said. Your instructor might even ask one student to keep notes of the class discussion for everyone. If you have computers and a printer in your classroom, the notes can be written on the computer and then printed and distributed after each discussion. This process can help to maintain continuity in the discussions over a number of class sessions. The group notes become a collaborative interpretation of the story that the class is studying and can be useful as you plan and draft your essay.

USING PREWRITING ACTIVITIES

Most of us have suffered from procrastination or writer's block when preparing to write a paper. One way of combating writer's block is to understand and to silence the internal critical voice that may discourage you from exploring your ideas and feelings. In her essay "The Watcher at the Gate," novelist and short-story writer Gail Godwin explains how she uses this critical energy in a positive way, visualizing her inner critic as a "Watcher":

> Get to know your Watcher. . . . Keep your Watcher in shape and he'll have less time to keep from shaping you. If he's really ruining your whole working day, sit down . . . and write him a letter. . . . "Dear Watcher," I wrote, "What is it you're so afraid I'll do?" Then I held his pen for him, and he replied instantly with a candor that has kept me from truly despising him. "Fail," he wrote back.

Like Godwin, you might write a letter to your Watcher, perhaps telling him or her to "get off your back."

Whereas your journal and drawings will help you to start thinking about a story and silencing your Watcher can free you to write, prewriting activities such as freewriting, invisible writing, brainstorming, and clustering can take you past feelings of anxiety and help you to understand better the story you are writing about while discovering and developing new ideas for your essay.

Freewriting. Freewriting involves writing rapidly for brief periods of time (five to ten minutes) without stopping. Freewriting can help you to get in touch with what you want to say about a story, with your thoughts and feelings about the characters, plot, and themes. After freewriting, reread what you have written and circle the phrases and ideas that interest you most. Then try a second freewriting using key words or ideas from the first freewriting to get you started. While freewriting is most frequently used to help a writer generate ideas when beginning a paper, it can be done at any stage of the writing process.

Here is student Kris Haeger's freewriting about "The Other Side of the Hedge."

> Perhaps the reason I found "The Other Side of the Hedge" so disturbing is that it touched too close to home. Even after reading only the first few paragraphs, I realized that I was unconsciously placing myself in the story as the narrator, and, similar to the narrator, became frustrated with the lack of direction in the laid-back society he has stumbled into. Many times in the past, I've become bored and felt useless when my actions had no direct consequence. Although everyone needs time to relax and rest, a strong part of my nature continually drives me forward and requires progress to be contented.

> From the moment the narrator saw the countryside and its carefree inhabitants' lackadaisical attitude toward progress and purpose, he sought an escape from "this prison." While the road for which he searched lacked the aesthetic beauty and simple contentment of the land he accidentally wandered into, he needed a purpose, a goal, an aspiration whose pursuit would bring him satisfaction.

> While I've always known myself to be ambitious and self-motivated, this particular story had me questioning the true value and actual need for my ambitions. What is real happiness, and how do I know when I've achieved it? "The Other Side of the Hedge" now has me wondering about the answer to a question I thought I'd answered long ago.

Kris Haeger's freewriting is not as long as Liz Scheps's journal entry, as Haeger was given a time limit. Both strategies for prewriting are useful, and you will need to decide which works best for you. Here's what Kris wrote about the advantages of using freewriting:

> This strategy works well because when forced to continue writing without stopping, a true and honest response comes out. There's no time to hide feelings with fancy words, and though the result may not be as coherent and structured all correctly as if there was time for revisions, a real reaction makes itself known to the writer who might not have even been aware of those feelings.

Invisible Writing.   If you have access to a computer, you can experiment with a prewriting strategy that may be new to you — invisible writing. For this strategy, dim your computer screen and then proceed as if you were freewriting. Without the words on the screen to guide you, and without those inevitable spelling or grammar mistakes to see and worry about, you may be able to express yourself more freely. Because you may be accustomed to looking at the words you have already written to prod your thinking, this may not be easy to do the first time. If you persist, though, invisible writing may help to increase your concentration, and you may find that, like drawing, this new approach can help you to overcome a sense of writer's block and to discover new thoughts and feelings.

The following invisible writing by Steve Lim demonstrates how this strategy helped him to think more deeply about "The Other Side of the Hedge":

> There are several problems tha ti have not fully understood--what is the significance in Eliza Dimbleby, whom he saw lyin gon the hill? Another thing that intrigues me is that people are running as fast as they can on this road to reach the goal, yet they have know idea where it leads. People who have stopped to notice the hedges and has crossed over are the ones who have really advanced the most. Io have another question--what is the significance in the watch failing to work on the other side? At the end of the storym when the protagonist meets this brother is an interesting ending. It gives the story more aof a personl ending, because having a sibling reaching the other isde says tha tanyone could make it to the end. Also, the brother was, int hte beginning of the story, was characterized as a singer who helped others. This characteristics impies a sense of non-competition, and provides a positive spin to the ending. Incidently, the protagonist claims to have left his brother far behind, but in reality, his brother had jumped way ahead of him.

Brainstorming.   To begin brainstorming, list on paper or on the computer screen whatever comes into your mind about the story: issues or ideas raised, a character's motivations or problems, a vivid image or symbol, or your personal responses and related experiences. When your list is complete, you might choose one particular item to develop with further brainstorming, or you might do further brainstorming on interesting groups of ideas. Use your revised, reordered brainstorming list to freewrite from or to develop a tentative outline for your essay.

Liz Scheps's brainstorming list on "The Other Side of the Hedge" shows how this strategy helps a student to develop ideas. Liz includes in her list observed details and key phrases from the story, questions of her own, and insights into the issues and meanings reflected in the story.

narrator--no identity, nameless
hedge--thick, ensnares narrator, barrier
moat--like hedge, keep people in, why not out?
road--dusty, dirty, brown
brown versus green road versus lawn
running, somewhere? nowhere?
fruit offered to narrator--Garden of Eden-beer-brother
singing--happy
narrator unhappy on other side of hedge
brother unhappy on road
competition
guide showing narrator around
competition--showing calm side is better than road--is it?
appearances deceive
circular path
lots of gates to road
illusion
Alice in Wonderlandesque
gates open inward
let people in not out
escape from reality
does narrator ever get out?
unresolved ending
think what you want
choose between hedge sides
so blatantly different
don't they blend?
The Other Side of the Hedge!!!
which side is other?

Whereas Liz Scheps's journal entry has an objective, more impersonal tone, her brainstorming explores her immediate thoughts about the story's meaning. The energy in her questions helped to motivate her to begin her paper.

Clustering.   Clustering (or mapping) is an effective strategy for developing and making connections between ideas and feelings. Like brainstorming, this process can help you to develop a plan or outline for your essay. Begin by writing in the center of a page a character's name, the title, or something else central to the story. Draw a circle around it and develop offshoots that represent associations from the original word or phrase. Like blossoms from the central stem of a flower, each of these major associations can in turn become the point of origin for a new cluster of associations.

In the following cluster, student Eric Yang tries to make sense of some of the conflicting symbols and ideas presented in "The Other Side of the Hedge":

the road versus the other side, nature versus humanity, nature versus science, progress versus the "life cycle," competition versus acceptance. Eric circled key symbols and concepts and connected the circles with lines that help create a kind of mental pathway toward a closer reading and interpretation of the story.

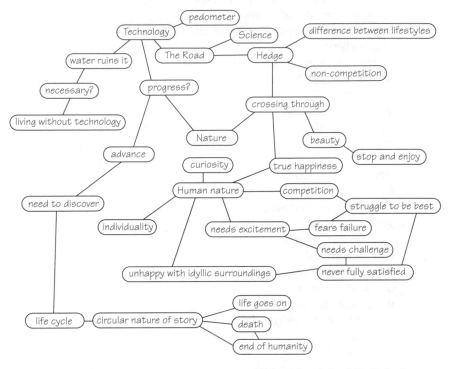

Student Eric Yang's interpretive map of "The Other Side of the Hedge"

Remember that all the prewriting strategies we have covered here can be useful; through exploration and experimentation you will be able to decide which work best for you in writing about stories.

Considering Your Audience

As you are developing a sense of purpose for your paper, you will also need to begin to think about your audience. When you first write about a story, you naturally want to clarify your ideas for yourself; the next step involves making sure that you can communicate your ideas to your readers. After working privately, it is necessary to imagine your audience; try to visualize them as open-minded and thoughtful, but don't assume that they will accept your opinions without convincing support and clarification. Writing for your classmates as audience rather than exclusively for your instructor will help you to find examples, evidence, and language closer to your own experience and also may help you to avoid overreliance on literary terminology that some students believe impresses instructors but that is seldom as effective as a direct expression of your own point of view. Always think carefully about how your readers may respond to your work. Asking yourself the following questions can help you to shape a paper that will be more easily understood and better received.

Questions about the Needs of Your Audience

1. How can I engage the reader's interest in my topic? In what ways will learning about my topic benefit my reader/audience?
2. What values do I share with my audience? How are my values different from those of my audience?
3. How can I anticipate the objections that my audience may have to my approach or point of view? How are these differences significant in relation to the issues that I am presenting? How can I overcome my audience's potential objections through ideas and support drawn from the story or outside readings?
4. What background knowledge about the story and its writer does my audience need in order to understand the issues covered in my paper?
5. Will any specialized critical words or concepts need to be defined or explained?

Organizing and Writing Your First Draft

Now you should be ready to compose a rough outline or to write a first draft. You might want to work from the journal entry or prewriting that has best helped you to express your ideas and feelings about your topic. Some writers work from an outline that puts the main ideas of their paper, expressed either in phrases or complete sentences, in a logical order. Remember that you don't need to follow your rough outline rigidly.

This rough outline was developed from Eric Chang's cluster map.

Difference between the Road and the Hedge World

Road: Science and Technology
   Struggle
   Competition and fear of failure
   Progress?

Hedge World: Nature
   Enjoyment
   Beauty and true happiness
   Circularity

Both Road and Hedge World are part of human nature
Narrator unhappy in idyllic world
Finally comes full circle
Seems to accept the natural life cycle of the world "on the other
side of the Hedge"

You might also create a more detailed outline, beginning by stating your main idea and then stating the ideas that will be discussed in your paragraphs to support the main idea. Many writers find that they discover more ideas as they draft and that they want to go back and modify their initial outline and main idea. In any case, it is best when possible to write your draft in one sitting to get the ideas flowing as you do in a freewriting; of course, you will need to refer often to your notes and outline as well as to the story you are writing about.

Here is the more detailed outline that Liz Scheps worked on before and after drafting her essay (her first draft appears in the next section).

Outline: The Inner Struggle of the Narrator
in "The Other Side of the Hedge"

I. *Main idea:*

The hedge represents the psychological boundary in the narrator, a repressed person who is unable to follow his true desires. The characters and setting of the story represent aspects of his inner struggle.

II. *Support from the story:*
A.   The old man who serves as the narrator's guide represents the narrator's inner voice that contradicts his external values.
B.   Eliza Dimbleby is seen at first as someone exactly like the narrator, constantly competing; he has trouble accepting that she can relax and enjoy herself on the other side, as he is attempting to do unconsciously--yet he cannot abandon his inner struggle.
C.   The narrator's loss of possessions in the story represents his realization that he can't explain everything and must shed his previous conceptions and ideas now that he is on "the other side."
D.   The narrator ends the story as he began it--resting on the ground. This position suggests that he is exploring through dreams a hidden part of himself, not only another physical community with different values.
E.   The thorny, overgrown Hedge is an important symbol in the story that represents the division in the narrator between the two sides of his personality; yet the fact that he is able to see light through it and crawl beneath it suggests that, with difficulty, he is moving toward a breakdown of the rigid separation within him.

III. *Conclusion:*

By submitting to the hedge, the narrator submits to an inner voice that urges him to take a break from stress and explore himself, his values, and his fears.

SHARING FIRST DRAFTS IN PEER GROUPS

Once you have a first draft written, sharing it in a small group will be very helpful. Getting responses from others can help you to develop a greater understanding of what you wanted to say and what you have written. Remember that cooperation and respect are necessary for successful communication. Arrive for your peer writing review sessions well prepared, with a substantial draft. When everyone pays attention to classmates' work as if it were his or her own and offers supportive and constructive suggestions, then much fruitful advice can be exchanged.

There are different ways to work together in a writing group. For example, your group might begin by just sharing one another's papers and responding orally to the feelings and ideas expressed. Alternatively, you could begin by defining some basic issues for evaluating the group's papers. If your group wants to do a more comprehensive critique, written evaluations are a good idea. The following questions will prove useful if you decide to try a more formal type of peer sharing. Consider working only with several issues per peer review session.

Peer Review Questions

1. Why did the paper engage your interest?
2. Are the paper's main ideas stated clearly, and is the paper's purpose apparent?
3. Is the paper well-focused and logical? Have all irrelevant details (however interesting) been deleted? Do any of the paragraphs need to be moved to tighten the paper's focus and logic?
4. Has the writer included enough support for his or her major points in the form of summaries of or brief quotations from the story? Does the evidence support the main points? Is the evidence convincing?
5. Does the essay have a voice that provides unity and personality? Are the quotations from other sources subordinate to the writer's voice?
6. What is the paper's greatest strength? In what ways and where could the paper be improved?

Liz Scheps's Early Draft.   Here is an early draft of Liz Scheps's essay. If your writing review group wants to practice peer editing, you might decide to start with Liz's draft. Be sure to take notes on your suggested changes. Then when you read the final draft, you will be able to compare your ideas about improving the paper with the ideas that Liz worked with after consulting with her peer writing group and her instructor.

The Inner Struggle of the Narrator
in "The Other Side of the Hedge"

Topic: The hedge is a psychological boundary for the narrator that
prevents him from exploring himself and from following his true desires.

Forster's short story "The Other Side of the Hedge" is generally considered to be the tale of a goal-oriented, competitive man who discovers the value of doing something simply for pleasure on the other side of a hedge. Everyday life, with all its stresses, is depicted as a dusty brown road, whereas the escape to relaxation and tranquillity is described as being almost a "park, or garden, if the words did not imply a certain triviality and constraint" (513). These strikingly different images seem to imply that conflict and progress are incompatible with art and leisure. Yet a closer inspection of the story reveals that it is quite likely that these two ideas are in fact quite compatible, and that both are embodied by the narrator, separated only by a psychological "hedge."

People often claim that they never lose their inner children, that there are always parts of them that remain immature. The narrator, although completely oriented toward the road on the surface, is one of these people, as exemplified on page 513. He states that his guide in this prison-like paradise is "a man of fifty or sixty--just the kind of age we mistrust on the road--but there was no anxiety in his manner, and his voice was that of a boy of eighteen." This guide can easily be interpreted as representing the inner voice of the narrator--that little part of him that doesn't want to be constantly moving, but that wishes instead to take time for the little things in life. The very fact that the narrator mistrusts him as much as he does lends strength to the idea that the guide is not a complete entity, or other person, but just a hidden fragment of the narrator, who dislikes him simply because he is the part of him that contradicts his values. In addition, the guide is old in appearance, but young in voice, which alludes to the often hasty maturing of those who are too competitive.

There is another much more obvious connection, in the form of Eliza Dimbleby, between the road that the narrator leaves behind, and the rolling hills that he enters. While the narrator is resting, "prostrate, with [his] face to the great parched hedge, praying that [he] might give up" (512), "Miss Eliza Dimbleby, the great educationist, [sweeps] past, exhorting [him] to persevere" (512). To the narrator, being passed by Miss Dimbleby represents a blow to his ego, because he is no longer beating her in the race of life. He sees her as someone exactly like him, who aims to get ahead and never slows down if she can help it. Later in the story, however, the narrator discovers her on the other side of the hedge, reclining with her feet in a fountain. This comes as a complete shock, because although the narrator has come through the hedge, he does not yet accept what he has found there, and he cannot believe that the motivated Miss Dimbleby would be relaxed and unproductive. In fact, he states that it is "impossible! I left her on the road, and she is due to lecture this evening" (515). As in dreams, when one finds himself envisioning someone that he knows in a completely unlikely status, the narrator cannot comprehend that Eliza, too, sometimes secretly longs for fun and peacefulness.

Not only does the narrator find someone he knows on the other side of the hedge, he also finds aspects of himself in those that he encounters. When Miss Dimbleby passes him on the road, he simply smiles, and lifts his hat to her. Similarly, when he finds himself in Eliza's place, unable to believe the scene in front of him, a few men on the hill "laugh and wave their caps" (513). Thus, Eliza's disbelief at finding him resting is replaced by the amusement of the man on the other side, who can't believe that he would be silly enough to ask where the place leads to. It is interesting to note that the narrator is actually more like the people in the paradiselike land when he is passed by Eliza on the road and tips his hat than when he is able to relax on the other side of the hedge.

Another parallel between the fast-paced world of the road and the laid-back side of the hedge may be seen in the losses of possessions that occur on both sides of the hedge. Toward the beginning of the story, the narrator states "I had already dropped several things--indeed, the road behind was strewn with the things we all had dropped" (512). This is akin to the other side of the hedge, where the narrator is forced to examine his values and leave behind many of his conceptions. Just as he drops material items on the road, he questions the continuity of science when he realizes that his pedometer and watch no longer work. He states soon after coming through the hedge that "the laws of science are universal in their application. . . . In normal conditions everything works. Science and the spirit of emulation--those are the forces that have made us what we are" (513). Yet, after touring the area, he no longer insists that it was water that made his watch stop, nor that it is inconceivable for his watch not to work. Subconsciously, he is beginning to realize that he can't explain everything, and that not all things are simple and straightforward like the road. Thus, just as he shed his belongings on the road, he must now shed his conceptions and ideas on the other side of the hedge.

In some ways, the narrator comes full circle by the end of the story. The narrative opens with him sitting on a milestone because he is too exhausted and fed up with competition to go any farther. Then, at the end of the story, a similar scene arises. He has journeyed through a beautiful land where everyone he meets is friendly, but because he cannot handle the fact that the people there do things for their own benefit and are completely unconcerned by the notion of getting ahead, he is tired and disoriented. Therefore, he ends his travels much as he began them, by resting on the ground. This cycle lends support to the idea that the narrator is not actually exploring another place with different values but simply a hidden part of himself, especially since the ending of the story is quite dreamlike and surreal.

Perhaps one of the most riveting questions is just how the separation of the competitive narrator from his inner voice is accomplished. The barrier is of course represented by the hedge, and so the characteristics of the hedge correspond to the narrator's inability to perceive the values of another way of life. It is nearly impossible for the narrator to make his way through, because it is thorny and overgrown. This is akin to the difficulty that the narrator feels in allowing himself to relax and enjoy the slow pace of the other side. In addition, when the narrator chooses to go through the hedge, he sees a light shining through, and then states, "The hedge could not be as thick as usual. . . . We of the road do not admit . . . that there is another side at all" (512). This statement demonstrates the breakdown of the narrator's mental block against the other side, but at the same time shows his reluctance to concede that he is not always naturally motivated, and sometimes he does long to merely drop all his obligations and relax. The very fact that he had to crawl through the hedge, rather than coming through the gate like much of the human race, shows that he cannot easily accept the way of the other side, and therefore must convince himself to investigate it, a process represented by his struggle through the hedge.

It is clear that the narrator is in fact undergoing a change in his way of thinking when he travels through the hedge. The physical actions of running on the road, crawling through the hedge, and walking around the other side are simply allegories to the mental processes of being strictly competitive, opening the mind to new ideas, and then exploring those ideas. Therefore, the narrator, by submitting to the other side of the hedge, actually submits to his inner voice, which urges him to take a break from stress and investigate the fun side of life. In exploring the other side of the hedge, he explores himself, his values, and his fears.

SUGGESTIONS FOR REVISION

Liz Scheps's classmates and instructor read this first draft and all agreed that the paper would benefit from some careful rewording and reordering of paragraphs and a combining of the ideas of her thesis statement into a single, unified sentence. One student reader observed that "not all of your paragraphs relate directly to your thesis statement; the last three paragraphs seem to rehash the same points over and over." Another student complimented the author on "some great and interesting ideas," particularly her "viewing the story as parts of the narrator." The instructor agreed that the paper's "portrait of division and conflict within the narrator" was sound and insightful but felt that the mention of the "inner child" needed defining or omission as a bit too much of a "psychobabble" concept. The instructor noted that the thesis needed rewording and clarification, and that there were places where the paper tended to ramble, sometimes losing track of the purpose announced in the thesis; transitions were advised to promote better linkage of ideas and a clearer overall direction. The instructor also felt that Liz needed to reorder her points to follow the flow of the story and to put more emphasis on the revelation contained in the story's powerful ending, with the reappearance of the narrator's brother.

Developing the Draft: Finding Support in the Text and Maintaining Your Voice

Once you have shared your essay with your peers, you will be ready to work on it again with a fresh point of view and new insights. In revising this time, you will want to support your interpretation through appropriate references to the story, as you saw Liz Scheps do in her draft. Quotations and summaries are essential, as they will help to convince the reader that your thoughts and feelings are based on the story itself.

Quotations and summaries that suggest the story's tone and themes are most effective when they are as brief as possible and are integrated into your text with clear and logical transitions. At the same time, it is important not to use too many quotations from the story or to summarize more than is necessary. The purpose of every quote and summary you include should be clear in relation to the ideas of your paragraph and of the paper as a whole: this can be achieved through strong topic sentences, transitional expressions, and repetition of key words and phrases. Integrating relevant biographical or historical information also can be effective. As you make decisions about what to paraphrase and what information to include, always consider the needs of your readers. Also return to the story itself, checking carefully to be sure that the plot, characters, and images or details support your position.

When you write about a story, remember to use language that is not only clear to your readers but also feels authentic to you. Choose words that you are sure of and that you believe accurately express your feelings and ideas. If you need to use a specialized academic or critical expression, define or clarify its meaning through example; otherwise, you may confuse your readers. When you are having trouble explaining an idea, try to create vivid images or comparisons using your imagination and experiences.

The Final Draft: Editing and Proofreading

The final stages of revision involve careful attention to language and style. Review the accuracy and length of your quotations and your transitions between paragraphs and into examples and quotes. Read your sentences aloud to hear and feel the flow and rhythm of your ideas and language; then fine-tune them for emphasis, variety, length, and rhythm. Next think carefully about the words you have chosen. Refer to a thesaurus or dictionary to replace words or expressions that are inaccurate, inappropriate, or unclear. Finally, check your grammar, punctuation, and spelling.

By the time you have finished the revision process, you will probably have composed a number of drafts of your paper. You should feel satisfied with what you have written and value what you have said. Liz Scheps was pleased with the development, content, and style of the final draft of her essay. Compare this version with her early draft. What makes this draft more effective? Do you see any possibilities for further improvement?

Final Draft of Liz Scheps's Paper

The Inner Struggle of the Narrator in "The Other Side of the Hedge"
by Liz Scheps

E. M. Forster's short story "The Other Side of the Hedge" is the tale of a goal-oriented, competitive man who discovers the value of living simply for pleasure. In this story, everyday life, with all its stresses, is depicted as a dusty brown road, whereas the escape to relaxation and tranquillity is described as "a park, or garden, if the words did not imply a certain triviality and constraint" (513). At first these strikingly different images seem to imply that conflict and progress are incompatible with art and leisure, but a closer inspection of the story reveals that all four of these ideas are in fact compatible, and that elements of all of them coexist within the narrator. They are separated only by a psychological hedge that must be cut back in order for them to mix and combine.

The characteristics of the barrier hedge correspond to the narrator's inability to perceive the values of another way of life. It is nearly impossible for the narrator to make his way through the hedge, because it is thorny and overgrown. The mental counterpart of this physical obstacle is the difficulty that the narrator feels in allowing himself to relax and enjoy the slow pace of the other side. In addition, when the narrator chooses to go through the hedge, he sees a light shining through, and then states, "The hedge could not be as thick as usual. . . . We of the road do not admit . . . that there is another side at all" (512). This statement demonstrates the breakdown of the narrator's mental block against the other side, but at the same time shows his reluctance to concede that he is not always motivated to struggle, and sometimes he does long to merely drop all his obligations and relax. The very fact that he had to crawl through the hedge, rather than coming through the gate like much of the human race, shows that he cannot easily accept the way of the other side, and therefore must convince himself to investigate it, a process represented by his struggle through the hedge.

It is clear that the narrator is in fact undergoing a change in his way of thinking when he travels through the hedge. The physical actions of running on the road, crawling through the hedge, and walking around the other side are comparable to the mental processes of being strictly competitive, opening the mind to new ideas, and then exploring those ideas. Therefore, the narrator, by submitting to the other side of the hedge, actually submits to his inner voice, which urges him to take a break from stress and investigate the slower-paced side of life. In exploring the other side of the hedge, the narrator explores himself, and begins to reconcile his values with his fears.

The guide whom the narrator meets following his journey through the hedge embodies the relaxed traits that would have allowed the narrator to enjoy the other side without his painful crawl through the undergrowth. The narrator states that his guide in this prisonlike paradise is a man of fifty or sixty, "just the kind of age we mistrust on the road--but there [is] no anxiety in his manner, and his voice [is] that of a boy of eighteen" (513). This guide represents the inner voice of the narrator, that part of him that doesn't want to be constantly moving, but wishes instead to take time for the simple things in life. His elderly appearance and young voice support the idea that he is the relaxed portion of the narrator that has been suppressed by the narrator's overbearing drive to succeed; as a result, the guide looks older than his years. The very fact that the narrator mistrusts the old man as much as he does lends strength to the idea that the guide is not a separate entity, another person, but rather a hidden fragment of the narrator, who dislikes the guide simply because he contradicts the narrator's values. According to popular wisdom, the qualities that people loathe in others can often be found in themselves. The narrator detests the guide because he enjoys relaxing and taking time for the little things--something that the narrator secretly longs to do. The guide embodies the characteristics that the narrator despised in his brother: he questions the purpose of racing, enjoys saying hello to others, and takes time to appreciate the world around him. Therefore, it troubles the narrator to discover that these attributes also appear in himself.

Eliza Dimbleby, like the guide, is a link between the road that the narrator leaves behind and the rolling hills that he enters. While the narrator is lying prostrate, "with [his] face to the great parched hedge, praying that [he] might give up . . . Miss Eliza Dimbleby, the great educationist, [sweeps] past, exhorting [him] to persevere" (512). To the narrator, being passed by Miss Dimbleby represents a blow to his ego because he is no longer beating her in the race of life. He sees her as someone similar to him, who aims to get ahead and never slows down if she can help it. Later in the story, however, the narrator discovers her on the other side of the hedge, reclining with her feet in a fountain. This comes as a complete shock, because although the narrator has come through the hedge, he does not yet accept what he has found there and cannot believe that the highly motivated Miss Dimbleby would be relaxed and unproductive. In fact, he states that it is "impossible! I left her on the road, and she is due to lecture this evening" (515). The narrator is quickly discovering that his ideals and beliefs from the road, which he believed were true and constant, are repeatedly being questioned and tested on the other side of the hedge. As in dreams, when one finds oneself envisioning someone that one knows in a completely unlikely situation, the narrator cannot comprehend that Eliza, like himself, sometimes secretly longs for repose and peacefulness.

Not only does the narrator find someone he knows on the other side of the hedge, but he also finds aspects of himself in those whom he encounters. When Miss Dimbleby passes him on the road, he simply smiles and lifts his hat to her. Similarly, when he finds himself in Eliza's place, unable to believe the scene in front of him, a few men on the hill laugh and wave their caps (513). Thus, Eliza's disbelief at finding him resting is replaced by the amusement of the man on the other side, who can't believe that he would be silly enough to ask where the place leads to. It is interesting to note that the narrator is actually more like the people in the paradise-like land when he is passed by Eliza on the road and tips his hat than when he is able to relax on the other side of the hedge. This indicates that he is more comfortable with his position on the road than with the one he holds on the other side of the hedge. He feels able to take a moment to say hello to Miss Dimbleby or rest his weary body when on the road, but he feels defensive when on the unfamiliar side of the hedge and therefore holds tightly to his strong willed, determined persona, even more tightly than he normally does on the road.

Another parallel between the fast-paced world of the road and the serene side of the hedge may be seen in the losses of possessions that occur on both sides of the hedge. Toward the beginning of the story, the narrator states, "I had already dropped several things--indeed, the road behind was strewn with the things we all had dropped" (512). This is an exact parallel to the other side of the hedge, where the narrator is forced to examine his values and leave behind many of his conceptions of the correct way to lead life. Just as he drops material items on the road, he questions the continuity of science when he realizes that his pedometer and watch no longer work. He states soon after coming through the hedge that "the laws of science are universal in their application. . . . In normal conditions everything works. Science and the spirit of emulation--those are the forces that have made us what we are" (513). Yet, after touring the area, he no longer insists that it was water that made his watch stop, nor that it is inconceivable for his watch not to work. Subconsciously, he is beginning to realize that he can't explain everything, and that not all things are simple and straightforward like they seem to be on the road. Thus, just as he shed his belongings on the road, he must now shed his conceptions and ideas on the other side of the hedge.

By the end of the story, the narrator comes full circle. The narrative opens with him sitting on a milestone because he is too exhausted and fed up with competition to go any farther; then, at the end of the story, a similar scene arises. He has journeyed through a beautiful land where everyone he meets is friendly, but because he cannot accept the fact that the people there do things for their own benefit and are completely unconcerned by the notion of getting ahead, he is tired and disoriented. Therefore, he ends his travels much as he began them, by resting on the ground, like the brother whom he had long since rejected as one who "wasted" himself through noncompetitive, playful behavior.

The cyclical nature of the story lends support to the idea that the narrator is not actually exploring another place with different values, but simply reentering a hidden part of himself. This is reinforced by the ending of the story, which is dreamlike and surreal: "Though my senses were sinking into oblivion, they seemed to expand ere they reached it" (517). Although it is questionable whether the narrator has embraced the lifestyle of the other side of the hedge and thereby fully heeded his inner voice, it is clear that at the very least he has recognized the power and presence of relaxation and tranquillity. The final words in the story imply an ability on the part of the narrator to accept the earliest, most intimate part of himself: "I saw that he was my brother" (517).

Varieties of Literary Papers

The kind of analytical/interpretive paper that Liz Scheps wrote is traditionally assigned in literature courses. Others include comparison papers, reflective papers, creative-writing papers, and research papers. As you begin any paper, try to find a topic that interests you while following the guidelines of your instructor's assignment. Ask yourself questions about the story — its plot, characters, symbols, point of view, tone, style, and themes — to discover what interests you. The most successful papers are developed by students who want to understand more about the story that they are reading, who are interested in what they are writing, and who have a genuine desire to share their insights with others.

ANALYTICAL/INTERPRETIVE PAPERS

Analytical writing breaks a subject — in this case a story — into parts in order to understand better how it works or what it means. In writing about stories, this could mean breaking the plot down into opening, development of conflict, climax, and resolution or examining a character's actions and motivations and the consequences of his or her actions. You might want to look at the way one or more literary strategies — such as point of view, symbolism, or setting — work together to build the story's theme. Alternatively, you might decide to focus more on what the story seems to represent in terms of philosophical, religious, cultural, gender-related, or political issues. An analytical paper can be rewarding to write, allowing you to examine in depth particular parts of a story and the way these parts are interrelated as a meaningful pattern.

The six casebooks developed in *A Web of Stories* provide you with a number of professional examples of analytical writing about short stories. In addition, each casebook includes one example of a student writing about a short story. For example, in the Edgar Allan Poe casebook, student Patrick Weekes analyzes "The Masque of the Red Death," joining the debate that critics over the decades have had about the meaning of the symbolism that structures the story.

COMPARISON PAPER

A comparison-and-contrast paper looks at two stories to present an interpretation of both. For example, you might compare two stories by the same writer or two stories on the same theme by different writers; you might compare and contrast the cultural perspectives of two writers in relation to a theme raised in two stories, or you might contrast stories from different historical periods written on an enduring social or philosophical issue.

When writing a comparison paper, it is important to keep your larger purpose in mind, or you may end up with a well-organized series of parallel points that do not lead to an interpretive statement. Consider, for example, whether you are comparing in order to evaluate, such as you might do for a review, or writing in order to clarify how different cultural assumptions shape characters, values, and choices. Are you comparing in order to interpret the influence of history or gender, or to show the influence of different literary styles? Start with a clear focus and a limited number of comparative points, depending on the length of your paper. Outlining a comparison paper will help you to balance your discussion of the two stories and to arrange your points clearly and logically. As you plan and outline your paper, you will need to decide on a structure: either point by point (topic by topic) or whole by whole (subject by subject). This type of paper is challenging in that you need to make logical transitions as you move between specific points or between major points and specific evidence from a story.

Two of the casebooks provide student examples of comparative essays. In the Anton Chekhov casebook, Joseph Hsieh contrasts Chekhov's stories "The Darling" and "The Schoolmistress." While both of these stories follow the thoughts and feelings of a middle-aged woman, the attitudes of the characters and the tones of the stories are very different. In the Katherine Mansfield casebook, Cathy Young compares and contrasts James Joyce's "Araby" with Mansfield's "The Garden-Party," focusing on the technique of the epiphany in each story as well as on issues of class.

REFLECTIVE PAPERS

Formal analytical and comparative essays with an argumentative and interpretive perspective are part of the tradition of literary criticism. Such essays are not the only way to write about literature, however. In the sixteenth century French writer Michel de Montaigne first used the term *essai* ("attempt" or "exploration") to describe his short prose writings. Since then authors have continued to write personal, reflective essays, often referring to stories and poems that have inspired and led them to unusual insights. A reflective paper normally focuses on philosophical, psychological, social, or personal issues that a story has raised for the reader. Such an essay allows you considerable freedom to develop your point of view.

The new genre of personal, "reader-response" criticism practiced by authors such as Norman Holland can be seen as a continuation of the tradition of the reflective essay. An effective approach to writing a reflective essay is to acknowledge openly that you are writing subjectively and then to examine various meanings of the story in relation to your own life and values, rather than arguing for one correct interpretation. At the same time, you do need to consider your readers; keep them interested through lively personal examples, specific references to the story, and a sense of humor or voice. In the James Baldwin casebook, student Zachary Roberts's reflective essay explores his response to "Sonny's Blues" by integrating his personal reflections on the nature of music and creation.

CREATIVE-WRITING PAPERS

By entering the text as a creative writer, producing your own story or a variation of an existing story, it is possible to gain a deeper understanding of a story's meaning, how it has been constructed, and the problems of interpreting literature. When writing this type of paper, you assume a role within the story, instead of just observing and analyzing it. *A Web of Stories* presents many ideas for this type of writing project. For example, you might be asked to retell a story from the point of view of another character. Alternatively, you might begin the story at an earlier time, further develop a scene that is only hinted at, expand the role of a minor character, or develop an alternative ending or a sequel.

Another type of creative approach to writing about stories is to use a literary technique developed in a story you have read. For example, after reading Ernest Hemingway's "Hills like White Elephants," you could write a dramatic scene between two estranged characters; similarly, after reading Katherine Anne Porter's "The Jilting of Granny Weatherall," you might create an interior monologue similar to that of the main character in the story. Creative written responses to fiction challenge your imagination and encourage you to read and to think very carefully. Such projects can teach you how writers solve the problems inherent in literary creation; at the same time, you will gain a deeper understanding of the stories you read. An example of a creative approach to writing about fiction can be found in the Eudora Welty casebook, where student Amanda Morgan develops a sequel to "A Worn Path" in which she imagines Phoenix Jackson returning to her rural home.

THE LITERARY RESEARCH PAPER

The literary research paper frequently uses the techniques of analysis, interpretation, and comparison, as well as a formal style of documentation. Some of the shorter student essays included in the casebooks, such as that by Cathy Young comparing Joyce's "Araby" with Mansfield's "The Garden-Party," are considered documented papers because they integrate information from two or three sources and include formal documentation (a works-cited list and parenthetical citations). A typical college research paper such as Sage Van Wing's "A Cultural Heritage: Louise Erdrich's Fiction" (in the Louise Erdrich casebook) is longer than Cathy Young's — ten pages or more in length — and requires more extensive support from a wider range of sources.

Finding Sources. Sources can be either *primary* (works by fiction writers, including their stories, as well as their letters, interviews, autobiographies, and essays) or *secondary* (works such as essays, reviews, editorial commentary, biographies, and longer studies by literary critics). Research sources on stories and writers can be found in reference works and bibliographies available through many college library systems. Electronic online catalog searches of authors or of the titles can also be very helpful. See Appendix B for a list of resources — literary journals, electronic and print indexes and bibliographies, literary histories of the short story, and anthologies of articles in literary criticism and theory.

Formal Documentation. Research papers also involve the use of formal documentation; in literary research the Modern Language Association format with a works-cited list and in-text parenthetical citations is most often used.

See Appendix B for examples of some typical works-cited entries and parenthetical citations that occur frequently in literary research papers, as well as for
some references to handbooks and guides to the MLA format for documentation. See the research paper by Sage Van Wing (in the Louise Erdrich casebook)
for an example of a full-length research paper using the MLA format.

Planning a Schedule for Research and Writing. Considerable time and
planning are needed for a successful research paper. Start early and budget
your time carefully using a calendar or timetable to guide yourself through the
stages of research and writing so that you complete an initial draft with time
for revision. The literary research paper often begins with a question you have
about a particular writer or story, then moves into a thorough examination of
available library resources. As you explore the library, you will begin to
develop a "working bibliography" that includes all necessary bibliographical
information on each interesting source encountered in your research. After
locating the desired research materials, the period of reading and note-taking
begins. Even at the earliest stages of research, you should take care to gather
all the information that will later be necessary to formally document the
sources you choose to use in your finished paper: complete author names; editor names in edited collections; exact full titles of all books, articles, and periodicals; exact dates of books and periodicals; volume numbers of periodicals;
city and publisher names for books; and exact page numbers of any material
you quote, including the stories you are interpreting. If you wish to record a
quotation from a source, you can scan it into your computer, cut it and paste
it from a photocopy of the original, or copy down the quotation exactly. You
can shorten longer quotes by using ellipses (. . .); you also will need to combine paraphrase and summary to tighten up longer passages. Go over your
paraphrased/summarized material to check for any inaccuracies or unintentionally copied text — any such text should be put in quotations or rewritten
in entirely your own words, even though the ideas are those of the source.

Organizing Research Material Using a Computer. Students preparing
research papers for any subject have traditionally kept card files of bibliographic data, quotations, and brief summaries of any source material they are
considering for their paper. Nowadays such files are being replaced by computer files, which save much time in the long run. With computer equipment,
you can copy or scan source material onto files, making sure to include the
right material to pinpoint the source and pages. Computer files also allow you
to cut and paste quotations and bibliographic data from document to document, as well as to organize your work into electronic "folders," the contents
of which can be automatically arranged in alphabetical order if desired.

Focusing, Outlining, and Revising. Next you need to begin to develop a
focus for your paper, perhaps in the form of an exploration of several possible

answers for the question that began your research. A focused topic in turn leads to a thesis and preliminary outline. A detailed outline for a research paper is important to get the sequence and proportions of the project under control. You can move from the outline to a draft, but at this point you may discover areas where you need to do further research and to modify your original plan somewhat according to where your research takes you. Write the first complete draft paper in rough form, with approximate documentation and most of your major quotations in place; then go back to insert more quotations and citations as needed, resolving any problems of documentation or form by checking reference books or asking questions of your instructor. Finally, you will need to spend considerable time revising and refining your central argument, word choice, supporting quotations, grammar, and mechanics.

Conclusion

With your own imagination and curiosity, effective strategies for close reading, efficient time management, and thorough writing and revising habits, you will be able to create thoughtful literary essays that contribute to your understanding of stories, ideas, and even yourself, as well as to your readers' enlightenment. You will find that this ability is one you can use often, and you will also come to realize that this ability enhances your enjoyment of literature enormously while it places you in the company of the greatest writers.

STORIES and CASEBOOKS

The Folk Story: Tricksters and Lies

The modern short story can trace its lineage back to folk tales and fairy tales. Folk tales were originally passed on orally by family members and village storytellers, who frequently would act out the parts in a dramatic sequence, whereas fairy tales such as Hans Christian Andersen's "The Emperor's New Clothes" are intended to be published and read to children. Although some folk and fairy tales were designed primarily to entertain, most contain dominant themes and moral lessons. Many folk stories and fairy tales reflect on the nature of deception and storytelling itself through plots that involve lying and trickery. The character of the trickster is, in fact, one of the most common, nearly universal figures in folk literature, and is a character that survives in modern fiction as well. The trickster succeeds by creating a real-seeming fictional world through lies and deceit. Such a character can be presented sympathetically, although these tales usually demonstrate the folly of lies that grow out of control, so that the carefully laid plans of the trickster sometimes result in a reversal of fortunes.

The following stories represent different countries — Germany (in the short folk story "Helping to Lie"), Burma ("The Tall Tales"), Israel ("A Dispute in Sign Language"), and Denmark (Hans Christian Andersen's "The Emperor's New Clothes") — plus the African-American culture of the United States ("The Barn Is Burning"). Each of these stories features a trickster as a central character, and each tale reflects on the art and consequences of deception.

Helping to Lie   (Germany)

The German folk tale "Helping to Lie" features a foolish master who attempts to tell lies but fails, while his clever servant helps him out. A similar story was told in tenth-century Persia by the poet Firdausi. The Bishop of Akkon included Firdausi's tale in his *Exempla* (from the twelfth century); from there it passed into European folklore.

There once was a nobleman who liked to tell terrible lies, but sometimes he got stuck. Once he wanted to hire a new servant. When one came to offer his services, the nobleman asked him if he could lie. "Well," he said, "if it's got to be!"

"Yes," said the nobleman, "I sometimes get stuck telling lies. Then you will have to help me."

One day they were in an inn, and the nobleman was as usual telling lies: "Once I went hunting and I shot three hares in the air."

"This is not possible," said the others.

"Then you better fetch my coachman," he said, "to bear witness." They fetched him. "Johann, listen, I have just been telling these gentlemen about the three hares I shot in the air. Now you tell them how that was."

"Yes, sir. We were in the meadow, and a hare came jumping through the hedge, and while it was jumping out, you shot and it was dead. Afterward, when it was cut open, there were two young hares inside." Of course the others could say nothing to this.

On their way home the nobleman said that it was well done.

"Well, sir," said Johann, "the next time you tell lies, try to keep out of the air. On firm ground it will be easier for me to help you."

The Tall Tales   (Burma)

"The Tall Tales" focuses on three brothers who attempt to tell winning stories but are "one-upped" by a sophisticated prince. This story makes a powerful statement on power and class relationships while raising the issue of the ethics and consequences of lying to achieve one's goals.

There once lived three brothers who were known throughout the land for the tall tales they told. They would travel from place to place telling their strange stories to whoever would listen. No one ever believed their tales and all who heard them would cry out with exclamations of disbelief.

One day while traveling very far from home the three brothers came upon a wealthy prince. The prince was dressed very elegantly and bedecked in jewels such as the three men had never seen in their lives. They thought how wonderful it would be to have such possessions so they devised a plan whereby they could use their storytelling ability to trick the prince out of his belongings.

They said to the prince: "Let's tell each other stories of past adventures and if anyone should doubt the truth of what the other is saying then that person must become a slave to the others." Now the brothers had no use for a slave but if they could make the prince their slave then they could take his clothes because they would then belong to them.

The prince agreed to their plan. The brothers were sure they would win because no one had ever heard their stories without uttering cries of disbelief. And so they found a passer-by and asked him to act as judge in the matter. All sat down under the shade of a tree and the storytelling began.

The first brother stood up to tell his tale. With a smile on his face he began to speak: "When I was a young boy I thought it would be fun to hide from my brothers so I climbed the tallest tree in our village and remained there all day while my brothers searched high and low for me. When night fell my brothers gave up the search and returned home. It was then that I realized that I was unable to climb down the tree. But I knew I could get down with the help of a rope, so I went to the nearest cottage and borrowed a rope and was then able to climb down the tree and return home."

When the prince heard this ridiculous story he did not make a comment but merely stood and waited for the next story to begin. The three brothers were quite surprised but were sure that the second story would not be believed by the prince. And so the second brother began his tale: "That day when my brother hid from us I was searching for him in the forest. I saw something run into the bushes and thinking it was my brother I ran in after it. When I got into the bushes I saw that it was not my brother but a huge hungry tiger. He opened his mouth to devour me and I jumped inside and crawled into his belly before he could chew me up. When inside I started jumping up and down and making loud, fierce noises. The beast did not know what was happening and became so frightened that he spit me out with such force that I traveled several hundred feet through the air and landed back in the middle of our village. And so though I was but a young lad I saved our whole village from the fearful tiger, because never again did the beast come near our village."

After this story the prince once again made no comment. He merely asked that the third story begin. The three brothers were quite upset by this and as the last brother began his tale he had quite a frown upon his face. But he was still quite determined to make up a story so absurd that the prince could not this time help but doubt its truthfulness. And so he began his tale: "One day as I was walking along the banks of the river I saw that all the fishermen seemed quite unhappy. I inquired as to why they seemed so sad. They therefore informed me that they had not caught one fish in a week and their families were going hungry as a result. I told them that I would try and help them. So I dove into the water and was immediately transformed into a fish. I swam around until I saw the source of the problem. A giant fish had eaten all the smaller fish and was himself avoiding the fishermen's nets. When this giant saw me he came toward me and was about to devour me, but I changed back to human form and slashed the fish open with my sword. The fish inside his belly were then able to escape. Many swam right into the waiting nets. When I returned to shore many of the fish were so thankful that I had saved them that they returned with me. When the fishermen saw all these fish jumping onto shore after me they were indeed pleased and rewarded me abundantly."

When this story was finished the prince did not doubt a word of it. The three brothers were quite upset, but at least they knew that they would not doubt the words of the prince. And so the prince began his tale: "I am a prince of great wealth and property. I am on the road in search of three slaves who have escaped from me. I have searched high and low for them as they were very valuable property. I was about to give up the search when I met you three fellows. But now my search is ended because I have found my missing slaves, because you gentlemen are they."

When the brothers heard these words they were shocked. If they agreed to the prince's story then they were admitting that they were his slaves, but if they doubted what he said then they lost the bet and became his slaves anyway. The brothers were so upset by the cleverness of the prince that they said not a word. The passer-by who was judging the contest nevertheless declared that the prince had won the wager.

The prince did not make slaves of these men but instead allowed them to return to their village with the promise that they would never tell tall tales again. And the three brothers were thereafter known throughout the land for their honesty and truthfulness.

A Dispute in Sign Language   (Israel)

This popular Israeli story tells of a powerful priest who is outsmarted by a humble Jewish poultry man. This story revolves around the interpretation of symbols and, despite its humor, resembles a religious allegory. A similar tale was included in *The Gloss of Accursius* in the thirteenth century. Variations of the plot are found in English, French (in the stories of François Rabelais), and Turkish folklore and literature.

Once there was a wicked priest who hated Jews. One day he summoned the chief rabbi and said to him, "I want to have a dispute with a Jew in the language of signs. I give you thirty days to prepare yourself, and if nobody appears to take part in the dispute, I shall order that all the Jews be killed."

What was the rabbi to do? He brought the bad tidings to his people and ordered them to fast and to pray in the synagogue. A week went by, two weeks, three weeks passed, but there was no one with the courage to accept the priest's challenge and the great responsibility. It was already the fourth week, and still there was no one to represent the Jews in the dispute.

Then along came a poultry dealer who had been away, bringing chickens from the nearby villages into the town. He had not heard what was going on there, but he noticed on his arrival that the market was closed, and at home he found his wife and children fasting, praying, and weeping.

"What is the matter?" asked the poultry dealer. His wife replied, "The wicked priest has ordered a Jew to hold a discussion with him in the language of signs. If there is no one who is able to do so, all of us will be killed."

"Is that all the matter?" wondered the poultry dealer in surprise. "Go to the rabbi, and tell him that I am ready to participate."

"What are you talking about? How can you understand the priest? Greater and wiser men than you have not been willing to take upon themselves this task!" cried his wife.

"Why should you worry? In any case we shall all be killed." And off they went together to the rabbi.

"Rabbi," said the man, "I am ready to meet the priest!"

The rabbi blessed him. "May God help you and bring you success."

So the priest was told that a Jew, sent by the rabbi, would hold a discussion with him in sign language.

"You have to understand my signs and to answer them in the same way," explained the priest to the Jew before a great assembly. Then he pointed a finger to him. In reply the Jew pointed two fingers. Then the priest took a piece of white cheese from his pocket. In reply the Jew took out an egg. Then the priest took the seeds of some grain and scattered them on the floor. In reply, the Jew set a hen free from the coop and let it eat up the seeds.

"Well done," exclaimed the priest in amazement. "You answered my questions correctly." And he gave the poultry dealer many gifts and ordered his servant to bathe him and to give him fine garments to wear.

"Now I know that the Jews are wise men, if the most humble among them was able to understand me," admitted the priest.

The town was in great excitement, and the people waited in suspense for the result of the dispute. When they saw the poultry dealer leaving the priest's house in fine garments and with a happy expression on his face, they understood that everything was in order, blessed be the Almighty.

"How did it go? What did the priest ask you?" all the people wanted to know. The rabbi called the poultry dealer to his home and asked him to relate what had happened.

And this is what the poultry dealer related: "The priest pointed with one finger to my eyes meaning to take out my eye. I pointed with two fingers to imply I would take out *both* his eyes. Then he took out a piece of cheese to show that I was hungry while he had cheese. So I took out an egg to show that I was not in need of his alms. Then he spilled some wheat grain on the floor. So I fed my hen knowing it was hungry and thinking what a pity to waste the grain."

At the same time the priest's friends questioned him: "What did you ask the Jew? What did he reply?"

The priest related: "At first I pointed one finger meaning that there is only one king. He pointed with two fingers meaning that there are two kings, the King in Heaven and the king on earth. Then I took out a piece of cheese, meaning, Is this cheese from a white or a black goat? In answer he took out an egg, meaning, Is this egg from a white or a brown hen? Finally I scattered some grain on the floor meaning that the Jews are spread all over the world. Whereupon he freed his hen which ate up all the grain, meaning that the Messiah will come and gather all the Jews from the four corners of the world."

The Barn Is Burning   (African American)

"The Barn Is Burning" is a slave narrative based on the English folk story "Master of All Masters." A similar plot can be found in several European and Mexican tales. In this story the slave (Old Tom) and the master both play the role of trickster, telling stories designed to deceive. As is often the case in the slave narrative, language differences between slave and master create deceptions and misunderstandings.

During slavery time, there was a rich old master in Brunswick County who owned more than three hundred slaves. Among them was one very smart slave named Tom. What I mean by smart is that he was a smooth operator — he knew what was happening. He came to be so smart because he would crawl under the master's house every night and listen to the master tell his wife what kind of work he was going to have the slaves do the next day. When the master would come out of the house the next morning and begin to tell the slaves what kind of work he wanted them to do that day, Old Tom would say, "Wait just a minute, Master. I know exactly what you're going to have us do." So the master would stop talking and let Old Tom tell the slaves what he had in mind for them to do that day. Old Tom could always tell the slaves exactly what the master wanted them to do, too; and the master was very surprised, because he didn't know how Old Tom was getting his information.

Old Tom wanted to prove to his master that he was the smartest slave on the plantation, because the smartest slave always got the easiest work — and Old Tom was tired of working so hard. Sometimes the masters let their smart slaves sleep in a bed in the big house, too; so Old Tom had been dreaming about how, one day maybe, he would get to sleep in a real bed instead of on an old quilt on his cabin floor. And it wasn't long before his dreams came to be true, because the next week after Old Tom had started prophesying what work the slaves were supposed to do that day, Old Master told his wife that he thought he was going to bring Old Tom to live in the house with them. And he did, and he gave him a room to sleep in with a big old bed and everything. Old Tom was so tickled he didn't know what to do with himself — just think, living in the same house with Old Master.

One winter night, when the master and his wife were seated around the fire, the master called Old Tom in to test his smartness. He pointed to the fire and said, "Tom, what is that?"

"That's a fire, Old Master," said Tom.

"No, it isn't either," replied Old Master. "That's a flame of evaporation."

Just then a cat passed in front of the fire, and Old Master said, "Tom, do you know what that was that just passed by in front of the fireplace?"

"That's a cat, sir," replied Tom.

Then Old Master said, "No, it's not either. That's a high-ball-a-sooner."

Old Tom was getting tired of answering questions by this time, so he went over to the window and started looking out. The old master walked over to the window where Tom was and said, "Tom, what is that you're looking at through the window?"

"I'm looking at a haystack," said Tom.

Then Old Master said, "That's not a haystack, that's a high tower."

Then Old Tom sat down in a chair and started getting ready to go to his room in the attic to go to bed for the night. He didn't want to get the carpet all spotted up with dirt in the living room, so he started unbuckling his shoes and taking them off. When the old man looked and saw Tom taking off his shoes, he said, "What are those, Tom?"

And Tom said, "Those are my shoes."

"No, they aren't either," said Old Master. "Those are your tramp-tramps."

Then the old master pointed through the archway to where a bed could be seen in his bedroom and said, "What's that I'm pointing to in there, Tom?"

"That's a bed," said Old Tom.

"No, it's not either," said Old Master. "That's a flowery bed of ease, and I'm going right now and get in it because we've all got a hard day's work coming up tomorrow."

So the old master and the old missus went into their bedroom and went to bed. Then Old Tom went on up to the attic room where they had him sleeping and he got in his big old bed. But just then the cat ran through the fire in the fireplace and caught on fire and started raising a howl. So Tom jumped out of bed and looked, and saw the cat run out to the haystack and set it on fire. Old Tom was there at the window, and when he saw the cat on fire and the haystack on fire, he started yelling as loud as he could, "Master, Master, you better get up out of your flowery bed of ease and put on your tramp-tramps because your high-ball-a-sooner has run through your flame of evaporation and set your high tower on fire."

Old Master didn't move a peg — he just chuckled to his wife and said, "Listen to that high-class slave up there using all that Latin."

Then once more Old Tom yelled out, "Master, Master, I said that you better get out of your flowery bed of ease, and put on your tramp-tramps, because your high-ball-a-sooner has run through your flame of evaporation and set your high tower on fire."

But Old Master just chuckled to his wife again, and said, "That sure is a smart slave, that Tom, isn't he? Just listen to him talking all that Latin up there again."

Old Tom went on yelling like this about five more times. But when he saw that Old Master wasn't getting out of bed, he yelled, "Master, you better get up out of that bed and put on your shoes and go out there and put out that haystack fire that your cat started, or else your whole damn farm's going to burn up!" I guess that got Old Master up pretty quick!

HANS CHRISTIAN ANDERSEN   (1805–1875)

The Emperor's New Clothes   (Denmark)

> This is the first of our stories to have a single originator. Hans Christian Andersen was a published author of fairy tales, poems, plays, novels, and travel books. As most of his tales (collected in *The Fairy Tales of Hans Christian Andersen* [1872]) were intended for children, they generally have a child as a central character, unlike earlier folk stories that feature adult characters. Like typical folk storytellers, Andersen, the son of an impoverished tailor, based many of his fairy tales on the oral narratives he heard around his home and community during his youth. But the college-educated Andersen revised his stories numerous times to achieve a high level of craft: his plots are more fully developed and tightly structured than those in oral folk narratives, and he used many of the techniques found in modern short stories. In "The Emperor's New Clothes" (1837) the trickster figure appears in the form of two swindlers who dupe the emperor and his court into believing that they are great weavers by appealing to people's fears of appearing stupid or incompetent. Ironically, only a child with no interest in being considered clever or sophisticated can see through the ruse.

Many, many years ago lived an emperor, who thought so much of new clothes that he spent all his money in order to obtain them; his only ambition was to be always well dressed. He did not care for his soldiers, and the theater did not amuse him; the only thing, in fact, he thought anything of was to drive out and show a new suit of clothes. He had a coat for every hour of the day; and as one would say of a king "He is in his cabinet," so one could say of him, "The emperor is in his dressing-room."

The great city where he resided was very gay; every day many strangers from all parts of the globe arrived. One day two swindlers came to this city; they made people believe that they were weavers, and declared they could manufacture the finest cloth to be imagined. Their colors and patterns, they said, were not only exceptionally beautiful, but the clothes made of their material possessed the wonderful quality of being invisible to any man who was unfit for his office or unpardonably stupid.

"That must be wonderful cloth," thought the emperor. "If I were to be dressed in a suit made of this cloth I should be able to find out which men in my empire were unfit for their places, and I could distinguish the clever from the stupid. I must have this cloth woven for me without delay." And he gave a large sum of money to the swindlers, in advance, that they should set to work without any loss of time. They set up two looms, and pretended to be very hard at work, but they did nothing whatever on the looms. They asked for the finest silk and the most precious gold-cloth; all they got they did away with, and worked at the empty looms till late at night.

"I should very much like to know how they are getting on with the cloth," thought the emperor. But he felt rather uneasy when he remembered that he who was not fit for his office could not see it. Personally, he was of the opinion that he had nothing to fear, yet he thought it advisable to send somebody else first to see how matters stood. Everybody in the town knew what a remarkable quality the stuff possessed, and all were anxious to see how bad or stupid their neighbors were.

"I shall send my honest old minister to the weavers," thought the emperor. "He can judge best how the stuff looks, for he is intelligent, and nobody understands his office better than he."

The good old minister went into the room where the swindlers sat before the empty looms. "Heaven preserve us!" he thought, and opened his eyes wide. "I cannot see anything at all," he thought, but he did not say so aloud. Both swindlers requested him to come near, and asked him if he did not admire the exquisite pattern and the beautiful colors, pointing to the empty looms. The poor old minister tried his very best, but he could see nothing, for there was nothing to be seen. "Oh dear," he thought, "can I be so stupid? I should never have thought so, and nobody must know it! Is it possible that I am not fit for my office? No, no, I cannot say that I was unable to see the cloth."

"Now, have you got nothing to say?" said one of the swindlers, while he pretended to be busily weaving.

"Oh, it is very pretty, exceedingly beautiful," replied the old minister looking through his glasses. "What a beautiful pattern, what brilliant colors! I shall tell the emperor that I like the cloth very much."

"We are pleased to hear that," said the two weavers, and described to him the colors and explained the curious pattern. The old minister listened attentively, that he might relate to the emperor what they said; and so he did.

Now the swindlers asked for more money, silk and gold-cloth, which they required for weaving. They kept everything for themselves, and not a thread came near the loom, but they continued, as hitherto, to work at the empty looms.

Soon afterwards the emperor sent another honest courtier to the weavers to see how they were getting on, and if the cloth was nearly finished. Like the old minister, he looked and looked but could see nothing, as there was nothing to be seen.

"Is it not a beautiful piece of cloth?" asked the two swindlers, showing and explaining the magnificent pattern, which, however, did not exist.

"I am not stupid," thought the man. "It is therefore my good appointment for which I am not fit. It is very strange, but I must not let anyone know it"; and he praised the cloth, which he did not see, and expressed his joy at the beautiful colors and the fine pattern. "It is very excellent," he said to the emperor.

Everybody in the whole town talked about the precious cloth. At last the emperor wished to see it himself, while it was still on the loom. With a number of courtiers, including the two who had already been there, he went to the two clever swindlers, who now worked as hard as they could, but without using any thread.

"Is it not magnificent?" said the two old statesmen who had been there before. "Your Majesty must admire the colors and the pattern." And then they pointed to the empty looms, for they imagined the others could see the cloth.

"What is this?" thought the emperor, "I do not see anything at all. That is terrible! Am I stupid? Am I unfit to be emperor? That would indeed be the most dreadful thing that could happen to me."

"Really," he said, turning to the weavers, "your cloth has our most gracious approval." And nodding contentedly he looked at the empty loom, for he did not like to say that he saw nothing. All his attendants, who were with him, looked and looked, and although they could not see anything more than the others, they said, like the emperor, "It is very beautiful." And all advised him to wear the new magnificent clothes at a great procession that was soon to take place. "It is magnificent, beautiful, excellent," one heard them say; everybody seemed to be delighted, and the emperor appointed the two swindlers "Imperial Court weavers."

The whole night previous to the day on which the procession was to take place, the swindlers pretended to work, and burned more than sixteen candles. People should see that they were busy to finish the emperor's new suit. They pretended to take the cloth from the loom, and worked about in the air with big scissors, and sewed with needles without thread, and said at last: "The emperor's new suit is ready now."

The emperor and all his barons then came to the hall; the swindlers held their arms up as if they held something in their hands and said: "These are the trousers!" "This is the coat!" and "Here is the cloak!" and so on. "They are all as light as a cobweb, and one must feel as if one had nothing at all upon the body; but that is just the beauty of them."

"Indeed!" said all the courtiers; but they could not see anything, for there was nothing to be seen.

"Does it please your Majesty now to graciously undress," said the swindlers, "that we may assist your Majesty in putting on the new suit before the large looking-glass?"

The emperor undressed, and the swindlers pretended to put the new suit upon him, one piece after another; and the emperor looked at himself in the glass from every side.

"How well they look! How well they fit!" said all. "What a beautiful pattern! What fine colors! That is a magnificent suit of clothes!"

The master of ceremonies announced that the bearers of the canopy, which was to be carried in the procession, were ready.

"I am ready," said the emperor. "Does not my suit fit me marvellously?" Then he turned once more to the looking-glass, that people should think he admired his garments.

The chamberlains, who were to carry the train, stretched their hands to the ground as if they lifted up a train, and pretended to hold something in their hands; they did not like people to know that they could not see anything.

The emperor marched in the procession under the beautiful canopy, and all who saw him in the street and out of the windows exclaimed: "Indeed, the emperor's new suit is incomparable! What a long train he has! How well it fits him!" Nobody wished to let others know he saw nothing, for then he would have been unfit for his office or too stupid. Never were the emperor's clothes more admired.

"But he has nothing on at all," said a little child at last. "Good heavens! listen to the voice of an innocent child," said the father, and one whispered to the other what the child had said. "But he has nothing on at all," cried at last the whole people. That made a deep impression upon the emperor, for it seemed to him that they were right; but he thought to himself, "Now I must bear up to the end." And the chamberlains walked with still greater dignity, as if they carried the train that did not exist.

Questions for Discussion

1. Make a simple plot outline of each story; identify the exposition, the major conflict, the climax, and the resolution of the conflict. How does the plot or story line of each tale help to make its main point or moral?

2. All of these stories involve a cunning character who tries to deceive others. How successful are these characters? What is implied or suggested about the true nature of power and wisdom by their success or failure?

3. Contrast the portraits of the "weaker" or lower-social-caste characters in these stories. In which stories do these "weaker" characters become stronger as the story develops, and what social commentary does this imply?

4. Several of these stories comment on the relationship between master and subject. Compare the portraits of the masters, the priest, the prince, and the king in these stories. Which seem like wise rulers? Which seem foolish in comparison to their subjects? Which are tricksters and which are tricked by their subjects?

5. How does each story use symbolic objects to advance its plot and to make its moral points? Which story uses the most symbolism? Which story is most "literal" in its use of physical objects?

6. Each of these tales can be read as a lesson in effective storytelling. What does each imply about a successful story in terms of its relationship to reality, to language, and to reader expectations?

Ideas for Writing

1. Write a modern trickster story in which you use some of the situations and techniques in these five tales.

2. Compare two or three of the stories and develop some of the issues raised in the preceding questions.

WASHINGTON IRVING (1783–1859)

The first American-born writer to be taken seriously by the European literary establishment, Washington Irving was also instrumental in bringing a distinctively American voice to the popular folk tale. The youngest child of a successful New York businessman, Irving spent his early career writing for popular Manhattan journals. His first literary success came in 1809 with the publication of *A History of New York, from the Beginning of the World to the End of the Dutch Dynasty*. A rollicking mixture of fact, fiction, and broad character sketch, *A History* was related in the voice of the fictional Diedrich Knickerbocker, a "historian" who seemingly never heard a tale he didn't believe. Ten years later came Irving's next great success, *The Sketch Book of Geoffrey Crayon, Gent.* (1819–20), a collection of observations Irving recorded of his experiences traveling in England, along with a few pieces on American themes. Irving's voice for Crayon was far more refined than his voice for Knickerbocker, and the book was seen by both American and European critics as establishing a new standard for American literature. Interestingly, however, the only two pieces from *The Sketch Book* that are well known today — "Rip Van Winkle" and "The Legend of Sleepy Hollow" — were both written in the less restrained voice of Diedrich Knickerbocker. Irving continued to publish biographies, travel sketches, and other works throughout his life.

The success of "Rip Van Winkle" has been attributed by one critic to its "juxtaposition of solid realism and tenuous myth, . . . the legendary . . . firmly woven with earthy realism."

Rip Van Winkle (1819)
A Posthumous Writing of Diedrich Knickerbocker

> By Woden, God of Saxons,
> From whence comes Wensday, that is Wodensday,
> Truth is a thing that ever I will keep
> Unto thylke day in which I creep into
> My sepulchre ——
> — *Cartwright*

[The following Tale was found among the papers of the late Diedrich Knickerbocker, an old gentleman of New York, who was very curious in the Dutch history of the province and the manners of the descendants from its primitive settlers. His historical researches, however, did not lie

72

so much among books as among men, for the former are lamentably scanty on his favorite topics, whereas he found the old burghers, and still more their wives, rich in that legendary lore so invaluable to true history. Whenever, therefore, he happened upon a genuine Dutch family, snugly shut up in its low-roofed farmhouse, under a spreading sycamore, he looked upon it as a little clasped volume of black letter and studied it with the zeal of a bookworm.

The result of all these researchers was a history of the province during the reign of the Dutch governors, which he published some years since. There have been various opinions as to the literary character of his work, and, to tell the truth, it is not a whit better than it should be. Its chief merit is its scrupulous accuracy, which indeed was a little questioned on its first appearance, but has since been completely established, and it is now admitted into all historical collections as a book of unquestionable authority.

The old gentleman died shortly after the publication of his work, and now that he is dead and gone, it cannot do much harm to his memory to say that his time might have been much better employed in weightier labors. He, however, was apt to ride his hobby his own way; and though it did now and then kick up the dust a little in the eyes of his neighbors and grieve the spirit of some friends, for whom he felt the truest deference and affection, yet his errors and follies are remembered "more in sorrow than in anger," and it begins to be suspected that he never intended to injure or offend. But however his memory may be appreciated by critics, it is still held dear by many folks, whose good opinion is well worth having; particularly by certain biscuit bakers, who have gone so far as to imprint his likeness on their new-year cakes, and have thus given him a chance for immortality, almost equal to being stamped on a Waterloo Medal, or a Queen Anne's Farthing.]

Whoever has made a voyage up the Hudson must remember the Kaatskill Mountains. They are a dismembered branch of the great Appalachian family, and are seen away to the west of the river, swelling up to a noble height and fording it over the surrounding country. Every change of season, every change of weather, indeed, every hour of the day produces some change in the magical hues and shapes of these mountains, and they are regarded by all the good wives, far and near, as perfect barometers. When the weather is fair and settled, they are clothed in blue and purple, and print their bold outlines on the clear evening sky; but, sometimes, when the rest of the landscape is cloudless, they will gather a hood of gray vapors about their summits, which, in the last rays of the setting sun, will glow and light up like a crown of glory.

At the foot of these fairy mountains, the voyager may have described the light smoke curling up from a village, whose shingle roofs gleam among the trees, just where the blue tints of the upland melt away into the fresh green of the nearer landscape. It is a little village of great antiquity, having been founded by some of the Dutch colonists in the early times of the province, just about the beginning of the government of the good Peter Stuyvesant (may he rest in peace!), and there were some of the houses of the original settlers standing within a few years, built of small yellow bricks brought from Holland, having latticed windows and gable fronts, surmounted with weathercocks.

In that same village, and in one of these very houses (which, to tell the precise truth, was sadly time-worn and weather-beaten), there lived many years since, while the country was yet a province of Great Britain, a simple, good-natured fellow of the name of Rip Van Winkle. He was a descendant of the Van Winkles who figured so gallantly in the chivalrous days of Peter Stuyvesant, and accompanied him to the siege of Fort Christina. He inherited, however, but little of the martial character of his ancestors. I have observed that he was a simple, good-natured man; he was, moreover, a kind neighbor, and an obedient, henpecked husband. Indeed, to the latter circumstance might be owing that meekness of spirit which gained him such universal popularity, for those men are most apt to be obsequious and conciliating abroad who are under the discipline of shrews at home. Their tempers, doubtless, are rendered pliant and malleable in the fiery furnace of domestic tribulation, and a curtain lecture is worth all the sermons in the world for teaching the virtues of patience and long-suffering. A termagant wife may, therefore, in some respects, be considered a tolerable blessing; and if so, Rip Van Winkle was thrice blessed.

Certain it is that he was a great favorite among all the good wives of the village, who, as usual with the amiable sex, took his part in all family squabbles and never failed, whenever they talked those matters over in their evening gossipings, to lay all the blame on Dame Van Winkle. The children of the village, too, would shout with joy whenever he approached. He assisted at their sports, made their playthings, taught them to fly kites and shoot marbles, and told them long stories of ghosts, witches, and Indians. Whenever he went dodging about the village, he was surrounded by a troop of them, hanging on his skirts, clambering on his back, and playing a thousand tricks on him with impunity; and not a dog would bark at him throughout the neighborhood.

The great error in Rip's composition was an insuperable aversion to all kinds of profitable labor. It could not be from the want of assiduity or perseverance, for he would sit on a wet rock, with a rod as long and heavy as a Tartar's lance, and fish all day without a murmur, even though he should not be encouraged by a single nibble. He would carry a fowling piece on his shoulder for hours together, trudging through woods and swamps and up hill and down dale to shoot a few squirrels or wild pigeons. He would never refuse to assist a neighbor even in the roughest toil, and was a foremost man at all country frolics for husking Indian corn or building stone fences; the women of the village, too, used to employ him to run their errands and to do such little odd jobs as their less obliging husbands would not do for them. In a word, <u>Rip was</u>

ready to attend to anybody's business but his own; but as to doing family duty and keeping his farm in order, he found it impossible.

In fact, he declared it was of no use to work on his farm; it was the most pestilent little piece of ground in the whole country; everything about it went wrong, and would go wrong, in spite of him. His fences were continually falling to pieces; his cow would either go astray or get among the cabbages; weeds were sure to grow quicker in his fields than anywhere else; the rain always made a point of setting in just as he had some outdoor work to do; so that though his patrimonial estate had dwindled away under his management, acre by acre, until there was little more left than a mere patch of Indian corn and potatoes, yet it was the worst-conditioned farm in the neighborhood.

His children, too, were as ragged and wild as if they belonged to nobody. His son Rip, an urchin begotten in his own likeness, promised to inherit the habits, with the old clothes, of his father. He was generally seen trooping like a colt at his mother's heels, equipped in a pair of his father's cast-off galligaskins, which he had much ado to hold up with one hand as a fine lady does her train in bad weather.

Rip Van Winkle, however, was one of those happy mortals of foolish, well-oiled dispositions who take the world easy, eat white bread or brown, whichever can be got with least thought or trouble, and would rather starve on a penny than work for a pound. If left to himself, he would have whistled life away in perfect contentment; but his wife kept continually dinning in his ears about his idleness, his carelessness, and the ruin he was bringing on his family. Morning, noon, and night, her tongue was incessantly going, and everything he said or did was sure to produce a torrent of household eloquence. Rip had but one way of replying to all lectures of the kind, and that, by frequent use, had grown into a habit. He shrugged his shoulders, shook his head, cast up his eyes, but said nothing. This, however, always provoked a fresh volley from his wife, so that he was fain to draw off his forces and take to the outside of the house — the only side which, in truth, belongs to a henpecked husband.

his wife nags him

Rip's sole domestic adherent was his dog, Wolf, who was as much henpecked as his master, for Dame Van Winkle regarded them as companions in idleness, and even looked upon Wolf with an evil eye as the cause of his master's going so often astray. True it is, in all points of spirit befitting an honorable dog, he was as courageous an animal as ever scoured the woods — but what courage can withstand the ever-during and all-besetting terrors of a woman's tongue? The moment Wolf entered the house his crest fell, his tail drooped to the ground, or curled between his legs, he sneaked about with a gallows air, casting many a sidelong glance at Dame Van Winkle, and at the least flourish of a broomstick or ladle he would fly to the door with yelping precipitation.

Times grew worse and worse with Rip Van Winkle as years of matrimony rolled on; a tart temper never mellows with age, and a sharp tongue is the only edged tool that grows keener with constant use. For a long while he used to console himself, when driven from home, by frequenting a kind of perpetual club of the sages, philosophers, and other idle personages of the village, which held its sessions on a bench before a small inn, designated by a rubicund portrait of His Majesty George the Third. Here they used to sit in the shade through a long, lazy summer's day talking listlessly over village gossip or telling endless sleepy stories about nothing. But it would have been worth any statesman's money to have heard the profound discussions that sometimes took place when by chance an old newspaper fell into their hands from some passing traveler. How solemnly they would listen to the contents, as drawled out by Derrick Van Bummel, the schoolmaster, a dapper, learned little man who was not to be daunted by the most gigantic word in the dictionary; and how sagely they would deliberate upon public events some months after they had taken place.

The opinions of this junto were completely controlled by Nicholas Vedder, a patriarch of the village and landlord of the inn, at the door of which he took his seat from morning till night, just moving sufficiently to avoid the sun and keep in the shade of a large tree, so that the neighbors could tell the hour by his movements as accurately as by a sundial. It is true he was rarely heard to speak, but smoked his pipe incessantly. His adherents, however (for every great man has his adherents), perfectly understood him, and knew how to gather his opinions. When anything that was read or related displeased him, he was observed to smoke his pipe vehemently and to send forth short, frequent, and angry puffs; but when pleased, he would inhale the smoke slowly and tranquilly and emit it in light and placid clouds, and sometimes, taking the pipe from his mouth and letting the fragrant vapor curl about his nose, would gravely nod his head in token of perfect approbation.

From even this stronghold the unlucky Rip was at length routed by his termagant wife, who would suddenly break in upon the tranquillity of the assemblage and call the members all to naught; nor was that august personage, Nicholas Vedder himself, sacred from the daring tongue of this terrible virago, who charged him outright with encouraging her husband in habits of idleness.

Poor Rip was at last reduced almost to despair, and his only alternative, to escape from the labor of the farm and clamor of his wife, was to take gun in hand and stroll away into the woods. Here he would sometimes seat himself at the foot of a tree and share the contents of his wallet with Wolf, with whom he sympathized as a fellow sufferer in persecution. "Poor Wolf," he would say, "thy mistress leads thee a dog's life of it; but never mind, my lad, whilst I live thou shalt never want a friend to stand by thee!" Wolf would wag his tail, look wistfully in his master's face, and if dogs can feel pity, I verily believe he reciprocated the sentiment with all his heart.

In a long ramble of the kind of a fine autumnal day, Rip had unconsciously scrambled to one of the highest parts of the Kaatskill Mountains. He was after his favorite sport of squirrel shooting, and the still solitudes had echoed and re-echoed with the reports of his gun. Panting and fatigued, he threw himself, late in the afternoon, on a green knoll, covered with mountain herbage, that crowned the brow of a precipice. From an opening between the trees he could overlook all the lower country for many a mile of rich woodland. He saw at a distance the lordly Hudson, far, far below him, moving on its silent but majestic course, with the reflection of a purple cloud or the sail of a lagging bark here and there sleeping on its glassy bosom, and at last losing itself in the blue highlands.

On the other side he looked down into a deep mountain glen, wild, lonely, and shagged, the bottom filled with fragments from the impending cliffs, and scarcely lighted by the reflected rays of the setting sun. For some time Rip lay musing on this scene. Evening was gradually advancing; the mountains began to throw their long blue shadows over the valleys. He saw that it would be dark long before he could reach the village, and he heaved a heavy sigh when he thought of encountering the terrors of Dame Van Winkle.

As he was about to descend, he heard a voice from a distance, hallooing, "Rip Van Winkle! Rip Van Winkle!" He looked around, but could see nothing but a crow winging its solitary flight across the mountain. He thought his fancy must have deceived him, and turned again to descend, when he heard the same cry ring through the still evening air, "Rip Van Winkle! Rip Van Winkle!" At the same time Wolf bristled up his back and, giving a low growl, skulked to his master's side, looking fearfully down into the glen. Rip now felt a vague apprehension stealing over him; he looked anxiously in the same direction and perceived a strange figure slowly toiling up the rocks, and bending under the weight of something he carried on his back. He was surprised to see any human being in this lonely and unfrequented place, but supposing it to be some one of the neighborhood in need of his assistance, he hastened down to yield it.

On nearer approach he was still more surprised at the singularity of the stranger's appearance. He was a short, square-built old fellow, with thick, bushy hair and a grizzled beard. His dress was of the antique Dutch fashion — a cloth jerkin strapped around the waist and several pairs of breeches, the outer one of ample volume, decorated with rows of buttons down the sides and bunches at the knees. He bore on his shoulder a stout keg that seemed full of liquor, and made signs for Rip to approach and assist him with the load. Though rather shy and distrustful of this new acquaintance, Rip complied with his usual alacrity, and mutually relieving one another, they clambered up a narrow gully, apparently the dry bed of a mountain torrent. As they ascended, Rip every now and then heard long rolling peals, like distant thunder, that seemed to issue out of a deep ravine, or rather cleft, between lofty rocks, toward which their rugged path conducted. He paused for an instant, but supposing it to be the muttering of one of those transient thunder showers which often take place in mountain heights, he proceeded. Passing through the ravine, they came to a hollow, like a small amphitheater, surrounded by perpendicular precipices, over the brinks of which impending trees shot their branches, so that you only caught glimpses of the azure sky and the bright evening cloud. During the whole time, Rip and his companion had labored on in silence, for though the former marveled greatly what could be the object of carrying a keg of liquor up this wild mountain, yet there was something strange and incomprehensible about the unknown that inspired awe and checked familiarity.

On entering the amphitheater, new objects of wonder were to be seen. On a level spot in the center was a company of odd-looking personages playing at ninepins. They were dressed in a quaint, outlandish fashion; some wore short doublets, others jerkins, with long knives in their belts, and most of them had enormous breeches, of similar style with that of the guide's. Their visages, too, were peculiar; one had a large beard, broad face, and small piggish eyes, the face of another seemed to consist entirely of nose and was surmounted by a white sugarloaf hat set off with a little red cock's tail. They all had beards, of various shapes and colors. There was one who seemed to be the commander. He was a stout old gentleman, with a weather-beaten countenance; he wore a laced doublet, broad belt and hanger, high-crowned hat and feather, red stockings, and high-heeled shoes, with roses in them. The whole group reminded Rip of the figures in an old Flemish painting, in the parlor of Dominie Van Shaick, the village parson, and which had been brought over from Holland at the time of the settlement.

What seemed particularly odd to Rip was that though these folks were evidently amusing themselves, yet they maintained the gravest faces, the most mysterious silence, and were, withal, the most melancholy party of pleasure he had ever witnessed. Nothing interrupted the stillness of the scene but the noise of the balls, which, whenever they were rolled, echoed along the mountains like rumbling peals of thunder.

As Rip and his companion approached them, they suddenly desisted from their play and stared at him with such fixed, statuelike gaze and such strange, uncouth, lackluster countenances that his heart turned within him and his knees smote together. His companion now emptied the contents of the keg into large flagons and made signs to him to wait upon the company. He obeyed with fear and trembling; they quaffed the liquor in profound silence and then returned to their game.

By degrees Rip's awe and apprehension subsided. He even ventured, when no eye was fixed upon him, to taste the beverage, which he found had much of the flavor of excellent Hollands. He was naturally a thirsty soul and was soon tempted to repeat the draft. One taste provoked another; and he reiterated his visits to the flagon so often that at length his senses were overpowered, his eyes swam in his head, his head gradually declined, and he fell into a deep sleep.

On waking, he found himself on the green knoll whence he had first seen the old man of the glen. He rubbed his eyes — it was a bright, sunny morning.

The birds were hopping and twittering among the bushes, and the eagle was wheeling aloft and breasting the pure mountain breeze. "Surely," thought Rip, "I have not slept here all night." He recalled the occurrences before he fell asleep. The strange man with a keg of liquor — the mountain ravine — the wild retreat among the rocks — the woebegone party at ninepins — the flagon — "Oh! That flagon! That wicked flagon!" thought Rip. "What excuse shall I make to Dame Van Winkle?"

He looked around for his gun, but in place of the clean, well-oiled fowling piece he found an old firelock lying by him, the barrel encrusted with rust, the lock falling off, and the stock worm-eaten. He now suspected that the grave roysters of the mountain had put a trick upon him, and, having dosed him with liquor, had robbed him of his gun. Wolf, too, had disappeared, but he might have strayed away after a squirrel or partridge. He whistled after him and shouted his name, but all in vain; the echoes repeated his whistle and shout, but no dog was to be seen.

He determined to revisit the scene of the last evening's gambol, and if he met with any of the party, to demand his dog and gun. As he rose to walk, he found himself stiff in the joints and wanting in his usual activity. "These mountain beds do not agree with me," thought Rip, "and if this frolic should lay me up with a fit of the rheumatism, I shall have a blessed time with Dame Van Winkle." With some difficulty he got down into the glen; he found the gully up which he and his companion had ascended the preceding evening, but to his astonishment a mountain stream was now foaming down it, leaping from rock to rock and filling the glen with babbling murmurs. He, however, made shift to scramble up its sides, working his toilsome way through thickets of birch, sassafras, and witch hazel, and sometimes tripped up or entangled by the wild grapevines that twisted their coils or tendrils from tree to tree and spread a kind of network in his path.

At length he reached to where the ravine had opened through the cliffs to the amphitheater, but no traces of such opening remained. The rocks presented a high, impenetrable wall over which the torrent came tumbling in a sheet of feathery foam and fell into a broad, deep basin, black from the shadows of the surrounding forest. Here, then, poor Rip was brought to a stand. He again called and whistled after his dog; he was only answered by the cawing of a flock of idle crows, sporting high in air about a dry tree that overhung a sunny precipice, and who, secure in their elevation, seemed to look down and scoff at the poor man's perplexities. What was to be done? The morning was passing away, and Rip felt famished for want of his breakfast. He grieved to give up his dog and gun, he dreaded to meet his wife, but it would not do to starve among the mountains. He shook his head, shouldered the rusty firelock, and, with a heart full of trouble and anxiety, turned his steps homeward.

As he approached the village he met a number of people, but none whom he knew, which somewhat surprised him, for he had thought himself acquainted with every one in the country around. Their dress, too, was of a different fashion from that to which he was accustomed. They all stared at him with equal marks of surprise, and whenever they cast their eyes upon him invariably stroked their chins. The constant recurrence of this gesture induced Rip, involuntarily, to do the same, when, to his astonishment, he found his beard had grown a foot long!

He had now entered the skirts of the village. A troop of strange children ran at his heels, hooting after him and pointing at his gray beard. The dogs, too, not one of which he recognized for an old acquaintance, barked at him as he passed. The very village was altered; it was larger and more populous. There were rows of houses which he had never seen before, and those which had been his familiar haunts had disappeared. Strange names were over the doors — strange faces at the windows — everything was strange. His mind now misgave him; he began to doubt whether both he and the world around him were not bewitched. Surely this was his native village, which he had left but the day before. There stood the Kaatskill Mountains — there ran the silver Hudson at a distance — there was every hill and dale precisely as it had always been. Rip was sorely perplexed. "That flagon last night," thought he, "has addled my poor head sadly!"

It was with some difficulty that he found the way to his own house, which he approached with silent awe, expecting every moment to hear the shrill voice of Dame Van Winkle. He found the house gone to decay — the roof fallen in, the windows shattered, and the doors off the hinges. A half-starved dog that looked like Wolf was skulking about it. Rip called him by name, but the cur snarled, showed his teeth, and passed on. This was an unkind cut indeed. "My very dog," sighed poor Rip, "has forgotten me!"

He entered the house, which, to tell the truth, Dame Van Winkle had always kept in neat order. It was empty, forlorn, and apparently abandoned. This desolateness overcame all his connubial fears — he called loudly for his wife and children; the lonely chambers rang for a moment with his voice, and then all again was silence.

He now hurried forth and hastened to his old resort, the village inn — but it too was gone. A large, rickety, wooden building stood in its place, with great gaping windows, some of them broken and mended with old hats and petticoats, and over the door was painted, "the Union Hotel, by Jonathan Doolittle." Instead of the great tree that used to shelter the quiet little Dutch inn of yore, there now was reared a tall, naked pole, with something on the top that looked like a red nightcap, and from it was fluttering a flag, on which was a singular assemblage of stars and stripes — all this was strange and incomprehensible. He recognized on the sign, however, the ruby face of King George, under which he had smoked so many a peaceful pipe; but even this was singularly metamorphosed. The red coat was changed for one of blue and buff, a sword was held in the hand instead of a scepter, the head was decorated with a cocked hat, and underneath was painted in large characters, GENERAL WASHINGTON.

There was, as usual, a crowd of folk about the door, but none that Rip recollected. The very character of the people seemed changed. There was a busy, bustling, disputatious tone about it, instead of the accustomed phlegm and drowsy tranquillity. He looked in vain for the sage Nicholas Vedder, with his broad face, double chin, and fair long pipe, uttering clouds of tobacco smoke instead of idle speeches; or Van Bummel, the schoolmaster, doling forth the contents of an ancient newspaper. In place of these, a lean, billious-looking fellow, with his pockets full of handbills, was haranguing vehemently about rights of citizens — elections — members of congress — liberty — Bunker's Hill — heroes of seventy-six — and other words which were a perfect Babylonish jargon to the bewildered Van Winkle.

new political ideas

The appearance of Rip, with his long, grizzled beard, his rusty fowling piece, his uncouth dress, and an army of women and children at his heels, soon attracted the attention of the tavern politicians. They crowded around him, eying him from head to foot with great curiosity. The orator bustled up to him and, drawing him partly aside, inquired "on which side he voted?" Rip stared in vacant stupidity. Another short but busy little fellow pulled him by the arm, and, rising on tiptoe, inquired in his ear, "whether he was Federal or Democrat?" Rip was equally at a loss to comprehend the question; when a knowing, self-important old gentleman in a sharp cocked hat made his way through the crowd, putting them to the right and left with his elbows as he passed, and, planting himself before Van Winkle, with one arm akimbo, the other resting on his cane, his keen eyes and sharp hat penetrating, as it were, into his very soul, demanded in an austere tone, "what brought him to the election with a gun on his shoulder, and a mob at his heels, and whether he meant to breed a riot in the village?" "Alas! Gentlemen," cried Rip, somewhat dismayed, "I am a poor, quiet man, a native of the place, and a loyal subject of the king, God bless him!"

Here a general shout burst from the bystanders. "A tory! A tory! A spy! A refugee! Hustle him! Away with him!" It was with great difficulty that the self-important man in the cocked hat restored order; and, having assumed a tenfold austerity of brow, demanded again of the unknown culprit what he came there for and whom he was seeking. The poor man humbly assured him that he meant no harm, but merely came there in search of some of his neighbors, who used to keep about the tavern.

"Well — who are they? Name them."

Rip bethought himself a moment, and inquired, "Where's Nicholas Vedder?"

There was a silence for a little while, when an old man replied, in a thin, piping voice, "Nicholas Vedder! Why, he is dead and gone these eighteen years! There was a wooden tombstone in the churchyard that used to tell all about him, but that's rotten and gone too."

"Where's Brom Dutcher?"

"Oh, he went off to the army in the beginning of the war; some say he was killed at the storming of Stony Point — others say he was drowned in a squall at the foot of Antony's Nose. I don't know — he never came back again."

"Where's Van Bummel, the schoolmaster?"

"He went off to the wars, too, was a great militia general, and is now in congress."

Rip's heart died away at hearing of these sad changes in his home and friends, and finding himself thus alone in the world. Every answer puzzled him, too, by treating of such enormous lapses of time and of matters which he could not understand: war — congress — Stony Point. He had no courage to ask after any more friends, but cried out in despair, "Does nobody here know Rip Van Winkle?"

"Oh, Rip Van Winkle!" exclaimed two or three. "Oh, to be sure! That's Rip Van Winkle yonder, leaning against the tree."

Rip looked, and beheld a precise counterpart of himself as he went up the mountain: apparently as lazy, and certainly as ragged. The poor fellow was now completely confounded. He doubted his own identity, and whether he was himself or another man. In the midst of his bewilderment, the man in the cocked hat demanded who he was, and what was his name?

"God knows," exclaimed he, at his wit's end. "I'm not myself — I'm somebody else — that's me yonder — no — that's somebody else got into my shoes — I was myself last night, but I fell asleep on the mountain, and they've changed my gun, and everything's changed, and I'm changed, and I can't tell what's my name, or who I am!"

The bystanders began now to look at each other, nod, wink significantly, and tap their fingers against their foreheads. There was a whisper also about securing the gun and keeping the old fellow from doing mischief, at the very suggestion of which the self-important man in the cocked hat retired with some precipitation. At this critical moment a fresh, comely woman pressed through the throng to get a peep at the gray-bearded man. She had a chubby child in her arms, which, frightened at his looks, began to cry. "Hush, Rip," cried she, "hush, you little fool; the old man won't hurt you." The name of the child, the air of the mother, the tone of her voice, all awakened a train of recollections in his mind. "What is your name, my good woman?" asked he.

"Judith Gardenier."

"And your father's name?"

"Ah, poor man, Rip Van Winkle was his name, but it's twenty years since he went away from home with his gun, and never has been heard of since — his dog came home without him, but whether he shot himself, or was carried away by the Indians, nobody can tell. I was then but a little girl."

Rip had but one question more to ask; but he put it with a faltering voice: "Where's your mother?"

"Oh, she too had died but a short time since; she broke a blood vessel in a fit of passion at a New England peddler."

There was a drop of comfort, at least, in this intelligence. The honest man could contain himself no longer. He caught his daughter and her child in his arms. "I am your father!" cried he. "Young Rip Van Winkle once — old Rip Van Winkle now! Does nobody know poor Rip Van Winkle?"

All stood amazed, until an old woman, tottering out from among the crowd, put her hand to her brow and, peering under it in his face for a moment, exclaimed, "Sure enough! It is Rip Van Winkle — it is himself! Welcome home again, old neighbor. Why, where have you been these twenty long years?"

Rip's story was soon told, for the whole twenty years had been to him but as one night. The neighbors stared when they heard it; some were seen to wink at each other and put their tongues in their cheeks, and the self-important man in the cocked hat, who, when the alarm was over, had returned to the field, screwed down the corners of his mouth and shook his head — upon which there was a general shaking of the head throughout the assemblage.

It was determined, however, to take the opinion of old Peter Vanderdonk, who was seen slowly advancing up the road. He was a descendant of the historian of that name, who wrote one of the earliest accounts of the province. Peter was the most ancient inhabitant of the village, and well versed in all the wonderful events and traditions of the neighborhood. He recollected Rip at once and corroborated his story in the most satisfactory manner. He assured the company that it was a fact, handed down from his ancestor the historian, that the Kaatskill Mountains had always been haunted by strange beings. That it was affirmed that the great Hendrick Hudson, the first discoverer of the river and country, kept a kind of vigil there every twenty years, with his crew of the *Half Moon*, being permitted in this way to revisit the scenes of his enterprise and keep a guardian eye upon the river and the great city called by his name. That his father had once seen them in their old Dutch dresses playing at ninepins in a hollow of the mountain, and that he himself had heard, one summer afternoon, the sound of their balls, like distant peals of thunder.

To make a long story short, the company broke up and returned to the more important concerns of the election. Rip's daughter took him home to live with her; she had a snug, well-furnished house, and a stout, cheery farmer for a husband, whom Rip recollected for one of the urchins that used to climb upon his back. As to Rip's son and heir, who was the ditto of himself, seen leaning against the tree, he was employed to work on the farm, but evinced a hereditary disposition to attend to anything else but his business.

Rip now resumed his old walks and habits; he soon found many of his former cronies, though all rather the worse for the wear and tear of time, and preferred making friends among the rising generation, with whom he soon grew into great favor.

[handwritten margin note: went back to old routine]

Having nothing to do at home, and being arrived at that happy age when a man can be idle with impunity, he took his place once more on the bench at the inn door and was reverenced as one of the patriarchs of the village, and a chronicle of the old times "before the war." It was some time before he could get into the regular track of gossip, or could be made to comprehend the strange events that had taken place during his torpor. How that there had been a revolutionary war — that the country had thrown off the yoke of old England — and that, instead of being a subject of his Majesty George the Third, he was now a free citizen of the United States. Rip, in fact, was no politician — the changes of states and empires made but little impression on him; but there was one species of despotism under which he had long groaned, and that was — petticoat government. Happily that was at an end; he had got his neck out of the yoke of matrimony and could go in and out whenever he pleased, without dreading the tyranny of Dame Van Winkle. Whenever her name was mentioned, however, he shook his head, shrugged his shoulders, and cast up his eyes, which might pass either for an expression of resignation to his fate or joy at his deliverance.

He used to tell his story to every stranger that arrived at Mr. Doolittle's hotel. He was observed, at first, to vary on some points every time he told it, which was, doubtless, owing to his having so recently awaked. It at last settled down precisely to the tale I have related, and not a man, woman, or child in the neighborhood but knew it by heart. Some always pretended to doubt the reality of it, and insisted that Rip had been out of his head, and that this was one point on which he always remained flighty. The old Dutch inhabitants, however, almost universally gave it full credit. Even to this day they never hear a thunderstorm of a summer afternoon about the Kaatskill but they say Hendrick Hudson and his crew are at their game of ninepins; and it is a common wish of all henpecked husbands in the neighborhood, when life hangs heavy on their hands, that they might have a quieting draft out of Rip Van Winkle's flagon.

NOTE

The foregoing Tale, one would suspect, had been suggested to Mr. Knickerbocker by a little German superstition about the Emperor Frederick *der Rothbart* and the Kypphaüser mountain. The subjoined note, however, which he had appended to the tale, shows that it is an absolute fact, narrated with his usual fidelity:

"The story of Rip Van Winkle may seem incredible to many, but nevertheless I give it my full belief, for I know the vicinity of our old Dutch settlements to have been very subject to marvelous events and appearances. Indeed, I have heard many stranger stories than this, in the villages along the Hudson, all of which were too well authenticated to admit of a doubt. I have even talked with Rip Van Winkle myself, who, when last I saw him, was a very venerable old man and so perfectly rational and consistent on every other point that I think no conscientious person could refuse to take this into the bargain; nay, I have seen a certificate on the subject taken before a country justice and signed with a cross, in the justice's own handwriting. The story, therefore, is beyond the possibility of doubt.

D. K."

POSTSCRIPT

The following are traveling notes from a memorandum book of Mr. Knickerbocker:

The Kaatsberg, or Catskill Mountains, have always been a region full of fable. The Indians considered them the abode of spirits, who influenced the weather, spreading sunshine or clouds over the landscape, and sending good or bad hunting seasons. They were ruled by an old squaw spirit, said to be their mother. She dwelt on the highest peak of the Catskills and had charge of the doors of day and night, to open and shut them at the proper hour. She hung up the new moons in the skies and cut up the old ones into stars. In times of drought, if properly propitiated, she would spin light summer clouds out of cobwebs and morning dew and send them off from the crest of the mountain, flake after flake, like flakes of carded cotton, to float in the air; until, dissolved by the heat of the sun, they would fall in gentle showers, causing the grass to spring, the fruits to ripen, and the corn to grow an inch an hour. If displeased, however, she would brew up clouds black as ink, sitting in the midst of them like a bottle-bellied spider in the midst of its web; and when these clouds broke, woe betide the valleys!

In old times, say the Indian traditions, there was a kind of Manitou or Spirit, who kept about the wildest recesses of the Catskill Mountains, and took a mischievous pleasure in wreaking all kinds of evils and vexations upon the red men. Sometimes he would assume the form of a bear, a panther, or a deer, lead the bewildered hunter a weary chase through tangled forests and among ragged rocks, and then spring off with a loud ho! ho! leaving him aghast on the brink of a beetling precipice or raging torrent.

The favorite abode of this Manitou is still shown. It is a great rock or cliff on the loneliest part of the mountains, and, from the flowering vines which clamber about it and the wild flowers which abound in its neighborhood, is known by the name of the Garden Rock. Near the foot of it is a small lake, the haunt of the solitary bittern, with water snakes basking in the sun on the leaves of the pond lilies which lie on the surface. This place was held in great awe by the Indians, insomuch that the boldest hunter would not pursue his game within its precincts. Once upon a time, however, a hunter who had lost his way penetrated to the Garden Rock, where he beheld a number of gourds placed in the crotches of trees. One of these he seized and made off with, but in the hurry of his retreat he let it fall among the rocks, when a great stream gushed forth, which washed him away and swept him down precipices, where he was dashed to pieces, and the stream made its way to the Hudson and continues to flow to the present day, being the identical stream known by the name of the Kaaters-kill.

Questions for Discussion

1. "Rip Van Winkle" begins with an epigraph and three-paragraph preface and ends with a brief note. What comment do these literary devices make about the story? How do they influence your reading and interpretation?
2. Irving based this story on a German folk tale, from which he drew its supernatural elements. But there is also evidence for reading the story more realistically. Can you relate the plot of "Rip Van Winkle" in a way that makes it more plausible as a "realistic" short story?
3. Irving has long been praised for his powers of description. What do his descriptions of setting — the village, before and after Rip's long sleep, and the natural wonders of the Kaatskills (Catskills) — contribute to the overall effect of the story?
4. Irving's characterization of Rip has been called a stereotype of the pre-Revolutionary American male as seen by eighteenth- and nineteenth-century Europeans. In addition, American life changed drastically over the course of Rip's sleep. Do you see any social or political implications in these elements of the story?

Ideas for Writing

1. Write an interpretation of the story that focuses on the layers of voices through which it is presented — the author of the three-paragraph preface and the concluding note; the historian Diedrich Knickerbocker, who tells the story proper; Knickerbocker's unnamed sources for the story; and Rip Van Winkle himself.
2. Write an updated version of "Rip Van Winkle," a story of someone "waking up" today after a twenty-year sleep.

NATHANIEL HAWTHORNE   (1804–1864)

Descended from a New England Puritan family, Nathaniel Hawthorne was born in Salem, Massachusetts, site of the infamous 1692 witch trials. He began writing stories as a youth, and throughout his career most of his fiction explored issues of guilt and historic responsibility for the repressive legacy of the Puritans — in part, perhaps, because one of his ancestors was a judge at the Salem trials. Hawthorne's first story collection, *Twice-Told Tales* (1837), was followed in 1846 by *Mosses from an Olde Manse*. Unsuccessful as a commercial writer, Hawthorne had to rely on government jobs and diplomatic positions to support himself and his family for most of his life. He achieved fame with his novel of adultery in Puritan society, *The Scarlet Letter* (1850), and in 1851 he published another powerful novel of the colonial past, *The House of the Seven Gables*. Hawthorne wrote several other volumes of stories and children's stories, as well as two more novels, *The Blithedale Romance* (1852) and *The Marble Faun* (1860). Many of Hawthorne's tales are set in colonial America, "in those strange old times when fantastic dreams and madmen's reveries were realized among the actual circumstances of life." Obsessed with issues of guilt, sin, and responsibility, Hawthorne often wrote in the form of the parable or allegory. Unlike traditional religious allegories, however, Hawthorne's tales cannot be decoded into simple "good versus evil" dichotomies, as the following two stories from *Twice-Told Tales* suggest.

Young Goodman Brown   (1835)

↳ the end: symbolic

two forces

Young Goodman Brown came forth at sunset into the street at Salem village; but put his head back, after crossing the threshold, to exchange a parting kiss with his young wife. And Faith, as the wife was aptly named, thrust her own pretty head into the street, letting the wind play with the pink ribbons of her cap while she called to Goodman Brown.   *↳ life, liveliness*

"Dearest heart," whispered she, softly and rather sadly, when her lips were close to his ear, "prithee put off your journey until sunrise and sleep in your own bed to-night. A lone woman is troubled with such dreams and such thoughts that she's afeared of herself sometimes. Pray tarry with me this night, dear husband, of all nights in the year."

"My love and my Faith," replied young Goodman Brown, "of all nights in the year, this one night must I tarry away from thee. My journey, as thou callest it, forth and back again, must needs be done 'twixt now and sunrise. What, my sweet, pretty wife, dost thou doubt me already, and we but three months married?"

wishful statement

"Then God bless you!" said Faith, with the pink ribbons; "and may you find all well when you come back."

"Amen!" cried Goodman Brown. "Say thy prayers, dear Faith, and go to bed at dusk, and no harm will come to thee."

So they parted; and the young man pursued his way until, being about to turn the corner by the meeting-house, he looked back and saw the head of

already + a look of uncertainty

Faith still peeping after him with a melancholy air, in spite of her pink ribbons.

"Poor little Faith!" thought he, for his heart smote him. "What a wretch am I to leave her on such an errand! She talks of dreams, too. Methought as she spoke there was trouble in her face, as if a dream had warned her what work is to be done tonight. But no, no; 'twould kill her to think it. Well, she's a blessed angel on earth; and after this one night I'll cling to her skirts and follow her to heaven."

fw

With this excellent resolve for the future, Goodman Brown felt himself justified in making more haste on his present evil purpose. He had taken a dreary road, darkened by all the gloomiest trees of the forest, which barely stood aside to let the narrow path creep through, and closed immediately behind. It was all as lonely as could be; and there is this peculiarity in such a solitude, that the traveller knows not who may be concealed by the innumerable trunks and the thick boughs overhead; so that with lonely footsteps he may yet be passing through an unseen multitude.

"There may be a devilish Indian behind every tree," said Goodman Brown to himself and he glanced fearfully behind him as he added, "What if the devil himself should be at my very elbow!"

His head being turned back, he passed a crook of the road, and, looking forward again, beheld the figure of a man, in grave and decent attire, seated at the foot of an old tree. He arose at Goodman Brown's approach and walked onward side by side with him.

"You are late, Goodman Brown," said he. "The clock of the Old South was striking as I came through Boston, and that is full fifteen minutes agone."

double meaning

"Faith kept me back a while," replied the young man, with a tremor in his voice, caused by the sudden appearance of his companion, though not wholly unexpected.

It was now deep dusk in the forest, and deepest in that part of it where these two were journeying. As nearly as could be discerned, the second traveller was about fifty years old, apparently in the same rank of life as Goodman Brown, and bearing a considerable resemblance to him, though perhaps more in expression than features. Still they might have been taken for father and son. And yet, though the elder person was as simply clad as the younger, and as simple in manner too, he had an indescribable air of one who knew the world, and who would not have felt abashed at the governor's dinner table or in King William's court, were it possible that his affairs should call him thither. But the only thing about him that could be fixed upon as remarkable was his staff, which bore the likeness of a great black snake, so curiously wrought that it might almost be seen to twist and wriggle itself like a living serpent. This, of course, must have been an ocular deception, assisted by the uncertain light.

"Come, Goodman Brown," cried his fellow-traveller, "this is a dull pace for the beginning of a journey. Take my staff, if you are so soon weary."

"Friend," said the other, exchanging his slow pace for a full stop, "having kept covenant by meeting thee here, it is my purpose now to return whence I came. I have scruples touching the matter thou wot'st of."

"Sayest thou so?" replied he of the serpent, smiling apart. "Let us walk on, nevertheless, reasoning as we go; and if I convince thee not thou shalt turn back. We are but a little way in the forest yet."

"Too far! too far!" exclaimed the goodman, unconsciously resuming his walk. "My father never went into the woods on such an errand, nor his father before him. We have been a race of honest men and good Christians since the days of the martyrs; and shall I be the first of the name of Brown that ever took this path and kept—"

"Such company, thou wouldst say," observed the elder person, interrupting his pause. "Well said, Goodman Brown! I have been as well acquainted with your family as with ever a one among the Puritans; and that's no trifle to say. I helped your grandfather, the constable, when he lashed the Quaker woman so smartly through the streets of Salem; and it was I that brought your father a pitch-pine knot, kindled at my own hearth, to set fire to an Indian village, in King Philip's war. They were my good friends, both; and many a pleasant walk have we had along this path, and returned merrily after midnight. I would fain be friends with you for their sake."

"If it be as thou sayest," replied Goodman Brown, "I marvel they never spoke of these matters; or, verily, I marvel not, seeing that the least rumor of the sort would have driven them from New England. We are a people of prayer, and good works to boot, and abide no such wickedness."

"Wickedness or not," said the traveller with the twisted staff, "I have a very general acquaintance here in New England. The deacons of many a church have drunk the communion wine with me; the selectmen of divers towns make me their chairman; and a majority of the Great and General Court are firm supporters of my interest. The governor and I, too—But these are state secrets."

"Can this be so?" cried Goodman Brown, with a stare of amazement at his undisturbed companion. "Howbeit, I have nothing to do with the governor and council; they have their own ways, and are no rule for a simple husbandman like me. But, were I to go on with thee, how should I meet the eye of that good old man, our minister, at Salem village? Oh, his voice would make me tremble both Sabbath day and lecture day."

Thus far the elder traveller had listened with due gravity; but now burst into a fit of irrepressible mirth, shaking himself so violently that his snake-like staff actually seemed to wriggle in sympathy.

"Ha! ha! ha!" shouted he again and again; then composing himself, "Well, go on, Goodman Brown, go on; but, prithee don't kill me with laughing."

"Well, then, to end the matter at once," said Goodman Brown, considerably nettled, "there is my wife, Faith. It would break her dear little heart; and I'd rather break my own."

"Nay, if that be the case," answered the other, "e'en go thy ways, Goodman Brown. I would not for twenty old women like the one hobbling before us that Faith should come to any harm."

As he spoke he pointed his staff at a female figure on the path, in whom Goodman Brown recognized a very pious and exemplary dame, who had taught him his catechism in youth, and was still his moral and spiritual adviser, jointly with the minister and Deacon Gookin.

"A marvel, truly, that Goody Cloyse should be so far in the wilderness at nightfall," said he. "But with your leave, friend, I shall take a cut through the woods until we have left this Christian woman behind. Being a stranger to you, she might ask whom I was consorting with and whither I was going."

"Be it so," said his fellow-traveller. "Betake you the woods, and let me keep the path."

Accordingly the young man turned aside, but took care to watch his companion, who advanced softly along the road until he had come within a staff's length of the old dame. She, meanwhile, was making the best of her way, with singular speed for so aged a woman, and mumbling some indistinct words — a prayer, doubtless — as she went. The traveller put forth his staff and touched her withered neck with what seemed the serpent's tail.

"The devil!" screamed the pious old lady.

"Then Goody Cloyse knows her old friend?" observed the traveller, confronting her and leaning on his writhing stick.

"Ah, forsooth, and is it your worship indeed?" cried the good dame. "Yea, truly is it, and in the very image of my old gossip, Goodman Brown, the grandfather of the silly fellow that now is. But — would your worship believe it? — my broomstick hath strangely disappeared, stolen, as I suspect, by that unhanged witch, Goody Cory, and that, too, when I was all anointed with the juice of smallage, and cinquefoil, and wolf's bane —"

"Mingled with fine wheat and the fat of a new-born babe," said the shape of old Goodman Brown.

"Ah, your worship knows the recipe," cried the old lady, cackling aloud. "So, as I was saying, being all ready for the meeting, and no horse to ride on, I made up my mind to foot it; for they tell me there is a nice young man to be taken into communion tonight. But now your good worship will lend me your arm, and we shall be there in a twinkling."

"That can hardly be," answered her friend. "I may not spare you my arm, Goody Cloyse; but here is my staff, if you will."

So saying, he threw it down at her feet, where, perhaps, it assumed life, being one of the rods which its owner had formerly lent to the Egyptian magi. Of this fact, however, Goodman Brown could not take cognizance. He had cast up his eyes in astonishment, and, looking down again, beheld neither Goody

Cloyse nor the serpentine staff but his fellow-traveller alone, who waited for him as calmly as if nothing had happened.

"That old woman taught me my catechism," said the young man; and there was a world of meaning in this simple comment.

They continued to walk onward, while the elder traveller exhorted his companion to make good speed and persevere in the path, discoursing so aptly that his arguments seemed rather to spring up in the bosom of his auditor than to be suggested by himself. As they went, he plucked a branch of maple to serve for a walking stick, and began to strip it of the twigs and little boughs, which were wet with evening dew. The moment his fingers touched them they became strangely withered and dried up as with a week's sunshine. Thus the pair proceeded, at a good free pace, until suddenly, in a gloomy hollow of the road, Goodman Brown sat himself down on the stump of a tree and refused to go any farther.

"Friend," said he, stubbornly, "my mind is made up. Not another step will I budge on this errand. What if a wretched old woman do choose to go to the devil when I thought she was going to heaven: is that any reason why I should quit my dear Faith and go after her?"

"You will think better of this by and by," said his acquaintance, composedly. "Sit here and rest yourself a while; and when you feel like moving again, there is my staff to help you along."

Without more words, he threw his companion the maple stick, and was as speedily out of sight as if he had vanished into the deepening gloom. The young man sat a few moments by the roadside, applauding himself greatly, and thinking with how clear a conscience he should meet the minister in his morning walk, nor shrink from the eye of good old Deacon Gookin. And what calm sleep would be his that very night, which was to have been spent so wickedly, but so purely and sweetly now, in the arms of Faith! Amidst these pleasant and praiseworthy meditations, Goodman Brown heard the tramp of horses along the road, and deemed it advisable to conceal himself within the verge of the forest, conscious of the guilty purpose that had brought him thither, though now so happily turned from it.

On came the hoof tramps and the voices of the riders, two grave old voices, conversing soberly as they drew near. These mingled sounds appeared to pass along the road, within a few yards of the young man's hiding-place; but, owing doubtless to the depth of the gloom at that particular spot, neither the travellers nor their steeds were visible. Though their figures brushed the small boughs by the wayside, it could not be seen that they intercepted, even for a moment, the faint gleam from the strip of bright sky athwart which they must have passed. Goodman Brown alternately crouched and stood on tiptoe, pulling aside the branches and thrusting forth his head as far as he durst without discerning so much as a shadow. It vexed him the more, because he could have sworn, were such a thing possible, that he recognized the voices of the minister and Deacon Gookin, jogging along quietly, as they were wont to do, when bound to some ordination or ecclesiastical council. While yet within hearing, one of the riders stopped to pluck a switch.

"Of the two, reverend sir," said the voice like the deacon's, "I had rather miss an ordination dinner than to-night's meeting. They tell me that some of our community are to be here from Falmouth and beyond, and others from Connecticut and Rhode Island, besides several of the Indian powwows, who, after their fashion, know almost as much deviltry as the best of us. Moreover, there is a goodly young woman to be taken into communion."

"Mighty well, Deacon Gookin!" replied the solemn old tones of the minister. "Spur up, or we shall be late. Nothing can be done, you know, until I get on the ground."

The hoofs clattered again; and the voices, talking so strangely in the empty air, passed on through the forest, where no church had ever been gathered or solitary Christian prayed. Whither, then, could these holy men be journeying so deep into the heathen wilderness? Young Goodman Brown caught hold of a tree for support, being ready to sink down on the ground, faint and overburdened with the heavy sickness of his heart. He looked up to the sky, doubting whether there really was a heaven above him. Yet there was the blue arch, and the stars brightening in it.

"With <u>heaven</u> above and <u>Faith</u> below, I will yet stand firm against the devil!" cried Goodman Brown.

While he still gazed upward into the deep arch of the firmament and had lifted his hands to pray, a cloud, though no wind was stirring, hurried across the zenith and hid the brightening stars. The blue sky was still visible, except directly overhead, where this black mass of cloud was sweeping swiftly northward. Aloft in the air, as if from the depths of the cloud, came a confused and doubtful sound of voices. Once the listener fancied that he could distinguish the accents of townspeople of his own, men and women, both pious and ungodly, many of whom he had met at the communion table, and had seen others rioting at the tavern. The next moment, so indistinct were the sounds, he doubted whether he had heard aught but the murmur of the old forest, whispering without a wind. Then came a stronger swell of those familiar tones, heard daily in the sunshine at Salem village, but never until now from a cloud of night. There was one voice, of a young woman, uttering lamentations, yet with an uncertain sorrow, and entreating for some favor, which, perhaps, it would grieve her to obtain; and all the unseen multitude, both saints and sinners, seemed to encourage her onward.

"Faith!" shouted Goodman Brown, in a voice of <u>agony</u> and <u>desperation</u>; and the echoes of the forest mocked him, crying, "Faith! Faith!" as if bewildered wretches were seeking her all through the wilderness.

The cry of grief, rage, and terror was yet piercing the night, when the unhappy husband held his breath for a response. There was a scream, drowned immediately in a louder murmur of voices, fading into far-off laughter, as the dark cloud swept away, leaving the clear and silent sky above Goodman

Brown. But something fluttered lightly down through the air and caught on the branch of a tree. The young man seized it, and beheld a <u>pink ribbon</u>. ○innocence

"My Faith is gone!" cried he, after one stupefied moment. "There is no good on earth; and sin is but a name. Come, devil; for to thee is this world given." } he questions the core of his faith.

And, maddened with despair, so that he laughed loud and long, did Goodman Brown grasp his staff and set forth again, at such a rate that he seemed to fly along the forest path rather than to walk or run. The road grew wilder and drearier and more faintly traced, and vanished at length, leaving him in the heart of the dark wilderness, still rushing onward with the instinct that guides mortal man to evil. The whole forest was peopled with frightful sounds — the creaking of the trees, the howling of wild beasts, and the yell of Indians; while sometimes the wind tolled like a distant church bell, and sometimes gave a broad roar around the traveller, as if all Nature were laughing him to scorn. But he was himself the chief horror of the scene, and shrank not from its other horrors.

"Ha! ha! ha!" roared Goodman Brown when the wind laughed at him. "Let us hear which will laugh loudest. Think not to frighten me with your deviltry. Come witch, come wizard, come Indian powwow, come devil himself, and here comes Goodman Brown. You may as well fear him as he fear you."

In truth, all through the haunted forest there could be nothing more frightful than the figure of Goodman Brown. On he flew among the black pines, brandishing his staff with frenzied gestures, now giving vent to an inspiration of horrid blasphemy, and now shouting forth such laughter as set all the echoes of the forest laughing like demons around him. The fiend in his own shape is less hideous than when he rages in the breast of man. Thus sped the demoniac on his course, until, quivering among the trees, he saw a red light before him, as when the felled trunks and branches of a clearing have been set on fire, and throw up their lurid blaze against the sky, at the hour of midnight. He paused, in a lull of the tempest that had driven him onward, and heard the swell of what seemed a hymn, rolling solemnly from a distance with the weight of many voices. He knew the tune; it was a familiar one in the choir of the village meeting-house. The verse died heavily away, and was lengthened by a chorus, not of human voices, but of all the sounds of the benighted wilderness pealing in awful harmony together. Goodman Brown cried out, and his cry was lost to his own ear by its unison with the cry of the desert.

In the interval of silence he stole forward until the light glared full upon his eyes. At one extremity of an open space, hemmed in by the dark wall of the forest, arose a rock, bearing some rude, natural resemblance either to an altar or a pulpit, and surrounded by four blazing pines, their tops aflame, their stems untouched, like candles at an evening meeting. The mass of foliage that had overgrown the summit of the rock was all on fire, blazing high into the night and fitfully illuminating the whole field. Each pendent twig and leafy festoon was in a blaze. As the red light arose and fell, a numerous congregation alternately shone forth, then disappeared in shadow, and again grew, as it were, out of the darkness, peopling the heart of the solitary woods at once.

"A grave and dark-clad company," quoth Goodman Brown.

In truth they were such. Among them, quivering to and fro between gloom and splendor, appeared faces that would be seen next day at the council board of the province, and others which, Sabbath after Sabbath, looked devoutly heavenward, and benignantly over the crowded pews, from the holiest pulpits in the land. Some affirm that the lady of the governor was there. At least there were high dames well known to her, and wives of honored husbands, and widows, a great multitude, and ancient maidens, all of excellent repute, and fair young girls, who trembled lest their mothers should espy them. Either the sudden gleams of light flashing over the obscure field bedazzled Goodman Brown, or he recognized a score of the church members of Salem village famous for their especial sanctity. Good old Deacon Gookin had arrived, and waited at the skirts of that venerable saint, his revered pastor. But, irreverently consorting with these grave, reputable, and pious people, these elders of the church, these chaste dames and dewy virgins, there were men of dissolute lives and women of spotted fame, wretches given over to all mean and filthy vice, and suspected even of horrid crimes. It was strange to see that the good shrank not from the wicked, nor were the sinners abashed by the saints. Scattered also among their pale-faced enemies were the Indian priests, or powwows, who had often scared their native forest with more hideous incantations than any known to English witchcraft.

"But where is Faith?" thought Goodman Brown; and, as hope came into his heart, he trembled.

Another verse of the hymn arose, a slow and mournful strain, such as the pious love, but joined to words which expressed all that our nature can conceive of sin, and darkly hinted at far more. Unfathomable to mere mortals is the lore of fiends. Verse after verse was sung; and still the chorus of the desert swelled between like the deepest tone of a mighty organ; and with the final peal of that dreadful anthem there came a sound, as if the roaring wind, the rushing streams, the howling beasts, and every other voice of the unconcerted wilderness were mingling and according with the voice of guilty man in homage to the prince of all. The four blazing pines threw up a loftier flame, and obscurely discovered shapes and visages of horror on the smoke wreaths above the impious assembly. At the same moment the fire on the rock shot redly forth and formed a glowing arch above its base, where now appeared a figure. With reverence be it spoken, the figure bore no slight similitude, both in garb and manner, to some grave divine of the New England churches.

"Bring forth the converts!" cried a voice that echoed through the field and rolled into the forest.

At the word, Goodman Brown stepped forth from the shadow of the trees and approached the congregation, with whom he felt a loathful brotherhood by the sympathy of all that was wicked in his heart. He could have well-nigh sworn that the shape of his own dead father beckoned him to advance, looking downward from a smoke wreath, while a woman, with dim features of despair, threw out her hand to warn him back. Was it his mother? But he had no power to retreat one step, nor to resist, even in thought, when the minister and good old Deacon Gookin seized his arms and led him to the blazing rock. Thither came also the slender form of a veiled female, led between Goody Cloyse, that pious teacher of the catechism, and Martha Carrier, who had received the devil's promise to be queen of hell. A rampant hag was she. And there stood the proselytes beneath the canopy of fire.

"Welcome, my children," said the dark figure, "to the communion of your race. Ye have found thus young your nature and your destiny. My children, look behind you!"

They turned; and flashing forth, as it were, in a sheet of flame, the fiend worshippers were seen; the smile of welcome gleamed darkly on every visage.

"There," resumed the sable form, "are all whom ye have reverenced from youth. Ye deemed them holier than yourselves, and shrank from your own sin, contrasting it with their lives of righteousness and prayerful aspirations heavenward. Yet here are they all in my worshipping assembly. This night it shall be granted you to know their secret deeds: how hoary-bearded elders of the church have whispered wanton words to the young maids of their households; how many a woman, eager for widows' weeds, has given her husband a drink at bedtime and let him sleep his last sleep in her bosom; how beardless youths have made haste to inherit their fathers' wealth; and how fair damsels — blush not, sweet ones — have dug little graves in the garden, and bidden me, the sole guest, to an infant's funeral. By the sympathy of your human hearts for sin ye shall scent out all the places — whether in church, bed-chamber, street, field, or forest — where crime has been committed, and shall exult to behold the whole earth one stain of guilt, one mighty blood spot. Far more than this. It shall be yours to penetrate, in every bosom, the deep mystery of sin, the fountain of all wicked arts, and which inexhaustibly supplies more evil impulses than human power — than my power at its utmost — can make manifest in deeds. And now, my children, look upon each other."

They did so; and, by the blaze of the hell-kindled torches, the wretched man beheld his Faith, and the wife her husband, trembling before that unhallowed altar.

"Lo, there ye stand, my children," said the figure, in a deep and solemn tone, almost sad with its despairing awfulness, as if his once angelic nature could yet mourn for our miserable race. "Depending upon one another's hearts, ye had still hoped that virtue were not all a dream. Now are ye undeceived. Evil is the nature of mankind. Evil must be your only happiness. Welcome again, my children, to the communion of your race."

"Welcome," repeated the fiend worshippers, in one cry of despair and triumph.

And there they stood, the only pair, as it seemed, who were yet hesitating on the verge of wickedness in this dark world. A basin was hollowed, naturally, in the rock. Did it contain water, reddened by the lurid light? or was it blood? or, perchance, a liquid flame? Herein did the shape of evil dip his hand and prepare to lay the mark of baptism upon their foreheads, that they might be partakers of the mystery of sin, more conscious of the secret guilt of others, both in deed and thought, than they could now be of their own. The husband cast one look at his pale wife, and Faith at him. What polluted wretches would the next glance show them to each other, shuddering alike at what they disclosed and what they saw!

double
meaning

"Faith! Faith!" cried the husband, "look up to heaven, and resist the wicked one."

Whether Faith obeyed he knew not. Hardly had he spoken when he found himself amid calm night and solitude, listening to a roar of the wind which died heavily away through the forest. He staggered against the rock, and felt it chill and damp; while a hanging twig, that had been all on fire, besprinkled his cheek with the coldest dew.

The next morning young Goodman Brown came slowly into the street of Salem village, staring around him like a bewildered man. The good old minister was taking a walk along the graveyard to get an appetite for breakfast and meditate his sermon, and bestowed a blessing, as he passed, on Goodman Brown. He shrank from the venerable saint as if to avoid an anathema. Old Deacon Gookin was at domestic worship, and the holy words of his prayer were heard through the open window. "What God doth the wizard pray to?" quoth Goodman Brown. Goody Cloyse, that excellent old Christian, stood in the early sunshine at her own lattice, catechizing a little girl who had brought her a pint of morning's milk. Goodman Brown snatched away the child as from the grasp of the fiend himself. Turning the corner by the meeting-house, he spied the head of Faith, with the pink ribbons, gazing anxiously forth, and bursting into such joy at sight of him that she skipped along the street and almost kissed her husband before the whole village. But Goodman Brown looked sternly and sadly into her face, and passed on without a greeting.

Had Goodman Brown fallen asleep in the forest and only dreamed a wild dream of a witch-meeting?

Be it so if you will; but, alas! it was a dream of evil omen for young Goodman Brown. A stern, a sad, a darkly meditative, a distrustful, if not a desperate man did he become from the night of that fearful dream. On the Sabbath day, when the congregation were singing a holy psalm, he could not listen because an anthem of sin rushed loudly upon his ear and drowned all the blessed strain. When the minister spoke from the pulpit with power and fervid eloquence, and, with his hand on the open Bible, of the sacred truths of our religion, and of saint-like lives and triumphant deaths, and of future bliss or misery unutterable, then did Goodman Brown turn pale, dreading lest the roof should thunder down upon the gray blasphemer and his hearers. Often, awaking suddenly at midnight, he shrank from the bosom of Faith; and at morning or eventide, when the family knelt down at prayer, he scowled and muttered to himself, and gazed sternly at his wife, and turned away. And when he had lived long, and was borne to his grave a hoary corpse, followed by Faith, an aged woman, and children and grandchildren, a goodly procession, besides neighbors not a few, they carved no hopeful verse upon his tombstone, for his dying hour was gloom.

Questions for Discussion

1. Why is Brown's wife named Faith? What is the significance of Faith's fear of young Goodman Brown's leaving on this particular night? What is his "wretched errand," and how can it be interpreted as a religious allegory?
2. How does the devil convince young Goodman Brown to continue on his journey? Why does the devil trust that Brown will not return home?
3. Interpret the symbolism of the forest setting where the nighttime conversions take place and the range of local "respectable" figures encountered there.
4. What is the significance of the fact that all of the people at the witches' meeting are equal regardless of their social standing in the community?
5. "Evil is the nature of mankind. Evil must be your only happiness." Does the devil lie here, or does the story as a whole support his assertion?
6. How is young Goodman Brown transformed by what he learns in the forest? What is the significance of his deterioration and the story's ending?

Ideas for Writing

1. Write an essay that discusses the kind of commentary the story is making on Brown's nocturnal experience and subsequent disillusionment. Is the evil that Brown perceives more deeply intertwined in the world at large or in his own heart? What evaluation of Brown's revelation and subsequent life does the story seem to make?
2. Create an alternative ending for the story: imagine Brown deciding to interpret his dreamlike experience from another perspective. What would his subsequent life be like?

The Maypole of Merry Mount   (1836)

There is an admirable foundation for a philosophic romance in the curious history of the early settlement of Mount Wollaston, or Merry Mount. In the slight sketch here attempted, the facts, recorded on the grave pages of our New England annalists, have wrought themselves, almost spontaneously, into a sort of allegory. The masques, mummeries, and festive customs described in the text are in accordance with the manners of the age. Authority on these points may be found in Strutt's *Book of English Sports and Pastimes*.

Bright were the days at Merry Mount when the Maypole was the banner staff of that gay colony! They who reared it, should their banner be triumphant, were to pour sunshine over New England's rugged hills, and scatter flower seeds throughout the soil. Jollity and gloom were contending for an empire. Midsummer eve had come, bringing deep verdure to the forest, and roses in her lap, of a more vivid hue than the tender buds of spring. But May, or her mirthful spirit, dwelt all the year round at Merry Mount, sporting with the summer months, and reveling with autumn, and basking in the glow of winter's fireside. Through a world of toil and care she flitted with a dreamlike smile, and came hither to find a home among the lightsome hearts of Merry Mount.

Never had the Maypole been so gaily decked as at sunset on Midsummer eve. This venerated emblem was a pine tree, which had preserved the slender grace of youth, while it equaled the loftiest height of the old wood monarchs. From its top streamed a silken banner colored like the rainbow. Down nearly to the ground the pole was dressed with birchen boughs, and others of the liveliest green, and some with silvery leaves, fastened by ribands that fluttered in fantastic knots of twenty different colors, but no sad ones. Garden flowers and blossoms of the wilderness laughed gladly forth amid the verdure, so fresh and dewy that they must have grown by magic on that happy pine tree. Where this green and flowery splendor terminated, the shaft of the Maypole was stained with the seven brilliant hues of the banner at its top. On the lowest green bough hung an abundant wreath of roses, some that had been gathered in the sunniest spots of the forest, and others, of still richer blush, which the colonists had reared from English seed. Oh, people of the Golden Age, the chief of your husbandry was to raise flowers!

But what was the wild throng that stood hand in hand about the Maypole? It could not be that the fauns and nymphs, when driven from their classic groves and homes of ancient fable, had sought refuge, as all the persecuted did, in the fresh woods of the West. These were Gothic monsters, though perhaps of Grecian ancestry. On the shoulders of a comely youth uprose the head and branching antlers of a stag; a second, human in all other points, had the grim visage of a wolf; a third, still with the trunk and limbs of a mortal man, showed the beard and horns of a venerable he-goat. There was the likeness of a bear erect, brute in all but his hind legs, which were adorned with pink silk stockings. And here again, almost as wondrous, stood a real bear of the dark forest, lending each of his forepaws to the grasp of a human hand, and as ready for the dance as any in that circle. His inferior nature rose halfway to meet his companions as they stooped. Other faces wore the similitude of man or woman, but distorted or extravagant, with red noses pendulous before their mouths, which seemed of awful depth, and stretched from ear to ear in an eternal fit of laughter. Here might be seen the salvage man, well known in heraldry, hairy as a baboon, and girdled with green leaves. By his side, a nobler figure, but still a counterfeit, appeared an Indian hunter, with feathery crest and wampum belt. Many of this strange company wore fools' caps, and had little bells appended to their garments tinkling with a silvery sound, responsive to the inaudible music of their gleesome spirits. Some youths and maidens were of soberer garb, yet well maintained their places in the irregular throng by the expression of wild revelry upon their features. Such were the colonists of Merry Mount, as they stood in the broad smile of sunset round their venerated Maypole.

Had a wanderer, bewildered in the melancholy forest, heard their mirth, and stolen a half-affrighted glance, he might have fancied them the crew of Comus, some already transformed to brutes, some midway between man and beast, and the others rioting in the flow of tipsy jollity that foreran the change. But a band of Puritans, who watched the scene, invisible themselves, compared the masquers to those devils and ruined souls with whom their superstition peopled the black wilderness.

Within the ring of monsters appeared the two airiest forms that had ever trodden on any more solid footing than a purple and golden cloud. One was a youth in glistening apparel, with a scarf of the rainbow pattern crosswise on his breast. His right hand held a gilded staff, the ensign of high dignity among the revelers, and his left grasped the slender fingers of a fair maiden, not less gaily decorated than himself. Bright roses glowed in contrast with the dark and glossy curls of each, and were scattered round their feet, or had sprung up spontaneously there. Behind this lightsome couple, so close to the Maypole that its boughs shaded his jovial face, stood the figure of an English priest, canonically dressed, yet decked with flowers in heathen fashion, and wearing a chaplet of the native vine leaves. By the riot of his rolling eye, and the pagan decorations of his holy garb, he seemed the wildest monster there, and the very Comus of the crew.

"Votaries of the Maypole," cried the flower-decked priest, "merrily all day long have the woods echoed to your mirth. But be this your merriest hour, my hearts! Lo, here stand the Lord and Lady of the May, whom I, a clerk of Oxford, and high priest of Merry Mount, am presently to join in holy matrimony. Up with your nimble spirits, ye morrice dancers, green men, and glee maidens, bears, wolves, and horned gentlemen! Come, a chorus now, rich with the old mirth of Merry England, and the wilder glee of this fresh forest; and then a dance to show the youthful pair what life is made of, and how airily they should go through it! All ye that love the Maypole, lend your voices to the nuptial song of the Lord and Lady of the May!"

This wedlock was more serious than most affairs of Merry Mount, where jest and delusion, trick and fantasy, kept up a continual carnival. The Lord and Lady of the May, though their titles must be laid down at sunset, were really and truly to be partners for the dance of life, beginning the measure that same bright eve. The wreath of roses that hung from the lowest green bough of the Maypole had been twined for them and would be thrown over both their heads, in symbol of their flowery union. When the priest had spoken, therefore, a riotous uproar burst from the rout of monstrous figures.

"Begin you the stave, reverend sir," cried they all; "and never did the woods ring to such a merry peal as we of the Maypole shall send up!"

Immediately a prelude of pipe, cittern, and viol, touched with practiced minstrelsy, began to play from a neighboring thicket, in such a mirthful cadence that the boughs of the Maypole quivered to the sound. But the May Lord, he of the gilded staff, chancing to look into his Lady's eyes, was wonderstruck at the almost pensive glance that met his own.

"Edith, sweet Lady of the May," whispered he reproachfully, "is yon wreath of roses a garland to hang above our graves, that you look so sad? Oh, Edith, this is our golden time! Tarnish it not by any pensive shadow of the mind; for it may be that nothing of futurity will be brighter than the mere remembrance of what is now passing."

"That was the very thought that saddened me! How came it in your mind too?" said Edith, in a still lower tone than he; for it was high treason to be sad at Merry Mount. "Therefore do I sigh amid this festive music. And besides, dear Edgar, I struggle as with a dream, and fancy that these shapes of our jovial friends are visionary, and their mirth unreal, and that we are no true Lord and Lady of the May. What is the mystery in my heart?"

Just then, as if a spell had loosened them, down came a little shower of withering rose leaves from the Maypole. Alas, for the young lovers! No sooner had their hearts glowed with real passion than they were sensible of something vague and unsubstantial in their former pleasures, and felt a dreary presentiment of inevitable change. From the moment that they truly loved, they had subjected themselves to earth's doom of care and sorrow, and troubled joy, and had no more a home at Merry Mount. That was Edith's mystery. Now leave we the priest to marry them, and the masquers to sport round the Maypole till the last sunbeam be withdrawn from its summit, and the shadows of the forest mingle gloomily in the dance. Meanwhile, we may discover who these gay people were.

Two hundred years ago, and more, the Old World and its inhabitants became mutually weary of each other. Men voyaged by thousands to the West; some to barter glass beads, and suchlike jewels, for the furs of the Indian hunter; some to conquer virgin empires; and one stern band to pray. But none of these motives had much weight with the colonists of Merry Mount. Their leaders were men who had sported so long with life that, when Thought and Wisdom came, even these unwelcome guests were led astray by the crowd of vanities which they should have put to flight. Erring Thought and perverted Wisdom were made to put on masques and play the fool. The men of whom we speak, after losing the heart's fresh gaiety, imagined a wild philosophy of pleasure, and came hither to act out their latest daydream. They gathered followers from all that giddy tribe whose whole life is like the festal days of soberer men. In their train were minstrels, not unknown in London streets; wandering players, whose theaters had been the halls of noblemen; mummers, ropedancers, and mountebanks, who would long be missed at wakes, church ales, and fairs; in a word, mirthmakers of every sort, such as abounded in that age, but now began to be discountenanced by the rapid growth of Puritanism. Light had their footsteps been on land, and as lightly they came across the sea. Many had been maddened by their previous troubles into a gay despair; others were as madly gay in the flush of youth, like the May Lord and his Lady; but whatever might be the quality of their mirth, old and young were gay at Merry Mount. The young deemed themselves happy. The elder spirits, if they knew that mirth was but the counterfeit of happiness, yet followed the false shadow willfully, because at least her garments glittered brightest. Sworn triflers of a lifetime, they would not venture among the sober truths of life, not even to be truly blessed.

All the hereditary pastimes of Old England were transplanted hither. The King of Christmas was duly crowned, and the Lord of Misrule bore potent sway. On the eve of Saint John, they felled whole acres of the forest to make bonfires, and danced by the blaze all night, crowned with garlands and throwing flowers into the flame. At harvesttime, though their crop was of the smallest, they made an image with the sheaves of Indian corn, and wreathed it with autumnal garlands, and bore it home triumphantly. But what chiefly characterized the colonists of Merry Mount was their veneration for the Maypole. It has made their true history a poet's tale. Spring decked the hallowed emblem with young blossoms and fresh green boughs; summer brought roses of the deepest blush, and the perfect foliage of the forest; autumn enriched it with that red and yellow gorgeousness which converts each wildwood leaf into a painted flower; and winter silvered it with sleet, and hung it round with icicles, till it flashed in the cold sunshine, itself a frozen sunbeam. Thus each alternate season did homage to the Maypole, and paid it a tribute of its own richest splendor. Its votaries danced round it, once, at least, in every month; sometimes they called it their religion, or their altar; but always it was the banner staff of Merry Mount.

Unfortunately, there were men in the new world of a sterner faith than these Maypole worshipers. Not far from Merry Mount was a settlement of Puritans, most dismal wretches, who said their prayers before daylight, and then wrought in the forest or the cornfield till evening made it prayer time again. Their weapons were always at hand, to shoot down the straggling savage. When they met in conclave, it was never to keep up the old English mirth, but to hear sermons three hours long, or to proclaim bounties on the heads of wolves and the scalps of Indians. Their festivals were fast days, and their chief pastime the singing of psalms. Woe to the youth or maiden who did but dream of a dance! The selectman nodded to the constable; and there sat the light-heeled reprobate in the stocks; or if he danced, it was round the whipping post, which might be termed the Puritan Maypole.

A party of these grim Puritans, toiling through the difficult woods, each with a horseload of iron armor to burden his footsteps, would sometimes draw near the sunny precincts of Merry Mount. There were the silken colonists, sporting

round their Maypole; perhaps teaching a bear to dance, or striving to communicate their mirth to the grave Indian; or masquerading in the skins of deer and
wolves, which they had hunted for that especial purpose. Often, the whole
colony were playing at blindman's buff, magistrates and all, with their eyes bandaged, except a single scapegoat, whom the blinded sinners pursued by the tinkling of the bells at his garments. Once, it is said, they were seen following a
flower-decked corpse, with merriment and festive music, to his grave. But did the
dead man laugh? In their quietest times they sang ballads and told tales, for the
edification of their pious visitors; or perplexed them with juggling tricks; or
grinned at them through horse collars; and when sport itself grew wearisome,
they made game of their own stupidity, and began a yawning match. At the very
least of these enormities, the men of iron shook their heads and frowned so
darkly that the revelers looked up, imagining that a momentary cloud had overcast the sunshine, which was to be perpetual there. On the other hand, the
Puritans affirmed that when a psalm was pealing from their place of worship, the
echo which the forest sent them back seemed often like the chorus of a jolly
catch, closing with a roar of laughter. Who but the fiend and his bond slaves, the
crew of Merry Mount, had thus disturbed them? In due time a feud arose, stern
and bitter on one side, and as serious on the other as anything could be among
such light spirits as had sworn allegiance to the Maypole. The future complexion
of New England was involved in this important quarrel. Should the grisly saints
establish their jurisdiction over the gay sinners, then would their spirits darken
all the clime, and make it a land of clouded visages, of hard toil, of sermon and
psalm forever. But should the banner staff of Merry Mount be fortunate, sunshine
would break upon the hills, and flowers would beautify the forest, and late posterity do homage to the Maypole.

    After these authentic passages from history, we return to the nuptials of
the Lord and Lady of the May. Alas! we have delayed too long, and must
darken our tale too suddenly. As we glance again at the Maypole, a solitary
sunbeam is fading from the summit and leaves only a faint golden tinge,
blended with the hues of the rainbow banner. Even that dim light is now withdrawn, relinquishing the whole domain of Merry Mount to the evening gloom,
which has rushed so instantaneously from the black surrounding woods. But
some of these black shadows have rushed forth in human shape.

    Yes, with the setting sun, the last day of mirth had passed from Merry Mount.
The ring of gay masquers was disordered and broken, the stag lowered his antlers
in dismay; the wolf grew weaker than a lamb; the bells of the morrice dancers tinkled with tremulous affright. The Puritans had played a characteristic part in the
Maypole mummeries. Their darksome figures were intermixed with the wild
shapes of their foes and made the scene a picture of the moment, when waking
thoughts start up amid the scattered fantasies of a dream. The leader of the hostile party stood in the center of the circle, while the rout of monsters cowered
around him, like evil spirits in the presence of a dread magician. No fantastic
foolery could look him in the face. So stern was the energy of his aspect that the

whole man, visage, frame, and soul, seemed wrought of iron, gifted with life and thought, yet all of one substance with his headpiece and breastplate. It was the Puritan of Puritans; it was Endicott[1] himself!

"Stand off, priest of Baal!" said he with a grim frown, and laying no reverent hand upon the surplice. "I know thee, Blackstone![2] Thou art the man who couldst not abide the rule even of thine own corrupted church, and hast come hither to preach iniquity, and to give example of it in thy life. But now shall it be seen that the Lord hath sanctified this wilderness for his peculiar people. Woe unto them that would defile it! And first, for this flower-decked abomination, the altar of thy worship!"

And with his keen sword, Endicott assaulted the hallowed Maypole. Nor long did it resist his arm. It groaned with a dismal sound; it showered leaves and rosebuds upon the remorseless enthusiast; and, finally, with all its green boughs, and ribands, and flowers, symbolic of departed pleasures, down fell the banner staff of Merry Mount. As it sank, tradition says, the evening sky grew darker, and the woods threw forth a more somber shadow.

"There," cried Endicott, looking triumphantly on his work, "there lies the only Maypole in New England! The thought is strong within me that by its fall is shadowed forth the fate of light and idle mirthmakers amongst us and our posterity. Amen, saith John Endicott."

"Amen!" echoed his followers.

But the votaries of the Maypole gave one groan for their idol. At the sound, the Puritan leader glanced at the crew of Comus, each a figure of broad mirth, yet, at this moment, strangely expressive of sorrow and dismay.

"Valiant captain," quoth Peter Palfrey, the Ancient of the band, "what order shall be taken with the prisoners?"

"I thought not to repent me of cutting down a Maypole," replied Endicott, "yet now I could find in my heart to plant it again, and give each of these bestial pagans one other dance round their idol. It would have served rarely for a whipping post!"

"But there are pine trees enow," suggested the lieutenant.

"True, good Ancient," said the leader. "Wherefore bind the heathen crew, and bestow on them a small matter of stripes apiece, as earnest of our future justice. Set some of the rogues in the stocks to rest themselves, so soon as Providence shall bring us to one of our well-ordered settlements, where such accommodations may be found. Further penalties, such as branding and cropping of ears, shall be thought of hereafter."

"How many stripes for the priest?" inquired Ancient Palfrey.

---

[1] John Endicott led the first group of Puritans to Massachusetts Bay and served as the colony's first governor. — Eds.

[2] Did Governor Endicott speak less positively, we should suspect a mistake here. The Rev. Mr. Blackstone, though an eccentric, is not known to have been an immoral man. We rather doubt his identity with the priest of Merry Mount. — Hawthorne's note.

"None as yet," answered Endicott, bending his iron frown upon the culprit. "It must be for the Great and General Court to determine whether stripes and long imprisonment and other grievous penalty may atone for his transgressions. Let him look to himself! For such as violate our civil order, it may be permitted us to show mercy. But woe to the wretch that troubleth our religion!"

"And this dancing bear," resumed the officer, "must he share the stripes of his fellows?"

"Shoot him through the head!" said the energetic Puritan. "I suspect witch-craft in the beast."

"Here be a couple of shining ones," continued Peter Palfrey, pointing his weapon at the Lord and Lady of the May. "They seem to be of high station among these misdoers. Methinks their dignity will not be fitted with less than a double share of stripes."

Endicott rested on his sword and closely surveyed the dress and aspect of the hapless pair. There they stood — pale, downcast, and apprehensive. Yet there was an air of mutual support and of pure affection, seeking aid and giving it, that showed them to be man and wife, with the sanction of a priest upon their love. The youth, in the peril of the moment, had dropped his gilded staff, and thrown his arm about the Lady of the May, who leaned against his breast, too lightly to burden him, but with weight enough to express that their destinies were linked together, for good or evil. They looked first at each other and then into the grim captain's face. There they stood, in the first hour of wedlock, while the idle pleasures, of which their companions were the emblems, had given place to the sternest cares of life, personified by the dark Puritans. But never had their youthful beauty seemed so pure and high as when its glow was chastened by adversity.

"Youth," said Endicott, "ye stand in an evil case, thou and thy maiden wife. Make ready presently; for I am minded that ye shall both have a token to remember your wedding day!"

"Stern man," cried the May Lord, "how can I move thee? Were the means at hand, I would resist to the death. Being powerless, I entreat! Do with me as thou wilt; but let Edith go untouched!"

"Not so," replied the immitigable zealot. "We are not wont to show an idle courtesy to that sex which requireth the stricter discipline. What sayest thou, maid? Shall thy silken bridegroom suffer thy share of the penalty, besides his own?"

"Be it death," said Edith, "and lay it all on me!"

Truly, as Endicott had said, the poor lovers stood in a woful case. Their foes were triumphant, their friends captive and abased, their home desolate, the benighted wilderness around them, and a rigorous destiny, in the shape of the Puritan leader, their only guide. Yet the deepening twilight could not altogether conceal that the iron man was softened; he smiled at the fair spectacle of early love; he almost sighed for the inevitable blight of early hopes.

"The troubles of life have come hastily on this young couple," observed Endicott. "We will see how they comport themselves under their present trials ere we burden them with greater. If, among the spoil, there be any garments of a more decent fashion, let them be put upon this May Lord and his Lady, instead of their glistening vanities. Look to it, some of you."

"And shall not the youth's hair be cut?" asked Peter Palfrey, looking with abhorrence at the love-lock and long glossy curls of the young man.

"Crop it forthwith, and that in the true pumpkin-shell fashion," answered the captain. "Then bring them along with us, but more gently than their fellows. There be qualities in the youth, which may make him valiant to fight, and sober to toil, and pious to pray; and in the maiden, that may fit her to become a mother in our Israel, bringing up babes in better nurture than her own hath been. Nor think ye, young ones, that they are the happiest, even in our lifetime of a moment, who mis-spend it in dancing round a Maypole!"

And Endicott, the severest Puritan of all who laid the rock foundation of New England, lifted the wreath of roses from the ruin of the Maypole, and threw it, with his own gauntleted hand, over the heads of the Lord and Lady of the May. It was a deed of prophecy. As the moral gloom of the world overpowers all systematic gayety, even so was their home of wild mirth made desolate amid the sad forest. They returned to it no more. But as their flowery garland was wreathed of the brightest roses that had grown there, so, in the tie that united them, were intertwined all the purest and best of their early joys. They went heavenward, supporting each other along the difficult path which it was their lot to tread, and never wasted one regretful thought on the vanities of Merry Mount.

Questions for Discussion

1. What mood is established in the first paragraph, which describes the story's setting? How does the idea that "jollity and gloom were contending for an empire" put the events described in a larger context of values and power?

2. How are the details that describe the maypole, the rainbow banner, and the animal costumes of the revelers allegorically significant?

3. How is the marriage of "the Lord and Lady of the May," Edgar and Edith, described? Does the ritual seem to be primarily a pagan rite, or does it integrate pagan and Christian values?

4. What "dreary presentiment of inevitable change" intrudes on the marriage celebration? What change is foreshadowed?

5. In relating the history of the Merry Mount colony, does the narrator appear more critical of Merry Mount's values or those of the Puritans? How does the conclusion contribute to your response?

Ideas for Writing

1. Examine the story's comment on both the short-lived colony of Merry Mount and the Puritans who destroy it. What did the Merry Mount colonists lack that the Puritans possessed, and vice versa? Might the example of Merry Mount, particularly the loving couple Edith and Edgar, have "softened" the Puritans?

2. Although "The Maypole of Merry Mount" is based on historical accounts, Hawthorne's version presents an allegory of life in the New World. Discuss the story's allegorical figures and interpret their meaning, particularly in terms of how the wilderness affected the American colonists.

EDGAR ALLAN POE   (1809–1849)

Edgar Allan Poe is respected internationally as one of the originators of the modern story and as a major influence on other fictional forms, including fantasy, science fiction, horror, and the modern detective story. Born to a family of traveling actors, Poe was orphaned at age two and adopted along with his sister by a wealthy Virginia merchant, John Allan. Sent away to boarding school in England, Poe developed habits of gambling and drinking at an early age, which affected the rest of his life. He attended the University of Virginia and enrolled at West Point, from which he was dismissed. His adoptive father died in 1834, leaving him nothing, so Poe turned to writing and editing for periodicals to earn his living. His marriage in 1835 to a fourteen-year-old cousin, Virginia Clemm, put him under mounting financial strains, and he moved back and forth between New York and Philadelphia, working for magazines. Between 1838 and 1846 Poe had his most productive years, publishing *Tales of the Grotesque and Arabesque* (1840) and his popular narrative poem "The Raven" (1845). With the death of his wife in 1847, Poe fell into a depression and wrote little, attempting suicide several times and indulging in heavy drinking. He died in a delirium on the streets of Baltimore.

Poe's reputation grew in Europe after his death, when his poems and stories were translated by the French poet Charles Baudelaire, who admired Poe's grotesque humor, fantastic imagination, and morbid fascination with death and decay. Poe contributed to a vision of the short story as a concentrated, imaginative popular form achieved artistically to create "a certain unique or single effect" from the "very initial sentence" and drawing on the poetic technique of rhythm to achieve its ends.

The Masque of the Red Death   (1842)

The "Red Death" had long devastated the country. No pestilence had ever been so fatal, or so hideous. Blood was its Avatar and its seal — the redness and the horror of blood. There were sharp pains, and sudden dizziness, and then profuse bleeding at the pores, with dissolution. The scarlet stains upon the body and especially upon the face of the victim, were the pest ban which shut him out from the aid and from the sympathy of his fellow-men. And the whole seizure, progress, and termination of the disease, were the incidents of half an hour.

But the Prince Prospero was happy and dauntless and sagacious. When his dominions were half depopulated, he summoned to his presence a thousand hale and light-hearted friends from among the knights and dames of his court, and with these retired to the deep seclusion of one of his castellated abbeys. This was an extensive and magnificent structure, the creation of the prince's own eccentric yet august taste. A strong and lofty wall girdled it in. This wall had gates of iron. The courtiers, having entered, brought furnaces and massy hammers and welded the bolts. They resolved to leave means neither of ingress nor egress to the sudden impulses of despair or of frenzy from within. The abbey was amply provisioned. With such precautions the courtiers might bid defiance to contagion. The external world could take care of itself. In the meantime it was folly to grieve, or to think. The prince had provided all the appliances of pleasure. There were buffoons, there were improvisatori, there were ballet-dancers, there were musicians, there was Beauty, there was wine. All these and security were within. Without was the "Red Death."

It was toward the close of the fifth or sixth month of his seclusion, and while the pestilence raged most furiously abroad, that the Prince Prospero entertained his thousand friends at a masked ball of the most unusual magnificence.

It was a voluptuous scene, that masquerade. But first let me tell of the rooms in which it was held. There were seven — an imperial suite. In many palaces, however, such suites form a long and straight vista, while the folding doors slide back nearly to the walls on either hand, so that the view of the whole extent is scarcely impeded. Here the case was very different; as might have been expected from the duke's love of the *bizarre*. The apartments were so irregularly disposed that the vision embraced but little more than one at a time. There was a sharp turn at every twenty or thirty yards, and at each turn a novel effect. To the right and left, in the middle of each wall, a tall and narrow Gothic window looked out upon a closed corridor which pursued the windings of the suite. These windows were of stained glass whose color varied in accordance with the prevailing hue of the decorations of the chamber into which it opened. That at the eastern extremity was hung, for example, in blue — and vividly blue were its windows. The second chamber was purple in its ornaments and tapestries, and here the panes were purple. The third was green throughout, and so were the casements. The fourth was furnished and lighted with orange — the fifth with white — the sixth with violet. The seventh apartment was closely shrouded in black velvet tapestries that hung all over the ceiling and down the walls, falling in heavy folds upon a carpet of the same material and hue. But in this chamber only, the color of the windows failed to correspond with the decorations. The panes here were scarlet — a deep blood color. Now in no one of the seven apartments was there any lamp or candelabrum, amid the profusion of golden ornaments that lay scattered to and fro or depended from the roof. There was no light of any kind emanating from lamp or candle within the suite of chambers. But in the corridors that followed the suite, there stood, opposite to each window, a heavy tripod, bearing a brazier of fire, that projected its rays through the tinted glass and so glaringly illumined the room. And thus were produced a multitude of gaudy and fantastic appearances. But in the western or black chamber the effect of the fire-light that streamed upon the dark hangings through the blood-tinted panes was ghastly in the extreme, and produced so wild a look upon the countenances of those who entered, that there were few of the company bold enough to set foot within its precincts at all.

It was in this apartment, also, that there stood against the western wall, a gigantic clock of ebony. Its pendulum swung to and fro with a dull, heavy, monotonous clang; and when the minute-hand made the circuit of the face, and the hour was to be stricken, there came from the brazen lungs of the clock a sound which was clear and loud and deep and exceedingly musical, but of so peculiar a note and emphasis that, at each lapse of an hour, the musicians of the orchestra were constrained to pause, momentarily, in their performance, to hearken to the sound; and thus the waltzers perforce ceased their evolutions; and there was a brief disconcert of the whole gay company; and, while the chimes of the clock yet rang, it was observed that the giddiest grew pale, and the more aged and sedate passed their hands over their brows as if in confused revery or meditation. But when the echoes had fully ceased, a light laughter at once pervaded the assembly; the musicians looked at each other and smiled as if at their own nervousness and folly, and made whispering vows, each to the other, that the next chiming of the clock should produce in them no similar emotion; and then, after the lapse of sixty minutes (which embrace three thousand and six hundred seconds of the Time that flies), there came yet another chiming of the clock, and then were the same disconcert and tremulousness and meditation as before.

But, in spite of these things, it was a gay and magnificent revel. The tastes of the duke were peculiar. He had a fine eye for colors and effects. He disregarded the *decora* of mere fashion. His plans were bold and fiery, and his conceptions glowed with barbaric lustre. There are some who would have thought him mad. His followers felt that he was not. It was necessary to hear and see and touch him to be *sure* that he was not.

He had directed, in great part, the movable embellishments of the seven chambers, upon occasion of this great *fête;* and it was his own guiding taste which had given character to the masqueraders. Be sure they were grotesque. There were much glare and glimmer and piquancy and phantasm — much of what has been since seen in "Hernani." There were arabesque figures with unsuited limbs and appointments. There were delirious fancies such as the madman fashions. There were much of the beautiful, much of the wanton, much of the *bizarre,* something of the terrible, and not a little of that which might have excited disgust. To and fro in the seven chambers there stalked, in fact, a multitude of dreams. And these — the dreams — writhed in and about, taking hue from the rooms, and causing the wild music of the orchestra to seem as the echo of their steps. And, anon, there strikes the ebony clock which stands in the hall of the velvet. And then, for a moment, all is still, and all is silent save the voice of the clock. The dreams are stiff-frozen as they stand. But the echoes of the chime die away — they have endured but an instant — and a light, half-subdued laughter floats after them as they depart. And now again the music swells, and the dreams live, and writhe to and fro more merrily than ever, taking hue from the many-tinted windows through which stream the rays from the tripods. But to the chamber which lies most westwardly of the seven there are now none of the maskers who venture; for the night is waning away; and there flows a ruddier light through the blood-colored panes; and the blackness of the sable drapery appals; and to him whose foot falls upon the sable carpet, there comes from the near clock of ebony a muffled peal more solemnly emphatic than any which reaches *their* ears who indulge in the more remote gaieties of the other apartments.

But these other apartments were densely crowded, and in them beat feverishly the heart of life. And the revel went whirlingly on, until at length there commenced the sounding of midnight upon the clock. And then the music ceased, as I have told; and the evolutions of the waltzers were quieted; and there was an uneasy cessation of all things as before. But now there were twelve strokes to be sounded by the bell of the clock; and thus it happened, perhaps, that more of thought crept, with more of time, into the meditations of the thoughtful among those who revelled. And thus too, it happened, perhaps, that before the last echoes of the last chime had utterly sunk into silence, there were many individuals in the crowd who had found leisure to become aware of the presence of a masked figure which had arrested the attention of no single individual before. And the rumor of this new presence having spread itself whisperingly around, there arose at length from the whole company a buzz, or murmur, expressive of disapprobation and surprise — then, finally, of terror, of horror, and of disgust.

In an assembly of phantasms such as I have painted, it may well be supposed that no ordinary appearance could have excited such sensation. In truth the masquerade license of the night was nearly unlimited; but the figure in question had out-Heroded Herod, and gone beyond the bounds of even the prince's indefinite decorum. There are chords in the hearts of the most reckless which cannot be touched without emotion. Even with the utterly lost, to whom life and death are equally jests, there are matters of which no jest can be made. The whole company, indeed, seemed now deeply to feel that in the costume and bearing of the stranger neither wit nor propriety existed. The figure was tall and gaunt, and shrouded from head to foot in the habiliments of the grave. The mask which concealed the visage was made so nearly to resemble the countenance of a stiffened corpse that the closest scrutiny must have had difficulty in detecting the cheat. And yet all this might have been endured, if not approved, by the mad revellers around. But the mummer had gone so far as to assume the type of the Red Death. His vesture was dabbled in *blood* — and his broad brow, with all the features of the face, was besprinkled with the scarlet horror.

When the eyes of Prince Prospero fell upon this spectral image (which, with a slow and solemn movement, as if more fully to sustain its *rôle*, stalked to and fro among the waltzers) he was seen to be convulsed, in the first moment with a strong shudder either of terror or distaste; but, in the next, his brow reddened with rage.

"Who dares" — he demanded hoarsely of the courtiers who stood near him — "who dares insult us with this blasphemous mockery? Seize him and unmask him that we may know whom we have to hang, at sunrise, from the battlements!"

It was in the eastern or blue chamber in which stood the Prince Prospero as he uttered these words. They rang throughout the seven rooms loudly and clearly, for the prince was a bold and robust man, and the music had become hushed at the waving of his hand.

It was in the blue room where stood the prince, with a group of pale courtiers by his side. At first, as he spoke, there was a slight rushing movement of this group in the direction of the intruder, who, at the moment was also near at hand, and now, with deliberate and stately step, made closer approach to the speaker. But from a certain nameless awe with which the mad assumptions of the mummer had inspired the whole party, there were found none who put forth hand to seize him; so that, unimpeded, he passed within a yard of the prince's person; and, while the vast assembly, as if with one impulse, shrank from the centres of the rooms to the walls, he made his way uninterruptedly, but with the same solemn and measured step which had distinguished him from the first, through the blue chamber to the purple — through the purple to the green — through the green to the orange — through this again to the white — and even thence to the violet, ere a decided movement had been made to arrest him. It was then, however, that the Prince Prospero, maddening with rage and the shame of his own momentary cowardice, rushed hurriedly through the six chambers, while none followed him on account of a deadly terror that had seized upon all. He bore aloft a drawn dagger, and had approached, in rapid impetuosity, to within three or four feet of the retreating figure, when the latter, having attained the extremity of the velvet apartment, turned suddenly and confronted his pursuer. There was a sharp cry — and the dagger dropped gleaming upon the sable carpet, upon which, instantly afterward, fell prostrate in death the Prince Prospero. Then, summoning the wild courage of despair, a throng of the revellers at once threw themselves into the black apartment, and, seizing the mummer, whose tall figure stood erect and motionless within the shadow of the ebony clock, gasped in unutterable horror at finding the grave cerements and corpse-like mask, which they handled with so violent a rudeness, untenanted by any tangible form.

And now was acknowledged the presence of the Red Death. He had come like a thief in the night. And one by one dropped the revellers in the blood-bedewed halls of their revel, and died each in the despairing posture of his fall. And the life of the ebony clock went out with that of the last of the gay. And the flames of the tripods expired. And Darkness and Decay and the Red Death held illimitable dominion over all.

Questions for Discussion

1. How does Poe describe Prospero's abbey? What is ironic about Prospero's court taking refuge from the plague in an abbey?
2. The prince is given the name Prospero, the outcast magician-ruler of the mystical island in Shakespeare's *The Tempest*. In what sense is Poe's Prospero a magician? an outcast?
3. Describe the "bizarre" interior of Prospero's palace. Why are the rooms shaped "irregularly"? How are they painted and illuminated? What do their shapes, colors, and east-west orientation reveal about the values of Prospero and his entourage?
4. What does the "gigantic clock of ebony" in the final chamber, with its peculiar hourly chime, represent? What impact does its sound have on the revelers?
5. Poe speaks of a "multitude of dreams" stalking the chambers of Prospero. Why are the masquers referred to as dreams?

Ideas for Writing

1. Write an essay about the story's perspective on madness. Is Prospero's decision to wall himself and his courtiers off from the reality of the plague essentially a mad act or a last grasp for life?
2. Write a story about a modern character or group of characters who attempt desperately to avoid death.

The Tell-Tale Heart   (1843)

True! — nervous — very, very dreadfully nervous I had been and am; but why *will* you say that I am mad? The disease had sharpened my senses — not destroyed — not dulled them. Above all was the sense of hearing acute. I heard all things in the heaven and in the earth. I heard many things in hell. How, then, am I mad? Hearken! and observe how healthily — how calmly I can tell you the whole story.

It is impossible to say how first the idea entered my brain; but once conceived, it haunted me day and night. Object there was none. Passion there was none. I loved the old man. He had never wronged me. He had never given me insult. For his gold I had no desire. I think it was his eye! yes, it was this! One of his eyes resembled that of a vulture — a pale blue eye, with a film over it. Whenever it fell upon me, my blood ran cold; and so by degrees — very gradually — I made up my mind to take the life of the old man, and thus rid myself of the eye for ever.

Now this is the point. You fancy me mad. Madmen know nothing. But you should have seen *me*. You should have seen how wisely I proceeded — with what caution — with what foresight — with what dissimulation I went to work! I was never kinder to the old man than during the whole week before I killed him. And every night, about midnight, I turned the latch of his door and opened it — oh, so gently! And then, when I had made an opening sufficient for my head, I put in a dark lantern, all closed, closed, so that no light shone out, and then I thrust in my head. Oh, you would have laughed to see how cunningly I thrust it in! I moved it slowly — very, very slowly, so that I might not disturb the old man's sleep. It took me an hour to place my whole head within the opening so far that I could see him as he lay upon his bed. Ha! — would a madman have been so wise as this? And then, when my head was well in the room, I undid the lantern cautiously — oh, so cautiously — cautiously (for the hinges creaked) — I undid it just so much that a single thin ray fell upon the vulture eye. And this I did for seven long nights — every night just at midnight — but I found the eye always closed; and so it was impossible to do the work; for it was not the old man who vexed me, but his Evil Eye. And every morning, when the day broke, I went boldly into the chamber, and spoke courageously to him, calling him by name in a hearty tone, and inquiring how he had passed the night. So you see he would have been a very profound old man, indeed, to suspect that every night, just at twelve, I looked in upon him while he slept.

Upon the eighth night I was more than usually cautious in opening the door. A watch's minute hand moves more quickly than did mine. Never before that night had I *felt* the extent of my own powers — of my sagacity. I could scarcely contain my feelings of triumph. To think that there I was, opening the door, little by little, and he not even to dream of my secret deeds or thoughts. I fairly chuckled at the idea; and perhaps he heard me; for he moved on the bed suddenly, as if startled. Now you may think that I drew back — but no. His room was as black as pitch with the thick darkness (for the shutters were close fastened, through fear of robbers), and so I knew that he could not see the opening of the door, and I kept pushing it on steadily, steadily.

I had my head in, and was about to open the lantern, when my thumb slipped upon the tin fastening, and the old man sprang up in the bed, crying out — "Who's there?"

I kept quite still and said nothing. For a whole hour I did not move a muscle, and in the meantime I did not hear him lie down. He was still sitting up in the bed listening; — just as I have done, night after night, hearkening to the death watches in the wall.

Presently I heard a slight groan, and I knew it was the groan of mortal terror. It was not a groan of pain or of grief — oh, no! — it was the low stifled sound that arises from the bottom of the soul when overcharged with awe. I knew the sound well. Many a night, just at midnight, when all the world slept, it has welled up from my own bosom, deepening, with its dreadful echo, the terrors that distracted me. I say I knew it well. I knew what the old man felt, and pitied him, although I chuckled at heart. I knew that he had been lying awake ever since the first slight noise, when he had turned in the bed. His fears had been ever since growing upon him. He had been trying to fancy them causeless, but could not. He had been saying to himself — "It is nothing but the wind in the chimney — it is only a mouse crossing the floor," or "it is merely a cricket which has made a single chirp." Yes, he has been trying to comfort himself with these suppositions; but he had found all in vain. *All in vain;* because Death, in approaching him, had stalked with his black shadow before him, and enveloped the victim. And it was the mournful influence of the unperceived shadow that caused him to feel — although he neither saw nor heard — to *feel* the presence of my head within the room.

When I had waited a long time, very patiently, without hearing him lie down, I resolved to open a little — a very, very little crevice in the lantern. So I opened it — you cannot imagine how stealthily, stealthily — until, at length, a single dim ray, like the thread of a spider, shot from out the crevice and full upon the vulture eye.

It was open — wide, wide open — and I grew furious as I gazed upon it. I saw it with perfect distinctness — all a dull blue, with a hideous veil over it that chilled the very marrow in my bones; but I could see nothing else of the old man's face or person: for I had directed the ray as if by instinct, precisely upon the damned spot.

And now have I not told you that what you mistake for madness is but over-acuteness of the senses? — now, I say, there came to my ears a low, dull, quick sound, such as a watch makes when enveloped in cotton. I knew *that* sound well too. It was the beating of the old man's heart. It increased my fury, as the beating of a drum stimulates the soldier into courage.

But even yet I refrained and kept still. I scarcely breathed. I held the lantern motionless. I tried how steadily I could maintain the ray upon the eye. Meantime the hellish tattoo of the heart increased. It grew quicker and quicker, and louder and louder every instant. The old man's terror *must* have been extreme! It grew louder, I say, louder every moment! — do you mark me well? I have told you that I am nervous: so I am. And now at the dead hour of the night, amid the dreadful silence of that old house, so strange a noise as this excited me to uncontrollable terror. Yet, for some minutes longer I refrained and stood still. But the beating grew louder, louder! I thought the heart must burst. And now a new anxiety seized me — the sound would be heard by a neighbor! The old man's hour had come! With a loud yell, I threw open the lantern and leaped into the room. He shrieked once — once only. In an instant I dragged him to the floor, and pulled the heavy bed over him. I then smiled gaily, to find the deed so far done. But, for many minutes, the heart beat on with a muffled sound. This, however, did not vex me; it would not be heard through the wall. At length it ceased. The old man was dead. I removed the bed and examined the corpse. Yes, he was stone, stone dead. I placed my hand upon the heart and held it there many minutes. There was no pulsation. He was stone dead. His eye would trouble me no more.

If still you think me mad, you will think so no longer when I describe the wise precautions I took for the concealment of the body. The night waned, and

I worked hastily, but in silence. First of all I dismembered the corpse. I cut off the head and the arms and the legs.

I then took up three planks from the flooring of the chamber, and deposited all between the scantlings. I then replaced the boards so cleverly, so cunningly, that no human eye — not even *his* — could have detected any thing wrong. There was nothing to wash out — no stain of any kind — no blood-spot whatever. I had been too wary for that. A tub had caught all — ha! ha!

When I had made an end of these labors, it was four o'clock — still dark as midnight. As the bell sounded the hour, there came a knocking at the street door. I went down to open it with a light heart, — for what had I *now* to fear? There entered three men, who introduced themselves, with perfect suavity, as officers of the police. A shriek had been heard by a neighbor during the night; suspicion of foul play had been aroused; information had been lodged at the police office, and they (the officers) had been deputed to search the premises.

I smiled, — for *what* had I to fear? I bade the gentlemen welcome. The shriek, I said, was my own in a dream. The old man, I mentioned, was absent in the country. I took my visitors all over the house. I bade them search — search *well*. I led them, at length, to *his* chamber. I showed them his treasures, secure, undisturbed. In the enthusiasm of my confidence, I brought chairs into the room, and desired them *here* to rest from their fatigues, while I myself, in the wild audacity of my perfect triumph, placed my own seat upon the very spot beneath which reposed the corpse of the victim.

The officers were satisfied. My *manner* had convinced them. I was singularly at ease. They sat, and while I answered cheerily, they chatted familiar things. But, ere long, I felt myself getting pale and wished them gone. My head ached, and I fancied a ringing in my ears: but still they sat and still they chatted. The ringing became more distinct: — it continued and became more distinct: I talked more freely to get rid of the feeling: but it continued and gained definitiveness — until, at length, I found that the noise was *not* within my ears.

No doubt I now grew *very* pale; — but I talked more fluently, and with a heightened voice. Yet the sound increased — and what could I do? It was *a low, dull, quick sound — much such a sound as a watch makes when enveloped in cotton.* I gasped for breath — and yet the officers heard it not. I talked more quickly — more vehemently; but the noise steadily increased. I arose and argued about trifles, in a high key and with violent gesticulations, but the noise steadily increased. Why *would* they not be gone? I paced the floor to and fro with heavy strides, as if excited to fury by the observation of the men — but the noise steadily increased. Oh God! what *could* I do? I foamed — I raved — I swore! I swung the chair upon which I had been sitting, and grated it upon the boards, but the noise arose over all and continually increased. It grew louder — louder — *louder!* And still the men chatted pleasantly, and smiled. Was it possible they heard not? Almighty God! — no, no! They heard! — they suspected! — they *knew!* — they were making a mockery of my horror! — this I thought, and this I think. But any thing was better than this agony! Any thing was more tolerable than this derision! I could bear those hypocritical smiles no longer! I felt that I must scream or die! — and now — again! — hark! louder! louder! louder! *louder!* —

"Villains!" I shrieked, "dissemble no more! I admit the deed! — tear up the planks! — here, here! — it is the beating of his hideous heart!"

Questions for Discussion

1. This is a story about what the French call an *idée fixe* — a fixed idea that takes possession and drives a person to an act of madness. How does Poe's plot develop the *idée fixe* of the narrator?

2. One of the pleasures of reading this story as well as others by Poe is the discovery that the narrator, although he thinks himself perfectly sane and rational in his perceptions and decisions, is in fact perfectly mad. Discuss distortions in the narrator's perceptions and the irrationality of his decisions that demonstrate his insanity.

3. Poe was a master of the sharply observed detail. How do such details contribute to the narrator's description of the "evil eye" of the old man? Do you feel the narrator is telling the truth when he blames the eye for his obsession and his crime?

4. Compare the image of the lantern that the narrator uses to shine into the old man's room with the "vulture eye" of the man. What does Poe achieve by juxtaposing these two "eyes" — one mechanical, one natural? What does each come to symbolize?

5. Why is the sound of the old man's heart particularly disturbing to the narrator? How does he describe it, both before and after the killing? Why does he compare its sound to that of a watch?

Ideas for Writing

1. Trace in an essay the narrator's descent into madness. How do the descriptive details and metaphors he uses help to reveal his insanity?

2. Write a story using a first-person narrator who gradually goes insane, although he or she tries to appear to be "in control."

Hop-Frog   (1850)

I never knew any one so keenly alive to a joke as the king was. He seemed to live only for joking. To tell a good story of the joke kind, and to tell it well, was the surest road to his favor. Thus it happened that his seven ministers were all noted for their accomplishments as jokers. They all took after the king, too, in being large, corpulent, oily men, as well as inimitable jokers. Whether people grow fat by joking, or whether there is something in fat itself which predisposes to a joke, I have never been quite able to determine; but certain it is that a lean joker is a *rara avis in terris*.[1]

About the refinements, or, as he called them, the "ghosts" of wit, the king troubled himself very little. He had an especial admiration for *breadth* in a jest, and would often put up with *length*, for the sake of it. Overniceties wearied him. He would have preferred Rabelais' *Gargantua* to the *Zadig* of Voltaire: and, upon the whole, practical jokes suited his taste far better than verbal ones.

At the date of my narrative, professing jesters had not altogether gone out of fashion at court. Several of the great continental "powers" still retained their "fools," who wore motley, with caps and bells, and who were expected to be always ready with sharp witticisms, at a moment's notice, in consideration of the crumbs that fell from the royal table.

Our king, as a matter of course, retained his "fool." The fact is, he *required* something in the way of folly — if only to counterbalance the heavy wisdom of the seven wise men who were his ministers — not to mention himself.

His fool, or professional jester, was not *only* a fool, however. His value was trebled in the eyes of the king, by the fact of his being also a dwarf and a cripple. Dwarfs were as common at court, in those days, as fools; and many monarchs would have found it difficult to get through their days (days are rather longer at court than elsewhere) without both a jester to laugh *with* and a dwarf to laugh *at*. But, as I have already observed, your jesters, in ninety-nine cases out of a hundred, are fat, round, and unwieldy — so that it was no small source of self-gratulation with our king that, in Hop-Frog (this was the fool's name), he possessed a triplicate treasure in one person.

I believe the name "Hop-Frog" was *not* that given to the dwarf by his sponsors at baptism, but it was conferred upon him, by general consent of the seven ministers, on account of his inability to walk as other men do. In fact, Hop-Frog could only get along by a sort of interjectional gait — something between a leap and a wriggle, — a movement that afforded illimitable amusement, and of course consolation, to the king, for (notwithstanding the protuberance of his stomach and a constitutional swelling of the head) the king, by his whole court, was accounted a capital figure.

But although Hop-Frog, through the distortion of his legs, could move only with great pain and difficulty along a road or floor, the prodigious muscular power which nature seemed to have bestowed upon his arms, by way of compensation for deficiency in the lower limbs, enabled him to perform many feats of wonderful dexterity, where trees or ropes were in question, or anything else to climb. At such exercises he certainly much more resembled a squirrel, or a small monkey, than a frog.

I am not able to say, with precision, from what country Hop-Frog originally came. It was from some barbarous region, however, that no person ever

---

[1] Rare, unusual species. — Eds.

heard of—a vast distance from the court of our king. Hop-Frog, and a young girl very little less dwarfish than himself (although of exquisite proportions and a marvellous dancer), had been forcibly carried off from their respective homes in adjoining provinces, and sent as presents to the king, by one of his ever-victorious generals.

Under these circumstances, it is not to be wondered at that a close intimacy arose between the two little captives. Indeed, they soon became sworn friends. Hop-Frog, who, although he made a great deal of sport, was by no means popular, had it not in his power to render Trippetta many services; but *she,* on account of her grace and exquisite beauty (although a dwarf), was universally admired and petted; so she possessed much influence; and never failed to use it, whenever she could, for the benefit of Hop-Frog.

On some grand state occasion — I forget what — the king determined to have a masquerade; and whenever a masquerade, or any thing of that kind, occurred at our court, then the talents both of Hop-Frog and Trippetta were sure to be called into play. Hop-Frog, in especial, was so inventive in the way of getting up pageants, suggesting novel characters, and arranging costume, for masked balls, that nothing could be done, it seems, without his assistance.

The night appointed for the *fête* had arrived. A gorgeous hall had been fitted up, under Trippetta's eye, with every kind of device which could possibly give *éclat* to a masquerade. The whole court was in a fever of expectation. As for costumes and characters, it might well be supposed that everybody had come to a decision on such points. Many had made up their minds (as to what *rôles* they should assume) a week, or even a month, in advance; and, in fact, there was not a particle of indecision anywhere — except in the case of the king and his seven ministers. Why *they* hesitated I never could tell, unless they did it by way of a joke. More probably, they found it difficult, on account of being so fat, to make up their minds. At all events, time flew; and, as a last resort, they sent for Trippetta and Hop-Frog.

When the two little friends obeyed the summons of the king, they found him sitting at his wine with the seven members of his cabinet council; but the monarch appeared to be in a very ill humor. He knew that Hop-Frog was not fond of wine; for it excited the poor cripple almost to madness; and madness is no comfortable feeling. But the king loved his practical jokes, and took pleasure in forcing Hop-Frog to drink and (as the king called it) "to be merry."

"Come here, Hop-Frog," said he, as the jester and his friend entered the room; "swallow this bumper to the health of your absent friends [here Hop-Frog sighed] and then let us have the benefit of your invention. We want characters — *characters,* man, — something novel — out of the way. We are wearied with this everlasting sameness. Come, drink! the wine will brighten your wits."

Hop-Frog endeavored, as usual, to get up a jest in reply to these advances from the king; but the effort was too much. It happened to be the poor dwarf's birthday, and the command to drink to his "absent friends" forced the tears to his eyes. Many large, bitter drops fell into the goblet as he took it, humbly, from the hand of the tyrant.

"Ah! ha! ha! ha!" roared the latter, as the dwarf reluctantly drained the beaker. "See what a glass of good wine can do! Why, your eyes are shining already!"

Poor fellow! his large eyes *gleamed,* rather than shone; for the effect of wine on his excitable brain was not more powerful than instantaneous. He placed the goblet nervously on the table, and looked round upon the company with a half-insane stare. They all seemed highly amused at the success of the king's "*joke.*"

"And now to business," said the prime minister, a *very* fat man.

"Yes," said the king. "Come, Hop-Frog, lend us your assistance. Characters, my fine fellow; we stand in need of characters — all of us — ha! ha! ha!" and as this was seriously meant for a joke, his laugh was chorused by the seven.

Hop-Frog also laughed, although feebly and somewhat vacantly.

"Come, come," said the king, impatiently, "have you nothing to suggest?"

"I am endeavoring to think of something *novel,*" replied the dwarf, abstractedly, for he was quite bewildered by the wine.

"Endeavoring!" cried the tyrant, fiercely; "what do you mean by *that?* Ah, I perceive. You are sulky, and want more wine. Here, drink this!" and he poured out another goblet full and offered it to the cripple, who merely gazed at it, gasping for breath.

"Drink, I say!" shouted the monster, "or by the fiends —— "

The dwarf hesitated. The king grew purple with rage. The courtiers smirked. Trippetta, pale as a corpse, advanced to the monarch's seat, and, falling on her knees before him, implored him to spare her friend.

The tyrant regarded her, for some moments, in evident wonder at her audacity. He seemed quite at a loss what to do or say — how most becomingly to express his indignation. At last, without uttering a syllable, he pushed her violently from him, and threw the contents of the brimming goblet in her face.

The poor girl got up as best she could, and, not daring even to sigh, resumed her position at the foot of the table.

There was a dead silence for about half a minute, during which the falling of a leaf, or of a feather, might have been heard. It was interrupted by a low, but harsh and protracted *grating* sound which seemed to come at once from every corner of the room.

"What — what — *what* are you making that noise for?" demanded the king, turning furiously to the dwarf.

The latter seemed to have recovered, in great measure, from his intoxication, and looking fixedly but quietly into the tyrant's face, merely ejaculated:

"I — I? How could it have been me?"

"The sound appeared to come from without," observed one of the courtiers. "I fancy it was the parrot at the window, whetting his bill upon his cage-wires."

"True," replied the monarch, as if much relieved by the suggestion; "but, on the honor of a knight, I could have sworn that it was the gritting of this vagabond's teeth."

Hereupon the dwarf laughed (the king was too confirmed a joker to object to any one's laughing), and displayed a set of large, powerful, and very repulsive teeth. Moreover, he avowed his perfect willingness to swallow as much wine as desired. The monarch was pacified; and having drained another bumper with no very perceptible ill effect, Hop-Frog entered at once, and with spirit, into the plans for the masquerade.

"I cannot tell what was the association of ideas," observed he, very tranquilly, and as if he had never tasted wine in his life, "but *just after* your majesty had struck the girl and thrown the wine in her face — *just after* your majesty had done this, and while the parrot was making that odd noise outside the window, there came into my mind a capital diversion — one of my own country frolics — often enacted among us, at our masquerades: but here it will be new altogether. Unfortunately, however, it requires a company of eight persons, and——"

"Here we *are!*" cried the king, laughing at his acute discovery of the coincidence; "eight to a fraction — I and my seven ministers. Come! what is the diversion?"

"We call it," replied the cripple, "the Eight Chained Ourang-Outangs, and it really is excellent sport if well enacted."

"*We* will enact it," remarked the king, drawing himself up, and lowering his eyelids.

"The beauty of the game," continued Hop-Frog, "lies in the fright it occasions among the women."

"Capital!" roared in chorus the monarch and his ministry.

"I will equip you as ourang-outangs," proceeded the dwarf; "leave all that to me. The resemblance shall be so striking that the company of masqueraders will take you for real beasts — and of course, they will be as much terrified as astonished."

"Oh, this is exquisite!" exclaimed the king. "Hop-Frog! I will make a man of you."

"The chains are for the purpose of increasing the confusion by their jangling. You are supposed to have escaped, *en masse,* from your keepers. Your majesty cannot conceive the *effect* produced, at a masquerade, by eight chained ourang-outangs, imagined to be real ones by most of the company; and rushing in with savage cries, among the crowd of delicately and gorgeously habited men and women. The *contrast* is inimitable."

"It *must* be," said the king: and the council arose hurriedly (as it was growing late), to put in execution the scheme of Hop-Frog.

His mode of equipping the party as ourang-outangs was very simple, but effective enough for his purposes. The animals in question had, at the epoch of my story, very rarely been seen in any part of the civilized world; and as the imitations made by the dwarf were sufficiently beast-like and more than sufficiently hideous, their truthfulness to nature was thus thought to be secured.

The king and his ministers were first encased in tight-fitting stockinet shirts and drawers. They were then saturated with tar. At this stage of the process, some one of the party suggested feathers; but the suggestion was at once overruled by the dwarf, who soon convinced the eight, by ocular demonstration, that the hair of such a brute as the ourang-outang was much more efficiently represented by *flax*. A thick coating of the latter was accordingly plastered upon the coating of tar. A long chain was now procured. First, it was passed about the waist of the king, *and tied*; then about another of the party, and also tied; then about all successively, in the same manner. When this chaining arrangement was complete, and the party stood as far apart from each other as possible, they formed a circle; and to make all things appear natural, Hop-Frog passed the residue of the chain, in two diameters, at right angles, across the circle, after the fashion adopted, at the present day, by those who capture chimpanzees, or other large apes, in Borneo.

The grand saloon in which the masquerade was to take place, was a circular room, very lofty, and receiving the light of the sun only through a single window at the top. At night (the season for which the apartment was especially designed) it was illuminated principally by a large chandelier, depending by a chain from the centre of the sky-light, and lowered, or elevated, by means of a counterbalance as usual; but (in order not to look unsightly) this latter passed outside the cupola and over the roof.

The arrangements of the room had been left to Trippetta's superintendence; but, in some particulars, it seems, she had been guided by the calmer judgment of her friend the dwarf. At his suggestion it was that, on this occasion, the chandelier was removed. Its waxen drippings (which, in weather so warm, it was quite impossible to prevent) would have been seriously detrimental to the rich dresses of the guests, who, on account of the crowded state of the saloon, could not *all* be expected to keep from out its centre — that is to say, from under the chandelier. Additional sconces were set in various parts of the hall, out of the way; and a flambeau, emitting sweet odor, was placed in the right hand of each of the Caryatides that stood against the wall — some fifty or sixty all together.

The eight ourang-outangs, taking Hop-Frog's advice, waited patiently until midnight (when the room was thoroughly filled with masqueraders) before making their appearance. No sooner had the clock ceased striking, however, than they rushed, or rather rolled in, all together — for the impediments of their chains caused most of the party to fall, and all to stumble as they entered.

The excitement among the masqueraders was prodigious, and filled the heart of the king with glee. As had been anticipated, there were not a few of the guests who supposed the ferocious-looking creatures to be beasts of *some* kind in reality, if not precisely ourang-outangs. Many of the women swooned with affright; and had not the king taken the precaution to exclude all weapons from the saloon, his party might soon have expiated their frolic in their blood. As it was, a general rush was made for the doors; but the king had ordered them to be locked immediately upon his entrance; and, at the dwarf's suggestion, the keys had been deposited with *him*.

While the tumult was at its height, and each masquerader attentive only to his own safety (for, in fact, there was much *real* danger from the pressure of the excited crowd), the chain by which the chandelier ordinarily hung, and which had been drawn up on its removal, might have been seen very gradually to descend, until its hooked extremity came within three feet of the floor.

Soon after this, the king and his seven friends having reeled about the hall in all directions, found themselves, at length, in its centre, and, of course, in immediate contact with the chain. While they were thus situated, the dwarf, who had followed noiselessly at their heels, inciting them to keep up the commotion, took hold of their own chain at the intersection of the two portions which crossed the circle diametrically and at right angles. Here, with the rapidity of thought, he inserted the hook from which the chandelier had been wont to depend; and, in an instant, by some unseen agency, the chandelier-chain was drawn so far upward as to take the hook out of reach, and, as an inevitable consequence, to drag the ourang-outangs together in close connection, and face to face.

The masqueraders, by this time, had recovered, in some measure, from their alarm; and, beginning to regard the whole matter as a well-contrived pleasantry, set up a loud shout of laughter at the predicament of the apes.

"Leave them to *me!*" now screamed Hop-Frog, his shrill voice making itself easily heard through all the din. "Leave them to *me*. I fancy *I* know them. If I can only get a good look at them, *I* can soon tell who they are."

Here, scrambling over the heads of the crowd, he managed to get to the wall; when, seizing a flambeau from one of the Caryatides, he returned, as he went, to the centre of the room — leaped, with the agility of a monkey, upon the king's head — and thence clambered a few feet up the chain — holding down the torch to examine the group of ourang-outangs, and still screaming: "*I* shall soon find out who they are!"

And now, while the whole assembly (the apes included) were convulsed with laughter, the jester suddenly uttered a shrill whistle; when the chain flew violently up for about thirty feet — dragging with it the dismayed and struggling ourang-outangs, and leaving them suspended in mid-air between the sky-light and the floor. Hop-Frog, clinging to the chain as it rose, still maintained his relative position in respect to the eight maskers, and still (as if nothing were the matter) continued to thrust his torch down toward them, as though endeavoring to discover who they were.

So thoroughly astonished was the whole company at this ascent, that a dead silence, of about a minute's duration, ensued. It was broken by just such a low, harsh, *grating* sound as had before attracted the attention of the king and his councillors when the former threw the wine in the face of Trippetta. But, on the present occasion, there could be no question as to *whence* the sound issued. It came from the fang-like teeth of the dwarf, who ground them and gnashed them as he foamed at the mouth, and glared, with an expression of maniacal rage, into the upturned countenances of the king and his seven companions.

"Ah, ha!" said at length the infuriated jester. "Ah, ha! I begin to see who these people *are*, now!" Here, pretending to scrutinize the king more closely, he held the flambeau to the flaxen coat which enveloped him, and which instantly burst into a sheet of vivid flame. In less than half a minute the whole eight ourang-outangs were blazing fiercely, amid the shrieks of the multitude who gazed at them from below, horror-stricken, and without the power to render them the slightest assistance.

At length the flames, suddenly increasing in virulence, forced the jester to climb higher up the chain, to be out of their reach; and, as he made this movement, the crowd again sank, for a brief instant, into silence. The dwarf seized his opportunity, and once more spoke:

"I now see *distinctly*," he said, "what manner of people these maskers are. They are a great king and his seven privy-councillors, — a king who does not scruple to strike a defenceless girl, and his seven councillors who abet him in the outrage. As for myself, I am simply Hop-Frog, the jester — and *this is my last jest.*"

Owing to the high combustibility of both the flax and the tar to which it adhered, the dwarf had scarcely made an end of his brief speech before the work of vengeance was complete. The eight corpses swung in their chains, a fetid, blackened, hideous, and indistinguishable mass. The cripple hurled his torch at them, clambered leisurely to the ceiling, and disappeared through the sky-light.

It is supposed that Trippetta, stationed on the roof of the saloon, had been the accomplice of her friend in his fiery revenge, and that, together, they effected their escape to their own country; for neither was seen again.

Questions for Discussion

1. What is the irony of the first line of the story, "I never knew any one so keenly alive to a joke as the king was"? What kind of joke does the king like best? What are the limits of his humor?

2. The king and his advisors are thought of as "wise men." How does the story reveal that their "wisdom" is a sham?

3. Poe's narrator uses many elements of the fairy-tale form, referring to "those days"

and alluding to vanished customs such as the keeping of jesters and dwarves for royal amusement. In what ways is "Hop-Frog" an ironic use of the fairy-tale form?

4. How does Poe invite his readers to perceive Hop-Frog differently from the way the king and his ministers see him? How is Hop-Frog's mind different from his body? How does the mysterious grating sound made by Hop-Frog's teeth reveal his true feelings?

5. What is the relationship between Hop-Frog and Trippetta? How does the offense to Trippetta trigger the events that occur in the latter part of the story?

Ideas for Writing

1. In an essay, discuss Hop-Frog's ingenious plan to get revenge on the king and his "wise men." Why is the plan successful, despite its outlandish nature? What does the form and success of the plan reveal about Hop-Frog's true nature and the story's moral perspective on his final act?

2. Write a story in which a despised character triumphs through ingenuity over others who have ridiculed him or her.

Edgar Allan Poe

Edgar Allan Poe's stories, like his life, have been the subject of much controversy. Nineteenth-century critics disagreed over whether Poe's stories were the ravings of a drunken hack, the inspired visions of a dark angel of literature, or the self-conscious creations of a deliberate artist. Today Poe's place in the evolution of the short story is secure, his artistry recognized internationally. Yet critics still find his bizarre, highly charged symbolism; his eccentric characters; and his strange plot lines subject to a wide range of interpretations. In his thoughtful and perceptive critical writings, which appeared mostly in the popular magazines of his day, Poe discussed the nature of both the story form and creative genius. In the first essay of the casebook, Poe's preface to his *Tales of the Grotesque and Arabesque* (1839), he defines his fiction as "the results of matured purpose and very careful elaboration," not merely as popular literature derived from the Germanic tales of the Romantic period. Poe emphasizes in the preface that his stories of terror are more archetypal, more deeply grounded in nature than some readers believe — that they are stories "of the soul." Another important piece of criticism by Poe is his 1841 review of Nathaniel Hawthorne's *Twice-Told Tales*. Here Poe sets out not merely to review a book but to define the "tale" as a literary form, emphasizing that the stories that Hawthorne and he himself were then creating constitute an exercise of "the highest genius," that they are superior to the novel in artistic unity and control and resemble the best poetry.

A number of Poe's shorter pieces were collected in *Marginalia* (1844–1849). In the excerpts included here, Poe addresses such issues as the role of intuition, the nature of genius, and the need for a preestablished purpose and a structured plot for the story. In one segment, "Between Waking and Dreams," he explains his method for finding creative material within the "fancies" or fleeting dreams that come into his mind in the state between sleep and waking — a method that sounds remarkably like the kind of focus on dream recording and "lucid dreaming" that is popular today.

From Poe's own critical writing we pass to a critical examination of his work by a number of critics and creative writers. The first of these, an excerpt from "Edgar Allan Poe" (1919) by D. H. Lawrence, emphasizes the theme of death and decomposition of the soul in Poe's life and writings. Lawrence sees Poe less as an artist than as a scientist who focused on creating in his tales "a concatenation of scientific cause and effect" rather than the "spontaneous emotion" that characterizes the true story. Also concerned with the theme of death in Poe's writing, critic Joseph Patrick Roppolo in his "Meaning and 'The Masque of the Red Death'" (1963) interprets the story as a "mythic parable . . . of man's fate, and of the fate of the universe." In his essay "The House of Poe" (1959), poet and critic Richard Wilbur interprets the writer more psychologically, perceiving Poe's stories as closely connected to the imagery of dreams, as "concrete representations of states of mind." Wilbur views stories such as "Hop-Frog" and "The Masque of the Red Death" as "prose allegories of psychic conflict" and examines dream symbolism underlying the peculiar architecture and furnishings used in the stories. In a lighter vein, student Patrick Weekes reflects in his essay "Looking Death in the Eye" on "The Masque of the Red Death" as a carnival story in which it is not death itself but the knowledge of death, like the knowledge of good and evil in the Garden of Eden, that brings the Edenic revels of Prince Prospero to a close.

EDGAR ALLAN POE

PREFACE TO *Tales of the Grotesque and Arabesque* (1839)

The epithets "Grotesque" and "Arabesque" will be found to indicate with sufficient precision the prevalent tenor of the tales here published. But from the fact that, during a period of some two or three years, I have written five-and-twenty short stories whose general character may be so briefly defined, it cannot be fairly inferred — at all events it is not truly inferred — that I have, for this species of writing, any inordinate, or indeed any peculiar taste or pre-possession. I may have written with an eye to this republication in volume form, and may, therefore, have desired to preserve, as far as a certain point, a certain unity of design. This is, indeed, the fact; and it may even happen that, in this manner, I shall never compose anything again. I speak of these things here, because I am led to think that it is this prevalence of the "Arabesque" in my serious tales, which has induced one or two critics to tax me, in all friendliness, with what they have been pleased to term "Germanism" and gloom. The charge is in bad taste, and the grounds of the accusation have not been sufficiently considered. Let us admit, for the moment, that the "phantasy-pieces" now given *are* Germanic, or what not. Then Germanism is "the vein" for the time being. Tomorrow I may be anything but German, as yesterday I was everything else. These many pieces are yet one book. My friends would be quite as wise in taxing an astronomer with too much astronomy, or an ethical author with treating too largely of morals. But the truth is that, with a single exception, there is no one of these stories in which the scholar should recognise the distinctive features of that species of pseudo-horror which we are taught to call Germanic, for no better reason than that some of the secondary names of German literature have become identified with its folly. If in many of my productions terror has been the thesis, I maintain that terror is not of Germany, but of the soul, — that I have deduced this terror only from its legitimate sources, and urged it only to its legitimate results. ~ *his theory*

There are one or two of the articles here, (conceived and executed in the purest spirit of extravaganza,) to which I expect no serious attention, and of which I shall speak no farther. But for the rest I cannot conscientiously claim indulgence on the score of hasty effort. I think it best becomes me to say, therefore, that if I have sinned, I have deliberately sinned. These brief compositions are, in chief part, the results of matured purpose and very careful elaboration.

EDGAR ALLAN POE

Review of Hawthorne's Twice-Told Tales   (1841)

We said a few hurried words about Mr. Hawthorne in our last number, with the design of speaking more fully in the present. We are still, however, pressed for room, and must necessarily discuss his volumes more briefly and more at random than their high merits deserve.

The book professes to be a collection of *tales*, yet is, in two respects, misnamed. These pieces are now in their third republication, and, of course, are thrice-told. Moreover, they are by no means *all* tales, either in the ordinary or in the legitimate understanding of the term. Many of them are pure essays. . . .

But it is of his tales that we desire principally to speak. The tale proper, in our opinion, affords unquestionably the fairest field for the exercise of the loftiest talent, which can be afforded by the wide domains of mere prose. Were we bidden to say how the highest genius could be most advantageously employed for the best display of its own powers, we should answer, without hesitation — in the composition of a rhymed poem, not to exceed in length what might be perused in an hour. . . .

Were we called upon, however, to designate that class of composition which, next to such a poem as we have suggested, should best fulfil the demands of high genius — should offer it the most advantageous field of exertion — we should unhesitatingly speak of the prose tale, as Mr. Hawthorne has here exemplified it. We allude to the short prose narrative, requiring from a half-hour to one or two hours in its perusal. The ordinary novel is objectionable, from its length, for reasons already stated in substance. As it cannot be read at one sitting, it deprives itself, of course, of the immense force derivable from *totality*. Worldly interests intervening during the pauses of perusal, modify, annul, or counteract, in a greater or less degree, the impressions of the book. But simple cessation in reading, would, of itself, be sufficient to destroy the true unity. In the brief tale, however, the author is enabled to carry out the fulness of his intention, be it what it may. During the hour of perusal the soul of the reader is at the writer's control. There are no external or extrinsic influences — resulting from weariness or interruption.

A skilful literary artist has constructed a tale. If wise, he has not fashioned his thoughts to accommodate his incidents; but having conceived, with deliberate care, a certain unique or single *effect* to be wrought out, he then invents such incidents — he then combines such events as may best aid him in establishing this preconceived effect. If his very initial sentence tend not to the outbringing of this effect, then he has failed in his first step. In the whole composition there should be no word written, of which the tendency, direct or indirect, is not to the one pre-established design. And by such means, with such care and skill, a picture is at length painted which leaves in the mind of him who contemplates it with a kindred art, a sense of the fullest satisfaction. The idea of the tale has been presented unblemished, because undisturbed; and this is an end unattainable by the novel. Undue brevity is just as exceptionable here as in the poem; but undue length is yet more to be avoided.

We have said that the tale has a point of superiority even over the poem. In fact, while the *rhythm* of this latter is an essential aid in the development of the poet's highest idea — the idea of the Beautiful — the artificialities of this rhythm are an inseparable bar to the development of all points of thought or expression which have their basis in *Truth*. But Truth is often, and in very great degree, the aim of the tale. Some of the finest tales are tales of ratiocination.[1] Thus the field of this species of composition, if not in so elevated a region on the mountain of Mind, is a table-land of far vaster extent than the domain of the mere poem. Its products are never so rich, but infinitely more numerous, and more appreciable by the mass of mankind. The writer of the prose tale, in short, may bring to his theme a vast variety of modes or inflections of thought and expression — (the ratiocinative, for example, the sarcastic, or the humorous) which are not only antagonistical to the nature of the poem, but absolutely forbidden by one of its most peculiar and indispensable adjuncts; we allude, of course, to rhythm. It may be added here, *par parenthèse,* that the author who aims at the purely beautiful in a prose tale is laboring at great disadvantage. For Beauty can be better treated in the poem. Not so with terror, or passion, or horror, or a multitude of such other points. And here it will be seen how full of prejudice are the usual animadversions against those *tales of effect,* many fine examples of which were found in the earlier numbers of Blackwood.[2] The impressions produced were wrought in a legitimate sphere of action, and constituted a legitimate although sometimes an exaggerated interest. They were relished by every man of genius: although there were found many men of genius who condemned them without just ground. The true critic will but demand that the design intended be accomplished, to the fullest extent, by the means most advantageously applicable.

---

[1] Logic, rationality. — Eds.
[2] British literary magazine. — Eds.

EDGAR ALLAN POE
FROM *Marginalia* (1844–1849)

"GREAT WIT TO MADNESS IS NEARLY ALLIED . . ."

Let a man succeed ever so evidently — ever so demonstrably — in many different displays of *genius*, the envy of criticism will agree with the popular voice in denying him more than *talent*, in any. Thus a poet who has achieved a great (by which I mean an effective) poem, should be cautious not to distinguish himself in any other walk of Letters. In especial — let him make no effort in Science — unless anonymously, or with the view of waiting patiently the judgment of posterity. Because universal or even versatile geniuses have rarely or never been known, *therefore*, thinks the world, none such can ever be. A "therefore" of this kind is, with the world, conclusive. But what is the *fact*, as taught us by analysis of mental powers? Simply, the *highest* genius — that the genius which all men instantaneously acknowledge as such — which acts upon individuals, as well as upon the mass, by a species of magnetism incomprehensible but irresistible and *never resisted* — that this genius which demonstrates itself in the simplest gesture — or even by the absence of all — this genius which speaks without a voice and flashes from the unopened eye — is but the result of generally large mental power existing in a state of *absolute proportion* — so that no one faculty has undue predominance. *That* factitious "genius" — that "genius" in the popular sense — which is but the manifestation of the abnormal predominance of some one faculty over all the others — and, of course, at the expense and to the detriment, of all the others — is a result of mental disease or rather, of organic malformation of mind:— it is this and nothing more. Not only will such "genius" fail, if turned aside from the path indicated by its predominant faculty; but, even when pursuing this path — when producing those works in which, certainly, it is *best* calculated to succeed — will give unmistakeable indications of *unsoundness*, in respect to general intellect. Hence, indeed, arises the just idea that

> "Great wit to madness nearly is allied."

I say "*just* idea"; for by "great wit," in this case, the poet intends precisely the pseudo-genius to which I refer. The true genius, on the other hand, is necessarily, if not universal in its manifestations, at least capable of universality; and if, attempting all things, it succeeds in one rather better than another, this is merely on account of a certain bias by which *Taste* leads it with more earnestness in the one direction than in the other. With equal zeal, it would succeed equally in all.

To sum up our results in respect to this very simple, but much *vexata quaestio:* — [1]

---

[1] Vexing question. — Eds.

What the world calls "genius" is the state of mental disease arising from the undue predominance of some one of the faculties. The works of such genius are never sound in themselves and, in especial, always betray the general mental insanity.

The proportion of the mental faculties, in a case where the general mental power is *not* inordinate, gives that result which we distinguish as *talent:*— and the talent is greater or less, first, as the general mental power is greater or less; and, secondly, as the proportion of the faculties is more or less absolute.

The proportion of the faculties, in a case where the mental power is inordinately great, gives that result which *is* the true *genius* (but which, on account of the proportion and seeming simplicity of its works, is seldom acknowledged to *be* so;) and the genius is greater or less, first, as the general mental power is more or less inordinately great; and, secondly, as the proportion of the faculties is more or less absolute.

An objection will be made:— that the greatest excess of mental power, however proportionate, does not seem to satisfy our idea of genius, unless we have, in addition, sensibility, passion, energy. The reply is, that the "absolute proportion" spoken of, when applied to inordinate mental power, gives, as a result, the appreciation of Beauty and a horror of Deformity which we call sensibility, together with that intense vitality, which is implied when we speak of "Energy" or "Passion."

ON INTUITION

There are few thinkers who will not be surprised to find, upon retrospect of the world of thought, how *very* frequently the first, or intuitive, impressions have been the true ones. A poem, for example, enraptures us in our childhood. In adolescence, we perceive it to be full of fault. In the first years of manhood, we utterly despise and condemn it; and it is not until mature age has given tone to our feelings, enlarged our knowledge, and perfected our understanding, that we recur to our original sentiment and primitive admiration, with the additional pleasure which is always deduced from knowing *how* it was that we once were pleased, and *why* it is that we still admire.

That the imagination has not been unjustly ranked as supreme among the mental faculties, appears from the intense consciousness, on the part of the imaginative man, that the faculty in question brings his soul often to a glimpse of things supernal and eternal— to the very verge of the *great secrets*. There are moments, indeed, in which he perceives the faint perfumes, and hears the melodies of a happier world. Some of the most profound knowledge— perhaps all *very* profound knowledge— has originated from a highly stimulated imagination. Great intellects guess well. The laws of Kepler were, professedly, *guesses*.

BETWEEN WAKING AND DREAMS

Some Frenchman— possibly Montaigne— says: "People talk about thinking, but for my part I never think except when I sit down to write." It is this never thinking, unless when we sit down to write, which is the cause of so much indifferent composition. But perhaps there is something more involved in the Frenchman's observation than meets the eye. It is certain that the mere act of inditing tends, in a great degree, to the logicalisation of thought. Whenever, on account of its vagueness, I am dissatisfied with a conception of the brain, I resort forthwith to the pen, for the purpose of obtaining, through its aid, the necessary form, consequence, and precision.

How very commonly we hear it remarked that such and such thoughts are beyond the compass of words! I do not believe that any thought, properly so called, is out of the reach of language. I fancy, rather, that where difficulty in expression is experienced, there is, in the intellect which experiences it, a want either of deliberateness or of method. For my own part, I have never had a thought which I could not set down in words, with even more distinctness than that with which I conceived it: as I have before observed, the thought is logicalised by the effort at (written) expression.

There is, however, a class of fancies, of exquisite delicacy, which are not thoughts, and to which, as yet, I have found it absolutely impossible to adapt language. I use the word *fancies* at random, and merely because I must use *some* word; but the idea commonly attached to the term is not even remotely applicable to the shadows of shadows in question. They seem to me rather psychal than intellectual. They arise in the soul (alas, how rarely!) only at its epochs of most intense tranquillity — when the bodily and mental health are in perfection — and at those mere points of time where the confines of the waking world blend with those of the world of dreams. I am aware of these "fancies" only when I am upon the very brink of sleep, with the consciousness that I am so. I have satisfied myself that this condition exists but for an inappreciable *point* of time — yet it is crowded with these "shadows of shadows"; and for absolute *thought* there is demanded time's *endurance*.

These "fancies" have in them a pleasurable ecstasy, as far beyond the most pleasurable of the world of wakefulness, or of dreams, as the Heaven of the Northman[2] theology is beyond its Hell. I regard the visions, even as they arise, with an awe which, in some measure moderates or tranquillises the ecstasy — so regard them, through a conviction (which seems a portion of the ecstasy itself) that this ecstasy, in itself, is of a character supernal to the Human Nature — is a glimpse of the spirit's outer world; and I arrive at this conclusion — if this term is at all applicable to instantaneous intuition — by a perception that the delight experienced has, as its element, but *the absoluteness of novelty*. I say the absoluteness — for in the fancies — let me now term them psychal impressions — there is really nothing even approximate in character to impressions ordinarily received. It is as if the five senses were supplanted by five myriad others alien to mortality.

---

[2] Norse. — Eds.

Now, so entire is my faith in the *power of words*, that at times I have believed it possible to embody even the evanescence of fancies such as I have attempted to describe. In experiments with this end in view, I have proceeded so far as, first, to control (when the bodily and mental health are good), the existence of the condition — that is to say, I can now (unless when ill), be sure that the condition will supervene, if I so wish it, at the point of time already described: of its supervention until lately I could never be certain even under the most favorable circumstances. I mean to say, merely, that now I can be sure, when all circumstances are favorable, of the supervention of the condition, and feel even the capacity of inducing or compelling it — the favorable circumstances, however, are not the less rare — else had I compelled already the Heaven into the Earth.

I have proceeded so far, secondly, as to prevent the lapse from *the point* of which I speak — the point of blending between wakefulness and sleep — as to prevent at will, I say, the lapse from this border-ground into the dominion of sleep. Not that I can *continue* the condition — not that I can render the point more than a point — but that I can startle myself from the point into wakefulness; *and thus transfer the point itself into the realm of Memory* — convey its impressions, or more properly their recollections, to a situation where (although still for a very brief period) I can survey them with the eye of analysis.

For these reasons — that is to say, because I have been enabled to accomplish thus much — I do not altogether despair of embodying in words at least enough of the fancies in question to convey to certain classes of intellect, a shadowy conception of their character.

In saying this I am not to be understood as supposing that the fancies or psychal impressions to which I allude are confined to my individual self — are not, in a word, common to all mankind — for on this point it is quite impossible that I should form an opinion — but nothing can be more certain than that even a partial record of the impressions would startle the universal intellect of mankind, by the *supremeness of the novelty* of the material employed, and of its consequent suggestions. In a word — should I ever write a paper on this topic, the world will be compelled to acknowledge that, at last, I have done an original thing.

PLOT—A DEFINITION

An excellent magazine paper might be written upon the subject of the progressive steps by which any great work of art — especially of literary art — attained completion. How vast a dissimilarity always exists between the germ and the fruit — between the work and its original conception! Sometimes the original conception is abandoned, or left out of sight altogether. Most authors sit down to write with *no* fixed design, trusting to the inspiration of the moment; it is not, therefore, to be wondered at, that *most* books are valueless. Pen should never touch paper, until at least a well-digested *general* purpose be established. In fiction, the *dénouement* — in all other composition the intended *effect,* should be definitely considered and arranged, before writing the first word; and no word should be then written which does not tend, or form a part of a sentence which tends to the development of the *dénouement,* or to the strengthening of the effect. Where *plot* forms a portion of the contemplated interest, too much preconsideration cannot be had. *Plot* is very imperfectly understood, and has never been rightly defined. Many persons regard it as mere complexity of incident. In its most rigorous acceptation, it is *that from which no component atom can be removed, and in which none of the component atoms can be displaced, without ruin to the whole;* and although a sufficiently good plot may be constructed, without attention to the whole rigor of this definition, still it is the definition which the true artist should always keep in view, and always endeavor to consummate in his works.

D. H. LAWRENCE

FROM *Edgar Allan Poe*   (1919)

It seems a long way from Fenimore Cooper to Poe. But in fact it is only a step. Leatherstocking is the last instance of the integral, progressive, soul of the white man in America. In the last conjunction between Leatherstocking and Chingachgook we see the passing out into the darkness of the interim, as a seed falls into the dark interval of winter. What remains is the old tree withering and seething down to the crisis of winterdeath, the great white race in America keenly disintegrating, seething back in electric decomposition, back to that crisis where the old soul, the old era, perishes in the denuded frame of man, and the first throb of a new year sets in.

The process of the decomposition of the body after death is slow and mysterious, a life process of post-mortem activity. In the same way, the great psyche, which we have evolved through two thousand years of effort, must die, and not only die, must be reduced back to its elements by a long, slow process of disintegration, living disintegration.

This is the clue to Edgar Allan Poe, and to the art that succeeds him, in America. When a tree withers, at the end of a year, then the whole life of the year is gradually driven out until the tissue remains elemental and almost null. Yet it is only reduced to that crisis of perfect quiescence which *must* intervene between life-cycle and life-cycle. Poe shows us the first vivid, seething reduction of the psyche, the first convulsive spasm that sets-in in the human soul, when the last impulse of creative love, creative conjunction, is finished. It is like a tree whose fruits are perfected, writhing now in the grip of the first frost.

For men who are born at the end of a great era or epoch nothing remains but the seething reduction back to the elements; just as for a tree in autumn nothing remains but the strangling-off of the leaves and the strange decomposition and arrest of the sap. It is useless to ask for perpetual spring and summer. Poe had to lead on to that winter-crisis when the soul is, as it were, denuded of itself, reduced back to the elemental state of a naked, arrested tree in midwinter. Man must be stripped of himself. And the process is slow and bitter and beautiful, too. But the beauty has its spark in anguish; it is the strange, expiring cry, the phosphorescence of decay.

Poe is a man writhing in the mystery of his own undoing. He is a great dead soul, progressing terribly down the long process of post-mortem activity in disintegration. This is how the dead bury their dead. This is how man must bury his own dead self: in pang after pang of vital, explosive self-reduction, back to the elements. This is how the seed must fall into the ground and perish before it can bring forth new life. For Poe the process was one of perishing in the old body, the old psyche, the old self. He leads us back, through pang after pang of disintegrative sensation, back towards the end of all things, where the beginning is: just as the year begins where the year is utterly dead. It is only perfect courage which can carry us through the extremity of death, through the crisis of our own nullification, the midwinter which is the end of the end and the beginning of the beginning.

Yet Poe is hardly an artist. He is rather a supreme scientist. Art displays the movements of the pristine self, the living conjunction or communion between the self and its context. Even in tragedy self meets self in supreme conjunction, a communion of passionate or creative death. But in Poe the self is finished, already stark. It would be true to say that Poe had no soul. He lives in the post-mortem reality, a living dead. He reveals the after-effects of life, the processes of organic disintegration. Arrested in himself, he cannot realise self or soul in any other human being. For him, the vital world is the sensational world. He is not sensual, he is sensational. The difference between these two is a difference between growth and decay. In Poe, sensationalism is a process of explosive disintegration, phosphorescent, electric, refracted. In him, sensation is that momentaneous state of consciousness which concurs with the sudden combustion and reduction of vital tissue. The combustion of his own most vital plasm liberates the white gleam of his sensational consciousness. Hence his addiction to alcohol and drugs, which are the common agents of reductive combustion.

It is for this reason that we would class the "tales" as science rather than art: because they reveal the workings of the great inorganic forces, disruptive within the organic psyche. The central soul or self is in arrest. And for this reason we cannot speak of the tales as stories or novels. A tale is a concatenation of scientific cause and effect. But in a story the movement depends on the sudden appearance of spontaneous emotion or gesture, causeless, arising out of the living self.

JOSEPH PATRICK ROPPOLO

FROM *Meaning and*
"The Masque of the Red Death"   (1963)

In Poe's imaginative prose, beginnings unfailingly are important. "The Masque of the Red Death" begins with these three short sentences:

> The "Red Death" had long devastated the country. No pestilence had even been so fatal or so hideous. Blood was its Avatar and its seal — the redness and horror of blood.

On one level, the reader is introduced to a disease, a plague, with hideous and terrifying symptoms, a remarkably rapid course, and inevitable termination in death. But Poe's heaviest emphasis is on blood, not as sign or symptom, but as avatar and seal. A seal is something that confirms or assures or ratifies. The appearance — the presence — of blood is confirmation or assurance of the existence of the Red Death or, more broadly, of Death itself. As avatar, blood is the incarnation, the bodily representation, of the Red Death. It is, further, something godlike, an eternal principle, for in Hindu myth, the word "avatar" referred to the descent of a god, in human form, to earth. Further, "avatar" can be defined as "a variant phase or version of a continuing entity."[1] A second level thus emerges: blood represents something invisible and eternal, a ruling principle of the universe. That principle, Poe seems to suggest, is death.

But is it? The Red Death, Poe tells us, "had long devastated the country." And then: "No pestilence had ever been so fatal" — surely a remarkable second sentence for a man so careful of grammar and logic as Poe. Is or is not the Red Death a pestilence? And does the word "fatal" permit of comparison? I should like to suggest that here Poe is being neither ungrammatical nor even carefully ambiguous, but daringly clear. The Red Death is not a pestilence, in the usual sense; it is unfailingly and universally fatal, as no mere disease or plague can be; and blood is its guarantee, its avatar and seal. Like itself, then, is the Red Death, the one "affliction" shared by all mankind.[2]

For purposes of commenting on life and of achieving his single effect, Poe chooses to emphasize death. He is aware not only of the brevity of all life and of its inevitable termination but also of men's isolation: blood, the visible

---

[1] Reference to the *OED* will show that all meanings given here for *seal* and *avator* were current in Poe's time.

[2] "For the life of all flesh is the blood thereof" (Leviticus 17:14). Poe knew the Bible well, and references to and quotations from the Bible are frequent in his works. In *Biblical Allusions in Poe* (New York: The Macmillan Company, 1928), William Mentzel Forrest says that Poe's views on death are "essentially Biblical" and points out that "Throughout the Old Testament death is looked upon not from the religious but from the natural viewpoint, as something to which all life is subject in harmony with the great laws of change" (p. 58).

sign of life, is, Poe says, "the pest ban which shuts him out from the aid and sympathy of his fellow man." In the trap of life and in his death, every man *is* an island. If there is a mutual bond, it is the shared horror of death.

Out of the chaos that has "long devastated" his dominions, Prince Prospero creates a new and smaller world for the preservation of life. A kind of demigod, Prospero can "create" his world, and he can people it; but time (the ebony clock) exists in his new world, and he is, of course, deluded in his belief that he can let in life and shut out death. Prospero's world of seven rooms, without "means [either] of ingress or egress," is a microcosm, as the parallel with the seven ages of man indicates, and its people are eminently human, with their predilection for pleasure and their susceptibility to "sudden impulses of despair or frenzy." In their masquerade costumes, the people are "in fact, a multitude of dreams," but they are fashioned like the inhabitants of the macrocosmic world. Many are beautiful, but many also are bizarre or grotesque. Some are wanton; some are "arabesque figures with unsuited limbs and appointments"; some are terrible, some are disgusting, and some are "delirious fancies such as the madman fashions" (and Prospero, the demigod, for all his "fine eye for colors and effects," may indeed be mad). But all of them are life, and in six of the seven apartments "the heart of life" beats "feverishly." And even here, by deliberate use of the word "feverishly," Poe links life with disease and death.

The seventh apartment is not the room of death; death occurs in fact in each of the rooms. It is, however, the room in which the reminders of death are strongest, and it is the room to which all must come who traverse the preceding six. Death's colors, red and black, are there; and there the ebony clock mercilessly measures Time, reminding the revelers hour after hour that life, like the course of the Red Death, is short.

When the clock strikes the dreaded hour of twelve, the revelers become aware suddenly of the presence of a masked figure which none has noted before:

> The figure was tall and gaunt, and shrouded from head to foot in the habiliments of the grave. The mask which concealed the visage was made so nearly to resemble the countenance of a stiffened corpse that the closest scrutiny must have had difficulty in detecting the cheat. And yet all this might have been endured, if not approved, by the mad revelers around. But the mummer had gone so far as to assume the type of the Red Death. His vesture was dabbled in *blood*—and his broad brow, with all the features of the face, was besprinkled with the scarlet horror.

Poe does not indicate in which room the awareness of the masked figure occurred first, but Prince Prospero sees this blood-sprinkled horror in the blue, or easternmost, room, which is usually associated with birth, rather than with death. The figure moves then through each of the apartments, and Prospero follows, to meet his own death in the room of black and red.

Not once does Poe say that the figure is the Red Death. Instead "this new presence" is called "the masked figure," "the stranger," "the mummer," "this spectral image," and "the intruder." He is "shrouded" in "the habiliments of the grave," the dress provided by the living for their dead and endowed by the living with all the horror and terror which they associate with death. The mask, fashioned to resemble "the countenance of a stiffened corpse," is but a mask, a "cheat." And all this, we are told, "might have been borne" had it not been for the blood, that inescapable reminder to life of the inevitability of death. The intruder is, literally, "The *Mask* of the Red Death,"[3] not the plague itself, nor even — as many would have it — the all-inclusive representation of Death.

There is horror in the discovery that "the grave-cerements and corpse-like mask" are "untenanted by any tangible form," but the horror runs more deeply than the supernatural interpretation allows, so deeply in fact that it washes itself clean to merge as Truth. Blood, Poe has been saying, is (or is symbolic of) the life force; but even as it suggests life, blood serves as a reminder of death.[4] Man himself invests death with elements of terror, and he clothes not death but the terror of death in garb of his own making — "the habiliments of the grave" — and then runs, foolishly, to escape it or, madly, to kill it, mistaking the mummer, the cheat, for death itself. The fear of death can kill: Prospero attempts to attack the masked figure and falls; but when man's image of death is confronted directly, it is found to be nothing. The vestments are empty. The intruder in "The Masque of the Red Death" is, then, not the plague, not death itself, but man's creation, his self-aroused and self-developed fear of his own mistaken concept of death.

Death is nevertheless present, as pervasive and as invisible as eternal law. He is nowhere and everywhere, not only near, about, and around man, but in him. And so it is, at last, that, having unmasked their unreasoning fear, the revelers acknowledge the presence of the Red Death. One by one, the revelers die — as everything endowed with life must; and, with the last of them, time, which is measured and feared only by man, dies, too.[5]

Poe might have stopped there, just as he might have ended "The Raven" with the sixteenth stanza. The narrative is complete, and there are even "morals" or "lessons" for those who demand them. But, as Poe says in "The Philosophy of Composition,"

---

[3] Poe's original title for this short prose piece, when it appeared in *Graham's Lady and Gentleman's Magazine* in May 1842, was "The Mask of the Red Death. A Fantasy."

[4] Charles O'Donnell, in "From Earth to Ether: Poe's Flight into Space," *PMLA*, LXXVII (March 1962), pp. 88, 89, makes much the same point in his discussion of *The Narrative of Arthur Gordon Pym*. O'Donnell speaks of blood as "the life force" and as "suggestive of life, mystery, suffering, terror — in general of the human situation."

[5] "The angel which I saw stand upon the sea and upon the earth . . . sware . . . that there should be time no longer" (Revelation 10:5, 6).

in subjects so handled, however skilfully, or with however vivid an array of incident, there is always a certain hardness or nakedness, which repels the artistical eye. Two things are invariably required — first, some amount of complexity, or more properly, adaptation; and, secondly, some amount of suggestiveness — some undercurrent, however indefinite, of meaning.

To achieve complexity and suggestiveness, Poe added two stanzas to "The Raven." To "The Masque of the Red Death" he added two sentences: "And the flames of the tripods expired. And Darkness and Decay and the Red Death held illimitable dominion over all."

"Let there be light" was one of the principles of Creation; darkness, then, is a principle of Chaos. And to Poe Chaos is synonymous with Nothingness, "which, to all finite perception, Unity must be." Decay occurs as matter "expels the ether" to return to or to sink into Unity. Prince Prospero's world, created out of a chaos ruled by the Red Death, returns to chaos, ruled by the trinity of Darkness and Decay and the Red Death. But, it will be remembered, Prince Prospero's world came into being *because of* the Red Death, which, although it includes death, is the principle of life. In Chaos, then, is the promise of new lives and of new worlds which will swell into existence and then, in their turn, subside into nothingness in the eternal process of contraction and expansion which Poe describes in *Eureka*.[6]

There are "morals" implicit and explicit in this interpretation of "The Masque of the Red Death," but they need not be underlined here. Poe, who had maintained in his "Review of Nathaniel Hawthorne's *Twice-Told Tales*" that "Truth is often, and in very great degree, the aim of the tale," was working with a larger, but surely not entirely inexpressible, truth than can be conveyed in a simple "Poor Richard" maxim; and in that task, it seems to me, he transcends the tale (into which classification most critics put "The Masque of the Red Death") to create a prose which, in its free rhythms, its diction, its compression, and its suggestion, approaches poetry.[7]

The ideas that were haunting Poe when he published *Eureka* were already haunting him in 1842, when he published "The Masque of the Red Death," and what emerged was not, certainly, a short story; nor was it, except by the freest definition, a tale. For either category, it is deficient in plot and in characterization. Instead, "The Masque of the Red Death" combines elements of the parable and of the myth. Not as explicit or as pointedly allegorical always

---

[6] Poe's theories of the universe, including his theory of the identity of Unity and Nothingness, are explained in detail in *Eureka*. Also pertinent is Poe's statement in *Eureka* that "In the Original Unity of the First Thing lies the Secondary Cause of All Things, with the Germ of their Inevitable Annihilation."

[7] Poe calls *Eureka* a prose poem, "Shadow" a parable, and "Silence" a fable. Both "Shadow" and "Silence" have many of the qualities of prose poetry. According to Buranelli (p. 113), Poe believed that "prose poetry is genuine poetry; intellectually inpoverished rhyme is not." Blair (p. 238) also notes that the indefiniteness and suggestiveness of "The Masque of the Red Death" are "calculated to elevate the soul" — and elevation of the soul is, according to Poe, the function of poetry.

as the parable, "The Masque of the Red Death" nevertheless can be (and has been) read as a parable of the inevitability and the universality of death; but it deals also with the feats of a hero or demigod — Prospero — and with Poe's concepts of universal principles, and it has the mystery and the remoteness of myth. What Poe has created, then, is a kind of mythic parable, brief and poetic, of the human condition, of man's fate, and of the fate of the universe.

RICHARD WILBUR

FROM *The House of Poe*   (1959)

Like many romantic poets, Poe identified imagination with dream. Where Poe differed from other romantic poets was in the literalness and absoluteness of the identification, and in the clinical precision with which he observed the phenomena of dream, carefully distinguishing the various states through which the mind passes on its way to sleep. A large number of Poe's stories derive their very structure from this sequence of mental states: "MS. Found in a Bottle," to give but one example, is an allegory of the mind's voyage from the waking world into the world of dreams, with each main step of the narrative symbolizing the passage of the mind from one state to another — from wakefulness to reverie, from reverie to the hypnagogic state, from the hypnagogic state to the deep dream. The departure of the narrator's ship from Batavia represents the mind's withdrawal from the waking world; the drowning of the captain and all but one of the crew represents the growing solitude of reverie; when the narrator is transferred by collision from a real ship to a phantom ship, we are to understand that he has passed from reverie, a state in which reality and dream exist in a kind of equilibrium, into the free fantasy of the hypnagogic state. And when the phantom ship makes its final plunge into the whirlpool, we are to understand that the narrator's mind has gone over the brink of sleep and descended into dreams.

What I am saying by means of this example is that the scenes and situations of Poe's tales are always concrete representations of states of mind. If we bear in mind Poe's fundamental plot — the effort of the poetic soul to escape all consciousness of the world in dream — we soon recognize the significance of certain scenic or situational motifs which turn up in story after story. The most important of these recurrent motifs is that of *enclosure* or *circumscription*; perhaps the latter term is preferable, because it is Poe's own word, and because Poe's enclosures are so often more or less circular in form. The heroes of Poe's tales and poems are violently circumscribed by whirlpools, or peacefully circumscribed by cloud-capped Paradisal valleys; they float upon circular pools ringed in by steep flowering hillsides; they dwell on islands, or voyage to them;

we find Poe's heroes also in coffins, in the cabs of balloons, or hidden away in the holds of ships; and above all we find them sitting alone in the claustral and richly furnished rooms of remote and mouldering mansions. . . .

Flickering candles, wavering torches, and censers full of writhing vari-colored flames furnish much of the illumination of Poe's rooms, and one can see the appropriateness of such lighting to the vague and shifting perceptions of the hypnagogic state. But undoubtedly the most important lighting-fixture in Poe's rooms—and one which appears in a good half of them—is the chandelier. It hangs from the lofty ceiling by a long chain, generally of gold, and it consists sometimes of a censer, sometimes of a lamp, sometimes of candles, sometimes of a glowing jewel (a ruby or a diamond), and once, in the macabre tale "King Pest," of a skull containing ignited charcoal. What we must understand about this chandelier, as Poe explains in his poem "Al Aaraaf," is that its chain does not stop at the ceiling: it goes right on through the ceiling, through the roof, and up to heaven. What comes down the chain from heaven is the divine power of imagination, and it is imagination's purifying fire which flashes or flickers from the chandelier. That is why the immaterial and angelic Ligeia makes her reappearance directly beneath the chandelier; and that is why Hop-Frog makes his departure for dream-land by climbing the chandelier chain and vanishing through the skylight.

The dreaming soul, then, has its own light—a light more spiritual, more divine, than that of the sun. And Poe's chamber of dream is autonomous in every other respect. No breath of air enters it from the outside world: either its atmosphere is dead, or its draperies are stirred by magical and intramural air currents. No earthly sound invades the chamber: either it is deadly still, or it echoes with a sourceless and unearthly music. Nor does any odor of flower or field intrude: instead, as Poe tells in "The Assignation," the sense of smell is "oppressed by mingled and conflicting perfumes, reeking up from strange convolute censers."

The point of all this is that the dreaming psyche separates itself wholly from the bodily senses—the "rudimental senses," as Poe called them. The bodily senses are dependent on objective stimuli—on the lights and sounds and odors of the physical world. But the sensuous life of dream is self-sufficient and immaterial, and consists in the imagination's Godlike enjoyment of its own creations.

I am reminded, at this point, of a paragraph of Santayana's, in which he describes the human soul as it was conceived by the philosopher Leibniz. Leibniz, says Santayana, assigned

> a mental seat to all sensible objects. The soul, he said, had no windows
> and, he might have added, no doors; no light could come to it from with-
> out; and it could not exert any transitive force or make any difference
> beyond its own insulated chamber. It was a *camera obscura*, with a uni-
> verse painted on its impenetrable walls. The changes which went on in it

were like those in a dream, due to the discharge of pent-up energies and fecundities within it.

Leibniz' chamber of the soul is identical with Poe's chamber of dream: but the solipsism which Leibniz saw as the normal human condition was for Poe an ideal state, a blessed state, which we may enjoy as children or as preexistent souls, but can reclaim in adult life only by a flight from everyday consciousness into hypnagogic trance.

The one thing which remains to be said about Poe's buildings is that cellars or catacombs, whenever they appear, stand for the irrational part of the mind; and that is so conventional an equation in symbolic literature that I think I need not be persuasive or illustrative about it. I had hoped, at this point, to discuss in a leisurely way some of the stories in which Poe makes use of his architectural properties, treating those stories as narrative wholes. But I have spoken too long about other things; and so, if you will allow me a few minutes more, I shall close by commenting briskly on two or three stories only.

The typical Poe story occurs *within* the mind of a poet; and its characters are not independent personalities, but allegorical figures representing the warring principles of the poet's divided nature. The lady Ligeia, for example, stands for that heavenly beauty which the poet's soul desires; while Rowena stands for that earthly, physical beauty which tempts the poet's passions. The action of the story is the dreaming soul's gradual emancipation from earthly attachments — which is allegorically expressed in the slow dissolution of Rowena. The result of this process is the soul's final, momentary vision of the heavenly Ligeia. Poe's typical story presents some such struggle between the visionary and the mundane; and the duration of Poe's typical story is the duration of a dream.

There are two tales in which Poe makes an especially clear and simple use of his architectural symbolism. The first is an unfamiliar tale called "The System of Dr. Tarr and Prof. Fether," and the edifice of that tale is a remote and dilapidated madhouse in southern France. What happens, in brief, is that the inmates of the madhouse escape from their cells in the basement of the building, overpower their keepers, and lock them up in their own cells. Having done this, the lunatics take possession of the upper reaches of the house. They shutter all the windows, put on odd costumes, and proceed to hold an uproarious and discordant feast, during which there is much eating and drinking of a disgusting kind, and a degraded version of Ligeia or Helen does a strip tease. At the height of these festivities, the keepers escape from their cells, break in through the barred and shuttered windows of the dining room, and restore order. . . .

You will recall how Prince Prospero [in "The Masque of the Red Death"], when his dominions are being ravaged by the plague, withdraws with a thousand of his knights and ladies into a secluded, impregnable and windowless abbey, where after a time he entertains his friends with a costume ball. The weird décor of the seven ballrooms expresses the Prince's own taste, and in strange costumes of the Prince's own design the company dances far into the night, looking, as Poe says, like "a multitude of dreams." The festivities are interrupted only by the hourly striking of a gigantic ebony clock which stands in the westernmost room; and the striking of this clock has invariably a sobering effect on the revellers. Upon the last stroke of twelve, as you will remember, there appears amid the throng a figure attired in the blood-dabbled graveclothes of a plague-victim. The dancers shrink from him in terror. But the Prince, infuriated at what he takes to be an insolent practical joke, draws his dagger and pursues the figure through all of the seven rooms. In the last and westernmost room, the figure suddenly turns and confronts Prince Prospero, who gives a cry of despair and falls upon his own dagger. The Prince's friends rush forward to seize the intruder, who stands now within the shadow of the ebony clock; but they find nothing there. And then, one after the other, the thousand revellers fall dead of the Red Death, and the lights flicker out, and Prince Prospero's ball is at an end.

In spite of its cast of one thousand and two, "The Masque of the Red Death" has only one character. Prince Prospero is one-half of that character, the visionary half; the nameless figure in graveclothes is the other, as we shall see in a moment.

More than once, in his dialogues or critical writings, Poe describes the earth-bound, time-bound rationalism of his age as a *disease*. And that is what the Red Death signifies. Prince Prospero's flight from the Red Death is the poetic imagination's flight from temporal and worldly consciousness into dream. The thousand dancers of Prince Prospero's costume ball are just what Poe says they are — "dreams" or "phantasms," veiled and vivid creatures of Prince Prospero's rapt imagination. Whenever there is a feast, or carnival, or costume ball in Poe, we may be sure that a dream is in progress.

But what is the gigantic ebony clock? For the answer to that, one need only consult a dictionary of slang: we call the human heart a *ticker,* meaning that it is the clock of the body; and that is what Poe means here. In sleep, our minds may roam beyond the temporal world, but our hearts tick on, binding us to time and mortality. Whenever the ebony clock strikes, the dancers of Prince Prospero's dream grow momentarily pale and still, in half-awareness that they and their revel must have an end; it is as if a sleeper should half-awaken, and know that he has been dreaming, and then sink back into dreams again.

The figure in blood-dabbled graveclothes, who stalks through the terrified company and vanishes in the shadow of the clock, is waking temporal consciousness, and his coming means the death of dreams. He breaks up Prince Prospero's ball as the keepers in "Dr. Tarr and Prof. Fether" break up the revels of the lunatics. The final confrontation between Prince Prospero and the shrouded figure is like the terrible final meeting between William Wilson and his double. Recognizing his adversary as his own worldly and mortal self, Prince Prospero gives a cry of despair which is also Poe's cry of despair:

despair at the realization that only by self-destruction could the poet fully free his soul from the trammels of this world.

Poe's aesthetic, Poe's theory of the nature of art, seems to me insane. To say that art should repudiate everything human and earthly, and find its subject matter at the flickering end of dreams, is hopelessly to narrow the scope and function of art. Poe's aesthetic points toward such impoverishments as *poésie pure* and the abstract expressionist movement in painting. And yet, despite his aesthetic, Poe is a great artist, and I would rest my case for him on his prose allegories of psychic conflict. In them, Poe broke wholly new ground, and they remain the best things of their kind in our literature. Poe's mind may have been a strange one; yet all minds are alike in their general structure; therefore we can understand him, and I think that he will have something to say to us as long as there is civil war in the palaces of men's minds.

STUDENT ESSAY

Looking Death in the Eye: Poe's "The Masque of the Red Death"
by Patrick Weekes

Upon reading Poe a reader might conclude that the author is unpleasantly ghoulish, with a sick, twisted vision. His stories usually focus on murder or death, often featuring the entombment of a person, animal, or organ; the stories often include a particularly grisly ending as well. What the reader may neglect if dismissing Poe as a mere horror writer, however, is that Poe, for all his ghoulishness, was also a dedicated philosopher. His ideas about life, death, and the varied realms in between are woven into his works, giving them a depth far beyond that of today's average suspense novel. While Poe's views may make us feel uncomfortable, they are powerful, indicative of the keen mind of one of America's most celebrated writers. In stories such as "The Masque of the Red Death," in addition to enjoying a frightening tale, readers learn of Poe's views on life, time, and death.

The setting of a novel or short story is usually just a background against which the characters are the main focus; in "The Masque of the Red Death," however, the characters are described in far less detail than the extravagant and sensual rooms in which the masque occurs. In such a short story, everything mentioned is mentioned for a reason, and since the description of the rooms and castle is so intense, it is reasonable to begin looking for Poe's deeper meaning in these settings. The room-by-room description begins "[The room] at the eastern extremity was hung, for example, in blue." The final room is described as "the western or black chamber."

Each room is characterized chiefly by a color, one of the most overtly symbolic devices in the story. Taking the black and red room as an obvious reference to death, it is then logical that the progression of rooms from east to west symbolizes a progression through life. Light is used first to illustrate time--the easternmost room is closest to the dawn, and symbolizes birth or the first stage in life, while the westernmost is closest to sunset and death. In addition the colors of the rooms can be seen as signifying each phase of life, although what each individual color symbolizes may be interpreted differently by every reader. For example, the fifth room, draped in white, could symbolize purity and the prime of life; it is equally possible that white signifies a lack of color, a sign of dullness or boredom in life. The similarity between the second room, done in purple, and the sixth, done in violet, could imply a regression, a return to innocence, but it could also portray a loss of strength, a return to childlike weakness. Once the symbolism of the rooms is recognized, one line by Poe seems to be particularly meaningful: "The apartments were so irregularly disposed that the vision embraced but little more than one at a time." This line implies that we can remember the rooms (or the moments of time) we have been in, but we cannot experience them while we are experiencing another moment, and the future will always be a surprise.

A second symbolic device in "The Masque of the Red Death," one which receives as much if not more attention than the rooms, is the clock located in the black room. At first it seems to be a simple horror element -- the gonging clock adds a gothic touch to the already fantastic and terrible party. When looked at more closely, however--the description of the clock situated on the westernmost wall of the westernmost--room--the clock can symbolize death. The words describing the clock ring with a gloomy sound: "dull, heavy, monotonous." These words seem to imply that the clock is a reminder of death, as does the reaction of the revellers when confronted with the clock's ringing. No musician can play, no partygoer can dance in the face of the ringing; each must stop and recognize their own mortality for one moment. Thus it seems logical to assume that the clock symbolizes death.

The last paragraph of the story, however, may be read as contradicting this symbolic interpretation: "And the life of the ebony clock went out with that of the last of the gay." Perhaps the clock does not symbolize death itself, but rather the *threat--the inevitability*--of death, which in some form or another rings through the lives of all the partygoers. Once they are dead, though, the threat itself is no more; it has been made a reality; there is no one left to fear it.

Finally, the reader needs to reflect upon the symbolic meaning of the Red Death himself, where the climax of the story occurs. The figure at first seems straightforward enough; he is dressed as a victim of the Red Death, complete with blood-speckled forehead, and is later revealed to be the living incarnation of the Red Death itself. But certain of his actions make the Red Death figure more than a mere melodramatic villain. Upon being threatened, the Red Death first approaches Prospero, who shrinks back in momentary cowardice. Rather than falling upon him then, though, the figure proceeds from the blue room through the castle, stopping in the room of death. Was it mere style that prevented Poe from writing Prospero's death in the easternmost room, or from having the figure appear in the black room from the beginning? Possibly a deeper meaning is suggested by the fact that Prospero "rushed hurriedly through the six chambers," to meet the Red Death, holding aloft a dagger. And how exactly does Prospero die, for there is no sign that the Red Death infected Prospero, or even touched him?

The procession of the Red Death through the seven rooms lends an air of completion to the story, as does Prospero's eagerness to follow immediately. If we take the Red Death to simply symbolize death, many of the above questions can be answered. Prospero, the large, bold, adventurous man, spends his life pursuing death. He is so eager to confront it, to control it, that everything in his life becomes a fight against death. This interpretation fits in well with Prospero's extravagant party, and with his brazen pursuit of the dark figure. When Prospero falls, it is not necessarily because he has contracted the Red Death, or even because the figure has killed him, but possibly because, in reaching the last room, Prospero has realized that death cannot be fought, dagger or no. Prospero dies because he loses what has kept him alive, the hope of a chance of avoiding death. It is similarly that lack of hope, the "wild courage of despair" that infects the crowd, and that leads to their deaths. They die because they are forced to realize that they cannot avoid death by locking themselves away in a castle. Wherever they go, however they try to forget it, some form of death will always await them.

The three images--the rooms, the clock, and the figure--combine to create a morbid but intriguing picture of Poe's philosophical views. A major sentiment through Poe's life was that one should live for the moment; using poetry as a metaphor, he stressed in *The Poetic Principle* the importance of the "poem for the poem's sake." In other words, Poe seems to ask readers to live for the dominant experience of the moment. Poe's belief that the literary work should be brief, unified, and focus on a single strong *effect* is represented by the partygoers who locked themselves in the castle, trying to forget the problem of death by reveling in an infinitely extended moment of bliss.

In another sense, however, the revellers did not follow Poe's philosophy, for had they truly been living for the party and not simply trying to avoid the plague, the ringing of the clock would not have bothered them. The clock is a reminder of mortality, and for most of us being reminded that we are going to die is unsettling. If, however, we truly live in the moment, for the experience, we may be so busy that we hardly glance up when the clock sounds. And from Poe's perspective, this is the safest way to exist. Had the revellers not stopped for the clock, they might not have seen the Red Death, and had they not seen him, they would not have confronted him. And had they not confronted him, they would not have lost all hope, and died in despair. Poe, a cynical philosopher, is warning the reader against staring at mortality face-to-face. And for some, certainly those who share Poe's moods, it is wise advice.

HERMAN MELVILLE   (1819–1891)

Now considered one of the greatest American writers of the nineteenth century, Herman Melville died in poverty and obscurity in large part because readers of the day refused to accept the troubled ambiguity about good and evil, right and wrong that lies at the heart of his best work. Born into an affluent family of New York City merchants that lost much of its fortune when he was eleven years old, Melville spent several years on whaling ships and in the United States Navy, traveling to the South Seas. After his discharge, he began to write and publish tales of his sea adventures — *Typee* (1846), *Omoo* (1847), *Mardi* (1849), and *White-Jacket* (1850) — that were greeted with great popular success. Ironically, his literary reputation and popularity began to decline with the publication of his greatest work, a moral and symbolic novel of the whaling trade, *Moby-Dick* (1852). Melville tried without success to get an appointment to a diplomatic post as his friend Hawthorne had done and so was forced to support himself and his family through lecturing and selling stories to magazines. Melville's best stories were published as *The Piazza Tales* (1856), in which "Bartleby, the Scrivener" appears. In 1866 he finally received a civil servant position at the New York Customs House, where he served for the next twenty years; he continued to write poetry and finished his great novella, *Billy Budd,* in 1891. Although Melville is best remembered for *Moby-Dick,* his short stories and *Billy Budd* also explore complex social, moral, and tragic dilemmas, presenting characters who are ignorant of their fates and unable to control their destinies, yet whose deepest motivations, like those of Bartleby, remain cloaked in mystery.

Bartleby, the Scrivener   (1853)

A Story of Wall Street

I am a rather elderly man. The nature of my avocations, for the last thirty years, has brought me into more than ordinary contact with what would seem an interesting and somewhat singular set of men, of whom, as yet, nothing, that I know of, has ever been written — I mean, the law-copyists, or scriveners. I have known very many of them, professionally and privately, and, if I pleased, could relate divers histories, at which good-natured gentlemen might smile, and sentimental souls might weep. But I waive the biographies of all other scriveners, for a few passages in the life of Bartleby, who was a scrivener, the strangest I ever saw, or heard of. While, of other law-copyists, I might write the complete life, of Bartleby nothing of that sort can be done. I believe that no materials exist, for a full and satisfactory biography of this man. It is an irreparable loss to literature. Bartleby was one of those beings of whom nothing is ascertainable, except from the original sources, and, in his case, those are very small. What my own astonished eyes saw of Bartleby, *that* is all I know of him, except, indeed, one vague report, which will appear in the sequel.

Ere introducing the scrivener, as he first appeared to me, it is fit I make some mention of myself, my *employés*, my business, my chambers, and general surroundings, because some such description is indispensable to an adequate understanding of the chief character about to be presented. Imprimis: I am a man who, from his youth upwards, has been filled with a profound conviction that the easiest way of life is the best. Hence, though I belong to a profession proverbially energetic and nervous, even to turbulence, at times, yet nothing of that sort have I ever suffered to invade my peace. I am one of those unambitious lawyers who never address a jury, or in any way draw down public applause; but, in the cool tranquillity of a snug retreat, do a snug business among rich men's bonds, and mortgages, and title-deeds. All who know me, consider me an eminently *safe* man. The late John Jacob Astor, a personage little given to poetic enthusiasm, had no hesitation in pronouncing my first grand point to be prudence; my next, method. I do not speak it in vanity, but simply record the fact, that I was not unemployed in my profession by the late John Jacob Astor; a name which, I admit, I love to repeat; for it hath a rounded and orbicular sound to it, and rings like unto bullion. I will freely add, that I was not insensible to the late John Jacob Astor's good opinion.

Some time prior to the period at which this little history begins, my avocations had been largely increased. The good old office, now extinct in the State of New York, of a Master in Chancery, had been conferred upon me. It was not a very arduous office, but very pleasantly remunerative. I seldom lose my temper; much more seldom indulge in dangerous indignation at wrongs and outrages; but I must be permitted to be rash here and declare, that I consider the sudden and violent abrogation of the office of Master in Chancery, by the new Constitution, as a —— premature act; inasmuch as I had counted upon a life-lease of the profits, whereas I only received those of a few short years. But this is by the way.

My chambers were up stairs, at No. — Wall Street. At one end, they looked upon the white wall of the interior of a spacious skylight shaft, penetrating the building from top to bottom.

This view might have been considered rather tame than otherwise, deficient in what landscape painters call "life." But, if so, the view from the other end of my chambers offered, at least, a contrast, if nothing more. In that direction, my windows commanded an unobstructed view of a lofty brick wall, black by age and everlasting shade; which wall required no spy-glass to bring out its lurking beauties, but, for the benefit of all near-sighted spectators, was pushed up to within ten feet of my window-panes. Owing to the great height of the surrounding buildings, and my chambers being on the second floor, the interval between this wall and mine not a little resembled a huge square cistern.

At the period just preceding the advent of Bartleby, I had two persons as copyists in my employment, and a promising lad as an office-boy. First, Turkey; second, Nippers; third, Ginger Nut. These may seem names, the like of which are not usually found in the Directory. In truth, they were nicknames, mutually conferred upon each other by my three clerks, and were deemed expressive of their respective persons or characters. Turkey was a short, pursy Englishman, of about my own age — that is, somewhere not far from sixty. In the morning, one might say, his face was of a fine florid hue, but after twelve o'clock, meridian — his dinner hour — it blazed like a grate full of Christmas coals; and continued blazing — but, as it were, with a gradual wane — till six o'clock P.M., or thereabouts; after which, I saw no more of the proprietor of the face, which, gaining its meridian with the sun, seemed to set with it, to rise, culminate, and decline the following day, with the like regularity and undiminished glory. There are many singular coincidences I have known in the course of my life, not the least among which was the fact, that, exactly when Turkey displayed his fullest beams from his red and radiant countenance, just then, too, at that critical moment, began the daily period when I considered his business capacities as seriously disturbed for the remainder of the twenty-four hours. Not that he was absolutely idle, or averse to business then; far from it. The difficulty was, he was apt to be altogether too energetic. There was a strange, inflamed, flurried, flighty recklessness of activity about him. He would be incautious in dipping his pen into his inkstand. All his blots upon my documents were dropped there after twelve o'clock, meridian. Indeed, not only would he be reckless, and sadly given to making blots in the afternoon, but, some days, he went further, and was rather noisy. At such times, too, his face flamed with augmented blazonry, as if cannel coal had been heaped on anthracite. He made an unpleasant racket with his chair; spilled his sand-box; in mending his pens, impatiently split them all to pieces, and threw them on the floor in a sudden passion; stood up, and leaned over his table, boxing his papers about in a most indecorous manner, very sad to behold in an elderly man like him. Nevertheless, as he was in many ways a most valuable person to me, and all the time before twelve o'clock, meridian, was the quickest, steadiest creature, too, accomplishing a great deal of work in a style not easily to be matched — for these reasons, I was willing to overlook his eccentricities, though, indeed, occasionally, I remonstrated with him. I did this very gently, however, because, though the civilest, nay, the blandest and most reverential of men in the morning, yet, in the afternoon, he was disposed, upon provocation, to be slightly rash with his tongue — in fact, insolent. Now, valuing his morning services as I did, and resolved not to lose them — yet, at the same time, made uncomfortable by his inflamed ways after twelve o'clock — and being a man of peace, unwilling by my admonitions to call forth unseemly retorts from him, I took upon me, one Saturday noon (he was always worse on Saturdays) to hint to him, very kindly, that, perhaps, now that he was growing old, it might be well to abridge his labors; in short, he need not come to my chambers after twelve o'clock, but, dinner over, had best go home to his lodgings, and rest himself till tea-time. But no; he insisted upon his afternoon devotions. His countenance became intolerably fervid, as he oratorically assured me — gesticulating with a long ruler at the other end of the room — that if his services in the morning were useful, how indispensable, then, in the afternoon?

"With submission, sir," said Turkey, on this occasion, "I consider myself your right-hand man. In the morning I but marshal and deploy my columns; but in the afternoon I put myself at their head, and gallantly charge the foe, thus" — and he made a violent thrust with the ruler.

"But the blots, Turkey," intimated I.

"True; but, with submission, sir, behold these hairs! I am getting old. Surely, sir, a blot or two of a warm afternoon is not to be severely urged against gray hairs. Old age — even if it blot the page — is honorable. With submission, sir, we *both* are getting old."

This appeal to my fellow-feeling was hardly to be resisted. At all events, I saw that go he would not. So, I made up my mind to let him stay, resolving, nevertheless, to see to it that, during the afternoon, he had to do with my less important papers.

Nippers, the second on my list, was a whiskered, sallow, and, upon the whole, rather piratical-looking young man, of about five-and-twenty. I always deemed him the victim of two evil powers — ambition and indigestion. The ambition was evinced by a certain impatience of the duties of a mere copyist, an unwarrantable usurpation of strictly professional affairs such as the original drawing up of legal documents. The indigestion seemed betokened in an occasional nervous testiness and grinning irritability, causing the teeth to audibly grind together over mistakes committed in copying; unnecessary maledictions, hissed, rather than spoken, in the heat of business; and especially by a continual discontent with the height of the table where he worked. Though of a very ingenious mechanical turn, Nippers could never get this table to suit him. He put chips under it, blocks of various sorts, bits of pasteboard, and at last went so far as to attempt an exquisite adjustment, by final pieces of folded blotting paper. But no invention would answer. If, for the sake of easing his back, he brought the table-lid at a sharp angle well up towards his chin, and wrote there like a man using the steep roof of a Dutch house for his desk, then he declared that it stopped the circulation in his arms. If now he lowered the table to his waistbands, and stooped over it in writing, then there was a sore aching in his back. In short, the truth of the matter was, Nippers knew not what he wanted. Or, if he wanted anything, it was to be rid of a scrivener's table altogether. Among the manifestations of his diseased ambition was a fondness he had for receiving visits from certain ambiguous-looking fellows in seedy coats, whom he called his clients. Indeed, I was aware that not only was he, at times, considerable of a ward-politician, but he occasionally did a little business at the justices' courts, and was not unknown on the steps of the Tombs. I have good reason to believe, however, that one individual who called upon him at my chambers, and who, with a grand air, he insisted was his client, was no other than a dun, and the alleged title-deed, a bill. But, with all his failings, and the annoyances he caused me, Nippers, like his compatriot Turkey, was a very useful man to me; wrote a neat, swift hand; and, when he chose, was not deficient in a gentlemanly sort of deportment. Added to this, he always dressed in a gentlemanly sort of way; and so, incidentally, reflected credit upon my chambers. Whereas, with respect to Turkey, I had much ado to keep him from being a reproach to me. His clothes were apt to look oily, and smell of eating-houses. He wore his pantaloons very loose and baggy in summer. His coats were execrable, his hat not to be handled. But while the hat was a thing of indifference to me, inasmuch as his natural civility and deference, as a dependent Englishman, always led him to doff it the moment he entered the room, yet his coat was another matter. Concerning his coats, I reasoned with him; but with no effect. The truth was, I suppose, that a man with so small an income could not afford to sport such a lustrous face and a lustrous coat at one and the same time. As Nippers once observed, Turkey's money went chiefly for red ink. One winter day, I presented Turkey with a highly respectable-looking coat of my own — a padded gray coat, of a most comfortable warmth, and which buttoned straight up from the knee to the neck. I thought Turkey would appreciate the favor, and abate his rashness and obstreperousness of afternoons. But no; I verily believe that buttoning himself up in so downy and blanket-like a coat had a pernicious effect upon him — upon the same principle that too much oats are bad for horses. In fact, precisely as a rash, restive horse is said to feel his oats, so Turkey felt his coat. It made him insolent. He was a man whom prosperity harmed.

Though, concerning the self-indulgent habits of Turkey, I had my own private surmises, yet, touching Nippers, I was well persuaded that, whatever might be his faults in other respects, he was, at least, a temperate young man. But, indeed, nature herself seemed to have been his vintner, and, at his birth, charged him so thoroughly with an irritable, brandy-like disposition, that all subsequent potations were needless. When I consider how, amid the stillness of my chambers, Nippers would sometimes impatiently rise from his seat, and stooping over his table, spread his arms wide apart, seize the whole desk, and move it, and jerk it, with a grim, grinding motion on the floor, as if the table were a perverse voluntary agent, intent on thwarting and vexing him, I plainly perceive that, for Nippers, brandy-and-water were altogether superfluous.

It was fortunate for me that, owing to its peculiar cause — indigestion — the irritability and consequent nervousness of Nippers were mainly observable in the morning, while in the afternoon he was comparatively mild. So that, Turkey's paroxysms only coming on about twelve o'clock, I never had to do with their eccentricities at one time. Their fits relieved each other, like guards. When Nippers' was on, Turkey's was off; and *vice versa*. This was a good natural arrangement, under the circumstances.

Ginger Nut, the third on my list, was a lad, some twelve years old. His father was a carman, ambitious of seeing his son on the bench instead of a cart, before he died. So he sent him to my office, as student at law, errand-boy, cleaner, and sweeper, at the rate of one dollar a week. He had a little desk to himself, but he did not use it much. Upon inspection, the drawer exhibited a great array of the shells of various sorts of nuts. Indeed, to this quick-witted youth, the whole noble science of the law was contained in a nutshell. Not the least among the employments of Ginger Nut, as well as one which he discharged with the most alacrity, was his duty as cake and apple purveyor for Turkey and Nippers. Copying lawpapers being proverbially a dry, husky sort of business, my two scriveners were fain to moisten their mouths very often with Spitzenbergs, to be had at the numerous stalls nigh the Custom House and Post Office. Also, they sent Ginger Nut very frequently for that peculiar cake — small, flat, round, and very spicy — after which he had been named by them. Of a cold morning, when business was but dull, Turkey would gobble up scores of these cakes, as if they were mere wafers — indeed, they sell them at the rate of six or eight for a penny — the scrape of his pen blending with the crunching of the crisp particles in his mouth. Of all the fiery afternoon blunders and flurried rashness of Turkey, was his once moistening a ginger-cake between his lips, and clapping it on to a mortgage, for a seal. I came within an ace of dismissing him then. But he mollified me by making an oriental bow, and saying —

"With submission, sir, it was generous of me to find you in stationery on my own account."

Now my original business — that of a conveyancer and title hunter, and drawer-up of recondite documents of all sorts — was considerably increased by receiving the Master's office. There was now great work for scriveners. Not only must I push the clerks already with me, but I must have additional help.

In answer to my advertisement, a motionless young man one morning stood upon my office threshold, the door being open, for it was summer. I can see that figure now — pallidly neat, pitiably respectable, incurably forlorn! It was Bartleby.

After a few words touching his qualifications, I engaged him, glad to have among my corps of copyists a man of so singularly sedate an aspect, which I thought might operate beneficially upon the flighty temper of Turkey, and the fiery one of Nippers.

I should have stated before that ground-glass folding-doors divided my premises into two parts, one of which was occupied by my scriveners, the other by myself. According to my humor, I threw open these doors, or closed them. I resolved to assign Bartleby a corner by the folding-doors, but on my side of them, so as to have this quiet man within easy call, in case any trifling thing was to be done. I placed his desk close up to a small side-window in that part of the room, a window which originally had afforded a lateral view of certain grimy brickyards and bricks, but which, owing to subsequent erections, commanded at present no view at all, though it gave some light. Within three feet of the panes was a wall, and the light came down from far above, between two lofty buildings, as from a very small opening in a dome. Still further to a satisfactory arrangement, I procured a high green folding screen, which might entirely isolate Bartleby from my sight, though not remove him from my voice. And thus, in a manner, privacy and society were conjoined.

At first, Bartleby did an extraordinary quantity of writing. As if long famishing for something to copy, he seemed to gorge himself on my documents. There was no pause for digestion. He ran a day and night line, copying by sunlight and by candle-light. I should have been quite delighted with his application, had he been cheerfully industrious. But he wrote on silently, palely, mechanically.

It is, of course, an indispensable part of a scrivener's business to verify the accuracy of his copy, word by word. Where there are two or more scriveners in an office, they assist each other in this examination, one reading from the copy, the other holding the original. It is a very dull, wearisome, and lethargic affair. I can readily imagine that, to some sanguine temperaments, it would be altogether intolerable. For example, I cannot credit that the mettlesome poet, Byron, would have contentedly sat down with Bartleby to examine a law document of, say five hundred pages, closely written in a crimpy hand.

Now and then, in the haste of business, it had been my habit to assist in comparing some brief document myself, calling Turkey or Nippers for this purpose. One object I had, in placing Bartleby so handy to me behind the screen, was, to avail myself of his services on such trivial occasions. It was on the third day, I think, of his being with me, and before any necessity had arisen for having his own writing examined, that, being much hurried to complete a small affair I had in hand, I abruptly called to Bartleby. In my haste and natural expectancy of instant compliance, I sat with my head bent over the original on my desk, and my right hand sideways, and somewhat nervously extended with the copy, so that, immediately upon emerging from his retreat, Bartleby might snatch it and proceed to business without the least delay.

In this very attitude did I sit when I called to him, rapidly stating what it was I wanted him to do—namely, to examine a small paper with me. Imagine my surprise, nay, my consternation, when, without moving from his privacy, Bartleby, in a singularly mild, firm voice, replied, "I would prefer not to."

I sat awhile in perfect silence, rallying my stunned faculties. Immediately it occurred to me that my ears had deceived me, or Bartleby had entirely misunderstood my meaning. I repeated my request in the clearest tone I could assume; but in quite as clear a one came the previous reply, "I would prefer not to."

"Prefer not to," echoed I, rising in high excitement, and crossing the room with a stride. "What do you mean? Are you moonstruck? I want you to help me compare this sheet here—take it," and I thrust it towards him.

"I would prefer not to," said he.

I looked at him steadfastly. His face was leanly composed; his gray eyes dimly calm. Not a wrinkle of agitation rippled him. Had there been the least uneasiness, anger, impatience, or impertinence in his manner; in other words, had there been anything ordinarily human about him, doubtless I should have violently dismissed him from the premises. But as it was, I should have as soon thought of turning my pale plaster-of-paris bust of Cicero out of doors. I stood gazing at him awhile, as he went on with his own writing, and then reseated myself at my desk. This is very strange, thought I. What had one best do? But my business hurried me. I concluded to forget the matter for the present, reserving it for my future leisure. So, calling Nippers from the other room, the paper was speedily examined.

A few days after this, Bartleby concluded four lengthy documents, being quadruplicates of a week's testimony taken before me in my High Court of Chancery. It became necessary to examine them. It was an important suit, and great accuracy was imperative. Having all things arranged, I called Turkey, Nippers, and Ginger Nut, from the next room, meaning to place the four copies in the hands of my four clerks, while I should read from the original. Accordingly, Turkey, Nippers, and Ginger Nut had taken their seats in a row, each with his document in his hand, when I called to Bartleby to join this interesting group.

"Bartleby! quick, I am waiting."

I heard a slow scrape of his chair legs on the uncarpeted floor, and soon he appeared standing at the entrance of his hermitage.

"What is wanted?" said he, mildly.

"The copies, the copies," said I, hurriedly. "We are going to examine them. There" — and I held towards him the fourth quadruplicate.

"I would prefer not to," he said, and gently disappeared behind the screen.

For a few moments I was fumed into a pillar of salt, standing at the head of my seated column of clerks. Recovering myself, I advanced towards the screen, and demanded the reason for such extraordinary conduct.

"*Why* do you refuse?"

"I would prefer not to."

With any other man I should have flown outright into a dreadful passion, scorned all further words, and thrust him ignominiously from my presence. But there was something about Bartleby that not only strangely disarmed me, but, in a wonderful manner, touched and disconcerted me. I began to reason with him.

"These are your own copies we are about to examine. It is labor saving to you, because one examination will answer for your four papers. It is common usage. Every copyist is bound to help examine his copy. Is it not so? Will you not speak? Answer!"

"I prefer not to," he replied in a flute-like tone. It seemed to me that, while I had been addressing him, he carefully revolved every statement that I made; fully comprehended the meaning; could not gainsay the irresistible conclusion;

but, at the same time, some paramount consideration prevailed with him to reply as he did.

"You are decided, then, not to comply with my request — a request made according to common usage and common sense?"

He briefly gave me to understand, that on that point my judgment was sound. Yes: his decision was irreversible.

It is not seldom the case that, when a man is browbeaten in some unprecedented and violently unreasonable way, he begins to stagger in his own plainest faith. He begins, as it were, vaguely to surmise that, wonderful as it may be, all the justice and all the reason is on the other side. Accordingly, if any disinterested persons are present, he turns to them for some reinforcement for his own faltering mind.

"Turkey," said I, "what do you think of this? Am I not right?"

"With submission, sir," said Turkey, in his blandest tone, "I think that you are."

"Nippers," said I, "what do *you* think of it?"

"I think I should kick him out of the office."

(The reader of nice perceptions will have perceived that, it being morning, Turkey's answer is couched in polite and tranquil terms, but Nippers replies in ill-tempered ones. Or, to repeat a previous sentence, Nippers' ugly mood was on duty, and Turkey's off.)

"Ginger Nut," said I, willing to enlist the smallest suffrage in my behalf, "what do *you* think of it?"

"I think, sir, he's a little *luny*," replied Ginger Nut, with a grin.

"You hear what they say," said I, turning towards the screen, "come forth and do your duty."

But he vouchsafed no reply. I pondered a moment in sore perplexity. But once more business hurried me. I determined again to postpone the consideration of this dilemma to my future leisure. With a little trouble we made out to examine the papers without Bartleby, though at every page or two Turkey deferentially dropped his opinion, that this proceeding was quite out of the common; while Nippers, twitching in his chair with a dyspeptic nervousness, ground out, between his set teeth, occasional hissing maledictions against the stubborn oaf behind the screen. And for his (Nippers') part, this was the first and the last time he would do another man's business without pay.

Meanwhile Bartleby sat in his hermitage, oblivious to everything but his own peculiar business there.

Some days passed, the scrivener being employed upon another lengthy work. His late remarkable conduct led me to regard his ways narrowly. I observed that he never went to dinner; indeed, that he never went anywhere. As yet I had never, of my personal knowledge, known him to be outside of my office. He was a perpetual sentry in the corner. At about eleven o'clock though, in the morning, I noticed that Ginger Nut would advance towards the opening in Bartleby's screen, as if silently beckoned thither by a gesture invisible to me where I sat. The boy would then leave the office, jingling a few pence, and reappear with a handful of ginger-nuts, which he delivered in the hermitage, receiving two of the cakes for his trouble.

He lives, then, on ginger-nuts, thought I; never eats a dinner, properly speaking; he must be a vegetarian, then, but no; he never eats even vegetables, he eats nothing but ginger-nuts. My mind then ran on in reveries concerning the probable effects upon the human constitution of living entirely on ginger-nuts. Ginger-nuts are so called, because they contain ginger as one of their peculiar constituents, and the final flavoring one. Now, what was ginger? A hot, spicy thing. Was Bartleby hot and spicy? Not at all. Ginger, then, had no effect upon Bartleby. Probably he preferred it should have none.

Nothing so aggravates an earnest person as a passive resistance. If the individual so resisted be of a not inhuman temper, and the resisting one perfectly harmless in his passivity, then, in the better moods of the former, he will endeavor charitably to construe to his imagination what proves impossible to be solved by his judgment. Even so, for the most part, I regarded Bartleby and his ways. Poor fellow! thought I, he means no mischief; it is plain he intends no insolence; his aspect sufficiently evinces that his eccentricities are involuntary. He is useful to me. I can get along with him. If I turn him away, the chances are he will fall in with some less indulgent employer, and then he will be rudely treated, and perhaps driven forth miserably to starve. Yes. Here I can cheaply purchase a delicious self-approval. To befriend Bartleby; to humor him in his strange wilfulness, will cost me little or nothing, while I lay up in my soul what will eventually prove a sweet morsel for my conscience. But this mood was not invariable with me. The passiveness of Bartleby sometimes irritated me. I felt strangely goaded on to encounter him in new opposition — to elicit some angry spark from him answerable to my own. But, indeed, I might as well have essayed to strike fire with my knuckles against a bit of Windsor soap. But one afternoon the evil impulse in me mastered me, and the following little scene ensued:

"Bartleby," said I, "when those papers are all copied, I will compare them with you."

"I would prefer not to."

"How? Surely you do not mean to persist in that mulish vagary?"

No answer.

I threw open the folding-doors nearby, and turning upon Turkey and Nippers, exclaimed:

"Bartleby a second time says, he won't examine his papers. What do you think of it, Turkey?"

It was afternoon, be it remembered. Turkey sat glowing like a brass boiler; his bald head steaming; his hands reeling among his blotted papers.

"Think of it?" roared Turkey. "I think I'll just step behind his screen, and black his eyes for him!"

So saying, Turkey rose to his feet and threw his arms into a pugilistic position. He was hurrying away to make good his promise, when I detained him, alarmed at the effect of incautiously rousing Turkey's combativeness after dinner.

"Sit down, Turkey," said I, "and hear what Nippers has to say. What do you think of it, Nippers? Would I not be justified in immediately dismissing Bartleby?"

"Excuse me, that is for you to decide, sir. I think his conduct quite unusual, and, indeed, unjust, as regards Turkey and myself. But it may only be a passing whim."

"Ah," exclaimed I, "you have strangely changed your mind, then — you speak very gently of him now."

"All beer," cried Turkey; "gentleness is effects of beer — Nippers and I dined together to-day. You see how gentle *I* am, sir. Shall I go and black his eyes?"

"You refer to Bartleby, I suppose. No, not to-day, Turkey," I replied; "pray, put up your fists."

I closed the doors, and again advanced towards Bartleby. I felt additional incentives tempting me to my fate. I burned to be rebelled against again. I remembered that Bartleby never left the office.

"Bartleby," said I, "Ginger Nut is away; just step around to the Post Office, won't you?" (it was but a three minutes' walk) "and see if there is anything for me."

"I would prefer not to."

"You *will* not?"

"I *prefer* not."

I staggered to my desk, and sat there in a deep study. My blind inveteracy returned. Was there any other thing in which I could procure myself to be ignominiously repulsed by this lean, penniless wight? — my hired clerk? What added thing is there, perfectly reasonable, that he will be sure to refuse to do?

"Bartleby!"

No answer.

"Bartleby," in a louder tone.

No answer.

"Bartleby," I roared.

Like a very ghost, agreeably to the laws of magical invocation, at the third summons, he appeared at the entrance of his hermitage.

"Go to the next room, and tell Nippers to come to me."

"I would prefer not to," he respectfully and slowly said, and mildly disappeared.

"Very good, Bartleby," said I, in a quiet sort of serenely-severe self-possessed tone, intimating the unalterable purpose of some terrible retribution very close at hand. At the moment I half intended something of the kind. But upon the whole, as it was drawing towards my dinner-hour, I thought it best to put on my hat and walk home for the day, suffering much from perplexity and distress of mind.

Shall I acknowledge it? The conclusion of this whole business was, that it soon became a fixed fact of my chambers, that a pale young scrivener, by the name of Bartleby, had a desk there; that he copied for me at the usual rate of four cents a folio (one hundred words); but he was permanently exempt from examining the work done by him, that duty being transferred to Turkey and Nippers, out of compliment, doubtless, to their superior acuteness; moreover, said Bartleby was never, on any account, to be dispatched on the most trivial errand of any sort; and that even if entreated to take upon him such a matter, it was generally understood that he would "prefer not to" — in other words, that he would refuse point blank.

As days passed on, I became considerably reconciled to Bartleby. His steadiness, his freedom from all dissipation, his incessant industry (except when he chose to throw himself into a standing revery behind his screen), his great stillness, his unalterableness of demeanor under all circumstances, made him a valuable acquisition. One prime thing was this — *he was always there* — first in the morning, continually through the day, and the last at night. I had a singular confidence in his honesty. I felt my most precious papers perfectly safe in his hands. Sometimes, to be sure, I could not, for the very soul of me, avoid falling into sudden spasmodic passions with him. For it was exceeding difficult to bear in mind all the time those strange peculiarities, privileges, and unheard-of exemptions, forming the tacit stipulations on Bartleby's part under which he remained in my office. Now and then, in the eagerness of dispatching pressing business, I would inadvertently summon Bartleby, in a short, rapid tone, to put his finger, say, on the incipient tie of a bit of red tape with which I was about compressing some papers. Of course, from behind the screen the usual answer, "I prefer not to," was sure to come; and then, how could a human creature, with the common infirmities of our nature, refrain from bitterly exclaiming upon such perverseness — such unreasonableness? However, every added repulse of this sort which I received only tended to lessen the probability of my repeating the inadvertence.

Here it must be said, that, according to the custom of most legal gentlemen occupying chambers in densely populated law buildings, there were several keys to my door. One was kept by a woman residing in the attic, which person weekly scrubbed and daily swept and dusted my apartments. Another was kept by Turkey for convenience sake. The third I sometimes carried in my own pocket. The fourth I knew not who had.

Now, one Sunday morning I happened to go to Trinity Church, to hear a celebrated preacher, and finding myself rather early on the ground I thought I would walk round to my chambers for a while. Luckily I had my key with me; but upon applying it to the lock, I found it resisted by something inserted from the inside. Quite surprised, I called out; when to my consternation a key was turned from within; and thrusting his lean visage at me, and holding the door ajar, the apparition of Bartleby appeared, in his shirt-sleeves, and otherwise in a strangely tattered *deshabille,* saying quietly that he was sorry, but he was deeply engaged just then, and — preferred not admitting me at present. In a brief word or two, he moreover added, that perhaps I had better walk round the block two or three times, and by that time he would probably have concluded his affairs.

Now, the utterly unsurmised appearance of Bartleby, tenanting my law-chambers of a Sunday morning, with his cadaverously gentlemanly *nonchalance,* yet withal firm and self-possessed, had such a strange effect upon me, that incontinently I slunk away from my own door, and did as desired. But not without sundry twinges of impotent rebellion against the mild effrontery of this unaccountable scrivener. Indeed, it was his wonderful mildness chiefly, which not only disarmed me, but unmanned me, as it were. For I consider that one, for the time, is sort of unmanned when he tranquilly permits his hired clerk to dictate to him, and order him away from his own premises. Furthermore, I was full of uneasiness as to what Bartleby could possibly be doing in my office in his shirt-sleeves, and in an otherwise dismantled condition on a Sunday morning. Was anything amiss going on? Nay, that was out of the question. It was not to be thought of for a moment that Bartleby was an immoral person. But what could he be doing there? — copying? Nay again, whatever might be his eccentricities, Bartleby was an eminently decorous person. He would be the last man to sit down to his desk in any state approaching to nudity. Besides, it was Sunday; and there was something about Bartleby that forbade the supposition that he would by any secular occupation violate the proprieties of the day.

Nevertheless, my mind was not pacified; and full of a restless curiosity, at last I returned to the door. Without hindrance I inserted my key, opened it, and entered. Bartleby was not to be seen. I looked round anxiously, peeped behind his screen; but it was very plain that he was gone. Upon more closely examining the place, I surmised that for an indefinite period Bartleby must have ate, dressed, and slept in my office, and that too without plate, mirror, or bed. The cushioned seat of a rickety old sofa in one corner bore the faint impress of a lean, reclining form. Rolled away under his desk, I found a blanket; under the empty grate, a blacking box and brush; on a chair, a tin basin, with soap and a ragged towel; in a newspaper a few crumbs of ginger-nuts and a morsel of cheese. Yes, thought I, it is evident enough that Bartleby has been making his home here, keeping bachelor's hall all by himself. Immediately then the thought came sweeping across me, what miserable friendlessness and loneliness are here revealed! His poverty is great; but his solitude, how horrible! Think of it. Of a Sunday, Wall Street is deserted as Petra; and every night of every day it is an emptiness. This building, too, which of week-days hums with industry and life, at nightfall echoes with sheer vacancy, and all through Sunday is forlorn. And here Bartleby makes his home; sole spectator of a solitude which he has seen all populous — a sort of innocent and transformed Marius brooding among the ruins of Carthage!

For the first time in my life a feeling of overpowering stinging melancholy seized me. Before, I had never experienced aught but a not unpleasing sadness. The bond of a common humanity now drew me irresistibly to gloom. A fraternal melancholy! For both I and Bartleby were sons of Adam. I remembered the bright silks and sparkling faces I had seen that day, in gala trim, swan-like sailing down the Mississippi of Broadway; and I contrasted them with the pallid copyist, and thought to myself, Ah, happiness courts the light, so we deem the world is gay; but misery hides aloof, so we deem that misery there is none. These sad fancyings — chimeras, doubtless, of a sick and silly brain — led on to other and more special thoughts, concerning the eccentricities of Bartleby. Presentiments of strange discoveries hovered round me. The scrivener's pale form appeared to me laid out, among uncaring strangers, in its shivering winding-sheet.

Suddenly I was attracted by Bartleby's closed desk, the key in open sight left in the lock.

I mean no mischief, seek the gratification of no heartless curiosity, thought I; besides, the desk is mine, and its contents, too, so I will make bold to look within. Everything was methodically arranged, the papers smoothly placed. The pigeon-holes were deep, and removing the files of documents, I groped into their recesses. Presently I felt something there, and dragged it out. It was an old bandanna handkerchief, heavy and knotted. I opened it, and saw it was a saving's bank.

I now recalled all the quiet mysteries which I had noted in the man. I remembered that he never spoke but to answer; that, though at intervals he had considerable time to himself, yet I had never seen him reading — no, not even a newspaper; that for long periods he would stand looking out, at his pale window behind the screen, upon the dead brick wall; I was quite sure he never visited any refectory or eating-house; while his pale face clearly indicated that he never drank beer like Turkey; or tea and coffee even, like other men; that he never went anywhere in particular that I could learn; never went out for a walk, unless, indeed, that was the case at present; that he had declined telling who he was, or whence he came, or whether he had any relatives in the world; that though so thin and pale, he never complained of ill-health. And more than all, I remembered a certain unconscious air of pallid — how shall I call it — of pallid haughtiness, say, or rather an austere reserve about him, which has positively awed me into my tame compliance with his eccentricities, when I had feared to ask him to do the slightest incidental thing for me, even though I might know, from his long-continued motionlessness, that behind his screen he must be standing in one of those dead-wall reveries of his.

Revolving all these things, and coupling them with the recently discovered fact, that he made my office his constant abiding place and home, and not forgetful of his morbid moodiness; revolving all these things, a prudential feeling began to steal over me. My first emotions had been those of pure melancholy and sincerest pity; but just in proportion as the forlornness of Bartleby grew and grew to my imagination, did that same melancholy merge into fear, that pity into repulsion. So true it is, and so terrible, too, that up to a certain point the thought or sight of misery enlists our best affections; but, in certain special cases, beyond that point it does not. They err who would assert that invariably this is owing to the inherent selfishness of the human heart. It rather proceeds from a certain hopelessness of remedying excessive and organic ill. To a sensitive being, pity is not seldom pain. And when at last it is perceived that such pity cannot lead to effectual succor, common sense bids the soul be rid of it. What I saw that morning persuaded me that the scrivener was the victim of innate and incurable disorder. I might give alms to his body; but his body did not pain him; it was his soul that suffered, and his soul I could not reach.

I did not accomplish the purpose of going to Trinity Church that morning. Somehow, the things I had seen disqualified me for the time from church-going. I walked homeward, thinking what I would do with Bartleby. Finally, I resolved upon this — I would put certain calm questions to him the next morning, touching his history, etc., and if he declined to answer them openly and unreservedly (and I supposed he would prefer not), then to give him a twenty dollar bill over and above whatever I might owe him, and tell him his services were no longer required; but that if in any other way I could assist him, I would be happy to do so, especially if he desired to return to his native place, wherever that might be, I would willingly help to defray the expenses. Moreover, if, after reaching home, he found himself at any time in want of aid, a letter from him would be sure of a reply.

The next morning came.

"Bartleby," said I, gently calling to him behind his screen.

No reply.

"Bartleby," said I, in a still gentler tone, "come here; I am not going to ask you to do anything you would prefer not to do — I simply wish to speak to you."

Upon this he noiselessly slid into view.

"Will you tell me, Bartleby, where you were born?"

"I would prefer not to."

"Will you tell me *anything* about yourself?"

"I would prefer not to."

"But what reasonable objection can you have to speak to me? I feel friendly towards you."

He did not look at me while I spoke, but kept his glance fixed upon my bust of Cicero, which, as I then sat, was directly behind me, some six inches above my head.

"What is your answer, Bartleby?" said I, after waiting a considerable time for a reply, during which his countenance remained immovable, only there was the faintest conceivable tremor of the white attenuated mouth.

"At present I prefer to give no answer," he said, and retired into his hermitage.

It was rather weak in me I confess, but his manner, on this occasion, nettled me. Not only did there seem to lurk in it a certain calm disdain, but his perverseness seemed ungrateful, considering the undeniable good usage and indulgence he had received from me.

Again I sat ruminating what I should do. Mortified as I was at his behavior, and resolved as I had been to dismiss him when I entered my office, nevertheless I strangely felt something superstitious knocking at my heart, and forbidding me to carry out my purpose, and denouncing me for a villain if I dared to breathe one bitter word against this forlornest of mankind. At last, familiarly drawing my chair behind his screen, I sat down and said: "Bartleby, never mind, then, about revealing your history; but let me entreat you, as a friend, to comply as far as may be with the usages of this office. Say now, you will help to examine papers tomorrow or next day: in short, say now, that in a day or two you will begin to be a little reasonable: — say so, Bartleby."

"At present I would prefer not to be a little reasonable," was his mildly cadaverous reply.

Just then the folding-doors opened, and Nippers approached. He seemed suffering from an unusually bad night's rest, induced by severer indigestion than common. He overheard those final words of Bartleby.

"*Prefer not,* eh?" gritted Nippers — "I'd *prefer* him, if I were you, sir," addressing me — "I'd *prefer* him; I'd give him preferences, the stubborn mule! What is it, sir, pray, that he *prefers* not to do now?"

Bartleby moved not a limb.

"Mr. Nippers," said I, "I'd prefer that you would withdraw for the present."

Somehow, of late, I had got into the way of involuntarily using this word "prefer" upon all sorts of not exactly suitable occasions. And I trembled to think that my contact with the scrivener had already and seriously affected me in a mental way. And what further and deeper aberration might it not yet produce? This apprehension had not been without efficacy in determining me to summary measures.

As Nippers, looking very sour and sulky, was departing, Turkey blandly and deferentially approached.

"With submission, sir," said he, "yesterday I was thinking about Bartleby here, and I think that if he would but prefer to take a quart of good ale every day, it would do much towards mending him, and enabling him to assist in examining his papers."

"So you have got the word, too," said I, slightly excited.

"With submission, what word, sir?" asked Turkey, respectfully crowding himself into the contracted space behind the screen, and by so doing, making me jostle the scrivener. "What word, sir?"

"I would prefer to be left alone here," said Bartleby, as if offended at being mobbed in his privacy.

"*That's* the word, Turkey," said I — "*that's* it."

"Oh, *prefer?* oh yes — queer word. I never use it myself. But, sir, as I was saying, if he would but prefer —"

"Turkey," interrupted I, "you will please withdraw."

"Oh certainly, sir, if you prefer that I should."

As he opened the folding-door to retire, Nippers at his desk caught a glimpse of me, and asked whether I would prefer to have a certain paper copied on blue paper or white. He did not in the least roguishly accent the word "prefer." It was plain that it involuntarily rolled from his tongue. I thought to myself, surely I must get rid of a demented man, who already has in some degree turned the tongues, if not the heads of myself and clerks. But I thought it prudent not to break the dismission at once.

The next day I noticed that Bartleby did nothing but stand at his window in his dead-wall revery. Upon asking him why he did not write, he said that he had decided upon doing no more writing.

"Why, how now? what next?" exclaimed I, "do no more writing?"

"No more."

"And what is the reason?"

"Do you not see the reason for yourself?" he indifferently replied.

I looked steadfastly at him, and perceived that his eyes looked dull and glazed. Instantly it occurred to me, that his unexampled diligence in copying by his dim window for the first few weeks of his stay with me might have temporarily impaired his vision.

I was touched. I said something in condolence with him. I hinted that of course he did wisely in abstaining from writing for a while; and urged him to embrace that opportunity of taking wholesome exercise in the open air. This, however, he did not do. A few days after this, my other clerks being absent, and being in a great hurry to dispatch certain letters by the mail, I thought that, having nothing else earthly to do, Bartleby would surely be less inflexible than usual, and carry these letters to the Post Office. But he blankly declined. So, much to my inconvenience, I went myself.

Still added days went by. Whether Bartleby's eyes improved or not, I could not say. To all appearance, I thought they did. But when I asked him if they did, he vouchsafed no answer. At all events, he would do no copying. At last, in replying to my urgings, he informed me that he had permanently given up copying.

"What!" exclaimed I; "suppose your eyes should get entirely well — better than ever before — would you not copy then?"

"I have given up copying," he answered, and slid aside.

He remained as ever, a fixture in my chamber. Nay — if that were possible — he became still more of a fixture than before. What was to be done? He would do nothing in the office; why should he stay there? In plain fact, he had now become a millstone to me, not only useless as a necklace, but afflictive to bear. Yet I was sorry for him. I speak less than truth when I say that, on his own account, he occasioned me uneasiness. If he would but have named a single relative or friend, I would instantly have written, and urged their taking the poor fellow away to some convenient retreat. But he seemed alone, absolutely alone in the universe. A bit of wreck in the mid-Atlantic. At length, necessities connected with my business tyrannized over all other considerations. Decently as I could, I told Bartleby that in six days' time he must unconditionally leave the office. I warned him to take measures, in the interval, for procuring some other abode. I offered to assist him in this endeavor, if he himself would but take the first step towards a removal. "And when you finally quit me, Bartleby," added I, "I shall see that you go not away entirely unprovided. Six days from this hour, remember."

At the expiration of that period, I peeped behind the screen, and lo! Bartleby was there.

I buttoned up my coat, balanced myself; advanced slowly towards him, touched his shoulder, and said, "The time has come; you must quit this place; I am sorry for you; here is money; but you must go."

"I would prefer not," he replied, with his back still towards me.

"You *must*."

He remained silent.

Now I had an unbounded confidence in this man's common honesty. He had frequently restored to me sixpences and shillings carelessly dropped upon the floor, for I am apt to be very reckless in such shirt-button affairs. The proceeding, then, which followed will not be deemed extraordinary.

"Bartleby," said I, "I owe you twelve dollars on account; here are thirty-two; the odd twenty are yours — Will you take it?" and I handed the bills towards him.

But he made no motion.

"I will leave them here, then," putting them under a weight on the table. Then taking my hat and cane and going to the door, I tranquilly turned and added — "After you have removed your things from these offices, Bartleby, you will of course lock the door — since every one is now gone for the day but you — and if you please, slip your key underneath the mat, so that I may have it in the morning. I shall not see you again; so good-bye to you. If, hereafter, in your new place of abode, I can be of any service to you, do not fail to advise me by letter. Good-bye, Bartleby, and fare you well."

But he answered not a word; like the last column of some ruined temple, he remained standing mute and solitary in the middle of the otherwise deserted room.

As I walked home in a pensive mood, my vanity got the better of my pity. I could not but highly plume myself on my masterly management in getting rid of Bartleby. Masterly I call it, and such it must appear to any dispassionate thinker. The beauty of my procedure seemed to consist in its perfect quietness. There was no vulgar bullying, no bravado of any sort, no choleric hectoring, and striding to and fro across the apartment, jerking out vehement commands for Bartleby to bundle himself off with his beggarly traps. Nothing of the kind. Without loudly bidding Bartleby depart — as an inferior genius might have done — I *assumed* the ground that depart he must; and upon that assumption built all I had to say. The more I thought over my procedure, the more I was charmed with it. Nevertheless, next morning, upon awakening, I had my doubts — I had somehow slept off the fumes of vanity. One of the coolest and wisest hours a man has, is just after he awakes in the morning. My procedure seemed as sagacious as ever — but only in theory. How it would prove in practice — there was the rub. It was truly a beautiful thought to have assumed Bartleby's departure; but, after all, that assumption was simply my own, and none of Bartleby's. The great point was, not whether I had assumed that he would quit me, but whether he would prefer to do so. He was more a man of preferences than assumptions.

After breakfast, I walked down town, arguing the probabilities *pro* and *con*. One moment I thought it would prove a miserable failure, and Bartleby would be found all alive at my office as usual; the next moment it seemed certain that I should find his chair empty. And so I kept veering about. At the corner of Broadway and Canal Street, I saw quite an excited group of people standing in earnest conversation.

"I'll take odds he doesn't," said a voice as I passed.

"Doesn't go? — done!" said I, "put up your money."

I was instinctively putting my hand in my pocket to produce my own, when I remembered that this was an election day. The words I had overheard bore no reference to Bartleby, but to the success or non-success of some candidate for the mayoralty. In my intent frame of mind, I had, as it were, imagined that all Broadway shared in my excitement, and were debating the same question with me. I passed on, very thankful that the uproar of the street screened my momentary absent-mindedness.

As I had intended, I was earlier than usual at my office door. I stood listening for a moment. All was still. He must be gone. I tried the knob. The door was locked. Yes, my procedure had worked to a charm; he indeed must be vanished. Yet a certain melancholy mixed with this: I was almost sorry for my brilliant success. I was fumbling under the door mat for the key, which Bartleby was to have left there for me, when accidentally my knee knocked against a panel, producing a summoning sound, and in response a voice came to me from within — "Not yet; I am occupied."

It was Bartleby.

I was thunderstruck. For an instant I stood like the man who, pipe in mouth, was killed one cloudless afternoon long ago in Virginia, by summer lightning; at his own warm open window he was killed, and remained leaning out there upon the dreamy afternoon, till someone touched him, when he fell.

"Not gone!" I murmured at last. But again obeying that wondrous ascendancy which the inscrutable scrivener had over me, and from which ascendancy, for all my chafing, I could not completely escape, I slowly went down stairs and out into the street, and while walking round the block, considered what I should next do in this unheard-of perplexity. Turn the man out by an actual thrusting I could not; to drive him away by calling him hard names would not do; calling in the police was an unpleasant idea; and yet, permit him to enjoy his cadaverous triumph over me — this, too, I could not think of. What was to be done? or, if nothing could be done, was there anything further that I could assume in the matter? Yes, as before I had prospectively assumed that Bartleby would depart, so now I might retrospectively assume that departed he was. In the legitimate carrying out of this assumption, I might enter my office in a great hurry, and pretending not to see Bartleby at all, walk straight against him as if he were air. Such a proceeding would in a singular degree have the appearance of a home-thrust. It was hardly possible that Bartleby could withstand such an application of the doctrine of assumption. But upon second thoughts the success of the plan seemed rather dubious. I resolved to argue the matter over with him again.

"Bartleby," said I, entering the office, with a quietly severe expression, "I am seriously displeased. I am pained, Bartleby. I had thought better of you. I had imagined you of such a gentlemanly organization, that in any delicate dilemma a slight hint would suffice — in short, an assumption. But it appears I am deceived. Why," I added, unaffectedly starting, "You have not even touched that money yet," pointing to it, just where I had left it the evening previous.

He answered nothing.

"Will you, or will you not, quit me?" I now demanded in a sudden passion, advancing close to him.

"I would prefer *not* to quit you," he replied, gently emphasizing the *not*.

"What earthly right have you to stay here? Do you pay any rent? Do you pay my taxes? Or is this property yours?"

He answered nothing.

"Are you ready to go on and write now? Are your eyes recovered? Could you copy a small paper for me this morning? or help examine a few lines? or step round to the Post Office? In a word, will you do anything at all, to give a coloring to your refusal to depart the premises?"

He silently retired into his hermitage.

I was now in such a state of nervous resentment that I thought it but prudent to check myself at present from further demonstrations. Bartleby and I were alone. I remembered the tragedy of the unfortunate Adams and the still more unfortunate Colt in the solitary office of the latter; and how poor Colt, being dreadfully incensed by Adams, and imprudently permitting himself to get wildly excited, was at unawares hurried into his fatal act — an act which certainly no man could possibly deplore more than the actor himself. Often it had occurred to me in my ponderings upon the subject that had that altercation taken place in the public street, or at a private residence, it would not have terminated as it did. It was the circumstance of being alone in a solitary office, up stairs, of a building entirely unhallowed by humanizing domestic associations — an uncarpeted office, doubtless, of a dusty, haggard sort of appearance — this it must have been, which greatly helped to enhance the irritable desperation of the hapless Colt.

But when this old Adam of resentment rose in me and tempted me concerning Bartleby, I grappled him and threw him. How? Why, simply by recalling the divine injunction: "A new commandment give I unto you, that ye love one another." Yes, this it was that saved me. Aside from higher considerations, charity often operates as a vastly wise and prudent principle — a great safeguard to its possessor. Men have committed murder for jealousy's sake, and anger's sake, and hatred's sake, and selfishness' sake, and spiritual pride's sake; but no man, that ever I heard of, ever committed a diabolical murder for sweet charity's sake. Mere self-interest, then, if no better motive can be enlisted, should, especially with high-tempered men, prompt all beings to charity and philanthropy. At any rate, upon the occasion in question, I strove to drown my exasperated feelings towards the scrivener by benevolently construing his conduct. Poor fellow, poor fellow! thought I, he don't mean anything; and besides, he has seen hard times, and ought to be indulged.

I endeavored, also, immediately to occupy myself, and at the same time to comfort my despondency. I tried to fancy, that in the course of the morning, at such time as might prove agreeable to him, Bartleby, of his own free accord, would emerge from his hermitage and take up some decided line of march in the direction of the door. But no. Halfpast twelve o'clock came; Turkey began to glow in the face, overturn his inkstand, and become generally obstreperous; Nippers abated down into quietude and courtesy; Ginger Nut munched his noon apple; and Bartleby remained standing at his window in one of his profoundest dead-wall reveries. Will it be credited? Ought I to acknowledge it? That afternoon I left the office without saying one further word to him.

Some days now passed, during which, at leisure intervals I looked a little into "Edwards on the Will," and "Priestley on Necessity." Under the circumstances, those books induced a salutary feeling. Gradually I slid into the persuasion that these troubles of mine, touching the scrivener, had been all predestined from eternity, and Bartleby was billeted upon me for some mysterious purpose of an all-wise Providence, which it was not for a mere mortal like me to fathom. Yes, Bartleby, stay there behind your screen, thought I; I shall persecute you no more; you are harmless and noiseless as any of these old chairs; in short, I never feel so private as when I know you are here. At last I see it, I feel it; I penetrate to the predestined purpose of my life. I am content. Others may have loftier parts to enact; but my mission in this world, Bartleby, is to furnish you with office-room for such period as you may see fit to remain.

I believe that this wise and blessed frame of mind would have continued with me, had it not been for the unsolicited and uncharitable remarks obtruded upon me by my professional friends who visited the rooms. But thus it often is, that the constant fraction of illiberal minds wears out at last the best resolves of the more generous. Though to be sure, when I reflected upon it, it was not strange that people entering my office should be struck by the peculiar aspect of the unaccountable Bartleby, and so be tempted to throw out some sinister observations concerning him. Sometimes an attorney, having business with me, and calling at my office, and finding no one but the scrivener there, would undertake to obtain some sort of precise information from him touching my whereabouts; but without heeding his idle talk, Bartleby would remain standing immovable in the middle of the room. So after contemplating him in that position for a time, the attorney would depart, no wiser than he came.

Also, when a reference was going on, and the room full of lawyers and witnesses, and business driving fast, some deeply-occupied legal gentleman present, seeing Bartleby wholly unemployed, would request him to run round to his (the legal gentleman's) office and fetch some papers for him. Thereupon, Bartleby would tranquilly decline, and yet remain idle as before. Then the lawyer would give a great stare, and turn to me. And what could I say? At last I was made aware that all through the circle of my professional acquaintance, a whisper of wonder was running round, having reference to the strange creature I kept at my office. This worried me very much. And as the idea came upon me of his possibly turning out a long-lived man, and keeping occupying my chambers, and denying my authority; and perplexing my visitors; and scandalizing my professional reputation; and casting a general gloom over the premises; keeping soul and body together to the last upon his savings (for doubtless he spent but half a dime a day), and in the end perhaps outlive me, and claim possession of my office by right of his perpetual occupancy: as all these dark anticipations crowded upon me more and more, and my friends continually intruded their relentless remarks upon the apparition in my room; a great change was wrought in me. I resolved to gather all my faculties together, and forever rid me of this intolerable incubus.

Ere revolving any complicated project, however, adapted to this end, I first simply suggested to Bartleby the propriety of his permanent departure. In a calm and serious tone, I commended the idea to his careful and mature consideration. But, having taken three days to meditate upon it, he apprised me, that his original determination remained the same; in short, that he still preferred to abide with me.

What shall I do? I now said to myself, buttoning up my coat to the last button. What shall I do? what ought I to do? what does conscience say I *should* do with this man, or, rather, ghost. Rid myself of him, I must; go, he shall. But how? You will not thrust him, the poor, pale, passive mortal — you will not thrust such a helpless creature out of your door? you will not dishonor yourself by such cruelty? No, I will not, I cannot do that. Rather would I let him live and die here, and then mason up his remains in the wall. What, then, will you do? For all your coaxing, he will not budge. Bribes he leaves under your own paperweight on your table; in short, it is quite plain that he prefers to cling to you.

Then something severe, something unusual must be done. What! surely you will not have him collared by a constable, and commit his innocent pallor to the common jail? And upon what ground could you procure such a thing to be done? — a vagrant, is he? What! he a vagrant, a wanderer, who refuses to budge? It is because he will not be a vagrant, then, that you seek to count him *as* a vagrant. That is too absurd. No visible means of support: there I have him. Wrong again: for indubitably he *does* support himself, and that is the only unanswerable proof that any man can show of his possessing the means so to do. No more, then. Since he will not quit me, I must quit him. I will change my offices; I will move elsewhere, and give him fair notice, that if I find him on my new premises I will then proceed against him as a common trespasser.

Acting accordingly, next day I thus addressed him: "I find these chambers too far from the City Hall; the air is unwholesome. In a word, I propose to remove my offices next week, and shall no longer require your services. I tell you this now, in order that you may seek another place."

He made no reply, and nothing more was said.

On the appointed day I engaged carts and men, proceeded to my chambers, and, having but little furniture, everything was removed in a few hours. Throughout, the scrivener remained standing behind the screen, which I directed to be removed the last thing. It was withdrawn; and, being folded up like a huge folio, left him the motionless occupant of a naked room. I stood in the entry watching him a moment, while something from within me upbraided me.

I re-entered, with my hand in my pocket — and — and my heart in my mouth.

"Good-bye, Bartleby; I am going — good-bye, and God some way bless you; and take that," slipping something in his hand. But it dropped upon the floor, and then — strange to say — I tore myself from him whom I had so longed to be rid of.

Established in my new quarters, for a day or two I kept the door locked, started at every footfall in the passages. When I returned to my rooms, after any little absence, I would pause at the threshold for an instant, and attentively listen, ere applying my key. But these fears were needless. Bartleby never came nigh me.

I thought all was going well, when a perturbed-looking stranger visited me, inquiring whether I was the person who had recently occupied rooms at No. — Wall Street.

Full of forebodings, I replied that I was.

"Then, sir," said the stranger, who proved a lawyer, "you are responsible for the man you left there. He refuses to do any copying; he refuses to do anything; he says he prefers not to; and he refuses to quit the premises."

"I am very sorry, sir," said I, with assumed tranquillity, but an inward tremor, "but, really, the man you allude to is nothing to me — he is no relation or apprentice of mine, that you should hold me responsible for him."

"In mercy's name, who is he?"

"I certainly cannot inform you. I know nothing about him. Formerly I employed him as a copyist; but he has done nothing for me now for some time past."

"I shall settle him, then — good morning, sir."

Several days passed, and I heard nothing more; and, though I often felt a charitable prompting to call at the place and see poor Bartleby, yet a certain squeamishness, of I know not what, withheld me.

All is over with him, by this time, thought I, at last, when, through another week, no further intelligence reached me. But, coming to my room the day after, I found several persons waiting at my door in a high state of nervous excitement.

"That's the man — here he comes," cried the foremost one, whom I recognized as the lawyer who had previously called upon me alone.

"You must take him away, sir, at once," cried a portly person among them, advancing upon me, and whom I knew to be the landlord of No. — Wall Street. "These gentlemen, my tenants, cannot stand it any longer; Mr. B——," pointing to the lawyer, "has turned him out of his room, and he now persists in haunting the building generally, sitting upon the banisters of the stairs by day, and sleeping in the entry by night. Everybody is concerned; clients are leaving the offices; some fears are entertained of a mob; something you must do, and that without delay."

Aghast at this torrent, I fell back before it, and would fain have locked myself in my new quarters. In vain I persisted that Bartleby was nothing to me — no more than to any one else. In vain — I was the last person known to have anything to do with him, and they held me to the terrible account. Fearful, then, of being exposed in the papers (as one person present obscurely threatened), I considered the matter, and, at length, said, that if the lawyer would give me a confidential interview with the scrivener, in his (the lawyer's) own room, I would, that afternoon, strive my best to rid them of the nuisance they complained of.

Going up stairs to my old haunt, there was Bartleby silently sitting upon the banister at the landing.

"What are you doing here, Bartleby?" said I.

"Sitting upon the banister," he mildly replied.

I motioned him into the lawyer's room, who then left us.

"Bartleby," said I, "are you aware that you are the cause of great tribulation to me, by persisting in occupying the entry after being dismissed from the office?"

No answer.

"Now one of two things must take place. Either you must do something, or something must be done to you. Now what sort of business would you like to engage in? Would you like to re-engage in copying for some one?"

"No; I would prefer not to make any change."

"Would you like a clerkship in a dry-goods store?"

"There is too much confinement about that. No, I would not like a clerkship; but I am not particular."

"Too much confinement," I cried, "why, you keep yourself confined all the time!"

"I would prefer not to take a clerkship," he rejoined, as if to settle that little item at once.

"How would a bar-tender's business suit you? There is no trying of the eye-sight in that."

"I would not like it at all; though, as I said before, I am not particular."

His unwonted wordiness inspirited me. I returned to the charge.

"Well, then, would you like to travel through the country collecting bills for the merchants? That would improve your health."

"No, I would prefer to be doing something else."

"How, then, would going as a companion to Europe, to entertain some young gentleman with your conversation — how would that suit you?"

"Not at all. It does not strike me that there is anything definite about that. I like to be stationary. But I am not particular."

"Stationary you shall be, then," I cried, now losing all patience, and, for the first time in all my exasperating connections with him, fairly flying into a passion. "If you do not go away from these premises before night, I shall feel bound — indeed, I *am* bound — to — to — to quit the premises myself!" I rather absurdly concluded, knowing not with what possible threat to try to frighten his immobility into compliance. Despairing of all further efforts, I was precipitately leaving him, when a final thought occurred to me — one which had not been wholly unindulged before.

"Bartleby," said I, in the kindest tone I could assume under such exciting circumstances, "will you go home with me now — not to my office, but my dwelling — and remain there till we can conclude upon some convenient arrangement for you at our leisure? Come, let us start now, right away."

"No: at present I would prefer not to make any change at all."

I answered nothing; but, effectually dodging every one by the suddenness and rapidity of my flight, rushed from the building, ran up Wall Street towards Broadway, and, jumping into the first omnibus, was soon removed from pursuit. As soon as tranquillity resumed, I distinctly perceived that I had now done all that I possibly could, both in respect to the demands of the landlord and his tenants, and with regard to my own desire and sense of duty, to benefit Bartleby, and shield him from rude persecution. I now strove to be entirely care-free and quiescent; and my conscience justified me in the attempt; though, indeed, it was not so successful as I could have wished. So fearful was I of being again hunted out by the incensed landlord and his exasperated tenants, that, surrendering my business to Nippers, for a few days, I drove about the upper part of the town and through the suburbs, in my rockaway; crossed over to Jersey City and Hoboken, and paid fugitive visits to Manhattanville and Astoria. In fact, I almost lived in my rockaway for the time.

When again I entered my office, lo, a note from the landlord lay upon the desk. I opened it with trembling hands. It informed me that the writer had sent to the police, and had Bartleby removed to the Tombs as a vagrant. Moreover, since I knew more about him than any one else, he wished me to appear at that place, and make a suitable statement of the facts. These tidings had a conflicting effect upon me. At first I was indignant; but, at last, almost approved. The landlord's energetic, summary disposition, had led him to adopt a procedure which I do not think I would have decided upon myself; and yet, as a last resort, under such peculiar circumstances, it seemed the only plan.

As I afterwards learned, the poor scrivener, when told that he must be conducted to the Tombs, offered not the slightest obstacle, but, in his pale, unmoving way, silently acquiesced.

Some of the compassionate and curious by-standers joined the party; and headed by one of the constables arm-in-arm with Bartleby, the silent procession filed its way through all the noise, and heat, and joy of the roaring thoroughfares at noon.

The same day I received the note, I went to the Tombs, or, to speak more properly, the Halls of Justice. Seeking the right officer, I stated the purpose of my call, and was informed that the individual I described was, indeed, within. I then assured the functionary that Bartleby was a perfectly honest man, and greatly to be compassionated, however unaccountably eccentric. I narrated all I knew, and closed by suggesting the idea of letting him remain in as indulgent confinement as possible, till something less harsh might be done — though, indeed, I hardly knew what. At all events, if nothing else could be decided upon, the alms-house must receive him. I then begged to have an interview.

Being under no disgraceful charge, and quite serene and harmless in all his ways, they had permitted him freely to wander about the prison, and, especially, in the inclosed grass-platted yards thereof. And so I found him there, standing all alone in the quietest of the yards, his face towards a high wall, while all around, from the narrow slits of the jail windows, I thought I saw peering out upon him the eyes of murderers and thieves.

"Bartleby!"

"I know you," he said, without looking round — "and I want nothing to say to you."

"It was not I that brought you here, Bartleby," said I, keenly pained at his implied suspicion. "And to you, this should not be so vile a place. Nothing reproachful attaches to you by being here. And see, it is not so sad a place as one might think. Look, there is the sky, and here is the grass."

"I know where I am," he replied, but would say nothing more, and so I left him.

As I entered the corridor again, a broad meat-like man, in an apron, accosted me, and, jerking his thumb over my shoulder, said — "Is that your friend?"

"Yes."

"Does he want to starve? If he does, let him live on the prison fare, that's all."

"Who are you?" asked I, not knowing what to make of such an unoffi-cially speaking person in such a place.

"I am the grub-man. Such gentlemen as have friends here, hire me to pro-vide them with something good to eat."

"Is this so?" said I, turning to the turnkey.

He said it was.

"Well, then," said I, slipping some silver into the grub-man's hands (for so they called him), "I want you to give particular attention to my friend there; let him have the best dinner you can get. And you must be as polite to him as possible."

"Introduce me, will you?" said the grub-man, looking at me with an expres-sion which seemed to say he was all impatience for an opportunity to give a specimen of his breeding.

Thinking it would prove of benefit to the scrivener, I acquiesced; and, ask-ing the grub-man his name, went up with him to Bartleby.

"Bartleby, this is a friend; you will find him very useful to you."

"Your servant, sir, your servant," said the grub-man, making a low saluta-tion behind his apron. "Hope you find it pleasant here, sir; nice grounds — cool apartments — hope you'll stay with us some time — try to make it agree-able. What will you have for dinner to-day?"

"I prefer not to dine to-day," said Bartleby, turning away. "It would dis-agree with me; I am unused to dinners." So saying, he slowly moved to the other side of the inclosure, and took up a position fronting the dead-wall.

"How's this?" said the grub-man, addressing me with a stare of astonish-ment. "He's odd, ain't he?"

"I think he is a little deranged," said I, sadly.

"Deranged? deranged is it? Well, now, upon my word, I thought that friend of yourn was a gentleman forger; they are always pale and genteel-like, them forgers. I can't help pity 'em — can't help it, sir. Did you know Monroe Edwards?" he added, touchingly, and paused. Then, laying his hand piteously on my shoulder, sighed, "he died of consumption at Sing-Sing. So you weren't acquainted with Monroe?"

"No, I was never socially acquainted with any forgers. But I cannot stop longer. Look to my friend yonder. You will not lose by it. I will see you again."

Some few days after this, I again obtained admission to the Tombs, and went through the corridors in quest of Bartleby; but without finding him.

"I saw him coming from his cell not long ago," said a turnkey, "may be he's gone to loiter in the yards."

So I went in that direction.

"Are you looking for the silent man?" said another turnkey, passing me. "Yonder he lies — sleeping in the yard there. 'Tis not twenty minutes since I saw him lie down."

The yard was entirely quiet. It was not accessible to the common prisoners. The surrounding walls, of amazing thickness, kept off all sounds behind them. The Egyptian character of the masonry weighed upon me with its gloom. But a soft imprisoned turf grew under foot. The heart of the eternal pyramids, it seemed, wherein, by some strange magic, through the clefts, grass-seed, dropped by birds, had sprung.

Strangely huddled at the base of the wall, his knees drawn up, and lying on his side, his head touching the cold stones, I saw the wasted Bartleby. But nothing stirred. I paused; then went close up to him; stooped over, and saw that his dim eyes were open; otherwise he seemed profoundly sleeping. Something prompted me to touch him. I felt his hand, when a tingling shiver ran up my arm and down my spine to my feet.

The round face of the grub-man peered upon me now. "His dinner is ready. Won't he dine to-day, either? Or does he live without dining?"

"Lives without dining," said I, and closed the eyes.

"Eh! — He's asleep, ain't he?"

"With kings and counselors," murmured I.

There would seem little need for proceeding further in this history. Imagination will readily supply the meagre recital of poor Bartleby's interment. But, ere parting with the reader, let me say, that if this little narrative has sufficiently interested him, to awaken curiosity as to who Bartleby was, and what manner of life he led prior to the present narrator's making his acquaintance, I can only reply, that in such curiosity I fully share, but am wholly unable to gratify it. Yet here I hardly know whether I should divulge one little item of rumor, which came to my ear a few months after the scrivener's decease. Upon what basis it rested, I could never ascertain; and hence, how true it is I cannot now tell. But, inasmuch as this vague report has not been without a certain suggestive interest to me, however sad, it may prove the same with some others; and so I will briefly mention it. The report was this: that Bartleby had been a subordinate clerk in the Dead Letter Office at Washington, from which he had been suddenly removed by a change in the administration. When I think over this rumor, hardly can I express the emotions which seize me. Dead letters! does it not sound like dead men? Conceive a man by nature and misfortune prone to a pallid hopelessness, can any business seem more fitted to heighten it than that of continually handling these dead letters, and assorting them for the flames? For by the cart-load they are annually burned. Sometimes from out the folded paper the pale clerk takes a ring — the finger it was meant for, perhaps, moulders in the grave; a bank-note sent in swiftest charity — he whom it would relieve, nor eats nor hungers any more; pardon for those who died despairing; hope for those who died unhoping; good tidings for those who died stifled by unrelieved calamities. On errands of life, these letters speed to death.

Ah, Bartleby! Ah, humanity!

Questions for Discussion

1. How would you characterize the narrator of the story, the elderly lawyer? What are his virtues as an employer? What are his limitations and inconsistencies as an employer and as a man?

2. What is the significance of the contrary and clashing personalities of Turkey, Nippers, and Ginger Nut? Why does the narrator continue to employ them? What is their attitude toward Bartleby?

3. How is the primary setting, the office where the story takes place, related physically and psychologically to the final setting, the yard in the Tombs where Bartleby is taken to die?

4. Bartleby is described as a sort of "human cipher." What motivates him? Why does he "prefer not to"? Is anything about his past revealed that helps you to understand his behavior? What makes Bartleby mysterious?

5. What is it about Bartleby that so touches the narrator's conscience? Trace the narrator's evolving attitude toward the scrivener. How have the narrator's values been transformed through his contact with Bartleby?

Ideas for Writing

1. In an essay, interpret the "cipher" Bartleby in light of the story's last sentences, "Ah, Bartleby! Ah, humanity!" In what sense is Bartleby a symbol for human destiny?

2. Analyze the character of the narrator, the old lawyer. What universal human qualities does he embody? What are his limits? How does he change? Contrast the purpose of his life to the purpose of Bartleby's.

LEO TOLSTOY   (1828–1910)

Leo Tolstoy is remembered chiefly for his great realist novels, *War and Peace* (1869) and *Anna Karenina* (1877). Although he was a master of realistic observation and detail as well as an imaginative fabulist who often wrote stories in the tradition of the Russian folk tale, Tolstoy was above all a moralist who believed that it is not artistic technique that produces true art but rather "the author's moral relation to the subject."

Tolstoy was born on his family's estate near Tula, Russia. In an early progressive reform, he established a school there for the children of peasants. Eventually, however, he turned away from the educational movement and married a young woman from a wealthy medical family, Sofia Beers. Sofia and Leo Tolstoy had a long marriage, if not a particularly happy one. She served as his copyist and raised a large family, but she could never accept Tolstoy's spiritual, antimaterialist views. Working among the poor and writing philosophical and religious tracts promoting nonviolence and antimaterialism, Tolstoy gained a large following in the 1880s, both in the city and among the rural peasants. By the end of the century, however, his works were banned and many of his followers imprisoned for refusing military service. As his career progressed, Tolstoy turned increasingly to philosophy and religious contemplation. His later works — *The Death of Ivan Ilyich* (1886) and *Resurrection* (1899) among them — reflect his disillusionment with worldly affairs and his unorthodox spirituality.

Three Deaths   (1859)

Translated by Arthur Mendel and Barbara Makandwitzky

1

It was fall. Two carriages were driving down the high-road at a fast trot. In the first carriage sat two women. One was a lady, thin and pale. The other, a chambermaid — shiny-red and plump. Short, dry locks of hair strayed from under the maid's faded cap and were impetuously straightened by her red hand in its torn glove. Her prominent bosom, covered with a thick shawl, exhaled good health; her lively, dark eyes first followed the fields rushing past the window, then glanced timidly at her mistress, then anxiously looked around the coach. The lady's hat, hung in a net, swung in front of the chambermaid's nose; on her knees lay a puppy; her feet drummed lightly on the boxes stacked on the floor with a sound barely audible in the midst of the jolting of springs and rattling of windows.

Her hands crossed in her lap and her eyes closed, the lady was swaying weakly on the cushions placed under her back, and frowning slightly as she coughed with her lips closed. She wore a white nightcap on her head and a blue kerchief around her pale, delicate neck. A straight part divided her dulled, pomaded, blond hair above the brow, and there was something dry and lifeless in the pallor of the skin in this wide part. Withered, somewhat yellowish skin hung loosely over the thin and beautiful features of the face and reddened over the cheeks and cheekbones. Her lips were dry and anxious, her thin lashes straight, and her cloth traveling gown fell in angular folds over her sunken chest. Although her eyes were closed, the lady's face expressed fatigue, vexation, and chronic suffering.

The lackey was leaning on his elbow and dozing on the coach-box; the coachman, shouting briskly, goaded the four sturdy sweating horses and glanced from time to time at the shouting coachman in the landau behind him. The wide, parallel tracks of the wheels spread evenly and quickly in the slimy mud of the road. The sky was gray and cold; a damp mist was sprinkling the roads and fields. It was stifling in the carriage and smelled of eau de cologne and dust. The invalid leaned her head back and opened her eyes slowly. Her eyes were large, shiny, and a beautiful, dark color.

"Again," she said, her lovely, slender hand nervously pushing away the edge of the maid's cloak which was barely touching her leg; and her mouth grimaced painfully. Matresha gathered up her cloak in both hands and lifted herself on her sturdy legs to sit down farther away. Her fresh face was bright red. The splendid, dark eyes of the invalid followed the maid's movements greedily. Bracing both hands on the seat, she tried to lift herself to sit up higher, but her strength failed her. Her mouth twisted and an expression of weak, spiteful irony distorted her whole face. "If you'd just help me! . . . Ah! Never mind! I can do it myself; just don't put your bags on top of me, if you please! . . . And don't tug at me if you can't help!" The lady closed her eyes, then quickly lifting her eyelids again, glanced at the maid. Matresha, looking at her, bit her red lower lip. A heavy sigh arose in the invalid's chest, but the incompleted sigh changed into a cough. She turned away, frowned, and clutched her chest with both hands. When the cough subsided, she closed her eyes again and sat motionless. The carriage and the landau entered a village. Matresha withdrew her stout hand from under the shawl and crossed herself.

"What's that?" asked the lady.

"The station, my lady."

"What are you crossing yourself for, I asked you?"

"A church, my lady."

The invalid turned toward the window and began to cross herself slowly, gazing with her full, large eyes at the big village church.

The coach and the landau both stopped at the station. The invalid's husband and the doctor climbed out of the landau and came up to the coach.

"How do you feel?" asked the doctor, taking her pulse.

"Well, now, you're not tired, my dear?" the husband asked in French. "You don't want to get out?"

Matresha, curled into a ball, pressed herself into her corner to avoid disturbing the conversation.

"All right; the same," answered the invalid. "I won't get out."

After a brief hesitation, the husband went into the station house. Matresha, jumping out of the carriage, ran on tiptoes through the mud past the gates.

"If I'm not well, it's no reason for you not to have breakfast," the invalid said with a faint smile to the doctor who had remained standing by the carriage window.

"None of them cares about me," she added to herself as soon as the doctor, after walking away from her slowly had run up to the steps of the station house at a trot. "They feel fine, so nothing else matters. Oh! My God!"

"Well, then, Eduard Ivanovich," said the husband, greeting the doctor and rubbing his hands with a jolly smile, "I ordered a lunch basket brought, what do you think of that?"

"It'll do," answered the doctor.

"Well, how is she?" the husband asked with a sigh, lowering his voice and raising his eyebrows.

"I say she can't reach, not only Italy, but Moscow, by God. Particularly in this weather."

"But what can one do? Ah, my God! My God!" The husband covered his eyes with his hand. "Over here," he added to the man carrying the lunch basket.

"She must not go," answered the doctor, shrugging his shoulders.

"But, tell me, what can I do?" exclaimed the husband. "Naturally I used every possible means of restraining her; I talked about the cost, the children we had to leave behind, my business — she didn't want to listen to anything. She's making plans about living abroad just as though she were well. But if she were told about her condition — you see, that would be her death."

"But she is already dead, you must know that, Vassily Dmitrich. A person can't live without lungs, and lungs can't grow back again. It's sad, it's hard, but what can one do? My duty and yours is simply to make her end as peaceful as possible. There must be a priest there."

"Ah, my God! But you understand my position if I were to remind her of her last testament. Happen what may, I won't tell her that. You know, of course, how good she is . . ."

"Just the same, try to persuade her to put off the trip until travel by sleigh is possible," the doctor said, nodding his head significantly; "otherwise, something bad might happen on the trip . . ."

"Aksyusha, oh Aksyusha!" shrieked the stationmaster's daughter, flinging a jacket over her head and trampling on the muddy back porch steps. "Let's go look at the Shirkinsky lady, they say they're taking her abroad for a sickness in the chest. I never saw somebody with consumption before."

Aksyusha jumped out the door, and holding hands the two girls ran through the gates. Shortening their steps as they went past the carriage, they glanced in the lowered window. The invalid turned her head toward them, but noticing their curiosity, frowned and turned away.

"Mm-mma-ma!" said the stationmaster's daughter, quickly averting her head. "She was once a wonderful beauty, and what has she become now? It's even frightening. Did you see, did you see, Aksyusha?"

"Yes, what a skinny woman!" seconded Aksyusha. "Let's go look again as though we were heading for the well. See, she turned away, but I still saw. How sad, Masha."

"Yes, and how muddy it is!" answered Masha, and they both ran back through the gates.

"Evidently I've become frightening," thought the invalid. "If only I can get abroad, quickly, I'll get well fast."

"How are you now, my dear?" said the husband, munching on something as he came up to the carriage.

"Always the same old question," thought the invalid; "and he eats!"

"All right," she let slip through her teeth.

"You know, my dear, I'm afraid you'll be worse for traveling in this weather, and Eduard Ivanich says so too. Shouldn't we turn back?"

She was angrily silent.

"The weather will right itself, perhaps the road will improve, and you would be better; and then we could all go together."

"Forgive me. If I hadn't listened to you long ago, I would be in Berlin now and completely well."

"What could I do, my angel? It was impossible, you know that. But if you wait a month now, you would get much better; and I'd finish my business, and we could take the children . . ."

"The children are well and I'm not."

"But you must understand, my dear, that in this weather, if you get worse on the road . . . there at least you'd be at home."

"At home for what? . . . To die at home?" the invalid flared in answer. But the word *die* clearly frightened her, and she looked at her husband questioningly and pleadingly. He dropped his eyes and was silent. The invalid's mouth suddenly twitched childishly and tears began streaming from her eyes. Her husband, covering his face with his handkerchief, walked silently away from the carriage.

"No, I'll get there," the invalid said, raising her eyes to the sky, crossing her arms, and whispering disconnected words. "My God! Why is it?" she said, and the tears poured faster. For a long time she prayed fervently, but her chest was congested and painful, and it was gray and gloomy in the sky, in the fields, and on the road, and the steady autumn mist kept sprinkling on the mud of the road, the roofs, the carriage, and the sheepskin coats of the coachmen, who, talking to each other in hearty, jolly voices, were greasing the carriage and getting it ready.

2

The carriage was harnessed; but the coachman lingered. He went into the drivers' hut. It was hot in the hut, stifling, dark, and heavy; it smelled of human habitation, of sheepskins, and the baking of bread, and cabbage. There were several drivers in the room; the cook was busy over the stove, and on the bunk over the stove lay a sick man, wrapped in sheepskins.

A young fellow, a driver in a sheepskin coat with a knout dangling from his belt entered the room and called to the sick man: "Uncle Fedor! Eh, Uncle Fedor!"

"What are you calling Fedka for, idiot?" said one of the drivers. "Look, they're waiting for you in the carriage."

"I want to ask for his boots; mine are worn out," the young fellow answered, tossing back his hair and shoving his mittens in his belt. "Is he asleep? Eh, Uncle Fedor?" he repeated, going up to the stove.

"What?" said a weak voice, and a red, thin face leaned down from the bunk. The old man's broad, emaciated, hairy white hand pulled his overcoat over the dirty shirt covering his angular shoulder. "Give me something to drink, brother; what do you want?"

The fellow brought him a dipper full of water.

"Well, then, Fedya," he said, shifting his feet uneasily; "look, you probably don't need new boots now; look, give them to me; you probably won't be walking."

The sick man, pressing his weary head against the shiny ladle and dipping his sparse, overhanging mustaches in the dark water, drank feebly but greedily. His lowered beard was dirty; his glazed, sunken eyes were raised with difficulty to the lad's face. Having finished drinking, he tried to raise his hand to wipe his wet lips, but, unable to, wiped them on the sleeves of his overcoat. Breathing with difficulty through his nose, gathering his forces, he looked directly and silently in the lad's eyes.

"Maybe you already promised somebody," said the lad; "then there's nothing doing. It's this way: it's wet in the yard, and I was just coming from work and I thought to myself: look, ask Fedka for his boots, he probably doesn't need them. Maybe you need them yourself—just say so . . ."

Something started fomenting and rising in the sick man's chest; he bent over and began choking on a throaty, erratic cough.

"And how would he need them," the voice of the cook shook the hut with an unexpectedly angry voice; "it's the second month he hasn't gotten down off the stove," she shouted. "See, he's finished; it makes your very insides hurt to hear him. How could he need boots? No point burying anybody in new boots.

And it was time long ago — Lord forgive me. See, he's finished. Take him to some other hut, or somewhere else! They say they have hospitals in towns; but here it's another story — he's been taking up the whole corner, and I've had enough! There's no room for you. And also, they like it clean here."

"Eh, Serega! Get out there, the passengers are waiting," the post overseer shouted from the doorway.

Serega was about to go out without waiting for an answer, but the sick man, still coughing, signaled with his eyes that he wanted to reply.

"Take the boots, Serega," he said, after suppressing the cough and resting a moment. "But, listen, buy me a stone when I die," he added hoarsely.

"Thanks, Uncle, then I'll take them; and I'll buy the stone for sure."

"There, children, you heard," the old man managed to blurt out, then again bent double and began choking.

"All right, we heard," said one of the drivers. "Go, Serega, get going or the overseer will be running back in here. The Shirkinsky lady is an invalid, you see."

Serega quickly pulled off his old, torn, unmatched boots and flung them under the bench. Uncle Fedor's new boots fit his feet perfectly, and Serega, glancing at them, went out to the carriage.

"What beautiful boots! Let me grease them," said a coachman with grease in his hands while Serega, climbing on the coach-box, sorted out the reins. "Did he give them free?"

"You're jealous," answered Serega, raising himself and wrapping the tails of his overcoat around his legs. "Let's go! Eh, my darlings!" he shouted, swinging his knout at the horses; and the two vehicles with their passengers, trunks and packages rolled swiftly over the wet road and disappeared in the gray fall fog.

The sick driver stayed in the bunk over the stove in the stifling hut, gasped, and painfully turning over on his other side, fell silent.

People came and went and ate in the hut until evening — the sick man was not to be heard. Before nightfall, the cook reached above the stove, over the sick man, to pull out her sheepskin coat.

"Don't be angry with me, Nastasya," said the sick man. "I'll soon free your corner."

"It's all right, all right, it doesn't matter," muttered Nastasya. "But what hurts you, Uncle? Tell me."

"My insides are all wasted. God knows what it is."

"Your chest hurts when you cough, I suppose?"

"It hurts everywhere. It's my death come — that's what. Oh, oh, oh!" groaned the sick man.

"You should cover your legs like that," said Nastasya, pulling the overcoat over him as she moved away from the stove.

Through the night, a feeble night-lamp flickered in the hut. Nastasya and ten drivers were sleeping with great snoring on the floor and the benches. Only the sick man groaned, coughed and tossed above the stove. Toward morning he became completely quiet.

"It's strange what I just dreamt," said the cook, preparing for another day, stretching herself in the half light. "I dreamt Uncle Fedor climbed down off the stove and went to chop wood. You know, he says, Nastasya, I'll help you; and I said to him: how could you chop wood, and he seizes the ax and begins chopping, so quickly, quickly that the chips just flew. But look, I say, you were sick. No, he says, I'm well, and he begins brandishing the ax so I got scared. When I screamed, I woke up. Is he dead? Uncle Fedor! Eh, Uncle!"

Fedor did not respond.

"Well then, is he dead? Go look," said one of the drivers, waking up.

Hanging down from the stove, his thin hand, covered with red hair, was cold and pale.

"Go tell the stationmaster it looks like he died," said the driver.

Fedor had no relatives — he came from far away. They buried him the following day in the new cemetery beyond the grove, and for several days Nastasya kept telling everyone about the dream she had had, and about how she had been the first to discover Uncle Fedor dead.

3

Spring came. Swift little streams coursed down the wet streets of the town between dung-covered lumps of ice; the people moving about had bright shades of clothing and tones of voice. The buds of the trees were swelling in the little gardens behind the fences, and their branches were swaying barely audibly in the fresh breeze. Everywhere, transparent drops dripped and trickled . . . the sparrows chirped and fluttered their little wings. In the sun, on the fences, houses, and trees, everything stirred and sparkled. Joy and youth were in the sky, the earth, and people's hearts.

Fresh straw was strewn in front of a nobleman's mansion on one of the main streets; in the house, the invalid who had been hurrying abroad was dying.

The invalid's husband was standing beside an elderly woman outside the closed doors of the sickroom. With lowered eyes, a priest sat on the couch, holding something twisted in his stole. In the corner, in a wing-backed armchair, an old woman — the mother of the invalid — lay crying bitterly. Next to her, a chambermaid held a clean handkerchief, waiting for the old woman to ask her for it; another maid was stroking the old woman's curls and blowing gently on the gray head under the nightcap.

"Come, God be with you, my dear," the husband said to the elderly woman, his cousin, standing by the doorway with him. "She has such confidence in you; you can talk to her and convince her, dear; go now." He was about to open the door for her, but she restrained him, put her handkerchief to her eyes several times and shook her head.

"Now I don't look as though I had been crying," she said, and opening the door herself, walked into the sickroom.

The husband was very agitated and seemed completely distraught. He was about to walk over to the old woman, but after two or three steps in her direction, turned around, crossed the room, and approached the priest. The priest looked at him, lifted his brows to heaven and sighed. His thick, grizzled beard also rose upward and then dropped.

"My God! My God!" said the husband.

"What can one do?" said the priest, sighing, and again his brows and beard rose and dropped.

"And with Mother here!" the husband said almost with despair. "She'll never endure this. How she loved, how she loved her, as if she . . . I don't know. If you, little Father, would only try to soothe her and persuade her to leave."

The priest got up and went over to the old woman.

"It's true, my lady, that no one can appreciate the maternal heart," he said, "but God is merciful."

The face of the old woman suddenly began to twitch all over, and she was overcome by hysterical hiccups.

"God is merciful," the priest continued when she had become a bit calmer. "I can tell you myself that someone was sick in my parish, much more gravely than Marya Dmitrievna; and this burgher was cured with herbs in a short time. And, the same burgher is now in Moscow. I told Vassily Dmitrievich about it — it could be tried. At the very least, it would be a comfort for the invalid. Everything is possible for God."

"No, she is no longer living," said the old woman; "if it were only I, but God took her." And the hysterical hiccuping became so violent that she fainted.

The invalid's husband covered his face with his hands and ran out of the room.

In the corridor, the first person he met was his six-year-old boy chasing his little girl at full speed.

"Don't you want the children taken to see their mother?" asked the nurse.

"No, she doesn't want to see them. It unsettles her."

The little boy stopped for a minute, looked fixedly at his father's face, and suddenly kicked up his legs and ran on with a merry shout.

"I'm pretending she's the black horse, Papasha!" the little boy shouted, pointing to his sister.

Meanwhile, in the sickroom, the cousin was sitting near the invalid, and by directing the conversation artfully, trying to prepare her to think of death. The doctor was mixing a potion by the window.

The invalid, in a white dressing gown, surrounded by pillows, sat on the bed and looked silently at her cousin.

"Ah, my dear," she said, unexpectedly interrupting her; "don't try to prepare me. Don't consider me a child. I am a Christian. I know. I know I haven't long to live; I know if my husband had listened to me earlier, I would be in Italy, and perhaps — even certainly — would be well. They all told him that. But what can you do; it's clear this was God's will. We all have many sins, I know that; but I trust that God in his mercy will forgive everyone, perhaps, everyone. I am trying to understand myself. And I have had many sins, my dear. But, in return, how much I have suffered. I have been trying to endure my sufferings with patience . . ."

"Shall I call the little Father, my dear? You will feel easier, after the Sacrament," said the cousin.

The invalid bent her head in agreement.

"God! Forgive me, a sinner," she whispered.

The cousin went out and nodded to the priest.

"She is an angel!" she told the husband with tears in her eyes.

The husband burst into tears; the priest walked in, the old woman was still unconscious, sitting motionless in the first room. Five minutes later the priest came out, removed his stole, and straightened his hair.

"Thanks be to God, she is calmer now," he said, "she wants to see you."

The cousin and husband went in. The invalid was crying quietly, looking at the holy image.

"I congratulate you, my dear," said the husband.

"Thank you! How well I am now, what an incomprehensible sweetness I feel," said the invalid, and a slight smile played on her thin lips. "How merciful is God! Is it not true that he is merciful and all-powerful?" And she again looked with eager entreaty and tear-filled eyes at the holy image.

Then she seemed to suddenly remember something. She called her husband to her by signs.

"You never want to do what I ask," she said in a feeble, discontented voice.

The husband, extending his neck, listened to her obediently.

"What is it, my dear?"

"How many times have I said these doctors don't know anything; they are simple healers, they cure . . . The little Father was just saying . . . the burgher . . . Send."

"For whom, my dear?"

"My God! He doesn't want to understand anything! . . ." and the invalid frowned and closed her eyes.

The doctor, approaching her, took her by the hand. The pulse was beating noticeably weaker and weaker. He nodded to the husband. The invalid noticed it and looked around in fright. The cousin turned away and burst into tears.

"Don't cry, don't torture me and yourself," said the invalid. "It takes away my remaining peace."

"You're an angel!" said the cousin, kissing her hand.

"No, kiss me here, only the dead are kissed on the hand. My God! My God!"

That same evening the invalid was a corpse, and the corpse stood in a coffin in the hall of the big house. In the big room with the closed doors, a deacon sat alone, reading in an even nasal voice the psalms of David. The bright waxen light from the high, silver candlesticks fell on the pale forehead of the deceased, on the pitiful, waxen hands and the stony folds of the shroud raised frighteningly over the knees and toes. The deacon read evenly, without understanding, and in the quiet room the words rang and died away. From time to time, the sounds of children's voices and trampling drifted from the far room.

"Thou hideth Thy face — they are troubled," said the Book of Psalms; "Thou taketh their spirit — they die and to dust return. Thou sendeth Thy spirit — they are created and renew the face of the earth. The glory of the Lord shall endure forever."

The face of the deceased was stern, calm, and majestic. On the clear, cold forehead, on the firmly compressed lips, nothing moved. She was all attention. But was she able to understand these solemn words even now?

4

A month later, a stone chapel was erected over the grave of the deceased woman. There was still no stone over the old coachman's grave, and the bright green grass sprouting on the mound was the sole testimony to the previous existence of a man.

"It'll be a sin, Serega, if you don't buy Fedor a stone," the cook once said. "You said: in winter, in winter; but, now why don't you keep your word? I was there, you know. He's already come to ask you once; if you don't do it, next time he comes, he'll strangle you."

"But why, unless I break my promise?" answered Serega. "I'll buy a stone, like I said. I'll buy one for a silver ruble and a half. I haven't forgotten, but I have to cart it here, you know. Next time I'm in town, I'll buy it."

"You should at least put a cross, that's what," retorted an old driver; "it's plain wrong, otherwise. You're wearing his boots."

"And where would I get a cross? Cut it out of firewood?"

"What are you talking about? Don't cut it out of firewood; take an ax and go in the woods early in the morning and cut something there. Chop down an ash or something. That'll make a little wood marker. You don't even have to give the forest guard a vodka. You haven't got enough money to treat for every nonsense. Look, I broke my splinter-bar a couple of days ago, chopped down a nice, big tree for a new one, nobody said a word."

Early in the morning when it was barely light, Serega took an ax and went to the forest.

A dull, cold veil of dew, not yet illuminated by the sun covered the ground. The East was barely brightening, reflecting its weak light on the vaulted sky, covered with thin clouds. Not a blade of grass, not a leaf on the treetops was stirring. Only the occasional whir of wings in the thick of the trees or a rustling along the ground broke the silence of the woods. Suddenly a strange, unnatural sound spread along the fringe of the forest and faded. But the sound rang out again and began being repeated rhythmically at the base of one of the motionless trees. One of the tops trembled oddly; its dry leaves whispered something, and a warbler, sitting on one of its branches, whistled as it flitted back and forth briefly, and with a twitch of its little tail, settled on another tree.

The ax down below sounded duller and duller; dry, white chips flew onto the dew-covered grass, and a slight crackling could be heard among the blows. The tree shuddered with its whole body, swayed and swiftly stood erect, shaking with fright to its roots. For an instant, everything was still. Then the tree swayed again, the crackling was heard again in its trunk, and snapping its branches and dropping its limbs, it fell on the damp ground. The sounds of the ax and the steps stopped. The warbler whistled and flitted higher. The branch she brushed with her wings quivered several times and became still like the rest. The trees flaunted their motionless branches still more joyously in the new space.

The first rays of the sun, penetrating the transparent cloud, gleamed in the sky and coursed over heaven and earth. The fog began to pour into the hollows in waves; the dew glimmering, played on the grass; the opaque, whitening clouds hurriedly scattered over the blue sky. The birds flitted in the thick brush, and frantically twittered something joyful; the dry leaves whispered happily and peacefully in the tops of the trees, and the branches of the living slowly, majestically rustled above the dead, fallen tree.

Questions for Discussion

1. How do the sections of the story contrast the characters and values of Old Fedor and the invalid? Which character is presented more sympathetically?
2. Tolstoy puts special emphasis on descriptions of physical objects and possessions in the passages about Fedor and the invalid's death. How do these descriptions of objects help to deepen and clarify the contrast between the characters and their values?
3. Contrast the attitudes of relatives and acquaintances toward the deaths of Fedor and the invalid. Which set of characters seems more genuine and less hypocritical in their responses?
4. What different religious perspectives toward death and the use of ritual to mourn death are portrayed in the death of the invalid, of Fedor, and of the tree at the end of the story? In which death is ritual most important?
5. How does the arrangement of the sections, concluding with the death of the tree, help to emphasize the story's moral?

Ideas for Writing

1. In an essay, discuss the story's perspective on spirituality and organized religion. For example, how does the description of the death of the tree imply a radical alternative to traditional religious practices?
2. Write a brief story in which a strong contrast is drawn between three people from different social classes at a crucial moment — perhaps at a death, a birth, or a marriage.

MARK TWAIN   (1835–1910)

Raised in Hannibal, Missouri on the Mississippi River, Mark Twain (born Samuel Langhorne Clemens) was America's first great humorist and satirist, with a style of his own.

Clemens left school when he was twelve to work as a printer, and traveled throughout the country, finding employment at various newspapers and print shops. Between 1856 and 1861, he piloted steamboats up and down the Mississippi. After a brief period of military service during the Civil War, Twain followed the great silver and gold strikes West to Nevada and California. There he found work in journalism and published many of his humorous sketches, such as "The Notorious Jumping Frog of Calaveras County" (1865), which brought him national renown as a humorist of the Wild West. After traveling as a journalist to both Hawaii and the Holy Land, he married in 1870 and settled in Hartford, Connecticut. Twain established a solid literary reputation for himself in the 1870s and 1880s with the publication of *The Adventures of Tom Sawyer* (1876), the autobiographical *Life on the Mississippi* (1883), and the classic satirical novel, *The Adventures of Huckleberry Finn* (1884).

Toward the end of his career, burdened by financial and personal losses, Twain's vision became darker and more pessimistic, although he remained popular as a lecturer and received many honorary degrees. In his autobiography, Twain referred to writing a narrative as a kind of journey, one without rules: ". . . always going, and always following at least one law, the law of *narrative* which has no law. Nothing to do but make the trip, the how of it is not important, so that the trip is made."

Political Economy   (1870)

Political Economy is the basis of all good government. The wisest men of all ages have brought to bear upon this subject the —

[Here I was interrupted and informed that a stranger wished to see me down at the door. I went and confronted him, and asked to know his business, struggling all the time to keep a tight rein on my seething political-economy ideas, and not let them break away from me or get tangled in their harness. And privately I wished the stranger was in the bottom of the canal with a cargo of wheat on top of him. I was all in a fever, but he was cool. He said he was sorry to disturb me, but as he was passing he noticed that I needed some lightning-rods. I said, "Yes, yes — go on — what about it?" He said there was nothing about it, in particular — nothing except that he would like to put them up for me.

I am new to housekeeping; have been used to hotels and boarding-houses all my life. Like anybody else of similar experience, I try to appear (to strangers) to be an old housekeeper; consequently I said in an offhand way that I had been intending for some time to have six or eight lightning-rods put up, but — The stranger started, and looked inquiringly at me, but I was serene. I thought that if I chanced to make any mistakes, he would not catch me by my countenance. He said he would rather have my custom than any man's in town. I said, "All right," and started off to wrestle with my great subject again, when he called me back and said it would be necessary to know exactly how many "points" I wanted put up, what parts of the house I wanted them on, and what quality of rod I preferred. It was close quarters for a man not used to the exigencies of housekeeping; but I went through creditably, and he probably never suspected that I was a novice. I told him to put up eight "points," and put them all on the roof, and use the best quality of rod. He said he could furnish the "plain" article at 20 cents a foot; "coppered," 25 cents; "zinc-plated spiral-twist," at 30 cents, that would stop a streak of lightning any time, no matter where it was bound, and "render its errand harmless and its further progress apocryphal." I said apocryphal was no slouch of a word, emanating from the source it did, but, philology aside, I liked the spiral-twist and would take that brand. Then he said he *could* make two hundred and fifty feet answer; but to do it right, and make the best job in town of it, and attract the admiration of the just and the unjust alike, and compel all parties to say they never saw a more symmetrical and hypothetical display of lightning-rods since they were born, he supposed he really couldn't get along without four hundred, though he was not vindictive, and trusted he was willing to try. I said, go ahead and use four hundred, and make any kind of a job he pleased out of it, but let me get back to my work. So I got rid of him at last; and now, after half an hour spent in getting my train of political-economy thoughts coupled together again, I am ready to go on once more.]

richest treasures of their genius, their experience of life, and their learning. The great lights of commercial jurisprudence, international, confraternity, and biological deviation, of all ages, all civilizations, and all nationalities, from Zoroaster down to Horace Greeley, have —

[Here I was interrupted again, and required to go down and confer further with that lightning-rod man. I hurried off, boiling and surging with prodigious thoughts wombed in words of such majesty that each one of them was in itself a straggling procession of syllables that might be fifteen minutes passing a given point, and once more I confronted him — he so calm and sweet, I so hot and frenzied. He was standing in the contemplative attitude of the Colossus of Rhodes, with one foot on my infant tuberose, and the other among my pansies, his hands on his hips, his hat-brim tilted forward, one eye shut and the other gazing critically and admiringly in the direction of my principal chimney. He said now *there* was a state of things to make a man glad to be alive; and added, "I leave it to *you* if you ever saw anything more deliriously picturesque than eight lightning-rods on one chimney?" I said I had no present recollection of anything that transcended it. He said that in his opinion nothing on earth but Niagara Falls was superior to it in the way of natural scenery. All that was needed now, he verily believed, to make my house a perfect balm to the eye, was to kind of touch up the other chimneys a little, and thus "add to the generous *coup d'œil* a soothing uniformity of achievement which would allay the excitement naturally consequent upon the *coup d'état*." I asked him if he learned to talk out of a book, and if I could borrow it anywhere? He smiled pleasantly, and said that his manner of speaking was not taught in books, and that nothing but familiarity with lightning could enable a man to handle his conversational style with impunity. He then figured up an estimate, and said that about eight more rods scattered about my roof would about fix me right, and he guessed five hundred feet of stuff would do it; and added that the first eight had got a little the start of him, so to speak, and used up a mere trifle of material more than he had calculated on — a hundred feet or along there. I said I was in a dreadful hurry, and I wished we could get this business permanently mapped out, so that I could go on with my work. He said, "I *could* have put up those eight rods, and marched off about my business — some men *would* have done it. But no; I said to myself, this man is a stranger to me, and I will die before I'll wrong him; there ain't lightning-rods enough on that house, and for one I'll never stir out of my tracks till I've done as I would be done by, and told him so. Stranger, my duty is accomplished; if the recalcitrant and dephlogistic messenger of heaven strikes your — " "There, now, there," I said, "put on the other eight — add five hundred feet of spiral-twist — do anything and everything you want to do; but calm your sufferings, and try to keep your feelings where you can reach them with the dictionary. Meanwhile, if we understand each other now, I will go to work again."

I think I have been sitting here a full hour this time, trying to get back to where I was when my train of thought was broken up by the last interruption; but I believe I have accomplished it at last, and may venture to proceed again.]

wrestled with this great subject, and the greatest among them have found it a worthy adversary, and one that always comes up fresh and smiling after every throw. The great Confucius said that he would rather be a profound political economist than chief of police. Cicero frequently said that political economy was the grandest consummation that the human mind was capable of consuming; and even our own Greeley had said vaguely but forcibly that "Political —

[Here the lightning-rod man sent up another call for me. I went down in a state of mind bordering on impatience. He said he would rather have died than interrupt me, but when he was employed to do a job, and that job was expected to be done in a clean, workmanlike manner, and when it was finished and fatigue urged him to seek the rest and recreation he stood so much in need of, and he was about to do it, but looked up and saw at a glance that all the calculations had been a little out, and if a thunder-storm were to come up, and that house, which he felt a personal interest in, stood there with nothing on earth to protect it but sixteen lightning-rods — "Let us have peace!" I shrieked. "Put up a hundred and fifty! Put some on the kitchen! Put a dozen on the barn! Put a couple on the cow — Put one on the cook! — scatter them all over the persecuted place till it looks like a zinc-plated, spiral-twisted, silver-mounted canebrake! Move! use up all the material you can get your hands on, and when you run out of lightning-rods put up ram-rods, cam-rods, stair-rods, piston-rods — *anything* that will pander to your dismal appetite for artificial scenery, and bring respite to my raging brain and healing to my lacerated soul!" Wholly unmoved — further than to smile sweetly — this iron being simply turned back his wristbands daintily, and said that he would now proceed to hump himself. Well, all that was nearly three hours ago. It is questionable whether I am calm enough yet to write on the noble theme of political economy, but I cannot resist the desire to try, for it is the one subject that is nearest to my heart and dearest to my brain of all this world's philosophy.]

— economy is heaven's best boon to man." *When the loose but gifted Byron lay in his Venetian exile he observed that, if it could be granted him to go back and live his misspent life over again, he would give his lucid and unintoxicated intervals to the composition, not of frivolous rhymes, but of essays upon political economy. Washington loved this exquisite science; such names as Baker, Beckwith, Judson, Smith, are imperishably linked with it; and even imperial Homer, in the ninth book of the* Iliad, *has said:*

> Fiat justitia, ruat cœlum,
> Post mortem unum, ante bellum,
> Hic jacet hoc, ex-parte res,
> Politicum e-conomico est.

The grandeur of these conceptions of the old poet, together with the felicity of the wording which clothes them, and the sublimity of the imagery whereby they are illustrated, have singled out that stanza, and made it more celebrated than any that ever —

["Now, not a word out of you — not a single word. Just state your bill and relapse into impenetrable silence for ever and ever on these premises. Nine hundred dollars? Is that all? This check for the amount will be honored at any respectable bank in America. What is that multitude of people gathered in the street for? How? — 'looking at the lightning-rods'! Bless my life, did they never see any lightning-rods before? Never saw 'such a stack of

them on one establishment,' did I understand you to say? I will step down
and critically observe this popular ebullition of ignorance."]

Three Days Later   We are all about worn out. For four-and-twenty
hours our bristling premises were the talk and wonder of the town. The theaters languished, for their happiest scenic inventions were tame and commonplace compared with my lightning-rods. Our street was blocked night
and day with spectators, and among them were many who came from the
country to see. It was a blessed relief on the second day when a thunder-
storm came up and the lightning began to "go for" my house, as the historian Josephus quaintly phrases it. It cleared the galleries, so to speak. In five
minutes there was not a spectator within half a mile of my place; but all the
high houses about that distance away were full, windows, roof, and all. And
well they might be, for all the falling stars and Fourth-of-July fireworks of a
generation, put together and rained down simultaneously out of heaven in
one brilliant shower upon one helpless roof, would not have any advantage
of the pyrotechnic display that was making my house so magnificently conspicuous in the general gloom of the storm. By actual count, the lightning
struck at my establishment seven hundred and sixty-four times in forty minutes, but tripped on one of those faithful rods every time, and slid down the
spiral-twist and shot into the earth before it probably had time to be surprised at the way the thing was done. And through all that bombardment
only one patch of slates was ripped up, and that was because, for a single
instant, the rods in the vicinity were transporting all the lightning they could
possibly accommodate. Well, nothing was ever seen like it since the world
began. For one whole day and night not a member of my family stuck his
head out of the window but he got the hair snatched off it as smooth as a
billiard-ball; and, if the reader will believe me, not one of us ever dreamt of
stirring abroad. But at last the awful siege came to an end — because there
was absolutely no more electricity left in the clouds above us within grap-
pling distance of my insatiable rods. Then I sallied forth, and gathered daring workmen together, and not a bite or a nap did we take till the premises
were utterly stripped of all their terrific armament except just three rods on
the house, one on the kitchen, and one on the barn — and, behold, these
remain there even unto this day. And then, and not till then, the people ventured to use our street again. I will remark here, in passing, that during that
fearful time I did not continue my essay upon political economy. I am not
even yet settled enough in nerve and brain to resume it.

To Whom It May Concern   Parties having need of three thousand two hundred and eleven feet of best quality zinc-plated spiral-twist lightning-rod stuff,
and sixteen hundred and thirty-one silver-tipped points, all in tolerable repair
(and, although much worn by use, still equal to any ordinary emergency), can
hear of a bargain by addressing the publisher.

Questions for Discussion

1. What point does the narrator make about political economy? Do you think he is a competent essayist? Why? Is his style in the italicized portions of the story consistent and logical?

2. What story does the essayist tell in brackets? How does this story reveal its narrator's weaknesses and gullibility?

3. How do the two opposed voices or narrative styles in the italicized and the bracketed "story" sections of the narrative illuminate each other? How is the story resolved? Does the narrator ever complete his essay? Why is the final section or voice of the story that of a newspaper advertisement?

4. In what ways is Twain's "Political Economy" more similar to Washington Irving's "Rip Van Winkle" than to other nineteenth-century stories included in this anthology?

Ideas for Writing

1. In an essay, discuss what the story reveals about the "real" nature of political economy as opposed to its theoretical nature. Consider the narrator's education at the hands of the lightning rod salesman and the story as a whole.

2. Write a story in which a character is writing an essay or letter that is interrupted from time to time by the "action" or conflict in the story; try to make the character's subject matter coincide with or in some way relate to the interruptions.

HENRY JAMES   (1843–1916)

A writer whose career spanned half a century and produced some twenty novels and more than one hundred stories, Henry James is noted for his meticulous style and psychological realism. His central concern throughout his work is the manners and morality of human behavior. James was born in New York City, into a wealthy, intellectual family. His father was a philosopher of religion; his brother, William, was a respected physician and philosopher and one of the founders of experimental psychology. James himself entered Harvard Law School when he was only nineteen and published his first short story when he was twenty-one. Acclaimed as a critic, novelist, and story writer, James had many friendships with other writers, including Gustave Flaubert, George Eliot, Ivan Turgenev, Edith Wharton, and Guy de Maupassant. A lifelong bachelor, James spent much of his time after 1875 in England, the setting of many of his best-known novels, including *The Wings of the Dove* (1902), *The Ambassadors* (1903), and *The Golden Bowl* (1904).

In his short stories, James was influenced by Maupassant's manipulation of the twist-ending plot, as can be seen in "Paste." His stories often elaborate on moral dilemmas, relying on a slow, patient unfolding of characters through a series of conversations that gradually build to a significant realization, often involving a sense of loss or a failure of will.

Paste   (1899)

"I've found a lot more things," her cousin said to her the day after the second funeral; "they're up in her room—but they're things I wish *you'd* look at."

The pair of mourners, sufficiently stricken, were in the garden of the vicarage together, before luncheon, waiting to be summoned to that meal, and Arthur Prime had still in his face the intention, she was moved to call it rather than the expression, of feeling something or other. Some such appearance was in itself of course natural within a week of his stepmother's death, within three of his father's; but what was most present to the girl, herself sensitive and shrewd, was that he seemed somehow to brood without sorrow, to suffer without what she in her own case would have called pain. He turned away from her after this last speech—it was a good deal his habit to drop an observation and leave her to pick it up without assistance. If the vicar's widow, now in her turn finally translated, had not really belonged to him it was not for want of her giving herself, so far as he ever would take her; and she had lain for three days all alone at the end of the passage, in the great cold chamber of hospitality, the dampish, greenish room where visitors slept and where several of the ladies of the parish had, without effect, offered, in pairs and successions, piously to watch with her. His personal connection with the parish was now slighter than ever, and he had really not waited for this opportunity to show the ladies what he thought of them. She felt that she herself had, during her doleful month's leave from Bleet, where she was governess, rather taken her place in the same snubbed order; but it was presently, none the less, with a better little hope of coming in for some remembrance, some relic, that she went up to look at the things he had spoken of, the identity of which, as a confused cluster of bright objects on a table in the darkened room, shimmered at her as soon as she had opened the door.

They met her eyes for the first time, but in a moment, before touching them, she knew them as things of the theatre, as very much too fine to have been, with any verisimilitude, things of the vicarage. They were too dreadfully good to be true, for her aunt had had no jewels to speak of, and these were coronets and girdles, diamonds, rubies, and sapphires. Flagrant tinsel and glass, they looked strangely vulgar, but if, after the first queer shock of them, she found herself taking them up, it was for the very proof, never yet so distinct to her, of a far-off faded story. An honest widowed cleric with a small son and a large sense of Shakespeare had, on a brave latitude of habit as well as of taste — since it implied his having in very fact dropped deep into the "pit" — conceived for an obscure actress, several years older than himself, an admiration of which the prompt offer of his reverend name and hortatory hand was the sufficiently candid sign. The response had perhaps, in those dim years, in the way of eccentricity, even bettered the proposal, and Charlotte, turning the tale over, had long since drawn from it a measure of the career renounced by the undistinguished *comédienne* — doubtless also tragic, or perhaps pantomimic, at a pinch — of her late uncle's dreams. This career could not have been eminent and must much more probably have been comfortless.

"You see what it is — old stuff of the time she never liked to mention."

Our young woman gave a start; her companion had, after all, rejoined her and had apparently watched a moment her slightly scared recognition. "So I said to myself," she replied. Then, to show intelligence, yet keep clear of twaddle: "How peculiar they look!"

"They look awful," said Arthur Prime. "Cheap gilt, diamonds as big as potatoes. These are trappings of a ruder age than ours. Actors do themselves better now."

"Oh now," said Charlotte, not to be less knowing, "actresses have real diamonds."

"Some of them." Arthur spoke drily.

"I mean the bad ones — the nobodies too."

"Oh, some of the nobodies have the biggest. But mamma wasn't of that sort."

"A nobody?" Charlotte risked.

example of
his denial

"Not a nobody to whom somebody — well, not a nobody with diamonds. It isn't all worth, this trash, five pounds."

There was something in the old gewgaws that spoke to her, and she continued to turn them over. "They're relics. I think they have their melancholy and even their dignity."

Arthur observed another pause. "Do you care for them?" he then asked. "I mean," he promptly added, "as a souvenir."

"Of you?" Charlotte threw off.

"Of me? What have I to do with it? Of your poor dead aunt who was so kind to you," he said with virtuous sternness.

"Well, I would rather have them than nothing."

"Then please take them," he returned in a tone of relief which expressed somehow more of the eager than of the gracious.

"Thank you." Charlotte lifted two or three objects up and set them down again. Though they were lighter than the materials they imitated they were so much more extravagant that they struck her in truth as rather an awkward heritage, to which she might have preferred even a matchbox or a penwiper. They were indeed shameless pinchbeck. "Had you any idea she had kept them?"

"I don't at all believe she had kept them or knew they were there, and I'm very sure my father didn't. They had quite equally worked off any tenderness for the connection. These odds and ends, which she thought had been given away or destroyed, had simply got thrust into a dark corner and been forgotten."

Charlotte wondered. "Where then did you find them?"

"In that old tin box" — and the young man pointed to the receptacle from which he had dislodged them and which stood on a neighbouring chair. "It's rather a good box still, but I'm afraid I can't give you *that.*"

The girl gave the box no look; she continued only to look at the trinkets. "What corner had she found?"

"She hadn't 'found' it," her companion sharply insisted; "she had simply lost it. The whole thing had passed from her mind. The box was on the top shelf of the old schoolroom closet, which, until one put one's head into it from a stepladder, looked, from below, quite cleared out. The door is narrow and the part of the closet to the left goes well into the wall. The box had stuck there for years."

Charlotte was conscious of a mind divided and a vision vaguely troubled, and once more she took up two or three of the subjects of this revelation; a big bracelet in the form of a gilt serpent with many twists and beady eyes, a brazen belt studded with emeralds and rubies, a chain, of flamboyant architecture, to which, at the Theatre Royal Little Peddlington, Hamlet's mother had probably been careful to attach the portrait of the successor to Hamlet's father. "Are you very sure they're not really worth something? Their mere weight alone — !" she vaguely observed, balancing a moment a royal diadem that might have crowned one of the creations of the famous Mrs. Jarley.

But Arthur Prime, it was clear, had already thought the question over and found the answer easy. "If they had been worth anything to speak of she would long ago have sold them. My father and she had unfortunately never been in a position to keep any considerable value locked up." And while his companion took in the obvious force of this he went on with a flourish just marked enough not to escape her: "If they're worth anything at all—why, you're only the more welcome to them."

Charlotte had now in her hand a small bag of faded, figured silk—one of those antique conveniences that speak to us, in the terms of evaporated camphor and lavender, of the part they have played in some personal history; but, though she had for the first time drawn the string, she looked much more at the young man than at the questionable treasure it appeared to contain. "I shall like them. They're all I have."

"All you have—?"

"That belonged to her."

He swelled a little, then looked about him as if to appeal—as against her avidity—to the whole poor place. "Well, what else do you want?"

"Nothing. Thank you very much." With which she bent her eyes on the article wrapped, and now only exposed, in her superannuated satchel—a necklace of large pearls, such as might once have graced the neck of a provincial Ophelia and borne company to a flaxen wig. "This perhaps *is* worth something. Feel it." And she passed him the necklace, the weight of which she had gathered for a moment into her hand.

He measured it in the same way with his own, but remained quite detached. "Worth at most thirty shillings."

"Not more?"

"Surely not if it's paste?"

"But *is* it paste?"

He gave a small sniff of impatience. "Pearls nearly as big as filberts?"

"But they're heavy," Charlotte declared.

"No heavier than anything else." And he gave them back with an allowance for her simplicity. "Do you imagine for a moment they're real?"

She studied them a little, feeling them, turning them round. "Mightn't they possibly be?"

"Of that size—stuck away with that trash?"

"I admit it isn't likely," Charlotte presently said. "And pearls are so easily imitated."

"That's just what—to a person who knows—they're not. These have no lustre, no play."

"No—they *are* dull. They're opaque."

"Besides," he lucidly inquired, "how could she ever have come by them?"

"Mightn't they have been a present?"

Arthur stared at the question as if it were almost improper. "Because actresses are exposed—?" He pulled up, however, not saying to what, and before she could supply the deficiency had, with the sharp ejaculation of "No, they mightn't!" turned his back on her and walked away. His manner made her feel that she had probably been wanting in tact, and before he returned to the subject, the last thing that evening, she had satisfied herself of the ground of his resentment. They had been talking of her departure the next morning, the hour of her train and the fly that would come for her, and it was precisely these things that gave him his effective chance. "I really can't allow you to leave the house under the impression that my stepmother was at *any* time of her life the sort of person to allow herself to be approached —"

"With pearl necklaces and that sort of thing?" Arthur had made for her somehow the difficulty that she couldn't show him she understood him without seeming pert.

It at any rate only added to his own gravity. "That sort of thing, exactly."

"I didn't think when I spoke this morning — but I see what you mean."

"I mean that she was beyond reproach," said Arthur Prime.

"A hundred times yes."

"Therefore if she couldn't, out of her slender gains, ever have paid for a row of pearls —"

"She couldn't, in that atmosphere, ever properly have had one? Of course she couldn't. I've seen perfectly since our talk," Charlotte went on, "that that string of beads isn't even, as an imitation, very good. The little clasp itself doesn't seem even gold. With false pearls, I suppose," the girl mused, "it naturally wouldn't be."

"The whole thing's rotten paste," her companion returned as if to have done with it. "If it were *not,* and she had kept it all these years hidden —"

"Yes?" Charlotte sounded as he paused.

"Why, I shouldn't know what to think!"

"Oh, I see." She had met him with a certain blankness, but adequately enough, it seemed, for him to regard the subject as dismissed; and there was no reversion to it between them before, on the morrow, when she had with difficulty made a place for them in her trunk, she carried off these florid survivals.

At Bleet she found small occasion to revert to them and, in an air charged with such quite other references, even felt, after she had laid them away, much enshrouded, beneath various piles of clothing, as if they formed a collection not wholly without its note of the ridiculous. Yet she was never, for the joke, tempted to show them to her pupils, though Gwendolen and Blanche, in particular, always wanted, on her return, to know what she had brought back; so that without an accident by which the case was quite changed they might have appeared to enter on a new phase of interment. The essence of the accident was the sudden illness, at the last moment, of Lady Bobby, whose advent had been so much counted on to spice the five days' feast laid out for the coming of age of the eldest son of the house; and its equally marked effect was the despatch of a pressing message, in quite another direction, to Mrs. Guy, who, could she by a miracle be secured — she was always engaged ten parties deep — might be trusted to supply, it was believed, an element of exuberance scarcely less active. Mrs. Guy was already known to several of the visitors already on the scene, but she was not yet known to our young lady, who found her, after many wires and counter-wires had at last determined the triumph of her arrival, a strange, charming little red-haired, black-dressed woman, with the face of a baby and the authority of a commodore. She took on the spot the discreet, the exceptional young governess into the confidence of her designs and, still more, of her doubts; intimating that it was a policy she almost always promptly pursued.

"To-morrow and Thursday are all right," she said frankly to Charlotte on the second day, "but I'm not half satisfied with Friday."

"What improvement then do you suggest?"

"Well, my strong point, you know, is *tableaux vivants*."

"Charming. And what is your favourite character?"

"Boss!" said Mrs. Guy with decision; and it was very markedly under that ensign that she had, within a few hours, completely planned her campaign and recruited her troop. Every word she uttered was to the point, but none more so than, after a general survey of their equipment, her final inquiry of Charlotte. She had been looking about, but half appeased, at the muster of decoration and drapery. "We shall be dull. We shall want more colour. You've nothing else?"

Charlotte had a thought. "No — I've *some* things."

"Then why don't you bring them?"

The girl hesitated. "Would you come to my room?"

"No," said Mrs. Guy — "bring them to-night to mine."

So Charlotte, at the evening's end, after candlesticks had flickered through brown old passages bedward, arrived at her friend's door with the burden of her aunt's relics. But she promptly expressed a fear. "Are they too garish?"

When she had poured them out on the sofa Mrs. Guy was but a minute, before the glass, in clapping on the diadem. "Awfully jolly — we can do Ivanhoe!"

"But they're only glass and tin."

"Larger than life they are, *rather!* — which is exactly what, for tableaux, is wanted. Our jewels, for historic scenes, don't tell — the real thing falls short. Rowena must have rubies as big as eggs. Leave them with me," Mrs. Guy continued — "they'll inspire me. Good-night."

The next morning she was in fact — yet very strangely — inspired. "Yes, I'll do Rowena. But I don't, my dear, understand."

"Understand what?"

Mrs. Guy gave a very lighted stare. "How you come to have such things."

Poor Charlotte smiled. "By inheritance."

"Family jewels?"

"They belonged to my aunt, who died some months ago. She was on the stage a few years in early life, and these are a part of her trappings."

"She left them to you?"

"No; my cousin, her stepson, who naturally has no use for them, gave them to me for remembrance of her. She was a dear kind thing, always so nice to me, and I was fond of her."

Mrs. Guy had listened with visible interest. "But it's *he* who must be a dear kind thing!"

Charlotte wondered. "You think so?"

"Is *he*," her friend went on, "also 'always so nice' to you?"

The girl, at this, face to face there with the brilliant visitor in the deserted breakfast-room, took a deeper sounding. "What is it?"

"Don't you know?"

Something came over her. "The pearls — ?" But the question fainted on her lips.

"Doesn't *he* know?"

Charlotte found herself flushing. "They're *not* paste?"

"Haven't you looked at them?"

She was conscious of two kinds of embarrassment. "*You* have?"

"Very carefully."

"And they're real?"

Mrs. Guy became slightly mystifying and returned for all answer: "Come again, when you've done with the children, to my room."

Our young woman found she had done with the children, that morning, with a promptitude that was a new joy to them, and when she reappeared before Mrs. Guy this lady had already encircled a plump white throat with the only ornament, surely, in all the late Mrs. Prime's — the effaced Miss Bradshaw's — collection, in the least qualified to raise a question. If Charlotte had never yet once, before the glass, tied the string of pearls about her own neck, this was because she had been capable of no such condescension to approved "imitation"; but she had now only to look at Mrs. Guy to see that, so disposed, the ambiguous objects might have passed for frank originals. "What in the world have you done to them?"

"Only handled them, understood them, admired them, and put them on. That's what pearls want; they want to be worn — it wakes them up. They're alive, don't you see? How *have* these been treated? They must have been buried, ignored, despised. They were half dead. Don't you *know* about pearls?" Mrs. Guy threw off as she fondly fingered the necklace.

"How *should* I? Do *you*?"

"Everything. These were simply asleep, and from the moment I really touched them — well," said their wearer lovingly, "it only took one's eye!"

"It took more than mine — though I did just wonder; and than Arthur's," Charlotte brooded. She found herself almost panting. "Then their value — ?"

"Oh, their value's excellent."

The girl, for a deep moment, took another plunge into the wonder, the beauty and mystery, of them. "Are you *sure?*"

Her companion wheeled round for impatience. "Sure? For what kind of an idiot, my dear, do you take me?"

It was beyond Charlotte Prime to say. "For the same kind as Arthur—and as myself," she could only suggest. "But my cousin didn't know. He thinks they're worthless."

"Because of the rest of the lot? Then your cousin's an ass. But what—if, as I understood you, he gave them to you—has he to do with it?"

"Why, if he gave them to me as worthless and they turn out precious—"

"You must give them back? I don't see that—if he was such a fool. He took the risk."

Charlotte fed, in fancy, on the pearls, which, decidedly, were exquisite, but which at the present moment somehow presented themselves much more as Mrs. Guy's than either as Arthur's or as her own. "Yes—he did take it; even after I had distinctly hinted to him that they looked to me different from the other pieces."

"Well, then!" said Mrs. Guy with something more than triumph—with a positive odd relief.

But it had the effect of making our young woman think with more intensity. "Ah, you see he thought they couldn't be different, because—so peculiarly—they shouldn't be."

"Shouldn't? I don't understand."

"Why, how would she have got them?"—so Charlotte candidly put it.

"She? Who?" There was a capacity in Mrs. Guy's tone for a sinking of persons—!

"Why, the person I told you of: his stepmother, my uncle's wife—among whose poor old things, extraordinarily thrust away and out of sight, he happened to find them."

Mrs. Guy came a step nearer to the effaced Miss Bradshaw. "Do you mean she may have stolen them?"

"No. But she had been an actress."

"Oh, well then," cried Mrs. Guy, "wouldn't that be just how?"

"Yes, except that she wasn't at all a brilliant one, nor in receipt of large pay." The girl even threw off a nervous joke. "I'm afraid she couldn't have been our Rowena."

Mrs. Guy took it up. "Was she very ugly?"

"No. She may very well, when young, have looked rather nice."

"Well, then!" was Mrs. Guy's sharp comment and fresh triumph.

"You mean it was a present? That's just what he so dislikes the idea of her having received—a present from an admirer capable of going such lengths."

"Because she wouldn't have taken it for nothing? *Speriamo*—that she wasn't a brute. The 'length' her admirer went was the length of a whole row. Let us hope she was just a little kind!"

"Well," Charlotte went on, "that she was 'kind' might seem to be shown by the fact that neither her husband, nor his son, nor I, his niece, knew or dreamed of her possessing anything so precious; by her having kept the gift all the rest of her life beyond discovery—out of sight and protected from suspicion."

"As if, you mean"—Mrs. Guy was quick—"she had been wedded to it and yet was ashamed of it? Fancy," she laughed while she manipulated the rare beads, "being ashamed of these!"

"But you see she had married a clergyman."

"Yes, she must have been 'rum.' But at any rate he had married *her*. What did he suppose?"

"Why, that she had never been of the sort by whom such offerings are encouraged."

"Ah, my dear, the sort by whom they are *not*—!" But Mrs. Guy caught herself up. "And her stepson thought the same?"

"Overwhelmingly."

"Was he, then, if only her stepson—"

"So fond of her as that comes to? Yes; he had never known, consciously, his real mother, and, without children of her own, she was very patient and nice with him. And I liked her so," the girl pursued, "that at the end of ten years, in so strange a manner, to 'give her away'—"

"Is impossible to you? Then don't!" said Mrs. Guy with decision.

"Ah, but if they're real I can't keep them!" Charlotte, with her eyes on them, moaned in her impatience. "It's too difficult."

"Where's the difficulty, if he has such sentiments that he would rather sacrifice the necklace than admit it, with the presumption it carries with it, to be genuine? You've only to be silent."

"And keep it? How can *I* ever wear it?"

"You'd have to hide it, like your aunt?" Mrs. Guy was amused. "You can easily sell it."

Her companion walked round her for a look at the affair from behind. The clasp was certainly, doubtless intentionally, misleading, but everything else was indeed lovely. "Well, I must think. Why didn't *she* sell them?" Charlotte broke out in her trouble.

Mrs. Guy had an instant answer. "Doesn't that prove what they secretly recalled to her? You've only to be silent!" she ardently repeated.

"I must think—I must think!"

Mrs. Guy stood with her hands attached but motionless. "Then you want them back?"

As if with the dread of touching them Charlotte retreated to the door. "I'll tell you to-night."

"But may I wear them?"

"Meanwhile?"

"This evening — at dinner."

It was the sharp, selfish pressure of this that really, on the spot, determined the girl; but for the moment, before closing the door on the question, she only said: "As you like!"

They were busy much of the day with preparation and rehearsal, and at dinner, that evening, the concourse of guests was such that a place among them for Miss Prime failed to find itself marked. At the time the company rose she was therefore alone in the schoolroom, where, towards eleven o'clock, she received a visit from Mrs. Guy. This lady's white shoulders heaved, under the pearls, with an emotion that the very red lips which formed, as if for the full effect, the happiest opposition of colour, were not slow to translate. "My dear, you should have seen the sensation — they've had a success!"

Charlotte, dumb a moment, took it all in. "It *is* as if they knew it — they're more and more alive. But so much the worse for both of us! I can't," she brought out with an effort, "be silent."

"You mean to return them?"

"If I don't I'm a thief."

Mrs. Guy gave her a long, hard look: what was decidedly not of the baby in Mrs. Guy's face was a certain air of established habit in the eyes. Then, with a sharp little jerk of her head and a backward reach of her bare beautiful arms, she undid the clasp and, taking off the necklace, laid it on the table. "If you do, you're a goose."

"Well, of the two — !" said our young lady, gathering it up with a sigh. And as if to get it, for the pang it gave, out of sight as soon as possible, she shut it up, clicking the lock, in the drawer of her own little table; after which, when she turned again, her companion, without it, looked naked and plain. "But what will you say?" it then occurred to her to demand.

"Downstairs — to explain?" Mrs. Guy was, after all, trying at least to keep her temper. "Oh, I'll put on something else and say that clasp is broken. And you won't of course name *me* to him," she added.

"As having undeceived me? No — I'll say that, looking at the thing more carefully, it's my own private idea."

"And does he know how little you really know?"

"As an expert — surely. And he has much, always, the conceit of his own opinion."

"Then he won't believe you — as he so hates to. He'll stick to his judgment and maintain his gift, and we shall have the darlings back!" With which reviving assurance Mrs. Guy kissed for good-night.

She was not, however, to be gratified or justified by any prompt event, for, whether or no paste entered into the composition of the ornament in question, Charlotte shrank from the temerity of despatching it to town by post. Mrs. Guy was thus disappointed of the hope of seeing the business settled — "by return," she had seemed to expect — before the end of the revels. The revels, moreover, rising to a frantic pitch, pressed for all her attention, and it was at last only in the general confusion of leave-taking that she made, parenthetically, a dash at her young friend.

"Come, what will you take for them?"

"The pearls! Ah, you'll have to treat with my cousin."

Mrs. Guy, with quick intensity, lent herself. "Where then does he live?"

"In chambers in the Temple. You can find him."

"But what's the use, if *you* do neither one thing nor the other?"

"Oh, I *shall* do the 'other,'" Charlotte said: "I'm only waiting till I go up. You want them so awfully?" She curiously, solemnly again, sounded her.

"I'm dying for them. There's a special charm in them — I don't know what it is: they tell so their history."

"But what do you know of that?"

"Just what they themselves say. It's all *in* them — and it comes out. They breathe a tenderness — they have the white glow of it. My dear," hissed Mrs. Guy in supreme confidence and as she buttoned her glove — "they're things of love!"

"Oh!" our young woman vaguely exclaimed.

"They're things of passion!"

"Mercy!" she gasped, turning short off. But these words remained, though indeed their help was scarce needed, Charlotte being in private face to face with a new light, as she by this time felt she must call it, on the dear dead, kind, colourless lady whose career had turned so sharp a corner in the middle. The pearls had quite taken their place as a revelation. She might have received them for nothing — admit that; but she couldn't have kept them so long and so unprofitably hidden, couldn't have enjoyed them only in secret, for nothing; and she had mixed them, in her reliquary, with false things, in order to put curiosity and detection off the scent. Over this strange fact poor Charlotte interminably mused: it became more touching, more attaching for her than she could now confide to any ear. How bad, or how happy — in the sophisticated sense of Mrs. Guy and the young man at the Temple — the effaced Miss Bradshaw must have been to have had to be so mute! The little governess at Bleet put on the necklace now in secret sessions; she wore it sometimes under her dress; she came to feel, verily, a haunting passion for it. Yet in her penniless state she would have parted with it for money; she gave herself also to dreams of what in this direction it would do for her. The sophistry of her so often saying to herself that Arthur had after all definitely pronounced her welcome to any gain from his gift that might accrue — this trick remained innocent, as she perfectly knew it for what it was. Then there was always the possibility of his — as she could only picture it — rising to the occasion. Mightn't he have a grand magnanimous moment? — mightn't he just say: "Oh, of course I couldn't have afforded to let you have it if I had known;

but since you *have* got it, and have made out the truth by your own wit, I really can't screw myself down to the shabbiness of taking it back"?

She had, as it proved, to wait a long time — to wait till, at the end of several months, the great house of Bleet had, with due deliberation, for the season, transferred itself to town; after which, however, she fairly snatched at her first freedom to knock, dressed in her best and armed with her disclosure, at the door of her doubting kinsman. It was still with doubt and not quite with the face she had hoped that he listened to her story. He had turned pale, she thought, as she produced the necklace, and he appeared, above all, disagreeably affected. Well, perhaps there was reason, she more than ever remembered; but what on earth was one, in close touch with the fact, to do? She had laid the pearls on his table, where, without his having at first put so much as a finger to them, they met his hard, cold stare.

"I don't believe in them," he simply said at last.

"That's exactly then," she returned with some spirit, "what I wanted to hear!"

She fancied that at this his colour changed; it was indeed vivid to her afterwards — for she was to have a long recall of the scene — that she had made him quite angrily flush. "It's a beastly unpleasant imputation, you know!" — and he walked away from her as he had always walked at the vicarage.

"It's none of *my* making, I'm sure," said Charlotte Prime. "If you're afraid to believe they're real — "

"Well?" — and he turned, across the room, sharp round at her.

"Why, it's not my fault."

He said nothing more, for a moment, on this; he only came back to the table. "They're what I originally said they were. They're rotten paste."

"Then I may keep them?"

"No. I want a better opinion."

"Than your own?"

"Than *your* own." He dropped on the pearls another queer stare, then, after a moment, bringing himself to touch them, did exactly what she had herself done in the presence of Mrs. Guy at Bleet — gathered them together, marched off with them to a drawer, put them in, and clicked the key. "You say I'm afraid," he went on as he again met her; "but I shan't be afraid to take them to Bond Street."

"And if the people say they're real — ?"

He hesitated — then had his strangest manner. "They won't say it! They shan't!"

There was something in the way he brought it out that deprived poor Charlotte, as she was perfectly aware, of any manner at all. "Oh!" she simply sounded, as she had sounded for her last word to Mrs. Guy; and, within a minute, without more conversation, she had taken her departure.

A fortnight later she received a communication from him, and towards the end of the season one of the entertainments in Eaton Square was graced by the presence of Mrs. Guy. Charlotte was not at dinner, but she came down afterwards, and this guest, on seeing her, abandoned a very beautiful young man on purpose to cross and speak to her. The guest had on a lovely necklace and had apparently not lost her habit of overflowing with the pride of such ornaments.

"Do you see?" She was in high joy.

They were indeed splendid pearls — so far as poor Charlotte could feel that she knew, after what had come and gone, about such mysteries. Charlotte had a sickly smile. "They're almost as fine as Arthur's."

"Almost? Where, my dear, are your eyes? They *are* 'Arthur's!'" After which, to meet the flood of crimson that accompanied her young friend's start: "I tracked them — after your folly, and, by miraculous luck, recognised them in the Bond Street window to which he had disposed of them."

"*Disposed* of them?" the girl gasped. "He wrote me that I had insulted his mother and that the people had shown him he was right — had pronounced them utter paste."

Mrs. Guy gave a stare. "Ah, I told you he wouldn't bear it! No. But I had, I assure you," she wound up, "to drive my bargain!"

Charlotte scarce heard or saw; she was full of her private wrong. "He wrote me," she panted, "that he had smashed them."

Mrs. Guy could only wonder and pity. "He's really morbid!" But it was not quite clear which of the pair she pitied; though Charlotte felt really morbid too after they had separated and she found herself full of thought. She even went the length of asking herself what sort of a bargain Mrs. Guy had driven and whether the marvel of the recognition in Bond Street had been a veracious account of the matter. Hadn't she perhaps in truth dealt with Arthur directly? It came back to Charlotte almost luridly that she had had his address.

Questions for Discussion

1. What is revealed about Arthur Prime's values through his feelings about his father's and stepmother's deaths?

2. What is the significance of Arthur's desire to believe that his stepmother forgot about her jewels and that they were only "paste"?

3. Why is Charlotte interested in the jewels? How is her response to the issue of the jewels different from Arthur's? Why does Charlotte think her aunt hid them, and what does her assumption reveal about Charlotte?

4. Interpret the significance of Arthur's giving the jewels to Charlotte. Why does he do this? Why does Charlotte accept them?

5. What motivates Charlotte to show Mrs. Guy the jewels? How is Mrs. Guy's appreciation of the jewels different from Charlotte's? Does Mrs. Guy deceive or take advantage of Charlotte?

6. Compare and contrast this story with Guy de Maupassant's "The Necklace." In what ways are the plots similar? How is James's story more morally complex?

Ideas for Writing

1. Analyze in an essay the character of Charlotte. What conflict in values does she experience? What are the strengths and weaknesses of her character? How does she change and grow in the story?

2. Write an interpretation of the way that James uses the jewels to reveal character. How is each character in the story — the aunt, Charlotte, Arthur, Mrs. Guy — defined or explored through his or her relationship to the jewels? Why is it significant that the story is entitled "Paste," although the jewels turn out (apparently) to be real?

SARAH ORNE JEWETT (1849–1909)

A native of the village of South Berwick, Maine, Sarah Orne Jewett is best known for her ability to capture the local color of the Maine region through details of landscape and the dialect and character of the common citizens. Because she inherited wealth, Jewett did not have to work or marry after graduating from private high school. Although her father had wanted her to follow his career and become a doctor, she did not attend college; instead she traveled extensively in the United States and Europe, developing friendships with American and European intellectuals, including Harriet Beecher Stowe, Henry James, Mark Twain, William Dean Howells, Christina Rossetti, and Alfred, Lord Tennyson. Jewett also maintained a long relationship with James T. Fields of Ticknor and Fields, a Boston publishing house. Jewett captured her father's strong character in her second novel, *The Country Doctor* (1884). Her best-known story collection is *A White Heron and Other Stories* (1886), in which "A White Heron" appears. Another of her books, *The Country of the Pointed Firs* (1896), can be read as either a novel or a collection of related stories, and *Old Friends and New* (1879) focuses on Jewett's friendships with women. In her essay "Looking Back on Girlhood," Jewett, who lived in and wrote about Maine for most of her life, speaks of the importance of knowing a few good things well: "If you have but a few good books, learn those to the very heart of them. Don't for one moment believe that if you had different surroundings and opportunities you would find the upward path any easier to climb."

A White Heron   (1886)

I

The woods were already filled with shadows one June evening, just before eight o'clock, though a bright sunset still glimmered faintly among the trunks of the trees. A little girl was driving home her cow, a plodding, dilatory, provoking creature in her behavior, but a valued companion for all that. They were going away from the western light, and striking deep into the dark woods, but their feet were familiar with the path, and it was no matter whether their eyes could see it or not.

There was hardly a night the summer through when the old cow could be found waiting at the pasture bars; on the contrary, it was her greatest pleasure to hide herself away among the high huckleberry bushes, and though she wore a loud bell she had made the discovery that if one stood perfectly still it would not ring. So Sylvia had to hunt for her until she found her and call Co'! Co'! with never an answering Moo, until her childish patience was quite spent. If the creature had not given good milk and plenty of it, the case would have seemed very different to her owners. Besides, Sylvia had all the time there was, and very little use to make of it. Sometimes in pleasant weather it was a consolation to look upon the cow's pranks as an intelligent attempt to play hide and seek, and as the child had no playmates she lent herself to this amusement with a good deal of zest. Though this chase had been so long that the wary animal herself had given an unusual signal of her whereabouts, Sylvia had only laughed when she came upon Mistress Moolly at the swamp-side, and urged her affectionately homeward with a twig of birch leaves. The old cow was not inclined to wander farther, she even turned in the right direction for once as they left the pasture, and stepped along the road at a good pace. She was quite ready to be milked now, and seldom stopped to browse. Sylvia wondered what her grandmother would say because they were so late. It was a great while since she had left home at half past five o'clock, but everybody knew the difficulty of making this errand a short one. Mrs. Tilley had chased the horned torment too many summer evenings herself to blame any one else for lingering, and was only thankful as she waited that she had Sylvia, nowadays, to give such valuable assistance. The good woman suspected that Sylvia loitered occasionally on her own account; there never was such a child for straying about out-of-doors since the world was made! Everybody said that it was a good change for a little maid who had tried to grow for eight years in a crowded manufacturing town, but, as for Sylvia herself, it seemed as if she never had been alive at all before she came to live at the farm. She thought often with wistful compassion of a wretched dry geranium that belonged to a town neighbor.

"'Afraid of folks,'" old Mrs. Tilley said to herself, with a smile, after she had made the unlikely choice of Sylvia from her daughter's houseful of children, and was returning to the farm. "'Afraid of folks,' they said! I guess she won't be troubled no great with 'em up to the old place!" When they reached the door of the lonely house and stopped to unlock it, and the cat came to purr loudly, and rub against them, a deserted pussy, indeed, but fat with young robins, Sylvia whispered that this was a beautiful place to live in, and she never should wish to go home.

The companions followed the shady wood-road, the cow taking slow steps, and the child very fast ones. The cow stopped long at the brook to drink, as if the pasture were not half a swamp, and Sylvia stood still and waited, letting her bare feet cool themselves in the shoal water, while the great twilight moths struck softly against her. She waded on through the brook as the cow moved away, and listened to the thrushes with a heart that beat fast with pleasure. There was a stirring in the great boughs overhead. They were full of little birds and beasts that seemed to be wide-awake, and going about their world, or else saying good-night to each other in sleepy twitters. Sylvia herself felt sleepy as she walked along. However, it was not much farther to the house, and the air was soft and sweet. She was not often in the woods so late as this, and it made her feel as if she were a part of the gray shadows and the moving leaves. She was just thinking how long it seemed since she first came to the farm a year ago, and wondering if everything went on in the noisy town just the same as when she was there; the thought of the great red-faced boy who used to chase and frighten her made her hurry along the path to escape from the shadow of the trees.

Suddenly this little woods-girl is horror-stricken to hear a clear whistle not very far away. Not a bird's whistle, which would have a sort of friendliness, but a boy's whistle, determined, and somewhat aggressive. Sylvia left the cow to whatever sad fate might await her, and stepped discreetly aside into the bushes, but she was just too late. The enemy had discovered her, and called out in a very cheerful and persuasive tone, "Halloa, little girl, how far is it to the road?" and trembling Sylvia answered almost inaudibly, "A good ways."

She did not dare to look boldly at the tall young man, who carried a gun over his shoulder, but she came out of her bush and again followed the cow, while he walked alongside.

"I have been hunting for some birds," the stranger said kindly, "and I have lost my way, and need a friend very much. Don't be afraid," he added gallantly. "Speak up and tell me what your name is, and whether you think I can spend the night at your house, and go out gunning early in the morning."

Sylvia was more alarmed than before. Would not her grandmother consider her much to blame? But who could have foreseen such an accident as this? It did not appear to be her fault, and she hung her head as if the stem of it were broken, but managed to answer, "Sylvy," with much effort when her companion again asked her name.

Mrs. Tilley was standing in the doorway when the trio came into view. The cow gave a loud moo by way of explanation.

"Yes, you'd better speak up for yourself, you old trial! Where'd she tucked herself away this time, Sylvy?" Sylvia kept an awed silence; she knew by instinct that her grandmother did not comprehend the gravity of the situation. She must be mistaking the stranger for one of the farmer-lads of the region.

The young man stood his gun beside the door, and dropped a heavy game-bag beside it; then he bade Mrs. Tilley good-evening, and repeated his way-farer's story, and asked if he could have a night's lodging.

"Put me anywhere you like," he said. "I must be off early in the morning, before day; but I am very hungry, indeed. You can give me some milk at any rate, that's plain."

"Dear sakes, yes," responded the hostess, whose long slumbering hospitality seemed to be easily awakened. "You might fare better if you went out on the main road a mile or so, but you're welcome to what we've got. I'll milk right off, and you make yourself at home. You can sleep on husks or feathers," she proffered graciously. "I raised them all myself. There's good pasturing for geese just below here towards the ma'sh. Now step round and set a plate for the gentleman, Sylvy!" And Sylvia promptly stepped. She was glad to have something to do, and she was hungry herself.

It was a surprise to find so clean and comfortable a little dwelling in this New England wilderness. The young man had known the horrors of its most primitive housekeeping, and the dreary squalor of that level of society which does not rebel at the companionship of hens. This was the best thrift of an old-fashioned farmstead, though on such a small scale that it seemed like a hermitage. He listened eagerly to the old woman's quaint talk, he watched Sylvia's pale face and shining gray eyes with ever growing enthusiasm, and insisted that this was the best supper he had eaten for a month; then, afterward, the new-made friends sat down in the doorway together while the moon came up.

Soon it would be berry-time, and Sylvia was a great help at picking. The cow was a good milker, though a plaguy thing to keep track of, the hostess gossiped frankly, adding presently that she had buried four children, so that Sylvia's mother, and a son (who might be dead) in California were all the children she had left. "Dan, my boy, was a great hand to go gunning," she explained sadly. "I never wanted for pa'tridges or gray squer'ls while he was to home. He's been a great wand'rer, I expect, and he's no hand to write letters. There, I don't blame him, I'd ha' seen the world myself if it had been so I could.

"Sylvia takes after him," the grandmother continued affectionately, after a minute's pause. "There ain't a foot o' ground she don't know her way over, and the wild creatur's counts her one o' themselves. Squer'ls she'll tame to come an' feed right out o' her hands, and all sorts o' birds. Last winter she got the jay-birds to bangeing here, and I believe she'd 'a' scanted herself of her own meals to have plenty to throw out amongst 'em, if I hadn't kep' watch. Anything but crows, I tell her, I'm willin' to help support, — though Dan he went an' tamed one o' them that did seem to have reason same as folks. It was round here a good spell after he went away. Dan an' his father they didn't hitch, — but he never held up his head ag'in after Dan had dared him an' gone off."

The guest did not notice this hint of family sorrows in his eager interest in something else.

"So Sylvy knows all about birds, does she?" he exclaimed, as he looked round at the little girl who sat, very demure but increasingly sleepy, in the moonlight. "I am making a collection of birds myself. I have been at it ever since I was a boy." (Mrs. Tilley smiled.) "There are two or three very rare ones I have been hunting for these five years. I mean to get them on my own ground if they can be found."

"Do you cage 'em up?" asked Mrs. Tilley doubtfully, in response to this enthusiastic announcement.

"Oh, no, they're stuffed and preserved, dozens and dozens of them," said the ornithologist, "and I have shot or snared every one myself. I caught a glimpse of a white heron three miles from here on Saturday, and I have followed it in this direction. They have never been found in this district at all. The little white heron, it is," and he turned again to look at Sylvia with the hope of discovering that the rare bird was one of her acquaintances.

But Sylvia was watching a hop-toad in the narrow footpath.

"You would know the heron if you saw it," the stranger continued eagerly. "A queer tall white bird with soft feathers and long thin legs. And it would have a nest perhaps in the top of a high tree, made of sticks, something like a hawk's nest."

Sylvia's heart gave a wild beat; she knew that strange white bird, and had once stolen softly near where it stood in some bright green swamp grass, away over at the other side of the woods. There was an open place where the sunshine always seemed strangely yellow and hot, where tall, nodding rushes grew, and her grandmother had warned her that she might sink in the soft black mud underneath and never be heard of more. Not far beyond were the salt marshes and beyond those was the sea, the sea which Sylvia wondered and dreamed about, but never had looked upon, though its great voice could often be heard above the noise of the woods on stormy nights.

"I can't think of anything I should like so much as to find that heron's nest," the handsome stranger was saying. "I would give ten dollars to anybody who could show it to me," he added desperately, "and I mean to spend my whole vacation hunting for it if need be. Perhaps it was only migrating, or had been chased out of its own region by some bird of prey."

Mrs. Tilley gave amazed attention to all this, but Sylvia still watched the toad, not divining, as she might have done at some calmer time, that the creature wished to get to its hole under the doorstep, and was much hindered by the unusual spectators at that hour of the evening. No amount of thought, that night, could decide how many wished-for treasures the ten dollars, so lightly spoken of, would buy.

The next day the young sportsman hovered about the woods, and Sylvia kept him company, having lost her first fear of the friendly lad, who proved to be most kind and sympathetic. He told her many things about the birds and what they knew and where they lived and what they did with themselves. And he gave her a jack-knife, which she thought as great a treasure as if she were a desert-islander. All day long he did not once make her troubled or afraid except when he brought down some unsuspecting singing creature from its bough. Sylvia would have liked him vastly better without his gun; she could not understand why he killed the very birds he seemed to like so much. But as the day waned, Sylvia still watched the young man with loving admiration. She had never seen anybody so charming and delightful; the woman's heart, asleep in the child, was vaguely thrilled by a dream of love. Some premonition of that great power stirred and swayed these young foresters who traversed the solemn woodlands with soft-footed silent care. They stopped to listen to a bird's song; they pressed forward again eagerly, parting the branches — speaking to each other rarely and in whispers; the young man going first and Sylvia following, fascinated, a few steps behind, with her gray eyes dark with excitement.

She grieved because the longed-for white heron was elusive, but she did not lead the guest, she only followed, and there was no such thing as speaking first. The sound of her own unquestioned voice would have terrified her — it was hard enough to answer yes or no when there was need of that. At last evening began to fall, and they drove the cow home together, and Sylvia smiled with pleasure when they came to the place where she heard the whistle and was afraid only the night before.

II

Half a mile from home, at the farther edge of the woods, where the land was highest, a great pine-tree stood, the last of its generation. Whether it was left for a boundary mark, or for what reason, no one could say; the woodchoppers who had felled its mates were dead and gone long ago, and a whole forest of sturdy trees, pines and oaks and maples, had grown again. But the stately head of this old pine towered above them all and made a landmark for sea and shore miles and miles away. Sylvia knew it well. She had always believed that whoever climbed to the top of it could see the ocean; and the little girl had often laid her hand on the great rough trunk and looked up wistfully at those dark boughs that the wind always stirred, no matter how hot and still the air might be below. Now she thought of the tree with a new excitement, for why, if one climbed it at break of day, could not one see all the world, and easily discover whence the white heron flew, and mark the place, and find the hidden nest?

What a spirit of adventure, what wild ambition! What fancied triumph and delight and glory for the later morning when she could make known the secret! It was almost too real and too great for the childish heart to bear.

All night the door of the little house stood open, and the whippoorwills came and sang upon the very step. The young sportsman and his old hostess were sound asleep, but Sylvia's great design kept her broad awake and watching. She forgot to think of sleep. The short summer night seemed as long as the winter darkness, and at last when the whippoorwills ceased, and she was afraid the morning would after all come too soon, she stole out of the house and followed the pasture path through the woods, hastening toward the open ground beyond, listening with a sense of comfort and companionship to the drowsy twitter of a half-awakened bird, whose perch she had jarred in passing. Alas, if the great wave of human interest which flooded for the first time this dull little life should sweep away the satisfactions of an existence heart to heart with nature and the dumb life of the forest!

There was the huge tree asleep yet in the paling moonlight, and small and hopeful Sylvia began with utmost bravery to mount to the top of it, with tingling, eager blood coursing the channels of her whole frame, with her bare feet and fingers, that pinched and held like bird's claws to the monstrous ladder reaching up, up, almost to the sky itself. First she must mount the white oak tree that grew alongside, where she was almost lost among the dark branches and the green leaves heavy and wet with dew; a bird fluttered off its nest, and a red squirrel ran to and fro and scolded pettishly at the harmless housebreaker. Sylvia felt her way easily. She had often climbed there, and knew that higher still one of the oak's upper branches chafed against the pine trunk, just where its lower boughs were set close together. There, when she made the dangerous pass from one tree to the other, the great enterprise would really begin.

She crept out along the swaying oak limb at last, and took the daring step across into the old pine-tree. The way was harder than she thought; she must reach far and hold fast, the sharp dry twigs caught and held her and scratched her like angry talons, the pitch made her thin little fingers clumsy and stiff as she went round and round the tree's great stem, higher and higher upward. The sparrows and robins in the woods below were beginning to wake and twitter to the dawn, yet it seemed much lighter there aloft in the pine-tree, and the child knew that she must hurry if her project were to be of any use.

The tree seemed to lengthen itself out as she went up, and to reach farther and farther upward. It was like a great main-mast to the voyaging earth; it must truly have been amazed that morning through all its ponderous frame as it felt this determined spark of human spirit creeping and climbing from higher branch to branch. Who knows how steadily the least twigs held themselves to advantage this light, weak creature on her way! The old pine must have loved his new dependent. More than all the hawks, and bats, and moths, and even the sweet-voiced thrushes, was the brave, beating heart of the solitary gray-eyed child. And the tree stood still and held away the winds that June morning while the dawn grew bright in the east.

Sylvia's face was like a pale star, if one had seen it from the ground, when the last thorny bough was past, and she stood trembling and tired but wholly triumphant, high in the tree-top. Yes, there was the sea with the dawning sun making a golden dazzle over it, and toward that glorious east flew two hawks with slow-moving pinions. How low they looked in the air from that height when before one had only seen them far up, and dark against the blue sky. Their gray feathers were as soft as moths; they seemed only a little way from the tree, and Sylvia felt as if she too could go flying away among the clouds. Westward, the woodlands and farms reached miles and miles into the distance; here and there were church steeples, and white villages; truly it was a vast and awesome world.

The birds sang louder and louder. At last the sun came up bewilderingly bright. Sylvia could see the white sails of ships out at sea, and the clouds that were purple and rose-colored and yellow at first began to fade away. Where was the white heron's nest in the sea of green branches, and was this wonderful sight and pageant of the world the only reward for having climbed to such a giddy height? Now look down again, Sylvia, where the green marsh is set among the shining birches and dark hemlocks; there where you saw the white heron once you will see him again; look, look! a white spot of him like a single floating feather comes up from the dead hemlock and grows larger, and rises, and comes close at last, and goes by the landmark pine with steady sweep of wing and outstretched slender neck and crested head. And wait! wait! do not move a foot or a finger, little girl, do not send an arrow of light and consciousness from your two eager eyes, for the heron has perched on a pine bough not far beyond yours, and cries back to his mate on the nest, and plumes his feathers for the new day!

The child gives a long sigh a minute later when a company of shouting cat-birds comes also to the tree, and vexed by their fluttering and lawlessness the solemn heron goes away. She knows his secret now, the wild, light, slender bird that floats and wavers, and goes back like an arrow presently to his home in the green world beneath. Then Sylvia, well satisfied, makes her perilous way down again, not daring to look far below the branch she stands on, ready to cry sometimes because her fingers ache and her lamed feet slip. Wondering over and over again what the stranger would say to her, and what he would think when she told him how to find his way straight to the heron's nest.

"Sylvy, Sylvy!" called the busy old grandmother again and again, but nobody answered, and the small husk bed was empty, and Sylvia had disappeared.

The guest waked from a dream, and remembering his day's pleasure hurried to dress himself that it might sooner begin. He was sure from the way the shy little girl looked once or twice yesterday that she had at least seen the white heron, and now she must really be persuaded to tell. Here she comes now, paler than ever, and her worn old frock is torn and tattered, and smeared with pine pitch. The grandmother and the sportsman stand in the door together and question her, and the splendid moment had come to speak of the dead hemlock-tree by the green marsh.

But Sylvia does not speak after all, though the old grandmother fretfully rebukes her, and the young man's kind appealing eyes are looking straight in her own. He can make them rich with money; he has promised it, and they are poor now. He is so well worth making happy, and he waits to hear the story she can tell.

No, she must keep silence! What is it that suddenly forbids her and makes her dumb? Has she been nine years growing, and now, when the great world for the first time puts out a hand to her, must she thrust it aside for a bird's sake? The murmur of the pine's green branches is in her ears, she remembers how the white heron came flying through the golden air and how they watched the sea and the morning together, and Sylvia cannot speak; she cannot tell the heron's secret and give its life away.

Dear loyalty, that suffered a sharp pang as the guest went away disappointed later in the day, that could have served and followed him and loved him as a dog loves! Many a night Sylvia heard the echo of his whistle haunting the pasture path as she came home with the loitering cow. She forgot even her sorrow at the sharp report of his gun and the piteous sight of thrushes and sparrows dropping silent to the ground, their songs hushed and their pretty feathers stained and wet with blood. Were the birds better friends than their hunter might have been, — who can tell? Whatever treasures were lost to her, woodlands and summer-time, remember! Bring your gifts and graces and tell your secrets to this lonely country child!

Questions for Discussion

1. What does Sylvia's treatment of the old cow, Mistress Moolly, suggest about her interests and concerns?

2. How are town and country life contrasted in the story? How has country life changed Sylvia?

3. Contrast Sylvia's attitude toward nature with the young ornithologist's. How does her attitude toward him change as the story develops? How is this change of attitude related to her belief in the natural world?

4. Why is it significant that Sylvia goes out at night to discover the heron's secret place? What "secret" does she discover on this adventure and over the course of the story?

5. Jewett makes use of the technique of personification in her portraits of the pine tree, the cow, and the birds. Why do you think she personifies these as "characters"? Is this technique effective?

Ideas for Writing

1. Write an essay about point of view in "A White Heron." Why does Jewett use an omniscient narrator, one who sees into the minds of several human and animal characters? How does the point of view contribute to the story's power and to our understanding of its meaning?

2. In an essay, discuss the conflict between science and nature that the story presents.

GUY DE MAUPASSANT (1850–1893)

Guy de Maupassant was one of the most influential short-story writers of his day: his work helped to define the style and form of the modern realistic short story. Much admired by critics, his stories were also popular with readers and were translated into many languages.

Born in rural Normandy to a stockbroker father and a culturally inclined mother, Maupassant moved to Paris when he was in his early twenties. There he studied with the great novelist Gustave Flaubert, and much of his later writing was based on Flaubert's literary precepts: close observation of character and detail, objective presentation, sympathy with ordinary people, and careful control of form. His style ranged from slice-of-life narratives focused on external detail to intense interior monologues, while his subjects ranged from the Parisian bourgeoisie to the peasants of his native Normandy. And he was no stranger to controversy: in 1880 his first published story, "Bouile du Suif" ("Ball of Fat"), created a sensation in its comparison of prostitution with bourgeois hypocrisy. Over the next ten years, Maupassant produced some three hundred stories, along with a number of longer works, before succumbing to the effects of syphilis and dying at the age of forty-three.

Maupassant is particularly known for his use of the "twist" ending, an unexpected plot development that produces an ironic conclusion. While his plots may sometimes stretch credibility, his restrained tone and impeccable use of detail make them nonetheless convincing.

The Necklace (1884)

Translated by Marjorie Laurie

She was one of those pretty and charming girls who are sometimes, as if by a mistake of destiny, born in a family of clerks. She had no dowry, no expectations, no means of being known, understood, loved, wedded by any rich and distinguished man; and she let herself be married to a little clerk at the Ministry of Public Instruction.

She dressed plainly because she could not dress well, but she was as unhappy as though she had really fallen from her proper station, since with women there is neither caste nor rank: and beauty, grace and charm act instead of family and birth. Natural fineness, instinct for what is elegant, suppleness of wit, are the sole hierarchy, and make from women of the people the equals of the very greatest ladies.

She suffered ceaselessly, feeling herself born for all the delicacies and all the luxuries. She suffered from the poverty of her dwelling, from the wretched look of the walls, from the worn-out chairs, from the ugliness of the curtains. All those things, of which another woman of her rank would never even have been conscious, tortured her and made her angry. The sight of the little Breton peasant who did her humble housework aroused in her regrets which were despairing, and distracted dreams. She thought of the silent antechambers hung with Oriental tapestry, lit by tall bronze candelabra, and of the two great footmen in knee breeches who sleep in the big armchairs, made drowsy by the heavy warmth of the hot-air stove. She thought of the long *salons* fitted up with ancient silk, of the delicate furniture carrying priceless curiosities, and of the coquettish perfumed boudoirs made for talks at five o'clock with intimate friends, with men famous and sought after, whom all women envy and whose attention they all desire.

When she sat down to dinner, before the round table covered with a tablecloth three days old, opposite her husband, who uncovered the soup tureen and declared with an enchanted air, "Ah, the good *pot-au-feu!* I don't know anything better than that," she thought of dainty dinners, of shining silverware, of tapestry which peopled the walls with ancient personages and with strange birds flying in the midst of a fairy forest; and she thought of delicious dishes served on marvelous plates, and of the whispered gallantries which you listen to with a sphinxlike smile, while you are eating the pink flesh of a trout or the wings of a quail.

She had no dresses, no jewels, nothing. And she loved nothing but that; she felt made for that. She would so have liked to please, to be envied, to be charming, to be sought after.

She had a friend, a former schoolmate at the convent, who was rich, and whom she did not like to go and see any more, because she suffered so much when she came back.

But one evening, her husband returned home with a triumphant air, and holding a large envelope in his hand.

"There," said he. "Here is something for you."

She tore the paper sharply, and drew out a printed card which bore these words:

"The Minister of Public Instruction and Mme. Georges Ramponneau request the honor of M. and Mme. Loisel's company at the palace of the Ministry on Monday evening, January eighteenth."

Instead of being delighted, as her husband hoped, she threw the invitation on the table with disdain, murmuring:

"What do you want me to do with that?"

"But, my dear, I thought you would be glad. You never go out, and this is such a fine opportunity. I had awful trouble to get it. Everyone wants to go; it is very select, and they are not giving many invitations to clerks. The whole official world will be there."

She looked at him with an irritated glance, and said, impatiently:

"And what do you want me to put on my back?"

He had not thought of that; he stammered:

"Why, the dress you go to the theater in. It looks very well to me."

He stopped, distracted, seeing his wife was crying. Two great tears descended slowly from the corners of her eyes toward the corners of her mouth. He stuttered:

"What's the matter? What's the matter?"

But, by violent effort, she had conquered her grief, and she replied with a calm voice, while she wiped her wet cheeks:

"Nothing. Only I have no dress and therefore I can't go to this ball. Give your card to some colleague whose wife is better equipped than I."

He was in despair. He resumed:

"Come, let us see, Mathilde. How much would it cost, a suitable dress, which you could use on other occasions, something very simple?"

She reflected several seconds, making her calculations and wondering also what sum she could ask without drawing on herself an immediate refusal and a frightened exclamation from the economical clerk.

Finally, she replied, hesitatingly:

"I don't know exactly, but I think I could manage it with four hundred francs."

He had grown a little pale, because he was laying aside just that amount to buy a gun and treat himself to a little shooting next summer on the plain of Nanterre, with several friends who went to shoot larks down there, of a Sunday.

But he said:

"All right. I will give you four hundred francs. And try to have a pretty dress."

The day of the ball drew near, and Mme. Loisel seemed sad, uneasy, anxious. Her dress was ready, however. Her husband said to her one evening:

"What is the matter? Come, you've been so queer these last three days."

And she answered:

"It annoys me not to have a single jewel, not a single stone, nothing to put on. I shall look like distress. I should almost rather not go at all."

He resumed:

"You might wear natural flowers. It's very stylish at this time of the year. For ten francs you can get two or three magnificent roses."

She was not convinced.

"No; there's nothing more humiliating than to look poor among other women who are rich."

But her husband cried:

"How stupid you are! Go look up your friend Mme. Forestier, and ask her to lend you some jewels. You're quite thick enough with her to do that."

She uttered a cry of joy:

"It's true. I never thought of it."

The next day she went to her friend and told of her distress.

Mme. Forestier went to a wardrobe with a glass door, took out a large jewel-box, brought it back, opened it, and said to Mme. Loisel:

"Choose, my dear."

She saw first of all some bracelets, then a pearl necklace, then a Venetian cross, gold and precious stones of admirable workmanship. She tried on the ornaments before the glass, hesitated, could not make up her mind to part with them, to give them back. She kept asking:

"Haven't you any more?"

"Why, yes. Look. I don't know what you like."

All of a sudden she discovered, in a black satin box, a superb necklace of diamonds, and her heart began to beat with an immoderate desire. Her hands trembled as she took it. She fastened it around her throat, outside her high-necked dress, and remained lost in ecstasy at the sight of herself.

Then she asked, hesitating, filled with anguish:

"Can you lend me that, only that?"

"Why, yes, certainly."

She sprang upon the neck of her friend, kissed her passionately, then fled with her treasure.

The day of the ball arrived. Mme. Loisel made a great success. She was prettier than them all, elegant, gracious, smiling, and crazy with joy. All the men looked at her, asked her name, endeavored to be introduced. All the attachés of the Cabinet wanted to waltz with her. She was remarked by the minister himself.

She danced with intoxication, with passion, made drunk by pleasure, forgetting all, in the triumph of her beauty, in the glory of her success, in a sort of cloud of happiness composed of all this homage, of all this admiration, of all these awakened desires, and of that sense of complete victory which is so sweet to a woman's heart.

She went away about four o'clock in the morning. Her husband had been sleeping since midnight, in a little deserted anteroom, with three other gentlemen whose wives were having a very good time. He threw over her shoulders the wraps which he had brought, modest wraps of common life, whose poverty contrasted with the elegance of the ball dress. She felt this, and wanted to escape so as not to be remarked by the other women, who were enveloping themselves in costly furs.

Loisel held her back.

"Wait a bit. You will catch cold outside. I will go and call a cab."

But she did not listen to him, and rapidly descended the stairs. When they were in the street they did not find a carriage; and they began to look for one, shouting after the cabmen whom they saw passing by at a distance.

They went down toward the Seine, in despair, shivering with cold. At last they found on the quay one of those ancient noctambulant coupés which, exactly as if they were ashamed to show their misery during the day, are never seen round Paris until after nightfall.

It took them to their door in the Rue des Martyrs, and once more, sadly, they climbed up homeward. All was ended, for her. And as to him, he reflected that he must be at the Ministry at ten o'clock.

She removed the wraps which covered her shoulders, before the glass, so as once more to see herself in all her glory. But suddenly she uttered a cry. She no longer had the necklace around her neck!

Her husband, already half undressed, demanded:

"What is the matter with you?"

She turned madly towards him:

"I have — I have — I've lost Mme. Forestier's necklace."

He stood up, distracted.

"What! — how? — impossible!"

And they looked in the folds of her dress, in the folds of her cloak, in her pockets, everywhere. They did not find it.

He asked:

"You're sure you had it on when you left the ball?"

"Yes, I felt it in the vestibule of the palace."

"But if you had lost it in the street we should have heard it fall. It must be in the cab."

"Yes. Probably. Did you take his number?"

"No. And you, didn't you notice it?"

"No."

They looked, thunderstruck, at one another. At last Loisel put on his clothes.

"I shall go back on foot," said he, "over the whole route which we have taken to see if I can find it."

And he went out. She sat waiting on a chair in her ball dress, without strength to go to bed, overwhelmed, without fire, without a thought.

Her husband came back about seven o'clock. He had found nothing.

He went to Police Headquarters, to the newspaper offices, to offer a reward; he went to the cab companies — everywhere, in fact, whither he was urged by the least suspicion of hope.

She waited all day, in the same condition of mad fear before this terrible calamity.

Loisel returned at night with a hollow, pale face; he had discovered nothing.

"You must write to your friend," said he, "that you have broken the clasp of her necklace and that you are having it mended. That will give us time to turn round."

She wrote at his dictation.

At the end of a week they had lost all hope.

And Loisel, who had aged five years, declared:

"We must consider how to replace that ornament."

The next day they took the box which had contained it, and they went to the jeweler whose name was found within. He consulted his books.

"It was not I, madame, who sold that necklace; I must simply have furnished the case."

Then they went from jeweler to jeweler, searching for a necklace like the other, consulting their memories, sick both of them with chagrin and anguish.

They found, in a shop at the Palais Royal, a string of diamonds which seemed to them exactly like the one they looked for. It was worth forty-thousand francs. They could have it for thirty-six.

So they begged the jeweler not to sell it for three days yet. And they made a bargain that he should buy it back for thirty-four thousand francs, in case they found the other one before the end of February.

Loisel possessed eighteen thousand francs which his father had left him. He would borrow the rest.

He did borrow, asking a thousand francs of one, five hundred of another, five louis[1] here, three louis there. He gave notes, took up ruinous obligations, dealt with usurers and all the race of lenders. He compromised all the rest of his life, risked his signature without even knowing if he could meet it; and, frightened by the pains yet to come, by the black misery which was about to fall upon him, by the prospect of all the physical privation and of all the moral tortures which he was to suffer, he went to get the new necklace, putting down upon the merchant's counter thirty-six thousand francs.

When Mme. Loisel took back the necklace, Mme. Forestier said to her, with a chilly manner:

"You should have returned it sooner; I might have needed it."

She did not open the case, as her friend had so much feared. If she had detected the substitution, what would she have thought, what would she have said? Would she not have taken Mme. Loisel for a thief?

Mme. Loisel now knew the horrible existence of the needy. She took her part, moreover, all of a sudden, with heroism. That dreadful debt must be paid. She would pay it. They dismissed their servant; they changed their lodgings; they rented a garret under the roof.

She came to know what heavy housework meant and the odious cares of the kitchen. She washed the dishes, using her rosy nails on the greasy pots and pans. She washed the dirty linen, the shirts, and the dishcloths, which she dried upon a line; she carried the slops down to the street every morning, and carried up the water, stopping for breath at every landing. And, dressed like a woman of the people, she went to the fruiterer, the grocer, the butcher, her basket on her arm, bargaining, insulted, defending her miserable money sou by sou.

Each month they had to meet some notes, renew others, obtain more time.

Her husband worked in the evening making a fair copy of some tradesman's accounts, and late at night he often copied manuscript for five sous a page.

And this life lasted for ten years.

---

[1] A louis is equal to twenty francs. — Eds.

At the end of ten years, they had paid everything, everything, with the rates of usury, and the accumulations of the compound interest.

Mme. Loisel looked old now. She had become the woman of impoverished households — strong and hard and rough. With frowsy hair, skirts askew, and red hands, she talked loud while washing the floor with great swishes of water. But sometimes, when her husband was at the office, she sat down near the window, and she thought of that gay evening of long ago, of the ball where she had been so beautiful and so fêted.

What would have happened if she had not lost that necklace? Who knows? Who knows? How life is strange and changeful! How little a thing is needed for us to be lost or to be saved!

But, one Sunday, having gone to take a walk in the Champs Elysées to refresh herself from the labor of the week, she suddenly perceived a woman who was leading a child. It was Mme. Forestier, still young, still beautiful, still charming.

Mme. Loisel felt moved. Was she going to speak to her? Yes, certainly. And now that she had paid, she was going to tell her all about it. Why not?

She went up.

"Good-day, Jeanne."

The other, astonished to be familiarly addressed by this plain good-wife, did not recognize her at all, and stammered:

"But — madam! — I do not know — You must be mistaken."

"No. I am Mathilde Loisel."

Her friend uttered a cry.

"Oh, my poor Mathilde! How you are changed!"

"Yes, I have had days hard enough, since I have seen you, days wretched enough — and that because of you!"

"Of me! How so?"

"Do you remember that diamond necklace which you lent me to wear at the ministerial ball?"

"Yes. Well?"

"Well, I lost it."

"What do you mean? You brought it back."

"I brought you back another just like it. And for this we have been ten years paying. You can understand that it was not easy for us, us who had nothing. At last it is ended, and I am very glad."

Mme. Forestier had stopped.

"You say that you bought a necklace of diamonds to replace mine?"

"Yes. You never noticed it, then! They were very like."

And she smiled with a joy which was proud and naïve at once.

Mme. Forestier, strongly moved, took her two hands.

"Oh, my poor Mathilde! Why, my necklace was paste. It was worth at most five hundred francs!"

Questions for Discussion

1. Within the rigid class and economic structure of nineteenth-century France, a young woman in Mathilde's position could have little hope of marrying above her position. What does it say about her that she believes herself deserving of a more luxurious and elegant lifestyle?
2. How would you characterize the Loisels' marriage? Do they seem to be a loving couple?
3. What does the borrowed necklace represent?
4. What was your response to the twist ending? Did it seem to emerge credibly from what preceded it? What might be the "moral" of the ending?
5. The Loisels would have been spared their misfortune if Mathilde had simply told Mme. Forestier the truth about losing the necklace. Why do she and her husband not even consider doing so? How does this affect your sympathy for them?

Ideas for Writing

1. Wirte an analysis of the narrator's attitude toward Mathilde Loisel, her husband, and the class-oriented, materialistic society they inhabit. How much criticism and how much sympathy for the characters seems to be implied?
2. Write a story of your own with a twist ending. You might model your plot on Maupassant's: an incident changes a life for the worse, and not until years later is it revealed that this misfortune was based on a misunderstanding.

Confessing (1884)

The noon sun poured fiercely down upon the fields. They stretched in undulating folds between the clumps of trees that marked each farmhouse; the different crops, ripe rye and yellowing wheat, pale-green oats, dark-green clover, spread a vast striped cloak, soft and rippling, over the naked body of the earth.

In the distance, on the crest of a slope, was an endless line of cows, ranked like soldiers, some lying down, others standing, their large eyes blinking in the burning light, chewing the cud and grazing on a field of clover as broad as a lake.

Two women, mother and daughter, were walking with a swinging step, one behind the other, towards this regiment of cattle. Each carried two zinc pails, slung outwards from the body on a hoop from a cask; at each step the metal sent out a dazzling white flash under the sun that struck full upon it.

The women did not speak. They were on their way to milk the cows. When they arrive, they set down one of their pails and approach the first two cows, making them stand up with a kick in the ribs from wooden-shod feet. The beast rises slowly, first on its forelegs, then with more difficulty raises its large hind quarters, which seem to be weighted down by the enormous udder of livid pendulous flesh.

The two Malivoires, mother and daughter, kneeling beneath the animal's belly, tug with a swift movement of their hands at the swollen teat, which at each squeeze sends a jet of milk into the pail. The yellowish froth mounts to the brim, and the women go from cow to cow until they reach the end of the long line.

As soon as they finish milking a beast, they change its position, giving it a fresh patch of grass on which to graze.

Then they start on their way home, more slowly now, weighed down by the load of milk, the mother in front, the daughter behind.

Abruptly the latter halts, sets down her burden, sits down, and begins to cry.

Mme. Malivoire, missing the sound of steps behind her, turns round and is quite amazed.

"What's the matter with you?" she said.

Her daughter Céleste, a tall girl with flaming red hair and flaming cheeks, flecked with freckles as though sparks of fire had fallen upon her face one day as she worked in the sun, murmurs, moaning softly like a beaten child:

"I can't carry the milk any further."

Her mother looked at her suspiciously.

"What's the matter with you?" she repeated.

"It drags too heavy, I can't," replied Céleste, who had collapsed and was lying on the ground between the two pails, hiding her eyes in her apron.

"What's the matter with you, then?" said her mother for the third time. The girl moaned:

"I guess there's a baby on the way." And she broke into sobs.

The old woman now in her turn set down her load, so amazed that she could find nothing to say. At last she stammered:

"You . . . you . . . you're going to have a baby, you clod! How can that be?"

The Malivoires were prosperous farmers, wealthy and of a certain position, widely respected, good business folk, of some importance in the district.

"I guess I am, all the same," faltered Céleste.

The frightened mother looked at the weeping girl groveling at her feet. After a few seconds she cried:

"You're going to have a baby! A baby! Where did you get it, you slut?"

Céleste, shaken with emotion, murmured:

"I guess it was in Polyte's coach."

The old woman tried to understand, tried to imagine, to realize who could have brought this misfortune upon her daughter. If the lad was well off and of decent position, an arrangement might be come to. It wasn't so bad, yet. Céleste was not the first to be in the same way, but it was annoying all the same, seeing their position and the way people talked.

"And who was it, you slut?" she repeated.

Céleste, resolved to make a clean breast of it, stammered:

"I guess it was Polyte."

At that Mme. Malivoire, mad with rage, rushed upon her daughter and began to beat her with such fury that her hat fell off in the effort.

With great blows of the fist she struck her on the head, on the back, all over her body; Céleste, prostrate between the two pails, which afforded her some slight protection, shielded just her face with her hands.

All the cows, disturbed, had stopped grazing and turned round, staring with their great eyes. The last one mooed, stretching out its muzzle towards the women.

After beating her daughter till she was out of breath, Mme. Malivoire stopped, exhausted; her spirits reviving a little, she tried to get a thorough understanding of the situation.

"——Polyte! Lord save us, it's not possible! How could you, with a carrier? You must have lost your wits. He must have played you a trick, the good-for-nothing!"

Céleste, still prostrate, murmured in the dust:

"I didn't pay my fare!"

And the old Norman woman understood.

Every week, on Wednesday and on Saturday, Céleste went to town with the farm produce, poultry, cream, and eggs.

She started at seven with her two huge baskets on her arm, the dairy produce in one, the chickens in the other, and went to the main road to wait for the coach to Yvetot.

She set down her wares and sat in the ditch, while the chickens with their short pointed beaks and the ducks with their broad flat bills thrust their heads between the wicker bars and looked about them with their round, stupid, surprised eyes.

Soon the bus, a sort of yellow box with a black leather cap on the top, came up, jerking and quivering with the trotting of the old white horse.

Polyte the coachman, a big jolly fellow, stout though still young, and so burned up by sun and wind, soaked by rain, and colored with brandy that his face and neck were brick-red, cracked his whip and shouted from the distance:

"Morning, Mam'selle Céleste. In good health, I hope?"

She gave him her baskets, one after the other, which he stowed in the boot; then she got in, lifting her leg high up to reach the step, and exposing a sturdy leg clad in a blue stocking.

Every time Polyte repeated the same joke: "Clumsy; it's not got any thinner."

She laughed, thinking it funny.

Then he uttered a "Gee up, old girl!" which started off the thin horse. Then Céleste, reaching for her purse in the depths of her pocket, slowly took out fivepence, threepence for herself and twopence for the baskets, and handed them to Polyte over his shoulder.

He took them, saying:

"Aren't we going to have our little bit of sport today?"

And he laughed heartily, turning round towards her so as to stare at her at his ease.

She found it a big expense, the half franc for a journey of two miles. And when she had no coppers she felt it still more keenly; it was hard to make up her mind to part with a silver coin.

One day, as she was paying, she asked:

"From a good customer like me you oughtn't to take more than three-pence."

He burst out laughing.

"Threepence, my beauty; why, you're worth more than that."

She insisted on the point.

"But you make a good two francs a month out of me."

He whipped up his horse and exclaimed:

"Look here, I'm an obliging fellow! We'll call it quits for a bit of sport."

"What do you mean?" she asked with an air of innocence.

He was so amused that he laughed till he coughed.

"A bit of sport is a bit of sport, damn it; a game for a lad and a lass, a dance for two without music."

She understood, blushed, and declared:

"I don't care for that sort of game, M. Polyte."

But he was in no way abashed, and repeated, with growing merriment:

"You'll come to it some day, my beauty, a bit of sport for a lad and a lass!"

And since that day he had taken to asking her, each time that she paid her fare:

"Aren't we going to have our bit of sport today?"

She, too, joked about it by this time, and replied:

"Not today, M. Polyte, but Saturday, for certain!"

And amid peals of laughter he answered:

"Saturday then, my beauty."

But inwardly she calculated that, during the two years the affair had been going on, she had paid Polyte forty-eight whole francs, and in the country forty-eight francs is not a sum which can be picked up on the roadside; she also calculated that in two more years she would have paid nearly a hundred francs.

To such purpose she meditated that, one spring day as they jogged on alone, when he made his customary inquiry: "Aren't we going to have our bit of sport yet?" she replied:

"Yes, if you like, M. Polyte."

He was not at all surprised, and clambered over the back of his seat, mur-muring with a complacent air:

"Come along, then. I knew you'd come to it some day."

The old white horse trotted so gently that she seemed to be dancing upon the same spot, deaf to the voice which cried at intervals, from the depths of the vehicle: "Gee up, old girl! Gee up, then!"

Three months later Céleste discovered that she was going to have a child.

All this she had told her mother in a tearful voice. Pale with fury, the old woman asked:

"Well, what did it cost?"

"Four months; that makes eight francs, doesn't it?" replied Céleste.

At that the peasant woman's fury was utterly unleashed, and, falling once more upon her daughter, she beat her a second time until she was out of breath. Then she rose and said:

"Have you told him about the baby?"

"No, of course not."

"Why haven't you told him?"

"Because very likely he'd have made me pay for all the free rides!"

The old woman pondered awhile, then picked up her milk pails.

"Come on, get up, and try to walk home," she said, and, after a pause, continued:

"And don't tell him as long as he doesn't notice anything, and we'll make six or eight months' fares out of him."

And Céleste, who had risen, still crying, disheveled and swollen round the eyes, started off again with dragging steps, murmuring:

"Of course I won't say a word."

Questions for Discussion

1. In what ways does the opening scene set the stage for the confession that will follow?
2. How does Mme. Malivoire get Céleste to tell why she is pregnant, and what does the mother's method reveal about her values and attitude toward her daughter?
3. Why does Céleste have sex with Polyte? What values did she affirm in agreeing to his demands?
4. What does Céleste's attitude toward her pregnancy imply about her ability to handle motherhood?
5. What do Mme. Malivoire's arguments for keeping the truth of Céleste's pregnancy from Polyte say about her values?

Ideas for Writing

1. Write a scene in which Céleste confesses to Polyte that she is pregnant with his child. What will his response be? Will he marry her?
2. Write an essay that addresses the attitudes toward sex and marriage implied through the characters and plot of "Confessing." Does the story seem moralistic or amoral, caring or cynical in its outlook?

KATE CHOPIN   (1851–1904)

Chopin's short fiction and novels are realistic in incident and psychology. At the same time, they provide compassionate and delicate portrayals of women's inner lives and the effects of late-nineteenth-century social constraints on their freedom and happiness.

Chopin was born Katherine O'Flaherty in St. Louis, Missouri, to a socially prominent family of French ancestry. In 1871 she married and moved to New Orleans, where her husband, Oscar Chopin, owned cotton plantations. It was only after her husband's death, when she was already in her late thirties, that Chopin began to write and to support her six children through the publication of her stories in popular magazines and in two successful collections, *Bayou Folk* (1894) and *A Night in Acadie* (1897). Using humor, dialect, and elements of local color, these stories capture the day-to-day lives of Louisiana's French Creoles and rural Acadians. Her short novel *The Awakening* (1899), because of its sympathetic portrayal of adultery, was widely criticized and banned from bookstores and libraries, and Chopin was shunned by many of her friends and social acquaintances. Her literary reputation diminished, and she was unable to get her third collection of stories published. In fact, "The Storm," which was written in 1898, was not published until 1969. Ironically, *The Awakening* has become Chopin's most highly acclaimed work — a small masterpiece rediscovered by feminist critics in the 1960s. Subsequently, her stories have all been reissued or published for the first time. Chopin's description of Maupassant's fiction and its impact describes her own goals in writing: "Here was life, not fiction; for where were the plots, the old fashioned mechanism and stage trapping[?]"

A Pair of Silk Stockings   (1897)

Little Mrs. Sommers one day found herself the unexpected possessor of fifteen dollars. It seemed to her a very large amount of money, and the way in which it stuffed and bulged her worn old *porte-monnaie* gave her a feeling of importance such as she had not enjoyed for years.

The question of investment was one that occupied her greatly. For a day or two she walked about apparently in a dreamy state, but really absorbed in speculation and calculation. She did not wish to act hastily, to do anything she might afterward regret. But it was during the still hours of the night when she lay awake revolving plans in her mind that she seemed to see her way clearly toward a proper and judicious use of the money.

A dollar or two should be added to the price usually paid for Janie's shoes, which would insure their lasting an appreciable time longer than they usually did. She would buy so and so many yards of percale for new shirt waists for the boys and Janie and Mag. She had intended to make the old ones do by skilful patching. Mag should have another gown. She had seen some beautiful patterns, veritable bargains in the shop windows. And still there would be left enough for new stockings — two pairs apiece — and what darning that would save for a while! She would get caps for the boys and sailor-hats for the girls. The vision of her little brood looking fresh and dainty and new for once in their lives excited her and made her restless and wakeful with anticipation.

The neighbors sometimes talked of certain "better days" that little Mrs. Sommers had known before she had ever thought of being Mrs. Sommers. She herself indulged in no such morbid retrospection. She had no time — no second of time to devote to the past. The needs of the present absorbed her every faculty. A vision of the future like some dim, gaunt monster sometimes appalled her, but luckily to-morrow never comes.

Mrs. Sommers was one who knew the value of bargains; who could stand for hours making her way inch by inch toward the desired object that was selling below cost. She could elbow her way if need be; she had learned to clutch a piece of goods and hold it and stick to it with persistence and determination till her turn came to be served, no matter when it came.

But that day she was a little faint and tired. She had swallowed a light luncheon — no! when she came to think of it, between getting the children fed and the place righted, and preparing herself for the shopping bout, she had actually forgotten to eat any luncheon at all!

She sat herself upon a revolving stool before a counter that was comparatively deserted, trying to gather strength and courage to charge through an eager multitude that was besieging breast-works of shirting and figured lawn. An all-gone limp feeling had come over her and she rested her hand aimlessly upon the counter. She wore no gloves. By degrees she grew aware that her hand had encountered something very soothing, very pleasant to touch. She looked down to see that her hand lay upon a pile of silk stockings. A placard near by announced that they had been reduced in price from two dollars and fifty cents to one dollar and ninety-eight cents; and a young girl who stood behind the counter asked her if she wished to examine their line of silk hosiery. She smiled, just as if she had been asked to inspect a tiara of diamonds with the ultimate view of purchasing it. But she went on feeling the soft, sheeny luxurious things — with both hands now, holding them up to see them glisten, and to feel them glide serpent-like through her fingers.

Two hectic blotches came suddenly into her pale cheeks. She looked up at the girl.

"Do you think there are any eights-and-a-half among these?"

There were any number of eights-and-a-half. In fact, there were more of that size than any other. Here was a light-blue pair; there were some lavender, some all black and various shades of tan and gray. Mrs. Sommers selected a black pair and looked at them very long and closely. She pretended to be examining their texture, which the clerk assured her was excellent.

"A dollar and ninety-eight cents," she mused aloud. "Well, I'll take this pair." She handed the girl a five-dollar bill and waited for her change and for her parcel. What a very small parcel it was. It seemed lost in the depths of her shabby old shopping-bag.

Mrs. Sommers after that did not move in the direction of the bargain counter. She took the elevator, which carried her to an upper floor into the region of the ladies' waiting-rooms. Here, in a retired corner, she exchanged her cotton stockings for the new silk ones which she had just bought. She was not going through any acute mental process or reasoning with herself, nor was she striving to explain to her satisfaction the motive of her action. She was not thinking at all. She seemed for the time to be taking a rest from that laborious and fatiguing function and to have abandoned herself to some mechanical impulse that directed her actions and freed her of responsibility.

How good was the touch of the raw silk to her flesh! She felt like lying back in the cushioned chair and reveling for a while in the luxury of it. She did for a little while. Then she replaced her shoes, rolled the cotton stockings together and thrust them into her bag. After doing this she crossed straight over to the shoe department and took her seat to be fitted.

She was fastidious. The clerk could not make her out; he could not reconcile her shoes with her stockings, and she was not too easily pleased. She held back her skirts and turned her feet one way and her head another way as she glanced down at the polished, pointed-tipped boots. Her foot and ankle looked very pretty. She could not realize that they belonged to her and were a part of herself. She wanted an excellent and stylish fit, she told the young fellow who served her, and she did not mind the difference of a dollar or two more in the price so long as she got what she desired.

It was a long time since Mrs. Sommers had been fitted with gloves. On rare occasions when she had bought a pair they were always "bargains," so cheap that it would have been preposterous and unreasonable to have expected them to be fitted to the hand.

Now she rested her elbow on the cushion of the glove counter, and a pretty, pleasant young creature, delicate and deft of touch, drew a long-wristed "kid" over Mrs. Sommers' hand. She smoothed it down over the wrist and buttoned it neatly, and both lost themselves for a second or two in admiring contemplation of the little symmetrical gloved hand. But there were other places where money might be spent.

There were books and magazines piled up in the window of a stall a few paces down the street. Mrs. Sommers bought two high-priced magazines such as she had been accustomed to read in the days when she had been accustomed to other pleasant things. She carried them without wrapping. As well as she could she lifted her skirts at the crossings. Her stockings and boots and well-fitting gloves had worked marvels in her bearing — had given her a feeling of assurance, a sense of belonging to the well-dressed multitude.

She was very hungry. Another time she would have stilled the cravings for food until reaching her own home, where she would have brewed herself a cup of tea and taken a snack of anything that was available. But the impulse that was guiding her would not suffer her to entertain any such thought.

There was a restaurant at the corner. She had never entered its doors; from the outside she had sometimes caught glimpses of spotless damask and shining crystal, and soft-stepping waiters serving people of fashion.

When she entered her appearance created no surprise, no consternation, as she had half feared it might. She seated herself at a small table alone, and an attentive waiter at once approached to take her order. She did not want a profusion; she craved a nice and tasty bite — a half dozen blue-points, a plump chop with cress, a something sweet — a crème-frappée, for instance; a glass of Rhine wine, and after all a small cup of black coffee.

While waiting to be served she removed her gloves very leisurely and laid them beside her. Then she picked up a magazine and glanced through it, cutting the pages with a blunt edge of her knife. It was all very agreeable. The damask was even more spotless than it had seemed through the window, and the crystal more sparkling. There were quiet ladies and gentlemen, who did not notice her, lunching at the small tables like her own. A soft, pleasing strain of music could be heard, and a gentle breeze was blowing through the window. She tasted a bite, and she read a word or two, and she sipped the amber wine and wiggled her toes in the silk stockings. The price of it made no difference. She counted the money out to the waiter and left an extra coin on his tray, whereupon he bowed before her as before a princess of royal blood.

There was still money in her purse, and her next temptation presented itself in the shape of a matinée poster.

It was a little later when she entered the theatre, the play had begun and the house seemed to her to be packed. But there were vacant seats here and there, and into one of them she was ushered, between brilliantly dressed women who had gone there to kill time and eat candy and display their gaudy attire. There were many others who were there solely for the play and acting. It is safe to say there was no one present who bore quite the attitude which Mrs. Sommers did to her surroundings. She gathered in the whole — stage and players and people in one wide impression, and absorbed it and enjoyed it. She laughed at the comedy and wept — she and the gaudy woman next to her wept over the tragedy. And they talked a little together over it. And the gaudy woman wiped her eyes and sniffled on a tiny square of filmy, perfumed lace and passed little Mrs. Sommers her box of candy.

The play was over, the music ceased, the crowd filed out. It was like a dream ended. People scattered in all directions. Mrs. Sommers went to the corner and waited for the cable car.

A man with keen eyes, who sat opposite to her, seemed to like the study of her small, pale face. It puzzled him to decipher what he saw there. In truth, he saw nothing — unless he were wizard enough to detect a poignant wish, a powerful longing that the cable car would never stop anywhere, but go on and on with her forever.

Questions for Discussion
1. What do the story's first paragraphs reveal about Mrs. Sommers's economic status and her feelings about wealth?
2. What initial plans for spending the fifteen dollars (equivalent to over one hundred dollars today) does Mrs. Sommers make? What leads her to change her plans?
3. How does Chopin let us know her character's intimate thoughts and concerns? Why is this technique effective?
4. What is the significance of the line "How good was the touch of the raw silk to her flesh!"? What chain of events does the pair of stockings set in motion?
5. What is implied by Mrs. Sommers's reluctance to return home and to think about her past or her future? What has Mrs. Sommers learned on her outing?

Ideas for Writing
1. Write a sequel to the story. Will Mrs. Sommers return from her spending spree to live her modest life as she has done before? Do you think she has been changed in a significant way through her experience?
2. In an essay, discuss what the story reveals about the economic and social status of single or widowed mothers in the late 1800s. You might also do some library research to support the evidence presented by the story. How much different are the lives of single and widowed mothers today?

The Storm   (1898)

I

The leaves were so still that even Bibi thought it was going to rain. Bobinôt, who was accustomed to converse on terms of perfect equality with his little son, called the child's attention to certain sombre clouds that were rolling with sinister intention from the west, accompanied by a sullen, threatening roar. They were at Friedheimer's store and decided to remain there till the storm had passed. They sat within the door on two empty kegs. Bibi was four years old and looked very wise.

"Mama'll be 'fraid, yes," he suggested with blinking eyes.

"She'll shut the house. Maybe she got Sylvie helpin' her this evenin'," Bobinôt responded reassuringly.

"No; she ent got Sylvie. Sylvie was helpin' her yistiday," piped Bibi.

Bobinôt arose and going across to the counter purchased a can of shrimps, of which Calixta was very fond. Then he returned to his perch on the keg and sat stolidly holding the can of shrimps while the storm burst. It shook the wooden store and seemed to be ripping great furrows in the distant field. Bibi laid his little hand on his father's knee and was not afraid.

II

Calixta, at home, felt no uneasiness for their safety. She sat at a side window sewing furiously on a sewing machine. She was greatly occupied and did not notice the approaching storm. But she felt very warm and often stopped to mop her face on which the perspiration gathered in beads. She unfastened her white sacque at the throat. It began to grow dark, and suddenly realizing the situation she got up hurriedly and went about closing windows and doors.

Out on the small front gallery she had hung Bobinôt's Sunday clothes to air and she hastened out to gather them before the rain fell. As she stepped outside, Alcée Laballière rode in at the gate. She had not seen him very often since her marriage, and never alone. She stood there with Bobinôt's coat in her hands, and the big rain drops began to fall. Alcée rode his horse under the shelter of a side projection where the chickens had huddled and there were plows and a harrow piled up in the corner.

"May I come and wait on your gallery till the storm is over, Calixta?" he asked.

"Come 'long in, M'sieur Alcée."

His voice and her own startled her as if from a trance, and she seized Bobinôt's vest. Alcée, mounting to the porch, grabbed the trousers and snatched Bibi's braided jacket that was about to be carried away by a sudden gust of wind. He expressed an intention to remain outside, but it was soon apparent that he might as well have been out in the open: the water beat in upon the boards in driving sheets, and he went inside, closing the door after him. It was even necessary to put something beneath the door to keep the water out.

"My! what a rain! It's good two years sence it rain' like that," exclaimed Calixta as she rolled up a piece of bagging and Alcée helped her to thrust it beneath the crack.

She was a little fuller of figure than five years before when she married; but she had lost nothing of her vivacity. Her blue eyes still retained their melting quality; and her yellow hair, dishevelled by the wind and rain, kinked more stubbornly than ever about her ears and temples.

The rain beat upon the low, shingled roof with a force and clatter that threatened to break an entrance and deluge them there. They were in the dining room — the sitting room — the general utility room. Adjoining was her bed room, with Bibi's couch along side her own. The door stood open, and the room with its white, monumental bed, its closed shutters, looked dim and mysterious.

Alcée flung himself into a rocker and Calixta nervously began to gather up from the floor the lengths of a cotton sheet which she had been sewing.

"If this keeps up, *Dieu sait*[1] if the levees goin' to stan' it!" she exclaimed.

"What have you got to do with the levees?"

"I got enough to do! An' there's Bobinôt with Bibi out in that storm — if he only didn' left Friedheimer's!"

"Let us hope, Calixta, that Bobinôt's got sense enough to come in out of a cyclone."

She went and stood at the window with a greatly disturbed look on her face. She wiped the frame that was clouded with moisture. It was stiflingly hot. Alcée got up and joined her at the window, looking over her shoulder. The rain was coming down in sheets obscuring the view of far-off cabins and enveloping the distant wood in a gray mist. The playing of the lightning was incessant. A bolt struck a tall chinaberry tree at the edge of the field. It filled all visible space with a blinding glare and the crash seemed to invade the very boards they stood upon.

Calixta put her hands to her eyes, and with a cry, staggered backward. Alcée's arm encircled her, and for an instant he drew her close and spasmodically to him.

"*Bonté*"[2] she cried, releasing herself from his encircling arm and retreating from the window, "the house'll go next! If I only knew w'ere Bibi was!" She would not compose herself; she would not be seated. Alcée clasped her shoulders and looked into her face. The contact of her warm, palpitating body when he had unthinkingly drawn her into his arms, had aroused all the old-time infatuation and desire for her flesh.

"Calixta," he said, "don't be frightened. Nothing can happen. The house is too low to be struck, with so many tall trees standing about. There! aren't you going to be quiet? say, aren't you?" He pushed her hair back from her face that was warm and steaming. Her lips were as red and moist as pomegranate seed. Her white neck and a glimpse of her full, firm bosom disturbed him powerfully. As she glanced up at him the fear in her liquid blue eyes had given place to a drowsy gleam that unconsciously betrayed a sensuous desire. He looked down into her eyes and there was nothing for him to do but to gather her lips in a kiss. It reminded him of Assumption.

"Do you remember — in Assumption, Calixta?" he asked in a low voice broken by passion. Oh! she remembered; for in Assumption he had kissed her and kissed and kissed her; until his senses would well nigh fail, and to save her he would resort to a desperate flight. If she was not an immaculate dove in those days, she was still inviolate; a passionate creature whose very defenselessness had made her defense, against which his honor forbade him to prevail. Now — well, now — her lips seemed in a manner free to be tasted, as well as her round, white throat and her whiter breasts.

They did not heed the crashing torrents, and the roar of the elements made

---

[1] "God knows." — Eds.
[2] "Goodness!" — Eds.

her laugh as she lay in his arms. She was a revelation in that dim, mysterious chamber; as white as the couch she lay upon. Her firm, elastic flesh that was knowing for the first time its birthright, was like a creamy lily that the sun invites to contribute its breath and perfume to the undying life of the world.

The generous abundance of her passion, without guile or trickery, was like a white flame which penetrated and found response in depths of his own sensuous nature that had never yet been reached.

When he touched her breasts they gave themselves up in quivering ecstasy, inviting his lips. Her mouth was a fountain of delight. And when he possessed her, they seemed to swoon together at the very borderland of life's mystery.

He stayed cushioned upon her, breathless, dazed, enervated, with his heart beating like a hammer upon her. With one hand she clasped his head, her lips lightly touching his forehead. The other hand stroked with a soothing rhythm his muscular shoulders.

The growl of the thunder was distant and passing away. The rain beat softly upon the shingles, inviting them to drowsiness and sleep. But they dared not yield.

The rain was over; and the sun was turning the glistening green world into a palace of gems. Calixta, on the gallery, watched Alcée ride away. He turned and smiled at her with a beaming face; and she lifted her pretty chin in the air and laughed aloud.

III

Bobinôt and Bibi, trudging home, stopped without at the cistern to make themselves presentable.

"My! Bibi, w'at will yo' mama say! You ought to be ashame'. You oughtn' put on those good pants. Look at 'em! An' that mud on yo' collar! How you got that mud on yo' collar, Bibi? I never saw such a boy!" Bibi was the picture of pathetic resignation. Bobinôt was the embodiment of serious solicitude as he strove to remove from his own person and his son's the signs of their tramp over heavy roads and through wet fields. He scraped the mud off Bibi's bare legs and feet with a stick and carefully removed all traces from his heavy brogans. Then, prepared for the worst — the meeting with an over-scrupulous housewife, they entered cautiously at the back door.

Calixta was preparing supper. She had set the table and was dripping coffee at the hearth. She sprang up as they came in.

"Oh, Bobinôt! You back! My! but I was uneasy. W'ere you been during the rain? An' Bibi? he ain't wet? he ain't hurt?" She had clasped Bibi and was kissing him effusively. Bobinôt's explanations and apologies which he had been composing all along the way, died on his lips as Calixta felt him to see if he were dry, and seemed to express nothing but satisfaction at their safe return.

"I brought you some shrimps, Calixta," offered Bobinôt, hauling the can from his ample side pocket and laying it on the table.

"Shrimps! Oh, Bobinôt! you too good fo' anything!" and she gave him a smacking kiss on the cheek that resounded. *J'vous réponds,*[3] we'll have a feas' to-night! umph-umph!"

Bobinôt and Bibi began to relax and enjoy themselves, and when the three seated themselves at table they laughed much and so loud that anyone might have heard them as far away as Laballière's.

IV

Alcée Laballière wrote to his wife, Clarisse, that night. It was a loving letter, full of tender solicitude. He told her not to hurry back, but if she and the babies liked it at Biloxi, to stay a month longer. He was getting on nicely; and though he missed them, he was willing to bear the separation a while longer—realizing that their health and pleasure were the first things to be considered.

V

As for Clarisse, she was charmed upon receiving her husband's letter. She and the babies were doing well. The society was agreeable; many of her old friends and acquaintances were at the bay. And the first free breath since her marriage seemed to restore the pleasant liberty of her maiden days. Devoted as she was to her husband, their intimate conjugal life was something which she was more than willing to forego for a while.

So the storm passed and every one was happy.

Questions for Discussion
1. Why does Alcée find himself alone with Calixta for the first time in five years? What is implied by his memories of her and his current feelings toward her?
2. How does Alcée feel that Calixta has changed? Contrast Bobinôt's expectations of Calixta to Alcée's expectations of Calixta.
3. Why doesn't the reader learn any more about Calixta's feelings about Alcée after the storm? What is the effect on the reader of leaving so much to the imagination?
4. What is the significance of Alcée's writing to his wife? Do you think he hopes to meet with Calixta again?
5. What does the storm signify? Why is it used as a setting for the couple's passion?

Ideas for Writing
1. Creole and Acadian dialect appears in many of Chopin's stories. Write an interpretation of the use of dialectical speech and other forms of nonstandard English in "The Storm." How does dialect emphasize class differences and reveal character?
2. Write a story about two former lovers who meet several years after they both have married yet still have feelings for each other.

---

[3] "I reply to you." — Eds.

JOSEPH CONRAD   (1857–1924)

A seaman, mate, and captain for thirty years, Joseph Conrad set many of his stories and novels on sailing ships or among the East Indian islands he often navigated. Because of their serious moral themes and critique of naval authority and colonialism, Conrad's books were not popular during much of his life but achieved considerable acclaim in later years.

Conrad was born in a Russian-ruled area of Poland to parents deeply involved with the Polish nationalist movement; both died before he was twelve. He was raised by relatives in Russia and Poland, studying at the University of Cracow before entering the French maritime service. After a career at sea, he published his first novel, *Almayer's Folly,* in 1895 and settled in England, where he married, lived, and wrote until his death. English was his third language, after Polish and French, and Conrad described the difficulty of writing his stories in English as "work[ing] like a coal miner in his pit quarrying all my English sentences out of a black night." Through practice and determination, he became so adept at his craft that he is acclaimed as one of the great English stylists. Among his works are the widely read novels *Lord Jim* (1900) and *The Secret Agent* (1907), and three classic novellas — *Youth* (1902), *Heart of Darkness* (1902), and *The Secret Sharer* (1912).

Conrad's goal in all of his fiction was to imaginatively reproduce his experiences in the most powerful narrative language available to him. As he said in his essay "Books," "In truth every novelist must begin by creating for himself a world, great or little, in which he can honestly believe."

The Secret Sharer   (1912)

1

On my right hand there were lines of fishing stakes resembling a mysterious system of half-submerged bamboo fences, incomprehensible in its division of the domain of tropical fishes, and crazy of aspect as if abandoned forever by some nomad tribe of fishermen now gone to the other end of the ocean; for there was no sign of human habitation as far as the eye could reach. To the left a group of barren islets, suggesting ruins of stone walls, towers, and blockhouses, had its foundations set in a blue sea that itself looked solid, so still and stable did it lie below my feet; even the track of light from the westering sun shone smoothly, without that animated glitter which tells of an imperceptible ripple. And when I turned my head to take a parting glance at the tug which had just left us anchored outside the bar, I saw the straight line of the flat shore joined to the stable sea, edge to edge, with a perfect and unmarked closeness, in one leveled floor half brown, half blue under the enormous dome of the sky. Corresponding in their insignificance to the islets of the sea, two small clumps of trees, one on each side of the only fault in the impeccable joint, marked the mouth of the river Meinam we had just left on the first preparatory stage of our homeward journey; and, far back on the inland level, a larger and loftier mass, the grove surrounding the great Paknam pagoda, was the only thing on which the eye could rest from the vain task of exploring the monotonous sweep of the horizon. Here and there gleams as of a few scattered pieces of silver marked the windings of the great river; and on the nearest of them, just within the bar, the tug steaming right into the land became lost to my sight, hull and funnel and masts, as though the impassive earth had swallowed her up without an effort, without a tremor. My eye followed the light cloud of her smoke, now here, now there, above the plain, according to the devious curves of the stream, but always fainter and farther away, till I lost it at last behind the miter-shaped hill of the great pagoda. And then I was left alone with my ship, anchored at the head of the Gulf of Siam.

She floated at the starting point of a long journey, very still in an immense stillness, the shadows of her spars flung far to the eastward by the setting sun. At that moment I was alone on her decks. There was not a sound in her—and around us nothing moved, nothing lived, not a canoe on the water, not a bird in the air, not a cloud in the sky. In this breathless pause at the threshold of a long passage we seemed to be measuring our fitness for a long and arduous enterprise, the appointed task of both our existences to be carried out, far from all human eyes, with only sky and sea for spectators and for judges.

There must have been some glare in the air to interfere with one's sight, because it was only just before the sun left us that my roaming eyes made out beyond the highest ridge of the principal islet of the group something which did away with the solemnity of perfect solitude. The tide of darkness flowed on swiftly; and with tropical suddenness a swarm of stars came out above the shadowy earth, while I lingered yet, my hand resting lightly on my ship's rail as if on the shoulder of a trusted friend. But, with all that multitude of celestial bodies staring down at one, the comfort of quiet communion with her was gone for good. And there were also disturbing sounds by this time — voices, footsteps forward; the steward flitted along the main deck, a busily ministering spirit; a hand bell tinkled urgently under the poop deck. . . .

I found my two officers waiting for me near the supper table, in the lighted cuddy. We sat down at once, and as I helped the chief mate, I said:

"Are you aware that there is a ship anchored inside the islands? I saw her mastheads above the ridge as the sun went down."

He raised sharply his simple face, overcharged by a terrible growth of whisker, and emitted his usual ejaculations: "Bless my soul, sir! You don't say so!"

My second mate was a round-cheeked, silent young man, grave beyond his years, I thought; but as our eyes happened to meet I detected a slight quiver on his lips. I looked down at once. It was not my part to encourage sneering on board my ship. It must be said, too, that I knew very little of my officers. In consequence of certain events of no particular significance, except to myself, I had been appointed to the command only a fortnight before. Neither did I know much of the hands forward. All these people had been together for eighteen months or so, and my position was that of the only stranger on board. I mention this because it has some bearing on what is to follow. But what I felt most was my being a stranger to the ship; and if all the truth must be told, I was somewhat of a stranger to myself. The youngest man on board (barring the second mate), and untried as yet by a position of the fullest responsibility, I was willing to take the adequacy of the others for granted. They had simply to be equal to their tasks; but I wondered how far I should turn out faithful to that ideal conception of one's own personality every man sets up for himself secretly.

Meantime the chief mate, with an almost visible effect of collaboration on the part of his round eyes and frightful whiskers, was trying to evolve a theory of the anchored ship. His dominant trait was to take all things into earnest consideration. He was of a painstaking turn of mind. As he used to say, he "liked to account to himself" for practically everything that came in his way, down to the miserable scorpion he had found in his cabin a week before. The why and the wherefore of that scorpion — how it got on board and came to select his room rather than the pantry (which was a dark place and more what a scorpion would be partial to), and how on earth it managed to drown itself in the inkwell of his writing desk — had exercised him infinitely. The ship within the islands was much more easily accounted for; and just as we were about to rise from the table he made his pronouncement. She was, he doubted not, a ship from home lately arrived. Probably she drew too much water to cross the bar except at the top of spring tides. Therefore she went into that natural harbor to wait for a few days in preference to remaining in an open roadstead.

"That's so," confirmed the second mate, suddenly, in his slightly hoarse voice. "She draws over twenty feet. She's the Liverpool ship *Sephora* with a cargo of coal. Hundred and twenty-three days from Cardiff."

We looked at him in surprise.

"The tugboat skipper told me when he came on board for your letters, sir," explained the young man. "He expects to take her up the river the day after tomorrow."

After thus overwhelming us with the extent of his information he slipped out of the cabin. The mate observed regretfully that he "could not account for that young fellow's whims." What prevented him telling us all about it at once, he wanted to know.

I detained him as he was making a move. For the last two days the crew had had plenty of hard work, and the night before they had very little sleep.

I felt painfully that I — a stranger — was doing something unusual when I directed him to tell all hands turn in without setting an anchor watch. I proposed to keep on deck myself till one o'clock or thereabouts. I would get the second mate to relieve me at that hour.

"He will turn out the cook and the steward at four," I concluded, "and then give you a call. Of course at the slightest sign of any sort of wind we'll have the hands up and make a start at once."

He concealed his astonishment. "Very well, sir." Outside the cuddy he put his head in the second mate's door to inform him of my unheard-of caprice to take a five hours' anchor watch on myself. I heard the other raise his voice incredulously: "What? The captain himself?" Then a few more murmurs, a door closed, then another. A few moments later I went on deck.

My strangeness, which had made me sleepless, had prompted that unconventional arrangement, as if I had expected in those solitary hours of the night to get on terms with the ship of which I knew nothing, manned by men of whom I knew very little more. Fast alongside a wharf, littered like any ship in port with a tangle of unrelated things, invaded by unrelated shore people, I had hardly seen her yet properly. Now, as she lay cleared for sea, the stretch of her main deck seemed to me very fine under the stars. Very fine, very roomy for her size, and very inviting. I descended the poop and paced the waist, my mind picturing to myself the coming passage through the Malay Archipelago, down the Indian Ocean, and up the Atlantic. All its phases were familiar enough to me, every characteristic, all the alternatives which were likely to face me on the high seas — everything! . . . except the novel responsibility of command. But I took heart from the reasonable thought that the ship was like other ships, the men like other men, and that the sea was not likely to keep any special surprises expressly for my discomfiture.

Arriving at that comforting conclusion, I bethought myself of a cigar and went below to get it. All was still down there. Everybody at the after end of the ship was sleeping profoundly. I came out again on the quarter-deck, agreeably at ease in my sleeping suit on that warm breathless night, barefooted, a glowing cigar in my teeth, and, going forward, I was met by the profound silence of the fore end of the ship. Only as I passed the door of the forecastle I heard a deep, quiet, trustful sigh of some sleeper inside. And suddenly I rejoiced in the great security of the sea as compared with the unrest of the land, in my choice of that untempted life presenting no disquieting problems, invested with an elementary moral beauty by the absolute straightforwardness of its appeal and by the singleness of its purpose.

The riding light in the fore-rigging burned with a clear, untroubled, as if symbolic, flame, confident and bright in the mysterious shades of the night. Passing on my way aft along the other side of the ship, I observed that the rope side ladder, put over, no doubt, for the master of the tug when he came to fetch away our letters, had not been hauled in as it should have been. I became annoyed at this, for exactitude in small matters is the very soul of discipline.

Then I reflected that I had myself peremptorily dismissed my officers from duty, and by my own act had prevented the anchor watch being formally set and things properly attended to. I asked myself whether it was wise ever to interfere with the established routine of duties even from the kindest of motives. My action might have made me appear eccentric. Goodness only knew how that absurdly whiskered mate would "account" for my conduct, and what the whole ship thought of that informality of their new captain. I was vexed with myself.

Not from compunction certainly, but, as it were mechanically, I proceeded to get the ladder in myself. Now a side-ladder of that sort is a light affair and comes in easily, yet my vigorous tug, which should have brought it flying on board, merely recoiled upon my body in a totally unexpected jerk. What the devil! . . . I was so astounded by the immovableness of that ladder that I remained stockstill, trying to account for it to myself like that imbecile mate of mine. In the end, of course, I put my head over the rail.

The side of the ship made an opaque belt of shadow on the darkling glassy shimmer of the sea. But I saw at once something elongated and pale floating very close to the ladder. Before I could form a guess a faint flash of phosphorescent light, which seemed to issue suddenly from the naked body of a man, flickered in the sleeping water with the elusive, silent play of summer lightning in a night sky. With a gasp I saw revealed to my stare a pair of feet, the long legs, a broad livid back immersed right up to the neck in a greenish cadaverous glow. One hand, awash, clutched the bottom rung of the ladder. He was complete but for the head. A headless corpse! The cigar dropped out of my gaping mouth with a tiny plop and a short hiss quite audible in the absolute stillness of all things under heaven. At that I suppose he raised up his face, a dimly pale oval in the shadow of the ship's side. But even then I could only barely make out down there the shape of his black-haired head. However, it was enough for the horrid, frost-bound sensation which had gripped me about the chest to pass off. The moment of vain exclamations was past, too. I only climbed on the spare spar and leaned over the rail as far as I could, to bring my eyes nearer to that mystery floating alongside.

As he hung by the ladder, like a resting swimmer, the sea lightning played about his limbs at every stir; and he appeared in it ghastly, silvery, fishlike. He remained as mute as a fish, too. He made no motion to get out of the water, either. It was inconceivable that he should not attempt to come on board, and strangely troubling to suspect that perhaps he did not want to. And my first words were prompted by just that troubled incertitude.

"What's the matter?" I asked in my ordinary tone, speaking down to the face upturned exactly under mine.

"Cramp," it answered, no louder. Then slightly anxious, "I say, no need to call anyone."

"I was not going to," I said.

"Are you alone on deck?"

"Yes."

I had somehow the impression that he was on the point of letting go the ladder to swim away beyond my ken — mysterious as he came. But, for the moment, this being appearing as if he had risen from the bottom of the sea (it was certainly the nearest land to the ship) wanted only to know the time. I told him. And he, down there, tentatively:

"I suppose your captain's turned in?"

"I am sure he isn't," I said.

He seemed to struggle with himself, for I heard something like the low, bitter murmur of doubt. "What's the good?" His next words came out with a hesitating effort.

"Look here, my man. Could you call him out quietly?"

I thought the time had come to declare myself.

"*I* am the captain."

I heard a "By Jove!" whispered at the level of the water. The phosphorescence flashed in the swirl of the water all about his limbs, his other hand seized the ladder.

"My name's Leggatt."

The voice was calm and resolute. A good voice. The self-possession of that man had somehow induced a corresponding state in myself. It was very quietly that I remarked:

"You must be a good swimmer."

"Yes. I've been in the water practically since nine o'clock. The question for me now is whether I am to let go this ladder and go on swimming till I sink from exhaustion, or — to come on board here."

I felt this was no mere formula of desperate speech, but a real alternative in the view of a strong soul. I should have gathered from this that he was young; indeed, it is only the young who are ever confronted by such clear issues. But at the time it was pure intuition on my part. A mysterious communication was established already between us two — in the face of that silent, darkened tropical sea. I was young, too; young enough to make no comment. The man in the water began suddenly to climb up the ladder, and I hastened away from the rail to fetch some clothes.

Before entering the cabin I stood still, listening in the lobby at the foot of the stairs. A faint snore came through the closed door of the chief mate's room. The second mate's door was on the hook, but the darkness in there was absolutely soundless. He, too, was young and could sleep like a stone. Remained the steward, but he was not likely to wake up before he was called. I got a sleeping suit out of my room and, coming back on deck, saw the naked man from the sea sitting on the main hatch, glimmering white in the darkness, his elbows on his knees and his head in his hands. In a moment he had concealed his damp body in a sleeping suit of the same gray-stripe pattern as the one I was wearing and followed me like my double on the poop. Together we moved right aft, barefooted, silent.

"What is it?" I asked in a deadened voice, taking the lighted lamp out of the binnacle, and raising it to his face.

"An ugly business."

He had rather regular features; a good mouth; light eyes under somewhat heavy, dark eyebrows; a smooth, square forehead, no growth on his cheeks; a small, brown mustache, and a well-shaped, round chin. His expression was concentrated, meditative, under the inspecting light of the lamp I held up to his face; such as a man thinking hard in solitude might wear. My sleeping suit was just right for his size. A well-knit young fellow of twenty-five at most. He caught his lower lip with the edge of white, even teeth.

"Yes," I said, replacing the lamp in the binnacle. The warm, heavy tropical night closed upon his head again.

"There's a ship over there," he murmured.

"Yes, I know. The *Sephora*. Did you know of us?"

"Hadn't the slightest idea. I am the mate of her —" He paused and corrected himself. "I should say I *was*."

"Aha! Something wrong?"

"Yes. Very wrong indeed. I've killed a man."

"What do you mean? Just now?"

"No, on the passage. Weeks ago. Thirty-nine south. When I say a man —"

"Fit of temper," I suggested, confidently.

The shadowy, dark head, like mine, seemed to nod imperceptibly above the ghostly gray of my sleeping suit. It was, in the night, as though I had been faced by my own reflection in the depths of a somber and immense mirror.

"A pretty thing to have to own up to for a Conway boy," murmured my double, distinctly.

"You're a Conway boy?"

"I am," he said, as if startled. Then, slowly . . . "Perhaps you too —"

It was so; but being a couple of years older I had left before he joined. After a quick interchange of dates a silence fell; and I thought suddenly of my absurd mate with his terrific whiskers and the "Bless my soul — you don't say so" type of intellect. My double gave me an inkling of his thoughts by saying:

"My father's a parson in Norfolk. Do you see me before a judge and jury on that charge? For myself I can't see the necessity. There are fellows that an angel from heaven — And I am not that. He was one of those creatures that are just simmering all the time with a silly sort of wickedness. Miserable devils that have no business to live at all. He wouldn't do his duty and wouldn't let anybody else do theirs. But what's the good of talking! You know well enough the sort of ill-conditioned snarling cur —"

He appealed to me as if our experiences had been as identical as our clothes. And I knew well enough the pestiferous danger of such a character where there are no means of legal repression. And I knew well enough also that my double there was no homicidal ruffian. I did not think of asking him for details, and he told me the story roughly in brusque, disconnected sentences.

I needed no more. I saw it all going on as though I were myself inside that other sleeping suit.

"It happened while we were setting a reefed foresail, at dusk. Reefed foresail! You understand the sort of weather. The only sail we had left to keep the ship running; so you may guess what it had been like for days. Anxious sort of job, that. He gave me some of his cursed insolence at the sheet. I tell you I was overdone with this terrific weather that seemed to have no end to it. Terrific, I tell you — and a deep ship. I believe the fellow himself was half crazed with funk. It was no time for gentlemanly reproof, so I turned around and felled him like an ox. He up and at me. We closed just as an awful sea made for the ship. All hands saw it coming and took to the rigging, but I had him by the throat, and went on shaking him like a rat, the men above us yelling, 'Look out! look out!' Then a crash as if the sky had fallen on my head. They say that for over ten minutes hardly anything was to be seen of the ship — just the three masts and a bit of the forecastle head and of the poop all awash driving along in a smother of foam. It was a miracle that they found us, jammed together behind the forebits. It's clear that I meant business, because I was holding him by the throat still when they picked us up. He was black in the face. It was too much for them. It seems they rushed us aft together, gripped as we were, screaming 'Murder!' like a lot of lunatics, and broke into the cuddy. And the ship running for her life, touch and go all the time, any minute her last in a sea fit to turn your hair gray only a-looking at it. I understand that the skipper, too, started raving like the rest of them. The man had been deprived of sleep for more than a week, and to have this sprung on him at the height of a furious gale nearly drove him out of his mind. I wonder they didn't fling me overboard after getting the carcass of their precious shipmate out of my fingers. They had rather a job to separate us, I've been told. A sufficiently fierce story to make an old judge and a respectable jury sit up a bit. The first thing I heard when I came to myself was the maddening howling of that endless gale, and on that the voice of the old man. He was hanging on to my bunk, staring into my face out of his sou'wester.

"'Mr. Leggatt, you have killed a man. You can act no longer as chief mate of this ship.'"

His care to subdue his voice made it sound monotonous. He rested a hand on the end of the skylight to steady himself with, and all that time did not stir a limb, so far as I could see. "Nice little tale for a quiet tea party," he concluded in the same tone.

One of my hands, too, rested on the end of the skylight; neither did I stir a limb, so far as I knew. We stood less than a foot from each other. It occurred to me that if old "Bless my soul — you don't say so" were to put his head up the companion and catch sight of us, he would think he was seeing double, or imagine himself come upon a scene of weird witchcraft; the strange captain having a quiet confabulation by the wheel with his own gray ghost. I became very much concerned to prevent anything of the sort. I heard the other's soothing undertone.

"My father's a parson in Norfolk," it said. Evidently he had forgotten he had told me this important fact before. Truly a nice little tale.

"You had better slip down into my stateroom now," I said, moving off stealthily. My double followed my movements; our bare feet made no sound; I let him in, closed the door with care, and, after giving a call to the second mate, returned on deck for my relief.

"Not much sign of any wind yet," I remarked when he approached.

"No, sir. Not much," he assented, sleepily, in his hoarse voice, with just enough deference, no more, and barely suppressing a yawn.

"Well, that's all you have to look out for. You have got your orders."

"Yes, sir."

I paced a turn or two on the poop and saw him take up his position face forward with his elbow in the ratlines of the mizzen-rigging before I went below. The mate's faint snoring was still going on peacefully. The cuddy lamp was burning over the table on which stood a vase with flowers, a polite attention from the ships' provision merchant — the last flowers we should see for the next three months at the very least. Two bunches of bananas hung from the beam symmetrically, one on each side of the rudder casing. Everything was as before in the ship — except that two of her captain's sleeping suits were simultaneously in use, one motionless in the cuddy, the other keeping very still in the captain's stateroom.

It must be explained here that my cabin had the form of the capital letter L, the door being within the angle and opening into the short part of the letter. A couch was to the left, the bed-place to the right; my writing desk and the chronometers' table faced the door. But anyone opening it, unless he stepped right inside, had no view of what I call the long (or vertical) part of the letter. It contained some lockers surmounted by a bookcase; and a few clothes, a thick jacket or two, caps, oilskin coat, and such like, hung on hooks. There was at the bottom of that part a door opening into my bathroom, which could be entered also directly from the saloon.[1] But that way was never used.

The mysterious arrival had discovered the advantage of this particular shape. Entering my room, lighted strongly by a big bulkhead lamp swung on gimbals above my writing desk, I did not see him anywhere till he stepped out quietly from behind the coats hung in the recessed part.

"I heard somebody moving about, and went in there at once," he whispered.

I, too, spoke under my breath.

"Nobody is likely to come in here without knocking and getting permission."

He nodded. His face was thin and the sunburn faded, as though he had been ill. And no wonder. He had been, I heard presently, kept under arrest in

---

[1] Captain's cabin, stateroom. — Eds.

his cabin for nearly seven weeks. But there was nothing sickly in his eyes or in his expression. He was not a bit like me, really; yet, as we stood leaning over my bed-place, whispering side by side, with our dark heads together and our backs to the door, anybody bold enough to open it stealthily would have been treated to the uncanny sight of a double captain busy talking in whispers with his other self.

"But all this doesn't tell me how you came to hang on to our side ladder," I inquired, in the hardly audible murmurs we used, after he had told me something more of the proceedings on board the *Sephora* once the bad weather was over.

"When we sighted Java Head I had had time to think all those matters out several times over. I had six weeks of doing nothing else, and with only an hour or so every evening for a tramp on the quarter-deck."

He whispered, his arms folded on the side of my bed-place, staring through the open port. And I could imagine perfectly the manner of this thinking out —a stubborn if not a steadfast operation; something of which I should have been perfectly incapable.

"I reckoned it would be dark before we closed with the land," he continued, so low that I had to strain my hearing, near as we were to each other, shoulder touching shoulder almost. "So I asked to speak to the old man. He always seemed very sick when he came to see me—as if he could not look me in the face. You know, that foresail saved the ship. She was too deep to have run long under bare poles. And it was I that managed to set it for him. Anyway, he came. When I had him in my cabin—he stood by the door looking at me as if I had the halter around my neck already—I asked him right away to leave my cabin door unlocked at night while the ship was going through Sunda Straits. There would be the Java coast within two or three miles, off Angier Point. I wanted nothing more. I've had a prize for swimming my second year in the Conway."

"I can believe it," I breathed out.

"God only knows why they locked me in every night. To see some of their faces you'd have thought they were afraid I'd go about at night strangling people. Am I a murdering brute? Do I look it? By Jove! if I had been he wouldn't have trusted himself like that into my room. You'll say I might have chucked him aside and bolted out, there and then—it was dark already. Well, no. And for the same reason I wouldn't think of trying to smash the door. There would have been a rush to stop me at the noise, and I did not mean to get into a confounded scrimmage. Somebody else might have got killed—for I would not have broken out only to get chucked back, and I did not want any more of that work. He refused, looking more sick than ever. He was afraid of the men, and also of that old second mate of his who had been sailing with him for years— a gray-headed old humbug; and his steward, too, had been with him devil knows how long—seventeen years or more—a dogmatic sort of loafer who hated me like poison, just because I was the chief mate. No chief mate ever made more than one voyage in the *Sephora,* you know. Those two old chaps ran the ship. Devil only knows what the skipper wasn't afraid of (all his nerve went to pieces altogether in that hellish spell of bad weather we had) — of what the law would do to him — of his wife, perhaps. Oh, yes! she's on board. Though I don't think she would have meddled. She would have been only too glad to have me out of the ship in any way. The 'brand of Cain' business, don't you see. That's all right. I was ready enough to go off wandering on the face of the earth — and that was price enough to pay for an Abel of that sort. Anyhow, he wouldn't listen to me. 'This thing must take its course. I represent the law here.' He was shaking like a leaf. 'So you won't?' 'No!' 'Then I hope you will be able to sleep on that,' I said, and turned my back on him. 'I wonder that *you* can,' cries he, and locks the door.

"Well, after that, I couldn't. Not very well. That was three weeks ago. We have had a slow passage through the Java Sea; drifted about Carimata for ten days. When we anchored here they thought, I suppose, it was all right. The nearest land (and that's five miles) is the ship's destination; the consul would soon set about catching me; and there would have been no object in bolting to these islets there. I don't suppose there's a drop of water on them. I don't know how it was, but tonight that steward, after bringing me my supper, went out to let me eat it, and left the door unlocked. And I ate it — all there was, too. After I had finished I strolled out on the quarter-deck. I don't know that I meant to do anything. A breath of fresh air was all I wanted, I believe. Then a sudden temptation came over me. I kicked off my slippers and was in the water before I had made up my mind fairly. Somebody heard the splash and they raised an awful hullabaloo. 'He's gone! Lower the boats! He's committed suicide! No, he's swimming.' Certainly I was swimming. It's not so easy for a swimmer like me to commit suicide by drowning. I landed on the nearest islet before the boat left the ship's side. I heard them pulling about in the dark, hailing, and so on, but after a bit they gave up. Everything quieted down and the anchorage became as still as death. I sat down on a stone and began to think. I felt certain they would start searching for me at daylight. There was no place to hide on those stony things — and if there had been, what would have been the good? But now I was clear of that ship, I was not going back. So after a while I took off all my clothes, tied them up in a bundle with a stone inside, and dropped them in the deep water on the outer side of that islet. That was suicide enough for me. Let them think what they liked, but I didn't mean to drown myself. I meant to swim till I sank — but that's not the same thing. I struck out for another of these little islands, and it was from that one that I first saw your riding light. Something to swim for. I went on easily, and on the way I came upon a flat rock a foot or two above water. In the daytime, I dare say, you might make it out with a glass from your poop. I scrambled up on it and rested myself for a bit. Then I made another start. That last spell must have been over a mile."

His whisper was getting fainter and fainter, and all the time he stared straight out through the porthole, in which there was not even a star to be seen. I had not interrupted him. There was something that made comment impossible in his narrative, or perhaps in himself; a sort of feeling, a quality, which I can't find a name for. And when he ceased, all I found was a futile whisper: "So you swam for our light?"

"Yes—straight for it. It was something to swim for. I couldn't see any stars low down because the coast was in the way, and I couldn't see the land, either. The water was like glass. One might have been swimming in a confounded thousand-feet deep cistern with no place for scrambling out anywhere; but what I didn't like was the notion of swimming round and round like a crazed bullock before I gave out; and as I didn't mean to go back . . . No. Do you see me being hauled back, stark naked, off one of these little islands by the scruff of the neck and fighting like a wild beast? Somebody would have got killed for certain, and I did not want any of that. So I went on. Then your ladder—"

"Why didn't you hail the ship?" I asked, a little louder.

He touched my shoulder lightly. Lazy footsteps came right over our heads and stopped. The second mate had crossed from the other side of the poop and might have been hanging over the rail, for all we knew.

"He couldn't hear us talking—could he?" My double breathed into my very ear, anxiously.

His anxiety was an answer, a sufficient answer, to the question I had put to him. An answer containing all the difficulty of that situation. I closed the porthole quietly, to make sure. A louder word might have been overheard.

"Who's that?" he whispered then.

"My second mate. But I don't know much more of the fellow than you do."

And I told him a little about myself. I had been appointed to take charge while I least expected anything of the sort, not quite a fortnight ago. I didn't know either the ship or the people. Hadn't had the time in port to look about me or size anybody up. And as to the crew, all they knew was that I was appointed to take the ship home. For the rest, I was almost as much of a stranger on board as himself, I said. And at the moment I felt it most acutely. I felt that it would take very little to make me a suspect person in the eyes of the ship's company.

He had turned about meantime; and we, the two strangers in the ship, faced each other in identical attitudes.

"Your ladder—" he murmured, after a silence. "Who'd have thought of finding a ladder hanging over at night in a ship anchored out here! I felt just then a very unpleasant faintness. After the life I've been leading for nine weeks, anybody would have got out of condition. I wasn't capable of swimming round as far as your rudder chains. And, lo and behold! there was a ladder to get hold of. After I gripped it I said to myself, 'What's the good?' When I saw a man's head looking over I thought I would swim away presently and leave him shouting—in whatever language it was. I didn't mind being looked at. I—I liked it. And then you speaking to me so quietly—as if you had expected me—made me hold on a little longer. It had been a confounded lonely time—I don't mean while swimming. I was glad to talk a little to somebody that didn't belong to the *Sephora*. As to asking for the captain, that was a mere impulse. It could have been no use, with all the ship knowing about me and the other people pretty certain to be round here in the morning. I don't know — I wanted to be seen, to talk with somebody, before I went on. I don't know what I would have said. . . . 'Fine night, isn't it?' or something of the sort."

"Do you think they will be round here presently?" I asked with some incredulity.

"Quite likely," he said, faintly.

He looked extremely haggard all of a sudden. His head rolled on his shoulders.

"H'm. We shall see then. Meantime get into that bed," I whispered. "Want help? There."

It was a rather high bed-place with a set of drawers underneath. This amazing swimmer really needed the lift I gave him by seizing his leg. He tumbled in, rolled over on his back, and flung one arm across his eyes. And then, with his face nearly hidden, he must have looked exactly as I used to look in that bed. I gazed upon my other self for a while before drawing across carefully the two green serge curtains which ran on a brass rod. I thought for a moment of pinning them together for greater safety, but I sat down on the couch, and once there I felt unwilling to rise and hunt for a pin. I would do it in a moment. I was extremely tired, in a peculiarly intimate way, by the strain of stealthiness, by the effort of whispering and the general secrecy of this excitement. It was three o'clock by now and I had been on my feet since nine, but I was not sleepy; I could not have gone to sleep. I sat there, fagged out, looking at the curtains, trying to clear my mind of the confused sensation of being in two places at once, and greatly bothered by an exasperating knocking in my head. It was a relief to discover suddenly that it was not in my head at all, but on the outside of the door. Before I could collect myself the words "Come in" were out of my mouth, and the steward entered with a tray, bringing in my morning coffee. I had slept, after all, and I was so frightened that I shouted, "This way! I am here, steward," as though he had been miles away. He put down the tray on the table next the couch and only then said, very quietly, "I can see you are here, sir." I felt him give me a keen look, but I dared not meet his eyes just then. He must have wondered why I had drawn the curtains of my bed before going to sleep on the couch. He went out, hooking the door open as usual.

I heard the crew washing decks above me. I knew I would have been told at once if there had been any wind. Calm, I thought, and I was doubly vexed. Indeed, I felt dual more than ever. The steward reappeared suddenly in the doorway. I jumped up from the couch so quickly that he gave a start.

"What do you want here?"

"Close your port, sir — they are washing decks."

"It is closed," I said, reddening.

"Very well, sir." But he did not move from the doorway and returned my stare in an extraordinary, equivocal manner for a time. Then his eyes wavered, all his expression changed, and in a voice unusually gentle, almost coaxingly:

"May I come in to take the empty cup away, sir?"

"Of course!" I turned my back on him while he popped in and out. Then I unhooked and closed the door and even pushed the bolt. This sort of thing could not go on very long. The cabin was as hot as an oven, too. I took a peep at my double, and discovered that he had not moved, his arm was still over his eyes; but his chest heaved; his hair was wet; his chin glistened with perspiration. I reached over him and opened the port.

"I must show myself on deck," I reflected.

Of course, theoretically, I could do what I liked, with no one to say nay to me within the whole circle of the horizon; but to lock my cabin door and take the key away I did not dare. Directly I put my head out of the companion I saw the group of my two officers, the second mate barefooted, the chief mate in long india-rubber boots, near the break of the poop, and the steward halfway down the poop ladder talking to them eagerly. He happened to catch sight of me and dived, the second ran down on the main deck shouting some order or other, and the chief mate came to meet me, touching his cap.

There was a sort of curiosity in his eye that I did not like. I don't know whether the steward had told them that I was "queer" only, or downright drunk, but I know the man meant to have a good look at me. I watched him coming with a smile which, as he got into point-blank range, took effect and froze his very whiskers. I did not give him time to open his lips.

"Square the yards by lifts and braces before the hands go to breakfast."

It was the first particular order I had given on board that ship; and I stayed on deck to see it executed, too. I had felt the need of asserting myself without loss of time. That sneering young cub got taken down a peg or two on that occasion, and I also seized the opportunity of having a good look at the face of every foremast man as they filed past me to go to the after braces. At breakfast time, eating nothing myself, I presided with such frigid dignity that the two mates were only too glad to escape from the cabin as soon as decency permitted; and all the time the dual working of my mind distracted me almost to the point of insanity. I was constantly watching myself, my secret self, as dependent on my actions as my own personality, sleeping in that bed, behind that door which faced me as I sat at the head of the table. It was very much like being mad, only it was worse because one was aware of it.

I had to shake him for a solid minute, but when at last he opened his eyes it was in the full possession of his senses, with an inquiring look.

"All's well so far," I whispered. "Now you must vanish into the bathroom."

He did so, as noiseless as a ghost, and I then rang for the steward, and facing him boldly, directed him to tidy up my stateroom while I was having my bath — "and be quick about it." As my tone admitted of no excuses, he said, "Yes, sir," and ran off to fetch his dustpan and brushes. I took a bath and did most of my dressing, splashing, and whistling softly for the steward's edification, while the secret sharer of my life stood drawn up bolt upright in that little space, his face looking very sunken in daylight, his eyelids lowered under the stern, dark line of his eyebrows drawn together by a slight frown.

When I left him there to go back to my room the steward was finishing dusting. I sent for the mate and engaged him in some insignificant conversation. It was, as it were, trifling with the terrific character of his whiskers; but my object was to give him an opportunity for a good look at my cabin. And then I could at last shut, with a clear conscience, the door of my stateroom and get my double back into the recessed part. There was nothing else for it. He had to sit still on a small folding stool, half smothered by the heavy coats hanging there. We listened to the steward going into the bathroom out of the saloon, filling the water bottles there, scrubbing the bath, setting things to rights, whisk, bang, clatter — out again into the saloon — turn the key — click. Such was my scheme for keeping my second self invisible. Nothing better could be contrived under the circumstances. And there we sat; I at my writing desk ready to appear busy with some papers, he behind me, out of sight of the door. It would not have been prudent to talk in daytime; and I could not have stood the excitement of that queer sense of whispering to myself. Now and then, glancing over my shoulder, I saw him far back there, sitting rigidly on the low stool, his bare feet close together, his arms folded, his head hanging on his breast — and perfectly still. Anybody would have taken him for me.

I was fascinated by it myself. Every moment I had to glance over my shoulder. I was looking at him when a voice outside the door said:

"Beg pardon, sir."

"Well!" . . . I kept my eyes on him, and so, when the voice outside the door announced, "There's a ship's boat coming our way, sir," I saw him give a start — the first movement he had made for hours. But he did not raise his bowed head.

"All right. Get the ladder over."

I hesitated. Should I whisper something to him? But what? His immobility seemed to have been never disturbed. What could I tell him he did not know already? . . . Finally I went on deck.

2

The skipper of the *Sephora* had a thin red whisker all round his face, and the sort of complexion that goes with hair of that color; also the particular, rather smeary shade of blue in the eyes. He was not exactly a showy figure; his shoulders were high, his stature but middling — one leg slightly more bandy than the other. He shook hands, looking vaguely around. A spiritless tenacity was his main characteristic, I judged. I behaved with a politeness which seemed to disconcert him. Perhaps he was shy. He mumbled to me as if he were ashamed of what he was saying: gave his name (it was something like Archbold — but at this distance of years I hardly am sure), his ship's name, and a few other particulars of that sort, in the manner of a criminal making a reluctant and doleful confession. He had had terrible weather on the passage out — terrible — terrible — wife aboard, too.

By this time we were seated in the cabin and the steward brought in a tray with a bottle and glasses. "Thanks! No." Never took liquor. Would have some water, though. He drank two tumblerfuls. Terrible thirsty work. Ever since daylight had been exploring the islands round his ship.

"What was that for — fun?" I asked, with an appearance of polite interest.

"No!" He sighed. "Painful duty."

As he persisted in his mumbling and I wanted my double to hear every word, I hit upon the notion of informing him that I regretted to say I was hard of hearing.

"Such a young man, too!" he nodded, keeping his smeary blue, unintelligent eyes fastened upon me. What was the cause of it — some disease? he inquired, without the least sympathy and as if he thought that, if so, I'd got no more than I deserved.

"Yes; disease," I admitted in a cheerful tone which seemed to shock him. But my point was gained, because he had to raise his voice to give me his tale. It is not worth while to record that version. It was just over two months since all this had happened, and he had thought so much about it that he seemed completely muddled as to its bearings, but still immensely impressed.

"What would you think of such a thing happening on board your own ship? I've had the *Sephora* for these fifteen years. I am a well-known shipmaster."

He was densely distressed — and perhaps I should have sympathized with him if I had been able to detach my mental vision from the unsuspected sharer of my cabin as though he were my second self. There he was on the other side of the bulkhead, four or five feet from us, no more, as we sat in the saloon. I looked politely at Captain Archbold (if that was his name), but it was the other I saw, in a gray sleeping suit, seated on a low stool, his bare feet close together, his arms folded, and every word said between us falling into the ears of his dark head bowed on his chest.

"I've been at sea now, man and boy, for seven-and-thirty years, and I've never heard of such a thing happening in an English ship. And that it should be my ship. Wife on board, too."

I was hardly listening to him.

"Don't you think," I said, "that the heavy sea which, you told me, came aboard just then might have killed the man? I have seen the sheer weight of a sea kill a man very neatly, by simply breaking his neck."

"Good God!" he uttered, impressively, fixing his smeary blue eyes on me. "The sea! No man killed by the sea ever looked like that." He seemed positively scandalized at my suggestion. And as I gazed at him, certainly not prepared for anything original on his part, he advanced his head close to mine and thrust his tongue out at me so suddenly that I couldn't help starting back.

After scoring over my calmness in this graphic way he nodded wisely. If I had seen the sight, he assured me, I would never forget it as long as I lived. The weather was too bad to give the corpse a proper sea burial. So next day at dawn they took it up on the poop, covering its face with a bit of bunting; he read a short prayer, and then, just as it was, in its oilskins and long boots, they launched it amongst those mountainous seas that seemed ready every moment to swallow up the ship herself and the terrified lives on board of her.

"That reefed foresail saved you," I threw in.

"Under God — it did," he exclaimed fervently. "It was by a special mercy, I firmly believe, that it stood some of those hurricane squalls."

"It was the setting of that sail which —" I began.

"God's own hand in it," he interrupted me. "Nothing less could have done it. I don't mind telling you that I hardly dared give the order. It seemed impossible that we could touch anything without losing it, and then our last hope would have been gone."

The terror of that gale was on him yet. I let him go on for a bit, then said, casually — as if returning to a minor subject:

"You were very anxious to give up your mate to the shore people, I believe?"

He was. To the law. His obscure tenacity on that point had in it something incomprehensible and a little awful; something, as it were, mystical, quite apart from his anxiety that he should not be suspected of "countenancing any doings of that sort." Seven-and-thirty virtuous years at sea, of which over twenty of immaculate command, and the last fifteen in the *Sephora*, seemed to have laid him under some pitiless obligation.

"And you know," he went on, groping shamefacedly amongst his feelings, "I did not engage that young fellow. His people had some interest with my owners. I was in a way forced to take him on. He looked very smart, very gentlemanly, and all that. But do you know — I never liked him, somehow. I am a plain man. You see, he wasn't exactly the sort for the chief mate of a ship like the *Sephora*."

I had become so connected in thoughts and impressions with the secret sharer of my cabin that I felt as if I, personally, were being given to understand that I, too, was not the sort that would have done for the chief mate of a ship like the *Sephora*. I had no doubt of it in my mind.

"Not at all the style of man. You understand," he insisted, superfluously, looking hard at me.

I smiled urbanely. He seemed at a loss for a while.

"I suppose I must report a suicide."

"Beg pardon?"

"Sui-cide! That's what I'll have to write to my owners directly I get in."

"Unless you manage to recover him before tomorrow," I assented, dispassionately. . . . "I mean, alive."

He mumbled something which I really did not catch, and I turned my ear to him in a puzzled manner. He fairly bawled:

"The land — I say, the mainland is at least seven miles off my anchorage."

"About that."

My lack of excitement, of curiosity, of surprise, of any sort of pronounced interest, began to arouse his distrust. But except for the felicitous pretense of deafness I had not tried to pretend anything. I had felt utterly incapable of playing the part of ignorance properly, and therefore was afraid to try. It is also certain that he had brought some ready-made suspicions with him, and that he viewed my politeness as a strange and unnatural phenomenon. And yet how else could I have received him? Not heartily! That was impossible for psychological reasons, which I need not state here. My only object was to keep off his inquiries. Surlily? Yes, but surliness might have provoked a point-blank question. From its novelty to him and from its nature, punctilious courtesy was the manner best calculated to restrain the man. But there was the danger of his breaking through my defense bluntly. I could not, I think, have met him by a direct lie, also for psychological (not moral) reasons. If he had only known how afraid I was of his putting my feeling of identity with the other to the test! But, strangely enough — (I thought of it only afterward) — I believe that he was not a little disconcerted by the reverse side of that weird situation, by something in me that reminded him of the man he was seeking — suggested a mysterious similitude to the young fellow he had distrusted and disliked from the first.

However that might have been, the silence was not very prolonged. He took another oblique step.

"I reckon I had no more than a two-mile pull to your ship. Not a bit more."

"And quite enough, too, in this awful heat," I said.

Another pause full of mistrust followed. Necessity, they say, is mother of invention, but fear, too, is not barren of ingenious suggestions. And I was afraid he would ask me point-blank for news of my other self.

"Nice little saloon, isn't it?" I remarked, as if noticing for the first time the way his eyes roamed from one closed door to the other. "And very well fitted out, too. Here, for instance," I continued, reaching over the back of my seat negligently and flinging the door open, "is my bathroom."

He made an eager movement, but hardly gave it a glance. I got up, shut the door of the bathroom, and invited him to have a look round, as if I were very proud of my accommodation. He had to rise and be shown round, but he went through the business without any raptures whatever.

"And now we'll have a look at my stateroom," I declared, in a voice as loud as I dared to make it, crossing the cabin to the starboard side with purposely heavy steps.

He followed me in and gazed around. My intelligent double had vanished. I played my part.

"Very convenient — isn't it?"

"Very nice. Very comf . . ." He didn't finish, and went out brusquely as if to escape from some unrighteous wiles of mine. But it was not to be. I had been too frightened not to feel vengeful; I felt I had him on the run, and I meant to keep him on the run. My polite insistence must have had something menacing in it, because he gave in suddenly. And I did not let him off a single item; mate's room, pantry, storerooms, the very sail locker which was also under the poop — he had to look into them all. When at last I showed him out on the quarter-deck he drew a long, spiritless sigh, and mumbled dismally that he must really be going back to his ship now. I desired my mate, who had joined us, to see to the captain's boat.

The man of whiskers gave a blast on the whistle which he used to wear hanging round his neck, and yelled, "*Sephoras away!*" My double down there in my cabin must have heard, and certainly could not feel more relieved than I. Four fellows came running out from somewhere forward and went over the side, while my own men, appearing on deck too, lined the rail. I escorted my visitor to the gangway ceremoniously, and nearly overdid it. He was a tenacious beast. On the very ladder he lingered, and in that unique, guiltily conscientious manner of sticking to the point.

"I say . . . you . . . you don't think that —"

I covered his voice loudly:

"Certainly not. . . . I am delighted. Good-by."

I had an idea of what he meant to say, and just saved myself by the privilege of defective hearing. He was too shaken generally to insist, but my mate, close witness of that parting, looked mystified and his face took on a thoughtful cast. As I did not want to appear as if I wished to avoid all communication with my officers, he had the opportunity to address me.

"Seems a very nice man. His boat's crew told our chaps a very extraordinary story, if what I am told by the steward is true. I suppose you had it from the captain, sir?"

"Yes. I had a story from the captain."

"A very horrible affair — isn't it, sir?"

"It is."

"Beats all these tales we hear about murders in Yankee ships."

"I don't think it beats them. I don't think it resembles them in the least."

"Bless my soul — you don't say so! But of course I've no acquaintance whatever with American ships, not I, so I couldn't go against your knowledge. It's horrible enough for me. . . . But the queerest part is that those fellows seemed to have some idea the man was hidden aboard here. They had really. Did you ever hear of such a thing?"

"Preposterous — isn't it?"

We were walking to and fro athwart the quarter-deck. No one of the crew forward could be seen (the day was Sunday), and the mate pursued:

"There was some little dispute about it. Our chaps took offense. 'As if we would harbor a thing like that,' they said. 'Wouldn't you like to look for him in our coal hole?' Quite a tiff. But they made it up in the end. I suppose he did drown himself. Don't you, sir?"

"I don't suppose anything."

"You have no doubt in the matter, sir?"

"None whatever."

I left him suddenly. I felt I was producing a bad impression, but with my double down there it was most trying to be on deck. And it was almost as trying to be below. Altogether a nerve-trying situation. But on the whole I felt less torn in two when I was with him. There was no one in the whole ship whom I dared take into my confidence. Since the hands had got to know his story, it would have been impossible to pass him off for anyone else, and an accidental discovery was to be dreaded now more than ever. . . .

The steward being engaged in laying the table for dinner, we could talk only with our eyes when I first went down. Later in the afternoon we had a cautious try at whispering. The Sunday quietness of the ship was against us; the stillness of air and water around her was against us; the elements, the men were against us — everything was against us in our secret partnership; time itself — for this could not go on forever. The very trust in Providence was, I suppose, denied to his guilt. Shall I confess that this thought cast me down very much? And as to the chapter of accidents which counts for so much in the book of success, I could only hope that it was closed. For what favorable accident could be expected?

"Did you hear everything?" were my first words as soon as we took up our position side by side, leaning over my bed-place.

He had. And the proof of it was his earnest whisper, "The man told you he hardly dared to give the order."

I understood the reference to be to that saving foresail.

"Yes. He was afraid of it being lost in the setting."

"I assure you he never gave the order. He may think he did, but he never gave it. He stood there with me on the break of the poop after the maintopsail blew away, and whimpered about our last hope — positively whimpered about it and nothing else — and the night coming on! To hear one's skipper go on like that in such weather was enough to drive any fellow out of his mind. It worked me up into a sort of desperation. I just took it into my own hands and went away from him, boiling, and—. But what's the use telling you? *You* know! . . . Do you think that if I had not been pretty fierce with them I should have got the men to do anything? Not it! The bosun perhaps? Perhaps! It wasn't a heavy sea — it was a sea gone mad! I suppose the end of the world will be something like that; and a man may have the heart to see it coming once and be done with it — but to have to face it day after day — I don't blame anybody. I was precious little better than the rest. Only — I was an officer of that old coal-wagon, anyhow —"

"I quite understand," I conveyed that sincere assurance into his ear. He was out of breath with whispering; I could hear him pant slightly. It was all very simple. The same strung-up force which had given twenty-four men a chance, at least, for their lives, had, in a sort of recoil, crushed an unworthy mutinous existence.

But I had no leisure to weigh the merits of the matter — footsteps in the saloon, a heavy knock. "There's enough wind to get under way with, sir." Here was the call of a new claim upon my thoughts and even upon my feelings.

"Turn the hands up," I cried through the door. "I'll be on deck directly."

I was going out to make the acquaintance of my ship. Before I left the cabin our eyes met — the eyes of the only two strangers on board. I pointed to the recessed part where the little campstool awaited him and laid my finger on my lips. He made a gesture — somewhat vague — a little mysterious, accompanied by a faint smile, as if of regret.

This is not the place to enlarge upon the sensations of a man who feels for the first time a ship move under his feet to his own independent word. In my case they were not unalloyed. I was not wholly alone with my command; for there was that stranger in my cabin. Or rather, I was not completely and wholly with her. Part of me was absent. That mental feeling of being in two places at once affected me physically as if the mood of secrecy had penetrated my very soul. Before an hour had elapsed since the ship had begun to move, having occasion to ask the mate (he stood by my side) to take a compass bearing of the Pagoda, I caught myself reaching up to his ear in whispers. I say I caught myself, but enough had escaped to startle the man. I can't describe it otherwise than by saying that he shied. A grave, preoccupied manner, as though he were in possession of some perplexing intelligence, did not leave him henceforth. A little later I moved away from the rail to look at the compass with such a stealthy gait that the helmsman noticed it — and I could not help noticing the unusual roundness of his eyes. These are trifling instances, though it's to no commander's advantage to be suspected of ludicrous eccentricities. But I was also more seriously affected. There are to a seaman certain words, gestures, that should in given conditions come as naturally, as instinctively as the winking of a menaced eye. A certain order should spring on to his lips without thinking; a certain sign should get itself made, so to speak, without reflection. But all unconscious alertness had abandoned me. I had to make an effort of will to recall myself back (from the cabin) to the conditions of the moment. I felt that I was appearing an irresolute commander to those people who were watching me more or less critically.

And, besides, there were the scares. On the second day out, for instance, coming off the deck in the afternoon (I had straw slippers on my bare feet) I stopped at the open pantry door and spoke to the steward. He was doing something there with his back to me. At the sound of my voice he nearly jumped out of his skin, as the saying is, and incidentally broke a cup.

"What on earth's the matter with you?" I asked, astonished.

He was extremely confused. "Beg your pardon, sir. I made sure you were in your cabin."

"You see I wasn't."

"No, sir. I could have sworn I had heard you moving in there not a moment ago. It's most extraordinary . . . very sorry, sir."

I passed on with an inward shudder. I was so identified with my secret double that I did not even mention the fact in those scanty, fearful whispers we exchanged. I suppose he had made some slight noise of some kind or other. It would have been miraculous if he hadn't at one time or another. And yet, haggard as he appeared, he looked always perfectly self-controlled, more than calm — almost invulnerable. On my suggestion he remained almost entirely in the bathroom, which, upon the whole, was the safest place. There could be really no shadow of an excuse for anyone ever wanting to go in there, once the steward had done with it. It was a very tiny place. Sometimes he reclined on the floor, his legs bent, his head sustained on one elbow. At others I would find him on the campstool, sitting in his gray sleeping suit and with his cropped dark hair like a patient, unmoved convict. At night I would smuggle him into my bed-place, and we would whisper together, with the regular footfalls of the officer of the watch passing and repassing over our heads. It was an infinitely miserable time. It was lucky that some tins of fine preserves were stowed in a locker in my stateroom; hard bread I could always get hold of; and so he lived on stewed chicken, paté de foie gras, asparagus, cooked oysters, sardines — on all sorts of abominable sham delicacies out of tins. My early morning coffee he always drank; and it was all I dared do for him in that respect.

Every day there was the horrible maneuvering to go through so that my room and then the bathroom should be done in the usual way. I came to hate the sight of the steward, to abhor the voice of that harmless man. I felt that it was he who would bring on the disaster of discovery. It hung like a sword over our heads.

The fourth day out, I think (we were then working down the east side of the Gulf of Siam, tack for tack, in light winds and smooth water) — the fourth day, I say, of this miserable juggling with the unavoidable, as we sat at our evening meal, that man, whose slightest movement I dreaded, after putting down the dishes ran up on deck busily. This could not be dangerous. Presently he came down again; and then it appeared that he had remembered a coat of mine which I had thrown over a rail to dry after having been wetted in a shower which had passed over the ship in the afternoon. Sitting stolidly at the head of the table I became terrified at the sight of the garment on his arm. Of course he made for my door. There was no time to lose.

"Steward," I thundered. My nerves were so shaken that I could not govern my voice and conceal my agitation. This was the sort of thing that made my terrifically whiskered mate tap his forehead with his forefinger. I had detected him using that gesture while talking on deck with a confidential air to the carpenter. It was too far to hear a word, but I had no doubt that this pantomime could only refer to the strange new captain.

"Yes, sir," the pale-faced steward turned resignedly to me. It was this maddening course of being shouted at, checked without rhyme or reason, arbitrarily chased out of my cabin, suddenly called into it, sent flying out of his pantry on incomprehensible errands, that accounted for the growing wretchedness of his expression.

"Where are you going with that coat?"

"To your room, sir."

"Is there another shower coming?"

"I'm sure I don't know, sir. Shall I go up again and see, sir?"

"No! never mind."

My object was attained, as of course my other self in there would have heard everything that passed. During this interlude my two officers never raised their eyes off their respective plates; but the lip of that confounded cub, the second mate, quivered visibly.

I expected the steward to hook my coat on and come out at once. He was very slow about it; but I dominated my nervousness sufficiently not to shout after him. Suddenly I became aware (it could be heard plainly enough) that the fellow for some reason or other was opening the door of the bathroom. It was the end. The place was literally not big enough to swing a cat in. My voice died in my throat and I went stony all over. I expected to hear a yell of surprise and terror, and made a movement, but had not the strength to get on my legs. Everything remained still. Had my second self taken the poor wretch by the throat? I don't know what I would have done next moment if I had not seen the steward come out of my room, close the door, and then stand quietly by the sideboard.

Saved, I thought. But, no! Lost! Gone! He was gone!

I laid my knife and fork down and leaned back in my chair. My head swam. After a while, when sufficiently recovered to speak in a steady voice, I instructed my mate to put the ship round at eight o'clock himself.

"I won't come on deck," I went on. "I think I'll turn in, and unless the wind shifts I don't want to be disturbed before midnight. I feel a bit seedy."

"You did look middling bad a little while ago," the chief mate remarked without showing any great concern.

They both went out, and I stared at the steward clearing the table. There was nothing to be read on that wretched man's face. But why did he avoid my eyes I asked myself. Then I thought I should like to hear the sound of his voice.

"Steward!"

"Sir!" Startled as usual.

"Where did you hang up that coat?"

"In the bathroom, sir." The usual anxious tone. "It's not quite dry yet, sir."

For some time longer I sat in the cuddy. Had my double vanished as he had come? But of his coming there was an explanation, whereas his disappearance would be inexplicable. . . . I went slowly into my dark room, shut the door, lighted the lamp, and for a time dared not turn round. When at last I did I saw him standing bolt upright in the narrow recessed part. It would not be true to say I had a shock, but an irresistible doubt of his bodily existence flitted through my mind. Can it be, I asked myself, that he is not visible to other eyes than mine? It was like being haunted. Motionless, with a grave face, he raised his hands slightly at me in a gesture which meant clearly, "Heavens! what a narrow escape!" Narrow indeed. I think I had come creeping quietly as near insanity as any man who has not actually gone over the border. That gesture restrained me, so to speak.

The mate with the terrific whiskers was now putting the ship on the other tack. In the moment of profound silence which follows upon the hands going to their stations I heard on the poop his raised voice: "Hard alee!" and the distant shout of the order repeated on the maindeck. The sails, in that light breeze, made but a faint fluttering noise. It ceased. The ship was coming round slowly; I held my breath in the renewed stillness of expectation; one wouldn't have thought that there was a single living soul on her decks. A sudden brisk shout, "Mainsail haul!" broke the spell, and in the noisy cries and rush overhead of the men running away with the main brace we two, down in my cabin, came together in our usual positions by the bed-place.

He did not wait for my question. "I heard him fumbling here and just managed to squat myself down in the bath," he whispered to me. "The fellow only opened the door and put his arm in to hang the coat up. All the same—"

"I never thought of that," I whispered back, even more appalled than before at the closeness of the shave, and marveling at that something unyielding in his character which was carrying him through so finely. There was no agitation in his whisper. Whoever was being driven distracted, it was not he. He was sane. And the proof of his sanity was continued when he took up the whispering again.

"It would never do for me to come to life again."

It was something that a ghost might have said. But what he was alluding to was his old captain's reluctant admission of the theory of suicide. It would obviously serve his turn—if I had understood at all the view which seemed to govern the unalterable purpose of his action.

"You must maroon me as soon as ever you can get amongst these islands off the Cambodje shore," he went on.

"Maroon you! We are not living in a boy's adventure tale," I protested. His scornful whispering took me up.

"We aren't indeed! There's nothing of a boy's tale in this. But there's nothing else for it. I want no more. You don't suppose I am afraid of what can be done to me? Prison or gallows or whatever they may please. But you don't see me coming back to explain such things to an old fellow in a wig and twelve respectable tradesmen, do you? What can they know whether I am guilty or not—or of *what* I am guilty, either? That's my affair. What does the Bible say? 'Driven off the face of the earth.' Very well. I am off the face of the earth now. As I came at night so I shall go."

"Impossible!" I murmured. "You can't."

"Can't? . . . Not naked like a soul on the Day of Judgment. I shall freeze on to this sleeping suit. The Last Day is not yet—and . . . you have understood thoroughly. Didn't you?"

I felt suddenly ashamed of myself. I may say truly that I understood—and my hesitation in letting that man swim away from my ship's side had been a mere sham sentiment, a sort of cowardice.

"It can't be done now till next night," I breathed out. "The ship is on the offshore tack and the wind may fail us."

"As long as I know that you understand," he whispered. "But of course you do. It's a great satisfaction to have got somebody to understand. You seem to have been there on purpose." And in the same whisper, as if we two whenever we talked had to say things to each other which were not fit for the world to hear, he added, "It's very wonderful."

We remained side by side talking in our secret way—but sometimes silent or just exchanging a whispered word or two at long intervals. And as usual he stared through the port. A breath of wind came now and again into our faces. The ship might have been moored in dock, so gently and on an even keel she slipped through the water, that did not murmur even at our passage, shadowy and silent like a phantom sea.

At midnight I went on deck, and to my mate's great surprise put the ship round on the other tack. His terrible whiskers flitted round me in silent criticism. I certainly should not have done it if it had been only a question of getting out of that sleepy gulf as quickly as possible. I believe he told the second mate, who relieved him, that it was a great want of judgment. The other only yawned. That intolerable cub shuffled about so sleepily and lolled against the rails in such a slack, improper fashion that I came down on him sharply.

"Aren't you properly awake yet?"

"Yes, sir! I am awake."

"Well, then, be good enough to hold yourself as if you were. And keep a lookout. If there's any current we'll be closing with some islands before daylight."

The east side of the gulf is fringed with islands, some solitary, others in groups. On the blue background of the high coast they seem to float on silvery patches of calm water, arid and gray, or dark green and rounded like clumps of evergreen bushes, with the larger ones, a mile or two long, showing the outlines of ridges, ribs of gray rock under the dark mantle of matted leafage. Unknown to trade, to travel, almost to geography, the manner of life they harbor is an unsolved secret. There must be villages—settlements of fishermen at least — on the largest of them, and some communication with the world is probably kept up by native craft. But all that forenoon, as we headed for them, fanned along by the faintest of breezes, I saw no sign of man or canoe in the field of the telescope I kept on pointing at the scattered group.

At noon I gave no orders for a change of course, and the mate's whiskers became much concerned and seemed to be offering themselves unduly to my notice. At last I said:

"I am going to stand right in. Quite in — as far as I can take her."

The stare of extreme surprise imparted an air of ferocity also to his eyes, and he looked truly terrific for a moment.

"We're not doing well in the middle of the gulf," I continued, casually. "I am going to look for the land breezes tonight."

"Bless my soul! Do you mean, sir, in the dark amongst the lot of all them islands and reefs and shoals?"

"Well — if there are any regular land breezes at all on this coast one must get close inshore to find them, mustn't one?"

"Bless my soul!" he exclaimed again under his breath. All that afternoon he wore a dreamy, contemplative appearance which in him was a mark of perplexity. After dinner I went into my stateroom as if I meant to take some rest. There we two bent our dark heads over a half-unrolled chart lying on my bed.

"There," I said. "It's got to be Koh-ring. I've been looking at it ever since sunrise. It has got two hills and a low point. It must be inhabited. And on the coast opposite there is what looks like the mouth of a biggish river — with some town, no doubt, not far up. It's the best chance for you that I can see."

"Anything. Koh-ring let it be."

He looked thoughtfully at the chart as if surveying chances and distances from a lofty height — and following with his eyes his own figure wandering on the blank land of Cochin-China, and then passing off that piece of paper clean out of sight into uncharted regions. And it was as if the ship had two captains to plan her course for her. I had been so worried and restless running up and down that I had not had the patience to dress that day. I had remained in my sleeping suit, with straw slippers and a soft floppy hat. The closeness of the heat in the gulf had been most oppressive, and the crew were used to see me wandering in that airy attire.

"She will clear the south point as she heads now," I whispered into his ear. "Goodness only knows when, though, but certainly after dark. I'll edge her in to half a mile, as far as I may be able to judge in the dark — "

"Be careful," he murmured, warningly — and I realized suddenly that all my future, the only future for which I was fit, would perhaps go irretrievably to pieces in any mishap to my first command.

I could not stop a moment longer in the room. I motioned him to get out of sight and made my way on the poop. That unplayful cub had the watch. I walked up and down for a while thinking things out, then beckoned him over.

"Send a couple of hands to open the two quarter-deck ports," I said, mildly.

He actually had the impudence, or else so forgot himself in his wonder at such an incomprehensible order, as to repeat:

"Open the quarter-deck ports! What for, sir?"

"The only reason you need concern yourself about is because I tell you to do so. Have them open wide and fastened properly."

He reddened and went off, but I believe made some jeering remark to the carpenter as to the sensible practice of ventilating a ship's quarter-deck. I know he popped into the mate's cabin to impart the fact to him because the whiskers came on deck, as it were by chance, and stole glances at me from below — for signs of lunacy or drunkenness, I suppose.

A little before supper, feeling more restless than ever, I rejoined, for a moment, my second self. And to find him sitting so quietly was surprising, like something against nature, inhuman.

I developed my plan in a hurried whisper.

"I shall stand in as close as I dare and then put her round. I shall presently find means to smuggle you out of here into the sail locker, which communicates with the lobby. But there is an opening, a sort of square for hauling the sails out, which gives straight on the quarter-deck and which is never closed in fine weather, so as to give air to the sails. When the ship's way is deadened in stays and all the hands are aft at the main braces you shall have a clear road to slip out and get overboard through the open quarter-deck port. I've had them both fastened up. Use a rope's end to lower yourself into the water so as to avoid a splash — you know. It could be heard and cause some beastly complication."

He kept silent for a while, then whispered, "I understand."

"I won't be there to see you go," I began with an effort. "The rest . . . I only hope I have understood, too."

"You have. From first to last," and for the first time there seemed to be a faltering, something strained in his whisper. He caught hold of my arm, but the ringing of the supper bell made me start. He didn't, though; he only released his grip.

After supper I didn't come below again till well past eight o'clock. The faint, steady breeze was loaded with dew; and the wet, darkened sails held all there was of propelling power in it. The night, clear and starry, sparkled darkly, and the opaque, lightless patches shifting slowly against the low stars were the drifting islets. On the port bow there was a big one more distant and shadowily imposing by the great space of sky it eclipsed.

On opening the door I had a back view of my very own self looking at a chart. He had come out of the recess and was standing near the table.

"Quite dark enough," I whispered.

He stepped back and leaned against my bed with a level, quiet glance. I sat on the couch. We had nothing to say to each other. Over our heads the officer of the watch moved here and there. Then I heard him move quickly. I knew what was meant. He was making for the companion; and presently his voice was outside my door.

"We are drawing in pretty fast, sir. Land looks rather close."

"Very well," I answered. "I am coming on deck directly."

I waited till he was gone out of the cuddy, then rose. My double moved too. The time had come to exchange our last whispers, for neither of us was ever to hear each other's natural voice.

"Look here!" I opened a drawer and took out three sovereigns. "Take this, anyhow. I've got six and I'd give you the lot, only I must keep a little money to buy some fruit and vegetables for the crew from native boats as we go through Sunda Straits."

He shook his head.

"Take it," I urged him, whispering desperately. "No one can tell what —"

He smiled and slapped meaningly the only pocket of the sleeping jacket. It was not safe, certainly. But I produced a large old sick handkerchief of mine, and tying the three pieces of gold in a corner, pressed it on him. He was touched, I suppose, because he took it at last and tied it quickly round his waist under the jacket, on his bare skin.

Our eyes met; several seconds elapsed, till, our glances still mingled, I extended my hand and turned the lamp out. Then I passed through the cuddy, leaving the door of my room wide open. . . . "Steward!"

He was still lingering in the pantry in the greatness of his zeal, giving a rub-up to a plated cruet stand the last thing before going to bed. Being careful not to wake up the mate, whose room was opposite, I spoke in an undertone.

He looked round anxiously. "Sir!"

"Can you get me a little hot water from the galley?"

"I am afraid, sir, the galley fire's been out for some time now."

"Go and see."

He fled up the stairs.

"Now," I whispered, loudly, into the saloon — too loudly, perhaps, but I was afraid I couldn't make a sound. He was by my side in an instant — the double captain slipped past the stairs — through the tiny dark passage . . . a sliding door. We were in the sail locker, scrambling on our knees over the sails. A sudden thought struck me. I saw myself wandering barefooted, bareheaded, the sun beating on my dark poll. I snatched off my floppy hat and tried hurriedly in the dark to ram it on my other self. He dodged and fended off silently. I wonder what he thought had come to me before he understood and suddenly desisted. Our hands met gropingly, lingered united in a steady, motionless clasp for a second. . . . No word was breathed by either of us when they separated.

I was standing quietly by the pantry door when the steward returned.

"Sorry, sir. Kettle barely warm. Shall I light the spirit lamp?"

"Never mind."

I came out on deck slowly. It was now a matter of conscience to shave the land as close as possible — for now he must go overboard whenever the ship was put in stays. Must! There could be no going back for him. After a moment I walked over to leeward and my heart flew into my mouth at the nearness of the land on the bow. Under any other circumstances I would not have held on a minute longer. The second mate had followed me anxiously.

I looked on till I felt I could command my voice.

"She will weather," I said then in a quiet tone.

"Are you going to try that, sir?" he stammered out incredulously.

I took no notice of him and raised my tone just enough to be heard by the helmsman.

"Keep her good full."

"Good full, sir."

The wind fanned my cheek, the sails slept, the world was silent. The strain of watching the dark loom of the land grow bigger and denser was too much for me. I had shut my eyes — because the ship must go closer. She must! The stillness was intolerable. Were we standing still?

When I opened my eyes the second view started my heart with a thump. The black southern hill of Koh-ring seemed to hang right over the ship like a towering fragment of the everlasting night. On that enormous mass of blackness there was not a gleam to be seen, not a sound to be heard. It was gliding irresistibly toward us and yet seemed already within reach of the hand. I saw the vague figures of the watch grouped in the waist, gazing in awed silence.

"Are you going on, sir?" inquired an unsteady voice at my elbow.

I ignored it. I had to go on.

"Keep her full. Don't check her way. That won't do now," I said warningly.

"I can't see the sails very well," the helmsman answered me, in strange, quavering tones.

Was she close enough? Already she was, I won't say in the shadow of the land, but in the very blackness of it, already swallowed up as it were, gone too close to be recalled, gone from me altogether.

"Give the mate a call," I said to the young man who stood at my elbow as still as death. "And turn all hands up."

My tone had a borrowed loudness reverberated from the height of the land. Several voices cried out together: "We are all on deck, sir."

Then stillness again, with the great shadow gliding closer, towering higher, without a light, without a sound. Such a hush had fallen on the ship that she might have been a bark of the dead floating in slowly under the very gate of Erebus.

"My God! Where are we?"

It was the mate moaning at my elbow. He was thunderstruck, and as it were deprived of the moral support of his whiskers. He clapped his hands and absolutely cried out, "Lost!"

"Be quiet," I said sternly.

He lowered his tone, but I saw the shadowy gesture of his despair. "What are we doing here?"

"Looking for the land wind."

He made as if to tear his hair, and addressed me recklessly.

"She will never get out. You have done it, sir. I knew it'd end in something like this. She will never weather, and you are too close now to stay. She'll drift ashore before she's round. O my God!"

I caught his arm as he was raising it to batter his poor devoted head, and shook it violently.

"She's ashore already," he wailed, trying to tear himself away.

"Is she? . . . Keep good full there!"

"Good full, sir," cried the helmsman in a frightened, thin, childlike voice.

I hadn't let go the mate's arm and went on shaking it. "Ready about, do you hear? You go forward" — shake — "and stop there" — shake — "and hold your noise" — shake — "and see these head sheets properly overhauled" — shake, shake — shake.

And all the time I dared not look toward the land lest my heart should fail me. I released my grip at last and he ran forward as if fleeing for dear life.

I wondered what my double there in the sail locker thought of this commotion. He was able to hear everything — and perhaps he was able to understand why, on my conscience, it had to be thus close — no less. My first order "Hard alee!" re-echoed ominously under the towering shadow of Koh-ring as if I had shouted in a mountain gorge. And then I watched the land intently. In that smooth water and light wind it was impossible to feel the ship coming-to. No! I could not feel her. And my second self was making now ready to slip out and lower himself overboard. Perhaps he was gone already . . . ?

The great black mass brooding over our very mastheads began to pivot away from the ship's side silently. And now I forgot the secret stranger ready to depart, and remembered only that I was a total stranger to the ship. I did not know her. Would she do it? How was she to be handled?

I swung the mainyard and waited helplessly. She was perhaps stopped, and her very fate hung in the balance, with the black mass of Koh-ring like the gate of the everlasting night towering over her taffrail. What would she do now? Had she way on her yet? I stepped to the side swiftly, and on the shadowy water I could see nothing except a faint phosphorescent flash revealing the glassy smoothness of the sleeping surface. It was impossible to tell — and I had not learned yet the feel of my ship. Was she moving? What I needed was something easily seen, a piece of paper, which I could throw overboard and watch. I had nothing on me. To run down for it I didn't dare. There was no time. All at once my strained, yearning stare distinguished a white object floating within a yard of the ship's side. White on the black water. A phosphorescent flash passed under it. What was that thing? . . . I recognized my own floppy hat. It must have fallen off his head . . . and he didn't bother. Now I had what I wanted — the saving mark for my eyes. But I hardly thought of my other self, now gone from the ship, to be hidden forever from all friendly faces, to be a fugitive and a vagabond on the earth, with no brand of the curse on his sane forehead to stay a slaying hand . . . too proud to explain.

And I watched the hat — the expression of my sudden pity for his mere flesh. It had been meant to save his homeless head from the dangers of the sun. And now — behold — it was saving the ship, by serving me for a mark to help out the ignorance of my strangeness. Ha! It was drifting forward, warning me just in time that the ship had gathered sternway.

"Shift the helm," I said in a low voice to the seaman standing still like a statue.

The man's eyes glistened wildly in the binnacle light as he jumped round to the other side and spun round the wheel.

I walked to the break of the poop. On the overshadowed deck all hands stood by the forebraces waiting for my order. The stars ahead seemed to be gliding from right to left. And all was so still in the world that I heard the quiet remark "She's round," passed in a tone of intense relief between two seamen.

"Let go and haul."

The foreyards ran round with a great noise amidst cheery cries. And now the frightful whiskers made themselves heard giving various orders. Already the ship was drawing ahead. And I was alone with her. Nothing! no one in the world should stand now between us, throwing a shadow on the way of silent knowledge and mute affection, the perfect communion of a seaman with his first command.

Walking to the taffrail, I was in time to make out, on the very edge of a darkness thrown by a towering black mass like the very gateway of Erebus — yes, I was in time to catch an evanescent glimpse of my white hat left behind to mark the spot where the secret sharer of my cabin and of my thoughts, as though he were my second self, had lowered himself into the water to take his punishment: a free man, a proud swimmer striking out for a new destiny.

Questions for Discussion

1. What mood and sense of values are created through the story's opening images: "lines of fishing stakes resembling a mysterious system of half-submerged bamboo fences, incomprehensible in its division of the domain of tropical fishes"? How do these images establish the narrator's ability to observe, as well as the quality of his imagination?

2. In the opening paragraph and at the end of the story, the narrator, a new captain, focuses on the feeling of being "alone with [his] ship." How does his understanding of being alone change over the course of the story?

3. How does the narrator relate to the other sailors on his ship, particularly the chief mate, the second mate, and the steward? What images does he use to describe them? Why and how do his relations with them change and develop?

4. Why does the narrator describe Leggatt as "fishlike" when he first spots him? How does this image relate back to the story's first image about "fishing stakes"?

5. What is Leggatt's crime? Why does the narrator respond to his account of the storm on the ship as he does? After the appearance of the skipper of the *Sephora*, is the narrator more or less inclined to value Leggatt's story and to perceive him as a "double"? Why?

6. After the near discovery of the double by the steward, the narrator reflects, "Can it be . . . that he is not visible to other eyes than mine? It was like being haunted." In what sense is Leggatt like a ghost, a haunting? Why does the narrator allow himself to be haunted?

7. What is the significance of the "floppy hat" that the narrator gives to Leggatt and of the fact that he is able to use it in the end as "the saving mark for my eyes"? What has the narrator learned about himself through his encounter with Leggatt?

Ideas for Writing

1. Write an essay in which you discuss what the narrator's experience with Leggatt has taught the narrator about himself, about the sea, about justice, and about power and command.

2. *The Secret Sharer* is an example of the "double" story popular in the nineteenth century. Write a story about a double figure who haunts a central character and comes to represent his or her hidden or "other self."

A major figure in African-American literature, Charles Waddell Chesnutt lived during a period of racial backlash, when the Ku Klux Klan was active and African Americans were denied fundamental civil rights. Thus racial prejudice and the need for justice are important themes in his fiction. Born in Cleveland, Ohio, Chesnutt attended grade school in Fayetteville, North Carolina, and taught high school before working as a journalist and court reporter in New York City. Upon moving back to Ohio, Chesnutt became a lawyer and practiced for several years before turning in the 1890s to writing stories, novels, and autobiography. Chesnutt's literary career was short-lived, however: he returned to the court-reporting business after the turn of the century and stopped writing fiction. Chesnutt wrote three novels: *The House behind the Cedars* (1901), *The Marrow of Tradition* (1901), and *The Colonel's Dreams* (1905). His short stories are collected in *The Conjure Woman* and *The Wife of His Youth and Other Stories of the Color Line,* both published in 1899. Chesnutt also wrote a biography of Frederick Douglass. In his fiction, Chesnutt hoped to reach an audience outside of the African-American community and saw his mission as "not so much the elevation of the colored people as the elevation of the whites."

The Web of Circumstance   (1899)

I

Within a low clapboarded hut, with an open front, a forge was glowing. In front a blacksmith was shoeing a horse, a sleek, well-kept animal with the signs of good blood and breeding. A young mulatto stood by and handed the blacksmith such tools as he needed from time to time. A group of negroes were sitting around, some in the shadow of the shop, one in the full glare of the sunlight. A gentleman was seated in a buggy a few yards away, in the shade of a spreading elm. The horse had loosened a shoe, and Colonel Thornton, who was a lover of fine horseflesh, and careful of it, had stopped at Ben Davis's blacksmith shop, as soon as he discovered the loose shoe, to have it fastened on.

"All right, Kunnel," the blacksmith called out. "Tom," he said, addressing the young man, "he'p me hitch up."

Colonel Thornton alighted from the buggy, looked at the shoe, signified his approval of the job, and stood looking on while the blacksmith and his assistant harnessed the horse to the buggy.

"Dat's a mighty fine whip yer got dere, Kunnel," said Ben, while the young man was tightening the straps of the harness on the opposite side of the horse. "I wush I had one like it. Where kin yer git dem whips?"

"My brother brought me this from New York," said the Colonel. "You can't buy them down here."

The whip in question was a handsome one. The handle was wrapped with interlacing threads of variegated colors, forming an elaborate pattern, the lash being dark green. An octagonal ornament of glass was set in the end of the handle. "It cert'n'y is fine," said Ben; "I wish I had one like it." He looked at the whip longingly as Colonel Thornton drove away.

"'Pears ter me Ben gittin' mighty blooded," said one of the bystanders, "drivin' a hoss an' buggy, an' wantin' a whip like Colonel Thornton's."

"What's de reason I can't hab a hoss an' buggy an' a whip like Kunnel Tho'nton's, ef I pay fer 'em?" asked Ben. "We colored folks never had no chance ter git nothin' befo' de wah, but ef eve'y nigger in dis town had a tuck keer er his money sence de wah, like I has, an' bought as much lan' as I has, de niggers might 'a' got half de lan' by dis time," he went on, giving a finishing blow to a horseshoe, and throwing it on the ground to cool.

Carried away by his own eloquence, he did not notice the approach of two white men who came up the street from behind him.

"An' ef you niggers," he continued, raking the coals together over a fresh bar of iron, "would stop wastin' yo' money on 'scursions to put money in w'ite folks' pockets, an' stop buildin' fine chu'ches, an' buil' houses fer yo'se'ves, you'd git along much faster."

"You're talkin' sense, Ben," said one of the white men. "Yo'r people will never be respected till they've got property."

The conversation took another turn. The white men transacted their business and went away. The whistle of a neighboring steam sawmill blew a raucous blast for the hour of noon, and the loafers shuffled away in different directions.

"You kin go ter dinner, Tom," said the blacksmith. "An' stop at de gate w'en yer go by my house, and tell Nancy I'll be dere in 'bout twenty minutes. I got ter finish dis yer plough p'int fus'."

The young man walked away. One would have supposed, from the rapidity with which he walked, that he was very hungry. A quarter of an hour later the blacksmith dropped his hammer, pulled off his leather apron, shut the front door of the shop, and went home to dinner. He came into the house out of the fervent heat, and, throwing off his straw hat, wiped his brow vigorously with a red cotton handkerchief.

"Dem collards smells good," he said, sniffing the odor that came in through the kitchen door, as his good-looking yellow wife opened it to enter the room where he was. "I've got a monst'us good appetite ter-day. I feels good, too. I paid Majah Ransom de intrus' on de mortgage dis mawnin' an' a hund'ed dollahs besides, an' I spec's ter hab de balance ready by de fust of nex' Jiniwary; an' den we won't owe nobody a cent. I tell yer dere ain' nothin' like propputy ter make a pusson feel like a man. But w'at's de matter wid yer, Nancy? Is sump'n' skeered yer?"

The woman did seem excited and ill at ease. There was a heaving of the full bust, a quickened breathing, that betokened suppressed excitement.

"I — I — jes' seen a rattlesnake out in de gyahden," she stammered.

The blacksmith ran to the door. "Which way? Whar wuz he?" he cried.

He heard a rustling in the bushes at one side of the garden, and the sound of a breaking twig, and, seizing a hoe which stood by the door, he sprang toward the point from which the sound came.

"No, no," said the woman hurriedly, "it wuz over here," and she directed her husband's attention to the other side of the garden.

The blacksmith, with the uplifted hoe, its sharp blade gleaming in the sunlight, peered cautiously among the collards and tomato plants, listening all the while for the ominous rattle, but found nothing.

"I reckon he's got away," he said, as he set the hoe up again by the door. "Whar's de chillen?" he asked with some anxiety. "Is dey playin' in de woods?"

"No," answered his wife, "dey've gone ter de spring."

The spring was on the opposite side of the garden from that on which the snake was said to have been seen, so the blacksmith sat down and fanned himself with a palm-leaf fan until the dinner was served.

"Yer ain't quite on time ter-day, Nancy," he said, glancing up at the clock on the mantel, after the edge of his appetite had been taken off. "Got ter make time ef yer wanter make money. Didn't Tom tell yer I'd be heah in twenty minutes?"

"No," she said; "I seen him goin' pas'; he didn' say nothin'."

"I dunno w'at's de matter wid dat boy," mused the blacksmith over his apple dumpling. "He's gittin' mighty keerless heah lately; mus' hab sump'n' on 'is min', — some gal, I reckon."

The children had come in while he was speaking, — a slender, shapely boy, yellow like his mother, a girl several years younger, dark like her father: both bright-looking children and neatly dressed.

"I seen cousin Tom down by de spring," said the little girl, as she lifted off the pail of water that had been balanced on her head. "He come out er de woods just ez we wuz fillin' our buckets."

"Yas," insisted the blacksmith, "he's got some gal on his min'."

II

The case of the State of North Carolina *vs.* Ben Davis was called. The accused was led into court, and took his seat in the prisoner's dock.

"Prisoner at the bar, stand up."

The prisoner, pale and anxious, stood up. The clerk read the indictment, in which it was charged that the defendant by force and arms had entered the barn of one G. W. Thornton, and feloniously taken therefrom one whip, of the value of fifteen dollars.

"Are you guilty or not guilty?" asked the judge.

"Not guilty, yo' Honah; not guilty, Jedge. I never tuck de whip."

The State's attorney opened the case. He was young and zealous. Recently elected to the office, this was his first batch of cases, and he was anxious to make as good a record as possible. He had no doubt of the prisoner's guilt. There had been a great deal of petty thieving in the county, and several gentlemen had suggested to him the necessity for greater severity in punishing it. The jury were all white men. The prosecuting attorney stated the case.

"We expect to show, gentlemen of the jury, the facts set out in the indictment, — not altogether by direct proof, but by a chain of circumstantial evidence which is stronger even than the testimony of eyewitnesses. Men might lie, but circumstances cannot. We expect to show that the defendant is a man of dangerous character, a surly, impudent fellow; a man whose views of property are prejudicial to the welfare of society, and who has been heard to assert that half the property which is owned in this county has been stolen, and that, if justice were done, the white people ought to divide up the land with the negroes; in other words, a negro nihilist, a communist, a secret devotee of Tom Paine and Voltaire, a pupil of the anarchist propaganda, which, if not checked by the stern hand of the law, will fasten its insidious fangs on our social system, and drag it down to ruin."

"We object, may it please your Honor," said the defendant's attorney. "The prosecutor should defer his argument until the testimony is in."

"Confine yourself to the facts, Major," said the court mildly.

The prisoner sat with half-open mouth overwhelmed by this flood of eloquence. He had never heard of Tom Paine or Voltaire. He had no conception of what a nihilist or an anarchist might be, and could not have told the difference between a propaganda and a potato.

"We expect to show, may it please the court, that the prisoner had been employed by Colonel Thornton to shoe a horse; that the horse was taken to the prisoner's blacksmith shop by a servant of Colonel Thornton's; that, this servant expressing a desire to go somewhere on an errand before the horse had been shod, the prisoner volunteered to return the horse to Colonel Thornton's stable; that he did so, and the following morning the whip in question was missing; that, from circumstances, suspicion naturally fell upon the prisoner, and a search was made of his shop, where the whip was found secreted; that the prisoner denied that the whip was there, but when confronted with the evidence of his crime, showed by his confusion that he was guilty beyond a peradventure."

The prisoner looked more anxious; so much eloquence could not but be effective with the jury.

The attorney for the defendant answered briefly, denying the defendant's guilt, dwelling upon his previous good character for honesty, and begging the jury not to pre-judge the case, but to remember that the law is merciful, and that the benefit of the doubt should be given to the prisoner.

The prisoner glanced nervously at the jury. There was nothing in their faces to indicate the effect upon them of the opening statements. It seemed to the disinterested listeners as if the defendant's attorney had little confidence in his client's cause.

Colonel Thornton took the stand and testified to his ownership of the whip, the place where it was kept, its value, and the fact that it had disappeared. The whip was produced in court and identified by the witness. He also testified to the conversation at the blacksmith shop in the course of which the prisoner had expressed a desire to possess a similar whip. The cross-examination was brief, and no attempt was made to shake the Colonel's testimony.

The next witness was the constable who had gone with a warrant to search Ben's shop. He testified to the circumstances under which the whip was found.

"He wuz brazen as a mule at fust, an' wanted ter git mad about it. But when we begun ter turn over that pile er truck in the cawner, he kinder begun ter trimble; when the whip-handle stuck out, his eyes commenced ter grow big, an' when we hauled the whip out he turned pale ez ashes, an' begun to swear he did n' take the whip an' did n' know how it got thar."

"You may cross-examine," said the prosecuting attorney triumphantly.

The prisoner felt the weight of the testimony, and glanced furtively at the jury, and then appealingly at his lawyer.

"You say that Ben denied that he had stolen the whip," said the prisoner's attorney, on cross-examination. "Did it not occur to you that what you took for brazen impudence might have been but the evidence of conscious innocence?"

The witness grinned incredulously, revealing thereby a few blackened fragments of teeth.

"I've tuck up more'n a hundred niggers fer stealin', Kurnel, an' I never seed one yit that did n' 'ny it ter the las'."

"Answer my question. Might not the witness's indignation have been a manifestation of conscious innocence? Yes or no?"

"Yes, it mought, an' the moon mought fall — but it don't."

Further cross-examination did not weaken the witness's testimony, which was very damaging, and every one in the court room felt instinctively that a strong defense would be required to break down the State's case.

"The State rests," said the prosecuting attorney, with a ring in his voice which spoke of certain victory.

There was a temporary lull in the proceedings, during which a bailiff passed a pitcher of water and a glass along the line of jurymen. The defense was then begun.

The law in its wisdom did not permit the defendant to testify in his own behalf. There were no witnesses to the facts, but several were called to testify to Ben's good character. The colored witnesses made him out possessed of all the virtues. One or two white men testified that they had never known anything against his reputation for honesty.

The defendant rested his case, and the State called its witnesses in rebuttal. They were entirely on the point of character. One testified that he had heard the prisoner say that, if the negroes had their rights, they would own at least half the property. Another testified that he had heard the defendant say that the negroes spent too much money on churches, and that they cared a good deal more for God than God had ever seemed to care for them.

Ben Davis listened to this testimony with half-open mouth and staring eyes. Now and then he would lean forward and speak perhaps a word, when his attorney would shake a warning finger at him, and he would fall back helplessly, as if abandoning himself to fate; but for a moment only, when he would resume his puzzled look.

The arguments followed. The prosecuting attorney briefly summed up the evidence, and characterized it as almost a mathematical proof of the prisoner's guilt. He reserved his eloquence for the closing argument.

The defendant's attorney had a headache, and secretly believed his client guilty. His address sounded more like an appeal for mercy than a demand for justice. Then the State's attorney delivered the maiden argument of his office, the speech that made his reputation as an orator, and opened up to him a successful political career.

The judge's charge to the jury was a plain, simple statement of the law as applied to circumstantial evidence, and the mere statement of the law foreshadowed the verdict.

The eyes of the prisoner were glued to the jury-box, and he looked more and more like a hunted animal. In the rear of the crowd of blacks who filled the back part of the room, partly concealed by the projecting angle of the fireplace, stood Tom, the blacksmith's assistant. If the face is the mirror of the soul, then this man's soul, taken off its guard in this moment of excitement, was full of lust and envy and all evil passions.

The jury filed out of their box, and into the jury room behind the judge's stand. There was a moment of relaxation in the court room. The lawyers fell into conversation across the table. The judge beckoned to Colonel Thornton, who stepped forward, and they conversed together a few moments. The prisoner was all eyes and ears in this moment of waiting, and from an involuntary gesture on the part of the judge he divined that they were speaking of him. It is a pity he could not hear what was said.

"How do you feel about the case, Colonel?" asked the judge.

"Let him off easy," replied Colonel Thornton. "He's the best blacksmith in the county."

The business of the court seemed to have halted by tacit consent, in anticipation of a quick verdict. The suspense did not last long. Scarcely ten minutes had elapsed when there was a rap on the door, the officer opened it, and the jury came out.

The prisoner, his soul in his eyes, sought their faces, but met no reassuring glance; they were all looking away from him.

"Gentlemen of the jury, have you agreed upon a verdict?"

"We have," responded the foreman. The clerk of the court stepped forward and took the fateful slip from the foreman's hand.

The clerk read the verdict: "We, the jury impaneled and sworn to try the issues in this cause, do find the prisoner guilty as charged in the indictment."

There was a moment of breathless silence. Then a wild burst of grief from the prisoner's wife, to which his two children, not understanding it all, but vaguely conscious of some calamity, added their voices in two long, discordant wails, which would have been ludicrous had they not been heart-rending.

The face of the young man in the back of the room expressed relief and badly concealed satisfaction. The prisoner fell back upon the seat from which he had half risen in his anxiety, and his dark face assumed an ashen hue. What he thought could only be surmised. Perhaps, knowing his innocence, he had not believed conviction possible; perhaps, conscious of guilt, he dreaded the punishment, the extent of which was optional with the judge, within very wide limits. Only one other person present knew whether or not he was guilty, and that other had slunk furtively from the court room.

Some of the spectators wondered why there should be so much ado about convicting a negro of stealing a buggy-whip. They had forgotten their own interest of the moment before. They did not realize out of what trifles grow the tragedies of life.

It was four o'clock in the afternoon, the hour for adjournment, when the verdict was returned. The judge nodded to the bailiff.

"Oyez, oyez! this court is now adjourned until ten o'clock tomorrow morning," cried the bailiff in a singsong voice. The judge left the bench, the jury filed out of the box, and a buzz of conversation filled the court room.

"Brace up, Ben, brace up, my boy," said the defendant's lawyer, half apologetically. "I did what I could for you, but you can never tell what a jury will do. You won't be sentenced till tomorrow morning. In the meantime I'll speak to the judge and try to get him to be easy with you. He may let you off with a light fine."

The negro pulled himself together, and by an effort listened.

"Thanky, Majah," was all he said. He seemed to be thinking of something far away.

He barely spoke to his wife when she frantically threw herself on him, and clung to his neck, as he passed through the side room on his way to jail. He kissed his children mechanically, and did not reply to the soothing remarks made by the jailer.

III

There was a good deal of excitement in town the next morning. Two white men stood by the post office talking.

"Did yer hear the news?"

"No, what wuz it?"

"Ben Davis tried ter break jail las' night."

"You don't say so! What a fool! He ain't be'n sentenced yit."

"Well, now," said the other, "I've knowed Ben a long time, an' he wuz a right good nigger. I kinder found it hard ter b'lieve he did steal that whip. But what's a man's feelin's ag'in' the proof?"

They spoke on awhile, using the past tense as if they were speaking of a dead man.

"Ef I know Jedge Hart, Ben 'll wish he had slep' las' night, 'stidder tryin' ter break out'n jail."

At ten o'clock the prisoner was brought into court. He walked with shambling gait, bent at the shoulders, hopelessly, with downcast eyes, and took his seat with several other prisoners who had been brought in for sentence. His wife, accompanied by the children, waited behind him, and a number of his friends were gathered in the court room.

The first prisoner sentenced was a young white man, convicted several days before of manslaughter. The deed was done in the heat of passion, under circumstances of great provocation, during a quarrel about a woman. The prisoner was admonished of the sanctity of human life, and sentenced to one year in the penitentiary.

The next case was that of a young clerk, eighteen or nineteen years of age, who had committed a forgery in order to procure the means to buy lottery tickets. He was well connected, and the case would not have been prosecuted if the judge had not refused to allow it to be nolled, and, once brought to trial, a conviction could not have been avoided.

"You are a young man," said the judge gravely, yet not unkindly, "and your life is yet before you. I regret that you should have been led into evil courses by the lust for speculation, so dangerous in its tendencies, so fruitful of crime and misery. I am led to believe that you are sincerely penitent, and that, after such punishment as the law cannot remit without bringing itself into contempt, you will see the error of your ways and follow the strict path of rectitude. Your fault has entailed distress not only upon yourself, but upon your relatives, people of good name and good family, who suffer as keenly from your disgrace as you yourself. Partly out of consideration for their feelings, and partly because I feel that, under the circumstances, the law will be satisfied by the penalty I shall inflict, I sentence you to imprisonment in the county jail for six months, and a fine of one hundred dollars and the costs of this action."

"The jedge talks well, don't he?" whispered one spectator to another.

"Yes, and kinder likes ter hear hisse'f talk," answered the other.

"Ben Davis, stand up," ordered the judge.

He might have said "Ben Davis, wake up," for the jailer had to touch the prisoner on the shoulder to rouse him from his stupor. He stood up, and something of the hunted look came again into his eyes, which shifted under the stern glance of the judge.

"Ben Davis, you have been convicted of larceny, after a fair trial before twelve good men of this county. Under the testimony, there can be no doubt of your guilt. The case is an aggravated one. You are not an ignorant, shiftless fellow, but a man of more than ordinary intelligence among your people, and one who ought to know better. You have not even the poor excuse of having stolen to satisfy hunger or a physical appetite. Your conduct is wholly without excuse, and I can only regard your crime as the result of a tendency to offenses of this nature, a tendency which is only too common among your people; a tendency which is a menace to civilization, a menace to society itself, for society rests upon the sacred right of property. Your opinions, too, have been given a wrong turn; you have been heard to utter sentiments which, if disseminated among an ignorant people, would breed discontent, and give rise to strained relations between them and their best friends, their old masters, who understand their real nature and their real needs, and to whose justice and enlightened guidance they can safely trust. Have you anything to say why sentence should not be passed upon you?"

"Nothin', suh, cep'n dat I did n' take de whip."

"The law, largely, I think, in view of the peculiar circumstances of your unfortunate race, has vested a large discretion in courts as to the extent of the punishment for offenses of this kind. Taking your case as a whole, I am convinced that it is one which, for the sake of the example, deserves a severe punishment. Nevertheless, I do not feel disposed to give you the full extent of the law, which would be twenty years in the penitentiary,[1] but, considering the fact that you have a family, and have heretofore borne a good reputation in the community, I will impose upon you the light sentence of imprisonment for five years in the penitentiary at hard labor. And I hope that this will be a warning to you and others who may be similarly disposed, and that after your sentence has expired you may lead the life of a law-abiding citizen."

"O Ben! O my husband! O God!" moaned the poor wife, and tried to press forward to her husband's side.

"Keep back, Nancy, keep back," said the jailer. "You can see him in jail."

Several people were looking at Ben's face. There was one flash of despair, and then nothing but a stony blank, behind which he masked his real feelings, whatever they were.

Human character is a compound of tendencies inherited and habits acquired. In the anxiety, the fear of disgrace, spoke the nineteenth century civilization with which Ben Davis had been more or less closely in touch during twenty years of slavery and fifteen years of freedom. In the stolidity with which he received this sentence for a crime which he had not committed, spoke who knows what trait of inherited savagery? For stoicism is a savage virtue.

---

[1] There are no degrees of larceny in North Carolina, and the penalty for any offense lies in the discretion of the judge, to the limit of twenty years.

IV

One morning in June, five years later, a black man limped slowly along the old Lumberton plank road; a tall man, whose bowed shoulders made him seem shorter than he was, and a face from which it was difficult to guess his years, for in it the wrinkles and flabbiness of age were found side by side with firm white teeth, and eyes not sunken, — eyes bloodshot, and burning with something, either fever or passion. Though he limped painfully with one foot, the other hit the ground impatiently, like the good horse in a poorly matched team. As he walked along, he was talking to himself: —

"I wonder what dey'll do w'en I git back? I wonder how Nancy's s'ported the fambly all dese years? Tuck in washin', I s'ppose, — she was a monst'us good washer an' ironer. I wonder ef de chillen 'll be too proud ter reco'nize deir daddy come back f'um de penetenchy? I 'spec' Billy must be a big boy by dis time. He won' b'lieve his daddy ever stole anything. I'm gwine ter slip roun' an' s'prise 'em."

Five minutes later a face peered cautiously into the window of what had once been Ben Davis's cabin, — at first an eager face, its coarseness lit up with the fire of hope; a moment later a puzzled face; then an anxious, fearful face as the man stepped away from the window and rapped at the door.

"Is Mis' Davis home?" he asked of the woman who opened the door.

"Mis' Davis don' live here. You er mistook in de house."

"Whose house is dis?"

"It b'longs ter my husban, Mr. Smith, — Primus Smith."

"'Scuse me, but I knowed de house some years ago, w'en I wuz here oncet on a visit, an' it b'longed ter a man name' Ben Davis."

"Ben Davis — Ben Davis? — oh yes, I 'member now. Dat wuz de gen'man w'at wuz sent ter de penitenchy fer sump'n er nuther, — sheep-stealin', I b'lieve. Primus," she called, "w'at wuz Ben Davis, w'at useter own dis yer house, sent ter de penitenchy fer?"

"Hoss-stealin'" came back the reply in sleepy accents, from the man seated by the fireplace.

The traveler went on to the next house. A neat-looking yellow woman came to the door when he rattled the gate, and stood looking suspiciously at him.

"W'at you want?" she asked

"Please, ma'am, will you tell me whether a man name' Ben Davis useter live in dis neighborhood?"

"Useter live in de nex' house; wuz sent ter de penitenchy fer killin' a man."

"Kin yer tell me w'at went wid Mis' Davis?"

"Umph! I's a 'spectable 'oman, I is, en don' mix wid dem kind er people. She wuz 'n' no better'n her husban'. She tuk up wid a man dat useter wuk fer Ben, an' dey're livin' down by de ole wagon-ya'd, where no 'spectable 'oman ever puts her foot."

"An' de chillen?"

"De gal's dead. Wuz'n no better'n she oughter be'n. She fell in de crick an' got drown'; some folks say she wuz'n' sober w'en it happen'. De boy tuck atter his pappy. He wuz 'rested las' week fer shootin' a w'ite man, an' wuz lynch' de same night. Dey wa'n't none of 'em no 'count after deir pappy went ter de penitenchy."

"What went wid de proputty?"

"Hit wuz sol' fer de mortgage, er de taxes, er de lawyer, er sump'n, — I don' know w'at. A w'ite man got it."

The man with the bundle went on until he came to a creek that crossed the road. He descended the sloping bank, and, sitting on a stone in the shade of a water-oak, took off his coarse brogans, unwound the rags that served him in lieu of stockings, and laved in the cool water the feet that were chafed with many a weary mile of travel.

After five years of unrequited toil, and unspeakable hardship in convict camps, — five years of slaving by the side of human brutes, and of nightly herding with them in vermin-haunted huts, — Ben Davis had become like them. For a while he had received occasional letters from home, but in the shifting life of the convict camp they had long since ceased to reach him, if indeed they had been written. For a year or two, the consciousness of his innocence had helped to make him resist the debasing influences that surrounded him. The hope of shortening his sentence by good behavior, too, had worked a similar end. But the transfer from one contractor to another, each interested in keeping as long as possible a good worker, had speedily dissipated any such hope. When hope took flight, its place was not long vacant. Despair followed, and black hatred of all mankind, hatred especially of the man to whom he attributed all his misfortunes. One who is suffering unjustly is not apt to indulge in fine abstractions, nor to balance probabilities. By long brooding over his wrongs, his mind became, if not unsettled, at least warped, and he imagined that Colonel Thornton had deliberately set a trap into which he had fallen. The Colonel, he convinced himself, had disapproved of his prosperity, and had schemed to destroy it. He reasoned himself into the belief that he represented in his person the accumulated wrongs of a whole race, and Colonel Thornton the race who had oppressed them. A burning desire for revenge sprang up in him, and he nursed it until his sentence expired and he was set at liberty. What he had learned since reaching home had changed his desire into a deadly purpose.

When he had again bandaged his feet and slipped them into his shoes, he looked around him, and selected a stout sapling from among the undergrowth that covered the bank of the stream. Taking from his pocket a huge clasp-knife, he cut off the length of an ordinary walking stick and trimmed it. The result was an ugly-looking bludgeon, a dangerous weapon when in the grasp of a strong man.

With the stick in his hand, he went on down the road until he approached a large white house standing some distance back from the street. The grounds were filled with a profusion of shrubbery. The negro entered the gate and secreted himself in the bushes, at a point where he could hear any one that might approach.

It was near midday, and he had not eaten. He had walked all night, and had not slept. The hope of meeting his loved ones had been meat and drink and rest for him. But as he sat waiting, outraged nature asserted itself, and he fell asleep, with his head on the rising root of a tree, and his face upturned.

And as he slept, he dreamed of his childhood; of an old black mammy taking care of him in the daytime, and of a younger face, with soft eyes, which bent over him sometimes at night, and a pair of arms which clasped him closely. He dreamed of his past, — of his young wife, of his bright children. Somehow his dreams all ran to pleasant themes for a while.

Then they changed again. He dreamed that he was in the convict camp, and, by an easy transition, that he was in hell, consumed with hunger, burning with thirst. Suddenly the grinning devil who stood over him with a barbed whip faded away, and a little white angel came and handed him a drink of water. As he raised it to his lips the glass slipped, and he struggled back to consciousness.

"Poo' man! Poo' man sick, an' sleepy. Dolly b'ing f'owers to cover poo' man up. Poo' man mus' be hungry. W'en Dolly get him covered up, she go b'ing poo' man some cake."

A sweet little child, as beautiful as a cherub escaped from Paradise, was standing over him. At first he scarcely comprehended the words the baby babbled out. But as they became clear to him, a novel feeling crept slowly over his heart. It had been so long since he had heard anything but curses and stern words of command, or the ribald songs of obscene merriment, that the clear tones of this voice from heaven cooled his calloused heart as the water of the brook had soothed his blistered feet. It was so strange, so unwonted a thing, that he lay there with half-closed eyes while the child brought leaves and flowers and laid them on his face and on his breast, and arranged them with little caressing taps.

She moved away, and plucked a flower. And then she spied another farther on, and then another, and, as she gathered them, kept increasing the distance between herself and the man lying there, until she was several rods away.

Ben Davis watched her through eyes over which had come an unfamiliar softness. Under the lingering spell of his dream, her golden hair, which fell in rippling curls, seemed like a halo of purity and innocence and peace, irradiating the atmosphere around her. It is true the thought occurred to Ben, vaguely, that through harm to her he might inflict the greatest punishment upon her father; but the idea came like a dark shape that faded away and vanished into nothingness as soon as it came within the nimbus that surrounded the child's person.

The child was moving on to pluck still another flower, when there came a sound of hoof-beats, and Ben was aware that a horseman, visible through the shrubbery, was coming along the curved path that led from the gate to the house. It must be the man he was waiting for, and now was the time to wreak his vengeance. He sprang to his feet, grasped his club, and stood for a moment irresolute. But either the instinct of the convict, beaten, driven, and debased, or the influence of the child, which was still strong upon him, impelled him, after the first momentary pause, to flee as though seeking safety.

His flight led him toward the little girl, whom he must pass in order to make his escape, and as Colonel Thornton turned the corner of the path he saw a desperate-looking negro, clad in filthy rags, and carrying in his hand a murderous bludgeon, running toward the child, who, startled by the sound of footsteps, had turned and was looking toward the approaching man with wondering eyes. A sickening fear came over the father's heart, and drawing the ever-ready revolver, which according to the Southern custom he carried always upon his person, he fired with unerring aim. Ben Davis ran a few yards farther, faltered, threw out his hands, and fell dead at the child's feet.

Some time, we are told, when the cycle of years has rolled around, there is to be another golden age, when all men will dwell together in love and harmony, and when peace and righteousness shall prevail for a thousand years. God speed the day, and let not the shining thread of hope become so enmeshed in the web of circumstance that we lose sight of it; but give us here and there, and now and then, some little foretaste of this golden age, that we may the more patiently and hopefully await its coming!

Questions for Discussion

1. In light of the events that follow, what is ironic about the initial description of Colonel Thornton as "a lover of fine horseflesh"? How does the story criticize Thornton's value system?
2. What are Ben Davis's values and aspirations? What does he feel would help his fellow African Americans to succeed? How and why is he misunderstood by others in the story?
3. Why does the case against Ben seem so strong? Is there any real evidence of his thievery other than "the web of circumstance" and the negative interpretation of his opinions presented by the prosecution?
4. Why is the attorney unable (or unwilling) to provide a strong defense? What is implied through the strong contrast between the judge's reprimand and sentencing of Ben and his comments to and sentencing of the two white defendants?
5. How has Ben deteriorated, physically and morally, during his years in prison? How is his diminished and distorted reputation in the community revealed?

Ideas for Writing

1. Write an essay in which you examine the story's final sequence of events, which begins with Ben's dream of paradise, includes his shooting, and ends in a discussion of the vision of a "golden age" of peace and righteousness. What is the effect of this ending? What does it imply about hope and the future of African Americans?
2. Write a story about an unjustly imprisoned man who returns home to find himself forgotten or negatively stereotyped.

ANTON CHEKHOV   (1860–1904)

Anton Chekhov is noted for his ability to construct stories that rely for their primary effect on mood and evocative description rather than on traditional narrative plot. Chekhov's short stories had a strong influence on the modernist movement of fiction, which valued experimental forms, subtle use of symbol and irony, and realistic characterization. They continue to be studied for their strong sense of craft and emotional insight.

Born in Taganrog, in southern Russia, Chekhov later moved to Moscow with his family and earned a medical degree at the University of Moscow in 1884. His first collection of stories, *Tales of Melopmene* (*The Motley Stories*), was published in 1886. Chekhov practiced as a doctor in small towns in Russia and helped to pay off his family's debts; by 1886 he was able to support himself by his writing. Many of his early stories were comic farces that he adapted as very successful sketches for the stage. His story "The Steppe" (1888) was awarded the Pushkin Prize, Russia's highest literary award, and he published numerous other collections over the next seven years. In the last years of his life, he revised his stories and wrote plays that have become classics of the modern theater: *The Seagull* (1898), *Uncle Vanya* (1899), *The Three Sisters* (1901), and *The Cherry Orchard* (1904).

In a letter to an early editor, Chekhov described himself as a "young man [who] squeezes the slave out of himself, drop by drop, and . . . on awaking one fine morning . . . feels that the blood coursing through his veins is no longer that of a slave but that of a real human being." According to one critic, Chekhov believed that his medical training "helped his writing, giving him a more perceptive and penetrating knowledge of men and women, guarding him against the pitfalls of subjectivity."

The Schoolmistress   (1897)

Translated by Constance Garnett

At half-past eight they drove out of the town.

The highroad was dry, a lovely April sun was shining warmly, but the snow was still lying in the ditches and in the woods. Winter, dark, long, and spiteful, was hardly over; spring had come all of a sudden. But neither the warmth nor the languid transparent woods, warmed by the breath of spring, nor the black flocks of birds flying over the huge puddles that were like lakes, nor the marvelous fathomless sky, into which it seemed one would have gone away so joyfully, presented anything new or interesting to Marya Vassilyevna who was sitting in the cart. For thirteen years she had been schoolmistress, and there was no reckoning how many times during all those years she had been to the town for her salary; and whether it were spring as now, or a rainy autumn evening, or winter, it was all the same to her, and she always—invariably—longed for one thing only, to get to the end of her journey as quickly as could be.

She felt as though she had been living in that part of the country for ages and ages, for a hundred years, and it seemed to her that she knew every stone, every tree on the road from the town to her school. Her past was here, her present was here, and she could imagine no other future than the school, the road to the town and back again, and again the school and again the road. . . .

She had got out of the habit of thinking of her past before she became a schoolmistress, and had almost forgotten it. She had once had a father and mother; they had lived in Moscow in a big flat near the Red Gate, but of all that life there was left in her memory only something vague and fluid like a dream. Her father had died when she was ten years old, and her mother had died soon after. . . . She had a brother, an officer; at first they used to write to each other, then her brother had given up answering her letters, he had got out of the way of writing. Of her old belongings, all that was left was a photograph of her mother, but it had grown dim from the dampness of the school, and now nothing could be seen but the hair and the eyebrows.

When they had driven a couple of miles, old Semyon, who was driving, turned round and said:

"They have caught a government clerk in the town. They have taken him away. The story is that with some Germans he killed Alexeyev, the Mayor, in Moscow."

"Who told you that?"

"They were reading it in the paper, in Ivan Ionov's tavern."

And again they were silent for a long time. Marya Vassilyevna thought of her school, of the examination that was coming soon, and of the girl and four boys she was sending up for it. And just as she was thinking about the examination, she was overtaken by a neighboring landowner called Hanov in a carriage with four horses, the very man who had been examiner in her school the year before. When he came up to her he recognized her and bowed.

"Good-morning," he said to her. " You are driving home, I suppose."

This Hanov, a man of forty with a listless expression and a face that showed signs of wear, was beginning to look old, but was still handsome and admired by women. He lived in his big homestead alone, and was not in the service; and people used to say of him that he did nothing at home but walk up and down the room whistling, or play chess with his old footman. People said, too, that he drank heavily. And indeed at the examination the year before the very papers he brought with him smelt of wine and scent. He had been dressed all in new clothes on that occasion, and Marya Vassilyevna thought him very attractive, and all the while she sat beside him she had felt embarrassed. She was accustomed to see frigid and sensible examiners at the school, while this one did not remember a single prayer, or know what to ask questions about, and was exceedingly courteous and delicate, giving nothing but the highest marks.

"I am going to visit Bakvist," he went on, addressing Marya Vassilyevna, "but I am told he is not at home."

They turned off the highroad into a by-road to the village, Hanov leading the way and Semyon following. The four horses moved at a walking pace, with effort dragging the heavy carriage through the mud. Semyon tacked from side to side, keeping to the edge of the road, at one time through a snowdrift, at another through a pool, often jumping out of the cart and helping the horse. Marya Vassilyevna was still thinking about the school, wondering whether the arithmetic questions at the examination would be difficult or easy. And she felt annoyed with the Zemstvo board at which she had found no one the day before. How unbusiness-like! Here she had been asking them for the last two years to dismiss the watchman, who did nothing, was rude to her, and hit the schoolboys; but no one paid any attention. It was hard to find the president at the office, and when one did find him he would say with tears in his eyes that he hadn't a moment to spare; the inspector visited the school at most once in three years, and knew nothing whatever about his work, as he had been in the Excise Duties Department, and had received the post of school inspector through influence. The School Council met very rarely, and there was no knowing where it met; the school guardian was an almost illiterate peasant, the head of a tanning business, unintelligent, rude, and a great friend of the watchman's — and goodness knows to whom she could appeal with complaints or inquiries. . . .

"He really is handsome," she thought, glancing at Hanov.

The road grew worse and worse. . . . They drove into the wood. Here there was no room to turn round, the wheels sank deeply in, water splashed and gurgled through them, and sharp twigs struck them in the face.

"What a road!" said Hanov, and he laughed.

The schoolmistress looked at him and could not understand why this queer man lived here. What could his money, his interesting appearance, his refined bearing do for him here, in this mud, in this God-forsaken, dreary place? He got no special advantages out of life, and here, like Semyon, was driving at a jog-trot on an appalling road and enduring the same discomforts. Why live here if one could live in Petersburg or abroad? And one would have thought it would be nothing for a rich man like him to make a good road instead of this bad one, to avoid enduring this misery and seeing the despair on the faces of his coachman and Semyon; but he only laughed, and apparently did not mind, and wanted no better life. He was kind, soft, naïve, and he did not understand this coarse life, just as at the examination he did not know the prayers. He subscribed nothing to the schools but globes, and genuinely regarded himself as a useful person and a prominent worker in the cause of popular education. And what use were his globes here?

"Hold on, Vassilyevna!" said Semyon.

The cart lurched violently and was on the point of upsetting; something heavy rolled on to Marya Vassilyevna's feet — it was her parcel of purchases. There was a steep ascent uphill through the clay; here in the winding ditches rivulets were gurgling. The water seemed to have gnawed away the road; and how could one get along here! The horses breathed hard. Hanov got out of his carriage and walked at the side of the road in his long overcoat. He was hot.

"What a road!" he said, and laughed again. "It would soon smash up one's carriage."

"Nobody obliges you to drive about in such weather," said Semyon surlily. "You should stay at home."

"I am dull at home, grandfather. I don't like staying at home."

Beside old Semyon he looked graceful and vigorous, but yet in his walk there was something just perceptible which betrayed in him a being already touched by decay, weak, and on the road to ruin. And all at once there was a whiff of spirits in the wood. Marya Vassilyevna was filled with dread and pity for this man going to his ruin for no visible cause or reason, and it came into her mind that if she had been his wife or sister she would have devoted her whole life to saving him from ruin. His wife! Life was so ordered that here he was living in his great house alone, and she was living in a God-forsaken village alone, and yet for some reason the mere thought that he and she might be close to one another and equals seemed impossible and absurd. In reality, life was arranged and human relations were complicated so utterly beyond all understanding that when one thought about it one felt uncanny and one's heart sank.

"And it is beyond all understanding," she thought, "why God gives beauty, this graciousness, and sad, sweet eyes to weak, unlucky, useless people — why they are so charming."

"Here we must turn off to the right," said Hanov, getting into his carriage. "Good-by! I wish you all things good!"

And again she thought of her pupils, of the examination, of the watchman, of the School Council; and when the wind brought the sound of the retreating carriage these thoughts were mingled with others. She longed to think of beautiful eyes, of love, of the happiness which would never be. . . .

His wife? It was cold in the morning, there was no one to heat the stove, the watchman disappeared; the children came in as soon as it was light, bringing in snow and mud and making a noise: it was all so inconvenient, so comfortless. Her abode consisted of one little room and the kitchen close by. Her head ached every day after her work, and after dinner she had heart-burn. She had to collect money from the school-children for wood and for the watchman, and to give it to the school guardian, and then to entreat him — that overfed, insolent peasant—for God's sake to send her wood. And at night she dreamed of examinations, peasants, snowdrifts. And this life was making her grow old and coarse, making her ugly, angular, and awkward, as though she were made of lead. She was always afraid, and she would get up from her seat and not venture to sit down in the presence of a member of the Zemstvo or the school guardian. And she used formal, deferential expressions when she spoke of any one of them. And no one thought her attractive, and life was passing drearily, without affection, without friendly sympathy, without interesting acquaintances. How awful it would have been in her position if she had fallen in love!

"Hold on, Vassilyevna!"

Again a sharp ascent uphill. . . .

She had become a schoolmistress from necessity, without feeling any vocation for it; and she had never thought of a vocation, of serving the cause of enlightenment; and it always seemed to her that what was most important in her work was not the children, nor enlightenment, but the examinations. And what time had she for thinking of vocation, of serving the cause of enlightenment? Teachers, badly paid doctors, and their assistants, with their terribly hard work, have not even the comfort of thinking that they are serving an idea or the people, as their heads are always stuffed with thoughts of their daily bread, of wood for the fire, of bad roads, of illnesses. It is a hard-working, an uninteresting life, and only silent, patient cart-horses like Marya Vassilyevna could put up with it for long; the lively, nervous, impressionable people who talked about a vocation and serving the idea were soon weary of it and gave up the work.

Semyon kept picking out the driest and shortest way, first by a meadow, then by the backs of the village huts; but in one place the peasants would not let them pass, in another it was the priest's land and they could not cross it, in another Ivan Ionov had bought a plot from the landowner and had dug a ditch round it. They kept having to turn back.

They reached Nizhneye Gorodistche. Near the tavern on the dung-strewn earth, where the snow was still lying, there stood wagons that had brought great bottles of crude sulphuric acid. There were a great many people in the tavern, all drivers, and there was a smell of vodka, tobacco, and sheepskins. There was a loud noise of conversation and the banging of the swing-door. Through the wall, without ceasing for a moment, came the sound of a concertina being played in the shop. Marya Vassilyevna sat down and drank some tea, while at the next table peasants were drinking vodka and beer, perspiring from the tea they had just swallowed and the stifling fumes of the tavern.

"I say, Kuzma!" voices kept shouting in confusion. "What there!" "The Lord bless us!" "Ivan Dementyitch, I can tell you that!" "Look out, old man!"

A little pock-marked man with a black beard, who was quite drunk, was suddenly surprised by something and began using bad language.

"What are you swearing at, you there?" Semyon, who was sitting some way off, responded angrily. "Don't you see the young lady?"

"The young lady!" someone mimicked in another corner.

"Swinish crow!"

"We meant nothing . . ." said the little man in confusion. "I beg your pardon. We pay with our money and the young lady with hers. Good-morning!"

"Good-morning," answered the schoolmistress.

"And we thank you most feelingly."

Marya Vassilyevna drank her tea with satisfaction, and she, too, began turning red like the peasants, and fell to thinking again about firewood, about the watchman. . . .

"Stay, old man," she heard from the next table, "it's the schoolmistress from Vyazovye. . . . We know her; she's a good young lady."

"She's all right!"

The swing-door was continually banging, some coming in, others going out. Marya Vassilyevna sat on, thinking all the time of the same things, while the concertina went on playing and playing. The patches of sunshine had been on the floor, then they passed to the counter, to the wall, and disappeared altogether; so by the sun it was past midday. The peasants at the next table were getting ready to go. The little man, somewhat unsteadily, went up to Marya Vassilyevna and held out his hand to her; following his example, the others shook hands, too, at parting, and went out one after another, and the swing-door squeaked and slammed nine times.

"Vassilyevna, get ready," Semyon called to her.

They set off. And again they went at a walking pace.

"A little while back they were building a school here in their Nizhneye Gorodistche," said Semyon, turning round. "It was a wicked thing that was done!"

"Why, what?"

"They say the president put a thousand in his pocket, and the school guardian another thousand in his, and the teacher five hundred."

"The whole school only cost a thousand. It's wrong to slander people, grandfather. That's all nonsense."

"I don't know, . . . I only tell you what folks say."

But it was clear that Semyon did not believe the schoolmistress. The peasants did not believe her. They always thought she received too large a salary, twenty-one roubles a month (five would have been enough), and that of the money that she collected from the children for the firewood and the watchman the greater part she kept for herself. The guardian thought the same as the peasants, and he himself made a profit off the firewood and received payments from the peasants for being a guardian — without the knowledge of the authorities.

The forest, thank God! was behind them, and now it would be flat, open ground all the way to Vyazovye, and there was not far to go now. They had to cross the river and then the railway line, and then Vyazovye was in sight.

"Where are you driving?" Marya Vassilyevna asked Semyon. "Take the road to the right to the bridge."

"Why, we can go this way as well. It's not deep enough to matter."

"Mind you don't drown the horse."

"What?"

"Look, Hanov is driving to the bridge," said Marya Vassilyevna, seeing the four horses far away to the right. "It is he, I think."

"It is. So he didn't find Bakvist at home. What a pig-headed fellow he is. Lord have mercy upon us! He's driven over there, and what for? It's fully two miles nearer this way."

They reached the river. In the summer it was a little stream easily crossed by wading. It usually dried up in August, but now, after the spring floods, it was a river forty feet in breadth, rapid, muddy, and cold; on the bank and right up to the water there were fresh tracks of wheels, so it had been crossed here.

"Go on!" shouted Semyon angrily and anxiously, tugging violently at the reins and jerking his elbows as a bird does its wings. "Go on!"

The horse went on into the water up to his belly and stopped, but at once went on again with an effort, and Marya Vassilyevna was aware of a keen chilliness in her feet.

"Go on!" she, too, shouted, getting up. "Go on!"

They got out on the bank.

"Nice mess it is, Lord have mercy upon us!" muttered Semyon, setting straight the harness. "It's a perfect plague with this Zemstvo. . . ."

Her shoes and goloshes were full of water, the lower part of her dress and of her coat and one sleeve were wet and dripping: the sugar and flour had got wet, and that was worst of all, and Marya Vassilyevna could only clasp her hands in despair and say:

"Oh, Semyon, Semyon! How tiresome you are, really! . . ."

The barrier was down at the railway crossing.

A train was coming out of the station. Marya Vassilyevna stood at the crossing waiting till it should pass, and shivering all over with cold. Vyazovye was in sight now, and the school with the green roof, and the church with its crosses flashing in the evening sun: and the station windows flashed too, and a pink smoke rose from the engine . . . and it seemed to her that everything was trembling with cold.

Here was the train; the windows reflected the gleaming light like the crosses on the church: it made her eyes ache to look at them. On the little platform between two first-class carriages a lady was standing, and Marya Vassilyevna glanced at her as she passed. Her mother! What a resemblance! Her mother had had just such luxuriant hair, just such a brow and bend of the head. And with amazing distinctness, for the first time in those thirteen years, there rose before her mind a vivid picture of her mother, her father, her brother, their flat in Moscow, the aquarium with little fish, everything to the tiniest detail; she heard the sound of the piano, her father's voice; she felt as she had been then, young, good-looking, well-dressed, in a bright warm room among her own people. A feeling of joy and happiness suddenly came over her, she pressed her hands to her temples in an ecstasy, and called softly, beseechingly:

"Mother!"

And she began crying, she did not know why. Just at that instant Hanov drove up with his team of four horses, and seeing him she imagined happiness such as she had never had, and smiled and nodded to him as an equal and a friend, and it seemed to her that her happiness, her triumph, was glowing in the sky and on all sides, in the windows and on the trees. Her father and mother had never died, she had never been a schoolmistress, it was a long, tedious, strange dream, and now she had awakened. . . .

"Vassilyevna, get in!"

And at once it all vanished. The barrier was slowly raised. Marya Vassilyevna, shivering and numb with cold, got into the cart. The carriage with the four horses crossed the railway line; Semyon followed it. The signalman took off his cap.

"And here is Vyazovye. Here we are."

Questions for Discussion

1. How do the story's action and setting — a journey by open cart on a sunny April day — help to reveal Marya's crisis?

2. How does Marya feel about her teaching? Does she care about her students? Does she think that she is a successful teacher, or is her work a burden she takes on in order to survive?

3. What is Marya's response to the landowner Hanov? What does he represent for her? Could any of her fantasies about him ever be realized?

4. How is Marya's status in the community emphasized by her encounter with the peasants in the tavern?

5. What is revealed by Marya's sudden remembrance about her life with her family in Moscow? Why does she mistake the woman on the first-class platform at the station in Vyazovye for her own mother? As the story ends, after her brief vision, how does Marya feel about her current existence and her relationship to her family?

Ideas for Writing

1. The story is structured according to a set of contrasts between Marya's life now and her life in the past, between Hanov with his heavy carriage and the peasant Semyon with his little cart in which Marya must ride, between Marya's tiny dwelling and Hanov's huge house. In an essay, discuss how Chekhov uses contrast in order to clarify Marya's concerns as well as to critique issues of economic and class status.

2. Write a sequel to the story that reveals how Marya has been changed by her journey in the cart.

The Bet   (1888)

Translated by Constance Garnet

I

It was a dark autumn night. The old banker was walking up and down his study and remembering how, fifteen years before, he had given a party one autumn evening. There had been many clever men there, and there had been interesting conversations. Among other things they had talked of capital punishment. The majority of the guests, among whom were many journalists and intellectual men, disapproved of the death penalty. They considered that form of punishment out of date, immoral, and unsuitable for Christian States. In the opinion of some of them the death penalty ought to be replaced everywhere by imprisonment for life.

"I don't agree with you," said their host the banker. "I have not tried either the death penalty or imprisonment for life, but if one may judge *à priori*, the death penalty is more moral and more humane than imprisonment for life. Capital punishment kills a man at once, but lifelong imprisonment kills him slowly. Which executioner is the more humane, he who kills you in a few minutes or he who drags the life out of you in the course of many years?"

"Both are equally immoral," observed one of the guests, "for they both have the same object — to take away life. The State is not God. It has not the right to take away what it cannot restore when it wants to."

Among the guests was a young lawyer, a young man of five-and-twenty. When he was asked his opinion, he said:

"The death sentence and the life sentence are equally immoral, but if I had to choose between the death penalty and imprisonment for life, I would certainly choose the second. To live anyhow is better than not at all."

A lively discussion arose. The banker, who was younger and more nervous in those days, was suddenly carried away by excitement; he struck the table with his fist and shouted at the young man:

"It's not true! I'll bet you two millions you wouldn't stay in solitary confinement for five years."

"If you mean that in earnest," said the young man, "I'll take the bet, but I would stay not five but fifteen years."

"Fifteen? Done!" cried the banker. "Gentlemen, I stake two millions!"

"Agreed! You stake your millions and I stake my freedom!" said the young man.

And this wild, senseless bet was carried out! The banker, spoilt and frivolous, with millions beyond his reckoning, was delighted at the bet. At supper he made fun of the young man, and said:

"Think better of it, young man, while there is still time. To me two millions are a trifle, but you are losing three or four of the best years of your life. I say three or four, because you won't stay longer. Don't forget either, you unhappy man, that voluntary confinement is a great deal harder to bear than compulsory. The thought that you have the right to step out in liberty at any moment will poison your whole existence in prison. I am sorry for you."

And now the banker, walking to and fro, remembered all this, and asked himself: "What was the object of that bet? What is the good of that man's losing fifteen years of his life and my throwing away two millions? Can it prove that the death penalty is better or worse than imprisonment for life? No, no. It was all nonsensical and meaningless. On my part it was the caprice of a pampered man, and on his part simple greed for money. . . ."

Then he remembered what followed that evening. It was decided that the young man should spend the years of his captivity under the strictest supervision in one of the lodges in the banker's garden. It was agreed that for fifteen years he should not be free to cross the threshold of the lodge, to see human beings, to hear the human voice, or to receive letters and newspapers. He was allowed to have a musical instrument and books, and was allowed to write letters, to drink wine, and to smoke. By the terms of the agreement, the only relations he could have with the outer world were by a little window made purposely for that object. He might have anything he wanted — books, music, wine, and so on — in any quantity he desired by writing an order, but could only receive them through the window. The agreement provided for every detail and every trifle that would make his imprisonment strictly solitary, and bound the young man to stay there *exactly* fifteen years, beginning from twelve o'clock of November 14, 1870, and ending at twelve o'clock of November 14, 1885. The slighest attempt on his part to break the conditions, if only two minutes before the end, released the banker from the obligation to pay him two millions.

For the first year of his confinement, as far as one could judge from his brief notes, the prisoner suffered severely from loneliness and depression. The sounds of the piano could be heard continually day and night from his lodge. He refused wine and tobacco. Wine, he wrote, excites the desires, and desires are the worst foes of the prisoner; and besides, nothing could be more dreary than drinking good wine and seeing no one. And tobacco spoilt the air of his room. In the first year the books he sent for were principally of a light character; novels with a complicated love plot, sensational and fantastic stories, and so on.

In the second year the piano was silent in the lodge, and the prisoner asked only for the classics. In the fifth year music was audible again, and the prisoner asked for wine. Those who watched him through the window said that all that year he spent doing nothing but eating and drinking and lying on his bed, frequently yawning and angrily talking to himself. He did not read books. Sometimes at night he would sit down to write; he would spend hours writing, and in the morning tear up all that he had written. More than once he could be heard crying.

In the second half of the sixth year the prisoner began zealously studying languages, philosophy, and history. He threw himself eagerly into these studies — so much so that the banker had enough to do to get him the books he ordered. In the course of four years some six hundred volumes were procured at his request. It was during this period that the banker received the following letter from his prisoner:

"My dear Jailer, I write you these lines in six languages. Show them to people who know the languages. Let them read them. If they find not one mistake I implore you to fire a shot in the garden. That shot will show me that my efforts have not been thrown away. The geniuses of all ages and of all lands speak different languages, but the same flame burns in them all. Oh, if you only knew what unearthly happiness my soul feels now from being able to understand them!" The prisoner's desire was fulfilled. The banker ordered two shots to be fired in the garden.

Then after the tenth year, the prisoner sat immovably at the table and read nothing but the Gospel. It seemed strange to the banker that a man who in four years had mastered six hundred learned volumes should waste nearly a year over one thin book easy of comprehension. Theology and histories of religion followed the Gospels.

In the last two years of his confinement the prisoner read an immense quantity of books quite indiscriminately. At one time he was busy with the natural sciences, then he would ask for Byron or Shakespeare. There were notes in which he demanded at the same time books on chemistry, and a manual of medicine, and a novel, and some treatise on philosophy or theology. His reading suggested a man swimming in the sea among the wreckage of his ship, and trying to save his life by greedily clutching first at one spar and then at another.

II

The old banker remembered all this, and thought:

"To-morrow at twelve o'clock he will regain his freedom. By our agreement I ought to pay him two millions. If I do pay him, it is all over with me: I shall be utterly ruined."

Fifteen years before, his millions had been beyond his reckoning; now he was afraid to ask himself which were greater, his debts or his assets. Desperate gambling on the Stock Exchange, wild speculation, and the excitability which he could not get over even in advancing years, had by degrees led to the decline of his fortune, and the proud, fearless, self-confident millionaire had become a banker of middling rank, trembling at every rise and fall in his investments. "Cursed bet!" muttered the old man, clutching his head in despair. "Why didn't the man die? He is only forty now. He will take my last penny from me, he will marry, will enjoy life, will gamble on the Exchange; while I shall look at him with envy like a beggar, and hear from him every day the same sentence: 'I am indebted to you for the happiness of my life, let me help you!' No, it is too much! The one means of being saved from bankruptcy and disgrace is the death of that man!"

It struck three o'clock, the banker listened; everyone was asleep in the house, and nothing could be heard outside but the rustling of the chilled trees. Trying to make no noise, he took from a fireproof safe the key of the door which had not been opened for fifteen years, put on his overcoat, and went out of the house.

It was dark and cold in the garden. Rain was falling. A damp cutting wind was racing about the garden, howling and giving the trees no rest. The banker strained his eyes, but could see neither the earth nor the white statues, nor the lodge, nor the trees. Going to the spot where the lodge stood, he twice called the watchman. No answer followed. Evidently the watchman had sought shelter from the weather, and was now asleep somewhere either in the kitchen or in the greenhouse.

"If I had the pluck to carry out my intention," thought the old man, "suspicion would fall first upon the watchman."

He felt in the darkness for the steps and the door, and went into the entry of the lodge. Then he groped his way into a little passage and lighted a match. There was not a soul there. There was a bedstead with no bedding on it, and in the corner there was a dark cast-iron stove. The seals on the door leading to the prisoner's rooms were intact.

When the match went out the old man, trembling with emotion, peeped through the little window. A candle was burning dimly in the prisoner's room. He was sitting at the table. Nothing could be seen but his back, the hair on his head, and his hands. Open books were lying on the table, on the two easy chairs, and on the carpet near the table.

Five minutes passed and the prisoner did not once stir. Fifteen years' imprisonment had taught him to sit still. The banker tapped at the window with his finger, and the prisoner made no movement whatever in response. Then the banker cautiously broke the seals off the door and put the key in the keyhole. The rusty lock gave a grating sound and the door creaked. The banker expected to hear at once footsteps and a cry of astonishment, but three minutes passed and it was as quiet as ever in the room. He made up his mind to go in.

At the table a man unlike ordinary people was sitting motionless. He was a skeleton with the skin drawn tight over his bones, with long curls like a woman's, and a shaggy beard. His face was yellow with an earthy tint in it, his cheeks were hollow, his back long and narrow, and the hand on which his shaggy head was propped was so thin and delicate that it was dreadful to look at it. His hair was already streaked with silver, and seeing his emaciated, aged-looking face, no one would have believed that he was only forty. He was asleep. . . . In front of his bowed head there lay on the table a sheet of paper on which there was something written in fine handwriting.

"Poor creature!" thought the banker, "he is asleep and most likely dreaming of the millions. And I have only to take this half-dead man, throw him on the bed, stifle him a little with the pillow, and the most conscientious expert would find no sign of a violent death. But let us first read what he has written here. . . ."

The banker took the page from the table and read as follows:

"To-morrow at twelve o'clock I regain my freedom and the right to associate with other men, but before I leave this room and see the sunshine, I think it necessary to say a few words to you. With a clear conscience I tell you, as before God, who beholds me, that I despise freedom and life and health, and all that in your books is called the good things of the world.

"For fifteen years I have been intently studying earthly life. It is true I have not seen the earth nor men, but in your books I have drunk fragrant wine, I have sung songs, I have hunted stags and wild boars in the forests, have loved women. . . . Beauties as ethereal as clouds, created by the magic of your poets and geniuses, have visited me at night, and have whispered in my ears wonderful tales that have set my brain in a whirl. In your books I have climbed to the peaks of Elburz and Mont Blanc, and from there I have seen the sun rise and have watched it at evening flood the sky, the ocean, and the mountain-tops with gold and crimson. I have watched from there the lightning flashing over my head and cleaving the storm-clouds. I have seen green forests, fields, rivers, lakes, towns. I have heard the singing of the sirens, and the strains of the shepherds' pipes; I have touched the wings of comely devils who flew down to converse with me of God. . . . In your books I have flung myself into the bottomless pit, performed miracles, slain, burned towns, preached new religions, conquered whole kingdoms. . . .

"Your books have given me wisdom. All that the unresting thought of man has created in the ages is compressed into a small compass in my brain. I know that I am wiser than all of you.

"And I despise your books, I despise wisdom and the blessings of this world. It is all worthless, fleeting, illusory, and deceptive, like a mirage. You may be proud, wise, and fine, but death will wipe you off the face of the earth as though you were no more than mice burrowing under the floor, and your posterity, your history, your immortal geniuses will burn or freeze together with the earthly globe.

"You have lost your reason and taken the wrong path. You have taken lies for truth, and hideousness for beauty. You would marvel if, owing to strange events of some sorts, frogs and lizards suddenly grew on apple and orange trees instead of fruit, or if roses began to smell like a sweating horse; so I marvel at you who exchange heaven for earth. I don't want to understand you.

"To prove to you in action how I despise all that you live by, I renounce the two millions of which I once dreamed as of paradise and which now I despise. To deprive myself of the right to the money I shall go out from here five hours before the time fixed, and so break the compact. . . ."

When the banker had read this he laid the page on the table, kissed the strange man on the head, and went out of the lodge, weeping. At no other time even when he had lost heavily on the Stock Exchange had he felt so great a contempt for himself. When he got home he lay on his bed, but his tears and emotion kept him for hours from sleeping.

Next morning the watchmen ran in with pale faces and told him they had seen the man who lived in the lodge climb out of the window into the garden, go to the gate, and disappear. The banker went at once with the servants to the lodge and made sure of the flight of his prisoner. To avoid arousing unnecessary talk, he took from the table the writing in which the millions were renounced, and when he got home locked it up in the fireproof safe.

Questions for Discussion
1. Define the issues raised in the initial debate over capital punishment. Does either character seem to have a stronger argument?
2. What were the lawyer's and the banker's motivations when making the bet? In what sense are they both naive?
3. In what ways does the lawyer adjust to his confinement? How does he fail to adjust? What does he learn, and how do his values change? Why does the lawyer leave before his confinement is finished and thus forfeit his money?
4. Why does the banker feel total contempt for himself upon reading the lawyer's letter? Does his contempt seem justified?
5. Note that much of the story is told as flashbacks recalled on the night before the lawyer is to be released. What effect does this structure have on the story's meanings?
6. What does the resolution of the story suggest about the dispute over whether capital punishment is more or less immoral than life imprisonment?

Ideas for Writing
1. Examine in an essay the character of the banker. How do his values change in the course of the story? What is the final impact of the lawyer's flight on the banker's sense of ethics?
2. Retell the story from the point of view of the lawyer, focusing on what he experienced and came to realize about the meaning and value of life during and after his imprisonment.

The Darling   (1899)

Translated by Constance Garnett

Olenka, the daughter of the retired collegiate assessor, Plemyanniakov, was sitting in her back porch, lost in thought. It was hot, the flies were persistent and teasing, and it was pleasant to reflect that it would soon be evening. Dark rainclouds were gathering from the east, and bringing from time to time a breath of moisture in the air.

Kukin, who was the manager of an open-air theatre called the Tivoli, and who lived in the lodge, was standing in the middle of the garden looking at the sky.

"Again!" he observed despairingly. "It's going to rain again! Rain every day, as though to spite me. I might as well hang myself! It's ruin! Fearful losses every day."

He flung up his hands, and went on, addressing Olenka:

"There! that's the life we lead, Olga Semyonovna. It's enough to make one cry. One works and does one's utmost; one wears oneself out, getting no sleep at night, and racks one's brain what to do for the best. And then what happens? To begin with, one's public is ignorant, boorish. I give them the very best operetta, a dainty masque, first rate music-hall artists. But do you suppose that's what they want! They don't understand anything of that sort. They want a clown; what they ask for is vulgarity. And then look at the weather! Almost every evening it rains. It started on the tenth of May, and it's kept it up all May and June. It's simply awful! The public doesn't come, but I've to pay the rent just the same, and pay the artists."

The next evening the clouds would gather again, and Kukin would say with an hysterical laugh:

"Well, rain away, then! Flood the garden, drown me! Damn my luck in this world and the next! Let the artists have me up! Send me to prison! — to Siberia! — the scaffold! Ha, ha, ha!"

And next day the same thing.

Olenka listened to Kukin with silent gravity, and sometimes tears came into her eyes. In the end his misfortunes touched her; she grew to love him. He was a small thin man, with a yellow face, and curls combed forward on his forehead. He spoke in a thin tenor; as he talked his mouth worked on one side, and there was always an expression of despair on his face; yet he aroused a deep and genuine affection in her. She was always fond of some one, and could not exist without loving. In earlier days she had loved her papa, who now sat in a darkened room, breathing with difficulty; she had loved her aunt who used to come every other year from Bryansk; and before that, when she was at school, she had loved her French master. She was a gentle, soft-hearted, compassionate girl, with mild, tender eyes and very good health. At the sight of her full rosy cheeks, her soft white neck with a little dark mole on it, and the kind, naïve smile, which came into her face when she listened to anything pleasant, men thought, "Yes, not half bad," and smiled too, while lady visitors could not refrain from seizing her hand in the middle of a conversation, exclaiming in a gush of delight, "You darling!"

The house in which she had lived from her birth upwards, and which was left her in her father's will, was at the extreme end of the town, not far from the Tivoli. In the evenings and at night she could hear the band playing, and the crackling and banging of fireworks, and it seemed to her that it was Kukin struggling with his destiny, storming the entrenchments of his chief foe, the indifferent public; there was a sweet thrill at her heart, she had no desire to sleep, and when he resumed home at daybreak, she tapped softly at her bedroom window, and showing him only her face and one shoulder through the curtain, she gave him a friendly smile. . . .

He proposed to her, and they were married. And when he had a closer view of her neck and her plump, fine shoulders, he threw up his hands, and said:

"You darling!"

He was happy, but as it rained on the day and night of his wedding, his face still retained an expression of despair.

They got on very well together. She used to sit in his office, to look after things in the Tivoli, to put down the accounts and pay the wages.

And her rosy cheeks, her sweet, naïve, radiant smile, were to be seen now at the office window, now in the refreshment bar or behind the scenes of the theatre. And already she used to say to her acquaintances that the theatre was the chief and most important thing in life, and that it was only through the drama that one could derive true enjoyment and become cultivated and humane.

"But do you suppose the public understands that?" she used to say. "What they want is a clown. Yesterday we gave 'Faust Inside Out,' and almost all the boxes were empty; but if Vanitchka and I had been producing some vulgar thing, I assure you the theatre would have been packed. Tomorrow Vanitchka and I are doing 'Orpheus in Hell.' Do come."

And what Kukin said about the theatre and the actors she repeated. Like him she despised the public for their ignorance and their indifference to art; she took part in the rehearsals, she corrected the actors, she kept an eye on the behaviour of the musicians, and when there was an unfavourable notice in the local paper, she shed tears, and then went to the editor's office to set things right.

The actors were fond of her and used to call her "Vanitchka and I," and "the darling"; she was sorry for them and used to lend them small sums of money, and if they deceived her, she used to shed a few tears in private, but did not complain to her husband.

They got on well in the winter too. They took the theatre in the town for the whole winter, and let it for short terms to a Little Russian company, or to a conjurer, or to a local dramatic society. Olenka grew stouter, and was always beaming with satisfaction, while Kukin grew thinner and yellower, and continually complained of their terrible losses, although he had not done badly all the winter. He used to cough at night, and she used to give him hot raspberry tea or lime-flower water, to rub him with eau-de-Cologne and to wrap him in her warm shawls.

"You're such a sweet pet!" she used to say with perfect sincerity, stroking his hair. "You're such a pretty dear!"

Towards Lent he went to Moscow to collect a new troupe, and without him she could not sleep, but sat all night at her window, looking at the stars, and she compared herself with the hens, who are awake all night and uneasy when the cock is not in the hen-house. Kukin was detained in Moscow, and wrote that he would be back at Easter, adding some instructions about the Tivoli. But on the Sunday before Easter, late in the evening, came a sudden ominous knock at the gate; some one was hammering on the gate as though on a barrel — boom, boom, boom! The drowsy cook went flopping with her bare feet through the puddles, as she ran to open the gate.

"Please open," said some one outside in a thick bass. "There is a telegram for you."

Olenka had received telegrams from her husband before, but this time for some reason she felt numb with terror. With shaking hands she opened the telegram and read as follows:

"Ivan Petrovitch died suddenly to-day. Awaiting immate instructions fufuneral Tuesday."

That was how it was written in the telegram — "fufuneral," and the utterly incomprehensible word "immate." It was signed by the stage manager of the operatic company.

"My darling!" sobbed Olenka. "Vanitchka, my precious, my darling! Why did I ever meet you! Why did I know you and love you! Your poor heart-broken Olenka is all alone without you!"

Kukin's funeral took place on Tuesday in Moscow, Olenka returned home on Wednesday, and as soon as she got indoors she threw herself on her bed and sobbed so loudly that it could be heard next door, and in the street.

"Poor darling!" the neighbours said, as they crossed themselves. "Olga Semyonovna, poor darling! How she does take on!"

Three months later Olenka was coming home from mass, melancholy and in deep mourning. It happened that one of her neighbours, Vassily Andreitch Pustovalov, returning home from church, walked back beside her. He was the manager at Babakayev's the timber merchant's. He wore a straw hat, a white waistcoat, and a gold watch-chain, and looked more like a country gentleman than a man in trade.

"Everything happens as it is ordained, Olga Semyonovna," he said gravely, with a sympathetic note in his voice; "and if any of our dear ones die, it must be because it is the will of God, so we ought to have fortitude and bear it submissively."

After seeing Olenka to her gate, he said good-bye and went on. All day afterwards she heard his sedately dignified voice, and whenever she shut her eyes she saw his dark beard. She liked him very much. And apparently she had made an impression on him too, for not long afterwards an elderly lady, with whom she was only slightly acquainted, came to drink coffee with her, and as soon as she was seated at table began to talk about Pustovalov, saying that he was an excellent man whom one could thoroughly depend upon, and that any girl would be glad to marry him. Three days later Pustovalov came himself. He did not stay long, only about ten minutes, and he did not say much, but when he left, Olenka loved him — loved him so much that she lay awake all night in a perfect fever, and in the morning she sent for the elderly lady. The match was quickly arranged, and then came the wedding.

Pustovalov and Olenka got on very well together when they were married.

Usually he sat in the office till dinner-time, then he went out on business, while Olenka took his place, and sat in the office till evening, making up accounts and booking orders.

"Timber gets dearer every year; the price rises twenty per cent," she would say to her customers and friends. "Only fancy we used to sell local timber, and now Vassitchka always has to go for wood to the Mogilev district. And the freight!" she would add, covering her cheeks with her hands in horror. "The freight!"

It seemed to her that she had been in the timber trade for ages and ages, and that the most important and necessary thing in life was timber; and there was something intimate and touching to her in the very sound of words such as "baulk," "post," "beam," "pole," "scantling," "batten," "lath," "plank," etc.

At night when she was asleep she dreamed of perfect mountains of planks and boards, and long strings of wagons, carting timber somewhere far away. She dreamed that a whole regiment of six-inch beams forty feet high, standing on end, was marching upon the timber-yard; that logs, beams, and boards knocked together with the resounding crash of dry wood, kept falling and getting up again, piling themselves on each other. Olenka cried out in her sleep, and Pustovalov said to her tenderly: "Olenka, what's the matter, darling? Cross yourself!"

Her husband's ideas were hers. If he thought the room was too hot, or that business was slack, she thought the same. Her husband did not care for entertainments, and on holidays he stayed at home. She did likewise.

"You are always at home or in the office," her friends said to her. "You should go to the theatre, darling, or to the circus."

"Vassitchka and I have no time to go to theatres," she would answer sedately. "We have no time for nonsense. What's the use of these theatres?"

On Saturdays Pustovalov and she used to go to the evening service; on holidays to early mass, and they walked side by side with softened faces as they came home from church. There was a pleasant fragrance about them both, and her silk dress rustled agreeably. At home they drank tea, with fancy bread and jams of various kinds, and afterwards they ate pie. Every day at twelve o'clock there was a savoury smell of beet-root soup and of mutton or duck in their yard, and on fast-days of fish, and no one could pass the gate without feeling hungry. In the office the samovar was always boiling, and customers were regaled with tea and cracknels. Once a week the couple went to the baths and returned side by side, both red in the face.

"Yes, we have nothing to complain of, thank God," Olenka used to say to her acquaintances. "I wish every one were as well off as Vassitchka and I."

When Pustovalov went away to buy wood in the Mogilev district, she missed him dreadfully, lay awake and cried. A young veterinary surgeon in the army, called Smirnin, to whom they had let their lodge, used sometimes to come in in the evening. He used to talk to her and play cards with her, and this entertained her in her husband's absence. She was particularly interested in what he told her of his home life. He was married and had a little boy, but was separated from his wife because she had been unfaithful to him, and now he hated her and used to send her forty roubles a month for the maintenance of their son. And hearing of all this, Olenka sighed and shook her head. She was sorry for him.

"Well, God keep you," she used to say to him at parting, as she lighted him down the stairs with a candle. "Thank you for coming to cheer me up, and may the Mother of God give you health."

And she always expressed herself with the same sedateness and dignity, the same reasonableness, in imitation of her husband. As the veterinary surgeon was disappearing behind the door below, she would say:

"You know, Vladimir Platonitch, you'd better make it up with your wife. You should forgive her for the sake of your son. You may be sure the little fellow understands."

And when Pustovalov came back, she told him in a low voice about the veterinary surgeon and his unhappy home life, and both sighed and shook their heads and talked about the boy, who, no doubt, missed his father, and by some strange connection of ideas, they went up to the holy ikons, bowed to the ground before them and prayed that God would give them children.

And so the Pustovalovs lived for six years quietly and peaceably in love and complete harmony.

But behold! one winter day after drinking hot tea in the office, Vassily Andreitch went out into the yard without his cap on to see about sending off some timber, caught cold, and was taken ill. He had the best doctors, but he grew worse and died after four months' illness. And Olenka was a widow once more.

"I've nobody, now you've left me, my darling," she sobbed, after her husband's funeral. "How can I live without you, in wretchedness and misery! Pity me, good people, all alone in the world!"

She went about dressed in black with long "weepers," and gave up wearing hat and gloves for good. She hardly ever went out, except to church, or to her husband's grave, and led the life of a nun. It was not till six months later that she took off the weepers and opened the shutters of the windows. She was sometimes seen in the mornings, going with her cook to market for provisions, but what went on in her house and how she lived now could only be surmised. People guessed, from seeing her drinking tea in her garden with the veterinary surgeon, who read the newspaper aloud to her, and from the fact that, meeting a lady she knew at the post-office, she said to her:

"There is no proper veterinary inspection in our town, and that's the cause of all sorts of epidemics. One is always hearing of people's getting infection from the milk supply, or catching diseases from horses and cows. The health of domestic animals ought to be as well cared for as the health of human beings."

She repeated the veterinary surgeon's words, and was of the same opinion as he about everything. It was evident that she could not live a year without some attachment, and had found new happiness in the lodge. In any one else this would have been censured, but no one could think ill of Olenka; everything she did was so natural. Neither she nor the veterinary surgeon said anything to other people of the change in their relations, and tried, indeed, to conceal it, but without success, for Olenka could not keep a secret. When he had visitors, men serving in his regiment, and she poured out tea or served the supper, she would begin talking of the cattle plague, of the foot and mouth disease, and of the municipal slaughter-houses. He was dreadfully embarrassed, and when the guests had gone, he would seize her by the hand and hiss angrily:

"I've asked you before not to talk about what you don't understand. When we veterinary surgeons are talking among ourselves, please don't put your word in. It's really annoying."

And she would look at him with astonishment and dismay, and ask him in alarm: "But, Voloditchka, what *am* I to talk about?"

And with tears in her eyes she would embrace him, begging him not to be angry, and they were both happy.

But this happiness did not last long. The veterinary surgeon departed, departed for ever with his regiment, when it was transferred to a distant place — to Siberia, it may be. And Olenka was left alone.

Now she was absolutely alone. Her father had long been dead, and his armchair lay in the attic, covered with dust and lame of one leg. She got thinner and plainer, and when people met her in the street they did not look at her as they used to, and did not smile to her; evidently her best years were over and left behind, and now a new sort of life had begun for her, which did not bear thinking about. In the evening Olenka sat in the porch, and heard the band playing and the fireworks popping in the Tivoli, but now the sound stirred no response. She looked into her yard without interest, thought of nothing, wished for nothing, and afterwards, when night came on she went to bed and dreamed of her empty yard. She ate and drank as it were unwillingly.

And what was worst of all, she had no opinions of any sort. She saw the objects about her and understood what she saw, but could not form any opinion about them, and did not know what to talk about. And how awful it is not to have any opinions! One sees a bottle, for instance, or the rain, or a peasant driving in his cart, but what the bottle is for, or the rain, or the peasant, and what is the meaning of it, one can't say, and could not even for a thousand roubles. When she had Kukin, or Pustovalov, or the veterinary surgeon, Olenka could explain everything, and give her opinion about anything you like, but now there was the same emptiness in her brain and in her heart as there was in her yard outside. And it was as harsh and as bitter as wormwood in the mouth.

Little by little the town grew in all directions. The road became a street, and where the Tivoli and the timber-yard had been, there were new turnings and houses. How rapidly time passes! Olenka's house grew dingy, the roof got rusty, the shed sank on one side, and the whole yard was overgrown with docks and stinging-nettles. Olenka herself had grown plain and elderly; in summer she sat in the porch, and her soul, as before, was empty and dreary and full of bitterness. In winter she sat at her window and looked at the snow. When she caught the scent of spring, or heard the chime of the church bells, a sudden rush of memories from the past came over her, there was a tender ache in her heart, and her eyes brimmed over with tears; but this was only for a minute, and then came emptiness again and the sense of the futility of life. The black kitten, Briska, rubbed against her and purred softly, but Olenka was not touched by these feline caresses. That was not what she needed. She wanted a love that would absorb her whole being, her whole soul and reason — that would give her ideas and an object in life, and would warm her old blood. And she would shake the kitten off her skirt and say with vexation:

"Get along; I don't want you!"

And so it was, day after day and year after year, and no joy, and no opinions. Whatever Mavra, the cook, said she accepted.

One hot July day, towards evening, just as the cattle were being driven away, and the whole yard was full of dust, some one suddenly knocked at the gate. Olenka went to open it herself and was dumbfounded when she looked out: she saw Smirnin, the veterinary surgeon, grey-headed, and dressed as a civilian. She suddenly remembered everything. She could not help crying and letting her head fall on his breast without uttering a word, and in the violence of her feeling she did not notice how they both walked into the house and sat down to tea.

"My dear Vladimir Platonitch! What fate has brought you?" she muttered, trembling with joy.

"I want to settle here for good, Olga Semyonovna," he told her. "I have resigned my post, and have come to settle down and try my luck on my own account. Besides, it's time for my boy to go to school. He's a big boy. I am reconciled with my wife, you know."

"Where is she?" asked Olenka.

"She's at the hotel with the boy, and I'm looking for lodgings."

"Good gracious, my dear soul! Lodgings? Why not have my house? Why shouldn't that suit you? Why, my goodness, I wouldn't take any rent!" cried Olenka in a flutter, beginning to cry again. "You live here, and the lodge will do nicely for me. Oh dear! how glad I am!"

Next day the roof was painted and the walls were whitewashed, and Olenka, with her arms akimbo, walked about the yard giving directions. Her face was beaming with her old smile, and she was brisk and alert as though she had waked from a long sleep. The veterinary's wife arrived — a thin, plain lady, with short hair and a peevish expression. With her was her little Sasha, a boy of ten, small for his age, blue-eyed, chubby, with dimples in his cheeks. And scarcely had the boy walked into the yard when he ran after the cat, and at once there was the sound of his gay, joyous laugh.

"Is that your puss, auntie?" he asked Olenka. "When she has little ones, do give us a kitten. Mamma is awfully afraid of mice."

Olenka talked to him, and gave him tea. Her heart warmed and there was a sweet ache in her bosom, as though the boy had been her own child. And when he sat at the table in the evening, going over his lessons, she looked at him with deep tenderness and pity as she murmured to herself:

"You pretty pet! . . . my precious! . . . Such a fair little thing, and so clever."

"'An island is a piece of land which is entirely surrounded by water,'" he read aloud.

"An island is a piece of land," she repeated, and this was the first opinion to which she gave utterance with positive conviction after so many years of silence and dearth of ideas.

Now she had opinions of her own, and at supper she talked to Sasha's parents, saying how difficult the lessons were at the high schools, but that yet the high-school was better than a commercial one, since with a high-school education all careers were open to one, such as being a doctor or an engineer.

Sasha began going to the high school. His mother departed to Harkov to her sister's and did not return; his father used to go off every day to inspect cattle, and would often be away from home for three days together, and it seemed to Olenka as though Sasha was entirely abandoned, that he was not wanted at home, that he was being starved, and she carried him off to her lodge and gave him a little room there.

And for six months Sasha had lived in the lodge with her. Every morning Olenka came into his bedroom and found him fast asleep, sleeping noiselessly with his hand under his cheek. She was sorry to wake him.

"Sashenka," she would say mournfully, "get up, darling. It's time for school."

He would get up, dress and say his prayers, and then sit down to breakfast, drink three glasses of tea, and eat two large cracknels and half a buttered roll. All this time he was hardly awake and a little ill-humored in consequence.

"You don't quite know your fable, Sashenka," Olenka would say, looking at him as though he were about to set off on a long journey. "What a lot of trouble I have with you! You must work and do your best, darling, and obey your teachers."

"Oh, do leave me alone!" Sasha would say.

Then he would go down the street to school, a little figure, wearing a big cap and carrying a satchel on his shoulder. Olenka would follow him noiselessly.

"Sashenka!" she would call after him, and she would pop into his hand a date or a caramel. When he reached the street where the school was, he would feel ashamed of being followed by a tall, stout woman; he would turn round and say:

"You'd better go home, auntie. I can go the rest of the way alone."

She would stand still and look after him fixedly till he had disappeared at the school-gate.

Ah, how she loved him! Of her former attachments not one had been so deep; never had her soul surrendered to any feeling so spontaneously, so disinterestedly, and so joyously as now that her maternal instincts were aroused. For this little boy with the dimple in his cheek and the big school cap, she would have given her whole life, she would have given it with joy and tears of tenderness. Why? Who can tell why?

When she had seen the last of Sasha, she returned home, contented and serene, brimming over with love; her face, which had grown younger during the last six months, smiled and beamed; people meeting her looked at her with pleasure.

"Good-morning, Olga Semyonovna, darling. How are you, darling?"

"The lessons at the high school are very difficult now," she would relate at the market. "It's too much; in the first class yesterday they gave him a fable to learn by heart, and a Latin translation and a problem. You know it's too much for a little chap."

And she would begin talking about the teachers, the lessons, and the school books, saying just what Sasha said.

At three o'clock they had dinner together: in the evening they learned their lessons together and cried. When she put him to bed, she would stay a long time making the Cross over him and murmuring a prayer; then she would go to bed and dream of that far-away misty future when Sasha would finish his studies and become a doctor or an engineer, would have a big house of his own with horses and a carriage, would get married and have children. . . . She would fall asleep still thinking of the same thing, and tears would run down her cheeks from her closed eyes, while the black cat lay purring beside her: "Mrr, mrr, mrr."

Suddenly there would come a loud knock at the gate.

Olenka would wake up breathless with alarm, her heart throbbing. Half a minute later would come another knock.

"It must be a telegram from Harkov," she would think, beginning to tremble from head to foot. "Sasha's mother is sending for him from Harkov. . . . Oh, mercy on us!"

She was in despair. Her head, her hands, and her feet would turn chill, and she would feel that she was the most unhappy woman in the world. But another minute would pass, voices would be heard: it would turn out to be the veterinary surgeon coming home from the club.

"Well, thank God!" she would think.

And gradually the load in her heart would pass off, and she would feel at ease. She would go back to bed thinking of Sasha, who lay sound asleep in the next room, sometimes crying out in his sleep:

"I'll give it you! Get away! Shut up!"

Questions for Discussion

1. Why is Olenka called "darling" by her husbands and neighbors? Why is the story entitled "The Darling"?

2. In what ways is Olenka's second marriage, to Pustovalov, similar to her marriage to Kukin? In what ways is it different?

3. How is Olenka's relationship with the veterinary surgeon similar to and yet different from her two previous relationships?

4. Interpret the meaning of Sasha's cries in his sleep as the story closes: "I'll give it you! Get away! Shut up!" Will Sasha also abandon Olenka? How do you imagine her future?

5. What is the narrative's tone toward Olenka? Is the story critical of her accommodating behavior, or is she presented sympathetically?

Ideas for Writing

1. In an essay, examine the possible causes and motivations for Olenka's self-sacrificing nature as well as for her lack of inner life.

2. Consider "The Darling" as an exploration of how to love or not to love. How does the story view the nature of love?

CASEBOOK

Anton Chekhov

Anton Chekhov continues to be an important influence on the short story, and many modern critics and fiction writers have acknowledged their respect for him and, in some cases, their debt to his innovations. We begin the casebook with a selection from Chekhov's letters. Although Chekhov wrote no formal criticism, his letters included much useful advice to younger writers on the craft of the story and provide some valuable insights into his own practice. Many of his letters were addressed to the publisher and critic Alexei Suvorin. In several of these, Chekhov defends his work, stating that his method involves asking questions about reality rather than providing answers; he perceives the latter to be the role of the reader. In a letter to Maxim Gorky (1898), Chekhov counsels the then unknown writer on the importance of stylistic precision and rhetorical restraint. Gorky was grateful for the help provided by Chekhov, and in his *Reminiscences* (1905) he wrote movingly of Chekhov as a melancholy critic of the "banality" of Russian life. The Russian novelist Leo Tolstoy, in an afterword to the 1905 edition of "The Darling," saw Chekhov as a writer interested in advancing a view of the "new woman," independent and educated. Tolstoy further believed that, in order to further this "new woman," Chekhov created in the character of "the darling" an image of all that is wrong in the traditional role of woman as helper and nurturer of men and children — a role that Tolstoy, a traditionalist in gender roles, strongly upheld.

The essays that follow are by creative writers and critics of the twentieth century. Poet and critic Conrad Aiken, in "Anton Chekhov" (1921), writes of Chekhov's stories as embodying "the quality of natural, seemingly artless, actuality." In "Chekhov's Prose" (1981), novelist and story writer Vladimir Nabokov describes Chekhov's tone as that of a person who found things "funny and sad at the same time," and his style as subdued, ordinary in diction, "all his words in the same dim light." Story writer Eudora Welty, in "Reality in Chekhov's Stories" (1978), likewise refers to the ordinary quality of daily life present in Chekhov's stories, but focuses more on his characters, commenting on how he manages to go deep within each of them and their life situations with an "exploratory and painstaking" candor that constituted his most important and revealing literary method.

A critic and historian of the story form, Charles E. May writes in "Chekhov and the Modern Short Story" (1985) of the influence of Chekhov's work on a wide range of writers and on the evolution of a concept of the story as a "lyrically charged fragment" with characters who are "embodiments of mood." May notices Chekhov's influence on writers such as James Joyce, Franz Kafka, Katherine Anne Porter, Ernest Hemingway, and Raymond Carver. A final critic,

Renato Poggioli, writes in his "Storytelling in a Double Key" (1957) of the character Olenka in "The Darling" and her parallels both with the merry widow motif in folklore and with Psyche, the character in Greek myth who was married to the god Eros but was never allowed to see him in the daytime. Student writer Joseph Hsieh also focuses on Chekhov's female characters, comparing Olenka in "The Darling" with Marya in "The Schoolmistress." Hsieh sees the two women as representing opposite extremes in response to the need for nurture and intimate relationships.

FROM *The Letters of Anton Chekhov* (1888, 1898)

TO ALEXEI SUVORIN, MOSCOW, MAY 30, 1888

. . . What you say about [my story] "Lights" is perfectly just. The "Nikolai and Masha" situation runs glaringly through it, but what can be done about it? Not being in the habit of writing long stories, I am over anxious. Each time I start writing, I am frightened by the thought that my story has no right to be as long as it is, and so I try to make it as short as possible. The final scene between Kisochka and the engineer seemed to me like an insignificant detail that only weighed down the story, so I threw it out and had no choice but to put "Nikolai and Masha" in its place.

You write that neither the conversation about pessimism nor Kisochka's story help to solve the problem of pessimism. In my opinion it is not the writer's job to solve such problems as God, pessimism, etc.; his job is merely to record who, under what conditions, said or thought what about God or pessimism. The artist is not meant to be a judge of his characters and what they say; his only job is to be an impartial witness. I heard two Russians in a muddled conversation about pessimism, a conversation that solved nothing; all I am bound to do is reproduce that conversation exactly as I heard it. Drawing conclusions is up to the jury, that is, the readers. My only job is to be talented, that is, to know how to distinguish important testimony from unimportant, to place my characters in the proper light and speak their language. Shcheglov-Leontyev criticizes me for finishing the story with "You can't figure anything out in this world!" To his mind, the artist who is a psychologist *must* figure things out because otherwise, why is he a psychologist? But I don't agree with him. It's about time that everyone who writes — especially genuine literary artists — admitted that in this world you can't figure anything out. Socrates admitted it once upon a time, and Voltaire was wont to admit it. The crowd thinks it knows and understands everything; the stupider it is, the broader it imagines its outlook. But, if a writer whom the crowd believes takes it upon himself to declare he understands nothing of what he sees, that alone will constitute a major gain in the realm of thought and a major step forward. . . .

TO ALEXEI SUVORIN, MOSCOW, OCTOBER 27, 1888

. . . I sometimes preach heresies, but I haven't once gone so far as to deny that problematic questions have a place in art. In conversations with my fellow writers I always insist that it is not the artist's job to try to answer narrowly specialized questions. It is bad for the artist to take on something he doesn't understand. We have specialists for dealing with special questions; it is their job to make judgments about the peasant communes, the fate of capitalism, the evils of intemperance, and about boots and female complaints. The artist must pass judgment only on what he understands; his range is as limited as that of any other specialist — that's what I keep repeating and insisting upon. Anyone who says the artist's field is all answers and no questions has never done any writing or had any dealings with imagery. The artist observes, selects, guesses and synthesizes. The very fact of these actions presupposes a question; if he hadn't asked himself a question at the start, he would have nothing to guess and nothing to select. To put it briefly, I will conclude with some psychiatry: if you deny that creativity involves questions and intent, you have to admit that the artist creates without premeditation or purpose, in a state of unthinking emotionality. And so if any author were to boast to me that he'd written a story from pure inspiration without first having thought over his intentions, I'd call him a madman.

You are right to demand that an author take conscious stock of what he is doing, but you are confusing two concepts: *answering the questions* and *formulating them correctly*. Only the latter is required of an author. There's not a single question answered in [Tolstoy's] *Anna Karenina* or [Pushkin's] *Eugene Onegin*, but they are still fully satisfying works because the questions they raise are all formulated correctly. It is the duty of the court to formulate the questions correctly, but it is up to each member of the jury to answer them according to his own preference. . . .

You write that the hero of my "Name-Day Party" is a figure worth developing. Good Lord, I'm not an insentient brute, I realize that. I realize I hack up my characters, ruin them, and I waste good material. To tell you the truth, I would have been only too glad to spend half a year on "The Name-Day Party." I like taking my own good time about things, and see nothing attractive about slapdash publication. I would gladly describe *all* of my hero, de-scribe him with feeling, understanding and deliberation, I'd describe his emotions while his wife was in labor, the trial, his sense of disgust after being acquitted, I'd describe the midwife and doctors having tea in the middle of the night, I'd describe the rain. . . . It would be sheer pleasure for me, because I love digging deep and rummaging. But what can I do? I began the story on September 10th with the thought that I have to finish it by October 5th at the latest; if I miss the deadline I'll be going back on my word and will be left without any money. I write the beginning calmly and don't hold myself back, but by the middle I start feeling uneasy and apprehensive that the story will come out too long. I have to keep in mind that the *Northern Herald* is low in funds and that

I am one of its more expensive contributors. That's why my beginning always seems as promising as if I'd started a novel, the middle is crumpled together and timid, and the end is all fireworks, like the end of a brief sketch. Whether you like it or not, the first thing you have to worry about when you're working up a story is its framework. From your mass of heroes and semi-heroes you choose one individual, a wife or a husband, place him against the background, and portray only that person and emphasize only him. The others you scatter in the background like so much small change. The result is something like the firmament: one large moon surrounded by a mass of tiny stars. But the moon doesn't work, because it can only be understood once the other stars are understandable, and the stars are not sufficiently delineated. So instead of literature I get a patchwork quilt. What can I do? I don't know. I have no idea. I'll just have to trust to all-healing time.

To tell the whole truth, even though I did receive the prize, I still have not begun my literary career. The plots for five stories and two novels are languishing away in my head. One of the novels I conceived so long ago that some of the characters have grown out of date before my ever getting them down on paper. I have a whole army of people in my head begging to be let out and ordered what to do. Everything I've written to date is nonsense compared with what I would like to have written and would be overjoyed to be writing. It doesn't make any difference to me whether I'm writing "The Name-Day Party," or "Lights," or a farce, or a letter to a friend — it's all boring, mechanical and vapid and at times I feel chagrined on behalf of some critic who ascribes great significance to, say, my "Lights," I feel as if I'm deceiving him with my writings, just as I deceive many people with my now serious, now inordinately cheerful face. I don't like being a success. The themes sitting around in my head are irritated by and jealous of what I've already written. It annoys me to think that all the nonsense has already been written, while all the good things lie abandoned in a stockroom like unsold books. Of course a great deal of my lament is exaggerated; much of it is only *my imagination*, but it does contain a measure of truth, a large measure. What do I call good? The images that I feel are best, that I love and jealously hold on to so as not to waste and mangle them on short-order "Name-Day Parties." If my love errs, then I am wrong, but it's also possible that it does not. I am either a conceited fool or an organism genuinely capable of being a fine writer. Everything now being written leaves me cold and indifferent, whereas everything stored in my head interests, moves and excites me, from which I conclude that everyone is on the wrong track and I alone know the secret of what needs to be done. That's most likely what all writers think. But the devil himself would break his neck over these problems.

Money won't help me figure out what I should do. An extra thousand rubles won't settle my problem, and a hundred thousand is a castle in the air. Besides, whenever I do have money (maybe because I'm so unused to it, I don't know), I become extremely carefree and lazy; I feel as if I could wade across the seas. I need privacy and time.

Forgive me for monopolizing your attention with my own person. My pen got the better of me. For some reason I can't get down to work these days.

Thank you for agreeing to print those little articles of mine. For God's sake, don't stand on ceremony; shorten them, lengthen them, change them around, throw them out, do whatever you like. As Korsh says, I give you *carte blanche*. I'll be glad If they don't take up someone else's place. . . .

TO MAXIM GORKY, YALTA, DECEMBER 3, 1898

. . . You ask what my opinion is about your stories. My opinion? Yours is an unmistakable talent, and a real, great talent. For instance, in your story "In the Steppe" it is expressed with extraordinary power, and I was even seized with envy that it was not I who wrote it. You are an artist, a wise man; you feel superbly, you are plastic; that is, when you describe a thing you see it and touch it with your hands. That is real art. There you have my opinion, and I am very glad to be able to express it to you. I repeat, I am very glad, and if we came to know each other and talk for an hour or two you would be convinced how highly I value you, and what hopes I build on your talent.

Shall I speak now of defects? But that is not so easy. To speak of the defects of a talent is like speaking of the defects of a great tree growing in the orchard; the chief consideration is not the tree itself, but the taste of the man who is looking at the tree. Is not that so?

I shall begin by saying that, in my opinion, you do not use sufficient restraint. You are like a spectator in the theatre who expresses his rapture so unreservedly that he prevents both himself and others from listening. Particularly is this lack of restraint felt in the descriptions of Nature with which you interrupt your dialogues; when one reads those descriptions one wishes they were more compact, shorter, put, say, into two or three lines. The frequent mention of tenderness, whispering, velvetiness, and so on, gives to these descriptions a certain character of rhetoric and monotony — and they chill the reader, almost tire him. Lack of restraint is felt also in the descriptions of women ("Malva," "On the Rafts") and in the love scenes. It is not vigour, nor breadth of touch, but plain unreserve. . . .

Are you a self-taught man? In your stories you are a complete artist, and a cultured one in the truest sense. Least of all is crudeness characteristic of you; you are wise, and your feelings are subtle and elegant. Your best things are "In the Steppe" and "On the Rafts" — did I write to you about that? These are superb things, models; one sees in them an artist who has passed through a very good school. I do not think I am mistaken. The only defect is lack of restraint, lack of grace. When a man spends the fewest number of movements on a certain definite action, that is grace. In your expenditure there is felt excess.

The descriptions of nature are artistic; you are a real landscape painter. But the frequent personification (anthropomorphism) — the sea breathes, the sky gazes, the steppe caresses, Nature whispers, speaks, mourns, and so on —

such personifications make the descriptions somewhat monotonous, at times sugary, at times vague. Colour and expressiveness in descriptions of Nature are attained only by simplicity, by such simple phrases as "the sun set," "it became dark," "it began to rain," and so on — and that simplicity is inherent in you to a high degree, rare to anyone among the novelists. . . .

MAXIM GORKY

FROM *Reminiscences*   (1905)

A delicate mockery always played about his melancholy gray eyes, but at times these eyes would grow cold, piercing, and hard; at such moments his melodious voice sounded harsher and then it seemed to me that this unpretentious, gentle man, if he had to, could stand up strongly and firmly against a hostile force and not give way before it. But now and then I seemed to sense in his attitude toward people a touch of some sort of hopelessness, almost of cold, quiet despair.

"What a strange being is the Russian man!" he said once. "He is like a sieve; nothing stays in him very long. In his youth he greedily fills up on everything that comes his way; but after the age of thirty all that's left is some sort of gray rubbish. To live well, to live as a human being, one must work! Work with passion, with faith. And we Russians can't do it. An architect builds two or three decent houses, then sits down to play cards and plays all the rest of his life or is always at the theater hanging around backstage. A doctor, if he has a practice, no longer keeps up with scientific developments, reads nothing but a medical journal, and at forty is seriously convinced that all illnesses are catarrhal in origin. I never met a single civil servant who understood the least little bit about the meaning of his work: usually he sits in the capital or in a provincial town, makes up regulations, and sends them to Zmiev and Smorgon to be carried out. But as to whose freedom of movement these papers restrict in Zmiev and Smorgon — the civil servant thinks as little about that as an atheist does of the torments of hell. Once a lawyer gets the reputation for being a successful defense attorney, he stops worrying about justice and defends only property rights, plays the horses, eats oysters, and passes himself off as a subtle connoisseur of all the arts. The actor plays two or three roles passably well and thereupon stops studying further roles but wears a top hat and thinks he is a genius. Russia is a land of greedy, lazy people; they eat and drink dreadfully much, love to sleep in the daytime, and snore in their sleep. They marry for the sake of order in the home and take a mistress for social prestige. They have a dog's psychology: beat them and they squeal piteously and hide in their kennels; fondle them — they turn over on their backs with their little paws in the air and wag their little tails —"

These words rang with an anguished and cold contempt. But while he scorned, he pitied, and when it happened that someone was abused in his presence, Anton Pavlovich immediately took his part: "Come now! After all, he's an old man. He's seventy—"

Or, "He's young yet; he does it out of ignorance—"

And when he talked that way I saw not a trace of smugness on his face.

In a young person, banality seems only funny and petty but after a while it envelops a man; it saturates his brain and blood with its gray shadow like poison and coal gas fumes and he becomes like an old signboard corroded with rust; as if something were written there—but what? You can't make it out.

Even in his earliest stories, Anton Pavlovich could already make out in the dreary sea of banality its somber absurdities with their tragic overtones. One need only read through his "humorous" stories attentively to convince oneself how much of the cruel and repulsive the author sorrowfully observed and, with a feeling of shame, concealed behind his droll words and situations.

He was in a way chastely modest; he never allowed himself to say to people loudly and openly: "Now, try to behave more decently," in the vain hope that they themselves would guess the urgent need for behaving decently. He hated everything banal and filthy; he described the abominations of life in the noble language of the poet, with the gentle smile of the humorist; and you hardly notice behind the outward beauty of his stories their inner meaning full of bitter reproach.

The very respectable public, when they read "Daughter of Albion," laugh and hardly see in that story the most vile mockery of a satiated gentleman, of a lonely being, a stranger to all and everything. And in every one of the humorous stories of Anton Pavlovich I hear the quiet, deep sigh of a pure, genuinely human spirit, the hopeless sigh of compassion for people who are unable to respect their own human worth and unresistingly submit to brute force, live like slaves, and believe in nothing but the need to gulp down as much greasy cabbage soup as possible and feel nothing but terror lest someone powerful and brazen should beat them.

Nobody understood so clearly and keenly as Anton Chekhov the tragedy of life's banalities; nobody before him could with such merciless truthtelling depict for people the shameful and painful picture of their life in the dreary chaos of petty bourgeois prosiness.

His enemy was banality; all his life he fought against it; he ridiculed it and portrayed it with a keen impassive pen; he could find the rot of banality even where at first glance everything seemed quite in order, even in splendid shape . . . and banality took revenge on him with a very nasty trick when it placed his corpse—the corpse of a poet—in a railway car for the transport of "oysters."

The yellowish-green stain of that car seems to me precisely the vast, triumphant smile of banality at its weary enemy while the hypocritical melancholy of the countless "reminiscences" in the daily papers conceal, I sense, the cold odorous breathing of all that banality, secretly gratified at the death of its enemy.

When you read the stories of Anton Chekhov, you feel just as if it were a melancholy day in late autumn when the air is so transparent you see sharply outlined in it bare trees, cramped little houses, and gray people. Everything is so strange — lonely, helpless, and still. The deepening blue distance is empty and, as it fades into the pale sky, breathes a dreary cold across the land, covered with frozen mud. The author's mind like an autumnal sun lights up with cruel clarity the scourged roads, the crooked streets, the cramped and filthy houses in which wretched little people are suffocating from boredom and laziness, flooding the house with their unintelligent, somnolent bustling. There anxiously, like a gray mouse, "the darling" scampers to and fro — she is a nice, gentle woman who loves so slavishly, so very much. You can even slap her in the face and she, meek slave that she is, will not even dare to groan aloud. Olga from *The Three Sisters* stands gloomily beside her; she also loves very much and unprotestingly submits to the whims of the depraved and banal wife of her lazy brother; before her eyes her sisters' lives are shattered; she weeps and cannot help anyone at all; in her heart there is not one vital, forceful word of protest against banality.

There is the lachrymose Ranevskaya and other former masters of *The Cherry Orchard* — egotistical, like children, and feeble, like old people. They are late in dying and they whine, seeing nothing around them, understanding nothing — parasites, without the strength to fix themselves to life again. The wretched little student Trofimov speaks eloquently about the need to work and — loafs and amuses himself out of boredom by stupid scoffing at Varya who is working indefatigably for the welfare of loafers.

Vershinin dreams of how fine life will be in three hundred years and goes on living without noticing that everything around him is decaying, that before his eyes, Solyony is prepared to kill poor Baron Tusenbach out of boredom and stupidity.

There file before us a long line of people — slaves to their love, their stupidity and laziness, their greed for the good things of this earth; there pass men who are slaves to a dark fear of life; they move along in clouded anxiety filling life with incoherent speeches about the future, feeling that there is no place for them in the present.

Sometimes in their gray mass, a shot rings out; some Ivanov or Treplev figured out what he had to do — and died.

Many of them dream gloriously about how good life will be after two hundred years, but one simple question never enters their heads: who will make it better if we do nothing but dream?

A great wise man, aware of everything, passed by this dull, gray crowd of feeble people, looked at the dreary inhabitants of his country. Then with a melancholy smile, in a tone of soft but profound reproach, with hopeless anguish on his face and in his heart, he said in his fine, honest voice:

"You live abominably, gentlemen!"

LEO TOLSTOY

FROM The Afterword to "The Darling"   (1905)

There is a story of profound significance in the Book of Numbers of how Balak, the King of Moab, summoned Balaam to curse the people of Israel who had pitched their tents in his plains. Balak promised Balaam many gifts, and Balaam, tempted, set off to go to Balak; but on his way he was stopped by an angel, whom the ass saw, but whom Balaam failed to see. In spite of that warning, Balaam came to Balak and they mounted a high place, on which was prepared an altar with offerings of oxen and rams, to curse Israel. Balak waited for the curse, but Balaam, instead of cursing, blessed Israel. . . .

What happened to Balaam, very often also happens to real poets, artists. Tempted by Balak's promises — by popularity or by his own false, assumed view, the poet does not see the angel who withholds him and whom even the ass sees; and the poet wants to curse, but, lo he blesses.

This very same thing happened to the real poet and artist Tchekhov, when he wrote his beautiful story "The Darling."

The author, evidently, wants to have a laugh at the pitiable — in his view, not in his feeling — creature of the Darling, who now shares Kookin's anxieties about his theatre, now is engrossed in the concerns of the timber trade, now, under the influence of the veterinary surgeon, believes the most important thing to be the fight against "pearl" disease, now is plunged in questions of grammar and in the interests of the schoolboy in the big peaked cap. There is fun in the very name Kookin, funny is his illness and the telegram announcing his death, funny is the timber merchant with his "worshipfulness," funny is the vet. and funny also is the schoolboy: but not funny and even sacred is the wonderful soul of Darling, with her capacity for giving herself with all her being to anyone she loves.

I think that in the mind, not in the feeling of the author, when he wrote "The Darling," there was floating a vague idea of the new woman, of her equal rights with man; of the educated, learned woman, working independently not worse, if not better than man, for the good of society; that very woman who has raised and upholds the woman question; and he, having begun to write "The Darling," meant to show what woman ought not to be. The Balak of public opinion called Tchekhov to curse the weak, submissive woman devoted to man, the uncultured woman, and Tchekhov mounted the high place, and there were prepared oxen and rams there; but, having begun to speak, the poet blessed what he had meant to curse. I, at any rate, in spite of the wonderful, happy fun of the whole story, can't read without tears certain passages of that marvellous story. I am moved by the description of how she, with complete self-abnegation, loves Kookin and everything loved by Kookin, and how she loves the timber merchant, and also the vet. and more still how she suffers, when she is left alone, when she has no one to love, and how she at last with all the strength of feminine and maternal feeling (of which she has had no direct experience) gives her boundless love to the future man, to the tiny schoolboy in the big cap.

The author makes her love the bold Kookin; the worthless timber-merchant, and the unpleasant vet.; but love is not the less sacred, whether its object be a Kookin, or a Spinoza, a Pascal, or a Schiller,[1] and whether its objects change as rapidly as with the Darling, or the object remains one and the same throughout life.

A long time ago I happened to read in the *Novoye Vremya* an excellent feuilleton by Ata on women. The author expressed in that feuilleton a remarkably wise and profound idea about women. "Women," he says, "try to prove to us that they can do everything which we, men, can. I not only don't dispute that," says the author, "but I am ready to agree that women can do everything which men do, and perhaps even do it better; but the unfortunate thing is that men cannot do anything, even slightly approaching what women can do."

Yes, doubtless it is so, and this refers not only to birthgiving, feeding, and the early upbringing of children; but men cannot perform the highest, the best work which brings man nearer to God — the work of love, of complete self-devotion to the person loved, which work has been so well and naturally done, is being done and will be done by good women. What would happen to the world, what would happen to us, men, if women did not possess that quality and did not manifest it? Without women as doctors, telegraphists, advocates, scholars, and authors we shall manage; but without mothers, helpmates, friends, comforters, who love in man all the best there is in him, and who, by imperceptible suggestion, evoke and sustain in him all the best in him — without such women it would be bad to live on earth. Christ would not have had Mary and the Magdalene, Francis of Assisi would not have had Clara, the wives of the Decembrists would not have gone into banishment, the Doukhobors would not have had their wives, who did not keep their husbands back, but supported them in their martyrdom for the truth; there would not exist thousands upon thousands of obscure women, the finest of all, as all that is obscure is fine, the comforters of drunken, weak, licentious men, those who more than anyone else need the consolation of love. In that love, whether it be directed to Kookin or to Christ, is the principal, great strength of woman, not to be replaced by anything else.

What an amazing misunderstanding is the whole so-called woman question, which has taken hold, as must be the case with every banality, of the majority of women and even of men!

"Woman wants to perfect herself" — can there be anything more lawful and just than that?

But surely the work of woman by her very destiny is other than the work

---

[1] The latter three are widely respected, intellectual men of letters. — Eds.

of man. And therefore the ideal of woman's perfection cannot be the same as the ideal of man's. Let us suppose that we do not know in what that ideal consists; at any rate there is no doubt that it is not the ideal of man's perfection. And yet to the attainment of that masculine ideal is being directed now all the ridiculous and mistaken activity of the fashionable feminist movement, which confuses women so much now.

I am afraid that Tchekhov, in writing "The Darling," was under the influence of that misunderstanding.

He, like Balaam, intended to curse, but the god of poesy forbade it him and commanded him to bless; and he blessed, and unwillingly he arrayed in such a wonderful light that darling creature, that she will for ever remain the model of what a woman can be, both to be happy herself as well as to make happy those with whom fate brings her closely together.

The story is so beautiful just because it came forth unconsciously.

I learnt to ride a bicycle in a riding school in which reviews of a military division were held. At the other end of the school a woman was learning to ride. It occurred to me that I might perhaps get in the woman's way, and I began looking at her. And, looking at her, I began unconsciously getting nearer and nearer to her, and in spite of the fact that she, having noticed the danger, hastened to get away, I rode into her and knocked her down, that is, I did the very opposite of what I wanted to do, only because I had fixed my strained attention on her.

The same, only the reverse, happened to Tchekhov: he wanted to knock the Darling down, and fixed on her the strained attention of the poet—and he exalted her.

CONRAD AIKEN

Anton Chekhov   (1921)

You are traveling from New York to Chicago, and the stranger with whom you have been talking leans with restrained excitement towards the car window, as the train passes a small town, and says: "I lived in that town for three years." It looks like any other town. But you stare at it as if it concealed something amazing, had some secret; and when, after a pause, he begins telling you the story of something odd that happened to him there, a story not very remarkable in itself nor involving very remarkable people, nevertheless the story, the people, the town all seem to you very extraordinary: you listen with an intensity of pleasure that is almost painful, you strive desperately to hold in mind the picture of that town with its small brick shops, dingy fences, white wooden church, to penetrate it, to live in it; and when the narrative is finished you have suddenly an overwhelming desire to tell the stranger a similar narrative, something real, convincing. You have, maybe, no such story at your disposal. You might tell him of something that happened to your friend S., but that, you feel, would not be so satisfactory: the effect of it would not be so powerful. What you desire to say is: "That reminds me of something that occurred when I was living in a small town in Vermont, two years ago. . . ." You are silent, and wonder why it is that the stranger's simple tale has so absorbed you.

Its charm, of course, is simply in the fact that it is actual, that it really happened. This charm is intensified by the fact that it is narrated by the protagonist himself, simply and artlessly, and by the fact that you have actually seen the town that served as a setting, two things that combine to make the reality overwhelming. You have been treated to a "slice of life," a "human document." . . . It is in this kind of actuality that we find, perhaps, a key to the work of Anton Chekhov, possibly the greatest writer of the short story who has ever lived. The stories of Chekhov have precisely this quality of natural, seemingly artless, actuality — casual and random in appearance, abrupt, discursive, alternately overcrowded and thin. Chekhov is the stranger who sits in the train beside us, who suddenly exclaims, "You see that town? I know a queer thing that happened there," and he tells us, in a normal, conversational tone, of the real things that happened there to real people. Observe his openings, taken in order from his volume, *The Schoolmistress and Other Stories*.

> At half-past eight they drove out of town.

> A medical student named Mayer, and a pupil of the Moscow School of Painting, Sculpture and Architecture, called Rybnikov, went one evening to see their friend Vasilyev, a law student, and suggested that he go with them to S Street.

> The twilight of evening. Big flakes of wet snow are whirling lazily about the street lamps, which have just been lighted.

> In the year in which my story begins I had a job at a little station on one of the south-western railways.

> Nadia Zelenin had just come back with her mamma from the theatre, where she had seen a performance of *Yevgeni Onegin*.

In every instance the pitch is at once plausibly colloquial. "I am not," Chekhov seems to say, "up to any literary tricks, I have no artistic designs upon you — literature bores me, with its exaggerations and flowerinesses. No, I simply happen to know about this case, and this is how it was." This disarms us — we are now ready to believe literally anything. The primitive desire to listen to a story has been aroused in us, but that is not all: we have been convinced a priori by the speaker's very tone of voice, by his calm, and above all by the absence, on his part, of any *desire* to convince, that what he is about to tell us is true. His audience is already half hypnotized with the first sentence.

In this regard, Chekhov is obviously in the tradition of the Goncourts, with their "human documents," and of Gogol: he was a contemporary of Maupassant in more than mere moment. The theory of the "slice of life" was, at that moment, the thing, and Chekhov, with Maupassant, remains as the chief exemplar, in the short story, of that theory. Yet that theory as it worked through Chekhov is not what it was as it worked through Maupassant: a world of difference sunders the two men. Basically, the difference lies in the fact that Maupassant was a logician of the short story, and Chekhov a poet. Maupassant's mere "mechanics" are superb; far better than Chekhov's. There is no waste, his items are well chosen and "clear"; he arranges them with precision and economy and in a sequence logically overwhelming; he makes his case with a miracle of cold dexterity. Grant his hypothesis, his Q.E.D. will punctually flower.

There is little of this in Chekhov. His stories have not this flat, swift trajectory, are not logically "rounded," do not move, as narratives, to an overwhelming provided conclusion, through an unalterable certainty which one has been permitted, or rather compelled, now and again terrifyingly to feel. Many of his stories do not, in this sense, conclude at all — they merely stop. In fact, the conclusion in itself did not interest Chekhov. He did not desire to emphasize, as Maupassant emphasized, the "final" event, nor, indeed, any single event; his method was more copious, and his concern was not so much with the possibility that in this copiousness a narrative current should be felt, as with the certainty that through it should be perceived a living being or group of beings, beings through whose rich consciousness, intense or palpable, we are enabled to live, backward and forward, in time, lives as appallingly genuine as our own.

Here we reach naturally the question of psychology, and must observe that while Maupassant's characters obey a logic in this regard, obey it mechanically, like marionettes, and have no life apart from it, Chekhov's characters are complex, indeterminate, diffuse a consciousness wider than the bounds of the particular event in which we see them participating: they come to it from "somewhere" (we know only vaguely where), and depart from it for somewhere else. This is due not merely to the fact that Chekhov is more concerned with the effect of "actuality" than with "story," but to the fact that, as was said above, he was a poet. His sensibilities were rich and of an immense range, had thrust their roots, one dares to think, almost as widely and deeply into life as Shakespeare's: his understanding was unsurpassed, and if he falls short of the greatest of artists it is not for a lack of that faculty. No artist has known, by introspection, more "states of mind," no artist has known better, by observation, what shapes they assume in talk or behavior. This, after all, is Chekhov's genius — he was a master of mood. His stories offer not only an extraordinary panorama of scenes, actions, situations but, more importantly, a range of states of consciousness which is perhaps unparalleled. It was this pluralism, this awareness of the many-sidedness of life, that sent him to the short story rather than to the novel, and made of his longer stories, as he himself says, mere accumulations. These accumulations — "A Dreary Story," "My Life," "The Steppe" — do not disintegrate, as the short stories do not, simply because, like the short stories, they depend for unity not on the formal working of a theme, but on verisimilitude, on the never-diminishing saturation of consciousness in the life to be "given": their unity is a unity of tone.

If we evade for the moment the question of the precise value, in fiction, of the "actual," and of the extent to which it may be permitted to supplant all other values, and evade, also for the moment, the question of the kind of actuality toward which Chekhov felt a compulsion, it is perhaps profitable to note how interesting are the aesthetic problems raised by the effort to capture, in fiction, that tone. We have already observed that Chekhov instinctively or consciously uses, at the outset of a story and throughout, a colloquial tone—he is never better than when he tells his story in the first person singular. He wishes, in other words, to keep the pitch of the story down, to diminish what is called "the psychic distance"; his picture is to be frameless and immediate, so close to us that we can touch it. He does not want us to be conscious of his style, nor of any arrangement. He wants us to see his people and scenes just as they are, neither larger nor smaller than life. Every trace of sympathy must therefore be excluded: "When you depict sad or unlucky people try to be colder—it gives their grief, as it were, a background. . . . Yes, you must be cold. . . . Every trace of stylization, of heightening, must be expunged. . . . Beauty and expressiveness in Nature are attained only by simplicity, by such simple phrases as 'The sun set,' 'It was dark,' 'It began to rain,' and so on. . . ." In everything we see the avoidance of the phrase, the detail, the attitude, the sense of "frame," of "scheme," which might mitigate the effect of immediacy. "But of the word 'art' I am terrified. . . ." No wonder—by art he meant conscious art, and Chekhov was only intermittently a conscious artist; he knew that he was at his best when, on a theme out of memory—a face, an incident—he gave himself up to rapid improvisation, an improvisation which took the form of a complete surrender to that face, that incident, a submersion of the senses.

This, of course, *was* his art—an art, of its sort, perfect. Yet we come back to question again the extent to which this effect of overwhelming actuality may be permitted to supplant other effects—the effects, for example, of an art more deliberate, more conscious. The two sorts of art ("two" if we take merely the extremes, say, Chekhov and Henry James) are not of course mutually exclusive, there will be room for both; the generation, like the individual, will make its natural choice and rationalize its choice ex post facto. Yet if we need not necessarily at the instant choose between them, it is none the less fruitful to observe their distinguishing characteristics, and we can do no better at the outset than to quote Henry James himself, speaking, in his essay on "The New Novel," of precisely this question of the degree in which mere immersion in the actual may be sufficient.

> Yes, yes—but is this all? These are the circumstances of the interest—we see, we see; but where is the interest itself, where and what is its center, and how are we to measure it in relation to that? . . . That appreciation is . . . a

mistake and a priggishness, being reflective and thereby corrosive, is another of the fond dicta which we are here concerned but to brush aside . . . appreciation, attentive and reflective, inquisitive and conclusive, is in this connection absolutely the golden *key* to our pleasure.

This is a statement of a theory of art so antithetical to that of Chekhov (insofar as he consciously entertained one), that it is reasonable to suppose that he simply would not have understood it. Here we have an artist who not only selects one from among many themes because it is richest in possibilities of being "worked," but also positively invites his reader to observe at every moment the "working" of it, to look, as it were, at the back of the clock no less often than at its face, so that he may know not merely what it says but how it says it. This is a pleasure to which Chekhov does not invite us: to make that invitation is, in the same breath, to take a deliberate step away from the "actual."

Compare Chekhov's *In the Ravine* with Turgenev's *A Lear of the Steppes*. The themes have much in common. But whereas Chekhov has richly and beautifully improvised, always in the key of the actual, giving us an immense number of scenes, dialogues, persons, all of them palpitantly real and caught in an exquisite, quiet beauty of tone, Turgenev has gone more deliberately to work: he strikes sharply, even artificially, his "theme" in the opening, giving us thus in advance a glimpse of the whole, and then proceeds to the fine development of this theme through a series of delicate exaggerations — he aims not at the immediate but at the distant, slightly distorted by a trick of atmosphere; not at the actual, but at the larger than the actual. One feels the artificiality, certainly; but one enjoys it, and in retrospect it is the Turgenev story that one clearly remembers, not the Chekhov story. Kharlov we still see, but we do not even recall the name of Chekhov's Lear, any more than we see him as a person. He was living as long as we read of him — more so perhaps than Kharlov. That whole life, in which Chekhov drowned us, how beautiful, resonant, full of echoes it was, how aromatically it ended! But it is our joy in the tone of it that we recall, and not the things that created that tone.

We come back, therefore, to the point from which we started, to a clear realization that Chekhov was in essence a poet, a poet of the actual, an improviser in the vivid. His compulsions drove him to seek character, perhaps — more precisely, to seek mood, state of mind; he profoundly knew the quality, the light, the timbre, the fluctuations of mood, particularly those of a melancholy tinge; and if, in retrospect, we find that his characters have an odd way of evaporating, it is because so often our view of them was never permitted for a moment to be external — we saw them only as infinitely fine and truthful sequences of mood. Chekhov was great because his sensibilities were of sufficient range to enable him to apply the method almost universally. His sympathy, his pity, his tenderness, were inexhaustible. He lived, and thus permitted us to live, everywhere.

VLADIMIR NABOKOV

FROM *Chekhov's Prose*   (1981)

Chekhov's books are sad books for humorous people; that is, only a reader with a sense of humor can really appreciate their sadness. There exist writers that sound like something between a titter and a yawn — many of these are professional humorists, for instance. There are others that are something between a chuckle and a sob — Dickens was one of these. There is also that dreadful kind of humor that is consciously introduced by an author in order to give a purely technical relief after a good tragic scene — but this is a trick remote from true literature. Chekhov's humor belonged to none of these types; it was purely Chekhovian. Things for him were funny and sad at the same time, but you would not see their sadness if you did not see their fun, because both were linked up.

Russian critics have noted that Chekhov's style, his choice of words and so on, did not reveal any of those special artistic preoccupations that obsessed, for instance, Gogol or Flaubert or Henry James. His dictionary is poor, his combination of words almost trivial — the purple patch, the juicy verb, the hothouse adjective, the crême-de-menthe epithet, brought in on a silver tray, these were foreign to him. He was not a verbal inventor in the sense that Gogol was; his literary style goes to parties clad in its everyday suit. Thus Chekhov is a good example to give when one tries to explain that a writer may be a perfect artist without being exceptionally vivid in his verbal technique or exceptionally preoccupied with the way his sentences curve. When Turgenev sits down to discuss a landscape, you notice that he is concerned with the trouser-crease of his phrase; he crosses his legs with an eye upon the color of his socks. Chekhov does not mind, not because these matters are not important — for some writers they are naturally and very beautifully important when the right temperament is there — but Chekhov does not mind because his temperament is quite foreign to verbal inventiveness. Even a bit of bad grammar or a slack newspaperish sentence left him unconcerned. The magical part of it is that in spite of his tolerating flaws which a bright beginner would have avoided, in spite of his being quite satisfied with the man-in-the-street among words, the word-in-the-street, so to say, Chekhov managed to convey an impression of artistic beauty far surpassing that of many writers who thought they knew what rich beautiful prose was. He did it by keeping all his words in the same dim light and of the same exact tint of gray, a tint between the color of an old fence and that of a low cloud. The variety of his moods, the flicker of his charming wit, the deeply artistic economy of characterization, the vivid detail, and the fade-out of human life — all the peculiar Chekhovian features — are enhanced by being suffused and surrounded by a faintly iridescent verbal haziness.

EUDORA WELTY

FROM *Reality in Chekhov's Stories*   (1978)

Chekhov's perception of our differing views of reality, with its capacity to understand them all, may have done more than anything else to bring about his revolutionizing of the short story. Surely it lay behind the fact that formal pattern imposed on the story by long tradition gave way to a treatment entirely different — something open to human meaning and answerable to that meaning in all its variety.

The story as Chekhov wrote it was set forth in simple terms of everyday life where it took place. The stuff of life was transmuted into the stuff of his story — the stuff of reality. All the same, "real," as in "the real world," does not, as we know, mean invariable, or static, or ironclad, or consistent, or even trustworthy. What is real in life — and what a Chekhov story was made to reflect with the utmost honesty — may be at the same time what is transient, ephemeral, contradictory, even on the point of vanishing before our eyes. So it isn't just *there*.

In Chekhov's stories, reality always has its origin: it comes to us through the living human being — and not anonymously. It lives, was born, in the particular — not in the general humanity but in this man, that woman, their child. What's real, like them, carries, as they do, the seed of change. It is perishable.

Chekhov shows no fondness for the abstract. Reality — along with good and evil, justice and love, and other subjects of fundamental importance to him — he dealt with in terms of the particular and personal meaning it took on for human beings in the course of their lives.

And so reality is no single, pure ray, no beacon against the dark. It might be thought of as a cluster of lesser lights, visible here on earth like the windows of a village at night, close together but not *one* — some are bright, some dim, some waywardly flickering. All imply people; there are people there for every light.

We can quickly think of a number of kinds of reality Chekhov shows us in his stories. Of course, they all bear some relationship to one another — it is, again, a matter of human connection, a state of kinship or at least of neighborliness. It is what "The Darling" has in common with "A Calamity," "The Name Day Party" with "The Duel" — each presents, or turns upon, its own emerging view of reality.

It was his plainest intention that we never should hear him telling us what we should think or feel or believe. He is not trying to teach us, through his characters; he only asks us to understand them.

Religion, government, science, education, the arts are not in themselves either moral or immoral, as he had cause to remark in his letters. Peasants, women, schoolteachers, the military, drunks, Turks, persons over forty or under two, revolutionaries, doctors, the raisers of their own gooseberries — none of them are good or evil in so being but in what they do to each other, the ways they treat their fellow human beings. A character in "A Dreary Story" remarks that "virtue and purity are not very different from vice if they are not free from evil feelings."

Chekhov is also the least self-obstrusive of story writers. It is the story he's written that has gained a self — a clear, unself-conscious identity, vigorous, purposeful, ongoing. This freeing of the form came from the deeps of his temperament, we might suppose. The abhorrence he felt toward coercion in human affairs must have had its own part in clearing away the confines of arbitrary plot, manipulated characters. As the grandson of a serf, who had "squeezed the slave out of himself drop by drop," Chekhov knew all the better what it meant to make himself free as an artist.

Thus he dared to make himself free to enter the body, spirit, mind and heart of a character, and free of any crippling wish to use him as a spokesman for himself, or as a moral example, or as a scapegoat. In the writing of his stories he conscientiously yielded only to the authority of his feeling for human beings as human beings.

And no human being is out of bounds to Chekhov. No state of health or stage of consciousness or time of life could have appeared strange to him. As a storyteller he is within any character he invents — a woman in her seventh month of pregnancy, an aged learned man suffering from insomnia and "strange and inappropriate thoughts," even a little dog being trained for a music-hall act, who "grew so used to the word 'talent,' that every time her master pronounced it, she jumped up as if it had been her name."

Neither did he hesitate to deal with any subject he wished. Chekhov wrote of sex with honesty and lack of fuss, as he wrote of all human experience. As always, it is a character's feelings that give it its meaning. Much ahead of his time, and perhaps of ours, in "The Duel" he treated with candor and seriousness a young woman of compelling sexuality. "The Lady with the Pet Dog" is a compassionate study of a cynical middle-aged man surprised when, almost against his will and against his belief, his sexual worldliness turns into the honesty and difficulty of belated love.

Chekhov's candor, which was natural to him, was more than a revulsion against lying and hypocrisy. It was a tool in his work. His candor was exploratory and painstaking — he might have used it as the doctor in him would know how, treating the need for truth between human beings as an emergency.

CHARLES E. MAY

FROM *Chekhov and the Modern Short Story*   (1985)

Anton Chekhov's short stories were first welcomed in England and America just after the turn of the century as examples of late nineteenth-century realism, but since they did not embody the social commitment or political convictions of the realistic novel, they were termed "realistic" primarily because they seemed to focus on fragments of everyday reality. Consequently, they were characterized as "sketches," "slices of life," "cross-sections of Russian life," and were often said to be lacking every element which constitutes a really good short story. However, at the same time, other critics saw that Chekhov's ability to dispense with a striking incident, his impressionism, and his freedom from the literary conventions of the highly plotted and formalized story marked the beginnings of a new or "modern" kind of short fiction that combined the specific details of realism with the poetic lyricism of romanticism.[1]

The primary characteristics of this new hybrid form are: character as mood rather than as either symbolic projection or realistic depiction; story as minimal lyricized sketch rather than as elaborately plotted tale; atmosphere as an ambiguous mixture of both external details and psychic projections; and a basic impressionistic apprehension of reality itself as a function of perspectival point of view. The ultimate result of these characteristics is the modernist and postmodernist focus on reality itself as a fictional construct and the contemporary trend to make fictional assumptions and techniques both the subject matter and theme of the novel and the short story.

CHARACTER AS MOOD

The most basic problem in understanding the Chekhovian shift to the "modern" short story involves a new definition of the notion of "story" itself, which, in turn, involves not only a new understanding of the kind of "experience" to be embodied in story but a new conception of character as well. Primarily this shift to the modern is marked by a transition from the romantic focus on a projective fiction, in which characters are functions in an essentially code-bound parabolic or ironic structure, to an apparently realistic episode in which plot is subordinate to "as-if-real" character. However, it should be noted that Chekhov's fictional figures are not realistic in the way that characters in the novel usually are. The short story is too short to allow for character to be created by the kind of dense detail and social interaction through duration typical of the novel.

Conrad Aiken was perhaps the first critic to recognize the secret of Chekhov's creation of character. Noting that Chekhov's stories offer an unparalleled "range of states of consciousness," Aiken says that whereas Poe manipulates plot and James manipulates thought, Chekhov "manipulates feeling or mood." If, says, Aiken, we find his characters have a strange way of evaporating, "it is because our view of them was never permitted for a moment to be

---

[1] Early reviews of Chekhov can be found in *Chekhov: The Critical Heritage*, ed. Victor Emeljanow (London: Routlege and Kagan Paul, 1981). See the twelfth essay in this volume by John Tulloch, "Chekhov Abroad: Western Criticism."

external — we saw them only as infinitely fine and truthful sequences of mood."[2] This apprehension of character as mood is closely related to D. S. Mirsky's understanding of the Chekhovian style, which he described as "bathed in a perfect and uniform haze," and the Chekhovian narrative method, which Mirsky says "allows nothing to 'happen,' but only smoothly and imperceptibly to 'become.'"[3]

Such a notion of character as mood and story as a hazy "eventless" becoming is characteristic of the modern artistic understanding of story. It is like Conrad's conception in *Heart of Darkness,* for to his story-teller Marlowe, "the meaning of an episode was not inside like a kernel but outside, enveloping the tale which brought it out only as a glow brings out a haze." More recently, Eudora Welty has suggested that the first thing we notice about the short story is "that we can't really see the solid outlines of it — it seems bathed in something of its own. It is wrapped in an atmosphere."[4] Once we see that the short story, by its very shortness, cannot deal with the denseness of detail and the duration of time typical of the novel, but rather focuses on a revelatory break-up of the rhythm of everyday reality, we can see how the form, striving to accommodate "realism" at the end of the nineteenth century, focused on an experience under the influence of a particular mood and therefore depended more on tone than on plot as a principle of unity.

In fact, "an experience" phenomenologically encountered, rather than "experience" discursively understood, is the primary focus of the modern short story, and, as John Dewey makes clear, "an experience" is recognized as such precisely because it has a unity, "a single *quality* that pervades the entire experience in spite of the variation of its constituent parts."[5] Rather than plot, what unifies the modern short story is an atmosphere, a certain tone of significance. The problem is to determine the source of this significance. On the one hand, it may be the episode itself, which, to use Henry James's phrase, seems to have a "latent value" that the artist tries to unveil.[6] It is this point of view that governs James Joyce's notion of the epiphany " — " a sudden spiritual manifestation, whether in the vulgarity of speech or of gesture or in a memorable phase of the mind itself."[7]

On the other hand, it may be the subjectivity of the teller, his perception that what seems trivial and everyday has, from his point of view, significance

[2] Conrad Aiken, "Anton Chekhov," 1921; reprinted in *Collected Criticism* (New York: Oxford University Press, 1968), pp. 148–53.

[3] D. S. Mirsky, "Chekhov and the English," 1927; reprinted in *Russian Literature and Modern English Fiction,* ed. Donald Davie (University of Chicago Press, 1965), pp. 203–213.

[4] Eudora Welty, "The Reading and Writing of Short Stories," 1949; reprinted in *Short Story Theories,* ed. Charles E. May (Athens: Ohio University Press, 1976), pp. 159–177.

[5] John Dewey, *Art of Experience* (New York: G. P. Putnam's Sons, 1934), p. 37.

[6] Quoted by Gorham Munson, "The Recapture of the Storyable," *The University Review* 10 (Autumn 1943): 37–44.

[7] *Stephen Hero,* ed. Theodore Spencer (New York: New Directions, 1944), p. 51.

and meaning. There is no way to distinguish between these two views of the source of the so-called "modern" short story, for it is by the teller's very choice of seemingly trivial details and his organization of them into a unified pattern that lyricizes the story and makes it seem natural and realistic even as it resonates with meaning. As Georg Lukács has suggested, lyricism in the short story is pure selection which hides itself behind the hard outlines of the event; it is "the most purely artistic form; it expresses the ultimate meaning of all artistic creation as *mood*."[8]

Although Chekhov's conception of the short story as a lyrically charged fragment in which characters are less fully rounded realistic figures than they are embodiments of mood has influenced all twentieth-century practitioners of the form, his most immediate impact has been on the three writers of the early twenties who have received the most critical attention for fully developing the so-called "modern" short story — James Joyce, Katherine Mansfield, and Sherwood Anderson. And because of the wide-spread influence of the stories of these three writers, Chekhov has thus had an effect on the works of such major twentieth-century short story writers as Katherine Anne Porter, Franz Kafka, Bernard Malamud, Ernest Hemingway, and Raymond Carver. . . .

Perhaps the contemporary short story writer who is closest to Chekhov is Raymond Carver. In Carver's most recent collection of stories, *What We Talk About When We Talk About Love,* language is used so sparingly and the plots are so minimal that the stories seem pallidly drained patterns with no flesh and life in them. The stories are so short and lean that they seem to have plot only as we reconstruct them in our memory. Whatever theme they may have is embodied in the bare outlines of the event and in the spare dialogue of characters who are so overcome by event and so lacking in language that the theme is unsayable. Characters often have no names or only first names and are so briefly described that they seem to have no physical presence at all; certainly they have no distinct identity but rather seem to be shadowy presences trapped in their own inarticulateness.

The charge lodged against Carver is the same one once lodged against Chekhov, that his fiction is dehumanized and therefore cold and unfeeling. In a typical Carver story, "Why Don't You Dance," plot is minimal; event is mysterious; character is negligible. A man puts all his furniture out in his front yard and runs an extension cord out so that things work just as they did when they were inside. A young couple stop by, look at the furniture, try out the bed, have a drink, and the girl dances with the owner. The conversation is functional, devoted primarily toward making purchases in a perfectly banal, garage-sale way. At the conclusion, the young wife tells someone about the event. "She kept talking. She told everyone. There was more to it, and she was trying to get

---

[8] Georg Lukács, *The Theory of the Novel,* trans. Anna Bostock (Cambridge, Mass.: MIT Press, 1971), p. 51.

it talked out. After a time, she quit trying." The problem of the story is that the event cannot be talked out; it is completely objectified in the spare description of the event itself. Although there is no exposition in the story, we know that a marriage is over, that the secret life of the house has been externalized on the front lawn, that the owner has made a desperate metaphor of his marriage, that the hopeful young couple play out a mock scenario of that marriage which presages their own, and that the event itself is a parody of events not told, but kept hidden, like the seven-eighths of the iceberg that Hemingway said could be left beneath the surface of prose if the writer knew his subject well enough.

THE WILL TO STYLE

From its beginnings as a separately recognized literary form, the short story has always been more closely associated with lyric poetry than with its overgrown narrative neighbor, the novel. Regardless of whether short fiction has clung to the legendary tale form of its early ancestry, as in Hawthorne, or whether it has moved toward the presentation of the single event, as in Chekhov, the form has always been a "much in little" proposition which conceals more than it reveals and leaves much unsaid. However, there are two basic means by which the short story has pursued its movement away from the linearity of prose toward the spatiality of poetry — either by using the metaphoric and plurasignative language of the poem or by radically limiting its selection of the presented event.

The result has been two completely different textures in short fiction — the former characterized by such writers as Eudora Welty in the forties and fifties and Bernard Malamud in the sixties and seventies whose styles are thick with metaphor and myth, and the latter characterized by such writers as Hemingway in the twenties and thirties and Raymond Carver in the seventies and eighties whose styles are thin to the point of disappearing. This second style, which could be said to have been started by Chekhov, became reaffirmed as the primary mode of the "literary" or "artistic" short story (as opposed to the still-popular tale form) in the twenties by Mansfield, Anderson, and Joyce; and it was later combined with the metaphoric mode by such writers as Faulkner, Katherine Anne Porter, Flannery O'Connor, and others to create a modern short story which still maintains some of the characteristics of the old romance form even as it seems to be a radically realistic depiction of a single crucial episode.

The charge often made against the Chekhovian story — that it is dehumanized and therefore cold and unfeeling — has been made about the short story as a form since Hawthorne was criticized for his "bloodless" parables. However, such a charge ignores the nature of art that has characterized Western culture since the early nineteenth century and which Ortega y Gasset so clearly delineated in *The Dehumanization of Art*. In their nostalgia for the bourgeois security of nineteenth-century realism, critics of the short story forget that the royal road to art, as Ortega delineates is, "the will to style." And to stylize "means to deform reality, to derealize: style involves dehumanization." Given this definition of art, it is easy to see that the short story as a form has always embodied "the will to style."[9] The short story writer realizes that the artist must not confuse reality with idea, that he must inevitably turn his back on alleged reality and, as Ortega insists, "take the ideas for what they are — mere subjective patterns — and make them live as such, lean and angular, but pure and transparent."

The lyricism of the Chekhovian short story lies in this will to style in which reality is derealized and ideas live solely as ideas. Thus Chekhov's stories are more "poetic," that is, more "artistic" than we usually expect fiction to be; they help define the difference between the loose and baggy monstrous novel and the taut, gemlike short story. One final implication of Chekhov's focus on the "will to style" is the inevitable self-consciousness of fiction as fiction. If the term "modernism" suggests, as most critics seem to agree, a reaction against nineteenth-century bourgeois realism, which, à la Chekhov, Joyce, Anderson, and others, manifested itself as a frustration of conventional expectations about the cause-and-effect nature of plot and the "as-if-real" nature of character; then postmodernism pushes this movement even further so that contemporary fiction is less and less about objective reality and more and more about its own creative processes.

The primary effect of this mode of thought on contemporary fiction is that the story has a tendency to loosen its illusion of reality to explore the reality of its illusion. Rather than presenting itself "as if" it were real — a mimetic mirroring of external reality — postmodernist fiction makes its own artistic conventions and devices the subject of the story as well as its theme. The underlying assumption is that the forms of art are explainable by the laws of art; literary language is not a proxy for something else, but rather an object of study itself. The short story as a genre has always been more apt to lay bare its fictionality than the novel, which has traditionally tried to cover it up. Fictional self-consciousness in the short story does not allow the reader to maintain the comfortable cover-up assumption that what is depicted is real; instead the reader is made uncomfortably aware that the only reality is the process of depiction itself — the fiction-making process, the language act.

Although Anton Chekhov could not have anticipated the far-reaching implications of his experimentation with the short story as a seemingly realistic, yet highly stylized, form in the work of John Barth, Donald Barthelme, Robert Coover, and Raymond Carver, it is clear that the contemporary short story, for all of its much complained-of "unreadability," owes a significant debt to the much-criticized "storyless" stories of Chekhov. For it is with Chekhov that the short story was liberated from its adherence to the parabolic exemplum and fiction generally was liberated from the tedium of the realistic novel. With Chekhov, the

[9] *The Dehumanization of Art and Other Writings on Art and Culture* (Garden City, N.Y.: Doubleday Anchor Books, 1956), p. 23.

short story took on a new respectability and began to be seen as the most appropriate narrative form to reflect the modern temperament. There can be no understanding of the short story as a genre without an understanding of Chekhov's contribution to the form. Conrad Aiken's assessment of him in 1921 has yet to be challenged: "Possibly the greatest writer of the short story who has ever lived."[10]

RENATO POGGIOLI

FROM *Storytelling in a Double Key*   (1957)

Chekhov wrote . . . ["The Darling"] in 1899, at the decline of his years, when his art was gradually changing the tragicomedy of life into something far too noble for pity, and far too pure for contempt. The change is particularly evident in this story, of which one could say, to paraphrase Milton's words, "nothing is here for tears." Nothing is here for laughter either, because "The Darling" ends by "saying yea" to life, by judging it "well and fair." Yet if the critic will go back to the text, so as to recapture the impression of his first reading, he will undoubtedly conclude that the final esthetic outcome transcends the tale's original intent. And he will do so even more confidently if he learns that his conclusion is supported by the authority of Leo Tolstoy, who was a great admirer of this story, as well as of Chekhov in general.

The protagonist, Olenka, is "a gentle, soft-hearted, compassionate girl, with mild, tender eyes, and very good health." Everyone feels captivated by her good nature, and exclaims: "You darling!" at the sight of her pleasant looks. She lives in her father's house, and watches from her back porch the tenant living in a lodge they rent. The tenant, whose name is Ivan Kukin, is thin and no longer young; he manages an open-air theater, and complains constantly about the rain which ruins his business, and about the public which fails to appreciate his shows. By listening to his misfortunes, the "darling" falls in love with him. She marries Kukin, works in his office, and accepts all his views as her own, repeating all he has to say about the theatrical arts. Despite her total identification with her husband, Olenka grows stouter and pinker, while Kukin grows thinner and paler. After a year has passed, he goes to Moscow on business, and within a few days Olenka receives a misspelled telegram informing her of Kukin's sudden death.

The poor widow loses all interest in life, but after a three-month interval she meets at mass Vasili Pustovalov, a dignified gentleman working at a timber merchant's. In a day or two Pustovalov proposes, and Olenka marries again.

---

[10] *Collected Criticism*, p. 149.

The "darling" helps her new husband in the shop, and absorbs herself in the timber trade as fully as she had previously done in the theater world. For six years, her husband's ideas become her ideas, but her mind returns to emptiness as soon as her second husband follows the first into the grave. Yet within half a year she finds happiness anew, this time with an army veterinary surgeon, by the name of Vladimir Smirnin, now renting her lodge. Smirnin is married and has a son, but lives separated from his wife and child. Everyone realizes what has happened as soon as Olenka goes around discussing sanitary questions and the dangers of animal epidemics. "It was evident," as Chekhov says, "that she could not live a year without an attachment," and yet nobody thinks ill of the "darling" for this.

But Smirnin is suddenly transferred to a distant place, and Olenka is left alone again. Time passes, and she becomes indifferent, sad, and old: "what is worst of all . . . she had no opinion of any sort." Like all old lonely women, she has a cat, but does not care for her pet. Suddenly her solitude is broken again: Smirnin, looking older and wearing a civilian suit, knocks again at her door. He has left the service and has come back with his family, to start life anew. Olenka yields her house to the newcomers, and retires to the lodge. With this change of perspective, her life seems to take a new turn. And this time she falls in love with the little Sasha, who is ten years old. Soon enough, the father starts working outside, and the mother departs to live elsewhere. Thus Olenka mothers the boy, who calls her auntie, and tells her about his studies, and his school experiences. Now the "darling" goes around discussing teachers and lessons, home assignments and class work. And everybody understands that there is another man in her house and in her life, even if this time he is another woman's child, whom she loves like the mother she was born to be.

This résumé fails to do justice to the story, and to point out the internal contradiction already alluded to. Tolstoy's commentary fulfills, however, both tasks almost perfectly. In the opening of the critique of this piece, which he collected in *Readings for Every Day of the Year,* Tolstoy recalls the biblical story of Balaam (Numbers, 22–24). The King of the Moabites ordered him to curse the people of Israel, and Balaam wanted to comply with this command. But while climbing the mountain, he was warned by an angel, who at first was invisible to him, while being visible to his ass. So, when he reached the altar at the top, Balaam, instead of cursing the Jews, blessed them. "This," Tolstoy concludes, "is just what happened with the true poet and artist Chekhov when he wrote his charming story, 'The Darling.'" Tolstoy then proceeds to develop his point:

> The author evidently wanted to laugh at this pitiful creature — as he
> judged her with his intellect, not with his heart — this "Darling," who,

after sharing Kukin's troubles about his theater, and then immersing herself in the interests of the timber business, under the influence of the veterinary surgeon considers the struggle against bovine tuberculosis to be the most important matter in the world, and is finally absorbed in questions of grammar and the interests of the little schoolboy in the big cap. Kukin's name is ridiculous, and so even is his illness and the telegram announcing his death. The timber dealer with his sedateness is ridiculous; but the soul of "Darling," with her capacity for devoting herself with her whole being to the one she loves, is not ridiculous but wonderful and holy.[1]

Nothing could be more exact, or better said; yet one may wonder whether Tolstoy is equally right in identifying the motive that had led the author of "The Darling" to take the pen. "When Chekhov began to write that story," says Tolstoy, "he wanted to show what woman ought not to be." In short, what Chekhov meant to do was to reassert his belief in the ideal of woman's emancipation, in her right and duty to have a mind and a soul of her own. While acknowledging the artistic miracle which had turned a satirical vignette into a noble human image, Tolstoy seems to enjoy as a good joke the implication that the author had to throw his beliefs overboard in the process. Being strongly adverse to the cause of woman's emancipation, Tolstoy speaks here *pro domo sua*,[2] but the reader has no compelling reason to prefer his anti-feminism to Chekhov's feminism. Tolstoy has an axe to grind, and his guess is too shrewd. One could venture to say that Chekhov sat down to write "The Darling" with neither polemical intentions nor ideological pretensions; what he wanted to do was perhaps to exploit again at the lowest level a commonplace type and a stock comic situation, which, however unexpectedly, develops into a vision of beauty and truth. If D. S. Mirsky is right in claiming that each Chekhov story follows a curve, then there is no tale where the curve of his art better overshoots its mark.

What must have attracted Chekhov was the idea of rewriting a half pathetic, half mocking version of the "merry widow" motif: of portraying in his own inimitable way the conventional character of the woman ready and willing to marry a new husband as soon as she has buried the preceding one. That such was the case may still be proven through many eloquent clues. No reader of "The Darling" will fail to notice that Olenka calls her successive mates with almost identical nicknames: Vanichka the first, Vassichka the second, and Volodichka the third. These familiar diminutives, although respectively deriving from such different names as Ivan, Vasili, and Vladimir, sound as if they were practically interchangeable, as if to suggest that the three men are interchangeable too.

---

[1] Quoted as translated by Aylmer Maude in his edition of Tolstoy's works (Oxford University Press).

[2] "For himself" (Latin). The literal translation is "about his own house." — Eds.

This runs true to type, since in the life scheme of the eternal, and eternally remarrying, widow, nothing really changes, while everything recurs: the bridal veil alternates regularly with the veil of mourning, and both may be worn in the same church. It is from this scheme that Chekhov derives the idea of the successive adoption, on Olenka's part, of the opinions and views of each one of her three men, and this detail is another proof that the story was originally conceived on the merry widow motif. Yet, if we look deeper, we realize that a merry widow does not look for happiness beyond wedded bliss: that she asks for no less than a ring, while offering nothing more than her hand. But Olenka gives and takes other, very different things. She receives her husbands' opinions, and makes them her own, while returning something far more solid and valuable in exchange. And when she loses the person she loves, she has no more use for his views, or for any views at all.

This cracks the merry widow pattern, which begins to break when she joins her third mate, who is a married man, without a wedding ceremony or the blessing of the Church. And the pattern visibly crumbles at the end, when Olenka finds her fourth and last love not in a man, but in a child, who is the son of her last friend. "Of her former attachments," says Chekhov, "not one had been so deep." Now we finally know Olenka for what she really is, and we better appraise in retrospect some of the story's earliest, unconscious hints. Now, for instance, we understand better her girlish infatuations for such unlikely objects as her father, her aunt, or her teacher of French. For her, almost any kind of person or any kind of love can do equally well, and it is because of this, not because of any old-maidish strain, that she fails to reduce love to sex alone.

Chekhov explains this better than we could, at that very point of the tale when the lonely Olenka is about to find her more lasting attachment: "She wanted a love that would absorb her whole being, and whole soul and reason — that could give her ideas and an object in life, and would warm her old blood." For all this one could never say of Olenka, as of Madame Bovary, that she is in love with love: she cares only for living beings like herself, as shown by the case with which she forgets all her husbands after their deaths. Her brain is never haunted by dreams or ghosts, and this is why it is either empty, or full of other people's thoughts. This does not mean that the "Darling" is a parrot or a monkey in woman's dress, although it is almost certain that Chekhov conceived her initially in such a form. She is more like the ass of Balaam, who sees the angel his master is unable to see. Olenka is poor in spirit and pure in heart, and this is why life curses her three times, only to bless her forever at the end.

Tolstoy is right when he reminds us that, unlike Olenka, her three men and even her foster-child are slightly ridiculous characters, and one must add that they remain unchangingly so from whatever standpoint we may look. The reminder is necessary: after all, the point of the story is that love is a grace proceeding from the lover's fullness of heart, not from the beloved's attractive qualities or high deserts. In the light of this, the parallel with Balaam's ass must be qualified by saying that Olenka sees angels where others see only men. Thus the double message of the story is that love is a matter of both blindness and insight.

While the whole story seems to emphasize Olenka's "insight," her "blindness" is intimated by a single hint, hidden, of all places, in the title itself. Since the latter is practically untranslatable, the foreign reader cannot help missing the hint. The "Darling" of the English translators is the Russian idiom *Dushechka,* meaning literally "little soul," and used colloquially as a term of endearment, a tribute of personal sympathy, a familiar and good-natured compliment. Chekhov never pays the compliment himself, except by indirection of implication: he merely repeats it again and again, in constant quotations from other people's direct speech. Thus the artist acts as an echo, reiterating that word as if it were a choral refrain, a suggestive *leitmotiv.* Yet, as we already know, everybody addresses Olenka in that way only when she is contented and happy, having someone to love and care for. As soon as she is left without a person on whom to pour the tenderness flowing from her heart, everybody ceases calling her Dushechka, as if she had lost her soul, as if she were no longer a soul.

Thus, even though intermittently used, that term becomes, so to say, Olenka's second name: and the reader finally finds it more right and true than the first. What one witnesses is a sort of transfiguration, both symbolic and literal: by changing into Dushechka, Olenka ends by personifying the very idea of the soul. We are suddenly faced by an allegory and a metamorphosis, turning the story into a fable, which, like all fables, partakes of the nature of myth. With startling awareness, we now realize that Dushechka, after all, is one of the Russian equivalents of the Greek Psyche, and that what Chekhov has written could be but a reinterpretation of the ancient legend about the girl who was named after the word meaning "soul."

The legend, which Apuleius first recorded for us,[3] tells how the youthful Psyche became the loving wife of a great god, who was Eros himself. Eros never showed her his face or person in the daylight; yet Psyche was happy as long as she could take care of her little house in the daytime, and share in night's darkness the bed and love of a husband she could neither know nor see. What the legend means to say is that love is blind, and must remain so, whether the loved one is mortal or an immortal creature. This is the truth which the Greek Psyche had to learn, while the Russian Dushechka seems to have known it, though unconsciously, all the time.

That Chekhov must have thought of this legend while writing "The Darling" may be proved by the fact that the name or word Dushechka is but a more

---

[3] In his Metamorphoses, better known under the title of The Golden Ass.

popular variant of the literary *Dushenka,* after which Bogdanovich, a minor Russian poet of the eighteenth century, entitled his own imitation of La Fontaine's *Psyché,* which, in its turn, is a rather frivolous version of the same old myth. This slight difference in the endings of what is practically the same noun may have greater significance than we think. Both endings are diminutive suffixes: but while in Bogdanovich's "-enka" there is a connotation of benevolent sympathy, in Chekhov's "-echka" there is an insinuation of pettiness, and a nuance of indulgent scorn. This obviously means that Chekhov's serious tale is as distant from Bogdanovich's light poem as from the original legend itself: the distance may be considered so great as to preclude any relationship. We realize this, and we realize as well that our proof that such a relationship exists may be considered a verbal coincidence and nothing more. In reply to this objection, we could observe that Chekhov testified elsewhere about his knowledge of the legend itself. As we already know, he did so in "Anyuta," by simply stating through the mouth of his student-painter that Psyche is "a fine subject."

The student-painter is right, even if he is fully unconscious of the irony in what he says. Aware as he was of the irony he himself had put in those words, Chekhov must have been equally aware of their truth. Yes, Psyche is a fine subject, even when the artist deals with it so freely as to completely change its background and situation, lowering its fabulous vision to the level of a bourgeois and provincial experience, and transcribing its poetic magic into the plain images and the flat language of modern realism. This does not imply that the tale is deprived of wonder: there is no greater wonder than to make luminous and holy the inner and outer darkness in which we live, even against our will. And there is no greater miracle than to have changed into a new Psyche, with no other sorcery but that of a single word, this heroine of the commonplace, this thrice-married little woman, neither clever nor beautiful, and no longer young.

STUDENT ESSAY

Inner and Outer Worlds:
A Comparison of Chekhov's "The Darling" and "The Schoolmistress"
by Joseph Hsieh

As Andrew Durkin notes in "Chekhov's Narrative Technique," "close identification with and emphasis on interior experience makes psychological rather than physical events the crucial action in Chekhov stories" (126). The meanings of Chekhov's stories are reflected through each character's experiences, as seen particularly in the inner suffering of the female protagonists in the "The Darling" and "The Schoolmistress." Both stories focus on exploration of the private worlds of the central characters, both record a discovery of painful disillusionment, and both lead to a final self-realization; at the same time, the psychological and social distinctions between the main characters in "The Darling" and "The Schoolmistress" lead to divergent conclusions and very different fates for the two women, Olenka and Marya.

There are clear similarities between the two stories. Both focus on a female protagonist's need for relationships, compassionate love, and personal adjustment. Olga Semyonovna, known in her community as Olenka or the Darling, alternates between years of wedded bliss--with Kukin the theater manager, Pustovalov the timber merchant, Smirnin the veterinary surgeon--and widowed grief after losing her loves. On the other hand, Marya Vassilyevna of "The Schoolmistress," a lonely middle-aged teacher, never believes that matrimony is anything but a daydream. While Olga Semyonovna has many experiences with love, Marya Vassilyevna finds love only in childhood memories of her family. The time-frame of the two stories also is quite different, with "The Darling" etching out many decades of Olenka's life, beginning with her father's illness and ending with her fourth and final love for the boy Sasha, while "The Schoolmistress" follows the pattern of Marya's day trip to town and back home. Chekhov brushes through the full years of Olenka's life as effortlessly as he details Marya's empty hours. The related questions remain: Why does the Darling find love as easily as falling off a limb, and why does the Schoolmistress hesitate to begin the climb?

The answers can be discovered through an analysis of each character's development and in the progression of thought in each story. For Olenka, psychological progression is as simple as the variation of husbands. With Kukin the theater manager, she operates the Tivoli theater while embodying her husband's disdain for public indifference to the arts. With Pustovalov the merchant, she dreams of "logs, beams, and boards knocked together with the resounding crash of dry wood" (327). With Smirnin, her speech turns to "cattle plague . . . foot and mouth disease . . . slaughter-houses" (329). Olenka repeats, rehashes, revocalizes her husband's thoughts as her own. Unlike the Darling's notions, the thoughts of the Schoolmistress are not borrowed. Marya recalls fond yet dimmed memories of her father, mother, and brother, and replays her annoyance with the unbusinesslike Zemstvo school board, with the president who lacked time for her, and with the illiterate peasant who moonlights as the school guardian. Not all of Marya's thoughts revolve around the past, however: she has fleeting hopes for the future, such as her fantasies of marrying the wealthy Hanov.

Social status and economics also play pivotal roles in the turn of events in the stories. Olenka's successive marriages do not bring her disgrace; her need for relationships is considered completely natural. Even her attempt to hide the affair with the married veterinary surgeon is ultimately accepted in her community; for, after all, she is the "Darling," fated to outlive her father and husbands and inherit their wealth. "The Schoolmistress," on the other hand, considers carefully the impact caused by social and economic disparity. Although Marya dreams of becoming Hanov's wife and relieving him from the coarse ruin offered by this "God-forsaken, dreary place" (7), Chekhov makes it clear that he is rich and she merely a "carthorse." The poor pub patrons of Nizhneye Gorodistche regard the schoolmistress with distrust because of their experience with educators as participants in a corrupt system. They begrudge her her twenty-one-ruble salary just as she begrudges the watchman's hold on firewood. "The Schoolmistress" is a much more class-oriented story than "The Darling," as social scrutiny and economic disadvantage make their impact felt through Marya's depressed mood and her negative interactions with the peasants and bureaucrats, while economic need and the analytical eyes of society are largely absent in "The Darling."

The combination of psychological and societal differences between the characters and their environments leads Chekhov to vary the causes of grief for the two protagonists. The causes of Olenka's desolation are swift and direct--Kukin's death is announced with a misspelled telegram, Pustovalov's pneumonia takes only two lines of Chekhov's prose, and Smirnin's departure occurs virtually overnight. These are quick strikes enacted to bring maximum grief in minimal time. Never does any responsibility other than love muddy Olenka's life. No such sharp division exists for Marya, who is plagued daily by painful thoughts of loneliness, loss, and annoyances related to her profession. The biting chill, the price of firewood, the students, the examination--these are perpetual realities of her life which offer no reprieve. The schoolmistress's fond memories of family or kind contemplation of Hanov collapse quickly under the constant necessity of work and social role.

As varied as the causes of each character's pain is the manner in which each expresses her grief. Olenka's emotional reactions are as extreme and abrupt as her losses. After Kukin's death, "as soon as she got indoors she threw herself on her bed and sobbed so loudly that it could be heard next door, and in the street" (326). After Pustovalov dies, she cries "How can I live without you, in wretchedness and misery! Pity me, good people, all alone in the world!" (328) Olenka's feeling of emptiness is most pronounced after Smirnin's abandonment. Her natural smiles and tenderness give way to an emptiness in both mind and emotion "as harsh and bitter as wormwood in the mouth" (330). Nettles overgrow her yard, the house crumbles by pieces, the roof rusts--her grief is physical and tangible.

In contrast, Marya's reactions are much more steady and in fact may be construed as a numbed lack of response. Life itself has made her "old and coarse, making her ugly, angular, and awkward, as though she were made of lead" (9). Chekhov's winter consumes her with bad roads and sickness. These ills are perpetual, not infrequent losses like Olenka's. From birth, Marya has been a survivor in a world where dreamers (one inevitably thinks of Olenka) flounder by the wayside. She has no love to cherish, no one to call her "darling," no warmth except for the tea at Nizhneye Gorodistche amid the patrons wary of another corrupt educator. It is no surprise that Olenka sheds tears far more freely than Marya. Olenka is deprived of both the joy of attachment and a source of opinion. Marya's deprivation is far more insidious--no joy departs, no opinions are stolen, but then again, what joy or kind opinion has she ever known?

The different revelations of the protagonists at the end of each story best reveal the divergence of their ultimate fates. Olenka yields her house to Smirnin's reunited family, accepting little Sasha under her motherly wing, gathering Sasha's thoughts as she once did her lovers'. Olenka devotes her conversation to teachers, the need of high school education, class work. Her love in the end is complete, sacred, all-encompassing. As Chekhov describes, "Ah how she loved him! Of her former attachments not one had been so deep; never had her soul surrendered to any feeling so spontaneously, so disinterestedly, and so joyously as now that her maternal instincts were aroused" (332). Likewise, Marya is also granted a moment of complete joy. A lady aboard a passing train triggers childhood memories of her family's comfortable flat in Moscow, the melody of piano and her father's voice, her mother's luxuriant hair. The emotional tidal wave of memories crests as Hanov pulls up beside her. For an instant, she escapes economic necessity and schoolroom into the fantasy of regained social status and matrimony with the charming man with the "sweet eyes" beside her: "It seemed to her," Chekhov narrates, "that her happiness, her triumph, was glowing in the sky and on all sides, in the windows and on the trees. Her father and mother had never died, she had never been a schoolmistress, it was a long, tedious, strange dream, and now she had awakened" (16). But unlike Olenka's Sasha, Marya's daydream disappears in a blink. She is stripped of this transcendental climax by Semyon's call, the bitter cold of Vyazovye, and again her responsibility to the examination. While Olenka discovers her best destiny in motherhood, Marya merely rediscovers her ever-present necessity to work and the emotional emptiness of her life.

Olenka is a character of pure attachment and love, Marya a character of economic need and social rules. "The Darling" is set in a romantic world seemingly without interaction and conflict beyond Olenka's all-encompassing love, while "The Schoolmistress" is a tale of love in a realistic world where love contends with the everyday necessity of survival. If Olenka and Marya were ever to meet, one could imagine that although Olenka would speak of the need to send Sasha to high school and Marya would assist with advice about the examination, neither woman would comprehend the other's experience in life and in love. Their worlds have made them alien to each other, and they are as different as Darlings and Schoolmistresses could possibly be.

Works Cited

Chekhov, Anton. "The Darling." Trans. Constance Garnett. *The Situation of the Story.* Ed. Diana Young. Boston: Bedford St. Martin's, 1993. 323–33.

---. "The Schoolmistress." *"The Schoolmistress" and Other Stories.* Trans. Constance Garnett. New York: The Ecco Press, 1986. 3–19.

Durkin, Andrew R. "Chekhov's Narrative Technique." *A Chekhov Companion.* Ed. Toby W. Clyman. Westport: Greenwood Press, 1985. 123–30.

CHARLOTTE PERKINS GILMAN   (1860–1935)

One of the earliest feminist thinkers and writers in the United States, Charlotte Perkins was raised in Hartford, Connecticut, by her mother, who had been abandoned by her husband when Charlotte was a child, and by the liberal and intellectual relatives of Harriet Beecher Stowe, the author of *Uncle Tom's Cabin*. Even as a young woman, Perkins was concerned about social injustice and the unequal social position of women. Attending the Rhode Island School of Design, she met her first husband, the artist Charles Stetson, but living within the confines of a conventional marriage was difficult for Gilman, and she suffered a serious depression after the birth of her daughter. In 1888 she moved by herself to California and made a living lecturing and writing about feminist ideals. She eventually divorced her husband, who gained custody of their daughter, and in 1900 she married her cousin George Gilman. Her best-known work, *Women and Economics* (1898), examines the negative effects that women's subordinate position had on society. Gilman started the Forerunner Press in 1909 in order to publish "important truths, needed yet unpopular." Her feminist utopian novel *Herland* (1915) speaks of a successful and peaceful world run and inhabited by women only.

Gilman is best remembered for her story "The Yellow Wallpaper," which first appeared in the *New England Magazine* in 1892. Although it was then read as a Gothic ghost story, "The Yellow Wallpaper" is based on Gilman's own agonizing experiences undergoing a common treatment for female depression and "nerves" that required complete isolation — even forbidding reading and writing. Gilman said about her story, "It was not intended to drive people crazy but to save people from being driven crazy, and it worked."

The Yellow Wallpaper   (1899)

It is very seldom that mere ordinary people like John and myself secure ancestral halls for the summer.

A colonial mansion, a hereditary estate, I would say a haunted house and reach the height of romantic felicity — but that would be asking too much of fate!

Still I will proudly declare that there is something queer about it.

Else, why should it be let so cheaply? And why have stood so long untenanted?

John laughs at me, of course, but one expects that.

John is practical in the extreme. He has no patience with faith, an intense horror of superstition, and he scoffs openly at any talk of things not to be felt and seen and put down in figures.

John is a physician, and *perhaps* — (I would not say it to a living soul, of course, but this is dead paper and a great relief to my mind) — *perhaps* that is one reason I do not get well faster.

You see, he does not believe I am sick! And what can one do?

If a physician of high standing, and one's own husband, assures friends and relatives that there is really nothing the matter with one but temporary nervous depression — a slight hysterical tendency — what is one to do?

My brother is also a physician, and also of high standing, and he says the same thing.

So I take phosphates or phosphites — whichever it is — and tonics, and air and exercise, and journeys, and am absolutely forbidden to "work" until I am well again.

Personally, I disagree with their ideas.

Personally, I believe that congenial work, with excitement and change, would do me good.

But what is one to do?

I did write for a while in spite of them; but it *does* exhaust me a good deal — having to be so sly about it, or else meet with heavy opposition.

I sometimes fancy that in my condition, if I had less opposition and more society and stimulus — but John says the very worst thing I can do is to think about my condition, and I confess it always makes me feel bad.

So I will let it alone and talk about the house.

The most beautiful place! It is quite alone, standing well back from the road, quite three miles from the village. It makes me think of English places that you read about, for there are hedges and walls and gates that lock, and lots of separate little houses for the gardeners and people.

There is a *delicious* garden! I never saw such a garden — large and shady, full of box-bordered paths, and lined with long grape-covered arbors with seats under them.

There were greenhouses, but they are all broken now.

There was some legal trouble, I believe, something about the heirs and co-heirs; anyhow, the place has been empty for years.

That spoils my ghostliness, I am afraid, but I don't care — there is something strange about the house — I can feel it.

I even said so to John one moonlight evening, but he said what I felt was a draught, and shut the window.

I get unreasonably angry with John sometimes. I'm sure I never used to be so sensitive. I think it is due to this nervous condition.

But John says if I feel so I shall neglect proper self-control; so I take pains to control myself — before him, at least, and that makes me very tired.

I don't like our room a bit. I wanted one downstairs that opened onto the piazza and had roses all over the window, and such pretty old-fashioned chintz hangings! But John would not hear of it.

He said there was only one window and not room for two beds, and no near room for him if he took another.

He is very careful and loving, and hardly lets me stir without special direction.

I have a schedule prescription of each hour in the day; he takes all care from me, and so I feel basely ungrateful not to value it more.

He said he came here solely on my account, that I was to have perfect rest and all the air I could get. "Your exercise depends on your strength, my dear," said he, "and your food somewhat on your appetite; but air you can absorb all the time." So we took the nursery at the top of the house.

It is a big, airy room, the whole floor nearly, with windows that look all ways, and air and sunshine galore. It was nursery first, and then playroom and gymnasium, I should judge, for the windows are barred for little children, and there are rings and things in the walls.

The paint and paper look as if a boys' school had used it. It is stripped off —the paper—in great patches all around the head of my bed, about as far as I can reach, and in a great place on the other side of the room low down. I never saw a worse paper in my life. One of those sprawling, flamboyant patterns committing every artistic sin.

It is dull enough to confuse the eye in following, pronounced enough constantly to irritate and provoke study, and when you follow the lame uncertain curves for a little distance they suddenly commit suicide—plunge off at outrageous angles, destroy themselves in unheard-of contradictions.

The color is repellent, almost revolting: a smouldering unclean yellow, strangely faded by the slow-turning sunlight. It is a dull yet lurid orange in some places, a sickly sulphur tint in others.

No wonder the children hated it! I should hate it myself if I had to live in this room long.

There comes John, and I must put this away—he hates to have me write a word.

We have been here two weeks, and I haven't felt like writing before, since that first day.

I am sitting by the window now, up in this atrocious nursery, and there is nothing to hinder my writing as much as I please, save lack of strength.

John is away all day, and even some nights when his cases are serious.

I am glad my case is not serious!

But these nervous troubles are dreadfully depressing.

John does not know how much I really suffer. He knows there is no reason to suffer, and that satisfies him.

Of course it is only nervousness. It does weigh on me so not to do my duty in any way!

I meant to be such a help to John, such a real rest and comfort, and here I am a comparative burden already!

Nobody would believe what an effort it is to do what little I am able — to dress and entertain, and order things.

It is fortunate Mary is so good with the baby. Such a dear baby!

And yet I *cannot* be with him, it makes me so nervous.

I suppose John never was nervous in his life. He laughs at me so about this wallpaper!

At first he meant to repaper the room, but afterward he said that I was letting it get the better of me, and that nothing was worse for a nervous patient than to give way to such fancies.

He said that after the wallpaper was changed it would be the heavy bedstead, and then the barred windows, and then that gate at the head of the stairs, and so on.

"You know the place is doing you good," he said, "and really, dear, I don't care to renovate the house just for a three months' rental."

"Then do let us go downstairs," I said. "There are such pretty rooms there."

Then he took me in his arms and called me a blessed little goose, and said he would go down cellar, if I wished, and have it whitewashed into the bargain.

But he is right enough about the beds and windows and things.

It is as airy and comfortable a room as anyone need wish, and, of course, I would not be so silly as to make him uncomfortable just for a whim.

I'm really getting quite fond of the big room, all but that horrid paper.

Out of one window I can see the garden — those mysterious deep-shaded arbors, the riotous old-fashioned flowers, and bushes and gnarly trees.

Out of another I get a lovely view of the bay and a little private wharf belonging to the estate. There is a beautiful shaded lane that runs down there from the house. I always fancy I see people walking in these numerous paths and arbors, but John has cautioned me not to give way to fancy in the least. He says that with my imaginative power and habit of story-making, a nervous weakness like mine is sure to lead to all manner of excited fancies, and that I ought to use my will and good sense to check the tendency. So I try.

I think sometimes that if I were only well enough to write a little it would relieve the press of ideas and rest me.

But I find I get pretty tired when I try.

It is so discouraging not to have any advice and companionship about my work. When I get really well, John says we will ask Cousin Henry and Julia down for a long visit; but he says he would as soon put fireworks in my pillowcase as to let me have those stimulating people about now.

I wish I could get well faster.

But I must not think about that. This paper looks to me as if it *knew* what a vicious influence it had!

There is a recurrent spot where the pattern lolls like a broken neck and two bulbous eyes stare at you upside down.

I get positively angry with the impertinence of it and the everlastingness. Up and down and sideways they crawl, and those absurd unblinking eyes are everywhere. There is one place where two breadths didn't match, and the eyes go all up and down the line, one a little higher than the other.

I never saw so much expression in an inanimate thing before, and we all know how much expression they have! I used to lie awake as a child and get more entertainment and terror out of blank walls and plain furniture than most children could find in a toy-store.

I remember what a kindly wink the knobs of our big old bureau used to have, and there was one chair that always seemed like a strong friend.

I used to feel that if any of the other things looked too fierce I could always hop into that chair and be safe.

The furniture in this room is no worse than inharmonious, however, for we had to bring it all from downstairs. I suppose when this was used as a play-room they had to take the nursery things out, and no wonder! I never saw such ravages as the children have made here.

The wallpaper, as I said before, is torn off in spots, and it sticketh closer than a brother — they must have had perseverance as well as hatred.

Then the floor is scratched and gouged and splintered, the plaster itself is dug out here and there, and this great heavy bed, which is all we found in the room, looks as if it had been through the wars.

But I don't mind it a bit — only the paper.

There comes John's sister. Such a dear girl as she is, and so careful of me! I must not let her find me writing.

She is a perfect and enthusiastic housekeeper, and hopes for no better pro-fession. I verily believe she thinks it is the writing which made me sick!

But I can write when she is out, and see her a long way off from these windows.

There is one that commands the road, a lovely shaded winding road, and one that just looks off over the country. A lovely country, too, full of great elms and velvet meadows.

This wallpaper has a kind of subpattern in a different shade, a particularly irritating one, for you can only see it in certain lights, and not clearly then.

But in the places where it isn't faded and where the sun is just so — I can see a strange, provoking, formless sort of figure that seems to skulk about behind that silly and conspicuous front design.

There's sister on the stairs!

Well, the Fourth of July is over! The people are all gone, and I am tired out. John thought it might do me good to see a little company, so we just had Mother and Nellie and the children down for a week.

Of course I didn't do a thing. Jennie sees to everything now.

But it tired me all the same.

John says if I don't pick up faster he shall send me to Weir Mitchell in the fall.

But I don't want to go there at all. I had a friend who was in his hands once, and she says he is just like John and my brother, only more so!

Besides, it is such an undertaking to go so far.

I don't feel as if it was worthwhile to turn my hand over for anything, and I'm getting dreadfully fretful and querulous.

I cry at nothing, and cry most of the time.

Of course I don't when John is here, or anybody else, but when I am alone.

And I am alone a good deal just now. John is kept in town very often by serious cases, and Jennie is good and lets me alone when I want her to.

So I walk a little in the garden or down that lovely lane, sit on the porch under the roses, and lie down up here a good deal.

I'm getting really fond of the room in spite of the wallpaper. Perhaps *because* of the wallpaper.

It dwells in my mind so!

I lie here on this great immovable bed — it is nailed down, I believe — and follow that pattern about by the hour. It is as good as gymnastics, I assure you. I start, we'll say, at the bottom, down in the corner over there where it has not been touched, and I determine for the thousandth time that I *will* follow that pointless pattern to some sort of a conclusion.

I know a little of the principle of design, and I know this thing was not arranged on any laws of radiation, or alternation, or repetition, or symmetry, or anything else that I ever heard of.

It is repeated, of course, by the breadths, but not otherwise.

Looked at in one way, each breadth stands alone; the bloated curves and flourishes — a kind of "debased Romanesque" with dilirium tremens go waddling up and down in isolated columns of fatuity.

But, on the other hand, they connect diagonally, and the sprawling outlines run off in great slanting waves of optic horror, like a lot of wallowing sea-weeds in full chase.

The whole thing goes horizontally, too, at least it seems so, and I exhaust myself trying to distinguish the order of its going in that direction.

They have used a horizontal breadth for a frieze, and that adds wonderfully to the confusion.

There is one end of the room where it is almost intact, and there, when the crosslights fade and the low sun shines directly upon it, I can almost fancy radiation after all — the interminable grotesque seems to form around a common center and rush off in headlong plunges of equal distraction.

It makes me tired to follow it. I will take a nap, I guess.

I don't know why I should write this.

I don't want to.

I don't feel able.

And I know John would think it absurd. But I *must* say what I feel and think in some way — it is such a relief!

But the effort is getting to be greater than the relief.

Half the time now I am awfully lazy, and lie down ever so much. John says I mustn't lose my strength, and has me take cod liver oil and lots of tonics and things, to say nothing of ale and wines and rare meat.

Dear John! He loves me very dearly, and hates to have me sick. I tried to have a real earnest reasonable talk with him the other day, and tell him how I wish he would let me go and make a visit to Cousin Henry and Julia.

But he said I wasn't able to go, nor able to stand it after I got there; and I did not make out a very good case for myself, for I was crying before I had finished.

It is getting to be a great effort for me to think straight. Just this nervous weakness, I suppose.

And dear John gathered me up in his arms, and just carried me upstairs and laid me on the bed, and sat by me and read to me till it tired my head.

He said I was his darling and his comfort and all he had, and that I must take care of myself for his sake, and keep well.

He says no one but myself can help me out of it, that I must use my will and self-control and not let any silly fancies run away with me.

There's one comfort — the baby is well and happy, and does not have to occupy this nursery with the horrid wallpaper.

If we had not used it, that blessed child would have! What a fortunate escape! Why, I wouldn't have a child of mine, an impressionable little thing, live in such a room for worlds.

I never thought of it before, but it is lucky that John kept me here after all; I can stand it so much easier than a baby, you see.

Of course I never mention it to them any more — I am too wise — but I keep watch for it all the same.

There are things in the wallpaper that nobody knows about but me, or ever will.

Behind that outside pattern the dim shapes get clearer every day.

It is always the same shape, only very numerous.

And it is like a woman stooping down and creeping about behind that pattern. I don't like it a bit. I wonder — I begin to think — I wish John would take me away from here!

It is so hard to talk with John about my case, because he is so wise, and because he loves me so.

But I tried it last night.

It was moonlight. The moon shines in all around just as the sun does.

I hate to see it sometimes, it creeps so slowly, and always comes in by one window or another.

John was asleep and I hated to waken him, so I kept still and watched the moonlight on that undulating wallpaper till I felt creepy.

The faint figure behind seemed to shake the pattern, just as if she wanted to get out.

I got up softly and went to feel and see if the paper *did* move, and when I came back John was awake.

"What is it, little girl?" he said. "Don't go walking about like that — you'll get cold."

I thought it was a good time to talk, so I told him that I really was not gaining here, and that I wished he would take me away.

"Why, darling!" said he. "Our lease will be up in three weeks, and I can't see how to leave before.

"The repairs are not done at home, and I cannot possibly leave town just now. Of course, if you were in any danger, I could and would, but you really are better, dear, whether you can see it or not. I am a doctor, dear, and I know. You are gaining flesh and color, your appetite is better, I feel really much easier about you."

"I don't weigh a bit more," said I, "nor as much; and my appetite may be better in the evening when you are here but it is worse in the morning when you are away!"

"Bless her little heart!" said he with a big hug. "She shall be as sick as she pleases! But now let's improve the shining hours by going to sleep, and talk about it in the morning!"

"And you won't go away?" I asked gloomily.

"Why, how can I, dear? It is only three weeks more and then we will take a nice little trip for a few days while Jennie is getting the house ready. Really, dear, you are better!"

"Better in body perhaps —" I began, and stopped short, for he sat up straight and looked at me with such a stern, reproachful look that I could not say another word.

"My darling," said he, "I beg you, for my sake and for our child's sake, as well as for your own, that you will never for one instant let that idea enter your mind! There is nothing so dangerous, so fascinating, to a temperament like yours. It is a false and foolish fancy. Can you trust me as a physician when I tell you so?"

So of course, I said no more on that score, and we went to sleep before long. He thought I was asleep first, but I wasn't, and lay there for hours trying to decide whether that front pattern and the back pattern really did move together or separately.

On a pattern like this, by daylight, there is a lack of sequence, a defiance of law, that is a constant irritant to a normal mind.

The color is hideous enough, and unreliable enough, and infuriating enough, but the pattern is torturing.

You think you have mastered it, but just as you get well under way in following, it turns a back-somersault and there you are. It slaps you in the face, knocks you down, and tramples upon you. It is like a bad dream.

The outside pattern is a florid arabesque, reminding one of a fungus. If you can imagine a toadstool in joints, an interminable string of toadstools, budding and sprouting in endless convolutions — why, that is something like it.

That is, sometimes!

There is one marked peculiarity about this paper, a thing nobody seems to notice but myself, and that is that it changes as the light changes.

When the sun shoots in through the east window — I always watch for that first long, straight ray — it changes so quickly that I never can quite believe it.

That is why I watch it always.

By moonlight — the moon shines in all night when there is a moon — I wouldn't know it was the same paper.

At night in any kind of light, in twilight, candlelight, lamplight, and worst of all by moonlight, it becomes bars! The outside pattern, I mean, and the woman behind it is as plain as can be.

I didn't realize for a long time what the thing was that showed behind, that dim subpattern, but now I am quite sure it is a woman.

By daylight she is subdued, quiet. I fancy it is the pattern that keeps her so still. It is so puzzling. It keeps me quiet by the hour.

I lie down ever so much now. John says it is good for me, and to sleep all I can.

Indeed he started the habit by making me lie down for an hour after each meal.

It is a very bad habit, I am convinced, for you see, I don't sleep.

And that cultivates deceit, for I don't tell them I'm awake — oh, no!

The fact is I am getting a little afraid of John.

He seems very queer sometimes, and even Jennie has an inexplicable look.

It strikes me occasionally, just as a scientific hypothesis, that perhaps it is the paper!

I have watched John when he did not know I was looking, and come into the room suddenly on the most innocent excuses, and I've caught him several times *looking at the paper!* And Jennie too. I caught Jennie with her hand on it once.

She didn't know I was in the room, and when I asked her in a quiet, a very quiet voice, and the most restrained manner possible, what she was doing with the paper, she turned around as if she had been caught stealing, and looked quite angry — asked me why I should frighten her so!

Then she said that the paper stained everything it touched, that she had found yellow smooches on all my clothes and John's and she wishes we would be more careful!

Did not that sound innocent? But I know she was studying that pattern, and I am determined that nobody shall find it out but myself!

Life is very much more exciting now than it used to be. You see, I have something more to expect, to look forward to, to watch. I really do eat better and am more quiet than I was.

John is so pleased to see me improve! He laughed a little the other day, and said I seemed to be flourishing in spite of my wallpaper.

I turned it off with a laugh. I had no intention of telling him it was *because* of the wallpaper — he would make fun of me. He might even want to take me away.

I don't want to leave now until I have found it out. There is a week more, and I think that will be enough.

I'm feeling so much better!

I don't sleep much at night, for it is so interesting to watch developments; but I sleep a good deal during the daytime.

In the daytime it is tiresome and perplexing.

There are always new shoots on the fungus, and new shades of yellow all over it. I cannot keep count of them, though I have tried conscientiously.

It is the strangest yellow, that wallpaper! It makes me think of all the yellow things I ever saw — not beautiful ones like buttercups, but old, foul, bad yellow things.

But there is something else about that paper — the smell! I noticed it the moment we came into the room, but with so much air and sun it was not bad. Now we have had a week of fog and rain, and whether the windows are open or not, the smell is here.

It creeps all over the house.

I find it hovering in the dining-room, skulking in the parlor, hiding in the hall, lying in wait for me on the stairs.

It gets into my hair.

Even when I go to ride, if I turn my head suddenly and surprise it — there is that smell!

Such a peculiar odor, too! I have spent hours in trying to analyze it, to find what it smelled like.

It is not bad — at first — and very gentle, but quite the subtlest, most enduring odor I ever met.

It used to disturb me at first. I thought seriously of burning the house — to reach the smell.

But now I am used to it. The only thing I can think of that it is like is the *color* of the paper! A yellow smell.

There is a very funny mark on this wall, low down, near the mopboard. A streak that runs round the room. It goes behind every piece of furniture, except the bed, a long, straight, even *smooch,* as if it had been rubbed over and over.

I wonder how it was done and who did it, and what they did it for. Round and round and round — round and round and round — it makes me dizzy!

I really have discovered something at last.

Through watching so much at night, when it changes so, I have finally found out.

The front pattern *does* move — and no wonder! The woman behind shakes it!

Sometimes I think there are a great many women behind, and sometimes only one, and she crawls around fast, and her crawling shakes it all over.

Then in the very bright spots she keeps still, and in the very shady spots she just takes hold of the bars and shakes them hard.

And she is all the time trying to climb through. But nobody could climb through that pattern—it strangles so; I think that is why it has so many heads.

They get through and then the pattern strangles them off and turns them upside down, and makes their eyes white!

If those heads were covered or taken off it would not be half so bad.

I think that woman gets out in the daytime!

And I'll tell you why—privately—I've seen her!

I can see her out of every one of my windows!

It is the same woman, I know, for she is always creeping, and most women do not creep by daylight.

I see her in that long shaded lane, creeping up and down. I see her in those dark grape arbors, creeping all round the garden.

I see her on that long road under the trees, creeping along, and when a carriage comes she hides under the blackberry vines.

I don't blame her a bit. It must be very humiliating to be caught creeping by daylight!

I always lock the door when I creep by daylight. I can't do it at night, for I know John would suspect something at once.

And John is so queer now that I don't want to irritate him. I wish he would take another room! Besides, I don't want anybody to get that woman out at night but myself.

I often wonder if I could see her out of all the windows at once.

But, turn as fast as I can, I can only see out of one at one time.

And though I always see her, she *may* be able to creep faster than I can turn! I have watched her sometimes away off in the open country, creeping as fast as a cloud shadow in a wind.

If only that top pattern could be gotten off from the under one! I mean to try it, little by little.

I have found out another funny thing, but I shan't tell it this time! It does not do to trust people too much.

There are only two more days to get this paper off, and I believe John is beginning to notice. I don't like the look in his eyes.

And I heard him ask Jennie a lot of professional questions about me. She had a very good report to give.

She said I slept a good deal in the daytime.

John knows I don't sleep very well at night, for all I'm so quiet!

He asked me all sorts of questions too, and pretended to be very loving and kind.

As if I couldn't see through him!

Still, I don't wonder he acts so, sleeping under this paper for three months. It only interests me, but I feel sure John and Jennie are affected by it.

Hurrah! This is the last day, but it is enough. John is to stay in town over night, and won't be out until this evening.

Jennie wanted to sleep with me — the sly thing; but I told her I should undoubtedly rest better for a night all alone.

That was clever, for really I wasn't alone a bit! As soon as it was moon-light and that poor thing began to crawl and shake the pattern, I got up and ran to help her.

I pulled and she shook. I shook and she pulled, and before morning we had peeled off yards of that paper.

A strip about as high as my head and half around the room.

And then when the sun came and that awful pattern began to laugh at me, I declared I would finish it today!

We go away tomorrow, and they are moving all my furniture down again to leave things as they were before.

Jennie looked at the wall in amazement, but I told her merrily that I did it out of pure spite at the vicious thing.

She laughed and said she wouldn't mind doing it herself, but I must not get tired.

How she betrayed herself that time!

But I am here, and no person touches this paper but Me — not *alive!*

She tried to get me out of the room — it was too patent! But I said it was so quiet and empty and clean now that I believed I would lie down again and sleep all I could, and not to wake me even for dinner — I would call when I woke.

So now she is gone, and the servants are gone, and the things are gone, and there is nothing left but that great bedstead nailed down, with the canvas mattress we found on it.

We shall sleep downstairs tonight, and take the boat home tomorrow.

I quite enjoy the room, now it is bare again.

How those children did tear about here!

This bedstead is fairly gnawed!

But I must get to work.

I have locked the door and thrown the key down into the front path.

I don't want to go out, and I don't want to have anybody come in, till John comes.

I want to astonish him.

I've got a rope up here that even Jennie did not find. If that woman does get out, and tries to get away, I can tie her!

But I forgot I could not reach far without anything to stand on!

This bed will *not* move!

I tried to lift and push it until I was lame, and then I got so angry I bit off a little piece at one corner — but it hurt my teeth.

Then I peeled off all the paper I could reach standing on the floor. It sticks horribly and the pattern just enjoys it! All those strangled heads and bulbous eyes and waddling fungus growths just shriek with derision!

I am getting angry enough to do something desperate. To jump out of the window would be admirable exercise, but the bars are too strong even to try.

Besides I wouldn't do it. Of course not. I know well enough that a step like that is improper and might be misconstrued.

I don't like to *look* out of the windows even — there are so many of those creeping women, and they creep so fast.

I wonder if they all come out of that wallpaper as I did!

But I am securely fastened now by my well-hidden rope — you don't get *me* out in the road there!

I suppose I shall have to get back behind the pattern when it comes night, and that is hard!

It is so pleasant to be out in this great room and creep around as I please!

I don't want to go outside. I won't, even if Jennie asks me to.

For outside you have to creep on the ground, and everything is green instead of yellow.

But here I can creep smoothly on the floor, and my shoulder just fits in that long smooch around the wall, so I cannot lose my way.

Why, there's John at the door!

It is no use, young man, you can't open it!

How he does call and pound!

Now he's crying to Jennie for an axe.

It would be a shame to break down that beautiful door!

"John, dear!" said I in the gentlest voice. "The key is down by the front steps, under a plantain leaf!"

That silenced him for a few moments.

Then he said, very quietly indeed, "Open the door, my darling!"

"I can't," said I. "The key is down by the front door under a plantain leaf!" And then I said it again, several times, very gently and slowly, and said it so often that he had to go and see, and he got it of course, and came in. He stopped short by the door.

"What is the matter?" he cried. "For God's sake, what are you doing!"

I kept on creeping just the same, but I looked at him over my shoulder.

"I've got out at last," said I, "in spite of you and Jane. And I've pulled off most of the paper, so you can't put me back!"

Now why should that man have fainted? But he did, and right across my path by the wall, so that I had to creep over him every time!

Questions for Discussion

1. What needs of the narrator does her husband's "treatment" fail to consider?
2. Discuss the symbolism of the large colonial house where the narrator goes to rest,

and the nursery room with its barred windows and restraints where she is confined. In what sense is the house a symbol of traditional marriage?

3. Why does the narrator become increasingly obsessed with the meaning of the wallpaper and with ripping it off? Why and how does she unravel the meaning of the wallpaper at night? In what ways is the narrator's relationship to the wallpaper similar to a nightmare, both literally and symbolically? Why?

4. How do you interpret the final scene of the story? Can the husband's fainting be seen as a sign of his weakness and his wife's strength? Is this victory only a temporary one? What will happen to the narrator? Has her condition improved?

5. How does the narrator's syntax and imagery help to create her voice? How does her voice change in the course of the story?

Ideas for Writing

1. In an essay, argue either that the narrator's complete break from her normal life has made her stronger psychologically or that she has had a nervous breakdown. You might consider the symbolism of the wallpaper, its patterns, and the hallucinatory "creeping" women.

2. Retell "The Yellow Wallpaper" from John's perspective, or from that of his sister.

EDITH WHARTON   (1862–1937)

Raised by her wealthy New York family and privately educated, Edith Wharton took as the subject of her fiction upper-class, well-educated characters involved in intense, if often intellectualized relationships and the passions and cruelties that often reside beneath their cultured surfaces. Born Edith Jones, she married a wealthy banker named Edward Wharton in 1885, and although she remained married to Wharton until 1913, she lived most of her life alone, traveling, entertaining, and writing. She moved to France in 1907, living there until her death.

Wharton began writing in her youth and continued for most of her life, publishing her early stories, collected in *The Greater Inclination,* in 1899 and her last novel, *The Gods Arrive,* in 1932. Wharton's best-known novels are *The House of Mirth* (1905), *Ethan Frome* (1911), and *The Age of Innocence* (1920), which won the Pulitzer Prize for Literature. Wharton published many story collections, most notably *Xingu and Other Stories* (1916). "The Dilettante" is included in *The Descent of Man* (1904).

In *The Writing of Fiction* (1925) Wharton explores the principles that underlie her writing, many of which can be traced to the theories of Henry James, a close friend who was her literary mentor and role model. From James, Wharton developed the idea that stories should reveal their insights through subtle nuances of dialogue and through what remains unspoken.

The Dilettante   (1903)

It was on an impulse hardly needing the arguments he found himself advancing in its favor, that Thursdale, on his way to the club, turned as usual into Mrs. Vervain's street.

The "as usual" was his own qualification of the act; a convenient way of bridging the interval — in days and other sequences — that lay between this visit and the last. It was characteristic of him that he instinctively excluded his call two days earlier, with Ruth Gaynor, from the list of his visits to Mrs. Vervain: the special conditions attending it had made it no more like a visit to Mrs. Vervain than an engraved dinner invitation is like a personal letter. Yet it was to talk over his call with Miss Gaynor that he was now returning to the scene of that episode; and it was because Mrs. Vervain could be trusted to handle the talking over as skillfully as the interview itself that, at her corner, he had felt the dilettante's irresistible craving to take a last look at a work of art that was passing out of his possession.

On the whole, he knew no one better fitted to deal with the unexpected than Mrs. Vervain. She excelled in the rare art of taking things for granted, and

Thursdale felt a pardonable pride in the thought that she owed her excellence to his training. Early in his career, Thursdale had made the mistake, at the outset of his acquaintance with a lady, of telling her that he loved her, and exacting the same avowal in return. The latter part of that episode had been like the long walk back from a picnic, when one has to carry all the crockery one has finished using: it was the last time Thursdale ever allowed himself to be encumbered with the debris of a feast. He thus incidentally learned that the privilege of loving her is one of the least favors that a charming woman can accord; and in seeking to avoid the pitfalls of sentiment he had developed a science of evasion in which the woman of the moment became a mere implement of the game. He owed a great deal of delicate enjoyment to the cultivation of this art. The perils from which it had been his refuge became naïvely harmless: was it possible that he who now took his easy way along the levels had once preferred to gasp on the raw heights of emotion? Youth is a high-colored season; but he had the satisfaction of feeling that he had entered earlier than most into that chiaroscuro of sensation where every half-tone has its value.

As a promoter of this pleasure no one he had known was comparable to Mrs. Vervain. He had taught a good many women not to betray their feelings, but he had never before had such fine material to work with. She had been surprisingly crude when he first knew her; capable of making the most awkward inferences, of plunging through thin ice, of recklessly undressing her emotions; but she had acquired, under the discipline of his reticences and evasions, a skill almost equal to his own, and perhaps more remarkable in that it involved keeping time with any tune he played and reading at sight some uncommonly difficult passages.

It had taken Thursdale seven years to form this fine talent, but the result justified the effort. At the crucial moment she had been perfect: her way of greeting Miss Gaynor had made him regret that he had announced his engagement by letter. It was an evasion that confessed a difficulty; a deviation implying an obstacle, where, by common consent, it was agreed to see none; it betrayed, in short, a lack of confidence in the completeness of his method. It had been his pride never to put himself in a position which had to be quitted, as it were, by the back door; but here, as he perceived, the main portals would have opened for him of their own accord. All this, and much more, he read in the finished naturalness with which Mrs. Vervain had met Miss Gaynor. He had never seen a better piece of work: there was no overeagerness, no suspicious warmth, above all (and this gave her art the grace of a natural quality) there were none of those damnable implications whereby a woman, in welcoming her friend's betrothed, may keep him on pins and needles while she laps the lady in complacency. So masterly a performance, indeed, hardly needed the offset of Miss Gaynor's doorstep words — "To be so kind to me, how she must have liked you!" — though he caught himself wishing it lay within the bounds of fitness to transmit them, as a final tribute, to the one woman he knew who was unfailingly certain to enjoy a good thing. It was perhaps the one drawback to his new situation that it might develop good things which it would be impossible to hand on to Margaret Vervain.

The fact that he had made the mistake of underrating his friend's powers, the consciousness that his writing must have betrayed his distrust of her efficiency, seemed an added reason for turning down her street instead of going on to the club. He would show her that he knew how to value her; he would ask her to achieve with him a feat infinitely rarer and more delicate than the one he had appeared to avoid. Incidentally, he would also dispose of the interval of time before dinner: ever since he had seen Miss Gaynor off, an hour earlier, on her return journey to Buffalo, he had been wondering how he should put in the rest of the afternoon. It was absurd, how he missed the girl. . . . Yes, that was it: the desire to talk about her was, after all, at the bottom of his impulse to call on Mrs. Vervain! It was absurd, if you like — but it was delightfully rejuvenating. He could recall the time when he had been afraid of being obvious: now he felt that his return to the primitive emotions might be as restorative as a holiday in the Canadian woods. And it was precisely by the girl's candor, her directness, her lack of complications, that he was taken. The sense that she might say something rash at any moment was positively exhilarating: if she had thrown her arms about him at the station he would not have given a thought to his crumpled dignity. It surprised Thursdale to find what freshness of heart he brought to the adventure; and though his sense of irony prevented his ascribing his intactness to any conscious purpose, he could but rejoice in the fact that his sentimental economies had left him such a large surplus to draw upon.

Mrs. Vervain was at home — as usual. When one visits the cemetery one expects to find the angel on the tombstone, and it struck Thursdale as another proof of his friend's good taste that she had been in no undue haste to change her habits. The whole house appeared to count on his coming; the footman took his hat and overcoat as naturally as though there had been no lapse in his visits; and the drawing room at once enveloped him in that atmosphere of tacit intelligence which Mrs. Vervain imparted to her very furniture.

It was a surprise that, in this general harmony of circumstances, Mrs. Vervain should herself sound the first false note.

"You?" she exclaimed; and the book she held slipped from her hand.

It was crude, certainly; unless it were a touch of the finest art. The difficulty of classifying it disturbed Thursdale's balance.

"Why not?" he said, restoring the book. "Isn't it my hour?" And as she made no answer, he added gently, "Unless it's someone else's?"

She laid the book aside and sank back into her chair. "Mine, merely," she said.

"I hope that doesn't mean that you're unwilling to share it?"

"With you? By no means. You're welcome to my last crust."

He looked at her reproachfully. "Do you call this the last?"

She smiled as he dropped into the seat across the hearth. "It's a way of giving it more flavor!"

He returned the smile. "A visit to you doesn't need such condiments."

She took this with just the right measure of retrospective amusement:

"Ah, but I want to put into this one a very special taste," she confessed.

Her smile was so confident, so reassuring, that it lulled him into the imprudence of saying: "Why should you want it to be different from what was always so perfectly right?"

She hesitated. "Doesn't the fact that it's the last constitute a difference?"

"The last — my last visit to you?"

"Oh, metaphorically, I mean — there's a break in the continuity."

Decidedly, she was pressing too hard: unlearning his arts already!

"I don't recognize it," he said. "Unless you make me — " he added with a note that slightly stirred her attitude of languid attention.

She turned to him with grave eyes. "You recognize no difference whatever?"

"None — except an added link in the chain."

"An added link?"

"In having one more thing to like you for — your letting Miss Gaynor see why I had already so many." He flattered himself that this turn had taken the least hint of fatuity from the phrase.

Mrs. Vervain sank into her former easy pose. "Was it that you came for?" she asked, almost gaily.

"If it is necessary to have a reason — that was one."

"To talk to me about Miss Gaynor?"

"To tell you how she talks about you."

"That will be very interesting — especially if you have seen her since her second visit to me."

"Her second visit?" Thursdale pushed his chair back with a start and moved to another. "She came to see you again?"

"This morning, yes — by appointment."

He continued to look at her blankly. "You sent for her?"

"I didn't have to — she wrote and asked me last night. But no doubt you have seen her since."

Thursdale sat silent. He was trying to separate his words from his thoughts, but they still clung together inextricably. "I saw her off just now at the station."

"And she didn't tell you that she had been here again?"

"There was hardly time, I suppose — there were people about — " he floundered.

"Ah, she'll write, then."

He regained his composure. "Of course she'll write: very often, I hope.

You know I'm absurdly in love," he cried audaciously.

She tilted her head back, looking up at him as he leaned against the chimney piece. He had leaned there so often that the attitude touched a pulse which set up a throbbing in her throat. "Oh, my poor Thursdale!" she murmured.

"I suppose it's rather ridiculous," he owned; and as she remained silent, he added, with a sudden break — "Or have you another reason for pitying me?"

Her answer was another question. "Have you been back to your rooms since you left her?"

"Since I left her at the station? I came straight here."

"Ah, yes — you *could:* there was no reason —" Her words passed into a silent musing.

Thursdale moved nervously nearer. "You said you had something to tell me?"

"Perhaps I had better let her do so. There may be a letter at your rooms."

"A letter? What do you mean? A letter from *her?* What has happened?"

His paleness shook her, and she raised a hand of reassurance. "Nothing has happened — perhaps that is just the worst of it. You always *hated,* you know," she added incoherently, "to have things happen: you never would let them."

"And now —"

"Well, that was what she came here for: I supposed you had guessed. To know if anything had happened."

"Had happened?" He gazed at her slowly. "Between you and me?" he said with a rush of light.

The words were so much cruder than any that had ever passed between them, that the color rose to her face; but she held his startled gaze.

"You know girls are not quite as unsophisticated as they used to be. Are you surprised that such an idea should occur to her?"

His own color answered hers: it was the only reply that came to him.

Mrs. Vervain went on smoothly: "I supposed it might have struck you that there were times when we presented that appearance."

He made an impatient gesture. "A man's past is his own!"

"Perhaps — it certainly never belongs to the woman who has shared it. But one learns such truths only by experience; and Miss Gaynor is naturally inexperienced."

"Of course — but — supposing her act a natural one —" he floundered lamentably among his innuendoes "— I still don't see — how there was anything —"

"Anything to take hold of? There wasn't —"

"Well, then — ?" escaped him, in undisguised satisfaction; but as she did not complete the sentence he went on with a faltering laugh: "She can hardly object to the existence of a mere friendship between us!"

"But she does," said Mrs. Vervain.

Thursdale stood perplexed. He had seen, on the previous day, no trace of jealousy or resentment in his betrothed: he could still hear the candid ring of the girl's praise of Mrs. Vervain. If she were such an abyss of insincerity as to dissemble distrust under such frankness, she must at least be more subtle than to bring her doubts to her rival for solution. The situation seemed one through which one could no longer move in a penumbra, and he let in a burst of light with the direct query: "Won't you explain what you mean?"

Mrs. Vervain sat silent, not provokingly, as though to prolong his distress, but as if, in the attenuated phraseology he had taught her, it was difficult to find words robust enough to meet his challenge. It was the first time he had ever asked her to explain anything; and she had lived so long in dread of offering elucidations which were not wanted, that she seemed unable to produce one on the spot.

At last she said slowly: "She came to find out if you were really free."

Thursdale colored again. "Free?" he stammered, with a sense of physical disgust at contact with such crassness.

"Yes — if I had quite done with you." She smiled in recovered security. "It seems she likes clear outlines; she has a passion for definitions."

"Yes — well?" he said, wincing at the echo of his own subtlety.

"Well — and when I told her that you had never belonged to me, she wanted me to define *my* status — to know exactly where I had stood all along."

Thursdale sat gazing at her intently; his hand was not yet on the clue. "And even when you had told her that —"

"Even when I had told her that I had had no status — that I had never stood anywhere, in any sense she meant," said Mrs. Vervain, slowly, "even then she wasn't satisfied, it seems."

He uttered an uneasy exclamation. "She didn't believe you, you mean?"

"I mean that she *did* believe me: too thoroughly."

"Well, then — in God's name, what did she want?"

"Something more — those were the words she used."

"Something more? Between — between you and me? Is it a conundrum?" He laughed awkwardly.

"Girls are not what they were in my day; they are no longer forbidden to contemplate the relation of the sexes."

"So it seems!" he commented. "But since, in this case, there wasn't any —" he broke off, catching the dawn of a revelation in her gaze.

"That's just it. The unpardonable offense has been — in our not offending."

He flung himself down despairingly. "I give up! What did you tell her?" he burst out with sudden crudeness.

"The exact truth. If I had only known," she broke off with a beseeching tenderness, "won't you believe that I would still have lied for you?"

"Lied for me? Why on earth should you have lied for either of us?"

"To save you — to hide you from her to the last! As I've hidden you from myself all these years!" She stood up with a sudden tragic import in her movement. "You believe me capable of that, don't you? If I had only guessed — but I have never known a girl like her; she had the truth out of me with a spring."

"The truth that you and I had never — "

"Had never — never in all these years! Oh, she knew why — she measured us both in a flash. She didn't suspect me of having haggled with you — her words pelted me like hail. 'He just took what he wanted — sifted and sorted you to suit his taste. Burnt out the gold and left a heap of cinders. And you let him — you let yourself be cut in bits' — she mixed her metaphors a little — 'be cut in bits, and used or discarded, while all the while every drop of blood in you belonged to him! But he's Shylock[1] — he's Shylock — and you have bled to death of the pound of flesh he has cut off you.' But she despises me the most, you know — far, far the most — " Mrs. Vervain ended.

The words fell strangely on the scented stillness of the room: they seemed out of harmony with its setting of afternoon intimacy, the kind of intimacy on which, at any moment, a visitor might intrude without perceptibly lowering the atmosphere. It was as though a grand opera singer had strained the acoustics of a private music room.

Thursdale stood up, facing his hostess. Half the room was between them, but they seemed to stare close at each other now that the veils of reticence and ambiguity had fallen.

His first words were characteristic: "She *does* despise me, then?" he exclaimed.

"She thinks the pound of flesh you took was a little too near the heart."

He was excessively pale. "Please tell me exactly what she said of me."

"She did not speak much of you: she is proud. But I gather that while she understands love or indifference, her eyes have never been opened to the many intermediate shades of feeling. At any rate, she expressed an unwillingness to be taken with reservations — she thinks you would have loved her better if you had loved someone else first. The point of view is original — she insists on a man with a past!"

"Oh, a past — if she's serious — I could rake up a past!" he said with a laugh.

"So I suggested: but she has her eyes on this particular portion of it. She insists on making it a test case. She wanted to know what you had done to me; and before I could guess her drift I blundered into telling her."

Thursdale drew a difficult breath. "I never supposed — your revenge is complete," he said slowly.

He heard a little gasp in her throat. "My revenge? When I sent for you to warn you — to save you from being surprised as I was surprised?"

---

[1] The money-lender in Shakespeare's *Merchant of Venice.* — Eds.

"You're very good — but it's rather late to talk of saving me." He held out his hand in the mechanical gesture of leave-taking.

"How you must care! — for I never saw you so dull," was her answer. "Don't you see that it's not too late for me to help you?" And as he continued to stare, she brought out sublimely: "Take the rest — in imagination! Let it at least be of that much use to you. Tell her I lied to her — she's too ready to believe it! And so, after all, in a sense, I shan't have been wasted."

His stare hung on her, widening to a kind of wonder. She gave the look back brightly, unblushingly, as though the expedient were too simple to need oblique approaches. It was extraordinary how a few words had swept them from an atmosphere of the most complex dissimulations to this contact of naked souls.

It was not in Thursdale to expand with the pressure of fate; but something in him cracked with it, and the rift let in new light. He went up to his friend and took her hand.

"You would do it — you would do it!"

She looked at him, smiling, but her hand shook.

"Good-bye," he said, kissing it.

"Good-bye? You are going — ?"

"To get my letter."

"Your letter? The letter won't matter, if you will only do what I ask."

He returned her gaze. "I might, I suppose, without being out of character. Only, don't you see that if your plan helped me it could only harm her?"

"Harm *her?*"

"To sacrifice you wouldn't make me different. I shall go on being what I have always been — sifting and sorting, as she calls it. Do you want my punishment to fall on *her?*"

She looked at him long and deeply. "Ah, if I had to choose between you — !"

"You would let her take her chance? But I can't, you see, I must take my punishment alone."

She drew her hand away, sighing. "Oh, there will be no punishment for either of you."

"For either of us? There will be the reading of her letter for me."

She shook her head with a slight laugh. "There will be no letter."

Thursdale faced about from the threshold with fresh life in his look. "No letter? You don't mean —"

"I mean that she's been with you since I saw her — she's seen you and heard your voice. If there *is* a letter, she has recalled it — from the first station, by telegraph."

He turned back to the door, forcing an answer to her smile. "But in the meanwhile I shall have read it," he said.

The door closed on him, and she hid her eyes from the dreadful emptiness of the room.

Questions for Discussion

1. Why is the story called "The Dilettante"? Who in the story is a dilettante, and how is this revealed?
2. What does his fiancée, Ruth Gaynor, represent for Thursdale, and how is his relationship with her different from the long-term relationship he has had with Mrs. Vervain, to whose drawing room he returns at the beginning of the story?
3. What do we learn about Thursdale's mood and thought processes through the complex, qualified sentences in the story's first seven paragraphs?
4. Discuss some of the key similes and metaphors used by and to describe the story's three characters. How do these figures of speech help to clarify their respective values and attitudes toward relationships?
5. Why does Ruth reject Thursdale? Does the story imply that she is wise to do so, based on what we know about Thursdale and his value system?

Ideas for Writing

1. Analyze Thursdale's character, taking into account the ending of the story as well as his responses to Mrs. Vervain's revelations about Ruth's rejection of him. Does Thursdale seem to have changed or grown in the course of the story? Will he continue to be merely a dilettante?
2. Except for the last sentence, most of "The Dilettante" is told from Thursdale's perspective. Rewrite the story from either Mrs. Vervain's or Ruth Gaynor's viewpoint.

STEPHEN CRANE   (1871–1900)

Like the authors of the French naturalist school of fiction (Gustave Flaubert, Emile Zola, and Guy de Maupassant among them), Stephen Crane often reflects in his fiction on how nature and social pressures affect the destiny of individuals and communities. Crane's characters are unique, however, because they exhibit strength, heroism, and the ability to cooperate in order to survive against overwhelming odds. The son of a Methodist minister and the youngest of fourteen children, Crane grew up in Asbury Park and Newark, New Jersey. His father died when Crane was very young, and his mother supported the family by writing news articles. Crane attended Syracuse University before moving to New York City, where he followed his mother's career as a freelance journalist. Although Crane died before he was thirty, he did an enormous amount of news writing in addition to completing nineteen books, which include novels and poetry and story collections. His best-known novels are *Maggie, a Girl of the Streets* (1893) and *The Red Badge of Courage* (1895), about the Civil War. His stories are collected in *The Open Boat and Other Tales of Adventure* (1898).

As a journalist, Crane traveled in the American West and in Florida, reporting on the Spanish-American War. On one journey to Florida in 1897, his steamship sank, and he survived in a lifeboat for more than thirty hours. He wrote of these experiences in the news article "The Sinking of the *Commodore*" which formed the basis for his best-known story, "The Open Boat," a work Crane considered a parable of human existence.

The Open Boat   (1898)

I

None of them knew the color of the sky. Their eyes glanced level, and were fastened upon the waves that swept toward them. These waves were of the hue of slate, save for the tops, which were of foaming white, and all of the men knew the colors of the sea. The horizon narrowed and widened, and dipped and rose, and at all times its edge was jagged with waves that seemed thrust up in points like rocks.

Many a man ought to have a bathtub larger than the boat which here rode upon the sea. These waves were most wrongfully and barbarously abrupt and tall, and each frothtop was a problem in small-boat navigation.

The cook squatted in the bottom, and looked with both eyes at the six inches of gunwale which separated him from the ocean. His sleeves were rolled over his fat forearms, and the two flaps of his unbuttoned vest dangled as he bent to bail out the boat. Often he said, "Gawd! that was a narrow clip." As he remarked it he invariably gazed eastward over the broken sea.

The oiler, steering with one of the two oars in the boat, sometimes raised himself suddenly to keep clear of water that swirled in over the stern. It was a thin little oar, and it seemed often ready to snap.

The correspondent, pulling at the other oar, watched the waves and wondered why he was there.

The injured captain, lying in the bow, was at this time buried in that profound dejection and indifference which comes, temporarily at least, to even the bravest and most enduring when, willy-nilly, the firm fails, the army loses, the ship goes down. The mind of the master of a vessel is rooted deep in the timbers of her, though he command for a day or a decade, and this captain had on him the stern impression of a scene in the grays of dawn of seven turned faces, and later a stump of a topmast with a white ball on it, that slashed to and fro at the waves, went low and lower, and down. Thereafter there was something strange in his voice. Although steady, it was deep with mourning, and of a quality beyond oration or tears.

"Keep 'er a little more south, Billie," said he.

"A little more south, sir," said the oiler in the stern.

A seat in this boat was not unlike a seat upon a bucking broncho, and by the same token a broncho is not much smaller. The craft pranced and reared and plunged like an animal. As each wave came, and she rose for it, she seemed like a horse making at a fence outrageously high. The manner of her scramble over these walls of water is a mystic thing, and, moreover, at the top of them were ordinarily these problems in white water, the foam racing down from the summit of each wave requiring a new leap, and a leap from the air. Then, after scornfully bumping a crest, she would slide and race and splash down a long incline, and arrive bobbing and nodding in front of the next menace.

A singular disadvantage of the sea lies in the fact that after successfully surmounting one wave you discover that there is another behind it just as important and just as nervously anxious to do something effective in the way of swamping boats. In a ten-foot dinghy one can get an idea of the resources of the sea in the line of waves that is not probable to the average experience which is never at sea in a dinghy. As each slaty wall of water approached, it shut all else from the view of the men in the boat, and it was not difficult to imagine that this particular wave was the final outburst of the ocean, the last effort of the grim water. There was a terrible grace in the move of the waves, and they came in silence, save for the snarling of the crests.

In the wan light the faces of the men must have been gray. Their eyes must have glinted in strange ways as they gazed steadily astern. Viewed from a balcony, the whole thing would doubtless have been weirdly picturesque. But the men in the boat had no time to see it, and if they had had leisure, there were other things to occupy their minds. The sun swung steadily up the sky, and they knew it was broad day because the color of the sea changed from slate to emerald green streaked with amber lights, and the foam was like tumbling snow. The process of the breaking day was unknown to them. They were aware only of this effect upon the color of the waves that rolled toward them.

In disjointed sentences the cook and the correspondent argued as to the difference between a life-saving station and a house of refuge. The cook had said: "There's a house of refuge just north of the Mosquito Inlet Light, and as soon as they see us they'll come off in their boat and pick us up."

"As soon as who see us?" said the correspondent.

"The crew," said the cook.

"Houses of refuge don't have crews," said the correspondent. "As I understand them, they are only places where clothes and grub are stored for the benefit of shipwrecked people. They don't carry crews."

"Oh, yes, they do," said the cook.

"No, they don't," said the correspondent.

"Well, we're not there yet, anyhow," said the oiler, in the stern.

"Well," said the cook, "perhaps it's not a house of refuge that I'm thinking of as being near Mosquito Inlet Light; perhaps it's a life-saving station."

"We're not there yet," said the oiler in the stern.

II

As the boat bounced from the top of each wave the wind tore through the hair of the hatless men, and as the craft plopped her stern down again the spray slashed past them. The crest of each of these waves was a hill, from the top of which the men surveyed for a moment a broad tumultuous expanse, shining and wind-riven. It was probably splendid, it was probably glorious, this play of the free sea, wild with lights of emerald and white and amber.

"Bully good thing it's an on-shore wind," said the cook. "If not, where would we be? Wouldn't have a show."

"That's right," said the correspondent.

The busy oiler nodded his assent.

Then the captain, in the bow, chuckled in a way that expressed humor, contempt, tragedy, all in one. "Do you think we've got much of a show now, boys?" said he.

Whereupon the three were silent, save for a trifle of hemming and hawing. To express any particular optimism at this time they felt to be childish and stupid, but they all doubtless possessed this sense of the situation in their minds. A young man thinks doggedly at such times. On the other hand, the ethics of their condition was decidedly against any open suggestion of hopelessness. So they were silent.

"Oh, well," said the captain, soothing his children, "we'll get ashore all right."

But there was that in his tone which made them think; so the oiler quoth, "Yes! if this wind holds."

The cook was bailing. "Yes! if we don't catch hell in the surf."

Canton-flannel gulls flew near and far. Sometimes they sat down on the sea, near patches of brown seaweed that rolled over the waves with a movement like carpets on a line in a gale. The birds sat comfortably in groups, and they were envied by some in the dinghy, for the wrath of the sea was no more to them than it was to a covey of prairie chickens a thousand miles inland. Often they came very close and stared at the men with black bead-like eyes. At these times they were uncanny and sinister in their unblinking scrutiny, and the men hooted angrily at them, telling them to be gone. One came, and evidently decided to alight on the top of the captain's head. The bird flew parallel to the boat and did not circle, but made short sidelong jumps in the air in chicken-fashion. His black eyes were wistfully fixed upon the captain's head. "Ugly brute," said the oiler to the bird. "You look as if you were made with a jacknife." The cook and the correspondent swore darkly at the creature. The captain naturally wished to knock it away with the end of the heavy painter, but he did not dare do it, because anything resembling an emphatic gesture would have capsized this freighted boat; and so, with his open hand, the captain gently and carefully waved the gull away. After it had been discouraged from the pursuit the captain breathed easier on account of his hair, and others breathed easier because the bird struck their minds at this time as being somehow gruesome and ominous.

In the meantime the oiler and the correspondent rowed. And also they rowed. They sat together in the same seat, and each rowed an oar. Then the oiler took both oars; then the correspondent took both oars; then the oiler; then the correspondent. They rowed and they rowed. The very ticklish part of the business was when the time came for the reclining one in the stern to take his turn at the oars. By the very last star of truth, it is easier to steal eggs from under a hen than it was to change seats in the dinghy. First the man in the stern slid his hand along the thwart and moved with care, as if he were of Sèvres. Then the man in the rowing-seat slid his hand along the other thwart. It was all done with the most extraordinary care. As the two sidled past each other, the whole party kept watchful eyes on the coming wave, and the captain cried: "Look out, now! Steady, there!"

The brown mats of seaweed that appeared from time to time were like islands, bits of earth. They were travelling, apparently, neither one way nor the other. They were, to all intents, stationary. They informed the men in the boat that it was making progress slowly toward the land.

The captain, rearing cautiously in the bow after the dinghy soared on a great swell, said that he had seen the lighthouse at Mosquito Inlet. Presently the cook remarked that he had seen it. The correspondent was at the oars then, and for some reason he too wished to look at the lighthouse; but his back was toward the far shore, and the waves were important, and for some time he could not seize an opportunity to turn his head. But at last there came a wave more gentle than the others, and when at the crest of it he swiftly scoured the western horizon.

"See it?" said the captain.

"No," said the correspondent, slowly; "I didn't see anything."

"Look again," said the captain. He pointed. "It's exactly in that direction."

At the top of another wave the correspondent did as he was bid, and this time his eyes chanced on a small, still thing on the edge of the swaying horizon. It was precisely like the point of a pin. It took an anxious eye to find a lighthouse so tiny.

"Think we'll make it, Captain?"

"If this wind holds and the boat don't swamp, we can't do much else," said the captain.

The little boat, lifted by each towering sea and splashed viciously by the crests, made progress that in the absence of seaweed was not apparent to those in her. She seemed just a wee thing wallowing, miraculously top up, at the mercy of five oceans. Occasionally a great spread of water, like white flames, swarmed into her.

"Bail her, cook," said the captain, serenely.

"All right, Captain," said the cheerful cook.

III

It would be difficult to describe the subtle brotherhood of men that was here established on the seas. No one said that it was so. No one mentioned it. But it dwelt in the boat, and each man felt it warm him. They were a captain, an oiler, a cook, and a correspondent, and they were friends — friends in a more curiously iron-bound degree than may be common. The hurt captain, lying against the water-jar in the bow, spoke always in a low voice and calmly; but he could never command a more ready and swiftly obedient crew than the motley three of the dinghy. It was more than a mere recognition of what was best for the common safety. There was surely in it a quality that was personal and heart-felt. And after this devotion to the commander of the boat, there was this comradeship, that the correspondent, for instance, who had been taught to be cynical of men, knew even at the time was the best experience of his life. But no one said that it was so. No one mentioned it.

"I wish we had a sail," remarked the captain. "We might try my overcoat on the end of an oar, and give you two boys a chance to rest." So the cook and the correspondent held the mast and spread wide the overcoat; the oiler steered; and the little boat made good way with her new rig. Sometimes the oiler had to scull sharply to keep a sea from breaking into the boat, but otherwise sailing was a success.

Meanwhile the lighthouse had been growing slowly larger. It had now almost assumed color, and appeared like a little gray shadow on the sky. The man at the oars could not be prevented from turning his head rather often to try for a glimpse of this little gray shadow.

At last, from the top of each wave, the men in the tossing boat could see land. Even as the lighthouse was an upright shadow on the sky, this land seemed but a long black shadow on the sea. It certainly was thinner than paper. "We must be about opposite New Smyrna," said the cook, who had coasted this shore often in schooners. "Captain, by the way, I believe they abandoned that life-saving station there about a year ago."

"Did they?" said the captain.

The wind slowly died away. The cook and the correspondent were not now obliged to slave in order to hold high the oar. But the waves continued their old impetuous swooping at the dinghy, and the little craft, no longer under way, struggled woundily over them. The oiler or the correspondent took the oars again.

Shipwrecks are apropos of nothing. If men could only train for them and have them occur when the men had reached pink condition, there would be less drowning at sea. Of the four in the dinghy none had slept any time worth mentioning for two days and two nights previous to embarking in the dinghy, and in the excitement of clambering about the deck of a foundering ship they had also forgotten to eat heartily.

For these reasons, and for others, neither the oiler nor the correspondent was fond of rowing at this time. The correspondent wondered ingenuously how in the name of all that was sane could there be people who thought it amusing to row a boat. It was not an amusement; it was a diabolical punishment, and even a genius of mental aberrations could never conclude that it was anything but a horror to the muscles and crime against the back. He mentioned to the boat in general how the amusement of rowing struck him, and the weary-faced oiler smiled in full sympathy. Previously to the foundering, by the way, the oiler had worked double watch in the engine-room of the ship.

"Take her easy now, boys," said the captain. "Don't spend yourselves. If we have to run a surf you'll need all your strength, because we'll sure have to swim for it. Take your time."

Slowly the land arose from the sea. From a black line it became a line of black and a line of white — trees and sand. Finally the captain said that he could make out a house on the shore. "That's the house of refuge, sure," said the cook. "They'll see us before long, and come out after us."

The distant lighthouse reared high. "The keeper ought to be able to make us out now, if he's looking through a glass," said the captain. "He'll notify the life-saving people."

"None of those other boats could have got ashore to give word of the wreck," said the oiler, in a low voice, "else the life-boat would be out hunting us."

Slowly and beautifully the land loomed out of the sea. The wind came again. It had veered from the north-east to the south-east. Finally a new sound struck the ears of the men in the boat. It was the low thunder of the surf on the shore. "We'll never be able to make the lighthouse now," said the captain. "Swing her head a little more north, Billie."

"A little more north, sir," said the oiler.

Whereupon the little boat turned her nose once more down the wind, and all but the oarsman watched the shore grow. Under the influence of this expansion doubt and direful apprehension were leaving the minds of the men. The management of the boat was still most absorbing, but it could not prevent a quiet cheerfulness. In an hour, perhaps, they would be ashore.

Their backbones had become thoroughly used to balancing in the boat, and they now rode this wild colt of a dinghy like circus men. The correspondent thought that he had been drenched to the skin, but happening to feel in the top pocket of his coat, he found therein eight cigars. Four of them were soaked with seawater; four were perfectly scatheless. After a search, somebody produced three dry matches; and thereupon the four waifs rode impudently in their little boat and, with an assurance of an impending rescue shining in their eyes, puffed at the big cigars, and judged well and ill of all men. Everybody took a drink of water.

IV

"Cook," remarked the captain, "there don't seem to be any signs of life about your house of refuge."

"No," replied the cook. "Funny they don't see us!"

A broad stretch of lowly coast lay before the eyes of the men. It was of low dunes topped with dark vegetation. The roar of the surf was plain, and sometimes they could see the white lip of a wave as it spun up the beach. A tiny house was blocked out black upon the sky. Southward, the slim lighthouse lifted its little gray length.

Tide, wind, and waves were swinging the dinghy northward. "Funny they don't see us," said the men.

The surf's roar was here dulled, but its tone was nevertheless thunderous and mighty. As the boat swam over the great rollers the men sat listening to this roar. "We'll swamp sure," said everybody.

It is fair to say here that there was not a life-saving station within twenty miles in either direction; but the men did not know this fact, and in consequence they made dark and opprobrious remarks concerning the eyesight of the nation's life-savers. Four scowling men sat in the dinghy and surpassed records in the invention of epithets.

"Funny they don't see us."

The light-heartedness of a former time had completely faded. To their sharpened minds it was easy to conjure pictures of all kinds of incompetency and blindness and, indeed, cowardice. There was the shore of the populous land, and it was bitter and bitter to them that from it came no sign.

"Well," said the captain, ultimately, "I suppose we'll have to make a try for ourselves. If we stay out here too long, we'll none of us have strength left to swim after the boat swamps."

And so the oiler, who was at the oars, turned the boat straight for the shore. There was a sudden tightening of muscles. There was some thinking. "If we don't all get ashore," said the captain — "if we don't all get ashore, I suppose you fellows know where to send news of my finish?"

They then briefly exchanged some addresses and admonitions. As for the reflections of the men, there was a great deal of rage in them. Perchance they might be formulated thus: "If I am going to be drowned — if I am going to be drowned — if I am going to be drowned, why, in the name of the seven mad gods who rule the sea, was I allowed to come thus far and contemplate sand and trees? Was I brought here merely to have my nose dragged away as I was about to nibble the sacred cheese of life? It is preposterous. If this old ninnywoman, Fate, cannot do better than this, she should be deprived of the management of men's fortunes. She is an old hen who knows not her intention. If she has decided to drown me, why did she not do it in the beginning and save me all this trouble? The whole affair is absurd. — But no; she cannot mean to drown me. She dare not drown me. She cannot drown me. Not after all this work." Afterward the man might have had an impulse to shake his fist at the clouds. "Just you drown me, now, and then hear what I call you!"

The billows that came at this time were more formidable. They seemed always just about to break and roll over the little boat in a turmoil of foam. There was a preparatory and long growl in the speech of them. No mind unused to the sea would have concluded that the dinghy could ascend these sheer heights in time. The shore was still afar. The oiler was a wily surfman. "Boys," he said swiftly, "she won't live three minutes more, and we're too far out to swim. Shall I take her to sea again, Captain?"

"Yes; go ahead!" said the captain.

This oiler, by a series of quick miracles and fast and steady oarsmanship, turned the boat in the middle of the surf and took her safely to sea again.

There was a considerable silence as the boat bumped over the furrowed sea to deeper water. Then somebody in gloom spoke: "Well, anyhow, they must have seen us from the shore by now."

The gulls went in slanting flight up the wind toward the gray, desolate east. A squall, marked by dinghy clouds and clouds brick-red like smoke from a burning building, appeared from the south-east.

"What do you think of those life-saving people? Ain't they peaches?"

"Funny they haven't seen us."

"Maybe they think we're out here for sport! Maybe they think we're fishin'. Maybe they think we're damned fools."

It was a long afternoon. A changed tide tried to force them southward, but wind and wave said northward. Far ahead, where coast-line, sea, and sky formed their mighty angle, there were little dots which seemed to indicate a city on the shore.

"St. Augustine?"

The captain shook his head. "Too near Mosquito Inlet."

And the oiler rowed, and then the correspondent rowed; then the oiler rowed. It was a weary business. The human back can become the seat of more aches and pains than are registered in books for the composite anatomy of a regiment. It is a limited area, but it can become the theatre of innumerable muscular conflicts, tangles, wrenches, knots, and other comforts.

"Did you ever like to row, Billie?" asked the correspondent.

"No," said the oiler; "hang it!"

When one exchanged the rowing-seat for a place in the bottom of the boat, he suffered a bodily depression that caused him to be careless of everything save an obligation to wiggle one finger. There was cold sea-water swashing to and fro in the boat, and he lay in it. His head, pillowed on a thwart, was within an inch of the swirl of a wave-crest, and sometimes a particularly obstreperous sea came inboard and drenched him once more. But these matters did not annoy him. It is almost certain that if the boat had capsized he would have tumbled comfortably upon the ocean as if he felt sure that it was a great soft mattress.

"Look! There's a man on the shore!"

"Where?"

"There! See 'im?"

"Yes, sure! He's walking along."

"Now he's stopped. Look! He's facing us!"

"He's waving at us!"

"So he is! By thunder!"

"Ah, now we're all right! Now we're all right! There'll be a boat out here for us in half an hour."

"He's going on. He's running. He's going up to that house there."

The remote beach seemed lower than the sea, and it required a searching glance to discern the little black figure. The captain saw a floating stick, and they rowed to it. A bath towel was by some weird chance in the boat, and, trying this on the stick, the captain waved it. The oarsman did not dare turn his head, so he was obliged to ask questions.

"What's he doing now?"

"He's standing still again. He's looking, I think. — There he goes again — toward the house. — Now he's stopped again."

"Is he waving at us?"

"No, not now; he was, though."

"Look! There comes another man!"

"He's running."

"Look at him go, would you!"

"Why, he's on a bicycle. Now he's met the other man. They're both waving at us. Look!"

"There comes something up the beach."

"What the devil is that thing?"

"Why, it looks like a boat."

"Why, certainly, it's a boat."

"No; it's on wheels."

"Yes, so it is. Well, that must be the life-boat. They drag them along shore on a wagon."

"That's the life-boat, sure."

"No, by God, it's — it's an omnibus."

"I tell you it's a life-boat."

"It is not! It's an omnibus. I can see it plain. See? One of these big hotel omnibuses."

"By thunder, you're right. It's an omnibus, sure as fate. What do you suppose they are doing with an omnibus? Maybe they are going around collecting the life-crew, hey?"

"That's it, likely. Look! There's a fellow waving a little black flag. He's standing on the steps of the omnibus. There come those other two fellows. Now they're all talking together. Look at the fellow with the flag. Maybe he ain't waving it!"

"That ain't a flag, is it? That's his coat. Why, certainly, that's his coat."

"So it is; it's his coat. He's taken it off and is waving it around his head. But would you look at him swing it!"

"Oh, say, there isn't any life-saving station there. That's just a winter-resort hotel omnibus that has brought over some of the boarders to see us drown."

"What's that idiot with the coat mean? What's he signalling, anyhow?"

"It looks as if he were trying to tell us to go north. There must be a life-saving station up there."

"No; he thinks we're fishing. Just giving us a merry hand. See? Ah, there, Willie!"

"Well, I wish I could make something out of those signals. What do you suppose he means?"

"He don't mean anything; he's just playing."

"Well, if he'd just signal us to try the surf again, or to go to sea and wait, or go north, or go south, or go to hell, there would be some reason in it. But look at him! He just stands there and keeps his coat revolving like a wheel. The ass!"

"There come more people."

"Now there's quite a mob. Look! Isn't that a boat?"

"Where? Oh, I see where you mean. No, that's no boat."

"That fellow is still waving his coat."

"He must think we like to see him do that. Why don't he quit it? It don't mean anything."

"I don't know. I think he is trying to make us go north. It must be that there's a life-saving station there somewhere."

"Say, he ain't tired yet. Look at 'im wave!"

"Wonder how long he can keep that up. He's been revolving his coat ever since he caught sight of us. He's an idiot. Why aren't they getting men to bring a boat out? A fishingboat — one of those big yawls — could come out here all right. Why don't he do something?"

"Oh, it's all right now."

"They'll have a boat out here for us in less than no time, now that they've seen us."

A faint yellow tone came into the sky over the low land. The shadows on the sea slowly deepened. The wind bore coldness with it, and the men began to shiver.

"Holy smoke!" said one, allowing his voice to express his impious mood, "If we keep on monkeying out here! If we've got to flounder out here all night!"

"Oh, we'll never have to stay here all night! Don't you worry. They've seen us now, and it won't be long before they'll come chasing out after us."

The shore grew dusky. The man waving a coat blended gradually into this gloom, and it swallowed in the same manner the omnibus and the group of people. The spray, when it dashed uproariously over the side, made the voyagers shrink and swear like men who were being branded.

"I'd like to catch the chump who waved the coat. I feel like socking him one, just for luck."

"Why? What did he do?"

"Oh, nothing, but then he seemed so damned cheerful."

In the meantime the oiler rowed, and then the correspondent rowed, and then the oiler rowed. Gray-faced and bowed forward, they mechanically, turn by turn, plied the leaden oars. The form of the lighthouse had vanished from the southern horizon, but finally a pale star appeared, just lifting from the sea. The streaked saffron in the west passed before the all-merging darkness, and the sea to the east was black. The land had vanished, and was expressed only by the low and dreary thunder of the surf.

"If I am going to be drowned — if I am going to be drowned — if I am going to be drowned, why, in the name of the seven gods who rule the sea, was I allowed to come thus far and contemplate sand and trees? Was I brought here merely to have my nose dragged away as I was about to nibble the sacred cheese of life?"

The patient captain, drooped over the water-jar, was sometimes obliged to speak to the oarsman.

"Keep her head up! Keep her head up!"

"Keep her head, up, sir." The voices were weary and low.

This was surely a quiet evening. All save the oarsman lay heavily and listlessly in the boat's bottom. As for him, his eyes were just capable of noting the tall black waves that swept forward in a most sinister silence, save for an occasional subdued growl of a crest.

The cook's head was on a thwart, and he looked without interest at the water under his nose. He was deep in other scenes. Finally he spoke. "Billie," he murmured, dreamfully, "what kind of pie do you like best?"

V

"Pie!" said the oiler and the correspondent, agitatedly. "Don't talk about those things, blast you!"

"Well," said the cook, "I was just thinking about ham sandwiches, and—"

A night on the sea in an open boat is a long night. As darkness settled finally, the shine of the light, lifting from the sea in the south, changed to full gold. On the northern horizon a new light appeared, a small bluish gleam on the edge of the waters. These two lights were the furniture of the world. Otherwise there was nothing but waves.

Two men huddled in the stern, and distances were so magnificent in the dinghy that the rower was enabled to keep his feet partly warm by thrusting them under his companions. Their legs indeed extended far under the rowing-seat until they touched the feet of the captain forward. Sometimes, despite the efforts of the tired oarsman, a wave came piling into the boat, an icy wave of the night, and the chilling water soaked them anew. They would twist their bodies for a moment and groan, and sleep the dead sleep once more, while the water in the boat gurgled about them as the craft rocked.

The plan of the oiler and the correspondent was for one to row until he lost the ability, and then arouse the other from his sea-water couch in the bottom of the boat.

The oiler plied the oars until his head drooped forward and the overpowering sleep blinded him; and he rowed yet afterward. Then he touched a man in the bottom of the boat, and called his name. "Will you spell me for a little while?" he said meekly.

"Sure, Billie," said the correspondent, awaking and dragging himself to a sitting position. They exchanged places carefully, and the oiler, cuddling down in the sea-water at the cook's side, seemed to go to sleep instantly.

The particular violence of the sea had ceased. The waves came without snarling. The obligation of the man at the oars was to keep the boat headed so that the tilt of the roller would not capsize her, and to preserve her from filling when the crests rushed past. The black waves were silent and hard to be seen in the darkness. Often one was almost upon the boat before the oarsman was aware.

In a low voice the correspondent addressed the captain. He was not sure that the captain was awake, although this iron man seemed to be always awake. "Captain, shall I keep her making for that light north, sir?"

The same steady voice answered him. "Yes. Keep it about two points off the port bow."

The cook had tied a life-belt around himself in order to get even the warmth which this clumsy cork contrivance could donate, and he seemed almost stove-like when a rower, whose teeth invariably chattered wildly as soon as he ceased his labor, dropped down to sleep.

The correspondent, as he rowed, looked down at the two men sleeping underfoot. The cook's arm was around the oiler's shoulders, and, with their fragmentary clothing and haggard faces, they were the babes of the sea — a grotesque rendering of the old babes in the wood.

Later he must have grown stupid at his work, for suddenly there was a growling of water, and a crest came with a roar and a swash into the boat, and it was a wonder that it did not set the cook afloat in his life-belt. The cook continued to sleep, but the oiler sat up, blinking his eyes and shaking with the new cold.

"Oh, I'm awful sorry, Billie," said the correspondent, contritely.

"That's all right, old boy," said the oiler, and lay down again and was asleep.

Presently it seemed that even the captain dozed, and the correspondent thought that he was the one man afloat on all the oceans. The wind had a voice as it came over the waves, and it was sadder than the end.

There was a long, loud swishing astern of the boat, and a gleaming trail of phosphorescence, like blue flame, was furrowed on the black waters. It might have been made by a monstrous knife.

Then there came a stillness, while the correspondent breathed with open mouth and looked at the sea.

Suddenly there was another swish and another long flash of bluish light, and this time it was alongside the boat, and might almost have been reached with an oar. The correspondent saw an enormous fin speed like a shadow through the water, hurling the crystalline spray and leaving the long glowing trail.

The correspondent looked over his shoulder at the captain. His face was hidden, and he seemed to be asleep. He looked at the babes of the sea. They certainly were asleep. So, being bereft of sympathy, he leaned a little way to one side and swore softly into the sea.

But the thing did not then leave the vicinity of the boat. Ahead or astern, on one side or the other, at intervals long or short, fled the long sparkling streak, and there was to be heard the *whirroo* of the dark fin. The speed and power of the thing was greatly to be admired. It cut the water like a gigantic and keen projectile.

The presence of this biding thing did not affect the man with the same horror that it would if he had been a picnicker. He simply looked at the sea dully and swore in an undertone.

Nevertheless, it is true that he did not wish to be alone with the thing. He wished one of his companions to awake by chance and keep him company with it. But the captain hung motionless over the water-jar, and the oiler and the cook in the bottom of the boat were plunged in slumber.

VI

"If I am going to be drowned — if I am going to be drowned — if I am going to be drowned, why, in the name of the seven mad gods who rule the sea, was I allowed to come thus far and contemplate sand and trees?"

During this dismal night, it may be remarked that a man would conclude that it was really the intention of the seven mad gods to drown him, despite the abominable injustice of it. For it was certainly an abominable injustice to drown a man who had worked so hard, so hard. The man felt it would be a crime most unnatural. Other people had drowned at sea since galleys swarmed with painted sails, but still —

When it occurs to a man that nature does not regard him as important, and that she feels she would not maim the universe by disposing of him, he at first wishes to throw bricks at the temple, and he hates deeply the fact that there are no bricks and no temples. Any visible expression of nature would surely be pelleted with his jeers.

Then, if there be no tangible thing to hoot, he feels, perhaps, the desire to confront a personification and indulge in pleas, bowed to one knee, and with hands supplicant, saying, "Yes, but I love myself."

A high cold star on a winter's night is the word he feels that she says to him. Thereafter he knows the pathos of his situation.

The men in the dinghy had not discussed these matters, but each had, no doubt, reflected upon them in silence and according to his mind. There was seldom any expression upon their faces save the general one of complete weariness. Speech was devoted to the business of the boat.

To chime the notes of his emotion, a verse mysteriously entered the correspondent's head. He had even forgotten that he had forgotten this verse, but it suddenly was in his mind.

A soldier of the Legion lay dying in Algiers;
There was lack of woman's nursing, there was dearth of woman's tears;
But a comrade stood beside him, and he took that comrade's hand,
And he said, "I never more shall see my own, my native land."

In his childhood the correspondent had been made acquainted with the fact that a soldier of the Legion lay dying in Algiers, but he had never regarded the fact as important. Myriads of his school-fellows had informed him of the soldier's plight, but the dinning had naturally ended by making him perfectly indifferent. He had never considered it his affair that a soldier of the Legion lay dying in Algiers, nor had it appeared to him as a matter for sorrow. It was less to him than the breaking of a pencil's point.

Now, however, it quaintly came to him as a human, living thing. It was no longer merely a picture of a few throes in the breast of a poet, meanwhile drinking tea and warming his feet at the grate; it was an actuality — stern, mournful, and fine.

The correspondent plainly saw the soldier. He lay on the sand with his feet out straight and still. While his pale left hand was upon his chest in an attempt to thwart the going of his life, the blood came between his fingers. In the far Algerian distance, a city of low square forms was set against a sky that was faint with the last sunset hues. The correspondent, plying the oars and dreaming of the slow and slower movements of the lips of the soldier, was moved by a profound and perfectly impersonal comprehension. He was sorry for the soldier of the Legion who lay dying in Algiers.

The thing which had followed the boat and waited had evidently grown bored at the delay. There was no longer to be heard the slash of the cutwater and there was no longer the flame of the long trail. The light in the north still glimmered, but it was apparently no nearer to the boat. Sometimes the boom of the surf rang in the correspondent's ears, and he turned the craft seaward then and rowed harder. Southward, some one had evidently built a watch-fire on the beach. It was too low and too far to be seen, but it made a shimmering, roseate reflection upon the bluff in back of it, and this could be discerned from the boat. The wind came stronger, and sometimes a wave suddenly raged out like a mountain cat, and there was to be seen the sheen and sparkle of a broken crest.

The captain, in the bow, moved on his water-jar and sat erect. "Pretty long night," he observed to the correspondent. He looked at the shore. "Those life-saving people take their time."

"Did you see that shark playing around?"

"Yes, I saw him. He was a big fellow, all right."

"Wish I had known you were awake."

Later the correspondent spoke into the bottom of the boat.

"Billie!" There was a slow and gradual disentanglement.

"Billie, will you spell me?"

"Sure," said the oiler.

As soon as the correspondent touched the cold, comfortable sea-water in the bottom of the boat and had huddled close to the cook's life-belt he was deep in sleep, despite the fact that his teeth played all the popular airs. This sleep was so good to him that it was but a moment before he heard a voice call his name in a tone that demonstrated the last stages of exhaustion. "Will you spell me?"

"Sure, Billie."

The light in the north had mysteriously vanished, but the correspondent took his course from the wide-awake captain.

Later in the night they took the boat farther out to sea, and the captain directed the cook to take one oar at the stern and keep the boat facing the seas. He was to call out if he should hear the thunder of the surf. This plan enabled the oiler and the correspondent to get respite together. "We'll give those boys a chance to get into shape again," said the captain. They curled down and, after a few preliminary chatterings and trembles, slept once more the dead sleep. Neither knew they had bequeathed to the cook the company of another shark, or perhaps the same shark.

As the boat caroused on the waves, spray occasionally bumped over the side and gave them a fresh soaking, but this had no power to break their repose. The ominous slash of the wind and the water affected them as it would have affected mummies.

"Boys," said the cook, with the notes of every reluctance in his voice, "she's drifted in pretty close. I guess one of you had better take her to sea again." The correspondent, aroused, heard the crash of the toppled crests.

As he was rowing, the captain gave him some whisky-and-water, and this steadied the chills out of him. "If I ever get ashore and anybody shows me even a photograph of an oar — "

At last there was a short conversation.

"Billie! — Billie, will you spell me?"

"Sure," said the oiler.

VII

When the correspondent again opened his eyes, the sea and sky were each of the gray hue of the dawning. Later, carmine and gold was painted upon the waters. The morning appeared finally, in its splendor, with a sky of pure blue, and the sunlight flamed on the tips of the waves.

On the distant dunes were set many little black cottages, and a tall white windmill reared above them. No man, nor dog, nor bicycle appeared on the beach. The cottages might have formed a deserted village.

The voyagers scanned the shore. A conference was held in the boat. "Well," said the captain, "if no help is coming, we might better try a run through the surf right away. If we stay out here much longer we will be too weak to do anything for ourselves at all." The others silently acquiesced in this reasoning. The boat was headed for the beach. The correspondent wondered if none ever ascended the tall wind-tower, and if they never looked seaward. This tower was a giant, standing with its back to the plight of the ants. It represented in a degree, to the correspondent, the serenity of nature amid the struggles of the individual — nature in the wind, and nature in the vision of men. She did not seem cruel to him then, nor beneficent, nor treacherous, nor wise. But she was indifferent, flatly indifferent. It is, perhaps, plausible that a man in this situation, impressed with the unconcern of the universe, should see the innumerable flaws of life, and have them taste wickedly in his mind, and wish for another chance. A distinction between right and wrong seems absurdly clear to him, then, in this new ignorance of the grave-edge, and he understands that if he were given another opportunity he would mend his conduct and his words, and be better and brighter during an introduction or at a tea.

"Now, boys," said the captain, "she is going to swamp sure. All we can do is to work her in as far as possible, and then when she swamps, pile out and scramble for the beach. Keep cool now, and don't jump until she swamps sure."

The oiler took the oars. Over his shoulders he scanned the surf. "Captain," he said, "I think I'd better bring her about and keep her head-on to the seas and back her in."

"All right, Billie," said the captain. "Back her in." The oiler swung the boat then, and, seated in the stern, the cook and the correspondent were obliged to look over their shoulders to contemplate the lonely and indifferent shore.

The monstrous inshore rollers heaved the boat high until the men were again enabled to see the white sheets of water scudding up the slanted beach. "We won't get in very close," said the captain. Each time a man could wrest his attention from the rollers, he turned his glance toward the shore, and in the expression of the eyes during this contemplation there was a singular quality. The correspondent, observing the others, knew that they were not afraid, but the full meaning of their glances was shrouded.

As for himself, he was too tired to grapple fundamentally with the fact. He tried to coerce his mind into thinking of it, but the mind was dominated at this time by the muscles, and the muscles said they did not care. It merely occurred to him that if he should drown it would be a shame.

There were no hurried words, no pallor, no plain agitation. The men simply looked at the shore. "Now, remember to get well clear of the boat when you jump," said the captain.

Seaward the crest of a roller suddenly fell with a thunderous crash, and the long white comber came roaring down upon the boat.

"Steady now," said the captain. The men were silent. They turned their eyes from the shore to the comber and waited. The boat slid up the incline, leaped at the furious top, bounced over it, and swung down the long back of the wave. Some water had been shipped, and the cook bailed it out.

But the next crest crashed also. The tumbling, boiling flood of white water caught the boat and whirled it almost perpendicular. Water swarmed in from all sides. The correspondent had his hands on the gunwale at this time, and when the water entered at that place he swiftly withdrew his fingers, as if he objected to wetting them.

The little boat, drunken with this weight of water, reeled and snuggled deeper into the sea.

"Bail her out, cook! Bail her out!" said the captain.

"All right, Captain," said the cook.

"Now, boys, the next one will do for us sure," said the oiler. "Mind to jump clear of the boat."

The third wave moved forward, huge, furious, implacable. It fairly swallowed the dinghy, and almost simultaneously the men tumbled into the sea. A piece of life-belt had lain in the bottom of the boat, and as the correspondent went overboard he held this to his chest with his left hand.

The January water was icy, and he reflected immediately that it was colder than he had expected to find it off the coast of Florida. This appeared to his dazed mind as a fact important enough to be noted at the time. The coldness of the water was sad; it was tragic. This fact was somehow mixed and confused with his opinion of his own situation, so that it seemed almost a proper reason for tears. The water was cold.

When he came to the surface he was conscious of little but the noisy water. Afterward he saw his companions in the sea. The oiler was ahead in the race. He was swimming strongly and rapidly. Off to the correspondent's left, the cook's great white and corked back bulged out of the water; and in the rear the captain was hanging with his one good hand to the keel of the overturned dinghy.

There is a certain immovable quality to a shore, and the correspondent wondered at it amid the confusion of the sea.

It seemed also very attractive; but the correspondent knew that it was a long journey, and he paddled leisurely. The piece of life-preserver lay under him, and sometimes he whirled down the incline of a wave as if he were on a handsled.

But finally he arrived at a place in the sea where travel was beset with difficulty. He did not pause swimming to inquire what manner of current had caught him, but there his progress ceased. The shore was set before him like a bit of scenery on a stage, and he looked at it and understood with his eyes each detail of it.

As the cook passed, much farther to the left, the captain was calling to him, "Turn over on your back, cook! Turn over on your back and use the oar."

"All right, sir." The cook turned on his back, and, paddling with an oar, went ahead as if he were a canoe.

Presently the boat also passed to the left of the correspondent, with the captain clinging with one hand to the keel. He would have appeared like a man raising himself to look over a board fence if it were not for the extraordinary gymnastics of the boat. The correspondent marvelled that the captain could still hold to it.

They passed on nearer to shore — the oiler, the cook, the captain — and following them went the water-jar, bouncing gaily over the seas.

The correspondent remained in the grip of this strange new enemy — a current. The shore, with its white slope of sand and its green bluff topped with little silent cottages, was spread like a picture before him. It was very near to him then, but he was impressed as one who, in a gallery, looks at a scene from Brittany or Algiers.

He thought: "I am going to drown? Can it be possible? Can it be possible? Can it be possible?" Perhaps an individual must consider his own death to be the final phenomenon of nature.

But later a wave perhaps whirled him out of this small deadly current, for he found suddenly that he could again make progress toward the shore. Later still he was aware that the captain, clinging with one hand to the keel of the dinghy, had his face turned away from the shore and toward him, and was calling his name. "Come to the boat! Come to the boat!"

In his struggle to reach the captain and the boat, he reflected that when one gets properly wearied drowning must really be a comfortable arrangement — a cessation of hostilities accompanied by a large degree of relief; and he was glad of it, for the main thing in his mind for some moments had been horror of the temporary agony. He did not wish to be hurt.

Presently he saw a man running along the shore. He was undressing with most remarkable speed. Coat, trousers, shirt, everything flew magically off him.

"Come to the boat!" called the captain.

"All right, Captain." As the correspondent paddled, he saw the captain let himself down to bottom and leave the boat. Then the correspondent performed his one little marvel of the voyage. A large wave caught him and flung him with ease and supreme speed completely over the boat and far beyond it. It struck him even then as an event in gymnastics and a true miracle of the sea. An overturned boat in the surf is not a plaything to a swimming man.

The correspondent arrived in water that reached only to his waist, but his condition did not enable him to stand for more than a moment. Each wave knocked him into a heap, and the undertow pulled at him.

Then he saw the man who had been running and undressing, and undressing and running, come bounding into the water. He dragged ashore the cook, and then waded toward the captain; but the captain waved him away and sent him to the correspondent. He was naked — naked as a tree in winter; but a halo was about his head, and he shone like a saint. He gave a strong pull, and a long drag, and a bully heave at the correspondent's hand. The correspondent, schooled in the minor formulae, said, "Thanks, old man." But suddenly the man cried, "What's that?" He pointed a swift finger. The correspondent said, "Go."

In the shallows, face downward, lay the oiler. His forehead touched sand that was periodically, between each wave, clear of the sea.

The correspondent did not know all that transpired afterward. When he achieved safe ground he fell, striking the sand with each particular part of his body. It was as if he had dropped from a roof, but the thud was grateful to him.

It seems that instantly the beach was populated with men with blankets, clothes, and flasks, and women with coffee-pots and all the remedies sacred to their minds. The welcome of the land to the men from the sea was warm and generous; but a still and dripping shape was carried slowly up the beach, and the land's welcome for it could only be the different and sinister hospitality of the grave.

When it came night, the white waves paced to and fro in the moonlight, and the wind brought the sound of the great sea's voice to the men on the shore, and they felt that they could then be interpreters.

Questions for Discussion

1. What is the effect of the description of the ocean in the opening paragraph? What does the story's first sentence — "None of them knew the color of the sky" — suggest?

2. How does Crane characterize the men on the open boat? In what ways are they different? Why do they become more similar as the story continues? What is the "subtle brotherhood" that develops among them?

3. How does Crane use metaphors to give personality to the boat, the waves and the ocean water, the shark, and the abstraction of fate?

4. Why do the men feel rage at fate? Who are the "seven mad gods"?

5. What is the significance of the poem about the dying soldier that the correspondent recites? How has the correspondent's understanding of the poem been shaped by his experiences?

6. What thoughts run through the correspondent's mind as he swims toward land after the boat capsizes? What does he seem to have learned from his experience?

Ideas for Writing

1. The story's final words are "they felt that they could then be interpreters." Write an essay in which you discuss the meaning of this phrase in the context of the story as a whole. What are the men interpreting here? What do you think their interpretation or conclusions might be?

2. Write a story or essay about an experience of survival through cooperation.

SHERWOOD ANDERSON (1876–1941)

Often set in small midwestern towns, the stories of Sherwood Anderson capture the frustrations and longings of ordinary people. The central theme in many of his stories is the deadening effects of modern life on what is truly valuable in the human spirit.

Born in Camden, Ohio, Anderson at fourteen left school to work as a laborer. He fought in the Spanish-American War in 1898 and then settled in Chicago, where he was in business and advertising, marrying in 1904. Gradually his business success allowed him to devote himself full time to his writing. Anderson became a literary celebrity with his first publication, a collection of portraits of troubled, isolated residents of a fictional midwestern community, *Winesburg Ohio* (1919), which includes the story "Hands." Other of his short-story collections are *The Triumph of the Egg* (1921), *Horses and Men* (1923), and *Death in the Woods* (1933). According to his editor, Martha Foley, Anderson's vision was his own; his characters were people into whose hearts and minds he seemed intuitively to peer; his prose was deceptively simple, sensuous, rich, and evocative."

Hands (1919)

Upon the half decayed veranda of a small frame house that stood near the edge of a ravine near the town of Winesburg, Ohio, a fat little old man walked nervously up and down. Across a long field that had been seeded for clover but that had produced only a dense crop of yellow mustard weeds, he could see the public highway along which went a wagon filled with berry pickers returning from the fields. The berry pickers, youths and maidens, laughed and shouted boisterously. A boy clad in a blue shirt leaped from the wagon and attempted to drag after him one of the maidens who screamed and protested shrilly. The feet of the boy in the road kicked up a cloud of dust that floated across the face of the departing sun. Over the long field came a thin girlish voice. "Oh, you Wing Biddlebaum, comb your hair, it's falling into your eyes," commanded the voice to the man, who was bald and whose nervous little hands fiddled about the bare white forehead as though arranging a mass of tangled locks.

Wing Biddlebaum, forever frightened and beset by a ghostly band of doubts, did not think of himself as in any way a part of the life of the town where he had lived for twenty years. Among all the people of Winesburg but one had come close to him. With George Willard, son of Tom Willard, the proprietor of the new Willard House, he had formed something like a friendship. George Willard was the reporter on the *Winesburg Eagle* and sometimes in the evenings he walked out along the highway to Wing Biddlebaum's house. Now as the old man walked up and down on the veranda, his hands moving nervously about, he was hoping that George Willard would come and spend the evening with him. After the wagon containing the berry pickers had passed, he went across the field through the tall mustard weeds and climbing a rail fence peered anxiously along the road to the town. For a moment he stood thus, rubbing his hands together and looking up and down the road, and then, fear overcoming him, ran back to walk again upon the porch of his own house.

In the presence of George Willard, Wing Biddlebaum, who for twenty years had been the town mystery, lost something of his timidity, and his shadowy personality, submerged in a sea of doubts, came forth to look at the world. With the young reporter at his side, he ventured in the light of day into Main Street or strode up and down on the rickety front porch of his own house, talking excitedly. The voice that had been low and trembling became shrill and loud. The bent figure straightened. With a kind of wriggle, like a fish returned to the brook by the fisherman, Biddlebaum the silent began to talk, striving to put into words the ideas that had been accumulated by his mind during long years of silence.

Wing Biddlebaum talked much with his hands. The slender expressive fingers, forever active, forever striving to conceal themselves in his pockets or behind his back, came forth and became the piston rods of his machinery of expression.

The story of Wing Biddlebaum is a story of hands. Their restless activity, like unto the beating of the wings of an imprisoned bird, had given him his name. Some obscure poet of the town had thought of it. The hands alarmed their owner. He wanted to keep them hidden away and looked with amazement at the quiet inexpressive hands of other men who worked beside him in the fields, or passed, driving sleepy teams on country roads.

When he talked to George Willard, Wing Biddlebaum closed his fists and beat with them upon a table or on the walls of his house. The action made him more comfortable. If the desire to talk came to him when the two were walking in the fields, he sought out a stump or the top board of a fence and with his hands pounding busily talked with renewed ease.

The story of Wing Biddlebaum's hands is worth a book itself. Sympathetically set forth it would tap many strange, beautiful qualities in obscure men. It is a job for a poet. In Winesburg the hands had attracted attention merely because of their activity. With them Wing Biddlebaum had picked as high as a hundred and forty quarts of strawberries in a day. They became his distinguishing feature, the source of his fame. Also they made more grotesque an already grotesque and elusive individuality. Winesburg was proud of the hands of Wing Biddlebaum in the same spirit in which it was proud of Banker White's new stone house and Wesley Moyer's bay stallion, Tony Tip, that had won the two-fifteen trot at the fall races in Cleveland.

As for George Willard, he had many times wanted to ask about the hands. At times an almost overwhelming curiosity had taken hold of him. He felt that there must be a reason for their strange activity and their inclination to keep hidden away and only a growing respect for Wing Biddlebaum kept him from blurting out the questions that were often in his mind.

Once he had been on the point of asking. The two were walking in the fields on a summer afternoon and had stopped to sit upon a grassy bank. All afternoon Wing Biddlebaum had talked as one inspired. By a fence he had stopped and beating like a giant woodpecker upon the top board had shouted at George Willard, condemning his tendency to be too much influenced by the people about him. "You are destroying yourself," he cried.

"You have the inclination to be alone and to dream and you are afraid of dreams. You want to be like others in town here. You hear them talk and you try to imitate them."

On the grassy bank Wing Biddlebaum had tried again to drive his point home. His voice became soft and reminiscent, and with a sigh of contentment he launched into a long rambling talk, speaking as one lost in a dream.

Out of the dream Wing Biddlebaum made a picture for George Willard. In the picture men lived again in a kind of pastoral golden age. Across a green open country came clean-limbed young men, some afoot, some mounted upon horses. In crowds the young men came to gather about the feet of an old man who sat beneath a tree in a tiny garden and who talked to them.

Wing Biddlebaum became wholly inspired. For once he forgot the hands. Slowly they stole forth and lay upon George Willard's shoulders. Something new and bold came into the voice that talked. "You must try to forget all you have learned," said the old man. "You must begin to dream. From this time on you must shut your ears to the roaring of the voices."

Pausing in his speech, Wing Biddlebaum looked long and earnestly at George Willard. His eyes glowed. Again he raised the hands to caress the boy and then a look of horror swept over his face.

With a convulsive movement of his body, Wing Biddlebaum sprang to his feet and thrust his hands deep into his trousers pockets. Tears came to his eyes. "I must be getting along home. I can talk no more with you," he said nervously.

Without looking back, the old man had hurried down the hillside and across a meadow, leaving George Willard perplexed and frightened upon the grassy slope. With a shiver of dread the boy arose and went along the road toward town. "I'll not ask him about his hands," he thought, touched by the memory of the terror he had seen in the man's eyes. "There's something wrong, but I don't want to know what it is. His hands have something to do with his fear of me and of everyone."

And George Willard was right. Let us look briefly into the story of the hands. Perhaps our talking of them will arouse the poet who will tell the hidden wonder story of the influence for which the hands were but fluttering pennants of promise.

In his youth Wing Biddlebaum had been a school teacher in a town in Pennsylvania. He was not then known as Wing Biddlebaum, but went by the less euphonic name of Adolph Myers. As Adolph Myers he was much loved by the boys of his school.

Adolph Myers was meant by nature to be a rare teacher of youth. He was one of those rare, little-understood men who rule by a power so gentle that it passes as a lovable weakness. In their feeling for the boys under their charge such men are not unlike the finer sort of women in their love of men.

And yet that is but crudely stated. It needs the poet there. With the boys of his school, Adolph Myers had walked in the evening or had sat talking until dusk upon the schoolhouse steps lost in a kind of dream. Here and there went his hands, caressing the shoulders of the boys, playing about the tousled heads. As he talked his voice became soft and musical. There was a caress in that also. In a way the voice and the hands, the stroking of the shoulders and the touching of the hair was a part of the schoolmaster's effort to carry a dream into the young minds. By the caress that was in his fingers he expressed himself. He was one of those men in whom the force that creates life is diffused, not centralized. Under the caress of his hands doubt and disbelief went out of the minds of the boys and they began also to dream.

And then the tragedy. A half-witted boy of the school became enamored of the young master. In his bed at night he imagined unspeakable things and in the morning went forth to tell his dreams as facts. Strange, hideous accusations fell from his loose-hung lips. Through the Pennsylvania town went a shiver. Hidden, shadowy doubts that had been in men's minds concerning Adolph Myers were galvanized into beliefs.

The tragedy did not linger. Trembling lads were jerked out of bed and questioned. "He put his arms about me," said one. "His fingers were always playing in my hair," said another.

One afternoon a man of the town, Henry Bradford, who kept a saloon, came to the schoolhouse door. Calling Adolph Myers into the school yard he began to beat him with his fists. As his hard knuckles beat down into the frightened face of the schoolmaster, his wrath became more and more terrible. Screaming with dismay, the children ran here and there like disturbed insects. "I'll teach you to put your hands on my boy, you beast," roared the saloon keeper, who, tired of beating the master, had begun to kick him about the yard.

Adolph Myers was driven from the Pennsylvania town in the night. With lanterns in their hands a dozen men came to the door of the house where he lived alone and commanded that he dress and come forth. It was raining and one of the men had a rope in his hands. They had intended to hang the schoolmaster, but something in his figure, so small, white, and pitiful, touched their hearts and they let him escape. As he ran away into the darkness they repented of their weakness and ran after him, swearing and throwing sticks and great balls of soft mud at the figure that screamed and ran faster and faster into the darkness.

For twenty years Adolph Myers had lived alone in Winesburg. He was but forty but looked sixty-five. The name Biddlebaum he got from a box of goods seen at a freight station as he hurried through an eastern Ohio town. He had an aunt in Winesburg, a black-toothed old woman who raised chickens, and with her he lived until she died. He had been ill for a year after the experience in Pennsylvania, and after his recovery worked as a day laborer in the fields, going timidly about and striving to conceal his hands. Although he did not understand what had happened he felt that the hands must be to blame. Again and again the fathers of the boys had talked of the hands. "Keep your hands to yourself," the saloon keeper had roared, dancing with fury in the schoolhouse yard.

Upon the veranda of his house by the ravine, Wing Biddlebaum continued to walk up and down until the sun had disappeared and the road beyond the field was lost in the grey shadows. Going into his house he cut slices of bread and spread honey upon them. When the rumble of the evening train that took away the express cars loaded with the day's harvest of berries had passed and restored the silence of the summer night, he went again to walk upon the veranda. In the darkness he could not see the hands and they became quiet. Although he still hungered for the presence of the boy, who was the medium through which he expressed his love of man, the hunger became again a part of his loneliness and his waiting. Lighting a lamp, Wing Biddlebaum washed the few dishes soiled by his simple meal and, setting up a folding cot by the screen door that led to the porch, prepared to undress for the night. A few stray white bread crumbs lay on the cleanly washed floor by the table; putting the lamp upon a low stool he began to pick up the crumbs, carrying them to his mouth one by one with unbelievable rapidity. In the dense blotch of light beneath the table, the kneeling figure looked like a priest engaged in some service of his church. The nervous expressive fingers, flashing in and out of the light, might well have been mistaken for the fingers of the devotee going swiftly through decade after decade of his rosary.

Questions for Discussion

1. Why was Adolph Myers driven from the town in Pennsylvania where he was a gifted teacher? How might parents today treat Myers?
2. Why does Myers change his name? In what ways are his new name and his process of choosing it symbolic?
3. What does the relationship between Biddlebaum and Willard reveal about them as individuals?
4. Why is Winesburg, Ohio, proud of Biddlebaum's hands? What is ironic about the town's pride?
5. What is the significance of the reference to "fingers of the devotee going swiftly through decade after decade of his rosary"?

Ideas for Writing

1. Explore in an essay the symbolism of hands in the story. Why is the story titled as such? How does Biddlebaum feel about his hands? Why does he express himself primarily through them?
2. Write a story involving a character whose personality is organized around an obsessive interest in a part of his or her body.

JAMES JOYCE   (1882–1941)

James Joyce was one of modern fiction's greatest innovators. Born in a Dublin suburb and educated at Jesuit-run schools and at home, he was a brilliant student; he won prizes for his essays and was given a full scholarship to Dublin's University College. Suffocated by the narrow Catholicism, provincialism, and middle-class hypocrisy of turn-of-the-century Ireland, Joyce left for Paris in 1902, returning to Dublin only for a short period the following year to care for his dying mother. On this trip Joyce kept a notebook of "epiphanies," overheard conversations and sharp insights into daily life that were similar to small moments of religious revelation. The idea of the epiphany was to become one of Joyce's major contributions to the modern story.

By 1904 Joyce had returned to the Continent, living in Paris, Zürich, and Trieste, where he wrote the fifteen innovative realist stories collected in *Dubliners* (1914), which includes "Araby" and "The Boarding House." His complex novels — *A Portrait of the Artist as a Young Man* (1916), *Ulysses* (1922), and *Finnegans Wake* (1939) — radically redefined the style and form of modern fiction. In *Ulysses* and *Finnegans Wake* Joyce developed a dense style that relies on complex literary allusion and word play, as well as on the use of mythological parallels and stream-of-consciousness narrative. Like the other stories in *Dubliners*, the following works explore the limits of imagination and desire within the constraints of everyday life.

Araby   (1914)

North Richmond Street, being blind, was a quiet street except at the hour when the Christian Brothers' School set the boys free. An uninhabited house of two storeys stood at the blind end, detached from its neighbours in a square ground. The other houses of the street, conscious of decent lives within them, gazed at one another with brown imperturbable faces.

The former tenant of our house, a priest, had died in the back drawing-room. Air, musty from having been long enclosed, hung in all the rooms, and the waste room behind the kitchen was littered with old useless papers. Among these I found a few paper-covered books, the pages of which were curled and damp: *The Abbot*, by Walter Scott, *The Devout Communicant* and *The Memoirs of Vidocq*. I liked the last best because its leaves were yellow. The wild garden behind the house contained a central apple-tree and a few straggling bushes under one of which I found the late tenant's rusty bicycle-pump. He had been a very charitable priest; in his will he had left all his money to institutions and the furniture of his house to his sister.

When the short days of winter came dusk fell before we had well eaten our dinners. When we met in the street the houses had grown sombre. The space of sky above us was the colour of ever-changing violet and towards it the lamps of the street lifted their feeble lanterns. The cold air stung us and we played till our bodies glowed. Our shouts echoed in the silent street. The career of our play brought us through the dark muddy lanes behind the houses where we ran the gauntlet of the rough tribes from the cottages, to the back doors of the dark dripping gardens where odours arose from the ashpits, to the dark odorous stables where a coachman smoothed and combed the horse or shook music from the buckled harness. When we returned to the street light from the kitchen windows had filled the areas. If my uncle was seen turning the corner we hid in the shadow until we had seen him safely housed. Or if Mangan's sister came out on the doorstep to call her brother in to his tea we watched her from our shadow peer up and down the street. We waited to see whether she would remain or go in and, if she remained, we left our shadow and walked up to Mangan's steps resignedly. She was waiting for us, her figure defined by the light from the half-opened door. Her brother always teased her before he obeyed and I stood by the railings looking at her. Her dress swung as she moved her body and the soft rope of her hair tossed from side to side.

Every morning I lay on the floor in the front parlour watching her door. The blind was pulled down to within an inch of the sash so that I could not be seen. When she came out on the doorstep my heart leaped. I ran to the hall, seized my books and followed her. I kept her brown figure always in my eye and, when we came near the point at which our ways diverged, I quickened my pace and passed her. This happened morning after morning. I had never spoken to her, except for a few casual words, and yet her name was like a summons to all my foolish blood.

Her image accompanied me even in places the most hostile to romance. On Saturday evenings when my aunt went marketing I had to go to carry some of the parcels. We walked through the flaring streets, jostled by drunken men and bargaining women, amid the curses of labourers, the shrill litanies of shop-boys who stood on guard by the barrels of pigs' cheeks, the nasal chanting of street-singers, who sang a *come-all-you* about O'Donovan Rossa, or a ballad about the troubles in our native land. These noises converged in a single sensation of life for me: I imagined that I bore my chalice safely through a throng of foes. Her name sprang to my lips at moments in strange prayers and praises which I myself did not understand. My eyes were often full of tears (I could not tell why) and at times a flood from my heart seemed to pour itself out into my bosom. I thought little of the future. I did not know whether I would ever speak to her or not or, if I spoke to her, how I could tell her of my confused adoration. But my body was like a harp and her words and gestures were like fingers running upon the wires.

One evening I went into the back drawing-room in which the priest had died. It was a dark rainy evening and there was no sound in the house. Through one of the broken panes I heard the rain impinge upon the earth, the fine incessant needles of water playing in the sodden beds. Some distant lamp or lighted window gleamed below me. I was thankful that I could see so little. All my senses seemed to desire to veil themselves and, feeling that I was about to slip from them, I pressed the palms of my hands together until they trembled, murmuring: *O love! O love!* many times.

At last she spoke to me. When she addressed the first words to me I was so confused that I did not know what to answer. She asked me was I going to *Araby*. I forget whether I answered yes or no. It would be a splendid bazaar, she said; she would love to go.

—And why can't you? I asked.

While she spoke she turned a silver bracelet round and round her wrist. She could not go, she said, because there would be a retreat that week in her convent. Her brother and two other boys were fighting for their caps and I was alone at the railings. She held one of the spikes, bowing her head towards me. The light from the lamp opposite our door caught the white curve of her neck, lit up her hair that rested there and, falling, lit up the hand upon the railing. It fell over one side of her dress and caught the white border of a petticoat, just visible as she stood at ease.

—It's well for you, she said.

—If I go, I said, I will bring you something.

What innumerable follies laid waste my waking and sleeping thoughts after that evening! I wished to annihilate the tedious intervening days. I chafed against the work of school. At night in my bedroom and by day in the classroom her image came between me and the page I strove to read. The syllables of the word *Araby* were called to me through the silence in which my soul luxuriated and cast an Eastern enchantment over me. I asked for leave to go to the bazaar Saturday night. My aunt was surprised and hoped it was not some Freemason affair. I answered few questions in class. I watched my master's face pass from amiability to sternness; he hoped I was not beginning to idle. I could not call my wandering thoughts together. I had hardly any patience with the serious work of life which, now that it stood between me and my desire, seemed to me child's play, ugly monotonous child's play.

On Saturday morning I reminded my uncle that I wished to go to the bazaar in the evening. He was fussing at the hallstand, looking for the hatbrush, and answered me curtly:

—Yes, boy, I know.

As he was in the hall I could not go into the front parlour and lie at the window. I left the house in bad humour and walked slowly towards the school. The air was pitilessly raw and already my heart misgave me.

When I came home to dinner my uncle had not yet been home. Still it was early. I sat staring at the clock for some time and, when its ticking began to irritate me, I left the room. I mounted the staircase and gained the upper part of the house. The high cold empty gloomy rooms liberated me and I went from room to room singing. From the front window I saw my companions playing below in the street. Their cries reached me weakened and indistinct and, leaning my forehead against the cool glass, I looked over at the dark house where she lived. I may have stood there for an hour, seeing nothing but the brown-clad figure cast by my imagination, touched discreetly by the lamp-light at the curved neck, at the hand upon the railings and at the border below the dress.

When I came downstairs again I found Mrs Mercer sitting at the fire. She was an old garrulous woman, a pawnbroker's widow, who collected used stamps for some pious purpose. I had to endure the gossip of the tea-table. The meal was prolonged beyond an hour and still my uncle did not come. Mrs Mercer stood up to go: she was sorry she couldn't wait any longer, but it was after eight o'clock and she did not like to be out late, as the night air was bad for her. When she had gone I began to walk up and down the room, clenching my fists. My aunt said:

— I'm afraid you may put off your bazaar for this night of Our Lord.

At nine o'clock I heard my uncle's latchkey in the halldoor. I heard him talking to himself and heard the hallstand rocking when it had received the weight of his overcoat. I could interpret these signs. When he was midway through his dinner I asked him to give me the money to go to the bazaar. He had forgotten.

— The people are in bed and after their first sleep now, he said.

I did not smile. My aunt said to him energetically:

— Can't you give him the money and let him go? You've kept him late enough as it is.

My uncle said he was very sorry he had forgotten. He said he believed in the old saying: *All work and no play makes Jack a dull boy.* He asked me where I was going and, when I had told him a second time he asked me did I know *The Arab's Farewell to his Steed.* When I left the kitchen he was about to recite the opening lines of the piece to my aunt.

I held a florin tightly in my hand as I strode down Buckingham Street towards the station. The sight of the streets thronged with buyers and glaring with gas recalled to me the purpose of my journey. I took my seat in a third-class carriage of a deserted train. After an intolerable delay the train moved out of the station slowly. It crept onward among ruinous houses and over the twinkling river. At Westland Row Station a crowd of people pressed to the carriage doors; but the porters moved them back, saying that it was a special train for the bazaar. I remained alone in the bare carriage. In a few minutes the train drew up beside an improvised wooden platform. I passed out on to the road and saw by the lighted dial of a clock that it was ten minutes to ten. In front of me was a large building which displayed the magical name.

I could not find any sixpenny entrance and, fearing that the bazaar would be closed, I passed in quickly through a turnstile, handing a shilling to a weary-looking man. I found myself in a big hall girdled at half its height by a gallery. Nearly all the stalls were closed and the greater part of the hall was in darkness. I recognised a silence like that which pervades a church after a service. I walked into the centre of the bazaar timidly. A few people were gathered about the stalls which were still open. Before a curtain, over which the words *Café Chantant* were written in coloured lamps, two men were counting money on a salver. I listened to the fall of the coins.

Remembering with difficulty why I had come I went over to one of the stalls and examined porcelain vases and flowered tea-sets. At the door of the stall a young lady was talking and laughing with two young gentlemen. I remarked their English accents and listened vaguely to their conversation.

— O, I never said such a thing!

— O, but you did!

— O, but I didn't!

— Didn't she say that?

— Yes, I heard her.

— O, there's a . . . fib!

Observing me the young lady came over and asked me did I wish to buy anything. The tone of her voice was not encouraging; she seemed to have spoken to me out of a sense of duty. I looked humbly at the great jars that stood like eastern guards at either side of the dark entrance to the stall and murmured:

— No, thank you.

The young lady changed the position of one of the vases and went back to the two young men. They began to talk of the same subject. Once or twice the young lady glanced at me over her shoulder.

I lingered before her stall, though I knew my stay was useless, to make my interest in her wares seem the more real. Then I turned away slowly and walked down the middle of the bazaar. I allowed the two pennies to fall against the sixpence in my pocket. I heard a voice call from one end of the gallery that the light was out. The upper part of the hall was now completely dark.

Gazing up into the darkness I saw myself as a creature driven and derided by vanity; and my eyes burned with anguish and anger.

Questions for Discussion

1. What is the effect of the opening descriptive details of North Richmond Street — its "blindness," the "brown imperturbable faces" of its houses, and the musty drawing-room formerly occupied by a now-deceased priest?

2. What is the significance of the story's title? What is the Araby bazaar on a literal level, and what is its meaning for the youthful narrator?

3. Who is Mangan's sister, and how does the narrator feel about her? How do his feelings for her and the meaning she holds for him change as the story develops?

4. How is the narrator's "patience with the serious work of life" as well as his relationship with his family and their rituals affected by his attempt to get a present for Mangan's sister at the bazaar?

5. How does the narrator's actual experience of the Araby bazaar contrast with his
   expectations? What is the significance of the conversation he overhears? Why is
   the silence of the half-deserted bazaar described as "like that which pervades a
   church after a service"?

Ideas for Writing

1. Explain in an essay why the narrator is full of "anguish and anger" at the end of
   the story. Why does he see himself as vain? Does his self-assessment seem realistic? Is the narrator too harsh on himself?
2. Write a scene in which the narrator of "Araby" fantasizes about developing a relationship with Mangan's sister. What would they talk about? What would they do?

The Boarding House   (1914)

Mrs. Mooney was a butcher's daughter. She was a woman who was quite
able to keep things to herself: a determined woman. She had married her
father's foreman and opened a butcher's shop near Spring Gardens. But as
soon as his father-in-law was dead Mr. Mooney began to go to the devil. He
drank, plundered the till, ran headlong into debt. It was no use making him
take the pledge: he was sure to break out again a few days after. By fighting his
wife in the presence of customers and by buying bad meat he ruined his business. One night he went for his wife with the cleaver and she had to sleep in
a neighbour's house.

After that they lived apart. She went to the priest and got a separation
from him with care of the children. She would give him neither money nor
food nor house-room; and so he was obliged to enlist himself as a sheriff's
man. He was a shabby stooped little drunkard with a white face and a white
moustache and white eyebrows, pencilled above his little eyes, which were
pink-veined and raw; and all day long he sat in the bailiff's room, waiting to
be put on a job. Mrs. Mooney, who had taken what remained of her money
out of the butcher business and set up a boarding house in Hardwicke Street,
was a big imposing woman. Her house had a floating population made up of
tourists from Liverpool and the Isle of Man and, occasionally, *artistes* from the
music halls. Its resident population was made up of clerks from the city. She
governed the house cunningly and firmly, knew when to give credit, when to
be stern and when to let things pass. All the resident young men spoke of her
as *The Madam*.

Mrs. Mooney's young men paid fifteen shillings a week for board and
lodgings (beer or stout at dinner excluded). They shared in common tastes
and occupations and for this reason they were very chummy with one another.
They discussed with one another the chances of favourites and outsiders. Jack
Mooney, the Madam's son, who was clerk to a commission agent in Fleet

Street, had the reputation of being a hard case. He was fond of using soldiers' obscenities: usually he came home in the small hours. When he met his friends he had always a good one to tell them and he was always sure to be on to a good thing — that is to say, a likely horse or a likely *artiste*. He was also handy with the mits and sang comic songs. On Sunday nights there would often be a reunion in Mrs. Mooney's front drawing-room. The music-hall *artistes* would oblige; and Sheridan played waltzes and polkas and vamped accompaniments. Polly Mooney, the Madam's daughter, would also sing. She sang:

> I'm a . . . naughty girl.
> You needn't sham:
> You know I am.

Polly was a slim girl of nineteen; she had light soft hair and a small full mouth. Her eyes, which were grey with a shade of green through them, had a habit of glancing upwards when she spoke with anyone, which made her look like a little perverse madonna. Mrs. Mooney had first sent her daughter to be a typist in a corn-factor's office but, as a disreputable sheriff's man used to come every other day to the office, asking to be allowed to say a word to his daughter, she had taken her daughter home again and set her to do house-work. As Polly was very lively the intention was to give her the run of the young men. Besides, young men like to feel that there is a young woman not very far away. Polly, of course, flirted with the young men but Mrs. Mooney, who was a shrewd judge, knew that the young men were only passing the time away: none of them meant business. Things went on so for a long time and Mrs. Mooney began to think of sending Polly back to typewriting when she noticed that something was going on between Polly and one of the young men. She watched the pair and kept her own counsel.

Polly knew that she was being watched, but still her mother's persistent silence could not be misunderstood. There had been no open complicity between mother and daughter, no open understanding but, though people in the house began to talk of the affair, still Mrs. Mooney did not intervene. Polly began to grow a little strange in her manner and the young man was evidently perturbed. At last, when she judged it to be the right moment, Mrs. Mooney intervened. She dealt with moral problems as a cleaver deals with meat: and in this case she had made up her mind.

It was a bright Sunday morning of early summer, promising heat, but with a fresh breeze blowing. All the windows of the boarding house were open and the lace curtains ballooned gently towards the street beneath the raised sashes. The belfry of George's Church sent out constant peals and worshippers, singly or in groups, traversed the little circus before the church, revealing their pur-pose by their self-contained demeanour no less than by the little volumes in their gloved hands. Breakfast was over in the boarding house and the table of the breakfast-room was covered with plates on which lay yellow streaks of eggs with morsels of bacon-fat and bacon-rind. Mrs. Mooney sat in the straw arm-chair and watched the servant Mary remove the breakfast things. She made Mary collect the crusts and pieces of broken bread to help to make Tuesday's bread-pudding. When the table was cleared, the broken bread collected, the sugar and butter safe under lock and key, she began to reconstruct the interview which she had had the night before with Polly. Things were as she had suspected: she had been frank in her questions and Polly had been frank in her answers. Both had been somewhat awkward, of course. She had been made awkward by her not wishing to receive the news in too cavalier a fashion or to seem to have connived and Polly had been made awkward not merely because allusions of that kind always made her awkward but also because she did not wish it to be thought that in her wise innocence she had divined the intention behind her mother's tolerance.

Mrs. Mooney glanced instinctively at the little gilt clock on the mantelpiece as soon as she had become aware through her revery that the bells of George's Church had stopped ringing. It was seventeen minutes past eleven: she would have lots of time to have the matter out with Mr. Doran and then catch short twelve at Marlborough Street. She was sure she would win. To begin with she had all the weight of social opinion on her side: she was an outraged mother. She had allowed him to live beneath her roof, assuming that he was a man of honour, and he had simply abused her hospitality. He was thirty-four or thirty-five years of age, so that youth could not be pleaded as his excuse; nor could ignorance be his excuse since he was a man who had seen something of the world. He had simply taken advantage of Polly's youth and inexperience: that was evident. The question was: What reparation would he make?

There must be reparation made in such case. It is all very well for the man: he can go his ways as if nothing had happened, having had his moment of pleasure, but the girl has to bear the brunt. Some mothers would be content to patch up such an affair for a sum of money; she had known cases of it. But she would not do so. For her only one reparation could make up for the loss of her daughter's honour: marriage.

She counted all her cards again before sending Mary up to Mr. Doran's room to say that she wished to speak with him. She felt sure she would win. He was a serious young man, not rakish or loud-voiced like the others. If it had been Mr. Sheridan or Mr. Meade or Bantam Lyons her task would have been much harder. She did not think he would face publicity. All the lodgers in the house knew something of the affair; details had been invented by some. Besides, he had been employed for thirteen years in a great Catholic winemerchant's office and publicity would mean for him, perhaps, the loss of his job. Whereas if he agreed all might be well. She knew he had a good screw for one thing and she suspected he had a bit of stuff put by.

Nearly the half-hour! She stood up and surveyed herself in the pier-glass. The decisive expression of her great florid face satisfied her and she thought of some mothers she knew who could not get their daughters off their hands.

Mr. Doran was very anxious indeed this Sunday morning. He had made two attempts to shave but his hand had been so unsteady that he had been obliged to desist. Three days' reddish beard fringed his jaws and every two or three minutes a mist gathered on his glasses so that he had to take them off and polish them with his pocket-handkerchief. The recollection of his confession of the night before was a cause of acute pain to him; the priest had drawn out every ridiculous detail of the affair and in the end had so magnified his sin that he was almost thankful at being afforded a loophole of reparation. The harm was done. What could he do now but marry her or run away? He could not brazen it out. The affair would be sure to be talked of and his employer would be certain to hear of it. Dublin is such a small city: everyone knows everyone else's business. He felt his heart leap warmly in his throat as he heard in his excited imagination old Mr. Leonard calling out in his rasping voice: "Send Mr. Doran here, please."

All his long years of service gone for nothing! All his industry and diligence thrown away! As a young man he had sown his wild oats, of course; he had boasted of his free-thinking and denied the existence of God to his companions in public-houses. But that was all passed and done with . . . nearly. He still bought a copy of *Reynolds's Newspaper* every week but he attended to his religious duties and for nine-tenths of the year lived a regular life. He had money enough to settle down on; it was not that. But the family would look down on her. First of all there was her disreputable father and then her mother's boarding house was beginning to get a certain fame. He had a notion that he was being had. He could imagine his friends talking of the affair and laughing. She *was* a little vulgar; some times she said "I seen" and "If I had've known." But what would grammar matter if he really loved her? He could not make up his mind whether to like her or despise her for what she had done. Of course he had done it too. His instinct urged him to remain free, not to marry. Once you are married you are done for, it said.

While he was sitting helplessly on the side of the bed in shirt and trousers she tapped lightly at his door and entered. She told him all, that she had made a clean breast of it to her mother and that her mother would speak with him that morning. She cried and threw her arms round his neck, saying:

"O Bob! Bob! What am I to do? What am I to do at all?"

She would put an end to herself, she said.

He comforted her feebly, telling her not to cry, that it would be all right, never fear. He felt against his shirt the agitation of her bosom.

It was not altogether his fault that it had happened. He remembered well, with the curious patient memory of the celibate, the first casual caresses her dress, her breath, her fingers had given him. Then late one night as he was undressing for bed she had tapped at his door, timidly. She wanted to relight her candle at his for hers had been blown out by a gust. It was her bath night. She wore a loose open combing-jacket of printed flannel. Her white instep shone in the opening of her furry slippers and the blood glowed warmly behind her perfumed skin. From her hands and wrists too as she lit and steadied her candle a faint perfume arose.

On nights when he came in very late it was she who warmed up his dinner. He scarcely knew what he was eating feeling her beside him alone, at night, in the sleeping house. And her thoughtfulness! If the night was anyway cold or wet or windy there was sure to be a little tumbler of punch ready for him. Perhaps they could be happy together. . . .

They used to go upstairs together on tiptoe, each with a candle, and on the third landing exchange reluctant goodnights. They used to kiss. He remembered well her eyes, the touch of her hand and his delirium. . . .

But delirium passes. He echoed her phrase, applying it to himself: *"What am I to do?"* The instinct of the celibate warned him to hold back. But the sin was there; even his sense of honour told him that reparation must be made for such a sin.

While he was sitting with her on the side of the bed Mary came to the door and said that the missus wanted to see him in the parlour. He stood up to put on his coat and waistcoat, more helpless than ever. When he was dressed he went over to her to comfort her. It would be all right, never fear. He left her crying on the bed and moaning softly: *"O my God!"*

Going down the stairs his glasses became so dimmed with moisture that he had to take them off and polish them. He longed to ascend through the roof and fly away to another country where he would never hear again of his trouble, and yet a force pushed him downstairs step by step. The implacable faces of his employer and of the Madam stared upon his discomfiture. On the last flight of stairs he passed Jack Mooney who was coming up from the pantry nursing two bottles of *Bass*. They saluted coldly; and the lover's eyes rested for a second or two on a thick bulldog face and a pair of thick short arms. When he reached the foot of the staircase he glanced up and saw Jack regarding him from the door of the return-room.

Suddenly he remembered the night when one of the music-hall *artistes*, a little blond Londoner, had made a rather free allusion to Polly. The reunion had been almost broken up on account of Jack's violence. Everyone tried to quiet him. The music-hall *artiste*, a little paler than usual, kept smiling and saying that there was no harm meant: but Jack kept shouting at him that if any fellow tried that sort of a game on with his sister he'd bloody well put his teeth down his throat, so he would.

Polly sat for a little time on the side of the bed, crying. Then she dried her eyes and went over to the looking-glass. She dipped the end of the towel in the water-jug and refreshed her eyes with the cool water. She looked at herself in profile and readjusted a hairpin above her ear. Then she went back to the bed again and sat at the foot. She regarded the pillows for a long time and the sight of them awakened in her mind secret, amiable memories. She rested the nape of her neck against the cool iron bed-rail and fell into a reverie. There was no longer any perturbation visible on her face.

She waited on patiently, almost cheerfully, without alarm, her memories gradually giving place to hopes and visions of the future. Her hopes and visions were so intricate that she no longer saw the white pillows on which her gaze was fixed or remembered that she was waiting for anything.

At last she heard her mother calling. She started to her feet and ran to the banisters.

"Polly! Polly!"

"Yes, mamma?"

"Come down, dear. Mr. Doran wants to speak to you."

Then she remembered what she had been waiting for.

Questions for Discussion

1. How has Mrs. Mooney's character been formed as a butcher's daughter? What is the significance of her nickname, "The Madam"?
2. What role do Jack and Polly play in the boardinghouse society? In what ways are they similar to their parents? to one another?
3. What conflicting emotions does Mr. Doran feel about his commitment to Polly? How does Joyce use physical detail to clarify Doran's anxieties?
4. What is revealed by Doran's fantasy as he descends the stairs to meet with Mrs. Mooney? What prevents him from acting on his fantasy?
5. What is the significance of Polly's dream at the end of the story? Why does her reverie cause her to forget "what she had been waiting for"?

Ideas for Writing

1. Doran reflects on his first romantic encounter with Polly: "It was not altogether his fault that it had happened." Whose fault was it? Examine in an essay the ways in which the story reflects on issues of responsibility and manipulation in romantic relationships.
2. Imitating Joyce's style, write a scene in which you create a day in the life of Doran and Polly after their marriage. How do you imagine their future together?

VIRGINIA WOOLF   (1882–1941)

Born into a prominent English family, Virginia Stephen was educated at home, in the library of her father, Leslie Stephen, a major literary critic and editor of the *Dictionary of National Biography*. After her parents died, Virginia lived with her siblings until her marriage to the writer Leonard Woolf in 1912. Starting with a small letter press in their home, the Woolfs founded the Hogarth Press, which published Virginia's early works, as well as many of the leading writers of the 1920s. Virginia and Leonard Woolf were also active members of the Bloomsbury Group of writers and artists, which included Virginia's sister, Vanessa Bell, as well as such authors as E. M. Forster, T. S. Eliot, and Lytton Strachey. After struggling with recurring periods of deep depression for many years, Woolf drowned herself in the river Ouse, near her home, in 1941. Leonard Woolf and Virginia's nephew Quentin Bell published much of her unfinished work, including diaries, letters, and a number of previously unpublished stories and essays. Woolf's most successful novels are *The Voyage Out* (1915), *Jacob's Room* (1922), *Mrs. Dalloway* (1925), *To the Lighthouse* (1927), and *The Waves* (1931). Her feminist essays, included in *A Room of One's Own* (1928) and *Three Guineas* (1938), have become classics in both England and America. Woolf's short stories are collected in *A Haunted House and Other Stories* (1953), which includes "The Symbol," and in *The Complete Shorter Fiction of Virginia Woolf* (1985). A major contributor to the modernist movement in fiction, Virginia Woolf developed a stream-of-consciousness narrative style that made use of a form of symbolism that at times reached beyond the individual consciousness of her characters to represent what she referred to as "moments of being."

The Symbol   (1941)

There was a little dent on the top of the mountain like a crater on the moon. It was filled with snow, iridescent like a pigeon's breast, or dead white. There was a scurry of dry particles now and again, covering nothing. It was too high for breathing flesh or fur covered life. All the same the snow was iridescent one moment; and blood red; and pure white, according to the day.

The graves in the valley — for there was a vast descent on either side; first pure rock; snow silted; lower a pine tree gripped a crag; then a solitary hut; then a saucer of pure green; then a cluster of eggshell roofs; at last, at the bottom, a village, an hotel, a cinema, and a graveyard — the graves in the churchyard near the hotel recorded the names of several men who had fallen climbing.

"The mountain," the lady wrote, sitting on the balcony of the hotel, "is a symbol . . ." She paused. She could see the topmost height through her glasses.

She focussed the lens, as if to see what the symbol was. She was writing to her elder sister at Birmingham.

The balcony overlooked the main street of the Alpine summer resort, like a box at a theatre. There were very few private sitting rooms, and so the plays — such as they were — the curtain raisers — were acted in public. They were always a little provisional; preludes, curtain raisers. Entertainments to pass the time; seldom leading to any conclusion, such as marriage; or even lasting friendship. There was something fantastic about them, airy, inconclusive. So little that was solid could be dragged to this height. Even the houses looked gimcrack. By the time the voice of the English Announcer had reached the village it too became unreal.

Lowering her glasses, she nodded at the young men who in the street below were making ready to start. With one of them she had a certain connection — that is, an Aunt of his had been Mistress of her daughter's school.

Still holding the pen, still tipped with a drop of ink, she waved down at the climbers. She had written the mountain was a symbol. But of what? In the forties of the last century two men, in the sixties four men had perished; the first party when a rope broke; the second when night fell and froze them to death. We are always climbing to some height; that was the cliché. But it did not represent what was in her mind's eye; after seeing through her glasses the virgin height.

She continued, inconsequently. "I wonder why it makes me think of the Isle of Wight? You remember when Mama was dying, we took her there. And I would stand on the balcony, when the boat came in and describe the passengers. I would say, I think that must be Mr Edwardes . . . He has just come off the gangway. Then, now all the passengers have landed. Now they have turned the boat . . . I never told you, naturally not — you were in India; you were going to have Lucy — how I longed when the doctor came, that he should say, quite definitely, She cannot live another week. It was very prolonged; she lived eighteen months. The mountain just now reminded me how when I was alone, I would fix my eyes upon her death, as a symbol. I would think if I could reach that point — when I should be free — we could not marry as you remember until she died — A cloud then would do instead of the mountain. I thought, when I reach that point — I have never told any one; for it seemed so heartless; I shall be at the top. And I could imagine so many sides. We come of course of an Anglo Indian family. I can still imagine, from hearing stories told, how people live in other parts of the world. I can see mud huts; and savages; I can see elephants drinking at pools. So many of our uncles and cousins were explorers. I have always had a great desire to explore for myself. But of course, when the time came it seemed more sensible, considering our long engagement, to marry."

She looked across the street at a woman shaking a mat on another balcony. Every morning at the same time she came out. You could have thrown a pebble into her balcony. They had indeed come to the point of smiling at each other across the street.

[handwritten margin note: cliché of symbol of mountain but not her representation]

"The little villas," she added, taking up her pen, "are much the same here as in Birmingham. Every house takes in lodgers. The hotel is quite full. Though monotonous, the food is not what you would call bad. And of course the hotel has a splendid view. One can see the mountain from every window. But then that's true of the whole place. I can assure you, I could shriek sometimes coming out of the one shop where they sell papers — we get them a week late — always to see that mountain. Sometimes it looks just across the way. At others, like a cloud; only it never moves. Somehow the talk, even among the invalids, who are every where, is always about the mountain. Either, how clear it is today, it might be across the street; or, how far away it looks; it might be a cloud. That is the usual cliché. In the storm last night, I hoped for once it was hidden. But just as they brought in the anchovies, The Rev. W. Bishop said, 'Look there's the mountain!'

"Am I being selfish? Ought I not to be ashamed of myself, when there is so much suffering? It is not confined to the visitors. The natives suffer dreadfully from goitre. Of course it could be stopped, if any one had enterprise, and money. Ought one not to be ashamed of dwelling upon what after all can't be cured? It would need an earthquake to destroy that mountain, just as, I suppose, it was made by an earthquake. I asked the Proprietor, Herr Melchior, the other day, if there were ever earthquakes now? No, he said, only landslides and avalanches. They have been known he said to blot out a whole village. But he added quickly, there's no danger here.

"As I write these words, I can see the young men quite plainly on the slopes of the mountain. They are roped together. One I think I told you was at the same school with Margaret. They are now crossing a crevasse. . . ."

The pen fell from her hand, and the drop of ink straggled in a zig zag line down the page. The young men had disappeared.

It was only late that night when the search party had recovered the bodies that she found the unfinished letter on the table on the balcony. She dipped her pen once more; and added, "The old clichés will come in very handy. They died trying to climb the mountain . . . And the peasants brought spring flowers to lay upon their graves. They died in an attempt to discover . . ."

There seemed no fitting conclusion. And she added, "Love to the children," and then her pet name.

Questions for Discussion

1. How is the mountain described in the story's first two paragraphs? What mood is created here by the word choice and color symbolism?
2. The woman writing the letter sees the mountain as a "symbol" and perceives the physical settings and human interactions she observes from her balcony as "curtain raisers . . . entertainments." What impression do you get of the woman and her values from her observations?

3. If the mountain is a "symbol," what different meaning does each character in the story find in it? Does any one interpretation seem more correct or complete than the others?
4. How does the letter writer construct a personal meaning for the symbol by drawing on key events in her life?
5. How does the letter writer's view of the mountain change at the end of the story? What does the ending imply about the nature of reading, writing, and the interpretation of symbols?

Ideas for Writing

1. The letter writer refers to the concept of cliché several times, ending by stating, "The old clichés will come in very handy." Examine in an essay what the story is saying about the relationship between symbolism, clichés, and real life.
2. Describe in the present tense a physical object you are observing. Provide one possible "meaning" for the object; then switch to another level of meaning or significance as you continue to observe.

FRANZ KAFKA (1883–1924)

In a letter to his friend Oskar Pollak, Franz Kafka spoke of his desire to write powerful stories and books — "like a disaster, that grieve us deeply, like the death of someone we loved more than ourselves, like being banished into forests far from everyone, like a suicide. A book must be the axe for the frozen sea inside us."

Born, raised, and educated in Prague, Czechoslovakia, Kafka remained there for most of his life; the city was the center of his personal and artistic universe. Kafka's father was a businessman, the son of a kosher butcher from a small village, whereas his mother came from a highly religious, educated, and cultured family. After attending rigorous schools, including the German Gymnasium, where he received a traditional education in the classics, Kafka went on to earn a doctorate in jurisprudence from the German University in Prague (1906). He was hired at the Workers Accident Insurance Institute in 1908, where he worked writing investigative reports on workers' health and accident prevention until 1922, when he was in the final stages of tuberculosis. Kafka never married and lived away from his parents' home for only short periods of time. He began writing in 1897 and always considered writing his true profession, although he had to write late at night after long days at the Insurance Institute.

Kafka had a number of close friends among the literary circle of Prague, most notably the novelist Max Brod. Although Kafka published only a few stories during his lifetime, he left the unfinished manuscripts of three novels, as well as a number of short stories, extensive diaries, and numerous letters. Almost all of Kafka's works were subsequently published by Max Brod, despite Kafka's orders in his will that they all be destroyed. His novels include *The Trial* (1925), *The Castle* (1926), and *Amerika* (1927); *The Complete Stories* appeared in 1971. Like his story "A Report to an Academy" (1917), Kafka's fiction draws on dreams and fantasies, traditional forms such as religious parables and animal fables, and his extensive experience with legal report writing.

A Report to an Academy (1917)

Translated by Willa and Edwin Muir

Honored members of the Academy!

You have done me the honor of inviting me to give your Academy an account of the life I formerly led as an ape.

I regret that I cannot comply with your request to the extent you desire. It is now nearly five years since I was an ape, a short space of time, perhaps, according to the calendar, but an infinitely long time to gallop through at full speed, as I have done, more or less accompanied by excellent mentors, good advice, applause, and orchestral music, and yet essentially alone, since all my escorters, to keep the image, kept well off the course. I could never have achieved what I have done had I been stubbornly set on clinging to my origins, to the remembrances of my youth. In fact, to give up being stubborn was the supreme commandment I laid upon myself; free ape as I was, I submitted myself to that yoke. In revenge, however, my memory of the past has closed the door against me more and more. I could have returned at first, had human beings allowed it, through an archway as wide as the span of heaven over the earth, but as I spurred myself on in my forced career, the opening narrowed and shrank behind me; I felt more comfortable in the world of men and fitted it better; the strong wind that blew after me out of my past began to slacken; today it is only a gentle puff of air that plays around my heels; and the opening in the distance, through which it comes and through which I once came myself, has grown so small that, even if my strength and my will power sufficed to get me back to it, I should have to scrape the very skin from my body to crawl through. To put it plainly, much as I like expressing myself in images, to put it plainly: your life as apes, gentlemen, insofar as something of that kind lies behind you, cannot be farther removed from you than mine is from me. Yet everyone on earth feels a tickling at the heels; the small chimpanzee and the great Achilles alike.

But to a lesser extent I can perhaps meet your demand, and indeed I do so with the greatest pleasure. The first thing I learned was to give a handshake; a handshake betokens frankness; well, today, now that I stand at the very peak of my career, I hope to add frankness in words to the frankness of that first handshake. What I have to tell the Academy will contribute nothing essentially new, and will fall far behind what you have asked of me and what with the best will in the world I cannot communicate — nonetheless, it should indicate the line an erstwhile ape has had to follow in entering and establishing himself in the world of men. Yet I could not risk putting into words even such insignificant information as I am going to give you if I were not quite sure of myself and if my position on all the great variety stages of the civilized world had not become quite unassailable.

I belong to the Gold Coast. For the story of my capture I must depend on the evidence of others. A hunting expedition sent out by the firm of Hagenbeck — by the way, I have drunk many a bottle of good red wine since then with the leader of that expedition — had taken up its position in the bushes by the shore when I came down for a drink at evening among a troop of apes. They shot at us; I was the only one that was hit; I was hit in two places.

Once in the cheek; a slight wound; but it left a large, naked, red scar which earned me the name of Red Peter, a horrible name, utterly inappropriate, which only some ape could have thought of, as if the only difference between me and the performing ape Peter, who died not so long ago and had some small local reputation, were the red mark on my cheek. This by the way.

The second shot hit me below the hip. It was a severe wound, it is the cause of my limping a little to this day. I read an article recently by one of the ten thousand windbags who vent themselves concerning me in the newspapers, saying: my ape nature is not yet quite under control; the proof being that when visitors come to see me, I have a predilection for taking down my trousers to show them where the shot went in. The hand which wrote that should have its fingers shot away one by one. As for me, I can take my trousers down before anyone if I like; you would find nothing but a well-groomed fur and the scar made — let me be particular in the choice of a word for this particular purpose, to avoid misunderstanding — the scar made by a wanton shot. Everything is open and aboveboard; there is nothing to conceal; when the plain truth is in question, great minds discard the niceties of refinement. But if the writer of the article were to take down his trousers before a visitor, that would be quite another story, and I will let it stand to his credit that he does not do it. In return, let him leave me alone with his delicacy!

After these two shots I came to myself — and this is where my own memories gradually begin — between decks in the Hagenbeck steamer, inside a cage. It was not a four-sided barred cage; it was only a three-sided cage nailed to a locker; the locker made the fourth side of it. The whole construction was too low for me to stand up in and too narrow to sit down in. So I had to squat with my knees bent and trembling all the time, and also, since probably for a time I wished to see no one, and to stay in the dark, my face was turned toward the locker while the bars of the cage cut into my flesh behind. Such a method of confining wild beasts is supposed to have its advantages during the first days of captivity, and out of my own experiences I cannot deny that from the human point of view this is really the case.

But that did not occur to me then. For the first time in my life I could see no way out; at least no direct way out; directly in front of me was the locker, board fitted close to board. True, there was a gap running right through the boards which I greeted with the blissful howl of ignorance when I first discovered it, but the hole was not even wide enough to stick one's tail through and not all the strength of an ape could enlarge it.

I am supposed to have made uncommonly little noise, as I was later informed, from which the conclusion was drawn that I would either soon die or if I managed to survive the first critical period would be very amenable to training. I did survive this period. Hopelessly sobbing, painfully hunting for fleas, apathetically licking a cocoanut, beating my skull against the locker, sticking out my tongue at anyone who came near me — that was how I filled in time at first in my new life. But over and above it all only the one feeling: no way out. Of course what I felt then as an ape I can represent now only in human terms, and therefore I misrepresent it, but although I cannot reach back to the truth of the old ape life, there is no doubt that it lies somewhere in the direction I have indicated.

Until then I had had so many ways out of everything, and now I had none. I was pinned down. Had I been nailed down, my right to free movement would not have been lessened. Why so? Scratch your flesh raw between your toes, but you won't find the answer. Press yourself against the bar behind you till it nearly cuts you in two, you won't find the answer. I had no way out but I had to devise one, for without it I could not live. All the time facing that locker — I should certainly have perished. Yet as far as Hagenbeck was concerned, the place for apes was in front of a locker — well then, I had to stop being an ape. A fine, clear train of thought, which I must have constructed somehow with my belly, since apes think with their bellies.

I fear that perhaps you do not quite understand what I mean by "way out." I use the expression in its fullest and most popular sense. I deliberately do not use the word "freedom." I do not mean the spacious feeling of freedom on all sides. As an ape, perhaps, I knew that, and I have met men who yearn for it. But for my part I desired such freedom neither then nor now. In passing: may I say that all too often men are betrayed by the word freedom. And as freedom is counted among the most sublime feelings, so the corresponding disillusionment can be also sublime. In variety theaters I have often watched, before my turn came on, a couple of acrobats performing on trapezes high in the roof. They swung themselves, they rocked to and fro, they sprang into the air, they floated into each other's arms, one hung by the hair from the teeth of the other. "And that too is human freedom," I thought, "self-controlled movement." What a mockery of holy Mother Nature! Were the apes to see such a spectacle, no theater walls could stand the shock of their laughter.

No, freedom was not what I wanted. Only a way out; right or left, or in any direction; I made no other demand; even should the way out prove to be an illusion; the demand was a small one, the disappointment could be no bigger. To get out somewhere, to get out! Only not to stay motionless with raised arms, crushed against a wooden wall.

Today I can see it clearly; without the most profound inward calm I could never have found my way out. And indeed perhaps I owe all that I have become to the calm that settled within me after my first few days in the ship. And again for that calmness it was the ship's crew I had to thank.

They were good creatures, in spite of everything. I find it still pleasant to remember the sound of their heavy footfalls which used to echo through my half-dreaming head. They had a habit of doing everything as slowly as possible. If one of them wanted to rub his eyes, he lifted a hand as if it were a drooping weight. Their jests were coarse, but hearty. Their laughter had always a gruff bark in it that sounded dangerous but meant nothing. They always had something in their mouths to spit out and did not care where they spat it. They always grumbled that they got fleas from me; yet they were not seriously angry about it; they knew that my fur fostered fleas, and that fleas jump; it was a simple matter of fact to them. When they were off duty some of them often used to sit down in a semicircle around me; they hardly spoke but only grunted to each other; smoked their pipes, stretched out on lockers; smacked their knees as soon as I made the slightest movement; and now and then one of them would take a stick and tickle me where I liked being tickled. If I were to be invited today to take a cruise on that ship I should certainly refuse the invitation, but just as certainly the memories I could recall between its decks would not all be hateful.

The calmness I acquired among these people kept me above all from trying to escape. As I look back now, it seems to me I must have had at least an inkling that I had to find a way out or die, but that my way out could not be reached through flight. I cannot tell now whether escape was possible, but I believe it must have been; for an ape it must always be possible. With my teeth as they are today I have to be careful even in simply cracking nuts, but at that time I could certainly have managed by degrees to bite through the lock of my cage. I did not do it. What good would it have done me? As soon as I had poked out my head I should have been caught again and put in a worse cage; or I might have slipped among the other animals without being noticed, among the pythons, say, who were opposite me, and so breathed out my life in their embrace; or supposing I had actually succeeded in sneaking out as far as the deck and leaping overboard, I should have rocked for a little on the deep sea and then been drowned. Desperate remedies. I did not think it out in this human way, but under the influence of my surroundings I acted as if I had thought it out.

I did not think things out; but I observed everything quietly. I watched these men go to and fro, always the same faces, the same movements, often it seemed to me there was only the same man. So this man or these men walked about unimpeded. A lofty goal faintly dawned before me. No one promised me that if I became like them the bars of my cage would be taken away. Such promises for apparently impossible contingencies are not given. But if one achieves the impossible, the promises appear later retrospectively precisely where one had looked in vain for them before. Now, these men in themselves had no great attraction for me. Had I been devoted to the aforementioned idea of freedom, I should certainly have preferred the deep sea to the way out that suggested itself in the heavy faces of these men. At any rate, I watched them for a long time before I even thought of such things, indeed, it was only the mass weight of my observations that impelled me in the right direction.

It was so easy to imitate these people. I learned to spit in the very first days. We used to spit in each other's faces; the only difference was that I licked my face clean afterwards and they did not. I could soon smoke a pipe like an old hand; and if I also pressed my thumb into the bowl of the pipe, a roar of appreciation went up between-decks; only it took me a very long time to understand the difference between a full pipe and an empty one.

My worst trouble came from the schnapps bottle. The smell of it revolted me; I forced myself to it as best I could; but it took weeks for me to master my repulsion. This inward conflict, strangely enough, was taken more seriously by the crew than anything else about me. I cannot distinguish the men from each other in my recollection, but there was one of them who came again and again, alone or with friends, by day, by night, at all kinds of hours; he would post himself before me with the bottle and give me instructions. He could not understand me, he wanted to solve the enigma of my being. He would slowly uncork the bottle and then look at me to see if I had followed him; I admit that I always watched him with wildly eager, too eager attention; such a student of humankind no human teacher ever found on earth. After the bottle was uncorked he lifted it to his mouth; I followed it with my eyes right up to his jaws; he would nod, pleased with me, and set the bottle to his lips; I, enchanted with my gradual enlightenment, squealed and scratched myself comprehensively wherever scratching was called for; he rejoiced, tilted the bottle, and took a drink; I, impatient and desperate to emulate him, befouled myself in my cage, which again gave him great satisfaction; and then, holding the bottle at arm's length and bringing it up with a swing, he would empty it at one draught, leaning back at an exaggerated angle for my better instruction. I, exhausted by too much effort, could follow him no farther and hung limply to the bars, while he ended his theoretical exposition by rubbing his belly and grinning.

After theory came practice. Was I not already quite exhausted by my theoretical instruction? Indeed I was; utterly exhausted. That was part of my destiny. And yet I would take hold of the proffered bottle as well as I was able; uncork it, trembling; this successful action would gradually inspire me with new energy; I would lift the bottle, already following my original model almost exactly; put it to my lips and — and then throw it down in disgust, utter disgust, although it was empty and filled only with the smell of the spirit, throw it down on the floor in disgust. To the sorrow of my teacher, to the greater sorrow of myself; neither of us being really comforted by the fact that I did not forget, even though I had thrown away the bottle, to rub my belly most admirably and to grin.

Far too often my lesson ended in that way. And to the credit of my teacher, he was not angry; sometimes indeed he would hold his burning pipe against my fur, until it began to smolder in some place I could not easily reach, but then he would himself extinguish it with his own kind, enormous hand; he was not angry with me, he perceived that we were both fighting on the same side against the nature of apes and that I had the more difficult task.

What a triumph it was then both for him and for me, when one evening before a large circle of spectators — perhaps there was a celebration of some kind, a gramophone was playing, an officer was circulating among the crew — when on this evening, just as no one was looking, I took hold of a schnapps bottle that had been carelessly left standing before my cage, uncorked it in the best style, while the company began to watch me with mounting attention, set it to my lips without hesitation, with no grimace, like a professional drinker, with rolling eyes and full throat, actually and truly drank it empty; then threw the bottle away, not this time in despair but as an artistic performer; forgot, indeed, to rub my belly; but instead of that, because I could not help it, because my senses were reeling, called a brief and unmistakable "Hallo!" breaking into human speech, and with this outburst broke into the human community, and felt its echo: "Listen, he's talking!" like a caress over the whole of my sweat-drenched body.

I repeat: there was no attraction for me in imitating human beings; I imitated them because I needed a way out, and for no other reason. And even that triumph of mine did not achieve much. I lost my human voice again at once; it did not come back for months; my aversion for the schnapps bottle returned again with even greater force. But the line I was to follow had in any case been decided, once for all.

When I was handed over to my first trainer in Hamburg I soon realized that there were two alternatives before me: the Zoological Gardens or the variety stage. I did not hesitate. I said to myself: do your utmost to get onto the variety stage; the Zoological Gardens means only a new cage; once there, you are done for.

And so I learned things, gentlemen. Ah, one learns when one has to; one learns when one needs a way out; one learns at all costs. One stands over oneself with a whip; one flays oneself at the slightest opposition. My ape nature fled out of me, head over heels and away, so that my first teacher was almost himself turned into an ape by it, had soon to give up teaching and was taken away to a mental hospital. Fortunately he was soon let out again.

But I used up many teachers, indeed, several teachers at once. As I became more confident of my abilities, as the public took an interest in my progress and my future began to look bright, I engaged teachers for myself, established them in five communicating rooms, and took lessons from them all at once by dint of leaping from one room to the other.

That progress of mine! How the rays of knowledge penetrated from all sides into my awakening brain! I do not deny it: I found it exhilarating. But I must also confess: I did not overestimate it, not even then, much less now. With an effort which up till now has never been repeated I managed to reach the cultural level of an average European. In itself that might be nothing to speak of, but it is something insofar as it has helped me out of my cage and opened a special way out for me, the way of humanity. There is an excellent idiom: to fight one's way through the thick of things; that is what I have done, I have fought through the thick of things. There was nothing else for me to do, provided always that freedom was not to be my choice.

As I look back over my development and survey what I have achieved so far, I do not complain, but I am not complacent either. With my hands in my trouser pockets, my bottle of wine on the table, I half lie and half sit in my rocking chair and gaze out of the window: if a visitor arrives, I receive him with propriety. My manager sits in the anteroom; when I ring, he comes and listens to what I have to say. Nearly every evening I give a performance, and I have a success that could hardly be increased. When I come home late at night from banquets, from scientific receptions, from social gatherings, there sits waiting for me a half-trained little chimpanzee and I take comfort from her as apes do. By day I cannot bear to see her; for she has the insane look of the bewildered half-broken animal in her eye; no one else sees it, but I do, and I cannot bear it. On the whole, at any rate, I have achieved what I set out to achieve. But do not tell me that was not worth the trouble. In any case, I am not appealing for any man's verdict, I am only imparting knowledge, I am only making a report. To you also, honored Members of the Academy, I have only made a report.

Questions for Discussion

1. What apologies does the ape make as he begins his report? What do these apologies reveal about his self-concept and his feelings about his past?
2. What is the significance of the ape's metaphor that "everyone on earth feels a tickling at the heels; the small chimpanzee and the great Achilles alike"?
3. What do the ape's scars and their placement represent?
4. What are the ape's views on freedom? Does he consider himself free? What do his comments on the "human freedom" of the acrobats reveal? Why would the apes laugh at them?
5. What is the ape's attitude toward the imitation of human beings? What has his successful imitation of humans brought him? Is he happy?

Ideas for Writing

1. In an essay, discuss the narrative's form and tone. Why is the ape's address delivered in the form of a report to a professional group rather than as an appeal "for any man's verdict"? Despite the ape's claim that he is objective, does the presentation have an emotional perspective or "appeal" behind it? If so, for what?
2. Write a "Report to an Academy" from either a human or animal perspective. As Kafka does in his story, give your "reporter" a distinct personality and emphasize how he or she has been transformed by a change of culture.

D. H. LAWRENCE (1885–1930)

> In both his short stories and novels, David Herbert Lawrence empha-
> sized the value of respect for the natural world, intuitive understanding, and
> physical passion, while criticizing materialism, excessive intellectualism, and
> sexual repression. His focus was often explicitly on the complex relationships
> between men and women.

Lawrence was born in Nottinghamshire, England, the son of a coal miner.
His mother, a former teacher, encouraged him to pursue a career in education,
and Lawrence did teach for a short time after his graduation from Nottingham
College. After publishing his first novel, *The White Peacock* (1909), however, he
decided to devote himself to writing full time. His novel *Sons and Lovers* (1913)
brought him modest acclaim. Other of his novels — such as *Women in Love*
(1920) and *Lady Chatterley's Lover* (1928), both of which celebrate natural
instincts and unconventional sexual relations — were subject to censorship in
England and America. Suffering from tuberculosis, Lawrence left England in
1919 with his wife, Frieda, to live abroad for the rest of his life, traveling to Italy,
France, Australia, Mexico, and the southwestern United States. His *Collected
Stories* appeared in 1933. A number of critics regard these tightly written, emotionally intense stories as artistically superior to Lawrence's sprawling novels.

Wintry Peacock (1922)

There was thin, crisp snow on the ground, the sky was blue, the wind very
cold, the air clear. Farmers were just turning out the cows for an hour or so
in the midday, and the smell of cowsheds was unendurable as I entered Tible.
I noticed the ash-twigs up in the sky were pale and luminous, passing into the
blue. And then I saw the peacocks. There they were in the road before me,
three of them, and tailless, brown, speckled birds, with dark-blue necks and
ragged crests. They stepped archly over the filigree snow, and their bodies
moved with slow motion, like small, light, flat-bottomed boats. I admired
them, they were curious. Then a gust of wind caught them, heeled them over
as if they were three frail boats, opening their feathers like ragged sails. They
hopped and skipped with discomfort, to get out of the draught of the wind.
And then, in the lee of the walls, they resumed their arch, wintry motion, light
and unballasted now their tails were gone, indifferent. They were indifferent
to my presence. I might have touched them. They turned off to the shelter of
an open shed.

As I passed the end of the upper house, I saw a young woman just coming out of the back door. I had spoken to her in the summer. She recognised
me at once, and waved to me. She was carrying a pail, wearing a white apron

that was longer than her preposterously short skirt, and she had on the cotton bonnet. I took off my hat to her and was going on. But she put down her pail and darted with a swift, furtive movement after me.

"Do you mind waiting a minute?" she said. "I'll be out in a minute."

She gave me a slight, odd smile, and ran back. Her face was long and sallow and her nose rather red. But her gloomy black eyes softened caressively to me for a moment, with that momentary humility which makes a man lord of the earth.

I stood in the road, looking at the fluffy, dark-red young cattle that mooed and seemed to bark at me. They seemed happy, frisky cattle, a little impudent, and either determined to go back into the warm shed, or determined not to go back. I could not decide which.

Presently the woman came forward again, her head rather ducked. But she looked up at me and smiled, with that odd, immediate intimacy, something witch-like and impossible.

"Sorry to keep you waiting," she said. "Shall we stand in this cart-shed — it will be more out of the wind."

So we stood among the shafts of the open cart-shed that faced the road. Then she looked down at the ground, a little sideways, and I noticed a small black frown on her brows. She seemed to brood for a moment. Then she looked straight into my eyes, so that I blinked and wanted to turn my face aside. She was searching me for something and her look was too near. The frown was still on her keen, sallow brow.

"Can you speak French?" she asked me abruptly.

"More or less," I replied.

"I was supposed to learn it at school," she said. "But I don't know a word." She ducked her head and laughed, with a slightly ugly grimace and a rolling of her black eyes.

"No good keeping your mind full of scraps," I answered.

But she had turned aside her sallow, long face, and did not hear what I said. Suddenly again she looked at me. She was searching. And at the same time she smiled at me, and her eyes looked softly darkly, with infinite trustful humility into mine. I was being cajoled.

"Would you mind reading a letter for me, in French," she said, her face immediately black and bitter-looking. She glanced at me, frowning.

"Not at all," I said.

"It's a letter to my husband," she said, still scrutinising.

I looked at her, and didn't quite realise. She looked too far into me, my wits were gone. She glanced round. Then she looked at me shrewdly. She drew a letter from her pocket, and handed it to me. It was addressed from France to Lance-Corporal Goyte, at Tible. I took out the letter and began to read it, as mere words. "*Mon chere* Alfred" — it might have been a bit of a torn newspaper. So I followed the script: the trite phrases of a letter from a French-speaking girl to an English soldier. "I think of you always, always. Do you think sometimes of me?" And then I vaguely realised that I was reading a man's private correspondence. And yet, how could one consider these trivial, facile French phrases private! Nothing more trite and vulgar in the world, than such a love-letter — no newspaper more obvious.

Therefore I read with a callous heart the effusions of the Belgian damsel. But then I gathered my attention. For the letter went on: "*Notre chere petit bébé* — our dear little baby was born a week ago. Almost I died, knowing you were far away, and perhaps forgetting the fruit of our perfect love. But the child comforted me. He has the smiling eyes and virile air of his English father. I pray to the Mother of Jesus to send me the dear father of my child, that I may see him with my child in his arms, and that we may be united in holy family love. Ah, my Alfred, can I tell you how I miss you, how I weep for you. My thoughts are with you always, I think of nothing but you, I live for nothing but you and our dear baby. If you do not come back to me soon, I shall die, and our child will die. But no, you cannot come back to me. But I can come to you, come to England with our child. If you do not wish to present me to your good mother and father, you can meet me in some town, some city, for I shall be so frightened to be alone in England with my child, and no one to take care of us. Yet I must come to you, I must bring my child, my little Alfred to his father, the big, beautiful Alfred that I love so much. Oh, write and tell me where I shall come. I have some money, I am not a penniless creature. I have money for myself and my dear baby ——"

I read to the end. It was signed: "Your very happy and still more unhappy Elise." I suppose I must have been smiling.

"I can see it makes you laugh," said Mrs. Goyte, sardonically. I looked up at her.

"It's a love-letter, I know that," she said. "There's too many 'Alfreds' in it."

"One too many," I said.

"Oh, yes —— And what does she say — Eliza ? We know her name's Eliza, that's another thing." She grimaced a little, looking up at me with a mocking laugh.

"Where did you get this letter?" I said.

"Postman gave it me last week."

"And is your husband at home?"

"I expect him home to-night. He's been wounded, you know, and we've been applying for him home. He was home about six weeks ago — he's been in Scotland since then. Oh, he was wounded in the leg. Yes, he's all right, a great strapping fellow. But he's lame, he limps a bit. He expects he'll get his discharge — but I don't think he will. We married? We've been married six years — and he joined up the first day of the war. Oh, he thought he'd like the life. He's been through the South African War. No, he was sick of it, fed up. I'm living with his father and mother — I've no home of my own now. My people had a big farm — over a thousand acres — in Oxfordshire. Not like here — no. Oh, they're very good to me, his father and mother. Oh, yes, they couldn't be better. They think more of me than of their own daughters. But it's not like being in a place of your own, is it? You can't *really* do as you like. No, there's only me and his father and mother at home. Before the war? Oh, he was anything. He had a good education—but he liked the farming better. Then he was a chauffeur. That's how he knew French. He was driving in France for a long time——"

At this point the peacocks came round the corner on a puff of wind.

"Hello, Joey!" she called, and one of the birds came forward, on delicate legs. Its grey speckled back was very elegant, it rolled its full, dark-blue neck as it moved to her. She crouched down. "Joey, dear," she said, in an odd, saturnine caressive voice, "you're bound to find me, aren't you?" She put her face forward, and the bird rolled his neck, almost touching her face with his beak, as if kissing her.

"He loves you," I said.

She twisted her face up at me with a laugh.

"Yes," she said, "he loves me, Joey does,"—then, to the bird—"and I love Joey, don't I. I *do* love Joey." And she smoothed his feathers for a moment. Then she rose, saying: "He's an affectionate bird."

I smiled at the roll of her "bir-rrd."

"Oh, yes, he is," she protested. "He came with me from my home seven years ago. Those others are his descendants—but they're not like Joey—*are they, dee-urr?*" Her voice rose at the end with a witch-like cry.

Then she forgot the bird in the cart-shed and turned to business again.

"Won't you read that letter?" she said. "Read it, so that I know what it says."

"It's rather behind his back," I said.

"Oh, never mind him," she cried. "He's been behind my back long enough —all these four years. If he never did no worse things behind my back than I do behind his, he wouldn't have cause to grumble. You read me what it says."

Now I felt a distinct reluctance to do as she bid, and yet I began—"My dear Alfred."

"I guessed that much," she said. "Eliza's dear Alfred." She laughed. "How do you say it in French? *Eliza?*"

I told her, and she repeated the name with great contempt—*Elise.*

"Go on," she said. "You're not reading."

So I began—"I have been thinking of you sometimes—have you been thinking of me——?"

"Of several others as well, beside her, I'll wager," said Mrs. Goyte.

"Probably not," said I, and continued. "A dear little baby was born here a week ago. Ah, can I tell you my feelings when I take my darling little brother into my arms——"

"I'll bet it's *his,*" cried Mrs. Goyte.

"No," I said. "It's her mother's."

"Don't you believe it," she cried. "It's a blind. You mark it's her own right enough—and his."

"No," I said, "it's her mother's." "He has sweet smiling eyes, but not like your beautiful English eyes——"

She suddenly struck her hand on her skirt with a wild motion, and bent down, doubled with laughter. Then she rose and covered her face with her hand.

"I'm forced to laugh at the beautiful English eyes," she said.

"Aren't his eyes beautiful?" I asked.

"Oh, yes — *very!* Go on! — *Joey, dear, dee-urr, Joey!*" — this to the peacock.

— "Er — We miss you very much. We all miss you. We wish you were here to see the darling baby. Ah, Alfred, how happy we were when you stayed with us. We all loved you so much. My mother will call the baby Alfred so that we shall never forget you——"

"Of course it's his right enough," cried Mrs. Goyte.

"No," I said. "It's the mother's." Er — "My mother is very well. My father came home yesterday — on leave. He is delighted with his son, my little brother, and wishes to have him named after you, because you were so good to us all in that terrible time, which I shall never forget. I must weep now when I think of it. Well, you are far away in England, and perhaps I shall never see you again. How did you find your dear mother and father? I am so happy that your wound is better, and that you can nearly walk——"

"How did he find his dear *wife?*" cried Mrs. Goyte. "He never told her he had one. Think of taking the poor girl in like that!"

"We are so pleased when you write to us. Yet now you are in England you will forget the family you served so well——"

"A bit too well — eh, *Joey?*" cried the wife.

"If it had not been for you we should not be alive now, to grieve and to rejoice in this life, that is so hard for us. But we have recovered some of our losses, and no longer feel the burden of poverty. The little Alfred is a great comfort to me. I hold him to my breast and think of the big, good Alfred, and I weep to think that those times of suffering were perhaps the times of a great happiness that is gone for ever."

"Oh, but isn't it a shame, to take a poor girl in like that!" cried Mrs. Goyte. "Never to let on that he was married, and raise her hopes — I call it beastly, I do."

"You don't know," I said. "You know how anxious women are to fall in love, wife or no wife. How could he help it, if she was determined to fall in love with him?"

"He could have helped it if he'd wanted."

"Well," I said, "we aren't all heroes."

"Oh, but that's different! The big, good Alfred! — did ever you hear such tommy-rot in your life! Go on — what does she say at the end?"

"Er — We shall be pleased to hear of your life in England. We all send many kind regards to your good parents. I wish you all happiness for your future days. Your very affectionate and ever-grateful, Elise."

There was silence for a moment, during which Mrs. Goyte remained with her head dropped, sinister and abstracted. Suddenly she lifted her face, and her eyes flashed.

"Oh, but I call it beastly, I call it mean, to take a girl in like that."

"Nay," I said. "Probably he hasn't taken her in at all. Do you think those French girls are such poor innocent things? I guess she's a great deal more downy than he."

"Oh, he's one of the biggest fools that ever walked," she cried.

"There you are!" said I.

"But it's his child right enough," she said.

"I don't think so," said I.

"I'm sure of it."

"Oh, well," I said, "if you prefer to think that way."

"What other reason has she for writing like that —— ?"

I went out into the road and looked at the cattle.

"Who is this driving the cows?" I said. She too came out.

"It's the boy from the next farm," she said.

"Oh, well," said I, "those Belgian girls! You never know where their letters will end. And, after all, it's his affair — you needn't bother."

"Oh —— !" she cried with scorn — "it's not *me* that bothers. But it's the nasty meanness of it — me writing him such loving letters" — she put her hand before her face and laughed malevolently — "and sending him parcels all the time. You bet he fed that gurrl on my parcels — I know he did. It's just like him. I'll bet they laughed together over my letters. I'll bet anything they did —— "

"Nay," said I. "He'd burn your letters for fear they'd give him away."

There was a black look on her yellow face. Suddenly a voice was heard calling. She poked her head out of the shed, and answered coolly:

"All right!" Then turning to me: "That's his mother looking after me."

She laughed into my face, witch-like, and we turned down the road.

When I awoke, the morning after this episode, I found the house darkened with deep, soft snow, which had blown against the large west windows, covering them with a screen. I went outside, and saw the valley all white and ghastly below me, the trees beneath black and thin-looking like wire, the rock-faces dark between the glistening shroud, and the sky above sombre, heavy, yellowish-dark, much too heavy for this world below of hollow bluey whiteness figured with black. I felt I was in a valley of the dead. And I sensed I was a prisoner, for the snow was everywhere deep, and drifted in places. So all the morning I remained indoors, looking up the drive at the shrubs so heavily plumed with snow, at the gate-posts raised high with a foot or more of extra whiteness. Or I looked down into the white-and-black valley that was utterly motionless and beyond life, a hollow sarcophagus.

Nothing stirred the whole day — no plume fell off the shrubs, the valley was as abstracted as a grove of death. I looked over at the tiny, half-buried farms away on the bare uplands beyond the valley hollow, and I thought of

Tible in the snow, of the black witch-like little Mrs. Goyte. And the snow seemed to lay me bare to influences I wanted to escape.

In the faint glow of the half-clear light that came about four o'clock in the afternoon, I was roused to see a motion in the snow away below, near where the thorn trees stood very black and dwarfed, like a little savage group, in the dismal white. I watched closely. Yes, there was a flapping and a struggle — a big bird, it must be, labouring in the snow. I wondered. Our biggest birds, in the valley, were the large hawks that often hung flickering opposite my windows, level with me, but high above some prey on the steep valley-side. This was much too big for a hawk — too big for any known bird. I searched in my mind for the largest English wild bird, geese, buzzards.

Still it laboured and strove, then was still, a dark spot, then struggled again. I went out of the house and down the steep slope, at risk of breaking my leg between the rocks. I knew the ground so well — and yet I got well shaken before I drew near the thorn trees.

Yes, it was a bird. It was Joey. It was the grey-brown peacock with a blue neck. He was snow-wet and spent.

"Joey — Joey, de-urr!" I said, staggering unevenly towards him. He looked so pathetic, rowing and struggling in the snow, too spent to rise, his blue neck stretching out and lying sometimes on the snow, his eye closing and opening quickly, his crest all battered.

"Joey dee-urr!" I said caressingly to him. And at last he lay still, blinking, in the surged and furrowed snow, whilst I came near and touched him, stroked him, gathering him under my arm. He stretched his long, wetted neck away from me as I held him, none the less he was quiet in my arm, too tired, perhaps, to struggle. Still he held his poor, crested head away from me, and seemed sometimes to droop, to wilt, as if he might suddenly die.

He was not so heavy as I expected, yet it was a struggle to get up to the house with him again. We set him down, not too near the fire, and gently wiped him with cloths. He submitted, only now and then stretched his soft neck away from us, avoiding us helplessly. Then we set warm food by him. I *put* it to his beak, tried to make him eat. But he ignored it. He seemed to be ignorant of what we were doing, recoiled inside himself inexplicably. So we put him in a basket with cloths, and left him crouching oblivious. His food we put near him. The blinds were drawn, the house was warm, it was night. Sometimes he stirred, but mostly he huddled still, leaning his queer crested head on one side. He touched no food, and took no heed of sounds or movements. We talked of brandy or stimulants. But I realised we had best leave him alone.

In the night, however, we heard him thumping about. I got up anxiously with a candle. He had eaten some food, and scattered more, making a mess. And he was perched on the back of a heavy arm-chair. So I concluded he was recovered, or recovering.

The next day was clear, and the snow had frozen, so I decided to carry him back to Tible. He consented, after various flappings, to sit in a big fish-bag with his battered head peeping out with wild uneasiness. And so I set off with him slithering down into the valley, making good progress down in the pale shadow beside the rushing waters, then climbing painfully up the arrested white valley-side, plumed with clusters of young pine trees, into the paler white radiance of the snowy, upper regions, where the wind cut fine. Joey seemed to watch all the time with wide, anxious, unseeing eye, brilliant and inscrutable. As I drew near to Tible township he stirred violently in the bag, though I do not know if he recognised the place. Then, as I came to the sheds, he looked sharply from side to side, and stretched his neck out long. I was a little afraid of him. He gave a loud, vehement yell, opening his sinister beak, and I stood still, looking at him as he struggled in the bag, shaken myself by his struggles, yet not thinking to release him.

Mrs. Goyte came darting past the end of the house, her head sticking forward in sharp scrutiny. She saw me, and came forward.

"Have you got Joey!" she cried sharply, as if I were a thief.

I opened the bag, and he flopped out, flapping as if he hated the touch of the snow now. She gathered him up, and put her lips to his beak. She was flushed and handsome, her eyes bright, her hair slack, thick, but more witch-like than ever. She did not speak.

She had been followed by a grey-haired woman with a round, rather sallow face and a slightly hostile bearing.

"Did you bring him with you, then?" she asked sharply. I answered that I had rescued him the previous evening.

From the background slowly approached a slender man with a grey moustache and large patches on his trousers.

"You've got 'im back 'gain, ah see," he said to his daughter-in-law. His wife explained how I had found Joey.

"Ah," went on the grey man. "It wor our Alfred scarred him off, back your life. He must'a flyed ower t'valley. Tha ma' thank thy stars as 'e wor fun, Maggie. 'E'd a bin froze. They a bit nesh, you know," he concluded to me.

"They are," I answered. "This isn't their country."

"No, it isna," replied Mr. Goyte. He spoke very slowly and deliberately, quietly, as if the soft pedal were always down in his voice. He looked at his daughter-in-law as she crouched, flushed and dark, before the peacock, which would lay its long blue neck for a moment along her lap. In spite of his grey moustache and thin grey hair, the elderly man had a face young and almost delicate, like a young man's. His blue eyes twinkled with some inscrutable source of pleasure, his skin was fine and tender, his nose delicately arched. His grey hair being slightly ruffled, he had a debonair look, as of a youth who is in love.

"We mun tell 'im it's come," he said slowly, and turning he called: "Alfred — Alfred! Wheer's ter gotten to?"

Then he turned again to the group.

"Get up then, Maggie, lass, get up wi' thee. Tha ma'es too much o' th' bod."

A young man approached, wearing rough khaki and knee-breeches. He was Danish-looking, broad at the loins.

"I's come back then," said the father to the son; "leastwise, he's bin browt back, flyed ower the Griff Low."

The son looked at me. He had a devil-may-care bearing, his cap on one side, his hands stuck in the front pockets of his breeches. But he said nothing.

"Shall you come in a minute, Master," said the elderly woman, to me.

"Ay, come in an' ha'e a cup o' tea or summat. You'll do wi' summat, carrin' that bod. Come on, Maggie wench, let's go in."

So we went indoors, into the rather stuffy, overcrowded living-room, that was too cosy, and too warm. The son followed last, standing in the doorway. The father talked to me. Maggie put out the tea-cups. The mother went into the dairy again.

"Tha'lt rouse thysen up a bit again, now, Maggie," the father-in-law said — and then to me: "'Ers not bin very bright sin' Alfred come whoam, an' the bod flyed awee. 'E come whoam a Wednesday night, Alfred did. But ay, you knowed, didna yer. Ay, 'e comed 'a Wednesday — an' I reckon there wor a bit of a to-do between 'em worn't there, Maggie?"

He twinkled maliciously to his daughter-in-law, who flushed, brilliant and handsome.

"Oh, be quiet, father. You're wound up, by the sound of you," she said to him, as if crossly. But she could never be cross with him.

"'Ers got 'er colour back this mornin'," continued the father-in-law slowly. "It's bin heavy weather wi' 'er this last two days. Ay — 'er's bin north-east sin' 'er seed you a Wednesday."

"Father, do stop talking. You'd wear the leg off an iron pot I can't think where you've found your tongue, all of a sudden," said Maggie, with caressive sharpness.

"Ah've found it wheer I lost it. Aren't goin' ter come in an' sit thee down, Alfred?"

But Alfred turned and disappeared.

"'E's got th' monkey on 'is back ower this letter job," said the father secretly to me. "Mother, 'er knows nowt about it. Lot o' tom-foolery, isn't it? Ay! What's good o'makkin' a peck o' trouble over what's far enough off, an' ned niver come no nigher. No — not a smite o' use. That's what I tell 'er. 'Er should ta'e no notice on't. Ty, what can y' expect."

The mother came in again, and the talk became general. Maggie flashed her eyes at me from time to time, complacent and satisfied, moving among the men. I paid her little compliments, which she did not seem to hear. She attended to me with a kind of sinister witch-like graciousness, her dark head ducked between her shoulders, at once humble and powerful. She was happy as a child attending to her father-in-law and to me. But there was something ominous between her eyebrows, as if a dark moth were settled there — and something ominous in her bent, hulking bearing.

She sat on a low stool by the fire, near her father-in-law. Her head was dropped, she seemed in a state of abstraction. From time to time she would suddenly recover, and look up at us, laughing and chatting. Then she would forget again. Yet in her hulked black forgetting she seemed very near to us.

The door having been opened, the peacock came slowly in, prancing calmly. He went near to her and crouched down, coiling his blue neck. She glanced at him, but almost as if she did not observe him. The bird sat silent, seeming to sleep, and the woman also sat hulked and silent, seemingly oblivious. Then once more there was a heavy step, and Alfred entered. He looked at his wife, and he looked at the peacock crouching by her. He stood large in the doorway, his hands stuck in front of him, in his breeches pockets. Nobody spoke. He turned on his heel and went out again.

I rose also to go. Maggie started as if coming to herself.

"Must you go?" she asked, rising and coming near to me, standing in front of me, twisting her head sideways and looking up at me. "Can't you stop a bit longer? We can all be cosy to-day, there's nothing to do outdoors." And she laughed, showing her teeth oddly. She had a long chin.

I said I must go. The peacock uncoiled and coiled again his long blue neck, as he lay on the hearth. Maggie still stood close in front of me, so that I was acutely aware of my waistcoat buttons.

"Oh, well," she said, "you'll come again, won't you? Do come again."

I promised.

"Come to tea one day — yes, do!"

I promised — one day.

The moment I went out of her presence I ceased utterly to exist for her — as utterly as I ceased to exist for Joey. With her curious abstractedness she forgot me again immediately. I knew it as I left her. Yet she seemed almost in physical contact with me while I was with her.

The sky was all pallid again, yellowish. When I went out there was no sun; the snow was blue and cold. I hurried away down the hill, musing on Maggie. The road made a loop down the sharp face of the slope. As I went crunching over the laborious snow I became aware of a figure striding down the steep scarp to intercept me. It was a man with his hands in front of him, half stuck in his breeches pockets, and his shoulders square — a real farmer of the hills; Alfred, of course. He waited for me by the stone fence.

"Excuse me," he said as I came up.

I came to a halt in front of him and looked into his sullen blue eyes. He had a certain odd haughtiness on his brows. But his blue eyes stared insolently at me.

"Do you know anything about a letter — in French — that my wife opened — a letter of mine —— ?"

"Yes," said I. "She asked me to read it to her."

He looked square at me. He did not know exactly how to feel.

"What was there in it?" he asked.

"Why?" I said. "Don't you know?"

"She makes out she's burnt it," he said.

"Without showing it to you?" I asked.

He nodded slightly. He seemed to be meditating as to what line of action he should take. He wanted to know the contents of the letter: he must know: and therefore he must ask me, for evidently his wife had taunted him. At the same time, no doubt, he would like to wreak untold vengeance on my unfortunate person. So he eyed me, and I eyed him, and neither of us spoke. He did not want to repeat his request to me. And yet I only looked at him, and considered.

Suddenly he threw back his head and glanced down the valley. Then he changed his position — he was a horse-soldier. Then he looked at me more confidentially.

"She burnt the blasted thing before I saw it," he said.

"Well," I answered slowly, "she doesn't know herself what was in it."

He continued to watch me narrowly. I grinned to myself.

"I didn't like to read her out what there was in it," I continued.

He suddenly flushed so that the veins in his neck stood out, and he stirred again uncomfortably.

"The Belgian girl said her baby had been born a week ago, and that they were going to call it Alfred," I told him.

He met my eyes. I was grinning. He began to grin, too.

"Good luck to her," he said.

"Best of luck," said I.

"And what did you tell *her*?" he asked.

"That the baby belonged to the old mother — that it was brother to your girl, who was writing to you as a friend of the family."

He stood smiling, with the long, subtle malice of a farmer.

"And did she take it in?" he asked.

"As much as she took anything else."

He stood grinning fixedly. Then he broke into a short laugh.

"Good for *her*!" he exclaimed cryptically.

And then he laughed aloud once more, evidently feeling he had won a big move in his contest with his wife.

"What about the other woman?" I asked.

"Who?"

"Elise."

"Oh" — he shifted uneasily — "she was all right —— "

"You'll be getting back to her," I said.

He looked at me. Then he made a grimace with his mouth.

"Not me," he said. "Back your life it's a plant."

"You don't think the *cher petit bébé* is a little Alfred?"

"It might be," he said.

"Only might?"

"Yes — an' there's lots of mites in a pound of cheese." He laughed boisterously but uneasily.

"What did she say, exactly?" he asked.

I began to repeat, as well as I could, the phrases of the letter: "*Mon cher Alfred — Figure-toi comme je suis desolée ——*"

He listened with some confusion. When I had finished all I could remember, he said:

"They know how to pitch you out a letter, those Belgian lasses."

"Practice," said I.

"They get plenty," he said.

There was a pause.

"Oh, well," he said. "I've never got that letter, anyhow."

The wind blew fine and keen, in the sunshine, across the snow. I blew my nose and prepared to depart.

"And *she* doesn't know anything?" he continued, jerking his head up the hill in the direction of Tible.

"She knows nothing but what I've said — that is, if she really burnt the letter."

"I believe she burnt it," he said, "for spite. She's a little devil, she is. But I shall have it out with her." His jaw was stubborn and sullen. Then suddenly he turned to me with a new note.

"Why?" he said. "Why didn't you wring that b—— peacock's neck — that b—— Joey?"

"Why?" I said. "What for?"

"I hate the brute," he said. "I had a shot at him —— "

I laughed. He stood and mused.

"Poor little Elise," he murmured

"Was she small — petite?" I asked. He jerked up his head.

"No," he said. "Rather tall."

"Taller than your wife, I suppose."

Again he looked into my eyes. And then once more he went into a loud burst of laughter that made the still, snow-deserted valley clap again.

"God, it's a knock-out!" he said, thoroughly amused. Then he stood at ease, one foot out, his hands in his breeches pockets, in front of him, his head thrown back, a handsome figure of a man.

"But I'll do that blasted Joey in —— " he mused.

I ran down the hill, shouting with laughter.

Questions for Discussion

1. What is revealed about the narrator's values and concerns through his description of the peacocks he encounters on a wintry day? Why does he admire them?

2. How is Maggie described? How would you characterize her personality and the narrator's response to her? What is suggested by his decision to lie to her about the contents of the letter?

3. How does the wife describe her husband to the narrator? What is the nature of the relationship she has with her husband?

4. How is the narrator's response to the peacock that blunders into his farmyard during the storm related to his earlier encounter with the farm wife? What is the significance of the narrator's comment to Mr. Goyte, "This isn't their country"?

5. Why does the narrator tell Alfred the truth about the letter's contents after lying to Maggie? What is the significance of the narrator's final run down the hill afterwards, "shouting with laughter"?

Ideas for Writing
1. In an essay, analyze the central symbol of the story, the "wintry peacock." What does the peacock represent to Maggie, to Alfred, to the narrator, and to the reader?

2. Write a scene between Alfred and Maggie in which he shares the true contents of the letter with her. How would he present this information, and how would she respond?

The Rocking-Horse Winner (1926)

There was a woman who was beautiful, who started with all the advantages, yet she had no luck. She married for love, and the love turned to dust. She had bonny children, yet she felt they had been thrust upon her, and she could not love them. They looked at her coldly, as if they were finding fault with her. And hurriedly she felt she must cover up some fault in herself. Yet what it was that she must cover up she never knew. Nevertheless, when her children were present, she always felt the center of her heart go hard. This troubled her, and in her manner she was all the more gentle and anxious for her children, as if she loved them very much. Only she herself knew that at the center of her heart was a hard little place that could not feel love, no, not for anybody. Everybody else said of her: "She is such a good mother. She adores her children." Only she herself, and her children themselves, knew it was not so. They read it in each other's eyes.

There were a boy and two little girls. They lived in a pleasant house, with a garden, and they had discreet servants, and felt themselves superior to anyone in the neighborhood.

Although they lived in style, they felt always an anxiety in the house. There was never enough money. The mother had a small income, and the father had a small income, but not nearly enough for the social position which they had to keep up. The father went into town to some office. But though he had good prospects, these prospects never materialized. There was always the grinding sense of the shortage of money, though the style was always kept up.

At last the mother said: "I will see if *I* can't make something." But she did not know where to begin. She racked her brains, and tried this thing and the other, but could not find anything successful. The failure made deep lines come into her face. Her children were growing up, they would have to go to school. There must be more money, there must be more money. The father, who was always very handsome and expensive in his tastes, seemed as if he never *would* be able to do anything worth doing. And the mother, who had a great belief in herself, did not succeed any better, and her tastes were just as expensive.

And so the house came to be haunted by the unspoken phrase: *There must be more money! There must be more money!* The children could hear it all the time though nobody said it aloud. They heard it at Christmas, when the expensive and splendid toys filled the nursery. Behind the shining modern rocking horse, behind the smart doll's house, a voice would start whispering: "There *must* be more money! There *must* be more money!" And the children would stop playing, to listen for a moment. They would look into each other's eyes, to see if they had all heard. And each one saw in the eyes of the other two that they too had heard. "There *must* be more money! There *must* be more money!"

It came whispering from the springs of the still-swaying rocking horse, and even the horse, bending his wooden, champing head, heard it. The big doll, sitting so pink and smirking in her new pram, could hear it quite plainly, and seemed to be smirking all the more self-consciously because of it. The foolish puppy, too, that took the place of the teddy bear, he was looking so extraordinarily foolish for no other reason but that he heard the secret whisper all over the house: "There *must* be more money!"

Yet nobody ever said it aloud. The whisper was everywhere, and therefore no one spoke it. Just as no one ever says: "We are breathing!" in spite of the fact that breath is coming and going all the time.

"Mother," said the boy Paul one day, "why don't we keep a car of our own? Why do we always use Uncle's, or else a taxi?"

"Because we're the poor members of the family," said the mother.

"But why *are* we, Mother?"

"Well — I suppose," she said slowly and bitterly, "it's because your father has no luck."

The boy was silent for some time.

"Is luck money, Mother?" he asked rather timidly.

"No, Paul. Not quite. It's what causes you to have money."

"Oh!" said Paul vaguely. "I thought when Uncle Oscar said *filthy lucker*, it meant money."

"*Filthy lucre* does not mean money," said the mother. "But it's lucre, not luck."

"Oh!" said the boy. "Then what *is* luck, Mother?"

"It's what causes you to have money. If you're lucky you have money. That's why it's better to be born lucky than rich. If you're rich, you may lose your money. But if you're lucky, you will always get more money."

"Oh! Will you? And is Father not lucky?"

"Very unlucky, I should say," she said bitterly.

The boy watched her with unsure eyes.

"Why?" he asked.

"I don't know. Nobody ever knows why one person is lucky and another unlucky."

"Don't they? Nobody at all? Does *nobody* know?"

"Perhaps God. But He never tells."

"He ought to, then. And aren't you lucky either, Mother?"

"I can't be, if I married an unlucky husband."

"But by yourself, aren't you?"

"I used to think I was, before I married. Now I think I am very unlucky indeed."

"Why?"

"Well — never mind! Perhaps I'm not really," she said.

The child looked at her, to see if she meant it. But he saw, by the lines of her mouth, that she was only trying to hide something from him.

"Well, anyhow," he said stoutly, "I'm a lucky person."

"Why?" said his mother, with a sudden laugh.

He stared at her. He didn't even know why he had said it.

"God told me," he asserted, brazening it out.

"I hope He did, dear!" she said, again with a laugh, but rather bitter.

"He did, Mother!"

"Excellent!" said the mother.

The boy saw she did not believe him; or, rather, that she paid no attention to his assertion. This angered him somewhat, and made him want to compel her attention.

He went off by himself, vaguely, in a childish way, seeking for the clue to "luck." Absorbed, taking no heed of other people, he went about with a sort of stealth, seeking inwardly for luck. He wanted luck, he wanted it, he wanted it. When the two girls were playing dolls in the nursery, he would sit on his big rocking horse, charging madly into space, with a frenzy that made the little girls peer at him uneasily. Wildly the horse careered, the waving dark hair of the boy tossed, his eyes had a strange glare in them. The little girls dared not speak to him.

When he had ridden to the end of his mad little journey, he climbed down and stood in front of his rocking horse, staring fixedly into its lowered face. Its red mouth was slightly open, its big eye was wide and glassy-bright.

Now! he could silently command the snorting steed. Now, take me to where there is luck! Now take me!

And he would slash the horse on the neck with the little whip he had asked Uncle Oscar for. He *knew* the horse could take him to where there was luck, if only he forced it. So he would mount again, and start on his furious ride, hoping at last to get there. He knew he could get there.

"You'll break your horse, Paul!" said the nurse.

"He's always riding like that! I wish he'd leave off!" said his elder sister Joan.

But he only glared down on them in silence. Nurse gave him up. She could make nothing of him. Anyhow he was growing beyond her.

One day his mother and his uncle Oscar came in when he was on one of his furious rides. He did not speak to them.

"Hallo, you young jockey! Riding a winner?" said his uncle.

"Aren't you growing too big for a rocking horse? You're not a very little boy any longer, you know," said his mother.

But Paul only gave a blue glare from his big, rather close-set eyes. He would speak to nobody when he was in full tilt. His mother watched him with an anxious expression on her face.

At last he suddenly stopped forcing his horse into the mechanical gallop, and slid down.

"Well, I got there!" he announced fiercely, his blue eyes still flaring, and his sturdy long legs straddling apart.

"Where did you get to?" asked his mother.

"Where I wanted to go," he flared back at her.

"That's right, son!" said Uncle Oscar. "Don't you stop till you get there. What's the horse's name?"

"He doesn't have a name," said the boy.

"Gets on without all right?" asked the uncle.

"Well, he has different names. He was called Sansovino last week."

"Sansovino, eh? Won the Ascot. How did you know his name?"

"He always talks about horse races with Bassett," said Joan.

The uncle was delighted to find that his small nephew was posted with all the racing news. Bassett, the young gardener, who had been wounded in the left foot in the war and had got his present job through Oscar Cresswell, whose batman he had been, was a perfect blade of the "turf." He lived in the racing events, and the small boy lived with him.

Oscar Cresswell got it all from Bassett.

"Master Paul comes and asks me, so I can't do more than tell him, sir," said Bassett, his face terribly serious, as if he were speaking of religious matters.

"And does he ever put anything on a horse he fancies?"

"Well — I don't want to give him away — he's a young sport, a fine sport, sir. Would you mind asking him himself? He sort of takes a pleasure in it, and perhaps he'd feel I was giving him away, sir, if you don't mind."

Bassett was serious as a church.

The uncle went back to his nephew and took him off for a ride in the car.

"Say, Paul, old man, do you ever put anything on a horse?" the uncle asked.

The boy watched the handsome man closely.

"Why, do you think I oughtn't to?" he parried.

"Not a bit of it! I thought perhaps you might give me a tip for the Lincoln."

The car sped on into the country, going down to Uncle Oscar's place in Hampshire.

"Honor bright?" said the nephew.

"Honor bright, son!" said the uncle.

"Well, then, Daffodil."

"Daffodil! I doubt it, sonny. What about Mirza?"

"I only know the winner," said the boy. "That's Daffodil."

"Daffodil, eh?"

There was a pause. Daffodil was an obscure horse comparatively.

"Uncle!"

"Yes, son?"

"You won't let it go any further, will you? I promised Bassett."

"Bassett be damned, old man! What's he got to do with it?"

"We're partners. We've been partners from the first. Uncle, he lent me my first five shillings, which I lost. I promised him, honor bright, it was only between me and him; only you gave me that ten-shilling note I started winning with, so I thought you were lucky. You won't let it go any further, will you?"

The boy gazed at his uncle from those big, hot, blue eyes, set rather close together. The uncle stirred and laughed uneasily.

"Right you are, son! I'll keep your tip private. Daffodil, eh? How much are you putting on him?"

"All except twenty pounds," said the boy. "I keep that in reserve."

The uncle thought it a good joke.

"You keep twenty pounds in reserve, do you, you young romancer? What are you betting, then?"

"I'm betting three hundred," said the boy gravely. "But it's between you and me, Uncle Oscar! Honor bright?"

The uncle burst into a roar of laughter.

"It's between you and me all right, you young Nat Gould," he said, laughing. "But where's your three hundred?"

"Bassett keeps it for me. We're partners."

"You are, are you! And what is Bassett putting on Daffodil?"

"He won't go quite as high as I do, I expect. Perhaps he'll go a hundred and fifty."

"What, pennies?" laughed the uncle.

"Pounds," said the child, with a surprised look at his uncle. "Bassett keeps a bigger reserve than I do."

Between wonder and amusement Uncle Oscar was silent. He pursued the matter no further, but he determined to take his nephew with him to the Lincoln races.

"Now, son," he said, "I'm putting twenty on Mirza, and I'll put five for you on any horse you fancy. What's your pick?"

"Daffodil, Uncle."

"No, not the fiver on Daffodil!"

"I should if it was my own fiver," said the child.

"Good! Good! Right you are! A fiver for me and a fiver for you on Daffodil."

The child had never been to a race meeting before, and his eyes were blue fire. He pursed his mouth tight, and watched. A Frenchman just in front had put his money on Lancelot. Wild with excitement, he flailed his arms up and down, yelling *"Lancelot! Lancelot!"* in his French accent.

Daffodil came in first, Lancelot second, Mirza third. The child, flushed and with eyes blazing, was curiously serene. His uncle brought him four five-pound notes, four to one.

"What am I to do with these?" he cried, waving them before the boy's eyes.

"I suppose we'll talk to Bassett," said the boy. "I expect I have fifteen hundred now; and twenty in reserve; and this twenty."

His uncle studied him for some moments.

"Look here, son!" he said. "You're not serious about Bassett and that fifteen hundred, are you?"

"Yes, I am. But it's between you and me, Uncle. Honor bright!"

"Honor bright all right, son! But I must talk to Bassett."

"If you'd like to be a partner, Uncle, with Bassett and me, we could all be partners. Only, you'd have to promise, honor bright, Uncle, not to let it go beyond us three. Bassett and I are lucky, and you must be lucky, because it was your ten shillings I started winning with. . . ."

Uncle Oscar took both Bassett and Paul into Richmond Park for an afternoon, and there they talked.

"It's like this, you see, sir," Bassett said. "Master Paul would get me talking about racing events, spinning yarns, you know, sir. And he was always keen on knowing if I'd made or if I'd lost. It's about a year since, now, that I put five shillings on Blush of Dawn for him — and we lost. Then the luck turned, with that ten shillings he had from you, that we put on Singhalese. And since then, it's been pretty steady, all things considering. What do you say, Master Paul?"

"We're all right when we're sure," said Paul. "It's when we're not quite sure that we go down."

"Oh, but we're careful then," said Bassett.

"But when are you *sure*?" Uncle Oscar smiled.

"It's Master Paul, sir," said Bassett, in a secret, religious voice. "It's as if he had it from heaven. Like Daffodil, now, for the Lincoln. That was as sure as eggs."

"Did you put anything on Daffodil?" asked Oscar Cresswell.

"Yes, sir. I made my bit."

"And my nephew?"

Bassett was obstinately silent, looking at Paul.

"I made twelve hundred, didn't I, Bassett? I told Uncle I was putting three hundred on Daffodil."

"That's right," said Bassett, nodding.

"But where's the money?" asked the uncle.

"I keep it safe locked up, sir. Master Paul he can have it any minute he likes to ask for it."

"What, fifteen hundred pounds?"

"And twenty! And *forty*, that is, with the twenty he made on the course."

"It's amazing!" said the uncle.

"If Master Paul offers you to be partners, sir, I would, if I were you; if you'll excuse me," said Bassett.

Oscar Cresswell thought about it.

"I'll see the money," he said.

They drove home again, and sure enough, Bassett came round to the garden house with fifteen hundred pounds in notes. The twenty pounds reserve was left with Joe Glee, in the Turf Commission deposit.

"You see, it's all right, Uncle, when I'm *sure!* Then we go strong, for all we're worth. Don't we, Bassett?"

"We do that, Master Paul."

"And when are you sure?" said the uncle, laughing.

"Oh, well, sometimes I'm *absolutely* sure, like about Daffodil," said the boy; "and sometimes I have an idea; and sometimes I haven't even an idea, have I, Bassett? Then we're careful, because we mostly go down."

"You do, do you! And when you're sure, like about Daffodil, what makes you sure, sonny?"

"Oh, well, I don't know," said the boy uneasily. "I'm sure, you know, Uncle; that's all."

"It's as if he had it from heaven, sir," Bassett reiterated.

"I should say so!" said the uncle.

But he became a partner. And when the Leger was coming on, Paul was "sure" about Lively Spark, which was a quite inconsiderable horse. The boy insisted on putting a thousand on the horse, Bassett went for five hundred, and Oscar Cresswell two hundred. Lively Spark came in first, and the betting had been ten to one against him. Paul had made ten thousand.

"You see," he said, "I was *absolutely* sure of him."

Even Oscar Cresswell had cleared two thousand.

"Look here, son," he said, "this sort of thing makes me nervous."

"It needn't, Uncle! Perhaps I shan't be sure again for a long time."

"But what are you going to do with your money?" asked the uncle.

"Of course," said the boy. "I started it for Mother. She said she had no luck, because Father is unlucky, so I thought if I was lucky, it might stop whispering."

"What might stop whispering?"

"Our house. I *hate* our house for whispering."

"What does it whisper?"

"Why — why" — the boy fidgeted — "why, I don't know. But it's always short of money, you know, Uncle."

"I know it, son, I know it."

"You know people send Mother writs, don't you, Uncle?"

"I'm afraid I do," said the uncle.

"And then the house whispers, like people laughing at you behind your back. It's awful, that is! I thought if I was lucky. . . ."

"You might stop it," added the uncle.

The boy watched him with big blue eyes, that had an uncanny cold fire in them, and he said never a word.

"Well, then!" said the uncle. "What are we doing?"

"I shouldn't like Mother to know I was lucky," said the boy.

"Why not, son?"

"She'd stop me."

"I don't think she would."

"Oh!" — and the boy writhed in an odd way — "I *don't* want her to know, Uncle."

"All right, son! We'll manage it without her knowing."

They managed it very easily. Paul, at the other's suggestion, handed over five thousand pounds to his uncle, who deposited it with the family lawyer, who was then to inform Paul's mother that a relative had put five thousand pounds into his hands. which sum was to be paid out a thousand pounds at a time, on the mother's birthday, for the next five years.

"So she'll have a birthday present of a thousand pounds for five successive years," said Uncle Oscar. "I hope it won't make it all the harder for her later."

Paul's mother had her birthday in November. The house had been "whispering" worse than ever lately, and, even in spite of his luck, Paul could not bear up against it. He was very anxious to see the effect of the birthday letter, telling his mother about the thousand pounds.

When there were no visitors, Paul now took his meals with his parents, as he was beyond the nursery control. His mother went into town nearly every day. She had discovered that she had an odd knack of sketching furs and dress materials, so she worked secretly in the studio of a friend who was the chief artist for the leading drapers. She drew the figures of ladies in furs and ladies in silk and sequins for the newspaper advertisements. This young woman artist earned several thousand pounds a year, but Paul's mother only made several hundred, and she was again dissatisfied. She so wanted to be first in something, and she did not succeed, even in making sketches for drapery advertisements.

She was down to breakfast on the morning of her birthday. Paul watched her face as she read her letters. He knew the lawyer's letter. As his mother read it, her face hardened and became more expressionless. Then a cold, determined look came on her mouth. She hid the letter under the pile of others, and said not a word about it.

"Didn't you have anything nice in the post for your birthday, Mother?" said Paul.

"Quite moderately nice," she said, her voice cold and absent.

She went away to town without saying more.

But in the afternoon Uncle Oscar appeared. He said Paul's mother had had a long interview with the lawyer, asking if the whole five thousand could not be advanced at once, as she was in debt.

"What do you think, Uncle?" said the boy.

"I leave it to you, son."

"Oh, let her have it, then! We can get some more with the other," said the boy.

"A bird in the hand is worth two in the bush, laddie!" said Uncle Oscar.

"But I'm sure to *know*, for the Grand National; or the Lincolnshire; or else the Derby. I'm sure to know for *one* of them," said Paul.

So Uncle Oscar signed the agreement, and Paul's mother touched the whole five thousand. Then something very curious happened. The voices in the house suddenly went mad, like a chorus of frogs on a spring evening. There were certain new furnishings, and Paul had a tutor. He was *really* going to Eton, his father's school, in the following autumn. There were flowers in the winter, and a blossoming of the luxury Paul's mother had been used to. And yet the voices in the house, behind the sprays of mimosa and almond blossom, and from under the piles of iridescent cushions, simply trilled and screamed in a sort of ecstasy: "There *must* be more money! Oh-h-h; there *must* be more money. Oh, now, now-w! Now-w-w — there *must* be more money! — more than ever! More than ever!"

It frightened Paul terribly. He studied away at his Latin and Greek. But his intense hours were spent with Bassett. The Grand National had gone by; he had not "known," and had lost a hundred pounds. Summer was at hand. He was in agony for the Lincoln. But even for the Lincoln he didn't "know," and he lost fifty pounds. He became wild-eyed and strange, as if something were going to explode in him.

"Let it alone, son! Don't you bother about it!" urged Uncle Oscar. But it was as if the boy couldn't really hear what his uncle was saying.

"I've got to know for the Derby! I've got to know for the Derby!" the child reiterated, his big blue eyes blazing with a sort of madness.

His mother noticed how overwrought he was.

"You'd better go to the seaside. Wouldn't you like to go now to the seaside, instead of waiting? I think you'd better," she said, looking down at him anxiously, her heart curiously heavy because of him.

But the child lifted his uncanny blue eyes. "I couldn't possibly go before the Derby, Mother!" he said. "I couldn't possibly!"

"Why not?" she said, her voice becoming heavy when she was opposed. "Why not? You can still go from the seaside to see the Derby with your uncle Oscar, if that's what you wish. No need for you to wait here. Besides, I think you care too much about these races. It's a bad sign. My family has been a gambling family, and you won't know till you grow up how much damage it has done. But it has done damage. I shall have to send Bassett away, and ask Uncle Oscar not to talk racing to you, unless you promise to be reasonable about it; go away to the seaside and forget it. You're all nerves!"

"I'll do what you like, Mother, so long as you don't send me away till after the Derby," the boy said.

"Send you away from where? Just from this house?"

"Yes," he said, gazing at her.

"Why, you curious child, what makes you care about this house so much, suddenly? I never knew you loved it."

He gazed at her without speaking. He had a secret within a secret, something he had not divulged, even to Bassett or to his uncle Oscar.

But his mother, after standing undecided and a little bit sullen for some moments, said:

"Very well, then! Don't go to the seaside till after the Derby, if you don't wish it. But promise me you won't let your nerves go to pieces. Promise you won't think so much about horse racing and *events,* as you call them!"

"Oh, no," said the boy casually. "I won't think much about them, Mother. You needn't worry. I wouldn't worry, Mother, if I were you."

"If you were me and I were you," said his mother, "I wonder what we *should* do!"

"But you know you needn't worry, Mother, don't you?" the boy repeated.

"I should be awfully glad to know it," she said wearily.

"Oh, well you *can,* you know. I mean, you *ought* to know you needn't worry," he insisted.

"Ought I? Then I'll see about it," she said.

Paul's secret of secrets was his wooden horse, that which had no name. Since he was emancipated from a nurse and a nursery governess, he had had his rocking horse removed to his own bedroom at the top of the house.

"Surely, you're too big for a rocking horse!" his mother had remonstrated.

"Well, you see, Mother, till I can have a *real* horse, I like to have *some* sort of animal about," had been his quaint answer.

"Do you feel he keeps you company?" She laughed.

"Oh, yes! He's very good, he always keeps me company, when I'm there," said Paul.

So the horse, rather shabby, stood in an arrested prance in the boy's bedroom.

The Derby was drawing near, and the boy grew more and more tense. He hardly heard what was spoken to him, he was very frail, and his eyes were really uncanny. His mother had sudden strange seizures of uneasiness about him.

Sometimes, for half an hour, she would feel a sudden anxiety about him that was almost anguish. She wanted to rush to him at once, and know he was safe.

Two nights before the Derby, she was at a big party in town, when one of her rushes of anxiety about her boy, her firstborn, gripped her heart till she could hardly speak. She fought with the feeling, might and main, for she believed in common sense. But it was too strong. She had to leave the dance and go downstairs to telephone to the country. The children's nursery governess was terribly surprised and startled at being rung up in the night.

"Are the children all right, Miss Wilmot?"

"Oh, yes, they are quite all right."

"Master Paul? Is he all right?"

"He went to bed as right as a trivet. Shall I run up and look at him?"

"No," said Paul's mother reluctantly. "No! Don't trouble. It's all right. Don't sit up. We shall be home fairly soon." She did not want her son's privacy intruded upon.

"Very good," said the governess.

It was about one o'clock when Paul's mother and father drove up to their house. All was still. Paul's mother went to her room and slipped off her white fur cloak. She had told her maid not to wait up for her. She heard her husband downstairs, mixing a whisky and soda.

And then, because of the strange anxiety at her heart, she stole upstairs to her son's room. Noiselessly she went along the upper corridor. Was there a faint noise? What was it?

She stood, with arrested muscles, outside his door, listening. There was a strange, heavy, and yet not loud noise. Her heart stood still. It was a soundless noise, yet rushing and powerful. Something huge, in violent, hushed motion. What was it? What in God's name was it? She ought to know. She felt that she knew the noise. She knew what it was.

Yet she could not place it. She couldn't say what it was. And on and on it went, like a madness.

Softly, frozen with anxiety and fear, she turned the door handle.

The room was dark. Yet in the space near the window, she heard and saw something plunging to and fro. She gazed in fear and amazement.

Then suddenly she switched on the light, and saw her son, in his green pajamas, madly surging on the rocking horse. The blaze of light suddenly lit him up, as he urged the wooden horse, and lit her up, as she stood, blonde, in her dress of pale green and crystal, in the doorway.

"Paul!" she cried. "Whatever are you doing?"

"It's Malabar!" he screamed, in a powerful, strange voice. "It's Malabar!"

His eyes blazed at her for one strange and senseless second, as he ceased urging his wooden horse. Then he fell with a crash to the ground, and she, all her tormented motherhood flooding upon her, rushed to gather him up.

But he was unconscious, and unconscious he remained, with some brain fever. He talked and tossed, and his mother sat stonily by his side.

"Malabar! It's Malabar! Bassett, Bassett, I *know!* It's Malabar!"

So the child cried, trying to get up and urge the rocking horse that gave him his inspiration.

"What does he mean by Malabar?" asked the heart-frozen mother.

"I don't know," said the father stonily.

"What does he mean by Malabar?" she asked her brother Oscar.

"It's one of the horses running for the Derby," was the answer.

And, in spite of himself, Oscar Cresswell spoke to Bassett, and himself put a thousand on Malabar: at fourteen to one.

The third day of the illness was critical: they were waiting for a change. The boy, with his rather long, curly hair, was tossing ceaselessly on the pillow. He never slept nor regained consciousness, and his eyes were like blue stones. His mother sat, feeling her heart had gone, turned actually into a stone.

In the evening, Oscar Cresswell did not come, but Bassett sent a message, saying could he come up for one moment, just one moment? Paul's mother was very angry at the intrusion, but on second thought she agreed. The boy was the same. Perhaps Bassett might bring him to consciousness.

The gardener, a shortish fellow with a little brown mustache, and sharp little brown eyes, tiptoed into the room, touched his imaginary cap to Paul's mother, and stole to the bedside, staring with glittering, smallish eyes at the tossing, dying child.

"Master Paul!" he whispered. "Master Paul! Malabar came in first all right, a clean win. I did as you told me. You've made over seventy thousand pounds, you have; you've got over eighty thousand. Malabar came in all right, Master Paul."

"Malabar! Malabar! Did I say Malabar, Mother? Did I say Malabar? Do you think I'm lucky, Mother? I knew Malabar, didn't I? Over eighty thousand pounds! I call that lucky, don't you, Mother? Over eighty thousand pounds! I knew, didn't I know I knew? Malabar came in all right. If I ride my horse till I'm sure, then I tell you, Bassett, you can go as high as you like. Did you go for all you were worth, Bassett?"

"I went a thousand on it, Master Paul."

"I never told you, Mother, that if I can ride my horse, and *get there*, then I'm absolutely sure — oh, absolutely! Mother, did I ever tell you? I *am* lucky!"

"No, you never did," said the mother.

But the boy died in the night.

And even as he lay dead, his mother heard her brother's voice saying to her: "My God, Hester, you're eighty-odd thousand to the good, and a poor devil of a son to the bad. But, poor devil, poor devil, he's best gone out of a life where he rides his rocking horse to find a winner."

Questions for Discussion

1. What is revealed about the mother through the description of her in the opening paragraphs of the story? How do her negative feelings about her life influence the outcome of the story?

2. How does the unspoken phrase "*There must be more money!*" influence the children? Why does the phrase remain unspoken?

3. How does the boy Paul come to understand the idea of "luck"? In what ways is this concept linked in his mind to the ideas of God and love? How does the concept of luck motivate him and transform his life?

4. In what ways does the central symbol of the story, the rocking horse, help to present the story's critique of materialism? Why is a toy horse an appropriate symbol here?

5. Discuss the characters of Uncle Oscar and Bassett, the young gardener and former servant of Oscar. How do they contribute to Paul's "luck" and to his self-destruction? What critique of their behavior does the story make?

Ideas for Writing

1. Interpret in an essay both the causes that lead to Paul's death and the larger significance of his death in relation to the story's themes and values.

2. Write a story about a child's response to the unhappiness and neediness of his or her parents.

KATHERINE MANSFIELD (1888–1923)

Influenced by Anton Chekhov, Katherine Mansfield departed in her stories from traditional author commentary on characters and their motivations. Instead, she relied on images, metaphors, brief exchanges of dialogue, interior monologue, and intensely felt moments of awareness to reveal character and theme.

Mansfield was born in Wellington, New Zealand, where her father was a successful banker. In 1903 he took his family to London, where Katherine studied music and literature at Queen's College. She revisited New Zealand in 1906 but felt restricted by the provincialism there and so returned to London in 1908 to pursue a career in music. Soon, however, she realized that she was more interested in writing. After an unhappy marriage and a thwarted love affair, Mansfield went to live and write in Germany for a year. Soon after her return to London she published her first collection of stories, *In a German Pension* (1911). At this time Mansfield met the editor and writer John Middleton Murry, who became her second husband and published her criticism in *Rhythm* magazine. Mansfield contracted tuberculosis in 1917 and never recovered; she died in 1923, when she was only thirty-four.

Mansfield's short-story collections include *Bliss and Other Stories* (1920), *The Garden-Party and Other Stories* (1922), and *The Dove's Nest and Other Stories* (1923). Much of her work — including criticism, unfinished stories, journals, and letters — was published after her death by Murry.

A Dill Pickle (1920)

And then, after six years, she saw him again. He was seated at one of those little bamboo tables decorated with a Japanese vase of paper daffodils. There was a tall plate of fruit in front of him, and very carefully, in a way she recognized immediately as his "special" way, he was peeling an orange.

He must have felt that shock of recognition in her for he looked up and met her eyes. Incredible! He didn't know her! She smiled; he frowned. She came towards him. He closed his eyes an instant, but opening them his face lit up as though he had struck a match in a dark room. He laid down the orange and pushed back his chair, and she took her little warm hand out of her muff and gave it to him.

"Vera!" he exclaimed. "How strange. Really, for a moment I didn't know you. Won't you sit down? You've had lunch? Won't you have some coffee?"

She hesitated, but of course she meant to.

"Yes, I'd like some coffee." And she sat down opposite him.

"You've changed. You've changed very much," he said, staring at her with that eager, lighted look. "You look so well. I've never seen you look so well before."

"Really?" She raised her veil and unbuttoned her high fur collar. "I don't feel very well. I can't bear this weather, you know."

"Ah, no. You hate the cold. . . ."

"Loathe it." She shuddered. "And the worst of it is that the older one grows . . ."

He interrupted her. "Excuse me," and tapped on the table for the waitress. "Please bring some coffee and cream." To her: "You are sure you won't eat anything? Some fruit, perhaps. The fruit here is very good."

"No, thanks. Nothing."

"Then that's settled." And smiling just a hint too broadly he took up the orange again. "You were saying — the older one grows — "

"The colder," she laughed. But she was thinking how well she remembered that trick of his — the trick of interrupting her — and of how it used to exasperate her six years ago. She used to feel then as though he, quite suddenly, in the middle of what she was saying, put his hand over her lips, turned from her, attended to something different, and then took his hand away, and with just the same slightly too broad smile, gave her his attention again. . . . Now we are ready. That is settled.

"The colder!" He echoed her words, laughing too. "Ah, ah. You still say the same things. And there is another thing about you that is not changed at all — your beautiful voice — your beautiful way of speaking." Now he was very grave; he leaned towards her, and she smelled the warm, stinging scent of the orange peel. "You have only to say one word and I would know your voice among all other voices. I don't know what it is — I've often wondered — that makes your voice such a — haunting memory. . . . Do you remember that first afternoon we spent together at Kew Gardens? You were so surprised because I did not know the names of any flowers. I am still just as ignorant for all your telling me. But whenever it is very fine and warm, and I see some bright colours — it's awfully strange — I hear your voice saying: 'Geranium, marigold and verbena.' And I feel those three words are all I recall of some forgotten, heavenly language. . . . You remember that afternoon?"

"Oh, yes, very well." She drew a long, soft breath, as though the paper daffodils between them were almost too sweet to bear. Yet, what had remained in her mind of that particular afternoon was an absurd scene over the tea table. A great many people taking tea in a Chinese pagoda, and he behaving like a maniac about the wasps — waving them away, flapping at them with his straw hat, serious and infuriated out of all proportion to the occasion. How delighted the sniggering tea drinkers had been. And how she had suffered.

But now, as he spoke, that memory faded. His was the truer. Yes, it had been a wonderful afternoon, full of geranium and marigold and verbena, and —

warm sunshine. Her thoughts lingered over the last two words as though she sang them.

In the warmth, as it were, another memory unfolded. She saw herself sitting on a lawn. He lay beside her, and suddenly, after a long silence, he rolled over and put his head in her lap.

"I wish," he said, in a low, troubled voice, "I wish that I had taken poison and were about to die — here now!"

At that moment a little girl in a white dress, holding a long, dripping water lily, dodged from behind a bush, stared at them, and dodged back again. But he did not see. She leaned over him.

"Ah, why do you say that? I could not say that."

But he gave a kind of soft moan, and taking her hand he held it to his cheek.

"Because I know I am going to love you too much — far too much. And I shall suffer so terribly, Vera, because you never, never will love me."

He was certainly far better looking now than he had been then. He had lost all that dreamy vagueness and indecision. Now he had the air of a man who has found his place in life, and fills it with a confidence and an assurance which was, to say the least, impressive. He must have made money, too. His clothes were admirable, and at that moment he pulled a Russian cigarette case out of his pocket.

"Won't you smoke?"

"Yes, I will." She hovered over them. "They look very good."

"I think they are. I get them made for me by a little man in St. James's Street. I don't smoke very much. I'm not like you — but when I do, they must be delicious, very fresh cigarettes. Smoking isn't a habit with me; it's a luxury — like perfume. Are you still so fond of perfumes? Ah, when I was in Russia . . ."

She broke in: "You've really been to Russia?"

"Oh, yes. I was there for over a year. Have you forgotten how we used to talk of going there?"

"No, I've not forgotten."

He gave a strange half laugh and leaned back in his chair. "Isn't it curious. I have really carried out all those journeys that we planned. Yes, I have been to all those places that we talked of, and stayed in them long enough to — as you used to say, 'air oneself' in them. In fact, I have spent the last three years of my life travelling all the time. Spain, Corsica, Siberia, Russia, Egypt. The only country left is China, and I mean to go there, too, when the war is over."

As he spoke, so lightly, tapping the end of his cigarette against the ash-tray, she felt the strange beast that had slumbered so long within her bosom stir, stretch itself, yawn, prick up its ears, and suddenly bound to its feet, and fix its longing, hungry stare upon those far away places. But all she said was, smiling gently: "How I envy you."

He accepted that. "It has been," he said, "very wonderful — especially

Russia. Russia was all that we had imagined, and far, far more. I even spent some days on a river boat on the Volga. Do you remember that boatman's song that you used to play?"

"Yes." It began to play in her mind as she spoke.

"Do you ever play it now?"

"No, I've no piano."

He was amazed at that. "But what has become of your beautiful piano?"

She made a little grimace. "Sold. Ages ago."

"But you were so fond of music," he wondered.

"I've no time for it now," said she.

He let it go at that. "That river life," he went on, "is something quite special. After a day or two you cannot realize that you have ever known another. And it is not necessary to know the language — the life of the boat creates a bond between you and the people that's more than sufficient. You eat with them, pass the day with them, and in the evening there is that endless singing."

She shivered, hearing the boatman's song break out again loud and tragic, and seeing the boat floating on the darkening river with melancholy trees on either side. . . . "Yes, I should like that," said she, stroking her muff.

"You'd like almost everything about Russian life," he said warmly. "It's so informal, so impulsive, so free without question. And then the peasants are so splendid. They are such human beings — yes, that is it. Even the man who drives your carriage has — has some real part in what is happening. I remember the evening a party of us, two friends of mine and the wife of one of them, went for a picnic by the Black Sea. We took supper and champagne and ate and drank on the grass. And while we were eating the coachman came up. 'Have a dill pickle,' he said. He wanted to share with us. That seemed to me so right, so — you know what I mean?"

And she seemed at that moment to be sitting on the grass beside the mysteriously Black Sea, black as velvet, and rippling against the banks in silent, velvet waves. She saw the carriage drawn up to one side of the road, and the little group on the grass, their faces and hands white in the moonlight. She saw the pale dress of the woman outspread and her folded parasol, lying on the grass like a huge pearl crochet hook. Apart from them, with his supper in a cloth on his knees, sat the coachman. "Have a dill pickle," said he, and although she was not certain what a dill pickle was, she saw the greenish glass jar with a red chili like a parrot's beak glimmering through. She sucked in her cheeks; the dill pickle was terribly sour. . . .

"Yes, I know perfectly what you mean," she said.

In the pause that followed they looked at each other. In the past when they had looked at each other like that they had felt such a boundless understanding between them that their souls had, as it were, put their arms round each other and dropped into the same sea, content to be drowned, like mournful lovers. But now, the surprising thing was that it was he who held back. He who said:

"What a marvellous listener you are. When you look at me with those wild eyes I feel that I could tell you things that I would never breathe to another human being."

Was there just a hint of mockery in his voice or was it her fancy? She could not be sure.

"Before I met you," he said, "I had never spoken of myself to anybody. How well I remember one night, the night that I brought you the little Christmas tree, telling you all about my childhood. And of how I was so miserable that I ran away and lived under a cart in our yard for two days without being discovered. And you listened, and your eyes shone, and I felt that you had even made the little Christmas tree listen too, as in a fairy story."

But of that evening she had remembered a little pot of caviar. It had cost seven and sixpence. He could not get over it. Think of it — a tiny jar like that costing seven and sixpence. While she ate it he watched her, delighted and shocked.

"No, really, that is eating money. You could not get seven shillings into a little pot that size. Only think of the profit they must make. . . ." And he had begun some immensely complicated calculations. . . . But now good-bye to the caviar. The Christmas tree was on the table, and the little boy lay under the cart with his head pillowed on the yard dog.

"The dog was called Bosun," she cried delightedly.

But he did not follow. "Which dog? Had you a dog? I don't remember a dog at all."

"No, no. I mean the yard dog when you were a little boy." He laughed and snapped the cigarette case to.

"Was he? Do you know I had forgotten that. It seems such ages ago. I cannot believe that it is only six years. After I had recognized you to-day — I had to take such a leap — I had to take a leap over my whole life to get back to that time. I was such a kid then." He drummed on the table. "I've often thought how I must have bored you. And now I understand so perfectly why you wrote to me as you did — although at the time that letter nearly finished my life. I found it again the other day, and I couldn't help laughing as I read it. It was so clever — such a true picture of me." He glanced up. "You're not going?"

She had buttoned her collar again and drawn down her veil.

"Yes, I am afraid I must," she said, and managed a smile. Now she knew that he had been mocking.

"Ah, no, please," he pleaded. "Don't go just for a moment," and he caught up one of her gloves from the table and clutched at it as if that would hold her. "I see so few people to talk to nowadays, that I have turned into a sort of barbarian," he said. "Have I said something to hurt you?"

"Not a bit," she lied. But as she watched him draw her glove through his fingers, gently, gently, her anger really did die down, and besides, at the moment he looked more like himself of six years ago. . . .

"What I really wanted then," he said softly, "was to be a sort of carpet — to make myself into a sort of carpet for you to walk on so that you need not be hurt by the sharp stones and the mud that you hated so. It was nothing more positive than that — nothing more selfish. Only I did desire, eventually, to turn into a magic carpet and carry you away to all those lands you longed to see."

As he spoke she lifted her head as though she drank something; the strange beast in her bosom began to purr. . . .

"I felt that you were more lonely than anybody else in the world," he went on, "and yet, perhaps, that you were the only person in the world who was really, truly alive. Born out of your time," he murmured, stroking the glove, "fated."

Ah, God! What had she done! How had she dared to throw away her happiness like this. This was the only man who had ever understood her. Was it too late? Could it be too late? *She* was that glove that he held in his fingers. . . .

"And then the fact that you had no friends and never had made friends with people. How I understood that, for neither had I. Is it just the same now?"

"Yes," she breathed. "Just the same. I am as alone as ever."

"So am I" he laughed gently, "just the same."

Suddenly with a quick gesture he handed her back the glove and scraped his chair on the floor. "But what seemed to me so mysterious then is perfectly plain to me now. And to you, too, of course. . . . It simply was that we were such egoists, so self-engrossed, so wrapped up in ourselves that we hadn't a corner in our hearts for anybody else. Do you know," he cried, naive and hearty, and dreadfully like another side of that old self again, "I began studying a Mind System when I was in Russia, and I found that we were not peculiar at all. It's quite a well known form of . . ."

She had gone. He sat there, thunder-struck, astounded beyond words. . . . And then he asked the waitress for his bill.

"But the cream has not been touched," he said. "Please do not charge me for it."

Questions for Discussion

1. Although they haven't seen each other for six years, Vera notices some familiar, exasperating behavior patterns in the young man. What particularly annoys her about him? Are these habits presented as genuinely annoying, or is Vera being oversensitive?

2. Vera flashes back in her mind to two previous encounters with the young man, both romantic yet disappointing. What was it about the young man in the past that made their relationship fail? Why is Vera's hope for them rekindled?

3. What do Vera's responses to the young man's wealth and travel reveal about her values and current economic status? Who or what is the "strange beast that had slumbered so long within her bosom"?

4. How does Vera's response to the story of the dill pickle reveal her feelings about the exotic experiences the young man is describing? How does the symbol of the

pickle parallel other sensory images associated with the man, such as the orange he peels, the remembered colors of flowers in Kew Gardens, his custom-made "fresh" cigarettes? What is the effect of this symbolism?

5. Why does Vera finally leave? Is she accurate in feeling that the young man has been "mocking"? How does the final scene and the young man's interaction with the waitress contribute to your evaluation of his character and Vera's decision?

Ideas for Writing

1. In an essay, evaluate Vera's character. You might consider her attire (muff, veil, high collar) as well as her thoughts about the young man and her decisions to reject him, six years earlier and at the time of the story. Does she have good common sense? Is she weary of falsehood and exaggeration? Is she overly guarded and fearful of experience and risk?

2. Rewrite the story from the young man's perspective. What would his real impressions of Vera be? How would he respond to her final rejection of him?

The Garden-Party   (1922)

And after all the weather was ideal. They could not have had a more perfect day for a garden-party if they had ordered it. Windless, warm, the sky without a cloud. Only the blue was veiled with a haze of light gold, as it is sometimes in early summer. The gardener had been up since dawn, mowing the lawns and sweeping them, until the grass and the dark flat rosettes where the daisy plants had been seemed to shine. As for the roses, you could not help feeling they understood that roses are the only flowers that impress people at garden-parties; the only flowers that everybody is certain of knowing. Hundreds, yes, literally hundreds, had come out in a single night; the green bushes bowed down as though they had been visited by archangels.

Breakfast was not yet over before the men came to put up the marquee.[1]

"Where do you want the marquee put, mother?"

"My dear child, it's no use asking me. I'm determined to leave everything to you children this year. Forget I am your mother. Treat me as an honoured guest."

But Meg could not possibly go and supervise the men. She had washed her hair before breakfast, and she sat drinking her coffee in a green turban, with a dark wet curl stamped on each cheek. Jose, the butterfly, always came down in a silk petticoat and a kimono jacket.

"You'll have to go, Laura; you're the artistic one."

---

[1] Open-sided tent. — Eds.

Away Laura flew, still holding her piece of bread-and-butter. It's so delicious to have an excuse for eating out of doors, and besides, she loved having to arrange things; she always felt she could do it so much better than anybody else.

Four men in their shirt-sleeves stood grouped together on the garden path. They carried staves covered with rolls of canvas, and they had big tool-bags slung on their backs. They looked impressive. Laura wished now that she had not got the bread-and-butter, but there was nowhere to put it, and she couldn't possibly throw it away. She blushed and tried to look severe and even a little bit short-sighted as she came up to them.

"Good morning," she said, copying her mother's voice. But that sounded so fearfully affected that she was ashamed, and stammered like a little girl, "Oh — er — have you come — is it about the marquee?"

"That's right, miss," said the tallest of the men, a lanky, freckled fellow, and he shifted his tool-bag, knocked back his straw hat and smiled down at her. "That's about it."

His smile was so easy, so friendly that Laura recovered. What nice eyes he had, small, but such a dark blue! And now she looked at the others, they were smiling too. "Cheer up, we won't bite," their smile seemed to say. How very nice workmen were! And what a beautiful morning! She mustn't mention the morning; she must be businesslike. The marquee.

"Well, what about the lily-lawn? Would that do?"

And she pointed to the lily-lawn with the hand that didn't hold the bread-and-butter. They turned, they stared in the direction. A little fat chap thrust out his under-lip, and the tall fellow frowned.

"I don't fancy it," said he. "Not conspicuous enough. You see, with a thing like a marquee," and he turned to Laura in his easy way, "you want to put it somewhere where it'll give you a bang slap in the eye, if you follow me."

Laura's upbringing made her wonder for a moment whether it was quite respectful of a workman to talk to her of bangs slap in the eye. But she did quite follow him.

"A corner of the tennis-court," she suggested. "But the band's going to be in one corner."

"H'm, going to have a band, are you?" said another of the workmen. He was pale. He had a haggard look as his dark eyes scanned the tennis-court. What was he thinking?

"Only a very small band," said Laura gently. Perhaps he wouldn't mind so much if the band was quite small. But the tall fellow interrupted.

"Look here, miss, that's the place. Against those trees. Over there. That'll do fine."

Against the karakas. Then the karaka trees would be hidden. And they were so lovely, with their broad, gleaming leaves, and their clusters of yellow fruit. They were like trees you imagined growing on a desert island, proud, solitary, lifting their leaves and fruits to the sun in a kind of silent splendour. Must they be hidden by a marquee?

They must. Already the men had shouldered their staves and were making for the place. Only the tall fellow was left. He bent down, pinched a sprig of lavender, put his thumb and forefinger to his nose and snuffed up the smell. When Laura saw that gesture she forgot all about the karakas in her wonder at him caring for things like that — caring for the smell of lavender. How many men that she knew would have done such a thing? Oh, how extraordinarily nice workmen were, she thought. Why couldn't she have workmen for friends rather than the silly boys she danced with and who came to Sunday night supper? She would get on much better with men like these.

It's all the fault, she decided, as the tall fellow drew something on the back of an envelope, something that was to be looped up or left to hang, of these absurd class distinctions. Well, for her part, she didn't feel them. Not a bit, not an atom. . . . And now there came the chock-chock of wooden hammers. Some one whistled, some one sang out, "Are you right there, matey?" "Matey!" The friendliness of it, the — the — Just to prove how happy she was, just to show the tall fellow how at home she felt, and how she despised stupid conventions, Laura took a big bite of her bread-and-butter as she stared at the little drawing. She felt just like a work-girl.

"Laura, Laura, where are you? Telephone, Laura!" a voice cried from the house.

"Coming!" Away she skimmed, over the lawn, up the path, up the steps, across the verandah, and into the porch. In the hall her father and Laurie were brushing their hats ready to go to the office.

"I say, Laura," said Laurie very fast, "you might just give a squiz at my coat before this afternoon. See if it wants pressing."

"I will," said she. Suddenly she couldn't stop herself. She ran at Laurie and gave him a small, quick squeeze. "Oh, I do love parties, don't you?" gasped Laura.

"Rather," said Laurie's warm, boyish voice, and he squeezed his sister too, and gave her a gentle push. "Dash off to the telephone, old girl."

The telephone. "Yes, yes; oh yes. Kitty? Good morning, dear. Come to lunch? Do, dear. Delighted of course. It will only be a very scratch meal — just the sandwich crusts and broken meringue-shells and what's left over. Yes, isn't it a perfect morning? Your white? Oh, I certainly should. One moment — hold the line. Mother's calling." And Laura sat back. "What, mother? Can't hear."

Mrs. Sheridan's voice floated down the stairs. "Tell her to wear that sweet hat she had on last Sunday."

"Mother says you're to wear that *sweet* hat you had on last Sunday. Good. One o'clock. Bye-bye."

Laura put back the receiver, flung her arms over her head, took a deep breath, stretched and let them fall. "Huh," she sighed, and the moment after the sigh she sat up quickly. She was still, listening. All the doors in the house seemed to open. The house was alive with soft, quick steps and running voices. The green baize door that led to the kitchen regions swung open and shut with a muffled thud. And now there came a long, chuckling absurd sound. It was the heavy piano being moved on its stiff castors. But the air! If you stopped to notice, was the air always like this? Little faint winds were playing chase, in at the tops of the windows, out at the doors. And there were two tiny spots of sun, one on the inkpot, one on a silver photograph frame, playing too. Darling little spots. Especially the one on the inkspot lid. It was quite warm. A warm little silver star. She could have kissed it.

The front door bell pealed, and there sounded the rustle of Sadie's print skirt on the stairs. A man's voice murmured; Sadie answered, careless, "I'm sure I don't know. Wait. I'll ask Mrs. Sheridan."

"What is it, Sadie?" Laura came into the hall.

"It's the florist, Miss Laura."

It was, indeed. There, just inside the door, stood a wide, shallow tray full of pots of pink lilies. No other kind. Nothing but lilies — canna lilies, big pink flowers, wide open, radiant, almost frighteningly alive on bright crimson stems.

"O-oh, Sadie!" said Laura, and the sound was like a little moan. She crouched down as if to warm herself at that blaze of lilies; she felt they were in her fingers, on her lips, growing in her breast.

"It's some mistake," she said faintly. "Nobody ever ordered so many. Sadie, go and find mother."

But at that moment Mrs. Sheridan joined them.

"It's quite right," she said calmly. "Yes, I ordered them. Aren't they lovely?" She pressed Laura's arm. "I was passing the shop yesterday, and I saw them in the window. And I suddenly thought for once in my life I shall have enough canna lilies. The garden-party will be a good excuse."

"But I thought you said you didn't mean to interfere," said Laura. Sadie had gone. The florist's man was still outside at his van. She put her arm round her mother's neck and gently, very gently, she bit her mother's ear.

"My darling child, you wouldn't like a logical mother, would you? Don't do that. Here's the man."

He carried more lilies still, another whole tray.

"Bank them up, just inside the door, on both sides of the porch, please," said Mrs. Sheridan. "Don't you agree, Laura?"

"Oh, I *do* mother."

In the drawing-room Meg, Jose and good little Hans had at last succeeded in moving the piano.

"Now, if we put this chesterfield against the wall and move everything out of the room except the chairs, don't you think?"

"Quite."

"Hans, move these tables into the smoking-room, and bring a sweeper to take these marks off the carpet and — one moment Hans — " Jose loved giving orders to the servants, and they loved obeying her. She always made them feel they were taking part in some drama. "Tell mother and Miss Laura to come here at once."

"Very good, Miss Jose."

She turned to Meg. "I want to hear what the piano sounds like, just in case I'm asked to sing this afternoon. Let's try over 'This Life is Weary.'"

Pom! Ta-ta-ta *Tee*-ta! The piano burst out so passionately that Jose's face changed. She clasped her hands. She looked mournfully and enigmatically at her mother and Laura as they came in.

> This Life is *Wee*-ary,
> A Tear — a Sigh.
> A Love that *Chan*-ges.
>   This life is *Wee*-ary,
> A Tear — a Sigh.
> A Love that *Chan*-ges,
> And then . . . Good-bye!

But at the word "Good-bye," and although the piano sounded more desperate than ever, her face broke into a brilliant, dreadfully unsympathetic smile. "Aren't I in good voice, mummy?" she beamed.

> This Life is *Wee*-ary,
> Hope comes to Die.
> A Dream — a *Wa*-kening.

But now Sadie interrupted them. "What is it, Sadie?"

"If you please, m'm, cook says have you got the flags[2] for the sandwiches?"

"The flags for the sandwiches, Sadie?" echoed Mrs. Sheridan dreamily. And the children knew by her face that she hadn't got them. "Let me see." And she said to Sadie firmly, "Tell cook I'll let her have them in ten minutes."

Sadie went.

"Now, Laura," said her mother quickly. "Come with me into the smoking-room. I've got the names somewhere on the back of an envelope. You'll have to write them out for me. Meg, go upstairs this minute and take that wet thing off your head. Jose, run and finish dressing this instant. Do you hear me, children, or shall I have to tell your father when he comes home to-night? And — and, Jose, pacify cook if you do go into the kitchen will you? I'm terrified of her this morning."

The envelope was found at last behind the dining-room clock, though how it had got there Mrs. Sheridan could not imagine.

"One of you children must have stolen it out of my bag, because I remember vividly — cream cheese and lemon-curd. Have you done that?"

"Yes."

"Egg and — " Mrs. Sheridan held the envelope away from her. "It looks like mice. It can't be mice, can it?"

"Olive, pet," said Laura, looking over her shoulder.

---

[2] Decorations made of paper, held on by toothpicks. — Eds.

"Yes, of course, olive. What a horrible combination it sounds. Egg and olive."

They were finished at last, and Laura took them off to the kitchen. She found Jose there pacifying the cook, who did not look at all terrifying.

"I have never seen such exquisite sandwiches," said Jose's rapturous voice. "How many kinds did you say there were, cook? Fifteen?"

"Fifteen, Miss Jose."

"Well, cook, I congratulate you."

Cook swept up crusts with the long sandwich knife, and smiled broadly.

"Godber's has come," announced Sadie, issuing out of the pantry. She had seen the man pass the window.

That meant the cream puffs had come. Godber's were famous for their cream puffs. Nobody ever thought of making them at home.

"Bring them in and put them on the table, my girl," ordered cook.

Sadie brought them in and went back to the door. Of course Laura and Jose were far too grown-up to really care about such things. All the same, they couldn't help agreeing that the puffs looked very attractive. Very. Cook began arranging them, shaking off the extra icing sugar.

"Don't they carry one back to all one's parties?" said Laura.

"I suppose they do," said practical Jose, who never liked to be carried back. "They look beautifully light and feathery, I must say."

"Have one each, my dears," said cook in her comfortable voice. "Yer ma won't know."

Oh, impossible. Fancy cream puffs so soon after breakfast. The very idea made one shudder. All the same, two minutes later Jose and Laura were licking their fingers with that absorbed inward look that only comes from whipped cream.

"Let's go into the garden, out by the back way," suggested Laura. "I want to see how the men are getting on with the marquee. They're such awfully nice men."

But the back door was blocked by cook, Sadie, Godber's man and Hans.

Something had happened.

"Tuk-tuk-tuk," clucked cook like an agitated hen. Sadie had her hand clapped to her cheek as though she had toothache. Hans's face was screwed up in the effort to understand. Only Godber's man seemed to be enjoying himself; it was his story.

"What's the matter? What's happened?"

"There's been a horrible accident," said cook. "A man killed."

"A man killed! Where? How? When?"

But Godber's man wasn't going to have his story snatched from under his very nose.

"Know those little cottages just below here, miss?" Know them? Of course, she knew them. "Well, there's a young chap living there, name of Scott, a carter. His horse shied at a traction-engine, corner of Hawke Street this morning, and he was thrown out on the back of his head. Killed."

"Dead!" Laura stared at Godber's man.

"Dead when they picked him up," said Godber's man with relish. "They were taking the body home as I come up here." And he said to the cook, "He's left a wife and five little ones."

"Jose, come here." Laura caught hold of her sister's sleeve and dragged her through the kitchen to the other side of the green baize door. There she paused and leaned against it. "Jose!" she said, horrified, "however, are we going to stop everything?"

"Stop everything, Laura!" cried Jose in astonishment. "What do you mean?"

"Stop the garden-party, of course." Why did Jose pretend?

But Jose was still more amazed. "Stop the garden-party? My dear Laura, don't be so absurd. Of course we can't do anything of the kind. Nobody expects us to. Don't be so extravagant."

"But we can't possibly have a garden-party with a man dead just outside the front gate."

That really was extravagant, for the little cottages were in a lane to themselves at the very bottom of a steep rise that led up to the house. A broad road ran between. True, they were far too near. They were the greatest possible eyesore, and they had no right to be in that neighbourhood at all. They were little mean dwellings painted a chocolate brown. In the garden patches there was nothing but cabbage stalks, sick hens and tomato cans. The very smoke coming out of their chimneys was poverty-stricken. Little rags and shreds of smoke, so unlike the great silvery plumes that uncurled from the Sheridan's chimneys. Washerwomen lived in the lane and sweeps and a cobbler, and a man whose house-front was studded all over with minute bird-cages. Children swarmed. When the Sheridans were little they were forbidden to set foot there because of the revolting language and of what they might catch. But since they were grown up, Laura and Laurie on their prowls sometimes walked through. It was disgusting and sordid. They came out with a shudder. But still one must go everywhere; one must see everything. So through they went.

"And just think of what the band would sound like to that poor woman," said Laura.

"Oh, Laura!" Jose began to be seriously annoyed. "If you're going to stop a band playing every time some one has an accident, you'll lead a very strenuous life. I'm every bit as sorry about it as you. I feel just as sympathetic." Her eyes hardened. She looked at her sister just as she used to when they were little and fighting together. "You won't bring a drunken workman back to life by being sentimental," she said softly.

"Drunk! Who said he was drunk?" Laura turned furiously on Jose. She said, just as they had used to say on those occasions, "I'm going straight up to tell mother."

"Do dear," cooed Jose.

"Mother, can I come into your room?" Laura turned the big glass door-knob.

"Of course, child. Why, what's the matter? What's given you such a colour?" And Mrs. Sheridan turned round from her dressing table. She was trying on a new hat.

"Mother, a man's been killed," began Laura.

"*Not* in the garden?" interrupted her mother.

"No, no!"

"Oh, what a fright you gave me!" Mrs. Sheridan sighed with relief, and took off the big hat and held it on her knees.

"But listen, mother," said Laura. Breathless, half-choking, she told the dreadful story. "Of course, we can't have our party, can we?" she pleaded. "The band and everybody arriving. They'd hear us, mother; they're nearly neighbours!"

To Laura's astonishment her mother behaved just like Jose, it was harder to bear because she seemed amused. She refused to take Laura seriously.

"But, my dear child, use your common sense. It's only by accident we've heard of it. If some one had died there normally — and I can't understand how they keep alive in those poky little holes — we should still be having our party, shouldn't we?"

Laura had to say "yes" to that, but she felt it was all wrong. She sat down on her mother's sofa and pinched the cushion frill.

"Mother, isn't it really terribly heartless of us?" she asked.

"Darling!" Mrs. Sheridan got up and came over to her, carrying the hat. Before Laura could stop her she had popped it on. "My child!" said her mother, "the hat is yours. It's made for you. It's much too young for me. I have never seen you look such a picture. Look at yourself!" And she held up her hand-mirror.

"But, mother," Laura began again. She couldn't look at herself; she turned aside.

This time Mrs. Sheridan lost patience just as Jose had done.

"You are being very absurd, Laura," she said coldly. "People like that don't expect sacrifices from us. And it's not very sympathetic to spoil everybody's enjoyment as you're doing now."

"I don't understand," said Laura, and she walked quickly out of the room into her own bedroom. There, quite by chance, the first thing she saw was this charming girl in the mirror, in her black hat trimmed with gold daisies, and a long black velvet ribbon. Never had she imagined she could look like that. Is mother right? she thought. And now she hoped her mother was right. Am I being extravagant? Perhaps it was extravagant. Just for a moment she had another glimpse of that poor woman and those little children, and the body being carried into the house. But it all seemed blurred, unreal, like a picture in the newspaper. I'll remember it again after the party's over, she decided. And somehow that seemed quite the best plan. . . .

Lunch was over by half past one. By half past two they were all ready for the fray. The green-coated band had arrived and was established in a corner of the tennis-court.

"My dear!" trilled Kitty Maitland, "aren't they too like frogs for words? You ought to have arranged them round the pond with the conductor in the middle on a leaf."

Laurie arrived and hailed them on his way to dress. At the sight of him Laura remembered the accident again. She wanted to tell him. If Laurie agreed with the others, then it was bound to be all right. And she followed him into the hall.

"Laurie!" "Hallo!" He was half-way upstairs, but when he turned round and saw Laura he suddenly puffed out his cheeks and goggled his eyes at her. "My word, Laura; you do look stunning," said Laurie. "What an absolutely topping hat!"

Laura said faintly "Is it?" and smiled up at Laurie, and didn't tell him after all.

Soon after that people began coming in streams. The band struck up; the hired waiters ran from the house to the marquee. Wherever you looked there were couples strolling, bending to the flowers, greeting, moving on over the lawn. They were like bright birds that had alighted in the Sheridan's garden for this one afternoon, on their way to — where? Ah, what happiness it is to be with people who all are happy, to press hands, press cheeks, smile into eyes.

"Darling Laura, how well you look!"

"What a becoming hat, child!"

"Laura, you look quite Spanish. I've never seen you look so striking."

And Laura, glowing, answered softly, "Have you had tea? Won't you have an ice? The passion-fruit ices really are rather special." She ran to her father and begged him. "Daddy darling, can't the band have something to drink?"

And the perfect afternoon slowly ripened, slowly faded, slowly its petals closed.

"Never a more delightful garden-party . . ." "The greatest success . . ." "Quite the most . . ."

Laura helped her mother with the good-byes. They stood side by side in the porch till it was all over.

"All over, all over, thank heaven," said Mrs. Sheridan. "Round up the others, Laura. Let's go and have some fresh coffee. I'm exhausted. Yes, it's been very successful. But oh, these parties, these parties! Why will you children insist on giving parties!" And they all of them sat down in the deserted marquee.

"Have a sandwich, daddy dear. I wrote the flag."

"Thanks." Mr. Sheridan took a bite and the sandwich was gone. He took another. "I suppose you didn't hear of a beastly accident that happened to-day?" he said.

"My dear," said Mrs. Sheridan, holding up her hand, "we did. It nearly ruined the party. Laura insisted we should put it off."

"Oh, mother!" Laura did not want to be teased about it.

"It was a horrible affair all the same," said Mr. Sheridan. "The chap was married too. Lived just below in the lane, and leaves a wife and a half a dozen kiddies, so they say."

An awkward little silence fell. Mrs. Sheridan fidgeted with her cup. Really, it was very tactless of father . . .

Suddenly she looked up. There on the table were all those sandwiches, cakes, puffs, all uneaten, all going to be wasted. She had one of her brilliant ideas.

"I know," she said. "Let's make up a basket. Let's send that poor creature some of this perfectly good food. At any rate, it will be the greatest treat for the children. Don't you agree? And she's sure to have neighbours calling in and so on. What a point to have it all ready prepared. Laura!" She jumped up. "Get me the big basket out of the stairs cupboard."

"But, mother, do you really think it's a good idea?" said Laura.

Again, how curious, she seemed to be different from them all. To take scraps from their party. Would the poor woman really like that?

"Of course! What's the matter with you to-day? An hour or two ago you were insisting on us being sympathetic, and now—"

Oh, well! Laura ran for the basket. It was filled, it was heaped by her mother.

"Take it yourself, darling," said she. "Run down just as you are. No, wait, take the arum lilies too. People of that class are so impressed by arum lilies."

"The stems will ruin her lace frock," said practical Jose.

So they would. Just in time. "Only the basket, then. And, Laura!"—her mother followed her out of the marquee—"don't on any account—"

"What, mother?"

No, better not put such ideas into the child's head! "Nothing! Run along."

It was just growing dusky as Laura shut their garden gates. A big dog ran by like a shadow. The road gleamed white, and down below in the hollow the little cottages were in deep shade. How quiet it seemed after the afternoon. Here she was going down the hill to somewhere where a man lay dead, and she couldn't realize it. Why couldn't she? She stopped a minute. And it seemed to her that kisses, voices, tinkling spoons, laughter, the smell of crushed grass were somehow inside her. She had no room for anything else. How strange! She looked up at the pale sky, and all she thought was, "Yes, it was the most successful party."

Now the broad road was crossed. The lane began, smoky and dark. Women in shawls and men's tweed caps hurried by. Men hung over the palings; the children played in the doorways. A low hum came from the mean little cottages. In some of them there was a flicker of light, and a shadow, crablike, moved across the window. Laura bent her head and hurried on. She wished now she had put on a coat. How her frock shone! And the big hat with the velvet streamer—if only it was another hat! Were the people looking at her? They must be. It was a mistake to have come; she knew all along it was a mistake. Should she go back even now?

No, too late. This was the house. It must be. A dark knot of people stood outside. Beside the gate an old, old woman with a crutch sat in a chair, watching. She had her feet on a newspaper. The voices stopped as Laura drew near. The group parted. It was as though she was expected, as though they had known she was coming here.

Laura was terribly nervous. Tossing the velvet ribbon over her shoulder, she said to a woman standing by, "Is this Mrs. Scott's house?" and the woman, smiling queerly, said, "It is, my lass."

Oh, to be away from this! She actually said, "Help me, God," as she walked up the tiny path and knocked. To be away from those staring eyes, or to be covered up in anything, one of those women's shawls even. I'll just leave the basket and go, she decided. I shan't even wait for it to be emptied.

Then the door opened. A little woman in black showed in the gloom.

Laura said, "Are you Mrs. Scott?" But to her horror the woman answered, "Walk in please, miss" and she was shut in the passage.

"No," said Laura, "I don't want to come in. I only want to leave this basket. Mother sent—"

The little woman in the gloomy passage seemed not to have heard her. "Step this way, please, miss," she said in an oily voice, and Laura followed her.

She found herself in a wretched little low kitchen, lighted by a smoky lamp. There was a woman sitting before the fire.

"Em," said the little creature who had let her in. "Em! It's a young lady." She turned to Laura. She said meaningly, "I'm 'er sister, miss. You'll excuse 'er won't you?"

"Oh, but of course!" said Laura. "Please, don't disturb her. I — I only want to leave—"

But at that moment the woman at the fire turned round. Her face, puffed up, red, with swollen eyes and swollen lips, looked terrible. She seemed as though she couldn't understand why Laura was there. What did it mean? Why was this stranger standing in the kitchen with a basket? What was it all about? And the poor face puckered up again.

"All right, my dear," said the other. "I'll thank the young lady."

And again she began, "You'll excuse her, miss, I'm sure" and her face, swollen too, tried an oily smile.

Laura only wanted to get out, to get away. She was back in the passage. The door opened. She walked straight through into the bedroom, where the dead man was lying.

"You'd like a look at 'im, wouldn't you?" said Em's sister, and she brushed past Laura over to the bed. "Don't be afraid, my lass, — " and now her voice sounded fond and sly, and fondly she drew down the sheet — "'e looks a picture. There's nothing to show. Come along, my dear."

Laura came.

There lay a young man, fast asleep — sleeping so soundly, so deeply, that he was far, far away from them both. Oh, so remote, so peaceful. He was dreaming. Never wake him up again. His head was sunk in the pillow, his eyes were closed; they were blind under the closed eyelids. He was given up to his dream. What did garden-parties and baskets and lace frocks matter to him? He was far from all those things. He was wonderful, beautiful. While they were laughing and while the band was playing, this marvel had come to the lane. Happy . . . happy. . . . All is well, said that sleeping face. This is just as it should be. I am content.

But all the same you had to cry, and she couldn't go out of the room without saying something to him. Laura gave a loud childish sob.

"Forgive my hat," she said.

And this time she didn't wait for Em's sister. She found her way out of the door, down the path, past all those dark people. At the corner of the land she met Laurie.

He stepped out of the shadow. "Is that you, Laura?"

"Yes."

"Mother was getting anxious. Was it all right?"

"Yes, quite. Oh, Laurie!" She took his arm, she pressed up against him.

"I say, you're not crying, are you?" asked her brother.

Laura shook her head. She was.

Laurie put his arm round her shoulder. "Don't cry," he said in his warm, loving voice. "Was it awful?"

"No," sobbed Laura. "It was simply marvellous. But. Laurie — " She stopped, she looked at her brother. "Isn't life," she stammered, "Isn't life — " But what life was she couldn't explain. No matter. He quite understood.

"*Isn't* it, darling?" said Laurie.

Questions for Discussion

1. Why does Mansfield begin the story with a description of the "ideal" weather and the impressive roses that have bloomed just before the day of the garden party? How does this description both prepare readers for and contrast ironically with the events that follow?

2. How does Laura feel about the workmen? How do her feelings about these men from a lower social class foreshadow her strong feelings about canceling the garden party? In what ways does the argument between Laura and her mother about canceling the garden party reveal the differences between Laura's values and those of her family?

3. What descriptive images and details are used to contrast life in the cottage where the dead man lived with the life that the Sheridans lead? What is the significance of the "velvet ribbon" on her hat that Laura feels self-conscious about?

4. When the mother compromises by sending Laura to the dead man's house with a basket of food, is she acting out of real sympathy for the dead man and his family or out of her personal and class interests?

5. Why does Laura feel that the dead man is "wonderful, beautiful," and that the experience of seeing him in his home "was simply marvellous"?

Ideas for Writing

1. Analyze the story focusing on Laura's growth. What has she learned from her day? How does she mature from her experiences? What would you predict for her future?

2. Although written in the third person, "The Garden-Party" is told from Laura's viewpoint. Retell one important scene, using a different point of view — that of one of the workmen, of Em Scott, of Mrs. Sheridan, or of Laura's brother Laurie.

Katherine Mansfield

Although she died very young, Katherine Mansfield left behind a number of impressive, beautifully written stories, modernist in style, that seem to grow directly out of her own life. Like Anton Chekhov, whom she greatly admired, Mansfield expressed many of her critical ideas in journal entries and in letters to friends and family members. We have included several of her letters and journal entries here, which give a sense of her consciousness of craft and creative struggle; they also suggest her method of reliving remembered scenes from her past and of becoming one with her characters, of living within them, to provide a more authentic sense of their existence. We next reprint a selection from the essay "Katherine Mansfield" (1959) by her husband, critic, and publisher John Middleton Murry, who describes Mansfield as endowed with an "experiencing nature," a person who never hesitated to take risks and who, in her art and life, worked through her own mortality to find serenity in the idea of the triumph of beauty and artistic creation. In the essay "A Living Writer" (1942), fiction writer Elizabeth Bowen describes Mansfield as one who allowed her stories to grow out of perception and vision, intuitively, rather than working from conscious construction or from the "love for experiment for its own sake." Bowen believes that what is most memorable in Mansfield's work is her sharp eye for detail that "provides a ballast . . . to . . . high-strung susceptibility."

In her book on Mansfield, *Illness, Gender, and Writing* (1994), critic Mary Burgan uses a biographical and psychological approach to understanding Mansfield's writing, pointing out how her tuberculosis was intimately linked to her creative process and her extensive use of the technique of the epiphany, a highly charged moment of daily experience in which a character achieves an emotional breakthrough or insight: "Mansfield used the ailing body in which she found herself to imagine and record . . . the unnoticed details of everyday existence." We also include analyses of two of Mansfield's stories, "A Dill Pickle" and "The Garden-Party," from Marvin Magalaner's *The Fiction of Katherine Mansfield* (1971). Magalaner traces "A Dill Pickle" from its origins in a journal entry, and shows how Mansfield went on to develop a simple idea of a couple who meet after a long separation into a story that captures "the perfume of relationship" through a set of complex sensory associations that move back and forth in time. In "The Garden-Party," Magalaner sees the main character, Laura, as wakening over the course of the story from a dream life of sheltered upper-middle-class superficiality to a recognition that mortality exists "above class." Our final reading, an essay by student Cathy Young, "The Epiphany of Adolescence," compares the use of the epiphany as a reflection of the spiritual growth of the preadolescent characters in Mansfield's "The Garden-Party" and James Joyce's "Araby."

FROM *Katherine Mansfield's Journal* (1916, 1919, 1921)

January 22, 1916; Villa Pauline, Bandol   Now, really, what is it that I do want to write? I ask myself, Am I less of a writer than I used to be? Is the need to write less urgent? Does it still seem as natural to me to seek that form of expression? Has speech fulfilled it? Do I ask anything more than to relate, to remember, to assure myself?

There are times when these thoughts half-frighten me and very nearly convince. I say: You are now so fulfilled in your own being, in being alive, in living, in aspiring towards a greater sense of life and a deeper loving, the other thing has gone out of you.

But no, at bottom I am not convinced, for at bottom never has my desire been so ardent. Only the form that I would choose has changed utterly. I feel no longer concerned with the same appearance of things. The people who lived or whom I wished to bring into my stories don't interest me any more. The plots of my stories leave me perfectly cold. Granted that these people exist and all the differences, complexities and resolutions are true to them — why should I write about them? They are not near me. All the false threads that bound me to them are cut away quite.

Now — now I want to write recollections of my own country. Yes, I want to write about my own country till I simply exhaust my store. Not only because it is "a sacred debt" that I pay to my country because my brother and I were born there, but also because in my thoughts I range with him over all the remembered places. I am never far away from them. I long to renew them in writing.

Ah, the people — the people we loved there — of them, too, I want to write. Another "debt of love." Oh, I want for one moment to make our undiscovered country leap into the eyes of the Old World. It must be mysterious, as though floating. It must take the breath. It must be "one of those islands. . . ." I shall tell everything, even of how the laundry-basket squeaked at 75. But all must be told with a sense of mystery, a radiance, an afterglow, because you, my little sun of it, are set. You have dropped over the dazzling brim of the world. Now I must play my part.

Then I want to write poetry. I feel always trembling on the brink of poetry. The almond tree, the birds, the little wood where you are, the flowers you do not see, the open window out of which I lean and dream that you are against my shoulder, and the times that your photograph "looks sad." But especially I want to write a kind of long elegy to you . . . perhaps not in poetry. Nor perhaps in prose. Almost certainly in a kind of *special prose*.

And, lastly, I want to keep a kind of *minute notebook,* to be published some day. That's all. No novels, no problem stories, nothing that is not simple, open.

February 13, 1916   I have written practically nothing yet, and now again the time is getting short. There is nothing done. I am no nearer my achievement than I was two months ago, and I keep half-doubting my will to perform anything. Each time I make a vow my demon says at almost the same moment: "Oh, yes, we've heard that before!" And then I hear R.D. in the Café Royal, "Do you still write?" If I went back to England without a book *finished* I should give myself up. I should know that, whatever I said, I was not really a writer and had no claim to "a table in my room." But if I go back with a book finished it will be a *profession de foi pour toujours.* Why do I hesitate so long? It is just idleness? Lack of will-power? Yes, I feel that's what it is, and that's why it's so immensely important that I should assert myself. I have put a table to-day in my room, facing a corner, but from where I sit I can see some top shoots of the almond-tree and the sea sounds loud. There is a vase of beautiful geraniums on the table. Nothing could be nicer than this spot, and it's so quiet and so high, like sitting up in a tree. I feel I shall be able to write here, especially towards twilight.

Ah, once fairly alight — how I'd blaze and burn! Here is a new fact. When I am not writing I feel my brother calling me, and he is not happy. Only when I write or am in a state of writing — a state of "inspiration" — do I feel that he is calm. . . . Last night I dreamed of him and Father Zossima. Father Zossima said: "Do not let the new man die." My brother[1] was certainly there. But last evening he called me while I sat down by the fire. At last I obeyed and came upstairs. I stayed in the dark and waited. The moon got very bright. There were stars outside, very bright twinkling stars, that seemed to move as I watched them. The moon shone. I could see the curve of the sea and the curve of the land embracing, and above in the sky there was a round sweep of cloud. Perhaps those three half-circles were very magic. But then, when I leaned out of the window I seemed to see my brother dotted all over the field — now on his back, now on his face, now huddled up, now half-pressed into the earth. Wherever I looked, there he lay. I felt that God showed him to me like that for some express purpose, and I knelt down by the bed. But I could not pray. I had done no work. I was not in an active state of grace. So I got up finally and went downstairs again. But I was terribly sad. . . . The night before, when I lay in bed, I felt suddenly passionate. I wanted J. to embrace me. But as I turned to speak to him or to kiss him I saw my brother lying fast asleep, and I got cold. That happens nearly always. Perhaps because I went to sleep thinking of him, I woke and was he, for quite a long time. I felt my face was his serious, sleepy face. I felt that the lines of my mouth were changed, and I blinked like he did on waking.

---

[1] Mansfield's brother was killed in WWI. — Eds.

This year I have to make money and get known. I want to make enough money to be able to give L.M. some. In fact, I want to provide for her. That's my idea, and to make enough so that J. and I shall be able to pay our debts and live honourably. I should like to have a book published and *numbers* of short stories ready. Ah, even as I write, the smoke of a cigarette seems to mount in a reflective way, and I feel nearer that kind of silent, crystallised being that used to be almost me.

May 31, 1919   Work. Shall I be able to express, one day, my love of work — my desire to be a better writer — my longing to take greater pains. And the passion I feel. It takes the place of religion — it *is* my religion — of people — I create my people: of "life" — it *is* Life. The temptation is to kneel before it, to adore, to prostrate myself, to stay too long in a state of ecstasy before the *idea* of it. I must be more busy about my master's business.

Oh, God! The sky is filled with the sun, and the sun is like music. The sky is full of music. Music comes streaming down these great beams. The wind touches the harp-like trees, shakes little jets of music — little shakes, little trills from the flowers. The shape of every flower is like a sound. My hands open like five petals. Praise Him! Praise Him! No, I am overcome; I am dazed; it is too much to bear.

A little fly has dropped by mistake into the huge sweet cup of magnolia. Isaiah (or was it Elisha?) was caught up into Heaven in a chariot of fire *once*. But when the weather is divine and I am free to work, such a journey is positively nothing.

December 1919   It often happens to me now that when I lie down to sleep at night, instead of getting drowsy, I get wakeful and, lying here in bed, I begin to *live* over either scenes from real life or imaginary scenes. It's not too much to say they are almost hallucinations: they are marvellously vivid. I lie on my right side and put my left hand up to my forehead as though I were praying. This seems to *induce* the state. Then, for instance, it is 10:30 p.m. on a big liner in mid-ocean. . . . People are beginning to leave the Ladies' Cabin. Father puts his head in and asks if "one of you women care for a walk before you turn in. It's glorious up on deck." That begins it. I am *there*. Details: Father rubbing his gloves, the cold air — the *night* air rather — he brings to the door, the pattern of everything, the feel of the brass stair-rail and the rubber stairs. Then the deck — the pause while the cigar is lighted, the look of all in the moonlight, the *steadying* hum of the ship, the first officer on the deck, so far aloft the bells, the steward going into the smoking-room with a tray, stepping over the high, brass-bound step. . . . All these things are far realer, more in detail, *richer* than life. And I believe I could go on until . . . There's *no end* to it.

I can do this about everything. Only there are no personalities. Neither am I there personally. People are only part of the silence, *not* of the pattern — vastly different from that — part of the *scheme.* I could always do this to a certain extent; but it's only since I was really ill that this — shall we call it? — "consolation prize" has been given to me. My God! it's a marvellous thing.

I can call up certain persons — Doctor S. for instance. And then I remember how I used to say to J. and R. "He was looking very beautiful to-day." I did not know what I was saying. But when I so summon him and see him "in relation," he *is* marvellously beautiful. There again he comes complete, to every detail, to the shape of his thumbs, to looking over his glasses, his lips as he writes, and particularly in all connected with putting the needle into the syringe. . . . I *relive* all this at will.

July 1921   I finished "Mr and Mrs Dove" yesterday. I am not altogether pleased with it. It's a little bit made up. It's not inevitable. I mean to imply that those two may not be happy together — that that is the kind of reason for which a young girl marries. But have I done so? I don't think so. Besides, it's not *strong* enough. I want to be nearer — far, far nearer than that. I want to use all my force even when I am taking a fine line. And I have a sneaking notion that I have, at the end, used the Doves *unwarrantably. Tu sais ce que je veux dire.* I used them to round off something — didn't I? Is that quite my game? No, it's not. It's not quite the kind of truth I'm after. Now for "Susannah." All must be *deeply felt.*

July 23, 1921   Finished "An Ideal Family" yesterday. It seems to me better than "The Doves," but still it's not good enough. I worked at it hard enough, God knows, and yet I didn't get the deepest truth out of the idea, even once. What *is* this feeling? I feel again that this kind of knowledge is too easy for me; it's even a kind of trickery. I know so much more. This looks and smells like a story, but I wouldn't buy it. I don't want to possess it — to live with it. NO. Once I have written two more, I shall tackle something different — a long story: "At the Bay," *with more difficult relationships. That's the whole problem.*

FROM *Katherine Mansfield's Letters*   (1917, 1921, 1922)

TO DOROTHY BRETT, 11 OCTOBER 1917

It seems to me so extraordinarily right that you should be painting Still Lives just now. What can one do, faced with this wonderful tumble of round bright fruits, but gather them and play with them — and *become them,* as it were. When I pass the apple stalls I cannot help stopping and staring until I feel that I, myself, am changing into an apple, too — and that at any moment I may produce an apple, miraculously, out of my own being like the conjuror produces the egg. When you paint apples do you feel that your breasts and your knees become apples, too? Or do you think this the greatest nonsense. I don't. I am *sure* it is not. When I write about ducks I swear that I am a white duck with a round eye, floating in a pond fringed with yellow blobs and taking an occasional dart at the other duck with the round eye, which floats upside down beneath me. In fact this whole process of becoming the duck (what [D. H.] Lawrence would, perhaps, call this "consummation with the duck or the apple") is so thrilling that I can hardly breathe, only to think about it. For although that is as far as most people can get, it is really only the "prelude." There follows the moment when you are *more* duck, *more* apple or *more* Natasha than any of these objects could ever possibly be, and so you *create* them anew. . . .

Forgive me. But that is why I believe in technique, too (you asked me if I did). I do, just because I don't see how art is going to make that divine *spring* into the bounding outlines of things if it hasn't passed through the process of trying to *become* these things before recreating them.

TO RICHARD MURRY, 17 JANUARY 1921

It's a very queer thing how *craft* comes into writing. I mean down to details. Par exemple. In "Miss Brill" I choose not only the length of every sentence, but even the sound of every sentence. I choose the rise and fall of every paragraph to fit her, and to fit her on that day at that very moment. After I'd written it I read it aloud — numbers of times — just as one would *play over* a musical composition — trying to get it nearer and nearer to the expression of Miss Brill — until it fitted her.

Don't think I'm vain about the little sketch. It's only the method I wanted to explain. I often wonder whether other writers do the same — If a thing has really come off it seems to me there mustn't be one single word out of place or one word that could be taken out. That's how I AIM at writing. It will take some time to get anywhere near there.

But you know, Richard, I was only thinking last night people have hardly begun to write yet. Put poetry out of it for a moment and leave out Shakespeare — now I mean prose. Take the very best of it. Aren't they still cutting up sections rather than tackling the whole of a mind? I had a moment of absolute terror in the night. I suddenly thought of *a living mind* — a whole mind — with absolutely nothing left out. With *all* that one knows how much does one not know? I used to fancy one knew all but some kind of mysterious core (or one could). But now I believe just the opposite. The unknown is far, far greater than the known. The known is only a mere shadow. This is a fearful thing and terribly hard to face. But it must be faced.

TO WILLIAM GERHARDI, 13 MARCH 1922

. . . I've been wanting to say — how strange, how delightful it is you should feel as you do about "The Voyage." No one has mentioned it to me but

Middleton Murry. But when I wrote that little story I felt that I was on that very boat, going down those stairs, smelling the smell of the saloon. And when the stewardess came in and said, "We're rather empty, we may pitch a little," I can't believe that my sofa did not pitch. And one moment I had a little bun of silk-white hair and a bonnet and the next I was Fenella hugging the swan neck umbrella. It was so vivid — terribly vivid — especially as they drove away and heard the sea as slowly it turned on the beach. Why — I don't know. It wasn't a memory of a real experience. It was a kind of *possession*. I might have remained the grandma for ever after if the wind had changed that moment. And that would have been a little bit embarrassing for Middleton Murry. . . .

And yes, that is what I tried to convey in "The Garden-Party." The diversity of life and how we try to fit in everything, Death included. That is bewildering for a person of Laura's age. She feels things ought to happen differently. First one and then another. But life isn't like that. We haven't the ordering of it. Laura says, "But all these things must not happen at once." And Life answers, "Why not? How are they divided from each other?" And they *do* all happen, it is inevitable. And it seems to me there is beauty in that inevitability. . . .

J. MIDDLETON MURRY

FROM *Katherine Mansfield*   (1959)

In scope Katherine Mansfield was a tiny artist; but because she was a perfectly pure, and perfectly submissive, artist she was a great one. In this order of artistic achievement, the small is veritably great, and the great no greater. In this order, achievement is absolute or not at all. There is Art, and there is not-Art; and between them is precisely the absolute difference which the philosophers of the Christian religion sought so often to express, between the descent of the divine grace and the utmost effort of the conscious personal being to achieve it. As Blake said — the great artist who was isolated because he knew the ultimate identity of Christianity and Art — "We in *ourselves* are nothing." And Katherine herself wrote to my brother:

> About religion. Did you mean "the study of life" or Christ's religion "Come unto me all ye that labour and are heavy laden and I will give you rest." The queer thing is that one does not seem to contradict the other, to me. *If I lose myself in the study of life, and give up Self, then I am at rest.* But the more I study the religion of Christ the more I marvel at it. (29.3.22.)

What may be the secret of this delicate and invincible integrity, no man dare say. It is perhaps enough that it should exist and that we should recognise and respond to it. But those who do recognise it see that it is manifest from the beginning in a strange compulsion to submit to experience. Between life and such natures the impact is not mitigated. It is naked all the while. Neither creed nor conception nor convention can interpose its comfortable medium. These natures are doomed, or privileged, to lead a life of "sensations rather than of thoughts." Such a life seemed, no doubt, good to Keats when he wrote those words, which after-generations have found it so easy to misunderstand; but he was to learn that as the joys of the immediate nature are incomparable, so are its sufferings; and that the time inevitably comes when the joy is suffering, and the suffering joy. For such natures, as though compelled by an inward law, return to the organic simplicity of the pre-conscious being; but in them that simplicity is enriched by all the subtleties of consciousness.

Of this simplicity in complexity — in life and art — Katherine Mansfield was a perfect example. She belonged, by birthright, to the "experiencing natures." They are sustained by some secret faith in life of which smaller souls are ignorant. They know what Blake meant when he proclaimed that "the road of excess leads to the palace of wisdom." They can take nothing in the matter of vital life-experience at second-hand. Always for them the truth must be proved as Keats said "on their pulses." And so, inevitably, in the eyes of the world they are not wise; for wisdom, in the world's eyes, consists precisely in refusing to expose ourselves to experience. The wise accept the report of others; of that great Other who is the worldly prudence of the race. They know that the Master of Life is a hard man, reaping where he did not sow, and they hide their talent in the earth. They take no risks with him.

And in this they *are* wise. But there is a greater wisdom than theirs. It is the wisdom which whispers "Take the risk! If that is truly the urge of your secret soul, obey it. No matter what the cost, obey!" Or as D. H. Lawrence cried in his last and most lovely poem: "Launch out, the fragile soul in the fragile ship of courage." The same — identically the same image — that Katherine Mansfield used to express *her* final discovery, when she said "The little boat enters the dark fearful gulf and our only cry is to escape — 'put me on land again.' But it's useless. Nobody listens. The shadowy figure rows on. One ought to sit still and uncover one's eyes." Of what were these two friends speaking — in the same image? Of the same thing. Of the acceptance of Death and Suffering. Uncovering one's eyes before the final dark shadow of all existence — the supreme sadness — the type of all that pain and evil from which the soul seeks to avert its head. The death of the ideal, the death of love, the death that comes through the never-ending discovery of the snail under the leaf, the death of Bertha Young's happiness in "Bliss," the death of Laura's happiness in "The Garden-Party" — these are all variations of the one unending theme.

But out of death always the birth of a new life: a new life doomed in turn to die, but destined always to be re-born, until the final acceptance of a complete self-surrender. Then, as Katherine said, "Everything for ever is changed." It is the final entry into what Blake called the world of true Imagination, which is

Spiritual Sensation — a world of sensation because it is a world of immediate experience; a spiritual world, because it is not discerned by the five senses or their ratio
which is the Intellect. It is beyond all these; yet it does not deny all these. The
world — one is driven back to the phrase — of the "beauty of the truth."

> It seems to me [she wrote nine months before her death] that if Beauty were
> Absolute it would no longer be the kind of Beauty it is. Beauty triumphs over
> ugliness in life. That's what I feel. And that marvellous *triumph* is what I long
> to express. . . . I sit in a waiting-room where all is ugly, where it's dirty, dull,
> dreadful, where sick people waiting with me to see the doctor are all
> marked by suffering and sorrow. And a very poor workman comes in, takes
> off his cap humbly, beautifully, walks on tiptoe, has a look as though he
> were in church, has a look as though he believed that behind that doctor's
> door shone the miracle of healing. *And all is changed, all is marvellous.* It's
> only then that one sees for the first time what is happening. Life is, all at
> one and the same time, far more mysterious and far simpler than we know.
> It's like religion in that. *If we want to have faith, and without faith we die, we
> must learn to accept.* That's how it seems to me.

And so it is that if I had to choose one adjective to describe the essential
quality of what she did and what she became, it would be the adjective
"serene." And it seems to me that those who are responsive to her writing
recognise this serenity — the serenity of a rainbow that shines through tears —
and know that it comes from a heart at peace "in spite of all." Katherine could
look back on her life, with all its miseries and all its brevity, and declare that
"in spite of all" it was good: that "in spite of all" suffering was a privilege, pain
the gateway to a deeper joy, sorrow the birth-pang of a new beauty. "In spite
of all" — the phrase, mysterious and simple as life, contains the secret of herself and her art. It is a phrase which more than any other echoes in my heart,
with the sweetness of a long familiar pain, when I think back on what she was,
and what she wrote from what she was. Beauty triumphs over Ugliness "in
spite of all." In spite of all, the little lamp glows gently and eternally in *The
Doll's House;* in spite of all, the sleeping face of the dead man in "The Garden-
Party" murmurs that All is well; and though Ma Parker has nowhere to cry out
her misery, she is beautiful for ever, in spite of all.

ELIZABETH BOWEN

FROM *A Living Writer: Katherine Mansfield* (1956)

"Katherine Mansfield's death, by coming so early, left her work still at the
experimental stage." This could be said — but would it be true? To me, such

a verdict would be misleading. First, her writing already *had* touched perfection a recognizable number of times; second, she would have been bound to
go on experimenting up to the end, however late that had come. One cannot
imagine her settling down to any one fixed concept of the short story — her
art was, by its very nature, tentative, responsive, exploratory. There are no
signs that she was casting about to find a formula: a formula would, in fact,
have been what she fled from. Her sense of the possibilities of the story was
bounded by no hard-and-fast horizons: she grasped that it is imperative for the
writer to expand his range, never contract his method. Perception and language could not be kept too fresh, too alert, too fluid. Each story entailed a
beginning right from the start, unknown demands, new risks, unforeseeable
developments. Often, she worked by trial-and-error.

So, ever on the move, she has left with us no "typical" Katherine Mansfield
story to anatomize. Concentrated afresh, each time, upon expression, she did
not envisage technique in the abstract. As it reached her, each idea for a story
had inherent within it its own shape: there could be for it no other. That shape,
it was for her to perceive, then outline — she thought (we learn from her letters and journal) far more of perception than of construction. The story *is*
there, but she has yet to come at it. One has the impression of a water-diviner,
pacing, halting, awaiting the twitch of the hazel twig. Also, to judge from her
writings about her writing, there were times when Katherine Mansfield believed a story to have a volition of its own — she seems to stand back watching
it take form. Yet this could not happen apart from her; the story drew her
steadily into itself.

All of her pieces, it seems clear, did not originate in the same order. Not
in all cases was there that premonitory stirring of an idea; sometimes the
external picture came to her first. She found herself seized upon by a scene,
an isolated incident or a face which, something told her, must *have* meaning,
though she had yet to divine what the meaning was. Appearances could in
themselves touch alight her creative power. It is then that we see her moving
into the story, from its visual periphery to its heart, recognizing the "why" as
she penetrates. (It could seem that her great scenic New Zealand stories came
into being by this process.) Her failures, as she uncompromisingly saw them,
together with her host of abandoned fragments, give evidence of the state of
mind she voices in anguished letters or journal entries — the sensation of having lost her way. She could finish a story by sheer craftsmanship but only, later,
to turn against the results.

Able and fine as was her intelligence, it was not upon that that she
depended: intuitive knowing, vision, had to be the thing. She was a writer
with whom there could be no secondary substitute for genius: genius was
vision. One might speak of her as having a burning gaze. But she faced this
trouble — vision at full intensity is not by nature able to be sustained; it is all
but bound to be intermittent. And for Katherine Mansfield those intermit-
tences set up an aesthetic disability, a bad, an antipathetic working condition.

Under such a condition, her work abounded, and well she knew it, in perils peculiar to itself. She dreaded sagging of tension, slackening of grip, flaws in interior continuity, numbness, and, most of all, a sort of synthetic quality which could creep in. She speaks of one bad day's work as "scrappy and dreamy." Dreaminess meant for her, dilution.

Subjects, to be ideal for Katherine Mansfield, had to attract, then hold, her power called vision. There occurred a false dawn, or false start, when a subject deceived her as to its possibilities — there were those which failed her, I feel, rather than she them. We must consider later which kind or what range of subject stood by her best, and why this may have been so. There was not a subject which did not tax her — raising, apart from anything else, exacting problems of treatment, focus, and angle. Her work was a succession of attempts to do what was only just not impossible. There is danger that in speaking of "attempts" one should call to mind those which have not succeeded: one forgets the no less attempt which is merged in victory. Katherine Mansfield's masterpiece stories cover their tracks; they have an air of serene inevitability, almost a touch of the miraculous. (But for the artist, remember, there are no miracles.) Her consummate achievements soar, like so many peaks, out of the foothills of her working life — spaced out, some nearer together in time than others. One asks oneself why the artist, requited thus, could not have been lastingly reassured, and how it could have happened that, after each, troughs of frustration, anxiety, dereliction should have awaited her once again?

The truth was, she implacably cut the cord between herself and any completed story. (She admits, in the journal: "It took me nearly a month to 'recover' from 'At the Bay.' I made at least three false starts. But I could not get away from the sound of the sea, and Beryl fanning her hair at the window. These things would not *die down*.") She must not look back; she must press forward. She had no time to form a consistent attitude to any one finished story: each stood to her as a milestone, passed, not as a destination arrived at. Let us say, she reacted to success (if in Katherine Mansfield's eyes there was such a thing) as others react to failure: there seemed to be nothing left but to try again.

To be compelled to experiment is one thing, to be in love with experiment quite another. Of love for experiment for its own sake, Katherine Mansfield shows not a sign. Conscious artist, she carries none of the marks of the self-consciously "experimental" writer. Nothing in her approach to people or nature is revolutionary; her story-telling is, on its own plane, not much less straightforward than Jane Austen's. She uses no literary shock tactics. The singular beauty of her language consists, partly, in its hardly seeming to *be* language at all, so glass-transparent is it to her meaning. Words had but one appeal for her, that of speakingness. (In her journal we find noted: "The *panting* of a saw.") She was to evolve from noun, verb, adjective, a marvellous sensory notation hitherto undreamed of outside poetry; nonetheless, she stayed subject to prose discipline. And her style, when the story-context requires, can

be curt, decisive, factual. It is a style generated by subject and tuned to mood
— so flexible as to be hardly *a* style at all. One would recognize a passage from
Katherine Mansfield not by the manner but by the content. There are no
eccentricities.

Katherine Mansfield was not a rebel, she was an innovator. Born into the
English traditions of prose narrative, she neither revolted against these nor
broke with them — simply, she passed beyond them. And now tradition,
extending, has followed her. Had she not written, written as she did, one form
of art might be still in infancy. One cannot attribute to Katherine Mansfield the
entire growth, in our century, of the short story. Its developments have been
speedy, inspired, various; it continues branching in a hundred directions many
of which show her influence not at all. What she did supply was an immense
impetus — also, did she not first see in the story the ideal reflector of the day?
We owe to her the prosperity of the "free" story: she untrammelled it from
conventions and, still more, gained for it a prestige till then unthought of.
How much ground Katherine Mansfield broke for her successors may not be
realized. Her imagination kindled unlikely matter; she was to alter for good
and all our ideas of what goes to make a story.

I have touched on Katherine Mansfield's alternatives: the evidences, that is,
in her early stories that she could have been a writer of more than one kind.
Alternations went on throughout her working life. In her letters appears a
brusque, formidable, masculine streak, which we must not overlook in the
stories. Her art has backbone. Her objectiveness, her quick, sharp observations,
her adept presentations — are these taken into account enough? Scenically, how
keen is her eye for the telling detail! The street, quayside, café, shop interior,
tea-time terrace, or public garden stand concretely forward into life. She is well
documented. Her liking for activity, for the crowd at play, for people going
about their work, her close interest in process and occupation, give an extra
vitality to stories. . . .

This factual firmness of Katherine Mansfield's provides a ballast, or anti-
dote, to her other side — the high-strung susceptibility, the almost hallucinatory floatingness. Nothing is more isolated, more claustrophobic than the
dream-fastness of a solitary person — no one knew the dangers better than she.
Yet rooted among those dangers was her genius; totally disinfected, wholly
adjusted, could she have written as she did? Perhaps there is no such thing as
"pure" imagination — all air must be breathed in, and some is tainting. Now
and then the emotional level of her writing drops: a whimsical, petulant little
girlishness disfigures a few of the lesser stories. Some others show a transferred
self-pity. She could not always keep up the guard. . . .

The writer was a woman of strong feeling. How quick were her sympathies, vehement her dislikes, total her angers, penitent her forgivingness, letters
and journal show. If we had not these, how much would we know of her from

her stories? Impersonality cannot but be the aim of a writer of anything like her calibre, and she fought to keep her stories clear of herself. But, human temperament and its workings being her subject, how could she wholly outlaw her own? And temperament played in her work an essential part — it was to provide as it were the climate in which ideas grew and came to flower. That throughout years of her creative life Katherine Mansfield was a sick woman, and that tuberculosis engenders a special temperament, or intensifies the one there already, must be allowed for. It has been more than allowed for — there is danger, in her case as in Keats's, that the medical history be overstressed. We are to marvel at the persistent strength with which Katherine Mansfield the artist threw off the sick-room. She was conscious only of her vocation — she *was* to write, she wrote, and wrote as she did. It may be that brutalities on the part of fate made her the more feel singled out, set apart. The battering at her health accounts for the inequalities of her accomplishment: that there was any trace of the pathological in the art itself, I imagine nobody could assert.

She was not by nature dispassionate. In the New Zealand, the "faraway people" stories, conflict seems stilled — there is an overruling harmony, the seer come to rest with the seen. Katherine Mansfield's ethics and partisanships come through far more in the English pieces (possibly because of their thinner fabric) and in some of those set in the South of France — though in "The Young Girl" and "The Doves' Nest" we again have a shining impartiality. She loved righteousness and hated iniquity: what, for her, constituted those two? She was on the side of innocence and honour: honesty, spontaneity, humbleness, trustfulness and forbearingness distinguish characters she is fond of. No less could she embody what she detested: cruelty or heartlessness, affectation, neurotic indulgence, cowardice, smugness. Indignation at injustice, from time to time, makes her no less inflammatory a writer than Charles Dickens. She concerns herself with bad cases rather than bad systems: political awareness or social criticism do not directly express themselves in the stories. How hard is her bearing against oppressors, how tender her leaning towards victims! Unimaginativeness, with regard to others, seem to her one of the grosser sins. The denial of love, the stunting of sorrow, or the cheating of joy was to her not short of an enormity — she had an intense regard for the human birthright.

How good is Katherine Mansfield's character-drawing? I have heard this named as her weak point. I feel one cannot insist enough upon what she instinctively grasped — that the short story, by reason of its aesthetics, is not and is not intended to be the medium either for exploration or long-term development of character. Character cannot be more than *shown* — it is there for use, the use is dramatic. Foreshortening is not only unavoidable, it is right. And with Katherine Mansfield there was another factor — her "stranger" outlook on so much of society. I revert to the restrictedness of her life in England, the eclecticism of her personal circle. She saw few people, saw them sometimes too often. This could account for her tendency to repeat certain types of character. This restless New Zealand woman writing of London deals with what was more than half a synthetic world: its denizens *are* types, and they remain so — to the impoverishment of the London stories. The divorce of the intelligentsia from real life tends to be with her an obsessive subject — aggravated more than she knew, perhaps, by her sense of being far from her home base. Her sophisticates are cut out sharply, with satire; they are animated, expressive but two-dimensional. . . .

Katherine Mansfield, we notice, seldom outlines and never dissects a character: instead, she causes the person to expose himself — and devastating may be the effect. The author's nominal impassivity is telling. I should not in the main call her a kind writer, though so often she is a pitiful one. Wholly benevolent are her comedies: high spirits, good humour no less than exquisite funniness endear to us "The Daughters of the Late Colonel," "The Doves' Nest," "The Singing Lesson." Nor is the laugh ever against a daydreamer. . . . The dauntless artist accomplished, if less than she hoped, more than she knew. Almost no writer's art has not its perishable fringes: light dust may settle on that margin. But against the core, the integrity, what can time do? Katherine Mansfield's deathless expectations set up a mark for us: no one has yet fulfilled them. Still at work, her genius rekindles faith; she is on our side in every further attempt. The effort she was involved in involves us — how can we feel her other than a contemporary?

MARY BURGAN

FROM *Illness, Gender, and Writing*   (1994)

The Case of Katherine Mansfield

Throughout this study, as a recurring formulation that unites the medical with the aesthetic, I have invoked a link between Katherine Mansfield's illness and writing which reflects Michel Foucault's suggestion that the clinical recognition of mortality and its causes can give rise to a "lyrical experience," a sense of the "obstinate, yet reassuring fact of . . . finitude" shared by the doctor and the poet alike as experts in the knowledge of death (*Birth*). To be sure, imminent death may concentrate the imagination decisively, but I do not want to suggest here that Mansfield wrote out of fear — in panic and terror. It seems, rather, that no matter how clear the inevitability of her death as her final disease progressed, her writing derived from an intensifying center of purpose *within* her illness. Her finitude was a "fact" that perhaps reassured by its refusal to succumb without a fight. More important, Mansfield seems to have found reassurance in facticity itself, in the plenitude of the external world to which her illness gave her extraordinary access.

Without succumbing to the romantic theory of tuberculosis as a "spiritual" disease, I have suggested that Katherine Mansfield used the ailing body in which she found herself to imagine and record experience with an unusual attention to the unnoticed details of everyday existence. She seems to have steadied herself upon these details, and in this application of physical sensation to psychic equilibrium, I believe that she exercised an imaginative form of "proprioception," which Oliver Sacks has defined as "that continuous but unconscious sensory flow from the movable parts of our body (muscles, tendons, joints), by which their position and tone and motion is continually monitored and adjusted, but hidden from us because it is automatic and unconscious." Ordinarily, our bodies engage in proprioception without conscious effort, but Sacks' story of "Christina," a young woman who lost that sense through a rare neurological catastrophe, emphasizes the courage as well as the imaginative ingenuity in adjustment by patients whose bodily damage requires a conscious relearning of the flowing grace of normal functioning. Damaged patients must understand their illness if they are to adjust to its deprivations, sometimes regaining the flow of their humanity only under the influence of long-forgotten music.

I make the analogy between the patient who must learn to hold herself in place and the afflicted artist, not to recall the Freudian concept of illness as the source of sublimation that gives rise to art, but to reiterate the notion of Mansfield's art as the result of an engagement of the total sensorium under the pressure to become conscious of its range in active struggle against dying. She confided to one of her sisters in a letter of 1922 that her sense of place had become both implicated in and transmuted by her suffering, and she made the confession of her attachment to the material world in images that accent the modest physicality of her own remains:

> How hard it is to escape from places. However carefully one goes they hold you — you leave little bits of yourself fluttering on the fences — little rags and shreds of your very life. But a queer thing it is — this is personal — however painful a thing has been when I look back it is no longer painful or more painful than music is. In fact it is just that. *Now* when I hear the sea at the Casetta [the Italian villa where she had felt most isolated in her illness exile the year before], it's unbearably beautiful. (Unpub. letter, Mar. 7, 1922, Berg)

In the process of her constant self-examination and its growing sensitivity to "sensory flow," then, and as the clinical manifestations of her final disease became more apparent, I believe that Mansfield sought to project the bodiliness of the self at a new degree of intimacy in her fiction, even as she managed to represent the materiality of the world — the "obstinate yet reassuring fact of finitude" — outside that self by expanding her already unusual command of imagery, prose rhythm, and spoken language in recollections of the crises of her life which became no "more painful than music is."

Whether or not there is a "genius" that is peculiar to victims of tuberculosis may remain an unanswerable question, but it seems clear to me that in her representation of the material world as framed by mortality, Mansfield manifested something of *spes phthisica,* the hectic savoring of "beauty that must die" which marked the romantic lyricism of tubercular poets such as Keats. Her fears that she might cease to be gave way to a steady contemplation of the finitude of the phenomenal world whose temporality inspired her emotion in re-collecting its smallest rags and shreds even as she projected the end of the future. Over and over again, the letters and journal entries of her illness years restate the hope that her words would be a stay against time. Thus she wrote to Mrs. Belloc-Lowndes in the summer of 1921: "I've seen the best man in Switzerland and he says I still have a chance. But I don't feel in the least die-away. Illness is a great deal more mysterious than doctors imagine. I simply can't afford to die with one very half-and-half little book and one bad one and a few . . . stories to my name. In spite of everything, in spite of all one knows and has felt — one has this longing to *praise life* — to sing one's minute song of praise, and it doesn't seem to matter whether its listened to or no" (unpub. letter, Texas).

The mode of Mansfield's praise was the epiphany, a characteristic modernist expression that George Steiner has described as the confrontation with "the facticity of death, a facticity wholly resistant to reason, to metaphor, to revelatory representation." In resistance against the modernist loading of all its faith into that moment, however, Steiner finds the epiphanic representation of time nihilistic — "an epistemology and ethics of spurious temporality." Steiner's nostalgia for a philosophical/theological basis for consonance between "word and world" underestimates the fact that the ontological satisfactions of facticity may coexist with the modernist's rejection of transcendence. The signification of the moment in Mansfield's writing will not be made manifest through systems or in plotted narratives that inevitably imply causality. The causality of Mansfield's stories is the causality of contingency. Milan Kundera explores this kind of causality in *The Unbearable Lightness of Being* when he comments on the fortuities, or coincidences, that are composed into "motifs" both by characters in novels and by people in life. The "beauty" is like music composed "even in times of greatest distress." The music of the slight perceptions that trigger epiphanies is an echo of time past made meaningful by a future that cannot be planned; it is an echo of significance which can only be played upon the instrument of the present, and it is therefore lyrical more than narrative in expression. As the unanswerable questions at the end of "The Daughters of the Late Colonel" suggest, Mansfield's modernist confrontation with death through the staging of the moment of revelation did not yield any final answer. But it posed the question in a fugue of memory and projection, registering the present as the only available repository of implication. As she wrote of Chekhov to Virginia Woolf, "What the writer does is not so much to *solve* the question but to *put* the question. There must be the question put" (*Collected Letters* [*CL*]).

For Katherine Mansfield, as for Virginia Woolf, the creativity of women was inflected by illness. As madness haunts the writing of Virginia Woolf, physical disease haunts Mansfield's fiction. For Mansfield, illness threatens not by driving women to suicide — an end of time — but by insidiously infecting them with the narcissistic self-absorption of invalidism — a waste of time. Both Virginia Woolf and Katherine Mansfield maintained that women's writing would have to work through such debilitating threats by expressing women's experience in all of its temporal confusions. Mansfield wrung out her epiphanies through the afflictions of a woman's body, but despite her own case history, Mansfield rarely wrote her illness directly into her fiction. Like Woolf, she had an ideal of narrative art as pure expression, unburdened by the special pleading of the writer's circumstances or by the regimenting abstraction of political or philosophical ambitions. This reliance on the present of the epiphany did not, however, embody a belief that the experience represented by her words was merely a surface materiality — what Ronald Schleifer has described as the material "metonymics" of modernism and postmodernism — marshaled ironically as a last resort against the facticity of death.

There was, of course, plenty of irony in Mansfield's fiction, but I believe that it was a tonic irony marshaled in defense of the authenticity of the epiphany. One of her last completed stories was "The Fly," one of her most ruthless satires upon the pretensions of the patriarchal father. It tells of "the boss" who, being reminded by an old retainer of the death of his son in the war, has every intention of spending an hour in solitude mourning the boy. But as he settles at his desk, he is distracted by the effort of a fly to recover from having fallen into the ink pot, and in playing with the creature's struggle, he finally causes it to die. He then tries to remember what he had been doing, but he cannot bring back the thought of his dead son. The piercing recognition in this story is that memory, the only memorial for the dead, is subject to lapse. Critics have belabored the symbolic possibilities in "The Fly," and biographers see in it Mansfield's anger against her father, who had lately remarried and who seemed to reject his daughter's achievements. Placed with her other final stories, however, "The Fly" enacts Mansfield's own main terror about death, her brother's and her own, that their lives should be forgotten. In the fragmentary "Six Years After," the dead son reproaches his mother, "Don't forget me! You are forgetting me, you know you are!" But the mother strives to hold the memory of the dead against her own voyage into darkness; she battles the ephemerality of the moment, unlike the boss, who fritters away his remembrance in the clutter of his self-endowed memorials — the new furniture of his office, his desk, his pen. His memory fails because it has been plotted as a dramatic episode: "The boss covered his face with his hands. He wanted, he intended, he had arranged to weep." The memorializations of women are spontaneous; they remain in the passing perceptions of dreams or of fleeting daily reminders. As the old woman who mourns her canary in Mansfield's very last story says of the sadness in life, "It is there, deep down, deep down, part of one, like one's breathing." Thus Mansfield's irony is gendered rather than general. The "hatred" (she used that word about herself in a marginal comment when she was writing "Six Years After") remained as one of the main "kick offs" in her writing. It has a specific object, however, in the carelessness of self-important authority.

Both Woolf and Mansfield launched their careers as writers under the brave flag of the freedom of women to write in expressive proclamation of the female self, and although each risked the trivialization by philosophical authorities for her efforts, in a different way, each was haunted by the image of the woman of genius as threatened by the finally fatal dissipation of her ambition to give voice to her experience through a lapse of confidence in its reality. Sounding Virginia Woolf's theme of the need for a writer, especially a sick writer, to have money and a room of her own—and the support of friends to help her along—Mansfield wrote to Murry in the dark days of 1919, "I wish I were a great deal more self-supporting. It's a thousand times harder for me to write reviews here where I have no one to talk things over with—I'm 'out of it' and see so few papers & never hear *talk*. I have to get into full diver's clothes & rake the floor of the unprofitable sea. All the same *it is my life: it saves me*" (*CL*). And then the next day, pulling her resources together out of despair, she writes about the memories that form the core of her past and her hope for the future, "It is all memories now—radiant, marvelous, faraway memories of happiness. Ah, how terrible life can be! I sometimes see an immense wall of black rock, shining in a place—just after death perhaps—and *smiling*—the *adamant of desire*. Let us live on memories, then, and when the time comes, let us live so fully that the memories are no nearer than faraway mountains" (*CL*).

The final question is how, in illness and in art, Katherine Mansfield managed the contradictions between her insight into the fragmentation of the self as the dependent subject of multiple roles and social determinations and her conviction of possessing a "self that is continuous and permanent" and so conscientious enough to exert the will to write even in isolation. It has been a running contention of this study that the conviction of selfhood is not only an intuitive and enabling artistic presumption but also an essential foundation for resistance to the threat of disease. In thinking about the hope, however feverish, which has traditionally been associated with the final stages of tuberculosis, I have come to believe that memory is the essential element in the psyche which turns subjectivity into identity. Mansfield's own meditation on the survival of the self is couched in an account of its organic development and of the use of consolidating the self through writing down its phases—creating as she says, a "rage for autobiography" (*Journal*). Oliver Sacks' accounts of the identity destruction that is the main psychic damage done by neurological amnesia show how important a role memory plays in providing the patient a sense of the continuity and meaning of his life. One pathetic case is that of "Jimmie G," a victim of amnesia whose memory is intact up to the age of nineteen and who therefore has always a sense of who he *was* but not who he *is*. An even more tragic case is that of "Mr. Thompson," a man whose Korsakov's syndrome has removed all memory function; this patient has no sense of what he ever was and so spends his days fabricating and narrating perpetually new stories about himself. In a sense, this man might seem to be the model of postmodern subjectivity unhitched from the illusion of continuity and in constant and immediate contact with the flux of his desire. But in a profound sense, the man is sick; he cannot work or love because the rush of stories, and frantic attempts at stabilizing himself through them, occupy every waking minute of his day. His day is full of discourse and there is no rest.

Mansfield's resource in the daily presence of her death was the restorative identity of memory recorded, relived, proprioceptively. Her experience of pain gave a sharp edge to her representation of physical sensation — breathing, eating, feeling the warmth of a cup of hot water on cold lips, searching out a spot of sun. These were the writerly instruments of her illness; with them she managed to live through her dying. Her acknowledgment of the limitations of the time available to her orchestrated her representations into a lyric art that made peace with the transitoriness of her moments while asserting their pattern in a life that mattered.

MARVIN MAGALANER

FROM *The Fiction of Katherine Mansfield*   (1971)

"A Dill Pickle," largely ignored or patronized by critics, reveals Mansfield on the brink of maturity. Fewer than seven pages in length, it yet establishes vividly the essence of a man and a woman, suggests the past, dramatizes the present, and implies the future by severe verbal economy and the sure employment of metaphorical devices hitherto reserved to poets like Eliot and Pound, whose portraits of ladies are called to mind.

An entry in Manfield's *Journal* may have been the point of departure for the plot. On August 21, 1917, Mansfield writes:

> I came home this afternoon and F. came in. . . . By and by we sat down and had tea and talk. This man is in many ways extraordinarily like me. I like him so much; I feel so *honest* with him. . . . I did not realize, until he was here and we ate together, how much I cared for him. . . . A real understanding. We might have spoken a different language — returned from a far country. I just felt all was well, and we understood each other. . . .
>
> We said good-bye at Vinden's. That is all. But I wanted to make a note of it.

I. They meet and just touch.

II. They come together and part.

III. They are separated and meet again.

IV. They realize their tie.

All that Mansfield needed to add to this bare outline is the fifth step of "A Dill Pickle": They also realize their incompatibility and therefore part.

The fashion in which the author transforms this simple narrative line — highly sentimental and almost banal — into a successful short story merits more attention than it has received. The story is built upon a then-and-now polarity, and the incidents move rapidly from one pole to the other. Connecting the two poles is a kind of perfume of relationship — a tenuous yet vividly recurring series of sense relationships that the author from time to time introduces. The peeling of an orange in an Oriental cafe recalls a similar manner of peeling fruit in earlier days. The present eating place with the Japanese vase and bamboo tables sets the woman's mind to thinking of an earlier scene in a Chinese pagoda tea shop. The paper daffodils on the table now are balanced by the real flowers the two admired in Kew Gardens years before.

It is almost as though the ability to enjoy, or to have enjoyed, this pleasure of the senses is directly related to the possibility of human compatibility. Thus, the man elicits from Vera the admission that she has given up the making of music:

> "Do you ever play it now?"
>
> "No, I've no piano."
>
> He was amazed at that. "But what has become of your beautiful piano?"
>
> She made a little grimace. "Sold. Ages ago." (p. 333)[1]

He remembers their visit to Kew Gardens on a "very fine and warm" (p. 332) day, but now Vera's principal concern appears to be the avoidance of the sensation of cold. Her high fur, her muff, her gloves, and all her thoughts on the weather attest to her apprehension. For her, the colorful and fragrant true flowers of the Gardens have been replaced by the "paper daffodils" (p. 330) of the restaurant, and even in breathing the air round these artificial flowers, she inhales "as though the paper daffodils between them were almost too sweet to bear" (p. 332). Nor does she answer the man's question when he asks whether she is "still so fond of perfumes" (p. 333) as in the old days. Instead she interrupts his question as he in earlier days had been accustomed to breaking in on her conversation.

---

[1] Mansfield, Katherine. *The Short Stories of Katherine Mansfield*. Ed. John Middleton Murry. New York: Knopf, 1941. All page numbers refer to this edition. — Eds.

The man, on the other hand, appears at least to savor the joys of the senses and thus to be ready now for human connection as he was not ready six years before. Mansfield has taken pains to delineate him as a younger man and a rather selfish, foolish person. His immature confession of a wish to die lest his growing love for Vera cause him pain is an obvious effort to mark his unwillingness for involvement. And the rather "absurd scene" in the Chinese tea shop when he behaves like a "maniac" (p. 332) in his frenzy to escape being stung by wasps further stresses his wish to avoid physical sensation — this time painful without the concomitant enjoyment of pleasure.

Now, however, the man has had six years of experience with life since his last encounter with Vera, six years in which to change. The alteration seems apparent. He enjoys, ostensibly, "the warm stinging scent of the orange peel" (p. 331). He recalls the colors and the names of the flowers they visited together. He considers smoking "delicious, very fresh cigarettes" a "luxury," and he talks of perfume, exotic places, and music.

These references in the story, scattered though they are, are central in importance, and they lead as they ought to a discussion of connection by the man. Speaking of his days on a river boat on the Volga River, he concludes that "the life of the boat creates a bond between you and the people that's more than sufficient" (p. 334). He reminds her that "it is not necessary to know the language" (p. 334), a particularly apposite reflection in the light of their own relationship, spoiled six years before by the words of a letter the woman had sent him and about to be spoiled again by the man's carelessly uttered remarks about his companion. A connection deeper than words can produce is made between the man and his Russian coachman (different from him in national-ity, language, social class, and environment) by the coachman's offer of a dill pickle at a picnic on the Black Sea. It will be noted that the offer is of a par-ticularly tantalizing, sharp sense experience that only eating a pickle provides. Yet Vera is "not certain what a dill pickle was" and only vicariously "sucked in her cheeks; the dill pickle was terribly sour . . ." (p. 334) [ellipsis marks Mansfield's]. Even at secondhand, this taste of life and involvement for Vera is "sour," for it would force her to forego her protective covering of gloves, muff, and the rest, for the dangers of exposure to life's sharp sensations. No wonder, then, with the realization that she is "as alone as ever" (p. 337), she disappears from the table and from her companion to avoid commitment.

The ending of the story is puzzling. The man reminds the waitress that he does not want to he charged for the cream inasmuch as it has not been con-sumed. The attempt seems to be to show that he has not changed greatly since the day, six years earlier, when he expressed doubt that Vera would pay seven and sixpence for a portion of caviar. It is quite possible that this throw-back in behavior to a former period would not have occurred had he not been deserted again by Vera — that six years of advancing maturity had been tem-porarily sloughed off by a repetition of the traumatic situation and that his concluding remark is meant to illustrate the reassumption of his earlier stance. This view is partially reinforced by the fact that just prior to his remark to the waitress, he has been talking at great length to a companion who is no longer there. The realization of his present role puts him precisely where he was before the experience of the dill pickle. To Vera also had come the realization that, except superficially, things had not changed for either of them.

One of the stories on which Katherine Mansfield's reputation as an artist chiefly rests is "The Garden-Party," which she completed on October 14, 1921. Aside from its merits as fiction, it provides an opportunity for its author to be at once her satirical earlier self, the gentle recorder of her New Zealand childhood, and the new, transfigured personality whose view of life is complex, warm, and utterly philosophical. Without self-consciousness, she writes to William Gerhardi in 1922 that she has tried to express in the story

> the diversity of life and how we try to fit in everything, Death included. That is bewildering for a person of Laura's age. She feels things ought to happen differently. First one and then another. But life isn't like that. We haven't the ordering of it. Laura says, "But all these things must not happen at once." And Life answers, "Why not? How are they divided from each other?" And they *do* all happen, it is inevitable. And it seems to me there is beauty in that inevitability.

Perhaps it is unfortunate that critics of "The Garden-Party" have dwelt so extensively on this excerpt from Mansfield's letter, for they have generally tended to see the story almost exclusively as a reconciliation of Death and Life: that is, the parenthetical "Death included" has been read as though it were "Death especially." Rather, the attempt is equally to reconcile reality and the dream, innocence and experience, and, with great concern, levels of society. That Mansfield could even hope to carry out so ambitious an enterprise within the limitations of the short story is testimony to the increasing self-confidence that she felt during the last year of her life.

The story itself seems simple, childishly unsophisticated, even obvious, but this view proves untenable. The narrative involves preparations for a garden party — Laura's first grown-up affair; a glimpse of the party itself; and the aftermath which describes an impulsive attempt to give the party leftovers to the bereaved family of an accident victim. Mansfield's "selective camera" centers upon Laura, a young and well-meaning girl trying to establish her own values in a world carefully arranged for her by the women in her family: her mother Mrs. Sheridan and her two older sisters. The camera follows Laura as she adopts the ways of her mother in talking to the workmen or to her friend Kitty; as she helps with the sandwiches; and as she confronts the insensitivity of her elders to the death which has happened nearby. The reader notes her wavering allegiance to the attitude of the family and, on the other hand, to her instinctive youthful sense of proportion and good taste that assumes the cancellation of the party out of respect for the other family's grief. The devices employed to divert Laura from her independent point of view and to set her firmly once again in the Sheridan orbit are described. The story ends with her visit to the home of the dead man bearing the party leftovers and with her enchantment with the appearance of death as she views the body. Her final "Isn't life . . . isn't life" (p. 649) represents not nearly as ambiguous and inconclusive an ending as has been charged to the author, but a deeper look at the story is necessary to demonstrate this.

Mansfield's choice of a garden party as the focus of action and attitude is obviously meaningful. No less than Joyce, who praised Ibsen for using "never a superfluous word or phrase," Katherine Mansfield insists on the inevitability of all elements in a successful story. (Her remarks on the writing of "Miss Brill" are particularly relevant here.) Clearly, a garden party offered the author a many-faceted symbol. Thus it may represent the Sheridan way of life: showy, superficial, upper class, ephemeral (almost before final preparations are made for the affair comes a description of its aftermath), and with little more substance than the cream puffs that are served. In a wider sense, the garden party is life itself, the brief moment men enjoy between cradle and grave. Perhaps this is why Mansfield required a party in the garden rather than in the drawing room of the Sheridan home. For a garden implies nature and natural development, a developing and growing into maturity, and, inevitably too, a withering and dying. It is no accident either that Laura's own name has associations with a growing plant or that, when the florist delivers a profusion of lilies to augment the attractions of the garden flowers, Laura "felt they were in her fingers, on her lips, growing in her breast" (p. 538).

Employment of the garden as a symbol of life, of natural growth and development, permits Mansfield to play upon the perversion of the natural too — whether with respect to nature or to man. Thus, in the first paragraph of the story, before the reader is introduced specifically to any character or to details of plot, the point of view of the opening description suggests the unnaturalness of what is to occur in a "natural" setting. Probably at Mrs. Sheridan's suggestion, the gardener has been "mowing the lawns and sweeping them" until the grass "seemed to shine" (p. 534). This attempt to "methodize" nature and bring it under control is implicit also in the line: "They could not have had a more perfect day for a garden-party *if they had ordered it*" (p. 534) [italics mine], in which climatic conditions are reduced to a matter of commercial transaction. Further, perhaps the height of perversity is reached in the turn of mind which conceives of roses blooming precisely in time for the party because they are the flowers most likely to "impress people at garden-parties" (p. 534) and the roses know it. The horror is that the point of view here must be attributed to the young and innocent Laura, though the reader quickly senses that the hands guiding the strings are the hands of the mother. Similarly, later in the story young Kitty Maitland's plans for the "green-coated band" bespeak the insensitivity of the older generation: "Aren't they too like frogs for words? You ought to have arranged them round the pond with the conductor in the middle on a leaf" (p. 544).

This afternoon affair is Laura's coming-out party — the first social occasion on which she is to play an adult role. It is, as others have pointed out, her initiation into the mature world. If she has hitherto been merely a bud on the parent stem, on this day she will have her opportunity to blossom. The question is, of course, whether she will grow into a simple, natural flower or whether, like her mother, she is doomed to artificiality, insensitivity, and falseness. The restricted view of the world that she and her sisters have been permitted by their mother has already made inroads into her spontaneity and natural freshness, as the first paragraph abundantly proves. Without a dramatic widening of horizons to force a reevaluation of basic elements, Laura's path, following in the footsteps of Meg and Jose and her mother, is clearly predictable.

Death makes the difference and, at least temporarily, forces Laura to see in the older women in her family the crystallized and hardened views which in herself are still vague and indefinite imitations of adult models. The most final of all human activities makes her own growth and development less certain than it was that morning. Knowledge of death means an end to innocence but it also heralds the possibility of a new kind of life. The death of Scott the carter postpones maybe forever the death of the heart in Laura — a death already suffered by the other Sheridan women.

Yet if the death itself and the subsequent reactions to it of the Sheridans can accomplish this new healthy growth for Laura, why does Mansfield bother to include the last section of the story? Is it necessary for Laura to see a corpse in order for the meaning of the day's lesson to sink in? Or can Mansfield not resist the emotional value of a child's confrontation with the physical presence of death? The answers to these questions require examination of the story from another point of view.

On the day of the party, Laura loses her innocence and her parent-fostered narrowness in more ways than one. The development of her attitude toward class distinction accelerates as the day advances, further widening the gap between her and the other Sheridan women. The progress of the development is put by Mansfield in terms of Laura's increasing difficulty in generalizing about the working-class group of whose lives she knows almost nothing as the story opens. Subtly, Mansfield encourages the reader to accept Laura's stereotyped impression of the workmen who have come to put up the marquee: "Four men in their shirt-sleeves stood grouped together on the garden path. They carried staves . . . and they had big tool-bags slung on their backs. They looked impressive" (p. 535). Through the repetition of "they," through the monotony of sentence structure and word order, and through her underlining of the fact that these shirt-sleeved men were "grouped together," Mansfield reinforces the generalization almost schematically, as though picturing on a social studies graph the distribution of laborers in the locality. And, though

Laura welcomes contact with this rarely encountered group, she embraces the generalization enthusiastically. If *a* workman has nice eyes, the corollary is "How very nice workmen were" (p. 535) [italics mine]. When an individual workman uses slang in conversing with her, she wonders whether such talk is quite respectful of *a* workman. When one smells a sprig of lavender, she approves of all workmen at the expense of all "the silly boys" of her own class at dances. And when in the garden she takes a bite of bread-and-butter, she feels "just like a work-girl" (p. 536).

Death, the Great Leveller, succeeds in making Laura wary of generalizations. Suddenly the girl who in the garden that morning could react only on that level discovers that in her elders' resort to generalization is a method of avoiding unpleasant confrontations, mental or physical — and her natural honesty is shocked into an awareness of the immorality of the process. To her sister's "You won't bring a drunken workman back to life by being sentimental," she counters, "Drunk! Who said he was drunk?" (p. 542). She is similarly outraged when her mother speaks nebulously of not understanding how "they" keep alive "in those poky little holes" (p 543).

But to Laura, if not to her family, a dead workman cannot be generalized away. In bringing the news of the accident, Godber's man has been deliberately particular. Though the dead man is hardly a character in the story, the protagonist and the reader are given his name, his profession, the nature of the accident, the name of the street on which it occurred, the location of the wound, his marital status, and the number of his children. Such detailed categorization is essential to the breaking down in Laura of the vague barrier between class and class. Now it is easier to see why Laura must make the post-party trip to Scott's cottage and look upon the carter not as just another dead workman to be subtracted from census statistics, but as an individual being. It becomes clear why Laura must ask the woman who opens the door at Scott's home whether she is Mrs. Scott and why she must discover that the woman is not. Identities count now, even among workpeople.

The final step in Laura's development on this day is her reaction to the dead Scott. He now transcends class. As Laura had lived in a different world from workmen hitherto, Scott inhabits a dream realm which removes him, in a sense, from his own former slum world and from her world too. His is the classless world of death to which Mrs. Sheridan and Mrs. Scott and Jose and Laura — everyone — must eventually come. It is no wonder that Laura's response to this new "marvel" should be a tearful, "Forgive my hat" (p. 548).

Hats had dominated the story as one image followed another from the beginning: the turban Meg wears, Laurie and his father brushing their hats, the carelessly worn hats of the workmen, Kitty Maitland's hat, and finally the hat of Laura's mother, hastily "popped" on her head by Mrs. Sheridan to make Laura forget the dead man and her opposition to holding the garden party. When the mother thus presents her daughter with her own party hat in typical

coronation fashion, she is symbolically transferring to Laura the Sheridan heritage of snobbery, restricted social views, narrowness of vision — the garden
party syndrome. It is not surprising that when Laura first sees herself in a mirror wearing the hat, she hardly recognizes "this charming girl" (p. 543) who
stares back at her. Certainly the hat is, as her mother tells her, "made for" her,
but she is not at all sure that she wishes to acquire her rightful legacy. In the
presence of Scott, the realization of the discrepancy between what the hat indicates and what Laura in her own dawning maturity is tending toward evokes
the involuntary cry. Laura has had her vision.

As several critics have shown, Mansfield has prepared the reader for this
epiphany through earlier introducing the "This Life is Weary" song, whose
tragic burden evokes only a "brilliant, dreadfully unsympathetic smile"
(p. 539) from the singer herself. The final line, "A Dream — a *Wa*-kening," is
echoed in the description of Scott at the end of the story: "He was dreaming.
Never wake him up again" (p. 548). In a sense, Laura has through contact
with death wakened from her dream-life, the existence of garden parties and
Sheridan exclusivity. And Scott has, in her eyes, awakened through death to
a life infinitely more desirable than that of the Sheridans. Both have a knowledge that puts them above class.

It is almost as though Katherine Mansfield dangles obscurely before the
reader the dim symbol of another garden — a false Eden this time — a dream
world of artificial delight and false security. The inhabitants of this fools' paradise tend the garden, "order" the appropriate weather, and regard themselves
as the center of the universe. Only when Laura is expelled from the garden
does she trade innocence for knowledge. Now she can see death in the world
and "all our woe," unwarned not to resist by the "archangels" who Mansfield
tells us had visited the garden on the evening before the party. Yet the confrontation with death is to the awakened Laura not only not frightening: it is
positively an ecstatic experience. For her protagonist at least, Mansfield has
been able to demonstrate that life and death may indeed coexist and that their
common existence in one world may be beautiful.

The final scene with Laurie appears much less ambiguous than critics
have allowed. The fairylike Laura who had, before the fact of death entered her
life, dealt with life largely in terms of comfortable generalizations, finds herself speechless now to sum up the complexity that the deeper view affords.
When she stammers, "Isn't life — ?" the generalizing predicate adjective will
not come, for no single word can encompass it. It would not matter, in this
regard, whether the question were completed by "good" or "bad," "ugly" or
"beautiful," "sad" or "happy." What matters is that no one word suffices in a
world that encompasses, though it may not always reconcile, all of them.

The unspoken communication here between Laura and Laurie is interesting.
Laurie "quite understood" (p. 549) although she "couldn't explain." Mansfield
chooses to associate brother and sister closely not only in their ages ostensibly,
but in Laurie's sympathy for his sister's point of view and his apparent humanity

when contrasted with the female Sheridans' coldness. Furthermore, by calling them Laura and Laurie, the author establishes an obvious similarity. It may be that they are intended to be male and female aspects of the same personality and that, therefore, their reactions would be identical. It is not necessary, though it is possible, to believe with one critic that Laurie had earlier been initiated into knowledge of death and thus can empathize with the new initiate.

Katherine Mansfield considered "The Garden-Party" "moderately successful," but had reservations about the quality of the ending. She had worked on parts of it during a period of at least five months, as her *Scrapbook* shows, though the episode given there in an earlier form survives in "The Garden-Party" as the song "This Life is Weary" and as very little else. Called "By Moonlight" in the *Scrapbook,* the episode of the song is treated discursively for over three pages as the focal point for a view of the Sheridans: "Mother," "Father," Meg, Laura, Laurie, and Francie (the Jose of the later story). Since there is no garden party and no dead man in the sketch, the significance of the song is considerably less, its employment being confined to pointing up attitudes of those who hear it. "Mother" especially is revealed as she deplores the trend toward the "tragic" and the "depressing" in contemporary lyrics. She states her preference for "songs about primroses and cheerful normal birds and . . . [ellipsis marks Mansfield's] and spring and so on." Thus the morbid and the lower class are excluded from her world here as they will be later in the "Garden-Party" story. As for Meg, she finds the song "fascinating." But to the reader, the fascination is in seeing how Mansfield surrounds the song with meaning in the later version as she is unable to do a few weeks earlier.

STUDENT ESSAY

Joyce's "Araby" and Mansfield's "The Garden-Party": The Epiphany of Adolescence
by Cathy Young

The two stories, "Araby" by James Joyce and "The Garden-Party" by Katherine Mansfield, have a similar theme and many common literary techniques. Both authors address the issue of adolescent awakening, describing it as a process of spiritual death and rebirth. They both show how ordinary circumstances and events can culminate in moments of deep insight and startling revelation, sometimes called *epiphanies.* They both pay tribute to a spirituality which is evoked by everyday experience rather than religious ritual and which allows one to transcend self-limiting conditions. The dissimilarities between the two stories stem from the different gender and social circumstances of the two protagonists. The young girl in "The Garden-Party" is from an upper-class background and the setting of the story is the garden of her estate, while the young boy in "Araby" is cast in an Irish working-class environment in the city of Dublin. Because of these differences in gender and class, as well as other distinctions of social circumstance, the two young people have different experiences and learn different lessons. However, they both undergo a process of spiritual growth through which they achieve a wider understanding of human experience, a deeper knowledge of themselves, and a greater possibility for self-transcendence. They exchange the veil of childhood innocence for the hope of a life built on a higher wisdom than that of the societies in which they were born and raised.

In both "Araby" and "The Garden-Party," the narrator expresses the point of view of the central character: a child on the threshold of adolescence. We are shown how each young person experiences the everyday world and how their experiences build toward a final moment of realization and self-awareness, an epiphany. In "The Garden-Party" Laura is poised between childhood innocence and an adulthood of false propriety and corrupt vanity. She is on the brink of sacrificing the immediacy of experience and the natural human sensitivity with which children are born, in order to follow a path of affectation, self-indulgence, and denial, as proscribed for her by her gender and social position. Laura escapes the certainty of this destiny as a result of her epiphany at the end of the story. Her world is widened to include an uglier side of reality when she confronts the poverty and death in the families who live on the lane below her house. She rejects her family's insensitive dismissal of the injustice and suffering caused by class distinctions, moves through her own denial and fear of human suffering, and encounters a world of authenticity and wholeness. In so doing, she finds truth and therefore beauty. Her veil of innocence and denial is lifted. Laura experiences a moment of spiritual death and rebirth. She grows beyond the limitations of her former self; the possibility of escaping the corruption of her heritage opens for her.

Similarly, the young boy in "Araby" stands at the brink of adolescence and confronts a wider world view than his usual, restrictive environment would allow. The depressing weight of a dreary existence is lifted by his dream of romantic love. An illusion of sexual love infuses his spirit with fresh determination and life, but he fails in his attempt to give form and substance to his dream. His realization of the illusive quality of love and his experience of personal failure fill him with "anger and anguish" in his moment of epiphany at the end of the story (Joyce 35). He has outgrown his former self, both the one that would repress love and sexuality and the one that would deny his own impotence and moral complacency. Like Laura, he is forever changed, having undergone a type of spiritual death and rebirth. Like Laura, he may escape the dreary restrictions and moral hypocrisy of his heritage and live a life of authenticity and wholeness.

In sharp contrast to the setting of "Araby" on the dismal streets of Dublin, Laura's world of wealth and privilege is filled with abundance and light. The atmosphere of "The Garden-Party" is only apparently vibrant; it emanates a false vitality (Magalaner 1130). The flowering garden's beauty is proscribed; even nature behaves somewhat unnaturally. The weather is so "ideal" that it appears to be "ordered" for the party, and the lawns have been "swept" until the grass "shines"

(Mansfield 65). Even the roses seem to know the role that they are called upon to play for the social occasion: "As for the roses, you could not help feeling they understood that roses are the only flowers that impress people at garden-parties; the only flowers that everybody is certain of knowing. Hundreds, yes, literally hundreds, had come out in a single night; the green bushes bowed down as though they had been visited by archangels" (65).

In contrast to this frivolity and artificial vibrancy, the initial setting of "Araby" is dark, spiritually repressive, and debilitating. North Richmond Street is "blind" and "quiet," except when the boys are "set free from school" (Joyce 29). The boys run through "dark muddy lanes," "dark dripping gardens," and "dark odorous stables" (30). A priest has died in the back room of the boy's house and his rusty bicycle pump is still in the yard. The air is "musty" throughout the house, "from having been long enclosed." Even the houses seem to experience the oppressive mood: "The other houses of the street, conscious of decent lives within them, gazed at one another with brown imperturbable faces" (29).

In both stories, the adult world of authority is presented as unworthy of the young people's respect and allegiance. Parents and other grown relatives are, for the most part, presented as selfish, insensitive, and hypocritical. The children in "Araby" fear and avoid the young boy's uncle. When the old man comes home late, spoiling the boy's plans to go to the fair, he is drunk and uncaring. He uses a platitude to justify his selfish and insensitive behavior: "'All work and no play makes Jack a dull boy'" (Joyce 34). Similarly, the older women who stand as role models for Laura in "The Garden-Party" are insensitive and hypocritical. They spill out morally twisted admonitions when Laura insists on cancelling the garden party because of the poor man's death in the lane below the house. Her sister tells Laura not to be so "extravagant" as to think of cancelling the party (Mansfield 76): "If you're going to stop a band playing every time some one has an accident, you'll lead a very strenuous life. I'm every bit as sorry about it as you. I feel just as sympathetic" (77). Laura's mother is equally false and self-centered. She tells Laura, "It's only by accident we've heard of it" and calls the girl "not very sympathetic to spoil everybody's enjoyment" by continuing to discuss the matter (78–79).

In both stories, the central character comes face to face with a view of reality which is very different from that of his or her background and environment. As a result, the young person experiences confusion and psychological conflict, and then a resolution that brings enlightenment and growth. This process is cast in a spiritual mold, with the moment of epiphany as a climax. The most universal lesson from each character's experiences is to value the spiritual life, to value the vitality of a life lived with openness of heart and mind, lived consciously and directly. In the case of "Araby," the boy's viewpoint is widened first by the dream of romantic love and then by disappointment and failure when he cannot implement his dream. Love awakens the young boy's heart and brings life to his dreary existence. The experience is described in spiritual, quasi-religious, and supernatural terms. The boy walks through the dark and noisy streets of Dublin, carrying his love like a "chalice" with strange "prayers and praises" on his lips (Joyce 31). As he walks and prays, "The syllables of the word *Araby* were called to [him] through the silence in which [his] soul luxuriated and cast an Eastern enchantment over [him]" (32). Arriving in the hall of the bazaar, in the lateness of his arrival at Araby and the darkness of the hall, he "recognized a silence like that which pervades a church after a service" (34). Finally, awestruck and unable to overcome his timidity before the flirtatious young sales lady with the English accent, he "looked humbly at the great jars that stood like eastern guards at either side of the dark entrance to the stall" (35). This time the boy would not overcome the oppression of family, church, and country, which Joyce felt pervaded Irish society and crippled the individual's will for change. However, the youth is transformed, both by his experience of the "confused adoration" and joy of romantic love and by the heartbreak of his self-betrayal and disappointment (31). He has come to realize that he is "a creature driven and derided by vanity" and although his eyes burn in "anguish and anger," at least they have been opened (35). One senses that he may yet find the courage and spiritual strength he needs to overcome the limitations of his society and build a brighter future for himself, as James Joyce did as an expatriate Irish writer.

Similarly, in "The Garden-Party," Laura encounters an opposing view of reality from that of her background, experiencing a spiritual transformation which may lead her away from the unjust and dehumanizing constraints and privileges of her class. Laura has a direct encounter with the injustice of premature death, that of the young man whose impoverished family depended on him for support. Still, on the man's dead body, Laura imagines a sleeping face: "He was dreaming. Never wake him up again" (Mansfield 86). She begs the dead man's forgiveness, with "a loud childish sob," for "her hat" (87). These words are like a religious confession of the injustice brought about by the role of her class, the "hat" that she wore in the social and economic system.

Yet Laura does not experience the "anguish and anger" of higher consciousness, as does the boy in "Araby." She has a sense of wonder and even equanimity in the moment of her epiphany. Despite her outrage at human suffering and victimization, Mansfield herself found beauty in direct, conscious experience, no matter what it brought. The kind of spiritual transformation and transcendence which Laura experiences in "The Garden-Party" is like that which Mansfield describes as her own after suffering years of painful, debilitating, and ultimately fatal tuberculosis. She wrote in a letter of 1920:

> And then bodily suffering such as I've known for three years. It has changed everything--even the *appearance* of the world is not the same -- something has been added. . . . If we set out on a journey, the more wonderful the treasure, the greater the temptations and perils to be overcome. . . . The little boat enters the dark fearful gulf and our only cry is to escape--"put me on land again." But it's useless. Nobody listens. The shadowy figure rows on. One ought to sit still and uncover one's eyes. (qtd. in Murry 88)

During the following year, 1921, Mansfield would express these ideas in "The Garden-Party"; the next year, at the age of thirty-four, she would die.

"Araby" and "The Garden-Party" are strikingly similar, despite the differences of gender, class, and social circumstance between the two protagonists. Both Joyce and Mansfield address the same issue--adolescent awakening--in much the same way. The two young people stand on the cusp between childhood and adulthood, a time of tremendous psychological change, when the values adopted and the choices made have lifetime implications. In the two stories, we are given a glimpse of the interior workings of the adolescent mind as the changes and choices crystallize. The young people observe with wide-eyed innocence the selfishness, repression, denial, and hypocrisy of the society in which they live. They try to understand and evaluate the world into which they were born and the people that they are called upon to emulate. They suffer conflict and confusion, which leads ultimately to their spiritual transformation, to their epiphany. They seem to exchange their childhood innocence not for the mantle of the corrupt society that they have inherited but for a way of being that is more open, conscious, compassionate, and authentic.

Works Cited

Joyce, James. "Araby." *Dubliners*. New York: Viking, 1953. 29–35.

Magalaner, Marvin. *The Fiction of Katherine Mansfield*. London and Amsterdam: Feffer & Simons, 1971.

Mansfield, Katherine. *The Garden-Party and Other Stories*. Middlesex, England: Penguin, 1951.

Murry, John Middleton. *"Katherine Mansfield" and Other Literary Studies*. London: Constable, 1959.

KATHERINE ANNE PORTER (1890–1980)

Like Katherine Mansfield and other modernist writers, Katherine Anne Porter frequently tried in her stories to capture a character's inner feelings about an important moment in his or her life instead of developing a complex plot line. The worlds she portrays are sometimes grotesque, but she always presents them with compassion.

Porter was born in Indian Creek, Texas, and after her mother died when Porter was two, she was raised by her grandmother, who remained the most influential woman in her life. She ran away from home at sixteen, married, and divorced three years later. The next year she left Texas. After writing for newspapers in a number of American cities, she chose New York as her base. In the 1920s she began working as a freelance writer but did not try to publish her short stories until she was well into her thirties. After the publication of *Flowering Judas and Other Stories* (1930), which includes "The Jilting of Granny Weatherall," Porter won a Guggenheim fellowship, which made it possible for her to live and write in Paris and Berlin. After a serious bout with influenza, she moved to Mexico to recover, to study art, and to write. The stories about her recovery from her illness provided material for her collection *Pale Horse, Pale Rider: Three Short Novels* (1939). When her *Collected Stories* was published in 1965, it received the National Book Award for Fiction and the Pulitzer Prize in Fiction. Porter's small-town southern roots provided the basis for many of her stories, including "The Jilting of Granny Weatherall."

The Jilting of Granny Weatherall (1929)

She flicked her wrist neatly out of Doctor Harry's pudgy careful fingers and pulled the sheet up to her chin. The brat ought to be in knee breeches. Doctoring around the country with spectacles on his nose! "Get along now, take your schoolbooks and go. There's nothing wrong with me."

Doctor Harry spread a warm paw like a cushion on her forehead where the forked green vein danced and made her eyelids twitch. "Now, now, be a good girl and we'll have you up in no time."

"That's no way to speak to a woman nearly eighty years old just because she's down. I'd have you respect your elders, young man."

"Well, Missy, excuse me." Doctor Harry patted her cheek. "But I've got to warn you, haven't I? You're a marvel, but you must be careful or you're going to be good and sorry."

"Don't tell me what I'm going to be. I'm on my feet now, morally speaking. It's Cornelia. I had to go to bed to get rid of her."

Her bones felt loose, and floated around in her skin, and Doctor Harry floated like a balloon around the foot of the bed. He floated and pulled down his waistcoat and swung his glasses on a cord. "Well, stay where you are, it certainly can't hurt you."

"Get along and doctor your sick," said Granny Weatherall. "Leave a well woman alone. I'll call for you when I want you. . . . Where were you forty years ago when I pulled through milk leg and double pneumonia? You weren't even born. Don't let Cornelia lead you on," she shouted, because Doctor Harry appeared to float up to the ceiling and out. "I pay my own bills, and I don't throw my money away on nonsense!"

She meant to wave good-by, but it was too much trouble. Her eyes closed of themselves, it was like a dark curtain drawn around the bed. The pillow rose and floated under her, pleasant as a hammock in a light wind. She listened to the leaves rustling outside the window. No, somebody was swishing newspapers: no, Cornelia and Doctor Harry were whispering together. She leaped broad awake, thinking they whispered in her ear.

"She was never like this, *never* like this!" "Well, what can we expect?" "Yes, eighty years old. . . ."

Well, and what if she was? She still had ears. It was like Cornelia to whisper around doors. She always kept things secret in such a public way. She was always being tactful and kind. Cornelia was dutiful; that was the trouble with her. Dutiful and good: "So good and dutiful," said Granny, "and I'd like to spank her." She saw herself spanking Cornelia and making a fine job of it.

"What'd you say, Mother?"

Granny felt her face tying up in hard knots.

"Can't a body think, I'd like to know?"

"I thought you might want something."

"I do. I want a lot of things. First off, go away and don't whisper."

She lay and drowsed, hoping in her sleep that the children would keep out and let her rest a minute. It had been a long day. Not that she was tired. It was always pleasant to snatch a minute now and then. There was always so much to be done, let me see: tomorrow.

Tomorrow was far away and there was nothing to trouble about. Things were finished somehow when the time came; thank God there was always a little margin over for peace: then a person could spread out the plan of life and tuck in the edges orderly. It was good to have everything clean and folded away, with the hair brushes and tonic bottles sitting straight on the white embroidered linen: the day started without fuss and the pantry shelves laid out with rows of jelly glasses and brown jugs and white stone-china jars with blue whirligigs and words painted on them: coffee, tea, sugar, ginger, cinnamon, allspice: and the bronze clock with the lion on top nicely dusted off. The dust that lion could collect in twenty-four hours! The box in the attic with all those letters tied up, she'd have to go through that tomorrow. All those letters — George's letters and John's letters and her letters to them both — lying around for the children to find afterwards made her uneasy. Yes, that would be tomorrow's business. No use to let them know how silly she had been once.

While she was rummaging around she found death in her mind and it felt clammy and unfamiliar. She had spent so much time preparing for death there was no need for bringing it up again. Let it take care of itself now. When she was sixty she had felt very old, finished, and went around making farewell trips to see her children and grandchildren, with a secret in her mind: This is the very last of your mother, children! Then she made her will and came down with a long fever. That was all just a notion like a lot of other things, but it was lucky too, for she had once for all got over the idea of dying for a long time. Now she couldn't be worried. She hoped she had better sense now. Her father had lived to be one hundred and two years old and had drunk a noggin of strong hot toddy on his last birthday. He told the reporters it was his daily habit, and he owed his long life to that. He had made quite a scandal and was very pleased about it. She believed she'd just plague Cornelia a little.

"Cornelia! Cornelia!" No footsteps, but a sudden hand on her cheek. "Bless you, where have you been?"

"Here, Mother."

"Well, Cornelia, I want a noggin of hot toddy."

"Are you cold, darling?"

"I'm chilly, Cornelia. Lying in bed stops the circulation. I must have told you that a thousand times."

Well, she could just hear Cornelia telling her husband that Mother was getting a little childish and they'd have to humor her. The thing that most annoyed her was that Cornelia thought she was deaf, dumb, and blind. Little hasty glances and tiny gestures tossed around her and over her head saying, "Don't cross her, let her have her way, she's eighty years old," and she sitting there as if she lived in a thin glass cage. Sometimes Granny almost made up her mind to pack up and move back to her own house where nobody could remind her every minute that she was old. Wait, wait, Cornelia, till your own children whisper behind your back!

In her day she had kept a better house and had got more work done. She wasn't too old yet for Lydia to be driving eighty miles for advice when one of the children jumped the track, and Jimmy still dropped in and talked things over: "Now, Mammy, you've a good business head, I want to know what you think of this? . . ." Old. Cornelia couldn't change the furniture around without asking. Little things, little things! They had been so sweet when they were little. Granny wished the old days were back again with the children young and everything to be done over. It had been a hard pull, but not too much for her. When she thought of all the food she had cooked, and all the clothes she had cut and sewed, and all the gardens she had made — well, the children showed it. There they were, made out of her, and they couldn't get away from that. Sometimes she wanted to see John again and point to them and say,

Well, I didn't do so badly, did I? But that would have to wait. That was for tomorrow. She used to think of him as a man, but now all the children were older than their father, and he would be a child beside her if she saw him now. It seemed strange and there was something wrong in the idea. Why, he couldn't possibly recognize her. She had fenced in a hundred acres once, digging the post holes herself and clamping the wires with just a negro boy to help. That changed a woman. John would be looking for a young woman with the peaked Spanish comb in her hair and the painted fan. Digging post holes changed a woman. Riding country roads in the winter when women had their babies was another thing: sitting up nights with sick horses and sick negroes and sick children and hardly ever losing one. John, I hardly ever lost one of them! John would see that in a minute, that would be something he could understand, she wouldn't have to explain anything!

It made her feel like rolling up her sleeves and putting the whole place to rights again. No matter if Cornelia was determined to be everywhere at once, there were a great many things left undone on this place. She would start tomorrow and do them. It was good to be strong enough for everything, even if all you made melted and changed and slipped under your hands, so that by the time you finished you almost forgot what you were working for. What was it I set out to do? she asked herself intently, but she could not remember. A fog rose over the valley, she saw it marching across the creek swallowing the trees and moving up the hill like an army of ghosts. Soon it would be at the near edge of the orchard, and then it was time to go in and light the lamps. Come in, children, don't stay out in the night air.

Lighting the lamps had been beautiful. The children huddled up to her and breathed like little calves waiting at the bars in the twilight. Their eyes followed the match and watched the flame rise and settle in a blue curve, then they moved away from her. The lamp was lit, they didn't have to be scared and hang on to mother any more. Never, never, never more. God, for all my life I thank Thee. Without Thee, my God, I could never have done it. Hail, Mary, full of grace.

I want you to pick all the fruit this year and see that nothing is wasted. There's always someone who can use it. Don't let good things rot for want of using. You waste life when you waste good food. Don't let things get lost. It's bitter to lose things. Now, don't let me get to thinking, not when I am tired and taking a little nap before supper. . . .

The pillow rose about her shoulders and pressed against her heart and the memory was being squeezed out of it: oh, push down the pillow, somebody: it would smother her if she tried to hold it. Such a fresh breeze blowing and such a green day with no threats in it. But he had not come, just the same. What does a woman do when she has put on the white veil and set out the white cake for a man and he doesn't come? She tried to remember. No, I swear he never harmed me but in that. He never harmed me but in that . . . and what if he did? There was the day, the day, but a whirl of dark smoke rose and covered it, crept up and over into the bright field where everything was planted so carefully in orderly rows. That was hell, she knew hell when she saw it. For sixty years she had prayed against remembering him and against losing her soul in the deep pit of hell, and now the two things were mingled in one and the thought of him was a smoky cloud from hell that moved and crept in her head when she had just got rid of Doctor Harry and was trying to rest a minute. Wounded vanity, Ellen, said a sharp voice in the top of her mind. Don't let your wounded vanity get the upper hand of you. Plenty of girls get jilted. You were jilted, weren't you? Then stand up to it. Her eyelids wavered and let in streamers of blue-gray light like tissue paper over her eyes. She must get up and pull the shades down or she'd never sleep. She was in bed again and the shades were not down. How could that happen? Better turn over, hide from the light, sleeping in the light gave you nightmares. "Mother, how do you feel now?" and a stinging wetness on her forehead. But I don't like having my face washed in cold water!

Hapsy? George? Lydia? Jimmy? No, Cornelia, and her features were swollen and full of little puddles. "They're coming, darling, they'll all be here soon." Go wash your face, child, you look funny.

Instead of obeying, Cornelia knelt down and put her head on the pillow. She seemed to be talking but there was no sound. "Well, are you tongue-tied? Whose birthday is it? Are you going to give a party?"

Cornelia's mouth moved urgently in strange shapes. "Don't do that, you bother me, daughter."

"Oh, no, Mother. Oh, no. . . ."

Nonsense. It was strange about children. They disputed your every word. "No what, Cornelia?"

"Here's Doctor Harry."

"I won't see that boy again. He just left five minutes ago."

"That was this morning, Mother. It's night now. Here's the nurse."

"This is Doctor Harry, Mrs. Weatherall. I never saw you look so young and happy!"

"Ah, I'll never be young again — but I'd be happy if they'd let me lie in peace and get rested."

She thought she spoke up loudly, but no one answered. A warm weight on her forehead, a warm bracelet on her wrist, and a breeze went on whispering, trying to tell her something. A shuffle of leaves in the everlasting hand of God. He blew on them and they danced and rattled. "Mother, don't mind, we're going to give you a little hypodermic." "Look here, daughter, how do ants get in this bed? I saw sugar ants yesterday." Did you send for Hapsy too?

It was Hapsy she really wanted. She had to go a long way back through a great many rooms to find Hapsy standing with a baby on her arm. She seemed to herself to be Hapsy also, and the baby on Hapsy's arm was Hapsy and himself and herself, all at once, and there was no surprise in the meeting. Then Hapsy melted from within and turned flimsy as gray gauze and the baby was a gauzy shadow, and Hapsy came up close and said, "I thought you'd never come," and looked at her very searchingly and said, "You haven't changed a bit!" They leaned forward to kiss, when Cornelia began whispering from a long way off, "Oh, is there anything you want to tell me? Is there anything I can do for you?"

Yes, she had changed her mind after sixty years and she would like to see George. I want you to find George. Find him and be sure to tell him I forgot him. I want him to know I had my husband just the same and my children and my house like any other woman. A good house too and a good husband that I loved and fine children out of him. Better than I hoped for even. Tell him I was given back everything he took away and more. Oh, no, oh, God, no, there was something else besides the house and the man and the children. Oh, surely they were not all? What was it? Something not given back. . . . Her breath crowded down under her ribs and grew into a monstrous frightening shape with cutting edges; it bored up into her head, and the agony was unbelievable: Yes, John, get the doctor now, no more talk, my time has come.

When this one was born it should be the last. The last. It should have been born first, for it was the one she had truly wanted. Everything came in good time. Nothing left out, left over. She was strong, in three days she would be as well as ever. Better. A woman needed milk in her to have her full health.

"Mother, do you hear me?"

"I've been telling you — "

"Mother, Father Connolly's here."

"I went to Holy Communion only last week. Tell him I'm not so sinful as all that."

"Father just wants to speak to you."

He could speak as much as he pleased. It was like him to drop in and inquire about her soul as if it were a teething baby, and then stay on for a cup of tea and a round of cards and gossip. He always had a funny story of some sort, usually about an Irishman who made his little mistakes and confessed them, and the point lay in some absurd thing he would blurt out in the confessional showing his struggles between native piety and original sin. Granny felt easy about her soul. Cornelia, where are your manners? Give Father Connolly a chair. She had her secret comfortable understanding with a few favorite saints who cleared a straight road to God for her. All as surely signed and sealed as the papers for the new Forty Acres. Forever . . . heirs and assigns forever. Since the day the wedding cake was not cut, but thrown out and wasted. The whole bottom dropped out of the world, and there she was blind and sweating with nothing under her feet and walls falling away. His hand had caught her under the breast, she had not fallen, there was the freshly polished floor with the green rug on it, just as before. He had cursed like a sailor's parrot and said, "I'll kill him for you." Don't lay a hand on him, for my sake leave something to God. "Now, Ellen, you must believe what I tell you. . . ."

So there was nothing, nothing to worry about any more, except sometimes in the night one of the children screamed in a nightmare, and they both
hustled out shaking and hunting for the matches and calling, "There, wait a
minute, here we are!" John, get the doctor now, Hapsy's time has come. But
there was Hapsy standing by the bed in a white cap. "Cornelia, tell Hapsy to
take off her cap. I can't see her plain."

Her eyes opened very wide and the room stood out like a picture she had
seen somewhere. Dark colors with the shadows rising towards the ceiling in
long angles. The tall black dresser gleamed with nothing on it but John's picture, enlarged from a little one, with John's eyes very black when they should
have been blue. You never saw him, so how do you know how he looked? But
the man insisted the copy was perfect, it was very rich and handsome. For a
picture, yes, but it's not my husband. The table by the bed had a linen cover
and a candle and a crucifix. The light was blue from Cornelia's silk lamp-
shades. No sort of light at all, just frippery. You had to live forty years with
kerosene lamps to appreciate honest electricity. She felt very strong and she
saw Doctor Harry with a rosy nimbus around him.

"You look like a saint, Doctor Harry, and I vow that's as near as you'll ever
come to it."

"She's saying something."

"I heard you, Cornelia. What's all this carrying on?"

"Father Connolly's saying — "

Cornelia's voice staggered and bumped like a cart in a bad road. It
rounded corners and turned back again and arrived nowhere. Granny stepped
up in the cart very lightly and reached for the reins, but a man sat beside her
and she knew him by his hands, driving the cart. She did not look in his face,
for she knew without seeing, but looked instead down the road where the
trees leaned over and bowed to each other and a thousand birds were singing
a Mass. She felt like singing too, but she put her hand in the bosom of her
dress and pulled out a rosary, and Father Connolly murmured Latin in a very
solemn voice and tickled her feet. My God, will you stop that nonsense? I'm a
married woman. What if he did run away and leave me to face the priest by
myself? I found another a whole world better. I wouldn't have exchanged my
husband for anybody except St. Michael himself, and you may tell him that for
me with a thank you in the bargain.

Light flashed on her closed eyelids, and a deep roaring shook her.
Cornelia, is that lightning? I hear thunder. There's going to be a storm. Close
all the windows. Call the children in. . . . "Mother, here we are, all of us." "Is
that you, Hapsy?" "Oh, no, I'm Lydia. We drove as fast as we could." Their
faces drifted above her, drifted away. The rosary fell out of her hands and Lydia
put it back. Jimmy tried to help, their hands fumbled together, and Granny
closed two fingers around Jimmy's thumb. Beads wouldn't do, it must be
something alive. She was so amazed her thoughts ran round and round.
So, my dear Lord, this is my death and I wasn't even thinking about it. My

children have come to see me die. But I can't, it's not time. Oh, I always hated surprises. I wanted to give Cornelia the amethyst set — Cornelia, you're to have the amethyst set, but Hapsy's to wear it when she wants, and, Doctor Harry, do shut up. Nobody sent for you. Oh, my dear Lord, do wait a minute. I meant to do something about the Forty Acres, Jimmy doesn't need it and Lydia will later on, with that worthless husband of hers. I meant to finish the altar cloth and send six bottles of wine to Sister Borgia for her dyspepsia. I want to send six bottles of wine to Sister Borgia, Father Connolly, now don't let me forget.

Cornelia's voice made short turns and tilted over and crashed, "Oh, Mother, oh, Mother, oh, Mother. . . ."

"I'm not going, Cornelia. I'm taken by surprise. I can't go."

You'll see Hapsy again. What about her? "I thought you'd never come." Granny made a long journey outward, looking for Hapsy. What if I don't find her? What then? Her heart sank down and down, there was no bottom to death, she couldn't come to the end of it. The blue light from Cornelia's lamp-shade drew into a tiny point in the center of her brain, it flickered and winked like an eye, quietly it fluttered and dwindled. Granny lay curled down within herself, amazed and watchful, staring at the point of light that was herself; her body was now only a deeper mass of shadow in an endless darkness and this darkness would curl around the light and swallow it up. God, give a sign!

For the second time there was no sign. Again no bridegroom and the priest in the house. She could not remember any other sorrow because this grief wiped them all away. Oh, no, there's nothing more cruel than this — I'll never forgive it. She stretched her self with a deep breath and blew out the light.

Questions for Discussion

1. How does Granny feel about Doctor Harry and Cornelia? What do her feelings reveal about her personality?
2. Does Granny realize that she is dying? How do her reflections reveal her preoccupations and unresolved conflicts?
3. What is the significance of Father Connolly? What role has he played in Granny's life?
4. To what extent has Granny been able to accept the fact that she was jilted on her wedding day? Why does she continue to feel bitter?
5. What does this story imply about how elderly people face death?

Ideas for Writing

1. Examine in an essay the ways in which Porter's narrative perspective and style, with its use of the stream of consciousness of the dying Granny, help to capture the meaning of Granny's life and her fundamental vitality.
2. Write a story that uses a stream-of-consciousness narrative such as Porter employs in this story. Develop a central character of your own whose voice is familiar to you.

ISAAC BABEL   (1894–1939)

Isaac Babel's writing is distinguished by its earthy, direct sensuality and a grotesque, at times ribald humor that is mixed with religious awe and with horror at the brutality of his unsettled times. Born in Odessa, Russia, the son of a devout Jewish merchant, Babel studied the Bible, Hebrew, and the Talmud while also taking lessons in French language and literature. He developed his literary style early by writing stories in French, and he particularly admired the work of Gustave Flaubert and Guy de Maupassant.

Babel was encouraged to continue writing by the Russian novelist and playwright Maxim Gorky, whom he met in St. Petersburg after moving there in 1915. Babel's literary career was interrupted by his service with the Red Army during World War I, his work as a press correspondent with the Soviet Cavalry, and his government service under the newly formed Bolshevik government. In 1924 he began to publish stories in the avant-garde periodical *Left*. His major collections include *The Story of My Dovecot* (1924) and *Red Cavalry* (1925). While Babel became a popular Soviet writer in the late 1920s, his family's emigration to Paris left him feeling increasingly isolated in Stalinist Russia. Tormented by the purges of writers who failed to follow the party line, he wrote little during the 1930s. Arrested in 1939, Babel vanished and is presumed to have died in a concentration camp. His collected stories were published in 1955.

Guy de Maupassant   (1920–1928)

In the winter of 1916 I found myself in St. Petersburg with a forged passport and not a cent to my name. Alexey Kazantsev, a teacher of Russian literature, took me into his house.

He lived on a yellow, frozen, evil-smelling street in the Peski district. The miserable salary he received was padded out a bit by doing translations from the Spanish. Blasco Ibáñez was just becoming famous at that time.

Kazantsev had never so much as passed through Spain, but his love for that country filled his whole being. He knew every castle, every garden, and every river in Spain. There were many other people huddling around Kazantsev, all of them, like myself, flung out of the round of ordinary life. We were half-starved. From time to time the yellow press would publish, in the smallest print, unimportant news-items we had written.

I spent my mornings hanging around the morgues and police stations.

Kazantsev was happier than any of us, for he had a country of his own — Spain.

In November I was given the chance to become a clerk at the Obukhov Mills. It was a rather good position, and would have exempted me from military service.

I refused to become a clerk.

Even in those days, when I was twenty years old, I had told myself: better starve, go to jail, or become a bum than spend ten hours every day behind a desk in an office.

There was nothing particularly laudable in my resolve, but I have never broken it and I never will. The wisdom of my ancestors was firmly lodged in my head: we are born to enjoy our work, our fights, and our love; we are born for that and for nothing else.

Listening to my bragging, Kazantsev ruffled the short yellow fluff on the top of his head. The horror in his stare was mixed with admiration.

At Christmastime we had luck. Bendersky the lawyer, who owned a publishing house called "Halcyon," decided to publish a new edition of Maupassant's works. His wife Raïsa tried her hand at the translation, but nothing came of her lofty ambition.

Kazantsev, who was known as a translator of Spanish, had been asked whether he could recommend someone to assist Raïsa Mikhaylovna. He told them of me.

The next day, in someone else's coat, I made my way to the Benderskys'. They lived at the corner of the Nevsky and the Moyka, in a house of Finland granite adorned with pink columns, crenellations and coats-of-arms worked in stone.

Bankers without a history and catapulted out of nowhere, converted Jews who had grown rich selling materials to the army, they put up these pretentious mansions in St. Petersburg before the war.

There was a red carpet on the stairs. On the landings, upon their hind legs, stood plush bears. Crystal lamps burned in their open mouths.

The Benderskys lived on the second floor. A high-breasted maid with a white cap on her head opened the door. She led me into a drawing-room decorated in the old Slav style. Blue paintings by Roerich depicting prehistoric stones and monsters hung on the walls. On stands in the corners stood ancestral icons.

The high-breasted maid moved smoothly and majestically. She had an excellent figure, was nearsighted and rather haughty. In her open gray eyes one saw a petrified lewdness. She moved slowly. I thought: when she makes love she must move with unheard-of agility. The brocade portiere over the doorway suddenly swayed, and a black-haired woman with pink eyes and a wide bosom entered the room. It was easy to recognize in Raïsa Bendersky one of those charming Jewesses who have come to us from Kiev and Poltava, from the opulent steppe-towns full of chestnut trees and acacias. The money made by their clever husbands is transformed by these women into a pink layer of fat on the belly, the back of the neck, and the well-rounded shoulders. Their subtle sleepy smiles drive officers from the local garrisons crazy.

"Maupassant," Raïsa said to me, "is the only passion of my life."

Trying to keep the swaying of her great hips under control, she left the room and returned with a translation of "Miss Harriet." In her translation not even a trace was left of Maupassant's free-flowing sentences with their fragrance of passion. Raïsa Bendersky took pains to write correctly and precisely, and all that resulted was something loose and lifeless, the way Jews wrote Russian in the old days.

I took the manuscript with me, and in Kazantsev's attic, among my sleeping friends, spent the night cutting my way through the tangled undergrowth of her prose. It was not such dull work as it might seem. A phrase is born into the world both good and bad at the same time. The secret lies in a slight, an almost invisible twist. The lever should rest in your hand, getting warm, and you can only turn it once, not twice.

Next morning I took back the corrected manuscript. Raïsa wasn't lying when she told me that Maupassant was her sole passion. She sat motionless, her hands clasped, as I read it to her. Her satin hands drooped to the floor, her forehead paled, and the lace between her constricted breasts danced and heaved.

"How did you do it?"

I began to speak of style, of the army of words, of the army in which all kinds of weapons may come into play. No iron can stab the heart with such force as a period put just at the right place. She listened with her head down and her painted lips half open. In her hair, pressed smooth, divided by a parting and looking like patent leather, shone a dark gleam. Her legs in tight-fitting stockings, with their strong soft calves, were planted wide apart on the carpet.

The maid, glancing to the side with her petrified wanton eyes, brought in breakfast on a tray.

The glassy rays of the Petersburg sun lay on the pale and uneven carpet. Twenty-nine volumes of Maupassant stood on the shelf above the desk. The sun with its fingers of melting dissolution touched the morocco backs of the books — the magnificent grave of a human heart.

Coffee was served in blue cups, and we started translating "Idyl." Everyone remembers the story of the youthful, hungry carpenter who sucked the breast of the stout nursing-mother to relieve her of the milk with which she was overladen. It happened in a train going from Nice to Marseille, at noon on a very hot day, in the land of roses, the birthplace of roses, where beds of flowers flow down to the seashore.

I left the Benderskys with a twenty-five rouble advance. That night our crowd at Peski got as drunk as a flock of drugged geese. Between drinks we spooned up the best caviar, and then changed over to liver sausage. Half-soused, I began to berate Tolstoy.

"He turned yellow, your Count; he was afraid. His religion was all fear. He was frightened by the cold, by old age, by death; and he made himself a warm coat out of his faith."

"Go on, go on," Kazantsev urged, swaying his birdlike head.

We fell asleep on the floor beside our beds. I dreamed of Katya, a forty-year-old washerwoman who lived a floor below us. We went to her every morning for our hot water. I had never seen her face distinctly, but in my dream we did god-awful things together. We almost destroyed each other with kisses. The very next morning I couldn't restrain myself from going to her for hot water.

I saw a wan woman, a shawl across her chest, with ash-gray hair and labor-worn, withered hands.

From then on I took my breakfast at the Benderskys' every day. A new stove, herrings, and chocolate appeared in our attic. Twice Raïsa took me out in her carriage for drives to the islands. I couldn't prevent myself from telling her all about my childhood. To my amazement the story turned out to be very sordid. From under her moleskin cowl her gleaming, frightened eyes stared at me. The rusty fringe of her eyelashes quivered with pity.

I met Raïsa's husband, a yellow-faced Jew with a bald skull and a flat, powerful body that seemed always poised obliquely, ready for flight.

There were rumors about his being close to Rasputin. The enormous profits he made from war supplies drove him almost crazy, giving him the expression of a person with a fixed hallucination. His eyes never remained still: it seemed that reality was lost to him for ever. Raïsa was embarrassed whenever she had to introduce him to new acquaintances. Because of my youth I noticed this a full week later than I should have.

After the New Year Raïsa's two sisters arrived from Kiev. One day I took along the manuscript of *"L'Aveu"* and, not finding Raïsa at home, returned that evening. They were at dinner. Silvery, neighing laughter and excited male voices came from the dining-room. In rich houses without tradition dinners are always noisy. It was a Jewish noise, rolling and tripping and ending up on a melodious, singsong note. Raïsa came out to me in evening dress, her back bare. Her feet stepped awkwardly in wavering patent-leather slippers.

"I'm drunk, darling," she said, and held out her arms, loaded with chains of platinum and emerald stars.

Her body swayed like a snake's dancing to music. She tossed her marcelled hair about, and suddenly, with a tinkle of rings, slumped into a chair with ancient Russian carvings. Scars glowed on her powered back.

Women's laughter again came from the dining-room. Raïsa's sisters, with delicate mustaches and as full-bosomed and round-bodied as Raïsa herself, entered the room. Their busts jutted out and their black hair fluttered. Both of them had their own Benderskys for husbands. The room was filled with disjointed, chaotic feminine merriment, the hilarity of ripe women. The husbands wrapped the sisters in their sealskins and Orenburg shawls and shod them in black boots. Beneath the snowy visors of their shawls only painted glowing cheeks, marble noses, and eyes with their myopic Jewish glitter could be seen. After making some more happy noise they left for the theater, where Chaliapin was singing *Judith*.

"I want to work," Raïsa lisped, stretching her bare arms to me, "we've skipped a whole week."

She brought a bottle and two glasses from the dining-room. Her breasts swung free beneath the sacklike gown, the nipples rose beneath the clinging silk.

"It's very valuable," said Raïsa, pouring out the wine. "Muscatel '83. My husband will kill me when he finds out."

I had never drunk Muscatel '83, and tossed off three glasses one after the other without thinking. They carried me swiftly away into alleys where an orange flame danced and sounds of music could be heard.

"I'm drunk, darling. What are we doing today?"

"Today it's '*L'Aveu*.' 'The Confession,' then. The sun is the hero of this story, *le soleil de France*. Molten drops of it pattering on the red-haired Céleste changed into freckles. The sun's direct rays and wine and apple-cider burnished the face of the coachman Polyte. Twice a week Céleste drove into town to sell cream, eggs and chickens. She gave Polyte ten sous for herself and four for her basket. And every time Polyte would wink at the red-haired Céleste and ask: 'When are we going to have some fun, *ma belle?*' — 'What do you mean, Monsieur Polyte?' Jogging up and down on the box, the coachman explained: 'To have some fun means . . . why, what the hell, to have some fun! A lad with a lass; no music necessary . . .'

"'I do not care for such jokes, Monsieur Polyte,' replied Céleste, moving further away the skirts that hung over her mighty calves in red stockings.

"But that devil Polyte kept right on guffawing and coughing: 'Ah, but one day we shall have our bit of fun, *ma belle*,' while tears of delight rolled down a face the color of brick-red wine and blood."

I downed another glass of the rare muscatel. Raïsa touched glasses with me. The maid with the stony eyes crossed the room and disappeared.

"*Ce diable de Polyte* . . . In the course of two years Céleste had paid him forty-eight francs; that is, two francs short of fifty! At the end of the second year, when they were alone in the carriage, Polyte, who had some cider before setting out, asked her his usual question: 'What about having some fun today, Mamselle Céleste?' And she replied, lowering her eyes: 'I am at your disposal, Monsieur Polyte.'"

Raïsa flung herself down on the table, laughing. "*Ce diable de Polyte* . . ."

"A white spavined mare was harnessed to the carriage. The white hack, its lips pink with age, went forward at a walking pace. The gay sun of France poured down on the ancient coach, screened from the world by a weather-beaten hood. A lad with a lass; no music necessary . . ."

Raïsa held out a glass to me. It was the fifth.

"*Mon vieux*, to Maupassant."

"And what about having some fun today, *ma belle?*"

I reached over to Raïsa and kissed her on the lips. They quivered and swelled.

"You're funny," she mumbled through her teeth, recoiling.

She pressed herself against the wall, stretching out her bare arms. Spots began to glow on her arms and shoulders. Of all the gods ever put on the crucifix, this was the most ravishing.

"Be so kind as to sit down, Monsieur Polyte."

She pointed to an oblique blue armchair done in Slavonic style. Its back was constructed of carved interlacing bands with colorful pendants. I groped my way to it, stumbling as I went.

Night had blocked the path of my famished youth with a bottle of Muscatel '83 and twenty-nine books, twenty-nine bombs stuffed with pity, genius and passion. I sprang up, knocking over the chair and banging against the shelf. The twenty-nine volumes crashed to the floor, their pages flew open, they fell on their edges . . . and the white mare of my fate went on at a walking pace.

"You are funny," growled Raïsa.

I left the granite house on the Moyka between eleven and twelve, before the sisters and the husband returned from the theater. I was sober and could have walked a chalk line, but it was pleasanter to stagger, so I swayed from side to side, singing in a language I had just invented. Through the tunnels of the streets bounded by lines of street lights the steamy fog billowed. Monsters roared behind the boiling walls. The roads amputated the legs of those walking on them.

Kazantsev was asleep when I got home. He slept sitting up, his thin legs extended in their felt boots. The canary fluff rose on his head. He had fallen asleep by the stove bending over a volume of *Don Quixote*, the edition of 1624. On the title-page of the book was a dedication to the Duc de Broglie. I got into bed quietly, so as not to wake Kazantsev; moved the lamp close to me and began to read a book by Edouard Maynial on Guy de Maupassant's life and work.

Kazantsev's lips moved; his head kept keeling over.

That night I learned from Edouard Maynial that Maupassant was born in 1850, the child of a Normandy gentleman and Laure Lepoiteven, Flaubert's cousin. He was twenty-five when he was first attacked by congenital syphilis. His productivity and *joie de vivre* withstood the onsets of the disease. At first he suffered from headaches and fits of hypochondria. Then the specter of blindness arose before him. His sight weakened. He became suspicious of everyone, unsociable and pettily quarrelsome. He struggled furiously, dashed about the Mediterranean in a yacht, fled to Tunis, Morocco, Central Africa . . . and wrote ceaselessly. He attained fame, and at forty years of age cut his throat; lost a great deal of blood, yet lived through it. He was then put away in a madhouse. There he crawled about on his hands and knees, devouring his own excrement. The last line in his hospital report read: *Monsieur de Maupassant va s'animaliser.* He died at the age of forty-two, his mother surviving him.

I read the book to the end and got out of bed. The fog came close to the window, the world was hidden from me. My heart contracted as the foreboding of some essential truth touched me with light fingers.

Questions for Discussion

1. What do we learn about the narrator as he journeys to St. Petersburg and then refuses to work in an office?
2. What is revealed about the narrator's values through his description of the Bendersky household, the maid, Mr. Bendersky, and the pupil, Raïsa? Why does the narrator feel the way he does about wealthy Jews?
3. As the narrator works with Raïsa to improve her translating style, a relationship develops between pupil and teacher. In what ways do the passages translated from Maupassant parallel and comment upon their evolving relationship?
4. After the narrator's attempted seduction of Raïsa, does she seem angry with him or simply amused? What does her attitude imply about her values?
5. Why does the narrator become obsessed with Maupassant's deterioration and early death from congenital syphilis? The story ends with the narrator being touched with "some essential truth." To what truth does the story refer?

Ideas for Writing

1. Write a sequel to the story. What will the narrator do next? Will he quit? Will he return to tutor and seduce Raïsa?
2. Read "Confessing" by Guy de Maupassant and write a comparison of these two stories. How does Babel draw on Maupassant's techniques and outlook on life as he reveals his own character's values and personal crisis?

F. SCOTT FITZGERALD · (1896–1940)

A major voice of the Jazz Age generation of the 1920s, F. Scott Fitzgerald often wrote about bright society people whose lives revolve around partying, drinking, and material display. Fitzgerald was born in St. Paul, Minnesota, and attended Princeton University, leaving school to join the army. He had a turbulent relationship with his wife, Zelda; both struggled with alcoholism and mental illness. In 1919 Fitzgerald completed his popular novel of the Jazz Age, *This Side of Paradise,* after which he wrote *The Beautiful and Damned* (1921), *The Great Gatsby* (1925), and *Tender Is the Night* (1934). Following this period of great success and European travel in the late 1920s, Fitzgerald experienced financial difficulties. He moved to Los Angeles in 1937 to try to revive his career by writing film scripts; this period of his life is chronicled in his final novel, *The Last Tycoon* (1941). Fitzgerald also published several volumes of short stories, including *Tales of the Jazz Age* (1922), *All the Sad Young Men* (1926), and *Taps at Reveille* (1935). Much of his fiction is rooted in his own glamour-seeking and troubled life, particularly his difficult relationship with Zelda.

Although he became cynical and disillusioned at the end of his life, Fitzgerald was essentially a romantic writer. In his essay "The Continuity of a Writer's Works" (1933), he confesses that he had only "two or three fundamental tales . . . to tell" and that in order to write authentically, he needed to rely on strong feeling: "I must start out with an emotion—one that's close to me and that I can understand."

The Baby Party (1925)

When John Andros felt old he found solace in the thought of life continuing through his child. The dark trumpets of oblivion were less loud at the patter of his child's feet or at the sound of his child's voice babbling mad non sequiturs to him over the telephone. The latter incident occurred every afternoon at three when his wife called the office from the country, and he came to look forward to it as one of the vivid minutes of his day.

He was not physically old, but his life had been a series of struggles up a series of rugged hills, and here at thirty-eight having won his battles against ill-health and poverty he cherished less than the usual number of illusions. Even his feeling about his little girl was qualified. She had interrupted his rather intense love-affair with his wife, and she was the reason for their living in a suburban town, where they paid for country air with endless servant troubles and the weary merry-go-round of the commuting train.

It was little Ede as a definite piece of youth that chiefly interested him. He liked to take her on his lap and examine minutely her fragrant, downy scalp and her eyes with their irises of morning blue. Having paid this homage John was content that the nurse should take her away. After ten minutes the very vitality of the child irritated him; he was inclined to lose his temper when things were broken, and one Sunday afternoon when she had disrupted a bridge game by permanently hiding up the ace of spades, he had made a scene that had reduced his wife to tears.

This was absurd and John was ashamed of himself. It was inevitable that such things would happen, and it was impossible that little Ede should spend all her indoor hours in the nursery up-stairs when she was becoming, as her mother said, more nearly a "real person" every day.

She was two and a half, and this afternoon, for instance, she was going to a baby party. Grown-up Edith, her mother, had telephoned the information to the office, and little Ede had confirmed the business by shouting "I yam going to a *pantry!*" into John's unsuspecting left ear.

"Drop in at the Markeys' when you get home, won't you, dear?" resumed her mother. "It'll be funny. Ede's going to be all dressed up in her new pink dress ―― "

The conversation terminated abruptly with a squawk which indicated that the telephone had been pulled violently to the floor. John laughed and decided to get an early train out; the prospect of a baby party in some one else's house amused him.

"What a peach of a mess!" he thought humorously. "A dozen mothers, and each one looking at nothing but her own child. All the babies breaking things and grabbing at the cake, and each mama going home thinking about the subtle superiority of her own child to every other child there."

He was in a good humor to-day―all the things in his life were going better than they had ever gone before. When he got off the train at his station he shook his head at an importunate taxi man, and began to walk up the long hill toward his house through the crisp December twilight. It was only six o'clock but the moon was out, shining with proud brilliance on the thin sugary snow that lay over the lawns.

As he walked along drawing his lungs full of cold air his happiness increased, and the idea of a baby party appealed to him more and more. He began to wonder how Ede compared to other children of her own age, and if the pink dress she was to wear was something radical and mature. Increasing his gait he came in sight of his own house, where the lights of a defunct Christmas-tree still blossomed in the window, but he continued on past the walk. The party was at the Markeys' next door.

As he mounted the brick step and rang the bell he. became aware of voices inside, and he was glad he was not too late. Then he raised his head and listened―the voices were not children's voices, but they were loud and pitched high with anger; there were at least three of them and one, which rose as he listened to a hysterical sob, he recognized immediately as his wife's.

"There's been some trouble," he thought quickly.

Trying the door, he found it unlocked and pushed it open.

The baby party began at half past four, but Edith Andros, calculating shrewdly that the new dress would stand out more sensationally against vestments already rumpled, planned the arrival of herself and little Ede for five. When they appeared it was already a flourishing affair. Four baby girls and nine baby boys, each one curled and washed and dressed with all the care of a proud and jealous heart, were dancing to the music of a phonograph. Never more than two or three were dancing at once, but as all were continually in motion running to and from their mothers for encouragement, the general effect was the same.

As Edith and her daughter entered, the music was temporarily drowned out by a sustained chorus, consisting largely of the word *cute* and directed toward little Ede, who stood looking timidly about and fingering the edges of her pink dress. She was not kissed — this is the sanitary age — but she was passed along a row of mamas each one of whom said "cu-u-ute" to her and held her pink little hand before passing her on to the next. After some encouragement and a few mild pushes she was absorbed into the dance, and became an active member of the party.

Edith stood near the door talking to Mrs. Markey, and keeping one eye on the tiny figure in the pink dress. She did not care for Mrs. Markey; she considered her both snippy and common, but John and Joe Markey were congenial and went in together on the commuting train every morning, so the two women kept up an elaborate pretense of warm amity. They were always reproaching each other for "not coming to see me," and they were always planning the kind of parties that began with "You'll have to come to dinner with us soon, and we'll go in to the theatre," but never matured further.

"Little Ede looks perfectly darling," said Mrs. Markey, smiling and moistening her lips in a way that Edith found particularly repulsive. "*So grown-up* — I can't *believe* it!"

Edith wondered if "little Ede" referred to the fact that Billy Markey, though several months younger, weighed almost five pounds more. Accepting a cup of tea she took a seat with two other ladies on a divan and launched into the real business of the afternoon, which of course lay in relating the recent accomplishments and insouciances of her child.

An hour passed. Dancing palled and the babies took to sterner sport. They ran into the dining-room, rounded the big table, and essayed the kitchen door, from which they were rescued by an expeditionary force of mothers. Having been rounded up they immediately broke loose, and rushing back to the dining-room tried the familiar swinging door again. The word "overheated" began to be used, and small white brows were dried with small white handkerchiefs. A general attempt to make the babies sit down began, but the babies squirmed off laps with peremptory cries of "Down! Down!" and the rush into the fascinating dining-room began anew.

This phase of the party came to an end with the arrival of refreshments, a large cake with two candles, and saucers of vanilla ice-cream. Billy Markey, a stout laughing baby with red hair and legs somewhat bowed, blew out the candles, and placed an experimental thumb on the white frosting. The refreshments were distributed, and the children ate, greedily but without confusion — they had behaved remarkably well all afternoon. They were modern babies who ate and slept at regular hours, so their dispositions were good, and their faces healthy and pink — such a peaceful party would not have been possible thirty years ago.

After the refreshments a gradual exodus began. Edith glanced anxiously at her watch — it was almost six, and John had not arrived. She wanted him to see Ede with the other children — to see how dignified and polite and intelligent she was, and how the only ice-cream spot on her dress was some that had dropped from her chin when she was joggled from behind.

"You're a darling," she whispered to her child, drawing her suddenly against her knee. "Do you know you're a darling? Do you *know* you're a darling?"

Ede laughed. "Bow-wow," she said suddenly.

"Bow-wow?" Edith looked around. "There isn't any bow-wow."

"Bow-wow," repeated Ede. "I want a bow-wow."

Edith followed the small pointing finger.

"That isn't a bow-wow, dearest, that's a teddy-bear."

"Bear?"

"Yes, that's a teddy-bear, and it belongs to Billy Markey. You don't want Billy Markey's teddy-bear, do you?"

Ede did want it.

She broke away from her mother and approached Billy Markey, who held the toy closely in his arms. Ede stood regarding him with inscrutable eyes, and Billy laughed.

Grown-up Edith looked at her watch again, this time impatiently.

The party had dwindled until, besides Ede and Billy, there were only two babies remaining — and one of the two remained only by virtue of having hidden himself under the dining-room table. It was selfish of John not to come. It showed so little pride in the child. Other fathers had come, half a dozen of them, to call for their wives, and they had stayed for a while and looked on.

There was a sudden wail. Ede had obtained Billy's teddy-bear by pulling it forcibly from his arms, and on Billy's attempt to recover it, she had pushed him casually to the floor.

"Why, Ede!" cried her mother, repressing an inclination to laugh.

Joe Markey, a handsome, broad-shouldered man of thirty-five, picked up his son and set him on his feet. "You're a fine fellow," he said jovially. "Let a girl knock you over! You're a fine fellow."

"Did he bump his head?" Mrs. Markey returned anxiously from bowing the next to last remaining mother out the door.

"No-o-o-o," exclaimed Markey. "He bumped something else, didn't you, Billy? He bumped something else."

Billy had so far forgotten the bump that he was already making an attempt to recover his property. He seized a leg of the bear which projected from Ede's enveloping arms and tugged at it but without success.

"No," said Ede emphatically.

Suddenly, encouraged by the success of her former half-accidental manoeuvre Ede dropped the teddy-bear, placed her hands on Billy's shoulders and pushed him backward off his feet.

This time he landed less harmlessly; his head hit the bare floor just off the rug with a dull hollow sound, whereupon he drew in his breath and delivered an agonized yell.

Immediately the room was in confusion. With an exclamation Markey hurried to his son, but his wife was first to reach the injured baby and catch him up into her arms.

"Oh, *Billy*," she cried, "what a terrible bump! She ought to be spanked."

Edith, who had rushed immediately to her daughter, heard this remark, and her lips came sharply together.

"Why, Ede," she whispered perfunctorily, "you bad girl!"

Ede put back her little head suddenly and laughed. It was a loud laugh, a triumphant laugh with victory in it and challenge and contempt. Unfortunately it was also an infectious laugh. Before her mother realized the delicacy of the situation, she too had laughed, an audible, distinct laugh not unlike the baby's, and partaking of the same overtones.

Then, as suddenly, she stopped.

Mrs. Markey's face had grown red with anger, and Markey, who had been feeling the back of the baby's head with one finger, looked at her, frowning.

"It's swollen already," he said with a note of reproof in his voice "I'll get some witch-hazel."

But Mrs. Markey had lost her temper. "I don't see anything funny about a child being hurt!" she said in a trembling voice.

Little Ede meanwhile had been looking at her mother curiously. She noted that her own laugh had produced her mother's and she wondered if the same cause would always produce the same effect. So she chose this moment to throw back her head and laugh again.

To her mother the additional mirth added the final touch of hysteria to the situation. Pressing her handkerchief to her mouth she giggled irrepressibly. It was more than nervousness — she felt that in a peculiar way she was laughing with her child — they were laughing together.

It was in a way a defiance — those two against the world.

While Markey rushed up-stairs to the bathroom for ointment, his wife was walking up and down rocking the yelling boy in her arms.

"Please go home!" she broke out suddenly. "The child's badly hurt, and if you haven't the decency to be quiet, you'd better go home."

"Very well," said Edith, her own temper rising. "I've never seen any one make such a mountain out of ——"

"Get out!" cried Mrs. Markey frantically. "There's the door, get out — I never want to see you in our house again. You or your brat either!"

Edith had taken her daughter's hand and was moving quickly toward the door, but at this remark she stopped and turned around, her face contracting with indignation.

"Don't you dare call her that!"

Mrs. Markey did not answer but continued walking up and down, muttering to herself and to Billy in an inaudible voice.

Edith began to cry.

"I will get out!" she sobbed, "I've never heard anybody so rude and c-common in my life. I'm glad your baby did get pushed down — he's nothing but a f-fat little fool anyhow."

Joe Markey reached the foot of the stairs just in time to hear this remark.

"Why, Mrs. Andros," he said sharply, "can't you see the child's hurt? You really ought to control yourself."

"Control m-myself!" exclaimed Edith brokenly. "You better ask her to c-control herself. I've never heard anybody so c- common in my life."

"She's insulting me!" Mrs. Markey was now livid with rage. "Did you hear what she said, Joe? I wish you'd put her out. If she won't go, just take her by the shoulders and put her out!"

"Don't you dare touch me!" cried Edith. "I'm going just as quick as I can find my c-coat!"

Blind with tears she took a step toward the hall. It was just at this moment that the door opened and John Andros walked anxiously in.

"John!" cried Edith, and fled to him wildly.

"What's the matter? Why, what's the matter?"

"They're — they're putting me out!" she wailed, collapsing against him. "He'd just started to take me by the shoulders and put me out. I want my coat!"

"That's not true," objected Markey hurriedly. "Nobody's going to put you out." He turned to John. "Nobody's going to put her out," he repeated. "She's ——"

"What do you mean 'put her out'?" demanded John abruptly. "What's all this talk, anyhow?"

"Oh, let's go!" cried Edith. "I want to go. They're so *common*, John!"

"Look here!" Markey's face darkened. "You've said that about enough. You're acting sort of crazy."

"They called Ede a brat!"

For the second time that afternoon little Ede expressed emotion at an inopportune moment. Confused and frightened at the shouting voices, she began to cry, and her tears had the effect of conveying that she felt the insult in her heart.

"What's the idea of this?" broke out John. "Do you insult your guests in your own house?"

"It seems to me it's your wife that's done the insulting!" answered Markey crisply. "In fact, your baby there started all the trouble."

John gave a contemptuous snort. "Are you calling names at a little baby?" he inquired. "That's a fine manly business!"

"Don't talk to him, John," insisted Edith. "Find my coat!"

"You must be in a bad way," went on John angrily, "if you have to take out your temper on a helpless little baby."

"I never heard anything so damn twisted in my life," shouted Markey. "If that wife of yours would shut her mouth for a minute —— "

"Wait a minute! You're not talking to a woman and child now —— "

There was an incidental interruption. Edith had been fumbling on a chair for her coat, and Mrs. Markey had been watching her with hot, angry eyes. Suddenly she laid Billy down on the sofa, where he immediately stopped crying and pulled himself upright, and coming into the hall she quickly found Edith's coat and handed it to her without a word. Then she went back to the sofa, picked up Billy, and rocking him in her arms looked again at Edith with hot, angry eyes. The interruption had taken less than half a minute.

"Your wife comes in here and begins shouting around about how common we are!" burst out Markey violently. "Well, if we're so damn common, you'd better stay away! And, what's more, you'd better get out now!"

Again John gave a short, contemptuous laugh.

"You're not only common," he returned, "you're evidently an awful bully — when there's any helpless women and children around." He felt for the knob and swung the door open. "Come on, Edith."

Taking up her daughter in her arms, his wife stepped outside and John, still looking contemptuously at Markey, started to follow.

"Wait a minute!" Markey took a step forward; he was trembling slightly, and two large veins on his temple were suddenly full of blood. "You don't think you can get away with that, do you? With me?"

Without a word John walked out the door, leaving it open.

Edith, still weeping, had started for home. After following her with his eyes until she reached her own walk, John turned back toward the lighted doorway where Markey was slowly coming down the slippery steps. He took off his overcoat and hat, tossed them off the path onto the snow. Then, sliding a little on the iced walk, he took a step forward.

At the first blow, they both slipped and fell heavily to the sidewalk, half rising then, and again pulling each other to the ground. They found a better foothold in the thin snow to the side of the walk and rushed at each other, both swinging wildly and pressing out the snow into a pasty mud underfoot.

The street was deserted, and except for their short tired gasps and the padded sound as one or the other slipped down into the slushy mud, they fought in silence, clearly defined to each other by the full moonlight as well as by the amber glow that shone out of the open door. Several times they both slipped down together, and then for a while the conflict threshed about wildly on the lawn.

For ten, fifteen, twenty minutes they fought there senselessly in the moonlight. They had both taken off coats and vests at some silently agreed upon interval and now their shirts dripped from their backs in wet pulpy shreds. Both were torn and bleeding and so exhausted that they could stand only when by their position they mutually supported each other — the impact, the mere effort of a blow, would send them both to their hands and knees.

But it was not weariness that ended the business, and the very meaning-lessness of the fight was a reason for not stopping. They stopped because once when they were straining at each other on the ground, they heard a man's foot-steps coming along the sidewalk. They had rolled somehow into the shadow, and when they heard these footsteps they stopped fighting, stopped moving, stopped breathing, lay huddled together like two boys playing Indian until the footsteps had passed. Then, staggering to their feet, they looked at each other like two drunken men.

"I'll be damned if I'm going on with this thing any more," cried Markey thickly.

"I'm not going on any more either," said John Andros. "I've had enough of this thing."

Again they looked at each other, sulkily this time, as if each suspected the other of urging him to a renewal of the fight. Markey spat out a mouthful of blood from a cut lip; then he cursed softly, and picking up his coat and vest, shook off the snow from them in a surprised way, as if their comparative dampness was his only worry in the world.

"Want to come in and wash up?" he asked suddenly.

"No, thanks," said John. "I ought to be going home — my wife'll be worried."

He too picked up his coat and vest and then his overcoat and hat. Soaking wet and dripping with perspiration, it seemed absurd that less than half an hour ago he had been wearing all these clothes.

"Well — good night," he said hesitantly.

Suddenly they both walked toward each other and shook hands. It was no perfunctory hand-shake: John Andros's arm went around Markey's shoulder, and he patted him softly on the back for a little while.

"No harm done," he said brokenly.

"No — you?"

"No, no harm done."

"Well," said John Andros after a minute, "I guess I'll say good night."

Limping slightly and with his clothes over his arm, John Andros turned away. The moonlight was still bright as he left the dark patch of trampled ground and walked over the intervening lawn. Down at the station, half a mile away, he could hear the rumble of the seven o'clock train.

"But you must have been crazy," cried Edith brokenly. "I thought you were going to fix it all up there and shake hands. That's why I went away."

"Did you want us to fix it up?"

"Of course not, I never want to see them again. But I thought of course that was what you were going to do." She was touching the bruises on his neck and back with iodine as he sat placidly in a hot bath. "I'm going to get the doctor," she said insistently. "You may be hurt internally."

He shook his head. "Not a chance," he answered. "I don't want this to get all over town."

"I don't understand yet how it all happened."

"Neither do I." He smiled grimly. "I guess these baby parties are pretty rough affairs."

"Well, one thing — " suggested Edith hopefully, "I'm certainly glad we have beefsteak in the house for to-morrow's dinner."

"Why ?"

"For your eye, of course. Do you know I came within an ace of ordering veal? Wasn't that the luckiest thing?"

Half an hour later, dressed except that his neck would accommodate no collar, John moved his limbs experimentally before the glass. "I believe I'll get myself in better shape," he said thoughtfully. "I must be getting old."

"You mean so that next time you can beat him?"

"I did beat him," he announced. "At least, I beat him as much as he beat me. And there isn't going to be any next time. Don't you go calling people common any more. If you get in any trouble, you just take your coat and go home. Understand?"

"Yes, dear," she said meekly. "I was very foolish and now I understand."

Out in the hall, he paused abruptly by the baby's door.

"Is she asleep?"

"Sound asleep. But you can go in and peek at her — just to say good night."

They tiptoed in and bent together over the bed. Little Ede, her cheeks flushed with health, her pink hands clasped tight together, was sleeping soundly in the cool, dark room. John reached over the railing of the bed and passed his hand lightly over the silken hair.

"She's asleep," he murmured in a puzzled way.

"Naturally, after such an afternoon."

"Miz Andros," the colored maid's stage whisper floated in from the hall, "Mr. and Miz Markey downstairs an' want to see you. Mr. Markey he's all cut up in pieces, ma'am. His face look like a roast beef. An' Miz Markey she 'pear mighty mad."

"Why, what incomparable nerve!" exclaimed Edith. "Just tell them we're not home. I wouldn't go down for anything in the world."

"You most certainly will." John's voice was hard and set.

"What?"

"You'll go down right now, and, what's more, whatever that other woman does, you'll apologize for what you said this afternoon. After that you don't ever have to see her again."

"Why — John, I can't."

"You've got to. And just remember that she probably hated to come over here just twice as much as you hate to go downstairs."

"Aren't you coming? Do I have to go alone?"

"I'll be down — in just a minute."

John Andros waited until she had closed the door behind her; then he reached over into the bed and picking up his daughter, blankets and all, sat down in the rocking-chair holding her tightly in his arms. She moved a little, and he held his breath, but she was sleeping soundly, and in a moment she was resting quietly in the hollow of his elbow. Slowly he bent his head until his cheek was against her bright hair. "Dear little girl," he whispered. "Dear little girl, dear little girl."

John Andros knew at length what it was he had fought for so savagely that evening. He had it now, he possessed it forever, and for some time he sat there rocking very slowly to and fro in the darkness.

Questions for Discussion

1. What type of crisis is John Andros experiencing at the beginning of the story? How do his feelings about his daughter, Ede, help to reveal this crisis?

2. What do Edith's feelings about attending the baby party suggest about her personality and values? How does she feel about the Markeys and their son Billy? Do her feelings seem justified?

3. What does Edith's response to Ede's behavior toward Billy suggest about her as a parent and her sense of responsibility as a mother?

4. How does John Andros respond to his wife's tears and accusations? Why doesn't he try to understand the cause of the conflict before responding as he does?

5. Why is the issue of the "commonness" of the Markeys such a concern in the conflict between the couples?

Ideas for Writing

1. Write an essay that interprets the significance of the fight between Andros and Markey. Which details and comparisons best help to reveal both the childishness and the passionate intensity of their struggle? How does this violent altercation, quite uncommon in a middle-class suburban neighborhood, reveal the characters of the two men while critiquing their values and lifestyles?

2. Write a sequel to the story focusing on John, Edith, and Ede. Emphasize how John's attitudes toward his neighbors, his wife, and his daughter have been changed through the fight and its aftermath.

WILLIAM FAULKNER   (1897–1962)

Nobel laureate William Faulkner lived for most of his life in Oxford, Mississippi, the town that he used as a model for his immortal fictional community, Jefferson, Yoknapatawpha County. Jefferson and the surrounding countryside make up the setting for most of Faulkner's novels and stories, which provide a cross-section of small-town Mississippi life.

Faulkner attended the University of Mississippi, leaving his native Oxford briefly to serve in the British Royal Air Force in Canada; he also spent some time traveling abroad and in the United States — to New York, New Orleans, and Hollywood, where he tried screenwriting. In the 1920s and 1930s Faulkner wrote his major novels: *The Sound and the Fury* (1929), *As I Lay Dying* (1930), *Light in August* (1932), and *Absalom, Absalom!* (1936); he received the Nobel Prize for Literature in 1949. His *Collected Stories*, which includes "A Rose for Emily" and "Barn Burning," won the National Book Award in 1950. Many of Faulkner's works — such as his most famous story, "A Rose for Emily" — move back and forth in time, giving a sense of the lived reality of history in a region that clings tenaciously to its past and its traditions. Faulkner also developed a stream-of-consciousness writing style that allows his readers access to the conscious and unconscious minds — the present thoughts and the memories — of a wide range of characters, young and old, wealthy and impoverished. This technique is exemplified in "Barn Burning," which focuses on the perceptions of Sarty, the son of a sharecropper.

A Rose for Emily   (1930)

I

When Miss Emily Grierson died, our whole town went to her funeral: the men through a sort of respectful affection for a fallen monument, the women mostly out of curiosity to see the inside of her house, which no one save an old manservant — a combined gardener and cook — had seen in at least ten years.

It was a big, squarish frame house that had once been white, decorated with cupolas and spires and scrolled balconies in the heavily lightsome style of the seventies, set on what had once been our most select street. But garages and cotton gins had encroached and obliterated even the august names of that neighborhood; only Miss Emily's house was left, lifting its stubborn and co-quettish decay above the cotton wagons and the gasoline pumps — an eyesore among eyesores. And now Miss Emily had gone to join the representatives of those august names where they lay in the cedar-bemused cemetery among the ranked and anonymous graves of Union and Confederate soldiers who fell at the battle of Jefferson.

Alive, Miss Emily had been a tradition, a duty, and a care; a sort of hereditary obligation upon the town, dating from that day in 1894 when Colonel Sartoris, the mayor — he who fathered the edict that no Negro woman should appear on the streets without an apron — remitted her taxes, the dispensation dating from the death of her father on into perpetuity. Not that Miss Emily would have accepted charity. Colonel Sartoris invented an involved tale to the effect that Miss Emily's father had loaned money to the town, which the town, as a matter of business, preferred this way of repaying. Only a man of Colonel Sartoris' generation and thought could have invented it, and only a woman could have believed it.

When the next generation, with its more modern ideas, became mayors and aldermen, this arrangement created some little dissatisfaction. On the first of the year they mailed her a tax notice. February came, and there was no reply. They wrote her a formal letter, asking her to call at the sheriff's office at her convenience. A week later the mayor wrote her himself, offering to call or to send his car for her, and received in reply a note on paper of an archaic shape, in a thin, flowing calligraphy in faded ink, to the effect that she no longer went out at all. The tax notice was also enclosed, without comment.

They called a special meeting of the Board of Aldermen. A deputation waited upon her, knocked at the door through which no visitor had passed since she ceased giving china-painting lessons eight or ten years earlier. They were admitted by the old Negro into a dim hall from which a stairway mounted into still more shadow. It smelled of dust and disuse — a close, dank smell. The Negro led them into the parlor. It was furnished in heavy, leather-covered furniture. When the Negro opened the blinds of one window, they could see that the leather was cracked; and when they sat down, a faint dust rose sluggishly about their thighs, spinning with slow motes in the single sun-ray. On a tarnished gilt easel before the fireplace stood a crayon portrait of Miss Emily's father.

They rose when she entered — a small, fat woman in black, with a thin gold chain descending to her waist and vanishing into her belt, leaning on an ebony cane with a tarnished gold head. Her skeleton was small and spare; perhaps that was why what would have been merely plumpness in another was obesity in her. She looked bloated, like a body long submerged in motionless water, and of that pallid hue. Her eyes, lost in the fatty ridges of her face, looked like two small pieces of coal pressed into a lump of dough as they moved from one face to another while the visitors stated their errand.

She did not ask them to sit. She just stood in the door and listened quietly until the spokesman came to a stumbling halt. Then they could hear the invisible watch ticking at the end of the gold chain.

Her voice was dry and cold. "I have no taxes in Jefferson. Colonel Sartoris explained it to me. Perhaps one of you can gain access to the city records and satisfy yourselves."

"But we have. We are the city authorities, Miss Emily. Didn't you get a notice from the sheriff, signed by him?"

"I received a paper, yes," Miss Emily said. "Perhaps he considers himself the sheriff . . . I have no taxes in Jefferson."

"But there is nothing on the books to show that, you see. We must go by the —"

"See Colonel Sartoris. I have no taxes in Jefferson."

"But, Miss Emily —"

"See Colonel Sartoris." (Colonel Sartoris had been dead almost ten years.) "I have no taxes in Jefferson. Tobe!" The Negro appeared. "Show these gentlemen out."

II

So she vanquished them, horse and foot, just as she had vanquished their fathers thirty years before about the smell. That was two years after her father's death and a short time after her sweetheart — the one we believed would marry her — had deserted her. After her father's death she went out very little; after her sweetheart went away, people hardly saw her at all. A few of the ladies had the temerity to call, but were not received, and the only sign of life about the place was the Negro man — a young man then — going in and out with a market basket.

"Just as if a man — any man — could keep a kitchen properly," the ladies said; so they were not surprised when the smell developed. It was another link between the gross, teeming world and the high and mighty Griersons.

A neighbor, a woman, complained to the mayor, Judge Stevens, eighty years old.

"But what will you have me do about it, madam?" he said.

"Why, send her word to stop it," the woman said. "Isn't there a law?"

"I'm sure that won't be necessary," Judge Stevens said. "It's probably just a snake or a rat that nigger of hers killed in the yard. I'll speak to him about it."

The next day he received two more complaints, one from a man who came in diffident deprecation. "We really must do something about it, Judge. I'd be the last one in the world to bother Miss Emily, but we've got to do something." That night the Board of Aldermen met — three graybeards and one younger man, a member of the rising generation.

"It's simple enough," he said. "Send her word to have her place cleaned up. Give her a certain time to do it in, and if she don't . . ."

"Dammit, sir," Judge Stevens said, "will you accuse a lady to her face of smelling bad?"

So the next night, after midnight, four men crossed Miss Emily's lawn and slunk about the house like burglars, sniffing along the base of the brickwork and at the cellar openings while one of them performed a regular sowing motion with his hand out of a sack slung from his shoulder. They broke open the cellar door and sprinkled lime there, and in all the outbuildings. As they recrossed the lawn, a window that had been dark was lighted and Miss Emily sat in it, the light behind her, and her upright torso motionless as that of an idol. They crept quietly across the lawn and into the shadow of the locusts that lined the street. After a week or two the smell went away.

That was when people had begun to feel really sorry for her. People in our town, remembering how old lady Wyatt, her great-aunt, had gone completely crazy at last, believed that the Griersons held themselves a little too high for what they really were. None of the young men were quite good enough for Miss Emily and such. We had long thought of them as a tableau, Miss Emily a slender figure in white in the background, her father a spraddled silhouette in the foreground, his back to her and clutching a horsewhip, the two of them framed by the back-flung front door. So when she got to be thirty and was still single, we were not pleased exactly, but vindicated; even with insanity in the family she wouldn't have turned down all of her chances if they had really materialized.

When her father died, it got about that the house was all that was left to her; and in a way, people were glad. At last they could pity Miss Emily. Being left alone, and a pauper, she had become humanized. Now she too would know the old thrill and the old despair of a penny more or less.

The day after his death all the ladies prepared to call at the house and offer condolence and aid, as is our custom. Miss Emily met them at the door, dressed as usual and with no trace of grief on her face. She told them that her father was not dead. She did that for three days, with the ministers calling on her, and the doctors, trying to persuade her to let them dispose of the body. Just as they were about to resort to law and force, she broke down, and they buried her father quickly.

We did not say she was crazy then. We believed she had to do that. We remembered all the young men her father had driven away, and we knew that with nothing left, she would have to cling to that which had robbed her, as people will.

III

She was sick for a long time. When we saw her again, her hair was cut short, making her look like a girl, with a vague resemblance to those angels in colored church windows — sort of tragic and serene.

The town had just let the contracts for paving the sidewalks, and in the summer after her father's death they began the work. The construction company came with niggers and mules and machinery, and a foreman named Homer Barron, a Yankee — a big, dark, ready man, with a big voice and eyes lighter than his face. The little boys would follow in groups to hear him cuss the niggers, and the niggers singing in time to the rise and fall of picks. Pretty soon he knew everybody in town. Whenever you heard a lot of laughing anywhere about the square, Homer Barron would be in the center of the group. Presently we began to see him and Miss Emily on Sunday afternoons driving in the yellow-wheeled buggy and the matched team of bays from the livery stable.

At first we were glad that Miss Emily would have an interest, because the ladies all said, "Of course a Grierson would not think seriously of a Northerner, a day laborer." But there were still others, older people, who said that even grief could not cause a real lady to forget *noblesse oblige* — without calling it *noblesse oblige*. They just said, "Poor Emily. Her kinsfolk should come to her." She had some kin in Alabama; but years ago her father had fallen out with them over the estate of old lady Wyatt, the crazy woman, and there was no communication between the two families. They had not even been represented at the funeral.

And as soon as the old people said, "Poor Emily," the whispering began. "Do you suppose it's really so?" they said to one another. "Of course it is. What else could . . ." This behind their hands; rustling of craned silk and satin behind jalousies closed upon the sun of Sunday afternoon as the thin, swift clop-clop-clop of the matched team passed: "Poor Emily."

She carried her head high enough — even when we believed that she was fallen. It was as if she demanded more than ever the recognition of her dignity as the last Grierson; as if it had wanted that touch of earthiness to reaffirm her imperviousness. Like when she bought the rat poison, the arsenic. That was over a year after they had begun to say "Poor Emily," and while the two female cousins were visiting her.

"I want some poison," she said to the druggist. She was over thirty then, still a slight woman, though thinner than usual, with cold, haughty black eyes in a face the flesh of which was strained across the temples and about the eye-sockets as you imagine a lighthouse-keeper's face ought to look. "I want some poison," she said.

"Yes, Miss Emily. What kind? For rats and such? I'd recom —"

"I want the best you have. I don't care what kind."

The druggist named several. "They'll kill anything up to an elephant. But what you want is — "

"Arsenic," Miss Emily said. "Is that a good one?"

"Is . . . arsenic? Yes, ma'am. But what you want — "

"I want arsenic."

The druggist looked down at her. She looked back at him, erect, her face like a strained flag. "Why, of course," the druggist said. "If that's what you want. But the law requires you to tell what you are going to use it for."

Miss Emily just stared at him, her head tilted back in order to look him eye for eye, until he looked away and went and got the arsenic and wrapped it up. The Negro delivery boy brought her the package; the druggist didn't come back. When she opened the package at home there was written on the box, under the skull and bones: "For rats."

IV

So the next day we all said, "She will kill herself"; and we said it would be the best thing. When she had first begun to be seen with Homer Barron, we had said, "She will marry him." Then we said, "She will persuade him yet," because Homer himself had remarked — he liked men, and it was known that he drank with the younger men in the Elks' Club — that he was not a marrying man. Later we said, "Poor Emily" behind the jalousies as they passed on Sunday afternoon in the glittering buggy, Miss Emily with her head high and Homer Barron with his hat cocked and a cigar in his teeth, reins and whip in a yellow glove.

Then some of the ladies began to say that it was a disgrace to the town and a bad example to the young people. The men did not want to interfere, but at last the ladies forced the Baptist minister — Miss Emily's people were Episcopal — to call upon her. He would never divulge what happened during that interview, but he refused to go back again. The next Sunday they again drove about the streets, and the following day the minister's wife wrote to Miss Emily's relations in Alabama.

So she had blood-kin under her roof again and we sat back to watch developments. At first nothing happened. Then we were sure that they were to be married. We learned that Miss Emily had been to the jeweler's and ordered a man's toilet set in silver, with the letters H. B. on each piece. Two days later we learned that she had bought a complete outfit of men's clothing, including a nightshirt, and we said, "They are married." We were really glad. We were glad because the two female cousins were even more Grierson than Miss Emily had ever been.

So we were not surprised when Homer Barron — the streets had been finished some time since — was gone. We were a little disappointed that there was not a public blowing-off, but we believed that he had gone on to prepare for Miss Emily's coming, or to give her a chance to get rid of the cousins. (By that time it was a cabal, and we were all Miss Emily's allies to help circumvent the cousins.) Sure enough, after another week they departed. And, as we had expected all along, within three days Homer Barron was back in town. A neighbor saw the Negro man admit him at the kitchen door at dusk one evening.

And that was the last we saw of Homer Barron. And of Miss Emily for some time. The Negro man went in and out with the market basket, but the front door remained closed. Now and then we would see her at a window for a moment, as the men did that night when they sprinkled the lime, but for almost six months she did not appear on the streets. Then we knew that this was to be expected too; as if that quality of her father which had thwarted her woman's life so many times had been too virulent and too furious to die.

When we next saw Miss Emily, she had grown fat and her hair was turning gray. During the next few years it grew grayer and grayer until it attained an even pepper-and-salt iron-gray, when it ceased turning. Up to the day of her death at seventy-four it was still that vigorous iron-gray, like the hair of an active man.

From that time on her front door remained closed, save for a period of six or seven years, when she was about forty, during which she gave lessons in china-painting. She fitted up a studio in one of the downstairs rooms, where the daughters and granddaughters of Colonel Sartoris' contemporaries were sent to her with the same regularity and in the same spirit that they were sent to church on Sundays with a twenty-five-cent piece for the collection plate. Meanwhile her taxes had been remitted.

Then the newer generation became the backbone and the spirit of the town, and the painting pupils grew up and fell away and did not send their children to her with boxes of color and tedious brushes and pictures cut from the ladies' magazines. The front door closed upon the last one and remained closed for good. When the town got free postal delivery, Miss Emily alone refused to let them fasten the metal numbers above her door and attach a mail-box to it. She would not listen to them.

Daily, monthly, yearly we watched the Negro grow grayer and more stooped, going in and out with the market basket. Each December we sent her a tax notice, which would be returned by the post office a week later, un-claimed. Now and then we would see her in one of the downstairs windows — she had evidently shut up the top floor of the house — like the carven torso of an idol in a niche, looking or not looking at us, we could never tell which. Thus she passed from generation to generation — dear, inescapable, impervi-ous, tranquil, and perverse.

And so she died. Fell ill in the house filled with dust and shadows, with only a doddering Negro man to wait on her. We did not even know she was sick; we had long since given up trying to get any information from the Negro. He talked to no one, probably not even to her, for his voice had grown harsh and rusty, as if from disuse.

She died in one of the downstairs rooms, in a heavy walnut bed with a curtain, her gray head propped on a pillow yellow and moldy with age and lack of sunlight.

V

The Negro met the first of the ladies at the front door and let them in, with their hushed, sibilant voices and their quick, curious glances, and then he disappeared. He walked right through the house and out the back and was not seen again.

The two female cousins came at once. They held the funeral on the sec-ond day, with the town coming to look at Miss Emily beneath a mass of bought flowers, with the crayon face of her father musing profoundly above the bier and the ladies sibilant and macabre; and the very old men — some

in their brushed Confederate uniforms — on the porch and the lawn, talking of Miss Emily as if she had been a contemporary of theirs, believing that
they had danced with her and courted her perhaps, confusing time with its
mathematical progression, as the old do, to whom all the past is not a
diminishing road but, instead, a huge meadow which no winter ever quite
touches, divided from them now by the narrow bottle-neck of the most
recent decade of years.

Already we knew that there was one room in that region above stairs which
no one had seen in forty years, and which would have to be forced. They waited
until Miss Emily was decently in the ground before they opened it.

The violence of breaking down the door seemed to fill this room with pervading dust. A thin, acrid pall as of the tomb seemed to lie everywhere upon
this room decked and furnished as for a bridal: upon the valance curtains of
faded rose color, upon the rose-shaded lights, upon the dressing table, upon
the delicate array of crystal and the man's toilet things backed with tarnished
silver, silver so tarnished that the monogram was obscured. Among them lay
collar and tie, as if they had just been removed, which, lifted, left upon the
surface a pale crescent in the dust. Upon a chair hung the suit, carefully
folded; beneath it the two mute shoes and the discarded socks.

The man himself lay in the bed.

For a long while we just stood there, looking down at the profound and
fleshless grin. The body had apparently once lain in the attitude of an
embrace, but now the long sleep that outlasts love, that conquers even the
grimace of love, had cuckolded him. What was left of him, rotted beneath
what was left of the nightshirt, had become inextricable from the bed in
which he lay; and upon him and upon the pillow beside him lay that even
coating of the patient and biding dust.

Then we noticed that in the second pillow was the indentation of a
head. One of us lifted something from it, and leaning forward, that faint
and invisible dust dry and acrid in the nostrils, we saw a long strand of
iron-gray hair.

Questions for Discussion

1. What do the descriptions of Miss Emily's house and the way it changes over the
   years suggest about her character, her slow decline, and the meaning of her life?
2. What does Colonel Sartoris's decision to remit Emily's taxes reveal about his values and those of his generation?
3. How is Emily described as the deputation comes to visit her to reinstate her taxes?
   What does the description suggest about her decline, her meaning as a symbolic
   character, and her continued power over the townspeople?
4. What type of relationship develops between Emily and Homer Barron? How does
   his social class differ from Emily's? Why is it significant, both socially and psychologically, that this relationship begins only after the death of Emily's father?
   Why is each involved in the relationship?

5. The story ends with a shocking revelation about Emily and Homer that comes only after Emily is "decently in the ground." What does the final image of the story reveal about Emily? Do you think the townspeople are surprised by this revelation?

Ideas for Writing

1. Write an essay on the themes of time and change as they are explored and related in the story. You might consider the plot line, which moves back and forth in time, and key images such as the older men's confused sense of time as reflected in their comments and observations at Emily's funeral.
2. Write a story that is not based on a linear time line but instead moves back and forth between different time periods, as Faulkner does in "A Rose for Emily."

Barn Burning   (1939)

The store in which the Justice of the Peace's court was sitting smelled of cheese. The boy, crouched on his nail keg at the back of the crowded room, knew he smelled cheese, and more: from where he sat he could see the ranked shelves close-packed with the solid, squat, dynamic shapes of tin cans whose labels his stomach read, not from the lettering which meant nothing to his mind but from the scarlet devils and the silver curve of fish — this, the cheese which he knew he smelled and the hermetic meat which his intestines believed he smelled coming in intermittent gusts momentary and brief between the other constant one, the smell and sense just a little of fear because mostly of despair and grief, the old fierce pull of blood. He could not see the table where the Justice sat and before which his father and his father's enemy (*our enemy he thought in that despair; ourn! mine and hisn both! He's my father!*) stood, but he could hear them, the two of them that is, because his father had said no word yet:

"But what proof have you, Mr. Harris?"

"I told you. The hog got into my corn. I caught it up and sent it back to him. He had no fence that would hold it. I told him so, warned him. The next time I put the hog in my pen. When he came to get it I gave him enough wire to patch up his pen. The next time I put the hog up and kept it. I rode down to his house and saw the wire I gave him still rolled on to the spool in his yard. I told him he could have the hog when he paid me a dollar pound fee. That evening a nigger came with the dollar and got the hog. He was a strange nigger. He said, 'He say to tell you wood and hay kin burn.' I said, 'What?' 'That whut he say to tell you,' the nigger said. 'Wood and hay kin burn.' That night my barn burned. I got the stock out but I lost the barn."

"Where is the nigger? Have you got him?"

"He was a strange nigger, I tell you. I don't know what became of him."

"But that's not proof. Don't you see that's not proof?"

"Get that boy up here. He knows." For a moment the boy thought too that the man meant his older brother until Harris said, "Not him. The little one. The boy," and, crouching, small for his age, small and wiry like his father, in patched and faded jeans even too small for him, with straight, uncombed, brown hair and eyes gray and wild as storm scud, he saw the men between himself and the table part and become a lane of grim faces, at the end of which he saw the Justice, a shabby, collarless, graying man in spectacles, beckoning him. He felt no floor under his bare feet; he seemed to walk beneath the palpable weight of the grim turning faces. His father, stiff in his black Sunday coat donned not for the trial but for the moving, did not even look at him. *He aims for me to lie,* he thought, again with that frantic grief and despair. *And I will have to do hit.*

"What's your name, boy?" the Justice said.

"Colonel Sartoris Snopes," the boy whispered.

"Hey?" the Justice said. "Talk louder. Colonel Sartoris? I reckon anybody named for Colonel Sartoris in this country can't help but tell the truth, can they?" The boy said nothing. *Enemy! Enemy!* he thought; for a moment he could not even see, could not see that the Justice's face was kindly nor discern that his voice was troubled when he spoke to the man named Harris: "Do you want me to question this boy?" But he could hear, and during those subsequent long seconds while there was absolutely no sound in the crowded little room save that of quiet and intent breathing it was as if he had swung outward at the end of a grape vine, over a ravine, and at the top of the swing had been caught in a prolonged instant of mesmerized gravity, weightless in time.

"No!" Harris said violently, explosively. "Damnation! Send him out of here!" Now time, the fluid world, rushed beneath him again, the voices coming to him again through the smell of cheese and sealed meat, the fear and despair and the old grief of blood:

"This case is closed. I can't find against you, Snopes, but I can give you advice. Leave this country and don't come back to it."

His father spoke for the first time, his voice cold and harsh, level without emphasis: "I aim to. I don't figure to stay in a country among people who . . ." he said something unprintable and vile, addressed to no one.

"That'll do," the Justice said. "Take your wagon and get out of this country before dark. Case dismissed."

His father turned, and he followed the stiff black coat, the wiry figure walking a little stiffly from where a Confederate provost's man's musket ball had taken him in the heel on a stolen horse thirty years ago, followed the two backs now, since his older brother had appeared from somewhere in the crowd, no taller than the father but thicker, chewing tobacco steadily, between the two lines of grim-faced men and out of the store and across the worn gallery and down the sagging steps and among the dogs and half-grown boys in the mild May dust, where as he passed a voice hissed:

"Barn burner!"

Again he could not see, whirling; there was a face in a red haze, moonlike, bigger than the full moon, the owner of it half again his size, he leaping in the red haze toward the face, feeling no blow, feeling no shock when his head struck the earth, scrabbling up and leaping again, feeling no blow this time either and tasting no blood, scrabbling up to see the other boy in full flight and himself already leaping into pursuit as his father's hand jerked him back, the harsh, cold voice speaking above him: "Go get in the wagon."

It stood in a grove of locusts and mulberries across the road. His two hulking sisters in their Sunday dresses and his mother and her sister in calico and sunbonnets were already in it, sitting on and among the sorry residue of the dozen and more movings which even the boy could remember — the battered stove, the broken beds and chairs, the clock inlaid with mother-of-pearl, which would not run, stopped at some fourteen minutes past two o'clock of a dead and forgotten day and time, which had been his mother's dowry. She was crying, though when she saw him she drew her sleeve across her face and began to descend from the wagon. "Get back," the father said.

"He's hurt. I got to get some water and wash his . . ."

"Get back in the wagon," his father said. He got in too, over the tail-gate. His father mounted to the seat where the older brother already sat and struck the gaunt mules two savage blows with the peeled willow, but without heat. It was not even sadistic; it was exactly that same quality which in later years would cause his descendants to over-run the engine before putting a motor car into motion, striking and reining back in the same movement. The wagon went on, the store with its quiet crowd of grimly watching men dropped behind; a curve in the road hid it. *Forever* he thought. *Maybe he's done satisfied now, now that he has* . . . stopping himself, not to say it aloud even to himself. His mother's hand touched his shoulder.

"Does hit hurt?" she said.

"Naw," he said. "Hit don't hurt. Lemme be."

"Can't you wipe some of the blood off before hit dries?"

"I'll wash to-night," he said. "Lemme be, I tell you."

The wagon went on. He did not know where they were going. None of them ever did or ever asked, because it was always somewhere, always a house of sorts waiting for them a day or two days or even three days away. Likely his father had already arranged to make a crop on another farm before he . . . Again he had to stop himself. He (the father) always did. There was something about his wolflike independence and even courage when the advantage was at least neutral which impressed strangers, as if they got from his latent ravening ferocity not so much a sense of dependability as a feeling that his ferocious conviction in the rightness of his own actions would be of advantage to all whose interest lay with his.

That night they camped, in a grove of oaks and beeches where a spring ran. The nights were still cool and they had a fire against it, of a rail lifted from a nearby fence and cut into lengths — a small fire, neat, niggard almost, a shrewd fire; such fires were his father's habit and custom always, even in freezing weather. Older, the boy might have remarked this and wondered why not a big one; why should not a man who had not only seen the waste and extravagance of war, but who had in his blood an inherent voracious prodigality with material not his own, have burned everything in sight? Then he might have gone a step farther and thought that that was the reason: that niggard blaze was the living fruit of nights passed during those four years in the woods hiding from all men, blue or gray, with his strings of horses (captured horses, he called them). And older still, he might have divined the true reason: that the element of fire spoke to some deep mainspring of his father's being, as the element of steel or of powder spoke to other men, as the one weapon for the preservation of integrity, else breath were not worth the breathing, and hence to be regarded with respect and used with discretion.

But he did not think this now and he had seen those same niggard blazes all his life. He merely ate his supper beside it and was already half asleep over his iron plate when his father called him, and once more he followed the stiff back, the stiff and ruthless limp, up the slope and on to the starlit road where, turning, he could see his father against the stars but without face or depth — a shape black, flat, and bloodless as though cut from tin in the iron folds of the frockcoat which had not been made for him, the voice harsh like tin and without heat like tin:

"You were fixing to tell them. You would have told him." He didn't answer. His father struck him with the flat of his hand on the side of the head, hard but without heat, exactly as he had struck the two mules at the store, exactly as he would strike either of them with any stick in order to kill a horse fly, his voice still without heat or anger: "You're getting to be a man. You got to learn. You got to learn to stick to your own blood or you ain't going to have any blood to stick to you. Do you think either of them, any man there this morning, would? Don't you know all they wanted was a chance to get at me because they knew I had them beat? Eh?" Later, twenty years later, he was to tell himself, "If I had said they wanted only truth, justice, he would have hit me again." But now he said nothing. He was not crying. He just stood there. "Answer me," his father said.

"Yes," he whispered. His father turned.

"Get on to bed. We'll be there to-morrow."

To-morrow they were there. In the early afternoon the wagon stopped before a paintless two-room house identical almost with the dozen others it had stopped before even in the boy's ten years, and again, as on the other dozen occasions, his mother and aunt got down and began to unload the wagon, although his two sisters and his father and brother had not moved.

"Likely hit ain't fitten for hawgs," one of the sisters said.

"Nevertheless, fit it will and you'll hog it and like it," his father said. "Get out of them chairs and help your Ma unload."

The two sisters got down, big, bovine, in a flutter of cheap ribbons; one of them drew from the jumbled wagon bed a battered lantern, the other a worn broom. His father handed the reins to the older son and began to climb stiffly over the wheel. "When they get unloaded, take the team to the barn and feed them." Then he said, and at first the boy thought he was still speaking to his brother: "Come with me."

"Me?" he said.

"Yes," his father said. "You."

"Abner," his mother said. His father paused and looked back — the harsh level stare beneath the shaggy, graying, irascible brows.

"I reckon I'll have a word with the man that aims to begin to-morrow owning me body and soul for the next eight months."

They went back up the road. A week ago — or before last night, that is — he would have asked where they were going, but not now. His father had struck him before last night but never before had he paused afterward to explain why; it was as if the blow and the following calm, outrageous voice still rang, repercussed, divulging nothing to him save the terrible handicap of being young, the light weight of his few years, just heavy enough to prevent his soaring free of the world as it seemed to be ordered but not heavy enough to keep him footed solid in it, to resist it and try to change the course of its events.

Presently he could see the grove of oaks and cedars and the other flowering trees and shrubs where the house would be, though not the house yet. They walked beside a fence massed with honeysuckle and Cherokee roses and came to a gate swinging open between two brick pillars, and now, beyond a sweep of drive, he saw the house for the first time and at that instant he forgot his father and the terror and despair both, and even when he remembered his father again (who had not stopped) the terror and despair did not return. Because, for all the twelve movings, they had sojourned until now in a poor country, a land of small farms and fields and houses, and he had never seen a house like this before. *Hit's big as a courthouse* he thought quietly, with a surge of peace and joy whose reason he could not have thought into words, being too young for that: *They are safe from him. People whose lives are a part of this peace and dignity are beyond his touch, he no more to them than a buzzing wasp: capable of stinging for a little moment but that's all; the spell of this peace and dignity rendering even the barns and stable and cribs which belong to it impervious to the puny flames he might contrive* . . . this, the peace and joy, ebbing for an instant as he looked again at the stiff black back, the stiff and implacable limp of the figure which was not dwarfed by the house, for the reason that it had never looked big anywhere and which now, against the serene columned backdrop, had more than ever that impervious quality of something cut ruthlessly from tin, depthless, as though, sidewise to the sun, it would cast no shadow. Watching him, the boy remarked the absolutely undeviating course which his father held and saw the stiff foot come squarely down in a pile of fresh droppings where a horse had stood in the drive and which his father could have avoided by a simple change of stride. But it ebbed only for a moment, though he could not have thought this into words either, walking on in the spell of the house, which he could even want but without envy, without sorrow, certainly never with that ravening and jealous rage which unknown to him walked in the ironlike black coat before him: *Maybe he will feel it too. Maybe it will even change him now from what maybe he couldn't help but be.*

They crossed the portico. Now he could hear his father's stiff foot as it came down on the boards with clocklike finality, a sound out of all proportion to the displacement of the body it bore and which was not dwarfed either by the white door before it, as though it had attained to a sort of vicious and ravening minimum not to be dwarfed by anything — the flat, wide, black hat, the formal coat of broadcloth which had once been black but which had now that friction-glazed greenish cast of the bodies of old house flies, the lifted sleeve which was too large, the lifted hand like a curled claw. The door opened so promptly that the boy knew the Negro must have been watching them all the time, an old man with neat grizzled hair, in a linen jacket, who stood barring the door with his body, saying, "Wipe yo foots, white man, fo you come in here. Major ain't home nohow."

"Get out of my way, nigger," his father said, without heat too, flinging the door back and the Negro also and entering, his hat still on his head. And now the boy saw the prints of the stiff foot on the doorjamb and saw them appear on the pale rug behind the machinelike deliberation of the foot which seemed to bear (or transmit) twice the weight which the body compassed. The Negro was shouting "Miss Lula! Miss Lula!" somewhere behind them, then the boy, deluged as though by a warm wave by a suave turn of carpeted stair and a pendant glitter of chandeliers and a mute gleam of gold frames, heard the swift feet and saw her too, a lady — perhaps he had never seen her like before either — in a gray, smooth gown with lace at the throat and an apron tied at the waist and the sleeves turned back, wiping cake or biscuit dough from her hands with a towel as she came up the hall, looking not at his father at all but at the tracks on the blond rug with an expression of incredulous amazement.

"I tried," the Negro cried. "I tole him to . . ."

"Will you please go away?" she said in a shaking voice. "Major de Spain is not at home. Will you please go away?"

His father had not spoken again. He did not speak again. He did not even look at her. He just stood stiff in the center of the rug, in his hat, the shaggy iron-gray brows twitching slightly above the pebble-colored eyes as he appeared to examine the house with brief deliberation. Then with the same deliberation he turned; the boy watched him pivot on the good leg and saw the stiff foot drag round the arc of the turning, leaving a final long and fading smear. His father never looked at it, he never once looked down at the rug. The Negro held the door. It closed behind them, upon the hysteric and indistinguishable woman-wail. His father stopped at the top of the steps and scraped his boot clean on the edge of it. At the gate he stopped again. He stood for a moment, planted stiffly on the stiff foot, looking back at the house. "Pretty and white, ain't it?" he said. "That's sweat. Nigger sweat. Maybe it ain't white enough yet to suit him. Maybe he wants to mix some white sweat with it."

Two hours later the boy was chopping wood behind the house within which his mother and aunt and the two sisters (the mother and aunt, not the two girls, he knew that; even at this distance and muffled by walls the flat loud voices of the two girls emanated an incorrigible idle inertia) were setting up the stove to prepare a meal, when he heard the hooves and saw the linen-clad man on a fine sorrel mare, whom he recognized even before he saw the rolled rug in front of the Negro youth following on a fat bay carriage horse — a suffused, angry face vanishing, still at full gallop, beyond the corner of the house where his father and brother were sitting in the two tilted chairs; and a moment later, almost before he could have put the axe down, he heard the hooves again and watched the sorrel mare go back out of the yard, already galloping again. Then his father began to shout one of the sisters' names, who presently emerged backward from the kitchen door dragging the rolled rug along the ground by one end while the other sister walked behind it.

"If you ain't going to tote, go on and set up the wash pot," the first said.

"You, Sarty!" the second shouted. "Set up the wash pot!" His father appeared at the door, framed against that shabbiness, as he had been against that other bland perfection, impervious to either, the mother's anxious face at his shoulder.

"Go on," the father said. "Pick it up." The two sisters stooped, broad, lethargic; stooping, they presented an incredible expanse of pale cloth and a flutter of tawdry ribbons.

"If I thought enough of a rug to have to git hit all the way from France I wouldn't keep hit where folks coming in would have to tromp on hit," the first said. They raised the rug.

"Abner," the mother said. "Let me do it."

"You go back and git dinner," his father said. "I'll tend to this."

From the woodpile through the rest of the afternoon the boy watched them, the rug spread flat in the dust beside the bubbling wash-pot, the two sisters stooping over it with that profound and lethargic reluctance, while the father stood over them in turn, implacable and grim, driving them though never raising his voice again. He could smell the harsh homemade lye they were using; he saw his mother come to the door once and look toward them with an expression not anxious now but very like despair; he saw his father turn, and he fell to with the axe and saw from the corner of his eye his father raise from the ground a flattish fragment of field stone and examine it and return to the pot, and this time his mother actually spoke: "Abner. Abner. Please don't. Please, Abner."

Then he was done too. It was dusk; the whippoorwills had already begun. He could smell coffee from the room where they would presently eat the cold food remaining from the mid-afternoon meal, though when he entered the house he realized they were having coffee again probably because there was a fire on the hearth, before which the rug now lay spread over the backs of the two chairs. The tracks of his father's foot were gone. Where they had been were now long, water-cloudy scoriations resembling the sporadic course of a lilliputian mowing machine.

It still hung there while they ate the cold food and then went to bed, scattered without order or claim up and down the two rooms, his mother in one bed, where his father would later lie, the older brother in the other, himself, the aunt, and the two sisters on pallets on the floor. But his father was not in bed yet. The last thing the boy remembered was the depthless, harsh silhouette of the hat and coat bending over the rug and it seemed to him that he had not even closed his eyes when the silhouette was standing over him, the fire almost dead behind it, the stiff foot prodding him awake. "Catch up the mule," his father said.

When he returned with the mule his father was standing in the black door, the rolled rug over his shoulder. "Ain't you going to ride?" he said.

"No. Give me your foot."

He bent his knee into his father's hand, the wiry, surprising power flowed smoothly, rising, he rising with it, on to the mule's bare back (they had owned a saddle once; the boy could remember it though not when or where) and with the same effortlessness his father swung the rug up in front of him. Now in the starlight they retraced the afternoon's path, up the dusty road rife with honeysuckle, through the gate and up the black tunnel of the drive to the lightless house, where he sat on the mule and felt the rough warp of the rug drag across his thighs and vanish.

"Don't you want me to help?" he whispered. His father did not answer and now he heard again that stiff foot striking the hollow portico with that wooden and clocklike deliberation, that outrageous overstatement of the weight it carried. The rug, hunched, not flung (the boy could tell that even in the darkness) from his father's shoulder struck the angle of wall and floor with a sound unbelievably loud, thunderous, then the foot again, unhurried and enormous; a light came on in the house and the boy sat, tense, breathing steadily and quietly and just a little fast, though the foot itself did not increase its beat at all, descending the steps now; now the boy could see him.

"Don't you want to ride now?" he whispered. "We kin both ride now," the light within the house altering now, flaring up and sinking. *He's coming down the stairs now,* he thought. He had already ridden the mule up beside the horse block; presently his father was up behind him and he doubled the reins over and slashed the mule across the neck, but before the animal could begin to trot the hard, thin arm came round him, the hard, knotted hand jerking the mule back to a walk.

In the first red rays of the sun they were in the lot, putting plow gear on the mules. This time the sorrel mare was in the lot before he heard it at all, the rider collarless and even bareheaded, trembling, speaking in a shaking voice as the woman in the house had done, his father merely looking up once before stooping again to the hame he was buckling, so that the man on the mare spoke to his stooping back:

"You must realize you have ruined that rug. Wasn't there anybody here, any of your women . . ." he ceased, shaking, the boy watching him, the older brother leaning now in the stable door, chewing, blinking slowly and steadily at nothing apparently. "It cost a hundred dollars. But you never had a hundred dollars. You never will. So I'm going to charge you twenty bushels of corn against your crop. I'll add it in your contract and when you come to the commissary you can sign it. That won't keep Mrs. de Spain quiet but maybe it will teach you to wipe your feet off before you enter her house again."

Then he was gone. The boy looked at his father, who still had not spoken or even looked up again, who was now adjusting the loggerhead in the hame.

"Pap," he said. His father looked at him — the inscrutable face, the shaggy brows beneath which the gray eyes glinted coldly. Suddenly the boy went toward him, fast, stopping as suddenly. "You done the best you could!" he cried. "If he wanted hit done differently why didn't he wait and tell you how? He won't git no twenty bushels! He won't git none! We'll gether hit and hide hit! I kin watch . . ."

"Did you put the cutter back in that straight stock like I told you?"

"No, sir," he said.

"Then go do it."

That was Wednesday. During the rest of that week he worked steadily, at what was within his scope and some which was beyond it, with an industry that did not need to be driven nor even commanded twice; he had this from his mother, with the difference that some at least of what he did he liked to do, such as splitting wood with the half-size axe which his mother and aunt had earned, or saved money somehow, to present him with at Christmas. In company with the two older women (and on one afternoon, even one of the sisters), he built pens for the shoat and the cow which were a part of his father's contract with the landlord, and one afternoon, his father being absent, gone somewhere on one of the mules, he went to the field.

They were running a middle buster now, his brother holding the plow straight while he handled the reins, and walking beside the straining mule, the rich black soil shearing cool and damp against his bare ankles, he thought *Maybe this is the end of it. Maybe even that twenty bushels that seems hard to have to pay for just a rag will be a cheap price for him to stop forever and always from being what he used to be;* thinking, dreaming now, so that his brother had to speak sharply to him to mind the mule: *Maybe he even won't collect the twenty bushels. Maybe it will all add up and balance and vanish — corn, rug, fire; the terror and grief, the being pulled two ways like between two teams of horses — gone, done with for ever and ever.*

Then it was Saturday; he looked up from beneath the mule he was harnessing and saw his father in the black coat and hat. "Not that," his father said. "The wagon gear." And then, two hours later, sitting in the wagon bed behind his father and brother on the seat, the wagon accomplished a final curve, and he saw the weathered paintless store with its tattered tobacco- and patent-medicine posters and the tethered wagons and saddle animals below the gallery. He mounted the gnawed steps behind his father and brother, and there again was the lane of quiet, watching faces for the three of them to walk through. He saw the man in spectacles sitting at the plank table and he did not need to be told this was a Justice of the Peace; he sent one glare of fierce, exultant, partisan defiance at the man in collar and cravat now, whom he had seen but twice before in his life, and that on a galloping horse, who now wore on his face an expression not of rage but of amazed unbelief which the boy could not have known was at the incredible circumstance of being sued by one of his own tenants, and came and stood against his father and cried at the Justice: "He ain't done it! He ain't burnt . . ."

"Go back to the wagon," his father said.

"Burnt?" the Justice said. "Do I understand this rug was burned too?"

"Does anybody here claim it was?" his father said. "Go back to the wagon." But he did not, he merely retreated to the rear of the room, crowded as that other had been, but not to sit down this time, instead, to stand pressing among the motionless bodies, listening to the voices:

"And you claim twenty bushels of corn is too high for the damage you did to the rug?"

"He brought the rug to me and said he wanted the tracks washed out of it. I washed the tracks out and took the rug back to him."

"But you didn't carry the rug back to him in the same condition it was in before you made the tracks on it."

His father did not answer, and now for perhaps half a minute there was no sound at all save that of breathing, the faint, steady suspiration of complete and intent listening.

"You decline to answer that, Mr. Snopes?" Again his father did not answer. "I'm going to find against you, Mr. Snopes. I'm going to find that you were responsible for the injury to Major de Spain's rug and hold you liable for it. But twenty bushels of corn seems a little high for a man in your circumstances to have to pay. Major de Spain claims it cost a hundred dollars. October corn will be worth about fifty cents. I figure that if Major de Spain can stand a ninety-five dollar loss on something he paid cash for, you can stand a five-dollar loss you haven't earned yet. I hold you in damages to Major de Spain to the amount of ten bushels of corn over and above your contract with him, to be paid to him out of your crop at gathering time. Court adjourned."

It had taken no time hardly, the morning was but half begun. He thought they would return home and perhaps back to the field, since they were late, far behind all other farmers. But instead his father passed on behind the wagon, merely indicating with his hand for the older brother to follow with it, and crossed the road toward the blacksmith shop opposite, pressing on after his father, overtaking him, speaking, whispering up at the harsh, calm face beneath the weathered hat: "He won't git no ten bushels neither. He won't git one. We'll . . ." until his father glanced for an instant down at him, the face absolutely calm, the grizzled eyebrows tangled above the cold eyes, the voice almost pleasant, almost gentle:

"You think so? Well, we'll wait till October anyway."

The matter of the wagon — the setting of a spoke or two and the tightening of the tires — did not take long either, the business of the tires accomplished by driving the wagon into the spring branch behind the shop and letting it stand there, the mules nuzzling into the water from time to time, and the boy on the seat with the idle reins, looking up the slope and through the sooty tunnel of the shed where the slow hammer rang and where his father sat on an upended cypress bolt, easily, either talking or listening, still sitting there when the boy brought the dripping wagon up out of the brand and halted it before the door.

"Take them on to the shade and hitch," his father said. He did so and returned. His father and the smith and a third man squatting on his heels inside the door were talking, about crops and animals; the boy, squatting too in the ammoniac dust and hoof-parings and scales of rust, heard his father tell a long and unhurried story out of the time before the birth of the older brother even when he had been a professional horsetrader. And then his father came up beside him where he stood before a tattered last year's circus poster on the other side of the store, gazing rapt and quiet at the scarlet horses, the incredible poising and convolutions of tulle and tights and the painted leers of comedians, and said, "It's time to eat."

But not at home. Squatting beside his brother against the front wall, he watched his father emerge from the store and produce from a paper sack a segment of cheese and divide it carefully and deliberately into three with his pocket knife and produce crackers from the same sack. They all three squatted on the gallery and ate, slowly, without talking; then in the store again, they drank from a tin dipper tepid water smelling of the cedar bucket and of living beech trees. And still they did not go home. It was a horse lot this time, a tall rail fence upon and along which men stood and sat and out of which one by one horses were led, to be walked and trotted and then cantered back and forth along the road while the slow swapping and buying went on and the sun began to slant westward, they — the three of them — watching and listening, the older brother with his muddy eyes and his steady, inevitable tobacco, the father commenting now and then on certain of the animals, to no one in particular.

It was after sundown when they reached home. They ate supper by lamplight, then, sitting on the doorstep, the boy watched the night fully accomplish, listening to the whippoorwills and the frogs, when he heard his mother's voice: "Abner! No! No! Oh, God. Oh, God. Abner!" and he rose, whirled, and saw the altered light through the door where a candle stub now burned in a bottle neck on the table and his father, still in the hat and coat, at once formal and burlesque as though dressed carefully for some shabby and ceremonial violence, emptying the reservoir of the lamp back into the five-gallon kerosene can from which it had been filled, while the mother tugged at his arm until he shifted the lamp to the other hand and flung her back, not savagely or viciously, just hard, into the wall, her hands flung out against the wall for balance, her mouth open and in her face the same quality of hopeless despair as had been in her voice. Then his father saw him standing in the door.

"Go to the barn and get that can of oil we were oiling the wagon with," he said. The boy did not move. Then he could speak.

"What . . ." he cried. "What are you . . ."

"Go get that oil," his father said. "Go."

Then he was moving, running, outside the house, toward the stable: this the old habit, the old blood which he had not been permitted to choose for himself, which had been bequeathed him willy nilly and which had run for so long (and who knew where, battening on what of outrage and savagery and lust) before it came to him. *I could keep on,* he thought. *I could run on and on and never look back, never need to see his face again. Only I can't. I can't,* the rusted can in his hand now, the liquid splshing in it as he ran back to the house and into it, into the sound of his mother's weeping in the next room, and handed the can to his father.

"Ain't you going to even send a nigger?" he cried. "At least you sent a nigger before!"

This time his father didn't strike him. The hand came even faster than the blow had, the same hand which had set the can on the table with almost excruciating care flashing from the can toward him too quick for him to follow it, gripping him by the back of his shirt and on to tiptoe before he had seen it quit the can, the face stooping at him in breathless and frozen ferocity, the cold, dead voice speaking over him to the older brother who leaned against the table, chewing with that steady, curious, sidewise motion of cows:

"Empty the can into the big one and go on. I'll catch up with you."

"Better tie him up to the bedpost," the brother said.

"Do like I told you," the father said. Then the boy was moving, his bunched shirt and the hard, bony hand between his shoulder-blades, his toes just touching the floor, across the room and into the other one, past the sisters sitting with spread heavy thighs in the two chairs over the cold hearth, and to where his mother and aunt sat side by side on the bed, the aunt's arms about his mother's shoulders.

"Hold him," the father said. The aunt made a startled movement. "Not you," the father said. "Lennie. Take hold of him. I want to see you do it." His mother took him by the wrist. "You'll hold him better than that. If he gets loose don't you know what he is going to do? He will go up yonder." He jerked his head toward the road. "Maybe I'd better tie him."

"I'll hold him," his mother whispered.

"See you do then." Then his father was gone, the stiff foot heavy and measured upon the boards, ceasing at last.

Then he began to struggle. His mother caught him in both arms, he jerking and wrenching at them. He would be stronger in the end, he knew that. But he had no time to wait for it. "Lemme go!" he cried. "I don't want to have to hit you!"

"Let him go!" the aunt said. "If he don't go, before God, I am going up there myself!"

"Don't you see I can't?" his mother cried. "Sarty! Sarty! No! No! Help me, Lizzie!"

Then he was free. His aunt grasped at him but it was too late. He whirled, running, his mother stumbled forward on to her knees behind him, crying to the nearer sister: "Catch him, Net! Catch him!" But that was too late too, the sister (the sisters were twins, born at the same time, yet either of them now gave the impression of being, encompassing as much living meat and volume and weight as any other two of the family) not yet having begun to rise from the chair, her head, face, alone merely turned, presenting to him in the flying instant an astonishing expanse of young female features untroubled by any surprise even, wearing only an expression of bovine interest. Then he was out of the room, out of the house, in the mild dust of the starlit road and the heavy rifeness of honeysuckle, the pale ribbon unspooling with terrific slowness under his running feet, reaching the gate at last and turning in, running, his heart and lungs drumming, on up the drive toward the lighted house, the lighted door. He did not knock, he burst in, sobbing for breath, incapable for the moment of speech; he saw the astonished face of the Negro in the linen jacket without knowing when the Negro had appeared.

"De Spain!" he cried, panted. "Where's . . ." then he saw the white man too emerging from a white door down the hall. "Barn!" he cried. "Barn!"

"What?" the white man said. "Barn?"

"Yes!" the boy cried. "Barn!"

"Catch him!" the white man shouted.

But it was too late this time too. The Negro grasped his shirt, but the entire sleeve, rotten with washing, carried away, and he was out that door and in the drive again, and had actually never ceased to run even while he was screaming into the white man's face.

Behind him the white man was shouting, "My horse! Fetch my horse!" and he thought for an instant of cutting across the park and climbing the fence into the road, but he did not know the park nor how high the vine-massed fence might be and he dared not risk it. So he ran down the drive, blood and breath roaring; presently he was in the road again though he could not see it. He could not hear either: the galloping mare was almost upon him before he heard her, and even then he held his course, as if the very urgency of his wild grief and need must in a moment more find him wings, waiting until the ultimate instant to hurl himself aside and into the weed-choked roadside ditch as the horse thundered past and on, for an instant in furious silhouette against the stars, the tranquil early summer night sky which, even before the shape of the horse and rider vanished, stained abruptly and violently upward: a long, swirling roar incredible and soundless, blotting the stars, and he springing up and into the road again, running again, knowing it was too late yet still running even after he heard the shot and, an instant later, two shots, pausing now without knowing he had ceased to run, crying, "Pap! Pap!," running again before he knew he had begun to run, stumbling, tripping over something and scrabbling up again without ceasing to run, looking backward over his shoulder at the glare as he got up, running on among the invisible trees, panting, sobbing, "Father! Father!"

At midnight he was sitting on the crest of a hill. He did not know it was midnight and he did not know how far he had come. But there was no glare behind him now and he sat now, his face toward the dark woods which he would enter when breath was strong again, small, shaking steadily in the chill darkness, hugging himself into the remainder of his thin, rotten shirt, the grief and despair now no longer terror and fear but just grief and despair. *Father. My father,* he thought. "He was brave!" he cried suddenly, aloud but not loud, no more than a whisper: "He was! He was in the war! He was in Colonel Sartoris' cav'ry!" not knowing that his father had gone to that war a private in the fine old European sense, wearing no uniform, admitting the authority of and giving fidelity to no man or army or flag, going to war as Malbrouck himself did: for booty — it meant nothing and less than nothing to him if it were enemy booty or his own.

The slow constellations wheeled on. It would be dawn and then sun-up after a while and he would be hungry. But that would be to-morrow and now he was only cold, and walking would cure that. His breathing was easier now and he decided to get up and go on, and then he found that he had been asleep because he knew it was almost dawn, the night almost over. He could tell that from the whippoorwills. They were everywhere now among the dark trees below him, constant and inflectioned and ceaseless, so that, as the instant for giving over to the day birds drew nearer and nearer, there was no interval at all between them. He got up. He was a little stiff, but walking would cure that too as it would the cold, and soon there would be the sun. He went on down the hill, toward the dark woods within which the liquid silver voices of the birds called unceasing — the rapid and urgent beating of the urgent and quiring heart of the late spring night. He did not look back.

Questions for Discussion

1. What impression do we get about the values and character of Sarty, the son of the accused man in the trial, at the beginning of the story? Why is the boy's name ironic?

2. How is Sarty's vision of Major de Spain's large house and the hope it gives him contrasted with his father's values?

3. What roles do the mother and sisters play in the barn burning? How well do we know them?

4. What does the incident of the ruined rug and the twenty bushels of corn reveal about the father's rage? What is significant about Sarty's response to his father's destructive behavior?

5. As Sarty sits alone on the hill at midnight, he reflects on his father's bravery as a soldier. How does the narrator's voice at this point and the natural description go beyond Sarty's internal voice and help to focus the values of the story?

Ideas for Writing

1. Write an essay about Sarty's father, the barn burner. How is this character revealed through action, speech, and the evaluations of other characters, as well as through the omniscient narrator? How have his experiences in the Civil War and the grinding poverty of the sharecropper's life shaped him? Does he have redeeming qualities or strengths?

2. Write a story or essay that predicts Sarty's future based on the story's events. Will he be successful and find happiness? Will he be haunted and limited by the anger and destructiveness of his father?

ERNEST HEMINGWAY (1899–1961)

Ernest Hemingway is remembered for his full and adventurous life as well as for his novels and stories. He influenced the form and style of the modern story by stripping his texts down to straightforward plots told in short, powerful sentences; his descriptions and dialogue are in everyday language that avoids explicit emotional or philosophical explanation.

Born in Oak Park, Illinois, Hemingway often went hunting and fishing with his father. After high school, he worked as a newspaper reporter for the *Kansas City Star* and the *Toronto Star;* he soon became a foreign correspondent, joining the community of expatriate writers in Paris. During World War I, Hemingway served with the Red Cross ambulance corps and was wounded in the leg; his war experiences and contacts with the expatriate community formed the basis for much of his early fiction, including the novels *The Sun Also Rises* (1926) and *A Farewell to Arms* (1929). Hemingway continued to write stories and novels in the 1930s and 1940s, often focusing on his experiences as a sportsman; his last significant novel was *The Old Man and the Sea* (1952). Hemingway was awarded the Nobel Prize for Literature in 1954. His first major story collection, *In Our Time* (1925), includes "Hills like White Elephants"; another major collection, *The Fifth Column and the First Forty-nine Stories,* was published in 1938.

Influenced by his journalistic experience, Hemingway saw himself primarily as a realist, in a way that went beyond surface appearances: "I'm trying in all my stories to get the feeling of the actual life across — not just to depict life — or criticize it — but to actually make it alive. So that when you have read something by me you actually experience the thing."

Hills like White Elephants (1927)

The hills across the valley of the Ebro were long and white. On this side there was no shade and no trees and the station was between two lines of rails in the sun. Close against the side of the station there was the warm shadow of the building and a curtain, made of strings of bamboo beads, hung across the open door into the bar, to keep out flies. The American and the girl with him sat at a table in the shade, outside the building. It was very hot and the express from Barcelona would come in forty minutes. It stopped at this junction for two minutes and went on to Madrid.

"What should we drink?" the girl asked. She had taken off her hat and put it on the table.

"It's pretty hot," the man said.

"Let's drink beer."

"*Dos cervezas,*" the man said into the curtain.

"Big ones?" a woman asked from the doorway.

"Yes. Two big ones."

The woman brought two glasses of beer and two felt pads. She put the felt pads and the beer glasses on the table and looked at the man and the girl. The girl was looking off at the line of hills. They were white in the sun and the country was brown and dry.

"They look like white elephants," she said.

"I've never seen one," the man drank his beer.

"No, you wouldn't have."

"I might have," the man said. "Just because you say I wouldn't have doesn't prove anything."

The girl looked at the bead curtain. "They've painted something on it," she said. "What does it say?"

"Anis del Toro. It's a drink,"

"Could we try it?"

The man called "Listen" through the curtain. The woman came out from the bar.

"Four reales."

"We want two Anis del Toro."

"With water?"

"Do you want it with water?"

"I don't know," the girl said. "Is it good with water?"

"It's all right."

"You want them with water?" asked the woman.

"Yes, with water."

"It tastes like licorice," the girl said and put the glass down.

"That's the way with everything."

"Yes," said the girl. "Everything tastes of licorice. Especially all the things you've waited so long for, like absinthe."

"Oh, cut it out."

"You started it," the girl said. "I was being amused. I was having a fine time."

"Well, let's try and have a fine time."

"All right. I was trying. I said the mountains looked like white elephants. Wasn't that bright?"

"That was bright."

"I wanted to try this new drink: That's all we do, isn't it — look at things and try new drinks?"

"I guess so."

The girl looked across at the hills.

"They're lovely hills," she said. "They don't really look like white elephants. I just meant the coloring of their skin through the trees."

"Should we have another drink?"

"All right."

The warm wind blew the bead curtain against the table.

"The beer's nice and cool," the man said.

"It's lovely," the girl said.

"It's really an awfully simple operation, Jig," the man said. "It's not really an operation at all."

The girl looked at the ground the table legs rested on.

"I know you wouldn't mind it, Jig. It's really not anything. It's just to let the air in."

The girl did not say anything.

"I'll go with you and I'll stay with you all the time. They just let the air in and then it's all perfectly natural."

"Then what will we do afterward?"

"We'll be fine afterward. Just like we were before."

"What makes you think so?"

"That's the only thing that bothers us. It's the only thing that's made us unhappy."

The girl looked at the bead curtain, put her hand out, and took hold of two of the strings of beads.

"And you think then we'll be all right and be happy."

"I know we will. You don't have to be afraid. I've known lots of people that have done it."

"So have I," said the girl. "And afterward they were all so happy."

"Well," the man said, "if you don't want to you don't have to. I wouldn't have you do it if you didn't want to. But I know it's perfectly simple."

"And you really want to?"

"I think it's the best thing to do. But I don't want you to do it if you don't really want to."

"And if I do it you'll be happy and things will be like they were and you'll love me?"

"I love you now. You know I love you."

"I know. But if I do it, then it will be nice again if I say things are like white elephants, and you'll like it?"

"I'll love it. I love it now but I just can't think about it. You know how I get when I worry."

"If I do it you won't ever worry?"

"I won't worry about that because it's perfectly simple."

"Then I'll do it. Because I don't care about me."

"What do you mean?"

"I don't care about me."

"Well, I care about you."

"Oh, yes. But I don't care about me. And I'll do it and then everything will be fine."

"I don't want you to do it if you feel that way."

The girl stood up and walked to the end of the station. Across, on the other side, were fields of grain and trees along the banks of the Ebro. Far away, beyond the river, were mountains. The shadow of a cloud moved across the field of grain and she saw the river through the trees.

"And we could have all this," she said. "And we could have everything and every day we make it more impossible."

"What did you say?"

"I said we could have everything."

"We can have everything."

"No, we can't."

"We can have the whole world."

"No, we can't."

"We can go everywhere."

"No, we can't. It isn't ours any more."

"It's ours."

"No, it isn't. And once they take it away, you never get it back."

"But they haven't taken it away."

"We'll wait and see."

"Come on back in the shade," he said. "You mustn't feel that way."

"I don't feel any way," the girl said. "I just know things."

"I don't want you to do anything that you don't want to do — "

"Nor that isn't good for me," she said. "I know. Could we have another beer?"

"All right. But you've got to realize — "

"I realize," the girl said. "Can't we maybe stop talking?"

They sat down at the table and the girl looked across at the hills on the dry side of the valley and the man looked at her and at the table.

"You've got to realize," he said, "that I don't want you to do it if you don't want to. I'm perfectly willing to go through with it if it means anything to you."

"Doesn't it mean anything to you? We could get along."

"Of course it does. But I don't want anybody but you. I don't want any one else. And I know it's perfectly simple."

"Yes, you know it's perfectly simple."

"It's all right for you to say that, but I do know it."

"Would you do something for me now?"

"I'd do anything for you."

"Would you please please please please please please please stop talking?"

He did not say anything but looked at the bags against the wall of the station. There were labels on them from all the hotels where they had spent nights.

"But I don't want you to," he said, "I don't care anything about it."

"I'll scream," the girl said.

The woman came out through the curtains with two glasses of beer and put them down on the damp felt pads. "The train comes in five minutes," she said.

"What did she say?" asked the girl.

"That the train is coming in five minutes."

The girl smiled brightly at the woman, to thank her.

"I'd better take the bags over to the other side of the station," the man said. She smiled at him.

"All right. Then come back and we'll finish the beer."

He picked up the two heavy bags and carried them around the station to the other tracks. He looked up the tracks but could not see the train. Coming back, he walked through the barroom, where people waiting for the train were drinking. He drank an Anis at the bar and looked at the people. They were all waiting reasonably for the train. He went out through the bead curtain. She was sitting at the table and smiled at him.

"Do you feel better?" he asked.

"I feel fine," she said. "There's nothing wrong with me. I feel fine."

Questions for Discussion

1. What mood is created through setting the story in a train-station bar in a foreign country with a view of the "long and white" hills across the Ebro River valley? Why does Jig admire the view of the mountains, the field of grain, and the river?

2. Why does Jig remark that the hills remind her of "white elephants"? What symbolism is suggested by the expression "a white elephant"?

3. What is the subject of the disagreement between the American and Jig? How are their personalities and outlooks on life contrasted?

4. Point out lines in the dialogue that seem to have a double or oblique meaning. For instance, what motivates Jig to remark "Everything tastes of licorice. Especially all the things you've waited so long for, like absinthe"? What does she mean by "It isn't ours any more"?

5. What is the irony of the American's line, "They just let the air in and then it's all perfectly natural"? Give examples of other unintended irony in the American's comments.

Ideas for Writing

1. At the end of the story, Jig remarks, "I feel fine." Do you think she actually feels fine, or is she being ironic? Has she made an important decision, or is she simply trying to get the American to leave her alone? Write an essay in which you interpret the meaning of Jig's remark based on the earlier conversation between the couple.

2. Write a story involving a conflict between two characters using the type of brief dialogue and simple, unadorned description that characterizes Hemingway's "Hills like White Elephants."

JORGE LUIS BORGES   (1899–1986)

The fiction of the Argentine writer Jorge Luis Borges explores issues of history, reality, knowledge, mysticism, and imagination in playful ways that often suggest hidden, occult meanings. Borges enjoyed inventing imaginary authors, books, and even parallel universes that exist only in the pages of his stories. From a wealthy Buenos Aires family, Borges was the son of a philosophy professor and studied at home in his family's extensive library before traveling abroad to study at the Collège de Genève in Switzerland. He was director of the Buenos Aires National Library for many years and a professor of literature at the University of Buenos Aires. Borges began to write in Europe; he later became a follower of *Ultraísme,* a Spanish literary movement that emphasized dense figurative language rather than realistic plots, descriptions, and characterizations. Borges was almost unknown as a writer outside of Argentina until he won the International Publishers Prize (Prix Formentor) in 1961; subsequently, many of his earlier works were translated and published internationally. His story collections published in English include *Ficciones* (1962), *Labyrinths* (1962), *The Aleph and Other Stories* (1970), and *The Book of Sand* (1977), in which the story "The Book of Sand" appears. Borges's postmodernist stories are often like philosophical puzzles or labyrinths that capture the reader's mind. One finds in many of them questions about the meaning of reality, written expression, and the limits of human understanding.

The Book of Sand   (1971)

Translated by Norman Thomas Di Giovanni

Thy rope of sands . . .
— *George Herbert*

The line is made up of an infinite number of points; the plane of an infinite number of lines; the volume of an infinite number of planes; the hypervolume of an infinite number of volumes. . . . No, unquestionably this is not — *more geometrico* — the best way of beginning my story. To claim that it is true is nowadays the convention of every made-up story. Mine, however, *is* true.

I live alone in a fourth-floor apartment on Belgrano Street, in Buenos Aires. Late one evening, a few months back, I heard a knock at my door. I opened it and a stranger stood there. He was a tall man, with nondescript features — or perhaps it was my myopia that made them seem that way. Dressed in gray and carrying a gray suitcase in his hand, he had an unassuming look about him. I saw at once that he was a foreigner. At first, he struck me as old; only later did I realize that I had been misled by his thin blond hair, which was, in a

535

Scandinavian sort of way, almost white. During the course of our conversation, which was not to last an hour, I found out that he came from the Orkneys.

I invited him in, pointing to a chair. He paused awhile before speaking. A kind of gloom emanated from him — as it does now from me.

"I sell Bibles," he said.

Somewhat pedantically, I replied, "In this house are several English Bibles, including the first — John Wiclif's. I also have Cipriano de Valera's, Luther's — which, from a literary viewpoint, is the worst — and a Latin copy of the Vulgate. As you see, it's not exactly Bibles I stand in need of."

After a few moments of silence, he said, "I don't only sell Bibles. I can show you a holy book I came across on the outskirts of Bikaner. It may interest you."

He opened the suitcase and laid the book on a table. It was an octavo volume, bound in cloth. There was no doubt that it had passed through many hands. Examining it, I was surprised by its unusual weight. On the spine were the words "Holy Writ" and, below them, "Bombay."

"Nineteenth century, probably," I remarked.

"I don't know," he said. "I've never found out."

I opened the book at random. The script was strange to me. The pages, which were worn and typographically poor, were laid out in double columns, as in a Bible. The text was closely printed, and it was ordered in versicles. In the upper corners of the pages were Arabic numbers. I noticed that one left-hand page bore the number (let us say) 40,514 and the facing right-hand page 999. I turned the leaf; it was numbered with eight digits. It also bore a small illustration, like the kind used in dictionaries — an anchor drawn with pen and ink, as if by a schoolboy's clumsy hand.

It was at this point that the stranger said, "Look at the illustration closely. You'll never see it again."

I noted my place and closed the book. At once, I reopened it. Page by page, in vain, I looked for the illustration of the anchor. "It seems to be a version of Scriptures in some Indian language, is it not?" I said to hide my dismay.

"No," he replied. Then, as if confiding a secret, he lowered his voice. "I acquired the book in a town out on the plain in exchange for a handful of rupees and a Bible. Its owner did not know how to read. I suspect that he saw the Book of Books as a talisman. He was of the lowest caste; nobody but other untouchables could tread his shadow without contamination. He told me his book was called the Book of Sand, because neither the book nor the sand has any beginning or end."

The stranger asked me to find the first page.

I laid my left hand on the cover and, trying to put my thumb on the flyleaf, I opened the book. It was useless. Every time I tried, a number of pages came between the cover and my thumb. It was as if they kept growing from the book.

"Now find the last page."

Again I failed. In a voice that was not mine, I barely managed to stammer, "This can't be."

Still speaking in a low voice, the stranger said, "It can't be, but it is. The number of pages in this book is no more or less than infinite. None is the first page, none the last. I don't know why they're numbered in this arbitrary way. Perhaps to suggest that the terms of an infinite series admit any number."

Then, as if he were thinking aloud, he said, "If space is infinite, we may be at any point in space. If time is infinite, we may be at any point in time."

His speculations irritated me. "You are religious, no doubt?" I asked him.

"Yes, I'm a Presbyterian. My conscience is clear. I am reasonably sure of not having cheated the native when I gave him the Word of God in exchange for his devilish book."

I assured him that he had nothing to reproach himself for, and I asked if he were just passing through this part of the world. He replied that he planned to return to his country in a few days. It was then that I learned that he was a Scot from the Orkney Islands. I told him I had a great personal affection for Scotland, through my love of Stevenson and Hume.

"You mean Stevenson and Robbie Burns," he corrected.

While we spoke, I kept exploring the infinite book. With feigned indifference, I asked, "Do you intend to offer this curiosity to the British Museum?"

"No. I'm offering it to you," he said, and he stipulated a rather high sum for the book.

I answered, in all truthfulness, that such a sum was out of my reach, and I began thinking. After a minute or two, I came up with a scheme.

"I propose a swap," I said. "You got this book for a handful of rupees and a copy of the Bible. I'll offer you the amount of my pension check, which I've just collected, and my black-letter Wiclif Bible. I inherited it from my ancestors."

"A black-letter Wiclif!" he murmured.

I went to my bedroom and brought him the money and the book. He turned the leaves and studied the title page with all the fervor of a true bibliophile.

"It's a deal," he said.

It amazed me that he did not haggle. Only later was I to realize that he had entered my house with his mind made up to sell the book. Without counting the money, he put it away.

We talked about India, about Orkney, and about the Norwegian jarls who once ruled it. It was night when the man left. I have not seen him again, nor do I know his name.

I thought of keeping the Book of Sand in the space left on the shelf by the Wiclif, but in the end I decided to hide it behind the volumes of a broken set of The Thousand and One Nights. I went to bed and did not sleep. At three or four in the morning, I turned on the light. I got down the impossible book and leafed through its pages. On one of them I saw engraved a mask. The upper corner of the page carried a number, which I no longer recall, elevated to the ninth power.

I showed no one my treasure. To the luck of owning it was added the fear of having it stolen, and then the misgiving that it might not truly be infinite. These twin preoccupations intensified my old misanthropy. I had only a few friends left; I now stopped seeing even them. A prisoner of the book, I almost never went out anymore. After studying its frayed spine and covers with a magnifying glass, I rejected the possibility of a contrivance of any sort. The small illustrations, I verified, came two thousand pages apart. I set about listing them alphabetically in a notebook, which I was not long in filling up. Never once was an illustration repeated. At night, in the meager intervals my insomnia granted, I dreamed of the book.

Summer came and went, and I realized that the book was monstrous. What good did it do me to think that I, who looked upon the volume with my eyes, who held it in my hands, was any less monstrous? I felt that the book was a nightmarish object, an obscene thing that affronted and tainted reality itself.

I thought of fire, but I feared that the burning of an infinite book might likewise prove infinite and suffocate the planet with smoke. Somewhere I recalled reading that the best place to hide a leaf is in a forest. Before retirement, I worked on Mexico Street, at the Argentine National Library, which contains nine hundred thousand volumes. I knew that to the right of the entrance a curved staircase leads down into the basement, where books and maps and periodicals are kept. One day I went there and, slipping past a member of the staff and trying not to notice at what height or distance from the door, I lost the Book of Sand on one of the basement's musty shelves.

Questions for Discussion

1. What relationship does the narrator establish between infinity and truth in the opening paragraph? While Borges does not expect the reader to accept the story as literally "true," what truths are illuminated through the story?

2. Why is it significant that the Bible salesman is a foreigner, from a rather exotic and underpopulated place, the Orkney Islands?

3. What is suggested by the fact that the book is acquired by both the salesman and the narrator in exchange for a Bible? Interpret the meaning of the book's title, the *Book of Sand.*

4. What leads to the narrator's obsession with the *Book of Sand?* What relationship between the two texts is implied when he hides the *Book of Sand* behind *The Thousand and One Nights?*

5. Why does the narrator eventually decide that the book is "monstrous"? What does his decision to abandon it in the basement of the National Library suggest?

Ideas for Writing

1. In an essay, explore what you think the *Book of Sand* symbolizes or represents in relation to truth, knowledge, and the act of reading itself.

2. Write a sequel to the story in which a character you create finds the book and develops a relationship with it.

JOHN STEINBECK   (1902–1968)

One of the most popular writers of his generation, John Steinbeck celebrated in all his work essential human dignity and decried those aspects of our social life that encourage exploitation and brutality. Steinbeck grew up in Salinas, California, where much of his fiction takes place. He attended Stanford University from 1919 to 1925, studying marine biology and English, but moved to New York City without finishing his degree, intending to develop his career as a professional writer. Disillusioned with life in New York, he moved back to California after only one year and began supporting himself with odd jobs. Steinbeck established his literary reputation with his fourth book, *Tortilla Flat* (1935), a novel that sympathetically portrays the lives of workingmen in Monterey. He was awarded the Pulitzer Prize for *The Grapes of Wrath* (1939), a novel about the oppression of migrant workers in the Southwest during the depression. Other of his well-known novels include *Of Mice and Men* (1937) and *East of Eden* (1952). Steinbeck was awarded the Nobel Prize for Literature in 1962.

The best of his short fiction, including the widely anthologized story "The Chrysanthemums," is collected in *The Long Valley* (1938). Steinbeck's stories are noted for characters who represent both rural, agricultural California and the depression years — migrant workers, political organizers, hobos, and small farmers. Steinbeck portrays his characters' inner worlds and frustrated yearning for a better life by focusing on key moments of insight or revelation.

The Chrysanthemums   (1937)

The high grey-flannel fog of winter closed off the Salinas Valley from the sky and from all the rest of the world. On every side it sat like a lid on the mountains and made of the great valley a closed pot. On the broad, level land floor the gang ploughs bit deep and left the black earth shining like metal where the shares had cut. On the foot-hill ranches across the Salinas River, the yellow stubble fields seemed to be bathed in pale cold sunshine, but there was no sunshine in the valley now in December. The thick willow scrub along the river flamed with sharp and positive yellow leaves.

It was a time of quiet and of waiting. The air was cold and tender. A light wind blew up from the southwest so that the farmers were mildly hopeful of a good rain before long; but fog and rain do not go together.

Across the river, on Henry Allen's foot-hill ranch there was little work to be done, for the hay was cut and stored and the orchards were ploughed up to receive the rain deeply when it should come. The cattle on the higher slopes were becoming shaggy and rough-coated.

Elisa Allen, working in her flower garden, looked down across the yard and saw Henry, her husband, talking to two men in business suits. The three of them stood by the tractor-shed, each man with one foot on the side of the little Fordson. They smoked cigarettes and studied the machine as they talked.

Elisa watched them for a moment and then went back to her work. She was thirty-five. Her face was lean and strong and her eyes were as clear as water. Her figure looked blocked and heavy in her gardening costume, a man's black hat pulled low down over her eyes, clod-hopper shoes, a figured print dress almost completely covered by a big corduroy apron with four big pockets to hold the snips, the trowel and scratcher, the seeds and the knife she worked with. She wore heavy leather gloves to protect her hands while she worked.

She was cutting down the old year's chrysanthemum stalks with a pair of short and powerful scissors. She looked down toward the men by the tractor-shed now and then. Her face was eager and mature and handsome; even her work with the scissors was overeager, over-powerful. The chrysanthemum stems seemed too small and easy for her energy.

She brushed a cloud of hair out of her eyes with the back of her glove, and left a smudge of earth on her cheek in doing it. Behind her stood the neat white farmhouse with red geraniums close-banked around it as high as the windows. It was a hard-swept-looking little house, with hard-polished windows, and a clean mud-mat on the front steps.

Elisa cast another glance toward the tractor-shed. The strangers were getting into their Ford coupé. She took off a glove and put her strong fingers down into the forest of new green chrysanthemum sprouts that were growing around the old roots. She spread the leaves and looked down among the close-growing stems. No aphids were there, no sow bugs or snails or cutworms. Her terrier fingers destroyed such pests before they could get started.

Elisa started at the sound of her husband's voice. He had come near quietly, and he leaned over the wire fence that protected her flower garden from cattle and dogs and chickens.

"At it again," he said. "You've get a strong new crop coming."

Elisa straightened her back and pulled on the gardening glove again. "Yes. They'll be strong this coming year." In her tone and on her face there was a little smugness.

"You've got a gift with things," Henry observed. "Some of those yellow chrysanthemums you had this year were ten inches across. I wish you'd work out in the orchard and raise some apples that big."

Her eyes sharpened. "Maybe I could do it, too. I've a gift with things, all right. My mother had it. She could stick anything in the ground and make it grow. She said it was having planters' hands that knew how to do it."

"Well, it sure works with flowers," he said.

"Henry, who were those men you were talking to?"

"Why, sure, that's what I came to tell you. They were from the Western

Meat Company. I sold those thirty head of three-year-olds steers. Got nearly my own price, too."

"Good," she said. "Good for you."

"And I thought," he continued, "I thought how it's Saturday afternoon, and we might go into Salinas for dinner at a restaurant, and then to a picture show — to celebrate, you see."

"Good," she repeated. "Oh, yes. That will be good."

Henry put on his joking tone. "There's fights tonight. How'd you like to go to the fights?"

"Oh, no," she said breathlessly. "No, I wouldn't like fights."

"Just fooling, Elisa. We'll go to a movie. Let's see. It's two now. I'm going to take Scotty and bring down those steers from the hill. It'll take us maybe two hours. We'll go in town about five and have dinner at the Cominos Hotel. Like that?"

"Of course I'll like it. It's good to eat away from home."

"All right, then. I'll go get up a couple of horses."

She said: "I'll have plenty of time to transplant some of these sets, I guess."

She heard her husband calling Scotty down by the barn. And a little later she saw the two men ride up the pale yellow hillside in search of the steers.

There was a little square sandy bed kept for rooting the chrysanthemums. With her trowel she turned the soil over and over, and smoothed it and patted it firm. Then she dug ten parallel trenches to receive the sets. Back at the chrysanthemum bed she pulled out the little crisp shoots, trimmed off the leaves of each one with her scissors and laid it on a small orderly pile.

A squeak of wheels and plod of hoofs came from the road. Elisa looked up. The country road ran along the dense bank of willows and cottonwoods that bordered the river, and up this road came a curious vehicle, curiously drawn. It was an old spring-wagon, with a round canvas top on it like the cover of a prairie schooner. It was drawn by an old bay horse and a little grey-and-white burro. A big stubble-bearded man sat between the cover flaps and drove the crawling team. Underneath the wagon, between the hind wheels, a lean and rangy mongrel dog walked sedately. Words were painted on the canvas, in clumsy, crooked letters. "Pots, pans, knives, scissors, lawn mores, Fixed." Two rows of articles, and the triumphantly definitive "Fixed" below. The black paint had run down in little sharp points beneath each letter.

[margin note: mismat- ched]

Elisa, squatting on the ground, watched to see the crazy, loose-jointed wagon pass by. But it didn't pass. It turned into the farm road in front of her house, crooked old wheels skirling and squeaking. The rangy dog darted from between the wheels and ran ahead. Instantly the two ranch shepherds flew out at him. Then all three stopped, and with stiff and quivering tails, with taut straight legs, with ambassadorial dignity, they slowly circled, sniffing daintily. The caravan pulled up to Elisa's wire fence and stopped. Now the newcomer dog, feeling out-numbered, lowered his tail and retired under the wagon with raised hackles and bared teeth.

The man on the wagon seat called out: "That's a bad dog in a fight when he gets started."

Elisa laughed. "I see he is. How soon does he generally get started?"

The man caught up her laughter and echoed it heartily. "Sometimes not for weeks and weeks," he said. He climbed stiffly down, over the wheel. The horse and the donkey drooped like unwatered flowers.

Elisa saw that he was a very big man. Although his hair and beard were greying, he did not look old. His worn black suit was wrinkled and spotted with grease. The laughter had disappeared from his face and eyes the moment his laughing voice ceased. His eyes were dark, and they were full of the brooding that gets in the eyes of teamsters and of sailors. The calloused hands he rested on the wire fence were cracked, and every crack was a black line. He took off his battered hat.

"I'm off my general road, ma'am," he said. "Does this dirt road cut over across the river to the Los Angeles highway?"

Elisa stood up and shoved the thick scissors in her apron pocket. "Well, yes, it does, but it winds around and then fords the river. I don't think your team could pull through the sand."

He replied with some asperity: "It might surprise you what them beasts can pull through."

"When they get started?" she asked.

He smiled for a second. "Yes. When they get started."

"Well,'" said Elisa, "I think you'll save time if you go back to the Salinas road and pick up the highway there."

He drew a big finger down the chicken wire and made it sing. "I ain't in any hurry, ma'am. I go from Seattle to San Diego and back every year. Takes all my time. About six months each way. I aim to follow nice weather."

Elisa took off her gloves and stuffed them in the apron pocket with the scissors. She touched the under edge of her man's hat, searching for fugitive hairs. "That sounds like a nice kind of way to live," she said.

He leaned confidentially over the fence. "Maybe you noticed the writing on my wagon. I mend pots and sharpen knives and scissors. You got any of them things to do?"

"Oh, no," she said quickly. "Nothing like that." Her eyes hardened with resistance.

"Scissors is the worst thing," he explained. "Most people just ruin scissors trying to sharpen 'em, but I know how. I got a special tool. It's a little bobbit kind of thing, and patented. But it sure does the trick."

"No. My scissors are all sharp."

"All right, then. Take a pot," he continued earnestly, "a bent pot, or a pot with a hole. I can make it like new so you don't have to buy no new ones.

That's a saving for you."

"No," she said shortly. "I tell you I have nothing like that for you to do."

His face fell to an exaggerated sadness. His voice took on a whining undertone. "I ain't had a thing to do today. Maybe I won't have no supper tonight. You see I'm off my regular road. I know folks on the highway clear from Seattle to San Diego. They save their things for me to sharpen up because they know I do it so good and save them money."

"I'm sorry," Elisa said irritably. "I haven't anything for you to do."

His eyes left her face and fell to searching the ground. They roamed about until they came to the chrysanthemum bed where she had been working. "What's them plants, ma'am?"

The irritation and resistance melted from Elisa's face. "Oh, those are chrysanthemums, giant whites and yellows. I raise them every year, bigger than anybody around here."

"Kind of a long-stemmed flower? Looks like a quick puff of colored smoke?" he asked.

"That's it. What a nice way to describe them."

"They smell kind of nasty till you get used to them," he said.

"It's a good bitter smell," she retorted, "not nasty at all."

He changed his tone quickly. "I like the smell myself."

"I had ten-inch blooms this year," she said.

The man leaned farther over the fence. "Look. I know a lady down the road a piece, has got the nicest garden you ever seen. Got nearly every kind of flower but no chrysanthemums. Last time I was mending a copper-bottom washtub for her (that's a hard job but I do it good), she said to me: 'If you ever run across some nice chrysanthemums I wish you'd try to get me a few seeds.' That's what she told me."

Elisa's eyes grew alert and eager. "She couldn't have known much about chrysanthemums. You *can* raise them from seed, but it's much easier to root the little sprouts you see here."

"Oh," he said. "I s'pose I can't take none to her, then."

"Why yes you can," Elisa cried. "I can put some in damp sand, and you can carry them right along with you. They'll take root in the pot if you keep them damp. And then she can transplant them."

"She'd sure like to have some, ma'am. You say they're nice ones?"

"Beautiful," she said. "Oh, beautiful." Her eyes shone. She tore off the battered hat and shook out her dark pretty hair. "I'll put them in a flowerpot, and you can take them right with you. Come into the yard."

While the man came through the picket gate Elisa ran excitedly along the geranium-bordered path to the back of the house. And she returned carrying a big red flower-pot. The gloves were forgotten now. She kneeled on the ground by the starting bed and dug up the sandy soil with her fingers and scooped it into the bright new flower-pot. Then she picked up the little pile of shoots she had prepared. With her strong fingers she pressed them into the sand and tamped around them with her knuckles. The man stood over her. "I'll tell you what to do," she said. "You remember so you can tell the lady."

"Yes, I'll try to remember."

"Well, look. These will take root in about a month. Then she must set them out, about a foot apart in good rich earth like this, see?" She lifted a handful of dark soil for him to look at. "They'll grow fast and tall. Now remember this: In July tell her to cut them down, about eight inches from the ground."

"Before they bloom?" he asked.

"Yes, before they bloom." Her face was tight with eagerness. "They'll grow right up again. About the last of September the buds will start."

She stopped and seemed perplexed. "It's the budding that takes the most care," she said hesitantly. "I don't know how to tell you." She looked deep into his eyes, searchingly. Her mouth opened a little, and she seemed to be listening. "I'll try to tell you," she said. "Did you ever hear of planting hands?"

"Can't say I have, ma'am."

"Well, I can only tell you what it feels like. It's when you're picking off the buds you don't want. Everything goes right down into your fingertips. You watch your fingers work. They do it themselves. You can feel how it is. They pick and pick the buds. They never make a mistake. They're with the plant. Do you see? Your fingers and the plant. You can feel that, right up your arm. They know. They never make a mistake. You can feel it. When you're like that you can't do anything wrong. Do you see that? Can you understand that?"

She was kneeling on the ground looking up at him. Her breast swelled passionately.

The man's eyes narrowed. He looked away self-consciously.

"Maybe I know," he said. "Sometimes in the night in the wagon there——"

Elisa's voice grew husky. She broke in on him: "I've never lived as you do, but I know what you mean. When the night is dark—why, the stars are sharp-pointed, and there's quiet. Why, you rise up and up! Every pointed star gets driven into your body. It's like that. Hot and sharp and—lovely."

Kneeling there, her hand went out toward his legs in the greasy black trousers. Her hesitant fingers almost touched the cloth. Then her hand dropped to the ground. She crouched low like a fawning dog.

He said: "It's nice, just like you say. Only when you don't have no dinner, it ain't."

She stood up then, very straight, and her face was ashamed. She held the flower-pot out to him and placed it gently in his arms. "Here. Put it in your wagon, on the seat, where you can watch it. Maybe I can find something for you to do."

At the back of the house she dug in the can pile and found two old and battered aluminum saucepans. She carried them back and gave them to him. "Here, maybe you can fix these."

His manner changed. He became professional. "Good as new I can fix them." At the back of his wagon he set a little anvil, and out of an oily tool-box dug a small machine hammer. Elisa came through the gate to watch him while he pounded out the dents in the kettles. His mouth grew sure and knowing. At a difficult part of the work he sucked his underlip.

"You sleep right in the wagon?" Elisa asked.

"Right in the wagon, ma'am. Rain or shine I'm dry as a cow in there."

"It must be nice," she said. "It must be very nice. I wish women could do such things."

"It ain't the right kind of a life for a woman."

Her upper lip raised a little, showing her teeth. "How do you know? How can you tell?" she said.

"I don't know, ma'am," he protested. "Of course I don't know. Now here's your kettles, done. You don't have to buy no new ones."

"How much?"

"Oh, fifty cents'll do. I keep my prices down and my work good. That's why I have all them satisfied customers up and down the highway."

Elisa brought him a fifty-cent piece from the house and dropped it in his hand. "You might be surprised to have a rival some time. I can sharpen scissors, too. And I can beat the dents out of little pots. I could show you what a woman might do."

He put his hammer back in the oily box and shoved the little anvil out of sight. "It would be a lonely life for a woman, ma'am, and a scarey life, too, with animals creeping under the wagon all night." He climbed over the single-tree, steadying himself with a hand on the burro's white rump. He settled himself in the seat, picked up the lines. "Thank you kindly ma'am," he said. "I'll do like you told me; I'll go back and catch the Salinas road."

"Mind," she called, "if you're long in getting there, keep the sand damp."

"Sand, ma'am? . . . Sand? Oh, sure. You mean around the chrysanthemums. Sure I will." He clucked his tongue. The beasts leaned luxuriously into their collars. The mongrel dog took his place between the back wheels. The wagon turned and crawled out the entrance road and back the way it had come, along the river.

Elisa stood in front of her wire fence watching the slow progress of the caravan. Her shoulders were straight, her head thrown back, her eyes half-closed, so that the scene came vaguely into them. Her lips moved silently, forming the words "Good-bye — good-bye." Then she whispered: "That's a bright direction. There's a glowing there." The sound of her whisper startled her. She shook herself free and looked about to see whether anyone had been listening. Only the dogs had heard. They lifted their heads toward her from their sleeping in the dust, and then stretched out their chins and settled asleep again. Elisa turned and ran hurriedly into the house.

In the kitchen she reached behind the stove and felt the water tank. It was

[handwritten marginalia: there's a glimmer of hope]

full of hot water from the noonday cooking. In the bathroom she tore off her soiled clothes and flung them into the corner. And then she scrubbed herself with a little block of pumice, legs and thighs, loins and chest and arms, until her skin was scratched and red. When she had dried herself she stood in front of a mirror in her bedroom and looked at her body. She tightened her stomach and threw out her chest. She turned and looked over her shoulders at her back.

After a while she began to dress slowly. She put on her newest under-clothing and her nicest stockings and the dress which was the symbol of her prettiness. She worked carefully on her hair, pencilled her eyebrows and rouged her lips.

Before she was finished she heard the little thunder of hoofs and the shouts of Henry and his helper as they drove the red steers into the corral. She heard the gate bang shut and set herself for Henry's arrival.

His step sounded on the porch. He entered the house calling: "Elisa, where are you?"

"In my room, dressing. I'm not ready. There's hot water for your bath. Hurry up. It's getting late."

When she heard him splashing in the tub, Elisa laid his dark suit on the bed, and shirt and socks and tie beside it. She stood his polished shoes on the floor beside the bed. Then she went to the porch and sat primly and stiffly down. She looked toward the river road where the willow-line was still yellow with frosted leaves so that under the high grey fog they seemed a thin band of sunshine. This was the only color in the grey afternoon. She sat unmoving for a long time. Her eyes blinked rarely.

Henry came banging out of the door, shoving his tie inside his vest as he came. Elisa stiffened and her face grew tight. Henry stopped short and looked at her. "Why — why, Elisa. You look so nice!"

"Nice? You think I look nice? What do you mean by 'nice'?"

Henry blundered on. "I don't know. I mean you look different, strong and happy."

"I am strong? Yes, strong. What do you mean 'strong'?"

He looked bewildered. "You're playing some kind of a game," he said helplessly. "It's a kind of a play. You look strong enough to break a calf over your knee, happy enough to eat it like a watermelon."

For a second she lost her rigidity. "Henry! Don't talk like that. You didn't know what you said." She grew complete again. "I'm strong," she boasted. "I never knew before how strong."

Henry looked down toward the tractor-shed, and when he brought his eyes back to her, they were his own again. "I'll get out the car. You can put on your coat while I'm starting."

Elisa went into the house. She heard him drive to the gate and idle down his motor, and then she took a long time to put on her hat. She pulled it here and pressed it there. When Henry turned the motor off she slipped into her coat and went out.

The little roadster bounced along on the dirt road by the river, raising the birds and driving the rabbits into the brush. Two cranes flapped heavily over the willow-line and dropped into the river-bed.

Far ahead on the road Elisa saw a dark speck. She knew.

She tried not to look as they passed it, but her eyes would not obey. She whispered to herself sadly: "He might have thrown them off the road. That wouldn't have been much trouble, not very much. But he kept the pot," she explained. "He had to keep the pot. That's why he couldn't get them off the road."

The roadster turned a bend and she saw the caravan ahead. She swung full around toward her husband so she could not see the little covered wagon and the mis-matched team as the car passed them.

In a moment it was over. The thing was done. She did not look back.

She said loudly, to be heard above the motor: "It will be good, tonight, a good dinner."

"Now you've changed again," Henry complained. He took one hand from the wheel and patted her knee. "I ought to take you in to dinner oftener. It would be good for both of us. We get so heavy out on the ranch."

"Henry," she asked, "could we have wine at dinner?"

"Sure we could. Say! That will be fine."

She was silent for a while; then she said: "Henry, at those prizefights, do the men hurt each other very much?"

"Sometimes a little, not often. Why?"

"Well, I've read how they break noses, and blood runs down their chests. I've read how the fighting gloves get heavy and soggy with blood."

He looked around at her. "What's the matter, Elisa? I didn't know you read things like that." He brought the car to a stop, then turned to the right over the Salinas River bridge.

"Do any women ever go to the fights?" she asked.

"Oh, sure, some. What's the matter, Elisa? Do you want to go? I don't think you'd like it, but I'll take you if you really want to go."

She relaxed limply in the seat. "Oh, no. No. I don't want to go. I'm sure I don't." Her face was turned away from him. "It will be enough if we can have wine. It will be plenty." She turned up her coat collar so he could not see that she was crying weakly—like an old woman. → despair/ post-modern element

Questions for Discussion

1. What mood and tone does the opening description of the Salinas Valley create?
2. What do Elisa's flowers and her skill at growing them represent for her and symbolize in the story?
3. What does the separation of Elisa's work area from that of Henry reveal about their relationship? Are they are a happy couple?
4. Why is Elisa interested in the peddler and his lifestyle? Why does she envy him?
5. Why does Elisa have trouble accepting Henry's compliment that she looks strong? Why does she say, "I'm strong. . . . I never knew before how strong"? Why is she

crying at the end of the story? What is significant about her desire to go to the prizefights?

Ideas for Writing

1. What long-term impact do you think the incident with the peddler will have on Elisa's marriage and her life? Write an essay or story in which you imagine Elisa's life at some point in the future.

2. Write an essay in which you discuss Steinbeck's use of everyday objects and the way the character Elisa interacts with these objects to reveal her values.

ISAAC BASHEVIS SINGER (1904–1991)

Written originally in Yiddish, the stories of Isaac Singer begin with realistic observation of detail and place, but he is primarily interested in showing how characters who have a fixed idea or obsession can also be open to the unexpected, to the miraculous, to the erotic, and to the spiritual.

Born in Radzymin, Poland, the son of a rabbi who also settled legal disputes, Singer grew up in Warsaw. After studying at the Rabbinical Seminary there, he went to work for the Yiddish press as a translator and proofreader. In 1935 he immigrated to America and continued working for Yiddish newspapers in New York City, writing news articles, short fiction, and autobiographical sketches. By 1950 he was working actively with translators such as the novelist Saul Bellow, who made his work available to a mainstream English-speaking audience. Singer's first novel, *The Family Moskat,* appeared in 1950. His first book of stories, *Gimpel the Fool,* was published in 1957. Other novels and story collections include *The Magician of Lublin* (1960), *Enemies: A Love Story* (1972), and *A Crown of Feathers* (1973), which won the National Book Award. In 1978 Singer received the Nobel Prize for Literature.

Singer has said that literature "informs while it entertains. It manages to be both clear and profound. It has the magical power of merging causality with purpose, doubt with faith, the passions of the flesh with the yearnings of the soul." Much of his early work is set in Central European Jewish shtetls of the nineteenth century. Later stories, like "The Séance," are set in twentieth-century immigrant communities in New York City.

The Séance (1982)

Translated by Roger H. Klein and Cecil Hemley

I

It was during the summer of 1946, in the living room of Mrs. Kopitzky on Central Park West. A single red bulb burned behind a shade adorned with one of Mrs. Kopitzky's automatic drawings — circles with eyes, flowers with mouths, goblets with fingers. The walls were all hung with Lotte Kopitzky's paintings, which she did in a state of trance and at the direction of her control — Bhaghavar Krishna, a Hindu sage supposed to have lived in the fourth century. It was he, Bhaghavar Krishna, who had painted the peacock with the golden tail, in the middle of which appeared the image of Buddha; the otherworldly trees hung with elflocks and fantastic fruits; the young women of the planet Venus with their branch-like arms and their ears from which stretched silver nets — organs of telepathy. Over the pictures, the old furniture, the shelves with books, there hovered reddish shadows. The windows were covered with heavy drapes.

At the round table on which lay a Ouija board, a trumpet, and a withered rose, sat Dr. Zorach Kalisher, small, broad-shouldered, bald in front and with sparse tufts of hair in the back, half yellow, half gray. From behind his yellow bushy brows peered a pair of small, piercing eyes. Dr. Kalisher had almost no neck — his head sat directly on his broad shoulders, making him look like a primitive African statue. His nose was crooked, flat at the top, the tip split in two. On his chin sprouted a tiny growth. It was hard to tell whether this was a remnant of a beard or just a hairy wart. The face was wrinkled, badly shaven, and grimy. He wore a black corduroy jacket, a white shirt covered with ash and coffee stains, and a crooked bow tie.

When conversing with Mrs. Kopitzky, he spoke an odd mixture of Yiddish and German. "What's keeping our friend Bhaghavar Krishna? Did he lose his way in the spheres of Heaven?"

"Dr. Kalisher, don't rush me," Mrs. Kopitzky answered. "We cannot give them orders . . . They have their motives and their moods. Have a little patience."

"Well, if one must, one must."

Dr. Kalisher drummed his fingers on the table. From each finger sprouted a little red beard. Mrs. Kopitzky leaned her head on the back of the uphol-stered chair and prepared to fall into a trance. Against the dark glow of the red bulb, one could discern her freshly dyed hair, black without luster, waved into tiny ringlets; her rouged face, the broad nose, high cheekbones, and eyes spread far apart and heavily lined with mascara. Dr. Kalisher often joked that she looked like a painted bulldog. Her husband, Leon Kopitzky, a dentist, had died eighteen years before, leaving no children. The widow supported herself on an annuity from an insurance company. In 1929 she had lost her fortune in the Wall Street crash, but had recently begun to buy securities again on the advice of her Ouija board, planchette, and crystal ball. Mrs. Kopitzky even asked Bhaghavar Krishna for tips on the races. In a few cases, he had divulged in dreams the names of winning horses.

Dr. Kalisher bowed his head and covered his eyes with his hands, mutter-ing to himself as solitary people often do. "Well, I've played the fool enough. This is the last night. Even from kreplech[1] one has enough."

"Did you say something, Doctor?"

"What? Nothing."

"When you rush me, I can't fall into the trance."

"Trance-shmance," Dr. Kalisher grumbled to himself. "The ghost is late, that's all. Who does she think she's fooling? Just crazy — meshugga."

Aloud, he said: "I'm not rushing you, I've plenty of time. If what the Americans say about time is right, I'm a second Rockefeller."

---

[1] Meat dumplings. — Eds.

As Mrs. Kopitzky opened her mouth to answer, her double chin, with all its warts, trembled, revealing a set of huge false teeth. Suddenly she threw back her head and sighed. She closed her eyes, and snorted once. Dr. Kalisher gaped at her questioningly, sadly. He had not yet heard the sound of the outside door opening, but Mrs. Kopitzky, who probably had the acute hearing of an animal, might have. Dr. Kalisher began to rub his temples and his nose, and then clutched at his tiny beard.

There was a time when he had tried to understand all things through his reason, but that period of rationalism had long passed. Since then, he had constructed an anti-rationalistic philosophy, a kind of extreme hedonism which saw in eroticism the *Ding an sich*,[2] and in reason the very lowest stage of being, the entropy which led to absolute death. His position had been a curious compound of Hartmann's idea of the Unconscious with the Cabala of Rabbi Isaac Luria, according to which all things, from the smallest grain of sand to the very Godhead itself, are Copulation and Union. It was because of this system that Dr. Kalisher had come from Paris to New York in 1939, leaving behind in Poland his father, a rabbi, a wife who refused to divorce him, and a lover, Nella, with whom he had lived for years in Berlin and later in Paris. It so happened that when Dr. Kalisher left for America, Nella went to visit her parents in Warsaw. He had planned to bring her over to the United States as soon as he found a translator, a publisher, and a chair at one of the American universities.

In those days Dr. Kalisher had still been hopeful. He had been offered a cathedra in the Hebrew University in Jerusalem; a publisher in Palestine was about to issue one of his books; his essays had been printed in Zurich and Paris. But with the outbreak of the Second World War, his life began to deteriorate. His literary agent suddenly died, his translator was inept and, to make matters worse, absconded with a good part of the manuscript, of which there was no copy. In the Yiddish press, for some strange reason, the reviewers turned hostile and hinted that he was a charlatan. The Jewish organizations which arranged lectures for him cancelled his tour. According to his own philosophy, he had believed that all suffering was nothing more than negative expressions of universal eroticism: Hitler, Stalin, the Nazis who sang the Horst Wessel song and made the Jews wear yellow armbands, were actually searching for new forms and variations of sexual salvation. But Dr. Kalisher began to doubt his own system and fell into despair. He had to leave his hotel and move into a cheap furnished room. He wandered about in shabby clothes, sat all day in cafeterias, drank endless cups of coffee, smoked bad cigars, and barely managed to survive on the few dollars that a relief organization gave him each month. The refugees whom he met spread all sorts of rumors about visas for those left behind in Europe, packages of food and medicines that could be sent them through various agencies, ways of bringing over relatives from Poland

[2] The thing in itself; the essential thing. — Eds.

through Honduras, Cuba, Brazil. But he, Zorach Kalisher, could save no one from the Nazis. He had received only a single letter from Nella.

Only in New York had Dr. Kalisher realized how attached he was to his mistress. Without her, he became impotent.

II

Everything was exactly as it had been yesterday and the day before. Bhaghavar Krishna began to speak in English with his foreign voice that was half male and half female, duplicating Mrs. Kopitzky's errors in pronunciation and grammar. Lotte Kopitzky came from a village in the Carpathian Mountains. Dr. Kalisher could never discover her nationality — Hungarian, Rumanian, Galician? She knew no Polish or German, and little English; even her Yiddish had been corrupted through her long years in America. Actually she had been left languageless and Bhaghavar Krishna spoke her various jargons. At first Dr. Kalisher had asked Bhaghavar Krishna the details of his earthly existence but had been told by Bhaghavar Krishna that he had forgotten everything in the heavenly mansions in which he dwelt. All he could recall was that he had lived in the suburbs of Madras. Bhaghavar Krishna did not even know that in that part of India Tamil was spoken. When Dr. Kalisher tried to converse with him about Sanskrit, the Mahabharata, the Ramayana, the Sakuntala, Bhaghavar Krishna replied that he was no longer interested in terrestrial literature. Bhaghavar Krishna knew nothing but a few theosophic and spiritualistic brochures and magazines which Mrs. Kopitzky subscribed to.

For Dr. Kalisher it was all one big joke; but if one lived in a bug-ridden room and had a stomach spoiled by cafeteria food, if one was in one's sixties and completely without family, one became tolerant of all kinds of crackpots. He had been introduced to Mrs. Kopitzky in 1942, took part in scores of her séances, read her automatic writings, admired her automatic paintings, listened to her automatic symphonies. A few times he had borrowed money from her which he had been unable to return. He ate at her house — vegetarian suppers, since Mrs. Kopitzky touched neither meat, fish, milk, nor eggs, but only fruit and vegetables which mother earth produces. She specialized in preparing salads with nuts, almonds, pomegranates, avocados.

In the beginning, Lotte Kopitzky had wanted to draw him into a romance. The spirits were all of the opinion that Lotte Kopitzky and Zorach Kalisher derived from the same spiritual origin: *The Great White Lodge.* Even Bhaghavar Krishna had a taste for matchmaking. Lotte Kopitzky constantly conveyed to Dr. Kalisher regards from the Masters, who had connections with Tibet, Atlantis, the Heavenly Hierarchy, the Shambala, the Fourth Kingdom of Nature and the Council of Sanat Kumara. In Heaven as on the earth, in the early forties, all kinds of crises were brewing. The Powers having realigned themselves, the members of the Ashrams were preparing a war on Cosmic Evil. The Hierarchy sent out projectors to light up the planet Earth, and to find esoteric men and women to serve special purposes. Mrs. Kopitzky assured Dr. Kalisher that he was ordained to play a huge part in the Universal Rebirth. But he had neglected his mission, disappointed the Masters. He had promised to telephone, but didn't. He spent months in Philadelphia without dropping her a postcard. He returned without informing her. Mrs. Kopitzky ran into him in an automat on Sixth Avenue and found him in a torn coat, a dirty shirt, and shoes worn so thin they no longer had heels. He had not even applied for United States citizenship, though refugees were entitled to citizenship without going abroad to get a visa.

Now, in 1946, everything that Lotte Kopitzky had prophesied had come true. All had passed over to the other side — his father, his brothers, his sisters, Nella. Bhaghavar Krishna brought messages from them. The Masters still remembered Dr. Kalisher, and still had plans for him in connection with the Centennial Conference of the Hierarchy. Even the fact that his family had perished in Treblinka, Maidanek, Stutthof[3] was closely connected with the Powers of Light, the Development of Karma, the New Cycle after Lemuria, and with the aim of leading humanity to a new ascent in Love and a new Aquatic Epoch.

During the last few weeks, Mrs. Kopitzky had become dissatisfied with summoning Nella's spirit in the usual way. Dr. Kalisher was given the rare opportunity of coming into contact with Nella's materialized form. It happened in this way: Bhaghavar Krishna would give a sign to Dr. Kalisher that he should walk down the dark corridor to Mrs. Kopitzky's bedroom. There in the darkness, near Mrs. Kopitzky's bureau, an apparition hovered which was supposed to be Nella. She murmured to Dr. Kalisher in Polish, spoke caressing words into his ear, brought him messages from friends and relatives. Bhaghavar Krishna had admonished Dr. Kalisher time and again not to try to touch the phantom, because contact could cause severe injury to both, to him and Mrs. Kopitzky. The few times that he sought to approach her, she deftly eluded him. But confused though Dr. Kalisher was by these episodes, he was aware that they were contrived. This was not Nella, neither her voice nor her manner. The messages he received proved nothing. He had mentioned all these names to Mrs. Kopitzky and had been questioned by her. But Dr. Kalisher remained curious: Who was the apparition? Why did she act the part? Probably for money. But the fact that Lotte Kopitzky was capable of hiring a ghost proved that she was not only a self-deceiver but a swindler of others as well. Every time Dr. Kalisher walked down the dark corridor, he murmured, "Crazy, meshugga, a ridiculous woman."

Tonight Dr. Kalisher could hardly wait for Bhaghavar Krishna's signal. He was tired of these absurdities. For years he had suffered from a prostate condition and now had to urinate every half hour. A Warsaw doctor who was not

---

[3] Sites of Nazi concentration camps. — Eds.

allowed to practice in America, but did so clandestinely nonetheless, had warned Dr. Kalisher not to postpone an operation, because complications might arise. But Kalisher had neither the money for the hospital nor the will to go there. He sought to cure himself with baths, hot-water bottles, and with pills he had brought with him from France. He even tried to massage his prostate gland himself. As a rule, he went to the bathroom the moment he arrived at Mrs. Kopitzky's, but this evening he had neglected to do so. He felt a pressure on his bladder. The raw vegetables which Mrs. Kopitzky had given him to eat made his intestines twist. "Well, I'm too old for such pleasures," he murmured. As Bhaghavar Krishna spoke, Dr. Kalisher could scarcely listen. "What is she babbling, the idiot? She's not even a decent ventriloquist."

The instant Bhaghavar Krishna gave his usual sign, Dr. Kalisher got up. His legs had been troubling him greatly but had never been as shaky as tonight. "Well, I'll go to the bathroom first," he decided. To reach the bathroom in the dark was not easy. Dr. Kalisher walked hesitantly, his hands outstretched, trying to feel his way. When he had reached the bathroom and opened the door, someone inside pulled the knob back. It is she, the girl, Dr. Kalisher realized. So shaken was he that he forgot why he was there. "She most probably came here to undress." He was embarrassed both for himself and for Mrs. Kopitzky. "What does she need it for, for whom is she playing this comedy?" His eyes had become accustomed to the dark. He had seen the girl's silhouette. The bathroom had a window giving on to the street, and the shimmer of the street lamp had fallen on to it. She was small, broadish, with a high bosom. She appeared to have been in her underwear. Dr. Kalisher stood there hypnotized. He wanted to cry out, "Enough, it's all so obvious," but his tongue was numb. His heart pounded and he could hear his own breathing.

After a while he began to retrace his steps, but he was dazed with blindness. He bumped into a clothes tree and hit a wall, striking his head. He stepped backwards. Something fell and broke. Perhaps one of Mrs. Kopitzky's otherworldly sculptures! At that moment the telephone began to ring, the sound unusually loud and menacing. Dr. Kalisher shivered. He suddenly felt a warmth in his underwear. He had wet himself like a child.

IV

"Well, I've reached the bottom," Dr. Kalisher muttered to himself. "I'm ready for the junkyard." He walked toward the bedroom. Not only his underwear, his pants also had become wet. He expected Mrs. Kopitzky to answer the telephone; it happened more than once that she awakened from her trance to discuss stocks, bonds, and dividends. But the telephone kept on ringing. Only now he realized what he had done — he had closed the living-room door, shutting out the red glow which helped him find his way. "I'm going home," he resolved. He turned toward the street door but found he had lost all sense of direction in that labyrinth of an apartment. He touched a knob and turned it. He heard a muffled scream. He had wandered into the bathroom again. There seemed to be no hook or chain inside. Again he saw the woman in a corset, but this time with her face half in the light. In that split second he knew she was middle-aged.

"Forgive, please." And he moved back.

The telephone stopped ringing, then began anew. Suddenly Dr. Kalisher glimpsed a shaft of red light and heard Mrs. Kopitzky walking toward the telephone. He stopped and said, half statement, half question: "Mrs. Kopitzky!"

Mrs. Kopitzky started. "Already finished?"

"I'm not well, I must go home."

"Not well? Where do you want to go? What's the matter? Your heart?"

"Everything."

"Wait a second."

Mrs. Kopitzky, having approached him, took his arm and led him back to the living room. The telephone continued to ring and then finally fell silent. "Did you get a pressure in your heart, huh?" Mrs. Kopitzky asked. "Lie down on the sofa, I'll get a doctor."

"No, no, not necessary."

"I'll massage you."

"My bladder is not in order, my prostate gland."

"What? I'll put on the light."

He wanted to ask her not to do so, but she had already turned on a number of lamps. The light glared in his eyes. She stood looking at him and at his wet pants. Her head shook from side to side. Then she said, "This is what comes from living alone."

"Really, I'm ashamed of myself."

"What's the shame? We all get older. Nobody gets younger. Were you in the bathroom?"

Dr. Kalisher didn't answer.

"Wait a moment, I still have *his* clothes. I had a premonition I would need them someday."

Mrs. Kopitzky left the room. Dr. Kalisher sat down on the edge of a chair, placing his handkerchief beneath him. He sat there stiff, wet, childishly guilty and helpless, and yet with that inner quiet that comes from illness. For years he had been afraid of doctors, hospitals, and especially nurses, who deny their feminine shyness and treat grownup men like babies. Now he was prepared for the last degradations of the body. "Well, I'm finished, *kaput*." He made a swift summation of his existence. "Philosophy? what philosophy? Eroticism? whose eroticism?" He had played with phrases for years, had come to no conclusions. What had happened to him, in him, all that had taken place in Poland, in Russia, on the planets, on the faraway galaxies, could not be reduced either to Schopenhauer's blind will or to his, Kalisher's, eroticism. It was explained neither by Spinoza's substance, Leibnitz's monads, Hegel's dialectic, or Heckel's monism. "They all just juggle words like Mrs. Kopitzky. It's better that I didn't publish all that scribbling of mine. What's the good of all these preposterous hypotheses? They don't help at all . . ." He looked up at Mrs. Kopitzky's pictures on the wall, and in the blazing light they resembled the smearings of school children. From the street came the honking of cars, the screams of boys, the thundering echo of the subway as a train passed. The door opened and Mrs. Kopitzky entered with a bundle of clothes: a jacket, pants, and shirt, and underwear. The clothes smelled of mothballs and dust. She said to him, "Have you been in the bedroom?"

"What? No."

"Nella didn't materialize?"

"No, she didn't materialize."

"Well, change your clothes. Don't let me embarrass you."

She put the bundle on the sofa and bent over Dr. Kalisher with the devotion of a relative. She said, "You'll stay here. Tomorrow I'll send for your things."

"No, that's senseless."

"I knew that this would happen the moment we were introduced on Second Avenue."

"How so? Well, it's all the same."

"*They* tell me things in advance. I look at someone, and I know what will happen to him."

"So? When am I going to go?"

"You still have to live many years. You're needed here. You have to finish your work."

"My work has the same value as your ghosts."

"There *are* ghosts, there are! Don't be so cynical. They watch over us from above, they lead us by the hand, they measure our steps. We are much more important to the Cyclic Revival of the Universe than you imagine."

He wanted to ask her: "Why then, did you have to hire a woman to deceive me?" but he remained silent. Mrs. Kopitzky went out again. Dr. Kalisher took off his pants and underwear and dried himself with his handkerchief. For a while he stood with his upper part fully dressed and his pants off like some mad jester. Then he stepped into a pair of loose drawers that were as cool as shrouds. He pulled on a pair of striped pants that were too wide and too long for him. He had to draw the pants up until the hem reached his knees. He gasped and snorted, had to stop every few seconds to rest. Suddenly he remembered! This was exactly how as a boy he had dressed himself in his father's clothes when his father napped after the Sabbath pudding: the old man's white trousers, his satin robe, his fringed garment, his fur hat. Now his father had become a pile of ashes somewhere in Poland, and he, Zorach, put on the musty clothes of a dentist. He walked to the mirror and looked at himself, even stuck out his tongue like a child. Then he lay down on the sofa. The telephone rang again, and Mrs. Kopitzky apparently answered it, because this time the ringing stopped immediately. Dr. Kalisher closed his eyes and lay quietly. He had nothing to hope for. There was not even anything to think about.

He dozed off and found himself in the cafeteria on Forty-second Street, near the Public Library. He was breaking off pieces of an egg cookie. A refugee was telling him how to save relatives in Poland by dressing them up in Nazi uniforms. Later they would be led by ship to the North Pole, the South Pole, and across the Pacific. Agents were prepared to take charge of them in Tierra del Fuego, in Honolulu and Yokohama. . . . How strange, but that smuggling had something to do with his, Zorach Kalisher's, philosophic system, not with his former version but with a new one, which blended eroticism with memory. While he was combining all these images, he asked himself in astonishment: "What kind of relationship can there be between sex, memory, and the redemption of the ego? And how will it work in infinite time? It's nothing but casuistry, casuistry. It's a way of explaining my own impotence. And how can I bring over Nella when she has already perished? Unless death itself is nothing but a sexual amnesia." He awoke and saw Mrs. Kopitzky bending over him with a pillow which she was about to put behind his head.

"How do you feel?"

"Has Nella left?" he asked, amazed at his own words. He must still be half asleep.

Mrs. Kopitzky winced. Her double chin shook and trembled. Her dark eyes were filled with motherly reproach.

"You're laughing, huh? There is no death, there isn't any. We live forever, and we love forever. This is the pure truth."

Questions for Discussion

1. How is Mrs. Kopitzky's apartment decorated? What do the hangings, paintings, decorative objects, and furniture reveal about her preoccupations and religious beliefs?
2. How is Dr. Zorach Kalisher described? What conflicting attitudes does he have about Mrs. Kopitzky's séances? Why does he continue to attend them?
3. What is Kalisher's "anti-rationalistic" philosophy? Why has he rejected reason, lost hope, and fallen into despair?
4. What is Kalisher's philosophical view of eroticism? Why has he become impotent? What romantic possibilities exist in the relationship he has with Lotte Kopitzky?
5. What does Kalisher discover about the "phantom" when he goes to the bathroom? Why doesn't he "cry out" his discovery of the fraud?

Ideas for Writing

1. Write an essay that explores the significance of ghosts and séances in the story. Consider the meaning of Mrs. Kopitzky's statement: "There is no death, there isn't any. We live forever, and we love forever. This is the pure truth."
2. Write a sequel to the story. How do you think that Kalisher will respond to Mrs. Kopitzky's final advice to him? Will they continue to have a relationship?

R. K. NARAYAN   (b. 1906)

Born in Madras, India, to a Hindu Brahmin family, Rasipuram Krishnaswami Narayan has written his stories and novels primarily in English, thus providing Western audiences with an inside view of Indian life, customs, and beliefs. He learned traditional Indian music, philosophy, and literature from his grandmother, who raised him and sent him to a Lutheran school. After graduating from Maharaja's College in Mysore in 1930, he began to write, supported by his family. One of India's best-known storytellers, Narayan has been writing actively for over sixty years, producing fourteen novels, a number of story collections, and a memoir, *My Days,* for which he won the English-Speaking Union Book Award. He has also translated Indian epic works such as the Ramayana. His better-known novels include *The Vendor of Sweets* (1967), *The Painter of Signs* (1976), and *The World of Nagaraj* (1990). Narayan's story collections include *An Astrologer's Day and Other Stories* (1947) and *Under the Banyan Tree and Other Stories* (1985). Narayan's stories, many of them written for the journal *Hindu,* are often set in a fictional south Indian city, Malgudi, which Narayan populates with a broad range of characters from all social classes and occupations.

An Astrologer's Day   (1947)

Punctually at midday he opened his bag and spread out his professional equipment, which consisted of a dozen cowrie shells, a square piece of cloth with obscure mystic charts on it, a notebook and a bundle of palmyra writing. His forehead was resplendent with sacred ash and vermilion, and his eyes sparkled with a sharp abnormal gleam which was really an outcome of a continual searching look for customers, but which his simple clients took to be a prophetic light and felt comforted. The power of his eyes was considerably enhanced by their position — placed as they were between the painted forehead and the dark whiskers which streamed down his cheeks: even a half-wit's eyes would sparkle in such a setting. To crown the effect he wound a saffron-coloured turban around his head. This colour scheme never failed. People were attracted to him as bees are attracted to cosmos or dahlia stalks. He sat under the boughs of a spreading tamarind tree which flanked a path running through the Town Hall Park. It was a remarkable place in many ways: a surging crowd was always moving up and down this narrow road morning till night. A variety of trades and occupations was represented all along its way: medicine-sellers, sellers of stolen hardware and junk, magicians and, above all, an auctioneer of cheap cloth, who created enough din all day to attract the whole town. Next to him in vociferousness came a vendor of fried groundnuts, who gave his ware a fancy name each day, calling it Bombay ice-cream one day, and on the next Delhi Almond, and on the third Raja's Delicacy, and so on and so forth, and people flocked to him. A considerable portion of this crowd dallied before the astrologer too. The astrologer transacted his business by the light of a flare which crackled and smoked up above the groundnut heap nearby. Half the enchantment of the place was due to the fact that it did not have the benefit of municipal lighting. The place was lit up by shop lights. One or two had missing gaslights, some had naked flares stuck on poles, some were lit up by old cycle lamps and one or two, like the astrologer's, managed without lights of their own. It was a bewildering criss-cross of light rays and moving shadows. This suited the astrologer very well, for the simple reason that he had not in the least intended to be an astrologer when he began life; and he knew no more of what was going to happen to others than he knew what was going to happen to himself the next minute. He was as much a stranger to the stars as were his innocent customers. Yet he said things which pleased and astonished everyone: that was more a matter of study, practice and shrewd guesswork. All the same, it was as much an honest man's labour as any other, and he deserved the wages he carried home at the end of a day.

He had left his village without any previous thought or plan. If he had continued there he would have carried on the work of his forefathers — namely, tilling the land, living, marrying and ripening in his cornfield and ancestral home. But that was not to be. He had to leave home without telling anyone, and he could not rest till he left it behind a couple of hundred miles. To a villager it is a great deal, as if an ocean flowed between.

He had a working analysis of mankind's troubles: marriage, money and the tangles of human ties. Long practice had sharpened his perception. Within five minutes he understood what was wrong. He charged three pies per question and never opened his mouth till the other had spoken for at least ten minutes, which provided him enough stuff for a dozen answers and advices. When he told the person before him, gazing at his palm, "In many ways you are not getting the fullest results for your efforts," nine out of ten were disposed to agree with him. Or he questioned: "Is there any woman in your family, maybe even a distant relative, who is not well disposed towards you?" Or he gave an analysis of character: "Most of your troubles are due to your nature. How can you be otherwise with Saturn where he is? You have an impetuous nature and a rough exterior." This endeared him to their hearts immediately, for even the mildest of us loves to think that he has a forbidding exterior.

The nuts-vendor blew out his flare and rose to go home. This was a signal for the astrologer to bundle up too, since it left him in darkness except for a little shaft of green light which strayed in from somewhere and touched the ground before him. He picked up his cowrie shells and paraphernalia and was putting them back into his bag when the green shaft of light was blotted out; he looked up and saw a man standing before him. He sensed a possible client and said: "You look so careworn. It will do you good to sit down for a while and chat with me." The other grumbled some vague reply. The astrologer pressed his invitation; whereupon the other thrust his palm under his nose, saying: "You call yourself an astrologer?" The astrologer felt challenged and said, tilting the other's palm towards the green shaft of light: "Yours is a nature . . ." "Oh, stop that," the other said. "Tell me something worthwhile . . ."

Our friend felt piqued. "I charge only three pies per question, and what you get ought to be good enough for your money . . ." At this the other withdrew his arm, took out an anna and flung it out to him, saying, "I have some questions to ask. If I prove you are bluffing, you must return the anna to me with interest."

"If you find my answers satisfactory, will you give me five rupees?"

"No."

"Or will you give me eight annas?"

"All right, provided you give me twice as much if you are wrong," said the stranger. This pact was accepted after a little further argument. The astrologer sent up a prayer to heaven as the other lit a cheroot. The astrologer caught a glimpse of his face by the matchlight. There was a pause as cars hooted on the road, *jutka* drivers swore at their horses and the babble of the crowd agitated the semi-darkness of the park. The other sat down, sucking his cheroot, puffing out, sat there ruthlessly. The astrologer felt very uncomfortable. "Here, take your anna back. I am not used to such challenges. It is late for me today. . . ." He made preparations to bundle up. The other held his wrist and said, "You can't get out of it now. You dragged me in while I was passing." The astrologer shivered in his grip; and his voice shook and became faint. "Leave me today. I will speak to you tomorrow." The other thrust his palm in his face and said, "Challenge is challenge. Go on." The astrologer proceeded with his throat drying up. "There is a woman . . ."

"Stop," said the other. "I don't want all that. Shall I succeed in my present search or not? Answer this and go. Otherwise I will not let you go till you disgorge all your coins." The astrologer muttered a few incantations and replied, "All right. I will speak. But will you give me a rupee if what I say is convincing? Otherwise I will not open my mouth, and you may do what you like." After a good deal of haggling the other agreed. The astrologer said, "You were left for dead. Am I right?"

"Ah, tell me more."

"A knife has passed through you once?" said the astrologer.

"Good fellow!" He bared his chest to show the scar. "What else?"

"And then you were pushed into a well nearby in the field. You were left for dead."

"I should have been dead if some passer-by had not chanced to peep into the well," exclaimed the other, overwhelmed by enthusiasm. "When shall I get at him?" he asked, clenching his fist.

"In the next world," answered the astrologer. "He died four months ago in a far-off town. You will never see any more of him." The other groaned on hearing it. The astrologer proceeded.

"Guru Nayak —"

"You know my name!" the other said, taken aback.

"As I know all other things. Guru Nayak, listen carefully to what I have to say. Your village is two days' journey due north of this town. Take the next train and be gone. I see once again great danger to your life if you go from home." He took out a pinch of sacred ash and held it out to him. "Rub it on your forehead and go home. Never travel southward again, and you will live to be a hundred."

"Why should I leave home again?" the other said reflectively. "I was only going away now and then to look for him and to choke out his life if I met him." He shook his head regretfully. "He has escaped my hands. I hope at least he died as he deserved." "Yes," said the astrologer. "He was crushed under a lorry." The other looked gratified to hear it.

The place was deserted by the time the astrologer picked up his articles and put them into his bag. The green shaft was also gone, leaving the place in darkness and silence. The stranger had gone off into the night, after giving the astrologer a handful of coins.

It was nearly midnight when the astrologer reached home. His wife was waiting for him at the door and demanded an explanation. He flung the coins at her and said, "Count them. One man gave all that."

"Twelve and a half annas," she said, counting. She was overjoyed. "I can buy some *jaggery* and coconut tomorrow. The child has been asking for sweets for so many days now. I will prepare some nice stuff for her."

"The swine has cheated me! He promised me a rupee," said the astrologer. She looked up at him. "You look worried. What is wrong?"

"Nothing."

After dinner, sitting on the *pyol*, he told her. "Do you know a great load is gone from me today? I thought I had the blood of a man on my hands all these years. That was the reason why I ran away from home, settled here and married you. He is alive."

She gasped. "You tried to kill!"

"Yes, in our village, when I was a silly youngster. We drank, gambled and quarrelled badly one day — why think of it now? Time to sleep," he said, yawning, and stretched himself on the *pyol*.

Questions for Discussion

1. How do we know from the first description of the astrologer that he is a fraud?
2. Why is the lighting of the bazaar — a "bewildering criss-cross of light rays and moving shadows" — a crucial factor in the story, on both a literal and symbolic level?

3. How does the astrologer succeed in pleasing and astonishing his customers, despite his lack of astrological knowledge? What satirical comment might this make about other types of spiritual and psychological healers?
4. What is implied by the astrologer's mysterious abandonment of his village, "without any previous thought or plan"?
5. Evaluate the advice the astrologer gives to Guru Nayak. Is the advice helpful, even if untruthful? Does Nayak find the advice reassuring?

Ideas for Writing

1. Write an essay that discusses the story's evaluation of the astrologer's profession, character, and values. Consider the astrologer's comments to his wife about his crime and his encounter with Nayak.
2. Write a story about a false prophet or fortune-teller who does good for his followers despite the fact that he has no real spiritual powers.

EUDORA WELTY   (b. 1909)

Widely admired for her sharp but sensitive depiction of a broad assortment of characters, Eudora Welty is, after Faulkner, the premier writer of the American South. Born and raised in Jackson, Mississippi, she was encouraged in her intellectual curiosity by her parents, who supported her decision to attend Mississippi State College for Women from 1925 to 1927. Welty continued her studies at the University of Wisconsin, where she earned a B.A. in 1929, and then moved to New York to study advertising at Columbia University's Business School. After her father's death in 1932, Welty returned home and began working as a photographer and writer for the Works Progress Administration. Her first collection of stories, *A Curtain of Green*, was published in 1941 and established her as a prominent southern writer. Other collections include *The Wide Net* (1943), *The Golden Apples* (1949), *The Bride of Innisfallen* (1955), and *The Collected Stories* (1980). Welty has published five novels, including *The Optimist's Daughter* which won the Pulitzer prize in 1972. She has also written a popular collection of essays on writing and writers, *The Eye of the Story* (1977); her autobiography, *One Writer's Beginnings*, was published in 1984.

Although most of Welty's stories are set in the South, particularly Mississippi where Welty still lives, her themes are universal. In the preface to her 1980 volume of collected stories, she states, "What I do in writing of any character is to try to enter into the mind, heart, and skin of a human being who is not myself. Whether this happens to be a man or a woman, old or young, with skin black or white, the primary challenge lies in making the jump itself."

A Visit of Charity   (1941)

It was mid-morning — a very cold, bright day. Holding a potted plant before her, a girl of fourteen jumped off the bus in front of the Old Ladies' Home, on the outskirts of town. She wore a red coat, and her straight yellow hair was hanging down loose from the pointed white cap all the little girls were wearing that year. She stopped for a moment beside one of the prickly dark shrubs with which the city had beautified the Home, and then proceeded slowly toward the building, which was of whitewashed brick and reflected the winter sunlight like a block of ice. As she walked vaguely up the steps she shifted the small pot from hand to hand; then she had to set it down and remove her mittens before she could open the heavy door.

"I'm a Campfire Girl. . . . I have to pay a visit to some old lady," she told the nurse at the desk. This was a woman in a white uniform who looked as if she were cold; she had close-cut hair which stood up on the very top of her head exactly like a sea wave. Marian, the little girl, did not tell her that this visit would give her a minimum of only three points in her score.

"Acquainted with any of our residents?" asked the nurse. She lifted one eyebrow and spoke like a man.

"With any old ladies? No — but — that is, any of them will do," Marian stammered. With her free hand she pushed her hair behind her ears, as she did when it was time to study Science.

The nurse shrugged and rose. "You have a nice *multiflora cineraria* there," she remarked as she walked ahead down the hall of closed doors to pick out an old lady.

There was loose, bulging linoleum on the floor. Marian felt as if she were walking on the waves, but the nurse paid no attention to it. There was a smell in the hall like the interior of a clock. Everything was silent until, behind one of the doors, an old lady of some kind cleared her throat like a sheep bleating. This decided the nurse. Stopping in her tracks, she first extended her arm, bent her elbow, and leaned forward from the hips — all to examine the watch strapped to her wrist; then she gave a loud double-rap on the door.

"There are two in each room," the nurse remarked over her shoulder.

"Two what?" asked Marian without thinking. The sound like a sheep's bleating almost made her turn around and run back.

One old woman was pulling the door open in short, gradual jerks, and when she saw the nurse a strange smile forced her old face dangerously awry. Marian, suddenly propelled by the strong, impatient arm of the nurse, saw next the side-face of another old woman, even older, who was lying flat in bed with a cap on and a counterpane drawn up to her chin.

"Visitor," said the nurse, and after one more shove she was off up the hall.

Marian stood tongue-tied; both hands held the potted plant. The old woman, still with that terrible, square smile (which was a smile of welcome) stamped on her bony face, was waiting. . . . Perhaps she said something. The old woman in bed said nothing at all, and she did not look around.

Suddenly Marian saw a hand, quick as a bird claw, reach up in the air and pluck the white cap off her head. At the same time, another claw to match drew her all the way into the room, and the next moment the door closed behind her.

"My, my, my," said the old lady at her side.

Marian stood enclosed by a bed, a washstand and a chair; the tiny room had altogether too much furniture. Everything smelled wet — even the bare floor. She held on to the back of the chair, which was wicker and felt soft and damp. Her heart beat more and more slowly, her hands got colder and colder, and she could not hear whether the old women were saying anything or not. She could not see them very clearly. How dark it was! The window shade was down, and the only door was shut. Marian looked at the ceiling. . . . It was like being caught in a robbers' cave, just before one was murdered.

"Did you come to be our little girl for a while?" the first robber asked.

Then something was snatched from Marian's hand — the little potted plant.

"Flowers!" screamed the old woman. She stood holding the pot in an undecided way. "Pretty flowers," she added.

Then the old woman in bed cleared her throat and spoke. "They are not pretty," she said, still without looking around, but very distinctly.

Marian suddenly pitched against the chair and sat down in it.

"Pretty flowers," the first old woman insisted. "Pretty — pretty . . ."

Marian wished she had the little pot back for just a moment — she had forgotten to look at the plant herself before giving it away. What did it look like?

"Stinkweeds," said the other old woman sharply. She had a bunchy white forehead and red eyes like a sheep. Now she turned them toward Marian. The fogginess seemed to rise in her throat again, and she bleated, "Who — are — you?"

To her surprise, Marian could not remember her name. "I'm a Campfire Girl," she said finally.

"Watch out for the germs," said the old woman like a sheep, not addressing anyone.

"One came out last month to see us," said the first old woman.

A sheep or a germ? wondered Marian dreamily, holding on to the chair.

"Did not!" cried the other old woman.

"Did so! Read to us out of the Bible, and we enjoyed it!" screamed the first.

"Who enjoyed it!" said the woman in bed. Her mouth was unexpectedly small and sorrowful, like a pet's.

"We enjoyed it," insisted the other. "You enjoyed it — I enjoyed it."

"We all enjoyed it," said Marian, without realizing that she had said a word.

The first old woman had just finished putting the potted plant high, high on the top of the wardrobe, where it could hardly be seen from below. Marian wondered how she had ever succeeded in placing it there, how she could ever have reached so high.

"You mustn't pay any attention to old Addie," she now said to the little girl. "She's ailing today."

"Will you shut your mouth?" said the woman in bed. "I am not."

"You're a story."

"I can't stay but a minute — really, I can't," said Marian suddenly. She looked down at the wet floor and thought that if she were sick in here they would have to let her go.

With much to-do the first old woman sat down in a rocking chair — still another piece of furniture! — and began to rock. With the fingers of one hand she touched a very dirty cameo pin on her chest. "What do you do at school?" she asked.

"I don't know . . ." said Marian. She tried to think but she could not.

"Oh, but the flowers are beautiful," the old woman whispered. She seemed to rock faster and faster; Marian did not see how anyone could rock so fast.

"Ugly," said the woman in bed.

"If we bring flowers —" Marian began, and then fell silent. She had almost said that if Campfire Girls brought flowers to the Old Ladies' Home, the visit would count one extra point, and if they took a Bible with them on the bus and read it to the old ladies, it counted double. But the old woman had not listened, anyway; she was rocking and watching the other one, who watched back from the bed.

"Poor Addie is ailing. She has to take medicine — see?" she said, pointing a horny finger at a row of bottles on the table, and rocking so high that her black comfort shoes lifted off the floor like a little child's.

"I am no more sick than you are," said the woman in bed.

"Oh, yes you are!"

"I just got more sense than you have, that's all," said the other old woman, nodding her head.

"That's only the contrary way she talks when *you all* come," said the first old lady with sudden intimacy. She stopped the rocker with a neat pat of her feet and leaned toward Marian. Her hand reached over — it felt like a petunia leaf, clinging and just a little sticky.

"Will you hush! Will you hush!" cried the other one.

Marian leaned back rigidly in her chair.

"When I was a little girl like you, I went to school and all," said the old woman in the same intimate, menacing voice. "Not here — another town . . ."

"Hush!" said the sick woman. "You never went to school. You never came and you never went. You never were anything — only here. You never were born! You don't know anything. Your head is empty, your heart and hands and your old black purse are all empty, even that little old box that you brought with you you brought empty — you showed it to me. And yet you talk, talk, talk, talk, talk all the time until I think I'm losing my mind! Who are you? You're a stranger — a perfect stranger! Don't you know you're a stranger? Is it possible that they have actually done a thing like this to anyone — sent them in a stranger to talk, and rock, and tell away her whole long rigmarole? Do they seriously suppose that I'll be able to keep it up, day in, day out, night in, night out, living in the same room with a terrible old woman — forever?"

Marian saw the old woman's eyes grow bright and turn toward her. This old woman was looking at her with despair and calculation in her face. Her small lips suddenly dropped apart, and exposed a half circle of false teeth with tan gums.

"Come here, I want to tell you something," she whispered. "Come here!"

Marian was trembling, and her heart nearly stopped beating altogether for a moment.

"Now, now, Addie," said the first old woman. "That's not polite. Do you know what's really the matter with old Addie today?" She, too, looked at Marian; one of her eyelids dropped low.

"The matter?" the child repeated stupidly. "What's the matter with her?"

"Why, she's mad because it's her birthday!" said the first old woman, beginning to rock again and giving a little crow as though she had answered her own riddle.

"It is not, it is not!" screamed the old woman in bed. "It is not my birthday, no one knows when that is but myself, and will you please be quiet and say nothing more, or I'll go straight out of my mind!" She turned her eyes toward Marian again, and presently she said in the soft, foggy voice, "When the worst comes to the worst, I ring this bell, and the nurse comes." One of her hands was drawn out from under the patched counterpane — a thin little hand with enormous black freckles. With a finger which would not hold still she pointed to a little bell on the table among the bottles.

"How old are you?" Marian breathed. Now she could see the old woman in bed very closely and plainly, and very abruptly, from all sides, as in dreams. She wondered about her — she wondered for a moment as though there was nothing else in the world to wonder about. It was the first time such a thing had happened to Marian.

"I won't tell!"

The old face on the pillow, where Marian was bending over it, slowly gathered and collapsed. Soft whimpers came out of the small open mouth. It was a sheep that she sounded like — a little lamb. Marian's face drew very close, the yellow hair hung forward.

"She's crying!" She turned a bright, burning face up to the first old woman.

"That's Addie for you," the old woman said spitefully.

Marian jumped up and moved toward the door. For the second time, the claw almost touched her hair, but it was not quick enough. The little girl put her cap on.

"Well, it was a real visit," said the old woman, following Marian through the doorway and all the way out into the hall. Then from behind she suddenly clutched the child with her sharp little fingers. In an affected, high-pitched whine she cried, "Oh, little girl, have you a penny to spare for a poor old woman that's not got anything of her own? We don't have a thing in the world — not a penny for candy — not a thing! Little girl, just a nickel — a penny —"

Marian pulled violently against the old hands for a moment before she was free. Then she ran down the hall, without looking behind her and without looking at the nurse, who was reading *Field & Stream* at her desk. The nurse, after another triple motion to consult her wrist watch, asked automatically the question put to visitors in all institutions: "Won't you stay and have dinner with *us*?"

Marian never replied. She pushed the heavy door open into the cold air and ran down the steps.

Under the prickly shrub she stooped and quickly, without being seen, retrieved a red apple she had hidden there.

Her yellow hair under the white cap, her scarlet coat, her bare knees all flashed in the sunlight as she ran to meet the big bus rocketing through the street.

"Wait for me!" she shouted. As though at an imperial command, the bus ground to a stop.

She jumped on and took a big bite out of the apple.

Questions for Discussion

1. What do the opening paragraphs of the story reveal about Marian's reasons for visiting the old women? Contrast Marian's and the nurse's attitudes toward the old women.
2. Being in the old women's room is to Marian "like being caught in a robbers' cave, just before being murdered." What does this simile reveal about Marian's fears and values?
3. What is the relationship between the two old women? For whom do you feel more sympathy?
4. What does the old woman's begging for money reveal about her character, needs, and life at the nursing home?
5. Evaluate the story's title: Was this really a visit of charity? In what sense is the title ironic?

Ideas for Writing

1. In an essay, discuss what Marian learns from her encounter with the women in the nursing home. Refer to specific passages, such as her immediate responses to the old women as well as to her final gestures as she leaves and boards the bus.
2. Write a story or a memory narrative from personal experience about a child's first visit to an unfamiliar, unsettling place in the adult world.

A Worn Path (1940)

It was December — a bright frozen day in the early morning. Far out in the country there was an old Negro woman with her head tied in a red rag, coming along a path through the pinewoods. Her name was Phoenix Jackson. She was very old and small and she walked slowly in the dark pine shadows, moving a little from side to side in her steps, with the balanced heaviness and lightness of a pendulum in a grandfather clock. She carried a thin, small cane made from an umbrella, and with this she kept tapping the frozen earth in front of her. This made a grave and persistent noise in the still air, that seemed meditative like the chirping of a solitary little bird.

She wore a dark striped dress reaching down to her shoe tops, and an equally long apron of bleached sugar sacks, with a full pocket: all neat and tidy, but every time she took a step she might have fallen over her shoelaces, which dragged from her unlaced shoes. She looked straight ahead. Her eyes were blue with age. Her skin had a pattern all its own of numberless branching wrinkles and as though a whole little tree stood in the middle of her forehead, but a golden color ran underneath, and the two knobs of her cheeks were illumined by a yellow burning under the dark. Under the red rag her hair came down on her neck in the frailest of ringlets, still black, and with an odor like copper.

Now and then there was a quivering in the thicket. Old Phoenix said, "Out of my way, all you foxes, owls, beetles, jack rabbits, coons and wild animals! . . . Keep out from under these feet, little bob-whites. . . . Keep the big wild hogs out of my path. Don't let none of those come running my direction. I got a long way." Under her small black-freckled hand her cane, limber as a buggy whip, would switch at the brush as if to rouse up any hiding things.

On she went. The woods were deep and still. The sun made the pine needles almost too bright to look at, up where the wind rocked. The cones dropped as light as feathers. Down in the hollow was the mourning dove — it was not too late for him.

The path ran up a hill. "Seem like there is chains about my feet, time I get this far," she said, in the voice of argument old people keep to use with themselves. "Something always take a hold of me on this hill — pleads I should stay."

After she got to the top she turned and gave a full, severe look behind her where she had come. "Up through pines," she said at length. "Now down through oaks."

Her eyes opened their widest, and she started down gently. But before she got to the bottom of the hill a bush caught her dress.

Her fingers were busy and intent, but her skirts were full and long, so that before she could pull them free in one place they were caught in another. It was not possible to allow the dress to tear. "I in the thorny bush," she said. "Thorns, you doing your appointed work. Never want to let folks pass, no sir. Old eyes thought you was a pretty little *green* bush."

Finally, trembling all over, she stood free, and after a moment dared to stoop for her cane.

"Sun so high!" she cried, leaning back and looking, while the thick tears went over her eyes. "The time getting all gone here."

At the foot of this hill was a place where a log was laid across the creek.

"Now comes the trial," said Phoenix.

Putting her right foot out, she mounted the log and shut her eyes. Lifting her skirt, leveling her cane fiercely before her, like a festival figure in some parade, she began to march across. Then she opened her eyes and she was safe on the other side.

"I wasn't as old as I thought," she said.

But she sat down to rest. She spread her skirts on the bank around her and folded her hands over her knees. Up above her was a tree in a pearly cloud of mistletoe. She did not dare to close her eyes, and when a little boy brought her a plate with a slice of marble-cake on it she spoke to him. "That would be acceptable," she said. But when she went to take it there was just her own hand in the air.

So she left that tree, and had to go through a barbed-wire fence. There she had to creep and crawl, spreading her knees and stretching her fingers like a baby trying to climb the steps. But she talked loudly to herself: she could not let her dress be torn now, so late in the day, and she could not pay for having her arm or her leg sawed off if she got caught fast where she was.

At last she was safe through the fence and risen up out in the clearing. Big dead trees, like black men with one arm, were standing in the purple stalks of the withered cotton field. There sat a buzzard.

"Who you watching?"

In the furrow she made her way along.

"Glad this not the season for bulls," she said, looking sideways, "and the good Lord made his snakes to curl up and sleep in the winter. A pleasure I don't see no two-headed snake coming around that tree, where it come once. It took a while to get by him, back in the summer."

She passed through the old cotton and went into a field of dead corn. It whispered and shook and was taller than her head. "Through the maze now," she said, for there was no path.

Then there was something tall, black, and skinny there, moving before her.

At first she took it for a man. It could have been a man dancing in the field. But she stood still and listened, and it did not make a sound. It was as silent as a ghost.

"Ghost," she said sharply, "who be you the ghost of? For I have heard of nary death close by."

But there was no answer — only the ragged dancing in the wind.

She shut her eyes, reached out her hand, and touched a sleeve. She found a coat and inside that an emptiness, cold as ice.

"You scarecrow," she said. Her face lighted. "I ought to be shut up for good," she said with laughter. "My senses is gone. I too old. I the oldest people I ever know. Dance, old scarecrow," she said, "while I dancing with you."

She kicked her foot over the furrow, and with mouth drawn down, shook her head once or twice in a little strutting way. Some husks blew down and whirled in streamers about her skirts.

Then she went on, parting her way from side to side with the cane, through the whispering field. At last she came to the end, to a wagon track where the silver grass blew between the red ruts. The quail were walking around like pullets, seeming all dainty and unseen.

"Walk pretty," she said. "This the easy place. This the easy going."

She followed the track, swaying through the quiet bare fields, through the little strings of trees silver in their dead leaves, past cabins silver from weather, with the doors and windows boarded shut, all like old women under a spell sitting there. "I walking in their sleep," she said, nodding her head vigorously.

In a ravine she went where a spring was silently flowing through a hollow log. Old Phoenix bent and drank. "Sweet-gum makes the water sweet," she said, and drank more. "Nobody know who made this well, for it was here when I was born."

The track crossed a swampy part where the moss hung as white as lace from every limb. "Sleep on, alligators, and blow your bubbles." Then the track went into the road.

Deep, deep the road went down between the high green-colored banks. Overhead the live-oaks met, and it was as dark as a cave.

A black dog with a lolling tongue came up out of the weeds by the ditch. She was meditating, and not ready, and when he came at her she only hit him a little with her cane. Over she went in the ditch, like a little puff of milkweed.

Down there, her senses drifted away. A dream visited her, and she reached her hand up, but nothing reached down and gave her a pull. So she lay there and presently went to talking. "Old woman," she said to herself, "that black dog come up out of the weeds to stall you off, and now there he sitting on his fine tail, smiling at you."

A white man finally came along and found her — a hunter, a young man, with his dog on a chain.

"Well, Granny!" he laughed. "What are you doing there?"

"Lying on my back like a June-bug waiting to be turned over, mister," she said, reaching up her hand.

He lifted her up, gave her a swing in the air, and set her down. "Anything broken, Granny?"

"No sir, them old dead weeds is springy enough," said Phoenix, when she had got her breath. "I thank you for your trouble."

"Where do you live, Granny?" he asked, while the two dogs were growling at each other.

"Away back yonder, sir, behind the ridge. You can't even see it from here."

"On your way home?"

"No sir, I going to town."

"Why, that's too far! That's as far as I walk when I come out myself, and I get something for my trouble." He patted the stuffed bag he carried, and there hung down a little closed claw. It was one of the bob-whites, with its beak hooked bitterly to show it was dead. "Now you go on home, Granny!"

"I bound to go to town, mister," said Phoenix. "The time come around."

He gave another laugh, filling the whole landscape. "I know you old colored people! Wouldn't miss going to town to see Santa Claus!"

But something held old Phoenix very still. The deep lines in her face went into a fierce and different radiation. Without warning, she had seen with her own eyes a flashing nickel fall out of the man's pocket onto the ground.

"How old are you, Granny?" he was saying.

"There is no telling, mister," she said, "no telling."

Then she gave a little cry and clapped her hands and said, "Git on away from here, dog! Look! Look at that dog!" She laughed as if in admiration. "He ain't scared of nobody. He a big black dog." She whispered, "Sic him!"

"Watch me get rid of that cur," said the man. "Sic him, Pete! Sic him!"

Phoenix heard the dogs fighting, and heard the man running and throwing sticks. She even heard a gunshot. But she was slowly bending forward by that time, further and further forward, the lids stretched down over her eyes, as if she were doing this in her sleep. Her chin was lowered almost to her knees. The yellow palm of her hand came out from the fold of her apron. Her fingers slid down and along the ground under the piece of money with the grace and care they would have in lifting an egg from under a setting hen. Then she slowly straightened up, she stood erect, and the nickel was in her apron pocket. A bird flew by. Her lips moved. "God watching me the whole time. I come to stealing."

The man came back, and his own dog panted about them. "Well, I scared him off that time," he said, and then he laughed and lifted his gun and pointed it at Phoenix.

She stood straight and faced him.

"Doesn't the gun scare you?" he said, still pointing it.

"No, sir, I seen plenty go off closer by, in my day, and for less than what I done," she said, holding utterly still.

He smiled, and shouldered the gun. "Well, Granny," he said, "you must be a hundred years old, and scared of nothing. I'd give you a dime if I had any money with me. But you take my advice and stay home, and nothing will happen to you."

"I bound to go on my way, mister," said Phoenix. She inclined her head in the red rag. Then they went in different directions, but she could hear the gun shooting again and again over the hill.

She walked on. The shadows hung from the oak trees to the road like curtains. Then she smelled wood-smoke, and smelled the river, and she saw a steeple and the cabins on their steep steps. Dozens of little black children whirled around her. There ahead was Natchez shining. Bells were ringing. She walked on.

In the paved city it was Christmas time. There were red and green electric lights strung and crisscrossed everywhere, and all turned on in the daytime. Old Phoenix would have been lost if she had not distrusted her eyesight and depended on her feet to know where to take her.

She paused quietly on the sidewalk where people were passing by. A lady came along in the crowd, carrying an armful of red-, green- and silver-wrapped presents; she gave off perfume like the red roses in hot summer, and Phoenix stopped her.

"Please, missy, will you lace up my shoe?" She held up her foot.

"What do you want, Grandma?"

"See my shoe," said Phoenix. "Do all right for out in the country, but wouldn't look right to go in a big building."

"Stand still then, Grandma," said the lady. She put her packages down on the sidewalk beside her and laced and tied both shoes tightly.

"Can't lace 'em with a cane," said Phoenix. "Thank you, missy. I doesn't mind asking a nice lady to tie up my shoe, when I gets out on the street."

Moving slowly and from side to side, she went into the big building, and into a tower of steps, where she walked up and around and around until her feet knew to stop.

She entered a door, and there she saw nailed up on the wall the document that had been stamped with the gold seal and framed in the gold frame, which matched the dream that was hung up in her head.

"Here I be," she said. There was a fixed and ceremonial stiffness over her body.

"A charity case, I suppose," said an attendant who sat at the desk before her.

But Phoenix only looked above her head. There was sweat on her face, the wrinkles in her skin shone like a bright net.

"Speak up, Grandma," the woman said. "What's your name? We must have your history, you know. Have you been here before? What seems to be the trouble with you?"

Old Phoenix only gave a twitch to her face as if a fly were bothering her.

"Are you deaf?" cried the attendant.

But then the nurse came in.

"Oh, that's just old Aunt Phoenix," she said. "She doesn't come for herself —she has a little grandson. She makes these trips just as regular as clockwork. She lives away back off the Old Natchez Trace." She bent down. "Well, Aunt Phoenix, why don't you just take a seat? We won't keep you standing after your long trip." She pointed.

The old woman sat down, bolt upright in the chair.

"Now, how is the boy?" asked the nurse.

Old Phoenix did not speak.

"I said, how is the boy?"

But Phoenix only waited and stared straight ahead, her face very solemn and withdrawn into rigidity.

"Is his throat any better?" asked the nurse. "Aunt Phoenix, don't you hear me? Is your grandson's throat any better since the last time you came for the medicine?"

With her hands on her knees, the old woman waited, silent, erect and motionless, just as if she were in armor.

"You mustn't take up our time this way, Aunt Phoenix," the nurse said. "Tell us quickly about your grandson, and get it over. He isn't dead, is he?"

At last there came a flicker and then a flame of comprehension across her face, and she spoke.

"My grandson. It was my memory had left me. There I sat and forgot why I made my long trip."

"Forgot?" The nurse frowned. "After you came so far?"

Then Phoenix was like an old woman begging a dignified forgiveness for waking up frightened in the night. "I never did go to school, I was too old at the Surrender," she said in a soft voice. "I'm an old woman without an education. It was my memory fail me. My little grandson, he is just the same, and I forgot it in the coming."

"Throat never heals, does it?" said the nurse, speaking in a loud, sure voice to old Phoenix. By now she had a card with something written on it, a little list. "Yes. Swallowed lye. When was it? —January— two, three years ago —"

Phoenix spoke unasked now. "No, missy, he not dead, he just the same. Every little while his throat begin to close up again, and he not able to swallow. He not get his breath. He not able to help himself. So the time come around, and I go on another trip for the soothing medicine."

"All right. The doctor said as long as you came to get it, you could have it," said the nurse. "But it's an obstinate case."

"My little grandson, he sit up there in the house all wrapped up, waiting by himself," Phoenix went on. "We is the only two left in the world. He suffer and it don't seem to put him back at all. He got a sweet look. He going to last. He wear a little patch quilt and peep out holding his mouth open like a little bird. I remembers so plain now. I not going to forget him again, no, the whole enduring time. I could tell him from all the others in creation."

"All right." The nurse was trying to hush her now. She brought her a bottle of medicine. "Charity," she said, making a check mark in a book.

Old Phoenix held the bottle close to her eyes, and then carefully put it into her pocket.

"I thank you," she said.

"It's Christmas time, Grandma," said the attendant. "Could I give you a few pennies out of my purse?"

"Five pennies is a nickel," said Phoenix stiffly.

"Here's a nickel," said the attendant.

Phoenix rose carefully and held out her hand. She received the nickel and then fished the other nickel out of her pocket and laid it beside the new one. She stared at her palm closely, with her head on one side.

Then she gave a tap with her cane on the floor.

"This is what come to me to do," she said. "I going to the store and buy my child a little windmill they sells, made out of paper. He going to find it hard to believe there such a thing in the world. I'll march myself back where he waiting, holding it straight up in this hand."

She lifted her free hand, gave a little nod, turned around, and walked out of the doctor's office. Then her slow step began on the stairs, going down.

Questions for Discussion

1. What impression of Phoenix Jackson's character and values is given in the first two paragraphs? Consider her clothing and type of movement and the description of her face and hair.
2. How does Phoenix relate to nature — to animals, trees, and terrain?
3. How does Welty use hallucination in the story? Consider Phoenix's vision of the boy with marble-cake and the ghost-scarecrow. Do these visions and Phoenix's admission at the end of the story imply that she is simply fatigued or that she is approaching senility?
4. Comment on the scenes in which Phoenix talks with condescending whites: the hunter, the nurse, and the attendant. How effectively does she communicate with them?
5. What does the windmill that Phoenix aims to purchase for her grandson at the end of the story symbolize?

Ideas for Writing

1. Critics have commented on the mythical parallels that Welty creates in her stories. Write an essay in which you discuss how "A Worn Path" draws upon the traditional stories and rituals of Christmas as well as on ancient myths such as the myth of the Phoenix, a bird that lives eternally, burning itself up in its nest and returning to life once every five hundred years.
2. Imitating Welty's style, write the story of Phoenix Jackson's return home. Will her grandson be there? Is he still alive?

Eudora Welty

One of America's best-loved story writers, Eudora Welty has given many interviews and written numerous critical essays, three of which we include here. Welty explains some of her thoughts about the creative process in her 1980 interview with critic Jo Brans, "Struggling against the Plaid." Here Welty explores the relationship between autobiography and writing, describes the origins of the character Phoenix Jackson in "A Worn Path," and discusses her reluctance to emphasize themes of race and white guilt in her fiction. Welty's three essays offer critical insights into the reading and composing processes and explain the author's intentions and influences in writing her most famous story, "A Worn Path." "Words into Fiction" (1965) examines the role that language and symbolism play in the writing and reading process. Welty rejects the tendency of some critics to overemphasize symbolism and meaning (the "in other words" of the interpretative gesture) at the expense of the lived experience that arises from the language and descriptive imagery of stories. She refers to the communication achieved between author and reader as the "reliability" of the story. In "Place in Fiction" (1974) Welty explores the significance of place, which she believes to be the very "life" of fiction. More limited in scope, "Is Phoenix Jackson's Grandson Really Dead?" (1974) explores the way that many readers have attempted to interpret "A Worn Path" as a portrayal of a delusional woman whose grandson is no longer alive, despite an elaborate fantasy on the part of Phoenix that she can still save him. Welty insists that the life or death of the child is not as significant to the story as the incredible journey that reveals Phoenix's tenacity; as Welty put it in this essay, "*Phoenix* is alive." Welty goes on to link Phoenix's journey to the archetypal journey of the writer in the act of creating a new work.

Ruth M. Vande Kieft's "Eudora Welty: Visited and Revisited" (1986) looks back on this critic's own early contacts with Welty's fiction and focuses on what she considers the basic appeal of the stories: their sense of mystery, of the complex contradiction and variety of human experience, and their suggestion that the author's voice is one in which readers could place their trust. The excerpt from Alfred Appel's *A Season of Dreams: The Fiction of Eudora Welty* (1965) analyzes the use of irony, myth, and religious significance in such stories as "A Visit of Charity" and "A Worn Path." The last item in the casebook is a story by student Amanda Morgan, whose alternative ending for "A Worn Path" has Phoenix return to her home with the medicine she has brought for her grandson.

JO BRANS

FROM *Struggling against the Plaid:*
An Interview with Eudora Welty (1980)

Brans: One thing that especially impressed me in the conversation yesterday was that you said you wrote because you loved language and you love using language. I know you are a photographer, and you've painted too.

Welty: Well, I was never a true or serious painter, just a childhood painter.

Brans: How does writing compare in your mind with those other art forms?

Welty: Oh, it's in the front. The others are just playthings. I didn't have any talent for photographs. I was strictly amateurish. I think the book I did [*One Time, One Place*] has a value in being a record, just because it was taken in the 1930s. And I was in the position of being perfectly accepted wherever I went, and everything was unselfconscious on the part of both the people and myself. There was no posing, and neither was there any pulling back or anything like that. Our relationship was perfectly free and open, so that I was able to get photographs of things really as they were. I think today it has a sort of historical value, which has nothing to do with any kind of professional expertise in taking pictures, which I knew I didn't have. But I am a professional writer. That is my work and my life, and I take it extremely seriously. It isn't just the love of language, or love of the written word, though that is certainly foremost, but the wish to use this language and written word in order to make something, which is what writing is. It's a tool. It's the tool, not the end result. So I guess that would be how you could describe what I'm trying to do.

Brans: To create a reality with words. Why is dialogue, spoken language, so important to you — say in *Losing Battles?*

Welty: I tried to see if I could do a whole novel completely without going inside the minds of my characters, which is the way I do in most of my writing. I didn't tell how anyone thought — I tried to show it by speech and action. I was deliberately trying to see if I could convey the same thing by speech and outward appearance, as I used to do by going inside people's minds.

Brans: It seems to me that in your writing you're hardly ever autobiographical. I've heard you say that you're working out of your feelings, but not your own experiences. Are there any stories that are autobiographical?

Welty: I don't deliberately avoid being autobiographical; it's just that when I'm writing a story I have to invent the things that best show my feelings about my own experience or about life, and I think most of us wouldn't be able to take our own experience and make a dramatic situation out of that without some aid. And I do much better with invented characters who can better carry out, act out, my feelings. I don't think you can describe emotion you have not felt. You know, you have to know what it's like — what it is to feel a certain thing — or your description or your use of these emotions will be artificial and shallow. So I certainly understand what my characters are feeling, but I try to show it in a way that is interesting dramatically.

And I don't lead a very dramatic life myself, outwardly. So it's not that I'm concealing myself, it's just that I'm using whatever — a lot of the details come out of my own life, things that I've observed. There was a scene in my novel, *The Optimist's Daughter*, about a three-year-old child in West Virginia, a whole section in there that I suppose you could call autobiographical, but actually it was my own memories of being at my grandmother's, on the farm, and all the things that the child felt — the rivers and the mountains and all those things. Nothing like that could be made up, you see. If you've never been in the mountains you wouldn't know how to say what it was like to be in the mountains. But it was not me as the character. It was my feelings, my memories, my experiences, but it was that character that was feeling them, not me. The character was not me. So, that's an example.

  Brans: You sort of projected your feelings into this creation.

  Welty: Yes, and use them to describe this character. I didn't use all that I had, I used just what would help me to explain the character.

  Brans: How do those characters come to your mind? Do they just spring full-blown into your mind? Or do you work them out . . . ?

  Welty: Well, it's just part of the whole process of making a story. I mean, they are all one with the plot and the atmosphere of the story and the weather and the location. They don't exist apart from the story — they're not even in the world outside the story. You can't take a character out of this story and put it into another.

  Brans: It doesn't work?

  Welty: Well, they wouldn't live. So the characters are all integral parts of the story in which they occur. Of course you use many sources to make a character — occupation, memory, knowledge, dreams, newspaper articles, many things. You may get little bits here and little bits there, because the character is a sort of magnet and attracts different kinds of observations. Not just any, you know; it's just what applies to the character. So how can you tell where they come from, any more than you can tell where anything comes from — where a tune comes from to a composer.

  Brans: Do you have any set pattern of working? That is, do the characters occur to you first, or a trick of plot, or some idea that you want to express? Is there any particular order that seems to be the same?

  Welty: It's different with every story. It just depends. Sometimes the story begins with the idea of a character and then you invent a plot which will bring this out. Take that one story that's used lots of times in schools called

"A Worn Path." That character called up the story. Such a person as that would take a trip like this to do something. That's a good simple case.

Brans: What I love about "A Worn Path" is not so much the endurance of the walker as the windmill or whatever you call it at the end. For me that was the beauty of the story, that all of a sudden old Phoenix does move above the . . . just the endurance . . .

Welty: I love that, too.

Brans: And walking all the way back down the path with the windmill. I have a clear picture of that. It made the trip into town worth the coming.

Welty: Absolutely.

Brans: In one of your essays you talk about Faulkner, and you say that Faulkner has this sense of blood guilt about the Indians and then about the blacks. In your own work you don't have that.

Welty: Well, it's not my theme. You know his work encompassed so much and so many books and so many generations and so much history, that that was an integral part of it. I don't write historically or anything. Most of the things that I write about can be translated into personal relationships. I've never gone into such things as guilt over the Indians or — it just hasn't been my subject. My stories, I think, reflect the racial relationships — guilt is just one aspect of that. Certainly I think any writer is aware of the complicated relationship between the races. It comes out in so many even domestic situations.

Brans: Very few of your stories deal directly with blacks, though. And those that do, I've wondered if the blackness is a necessary part of the character. For example, old Phoenix. Why is she black?

Welty: It's not a deliberate thing, like, "I am now going to write about the black race." I write about all people. I think my characters are about half and half black and white.

Brans: Really?

Welty: I would guess. Considering the novels and everything. I think it's the same challenge to a writer. It doesn't matter about color of skin or their age or anything else. Then again, I never have thought about "A Worn Path" as being anything but what it was; but one thing may be that when I wrote that story, what started me writing it was the sight of a figure like Phoenix Jackson. I never got close to her, just saw her crossing a distant field early one afternoon in the fall. Just her figure. I couldn't see her up close, but you could tell it was an old woman going somewhere, and I thought, she is bent on an errand. And I know it isn't for herself. It was just the look of her figure.

Brans: It's not true, then, what I read — that you were the lady old Phoenix asked to tie her shoe.

Welty: Oh, no. I was out with a painter who was painting his landscape and so we were sitting under a tree. I was reading, and I watched her cross the landscape in the half-distance, and when I got home I wrote that story that she had made me think of. She was a black woman. But then I suppose it would be more likely to be a black woman who would be in such desperate need and live so remotely away from help and who would have so far to go. I don't think that story would be the same story with a white person. The white person could have the same character, of course, and do the same thing, but it wouldn't have the same urgency about it.

Brans: Well, old Phoenix does fox white people. You know, she takes the nickel from the hunter, then asks the lady to tie her shoe.

Welty: It wasn't because they were white, though. Those are two different things altogether. It was the desperate need for the money and for the child that she needed that nickel — she knew it was a sin, too. But asking the lady to tie her shoe — she knew who would be nice to her. She picked a nice person, because she was a nice person, and she picked one. Those are two entirely different motives, taking the nickel from this really nasty white man and asking a favor of a nice lady. She knew in both cases.

Brans: She had a wonderful graciousness.

Welty: She knew how to treat both.

Brans: One of my students went to your reading Sunday night, and she came in with a paper on it. She had misunderstood the title of the story called "Livvie," and she referred to it as "Living," which showed she understood the story anyway.

Welty: That's very cute. I'm glad to hear that.

Brans: A misprision, I guess, but a nice one. What I'm saying is, I know sometimes I fix interpretations on the things I've read.

Welty: Well, I do too. We all do that. And I don't feel a thing bad about it, because a story writer hopes to suggest all kinds of possibilities. Even though it may not have been in the writer's mind, if something in the story suggests it, I think it's legitimate. You know, it doesn't have to be exact. The only way I think to err is to be completely out of tone or out of the scope of the story or its intention. No, it doesn't bother me one bit if someone interprets something in a different way, if I think the story can just as well suggest that as not, because you try to make it full of suggestions, not just one.

Brans: As a teacher I'm very sensitive to this whole question, because students frequently say, at the end of the discussion of the story where you really are trying to get at all the things that make the story possible, "Now do you think that Eudora Welty really intended all of that?" And of course there's no defense for a teacher, and all I can say is "How do I know?"

Welty: That's all we say when we read anybody's work.

Brans: How can I know what she intended? But if we find it here in the story, the story belongs to us when we're reading it.

Welty: Exactly. The only thing that I know bogs a lot of students down, because I get letters all the time, is in the case of that dread subject, symbols. You know, if they get to thinking, this equals this and this equals that, the whole story is destroyed. Symbols are important, I think, but only if they're organic — you know, occur in the course of the story, are not dragged in to equal something.

Brans: No, no. It takes all the life out to do that.

Welty: Of course. And symbols aren't equivalents.

Brans: — not algebraic equations!

Welty: I know it. But, you know, some students get the idea, and it's very troubling to them. And what I hate about it is it might discourage them from ever enjoying reading stories, if they think they're supposed to make an algebraic interpretation, as you said.

EUDORA WELTY

Words into Fiction   (1965)

We start from scratch, and words don't; which is the thing that matters — matters over and over again. For though we grow up in the language, when we begin using words to make a piece of fiction, that is of course as different from using even the same words to say hello on the telephone as putting paint on canvas is. This very leap in the dark is exactly what writers write fiction in order to try. And surely they discovered that daring, and developed that wish, from reading. My feeling is that it's when reading begins to impress on us what degrees and degrees and degrees of communication are possible between novelists and ourselves as readers that we surmise what it has meant, can mean, to write novels.

Indeed, learning to write may be a part of learning to read. For all I know, writing comes out of a superior devotion to reading. I feel sure that serious writing does come, must come, out of devotion to the thing itself, to fiction as an art. Both reading and writing are experiences — lifelong — in the course of which we who encounter words used in certain ways are persuaded by them to be brought mind and heart within the presence, the power, of the imagination. This we find to be above all the power to reveal, with nothing barred.

But of course writing fiction, which comes out of life and has the object of showing it, can't be learned from copying out of books. Imitation, or what is in any respect secondhand, is precisely what writing is not. How it is learned can only remain in general — like all else that is personal — an open question; and if ever it's called settled, or solved, the day of fiction is already over. The solution will be the last rites at the funeral. Only the writing of fiction keeps fiction alive. Regardless of whether or not it is reading that gives writing birth, a society that no longer writes novels is not very likely to read any novels at all.

Since we must and do write each our own way, we may during actual writing get more lasting instruction not from another's work, whatever its blessings, however better it is than ours, but from our own poor scratched-over pages. For these we can hold up to life. That is, we are born with a mind and heart to hold each page up to, and to ask: is it valid?

Reading the work of other writers and in the whole, and our long thoughts in retrospect, can tell us all we are able to know of fiction and at firsthand, but this is about *reading*.

The writer himself studies intensely how to do it while he is in the thick of doing it; then when the particular novel or story is done, he is likely to forget how; he does well to. Each work is new. Mercifully, the question of *how* abides less in the abstract, and less in the past, than in the specific, in the work at hand; I chance saying this is so with most writers. Maybe some particular problems, with their confusions and might-have-beens, could be seen into with profit just at the windup, but more likely it's already too late. Already the *working* insight, which is what counts, is gone — along with the story it made, that made it.

And rightly. Fiction finished has to bear the responsibility of its own meaning, it is its own memory. It is now a thing apart from the writer; like a letter mailed, it is nearer by now to its reader. If the writer has had luck, it has something of its own to travel on, something that can make it persist for a while, an identity, before it must fade.

How can I express outside fiction what I think this reality of fiction is?

As a child I was led, an unwilling sightseer, into Mammoth Cave in Kentucky, and after our party had been halted in the blackest hole yet and our guide had let us wait guessing in cold dark what would happen to us, suddenly a light was struck. And we stood in a prism. The chamber was bathed in color, and there was nothing else, we and our guide alike were blotted out by radiance. As I remember, nobody said boo. Gradually we could make out that there was a river in the floor, black as night, which appeared to come out of a closet in the wall; and then, on it, a common rowboat, with ordinary countrified people like ourselves sitting in it, mute, wearing hats, came floating out and on by, and exited into the closet in the opposite wall. I suppose they were simply a party taking the more expensive tour. As we tourists mutually and silently stared, our guide treated us to a recitation on bats, how they lived in uncounted numbers down here and reached light by shooting up winding mile-high chimneys through rock, never touching by so much as the crook of a wing. He had memorized the speech, and we didn't see a bat. Then the light was put out — just as it is after you've had your two cents' worth in the Baptistry of Florence, where of course more happens: the thing I'm trying here to leave out. As again we stood damp and cold and not able to see our feet, while we each now had something of our own out of it, presumably, what I for one remember is how right I had been in telling my parents it would be a bore. For I was too ignorant to know there might be more, or even less, in there than I could see unaided.

Fiction is not the cave; and human life, fiction's territory, merely contains caves. I am only trying to express what I think the so-called raw material is *without its interpretation;* without its artist. Without the act of human understanding — and it is a double act through which we make sense to each other — experience is the worst kind of emptiness; it is obliteration, black or prismatic, as meaningless as was indeed that loveless cave. Before there is meaning, there has to occur some personal act of vision. And it is this that is continuously projected as the novelist writes, and again as we, each to ourselves, read.

If this makes fiction sound full of mystery, I think it's fuller than I know how to say. Plot, characters, setting, and so forth, are not what I'm referring to now; we all deal with those as best we can. The mystery lies in the use of language to express human life.

In writing, do we try to solve this mystery? No, I think we take hold of the other end of the stick. In very practical ways, we rediscover the mystery. We even, I might say, take advantage of it.

As we know, a body of criticism stands ready to provide its solution, which is a kind of translation of fiction into another language. It offers us close analysis, like a headphone we can clamp on at the U.N. when they are speaking the Arabian tongue. I feel that we can accept this but only with distinct reservations — not about its brilliance or its worth, but about its time and place of application. While we are in the middle of reading some novel, the possibility of the critical phrase "in other words" is one to destroy, rather than make for, a real — that is, imaginative — understanding of the author. Indeed, it is one sure way to break off his carefully laid connection.

Fiction is made to show forth human life, in some chosen part and aspect. A year or so of one writer's life has gone into the writing of a novel, and then to the reader — so long at least as he is reading it — it may be something in his life. There is a remarkable chance of give-and-take. Does this not suggest that, in the novel at least, words have been found for which there may be no other words? If fiction matters — and many lives are at stake that it does — there can be, for the duration of the book, *no* other words.

The point for us if we write is that nearly everything we can learn about writing can be set down only in fiction's terms. What we know about writing the novel *is* the novel.

Try to tear it down, take it back to its beginning, and you are not so much lost as simply nowhere. Some things once done you can't undo, and I hope and believe fiction is one of them. What its own author knows about a novel is flexible till the end; it changes as it goes, and more than that, it will not be the same knowledge he has by the time the work ends as he had when it began. There is a difference not so much in measure of knowledge, which you would take for granted, as in kind of knowledge. The idea is now the object. The idea is something that you or I might just conceivably have had in common with the author, in the vague free air of the everyday. But not by the wildest chance should we be able to duplicate by one sentence what happened to the idea; neither could the author himself write the same novel again. As he works, his own revision, even though he throws away his changes, can never be wholly undone. The novel has passed through that station on its track. And as readers, we too proceed by the author's arbitrary direction to his one-time-only destination: a journey rather strange, hardly in a straight line, altogether personal.

There has occurred the experience of the writer in writing the novel, and now there occurs the experience of the reader in reading it. More than one mind and heart go into this. We may even hope to follow into a kind of future with a novel that to us seems good, drawn forward by what the long unfolding has promised and so far revealed. By yielding to what has been, by all his available means, *suggested,* we are able to see for ourselves a certain distance beyond what is possible for him simply to *say.* So that, although nobody else ought to say this, the novelist *has* said, "In other words . . ."

Thus all fiction may be seen as a symbol, if this is desired — and how often it is, so it seems. But surely the novel exists within the big symbol of fiction itself — not the other way round, as a conglomeration of little symbols. I think that fiction is the hen, not the egg, and that the good live hen came first.

Certainly symbols fill our daily lives, our busily communicative, if not always communicating, world; and any number of them come with perfect naturalness into our daily conversation and our behavior. And they are a legitimate part of fiction, as they have always been of every art — desirable as any device is, so long as it serves art. Symbols have to spring from the work direct, and stay alive. Symbols for the sake of symbols are counterfeit, and were they all stamped on the page in red they couldn't any more quickly give themselves away. So are symbols failing their purpose when they don't keep to proportion in the book. However alive they are, they should never call for an emphasis greater than the emotional reality they serve, in their moment, to illuminate. One way of looking at Moby Dick is that his task as a symbol was so big and strenuous that he *had* to be a whale.

Most symbols that a fiction writer uses, however carefully, today are apt to be as swiftly spotted by his reader as the smoke signals that once crossed our plains from Indian to Indian. Using symbols and — still worse — finding symbols is such a habit. It follows that too little comes to be suggested, and this, as can never be affirmed often enough, is the purpose of every word that goes into a piece of fiction. The imagination has to be involved, and more — ignited.

How much brighter than the symbol can be the explicit observation that springs firsthand from deep and present feeling in one breast. Indeed, it is something like this, spontaneous in effect, pure in effect, that takes on the emotional value of a symbol when it was first minted, but which as time passes shrinks to become only a counter.

When Chekhov says there were so many stars out that one could not have put a finger between them, he gives us more than night, he gives us *that* night.

For symbols can only grow to be the same when the same experiences on which fiction is based are more and more partaken of by us all. But Chekhov's stars, some as large as a goose's egg and some as small as hempseed, are still exactly where they were, in the sky of his story "Easter Eve." And from them to us that night still travels — for so much more than symbols, they are Chekhov looking at his sky.

Communication through fiction frequently happens, I believe, in ways that are small — a word is not too small; that are unannounced; that are less direct than we might first suppose on seeing how important they are. It isn't communication happening when you as the reader follow or predict the novel's plot or agree with, or anticipate, or could even quote the characters; when you hail the symbols; even when its whole landscape and climate have picked you up and transported you where it happens. But communication is going on, and regardless of all the rest, when you believe the writer.

Then is plausibility at the bottom of it? When we can read and say, "Oh, how right, I think so too," has the writer come through? Only stop to think how often simple plausibility, if put to measure a good story, falls down, while the story stands up, never wavers. And agreement isn't always, by any means, a mark of having been reached.

As a reader who never held a gun, I risk saying that it isn't exactly plausible that Old Ben, the bear in Faulkner's story, when he was finally brought down by a knife-thrust, had already in him fifty-two little hard lumps which were old bullets that had had no effect on him. Yet as a reader caught in the story, I think I qualify to bear witness that nothing less than fifty-two bullets could have been embedded in Old Ben or Old Ben he would not be. Old Ben and every one of his bullets along with him are parts of the truth in this story, William Faulkner's particular truth.

Belief doesn't depend on plausibility, but it seems to be a fact that validity of a kind, and this is of course a subjective kind, gained in whatever way that had to be, is the quality that makes a work reliable as art. This reliability comes straight out of the writer himself. In the end, it is another personal quotient in writing fiction; it is something inimitable. It is that by which each writer *lets us believe* — doesn't ask us to, can't make us, simply lets us.

EUDORA WELTY

Place in Fiction   (1974)

Place is one of the lesser angels that watch over the racing hand of fiction, perhaps the one that gazes benignly enough from off to one side, while others, like character, plot, symbolic meaning, and so on, are doing a good deal of wing-beating about her chair, and feeling, who in my eyes carries the crown, soars highest of them all and rightly relegates place into the shade. Nevertheless, it is this lowlier angel that concerns us here. There have been signs that she has been rather neglected of late; maybe she could do with a little petitioning.

What place has place in fiction? It might be thought so modest a one that it can be taken for granted: the location of a novel; to use a term of the day, it may make the novel "regional." The term, like most terms used to pin down a novel, means little; and Henry James said there isn't any difference between "the English novel" and "the American novel," since there are only two kinds of novels at all, the good and the bad. Of course Henry James didn't stop there, and we all hate generalities, and so does place. Yet as soon as we step down from the general view to the close and particular, as writers must and readers may and teachers well know how to, and consider what good writing may be, place can be seen, in her own way, to have a great deal to do with that goodness, if not to be responsible for it. How so?

First, with the goodness — validity — in the raw material of writing. Second, with the goodness in the writing itself — the achieved world of appearance, through which the novelist has his whole say and puts his whole case. There will still be the lady, always, who dismissed *The Ancient Mariner* on grounds of implausibility. Third, with the goodness — the worth — in the writer himself: place is where he has his roots, place is where he stands; in his experience out of which he writes, it provides the base of reference; in his work, the point of view. Let us consider place in fiction in these three wide aspects.

Wide, but of course connected — vitally so. And if in some present-day novels the connection has apparently slipped, that makes a fresh reason for us to ponder the subject of place. For novels, besides being the pleasantest things imaginable, are powerful forces on the side. Mutual understanding in the world being nearly always, as now, at low ebb, it is comforting to remember that it is through art that one country can nearly always speak reliably to another, if the other can hear at all. Art, though, is never the voice of a country; it is an even more precious thing, the voice of the individual, doing its best to speak, not comfort of any sort, indeed, but truth. And the art that speaks it most unmistakably, most directly, most variously, most fully, is fiction; in particular, the novel.

Why? Because the novel from the start has been bound up in the local, the "real," the present, the ordinary day-to-day of human experience. Where the imagination comes in is in directing the use of all this. That use is endless, and there are only four words, of all the millions we've hatched, that a novel rules out: "Once upon a time." They make a story a fairy tale by the simple sweep of the remove — by abolishing the present and the place where we are instead of conveying them to us. Of course we shall have some sort of fairy tale with us always — just now it is the historical novel. Fiction is properly at work on the here and now, or the past made here and now; for in novels *we* have to be there. Fiction provides the ideal texture through which the feeling and meaning that permeate our own personal, present lives will best show through. For in his theme — the most vital and important part of the work at hand — the novelist has the blessing of the inexhaustible subject: you and me. You and me, here. Inside that generous scope and circumference — who could ask for anything more? — the novel can accommodate practically anything on earth; and has abundantly done so. The novel so long as it be *alive* gives pleasure, and must always give pleasure, enough to stave off the departure of the Wedding Guest forever, except for that one lady.

It is by the nature of itself that fiction is all bound up in the local. The internal reason for that is surely that *feelings* are bound up in place. The human mind is a mass of associations — associations more poetic even than actual. I say, "The Yorkshire Moors," and you will say, "*Wuthering Heights*," and I have only to murmur, "If Father were only alive — " for you to come back with "We could go to Moscow," which certainly is not even so. The truth is, fiction depends for its life on place. Location is the crossroads of circumstance, the proving ground of "What happened? Who's here? Who's coming?" — and that is the heart's field.

Unpredictable as the future of any art must be, one condition we may hazard about writing: of all the arts, it is the one least likely to cut the cord that binds it to its source. Music and dancing, while originating out of place — groves! — and perhaps invoking it still to minds pure or childlike, are no longer bound to dwell there. Sculpture exists out in empty space: that is what it commands and replies to. Toward painting, place, to be so highly visible, has had a curious and changing relationship. Indeed, wasn't it when landscape invaded painting, and painting was given, with the profane content, a narrative content, that this worked to bring on a revolution to the art? Impressionism brought not the likeness-to-life but the mystery of place onto canvas; it was the method, not the subject, that told this. Painting and writing, always the closest two of the sister arts (and in ancient Chinese days only the blink of an eye seems to have separated them), have each a still closer connection with place than they have with each other; but a difference lies in their respective requirements of it, and even further in the way they use it — the written word being ultimately as different from the pigment as the note of the scale is from the chisel.

One element, which has just been mentioned, is surely the underlying bond that connects all the arts with place. All of them celebrate its mystery. Where does this mystery lie? Is it in the fact that place has a more lasting identity than we have, and we unswervingly tend to attach ourselves to identity? Might the magic lie partly, too, in the *name* of the place — since that is what *we* gave it? Surely, once we have it named, we have put a kind of poetic claim on its existence; the claim works even out of sight — may work forever sight unseen. The Seven Wonders of the World still give us this poetic kind of gratification. And notice we do not say simply "The Hanging Gardens" — that would leave them dangling out of reach and dubious in nature; we say "The Hanging Gardens of Babylon," and there they are, before our eyes, shimmering and garlanded and exactly elevated to the Babylonian measurement.

EUDORA WELTY
"Is Phoenix Jackson's Grandson Really Dead?" (1974)

A story writer is more than happy to be read by students; the fact that these serious readers think and feel something in response to his work he finds life-giving. At the same time he may not always be able to reply to their specific questions in kind. I wondered if it might clarify something, for both the questioners and myself, if I set down a general reply to the question that comes to me most often in the mail, from both students and their teachers, after some classroom discussion. The unrivaled favorite is this: "Is Phoenix Jackson's grandson really *dead?*"

It refers to a short story I wrote years ago called "A Worn Path," which tells of a day's journey an old woman makes on foot from deep in the country into town and into a doctor's office on behalf of her little grandson; he is at home, periodically ill, and periodically she comes for his medicine; they give it to her as usual, she receives it and starts the journey back.

I had not meant to mystify readers by withholding any fact; it is not a writer's business to tease. The story is told through Phoenix's mind as she undertakes her errand. As the author at one with the character as I tell it, I must assume that the boy is alive. As the reader, you are free to think as you like, of course: the story invites you to believe that no matter what happens, Phoenix for as long as she is able to walk and can hold to her purpose will make her journey. The *possibility* that she would keep on even if he were dead is there in her devotion and its single-minded, single-track errand. Certainly the *artistic* truth, which should be good enough for the fact, lies in Phoenix's own answer to that question. When the nurse asks, "He isn't dead, is he?" she speaks for herself: "He still the same. He going to last."

The grandchild is the incentive. But it is the journey, the going of the errand, that is the story, and the question is not whether the grandchild is in reality alive or dead. It doesn't affect the outcome of the story or its meaning from start to finish. But it is not the question itself that has struck me as much as the idea, almost without exception implied in the asking, that for Phoenix's grandson to be dead would somehow make the story "better."

It's *all right,* I want to say to the students who write to me, for things to be what they appear to be, and for words to mean what they say. It's all right, too, for words and appearances to mean more than one thing—ambiguity is a fact of life. A fiction writer's responsibility covers not only what he presents as the facts of a given story but what he chooses to stir up as their implications; in the end, these implications, too, become facts, in the larger, fictional sense. But it is not all right, not in good faith, for things *not* to mean what they say.

The grandson's plight was real and it made the truth of the story, which is the story of an errand of love carried out. If the child no longer lived, the truth would persist in the "wornness" of the path. But his being dead can't increase the truth of the story, can't affect it one way or the other. I think I signal this, because the end of the story has been reached before old Phoenix gets home again: she simply starts back. To the question "Is the grandson really dead?" I could reply that it doesn't make any difference. I could also say that I did not make him up in order to let him play a trick on Phoenix. But my best answer would be: "*Phoenix* is alive."

The origin of a story is sometimes a trustworthy clue to the author — or can provide him with the clue — to its key image; maybe in this case it will do the same for the reader. One day I saw a solitary old woman like Phoenix. She was walking; I saw her, at middle distance, in a winter country landscape, and watched her slowly make her way across my line of vision. That sight of her made me write the story. I invented an errand for her, but that only seemed a living part of the figure she was herself: what errand other than for someone else could be making her go? And her going was the first thing, her persisting in her landscape was the real thing, and the first and the real were what I wanted and worked to keep. I brought her up close enough, by imagination, to describe her face, make her present to the eyes, but the full-length figure moving across the winter fields was the indelible one and the image to keep, and the perspective extending into the vanishing distance the true one to hold in mind.

I invented for my character, as I wrote, some passing adventures — some dreams and harassments and a small triumph or two, some jolts to her pride, some flights of fancy to console her, one or two encounters to scare her, a moment that gave her cause to feel ashamed, a moment to dance and preen — for it had to be a *journey*, and all these things belonged to that, parts of life's uncertainty.

A narrative line is in its deeper sense, of course, the tracing out of a meaning, and the real continuity of a story lies in this probing forward. The real dramatic force of a story depends on the strength of the emotion that has set it going. The emotional value is the measure of the reach of the story. What gives any such content to "A Worn Path" is not its circumstances but its *subject*: the deep-grained habit of love.

What I hoped would come clear was that in the whole surround of this story, the world it threads through, the only certain thing at all is the worn path. The habit of love cuts through confusion and stumbles or contrives its way out of difficulty, it remembers the way even when it forgets, for a dumbfounded moment, its reason for being. The path is the thing that matters.

Her victory — old Phoenix's — is when she sees the diploma in the doctor's office, when she finds "nailed up on the wall the document that had been stamped with the gold seal and framed in the gold frame, which matched the dream that was hung up in her head." The return with the medicine is just a matter of retracing her own footsteps. It is the part of the journey, and of the story, that can now go without saying.

In the matter of function, old Phoenix's way might even do as a sort of parallel to your way of work if you are a writer of stories. The way to get there is the all-important, all-absorbing problem, and this problem is your reason for undertaking the story. Your only guide, too, is your sureness about your subject, about what this subject is. Like Phoenix, you work all your life to find your way, through all the obstructions and the false appearances and the upsets you may have brought on yourself, to reach a meaning — using inventions of your imagination, perhaps helped out by your dreams and bits of good luck. And finally too, like Phoenix, you have to assume that what you are working in aid of is life, not death.

But you would make the trip anyway — wouldn't you? — just on hope.

RUTH M. VANDE KIEFT

FROM *Eudora Welty: Visited and Revisited*   (1986)

It was strange, and prophetic, that although I lived in the South for three and a half years and graduated from a Southern woman's college, my first introduction to Eudora Welty's fiction was not as a reader, but as an instructor of English at a Northern woman's college. A few farsighted, discriminating colleagues at Wellesley had selected the Modern Library edition of Eudora Welty's *Collected Stories* (then the first two volumes only) to teach in an introductory literature course, along with Shakespeare's sonnets, Donne, James (*Portrait of a Lady*), Ibsen, and Yeats. The stature of the authors, the dedication of the students ("good," bright young women though rather anxious readers), the critical brilliance and commitment to teaching of my colleagues — "close readers" who loved literature and believed it meant something complex, subtle, and beautiful that could be put into words appropriately complex, vigorous, and clear — lent a certain strenuousness to our class discussions and informal literary talk; but it was a serious and fruitful activity in which this relatively unknown contemporary writer seemed in no way diminished by tests of comparison, while her stories challenged our combined talent, moved and delighted us as readers.

I think I must always have had the "right eyes" for looking at Eudora Welty's work (to borrow Rilke's phrase for his viewing of Cézanne's paintings), though at first I did not know why; and I had some difficulty articulating even *what* I saw there, still less why the stories so intrigued and pleased me. This has been a slow process of discovery, still continuing in my present writing, though I can now trace the disclosures in terms of affinities of temperament and experience, a "confluence" of spirit and process of life development as her reader, critic, and friend, much as in *One Writer's Beginnings* she traces the significance of events in her early life to her development as a fiction writer. In my earliest impressions of her stories, four things were central. Primary was the *mystery* I found there, and with it, the awareness that the revelation in them was paradoxical — part disclosure, part concealment. The stories were charged with the burden, or joy, of something hidden that cried out to be expressed, as impossible to be repressed. In every stage of its "growing up" — from the child's delight in its cherished secrets, its devouring curiosity and thirst for "grown-up" knowledge and experience; to the adolescent's romantic hope and dream of finding in love the answer (ah!) to life's "sweet mystery"; to the mature adult's awareness of the enigma that confronts him as loved ones misunderstand and often unintentionally hurt each other, as nature keeps her green curtains closed and fate pours blow after blow upon our naked heads — it was mystery that blessed and cursed human existence, in her stories as in life. The stories were bright but elusive, baffling and sometimes terrifying, leading to disclosures as often joyful as sorrowful, but still inscrutable. Robert Heilman spoke of "the penumbra of mystery — a mystery to be accepted, not solved — always bordering the clean light of Welty's characters and scenes": that seemed a fine summation of what I saw there.

Closely related to this quality of mystery was the "doubleness" of Eudora Welty's vision. Love and separateness (a pervasive theme discovered by Robert Penn Warren) were two sides of the same coin. Victim and conquerer were one, for "did it matter which poor, avid life took the gaze and which gave it?" (this is a cat's stalking vision in "Music from Spain"). "The excursion is the same when you go looking for your sorrow as when you go looking for your joy" (this is Doc in "The Wide Net"). "Virgie never saw it differently, never doubted that all the opposites on earth were close together, love close to hate, living to dying; but of them all, hope and despair were the closest blood — unrecognizable one from the other sometimes, making moments double upon themselves, and in the doubling double again, amending but never taking back" ("The Wanderers"). Every impulse of the heart proclaimed that also to be true. And in Eudora Welty's fiction it was a vision everywhere fleshed out in the persons, events, places necessary to give it solidity.

Then there was the variety — God's plenty, at least one story for every reader, every mood; experimentation in point of view, freshness, spontaneity. This variety eminently suited her stories to the classroom, where consideration of her use of the genre, her fictional technique, her subtle control and flexibility of tone, clarity of language, lovely surfaces and textures, fidelity to speech idiom, provided a wealth of possibilities for introducing students to the art of fiction. As part of this variety I count Eudora Welty's effectiveness in tragedy and comedy, satire, fantasy, sometimes "pure," sometimes "mixed" (or "streaked," as I like to think of it). In this respect she is like the greatest modern writers, such as Chekhov or Beckett, masters of "mixed" forms.

Finally I cherished the stories because behind them I intuited a writer whom I could *trust*. "Never trust the artist. Trust the tale," Lawrence famously advised in his *Studies in Classic American Literature*. "The proper function of a critic is to save the tale from the artist who created it." He was like a superior hound sniffing through the forest of our national literature for the freedom he thought our writers were denying by acts of subterfuge. *Blood-consciousness* he craved, and we have had to heed his advice in reading his own fiction. But that advice must fall on deaf ears, I think, to a reader of Eudora Welty's fiction. For teller and tale are here so seamless in their integrity that a critic's best office to her fiction can only be that of keeping the analysis as close to her as possible in artistic spirit and intention, true to each story's perceived fidelity to human experience, and thus returning it to her, giving beauty back to beauty's giver, with the self as an assimilated part of the gift.

Communication has been her goal from the first, even though her methods of achieving it have not been the easy or obvious ones. It is still her purpose, constantly stressed throughout the years and recently repeated to a wide television audience on NBC's *1986* in an interview with Roger Mudd: "I hope the characters will reveal themselves so that the reader will think what I think." To which Roger Mudd added a further truth of her intention, "You hope you're speaking for all human beings."

We have come a long way since Lawrence gave his advice and now many critics trust the tale no more than the teller — its very language, the kind of wholeness the teller tried to give it from truth wooed, won, pressed into words. The divorce is more thoroughgoing than that between and among tellers, tales, and reader-critics. But I was fortunate to come upon Eudora Welty's stories at a time when "the text" was trusted and the writer trusted language, when signifier and signified were not divided, and the complexity of language was part of its interest and beauty, giving pleasure to interpretation. The words were not trapped in their several closed systems or contexts, so many pigment oils locked in their cool little tubes. Seized from a rich variety of vernacular and literary sources, the words, the colors, had already been squeezed out onto her artist's palette and put up there on her canvas, *in the world*, the transformations wrought by her imagination for all to see. The light broke through, on them, from them.

ALFRED APPEL, JR.

FROM *A Season of Dreams: The Fiction of Eudora Welty*   (1965)

Irony is one of Miss Welty's most persistent moods in *A Curtain of Green*. In stories such as "Keela, the Outcast Indian Maiden," "A Worn Path," "Lily Daw and the Three Ladies," and "A Visit of Charity," the unfortunate and isolated characters not only withstand but even become ironically superior to their situations and tormentors. In "A Visit of Charity," Marian, a fourteen-year-old Campfire Girl, visits an Old Ladies' Home. The tone is satiric and ironic. "I have to pay a visit to some old lady," she tells the nurse at the desk. "'Any of them will do,' Marian stammered. With her free hand she pushed her hair behind her ears, as she did when it was time to study science." She "did not tell [the nurse] that this visit would give her a minimum of only three points in her score," although she has brought a potted plant as a gift; her points would have been doubled if she had brought a Bible to read to the "residents." The nurse "walked ahead down the hall of closed doors to pick out an old lady." However satiric the tone, there are also several forebodings of terror. The Old Ladies' Home is isolated—it is "on the outskirts of town"—and Marian had to "remove her mittens before she could open the heavy door" of the building, "which was of whitewashed brick and reflected the winter sunlight like a block of ice." The nurse "was a woman in a white uniform who looked as if she were cold; she had close-cut hair"; "she spoke like a man," and later is seen reading a copy of *Field and Stream.* "There was a smell in the hall like the interior of a clock." The girl hears a "sound like a sheep bleating," which "decides the nurse. Stopping in her tracks, she first extended her arm, bent her elbow, and leaned forward from the hips—all to examine the watch strapped to her wrist. . . ." At the end of the story she makes "another triple motion to consult her wrist watch." The portentousness of her gestures suggest, ominously enough, that she is the guardian of "time" in a place where all conceptions of time have become meaningless.

The nurse shoves Marian into a tiny, cluttered room. Hardly realizing what has happened, Marian finds herself closeted with two old women. There is an imperceptible shift in tone as the satiric sense gives way to a realization of the earlier forebodings; nightmare images are now predominant. One old woman has a "terrible, square smile (which was a smile of welcome) stamped on her bony face . . . a strange smile [that] forced her old face dangerously awry." The other old woman, even older, is "lying flat in bed with a cap on and a counterpane drawn up to her chin"; she has "a bunchy white forehead and red eyes like a sheep."

> Suddenly Marian saw a hand, quick as a bird claw, reach up in the air and pluck the white cap off her head. At the same time, another claw to match drew her all the way into the room, and the next moment the door closed behind her. . . . Everything smelled wet—even the bare floor. She held onto the back of the chair, which was wicker and felt soft and damp. Her heart beat more and more slowly, her hands got colder and colder, and she could not hear whether the old women were saying anything or not. She could not see them very clearly. How dark it was! The window shade was down, and the only door was shut. Marian looked at the ceiling. . . . It was like . . . a . . . cave.

Marian seems to have entered another world—or, more specifically, an underworld.

Although the story's beautifully controlled irony is its most evident source of appeal, its richest overtones may derive from the myth of the descent to the Underworld and the confrontation of the living with the living dead. Miss Welty seems to have made instinctive, perhaps unconscious, use of this widespread myth; the accounts of Virgil and Dante and the Proserpina story come to mind. Yet the reader can still sense the horror of the Old Ladies' Home and its removal from everyday reality without any knowledge of its possible antecedents in legend and literature. Miss Welty accomplishes this through the story's dream perspective, for Marian loses her sense of reality in the room. Marian's shock is expressed by her sudden inability to perceive what is happening around her. After giving up the potted plant, she wonders, "What did it look like?" The old woman bleats, "Who — are — you?" and, "to her surprise, Marian could not remember her name." When the old women argue over whether or not they had enjoyed the previous visit of another Campfire Girl, Marian — "without realizing that she had said a word" — blurts out, "We all enjoyed it." Marian's dissociated reactions underline the story's otherworldly atmosphere.

The two old women at first present comic contrasts. One is consistently ingratiating to Marian, while every reaction of the other is hostile. "'Pretty flowers,' the first old woman insisted" when she saw the potted plant, "'pretty — pretty. . . .'" But the other "old woman in bed cleared her throat and spoke. 'They are not pretty . . . ,'" adding, a moment later, "'Stinkweeds.'" But the comic perspective shifts quickly as the second old woman gives vent to her despair, protesting against her lack of privacy, her roommate's intolerable presence, and the indignities and terrifying loneliness of their lives in the dark confines of the home:

> "Hush!" said the sick woman [to the first old woman]. "You never went to school. You never came and you never went. You never were anything — only here. You never were born! You don't know anything. Your head is empty, your heart and hands and your old black purse are all empty, even that little old box that you brought with you you brought empty — you showed it to me. And yet you talk, talk, talk, talk, talk all the time until I think I'm losing my mind! Who are you? You're a stranger — a perfect stranger! Don't you know you're a stranger? Is it possible that they have actually done a thing like this to anyone — sent them in a stranger to talk, and rock, and tell away her whole long rigamarole? Do they seriously suppose that I'll be able to keep it up day in, day out, night in, night out, living in the same room with a terrible old woman — forever?"

This passage justifies the allusion to Dante; like the sinners in the Inferno, the two women seem ready to endure this horror forever; to use Sartre's title, there is "No Exit" from the hell they inflict upon each other. When Marian entered the home, the nurse looked at the plant, "'You have a nice *multiflora cineraria* there,' she remarked"; similarly, the old women have been coldly "classified" and filed away, seemingly for all time.

Rather than an understanding of the reality of the shut-in's world, the insensitive and point-seeking Campfire Girl has brought with her a sense of the callous indifference and unconscious cruelty with which the young too often treat the aged. But when the first old woman tells Marian "what's the matter with" the second—"Why, she's mad because it's her birthday!"—Marian trembles, and perhaps for the first time in her life shows a genuine interest in another human being:

> "How old are you?" Marian breathed. Now she could see the old woman in bed very closely and plainly, and very abruptly, from all sides, as in dreams. She wondered about her—she wondered for a moment as though there was nothing else in the world to wonder about. It was the first time such a thing had happened to Marian.
>
> "I won't tell!"

The old woman begins to cry softly and Marian, her face burning, flees from her confrontation of human misery. Struggling out of the clutching "claws" of the first old woman, who begs for a penny, Marian runs out of the room, down the hall and past the nurse, and pushing the heavy door open, she runs out of the "underworld" and into the cold air and bright sunlight of the "real" world. She retrieves a red apple she had hidden by the prickly shrub, and the story ends as she hails a bus.

> "Wait for me!" she shouted. As though at an imperial command, the bus ground to a stop.
>
> She jumped on and took a big bite out of the apple.

Her composure has returned; the egoism of the child reasserts itself. She is once again "protected" against human involvement. The isolated old women are ironically superior to the girl because of her total inability to cope with the situation. The story's controlling irony is implicit in its title; Marian's visit is not in the least "charitable," and the home—supposedly a haven—is rather a hell. "A Visit of Charity" is remarkable for the way in which its comic, satiric, and grotesque effects all contribute to a deeply felt sense of pathos. . . .

"Pageant of Birds," "Ida M'Toy," and the stories, "The Burning," "Livvie," and "A Worn Path," suggest that Miss Welty has a special sympathy and respect for the Southern Negro woman and that, like writers as various as Faulkner and James Baldwin, she seems to feel that the Negro's endurance in the South has had much to do with the strength of the Negro woman. "A Worn Path" is an effort at telescoping the history of the Negro woman. The setting is the "worn path" of the ancient Natchez Trace, and the story presents the greatest myths in the context of a folk tradition.

Its action concerns an old Negro woman, Phoenix Jackson, who, on a cold December day, makes an arduous trip from deep within the backcountry to the town of Natchez to get medicine for her sick grandson. She has been making the trip regularly since he swallowed lye two or three years before. Phoenix is not merely any old woman, as the story proves. It is no accident that she is named "Phoenix," for Miss Welty presents her as a symbol of the immortality of the Negro's spirit of endurance. Her cane, tapping the frozen earth, "made a grave and persistent noise . . . that seemed meditative like the chirping of a *solitary little bird*" [italics mine]. At the end of the story she refers to her grandson as "a little bird." Her endurance is etched in her wrinkled face, which seems to glow with an inner splendor: the "golden coloring" of her skin and the "yellow burning" which illuminates the two knobs of her cheeks remind us that her namesake was the legendary, self-perpetuating embodiment of the Egyptian sun god. When her weak eyes mistake a scarecrow for a ghost, she asks, "Who be you the ghost of? For I have heard of nary death close by." "I the oldest people I ever know," she tells the scarecrow. She never went to school because "I was too old at the Surrender." When she drinks from a spring flowing through a hollow log, she says, "Nobody know who made this well, for it was here when I was born." She is ageless. In fact, she *defies* death. When she sees a buzzard, she asks him, "Who you watching?" Like the clay bed of the Natchez Trace, Phoenix seems to disappear back into time. One might almost imagine her as an aged Florabel, the Negro slave who rose out of the ashes in "The Burning," a Phoenix emerging from the Civil War cinders.

Like "Keela" and "Powerhorse," "A Worn Path" provides an excellent example of how an eminently "modern" story teller makes use of folk materials. Miss Welty avoids confusing the folk with the *folksy* — of parodying her material. She seems to have discovered that the important relationship of formal art to folk art rests in the archetypes of primitive ritual, in the great world myths, rather than in reproductions of the "picturesque" surface texture of folk life. In "A Worn Path," these great myths are embedded within the folk context. Phoenix's journey is thus rendered as a minor-scale *Odyssey*. In the frozen, forbidding backcountry of the Natchez Trace, Phoenix is faced with at least twelve obstacles which require a heroic exertion on her part to surmount. Phoenix knows no fear: "Out of my way," she cautions all the animals that lurk in the thickets, "keep the wild hogs out of my path. Don't let none of those come running my direction. I got a long way." The rhythm of her speech communicates her determination; the tone of "I got a long way" is biblical. She struggles up a steep hill ("seem like there is chains about my feet.") In the valley she gets caught up in a "thorny bush." With eyes closed ("now comes the trial"), she bravely mounts a log that crosses a creek. The strain of this effort causes an hallucination. Then she encounters and survives a barbed-wire fence. Phoenix sees a buzzard and recalls the obstacles she had to bypass on previous journeys: "Glad this ain't the season for bulls . . . and the good Lord made his snakes to curl up and sleep, in the winter." She makes her way through the pathless maze of a dead cornfield, the stalks rising "taller than her head." She follows the track across a dark swamp ("sleep on Alligators, and blow your bubbles"). A stray dog knocks her over and into a ditch, "like a little puff of milkweed." She is dazed and helpless; a white hunter finds her. He helps Phoenix up and urges her to "go on home, Granny!" She explains, portentously, "'I bound to go to town . . . the time come around.' He gave another laugh, filling [and, in Miss Welty's view, desecrating] the whole landscape. 'I know you old colored people! Wouldn't miss going to town to see Santa Claus!'" But Phoenix ignores this patronization and asserts her dignity. When a nickel falls out of the man's pocket onto the ground, she shrewdly tricks him into turning his attention to the dogs and then, with painstaking effort, manages to get the nickel into her apron pocket. Unaware of his "loss" the man returns from chasing the dogs. He teases Phoenix by pointing his rifle at her, giving her another opportunity to show her courage. "I'd give you a dime if I had any money on me," he says. The irony complete, they go their separate ways. Phoenix arrives in Natchez — it is Christmas time — and asks a passerby to lace up her shoe: "Do all right for the country," she says, "but wouldn't look right to go in a big building." When she finally arrives at the hospital, she encounters her final obstacles: a temporary loss of memory and the hospital nurses. Miss Welty has not wasted a detail; theme and action are woven together intricately.

Phoenix's safe arrival expresses one level of her triumph: her courage. Her encounters with the hunter and the hospital nurses present another kind of triumph, for they establish Phoenix's moral superiority, ironically so, since the whites treat her as an inferior: when she presents herself at the hospital desk — "Here I be!" — the nurse answers, "A charity case, I suppose." Phoenix then loses her memory. The first nurse is impatient, and, although the second nurse is initially polite, she is cruelly blunt when Phoenix fails to regain her memory immediately: "You mustn't take up our time this way. . . . Tell us quickly about your grandson and get it over with. He isn't dead is he?" When Phoenix speaks, the nurse interrupts her:

> "All right. The doctor said as long as you came to get it, you could have it," said the nurse. "But it's an obstinate case."
>
> "My little grandson, he sit up there in the house *all wrapped up, waiting by himself*," Phoenix went on. "*We is the only two left in the world. He suffer and it don't seem to put him back at all. He got a sweet look. He going to last.* He wear a little patch quilt and peep out holding his mouth open like a little bird. I remembers so plain now. I not going to forget him again, no, *the whole enduring time, I could tell him from all the others in creation*" [italics mine].
>
> "All right." The nurse was trying to hush her now. She brought her a bottle of medicine. "Charity," she said, making a check mark in the book.

The hospital staff's lack of compassion highlights Phoenix's moral superiority. She is also "an obstinate case"; the nurses become aware of a mysterious barrier when they are unable to patronize Phoenix. The nurse gives Phoenix a nickel for Christmas but, like the hunter, is unsuccessful in patronizing Phoenix because, simply enough, she has a good use for the money: "I going to the store and buy my child a little windmill they sells, made out of paper. He going to find it hard to believe there such a thing in the world." Phoenix retains great dignity before the nurses because of her simplicity and devotion and, though illiterate, by her imagination and shrewdness. The joy that the little windmill will bring her grandson is the antithesis of the false Christmas spirit found in the town — from its electric light decor to the "charity" of its nurses. Phoenix is superior to the hunter and the nurses because of their complete inability to comprehend the profound source of her dignity and courage. That source is Phoenix's faith.

There is a deeply religious feeling manifest in "A Worn Path." Several times we are reminded that the story occurs at Christmas. Phoenix says, "God watching me the whole time." She marches across the treacherous log "like a festival figure in some parade"; when she presents herself at the hospital, "there was a fixed and ceremonial stiffness over her body"; and near the end of the story, she says, "I'll march myself straight back where he waiting, holding [the windmill] straight up in this hand" — the little toy assuming the attitude and importance of some religious banner, effigy, or offering. Her act of love is virtually ceremonial: the story opens with Phoenix coming along a path, walking "slowly in the dark pine shadows," and ends as "her slow step began on the stairs, going down." The landscape is strangely muted. Phoenix's cane makes a grave noise in the still air; "the sun made the pine needles almost too bright to look at"; "the cones dropped as light as feathers." Phoenix goes through silver grass, and through "the little strings of trees silver in their dead leaves, past cabins silver from weather, with the doors and windows boarded shut, *all like old women under a spell* sitting there. *'I walking in their sleep,'* she said, nodding her head vigorously" [italics mine]. Like a figure in a religious pageant, she sees herself as representative, as a personification: "I walking in their sleep." Phoenix's journey is presented as a kind of Christmas pageant or pilgrimage. When she sits down to rest, she sees up above her "a tree in a pearly cloud of mistletoe." But the setting and atmosphere of the backcountry are more than just seasonal; with their suspended, otherworldly quality they perhaps suggest the first Christmas season. When Phoenix begins her return journey, carrying the medicine and windmill, she is a kind of Magi, bringing gifts to a little grandson who, waiting alone, all wrapped up in a quilt, recalls the Christ child in the manger: "He got a sweet look . . . I could tell him from all the others in creation." Although the Christmas imagery need not be insisted upon, it is compatible with the story's extra Christian mythic elements and reinforces our sense of "A Worn Path" as a celebration of life out of death. "I bound to go. . . . The time come around," Phoenix tells the hunter, referring not only to her trip for the medicine, but to her own mortality; "My senses is gone. I too old"; "Sun so high. . . . The time getting all gone here." With her death approaching, all of Phoenix's remaining energies go toward perpetuating the life of her grandson: "He going to last."

There is a sudden shift in tone from the poetic to the prosaic when Phoenix moves from the legendary, dreamlike backcountry world into the world of the town. As she enters the town, the rich nature imagery gives way to a blunt, drab, journalistic style. The shift in tone complements the setting and Phoenix's reaction to it: she "would have been lost if she had not distrusted her eyesight and depended on her feet to know where to take her." The red and green electric lights are strung and crisscrossed everywhere. The garish is revealed with quick, deft strokes: all the lights are turned on in the daytime, and the lady passerby who ties Phoenix's laces gives off perfume "like the red roses in hot summer." The town and its inhabitants are presented in contrast to Phoenix and the Natchez Trace. The Christmas color scheme on the lady's "armful of red-, green- and silver-wrapped presents" and in the tangles of electric lights is only a corruption of the red-green-and-silver tones that "decorate" the backcountry — just as the insensitive hunter and nurses are only shadows next to Phoenix and her deep, instinctual humanity, her serene acceptance of the death on which all future life is based.

"A Worn Path" passes far beyond its regionalism because of its remarkable fusion of various elements of myth and legend, which invest the story with a religious meaning that can be universally felt. The "worn path" Phoenix travels is the same one that man has always had to contend with — the well-traveled road of human suffering and isolation. But Phoenix, like the Hebrews and the early Christians, meets and endures her many tribulations, and through her courage and single-minded devotion, her buoyancy, serenity, and strength, she experiences something akin to God: "We is the only two left in the world," she says of her grandson; "he suffers and it don't seem to put him back at all. He got a sweet look. He going to last." Phoenix is as indomitable as the Natchez Trace, one of the last regions to preserve its identity. The Negroes are part of their tragic history and living folk tradition just as the Trace stretches into the past. They *both* represent values that have been obscured in the confusion of modern life. In "Some Notes on River Country," Miss Welty writes: "Whatever is significant and whatever is tragic in a place live as long as the place does. . . . Though they are unseen . . . the new life will be built upon those things, regardless of commerce and the way of rivers and roads and other vagrancies."

Created in the spirit of the "place," ageless Phoenix seems to span the years that extend from the death of the white heron ("A Still Moment") to the emergence of the modern town ("Petrified Man"). She transcends her region's geographical boundaries, for her celebration of life and her endurance — and that of the Negroes in the other stories and sketches — are presented by Eudora Welty as human qualities that man, whether Southerner or Northerner, Negro or white, must possess if, as Phoenix says of her grandson, "He going to last."

STUDENT ESSAY

The Shadow Child: A Sequel to "A Worn Path"
by Amanda Morgan

Now with two unexpected nickels in her apron, old Phoenix walked haltingly across the avenue.

"I'm hurrin'. I'm hurrin'," she muttered beneath her breath as a shiny new motor car slowed to a stop, anticipating her progress.

"Just one last errand I got to do 'fore I follow my ol' footsteps home." She remembered exactly where to find him, that nice-looking young man.

"He had himself a beard, latest style, as I recalls it, a fine, fine beard."

She had passed his street corner one previous odyssey, where she had admired the colorful little windmills and paper kites. "Didn't have so much as a nickel. No, sir, not even a nickel," she thought to herself, and a little girl, her blond curls bobbing, couldn't keep from staring at the sight of such an old woman, shuffling up the shallow sidewalk incline as if it were a stairway to heaven, all the while muttering to herself.

"Just one more block I got to go, to find a little plaything for my sweet boy. I can already see the surprise in his eye." She completed her ascent, smiling to see the quaint little toy store, brightly lit with seasonal lights.

"My baby ain't never seen such a place," she sighed as she pulled on the door.

"How can I help you today, grandma?" asked the pleasant-looking man.

"I come for a windmill, for my sick lil' granchild, sir. I got with me ten whole cents, today," she offered, as she pulled two coins from her apron and placed them ceremoniously on the counter.

"Well, you came to the right place, we've got 'em in every color of the rainbow. What do you think of this one? It's a nice cheerful color for a sick little boy," he mused as he pulled out a bright red windmill from underneath the counter, and blew directly into the poinsettia bud. The crisp paper twirled in delight. Round and round. "It'll only cost you nine cents. You'll have a whole penny to spare!" Phoenix hardly heard him as she gazed through the glass display counter, her eyes resting on red, white, and blue stripes.

"Sir, that's the one I wants for my lil' boy," Phoenix exclaimed as she pointed at the windmill. "It looks just like a little flag!"

"Em, well, ma'm, you see, the striped ones cost fifteen cents. But the solid wind-mills are just as cheerful, and . . ."

"But, sir, you don't understand," Phoenix interrupted. "My lil' boy is sick. Swallowed himself nearly a cupful of lye, he did. He can't even leave home, and he ain't never seen such a sight as a windmill that's painted just like a flag."

"OK, OK, hush now, grandma. I'll give you the striped one for a dime. After all, it is the holidays. But don't you tell anyone. It must be our little secret, you hear. If my wife hears, she'll have an absolute fit. Says I give away everything we own. So you can't tell anyone. It's a Christmas secret."

"All right then, sir, I won't tell nobody, 'specially not your wife." The man chuckled, despite himself.

"Here you go, grandma. You have yourself a merry holiday. And don't forget your penny change."

Phoenix held her head high as she walked out of the store and down the avenue, the new windmill clutched at her side, spinning in time with the insistent breeze.

"I don't feel bad 'bout taken a lil' charity time and again," she muttered. "Don't feel one bit bad. There's no shame in an old woman buying the best windmill there is for her lil' lamb. He ain't never had a thing of his own. Well, don't you worry none. I's comin' home to soothe your lil' throat, I am."

By the time Phoenix retraced her steps, deftly avoiding the eager thorn bush, dusk had long since set in, and the last rays of light slanted out from the very edge of the sky. She came to the crest of a hill and gazed down to the little home where her grandson was waiting. Down the familiar incline, her heel slipped a bit on the frozen ground. "Seems that the North Pole came here and took roost," she uttered, a little out of breath from her near fall. Regaining her balance, she continued on her way.

"I will pick and choose where I go," she said emphatically to the stiff, crunchy grass. The sloped ground relaxed gracefully into the valley where a brood of three little ones tumbled and shrieked. "What you doin' out in this cold?" Phoenix called to them. "Foolish children I'm raising. Get yourselves into that house. Playing like that with the sun so long gone. You hear me now?" Three little heads looked up from their game, but as Phoenix opened her mouth, taking a deep breath to recommence her admonishment, the three figures dissolved into the frostbitten air from which they materialized. Phoenix blinked, and squinted just a little more fiercely than usual.

"Seems like just last summer," she sighed.

Leaning a little harder on the top of her cane, like a tree branch bent from years of wind and weather, she allowed her feet to pull her toward the house that had outlived several generations. She paused for a moment at a small cluster of well-groomed graves, marked with wooden crosses, still standing mostly straight, like a line of uniformed soldiers. Directing her attention to one of the graves, she took to the task of family business.

"I made the journey for the soothing medicine. Seems like every time, the hospital wants to be just a little farther away. But I always find it. Not much news I need to relate. The news all stays the same around here, 'cept my bones have taken to creaking a might earlier this year, and the winters keep getting colder and colder. But we've been here since the beginning of time. Since the beginning of time," she mused. "Well, I better be on my way. My boy has been waiting on me the whole long day."

Turning, she walked toward the back of the house. As she made her way around the side, she felt a chill, as if drafts were escaping from between the boards of the drab walls to cool the night air. She opened the creaking door, and the brightly striped windmill twirled furiously, causing the red, white, and blue to be woven together into a symphony of color. It took all her strength to push the door shut behind her. She walked through the gray little kitchen, pausing to lift the lid of a pot of broth, and light a meager fire underneath it. She walked into the main den of the dwelling, past a faded quilt, which was still proudly sagging on the same wall where it had been hung for display, sometime during the decade of the Surrender. With the little windmill hidden behind her back, she made her way, a little more slowly than before, to a door, concealed by shadows eternally slouched in the corner. She turned the handle, and struggled, one-handedly, with the stubbornness of the old crabby door that had grown sick and tired of being pushed and pulled on for the better part of a century. Squinting with her ancient eyes, she peered into the darkness of the sleeping room.

From within the great depth, she heard a faint stirring.

"Mammy?" questioned a frail little bird voice.

NAGUIB MAHFOUZ (b. 1911)

Long considered Egypt's finest writer, Naguib Mahfouz was almost unknown in English-speaking countries until 1988, when he was awarded the
Nobel Prize for Literature as an author who, "through works rich in nuance
— now clearsightedly realistic, now evocatively ambiguous — has formed an
Arabian narrative art that applies to all of mankind." Born in Cairo, where he
has spent his entire life, Mahfouz studied philosophy at Cairo University and
worked until his retirement as a civil servant. He began to write in the late
1930s, publishing his stories in local journals. Many of his thirty novels have
been translated into English, most notably his masterwork, *The Cairo Trilogy*
(1956–57), a history of several generations in an Egyptian family. His novel
Children of Our Alley (1959) was banned in the Middle East because it was
believed to be critical of Islam. By the 1960s, Mahfouz began to turn to shorter
novels, such as *The Thief and the Dogs* (1962). Among his numerous story collections are the experimental *Love in the Rain* (1973) and *The Time and the
Place and Other Stories* (1991), which includes "The Norwegian Rat."

Always a reader of European literature, Mahfouz has done much to pop-
ularize the novel and short-story forms in the Arab world, where poetry has
traditionally held sway. He is also deeply involved with religious, cultural, and
political issues in the Middle East.

The Norwegian Rat (1984)

Translated by Denys Johnson-Davies

Fortunately we were not alone in this affliction. Mr. A.M., being the senior
householder in the building, had invited us to a meeting in his flat for an
exchange of opinions. There were not more than ten people present, including Mr. A.M., who, in addition to being the oldest among us, held the most
senior position and was also the most well off. No one failed to show up —
and how could they, seeing that it had to do with the rats and their likely invasion of our homes and their threat to our safety? Mr. A.M. began in a voice of
great gravity with "As you all know . . ." and then set forth what the papers
had been reiterating about the advance of the rats, their vast numbers, and the
terrible destruction that would be wrought by them. Voices were raised around
the room.

"What is being said is quite beyond belief."

"Have you seen the television coverage?"

"They're not ordinary rats; they're even attacking cats and people."

"Isn't it likely that things are a bit exaggerated?"

"No . . . no, the facts are beyond any exaggeration."

Then, calmly and with pride in being the chairman, Mr. A.M. said, "It has in any case been established that we are not alone. This has been confirmed to me by the Governor."

"It's good to hear that."

"So all we have to do is carry out instructions meticulously, both those that come directly through me and those that come by way of the authorities."

"And will this cost us a great deal?" it occurred to one of us to inquire.

He resorted to the Koran for a reply. "'God does not charge a soul beyond its scope.'"

"The main thing is that the costs should not be excessive."

This time he resorted to a maxim. "An evil is not warded off by something worse."

At which more than one voice said, "We would hope that you will find us cooperative."

"We are with you," said Mr. A.M., "but do not rely upon us wholly. Rely too upon yourselves, starting at least with the obvious things."

"Absolutely so, but what are the obvious things?"

"Having traps and the traditional poisons."

"Fine."

"Having as many cats as possible in the stairwell and on the roofs. Also inside the flats if circumstances permit."

"But it's said that the Norwegian rat attacks cats."

"Cats are not without their use."

We returned to our homes in high spirits and with a sincere resolve. Soon, rats predominated over the rest of our worries. They made frequent appearances in our dreams, occupied the most time in our conversations, and came to engross us as life's main difficulty. We proceeded to take the precautions we had promised to, as we awaited the coming of the enemy. Some of us were saying that there was not long to go, while others said that one day we'd spot a rat darting past and that this would be the harbinger of imminent danger.

Many different explanations were given for the proliferation of rats. One opinion was that it was due to the Canal towns being empty after the evacuation, another attributed it to the negative aspects of the High Dam, others blamed it on the system of government, while many saw in it God's wrath at His servants for their refusal to accept His guidance. We expended laudable efforts in making rational preparations, about which no one was negligent. At a further meeting held at his home, the estimable Mr. A.M., may God preserve him, said, "I am happy with the preventive measures you have taken, and I am pleased to see the entrance to our building swarming with cats. Certainly there are those who complain about the expense of feeding them, but this is of little importance when we think of our safety and security." He scrutinized our faces with satisfaction, then asked, "What news of the traps?"

One of us (an eminent educator) answered. "I caught a skinny specimen — one of our local rats."

"Whatever a rat's identity, it's still harmful. Anyway, today I must inform you of the necessity, with the enemy at our gates, for being even more on your guard. Quantities of the new poison ground up in corn will be distributed to us. It is to be placed in vulnerable places such as the kitchen, though extreme care should be taken to protect children, poultry, and pets."

Everything happened just as the man said, and we told ourselves that we were truly not alone in the battle. Gratitude welled up in us for our solicitous neighbor and our revered Governor. Certainly all this had required of us a lot of care on top of our daily worries. And unavoidable mistakes did occur. Thus a cat was killed in one home and a number of chickens in another, but there were no losses in terms of human life. As time went on we became more and more tense and alert, and the suspense weighed heavily on us. We told ourselves that the happening of a calamity was preferable to the waiting for it. Then, one day, I met a neighbor at the bus stop, and he said, "I heard from a reliable source the rats have annihilated an entire village."

"There was not a thing about this in the papers!"

He gave me a scornful look and said nothing. I imagined the earth heaving with hordes of rats as far as the eye could see and crowds of refugees wandering aimlessly in the desert. Good God, could such a thing come about? But what was so impossible about it? Had not God previously sent the Flood and the flocks of birds as mentioned in the Koran? Would people tomorrow cease their daily struggle and throw all they possessed into the raging fires of battle? And would they be victorious, or would this spell the end?

At the third meeting, Mr. A.M. appeared in cheerful mood. "Congratulations, gentlemen," he said. "We are as active as can be. The losses are slight and will not, one hopes, recur. We shall become experts in matters of fighting rats, and perhaps we shall be called upon in the future in other places. His Excellency the Governor is extremely happy."

One of our number began to complain. "The fact is that our nerves — ."

But he was cut short by Mr. A.M. "Our nerves? Do you want to spoil our success with a thoughtless word?"

"When will the rats begin their attack?"

"No one can give a definite answer to that, and it is of no consequence so long as we are prepared for the battle." Then, after a pause, he continued. "Latest instructions are of special importance, relating as they do to windows, doors, and any apertures in walls or elsewhere. Close all doors and windows and examine in particular the lower part of any door. If any space is found through which a mere straw could pass, seal it up completely with wooden planks. When doing the morning cleaning, the windows of one room should be opened, and while one person sweeps, another, armed with a stick, should stand at the ready. Then you should close the windows and move to the next room, where the same procedure should be followed.

On finishing the cleaning, the flat should be left like a firmly closed box, whatever the weather."

We exchanged looks in glum silence.

"It's impossible to go on like that," said a voice.

"No, you must maintain the utmost precision in carrying out . . ."

"Even in a prison cell there's . . ."

"We are at war, that is to say in a state of emergency. We are threatened not only with destruction but also with epidemics — God spare us. We must reckon with that."

We went on submissively carrying out what we had been ordered to do. We became more deeply submerged in a morass of anticipation and wariness, with the boredom and depression that accompany them. The nervous tension increased and was translated into sharp daily quarrels between the man of the house and his wife and children. We continued to follow the news, while the Norwegian rat, with its huge body, long whiskers, and alarming glassy look, became a star of evil that roamed in our imaginations and dreams and occupied the major part of our conversation.

At the last meeting Mr. A.M. had said, "I've got some good news — a team of experts has been assigned to the task of checking the buildings, flats and locations exposed to risk, and all without any demand for additional rates."

It was indeed good news, and we received it with universal delight, the hope being that we would be able to relieve ourselves of some of the distress we had been suffering. Then one day the concierge informed us that a bureaucrat had inspected the entrance to the building, the stairwell, the roof, and the garage, and had pronounced favorably on the large bands of cats roaming about here and there. He had instructed the concierge to be extra vigilant and to inform him of any rat that might make its appearance, be it Norwegian or Egyptian.

One week after the meeting, the doorbell of our flat rang and the concierge gave us the good news that the bureaucrat was on his way and wished to have permission to make an inspection. The time was not convenient, because my wife had just finished preparing lunch, but I nevertheless hurried out to greet him. I found myself standing before a middle-aged, sturdily built man with a thick mustache, his square face with its short snub nose and glassy stare reminding me of a cat. I greeted him, concealing a smile that almost transformed itself into a laugh, and told myself that they really did have a flair for choosing their men. I walked ahead of him, and he proceeded to examine the traps and poisons, the windows and doors, nodding his head in approval. He did, however, find in the kitchen a small window covered over with a wire mesh of tiny holes, at which he said firmly, "Close the window."

My wife was on the point of protesting, but he snapped at her. "The Norwegian rat can gnaw through wire."

Satisfied that his order had been carried out, he sniffed at the smell of food, thus proclaiming his commendation. I therefore invited him to eat.

"Only a mean man refuses generosity," he answered simply.

Immediately we prepared a table for him alone, telling him that we had already eaten. He sat down as though in his own home and began gobbling up the food without any restraint or shyness — and with quite extraordinary voracity. Out of politeness, we left him to it. However, after a while I thought it best to check on him in case he might be in need of something. I gave him another helping, and while doing so I became aware of a dramatic change in his appearance. It seemed that his face reminded me no longer of a cat but of a rat, in fact of the Norwegian rat itself. I returned to my wife with my head spinning. I did not tell her what I had noticed but asked her to be pleasant to him and make him welcome. She was away for a minute or two, then returned, pallid, and stared at me in stupefaction. "Did you see what he looks like when he eats?" she breathed.

I nodded, and she whispered, "It's quite amazing, unbelievable."

I indicated my agreement with a movement of my spinning head. It seems that our utter astonishment caused us to forget the passage of time, and we only came to when we heard his voice from the hallway calling joyfully, "May your house ever prosper!"

We rushed out, but he had reached the front door before us and had gone. All we glimpsed of him was his swaying back, then a swift about-face as he bade us farewell with a fleeting Norwegian smile. We stood behind the closed door looking at each other in bewilderment.

Questions for Discussion

1. What is the significance of the "rat problem" that supposedly plagues the city? What exactly is a Norwegian rat? On what evidence do the people in the building and elsewhere in the city base their belief that these rats are in fact a "problem"?

2. Who is Mr. A.M., and what does he represent? Why do the neighbors perceive him as an authority figure and a leader? Does the narrator present him as a reliable source of information on the rat problem?

3. Why is it significant that Mr. A.M. relies so extensively on religious aphorisms such as "God does not charge a soul beyond its scope"?

4. Is Mr. A.M.'s advice for fighting the rats in fact helpful? What contradictions emerge both in his advice and in the reports of the invasion?

5. When the bureaucrat comes to inspect the narrator's flat, how is he described? Why does he seem suspicious? Why is he compared first to a cat? At what point does he seem to transform into a rat, and what does this transformation suggest?

Ideas for Writing

1. Write an essay in which you interpret the story as a modern satirical parable. What is its "moral," and what aspects of contemporary society does it satirize? Does the story's satire seem universal or more focused on issues of Egyptian bureaucracy?

2. Write a story that satirizes elements of municipal bureaucracy, using references to animals and elements of the fable or fairy tale.

(1912–1982)

Much of John Cheever's work focuses on the divided, alienated lives of upper-middle-class suburbanites who commute to Manhattan from Westchester County and Connecticut or of high-rise apartment dwellers who sometimes reveal their private lives in their buildings' public spaces. Realistic, sometimes affectionate, and often satirical, his stories are particularly attentive to the desperation and madness that often underlie the placid surface of urban and suburban existence.

Although Cheever was born into a well-to-do family in Quincy, Massachusetts, his father lost most of his money in the stock market crash of 1929. After being expelled from the prestigious Thayer Academy for smoking, Cheever moved to New York City to begin his life as a writer, publishing stories about his prep-school experiences in the *New Republic*. Most of his early stories first appeared in the *New Yorker*. Cheever went on to publish five novels — including *The Wapshot Chronicle* (1957), *Bullet Park* (1969), and *Falconer* (1977) — and seven collections of fiction. *The Stories of John Cheever* (1978), which includes "Clancy in the Tower of Babel" and "The Five-Forty-Eight," was awarded the Pulitzer prize. Plagued by alcoholism and deeply ambivalent about his sexuality, Cheever often seems to view his characters' foibles with an ironic ambiguity.

Clancy in the Tower of Babel   (1953)

James and Nora Clancy came from farms near the little town of Newcastle. Newcastle is near Limerick. They had been poor in Ireland and they were not much better off in the new country, but they were cleanly and decent people. Their home farms had been orderly places, long inhabited by the same families, and the Clancys enjoyed the grace of a tradition. Their simple country ways were so deeply ingrained that twenty years in the New World had had little effect on them. Nora went to market with a straw basket under her arm, like a woman going out to a kitchen garden, and Clancy's pleasant face reflected a simple life. They had only one child, a son named John, and they had been able to pass on to him their peaceable and contented views. They were people who centered their lives in half a city block, got down on their knees on the floor to say "Hail Mary, full of grace," and took turns in the bathtub in the kitchen on Saturday night.

When Clancy was still a strong man in his forties, he fell down some stairs in the factory and broke his hip. He was out of work for nearly a year, and while he got compensation for this time, it was not as much as his wages had been and he and his family suffered the pain of indebtedness and need. When Clancy recovered, he was left with a limp and it took him a long time to find another job. He went to church every day, and in the end it was the intercession of a priest that got work for him, running an elevator in one of the big apartment houses on the East Side. Clancy's good manners and his clean and pleasant face pleased the tenants, and with his salary and the tips they gave him he made enough to pay his debts and support his wife and son.

The apartment house was not far from the slum tenement where James and Nora had lived since their marriage, but financially and morally it was another creation, and Clancy at first looked at the tenants as if they were made out of sugar. The ladies wore coats and jewels that cost more than Clancy would make in a lifetime of hard work, and when he came home in the evenings, he would, like a returned traveler, tell Nora what he had seen. The poodles, the cocktail parties, the children and their nursemaids interested him, and he told Nora that it was like the Tower of Babel.

It took Clancy a while to memorize the floor numbers to which his tenants belonged, to pair the husbands and wives, to join the children to their parents, and the servants (who rode on the back elevators) to these families, but he managed at last and was pleased to have everything straight. Among his traits was a passionate sense of loyalty, and he often spoke of the Building as if it were a school or a guild, the product of a community of sentiment and aspiration. "Oh, I wouldn't do anything to harm the Building," he often said. His manner was respectful but he was not humorless, and when 11-A sent his tailcoat out to the dry cleaner's, Clancy put it on and paraded up and down the back hall. Most of the tenants were regarded by Clancy with an indiscriminate benevolence, but there were a few exceptions. There was a drunken wife-beater. He was a bulky, duck-footed lunkhead, in Clancy's eyes, and he did not belong in the Building. Then there was a pretty girl in 11-B who went out in the evenings with a man who was a weak character — Clancy could tell because he had a cleft chin. Clancy warned the girl, but she did not act on his advice. But the tenant about whom he felt most concerned was Mr. Rowantree.

Mr. Rowantree, who was a bachelor, lived in 4-A. He had been in Europe when Clancy first went to work, and he had not returned to New York until winter. When Mr. Rowantree appeared, he seemed to Clancy to be a well-favored man with graying hair who was tired from his long voyage. Clancy waited for him to re-establish himself in the city, for friends and relatives to start telephoning and writing, and for Mr. Rowantree to begin the give-and-take of parties in which most of the tenants were involved.

Clancy had discovered by then that his passengers were not made of sugar. All of them were secured to the world intricately by friends and lovers, dogs and songbirds, debts, inheritances, trusts, and jobs, and he waited for Mr. Rowantree to put out his lines. Nothing happened. Mr. Rowantree went to work at ten in the morning and returned home at six; no visitors appeared. A month passed in which he did not have a single guest. He sometimes went out in the evening, but he always returned alone, and for all Clancy knew he might have continued his friendless state in the movies around the corner. The man's lack of friends amazed and then began to aggravate and trouble Clancy. One night when he was on the evening shift and Mr. Rowantree came down alone, Clancy stopped the car between floors.

"Are you going out for dinner, Mr. Rowantree?" he asked.

"Yes," the man said.

"Well, when you're eating in this neighborhood, Mr. Rowantree," Clancy said, "you'll find that Bill's Clam Bar is the only restaurant worth speaking of. I've been living around here for twenty years and I've seen them come and go. The others have fancy lighting and fancy prices, but you won't get anything to eat that's worth sticking to your ribs excepting at Bill's Clam Bar."

"Thank you, Clancy," Mr. Rowantree said. "I'll keep that in mind."

"Now, Mr. Rowantree," Clancy said, "I don't want to sound inquisitive, but would you mind telling me what kind of a business you're in?"

"I have a store on Third Avenue," Mr. Rowantree said. "Come over and see it someday."

"I'd like to do that," Clancy said. "But now, Mr. Rowantree, I should think you'd want to have dinner with your friends and not be alone all the time." Clancy knew that he was interfering with the man's privacy, but he was led on by the thought that his soul might need help. "A good-looking man like you must have friends," he said, "and I'd think you'd have your supper with them."

"I'm going to have supper with a friend, Clancy," Mr. Rowantree said.

This reply made Clancy feel easier, and he put the man out of his mind for a while. The Building gave him the day off on St. Patrick's, so that he could march in the parade, and when the parade had disbanded and he was walking home, he decided to look for the store. Mr. Rowantree had told him which block it was in. It was easy to find. Clancy was pleased to see that it was a big store. There were two doors to go in by, separated by a large glass window. Clancy looked through the window to see if Mr. Rowantree was busy with a customer, but there was no one there. Before he went in, he looked at the things in the window. He was disappointed to see that it was not a clothing store or a delicatessen. It looked more like a museum. There were glasses and candlesticks, chairs and tables, all of them old. He opened the door. A bell attached to the door rang and Clancy looked up to see the old-fashioned bell on its string. Mr. Rowantree came out from behind a screen and greeted him cordially.

Clancy did not like the place. He felt that Mr. Rowantree was wasting his time. It troubled him to think of the energy in a man's day being spent in this place. A narrow trail, past tables and desks, urns and statues, led into the store and then branched off in several directions. Clancy had never seen so much junk. Since he couldn't imagine it all being manufactured in any one country, he guessed that it had been brought there from the four corners of the world. It seemed to Clancy a misuse of time to have gathered all these things into a dark store on Third Avenue. But it was more than the confusion and the waste that troubled him; it was the feeling that he was surrounded by the symbols of frustration and that all the china youths and maidens in their attitudes of love were the company of bitterness. It may have been because he had spent his happy life in bare rooms that he associated goodness with ugliness.

He was careful not to say anything that would offend Mr. Rowantree. "Do you have any clerks to help you?" he asked.

"Oh, yes," Mr. Rowantree said. "Miss James is here most of the time. We're partners."

That was it, Clancy thought. Miss James. That was where he went in the evenings. But why, then, wouldn't Miss James marry him? Was it because he was already married? Perhaps he had suffered some terrible human misfortune like having his wife go crazy or having his children taken away from him.

"Have you a snapshot of Miss James?" Clancy asked.

"No," Mr. Rowantree said.

"Well, I'm glad to have seen your store and thank you very much," Clancy said. The trip had been worth his while, because he took away from the dark store a clear image of Miss James. It was a good name, an Irish name, and now in the evenings when Mr. Rowantree went out, Clancy would ask him how Miss James was.

Clancy's son, John, was a senior in high school. He was captain of the basketball team and a figure in school government, and that spring he entered an essay he had written on democracy in a contest sponsored by a manufacturer in Chicago. There were millions of entries, but John won honorable mention, which entitled him to a trip to Chicago in an airplane and a week's visit there with all expenses paid. The boy was naturally excited by this bonanza and so was his mother, but Clancy was the one who seemed to have won the prize. He told all the tenants in the Building about it and asked them what kind of city Chicago was and if traveling in airplanes was safe. He would get up in the middle of the night and go into John's room to look at the wonderful boy while he slept. The boy's head was crammed with knowledge, Clancy thought. His heart was kind and strong. It was sinful, Clancy knew, to confuse the immortality of the Holy Spirit and earthly love, but when he realized that John was his flesh and blood, that the young man's face was *his* face improved with mobility and thought, and that when he, Clancy, was dead, some habit or taste of his would live on in the young man, he felt that there was no pain in death.

John's plane left for Chicago late one Saturday afternoon. He went to confession and then walked over to the Building to say goodbye to his father. Clancy kept the boy in the lobby as long as he could and introduced him to the tenants who came through. Then it was time for the boy to go. The doorman took the elevator, and Clancy walked John up to the corner. It was a clear, sunny afternoon in Lent. There wasn't a cloud in the sky. The boy had on his best suit and he looked like a million dollars. They shook hands at the corner, and Clancy limped back to the Building. Traffic was slow on the elevator, and he stood at the front door, watching the people on the sidewalk. Most of them were dressed in their best clothes and they were off to enjoy themselves. Clancy's best wishes followed them all. At the far end of the street he saw Mr. Rowantree's head and shoulders and saw that he was with a young man. Clancy waited and opened the door for them.

"Hello, Clancy," Mr. Rowantree said. "I'd like to have you meet my friend Bobbie. He's going to live here now."

Clancy grunted. The young man was not a young man. His hair was cut short and he wore a canary-yellow sweater and a padded coat but he was as old as Mr. Rowantree, he was nearly as old as Clancy. All the qualities and airs of youth, which a good man puts aside gladly when the time comes, had been preserved obscenely in him. He had dope in his eyes to make them shine and he smelled of perfume, and Mr. Rowantree took his arm to help him through the door, as if he were a pretty girl. As soon as Clancy saw what he had to deal with, he took a stand. He stayed at the door. Mr. Rowantree and his friend went through the lobby and got into the elevator. They reached out and rang the bell.

"I'm not taking you up in my car!" Clancy shouted down the lobby.

"Come here, Clancy," Mr. Rowantree said.

"I'm not taking that up in my car," Clancy said.

"I'll have you fired for this," Mr. Rowantree said.

"That's no skin off my nose," Clancy said. "I'm not taking you up in my car."

"Come here, Clancy," Mr. Rowantree said. Clancy didn't answer. Mr. Rowantree put his finger on the bell and held it there. Clancy didn't move. He heard Mr. Rowantree and his friend talking. A moment later, he heard them climb the stairs. All the solicitude he had felt for Mr. Rowantree, the times he had imagined him walking in the Park with Miss James, seemed like money lost in a terrible fraud. He was hurt and bitter. The idea of Bobbie's being in the Building was a painful one for him to take, and he felt as if it contested his own simple view of life. He was curt with everyone for the rest of the day. He even spoke sharply to the children. When he went to the basement to take off his uniform, Mr. Coolidge, the superintendent, called him into his office.

"Rowantree's been trying to get you fired for the last hour, Jim," he said. "He said you wouldn't take him up in your car. I'm not going to fire you, because you're a good, steady man, but I'm warning you now. He knows a lot of rich and influential people, and if you don't mind your own business, it won't be hard for him to get you kicked out." Mr. Coolidge was surrounded by all the treasures he had extricated from the rubbish baskets in the back halls — broken lamps, broken vases, a perambulator with three wheels.

"But he —" Clancy began.

"It's none of your business, Jim," Mr. Coolidge said. "He's been very quiet since he come back from Europe. You're a good, steady man, Clancy, and I don't want to fire you, but you got to remember that you aren't the boss around here."

The next day was Palm Sunday, and, by the grace of God, Clancy did not see Mr. Rowantree. On Monday, Clancy joined his bitterness at having to live in Sodom to the deep and general grief he always felt at the commencement of those events that would end on Golgotha. It was a gloomy day. Clouds and darkness were over the city. Now and then it rained. Clancy took Mr. Rowantree down at ten. He didn't say anything, but he gave the man a scornful look. The ladies began going off for lunch around noon. Mr. Rowantree's friend Bobbie went out then.

About half past two, one of the ladies came back from lunch, smelling of gin. She did a funny thing. When she got into the elevator, she stood with her face to the wall of the car, so that Clancy couldn't see it. He was not a man to look into somebody's face if they wanted to hide it, and this made him angry. He stopped the car. "Turn around," he said. "Turn around. I'm ashamed of you, a woman with three grown children, standing with your face to the wall like a crybaby." She turned around. She was crying about something. Clancy put the car into motion again. "You ought to fast," he mumbled. "You ought to go without cigarettes or meat during Lent. It would give you something to think about." She left the car, and he answered a ring from the first floor. It was Mr. Rowantree. He took him up. Then he took Mrs. DePaul up to 9. She was a nice woman, and he told her about John's trip to Chicago. On the way down, he smelled gas.

For a man who has lived his life in a tenement, gas is the odor of winter, sickness, need, and death. Clancy went up to Mr. Rowantree's floor. That was it. He had the master key and he opened the door and stepped into that hellish breath. It was dark. He could hear the petcocks[1] hissing in the kitchen. He put a rug against the door to keep it open and threw up a window in the hall. He stuck his head out for some air. Then, in terror of being blown into hell himself, and swearing and praying and half closing his eyes as if the poisonous air might blind him, he started for the kitchen and gave himself a cruel bang against the doorframe that made him cold all over with pain. He stumbled into the kitchen and turned off the gas and opened the doors and windows. Mr. Rowantree was on his knees with his head in the oven. He sat up. He was crying. "Bobbie's gone, Clancy," he said. "Bobbie's gone."

Clancy's stomach turned over, his gorge opened and filled up with bitter spit. "Dear Jesus!" he shouted. "Dear Jesus!" He stumbled out of the apartment. He was shaking all over. He took the car down and shouted for the doorman and told him what had happened.

---

[1] Valves. — Eds.

The doorman took the elevator, and Clancy went into the locker room and sat down. He didn't know how long he had been there when the doorman came in and said that he smelled more gas. Clancy went up to Mr. Rowantree's apartment again. The door was shut. He opened it and stood in the hall and heard the petcocks. "Take your God-damned fool head out of that oven, Mr. Rowantree!" he shouted. He went into the kitchen and turned off the gas. Mr. Rowantree was sitting on the floor. "I won't do it again, Clancy," he said. "I promise, I promise."

Clancy went down and got Mr. Coolidge, and they went into the basement together and turned off Mr. Rowantree's gas. He went up again. The door was shut. When he opened it, he heard the hissing of the gas. He yanked the man's head out of the oven. "You're wasting your time, Mr. Rowantree!" he shouted. "We've turned off your gas! You're wasting your time!" Mr. Rowantree scrambled to his feet and ran out of the kitchen. Clancy heard him running through the apartment, slamming doors. He followed him and found him in the bathroom, shaking pills out of a bottle into his mouth. Clancy knocked the pill bottle out of his hand and knocked the man down. Then he called the precinct station on Mr. Rowantree's phone. He waited there until a policeman, a doctor, and a priest came.

Clancy walked home at five. The sky was black. It was raining soot and ashes. Sodom, he thought, the city undeserving of clemency, the unredeemable place, and, raising his eye to watch the rain and the ashes fall through the air, he felt a great despair for his kind. They had lost the warrants for mercy, there was no movement in the city around him but toward self-destruction and sin. He longed for the simple life of Ireland and the City of God, but he felt that he had been contaminated by the stink of gas.

He told Nora what had happened, and she tried to comfort him. There was no letter or card from John. In the evening, Mr. Coolidge telephoned. He said it was about Mr. Rowantree.

"Is he in the insane asylum?" Clancy asked.

"No," Mr. Coolidge said. "His friend came back and they went out together. But he's been threatening to get you fired again. As soon as he felt all right again, he said he was going to get you fired. I don't want to fire you, but you got to be careful, you got to be careful." This was the twist that Clancy couldn't follow, and he felt sick. He asked Mr. Coolidge to get a man from the union to take his place for a day or so, and he went to bed.

Clancy stayed in bed the next morning. He got worse. He was cold. Nora lighted a fire in the range, but he shivered as if his heart and his bones were frozen. He doubled his knees up to his chest and snagged the blankets around him, but he couldn't keep warm. Nora finally called the doctor, a man from Limerick. It was after ten before he got there. He said that Clancy should go to the hospital. The doctor left to make the arrangements, and Nora got Clancy's best clothes together and helped him into them. There was still a price tag on his long underwear and there were pins in his shirt. In the end, nobody saw the new underwear and the clean shirt. At the hospital, they drew a curtain around his bed and handed the finery out to Nora. Then he stretched out in bed, and Nora gave him a kiss and went away.

He groaned, he moaned for a while, but he had a fever and this put him to sleep. He did not know or care where he was for the next few days. He slept most of the time. When John came back from Chicago, the boy's company and his story of the trip picked Clancy's spirits up a little. Nora visited him every day, and one day, a couple of weeks after Clancy entered the hospital, she brought Frank Quinn, the doorman, with her. Frank gave Clancy a narrow manila envelope, and when Clancy opened it, asking crossly what it was, he saw that it was full of currency.

"That's from the tenants, Clancy," Frank said.

"Now, why did they do this?" Clancy said. He was smitten. His eyes watered and he couldn't count the money. "Why did they do this?" he asked weakly. "Why did they go to this trouble? I'm nothing but an elevator man."

"It's nearly two hundred dollars," Frank said.

"Who took up the collection?" Clancy said. "Was it you, Frank?"

"It was one of the tenants," Frank said.

"It was Mrs. DePaul," Clancy said. "I'll bet it was that Mrs. DePaul."

"One of the tenants," Frank said.

"It was you, Frank," Clancy said warmly. "You was the one who took up the collection."

"It was Mr. Rowantree," Frank said sadly. He bent his head.

"You're not going to give the money back, Jim?" Nora asked.

"I'm not a God-damned fool!" Clancy shouted. "When I pick up a dollar off the street, I'm not the man to go running down to the lost-and-found department with it!"

"Nobody else could have gotten so much, Jim," Frank said. "He went from floor to floor. They say he was crying."

Clancy had a vision. He saw the church from the open lid of his coffin, before the altar. The sacristan had lighted only a few of the Vaseline-colored lamps, for the only mourners were those few people, all of them poor and old, who had come from Limerick with Clancy on the boat. He heard the priest's youthful voice mingling with the thin music of the bells. Then in the back of the church he saw Mr. Rowantree and Bobbie. They were crying and crying. They were crying harder than Nora. He could see their shoulders rise and fall, and hear their sighs.

"Does he think I'm dying, Frank?" Clancy asked.

"Yes, Jim. He does."

"He thinks I'm dying," Clancy said angrily. "He's got one of them soft heads. Well, I ain't dying. I'm not taking any of his grief. I'm getting out of here." He climbed out of bed. Nora and Frank tried unsuccessfully to push him back. Frank ran out to get a nurse. The nurse pointed a finger at Clancy and commanded him to get back into bed, but he had put on his pants and was tying his shoelaces. She went out and got another nurse, and the two young women tried to hold him down, but he shook them off easily. The first nurse went to get a doctor. The doctor who returned with her was a young man, much smaller than Clancy. He said that Clancy could go home. Frank and Nora took him back in a taxi, and as soon as he got into the tenement, he telephoned Mr. Coolidge and said that he was coming back to work in the morning. He felt a lot better, surrounded by the smells and lights of his own place. Nora cooked him a nice supper and he ate it in the kitchen.

After supper, he sat by the window in his shirtsleeves. He thought about going back to work, about the man with the cleft chin, the wife-beater, Mr. Rowantree and Bobbie. Why should a man fall in love with a monster? Why should a man try to kill himself? Why should a man try to get a man fired and then collect money for him with tears in his eyes, and then perhaps, a week later, try to get him fired again? He would not return the money, he would not thank Mr. Rowantree, but he wondered what kind of judgment he should pass on the pervert. He began to pick the words he would say to Mr. Rowantree when they met. "It's my suggestion, Mr. Rowantree," he would say, "that the next time you want to kill yourself, you get a rope or a gun. It's my suggestion, Mr. Rowantree," he would say, "that you go to a good doctor and get your head examined."

The spring wind, the south wind that in the city smells of drains, was blowing. Clancy's window looked onto an expanse of clotheslines and ailanthus trees, yards that were used as dumps, and the naked backs of tenements, with their lighted and unlighted windows. The symmetry, the reality of the scene heartened Clancy, as if it conformed to something good in himself. Men with common minds like his had built these houses. Nora brought him a glass of beer and sat near the window. He put an arm around her waist. She was in her slip, because of the heat. Her hair was held down with pins. She appeared to Clancy to be one of the glorious beauties of his day, but a stranger, he guessed, might notice the tear in her slip and that her body was bent and heavy. A picture of John hung on the wall. Clancy was struck with the strength and intelligence of his son's face, but he guessed that a stranger might notice the boy's glasses and his bad complexion. And then, thinking of Nora and John and that this half blindness was all that he knew himself of mortal love, he decided not to say anything to Mr. Rowantree. They would pass in silence.

Questions for Discussion

1. What is Clancy's background? In what religious, cultural, and family values does he believe? Why is it significant that he is an immigrant?

2. How does Clancy feel about the building and the individual tenants he serves? Do his feelings seem justified?

3. Why does Clancy think that Rowantree's "soul might need help"? What is revealed about Clancy's values through his obsession with Rowantree?

4. What is revealed about Clancy's values through his feelings about his son and his son's success? Does his attitude toward his son seem normal?

5. What is the importance of Clancy's saving Rowantree twice, despite his loathing of the man's lifestyle? Why does Clancy finally accept the collection Rowantree takes up for him?

Ideas for Writing

1. Evaluate Clancy's character in an essay. How does he grow and change in the course of the story? Does he become genuinely more tolerant? Is he worn down by his experiences?
2. Write a story about an intolerant person who, owing to circumstance, must save or assist a person who is a member of a group that this intolerant person despises. Show how the character is changed by the experience.

The Five-Forty-Eight (1958)

When Blake stepped out of the elevator, he saw her. A few people, mostly men waiting for girls, stood in the lobby watching the elevator doors. She was among them. As he saw her, her face took on a look of such loathing and purpose that he realized she had been waiting for him. He did not approach her. She had no legitimate business with him. They had nothing to say. He turned and walked toward the glass doors at the end of the lobby, feeling that faint guilt and bewilderment we experience when we bypass some old friend or classmate who seems threadbare, or sick, or miserable in some other way. It was five-eighteen by the clock in the Western Union office. He could catch the express. As he waited his turn at the revolving doors, he saw that it was still raining. It had been raining all day, and he noticed now how much louder the rain made the noises of the street. Outside, he started walking briskly east toward Madison Avenue. Traffic was tied up, and horns were blowing urgently on a crosstown street in the distance. The sidewalk was crowded. He wondered what she had hoped to gain by a glimpse of him coming out of the office building at the end of the day. Then he wondered if she was following him.

Walking in the city, we seldom turn and look back. The habit restrained Blake. He listened for a minute — foolishly — as he walked, as if he could distinguish her footsteps from the worlds of sound in the city at the end of a rainy day. Then he noticed, ahead of him on the other side of the street, a break in the wall of buildings. Something had been torn down; something was being put up, but the steel structure had only just risen above the sidewalk fence and daylight poured through the gap. Blake stopped opposite here and looked into a store window. It was a decorator's or an auctioneer's. The window was arranged like a room in which people live and entertain their friends. There were cups on the coffee table, magazines to read, and flowers in the vases, but the flowers were dead and the cups were empty and the guests had not come.

In the plate glass, Blake saw a clear reflection of himself and the crowds that were passing, like shadows, at his back. Then he saw her image — so close to him that it shocked him. She was standing only a foot or two behind him. He could have turned then and asked her what she wanted, but instead of recognizing her, he shied away abruptly from the reflection of her contorted face and went along the street. She might be meaning to do him harm — she might be meaning to kill him.

The suddenness with which he moved when he saw the reflection of her face tipped the water out of his hat brim in such a way that some of it ran down his neck. It felt unpleasantly like the sweat of fear. Then the cold water falling into his face and onto his bare hands, the rancid smell of the wet gutters and paving, the knowledge that his feet were beginning to get wet and that he might catch cold — all the common discomforts of walking in the rain — seemed to heighten the menace of his pursuer and to give him a morbid consciousness of his own physicalness and of the ease with which he could be hurt. He could see ahead of him the corner of Madison Avenue, where the lights were brighter. He felt that if he could get to Madison Avenue he would be all right. At the corner, there was a bakery shop with two entrances, and he went in by the door on the crosstown street, bought a coffee ring, like any other commuter, and went out the Madison Avenue door. As he started down Madison Avenue, he saw her waiting for him by a hut where newspapers were sold.

She was not clever. She would be easy to shake. He could get into a taxi by one door and leave by the other. He could speak to a policeman. He could run — although he was afraid that if he did run, it might precipitate the violence he now felt sure she had planned. He was approaching a part of the city that he knew well and where the maze of street-level and underground passages, elevator banks, and crowded lobbies made it easy for a man to lose a pursuer. The thought of this, and a whiff of sugary warmth from the coffee ring, cheered him. It was absurd to imagine being harmed on a crowded street. She was foolish, misled, lonely perhaps — that was all it could amount to. He was an insignificant man, and there was no point in anyone's following him from his office to the station. He knew no secrets of any consequence. The reports in his briefcase had no bearing on war, peace, the dope traffic, the hydrogen bomb, or any of the other international skulduggeries that he associated with pursuers, men in trench coats, and wet sidewalks. Then he saw ahead of him the door of a men's bar. Oh, it was so simple!

He ordered a Gibson and shouldered his way in between two other men at the bar, so that if she should be watching from the window she would lose sight of him. The place was crowded with commuters putting down a drink before the ride home. They had brought in on their clothes — on their shoes and umbrellas — the rancid smell of the wet dusk outside, but Blake began to relax as soon as he tasted his Gibson and looked around at the common, mostly not-young faces that surrounded him and that were worried, if they were worried at all, about tax rates and who would be put in charge of mer-chandising. He tried to remember her name — Miss Dent, Miss Bent, Miss Lent — and he was surprised to find that he could not remember it, although he was proud of the retentiveness and reach of his memory and it had only been six months ago.

Personnel had sent her up one afternoon — he was looking for a secre-tary. He saw a dark woman — in her twenties, perhaps — who was slender and shy. Her dress was simple, her figure was not much, one of her stockings was crooked, but her voice was soft and he had been willing to try her out. After she had been working for him a few days, she told him that she had been in the hospital for eight months and that it had been hard after this for her to find work, and she wanted to thank him for giving her a chance. Her hair was dark, her eyes were dark; she left with him a pleasant impression of darkness. As he got to know her better, he felt that she was oversensitive and, as a consequence, lonely. Once, when she was speaking to him of what she imagined his life to be — full of friendships, money, and a large and loving family — he had thought he recognized a peculiar feeling of deprivation. She seemed to imagine the lives of the rest of the world to be more brilliant than they were. Once, she had put a rose on his desk, and he had dropped it into the wastebasket. "I don't like roses," he told her.

She had been competent, punctual, and a good typist, and he had found only one thing in her that he could object to — her handwriting. He could not associate the crudeness of her handwriting with her appearance. He would have expected her to write a rounded backhand, and in her writing there were intermittent traces of this, mixed with clumsy printing. Her writing gave him the feeling that she had been the victim of some inner — some emotional — conflict that had in its violence broken the continuity of the lines she was able to make on paper. When she had been working for him three weeks — no longer — they stayed late one night and he offered, after work, to buy her a drink. "If you really want a drink," she said, "I have some whiskey at my place."

She lived in a room that seemed to him like a closet. There were suit boxes and hatboxes piled in a corner, and although the room seemed hardly big enough to hold the bed, the dresser, and the chair he sat in, there was an upright piano against one wall, with a book of Beethoven sonatas on the rack. She gave him a drink and said that she was going to put on something more comfortable. He urged her to; that was, after all, what he had come for. If he had any qualms, they would have been practical. Her diffidence, the feeling of deprivation in her point of view, promised to protect him from any conse-quences. Most of the many women he had known had been picked for their lack of self-esteem.

When he put on his clothes again, an hour or so later, she was weeping. He felt too contented and warm and sleepy to worry much about her tears. As he was dressing, he noticed on the dresser a note she had written to a cleaning woman. The only light came from the bathroom — the door was ajar — and in this half light the hideously scrawled letters again seemed entirely wrong for her, and as if they must be the handwriting of some other and very gross woman. The next day, he did what he felt was the only sensible thing. When she was out for lunch, he called personnel and asked them to fire her. Then he took the afternoon off. A few days later, she came to the office, asking to see him. He told the switchboard girl not to let her in. He had not seen her again until this evening.

Blake drank a second Gibson and saw by the clock that he had missed the express. He would get the local — the five-forty-eight. When he left the bar the sky was still light; it was still raining. He looked carefully up and down the street and saw that the poor woman had gone. Once or twice, he looked over his shoulder, walking to the station, but he seemed to be safe. He was still not quite himself, he realized, because he had left his coffee ring at the bar, and he was not a man who forgot things. This lapse of memory pained him.

He bought a paper. The local was only half full when he boarded it, and he got a seat on the river side and took off his raincoat. He was a slender man with brown hair — undistinguished in every way, unless you could have divined in his pallor or his gray eyes his unpleasant tastes. He dressed — like the rest of us — as if he admitted the existence of sumptuary laws.[1] His raincoat was the pale buff color of a mushroom. His hat was dark brown; so was his suit. Except for the few bright threads in his necktie, there was a scrupulous lack of color in his clothing that seemed protective.

He looked around the car for neighbors. Mrs. Compton was several seats in front of him, to the right. She smiled, but her smile was fleeting. It died swiftly and horribly. Mr. Watkins was directly in front of Blake. Mr. Watkins needed a haircut, and he had broken the sumptuary laws; he was wearing a corduroy jacket. He and Blake had quarreled, so they did not speak.

The swift death of Mrs. Compton's smile did not affect Blake at all. The Comptons lived in the house next to the Blakes, and Mrs. Compton had never understood the importance of minding her own business. Louise Blake took her troubles to Mrs. Compton, Blake knew, and instead of discouraging her crying jags, Mrs. Compton had come to imagine herself a sort of confessor and had developed a lively curiosity about the Blakes' intimate affairs. She had probably been given an account of their most recent quarrel. Blake had come home one night, overworked and tired, and had found that Louise had done nothing about getting supper. He had gone into the kitchen, followed by Louise, and had pointed out to her that the date was the fifth. He had drawn a circle around the date on the kitchen calendar. "One week is the twelfth," he had said. "Two weeks will be the nineteenth." He drew a circle around the nineteenth. "I'm not

---

[1] Laws regulating lavish spending and display. — Eds.

going to speak to you for two weeks," he had said. "That will be the nine-teenth." She had wept, she had protested, but it had been eight or ten years since she had been able to touch him with her entreaties. Louise had got old. Now the lines in her face were ineradicable, and when she clapped her glasses onto her nose to read the evening paper, she looked to him like an unpleasant stranger. The physical charms that had been her only attraction were gone. It had been nine years since Blake had built a bookshelf in the doorway that con-nected their rooms and had fitted into the bookshelf wooden doors that could be locked, since he did not want the children to see his books. But their pro-longed estrangement didn't seem remarkable to Blake. He had quarreled with his wife, but so did every other man born of woman. It was human nature. In any place where you can hear their voices — a hotel courtyard, an air shaft, a street on a summer evening — you will hear harsh words.

The hard feeling between Blake and Mr. Watkins also had to do with Blake's family, but it was not as serious or as troublesome as what lay behind Mrs. Compton's fleeting smile. The Watkinses rented. Mr. Watkins broke the sumptuary laws day after day — he once went to the eight-fourteen in a pair of sandals — and he made his living as a commercial artist. Blake's oldest son — Charlie was fourteen — had made friends with the Watkins boy. He had spent a lot of time in the sloppy rented house where the Watkinses lived. The friendship had affected his manners and his neatness. Then he had be-gun to take some meals with the Watkinses, and to spend Saturday nights there. When he had moved most of his possessions over to the Watkinses' and had begun to spend more than half his nights there, Blake had been forced to act. He had spoken not to Charlie but to Mr. Watkins, and had, of necessity, said a number of things that must have sounded critical. Mr. Watkins' long and dirty hair and his corduroy jacket reassured Blake that he had been in the right.

But Mrs. Compton's dying smile and Mr. Watkins' dirty hair did not lessen the pleasure Blake took in setting himself in an uncomfortable seat on the five-forty-eight deep underground. The coach was old and smelled oddly like a bomb shelter in which whole families had spent the night. The light that spread from the ceiling down onto their heads and shoulders was dim. The filth on the window glass was streaked with rain from some other journey, and clouds of rank pipe and cigarette smoke had begun to rise from behind each newspaper, but it was a scene that meant to Blake that he was on a safe path, and after his brush with danger he even felt a little warmth toward Mrs. Compton and Mr. Watkins.

The train traveled up from underground into the weak daylight, and the slums and the city reminded Blake vaguely of the woman who had fol-lowed him. To avoid speculation or remorse about her, he turned his atten-tion to the evening paper. Out of the corner of his eye he could see the landscape. It was industrial and, at that hour, sad. There were machine sheds and warehouses, and above these he saw a break in the clouds — a piece of yellow light. "Mr. Blake," someone said. He looked up. It was she. She was standing there holding one hand on the back of the seat to steady herself in the swaying coach. He remembered her name then — Miss Dent. "Hello, Miss Dent," he said.

"Do you mind if I sit here?"

"I guess not."

"Thank you. It's very kind of you. I don't like to inconvenience you like this. I don't want to . . ." He had been frightened when he looked up and saw her, but her timid voice rapidly reassured him. He shifted his hands — that futile and reflexive gesture of hospitality — and she sat down. She sighed. He smelled her wet clothing. She wore a formless black hat with a cheap crest stitched onto it. Her coat was thin cloth, he saw, and she wore gloves and carried a large pocketbook.

"Are you living out in this direction now, Miss Dent?"

"No."

She opened her purse and reached for her handkerchief. She had begun to cry. He turned his head to see if anyone in the car was looking, but no one was. He had sat beside a thousand passengers on the evening train. He had noticed their clothes, the holes in their gloves; and if they fell asleep and mumbled he had wondered what their worries were. He had classified almost all of them briefly before he buried his nose in the paper. He had marked them as rich, poor, brilliant or dull, neighbors or strangers, but no one of the thousand had ever wept. When she opened her purse, he remembered her perfume. It had clung to his skin the night he went to her place for a drink.

"I've been very sick," she said. "This is the first time I've been out of bed in two weeks. I've been terribly sick."

"I'm sorry that you've been sick, Miss Dent," he said in a voice loud enough to be heard by Mr. Watkins and Mrs. Compton. "Where are you working now?"

"What?"

"Where are you working now?"

"Oh, don't make me laugh," she said softly.

"I don't understand."

"You poisoned their minds."

He straightened his neck and braced his shoulders. These wrenching movements expressed a brief — and hopeless — longing to be in some other place. She meant trouble. He took a breath. He looked with deep feeling at the half-filled, half-lighted coach to affirm his sense of actuality, of a world in which there was not very much bad trouble after all. He was conscious of her heavy breathing and the smell of her rain-soaked coat. The train stopped. A nun and a man in overalls got off. When it started again, Blake put on his hat and reached for his raincoat.

"Where are you going?" she said.

"I'm going to the next car."

"Oh, no," she said. "No, no, no." She put her white face so close to his ear that he could feel her warm breath on his cheek. "Don't do that," she whispered. "Don't try and escape me. I have a pistol and I'll have to kill you and I don't want to. All I want to do is to talk with you. Don't move or I'll kill you. Don't, don't, don't!"

Blake sat back abruptly in his seat. If he had wanted to stand and shout for help, he would not have been able to. His tongue had swelled to twice its size, and when he tried to move it, it stuck horribly to the roof of his mouth. His legs were limp. All he could think of to do then was to wait for his heart to stop its hysterical beating, so that he could judge the extent of his danger. She was sitting a little sidewise, and in her pocketbook was the pistol, aimed at his belly.

"You understand me now, don't you?" she said. "You understand that I'm serious?" He tried to speak but he was still mute. He nodded his head. "Now we'll sit quietly for a little while," she said. "I got so excited that my thoughts are all confused. We'll sit quietly for a little while, until I can get my thoughts in order again."

Help would come, Blake thought. It was only a question of minutes. Someone, noticing the look on his face or her peculiar posture, would stop and interfere, and it would all be over. All he had to do was to wait until someone noticed his predicament. Out of the window he saw the river and the sky. The rain clouds were rolling down like a shutter, and while he watched, a streak of orange light on the horizon became brilliant. Its brilliance spread — he could see it move — across the waves until it raked the banks of the river with a dim firelight. Then it was put out. Help would come in a minute, he thought. Help would come before they stopped again; but the train stopped, there were some comings and goings, and Blake still lived on, at the mercy of the woman beside him. The possibility that help might not come was one that he could not face. The possibility that his predicament was not noticeable, that Mrs. Compton would guess that he was taking a poor relation out to dinner at Shady Hill, was something he would think about later. Then the saliva came back into his mouth and he was able to speak.

"Miss Dent?"

"Yes."

"What do you want?"

"I want to talk to you."

"You can come to my office."

"Oh, no. I went there every day for two weeks."

"You could make an appointment."

"No," she said. "I think we can talk here. I wrote you a letter but I've been too sick to go out and mail it. I've put down all my thoughts. I like to travel. I like trains. One of my troubles has always been that I could never afford to travel. I suppose you see this scenery every night and don't notice it any more, but it's nice for someone who's been in bed a long time. They say that He's not in the river and the hills but I think He is. 'Where shall wisdom be found?' it says. 'Where is the place of understanding? The depth saith it is not in me; the sea saith it is not with me. Destruction and death say we have heard the force with our ears.'

"Oh, I know what you're thinking," she said. "You're thinking that I'm crazy, and I have been very sick again but I'm going to be better. It's going to make me better to talk with you. I was in the hospital all the time before I came to work for you but they never tried to cure me, they only wanted to take away my self-respect. I haven't had any work now for three months. Even if I did have to kill you, they wouldn't be able to do anything to me except put me back in the hospital, so you see I'm not afraid. But let's sit quietly for a little while longer. I have to be calm."

The train continued its halting progress up the bank of the river, and Blake tried to force himself to make some plans for escape, but the immediate threat to his life made this difficult, and instead of planning sensibly, he thought of the many ways in which he could have avoided her in the first place. As soon as he had felt these regrets, he realized their futility. It was like regretting his lack of suspicion when she first mentioned her months in the hospital. It was like regretting his failure to have been warned by her shyness, her diffidence, and the handwriting that looked like the marks of a claw. There was no way of rectifying his mistakes, and he felt — for perhaps the first time in his mature life — the full force of regret. Out of the window, he saw some men fishing on the nearly dark river, and then a ramshackle boat club that seemed to have been nailed together out of scraps of wood that had been washed up on the shore.

Mr. Watkins had fallen asleep. He was snoring. Mrs. Compton read her paper. The train creaked, slowed, and halted infirmly at another station. Blake could see the southbound platform, where a few passengers were waiting to go into the city. There was a workman with a lunch pail, a dressed-up woman, and a woman with a suitcase. They stood apart from one another. Some advertisements were posted on the wall behind them. There was a picture of a couple drinking a toast in wine, a picture of a Cat's Paw rubber heel, and a picture of a Hawaiian dancer. Their cheerful intent seemed to go no farther than the puddles of water on the platform and to expire there. The platform and the people on it looked lonely. The train drew away from the station into the scattered lights of a slum and then into the darkness of the country and the river.

"I want you to read my letter before we get to Shady Hill," she said. "It's on the seat. Pick it up. I would have mailed it to you, but I've been too sick to go out. I haven't gone out for two weeks. I haven't had any work for three months. I haven't spoken to anybody but the landlady. Please read my letter."

He picked up the letter from the seat where she had put it. The cheap paper felt abhorrent and filthy to his fingers. It was folded and refolded.

"Dear Husband," she had written, in that crazy, wandering hand, "they say that human love leads us to divine love, but is this true? I dream about you every night. I have such terrible desires. I have always had a gift for dreams. I dreamed on Tuesday of a volcano erupting with blood. When I was in the hospital they said they wanted to cure me but they only wanted to take away my self-respect. They only wanted me to dream about sewing and basketwork but I protected my gift for dreams. I'm clairvoyant. I can tell when the telephone is going to ring. I've never had a true friend in my whole life. . . ."

The train stopped again. There was another platform, another picture of the couple drinking a toast, the rubber heel, and the Hawaiian dancer. Suddenly she pressed her face close to Blake's again and whispered in his ear. "I know what you're thinking. I can see it in your face. You're thinking you can get away from me in Shady Hill, aren't you? Oh, I've been planning this for weeks. It's all I've had to think about. I won't harm you if you'll let me talk. I've been thinking about devils. I mean, if there are devils in the world, if there are people in the world who represent evil, is it our duty to exterminate them? I know that you always prey on weak people. I can tell. Oh, sometimes I think I ought to kill you. Sometimes I think you're the only obstacle between me and my happiness. Sometimes . . ."

She touched Blake with the pistol. He felt the muzzle against his belly. The bullet, at that distance, would make a small hole where it entered, but it would rip out of his back a place as big as a soccer ball. He remembered the unburied dead he had seen in the war. The memory came in a rush; entrails, eyes, shattered bone, ordure, and other filth.

"All I've ever wanted in life is a little love," she said. She lightened the pressure of the gun. Mr. Watkins still slept. Mrs. Compton was sitting calmly with her hands folded in her lap. The coach rocked gently, and the coats and mushroom-colored raincoats that hung between the windows swayed a little as the car moved. Blake's elbow was on the window sill and his left shoe was on the guard above the steampipe. The car smelled like some dismal classroom. The passengers seemed asleep and apart, and Blake felt that he might never escape the smell of heat and wet clothing and the dimness of the light. He tried to summon the calculated self-deceptions with which he sometimes cheered himself, but he was left without any energy for hope of self-deception.

The conductor put his head in the door and said, "Shady Hill, next, Shady Hill."

"Now," she said. "Now you get out ahead of me."

Mr. Watkins waked suddenly, put on his coat and hat, and smiled at Mrs. Compton, who was gathering her parcels to her in a series of maternal gestures. They went to the door. Blake joined them, but neither of them spoke to him or seemed to notice the woman at his back. The conductor threw open the door, and Blake saw on the platform of the next car a few other neighbors who had missed the express, waiting patiently and tiredly in the wan light for their trip to end. He raised his head to see through the open door the abandoned mansion out of town, a NO TRESPASSING sign nailed to a tree, and then the oil tanks. The concrete abutments of the bridge passed, so close to the open door that he could have touched them. Then he saw the first of the lampposts on the northbound platform, the sign SHADY HILL in black and gold, and the little lawn and flower bed kept up by the Improvement Association, and then the cab stand and a corner of the old-fashioned depot. It was raining again; it was pouring. He could hear the splash of water and see the lights reflected in puddles and in the shining pavement, and the idle sound of splashing and dripping formed in his mind a conception of shelter, so light and strange that it seemed to belong to a time of his life that he could not remember.

He went down the steps with her at his back. A dozen or so cars were waiting by the station with their motors running. A few people got off from each of the other coaches; he recognized most of them, but none of them offered to give him a ride. They walked separately or in pairs — purposefully out of the rain to the shelter of the platform, where the car horns called to them. It was time to go home, time for a drink, time for love, time for supper, and he could see the lights on the hill — lights by which children were being bathed, meat cooked, dishes washed — shining in the rain. One by one, the cars picked up the heads of families, until there were only four left. Two of the stranded passengers drove off in the only taxi the village had. "I'm sorry, darling," a woman said tenderly to her husband when she drove up a few minutes later. "All our clocks are slow." The last man looked at his watch, looked at the rain, and then walked off into it, and Blake saw him go as if they had some reason to say goodbye — not as we say goodbye to friends after a party but as we say goodbye when we are faced with an inexorable and unwanted parting of the spirit and the heart. The man's footsteps sounded as he crossed the parking lot to the sidewalk, and then they were lost. In the station, a telephone began to ring. The ringing was loud, evenly spaced, and unanswered. Someone wanted to know about the next train to Albany, but Mr. Flanagan, the stationmaster, had gone home an hour ago. He had turned on all his lights before he went away. They burned in the empty waiting room. They burned, tin-shaded, at intervals up and down the platform and with the peculiar sadness of dim and purposeless lights. They lighted the Hawaiian dancer, the couple drinking a toast, the rubber heel.

"I've never been here before," she said. "I thought it would look different. I didn't think it would look so shabby. Let's get out of the light. Go over there."

His legs felt sore. All his strength was gone. "Go on," she said.

North of the station there were a freight house and a coalyard and an inlet where the butcher and the baker and the man who ran the service station moored the dinghies, from which they fished on Sundays, sunk now to the gunwales with the rain. As he walked toward the freight house, he saw a movement on the ground and heard a scraping sound, and then he saw a rat take its head out of a paper bag and regard him. The rat seized the bag in its teeth and dragged it into a culvert.

"Stop," she said. "Turn around. Oh, I ought to feel sorry for you. Look at your poor face. But you don't know what I've been through. I'm afraid to go out in the daylight. I'm afraid the blue sky will fall down on me. I'm like poor Chicken-Licken. I only feel like myself when it begins to get dark. But still and all I'm better than you. I still have good dreams sometimes. I dream about picnics and heaven and the brotherhood of man, and about castles in the moonlight and a river with willow trees all along the edge of it and foreign cities, and after all I know more about love than you."

He heard from off the dark river the drone of an outboard motor, a sound that drew slowly behind it across the dark water such a burden of clear, sweet memories of gone summers and gone pleasures that it made his flesh crawl, and he thought of dark in the mountains and the children singing. "They never wanted to cure me," she said. "They . . ." The noise of a train coming down from the north drowned out her voice, but she went on talking. The noise filled his ears, and the windows where people ate, drank, slept, and read flew past. When the train had passed beyond the bridge, the noise grew distant, and he heard her screaming at him, "*Kneel down! Kneel down! Do what I say. Kneel down!*"

He got to his knees. He bent his head. "There," she said. "You see, if you do what I say, I won't harm you, because I really don't want to harm you, I want to help you, but when I see your face it sometimes seems to me that I can't help you. Sometimes it seems to me that if I were good and loving and sane — oh, much better than I am — sometimes it seems to me that if I were all these things and young and beautiful, too, and if I called to show you the right way, you wouldn't heed me. Oh, I'm better than you, I'm better than you, and I shouldn't waste my time or spoil my life like this. Put your face in the dirt. *Put your face in the dirt!* Do what I say. Put your face in the dirt."

He fell forward in the filth. The coal skinned his face. He stretched out on the ground, weeping. "Now I feel better," she said. "Now I can wash my hands of you, I can wash my hands of all this, because you see there is some kindness, some saneness in me that I can find and use. I can wash my hands." Then he heard her footsteps go away from him, over the rubble. He heard the clearer and more distant sound they made on the hard surface of the platform. He heard them diminish. He raised his head. He saw her climb the stairs of the wooden footbridge and cross it and go down to the other platform, where her figure in the dim light looked small, common, and harmless. He raised himself out of the dust — warily at first, until he saw by her attitude, her looks, that she had forgotten him; that she had completed what she had wanted to do, and that he was safe. He got to his feet and picked up his hat from the ground where it had fallen and walked home.

Questions for Discussion

1. Describe the story's tone and point of view. How does the narrator manage to suggest a critical attitude while concentrating primarily on Blake's thoughts and feelings?

2. What does the narrator's first comment about Miss Dent ("She had no legitimate business with him") reveal about Blake's character and values? Give examples of other comments, judgments, and action that seem critical of Blake.

3. What is suggested about Blake and his values by his manner of dress and grooming, and by the decorator's window into which he stares before noticing the reflection of Miss Dent?

4. What quality of Blake's character is suggested by his retreat into the bar? Why does Blake select his women for their "lack of self-esteem"? How does he relate to his wife and son?

5. In the scene in which she confronts Blake and asks him to "kneel down," what ideas does Miss Dent express about love, madness, and religion? How would you evaluate her gesture and her ideas? Is she simply insane? Is she in any sense inspired?

Ideas for Writing

1. Write an essay in which you evaluate Blake's final realization: has he been reformed through his encounter with Miss Dent, or is he exactly the same?

2. Write a story about a character who confronts and humiliates a former supervisor or ex-lover who has taken advantage of him or her at some point in the past.

TILLIE OLSEN   (b. 1913)

Because of the demands of motherhood and work, Tillie Olsen didn't write seriously until she was in her early forties, when her youngest daughter started school. Time to write came as "stolen moments . . . in the deep night hours for as long as I could stay awake, after the kids were in bed, after the household tasks were done, sometimes during. It is no accident that the first work I considered publishable began: 'I stand here ironing.'"

Olsen was born and raised in Omaha, Nebraska, by parents who were political refugees of the 1905 Russian Revolution; her father was a socialist. Olsen left high school in eleventh grade to work to help support her family. Married twice, she raised four children with her husband Jack Olsen, a printer, and continued the family tradition of labor organizing. Olsen won the O. Henry Award for the best American short story of 1961 with "Tell Me a Riddle," which, along with "I Stand Here Ironing," is included in her story collection *Tell Me a Riddle*. Because of the success of this collection, Olsen was awarded writing grants that made it possible for her to complete *Yonnondio: From the Thirties* (1974), a novel about a poor, working-class family. *Silences* (1978), a volume of prose, explores how the work situations and family obligations in women's lives affect their creativity. Olsen has spoken of her subject matter in her writing as "the unnatural thwarting of what struggles to come into being but cannot."

I Stand Here Ironing   (1956)

I stand here ironing, and what you asked me moves tormented back and forth with the iron.

"I wish you would manage the time to come in and talk with me about your daughter. I'm sure you can help me understand her. She's a youngster who needs help and whom I'm deeply interested in helping."

"Who needs help." Even if I came, what good would it do? You think because I am her mother I have a key, or that in some way you could use me as a key? She has lived for nineteen years. There is all that life that has happened outside of me, beyond me.

And when is there time to remember, to sift, to weigh, to estimate, to total? I will start and there will be an interruption and I will have to gather it all together again. Or I will become engulfed with all I did or did not do, with what should have been and what cannot be helped.

She was a beautiful baby. The first and only one of our five that was beautiful at birth. You do not guess how new and uneasy her tenancy in her now-loveliness. You did not know her all those years she was thought homely, or see her poring over her baby pictures, making me tell her over and over how beautiful she had been — and would be, I would tell her — and was now, to the seeing eye. But the seeing eyes were few or non-existent. Including mine.

I nursed her. They feel that's important nowadays. I nursed all the children, but with her, with all the fierce rigidity of first motherhood, I did like the books then said. Though her cries battered me to trembling and my breasts ached with swollenness, I waited till the clock decreed.

Why do I put that first? I do not even know if it matters, or if it explains anything.

She was a beautiful baby. She blew shining bubbles of sound. She loved motion, loved light, loved color and music and textures. She would lie on the floor in her blue overalls patting the surface so hard in ecstasy her hands and feet would blur. She was a miracle to me, but when she was eight months old I had to leave her daytimes with the woman downstairs to whom she was no miracle at all, for I worked or looked for work and for Emily's father, who "could no longer endure" (he wrote in his good-bye note) "sharing want with us."

I was nineteen. It was the pre-relief, pre-WPA world of the depression. I would start running as soon as I got off the streetcar, running up the stairs, the place smelling sour, and awake or asleep to startle awake, when she saw me she would break into a clogged weeping that could not be comforted, a weeping I can hear yet.

After a while I found a job hashing at night so I could be with her days, and it was better. But it came to where I had to bring her to his family and leave her.

It took a long time to raise the money for her fare back. Then she got chicken pox and I had to wait longer. When she finally came, I hardly knew her, walking quick and nervous like her father, looking like her father, thin, and dressed in a shoddy red that yellowed her skin and glared at the pockmarks. All the baby loveliness gone.

She was two. Old enough for nursery school they said, and I did not know then what I know now — the fatigue of the long day, and the lacerations of group life in the nurseries that are only parking places for children.

Except that it would have made no difference if I had known. It was the only place there was. It was the only way we could be together, the only way I could hold a job.

And even without knowing, I knew. I knew the teacher that was evil because all these years it has curdled into my memory, the little boy hunched in the corner, her rasp, "why aren't you outside, because Alvin hits you? that's no reason, go out, scaredy." I knew Emily hated it even if she did not clutch and implore "don't go Mommy" like the other children, mornings.

She always had a reason why she should stay home. Momma, you look sick, Momma. I feel sick. Momma, the teachers aren't there today, they're sick. Momma, we can't go, there was a fire there last night. Momma, it's a holiday today, no school, they told me.

But never a direct protest, never rebellion. I think of our others in their three-, four-year-oldness — the explosions, the tempers, the denunciations, the demands — and I feel suddenly ill. I put the iron down. What in me demanded that goodness in her? And what was the cost, the cost to her of such goodness?

The old man living in the back once said in his gentle way: "You should smile at Emily more when you look at her." What *was* in my face when I looked at her? I loved her. There were all the acts of love.

It was only with the others I remembered what he said, and it was the face of joy, and not of care or tightness or worry I turned to them — too late for Emily. She does not smile easily, let alone almost always as her brothers and sisters do. Her face is closed and sombre, but when she wants, how fluid. You must have seen it in her pantomimes, you spoke of her rare gift for comedy on the stage that rouses a laughter out of the audience so dear they applaud and applaud and do not want to let her go.

Where does it come from, that comedy? There was none of it in her when she came back to me that second time, after I had had to send her away again. She had a new daddy now to learn to love, and I think perhaps it was a better time.

Except when we left her alone nights, telling ourselves she was old enough.

"Can't you go some other time, Mommy, like tomorrow?" she would ask. "Will it be just a little while you'll be gone? Do you promise?"

The time we came back, the front door open, the clock on the floor in the hall. She rigid awake. "It wasn't just a little while. I didn't cry. Three times I called you, just three times, and then I ran downstairs to open the door so you could come faster. The clock talked loud. I threw it away, it scared me what it talked."

She said the clock talked loud again that night I went to the hospital to have Susan. She was delirious with the fever that comes before red measles, but she was fully conscious all the week I was gone and the week after we were home when she could not come near the new baby or me.

She did not get well. She stayed skeleton thin, not wanting to eat, and night after night she had nightmares. She would call for me, and I would rouse from exhaustion to sleepily call back: "You're all right, darling, go to sleep, it's just a dream," and if she still called, in a sterner voice, "now go to sleep, Emily, there's nothing to hurt you." Twice, only twice, when I had to get up for Susan anyhow, I went in to sit with her.

Now when it is too late (as if she would let me hold and comfort her like I do the others) I get up and go to her at once at her moan or restless stirring. "Are you awake, Emily? Can I get you something?" And the answer is always the same: "No, I'm all right, go back to sleep, Mother."

They persuaded me at the clinic to send her away to a convalescent home in the country where "she can have the kind of food and care you can't manage for her, and you'll be free to concentrate on the new baby." They still send children to that place. I see pictures on the society page of sleek young women planning affairs to raise money for it, or dancing at the affairs, or decorating Easter eggs or filling Christmas stockings for the children.

They never have a picture of the children so I do not know if the girls still wear those gigantic red bows and the ravaged looks on the every other Sunday when parents can come to visit "unless otherwise notified" — as we were notified the first six weeks.

Oh it is a handsome place, green lawns and tall trees and fluted flower beds. High up on the balconies of each cottage the children stand, the girls in their red bows and white dresses, the boys in white suits and giant red ties. The parents stand below shrieking up to be heard and the children shriek down to be heard, and between them the invisible wall "Not To Be Contaminated by Parental Germs or Physical Affection."

There was a tiny girl who always stood hand in hand with Emily. Her parents never came. One visit she was gone. "They moved her to Rose College," Emily shouted in explanation. "They don't like you to love anybody here."

She wrote once a week, the labored writing of a seven-year-old. "I am fine. How is the baby. If I write my leter nicly I will have a star. Love." There never was a star. We wrote every other day, letters she could never hold or keep but only hear read — once. "We simply do not have room for children to keep any personal possessions," they patiently explained when we pieced one Sunday's shrieking together to plead how much it would mean to Emily, who loved so to keep things, to be allowed to keep her letters and cards.

Each visit she looked frailer. "She isn't eating," they told us.

(They had runny eggs for breakfast or mush with lumps, Emily said later, I'd hold it in my mouth and not swallow. Nothing ever tasted good, just when they had chicken.)

It took us eight months to get her released home, and only the fact that she gained back so little of her seven lost pounds convinced the social worker.

I used to try to hold and love her after she came back, but her body would stay stiff, and after a while she'd push away. She ate little. Food sickened her, and I think much of life too. Oh she had physical lightness and brightness, twinkling by on skates, bouncing like a ball up and down up and down over the jump rope, skimming over the hill; but these were momentary.

She fretted about her appearance, thin and dark and foreign-looking at a time when every little girl was supposed to look or thought she should look a chubby blonde replica of Shirley Temple. The doorbell sometimes rang for her, but no one seemed to come and play in the house or be a best friend. Maybe because we moved so much.

There was a boy she loved painfully through two school semesters. Months later she told me how she had taken pennies from my purse to buy him candy. "Licorice was his favorite and I brought him some every day, but he still like Jennifer better'n me. Why, Mommy?" The kind of question for which there is no answer.

School was a worry to her. She was not glib or quick in a world where glibness and quickness were easily confused with ability to learn. To her overworked and exasperated teachers she was an overconscientious "slow learner" who kept trying to catch up and was absent entirely too often.

I let her be absent, though sometimes the illness was imaginary. How different from my now-strictness about attendance with the others. I wasn't working. We had a new baby, I was home anyhow. Sometimes, after Susan grew old enough, I would keep her home from school, too, to have them all together.

Mostly Emily had asthma, and her breathing, harsh and labored, would fill the house with a curiously tranquil sound. I would bring the two old dresser mirrors and her boxes of collections to her bed. She would select beads and single earrings, bottle tops and shells, dried flowers and pebbles, old postcards and scraps, all sorts of oddments; then she and Susan would play Kingdom, setting up landscapes and furniture, peopling them with action.

Those were the only times of peaceful companionship between her and Susan. I have edged away from it, that poisonous feeling between them, that terrible balancing of hurts and needs I had to do between the two, and did so badly, those earlier years.

Oh there are conflicts between the others too, each one human, needing, demanding, hurting, taking—but only between Emily and Susan, no, Emily toward Susan that corroding resentment. It seems so obvious on the surface, yet it is not obvious. Susan, the second child, Susan, golden- and curly-haired and chubby, quick and articulate and assured, everything in appearance and manner Emily was not; Susan, not able to resist Emily's precious things, losing or sometimes clumsily breaking them; Susan telling jokes and riddles to company for applause while Emily sat silent (to say to me later: that was *my* riddle, Mother, I told it to Susan); Susan, who for all the five years' difference in age was just a year behind Emily in developing physically.

I am glad for that slow physical development that widened the difference between her and her contemporaries, though she suffered over it. She was too vulnerable for that terrible world of youthful competition, of preening and parading, of constant measuring of yourself against every other, of envy, "If I had that copper hair," "If I had that skin. . . ." She tormented herself enough about not looking like the others, there was enough of the unsureness, the having to be conscious of words before you speak, the constant caring—what are they thinking of me? without having it all magnified by the merciless physical drives.

Ronnie is calling. He is wet and I change him. It is rare there is such a cry now. That time of motherhood is almost behind me when the ear is not one's own but must always be racked and listening for the child cry, the child call. We sit for a while and I hold him, looking out over the city spread in charcoal with its soft aisles of light *"Shoogily,"* he breathes and curls closer. I carry him back to bed, asleep. *Shoogily.* A funny word, a family word, inherited from Emily, invented by her to say: *comfort.*

In this and other ways she leaves her seal, I say aloud. And startle at my saying it. What do I mean? What did I start to gather together, to try and make coherent? I was at the terrible, growing years. War years. I do not remember them well. I was working, there were four smaller ones now, there was not time for her. She had to help be a mother, and housekeeper, and shopper. She had to set her seal. Mornings of crisis and near hysteria trying to get lunches packed, hair combed, coats and shoes found, everyone to school or Child Care on time, the baby ready for transportation. And always the paper scribbled on by a smaller one, the book looked at by Susan then mislaid, the homework not done. Running out to that huge school where she was one, she was lost, she was a drop; suffering over the unpreparedness, stammering and unsure in her classes.

There was so little time left at night after the kids were bedded down. She would struggle over books, always eating (it was in those years she developed her enormous appetite that is legendary in our family) and I would be ironing, or preparing food for the next day, or writing V-mail to Bill, or tending the baby. Sometimes, to make me laugh, or out of her despair, she would imitate happenings or types at school.

I think I said once: "Why don't you do something like this in the school amateur show?" One morning she phoned me at work, hardly understandable through the weeping: "Mother, I did it. I won, I won; they gave me first prize; they clapped and clapped and wouldn't let me go."

Now suddenly she was Somebody, and as imprisoned in her difference as she had been in anonymity.

She began to be asked to perform at other high schools, even in colleges, then at city and statewide affairs. The first one we went to, I only recognized her that first moment when thin, shy, she almost drowned herself into the curtains. Then: Was this Emily? The control, the command, the convulsing and deadly clowning, the spell, then the roaring, stamping audience, unwilling to let this rare and precious laughter out of their lives.

Afterwards: You ought to do something about her with a gift like that — but without money or knowing how, what does one do? We have left it all to her, and the gift has as often eddied inside, clogged and clotted, as been used and growing.

She is coming. She runs up the stairs two at a time with her light graceful step, and I know she is happy tonight. Whatever it was that occasioned your call did not happen today.

"Aren't you ever going to finish the ironing, Mother? Whistler painted his mother in a rocker. I'd have to paint mine standing over an ironing board." This is one of her communicative nights and she tells me everything and nothing as she fixes herself a plate of food out of the icebox.

She is so lovely. Why did you want me to come in at all? Why were you concerned? She will find her way.

She starts up the stairs to bed. "Don't get me up with the rest in the morning." "But I thought you were having midterms." "Oh, those," she comes back in, kisses me, and says quite lightly, "in a couple of years when we'll all be atom-dead they won't matter a bit."

She has said it before. She *believes* it. But because I have been dredging the past, and all that compounds a human being is so heavy and meaningful in me, I cannot endure it tonight.

I will never total it all. I will never come in to say: She was a child seldom smiled at. Her father left me before she was a year old. I had to work her first six years when there was work, or I sent her home and to his relatives. There were years she had care she hated. She was dark and thin and foreign-looking in a world where the prestige went to blondeness and curly hair and dimples, she was slow where glibness was prized. She was a child of anxious, not proud, love. We were poor and could not afford for her the soil of easy growth. I was a young mother, I was a distracted mother. There were the other children pushing up, demanding. Her younger sister seemed all that she was not. There were years she did not want me to touch her. She kept too much in herself, her life was such she had to keep too much in herself. My wisdom came too late. She has much to her and probably nothing will come of it. She is a child of her age, of depression, of war, of fear.

Let her be. So all that is in her will not bloom — but in how many does it? There is still enough left to live by. Only help her to know — help make it so there is cause for her to know — that she is more than this dress on the ironing board, helpless before the iron.

[handwritten margin note: blaming external circumstances?]

Questions for Discussion

1. Why does Olsen open and close her story with an image of the mother sifting through the experiences of her daughter's life while standing and ironing? What symbolism does ironing come to have in the story?

2. The narrator's monologue is in part a response to a note from her daughter's high school counselor, who believes that Emily "needs help." What effect does the counselor's implied criticism have on the narrator's response? *[handwritten: defensive]*

3. What tone of voice do you hear through the narrator's sentence structure and rhythms of speech? What do the narrator's speech patterns reveal about her level of education and her feelings about her daughter?

4. Why is the mother mistrustful of social institutions that are supposed to help parents to raise their children? What evidence does she provide to support her criticism of "helping" institutions? Is she convincing?

5. The mother asks, "Where does it come from, that comedy?" Why does Emily become a comedian? *[handwritten: glimmer of hope. human nature is strong]*

Ideas for Writing

1. Retell the story from Emily's point of view. Would she come across as more or less troubled and rebellious than the counselor believes her to be?

2. Write an essay that discusses the mother's monologue as a statement about her parenting. Do you think that she was and is a "good mother"?

BERNARD MALAMUD   (1914–1986)

One of the most widely read urban Jewish writers of our time, Bernard Malamud created stories that combine fantasy and realism, suffering and hope, comedy and pathos, success and failure, happiness and despair. Malamud grew up in Brooklyn, New York, where his Russian immigrant parents owned a small grocery store. After earning his B.A. from City College in 1936, Malamud worked at odd jobs while completing a graduate degree in English at Columbia University. He taught night school in New York City from 1940 to 1945, then joined the faculty of Oregon State University and later moved to Bennington College in Vermont. Malamud also traveled and lectured in the United States and throughout the world. His novels include *The Natural* (1952) and *The Fixer* (1966), which won the National Book Award and the Pulitzer prize. Malamud's several story collections include *The Magic Barrel* (1958), winner of the National Book Award; "Angel Levine" is from that collection. His *Collected Stories* was published in 1983.

Of the stories in *The Magic Barrel,* one critic wrote, "These are sparse, densely concentrated tales . . . dealing most often with the possibility of spiritual growth, and characterized by a conversational directness that owes a great deal to the Yiddish tradition of oral storytelling."

Angel Levine   (1955)

Manischevitz, a tailor, in his fifty-first year suffered many reverses and indignities. Previously a man of comfortable means, he overnight lost all he had, when his establishment caught fire, after a metal container of cleaning fluid exploded, and burned to the ground. Although Manischevitz was insured against fire, damage suits by two customers who had been hurt in the flames deprived him of every penny he had saved. At almost the same time, his son, of much promise, was killed in the war, and his daughter, without so much as a word of warning, married a lout and disappeared with him as off the face of the earth. Thereafter Manischevitz was victimized by excruciating backaches and found himself unable to work even as a presser — the only kind of work available to him — for more then an hour or two daily, because beyond that the pain from standing was maddening. His Fanny, a good wife and mother, who had taken in washing and sewing, began before his eyes to waste away. Suffering shortness of breath, she at last became seriously ill and took to her bed. The doctor, a former customer of Manischevitz, who out of pity treated them, at first had difficulty diagnosing her ailment, but later put it down as hardening of the arteries at an advanced age. He took Manischevitz aside, prescribed complete rest for her, and in whispers gave him to know there was little hope.

Throughout his trials Manischevitz had remained somewhat stoic, almost unbelieving that all this had descended on his head, as if it were happening, let us say, to an acquaintance or some distant relative; it was in sheer quantity of woe, incomprehensible. It was also ridiculous, unjust, and because he had always been a religious man, an affront to God. Manischevitz believed this in all his suffering. When his burden had grown too crushingly heavy to be borne he prayed in his chair with shut hollow eyes: "My dear God, sweetheart, did I deserve that this should happen to me?" Then recognizing the worthlessness of it, he set aside the complaint and prayed humbly for assistance: "Give Fanny back her health, and to me for myself that I shouldn't feel pain in every step. Help now or tomorrow is too late." And Manischevitz wept.

Manischevitz's flat, which he had moved into after the disastrous fire, was a meager one, furnished with a few sticks of chairs, a table, and bed, in one of the poorer sections of the city. There were three rooms: a small, poorly papered living room; an apology for a kitchen with a wooden icebox; and the comparatively large bedroom where Fanny lay in a sagging secondhand bed, gasping for breath. The bedroom was the warmest room in the house and it was here, after his outburst to God, that Manischevitz, by the light of two small bulbs overhead, sat reading his Jewish newspaper. He was not truly reading because his thoughts were everywhere; however the print offered a convenient resting place for his eyes, and a word or two, when he permitted himself to comprehend them, had the momentary effect of helping him forget his troubles. After a short while he discovered, to his surprise, that he was actively scanning the news, searching for an item of great interest to him. Exactly what he thought he would read he couldn't say — until he realized, with some astonishment, that he was expecting to discover something about himself. Manischevitz put his paper down and looked up with the distinct impression that someone had come into the apartment, though he could not remember having heard the sound of the door opening. He looked around: the room was very still, Fanny sleeping, for once, quietly. Half frightened, he watched her until he was satisfied she wasn't dead; then, still disturbed by the thought of an unannounced visitor, he stumbled into the living room and there had the shock of his life, for at the table sat a black man reading a newspaper he had folded up to fit into one hand.

"What do you want here?" Manischevitz asked in fright.

The Negro put down the paper and glanced up with a gentle expression. "Good evening." He seemed not to be sure of himself, as if he had got into the wrong house. He was a large man, bonily built, with a heavy head covered by a hard derby, which he made no attempt to remove. His eyes seemed sad, but his lips, about which he wore a slight mustache, sought to smile; he was not otherwise prepossessing. The cuffs of his sleeves, Manischevitz noted, were frayed to the lining, and the dark suit was badly fitted. He had very large feet. Recovering from his fright, Manischevitz guessed he had left the door open and was being visited by a case worker from the Welfare Department—some came at night—for he had recently applied for welfare. Therefore he lowered himself into a chair opposite the Negro, trying, before the man's uncertain smile, to feel comfortable. The former tailor sat stiffly but patiently at the table, waiting for the investigator to take out his pad and pencil and begin asking questions; but before long he became convinced the man intended to do nothing of the sort.

"Who are you?" Manischevitz at last asked uneasily.

"If I may, insofar as one is able to, identify myself, I bear the name of Alexander Levine."

In spite of his troubles, Manischevitz felt a smile growing on his lips. "You said Levine?" he politely inquired.

The Negro nodded. "That is exactly right."

Carrying the jest further, Manischevitz asked, "You are maybe Jewish?"

"All my life I was, willingly."

The tailor hesitated. He had heard of black Jews but had never met one. It gave an unusual sensation.

Recognizing in afterthought something odd about the tense of Levine's remark, he said doubtfully, "You ain't Jewish any more?"

Levine at this point removed his hat, reveling a white part in his black hair, but quickly replaced it. He replied, "I have recently been disincarnated into an angel. As such, I offer you my humble assistance, if to offer is within my province and power — in the best sense." He lowered his eyes in apology. "Which calls for added explanation: I am what I am granted to be, and at present the completion is in the future."

"What kind of angel is this?" Manischevitz gravely asked.

"A bona fide angel of God, within prescribed limitations," answered Levine, "not to be confused with the members of any particular sect, order, or organization here on earth operating under a similar name."

Manischevitz was thoroughly disturbed. He had been expecting something, but not this. What sort of mockery was it — provided that Levine was an angel — of a faithful servant who had from childhood lived in the synagogues, concerned with the word of God?

To test Levine he asked, "Then where are your wings?"

The Negro blushed as well as he could. Manischevitz understood this from his altered expression. "Under certain circumstances we lose privileges and prerogatives upon returning to earth, no matter for what purpose or endeavoring to assist whomsoever."

"So tell me," Manischevitz said triumphantly, "how did you get here?"

"I was translated."

Still troubled, the tailor said, "If you are a Jew, say the blessing for bread."

Levine recited it in sonorous Hebrew.

Although moved by the familiar words Manischevitz still felt doubt he was dealing with an angel.

"If you are an angel," he demanded somewhat angrily, "give me the proof."

Levine wet his lips. "Frankly, I cannot perform either miracles or near-miracles, due to the fact that I am in a condition of probation. How long that will persist or even consist depends on the outcome."

Manischevitz racked his brains for some means of causing Levine positively to reveal his true identity, when the Negro spoke again:

"It was given me to understand that both your wife and you require assistance of a salubrious nature?"

The tailor could not rid himself of the feeling that he was the butt of a jokester. Is this what a Jewish angel looks like? he asked himself. This I am not convinced.

He asked a last question. "So if God sends to me an angel, why a black? Why not a white that there are so many of them?"

"It was my turn to go next," Levine explained.

Manischevitz could not be persuaded. "I think you are a faker."

Levine slowly rose. His eyes indicated disappointment and worry. "Mr. Manischevitz," he said tonelessly, "if you should desire me to be of assistance to you any time in the near future, or possibly before, I can be found" — he glanced at his fingernails — "in Harlem."

He was by then gone.

The next day Manischevitz felt: some relief from his backache and was able to work four hours at pressing. The day after, he put in six hours; and the third day four again. Fanny sat up a little and asked for some halvah to suck. But after the fourth day the stabbing, breaking ache afflicted his back, and Fanny again lay supine, breathing with bluelipped difficulty.

Manischevitz was profoundly disappointed at the return of his active pain and suffering. He had hoped for a longer interval of easement, long enough to have a thought other than of himself and his troubles. Day by day, minute after minute, he lived in pain, pain his only memory, questioning the necessity of it, inveighing, though with affection, against God. Why *so much*, Gottenyu? If He wanted to teach His servant a lesson for some reason, some cause — the nature of His nature — to teach him, say, for reasons of his weakness, his pride, perhaps, during his years of prosperity, his frequent neglect of God — to give him a little lesson, why then any of the tragedies that had happened to him, any *one* would have sufficed to chasten him. But *all together* — the loss of both his children, his means of livelihood, Fanny's health and his — that was too much to ask one frail-boned man to endure. Who, after all, was Manischevitz that he had been given so much to suffer? A tailor. Certainly not a man of talent. Upon him suffering was largely wasted. It went nowhere, into nothing: into more suffering. His pain did not earn him bread, nor fill the cracks in the wall, nor lift, in the middle of the night, the kitchen table; only lay upon him, sleepless, so sharply oppressive that he could many times have cried out yet not heard himself this misery.

In this mood he gave no thought to Mr. Alexander Levine, but at moments which the pain wavered, slightly diminishing, he sometimes wondered if he had been mistaken to dismiss him. A black Jew and angel to boot — very hard to believe, but suppose he had been sent to succor him, and he, Manischevitz, was in his blindness too blind to understand? It was this thought that put him on the knife-point of agony.

Therefore the tailor, after much self-questioning and continuing doubt, decided he would seek the self-styled angel in Harlem. Of course he had great difficulty because he had not asked for specific directions, and movement was tedious to him. The subway took him to 116th Street, and from there he wandered in the open dark world. It was vast and its lights lit nothing. Everywhere were shadows, often moving. Manischevitz hobbled along with the aid of a cane, and not knowing where to seek in the blackened tenement buildings, would look fruitlessly through store windows. In the stores he saw people and everybody was black. It was an amazing thing to observe. When he was too tired, too unhappy to go farther, Manischevitz stopped in front of a tailor's shop. Out of familiarity with the appearance of it, with some sadness he entered. The tailor, an old skinny man with a mop of woolly gray hair, was sitting cross-legged on his workbench, sewing a pair of tuxedo pants that had a razor slit all the way down the seat.

"You'll excuse me, please, gentleman," said Manischevitz, admiring the tailor's deft thimbled fingerwork, "but you know maybe somebody by the name Alexander Levine?"

The tailor, who, Manischevitz thought, seemed a little antagonistic to him, scratched his scalp.

"Cain't say I ever heared dat name."

"Alex-ander Lev-ine," Manischevitz repeated it.

The man shook his head. "Cain's say I heared."

Manischevitz remembered to say: "He is an angel, maybe."

"Oh *him*" said the tailor, clucking. "He hang out in dat honky-tonk down here a ways." He pointed with his skinny finger and returned to sewing the pants.

Manischevitz crossed the street against a red light and was almost run down by a taxi. On the block after the next, the sixth store from the corner was a cabaret, and the name in sparkling lights was Bella's. Ashamed to go in, Manischevitz gazed through the neon-lit window, and when the dancing couples had parted and drifted away, he discovered at a table on the side, toward the rear, Alexander Levine.

He was sitting alone, a cigarette butt hanging from the corner of his mouth, playing solitaire with a dirty pack of cards, and Manischevitz felt a touch of pity for him, because Levine had deteriorated in appearance. His derby hat was dented and had a gray smudge. His ill-fitting suit was shabbier, as if he had been sleeping in it. His shoes and trouser cuffs were muddy, and his face covered with an impenetrable stubble the color of licorice.

Manischevitz, though disappointed, was about to enter, when a big-breasted Negress in a purple evening gown appeared before Levine's table, and with much laughter through many white teeth, broke into a vigorous shimmy. Levine looked at Manischevitz with a haunted expression, but the tailor was too paralyzed to move or acknowledge it. As Bella's gyrations continued Levine rose, his eyes lit in excitement. She embraced him with vigor, both his hands clasped around her restless buttocks, and they tangoed together across the floor, loudly applauded by the customers. She seemed to have lifted Levine off his feet and his large shoes hung lip as they danced. They slid past the windows where Manischevitz, white-faced, stood staring in. Levine walked slyly and the tailor left for home.

Fanny lay at death's door. Through shrunken lips she muttered concerning her childhood, the sorrows of the marriage bed, the loss of her children; yet wept to live. Manischevitz tried not to listen, but even without ears he would have heard. It was not a gift. The doctor panted up the stairs, a broad but bland, unshaven man (it was Sunday), and soon shook his head. A day at most, or two. He left at once to spare himself Manischevitz's multiplied sorrow; the man who never stopped hurting. He would someday get him into a public home.

Manischevitz visited a synagogue and there spoke to God, but God had absented himself. The tailor searched his heart and found no hope. When she died, he would live dead. He considered taking his life although he knew he wouldn't. Yet it was something to consider. Considering, you existed. He railed against God — Can you love a rock, a broom, an emptiness? Baring his chest, he smote the naked bones, cursing himself for having, beyond belief, believed.

Asleep in a chair that afternoon, he dreamed of Levine. He was standing before a faded mirror, preening small decaying opalescent wings. "This means," mumbled Manischevitz, as he broke out of sleep, "that it is possible he could be an angel." Begging a neighbor lady to look in on Fanny and occasionally wet her lips with water, he drew on his thin coat, gripped his walking stick, exchanged some pennies for a subway token, and rode to Harlem. He knew this act was the last desperate one of his woe: to go seeking a black magician to restore his wife to invalidism. Yet if there was no choice, he did at least what was chosen.

He hobbled to Bella's, but the place seemed to have changed hands. It was now, as he breathed, a synagogue in a store. In the front, toward him, were several rows of empty wooden benches. In the rear stood the Ark, its portals of rough wood covered with rainbows of sequins; under it a long table on which lay the sacred scroll unrolled, illuminated by the dim light from a bulb on a chain overhead. Around the table, as if frozen to it and the scroll, which they all touched with their fingers, sat four Negroes wearing skullcaps. Now as they read the Holy Word, Manischevitz could, through the plate-glass window, hear the singsong chant of their voices. One of them was old, with a gray beard. One was bubble-eyed. One was humpbacked. The fourth was a boy, no older than thirteen. Their heads moved in rhythmic swaying. Touched by this sight from his childhood and youth, Manischevitz entered and stood silent in the rear.

"Neshoma," said bubble eyes, pointing to the word with a stubby finger. "Now what dat mean?"

"That's the word that means soul," said the boy. He wore eyeglasses.

"Let's git on wid de commentary," said the old man.

"Ain't necessary," said the humpback. "Souls is immaterial substance. That's all. The soul is derived in that manner. The immateriality is derived from the substance, and they both, causally an' otherwise, derived from the soul. There can be no higher."

"That's the highest."

"Over de top."

"Wait a minute," said bubble eyes. "I don't see what is dat immaterial substance. How come de one gits hitched up to de odder?" He addressed the humpback.

"Ask me somethin' hard. Because it is substanceless immateriality. It couldn't be closer together, like all the parts of the body under one skin — closer."

"Hear now," said the old man.

"All you done is switched de words."

"It's the premium mobile, the substanceless substance from which comes all things that were incepted in the idea — you, me, and everything and -body else."

"Now how did all dat happen? Make it sound simple."

"It de speerit," said the old man. "On de face of de water moved de speerit. An' dat was good. It say so in de Book. From de speerit ariz de man."

"But now listen here. How come it become substance if it all de time a spirit?"

"God alone done dat."

"Holy! Holy! Praise His Name."

"But has dis spirit got some kind of a shade or color?" asked bubble eyes, deadpan.

"Man, of course not. A spirit is a spirit."

"Then how come we is colored?" he said with a triumphant glare.

"Ain't got nothing to do wid dat."

"I still like to know."

"God put the spirit in all things," answered the boy. "He put it in the green leaves and the yellow flowers. He put it with the gold in the fishes and the blue in the sky. That's how come it came to us."

"Amen."

"Praise Lawd and utter loud His speechless Name."

"Blow de bugle till it bust the sky."

They fell silent, intent upon the next word. Manischevitz, with doubt, approached them.

"You'll excuse me," he said. "I am looking for Alexander Levine. You know him maybe?"

"That's the angel," said the boy.

"Oh *him*," snuffed bubble eyes.

"You'll find him at Bella's. It's the establishment right down the street," the humpback said.

Manischevitz said he was sorry that he could not stay, thanked them, and limped across the street. It was already night. The city was dark and he could barely find his way.

But Bella's was bursting with jazz and the blues. Through the window Manischevitz recognized the dancing crowd and among them sought Levine. He was sitting loose-lipped at Bella's side table. They were tippling from an almost empty whiskey fifth. Levine had shed his old clothes, wore a shiny new checkered suit, pearl-gray derby hat, cigar, and big, two-tone, button shoes. To the tailor's dismay, a drunken look had settled upon his formerly dignified face. He leaned toward Bella, tickled her earlobe with his pinky while whispering words that sent her into gales of raucous laughter. She fondled his knee.

Manischevitz, girding himself, pushed open the door and was not welcomed.

"This place reserved."

"Beat it, pale puss."

"Exit, Yankel, semitic trash."

But he moved toward the table where Levine sat, the crowd breaking before him as he hobbled forward.

"Mr. Levine," he spoke in a trembly voice. "Is here Manischevitz."

Levine glared blearily. "Speak yo' piece, son."

Manischevitz shivered. His back plagued him. Tremors tormented his legs. He looked around, everybody was all ears.

"You'll excuse me. I would like to talk to you in a private place."

"Speak, Ah is a private pusson."

Bella laughed piercingly. "Stop it, boy, you killin' me."

Manischevitz, no end disturbed, considered fleeing but Levine addressed him:

"Kindly state the pu'pose of yo' communication with yo's truly."

The tailor wet cracked lips. "You are Jewish. This I am sure."

Levine rose, nostrils flaring. "Anythin' else yo' got to say?"

Manischevitz's tongue lay like a slab of stone.

"Speak now or fo'ever hold off."

Tears blinded the tailor's eyes. Was ever man so tried? Should he say he believed a half-drunk Negro was an angel?

The silence slowly petrified.

Manischevitz was recalling scenes of his youth as a wheel in his mind whirred: believe, do not, yes, no, yes, no. The pointer pointed to yes, to between yes and no, to no, no it was yes. He sighed. It moved but one still had to make a choice.

"I think you are an angel from God." He said it in a broken voice, thinking, If you said it it was said. If you believed it you must say it. If you believed, you believed.

The hush broke. Everybody talked but the music began and they went on dancing. Bella, grown bored, picked up the cards and dealt herself a hand.

Levine burst into tears. "How you have humiliated me."

Manischevitz apologized.

"Wait'll I freshen up." Levine went to the men's room and returned in his old suit.

No one said goodbye as they left.

They rode to the flat via subway. As they walked up the stairs Manischevitz pointed with his cane at his door.

"That's all been taken care of," Levine said. "You go in while I take off."

Disappointed that it was so soon over, but torn by curiosity, Manischevitz followed the angel up three flights to the roof. When he got there the door was already padlocked.

Luckily he could see through a small broken window. He heard an odd noise, as though of a whirring of wings, and when he strained for a wider view, could have sworn he saw a dark figure borne aloft on a pair of strong black wings.

A feather drifted down. Manischevitz gasped as it turned white, but it was only snowing.

He rushed downstairs. In the flat Fanny wielded a dust mop under the bed, and shell upon the cobwebs on the wall.

"A wonderful thing, Fanny," Manischevitz said. "Believe me, there are Jews everywhere."

Questions for Discussion

1. What is revealed about Manischevitz and his conflicts in the two-paragraph summary of his misfortunes that begins the story?

2. What is suggested about Manischevitz's sophistication and self-awareness through his reading the news to discover something about himself?

3. Why is Angel Levine sent to help Manischevitz? What does the angel and Manischevitz's response to him indicate about the religious and cultural conflicts underlying the story? What social comment is made by the angel's race?

4. Why has God chosen Manischevitz to suffer? In what ways is his suffering both a punishment and a blessing? What does Manischevitz learn from his suffering?

5. Interpret the meaning of the dialogue between the four characters whom Manischevitz meets at the synagogue store.

Ideas for Writing

1. Write an interpretation of the story based on its themes of the power of suffering and of faith, focusing on the relationship between Manischevitz and the angel.

2. Write about the story as a commentary on the relationship between Jews and African Americans. In what ways are Levine and Manischevitz dependent on each other? How are they similar?

RALPH ELLISON   (1914–1994)

Influenced by Joyce, Hemingway, and other modernists, Ralph Ellison adapted their techniques to describe the black experience in America, incorporating elements of folklore as well as the rhythms of jazz. Ellison was born in Oklahoma City; his father died when Ellison was three, and he was raised by his mother, a domestic servant who encouraged him to become a political activist through her work for the Socialist party and nurtured his love of books and music. From 1933 to 1936 Ellison studied music at the Tuskegee Institute in Alabama; then he moved to New York City where he met Richard Wright and Langston Hughes, who encouraged his writing career.

Ellison's first short stories were published in 1939, and in 1942 he became the managing editor of the *Negro Quarterly*. Ellison taught at many colleges and universities, including New York University, where he was the Albert Schweitzer Professor of Contemporary Literature and Culture. Ellison published only one novel in his lifetime, *Invisible Man* (1952), which won the National Book Award in 1953. This much-acclaimed novel uses the metaphor of invisibility to define the status of black men in white America, beginning with the statement "I am a man of substance, of flesh and bone, fiber and liquids — and I might even be said to possess a mind. I am invisible, understand, simply because people refuse to see me." Ellison's short stories are collected in *Flying Home and Other Stories* (1996).

King of the Bingo Game   (1944)

The woman in front of him was eating roasted peanuts that smelled so good that he could barely contain his hunger. He could not even sleep and wished they'd hurry and begin the bingo game. There, on his right, two fellows were drinking wine out of a bottle wrapped in a paper bag, and he could hear soft gurgling in the dark. His stomach gave a low, gnawing growl. "If this was down South," he thought, "all I'd have to do is lean over and say, 'Lady, gimme a few of those peanuts, please ma'm,' and she'd pass me the bag and never think nothing of it." Or he could ask the fellows for a drink in the same way. Folks down South stuck together that way; they didn't even have to know you. But up here it was different. Ask somebody for something, and they'd think you were crazy. Well, I ain't crazy. I'm just broke, 'cause I got no birth certificate to get a job, and Laura 'bout to die 'cause we got no money for a doctor. But I ain't crazy. And yet a pinpoint of doubt was focused in his mind as he glanced toward the screen and saw the hero stealthily entering a dark room and sending the beam of a flashlight along a wall of bookcases. This is where he finds the trapdoor, he remembered. The man would pass abruptly through the wall and find the girl tied to a bed, her legs and arms spread wide, and her clothing torn to rags. He laughed softly to himself. He had seen the picture three times, and this was one of the best scenes.

On his right the fellow whispered wide-eyed to his companion. "Man, look a-yonder!"

"Damn!"

"Wouldn't I like to have her tied up like that . . ."

"Hey! That fool's letting her loose!"

"Aw, man, he loves her."

"Love or no love!"

The man moved impatiently beside him, and he tried to involve himself in the scene. But Laura was on his mind. Tiring quickly of watching the picture he looked back to where the white beam filtered from the projection room above the balcony. It started small and grew large, specks of dust dancing in its whiteness as it reached the screen. It was strange how the beam always landed right on the screen and didn't mess up and fall somewhere else. But they had it all fixed. Everything was fixed. Now suppose when they showed that girl with her dress torn the girl started taking off the rest of her clothes, and when the guy came in he didn't untie her but kept her there and went to taking off his own clothes? *That* would be something to see. If a picture got out of hand like that those guys up there would go nuts. Yeah, and there'd be so many folks in here you couldn't find a seat for nine months! A strange sensation played over his skin. He shuddered. Yesterday he'd seen a bedbug on a woman's neck as they walked out into the bright street. But exploring his thigh through a hole in his pocket he found only goose pimples and old scars.

The bottle gurgled again. He closed his eyes. Now a dreamy music was accompanying the film and train whistles were sounding in the distance, and he was a boy again walking along a railroad trestle down South, and seeing the train coming, and running back as fast as he could go, and hearing the whistle blowing, and getting off the trestle to solid ground just in time, with the earth trembling beneath his feet, and feeling relieved as he ran down the cinder-strewn embankment onto the highway, and looking back and seeing with terror that the train had left the track and was following him right down the middle of the street, and all the white people laughing as he ran screaming . . .

"Wake up there, buddy! What the hell do you mean hollering like that! Can't you see we trying to enjoy this here picture?"

He stared at the man with gratitude.

"I'm sorry, old man," he said. "I musta been dreaming."

"Well, here, have a drink. And don't be making no noise like that, damn!"

His hands trembled as he tilted his head. It was not wine, but whiskey. Cold rye whiskey. He took a deep swoller, decided it was better not to take another, and handed the bottle back to its owner.

"Thanks, old man," he said.

Now he felt the cold whiskey breaking a warm path straight through the middle of him, growing hotter and sharper as it moved. He had not eaten all day, and it made him light-headed. The smell of the peanuts stabbed him like a knife, and he got up and found a seat in the middle aisle. But no sooner did he sit than he saw a row of intense-faced young girls, and got up again, thinking, "You chicks musta been Lindy-hopping somewhere." He found a seat several rows ahead as the lights came on, and he saw the screen disappear behind a heavy red and gold curtain; then the curtain rising, and the man with the microphone and a uniformed attendant coming on the stage.

He felt for his bingo cards, smiling. The guy at the door wouldn't like it if he knew about his having *five* cards. Well, not everyone played the bingo game; and even with five cards he didn't have much of a chance. For Laura, though, he had to have faith. He studied the cards, each with its different numerals, punching the free center hole in each and spreading them neatly across his lap; and when the lights faded he sat slouched in his seat so that he could look from his cards to the bingo wheel with but a quick shifting of his eyes.

Ahead, at the end of the darkness, the man with the microphone was pressing a button attached to a long cord and spinning the bingo wheel and calling out the number each time the wheel came to rest. And each time the voice rang out his finger raced over the cards for the number. With five cards he had to move fast. He became nervous; there were too many cards, and the man went too fast with his grating voice. Perhaps he should just select one and throw the others away. But he was afraid. He became warm. Wonder how much Laura's doctor would cost? Damn that, watch the cards! And with despair he heard the man call three in a row which he missed on all five cards. This way he'd never win . . .

When he saw the row of holes punched across the third card, he sat paralyzed and heard the man call three more numbers before he stumbled forward, screaming.

"Bingo! Bingo!"

"Let that fool up there," someone called.

"Get up there, man!"

He stumbled down the aisle and up the steps to the stage into a light so sharp and bright that for a moment it blinded him, and he felt that he had moved into the spell of some strange, mysterious power. Yet it was as familiar as the sun, and he knew it was the perfectly familiar bingo.

The man with the microphone was saying something to the audience as he held out his card. A cold light flashed from the man's finger as the card left his hand. His knees trembled. The man stepped closer, checking the card against the numbers chalked an the board. Suppose he had made a mistake? The pomade on the man's hair made him feel faint, and he backed away. But the man was checking the card over the microphone now, and he had to stay. He stood tense, listening.

"Under the O, forty-four," the man chanted. "Under the I, seven. Under the G, three. Under the B, ninety-six. Under the N, thirteen!"

His breath came easier as the man smiled at the audience.

"Yessir, ladies and gentlemen, he's one of the chosen people!"

The audience rippled with laughter and applause.

"Step right up to the front of the stage."

He moved slowly forward, wishing that the light was not so bright.

"To win tonight's jackpot of $36.90 the wheel must stop between the double zero, understand?"

He nodded, knowing the ritual from the many days and nights he had watched the winners march across the stage to press the button that controlled the spinning wheel and receive the prizes. And now he followed the instructions as though he'd crossed the slippery stage a million prize-winning times.

The man was making some kind of a joke, and he nodded vacantly. So tense had he become that he felt a sudden desire to cry and shook it away. He felt vaguely that his whole life was determined by the bingo wheel; not only that which would happen now that he was at last before it, but all that had gone before, since his birth, and his mother's birth and the birth of his father. It had always been there, even though he had not been aware of it, handing out the unlucky cards and numbers of his days. The feeling persisted, and he started quickly away. I better get down from here before I make a fool of myself, he thought.

"Here, boy," the man called. "You haven't started yet."

Someone laughed as he went hesitantly back.

"Are you all reet?"

He grinned at the man's jive talk, but no words would come, and he knew it was not a convincing grin. For suddenly he knew that he stood on the slippery brink of some terrible embarrassment.

"Where are you from, boy?" the man asked.

"Down South."

"He's from down South, ladies and gentlemen," the man said. "Where from? Speak right into the mike."

"Rocky Mont," he said. "Rock' Mont, North Car'lina."

"So you decided to come down off that mountain to the U.S.," the man laughed. He felt that the man was making a fool of him, but then something cold was placed in his hand, and the lights were no longer behind him.

Standing before the wheel he felt alone, but that was somehow right, and he remembered his plan. He would give the wheel a short quick twirl. Just a touch of the button. He had watched it many times, and always it came close to double zero when it was short and quick. He steeled himself; the fear had left, and he felt a profound sense of promise, as though he were about to be repaid for all the things he'd suffered all his life. Trembling, he pressed the button. There was a whirl of lights, and in a second he realized with finality that though he wanted to, he could not stop. It was as though he held a high-powered line in his naked hand. His nerves tightened. As the wheel increased its speed it seemed to draw him more and more into its power, as though it held his fate; and with it came a deep need to submit, to whirl, to lose himself in its swirl of color. He could not stop it now, he knew. So let it be.

The button rested snugly in his palm where the man had placed it. And now he became aware of the man beside him, advising him through the microphone, while behind the shadowy audience hummed with noisy voices. He shifted his feet. There was still that feeling of helplessness within him, making part of him desire to turn back, even now that the jackpot was right in his hand. He squeezed the button until his fist ached. Then, like the sudden shriek of a subway whistle, a doubt tore through his head. Suppose he did not spin the wheel long enough? What could he do, and how could he tell? And then he knew, even as he wondered, that as long as he pressed the button, he could control the jackpot. He and only he could determine whether or not it was to be his. Not even the man with the microphone could do anything about it now. He felt drunk. Then, as though he had come down from a high hill into a valley of people, he heard the audience yelling.

"Come down from there, you jerk!"

"Let somebody else have a chance . . ."

"Ole Jack thinks he done found the end of the rainbow . . ."

The last voice was not unfriendly, and he turned and smiled dreamily into the yelling mouths. Then he turned his back squarely on them.

"Don't take too long, boy," a voice said.

He nodded. They were yelling behind him. Those folks did not understand what had happened to him. They had been playing the bingo game day in and night out for years, trying to win rent money or hamburger change. But not one of those wise guys had discovered this wonderful thing. He watched the wheel whirling past the numbers and experienced a burst of exaltation: This is God! This is the really truly God! He said it aloud, "This is God!"

He said it with such absolute conviction that he feared he would fall fainting into the footlights. But the crowd yelled so loud that they could not hear. Those fools, he thought. I'm here trying to tell them the most wonderful secret in the world, and they're yelling like they gone crazy. A hand fell upon his shoulder.

"You'll have to make a choice now, boy. You've taken too long."

He brushed the hand violently away.

"Leave me alone, man. I know what I'm doing!"

The man looked surprised and held on to the microphone for support. And because he did not wish to hurt the man's feelings he smiled, realizing with a sudden pang that there was no way of explaining to the man just why he had to stand there pressing the button forever.

"Come here," he called tiredly.

The man approached, rolling the heavy microphone across the stage.

"Anybody can play this bingo game, right?" he said.

"Sure, but . . ."

He smiled, feeling inclined to be patient with this slick looking white man with his blue sport shirt and his sharp gabardine suit.

"That's what I thought," he said. "Anybody can win the jackpot as long as they get the lucky number, right?"

"That's the rule, but after all . . ."

"That's what I thought," he said. "And the big prize goes to the man who knows how to win it?"

The man nodded speechlessly.

"Well then, go on over there and watch me win like I want to. I ain't going to hurt nobody," he said, "and I'll show you how to win. I mean to show the whole world how it's got to be done."

And because he understood, he smiled again to let the man know that he held nothing against him for being white and impatient. Then he refused to see the man any longer and stood pressing the button, the voices of the crowd reaching him like sounds in distant streets. Let them yell. All the Negroes down there were just ashamed because he was black like them. He smiled inwardly, knowing how it was. Most of the time he was ashamed of what Negroes did himself. Well, let them be ashamed for something this time. Like him. He was like a long thin black wire that was being stretched and wound upon the bingo wheel; wound until he wanted to scream; wound, but this time himself controlling the winding and the sadness and the shame, and because he did, Laura would be all right. Suddenly the lights flickered. He staggered backwards. Had something gone wrong? All this noise. Didn't they know that although he controlled the wheel, it also controlled him, and unless he pressed the button forever and forever and ever it would stop, leaving him high and dry, dry and high on this hard high slippery hill and Laura dead? There was only one chance; he had to do whatever the wheel demanded. And gripping the button in despair, he discovered with surprise that it imparted a nervous energy. His spine tingled. He felt a certain power.

Now he faced the raging crowd with defiance, its screams penetrating his eardrums like trumpets shrieking from a jukebox. The vague faces glowing in the bingo lights gave him a sense of himself that he had never known before. He was running the show, by God! They had to react to him, for he was their luck. This is *me*, he thought. Let the bastards yell. Then someone was laughing inside him, and he realized that somehow he had forgotten his own name. It was a sad, lost feeling to lose your name, and a crazy thing to do. That name had been given him by the white man who had owned his grandfather a long lost time ago down South. But maybe those wise guys knew his name.

"Who am I?" he screamed.

"Hurry up and bingo, you jerk!"

They didn't know either, he thought sadly. They didn't even know their own names, they were all poor nameless bastards.

Well, he didn't need that old name; he was reborn. For as long as he pressed the button he was The-man-who-pressed-the-button-who-held-the-prize-who-was-the-King-of-Bingo. That was the way it was, and he'd have to press the button even if nobody understood, even though Laura did not understand.

"Live!" he shouted.

The audience quieted like the dying of a huge fan.

"Live, Laura, baby. I got holt of it now, sugar. Live!"

He screamed it, tears streaming down his face. "I got nobody but YOU!"

The screams tore from his very guts. He felt as though the rush of blood to his head would burst out in baseball seams of small red droplets, like a head beaten by police clubs. Bending over he saw a trickle of blood splashing the toe of his shoe. With his free hand he searched his head. It was his nose. God, suppose something has gone wrong? He felt that the whole audience had somehow entered him and was stamping its feet in his stomach, and he was unable to throw them out. They wanted the prize, that was it. They wanted the secret for themselves. But they'd never get it; he would keep the bingo wheel whirling forever, and Laura would be safe in the wheel. But would she? It had to be, because if she were not safe the wheel would cease to turn; it could not go on. He had to get away, *vomit* all, and his mind formed an image of himself running with Laura in his arms down the tracks of the subway just ahead of an A train, running desperately *vomit* with people screaming for him to come out but knowing no way of leaving the tracks because to stop would bring the train crushing down upon him and to attempt to leave across the other tracks would mean to run into a hot third rail as high as his waist which threw blue sparks that blinded his eyes until he could hardly see.

He heard singing and the audience was clapping its hands.

> Shoot the liquor to him, Jim, boy!
> Clap-clap-clap
> Well a-calla the cop
> He's blowing his top!
> Shoot the liquor to him, Jim, boy!

Bitter anger grew within him at the singing. They think I'm crazy. Well let 'em laugh. I'll do what I got to do.

He was standing in an attitude of intense listening when he saw that they were watching something on the stage behind him. He felt weak. But when he turned he saw no one. If only his thumb did not ache so. Now they were applauding. And for a moment he thought that the wheel had stopped. But that was impossible, his thumb still pressed the button. Then he saw them. Two men in uniform beckoned from the end of the stage. They were coming toward him, walking in step, slowly, like a tap-dance team returning for a third encore. But their shoulders shot forward, and he backed away, looking wildly about. There was nothing to fight them with. He had only the long black cord which led to a plug somewhere back stage, and he couldn't use that because it operated the bingo wheel. He backed slowly, fixing the men with his eyes as his lips stretched over his teeth in a tight, fixed grin; moved toward the end of the stage and realizing that he couldn't go much further, for suddenly the cord became taut and he couldn't afford to break the cord. But he had to do something. The audience was howling. Suddenly he stopped dead, seeing the men halt, their legs lifted as in an interrupted step of a slow-motion dance. There was nothing to do but run in the other direction and he dashed forward, slipping and sliding. The men fell back, surprised. He struck out violently going past.

"Grab him!"

He ran, but all too quickly the cord tightened, resistingly, and he turned and ran back again. This time he slipped them, and discovered by running in a circle before the wheel he could keep the cord from tightening. But this way he had to flail his arms to keep the men away. Why couldn't they leave a man alone? He ran, circling.

"Ring down the curtain," someone yelled. But they couldn't do that. If they did the wheel flashing from the projection room would be cut off. But they had him before he could tell them so, trying to pry open his fist, and he was wrestling and trying to bring his knees into the fight and holding on the button, for it was his life. And now he was down, seeing a foot coming down, crushing his wrist cruelly, down, as he saw the wheel whirling serenely above.

"I can't give it up," he screamed. Then quietly, in a confidential tone, "Boys, I really can't give it up."

It landed hard against his head. And in the blank moment they had it away from him, completely now. He fought them trying to pull him up from the stage as he watched the wheel spin slowly to a stop. Without surprise he saw it rest at double zero.

"You see," he pointed bitterly.

"Sure, boy, sure, it's O.K.," one of the men said smiling.

And seeing the man bow his head to someone he could not see, he felt very, very happy; he would receive what all the winners received.

But as he warmed in the justice of the man's tight smile he did not see the man's slow wink, nor see the bow-legged man behind him step clear of the swiftly descending curtain and set himself for a blow. He only felt the dull pain exploding in his skull, and he knew even as it slipped out of him that his luck had run out on the stage.

Questions for Discussion

1. What does winning the bingo game represent for the narrator?
2. What do the narrator's responses to the movie tell you about his life?

3. What is suggested by the main character's uncomfortable feelings about the people at the bingo game?

4. Why is the narrator unable to let go of the button operating the bingo wheel? What does the bingo wheel symbolize for the narrator, for the crowd, and for the reader?

5. Discuss the tone of the story. Does the narrator's perspective lead you to feel sympathy for the main character?

Ideas for Writing

1. Write a story about desperate people engaging in a form of legalized gambling today — for instance, horse racing, bingo, or the lottery.

2. Interpret the story as an allegory, using the setting and the bingo game itself as symbols.

DORIS LESSING   (b. 1919)

While the scope of her work is quite broad, Doris Lessing most consistently focuses on equal rights for women and the humane treatment of children. Her work also emphasizes the search for self-knowledge and inner balance, and the belief that individuals have a responsibility to society and that social institutions need to change for the betterment of humankind.

Lessing spent her childhood in Southern Rhodesia (now called Zimbabwe). Unhappy at her Catholic convent high school, she dropped out when she was fourteen and became interested in politics, joining the Communist party, then moving to London in 1950. Lessing left the Communist party in 1956 and became deeply interested in the mystical teachings of Indries Shah and Sufism. In her long and distinguished writing career, she has published more than twenty-five novels; her better-known works include *The Golden Notebook* (1962), *The Diaries of Jane Somers* (1984), *The Good Terrorist* (1985), *The Fifth Child* (1988), and *Love Again* (1996). Lessing has also published more than fifteen short-story collections. "How I Finally Lost My Heart" is included in *A Man and Two Women* (1975), and "The Mother of the Child in Question" is included in *The Real Thing* (1992). Lessing's work varies stylistically from the dreamlike fantasy of "How I Finally Lost My Heart" to the straightforward, almost "case-history" realism of "The Mother of the Child in Question."

How I Finally Lost My Heart   (1958)

It would be easy to say that I picked up a knife, slit open my side, took my heart out, and threw it away; but unfortunately it wasn't as easy as that. Not that I, like everybody else, had not often wanted to do it. No, it happened differently, and not as I expected.

It was just after I had had a lunch and a tea with two different men. My lunch partner I had lived with for (more or less) four and seven-twelfths years. When he left me for new pastures, I spent two years, or was it three, half dead, and my heart was a stone, impossible to carry about, considering all the other things weighing on one. Then I slowly, and with difficulty, got free, because my heart cherished a thousand adhesions to my first love — though from another point of view he could be legitimately described as either my second *real* love (my father being the first) or my third (my brother interventing).

As the folk song has it:

> I have loved but three men in my life,
> My father, my brother, and the man that took my life.

But if one were going to look at the thing from outside, without insight, he could be seen as (perhaps, I forget) the thirteenth, but to do that means disregarding the inner emotional truth. For we all know that those affairs or entanglements one has between *serious* loves, though they may number dozens and stretch over years, *don't really count.*

This way of looking at things creates a number of unhappy people, for it is well known that what doesn't really count for me might very well count for you. But there is no way of getting over this difficulty, for a *serious* love is the most important business in life, or nearly so. At any rate, most of us are engaged in looking for it. Even when we are in fact being very serious indeed with one person we still have an eighth of an eye cocked in case some stranger unexpectedly encountered might turn out to be even more serious. We are all entirely in agreement that we are in the right to taste, test, sip and sample a thousand people on our way to the *real* one. It is not too much to say that in our circles tasting and sampling is probably the second most important activity, the first being earning money. Or to put it another way, "If you are serious about this thing, you go on laying everybody that offers until something clicks and you're all set to go."

I have digressed from an earlier point: that I regarded this man I had lunch with (we will call him A) as my first love; and still do, despite the Freudians, who insist on seeing my father as A and possibly my brother as B, making my (real) first love C. And despite, also, those who might ask: What about your two husbands and all those affairs?

What about them? I did not *really* love them, the way I loved A.

I had lunch with him. Then, quite by chance, I had tea with B. When I say B, here, I mean my *second* serious love, not my brother, or the little boys I was in love with between the ages of five and fifteen, if we are going to take fifteen (arbitrarily) as the point of no return . . . which last phrase is in itself a pretty brave defiance of the secular arbiters.

In between A and B (my count) there were a good many affairs, or samples, but they didn't score. B and I *clicked,* we went off like a bomb, though not quite as simply as A and I had clicked, because my heart was bruised, sullen, and suspicious because of A's throwing me over. Also there were all those ligaments and adhesions binding me to A still to be loosened, one by one. However, for a time B and I got on like a house on fire, and then we came to grief. My heart was again a ton weight in my side.

> If this were a stone in my side, a stone,
> I could pluck it out and be free. . . .

Having lunch with A, then tea with B, two men who between them had consumed a decade of my previous years (I am not counting the test or trial affairs in between) and, it is fair to say, had balanced all the delight (plenty and intense) with misery (oh Lord, Lord) — moving from one to the other, in the course of an afternoon, conversing amiably about this and that, with meanwhile my heart giving no more than slight reminiscent tugs, the fish of memory at the end of a long slack line. . . .

To sum up, it was salutary.

Particularly as that evening I was expecting to meet C, or someone who might very well turn out to be C — though I don't want to give too much emphasis to C, the truth is I can hardly remember what he looked like, but one can't be expected to remember the unimportant ones one has sipped or tasted in between. But after all, he might have turned out to be C, we might have *clicked,* and I was in that state of mind (in which we all so often are) of thinking: He might turn out to be the one. (I use a woman's magazine phrase deliberately here, instead of saying, as I might, *Perhaps it will be serious.*)

So there I was (I want to get the details and atmosphere right) standing at a window looking into a street (Great Portland Street, as a matter of fact) and thinking that while I would not dream of regretting my affairs, or experiences, with A and B (it is better to have loved and lost than never to have loved at all), my anticipation of the heart because of spending an evening with a possible C had a certain unreality, because there was no doubt that both A and B had caused me unbelievable pain. Why, therefore, was I looking forward to C? I should rather be running away as fast as I could.

It suddenly occurred to me that I was looking at the whole phenomenon quite inaccurately. My (or perhaps I am permitted to say our?) way of looking at it is that one must search for an A, or a B, or a C or a D with a certain combination of desirable or sympathetic qualities so that one may click, or spontaneously combust: or to put it differently, one needs a person who, like a saucer of water, allows one to float off on him/her, like a transfer. But this wasn't so at all. Actually one carries with one a sort of burning spear stuck in one's side, that one waits for someone else to pull out; it is something painful, like a sore or a wound, that one cannot wait to share with someone else.

I saw myself quite plainly in a moment of truth: I was standing at a window (on the third floor) with A and B (to mention only the mountain peaks of my emotional experience) behind me, a rather attractive woman, if I may say so, with a mellowness that I would be the first to admit is the sad harbinger of age, but is attractive by definition, because it is a testament to the amount of sampling and sipping (I nearly wrote simpling and sapping) I have done in my time . . . there I stood, brushed, dressed, red-lipped, kohl-eyed, all waiting for an evening with a possible C. And at another window overlooking (I think I am right in saying) Margaret Street, stood C, brushed, washed, shaved, smiling: an attractive man (I think), and *he* was thinking: Perhaps she will turn out to be D (or A or 3 or ? or %, or whatever symbol he used). We stood, separated by space, certainly, in identical conditions of pleasant uncertainty and anticipation, and we both held our hearts in our hands, all pink and palpitating and ready for pleasure and pain, and we were about to throw these hearts in each other's face like snowballs, or cricket balls (How's that?) or, more accurately, like great bleeding wounds: "Take my wound." Because the last thing one ever thinks at such moments is that he (or she) will say: Take *my* wound, please remove the spear from *my* side. No, not at all, only simply expects to get rid of one's own.

I decided I must go to the telephone and say C! — You know that joke about the joke-makers who don't trouble to tell each other jokes, but simply say Joke 1, or Joke 2, and everyone roars with laughter, or snickers, or giggles appropriately. . . . Actually one could reverse the game by guessing whether it was Joke C (b) or Joke A (d) according to what sort of laughter a person made to match the silent thought. . . . Well, C (I imagined myself saying), the analogy is for our instruction: Let's take the whole thing as read or said. Let's not lick each other's sores; let's keep our hearts to ourselves. Because just consider it, C, how utterly absurd — here we stand at our respective windows with our palpitating hearts in our hands. . . .

At this moment, dear reader, I was forced simply to put down the telephone with an apology. For I felt the fingers of my left hand push outwards around something rather large, light, and slippery — hard to describe this sensation, really. My hand is not large, and my heart was in a state of inflation after having had lunch with A, tea with B, and then looking forward to C. . . . Anyway, my fingers were stretching out rather desperately to encompass an unknown, largish, lightish object, and I said: Excuse me a minute, to C, looked down, and there was my heart, in my hand.

I had to end the conversation there.

For one thing, to find that one has achieved something so often longed for, so easily, is upsetting. It's not as if I had been trying. To get something one wants simply by accident — no, there's no pleasure in it, no feeling of achievement. So to find myself heart-whole, or, more accurately, heart-less, or at any rate, rid of the damned thing, and at such an awkward moment, in the middle of an imaginary telephone call with a man who might possibly turn out to be C, well, it was irritating rather than not.

For another thing, a heart, raw and bleeding and fresh from one's side, is not the prettiest sight. I'm not going into that at all. I was appalled, and indeed embarrassed that *that* was what had been loving and beating away all those years, because if I'd had any idea at all — well, enough of that.

My problem was how to get rid of it.

Simple, you'll say, drop it into the waste bucket.

Well, let me tell you, that's what I tried to do. I took a good look at this object, nearly died with embarrassment, and walked over to the rubbish can, where I tried to let it roll off my fingers. It wouldn't. It was stuck. There was my heart, a large red pulsing bleeding repulsive object, stuck to my fingers. What was I going to do? I sat down, lit a cigarette (with one hand, holding the matchbox between my knees), held my hand with the heart stuck on it over the side of the chair so that it could drip into a bucket, and considered.

> If this were a stone in my hand, a stone,
> I could throw it over a tree. . . .

When I had finished the cigarette, I carefully unwrapped some tin foil, of the kind used to wrap food in when cooking, and I fitted a sort of cover around my heart. This was absolutely and urgently necessary. First, it was smarting badly. After all, it had spent some forty years protected by flesh and ribs and the air was too much for it. Secondly, I couldn't have any Tom, Dick and Harry walking in and looking at it. Thirdly, I could not look at it for too long myself, it filled me with shame. The tin foil was effective, and indeed rather striking. It is quite pliable and now it seemed as if there were a stylised heart balanced on my palm, like a globe in glittering, silvery substance. I almost felt I needed a sceptre in the other hand to balance it. . . . But the thing was, there is no other word for it, in bad taste. I then wrapped a scarf around hand and tin-foiled heart, and felt safer. Now it was a question of pretending to have hurt my hand until I could think of a way of getting rid of my heart altogether, short of amputating my hand.

Meanwhile I telephoned (really, not in imagination) C, who now would never be C. I could feel my heart, which was stuck so close to my fingers that I could feel every beat or tremor, give a gulp of resigned grief at the idea of this beautiful experience now never to be. I told him some idiotic lie about having flu. Well, he was all stiff and indignant, but concealing it urbanely, as I would have done, making a joke but allowing a tiny barb of sarcasm to rankle in the last well-chosen phrase. Then I sat down again to think out my whole situation.

There I sat.

What was I going to do?

There I sat.

I am going to have to skip about four days here, vital enough in all conscience, because I simply cannot go heartbeat by heartbeat through my memories. A pity, since I suppose this is what this story is about; but in brief: I drew the curtains, I took the telephone off the hook, I turned on the lights, I took the scarf off the glittering shape, then the tin foil, then I examined the heart. There were two-fifths of a century's experiences to work through, and before I had even got through the first night, I was in a state hard to describe. . . .

> Or if I could pull the nerves from my skin
> A quick red net to drag through a sea for fish. . . .

By the end of the fourth day I was worn out. By no act of will, or intention, or desire, could I move that heart by a fraction — on the contrary, it was not only stuck to my fingers, like a sucked boiled sweet, but was actually growing to the flesh of my fingers and my palm.

I wrapped it up again in the foil and scarf, and turned out the lights and pulled up the blinds and opened the curtains. It was about ten in the morning, an ordinary London day, neither hot nor cold nor clear nor clouded nor wet nor fine. And while the street is interesting, it is not exactly beautiful, so I wasn't looking at it so much as waiting for something to catch my attention while thinking of something else.

Suddenly I heard a tap-tap-tapping that got louder, sharp and clear, and I knew before I saw her that this was the sound of high heels on a pavement though it might just as well have been a hammer against stone. She walked fast opposite my window and her heels hit the pavement so hard that all the noises of the street seemed absorbed into that single tap-tap-clang-clang. As she reached the corner at Great Portland Street two London pigeons swooped diagonally from the sky very fast, as if they were bullets aimed to kill her; and then as they saw her they swooped up and off at an angle. Meanwhile she had turned the corner. All this has taken time to write down, but the thing happening took a couple of seconds: the woman's body hitting the pavement bang-bang through her heels then sharply turning the corner in a right angle; and the pigeons making another acute angle across hers and intersecting it in a fast swoop of displaced air. Nothing to all that, of course, nothing—she had gone off down the street, her heels tip-tapping, and the pigeons landed on my windowsill and began cooing. All gone, all vanished, the marvellous exact coordination of sound and movement, but it had happened, it had made me happy and exhilarated, I had no problems in this world, and I realized that the heart stuck to my fingers was quite loose. I couldn't get it off altogether, though I was tugging at it under the scarf and the tin foil, but almost.

I understood that sitting and analysing each movement or pulse or beat of my heart through forty years was a mistake. I was on the wrong track altogether: this was the way to attach my red, bitter, delighted heart to my flesh forever and ever. . . .

> Ha! So you think I'm done! You think. . . .
> Watch, I'll roll my heart in a mesh of rage
> And bounce it like a handball off
> Walls, faces, railings, umbrellas and pigeons' backs. . . .

No, all that was no good at all, it just made things worse. What I must do is to take myself by surprise, as it were, the way I was taken by surprise over the woman and the pigeons and the sharp sounds of heels and silk wings.

I put on my coat, held my lumpy scarfed arm across my chest, so that if anyone said: What have you done with your hand? I could say: I've banged my finger in the door. Then I walked down into the street.

It wasn't easy to go among too many people, when I was worried that they were thinking: What has that woman done to her hand? because that made it hard to forget myself. And all the time it tingled and throbbed against my fingers, reminding me.

Now I was out I didn't know what to do. Should I go and have lunch with someone? Or wander in the park? Or buy myself a dress? I decided to go to the Round Pond, and walk around it by myself. I was tired after four days and nights without sleep. I went down into the Underground at Oxford Circus. Midday. Crowds of people. I felt self-conscious, but of course need not have worried. I swear you could walk naked down the street in London and no one would even turn round.

So I went down the escalator and looked at the faces coming up past me on the other side, as I always do; and wondered, as I always do, how strange it is that those people and I should meet by chance in such a way, and how odd that we would never see each other again, or, if we did, we wouldn't know it. And I went on to the crowded platform and looked at the faces as I always do, and got into the train, which was very full, and found a seat. It wasn't as bad as at rush hour, but all the seats were filled. I leaned back and closed my eyes, deciding to sleep a little, being so tired. I was just beginning to doze off, when I heard a woman's voice muttering, or rather, declaiming:

"A gold cigarette case, well, that's a nice thing, isn't it, I must say, a gold case, yes. . . ."

There was something about this voice which made me open my eyes: on the other side of the compartment, about eight persons away, sat a youngish woman, wearing a cheap green cloth coat, gloveless hands, flat brown shoes, and lisle stockings. She must be rather poor — a woman dressed like this is a rare sight, these days. But it was her posture that struck me. She was sitting half twisted in her seat, so that her head was turned over her left shoulder, and she was looking straight at the stomach of an elderly man next to her. But it was clear she was not seeing it: her young staring eyes were sightless, she was looking inwards.

She was so clearly alone, in the crowded compartment, that it was not as embarrassing as it might have been. I looked around, and people were smiling, or exchanging glances, or winking, or ignoring her, according to their natures, but she was oblivious of us all.

She suddenly aroused herself, turned so that she sat straight in her seat, and directed her voice and her gaze to the opposite seat:

"Well so that's what you think, you think that, you think that do you, well, you think I'm just going to wait at home for you, but you gave her a gold case and . . . ."

And with a clockwork movement of her whole thin person, she turned her narrow pale-haired head sideways over her left shoulder, and resumed her stiff empty stare at the man's stomach. He was grinning uncomfortably. I leaned forward to look along the line of people in the row of seats I sat in, and the man opposite her, a young man, had exactly the same look of discomfort which he was determined to keep amused. So we all looked at her, the young, thin, pale woman in her private drama of misery, who was so completely unconscious of us that she spoke and thought out loud. And again, without particular warning or reason, in between stops, so it wasn't that she was disturbed from her dream by the train stopping at Bond Street, and then jumping forward again, she twisted her body frontways, and addressed the seat opposite her (the young man had got off, and a smart gray-curled matron had got in):

"Well I know about it now, don't I, and if you come in all smiling and pleased well then I know, don't I, you don't have to tell me, I know, and I've said to her, I've said, I know he gave you a gold cigarette case. . . ."

At which point, with the same clockwork impulse, she stopped, or was checked, or simply ran out, and turned herself half around to stare at the stomach — the same stomach, for the middle-aged man was still there. But we stopped at Marble Arch and he got out, giving the compartment, rather than the people in it, a tolerant half-smile which said: I am sure I can trust you to realize that this unfortunate woman is stark staring mad. . . .

His seat remained empty. No people got in at Marble Arch, and the two people standing waiting for seats did not want to sit by her to receive her stare.

We all sat, looking gently in front of us, pretending to ourselves and to each other that we didn't know the poor woman was mad and that in fact we ought to be doing something about it. I even wondered what I should say: Madam, you're mad — shall I escort you to your home? Or: Poor thing, don't go on like that, it doesn't do any good, you know — just leave him, that'll bring him to his senses. . . .

And behold, after the interval that was regulated by her inner mechanism had elapsed, she turned back and said to the smart matron who received this statement of accusation with perfect self-command:

"Yes, I know! Oh, yes! And what about my shoes, what about them, a golden cigarette case is what she got, the filthy bitch, a golden case. . . ."

Stop. Twist. Stare. At the empty seat by her.

Extraordinary. Because it was a frozen misery, how shall I put it? A passionless passion — we were seeing unhappiness embodied, we were looking at the essence of some private tragedy — rather, Tragedy. There was no emotion in it. She was like an actress doing Accusation, or Betrayed Love, or Infidelity, when she has only just learned her lines and is not bothering to do more than get them right.

And whether she sat in her half-twisted position, her unblinking eyes staring at the greenish, furry, ugly covering of the train seat, or sat straight, directing her accusation to the smart woman opposite, there was a frightening immobility about her — yes, that was why she frightened us. For it was clear that she might very well (if the inner machine ran down) stay silent, forever, in either twisted or straight position, or at any point between them — yes, we could all imagine her, frozen perpetually in some arbitrary pose. It was as if we watched the shell of some woman going through certain predetermined motions.

For *she* was simply not there. *What* was there, who she was, it was impossible to tell, though it was easy to imagine her thin, gentle little face breaking into a smile in total forgetfulness of what she was enacting now. She did not know she was in a train between Marble Arch and Queensway, nor that she was publicly accusing her husband or lover, nor that we were looking at her.

And we, looking at her, felt an embarrassment and shame that was not on her account at all. . . .

Suddenly I felt, under the scarf and the tin foil, a lightening of my fingers, as my heart rolled loose.

I hastily took it off my palm, in case it decided to adhere there again, and I removed the scarf, leaving balanced on my knees a perfect stylised heart, like a silver heart on a Valentine card, though of course it was three-dimensional. This heart was not so much harmless, no that isn't the word, as artistic, but in very bad taste, as I said. I could see that the people in the train, now looking at me and the heart, and not at the poor madwoman, were pleased with it.

I got up, took the four or so paces to where she was, and laid the tin-foiled heart down on the seat so that it received her stare.

For a moment she did not react, then with a groan or a mutter of relieved and entirely theatrical grief, she leaned forward, picked up the glittering heart, and clutched it in her arms, hugging it and rocking it back and forth, even laying her cheek against it, while staring over its top at her husband as if to say: "Look what I've got, I don't care about you and your cigarette case, I've got a silver heart."

I got up, since we were at Notting Hill Gate, and, followed by the pleased congratulatory nods and smiles of the people left behind, I went out onto the platform, up the escalators, into the street, and along to the park.

No heart. No heart at all. What bliss. What freedom. . . .

> Hear that sound? That's laughter, yes.
> That's me laughing, yes, that's me.

Questions for Discussion

1. What view of love dominates in the first half of the story, and what images and experiences from the narrator's life support this view? In contrast, what definition of love is implied by the final scene of the story?

2. Discuss the metaphor of the heart: How is this metaphor developed from its initial comparison to a wound?

3. Why does the narrator finally decide to leave her room and take a train ride? Why is this a significant decision?

4. Characterize the woman the narrator sees on the train. Why does the narrator become interested in her? In what ways are they quite different? In what ways might the narrator identify with the woman's problems?

5. The song that runs through the story is completed only in the last two lines of the story. Who is singing the song? How does the song comment on the action and meaning of the story?

Ideas for Writing
1. Write an essay in which you discuss what the story is saying about the relation-ship between love and giving. Is the narrator's final gesture of giving away her heart to a stranger positive or cynical? Why?
2. Write a story in which a character's attitude toward love or some other strong emotion is radically changed, so that the character ends by performing an action that would have been impossible for him or her at the beginning of the story.

The Mother of the Child in Question   (1992)

High on a walkway connecting two tower blocks Stephen Bentley, social worker, stopped to survey the view. Cement, everywhere he looked. Stained grey piles went up into the sky, and down below lay grey acres where only one person moved among puddles, soft drink cans and bits of damp paper. This was an old man with a stick and a shopping bag. In front of Stephen, hori-zontally dividing the heavy building from pavement to low cloud, were rows of many-coloured curtains where people kept out of sight. They were proba-bly watching him, but he had his credentials, the file under his arm. The end of this walkway was on the fourth floor. The lift smelled bad: someone had been sick in it. He walked up grey urine-smelling stairs to the eighth floor, Number 15. The very moment he rang, the door was opened by a smiling brown boy. This must be Hassan, the twelve-year-old. His white teeth, his bright blue jersey, the white collar of his shirt, all dazzled, and behind him the small room crammed with furniture was too tidy for a family room, everything just so, polished, shining. Thorough preparations had been made for this visit. In front of a red plush sofa was the oblong of a low table, and on it waited cups, saucers and a sugar bowl full to the brim. A glinting spoon stood upright in it. Hassan sat down on the sofa, smiling hard. Apart from the sofa, there were three chairs, full of shiny cushions. In one of them sat Mrs. Khan, a plump pretty lady wearing the outfit Stephen thought of as "pyjamas" — trousers and tunic in flowered pink silk. They looked like best clothes, and the ten-year-old girl in the other chair wore a blue tunic and trousers, with ear-rings, bangles and rings. Mother wore a pink gauzy scarf, the child a blue one. These, in Pakistan, would be there ready to be pulled modestly up at the sight of a man, but here they added to the festive atmosphere. Stephen sat down in the empty chair at Mrs. Khan's (Stephen particularly noted) peremptory ges-ture. But she smiled. Hassan smiled and smiled. The little girl had not, it seemed, noticed the visitor, but she smiled too. She was pretty, like a kitten.

"Where is Mr. Khan?" asked Stephen of Mrs. Khan, who nodded com-mandingly at her son. Hassan at once said, "No, he cannot come, he is at work."

"But he told me he would be here. I spoke to him on the telephone yesterday."

Again the mother gave Hassan an order with her eyes, and he said, smiling with all his white teeth, "No, he is not here."

In the file that had the name Shireen Khan on the front, the last note, dated nine months before, said, "Father did not keep appointment. His presence essential."

Mrs. Khan said something in a low voice to her son, who allowed the smile to have a rest just as long as it took to fetch a tray with a pot of tea on it, and biscuits, from the sideboard. They must have been watching from the windows and made the tea when they saw him down there, file under his arm. Hassan put the smile back on his face when he sat down again. Mrs. Khan poured strong tea. The boy handed Stephen a cup, and the plate of biscuits. Mrs. Khan set a cup before her daughter, and counted five biscuits on to a separate plate and put this near the cup. The little girl was smiling at — it seemed — attractive private fancies. Mrs. Khan clicked her tongue with annoyance and said something to her in Urdu. But Shireen took no notice. She was bursting with internal merriment, and the result of her mother's prompting was that she tried to share this with her brother, reaching out to poke him mischievously, and laughing. Hassan could not prevent a real smile at her, tender, warm, charmed. He instantly removed this smile and put back the polite false one.

"Five," said Mrs. Khan in English. "She can count. Say five, Shireen." It was poor English, and she repeated the command in Urdu.

The little girl smiled delightfully and began breaking up the biscuits and eating them.

"If your husband would agree to it, Shireen could go to the school we discussed — my colleague William Smith discussed with you — when he came last year. It is a good school. It would cost a little but not much. It is Government-funded but there is a small charge this year. Unfortunately."

Mrs. Khan said something sharp and the boy translated. His English was fluent. "It is not money. My father has the money."

"Then I am sorry but I don't understand. The school would be good for Shireen."

Well, within limits. In the file was a medical report, part of which read, "The child in question would possibly benefit to a limited extent from special tuition."

Mrs. Khan said something loud and angry. Her amiable face was twisted with anger. Anxiety and anger had become the air in this small overfilled overclean room, and now the little girl's face was woeful and her lips quivered. Hassan at once put out his hand to her and made soothing noises. Mrs. Khan tried simultaneously to smile at the child and show a formal cold face to the intrusive visitor.

Hassan said, "My mother says Shireen must go to the big school, Beavertree School."

"Is that where you go, Hassan?"

"Yes, sir."

"My name is Stephen, Stephen Bentley."

"Yes, sir."

"Your father should be here," said Stephen, trying not to sound peevish. There was something going on, but he could not make out what. If it wasn't that two daughters were doing well at school Stephen would have thought perhaps Mr. Khan was old-fashioned and didn't want Shireen educated. (The two girls were both older than Hassan, but being girls did not count. It was the oldest son who had to be here representing the father.) Not that there was any question of "educating" Shireen. So what was it? Certainly he had sounded perfunctory yesterday on the telephone, agreeing to be here today.

Mrs. Khan now took out a child's picture book she had put down the side of the armchair for this very moment, and held it in front of Shireen. It was a brightly coloured book, for a three-year-old, perhaps. Shireen smiled at it in a vacant willing way. Mrs. Khan turned the big pages, frowning and nodding encouragingly at Shireen. Then she made herself smile. The boy was smiling away like anything. Shireen was happy and smiling.

"Look," said Stephen, smiling but desperate, "I'm not saying that Shireen will learn to read well, or anything like that, but . . ."

At this Mrs. Khan slammed the book shut and faced him. No smiles. A proud, cold, stubborn woman, eyes flashing, she demolished him in Urdu.

Hassan translated the long tirade thus. "My mother says Shireen must go to the big school with the rest of us."

"But, Mrs. Khan, she can't go to the big school. How can she?" As Mrs. Khan did not seem to have taken this in, he addressed the question again to Hassan. "How can she go to the big school? It's not possible!"

Hassan's smile was wan, and Stephen could swear there were tears in his eyes. But he turned his face away.

Another angry flood from Mrs. Khan, but Hassan did not interpret. He sat silent and looked sombrely at the chuckling and delighted little girl who was stirring biscuit crumbs around her plate with her finger. Mrs. Khan got up, full of imperious anger, pulled Shireen up from her chair, and went stormily out of the room, tugging the child after her by the hand. Stephen could hear her exclaiming and sighing and moving around the next room, and addressing alternately admonishing and tender remarks to the child. Then she wept loudly.

Hassan said, "Excuse me, sir, but I must go to my school. I asked permission to be here, and my teacher said yes, but I must go back quickly."

"Did your father tell you to be here?"

Hassan hesitated. "No, sir. My mother said I must be here."

For the first time Hassan was really looking at him. It even seemed that he might say something, explain . . . His eyes were full of a plea. For understanding? There was pride there, hurt.

"Thank you for staying to interpret, Hassan," said the social worker. "I wish I could talk to your father . . ."

"Excuse me, excuse me," said Hassan, and went running out. Stephen called, "Goodbye, Mrs. Khan," got no reply, and followed the boy. Along the dismal, stained and smelly corridors. Down the grey cement stairs. On to the walkway. A wind was blowing, fresh and strong. He looked down and saw Hassan four storeys below, a small urgent figure racing across the cement, leaping puddles, kicking bits of paper. He reached the street and vanished. He was running from a situation he hated: his whole body shouted it. What on earth . . . Just *what* was all that about?

And then Stephen understood. Suddenly. Just like that. But he couldn't believe it. But yes, he had to believe it. No, it wasn't possible . . .

Not impossible. It was true.

Mrs. Khan did not know that Shireen was "subnormal" as the medical record put it. She was not going to admit it. Although she had two normal sons and two normal daughters, all doing well at school, and she knew what normal bright children were like, she was not going to make the comparison. For her, Shireen was normal. No good saying this was impossible. For Stephen was muttering, "No, it simply isn't *on*, it's crazy." Anyway, he found these 'impossibilities' in his work every day. A rich and various lunacy inspired the human race and you could almost say the greater part of his work was dealing with this lunacy.

Stephen stood clutching the balustrade and gripping the file, because the wind was swirling noisily around the high walkway. His eyes were shut because he was examining in his mind's eye the picture of Mrs. Khan's face, that proud, cold, refusing look. So would a woman look while her husband shouted at her, "You stupid woman, she can't go to the big school with the others, why are you so stubborn? Do I have to explain it to you again?" She must have confronted her husband with this look and her silence a hundred times! And so he had not turned up for the appointment, or for the other appointment, because he knew it was no good. He didn't want to have to say to some social worker, "My wife's a fine woman, but she has this little peculiarity!" And Hassan wasn't going to say, "You see, sir, there's a little problem with my mother."

Stephen, eyes still shut, went on replaying what he had seen in that room: the tenderness on Mrs. Khan's face for her afflicted child, the smile on the boy's face, the real, warm, affectionate smile, at his sister. The little girl was swaddled in their tenderness, the family adored her, what was she going to learn at the special school better than she was getting from her family?

Stephen found he was filling with emotions that threatened to lift him off the walkway with the wind and float him off into the sky like a balloon. He wanted to laugh, or clap his hands, or sing with exhilaration. That woman, that *mother*, would not admit her little girl was simple. She just wouldn't agree to it! Why, it was a wonderful thing, a miracle! Good for you, Mrs. Khan, said Stephen Bentley opening his eyes, looking at the curtained windows four floors above him where he had no doubt Mrs. Khan was watching him, proud she had won yet another victory against those busybodies who would class her Shireen as stupid.

"Bloody marvellous," shouted the social worker into the wind. He opened his file against his knee then and there and wrote, "Father did not turn up as arranged. His presence essential." The date. His own name.

Questions for Discussion

1. What is the effect of the contrast between the neighborhood that social worker Stephen Bentley walks through and the inside of Mrs. Khan's apartment, where the interview takes place?
2. Why isn't the father present at the interview? What is implied by Hassan's reluctant performance of his father's role?
3. How are Mrs. Khan's strong personality and values revealed in her treatment of the social worker and in her appeals to him?
4. Why is Stephen Bentley initially confused by Mrs. Khan's behavior and her responses to him? Why does he finally accept her decision? What do his confusion and final concession reveal about his ability as a social worker?
5. What impact might the immigrant status of Mrs. Khan have on her attitudes toward social workers and the school system?

Ideas for Writing

1. In an essay, explore the reasons that Mrs. Khan decides not to send her daughter to the special school. Do you think that she has made the best decision for her daughter? Why or why not?
2. Write a story in which a parent or a couple makes a difficult decision about a child's education.

GRACE PALEY   (b. 1922)

Known for her minimalist style, Grace Paley relies not on plot but on the interplay of voice to carry her stories forward. At the same time, however, Paley's stories explore traditional themes of love, motherhood, and family companionship.

The daughter of Russian-Jewish political exiles, Paley grew up in the Bronx. She studied at Hunter College and New York University but eventually left college to marry. After separating from her husband, she raised two children while working as a typist, a writer, and a teacher at Columbia University, Syracuse University, and Sarah Lawrence College. She is a committed political activist who has participated in many formal protests: she was part of a mission to Vietnam in 1969 to negotiate for the release of prisoners of war, she has joined demonstrations against nuclear weapons, and she has protested against U.S. policies in Central America. Although she started out writing poetry, Paley is best known for her short-story collections *The Little Disturbances of Man: Stories of Men and Women In Love* (1959) and *Enormous Changes at the Last Minute* (1974), which includes "A Conversation with My Father." Her most recent collections are *Later the Same Day* (1985), *Long Walks and Intimate Talks* (1991), and *Collected Stories* (1994).

Believing that her roles as political activist, devoted mother, and teacher are complementary, Paley has said, "It may come from my political feelings, but I think art, literature, fiction, poetry, whatever it is, makes justice in the world."

A Conversation with My Father   (1974)

My father is eighty-six years old and in bed. His heart, that bloody motor, is equally old and will not do certain jobs any more. It still floods his head with brainy light. But it won't let his legs carry the weight of his body around the house. Despite my metaphors, this muscle failure is not due to his old heart, he says, but to a potassium shortage. Sitting on one pillow, leaning on three, he offers last-minute advice and makes a request.

"I would like you to write a simple story just once more," he says, "the kind de Maupassant wrote, or Chekhov, the kind you used to write. Just recognizable people and then write down what happened to them next."

I say, "Yes, why not? That's possible." I want to please him, though I don't remember writing that way. I *would* like to try to tell such a story, if he means the kind that begins: "There was a woman . . ." followed by plot, the absolute line between two points which I've always despised. Not for literary reasons, but because it takes all hope away. Everyone, real or invented, deserves the open destiny of life.

Finally I thought of a story that had been happening for a couple of years right across the street. I wrote it down, then read it aloud. "Pa," I said, "how about this? Do you mean something like this?"

> Once in my time there was a woman and she had a son. They lived nicely, in a small apartment in Manhattan. This boy at about fifteen became a junkie, which is not unusual in our neighborhood. In order to maintain her close friendship with him, she became a junkie too. She said it was part of the youth culture, with which she felt very much at home. After a while, for a number of reasons, the boy gave it all up and left the city and his mother in disgust. Hopeless and alone, she grieved. We all visit her.

"O.K., Pa, that's it," I said, "an unadorned and miserable tale."

"But that's not what I mean," my father said. "You misunderstood me on purpose. You know there's a lot more to it. You know that. You left everything out. Turgenev wouldn't do that. Chekhov wouldn't do that. There are in fact Russian writers you never heard of, you don't have an inkling of, as good as anyone, who can write a plain ordinary story, who would not leave out what you have left out. I object not to facts but to people sitting in trees talking senselessly, voices from who knows where. . . ."

"Forget that one, Pa, what have I left out now? In this one?"

"Her looks, for instance."

"Oh. Quite handsome, I think. Yes."

"Her hair?"

"Dark, with heavy braids, as though she were a girl or a foreigner."

"What were her parents like, her stock? That she became such a person. It's interesting, you know."

"From out of town. Professional people. The first to be divorced in their county. How's that? Enough?" I asked.

"With you, it's all a joke," he said. "What about the boy's father? Why didn't you mention him? Who was he? Or was the boy born out of wedlock?"

"Yes," I said. "He was born out of wedlock."

"For Godsakes, doesn't anyone in your stories get married? Doesn't anyone have the time to run down to City Hall before they jump into bed?"

"No," I said. "In real life, yes. But in my stories, no."

"Why do you answer me like that?"

"Oh, Pa, this is a simple story about a smart woman who came to N.Y.C. full of interest love trust excitement very up to date, and about her son, what a hard time she had in this world. Married or not, it's of small consequence."

"It is of great consequence," he said.

"O.K.," I said.

"O.K. O.K. yourself," he said, "but listen. I believe you that she's good-looking, but I don't think she was so smart."

"That's true," I said. "Actually that's the trouble with stories. People start out fantastic. You think they're extraordinary, but it turns out as the work goes along, they're just average with a good education. Sometimes the other way around, the person's a kind of dumb innocent, but he outwits you and you can't even think of an ending good enough."

"What do you do then?" he asked. He had been a doctor for a couple of decades and then an artist for a couple of decades and he's still interested in details, craft, technique.

"Well, you just have to let the story lie around till some agreement can be reached between you and the stubborn hero."

"Aren't you talking silly now?" he asked. "Start again," he said. "It so happens I'm not going out this evening. Tell the story again. See what you can do this time."

"O.K.," I said. "But it's not a five-minute job." Second attempt:

Once, across the street from us, there was a fine handsome woman, our neighbor. She had a son whom she loved because she'd known him since birth (in helpless chubby infancy, and in the wrestling, hugging ages, seven to ten, as well as earlier and later). This boy, when he fell into the fist of adolescence, became a junkie. He was not a hopeless one. He was in fact hopeful, an ideologue and successful converter. With his busy brilliance, he wrote persuasive articles for his high-school newspaper. Seeking a wider audience, using important connections, he drummed into Lower Manhattan newsstand distribution a periodical called *Oh! Golden Horse!*

In order to keep him from feeling guilty (because guilt is the stony heart of nine tenths of all clinically diagnosed cancers in America today, she said), and because she had always believed in giving bad habits room at home where one could keep an eye on them, she too became a junkie. Her kitchen was famous for a while — a center for intellectual addicts who knew what they were doing. A few felt artistic like Coleridge and others were scientific and revolutionary like Leary. Although she was often high herself, certain good mothering reflexes remained, and she saw to it that there was lots of orange juice around and honey and milk and vitamin pills. However, she never cooked anything but chili, and that no more than once a week. She explained, when we talked to her, seriously, with neighborly concern, that it was her part in the youth culture and she would rather be with the young, it was an honor, than with her own generation.

One week, while nodding through an Antonioni film, this boy was severely jabbed by the elbow of a stern and proselytizing girl, sitting beside him. She offered immediate apricots and nuts for his sugar level, spoke to him sharply, and took him home.

She had heard of him and his work and she herself published, edited, and wrote a competitive journal called *Man Does Live by Bread Alone*. In the organic heat of her continuous presence he could not help but become interested once more in his muscles, his arteries, and nerve connections. In fact he began to love them, treasure them, praise them with funny little songs in *Man Does Live*. . . .

> the fingers of my flesh transcend
> my transcendental soul
> the tightness in my shoulders end
> my teeth have made me whole

To the mouth of his head (that glory of will and determination) he brought hard apples, nuts, wheat germ, and soybean oil. He said to his old friends, From now on, I guess I'll keep my wits about me. I'm going on the natch. He said he was about to begin a spiritual deep-breathing journey. How about you too, Mom? he asked kindly.

His conversion was so radiant, splendid, that neighborhood kids his age began to say that he had never been a real addict at all, only a journalist along for the smell of the story. The mother tried several times to give up what had become without her son and his friends a lonely habit. This effort only brought it to supportable levels. The boy and his girl took their electronic mimeograph and moved to the bushy edge of another borough. They were very strict. They said they would not see her again until she had been off drugs for sixty days.

At home alone in the evening, weeping, the mother read and reread the seven issues of *Oh! Golden Horse!* They seemed to her as truthful as ever. We often crossed the street to visit and console. But if we mentioned any of our children who were at college or in the hospital or dropouts at home, she would cry out, My baby! My baby! and burst into terrible, face-scarring, time-consuming tears. The End.

First my father was silent, then he said, "Number One: You have a nice sense of humor. Number Two: I see you can't tell a plain story. So don't waste time." Then he said sadly, "Number Three: I suppose that means she was alone, she was left like that, his mother. Alone. Probably sick?"

I said, "Yes."

"Poor woman. Poor girl, to be born in a time of fools, to live among fools. The end. The end. You were right to put that down. The end."

I didn't want to argue, but I had to say, "Well, it is not necessarily the end, Pa."

"Yes," he said, "what a tragedy. The end of a person."

"No, Pa," I begged him. "It doesn't have to be. She's only about forty. She could be a hundred different things in this world as time goes on. A teacher or a social worker. An ex-junkie! Sometimes it's better than having a master's in education."

"Jokes," he said. "As a writer that's your main trouble. You don't want to recognize it. Tragedy! Plain tragedy! Historical tragedy! No hope. The end."

"Oh, Pa," I said. "She could change."

"In your own life, too, you have to look it in the face." He took a couple of nitroglycerin. "Turn to five," he said, pointing to the dial on the oxygen tank. He inserted the tubes into his nostrils and breathed deep. He closed his eyes and said, "No."

I had promised the family to always let him have the last word when arguing, but in this case I had a different responsibility. That woman lives across the street. She's my knowledge and my invention. I'm sorry for her. I'm not going to leave her there in that house crying. (Actually neither would Life, which unlike me has no pity.)

Therefore: She did change. Of course her son never came home again. But right now, she's the receptionist in a storefront community clinic in the East Village. Most of the customers are young people, some old friends. The head doctor has said to her, "If we only had three people in this clinic with your experiences. . . ."

"The doctor said that?" My father took the oxygen tubes out of his nostrils and said, "Jokes. Jokes again."

"No, Pa, it could really happen that way, it's a funny world nowadays."

"No," he said. "Truth first. She will slide back. A person must have character. She does not."

"No, Pa," I said. "That's it. She's got a job. Forget it. She's in that storefront working."

"How long will it be?" he asked. "Tragedy! You too. When will you look it in the face?"

Questions for Discussion

1. What does the father's wish for his daughter to write a traditional short story such as those of Chekhov or Maupassant and the daughter's rejection of the traditional plotline reveal about each one's values and outlook on life?
2. What is the basis of the father's objections to the first two versions of his daughter's story? Do his objections seem appropriate or fair?
3. What concepts about the story-writing process are demonstrated through the dialogue between father and daughter?
4. Why does the daughter have a comic view of life and art while her father has a tragic view? Which perspective is better supported by the story itself and the story-within-a-story that the daughter is writing? How does the father's illness affect the positions he takes and the themes of the story?
5. How do the style and structure of the story help Paley to make her point about the role of storytelling in life?

Ideas for Writing

1. Write an essay that discusses the relationship that Paley presents in the story between life and storytelling, between life and art.
2. Write a story that is focused on a disagreement between two relatives or friends over a piece of writing that one of them is working on. Include the work-in-progress and demonstrate through your characters' disagreement their different values, especially their attitudes about the role of a writer's work.

ITALO CALVINO   (1923–1985)

Early in his career, Italian writer Italo Calvino made a direct connection between narrative and the fable. Many of his subsequent works can be seen as fables for adults, set against playful imagined landscapes and generally offering moral instruction in the form of fantasy. Calvino was born in Cuba, but his family of scientists returned to Italy when he was very young, settling in a small town on the Italian Riviera, where Calvino grew up. After fighting with the Resistance movement during World War II, he attended the University of Turin, graduating in 1947. He was associated with the Italian Communist party for the next ten years and wrote his early novels in the neorealist tradition. After his break with communism, he traveled extensively and turned to an increasingly wide range of literary sources, including folk tales. He began to draw on literary and scientific theory for his inspiration, eventually becoming known as postwar Italy's most intellectual and cosmopolitan writer. His later works include *Italian Folktales* (1956), *Cosmicomics* (1965), *If on a Winter's Night a Traveller* (1979), and *Difficult Loves* (1984), which includes "The Adventure of a Reader." Calvino's works are distinguished by their wit, imagination, and craftsmanship. They illuminate the complexities of the human condition, offering a refreshing outlook on sometimes conventional themes.

The Adventure of a Reader   (1949)

Translated by D. M. Low

The coast road ran high above the cape; the sea was below, a sheer drop, and on all sides, as far as the hazy mountainous horizon. The sun was on all sides, too, as if the sky and the sea were two glasses magnifying it. Down below, against the jagged, irregular rocks of the cape, the calm water slapped without making foam. Amedeo Oliva climbed down a steep flight of steps, shouldering his bicycle, which he then left in a shady place, after closing the padlock. He continued down the steps amid spills of dry yellow earth and agaves jutting into the void, and he was already looking around for the most comfortable stretch of rock to lie down. Under his arm he had a rolled-up towel and, inside the towel, his bathing trunks and a book.

The cape was a solitary place: only a few groups of bathers dived into the water or took the sun, hidden from one another by the irregular conformation of the place. Between two boulders that shielded him from view, Amedeo undressed, put on his trunks, and began jumping from the top of one rock to the next. Leaping in this way on his skinny legs, he crossed half the rocky shore, sometimes almost grazing the faces of half-hidden pairs of bathers stretched out on beach towels. Having gone past an outcrop of sandy rock, its surface porous and irregular, he came upon smooth stones, with rounded corners; Amedeo took off his sandals, held them in his hand, and continued running barefoot, with the confidence of someone who can judge distances between rocks and whose soles nothing can hurt. He reached a spot directly above the sea; there was a kind of shelf running around the cliff at the halfway point. There Amedeo stopped. On a flat ledge he arranged his clothes, carefully folded, and set the sandals on them, soles up, so no gust of wind would carry everything off (in reality, only the faintest breath of air was stirring, from the sea; but this precaution was obviously a habit with him). A little bag he was carrying turned into a rubber cushion; he blew into it until it had filled out, then set it down; and below it, at a point slightly sloping from that rocky ledge, he spread out his towel. He flung himself on it supine, and already his hands were opening his book at the marked page. So he lay stretched out on the ledge, in that sun glaring on all sides, his skin dry (his tan was opaque, irregular, as of one who takes the sun without any method but doesn't burn); on the rubber cushion he set his head sheathed in a white canvas cap, moistened (yes, he had also climbed down to a low rock, to dip his cap in the water), immobile except for his eyes (invisible behind his dark glasses), which followed along the black and white lines the horse of Fabrizio del Dongo. Below him opened a little cove of greenish-blue water, transparent almost to the bottom. The rocks, according to their exposure, were bleached white or covered with algae. A little pebble beach was at their foot. Every now and then Amedeo raised his eyes to that broad view, lingered on a glinting of the surface, on the oblique dash of a crab; then he went back, gripped, to the page where Raskolnikov counted the steps that separated him from the old woman's door, or where Lucien de Rubempré, before sticking his head into the noose, gazed at the towers and roofs of the Conciergerie.

For some time Amedeo had tended to reduce his participation in active life to the minimum. Not that he didn't like action: on the contrary, love of action nourished his whole character, all his tastes; and yet, from one year to the next, the yearning to be someone who did things declined, declined, until he wondered if he had ever really harbored that yearning. His interest in action survived, however, in his pleasure in reading; his passion was always the narration of events, the stories, the tangle of human situations — nineteenth-century novels especially, but also memoirs and biographies, and so on down to thrillers and science fiction, which he didn't disdain but which gave him less satisfaction because they were short. Amedeo loved thick tomes, and in tackling them he felt the physical pleasure of undertaking a great task. Weighing them in his hand, thick, closely printed, squat, he would consider with some apprehension the number of pages, the length of the chapters, then venture into them, a bit reluctant at the beginning, without any desire to perform the initial chore of remembering the names, catching the drift of the story; then he would entrust himself to it, running along the lines, crossing the grid of the uniform page, and beyond the leaden print the flame and fire of battle appeared, the cannonball that, whistling through the sky, fell at the feet of Prince Andrei, and the shop filled with engravings and statues where Frédéric Moreau, his heart in his mouth, was to meet the Arnoux family. Beyond the surface of the page you entered a world where life was more alive than here on this side: like the surface of the water that separates us from that blue-and-green world, rifts as far as the eye can see, expanses of fine, ribbed sand, creatures half animal and half vegetable.

The sun beat down hard, the rock was burning, and after a while Amedeo felt he was one with the rock. He reached the end of the chapter, closed the book, inserted an advertising coupon to mark his place, took off his canvas cap and his glasses, stood up half dazed, and with broad leaps went down to the far end of the rock, where a group of kids were constantly, at all hours, diving in and climbing out. Amedeo stood erect on a shelf over the sea, not too high, a couple of yards above the water; his eyes, still dazzled, contemplated the luminous transparence below him, and all of a sudden he plunged. His dive was always the same: headlong, fairly correct, but with a certain stiffness. The passage from the sunny air to the tepid water would have been almost unnoticeable if it hadn't been abrupt. He didn't surface immediately: he liked to swim underwater, down, down, his belly almost scraping bottom, as long as his breath held out. He very much enjoyed physical effort, setting himself difficult assignments (for this he came to read his book at the cape, making the climb on his bicycle, pedaling up furiously under the noonday sun). Every time, swimming underwater, he tried to reach a wall of rocks that rose at a certain point from the sandy bed and was covered by a thick patch of sea grasses. He surfaced among those rocks and swam around a bit; he began to do "the Australian crawl" methodically, but expending more energy than necessary; soon, tired of swimming with his face in the water, as if blind, he took to a freer side stroke; sight gave him more satisfaction than movement, and in a little while he gave up the side stroke to drift on his back, moving less and less regularly and steadily, until he stopped altogether, in a dead-man's-float. And so he turned and twisted in that sea as in a bed without sides; he would set himself the goal of a sandbar to be reached, or limit the number of strokes, and he couldn't rest until he had carried out that task. For a while he would dawdle lazily, then he would head out to sea, taken by the desire to have nothing around him but sky and water; for a while he would move close to the rocks scattered along the cape, not to overlook any of the possible itineraries of that little archipelago. But as he swam, he realized that the curiosity occupying more and more of his mind was to know the outcome — for example — of the story of Albertine. Would Marcel find her again, or not? He swam furiously or floated idly, but his heart was between the pages of the book left behind on shore. And so, with rapid strokes, he would regain his rock, seek the place for climbing up, and, almost without realizing it, he would be up there again, rubbing the Turkish towel on his back. Sticking the canvas cap on his head once more, he would lie in the sun again, to begin the next chapter.

He was not, however, a hasty, voracious reader. He had reached the age when rereading a book — for the second, third, or fourth time — affords more pleasure than a first reading. And yet he still had many continents to discover. Every summer, the most laborious packing before his departure for the sea involved the heavy suitcase to be filled with books. Following the whims and dictates of the months of city life, each year Amedeo would choose certain famous books to reread and certain authors to essay for the first time. And there, on the rock, he went through them, lingering over sentences, often raising his eyes from the page to ponder, to collect his thoughts. At a certain point, raising his eyes in this way, he saw that on the little pebble beach below, in the cove, a woman had appeared and was lying there.

She was deeply tanned, thin, not very young or particularly beautiful, but nakedness became her (she wore a very tiny "two-piece," rolled up at the edges to get as much sun as she could), and Amedeo's eye was drawn to her. He realized that as he read he was raising his eyes more and more often from the book to gaze into the air; this air was the air that lay between that woman and himself. Her face (she was stretched out on the sloping shore, on a rubber mattress, and at every flicker of his pupils Amedeo saw her legs, not shapely but harmonious, the excellently smooth belly, the bosom slim in a perhaps not unpleasant way but probably sagging a bit, the shoulders a bit too bony, and then the neck and the arms, and the face masked by the sunglasses and by the brim of the straw hat) was slightly lined, lively, aware, and ironic. Amedeo classified the type: the independent woman, on holiday by herself, who dislikes crowded beaches and prefers the more deserted rocks, and likes to lie there and become black as coal; he evaluated the amount of lazy sensuality and of chronic frustration there was in her; he thought fleetingly of the likelihood of a rapidly consummated fling, measured it against the prospect of a trite conversation, a program for the evening, probable logistic difficulties, the effort of concentration always required to become acquainted, even superficially, with a person; and he went on reading, convinced that this woman couldn't interest him at all.

But he had been lying on that stretch of rock for too long, or else those fleeting thoughts had left a wake of restlessness in him; anyway, he felt an ache, the hardness of the rock under the towel that was his only pallet began to chafe him. He got up to look for another spot where he could stretch out. For a moment, he hesitated between two places that seemed equally comfortable to him: one more distant from the little beach where the tanned lady was lying (actually behind an outcrop of rock that blocked the sight of her), the other closer. The thought of approaching and of then perhaps being led by some unforeseeable circumstance to start a conversation, and thus perforce to interrupt his reading, made him immediately prefer the farther spot; but when he thought it over, it really would look as if, the moment that lady had arrived, he wanted to run off, and this might seem a bit rude; so he picked the closer spot, since his reading absorbed him so much anyway that the view of the lady — not specially beautiful, for that matter — could hardly distract him. He lay on one side, holding the book so that it blocked the sight of her, but it was awkward to keep his arm at that height, and in the end he lowered it. Now, every time he had to start a new line, the same gaze that ran along the lines encountered, just beyond the edge of the page, the legs of the solitary vacationer. She, too, had shifted slightly, looking for a more comfortable position, and the fact that she had raised her knees and crossed her legs precisely in Amedeo's direction allowed him to observe better her proportions, not unattractive. In short, Amedeo (though a shaft of rock was sawing at his hip) couldn't have found a finer position: the pleasure he could derive from the sight of the tanned lady — a marginal pleasure, something extra, but not for that reason to be discarded, since it could be enjoyed with no effort — did not mar the pleasure of reading, but was inserted into its normal process, so that now he was sure he could go on reading without being tempted to look away.

Everything was calm; only the course of his reading flowed on, with the motionless landscape serving as frame; the tanned lady had become a necessary part of this landscape. Amedeo was naturally relying on his own ability to remain absolutely still for a long time, but he hadn't taken into account the woman's restlessness: now she rose, was standing, making her way among the stones toward the water. She had moved — Amedeo understood immediately — to get a closer look at a great medusa that a group of boys were bringing ashore, poking at it with lengths of reed. The tanned lady bent toward the overturned body of the medusa and was questioning the boys; her legs rose from wooden clogs with very high heels, unsuited to those rocks; her body, seen from behind as Amedeo now saw it, was that of a more attractive younger woman than she had first seemed to him. He thought that, for a man seeking a romance, that dialogue between her and the fisher-boys would have been a "classic" opening: approach, also remark on the capture of the medusa, and in that way engage her in conversation. The very thing he wouldn't have done for all the gold in the world! he added to himself, plunging again into his reading.

To be sure, this rule of conduct of his also prevented him from satisfying a natural curiosity concerning the medusa, which seemed, as he saw it there, of unusual dimensions, and also of a strange hue between pink and violet. This curiosity about marine animals was in no way a sidetrack, either; it was coherent with the nature of his passion for reading. At that moment, in any case, his concentration on the page he was reading — a long descriptive passage — had been relaxing; in short, it was absurd that to protect himself against the danger of starting a conversation with that woman he should also deny himself spontaneous and quite legitimate impulses such as that of amusing himself for a few minutes by taking a close look at a medusa. He shut his book at the marked page and stood up. His decision couldn't have been more timely: at that same moment the lady moved away from the little group of boys, preparing to return to her mattress. Amedeo realized this as he was approaching and felt the need of immediately saying something in a loud voice. He shouted to the kids, "Watch out! It could be dangerous!"

The boys, crouched around the animal, didn't even look up: they continued, with the lengths of reed they held in their hands, to try to raise it and turn it over; but the lady turned abruptly and went back to the shore, with a half-questioning, half-fearful air. "Oh, how frightening! Does it bite?"

"If you touch it, it stings," he explained and realized he was heading not toward the medusa but toward the lady, who, for some reason, covered her bosom with her arms in a useless shudder and cast almost furtive glances, first at the supine animal, then at Amedeo. He reassured her, and so, predictably, they started conversing; but it didn't matter, because Amedeo would soon be going back to the book awaiting him: he only wanted to take a glance at the medusa. He led the tanned lady over, to lean into the center of the circle of boys. The lady was now observing with revulsion, her knuckles against her teeth, and at a certain point, as she and he were side by side, their arms came into contact and they delayed a moment before separating them. Amedeo then started talking about medusas. His direct experience wasn't great, but he had read some books by famous fishermen and underwater explorers, so, — skipping the smaller fauna — he began promptly talking about the famous manta. The lady listened to him, displaying great interest and interjecting something from time to time, always irrelevantly, the way women will. "You see this red spot on my arm? That wasn't a medusa, was it?" Amedeo touched the spot, just above the elbow, and said no. It was a bit red because she had been leaning on it while lying down.

With that, it was all over. They said good-bye; she went back to her place, and he to his, where he resumed reading. It had been an interval lasting the right amount of time, neither more nor less, a human encounter, not unpleasant (the lady was polite, discreet, unassuming) precisely because it was barely adumbrated. In the book he now found a far fuller and more concrete attachment to reality, where everything had a meaning, an importance, a rhythm. Amedeo felt himself in a perfect situation: the printed page opened true life to him, profound and exciting, and, raising his eyes, he found a pleasant but casual juxtaposition of colors and sensations, an accessory and decorative world that couldn't commit him to anything. The tanned lady, from her mattress, gave him a smile and a wave; he replied also with a smile and a vague gesture, and immediately lowered his eyes. But the lady had said something.

"Eh?"

"You're reading. Do you read all the time?"

"Mmm . . ."

"Interesting?"

"Yes."

"Enjoy yourself!"

"Thank you."

He mustn't raise his eyes again. At least not until the end of the chapter. He read it in a flash. The lady now had a cigarette in her mouth and motioned to him, as she pointed to it. Amedeo had the impression that for some time she had been trying to attract his attention. "I beg your pardon?"

". . . match. Forgive me. . . ."

"Oh, I'm very sorry. I don't smoke. . . ."

The chapter was finished. Amedeo rapidly read the first lines of the next one, which he found surprisingly attractive, but to begin the next chapter without anxiety he had to resolve as quickly as possible the matter of the match. "Wait!" He stood up, began leaping among the rocks, half dazed by the sun, until he found a little group of people smoking. He borrowed a box of matches, ran to the lady, lighted her cigarette, ran back to return the matches; and they said to him, "Keep them, you can keep them." He ran again to the lady to leave the matches with her, and she thanked him; he waited a moment before leaving her, but realized that after this delay he had to say something, and so he said, "You aren't swimming?"

"In a little while," the lady said. "What about you?"

"I've already had my swim."

"And you're not going to take another dip?"

"Yes, I'll read one more chapter, then have a swim again."

"Me, too, when I finish my cigarette, I'll dive in."

"See you later then."

"Later . . ."

This kind of appointment restored to Amedeo a calm such as he — now he realized — had not known since the moment he became aware of the solitary lady: now his conscience was no longer oppressed by the thought of having to have any sort of relationship with that lady; everything was postponed to the moment of their swim — a swim he would have taken anyway, even if the lady hadn't been there — and for now he could abandon himself without remorse to the pleasure of reading. So thoroughly that he didn't notice when, at a certain point — before he had reached the end of the chapter — the lady finished her cigarette, stood up, and approached him to invite him to go swimming. He saw the clogs and the straight legs just beyond the book; his eyes moved up; he lowered them again to the page — the sun was dazzling — and read a few lines in haste, looked up again, and heard her say, "Isn't your head about to explode? I'm going to have a dip!" It was nice to stay there, to go on reading and look up every now and then. But since he could no longer put it off, Amedeo did something he never did: he skipped almost half a page, to the conclusion of the chapter, which he read, on the other hand, with great attention, and then he stood up. "Let's go. Shall we dive from the point there?"

After all the talk of diving, the lady cautiously slipped into the water from a ledge on a level with it. Amedeo plunged headlong from a higher rock than usual. It was the hour of the still slow inclining of the sun. The sea was golden. They swam in that gold, somewhat separated: Amedeo at times sank for a few strokes underwater and amused himself by frightening the lady, swimming beneath her. Amused himself, after a fashion: it was kid stuff, of course, but for that matter, what else was there to do, anyway? Swimming with another person was slightly more tiresome than swimming alone, but the difference was minimal. Beyond the gold glints, the water's blue deepened, as if from down below rose an inky darkness. It was useless: nothing equaled the savor of life found in books. Skimming over some bearded rocks in mid-water and leading her, frightened (to help her onto a sandbar, he also clasped her hips and bosom, but his hands, from the immersion, had become almost insensitive, with white wrinkled pads), Amedeo turned his gaze more and more often toward land, where the colored jacket of his book stood out. There was no other story, no other possible expectation beyond what he had left suspended, between the pages where his bookmark was; all the rest was an empty interval.

However, returning to shore, giving her a hand, drying himself, then each rubbing the other's back, finally created a kind of intimacy, so that Amedeo felt it would have been impolite to go off on his own once more. "Well," he said, "I'll stretch out and read here; I'll go get my book and pillow." And *read:* he had taken care to warn her. She said, "Yes, fine. I'll smoke a cigarette and read *Annabella* a bit myself." She had one of those women's magazines with her, and so both of them could lie and read, each on his own. Her voice struck him like a drop of cold water on the nape of the neck, but she was only saying, "Why do you want to lie there on that hard rock? Come onto the mattress: I'll make room for you." The invitation was polite, the mattress was comfortable, and Amedeo gladly accepted. They lay there, he facing in one direction and she in the other. She didn't say another word, she leafed through those illustrated pages, and Amedeo managed to sink completely into his reading. It was a lingering sunset, when the heat and light hardly decline but remain only barely, sweetly attenuated. The novel Amedeo was reading had reached the point where the darkest secrets of characters and plot are revealed, and you move in a familiar world, and you achieve a kind of parity, an ease between author and reader: you proceed together, and you would like to go on forever.

On the rubber mattress it was possible to make those slight movements necessary to keep the limbs from going to sleep, and one of his legs, in one direction, came to graze a leg of hers, in the other. He didn't mind this, and kept his leg there; and obviously she didn't mind, either, because she also refrained from moving. The sweetness of the contact mingled with the reading and, as far as Amedeo was concerned, made it the more complete; but for the lady it must have been different, because she rose, sat up, and said, "Really . . ."

Amedeo was forced to raise his head from the book. The woman was looking at him, and her eyes were bitter.

"Something wrong?" he asked.

"Don't you ever get tired of reading?" she asked. "You could hardly be called good company! Don't you know that, with women, you're supposed to make conversation?" she added; her half smile was perhaps meant only to be ironic, though to Amedeo, who at that moment would have paid anything rather than give up his novel, it seemed downright threatening. What have I got myself into, moving down here? he thought. Now it was clear that with this woman beside him he wouldn't read a line.

I must make her realize she's made a mistake, he thought, that I'm not at all the type for a beach courtship, that I'm the sort it's best not to pay too much attention to. "Conversation," he said, aloud, "what kind of conversation?" and he extended his hand toward her. There, now: if I lay a hand on her, she will surely be insulted by such an unsuitable action, maybe she'll give me a slap and go away. But whether it was his own natural reserve, or there was a different, sweeter yearning that in reality he was pursuing, the caress, instead of being brutal and provocatory, was shy, melancholy, almost entreating: he grazed her throat with his fingers, lifted a little necklace she was wearing, and let it fall. The woman's reply consisted of a movement, first slow, as if resigned and a bit ironic — she lowered her chin to one side, to trap his hand — then rapid, as if in a calculated, aggressive spring: she bit the back of his hand. "Ow!" Amedeo cried. They moved apart.

"Is this how you make conversation?" the lady said.

There, Amedeo quickly reasoned, my way of making conversation doesn't suit her, so there won't be any conversing, and now I can read; he had already started a new paragraph. But he was trying to deceive himself: he understood clearly that by now they had gone too far, that between him and the tanned lady a tension had been created that could no longer be interrupted; he also understood that he was the first to wish not to interrupt it, since in any case he wouldn't be able to return to the single tension of his reading, all intimate and interior. He could, on the contrary, try to make this exterior tension follow, so to speak, a course parallel to the other, so that he would not be obliged to renounce either the lady or the book.

Since she had sat up, with her back propped against a rock, he sat beside her, put his arm around her shoulders, keeping his book on his knees. He turned toward her and kissed her. They moved apart, then kissed again. Then he lowered his head toward the book and resumed reading.

As long as he could, he wanted to continue reading. His fear was that he wouldn't be able to finish the novel: the beginning of a summer affair could be considered the end of his calm hours of solitude, for a completely different rhythm would dominate his days of vacation; and obviously, when you are completely lost in reading a book, if you have to interrupt it, then pick it up again some time later, most of the pleasure is lost: you forget so many details, you never manage to become immersed in it as before.

The sun was gradually setting behind the next promontory, and then the next, and the one after that, leaving remnants of color against the light. From the little coves of the cape, all the bathers had gone. Now the two of them were alone. Amedeo had his arm around the woman's shoulders, he was reading, he gave her kisses on the neck and on the ears — which it seemed to him she liked — and every now and then, when she turned, on the mouth; then he resumed reading. Perhaps this time he had found the ideal equilibrium: he could go on like this for a hundred pages or so. But once again it was she who wanted to change the situation. She began to stiffen, almost to reject him, and then said, "It's late. Let's go. I'm going to dress."

This abrupt decision opened up quite different prospects. Amedeo was a bit disoriented, but he didn't stop to weigh the pros and cons. He had reached a climax in the book, and her dimly heard words, "I'm going to dress," had, in his mind, immediately been translated into these others: While she dresses, I'll have time to read a few pages without being disturbed.

But she said, "Hold up the towel, please," addressing him as *tu* for perhaps the first time. "I don't want anyone to see me." The precaution was useless because the shore by now was deserted, but Amedeo consented amiably, since he could hold up the towel while remaining seated and so continue to read the book on his knees.

On the other side of the towel, the lady had undone her halter, paying no attention to whether he was looking at her or not. Amedeo didn't know whether to look at her, pretending to read, or to read, pretending to look at her. He was interested in the one thing and the other, but looking at her seemed too indiscreet, while going on reading seemed too indifferent. The lady did not follow the usual method used by bathers who dress outdoors, first putting on clothes and then removing the bathing suit underneath them. No: now that her bosom was bared, she also took off the bottom of her suit. This was when, for the first time, she turned her face toward him; and it was a sad face, with a bitter curl to the mouth, and she shook her head, shook her head and looked at him.

Since it has to happen, it might as well happen immediately, Amedeo thought, diving forward, book in hand, one finger between the pages; but what he read in that gaze — reproach, commiseration, dejection, as if to say: Stupid, all right, we'll do it if it has to be done like this, but you don't understand a thing, any more than the others — or, rather, what he did *not* read, since he didn't know how to read gazes, but only vaguely sensed, roused in him a moment of such transport toward the woman that, embracing her and falling onto the mattress with her, he only slightly turned his head toward the book to make sure it didn't fall into the sea.

It had fallen, instead, right beside the mattress, open, but a few pages had flipped over; and Amedeo, even in the ecstasy of his embraces, tried to free one hand to put the bookmark at the right page. Nothing is more irritating when you're eager to resume reading than to have to search through the book, unable to find your place.

Their lovemaking was a perfect match. It could perhaps have been extended a bit longer: but, then, hadn't everything been lightning-fast in their encounter?

Dusk was falling. Below, the rocks opened out, sloping, into a little harbor. Now she had gone down there and was halfway into the water. "Come down: we'll have a last swim. . . ." Amedeo, biting his lip, was counting how many pages were left till the end.

Questions for Discussion

1. How does the opening description set the tone for the story and introduce Amedeo's character? What does the presentation of his descent and bathing preparations in such painstaking detail reveal?

2. What type of books does Amedeo like to read? What do his choices of books as well as his absorption in the act of reading suggest about his character? Does his interest in reading seem obsessive or unhealthy?

3. How does Amedeo "read" the woman on the beach? What is implied about his relationship with women and with people in general through the way he communicates with her? If Amedeo is so involved in his reading, why does he find it hard to "renounce the lady"?

4. As Amedeo begins to make love to the woman, the metaphor of reading is continued: "He didn't know how to read gazes." Why is this metaphor of "reading gazes" ironic?

5. What comparison between the course of a relationship and the reading of a book is made with the story's concluding statement, "Amedeo, biting his lip, was counting how many pages were left till the end"? In what ways are reading and lovemaking similar?

Ideas for Writing

1. Write an essay in which you analyze the different kinds of "reading" that take place in relationships between men and women. In what ways do men and women get to know and to "read" each other differently? How are these differences embodied in "The Adventure of a Reader"?

2. Write a story about an introverted character like Amedeo who is obsessed with reading.

A white native of South Africa, Nadine Gordimer explores the moral and social questions that have made equality and justice compelling issues there. She has been praised for the delicacy and compassion with which she renders her characters' relationships.

Gordimer was born and raised in a small gold-mining town near Johannesburg. As a teenager, she decided that she wanted to become a writer. While studying at the University of the Witwatersrand, she was strongly influenced by modern British and American writers such as Katherine Mansfield, D. H. Lawrence, Henry James, Ernest Hemingway, and Eudora Welty. Although she still lives in Johannesburg, Gordimer has traveled all over the world and has lectured at major universities in America. In 1991 she was honored with the Nobel Prize for Literature. She has written ten novels, the best known of which are *The Conversationalist* (1974), *A Sport of Nature* (1987), and *My Son's Story* (1990). She is chiefly noted, however, for her story collections, the first of which, *Face to Face,* appeared in 1949. She has subsequently published ten collections, including *The Soft Voice of the Serpent and Other Stories* (1952) and *Friday's Footprint and Other Stories* (1960). Her *Selected Stories, 1950–1972* appeared in 1993.

Gordimer believes that her ideas can be best expressed in the short-story form, which she describes as "a fragmented and a restless form, a matter of hit or miss, and it is perhaps for this reason that it suits modern consciousness."

Crimes of Conscience   (1981)

Apparently they noticed each other at the same moment, coming down the steps of the Supreme Court on the third day of the trial. By then casual spectators who come for a look at the accused — to see for themselves who will risk prison walls round their bodies for ideas in their heads — have satisfied curiosity; only those who have some special interest attend day after day. He could have been a journalist; or an aide to the representative of one of the Western powers who 'observe' political trials in countries problematic for foreign policy and subject to human rights lobbying back in Western Europe and America. He wore a corduroy suit of unfamiliar cut. But when he spoke it was clear he was, like her, someone at home — he had the accent, and the casual, colloquial turn of phrase. "What a session! I don't know . . . After two hours of that . . . feel like I'm caught in a roll of sticky tape . . . unreal . . ."

There was no mistaking her. She was a young woman whose cultivated gentleness of expression and shabby homespun style of dress, in the context in which she was encountered, suggested not transcendental meditation centre or environmental concern group or design studio, but a sign of identification with the humanity of those who had nothing and risked themselves. Her only adornment, a necklace of ostrich-shell discs stacked along a thread, moved tight at the base of her throat tendons as she smiled and agreed. "Lawyers work like that . . . I've noticed. The first few days, it's a matter of people trying each to confuse the other side."

Later in the week, they had coffee together during the court's lunch adjournment. He expressed some naïve impressions of the trial, but as if fully aware of gullibility. Why did the State call witnesses who came right out and said the regime oppressed their spirits and frustrated their normal ambitions? Surely that kind of testimony favoured the Defence, when the issue was a crime of conscience? She shook fine hair, ripply as a mohair rug. "Just wait. Just wait. That's to establish credibility. To prove their involvement with the accused, their intimate knowledge of what the accused said and did, to *inculpate* the accused in what the Defence's going to deny. Don't you see?"

"Now I see." He smiled to himself. "When I was here before, I didn't take much interest in political things . . . activist politics, I suppose you'd call it? It's only since I've been back from overseas . . ."

She asked conversationally what was expected of her: how long had he been away?

"Nearly five years. Advertising then computers . . ." The dying-out of the sentence suggested the lack of interest in which these careers had petered. "Two years ago I just felt I wanted to come back. I couldn't give myself a real reason. I've been doing the same sort of work here — actually, I ran a course at the business school of a university, this year — and I'm slowly beginning to find out *why* I wanted to. To come back. It seems it's something to do with things like *this*."

She had a face that showed her mind following another's; eyebrows and mouth expressed quiet understanding.

"I imagine all this sounds rather feeble to you. I don't suppose you're someone who stands on the sidelines."

Her thin, knobbly little hands were like tools laid upon the formica counter of the coffee bar. In a moment of absence from their capability, they fiddled with the sugar sachets while she answered. "What makes you think that."

"You seem to know so much. As if you'd been through it yourself . . . Or maybe . . . you're a law student?"

"Me? Good lord, no." After one or two swallows of coffee, she offered a friendly response. "I work for a correspondence college."

"Teacher."

Smiling again: "Teaching people I never see."

"That doesn't fit too well. You look the kind of person who's more involved."

For the first time, polite interest changed, warmed. "That's what you missed, in London? Not being involved . . . ?"

At that meeting he gave her a name, and she told him hers.

The name was Derek Felterman. It was his real name. He *had* spent five years in London; he *had* worked in an advertising company and then studied computer science at an appropriate institution, and it was in London that he was recruited by someone from the Embassy who wasn't a diplomat but a representative of the internal security section of State security in his native country. Nobody knows how secret police recognize likely candidates; it is as mysterious as sexing chickens. But if the definitive characteristic sought is there to be recognized, the recruiting agent will see it, no matter how deeply the individual may hide his likely candidacy from himself.

He was not employed to infiltrate refugee circles plotting abroad. It was decided that he would come home "clean," and begin work in the political backwater of a coastal town, on a university campus. Then he was sent north to the mining and industrial centre of the country, told to get himself an ordinary commercial job without campus connections, and, as a new face, seek contacts wherever the information his employers wanted was likely to be let slip — left-wing cultural gatherings, poster-waving protest groups, the public gallery at political trials. His employers trusted him to know how to ingratiate himself; that was one of the qualities he had been fancied for, as a woman might fancy him for some other characteristic over which he had no volition — the way one corner of his mouth curled when he smiled, or the brown gloss of his eyes.

He, in turn, had quickly recognized her — first as a type, and then, the third day, when he went away from the court for verification of her in police files, as the girl who had gone secretly to visit a woman friend who was under House Arrest, and subsequently had served a three-month jail sentence for refusing to testify in a case brought against the woman for breaking her isolation ban. Aly, she had called herself. Alison Jane Ross. There was no direct connection to be found between Alison Jane Ross's interest in the present trial and the individuals on trial; but from the point of view of his avocation this did not exclude her possible involvement with a master organization or back-up group involved in continuing action of the subversive kind the charges named.

Felterman literally moved in to friendship with her, carrying a heavy case of books and a portable grill. He had asked if she would come to see a play with him on Saturday night. Alas, she was moving house that Saturday; perhaps he'd like to come and help, instead? The suggestion was added, tongue-in-cheek at her own presumption. He was there on time. Her family of friends, introduced by diminutives of their names, provided a combined service of old combi, springless station-wagon, take-away food and affectionate energy to fuel and accomplish the move from a flat to a tiny house with an ancient palm tree filling a square of garden, grating its dried fronds in the wind with the sound of a giant insect rubbing its legs together. To the night-song of that creature they made love for the first time a month later. Although all the Robs,

Jimbos and Ricks, as well as the Jojos, Bets and Lils, kissed and hugged their friend Aly, there seemed to be no lover about who had therefore been supplanted. On the particular, delicate path of intimacy along which she drew him or that he laid out before her, there was room only for the two of them. At the beginning of ease between them, even before they were lovers, she had come of herself to the stage of mentioning that experience of going to prison, but she talked of it always in banal surface terms — how the blankets smelled of disinfectant and the Chief Wardress's cat used to do the inspection round with its mistress. Now she did not ask him about other women, although he was moved, occasionally, in some involuntary warm welling-up complementary to that other tide — of sexual pleasure spent — to confess by the indirection of an anecdote, past affairs, women who had had their time and place. When the right moment came naturally to her, she told without shame, resentment or vanity that she had just spent a year "on her own" as something she felt she needed after living for three years with someone who, in the end, went back to his wife. Lately there had been one or two brief affairs — "Sometimes — don't you find — an old friend suddenly becomes something else . . . just for a little while, as if a face is turned to another angle . . . ? And next day, it's the same old one again. Nothing's changed."

"Friends are the most important thing for you, aren't they? I mean, everybody has friends, but you . . . You'd really do *anything*. For your friends. Wouldn't you?"

There seemed to come from her reaction rather than his words a reference to the three months she had spent in prison. She lifted the curly pelmet of hair from her forehead and the freckles faded against a flush colouring beneath: "And they for me."

"It's not just a matter of friendship, either — of course, I see that. Comrades — a band of brothers . . ."

She saw him as a child staring through a window at others playing. She leant over and took up his hand, kissed him with the kind of caress they had not exchanged before, on each eyelid.

Nevertheless her friends were a little neglected in favour of him. He would have liked to have been taken into the group more closely, but it is normal for two people involved in a passionate love affair to draw apart from others for a while. It would have looked unnatural to press to behave otherwise. It was also understood between them that Felterman didn't have much more than acquaintances to neglect; five years abroad and then two in the coastal town accounted for that. He revived for her pleasures she had left behind as a schoolgirl: took her water-skiing and climbing. They went to see indigenous people's theatre together, part of a course in the politics of culture she was giving him not by correspondence, without being aware of what she was doing and without giving it any such pompous name. She was not to be persuaded to go to a discothèque, but one of the valuable contacts he did have with her group of friends of different races and colours was an assumption that he would be with her at their parties, where she out-danced him, having been taught by blacks how to use her body to music. She was wild and nearly lovely, in this transformation, from where he drank and watched her and her associates at play. Every now and then she would come back to him: an offering, along with the food and drink she carried. As months went by, he was beginning to distinguish certain patterns in her friendships; these were extended beyond his life with her into proscribed places and among people restricted by law from contact, like the woman for whom she had gone to prison. Slowly she gained the confidence to introduce him to risk, never discussing but evidently always sensitively trying to gauge how much he really wanted to find out if "why he wanted to come back" had to do with "things like this."

It was more and more difficult to leave her, even for one night, going out late, alone under the dry, chill agitation of the old palm tree, rustling through its files. But although he knew his place had been made for him to live in the cottage with her, he had to go back to his flat that was hardly more than an office, now, unoccupied except for the chair and dusty table at which he sat down to write his reports: he could hardly write them in the house he shared with her.

She spoke often of her time in prison. She herself was the one to find openings for the subject. But even now, when they lay in one another's arms, out of reach, undiscoverable to any investigation, out of scrutiny, she did not seem able to tell of the experience what there really was in her being, necessary to be told: why she risked, for whom and what she was committed. She seemed to be waiting passionately to be given the words, the key. From him.

It was a password he did not have. It was a code that was not supplied him.

And then one night it came to him; he found a code of his own; that night he had to speak. "I've been spying on you."

Her face drew into a moment of concentration akin to the animal world, where a threatened creature can turn into a ball of spikes or take on a fearsome aspect of blown-up muscle and defensive garishness.

The moment left her face instantly as it had taken her. He had turned away before it as a man does with a gun in his back.

She shuffled across the bed on her haunches and took his head in her hands, holding him.

Questions for Discussion

1. What details of dress and speech seem most important in the opening paragraphs that introduce and contrast the characters?

2. What does the reader learn about Derek Felterman's life before the action of the story? How does this history help to explain his "recruitment" and current "avocation"?

3. What is implied by the line "[Alison] saw him as a child staring through a window at others playing"? Do you think this line characterizes Derek accurately?

4. What is Derek's first impression of Alison? How do his perceptions and feelings for her change as their relationship develops? Why is he attracted to her?

5. What relationship do you see between Alison's analysis of the lawyers' strategies in the opening scenes of the story and her response to Derek's admission that he is a spy? Do you think she was suspicious of him earlier?

Ideas for Writing

1. In an essay, interpret the conclusion of the story. What does Derek mean when he says, "I've been spying on you"? What is his real intention in making the "confession"? Why does Alison perceive his declaration as a "key" or password? What does this password allow her to do for Derek? for herself? What will happen next between the couple?

2. Write an essay in which you interpret the title "Crimes of Conscience" from both a political and a personal perspective. How does the title help to distance the reader from Derek and Alison? In what ways do both Derek and Alison commit "crimes of conscience"?

JAMES BALDWIN   (1924–1987)

James Baldwin was born in Harlem, into an impoverished family of nine children. Even as a young man he was interested in becoming a writer; an excellent student, he read as much as he could during his high school years. Following in the footsteps of his stepfather, an evangelical preacher, Baldwin was a junior minister at the Fireside Pentecostal Assembly from the age of fourteen to seventeen. He draws on many of these experiences in his first novel, *Go Tell It on the Mountain* (1953), and in the essays he published in *Notes of a Native Son* (1955).

After giving up the ministry, Baldwin lived in New Jersey and then Greenwich Village for six years. During these years he met Richard Wright, who encouraged him to apply for a fellowship that allowed him to begin his career as a writer. In 1948 Baldwin became an expatriate in Europe, where he met a number of international writers. Some of his best work was completed during his first stay in Paris, including the novel *Giovanni's Room* (1956), which presents a frank portrait of homosexual relationships. When Baldwin returned to the United States in 1957, he traveled in the South and became a spokesman for the civil rights movement.

The essay collections *Nobody Knows My Name* (1961) and *The Fire Next Time* (1963), as well as the story collection *Going to Meet the Man* (1965), which includes "The Rockpile" and "Sonny's Blues," reflect Baldwin's deep concern for race issues in the United States. Baldwin believed that "you write in order to change the world." Critic Robert A. Bone has said that Baldwin's writing "succeeded in transposing the entire discussion of American race relations to the interior plan; it is a major breakthrough for the American Imagination."

The Rockpile   (1957)

Across the street from their house, in an empty lot between two houses, stood the rockpile. It was a strange place to find a mass of natural rock jutting out of the ground; and someone, probably Aunt Florence, had once told them that the rock was there and could not be taken away because without it the subway cars underground would fly apart, killing all the people. This, touching on some natural mystery concerning the surface and the center of the earth, was far too intriguing an explanation to be challenged, and it invested the rockpile, moreover, with such mysterious importance that Roy felt it to be his right, not to say his duty, to play there.

Other boys were to be seen there each afternoon after school and all day Saturday and Sunday. They fought on the rockpile. Sure footed, dangerous, and reckless, they rushed each other and grappled on the heights, sometimes disappearing down the other side in a confusion of dust and screams and upended, flying feet. "It's a wonder they don't kill themselves," their mother said, watching sometimes from the fire escape. "You children stay away from there, you hear me?" Though she said "children" she was looking at Roy, where he sat beside John on the fire escape. "The good Lord knows," she continued, "I don't want you to come home bleeding like a hog every day the Lord sends." Roy shifted impatiently, and continued to stare at the street, as though in this gazing he might somehow acquire wings. John said nothing. He had not really been spoken to: he was afraid of the rockpile and of the boys who played there.

Each Saturday morning John and Roy sat on the fire escape and watched the forbidden street below. Sometimes their mother sat in the room behind them, sewing, or dressing their younger sister, or nursing the baby, Paul. The sun fell across them and across the fire escape with a high, benevolent indifference; below them, men and women, and boys and girls, sinners all, loitered; sometimes one of the church-members passed and saw them and waved. Then, for the moment that they waved decorously back, they were intimidated. They watched the saint, man or woman, until he or she had disappeared from sight. The passage of one of the redeemed made them consider, however vacantly, the wickedness of the street, their own latent wickedness in sitting where they sat; and made them think of their father, who came home early on Saturdays and who would soon be turning this corner and entering the dark hall below them.

But until he came to end their freedom, they sat, watching and longing above the street. At the end of the street nearest their house was the bridge which spanned the Harlem River and led to a city called the Bronx; which was where Aunt Florence lived. Nevertheless, when they saw her coming, she did not come from the bridge, but from the opposite end of the street. This, weakly, to their minds, she explained by saying that she had taken the subway, not wishing to walk, and that, besides, she did not live in *that* section of the Bronx. Knowing that the Bronx was across the river, they did not believe this story ever, but, adopting toward her their father's attitude, assumed that she had just left some sinful place which she dared not name, as, for example, a movie palace.

In the summertime boys swam in the river, diving off the wooden dock, or wading in from the garbage-heavy bank. Once a boy, whose name was Richard, drowned in the river. His mother had not known where he was; she had even come to their house, to ask if he was there. Then, in the evening, at six o'clock, they had heard from the street a woman screaming and wailing; and they ran to the windows and looked out. Down the street came the woman, Richard's mother, screaming, her face raised to the sky and tears running down her face. A woman walked beside her, trying to make her quiet and trying to hold her up. Behind them walked a man, Richard's father, with Richard's body in his arms. There were two white policemen walking in the gutter, who did not seem to know what should be done. Richard's father and Richard were wet, and Richard's body lay across his father's arms like a cotton baby. The woman's screaming filled all the street; cars slowed down and the people in the cars stared; people opened their windows and looked out and came rushing out of doors to stand in the gutter, watching. Then the small procession disappeared within the house which stood beside the rockpile. Then, *"Lord, Lord, Lord!"* cried Elizabeth, their mother, and slammed the window down.

One Saturday, an hour before his father would be coming home, Roy was wounded on the rockpile and brought screaming upstairs. He and John had been sitting on the fire escape and their mother had gone into the kitchen to sip tea with Sister McCandless. By and by Roy became bored and sat beside John in restless silence; and John began drawing into his schoolbook a newspaper advertisement which featured a new electric locomotive. Some friends of Roy passed beneath the fire escape and called him. Roy began to fidget, yelling down to them through the bars. Then a silence fell. John looked up. Roy stood looking at him.

"I'm going downstairs," he said.

"You better stay where you is, boy. You know Mama don't want you going downstairs."

"I be right *back*. She won't even know I'm gone, less you run and tell her."

"I ain't *got* to tell her. What's going to stop her from coming in here and looking out the window?"

"She's talking," Roy said. He started into the house.

"But Daddy's going to be home soon!"

"I be back before *that*. What you all the time got to be so *scared* for?" He was already in the house and he now turned, leaning on the windowsill, to swear impatiently, "I be back in *five* minutes."

John watched him sourly as he carefully unlocked the door and disappeared. In a moment he saw him on the sidewalk with his friends. He did not dare to go and tell his mother that Roy had left the fire escape because he had practically promised not to. He started to shout, *Remember, you said five minutes!* but one of Roy's friends was looking up at the fire escape. John looked down at his schoolbook: he became engrossed again in the problem of the locomotive.

When he looked up again he did not know how much time had passed, but now there was a gang fight on the rockpile. Dozens of boys fought each other in the harsh sun: clambering up the rocks and battling hand to hand, scuffed shoes sliding on the slippery rock; filling the bright air with curses and jubilant cries. They filled the air, too, with flying weapons: stones, sticks, tin cans, garbage, whatever could be picked up and thrown. John watched in a kind of absent amazement—until he remembered that Roy was still downstairs and that he was one of the boys on the rockpile. Then he was afraid; he could not see his brother among the figures in the sun; and he stood up, leaning over the fire-escape railing. Then Roy appeared from the other side of the rocks; John saw that his shirt was torn; he was laughing. He moved until he stood at the very top of the rockpile. Then, something, an empty tin can, flew out of the air and hit him on the forehead, just above the eye. Immediately, one side of Roy's face ran with blood, he fell and rolled on his face down the rocks. Then for a moment there was no movement at all, no sound, the sun, arrested, lay on the street and the sidewalk and the arrested boys. Then someone screamed or shouted; boys began to run away, down the street, toward the bridge. The figure on the ground, having caught its breath and felt its own blood, began to shout. John cried, "Mama! Mama!" and ran inside.

"Don't fret, don't fret," panted Sister McCandless as they rushed down the dark, narrow, swaying stairs, "don't fret. Ain't a boy been born don't get his knocks every now and again. *Lord!*" they hurried into the sun. A man had picked Roy up and now walked slowly toward them. One or two boys sat silent on their stoops; at either end of the street there was a group of boys watching. "He ain't hurt bad," the man said, "wouldn't be making this kind of noise if he was hurt real bad."

Elizabeth, trembling, reached out to take Roy, but Sister McCandless, bigger, calmer, took him from the man and threw him over her shoulder as she once might have handled a sack of cotton. "God bless you," she said to the man, "God bless you, son." Roy was still screaming. Elizabeth stood behind Sister McCandless to stare at his bloody face.

"It's just a flesh wound," the man kept saying, "just broke the skin, that's all." They were moving across the sidewalk, toward the house. John, not now afraid of the staring boys, looked toward the corner to see if his father was yet in sight.

Upstairs, they hushed Roy's crying. They bathed the blood away, to find, just above the left eyebrow, the jagged, superficial scar. "Lord, have mercy," murmured Elizabeth, "another inch and it would've been his eye." And she looked with apprehension toward the clock. "Ain't it the truth," said Sister McCandless, busy with bandages and iodine.

"When did he go downstairs?" his mother asked at last.

Sister McCandless now sat fanning herself in the easy chair, at the head of the sofa where Roy lay, bound and silent. She paused for a moment to look sharply at John. John stood near the window, holding the newspaper advertisement and the drawing he had done.

"We was sitting on the fire escape," he said. "Some boys he knew called him."

"When?"

"He said he'd be back in five minutes."

"Why didn't you tell me he was downstairs?"

He looked at his hands, clasping his notebook, and did not answer.

"Boy," said Sister McCandless, "you hear your mother a-talking to you?"

He looked at his mother. He repeated:

"He said he'd be back in five minutes."

"He said he'd be back in five minutes," said Sister McCandless with scorn, "don't look to me like that's no right answer. You's the man of the house, you supposed to look after your baby brothers and sisters — you ain't supposed to let them run off and get half-killed. But I expect," she added, rising from the chair, dropping the cardboard fan, "your Daddy'll make you tell the truth. Your Ma's way too soft with you."

He did not look at her, but at the fan where it lay in the dark red, depressed seat where she had been. The fan advertised a pomade for the hair and showed a brown woman and her baby, both with glistening hair, smiling happily at each other.

"Honey," said Sister McCandless, "I got to be moving along. Maybe I drop in later tonight. I don't reckon you going to be at Tarry Service tonight?"

Tarry Service was the prayer meeting held every Saturday night at church to strengthen believers and prepare the church for the coming of the Holy Ghost on Sunday.

"I don't reckon," said Elizabeth. She stood up; she and Sister McCandless kissed each other on the cheek. "But you be sure to remember me in your prayers."

"I surely will do that." She paused, with her hand on the door knob, and looked down at Roy and laughed. "Poor little man," she said, "reckon he'll be content to sit on the fire escape *now*."

Elizabeth laughed with her. "It sure ought to be a lesson to him. You don't reckon," she asked nervously, still smiling, "he going to keep that scar, do you?"

"Lord, no," said Sister McCandless, "ain't nothing but a scratch. I declare, Sister Grimes, you worse than a child. Another couple of weeks and you won't be able to *see* no scar. No, you go on about your housework, honey, and thank the Lord it weren't no worse." She opened the door; they heard the sound of feet on the stairs. "I expect that's the Reverend," said Sister McCandless, placidly, "I *bet* he going to raise cain."

"Maybe it's Florence," Elizabeth said. "Sometimes she get here about this time." They stood in the doorway, staring, while the steps reached the landing below and began again climbing to their floor. "No," said Elizabeth then, "that ain't her walk. That's Gabriel."

"Well, I'll just go on," said Sister McCandless, "and kind of prepare his mind." She pressed Elizabeth's hand as she spoke and started into the hall, leaving the door behind her slightly ajar. Elizabeth turned slowly back into the room. Roy did not open his eyes, or move; but she knew that he was not sleeping; he wished to delay until the last possible moment any contact with his father. John put his newspaper and his notebook on the table and stood, leaning on the table, staring at her.

"It wasn't my fault," he said. "I couldn't stop him from going downstairs."

"No," she said, "you ain't got nothing to worry about. You just tell your Daddy the truth."

He looked directly at her, and she turned to the window, staring into the street. What was Sister McCandless saying? Then from her bedroom she heard Delilah's thin wail and she turned, frowning, looking toward the bedroom and toward the still open door. She knew that John was watching her. Delilah continued to wail, she thought, angrily, *Now that girl's getting too big for that,* but she feared that Delilah would awaken Paul and she hurried into the bedroom. She tried to soothe Delilah back to sleep. Then she heard the front door open and close — too loud, Delilah raised her voice, with an exasperated sigh Elizabeth picked the child up. Her child and Gabriel's, her children and Gabriel's: Roy, Delilah, Paul. Only John was nameless and a stranger, living, unalterable testimony to his mother's days in sin.

"What happened?" Gabriel demanded. He stood, enormous, in the center of the room, his black lunchbox dangling from his hand, staring at the sofa where Roy lay. John stood just before him, it seemed to her astonished vision just below him, beneath his fist, his heavy shoe. The child stared at the man in fascination and terror — when a girl down home she had seen rabbits stand so paralyzed before the barking dog. She hurried past Gabriel to the sofa, feeling the weight of Delilah in her arms like the weight of a shield, and stood over Roy, saying:

"Now, ain't a thing to get upset about, Gabriel. This boy sneaked downstairs while I had my back turned and got hisself hurt a little. He's alright now."

Roy, as though in confirmation, now opened his eyes and looked gravely at his father. Gabriel dropped his lunchbox with a clatter and knelt by the sofa.

"How you feel, son? Tell your Daddy what happened?"

Roy opened his mouth to speak and then, relapsing into panic, began to cry. His father held him by the shoulder.

"You don't want to cry. You's Daddy's little man. Tell your Daddy what happened."

"He went downstairs," said Elizabeth, "where he didn't have no business to be, and got to fighting with them bad boys playing on that rockpile. That's what happened and it's a mercy it weren't nothing worse."

He looked up at her. "Can't you let this boy answer me for hisself?"

Ignoring this, she went on, more gently: "He got cut on the forehead, but it ain't nothing to worry about."

"You call a doctor? How you know it ain't nothing to worry about?"

"Is you got money to be throwing away on doctors? No, I ain't called no doctor. Ain't nothing wrong with my eyes that I can't tell whether he's hurt bad or not. He got a fright more'n anything else, and you ought to pray God it teaches him a lesson."

"You got a lot to say *now,*" he said, "but I'll have *me* something to say in a minute. I'll be wanting to know when all this happened, what you was doing with your eyes *then.*" He turned back to Roy, who had lain quietly sobbing eyes wide open and body held rigid: and who now, at his father's touch, remembered the height, the sharp, sliding rock beneath his feet, the sun, the

explosion of the sun, his plunge into darkness and his salty blood; and recoiled, beginning to scream, as his father touched his forehead. "Hold still,
hold still," crooned his father, shaking, "hold still. Don't cry. Daddy ain't going
to hurt you, he just wants to see this bandage, see what they've done to his little man." But Roy continued to scream and would not be still and Gabriel
dared not lift the bandage for fear of hurting him more. And he looked at
Elizabeth in fury: "Can't you put that child down and help me with this boy?
John, take your baby sister from your mother — don't look like neither of you
got good sense."

John took Delilah and sat down with her in the easy chair. His mother
bent over Roy, and held him still, while his father, carefully — but still Roy
screamed — lifted the bandage and stared at the wound. Roy's sobs began to
lessen. Gabriel readjusted the bandage. "You see," said Elizabeth, finally, "he
ain't nowhere near dead."

"It sure ain't your fault that he ain't dead." He and Elizabeth considered
each other for a moment in silence. "He came mightly close to losing an eye.
Course, his eyes ain't as big as your'n, so I reckon you don't think it matters
so much." At this her face hardened; he smiled. "Lord, have mercy," he said,
"you think you ever going to learn to do right? Where was you when all this
happened? Who let him go downstairs?"

"Ain't nobody let him go downstairs, he just went. He got a head just like
his father, it got to be broken before it'll bow. I was in the kitchen."

"Where was Johnnie?"

"He was in here?"

"Where?"

"He was on the fire escape."

"Didn't he know Roy was downstairs?"

"I reckon."

"What you mean, you reckon? He ain't got your big eyes for nothing, does
he?" He looked over at John. "Boy, you see your brother go downstairs?"

"Gabriel, ain't no sense in trying to blame Johnnie. You know right well if
you have trouble making Roy behave, he ain't going to listen to his brother. He
don't hardly listen to me."

"How come you didn't tell your mother Roy was downstairs?"

John said nothing, staring at the blanket which covered Delilah.

"Boy, you hear me? You want me to take a strap to you?"

"No, you ain't," she said. "You ain't going to take no strap to this boy, not
today you ain't. Ain't a soul to blame for Roy's lying up there now but you —
you because you done spoiled him so that he thinks he can do just anything
and get away with it. I'm here to tell you that ain't no way to raise no child.
You don't pray to the Lord to help you do better than you been doing, you
going to live to shed bitter tears that the Lord didn't take his soul today." And
she was trembling. She moved, unseeing, toward John and took Delilah from
his arms. She looked back at Gabriel, who had risen, who stood near the sofa,

staring at her. And she found in his face not fury alone, which would not have surprised her; but hatred so deep as to become insupportable in its lack of personality. His eyes were struck alive, unmoving, blind with malevolence — she felt, like the pull of the earth at her feet, his longing to witness her perdition. Again, as though it might be propitiation, she moved the child in her arms. And at this his eyes changed, he looked at Elizabeth, the mother of his children, the helpmeet given by the Lord. Then her eyes clouded; she moved to leave the room; her foot struck the lunchbox lying on the floor.

"John," she said, "pick up your father's lunchbox like a good boy."

She heard, behind her, his scrambling movement as he left the easy chair, the scrape and jangle of the lunchbox as he picked it up, bending his dark head near the toe of his father's heavy shoe.

Questions for Discussion

1. Why do the children feel that the rockpile is mysterious and important? What does the rockpile symbolize for the adults in the community and for readers of the story?

2. What is Sister McCandless's relationship to Elizabeth and the family? How does Aunt Florence contribute to the family conflict?

3. How is John contrasted to his brother Roy? What is John's position in the family? What is the significance of his drawing and his final gesture of humiliation at the end of the story?

4. Who feels guilty for Roy's getting hurt? Who is actually to blame?

5. Why is Gabriel so angry at Elizabeth when she tells him not to punish John? What are Gabriel's conflicts and limitations as a parent? How has his religion influenced his family?

Ideas for Writing

1. Write a sequel to the story or an essay in which you imagine John's future. Will he be able to overcome the scars of his childhood and lead a fulfilling life?

2. Compare the family and the relationship between the brothers in this story with family and the relationship between the older brother and Sonny in "Sonny's Blues."

Sonny's Blues   (1957)

I read about it in the paper, in the subway, on my way to work. I read it, and I couldn't believe it, and I read it again. Then perhaps I just stared at it, at the newsprint spelling out his name, spelling out the story. I stared at it in the swinging lights of the subway car, and in the faces and bodies of the people, and in my own face, trapped in the darkness which roared outside.

It was not to be believed and I kept telling myself that, as I walked from the subway station to the high school. And at the same time I couldn't doubt it. I was scared, scared for Sonny. He became real to me again. A great block of ice got settled in my belly and kept melting there slowly all day long, while I taught my classes algebra. It was a special kind of ice. It kept melting, sending trickles of ice water all up and down my veins, but it never got less. Sometimes it hardened and seemed to expand until I felt my guts were going to come spilling out or that I was going to choke or scream. This would always be at a moment when I was remembering some specific thing Sonny had once said or done.

When he was about as old as the boys in my classes his face had been bright and open, there was a lot of copper in it; and he'd had wonderfully direct brown eyes, and great gentleness and privacy. I wondered what he looked like now. He had been picked up, the evening before, in a raid on an apartment downtown, for peddling and using heroin.

I couldn't believe it: but what I mean by that is that I couldn't find any room for it anywhere inside me. I had kept it outside me for a long time. I hadn't wanted to know. I had had suspicions, but I didn't name them, I kept putting them away. I told myself that Sonny was wild, but he wasn't crazy. And he'd always been a good boy, he hadn't ever turned hard or evil or disrespectful, the way kids can, so quick, so quick, especially in Harlem. I didn't want to believe that I'd ever see my brother going down, coming to nothing, all that light in his face gone out, in the condition I'd already seen so many others. Yet it had happened and here I was, talking about algebra to a lot of boys who might, every one of them for all I knew, be popping off needles every time they went to the head. Maybe it did more for them than algebra could.

I was sure that the first time Sonny had ever had horse, he couldn't have been much older than these boys were now. These boys, now, were living as we'd been living then, they were growing up with a rush and their heads bumped abruptly against the low ceiling of their actual possibilities. They were filled with rage. All they really knew were two darknesses, the darkness of their lives, which was now closing in on them, and the darkness of the movies, which had blinded them to that other darkness, and in which they now, vindictively, dreamed, at once more together than they were at any other time, and more alone.

When the last bell rang, the last class ended, I let out my breath. It seemed I'd been holding it for all that time. My clothes were wet — I may have looked as though I'd been sitting in a steam bath, all dressed up, all afternoon. I sat alone in the classroom a long time. I listened to the boys outside, downstairs, shouting and cursing and laughing. Their laughter struck me for perhaps the first time. It was not the joyous laughter which — God knows why — one associates with children. It was mocking and insular, its intent to denigrate. It was disenchanted, and in this, also, lay the authority of their curses. Perhaps I was listening to them because I was thinking about my brother and in them I heard my brother. And myself.

One boy was whistling a tune, at once very complicated and very simple, it seemed to be pouring out of him as though he were a bird, and it sounded very cool and moving through all that harsh, bright air, only just holding its own through all those other sounds.

I stood up and walked over to the window and looked down into the courtyard. It was the beginning of the spring and the sap was rising in the boys. A teacher passed through them every now and again, quickly, as though he or she couldn't wait to get out of that courtyard, to get those boys out of their sight and off their minds. I started collecting my stuff. I thought I'd better get home and talk to Isabel.

The courtyard was almost deserted by the time I got downstairs. I saw this boy standing in the shadow of a doorway, looking just like Sonny. I almost called his name. Then I saw that it wasn't Sonny, but somebody we used to know, a boy from around our block. He'd been Sonny's friend. He'd never been mine, having been too young for me, and, anyway, I'd never liked him. And now, even though he was a grown-up man, he still hung around that block, still spent hours on the street corners, was always high and raggy. I used to run into him from time to time and he'd often work around to asking me for a quarter or fifty cents. He always had some real good excuse, too, and I always gave it to him, I don't know why.

But now, abruptly, I hated him. I couldn't stand the way he looked at me, partly like a dog, partly like a cunning child. I wanted to ask him what the hell he was doing in the school courtyard.

He sort of shuffled over to me, and he said, "I see you got the papers. So you already know about it."

"You mean about Sonny? Yes, I already know about it. How come they didn't get you?"

He grinned. It made him repulsive and it also brought to mind what he'd looked like as a kid. "I wasn't there. I stay away from them people."

"Good for you." I offered him a cigarette and I watched him through the smoke. "You come all the way down here just to tell me about Sonny?"

"That's right." He was sort of shaking his head and his eyes looked strange, as though they were about to cross. The bright sun deadened his damp dark brown skin and it made his eyes look yellow and showed up the dirt in his kinked hair. He smelled funky. I moved a little away from him and I said, "Well, thanks. But I already know about it and I got to get home."

"I'll walk you a little ways," he said. We started walking. There were a couple of kids still loitering in the courtyard and one of them said goodnight to me and looked strangely at the boy beside me.

"What're you going to do?" he asked me. "I mean, about Sonny?"

"Look. I haven't seen Sonny for over a year. I'm not sure I'm going to do anything. Anyway, what the hell *can* I do?"

"That's right," he said quickly, "ain't nothing you can do. Can't much help old Sonny no more, I guess."

It was what I was thinking and so it seemed to me he had no right to say it.

"I'm surprised at Sonny, though," he went on — he had a funny way of talking, he looked straight ahead as though he were talking to himself — "I thought Sonny was a smart boy, I thought he was too smart to get hung."

"I guess he thought so too," I said sharply, "and that's how he got hung. And how about you? You're pretty goddamn smart, I bet."

Then he looked directly at me, just for a minute. "I ain't smart," he said. "If I was smart, I'd have reached for a pistol a long time ago."

"Look. Don't tell *me* your sad story, if it was up to me, I'd give you one." Then I felt guilty — guilty, probably, for never having supposed that the poor bastard *had* a story of his own, much less a sad one, and I asked, quickly, "What's going to happen to him now?"

He didn't answer this. He was off by himself some place. "Funny thing," he said, and from his tone we might have been discussing the quickest way to get to Brooklyn, "when I saw the papers this morning, the first thing I asked myself was if I had anything to do with it. I felt sort of responsible."

I began to listen more carefully. The subway station was on the corner, just before us, and I stopped. He stopped, too. We were in front of a bar and he ducked slightly, peering in, but whoever he was looking for didn't seem to be there. The juke box was blasting away with something black and bouncy and I half watched the barmaid as she danced her way from the juke box to her place behind the bar. And I watched her face as she laughingly responded to something someone said to her, still keeping time to the music. When she smiled one saw the little girl, one sensed the doomed, still-struggling woman beneath the battered face of the semi-whore.

"I never *give* Sonny nothing," the boy said finally, "but a long time ago I come to school high and Sonny asked me how it felt." He paused, I couldn't bear to watch him, I watched the barmaid, and I listened to the music which seemed to be causing the pavement to shake. "I told him it felt great." The music stopped, the barmaid paused and watched the juke box until the music began again. "It did."

All this was carrying me some place I didn't want to go. I certainly didn't want to know how it felt. It filled everything, the people, the houses, the music, the dark, quicksilver barmaid, with menace; and this menace was their reality.

"What's going to happen to him now?" I asked again.

"They'll send him away some place and they'll try to cure him." He shook his head. "Maybe he'll even think he's kicked the habit. Then they'll let him loose" — he gestured, throwing his cigarette into the gutter. "That's all."

"What do you mean, that's *all*?"

But I knew what he meant.

"I *mean*, that's *all*." He turned his head and looked at me, pulling down the corners of his mouth. "Don't you know what I mean?" he asked, softly.

"How the hell *would* I know what you mean?" I almost whispered it, I don't know why.

"That's right," he said to the air, "how would *he* know what I mean?" He turned toward me again, patient and calm, and yet I somehow felt him shaking, shaking as though he were going to fall apart. I felt that ice in my guts again, the dread I'd felt all afternoon; and again I watched the barmaid, moving about the bar, washing glasses, and singing. "Listen. They'll let him out and then it'll just start all over again. That's what I mean."

"You mean — they'll let him out. And then he'll just start working his way back in again. You mean he'll never kick the habit. Is that what you mean?"

"That's right," he said, cheerfully. "*You* see what I mean."

"Tell me," I said at last, "why does he want to die? He must want to die, he's killing himself, why does he want to die?"

He looked at me in surprise. He licked his lips. "He don't want to die. He wants to live. Don't nobody want to die, ever."

Then I wanted to ask him — too many things. He could not have answered, or if he had, I could not have borne the answers. I started walking. "Well, I guess it's none of my business."

"It's going to be rough on old Sonny," he said. We reached the subway station. "This is your station?" he asked. I nodded. I took one step down. "Damn!" he said, suddenly. I looked up at him. He grinned again. "Damn it if I didn't leave all my money home. You ain't got a dollar on you, have you? Just for a couple of days, is all."

All at once something inside gave and threatened to come pouring out of me. I didn't hate him any more. I felt that in another moment I'd start crying like a child.

"Sure," I said. "Don't sweat." I looked in my wallet and didn't have a dollar, I only had a five. "Here," I said. "That hold you?"

He didn't look at it — he didn't want to look at it. A terrible closed look came over his face, as though he were keeping the number on the bill a secret from him and me. "Thanks," he said, and now he was dying to see me go. "Don't worry about Sonny. Maybe I'll write him or something."

"Sure," I said. "You do that. So long."

"Be seeing you," he said. I went on down the steps.

And I didn't write Sonny or send him anything for a long time. When I finally did, it was just after my little girl died, he wrote me back a letter which made me feel like a bastard.

Here's what he said:

> Dear brother,
> You don't know how much I needed to hear from you. I wanted to write you many a time but I dug how much I must have hurt you and so I didn't write. But now I feel like a man who's been trying to climb up out of some deep, real deep and funky hole and just saw the sun up there, outside. I got to get outside.

I can't tell you much about how I got here. I mean I don't know how to tell you. I guess I was afraid of something or I was trying to escape from something and you know I have never been very strong in the head (smile). I'm glad Mama and Daddy are dead and can't see what's happened to their son and I swear if I'd known what I was doing I would never have hurt you so, you and a lot of other fine people who were nice to me and who believed in me.

I don't want you to think it had anything to do with me being a musician. It's more than that. Or maybe less than that. I can't get anything straight in my head down here and I try not to think about what's going to happen to me when I get outside again. Sometime I think I'm going to flip and *never* get outside and sometime I think I'll come straight back. I tell you one thing, though, I'd rather blow my brains out than go through this again. But that's what they all say, so they tell me. If I tell you when I'm coming to New York and if you could meet me, I sure would appreciate it. Give my love to Isabel and the kids and I was sure sorry to hear about little Gracie. I wish I could be like Mama and say the Lord's will be done, but I don't know it seems to me that trouble is the one thing that never does get stopped and I don't know what good it does to blame it on the Lord. But maybe it does some good if you believe it.

> Your brother,
> Sonny

Then I kept in constant touch with him and I sent him whatever I could and I went to meet him when he came back to New York. When I saw him many things I thought I had forgotten came flooding back to me. This was because I had begun, finally, to wonder about Sonny, about the life that Sonny lived inside. This life, whatever it was, had made him older and thinner and it had deepened the distant stillness in which he had always moved. He looked very unlike my baby brother. Yet, when he smiled, when we shook hands, the baby brother I'd never known looked out from the depths of his private life, like an animal waiting to be coaxed into the light.

"How you been keeping?" he asked me.

"All right. And you?"

"Just fine." He was smiling all over his face. "It's good to see you again."

"It's good to see you."

The seven years' difference in our ages lay between us like a chasm: I wondered if these years would ever operate between us as a bridge. I was remembering, and it made it hard to catch my breath, that I had been there when he was born; and I had heard the first words he had ever spoken. When he started to walk, he walked from our mother straight to me. I caught him just before he fell when he took the first steps he ever took in this world.

"How's Isabel?"

"Just fine. She's dying to see you."

"And the boys?"

"They're fine, too. They're anxious to see their uncle."

"Oh, come on. You know they don't remember me."

"Are you kidding? Of course they remember you."

He grinned again. We got into a taxi. We had a lot to say to each other, far too much to know how to begin.

As the taxi began to move, I asked, "You still want to go to India?"

He laughed. "You still remember that. Hell, no. This place is Indian enough for me."

"It used to belong to them," I said.

And he laughed again. "They damn sure knew what they were doing when they got rid of it."

Years ago, when he was around fourteen, he'd been all tripped on the idea of going to India. He read books about people sitting on rocks, naked, in all kinds of weather, but mostly bad, naturally, and walking barefoot through hot coals and arriving at wisdom. I used to say that it sounded to me as though they were getting away from wisdom as fast as they could. I think he sort of looked down on me for that.

"Do you mind," he asked, "if we have the driver drive alongside the park? On the west side — I haven't seen the city in so long."

"Of course not," I said. I was afraid that I might sound as though I were humoring him, but I hoped he wouldn't take it that way.

So we drove along, between the green of the park and the stony, lifeless elegance of hotels and apartment buildings, toward the vivid, killing streets of our childhood. These streets hadn't changed, though housing projects jutted up out of them now like rocks in the middle of a boiling sea. Most of the houses in which we had grown up had vanished, as had the stores from which we had stolen, the basements in which we had first tried sex, the rooftops from which we had hurled tin cans and bricks. But houses exactly like the houses of our past yet dominated the landscape, boys exactly like the boys we once had been found themselves smothering in these houses, came down into the streets for light and air and found themselves encircled by disaster. Some escaped the trap, most didn't. Those who got out always left something of themselves behind, as some animals amputate a leg and leave it in the trap. It might be said, perhaps, that I had escaped, after all, I was a school teacher; or that Sonny had, he hadn't lived in Harlem for years. Yet, as the cab moved uptown through streets which seemed, with a rush, to darken with dark people, and as I covertly studied Sonny's face, it came to me that what we both were seeking through our separate cab windows was that part of ourselves which had been left behind. It's always at the hour of trouble and confrontation that the missing member aches.

We hit 110th Street and started rolling up Lenox Avenue. And I'd known this avenue all my life, but it seemed to me again, as it had seemed on the day

I'd first heard about Sonny's trouble, filled with a hidden menace which was its very breath of life.

"We almost there," said Sonny.

"Almost." We were both too nervous to say anything more.

We live in a housing project. It hasn't been up long. A few days after it was up it seemed uninhabitably new, now, of course, it's already rundown. It looks like a parody of the good, clean, faceless life — God knows the people who live in it do their best to make it a parody. The beat-looking grass lying around isn't enough to make their lives green, the hedges will never hold out the streets, and they know it. The big windows fool no one, they aren't big enough to make space out of no space. They don't bother with the windows, they watch the TV screen instead. The playground is most popular with the children who don't play at jacks, or skip rope, or roller skate, or swing, and they can be found in it after dark. We moved in partly because it's not too far from where I teach, and partly for the kids; but it's really just like the houses in which Sonny and I grew up. The same things happen, they'll have the same things to remember. The moment Sonny and I started into the house I had the feeling that I was simply bringing him back into the danger he had almost died trying to escape.

Sonny has never been talkative. So I don't know why I was sure he'd be dying to talk to me when supper was over the first night. Everything went fine, the oldest boy remembered him, and the youngest boy liked him, and Sonny had remembered to bring something for each of them; and Isabel, who is really much nicer than I am, more open and giving, had gone to a lot of trouble about dinner and was genuinely glad to see him. And she's always been able to tease Sonny in a way that I haven't. It was nice to see her face so vivid again and to hear her laugh and watch her make Sonny laugh. She wasn't, or, anyway, she didn't seem to be, at all uneasy or embarrassed. She chatted as though there were no subject which had to be avoided and she got Sonny past his first, faint stiffness. And thank God she was there, for I was filled with that icy dread again. Everything I did seemed awkward to me, and everything I said sounded freighted with hidden meaning. I was trying to remember everything I'd heard about dope addiction and I couldn't help watching Sonny for signs. I wasn't doing it out of malice. I was trying to find out something about my brother. I was dying to hear him tell me he was safe.

"Safe!" my father grunted, whenever Mama suggested trying to move to a neighborhood which might be safer for children. "Safe, hell! Ain't no place safe for kids, nor nobody."

He always went on like this, but he wasn't, ever, really as bad as he sounded, not even on weekends, when he got drunk. As a matter of fact, he was always on the lookout for "something a little better," but he died before he found it. He died suddenly, during a drunken weekend in the middle of the war, when Sonny was fifteen. He and Sonny hadn't ever got on too well. And this was partly because Sonny was the apple of his father's eye. It was because he loved Sonny so much and was frightened for him, that he was always fighting with him. It doesn't do any good to fight with Sonny. Sonny just moves back, inside himself, where he can't be reached. But the principal reason that they never hit it off is that they were so much alike. Daddy was big and rough and loud-talking, just the opposite of Sonny, but they both had—that same privacy.

Mama tried to tell me something about this, just after Daddy died. I was home on leave from the army.

This was the last time I ever saw my mother alive. Just the same, this picture gets all mixed up in my mind with pictures I had of her when she was younger. The way I always see her is the way she used to be on a Sunday afternoon, say, when the old folks were talking after the big Sunday dinner. I always see her wearing pale blue. She'd be sitting on the sofa. And my father would be sitting in the easy chair, not far from her. And the living room would be full of church folks and relatives. There they sit, in chairs all around the living room, and the night is creeping up outside, but nobody knows it yet. You can see the darkness growing against the windowpanes and you hear the street noises every now and again, or maybe the jangling beat of a tambourine from one of the churches close by, but it's real quiet in the room. For a moment nobody's talking, but every face looks darkening, like the sky outside. And my mother rocks a little from the waist, and my father's eyes are closed. Everyone is looking at something a child can't see. For a minute they've forgotten the children. Maybe a kid is lying on the rug, half asleep. Maybe somebody's got a kid in his lap and is absent-mindedly stroking the kid's head. Maybe there's a kid, quiet and big-eyed, curled up in a big chair in the corner. The silence, the darkness coming, and the darkness in the faces frightens the child obscurely. He hopes that the hand which strokes his forehead will never stop—will never die. He hopes that there will never come a time when the old folks won't be sitting around the living room, talking about where they've come from, and what they've seen, and what's happened to them and their kinfolk.

But something deep and watchful in the child knows that this is bound to end, is already ending. In a moment someone will get up and turn on the light. Then the old folks will remember the children and they won't talk any more that day. And when light fills the room, the child is filled with darkness. He knows that every time this happens he's moved just a little closer to that darkness outside. The darkness outside is what the old folks have been talking about. It's what they've come from. It's what they endure. The child knows that they won't talk any more because if he knows too much about what's happened to *them,* he'll know too much too soon, about what's going to happen to *him.*

The last time I talked to my mother, I remember I was restless. I wanted to get out and see Isabel. We weren't married then and we had a lot to straighten out between us.

There Mama sat, in black, by the window. She was humming an old church song, *Lord you brought me from a long ways off.* Sonny was out somewhere. Mama kept watching the streets.

"I don't know," she said, "if I'll ever see you again, after you go off from here. But I hope you'll remember the things I tried to teach you."

"Don't talk like that," I said, and smiled. "You'll be here a long time yet."

She smiled, too, but she said nothing. She was quiet for a long time. And I said, "Mama, don't you worry about nothing. I'll be writing all the time, and you be getting the checks. . . ."

"I want to talk to you about your brother," she said, suddenly. "If anything happens to me he ain't going to have nobody to look out for him."

"Mama," I said, "ain't nothing going to happen to you *or* Sonny. Sonny's all right. He's a good boy and he's got good sense."

"It ain't a question of his being a good boy," Mama said, "nor of his having good sense. It ain't only the bad ones, nor yet the dumb ones that gets sucked under." She stopped, looking at me. "Your Daddy once had a brother," she said, and she smiled in a way that made me feel she was in pain. "You didn't never know that, did you?"

"No," I said, "I never knew that," and I watched her face.

"Oh, yes," she said, "your Daddy had a brother." She looked out of the window again. "I know you never saw your Daddy cry. But I did — many a time, through all these years."

I asked her, "What happened to his brother? How come nobody's ever talked about him?"

This was the first time I ever saw my mother look old.

"His brother got killed," she said, "when he was just a little younger than you are now. I knew him. He was a fine boy. He was maybe a little full of the devil, but he didn't mean nobody no harm."

Then she stopped and the room was silent, exactly as it had sometimes been on those Sunday afternoons. Mama kept looking out into the streets.

"He used to have a job in the mill," she said, "and, like all young folks, he just liked to perform on Saturday nights. Saturday nights, him and your father would drift around to different places, go to dances and things like that, or just sit around with people they knew, and your father's brother would sing, he had a fine voice, and play along with himself on his guitar. Well, this particular Saturday night, him and your father was coming home from some place, and they were both a little drunk and there was a moon that night, it was bright like day. Your father's brother was feeling kind of good, and he was whistling to himself, and he had his guitar slung over his shoulder. They was coming down a hill and beneath them was a road that turned off from the highway. Well, your father's brother, being always kind of frisky, decided to run down this hill, and he did, with that guitar banging and clanging behind him, and he ran across the road, and he was making water behind a tree. And your father was sort of amused at him and he was still coming down the hill, kind of slow. Then he heard a car motor and that same minute his brother stepped from behind the tree, into the road, in the moonlight. And he started to cross the road. And your father started to run down the hill, he says he don't know why. This car was full of white men. They was all drunk, and when they seen your father's brother they let out a great whoop and holler and they aimed the car straight at him. They was having fun, they just wanted to scare him, the way they do sometimes, you know. But they was drunk. And I guess the boy, being drunk, too, and scared, kind of lost his head. By the time he jumped it was too late. Your father says he heard his brother scream when the car rolled over him, and he heard the wood of that guitar when it give, and he heard them strings go flying, and he heard them white men shouting, and the car kept on a-going and it ain't stopped till this day. And, time your father got down the hill, his brother weren't nothing but blood and pulp."

Tears were gleaming on my mother's face. There wasn't anything I could say.

"He never mentioned it," she said, "because I never let him mention it before you children. Your Daddy was like a crazy man that night and for many a night thereafter. He says he never in his life seen anything as dark as that road after the lights of that car had gone away. Weren't nothing, weren't nobody on that road, just your Daddy and his brother and that busted guitar. Oh, yes. Your Daddy never did really get right again. Till the day he died he weren't sure but that every white man he saw was the man that killed his brother."

She stopped and took out her handkerchief and dried her eyes and looked at me.

"I ain't telling you all this," she said, "to make you scared or bitter or to make you hate nobody. I'm telling you this because you got a brother. And the world ain't changed."

I guess I didn't want to believe this. I guess she saw this in my face. She turned away from me, toward the window again, searching those streets.

"But I praise my Redeemer," she said at last, "that He called your Daddy home before me. I ain't saying it to throw no flowers at myself, but, I declare, it keeps me from feeling too cast down to know I helped your father get safely through this world. Your father always acted like he was the roughest, strongest man on earth. And everybody took him to be like that. But if he hadn't had *me* there — to see his tears!"

She was crying again. Still, I couldn't move. I said, "Lord, Lord, Mama, I didn't know it was like that."

"Oh, honey," she said, "there's a lot that you don't know. But you are going to find it out." She stood up from the window and came over to me. "You got to hold on to your brother," she said, "and don't let him fall, no matter what it looks like is happening to him and no matter how evil you gets with him. You going to be evil with him many a time. But don't you forget what I told you, you hear?"

"I won't forget," I said. "Don't you worry, I won't forget. I won't let nothing happen to Sonny."

My mother smiled as though she were amused at something she saw in my face. Then, "You may not be able to stop nothing from happening. But you got to let him know you's *there*."

Two days later I was married, and then I was gone. And I had a lot of things on my mind and I pretty well forgot my promise to Mama until I got shipped home on a special furlough for her funeral.

And, after the funeral, with just Sonny and me alone in the empty kitchen, I tried to find out something about him.

"What do you want to do?" I asked him.

"I'm going to be a musician," he said.

For he had graduated, in the time I had been away, from dancing to the juke box to finding out who was playing what, and what they were doing with it, and he had bought himself a set of drums.

"You mean, you want to be a drummer?" I somehow had the feeling that being a drummer might be all right for other people but not for my brother Sonny.

"I don't think," he said, looking at me very gravely, "that I'll ever be a good drummer. But I think I can play a piano."

I frowned. I'd never played the role of the older brother quite so seriously before, had scarcely ever, in fact, *asked* Sonny a damn thing. I sensed myself in the presence of something I didn't really know how to handle, didn't understand. So I made my frown a little deeper as I asked: "What kind of musician do you want to be?"

He grinned. "How many kinds do you think there are?"

"Be *serious*," I said.

He laughed, throwing his head back, and then looked at me. "I *am* serious."

"Well, then, for Christ's sake, stop kidding around and answer a serious question. I mean, do you want to be a concert pianist, you want to play classical music and all that, or — or what?" Long before I finished he was laughing again. "For Christ's *sake*, Sonny!"

He sobered, but with difficulty. "I'm sorry. But you sound so — *scared!*" and he was off again.

"Well, you may think it's funny now, baby, but it's not going to be so funny when you have to make your living at it, let me tell you *that*." I was furious because I knew he was laughing at me and I didn't know why.

"No," he said, very sober now, and afraid, perhaps, that he'd hurt me, "I don't want to be a classical pianist. That isn't what interests me. I mean" — he paused, looking hard at me, as though his eyes would help me to understand, and then gestured helplessly, as though perhaps his hand would help — "I mean, I'll have a lot of studying to do, and I'll have to study *everything*, but, I mean, I want to play *with* — jazz musicians." He stopped. "I want to play jazz," he said.

Well, the word had never before sounded as heavy, as real, as it sounded that afternoon in Sonny's mouth. I just looked at him and I was probably frowning a real frown by this time. I simply couldn't see why on earth he'd want to spend his time hanging around nightclubs, clowning around on bandstands, while people pushed each other around a dance floor. It seemed —

beneath him, somehow. I had never thought about it before, had never been forced to, but I suppose I had always put jazz musicians in a class with what Daddy called "good-time people."

"Are you *serious?*"

"Hell, *yes,* I'm serious."

He looked more helpless than ever, and annoyed, and deeply hurt.

I suggested, helpfully: "You mean — like Louis Armstrong?"

His face closed as though I'd struck him. "No. I'm not talking about none of that old-time, down home crap."

"Well, look, Sonny, I'm sorry, don't get mad. I just don't altogether get it, that's all. Name somebody — you know, a jazz musician you admire."

"Bird."

"Who?"

"Bird! Charlie Parker! Don't they teach you nothing in the goddamn army?"

I lit a cigarette. I was surprised and then a little amused to discover that I was trembling. "I've been out of touch," I said. "You'll have to be patient with me. Now. Who's this Parker character?"

"He's just one of the greatest jazz musicians alive," said Sonny, sullenly, his hands in his pockets, his back to me. "Maybe *the* greatest," he added, bitterly, "that's probably why *you* never heard of him."

"All right," I said, "I'm ignorant. I'm sorry. I'll go out and buy all the cat's records right away, all right?"

"It don't," said Sonny, with dignity, "make any difference to me. I don't care what you listen to. Don't do me no favors."

I was beginning to realize that I'd never seen him so upset before. With another part of my mind I was thinking that this would probably turn out to be one of those things kids go through and that I shouldn't make it seem important by pushing it too hard. Still, I didn't think it would do any harm to ask: "Doesn't all this take a lot of time? Can you make a living at it?"

He turned back to me and half leaned, half sat, on the kitchen table. "Everything takes time," he said, "and — well, yes, sure, I can make a living at it. But what I don't seem to be able to make you understand is that it's the only thing I want to do."

"Well, Sonny," I said, gently, "you know people can't always do exactly what they *want* to do — "

"*No,* I don't know that," said Sonny, surprising me. "I think people *ought* to do what they want to do, what else are they alive for?"

"You getting to be a big boy," I said desperately, "it's time you started thinking about your future."

"I'm thinking about my future," said Sonny, grimly. "I think about it all the time."

I gave up. I decided, if he didn't change his mind, that we could always talk about it later. "In the meantime," I said, "you got to finish school." We had already decided that he'd have to move in with Isabel and her folks. I knew this wasn't the ideal arrangement because Isabel's folks are inclined to be dicey and they hadn't especially wanted Isabel to marry me. But I didn't know what else to do. "And we have to get you fixed up at Isabel's."

There was a long silence. He moved from the kitchen table to the window. "That's a terrible idea. You know it yourself."

"Do you have a *better* idea?"

He just walked up and down the kitchen for a minute. He was as tall as I was. He had started to shave. I suddenly had the feeling that I didn't know him at all.

He stopped at the kitchen table and picked up my cigarettes. Looking at me with a kind of mocking, amused defiance, he put one between his lips. "You mind?"

"You smoking already?"

He lit the cigarette and nodded, watching me through the smoke. "I just wanted to see if I'd have the courage to smoke in front of you." He grinned and blew a great cloud of smoke to the ceiling. "It was easy." He looked at my face. "Come on, now. I bet you was smoking at my age, tell the truth."

I didn't say anything but the truth was on my face, and he laughed. But now there was something very strained in his laugh. "Sure. And I bet that ain't all you was doing."

He was frightening me a little. "Cut the crap," I said. "We already decided that you was going to go and live at Isabel's. Now what's got into you all of a sudden?"

"*You* decided it," he pointed out. "*I* didn't decide nothing." He stopped in front of me, leaning against the stove, arms loosely folded. "Look, brother. I don't want to stay in Harlem no more, I really don't." He was very earnest. He looked at me, then over toward the kitchen window. There was something in his eyes I'd never seen before, some thoughtfulness, some worry all his own. He rubbed the muscle of one arm. "It's time I was getting out of here."

"Where do you want to *go*, Sonny?"

"I want to join the army. Or the navy, I don't care. If I say I'm old enough, they'll believe me."

Then I got mad. It was because I was so scared. "You must be crazy. You goddamn fool, what the hell do you want to go and join the *army* for?"

"I just told you. To get out of Harlem."

"Sonny, you haven't even finished *school*. And if you really want to be a musician, how do you expect to study if you're in the *army*?"

He looked at me, trapped, and in anguish. "There's ways. I might be able to work out some kind of deal. Anyway, I'll have the G.I. Bill when I come out."

"*If* you come out." We stared at each other. "Sonny, please. Be reasonable. I know the setup is far from perfect. But we got to do the best we can."

"I ain't learning nothing in school," he said. "Even when I go." He turned away from me and opened the window and threw his cigarette out into the narrow alley. I watched his back. "At least, I ain't learning nothing you'd want me to learn." He slammed the window so hard I thought the glass would fly out, and turned back to me. "And I'm sick of the stink of these garbage cans!"

"Sonny," I said, "I know how you feel. But if you don't finish school now, you're going to be sorry later that you didn't." I grabbed him by the shoulders. "And you only got another year. It ain't so bad. And I'll come back and I swear I'll help you do *whatever* you want to do. Just try to put up with it till I come back. Will you please do that? For me?"

He didn't answer and he wouldn't look at me.

"Sonny. You hear me?"

He pulled away. "I hear you. But you never hear anything *I* say."

I didn't know what to say to that. He looked out of the window and then back at me. "OK," he said, and sighed. "I'll try."

Then I said, trying to cheer him up a little, "They got a piano at Isabel's. You can practice on it."

And as a matter of fact, it did cheer him up for a minute. "That's right," he said to himself. "I forgot that." His face relaxed a little. But the worry, the thoughtfulness, played on it still, the way shadows play on a face which is staring into the fire.

But I thought I'd never hear the end of that piano. At first, Isabel would write me, saying how nice it was that Sonny was so serious about his music and how, as soon as he came in from school, or wherever he had been when he was supposed to be at school, he went straight to that piano and stayed there until suppertime. And, after supper, he went back to that piano and stayed there until everybody went to bed. He was at the piano all day Saturday and all day Sunday. Then he bought a record player and started playing records. He'd play one record over and over again, all day long sometimes, and he'd improvise along with it on the piano. Or he'd play one section of the record, one chord, one change, one progression, then he'd do it on the piano. Then back to the record. Then back to the piano.

Well, I really don't know how they stood it. Isabel finally confessed that it wasn't like living with a person at all, it was like living with sound. And the sound didn't make any sense to her, didn't make any sense to any of them — naturally. They began, in a way, to be afflicted by this presence that was living in their home. It was as though Sonny were some sort of god, or monster. He moved in an atmosphere which wasn't like theirs at all. They fed him and he ate, he washed himself, he walked in and out of their door; he certainly wasn't nasty or unpleasant or rude, Sonny isn't any of those things; but it was as though he were all wrapped up in some cloud, some fire, some vision all his own; and there wasn't any way to reach him.

At the same time, he wasn't really a man yet, he was still a child, and they had to watch out for him in all kinds of ways. They certainly couldn't throw him out. Neither did they dare to make a great scene about that piano because even they dimly sensed, as I sensed, from so many thousands of miles away, that Sonny was at that piano playing for his life.

But he hadn't been going to school. One day a letter came from the school board and Isabel's mother got it—there had, apparently, been other letters but Sonny had torn them up. This day, when Sonny came in, Isabel's mother showed him the letter and asked where he'd been spending his time. And she finally got it out of him that he'd been down in Greenwich Village, with musicians and other characters, in a white girl's apartment. And this scared her and she started to scream at him and what came up, once she began—though she denies it to this day—was what sacrifices they were making to give Sonny a decent home and how little he appreciated it.

Sonny didn't play the piano that day. By evening, Isabel's mother had calmed down but then there was the old man to deal with, and Isabel herself. Isabel says she did her best to be calm but she broke down and started crying. She says she just watched Sonny's face. She could tell, by watching him, what was happening with him. And what was happening was that they penetrated his cloud, they had reached him. Even if their fingers had been a thousand times more gentle than human fingers ever are, he could hardly help feeling that they had stripped him naked and were spitting on that nakedness. For he also had to see that his presence, that music, which was life or death to him, had been torture for them and that they had endured it, not at all for his sake, but only for mine. And Sonny couldn't take that. He can take it a little better today than he could then but he's still not very good at it and, frankly, I don't know anybody who is.

The silence of the next few days must have been louder than the sound of all the music ever played since time began. One morning, before she went to work, Isabel was in his room for something and she suddenly realized that all of his records were gone. And she knew for certain that he was gone. And he was. He went as far as the navy would carry him. He finally sent me a postcard from some place in Greece and that was the first I knew that Sonny was still alive. I didn't see him any more until we were both back in New York and the war had long been over.

He was a man by then, of course, but I wasn't willing to see it. He came by the house from time to time, but we fought almost every time we met. I didn't like the way he carried himself, loose and dreamlike all the time, and I didn't like his friends, and his music seemed to be merely an excuse for the life he led. It sounded just that weird and disordered.

Then we had a fight, a pretty awful fight, and I didn't see him for months. By and by I looked him up, where he was living, in a furnished room in the Village, and I tried to make it up. But there were lots of people in the room and Sonny just lay on his bed, and he wouldn't come downstairs with me, and he treated these other people as though they were his family and I weren't. So I got mad and then he got mad, and then I told him that he might just as well be dead as live the way he was living. Then he stood up and he told me not to worry about him any more in life, that he *was* dead as far as I was concerned. Then he pushed me to the door and the other people looked on as though nothing were happening, and he slammed the door behind me. I stood in the hallway, staring at the door. I heard somebody laugh in the room and then the tears came to my eyes. I started down the steps, whistling to keep from crying, I kept whistling to myself, *You going to need me, baby, one of these cold, rainy days.*

I read about Sonny's trouble in the spring. Little Grace died in the fall. She was a beautiful little girl. But she only lived a little over two years. She died of polio and she suffered. She had a slight fever for a couple of days, but it didn't seem like anything and we just kept her in bed. And we would certainly have called the doctor, but the fever dropped, she seemed to be all right. So we thought it had just been a cold. Then, one day, she was up, playing, Isabel was in the kitchen fixing lunch for the two boys when they'd come in from school, and she heard Grace fall down in the living room. When you have a lot of children you don't always start running when one of them falls, unless they start screaming or something. And, this time, Grace was quiet. Yet, Isabel says that when she heard that *thump* and then that silence, something happened in her to make her afraid. And she ran to the living room and there was little Grace on the floor, all twisted up, and the reason she hadn't screamed was that she couldn't get her breath. And when she did scream, it was the worst sound, Isabel says, that she'd ever heard in all her life, and she still hears it sometimes in her dreams. Isabel will sometimes wake me up with a low, moaning, strangled sound and I have to be quick to awaken her and hold her to me and where Isabel is weeping against me seems a mortal wound.

I think I may have written Sonny the very day that little Grace was buried. I was sitting in the living room in the dark, by myself, and I suddenly thought of Sonny. My trouble made his real.

One Saturday afternoon, when Sonny had been living with us, or, anyway, been in our house, for nearly two weeks, I found myself wandering aimlessly about the living room, drinking from a can of beer, and trying to work up the courage to search Sonny's room. He was out, he was usually out whenever I was home, and Isabel had taken the children to see their grandparents. Suddenly I was standing still in front of the living room window, watching Seventh Avenue. The idea of searching Sonny's room made me still. I scarcely dared to admit to myself what I'd be searching for. I didn't know what I'd do if I found it. Or if I didn't.

On the sidewalk across from me, near the entrance to a barbecue joint, some people were holding an old-fashioned revival meeting. The barbecue cook, wearing a dirty white apron, his conked hair reddish and metallic in the pale sun, and a cigarette between his lips, stood in the doorway, watching them. Kids and older people paused in their errands and stood there, along with some older men and a couple of very tough-looking women who watched everything that happened on the avenue, as though they owned it, or were maybe owned by it. Well, they were watching this, too. The revival was being carried on by three sisters in black, and a brother. All they had were their voices and their Bibles and a tambourine. The brother was testifying and while he testified two of the sisters stood together, seeming to say, amen, and the third sister walked around with the tambourine outstretched and a couple of people dropped coins into it. Then the brother's testimony ended and the sister who had been taking up the collection dumped the coins into her palm and transferred them to the pocket of her long black robe. Then she raised both hands, striking the tambourine against the air, and then against one hand, and she started to sing. And the two other sisters and the brother joined in.

It was strange, suddenly, to watch, though I had been seeing these street meetings all my life. So, of course, had everybody else down there. Yet, they paused and watched and listened and I stood still at the window. *"Tis the old ship of Zion,"* they sang, and the sister with the tambourine kept a steady, jangling beat, *"it has rescued many a thousand!"* Not a soul under the sound of their voices was hearing this song for the first time, not one of them had been rescued. Nor had they seen much in the way of rescue work being done around them. Neither did they especially believe in the holiness of the three sisters and the brother, they knew too much about them, knew where they lived, and how. The woman with the tambourine, whose voice dominated the air, whose face was bright with joy, was divided by very little from the woman who stood watching her, a cigarette between her heavy, chapped lips, her hair a cuckoo's nest, her face scarred and swollen from many beatings, and her black eyes glittering like coal. Perhaps they both knew this, which was why, when, as rarely, they addressed each other, they addressed each other as Sister. As the singing filled the air the watching, listening faces underwent a change, the eyes focusing on something within; the music seemed to soothe a poison out of them; and time seemed, nearly, to fall away from the sullen, belligerent, battered faces, as though they were fleeing back to their first condition, while dreaming of their last. The barbecue cook half shook his head and smiled, and dropped his cigarette and disappeared into his joint. A man fumbled in his pockets for change and stood holding it in his hand impatiently, as though he had just remembered a pressing appointment further up the avenue. He looked furious. Then I saw Sonny, standing on the edge of the crowd. He was carrying a wide, flat notebook with a green cover, and it made him look, from where I was standing, almost like a schoolboy. The coppery sun brought out the copper in his skin, he was very faintly smiling, standing very still. Then the singing stopped, the tambourine turned into a collection plate again. The furious man dropped in his coins and vanished, so did a couple of the women, and Sonny dropped some change in the plate, looking directly at the woman with a little smile. He started across the avenue, toward the house. He has a slow, loping walk, something like the way Harlem hipsters walk, only he's imposed on this his own half-beat. I had never really noticed it before.

I stayed at the window, both relieved and apprehensive. As Sonny disappeared from my sight, they began singing again. And they were still singing when his key turned in the lock.

"Hey," he said.

"Hey, yourself. You want some beer?"

"No. Well, maybe." But he came up to the window and stood beside me, looking out. "What a warm voice," he said.

They were singing *If I could only hear my mother pray again!*

"Yes," I said, "and she can sure beat that tambourine."

"But what a terrible song," he said, and laughed. He dropped his notebook on the sofa and disappeared into the kitchen. "Where's Isabel and the kids?"

"I think they went to see their grandparents. You hungry?"

"No." He came back into the living room with his can of beer. "You want to come some place with me tonight?"

I sensed, I don't know how, that I couldn't possibly say no. "Sure. Where?"

He sat down on the sofa and picked up his notebook and started leafing through it. "I'm going to sit in with some fellows in a joint in the Village."

"You mean, you're going to play, tonight?"

"That's right." He took a swallow of his beer and moved back to the window. He gave me a sidelong look. "If you can stand it."

"I'll try," I said.

He smiled to himself and we both watched as the meeting across the way broke up. The three sisters and the brother, heads bowed, were singing *God be with you till we meet again.* The faces around them were very quiet. Then the song ended. The small crowd dispersed. We watched the three women and the lone man walk slowly up the avenue.

"When she was singing before," said Sonny, abruptly, "her voice reminded me for a minute of what heroin feels like sometimes — when it's in your veins. It makes you feel sort of warm and cool at the same time. And distant. And — and sure." He sipped his beer, very deliberately not looking at me. I watched his face. "It makes you feel — in control. Sometimes you've got to have that feeling."

"Do you?" I sat down slowly in the easy chair.

"Sometimes." He went to the sofa and picked up his notebook again. "Some people do."

"In order," I asked, "to play?" And my voice was very ugly, full of contempt and anger.

"Well" — he looked at me with great, troubled eyes, as though, in fact, he hoped his eyes would tell me things he could never otherwise say — "they *think* so. And *if* they think so — !"

"And what do *you* think?" I asked.

He sat on the sofa and put his can of beer on the floor. "I don't know," he said, and I couldn't be sure if he were answering my question or pursuing his thoughts. His face didn't tell me. "It's not so much to *play*. It's to *stand* it, to be able to make it at all. On any level." He frowned and smiled: "In order to keep from shaking to pieces."

"But these friends of yours," I said, "they seem to shake themselves to pieces pretty goddamn fast."

"Maybe." He played with the notebook. And something told me that I should curb my tongue, that Sonny was doing his best to talk, that I should listen. "But of course you only know the ones that've gone to pieces. Some don't — or at least they haven't *yet* and that's just about all *any* of us can say." He paused. "And then there are some who just live, really, in hell, and they know it and they see what's happening and they go right on. I don't know." He sighed, dropped the notebook, folded his arms. "Some guys, you can tell from the way they play, they on something *all* the time. And you can see that, well, it makes something real for them. But of course," he picked up his beer from the floor and sipped it and put the can down again, "they *want* to, too, you've got to see that. Even some of them that say they don't — *some*, not all."

"And what about you?" I asked — I couldn't help it. "What about you? Do *you* want to?"

He stood up and walked to the window and remained silent for a long time. Then he sighed. "Me," he said. Then: "While I was downstairs before, on my way here, listening to that woman sing, it struck me all of a sudden how much suffering she must have had to go through — to sing like that. It's *repulsive* to think you have to suffer that much."

I said: "But there's no way not to suffer — is there, Sonny?"

"I believe not," he said and smiled, "but that's never stopped anyone from trying." He looked at me. "Has it?" I realized, with this mocking look, that there stood between us, forever, beyond the power of time or forgiveness, the fact that I had held silence — so long! — when he had needed human speech to help him. He turned back to the window. "No, there's no way not to suffer. But you try all kinds of ways to keep from drowning in it, to keep on top of it, and to make it seem — well, like *you*. Like you did something, all right, and now you're suffering for it. You know?" I said nothing. "Well you know," he said, impatiently, "why *do* people suffer? Maybe it's better to do something to give it a reason, *any* reason."

"But we just agreed," I said "that there's no way not to suffer. Isn't it better, then, just to — take it?"

"But nobody just takes it," Sonny cried, "that's what I'm telling you! *Everybody* tries not to. You're just hung up on the *way* some people try — it's not *your* way!"

The hair on my face began to itch, my face felt wet. "That's not true," I said, "that's not true. I don't give a damn what other people do, I don't even care how they suffer. I just care how *you* suffer." And he looked at me. "Please believe me," I said, "I don't want to see you — die — trying not to suffer."

"I won't," he said, flatly, "die trying not to suffer. At least, not any faster than anybody else."

"But there's no need," I said, trying to laugh, "is there? in killing yourself."

I wanted to say more, but I couldn't. I wanted to talk about will power and how life could be — well, beautiful. I wanted to say that it was all within; but was it? or, rather, wasn't that exactly the trouble? And I wanted to promise that I would never fail him again. But it would all have sounded — empty words and lies.

So I made the promise to myself and prayed that I would keep it.

"It's terrible sometimes, inside," he said, "that's what's the trouble. You walk these streets, black and funky and cold, and there's not really a living ass to talk to, and there's nothing shaking, and there's no way of getting it out — that storm inside. You can't talk it and you can't make love with it, and when you finally try to get with it and play it, you realize *nobody's* listening. So *you've* got to listen. You got to find a way to listen."

And then he walked away from the window and sat on the sofa again, as though all the wind had suddenly been knocked out of him. "Sometimes you'll do *anything* to play, even cut your mother's throat." He laughed and looked at me. "Or your brother's." Then he sobered. "Or your own." Then: "Don't worry. I'm all right now and I think I'll *be* all right. But I can't forget — where I've been. I don't mean just the physical place I've been, I mean where I've *been*. And *what* I've been."

"What have you been, Sonny?" I asked.

He smiled — but sat sideways on the sofa, his elbow resting on the back, his fingers playing with his mouth and chin, not looking at me. "I've been something I didn't recognize, didn't know I could be. Didn't know anybody could be." He stopped, looking inward, looking helplessly young, looking old. "I'm not talking about it now because I feel *guilty* or anything like that — maybe it would be better if I did, I don't know. Anyway, I can't really talk about it. Not to you, not to anybody," and now he turned and faced me. "Sometimes, you know, and it was actually when I was most *out* of the world, I felt that I was in it, that I was *with* it, really, and I could play or I didn't really have to *play,* it just came out of me, it was there. And I don't know how I played, thinking about it now, but I know I did awful things, those times, sometimes, to people. Or it wasn't that I *did* anything to them — it was that they weren't real." He picked up the beer can; it was empty; he rolled it between his palms: "And other times — well, I needed a fix, I needed to find a place to lean, I needed to clear a space to *listen* — and I couldn't find it, and I — went crazy, I did terrible things to *me,* I was terrible *for* me." He began pressing the beer can between his hands, I watched the metal begin to give. It glittered, as he played with it, like a knife, and I was afraid he would cut himself, but I said nothing. "Oh well. I can never tell you. I was all by myself at the bottom of something, stinking and sweating and crying and shaking, and I smelled it, you know? *my* stink, and I thought I'd die if I couldn't get away from it and yet, all the same, I knew that everything I was doing was just locking me in with it. And I didn't know," he paused, still flattening the beer can, "I didn't know, I still *don't* know, something kept telling me that maybe it was good to

smell your own stink, but I didn't think that *that* was what I'd been trying to do
—and—who can stand it?" and he abruptly dropped the ruined beer can, looking at me with a small, still smile, and then rose, walking to the window as
though it were the lodestone rock. I watched his face, he watched the avenue. "I
couldn't tell you when Mama died—but the reason I wanted to leave Harlem so
bad was to get away from drugs. And then, when I ran away, that's what I was
running from — really. When I came back, nothing had changed, *I* hadn't
changed, I was just—older." And he stopped, drumming with his fingers on the
windowpane. The sun had vanished, soon darkness would fall. I watched his
face. "It can come again," he said, almost as though speaking to himself. Then he
turned to me. "It can come again," he repeated. "I just want you to know that."

"All right," I said, at last. "So it can come again. All right."

He smiled, but the smile was sorrowful. "I had to try to tell you," he said.

"Yes," I said. "I understand that."

"You're my brother," he said, looking straight at me, and not smiling at all.

"Yes," I repeated, "yes. I understand that."

He turned back to the window, looking out. "All that hatred down there,"
he said, "all that hatred and misery and love. It's a wonder it doesn't blow the
avenue apart."

We went to the only nightclub on a short, dark street, downtown. We
squeezed through the narrow, chattering, jam-packed bar to the entrance of
the big room, where the bandstand was. And we stood there for a moment, for
the lights were very dim in this room and we couldn't see. Then, "Hello, boy,"
said a voice and an enormous black man, much older than Sonny or myself,
erupted out of all that atmospheric lighting and put an arm around Sonny's
shoulder. "I been sitting right here," he said, "waiting for you."

He had a big voice, too, and heads in the darkness turned toward us.

Sonny grinned and pulled a little away, and said, "Creole, this is my
brother. I told you about him."

Creole shook my hand. "I'm glad to meet you, son," he said, and it was
clear that he was glad to meet me *there,* for Sonny's sake. And he smiled, "You
got a real musician in *your* family," and he took his arm from Sonny's shoulder and slapped him, lightly, affectionately, with the back of his hand.

"Well. Now I've heard it all," said a voice behind us. This was another
musician, and a friend of Sonny's, a coal-black, cheerful-looking man, built
close to the ground. He immediately began confiding to me, at the top of his
lungs, the most terrible things about Sonny, his teeth gleaming like a lighthouse
and his laugh coming up out of him like the beginning of an earthquake. And
it turned out that everyone at the bar knew Sonny, or almost everyone; some
were musicians, working there, or nearby, or not working, some were simply
hangers-on, and some were there to hear Sonny play. I was introduced to all of
them and they were all very polite to me. Yet, it was clear that, for them, I was
only Sonny's brother. Here, I was in Sonny's world. Or, rather: his kingdom.
Here, it was not even a question that his veins bore royal blood.

They were going to play soon and Creole installed me, by myself, at a table in a dark corner. Then I watched them, Creole, and the little black man, and Sonny, and the others, while they horsed around, standing just below the bandstand. The light from the bandstand spilled just a little short of them and, watching them laughing and gesturing and moving about, I had the feeling that they, nevertheless, were being most careful not to step into that circle of light too suddenly: that if they moved into the light too suddenly, without thinking, they would perish in flame. Then, while I watched, one of them, the small, black man, moved into the light and crossed the bandstand and started fooling around with his drums. Then — being funny and being, also, extremely ceremonious — Creole took Sonny by the arm and led him to the piano. A woman's voice called Sonny's name and a few hands started clapping. And Sonny, also being funny and being ceremonious, and so touched, I think, that he could have cried, but neither hiding it nor showing it, riding it like a man, grinned, and put both hands to his heart and bowed from the waist.

Creole then went to the bass fiddle and a lean, very bright-skinned brown man jumped up on the bandstand and picked up his horn. So there they were, and the atmosphere on the bandstand and in the room began to change and tighten. Someone stepped up to the microphone and announced them. Then there were all kinds of murmurs. Some people at the bar shushed others. The waitress ran around, frantically getting in the last orders, guys and chicks got closer to each other, and the lights on the bandstand, on the quartet, turned to a kind of indigo. Then they all looked different there. Creole looked about him for the last time, as though he were making certain that all his chickens were in the coop, and then he — jumped and struck the fiddle. And there they were.

All I know about music is that not many people ever really hear it. And even then, on the rare occasions when something opens within, and the music enters, what we mainly hear, or hear corroborated, are personal, private, vanishing evocations. But the man who creates the music is hearing something else, is dealing with the roar rising from the void and imposing order on it as it hits the air. What is evoked in him, then, is of another order, more terrible because it has no words, and triumphant, too, for that same reason. And his triumph, when he triumphs, is ours. I just watched Sonny's face. His face was troubled, he was working hard, but he wasn't with it. And I had the feeling that, in a way, everyone on the bandstand was waiting for him, both waiting for him and pushing him along. But as I began to watch Creole, I realized that it was Creole who held them all back. He had them on a short rein. Up there, keeping the beat with his whole body, wailing on the fiddle, with his eyes half closed, he was listening to everything, but he was listening to Sonny. He was having a dialogue with Sonny. He wanted Sonny to leave the shoreline and strike out for the deep water. He was Sonny's witness that deep water and drowning were not the same thing — he had been there, and he knew. And he wanted Sonny to know. He was waiting for Sonny to do the things on the keys which would let Creole know that Sonny was in the water.

And, while Creole listened, Sonny moved, deep within, exactly like someone in torment. I had never before thought of how awful the relationship must be between the musician and his instrument. He has to fill it, this instrument, with the breath of life, his own. He has to make it do what he wants it to do. And a piano is just a piano. It's made out of so much wood and wires and little hammers and big ones, and ivory. While there's only so much you can do with it, the only way to find this out is to try; to try and make it do everything.

And Sonny hadn't been near a piano for over a year. And he wasn't on much better terms with his life, not the life that stretched before him now. He and the piano stammered, started one way, got scared, stopped; started another way, panicked, marked time, started again; then seemed to have found a direction, panicked again, got stuck. And the face I saw on Sonny I'd never seen before. Everything had been burned out of it, and, at the same time, things usually hidden were being burned in, by the fire and fury of the battle which was occurring in him up there.

Yet, watching Creole's face as they neared the end of the first set, I had the feeling that something had happened, something I hadn't heard. Then they finished, there was scattered applause, and then, without an instant's warning, Creole started into something else, it was almost sardonic, it was *Am I Blue.* And, as though he commanded, Sonny began to play. Something began to happen. And Creole let out the reins. The dry, low, black man said something awful on the drums, Creole answered, and the drums talked back. Then the horn insisted, sweet and high, slightly detached perhaps, and Creole listened, commenting now and then, dry, and driving, beautiful and calm and old. Then they all came together again, and Sonny was part of the family again. I could tell this from his face. He seemed to have found, right there beneath his fingers, a damn brand-new piano. It seemed that he couldn't get over it. Then, for awhile, just being happy with Sonny, they seemed to be agreeing with him that brand-new pianos certainly were a gas.

Then Creole stepped forward to remind them that what they were playing was the blues. He hit something in all of them, he hit something in me, myself, and the music tightened and deepened, apprehension began to beat the air. Creole began to tell us what the blues were all about. They were not about anything very new. He and his boys up there were keeping it new, at the risk of ruin, destruction, madness, and death, in order to find new ways to make us listen. For, while the tale of how we suffer, and how we are delighted, and how we may triumph is never new, it always must be heard. There isn't any other tale to tell, it's the only light we've got in all this darkness.

And this tale, according to that face, that body, those strong hands on those strings, has another aspect in every country, and a new depth in every generation. Listen, Creole seemed to be saying, listen. Now these are Sonny's blues. He made the little black man on the drums know it, and the bright, brown man on the horn. Creole wasn't trying any longer to get Sonny in the water. He was wishing him Godspeed. Then he stepped back, very slowly, filling the air with the immense suggestion that Sonny speak for himself.

Then they all gathered around Sonny and Sonny played. Every now and again one of them seemed to say, amen. Sonny's fingers filled the air with life, his life. But that life contained so many others. And Sonny went all the way back, he really began with the spare, flat statement of the opening phrase of the song. Then he began to make it his. It was very beautiful because it wasn't hurried and it was no longer a lament. I seemed to hear with what burning he had made it his, with what burning we had yet to make it ours, how we could cease lamenting. Freedom lurked around us and I understood, at last, that he could help us to be free if we would listen, that he would never be free until we did. Yet, there was no battle in his face now. I heard what he had gone through, and would continue to go through until he came to rest in earth. He had made it his: that long line, of which we knew only Mama and Daddy. And he was giving it back, as everything must be given back, so that, passing through death, it can live forever. I saw my mother's face again, and felt, for the first time, how the stones of the road she had walked on must have bruised her feet. I saw the moonlit road where my father's brother died. And it brought something else back to me, and carried me past it. I saw my little girl again and felt Isabel's tears again, and I felt my own tears begin to rise. And I was yet aware that this was only a moment, that the world waited outside, as hungry as a tiger, and that trouble stretched above us, longer than the sky.

Then it was over. Creole and Sonny let out their breath, both soaking wet, and grinning. There was a lot of applause and some of it was real. In the dark, the girl came by and I asked her to take drinks to the bandstand. There was a long pause, while they talked up there in the indigo light and after awhile I saw the girl put a Scotch and milk on top of the piano for Sonny. He didn't seem to notice it, but just before they started playing again, he sipped from it and looked toward me, and nodded. Then he put it back on top of the piano. For me, then, as they began to play again, it glowed and shook above my brother's head like the very cup of trembling.

Questions for Discussion

1. What images does the narrator use to describe his shock upon learning of Sonny's drug problem? What do these images reveal about the narrator's personality and relationship with his brother?

2. Why does the narrator believe that Sonny has made a mistake in deciding to become a jazz musician? How and why does the narrator come to change his feelings about jazz and jazz musicians?

3. What does the story imply about the causes of drug addiction? How is the issue of drugs related both to music and to the community in which the story is set? Does Sonny seem "safe" from future addiction at the end of the story?

4. How does the death of Gracie, the narrator's child, affect the narrator's relationship with Sonny? What does Sonny's letter about Gracie's death suggest about Sonny and his relationship with his family?

5. What does the story the mother tells about the father's brother reveal about the legacy of close relationships in the narrator's family? Knowing this story, what special burden of responsibility does the narrator feel?

6. What does the conversation between the two brothers immediately following the street scene where Sonny watches the revival singers reveal about the brothers' relationship and attitudes toward music, drugs, and suffering?

Ideas for Writing

1. Write an essay in which you analyze the final scene in which the narrator hears Sonny play. How does the scene reveal a major change in the narrator's understanding of Sonny? What does the narrator realize about African-American family relationships and cultural traditions as he listens? What is the significance of the final image in the story, the "cup of trembling" above Sonny's piano?

2. Write a story about two siblings with different lifestyles who come to understand each other after a period of conflict and separation.

James Baldwin

James Baldwin attracted considerable critical attention in his lifetime for his strong views on race and American society as well as for his stories, novels, and plays. The first piece in the casebook, "The Art of Fiction" (1984), is an interview with Baldwin by Jordan Elgrably and George Plimpton focusing on Baldwin's difficult early life in Harlem, his apprenticeship as a writer, his struggle to survive as an expatriate in Paris, and his writing process. The second selection, "Autobiographical Notes" (1955), is an essay Baldwin wrote fairly early in his career. In it he examines the dilemma of the "Negro" writer in America, along with the social forces that led him to become an expatriate and to "hat[e] and fea[r] the world." A second essay by Baldwin, "The Creative Process" (1962), speaks of the artist as one who "must actively cultivate . . . the state of being alone." In this essay Baldwin also speaks of American writers' obligation to move "beyond the Old World concepts of race and class" and, through the revelatory power of art to help "to make freedom real."

In an essay on "Sonny's Blues," "James Baldwin's Image of Black Community" (1970), John M. Reilly sees Baldwin's story as representing, for its middle-class narrator, a discovery of "the value of a characteristically Afro-American assertion of life-force." In contrast, Keith E. Byerman's structuralist analysis in "Words and Music: Narrative Ambiguity in 'Sonny's Blues'" (1982) focuses on the narrator's use of formal and at times ambiguous and evasive figurative language. Another viewpoint is offered by Pancho Savery, whose "Baldwin, Bebop, and 'Sonny's Blues'" (1990) emphasizes the music Sonny plays and its relationship to African-American cultural history and values, particularly to the urge to revolt and the new militancy that urban African Americans began to experience in the 1940s.

We conclude the casebook with student writer Zachary Roberts's reflective essay, "Listening to Sonny's Blues," in which he contrasts his own involvement with music and his sense of music's cultural and metaphysical significance with the concerns expressed by Sonny and the narrator in Baldwin's story.

JORDAN ELGRABLY AND GEORGE PLIMPTON

FROM The Art of Fiction: An Interview with James Baldwin (1984)

Interviewer: Was there an instant you knew you were going to write, to be a writer rather than anything else?

Baldwin: Yes. The death of my father. Until my father died I thought I could do something else. I had wanted to be a musician, thought of being a painter, thought of being an actor. This was all before I was nineteen. Given the conditions in this country to be a black writer was impossible. When I was young, people thought you were not so much wicked as sick, they gave up on you. My father didn't think it was possible — he thought I'd get killed, get murdered. He said I was contesting the white man's definitions, which was quite right. But I had also learned from my father what he thought of the white man's definitions. He was a pious, very religious and in some ways a very beautiful man, and in some ways a terrible man. He died when his last child was born and I realized I had to make a jump — a leap. I'd been a preacher for three years, from age fourteen to seventeen. Those were three years which probably turned me to writing.

Interviewer: Were the sermons you delivered from the pulpit very carefully prepared, or were they absolutely off the top of your head?

Baldwin: I would improvise from the texts, like a jazz musician improvises from a theme. I never wrote a sermon — I studied the texts. I've never written a speech. I can't *read* a speech. It's kind of give and take. You have to sense the people you're talking to. You have to respond to what they hear.

Interviewer: Do you have a reader in your mind when you write?

Baldwin: No, you can't have that.

Interviewer: So it's quite unlike preaching?

Baldwin: Entirely. The two roles are completely unattached. When you are standing in the pulpit, you must sound as though you know what you're talking about. When you're writing, you're trying to find out something which you don't know. The whole language of writing for me is finding out what you don't want to know, what you don't want to find out. But something forces you to anyway.

Interviewer: Is that one of the reasons you decided to be a writer — to find out about yourself?

Baldwin: I'm not sure I decided. It was that or nothing, since in my own mind I was the father of my family, That's not quite the way *they* saw it, but still I was the oldest brother, and I took it very seriously, I had to set an example. I couldn't allow anything to happen to me because what then would happen to them? I could have become a junkie. On the roads I traveled and the streets I ran, anything could have happened to a boy like me — in New York. Sleeping on rooftops and in the subways. Until this day I'm terrified of the public toilet. In any case . . . my father died, and I sat down and figured out what I had to do.

Interviewer: When did you find time to write?

Baldwin: I was very young then. I could write *and* hold a few jobs. I was for a time a waiter . . . like George Orwell in *Down and Out in Paris and London.* I couldn't do it now. I worked on the Lower East Side and in what we now call Soho.

Interviewer: Was there anyone to guide you?

Baldwin: I remember standing on a street corner with the black painter Beauford Delaney down in the Village, waiting for the light to change, and he pointed down and said, "Look." I looked and all I saw was water. And he said, "Look again," which I did, and I saw oil on the water and the city reflected in the puddle. It was a great revelation to me. I can't explain it. He taught me how to see, and how to trust what I saw. Painters have often taught writers how to see. And once you've had that experience, you see differently.

Interviewer: Do you think painters would help a fledgling writer more than another writer might? Did you read a great deal?

Baldwin: I read everything. I read my way out of the two libraries in Harlem by the time I was thirteen. One does learn a great deal about writing this way. First of all, you learn how little you know. It is true that the more one learns the less one knows. I'm still learning how to write. I don't know what technique is. All I know is that you have to make the reader *see* it. This I learned from Dostoyevsky, from Balzac. I'm sure that my life in France would have been very different had I not met Balzac. Even though I hadn't experienced it yet, I understood something about the concierge, all the French institutions and personalities. The way that country and its society works. How to find my way around in it, not get lost in it, and not feel rejected by it. The French gave me what I could not get in America, which was a sense of "If I can do it, I may do it." I won't generalize, but in the years I grew up in the U.S., I could not do that. I'd already been defined.

Interviewer: Did what you wanted to write about come easy to you from the start?

Baldwin: I had to be released from a terrible shyness — an illusion that I could hide anything from anybody.

Interviewer: I would think that anyone who could time after time, and without notes, address a congregation would never be shy again.

Baldwin: I was scared then and I'm scared now. Communication is a two-way street, really, it's a matter of listening to one another. During the civil rights movement I was in the back of a church in Tallahassee and the pastor, who recognized me, called my name and asked me to say a few words. I was thirty-four and had left the pulpit seventeen years before. The moment in which I had to stand up and walk down the aisle and stand in that pulpit was the strangest moment in my life up to that time. I managed to get through it and when I walked down from the pulpit and back up the aisle, a little old black lady in the congregation said to a friend of hers, "He's little, but he's loud!"

Interviewer: What was the process whereby you were able to write?

Baldwin: I had to go through a time of isolation in order to come to terms with who and what I was, as distinguished from all the things I'd been told I was. Right around 1950 I remember feeling that I'd come through *something*, shed a dying skin and was naked again. I wasn't, perhaps, but I certainly felt more at ease with myself. And then I was able to write. Throughout 1948 and 1949 I just tore up paper.

Interviewer: Those years were difficult, and yet you received four writing grants between 1945 and 1956. How much encouragement did they afford you?

Baldwin: Well, the first one was the most important in terms of morale — the Saxton Fellowship in 1945. I was twenty-one. I was launched into the publishing world, so to speak. And there was the novel, which became *Go Tell It on the Mountain* several years later.

Interviewer: The Saxton was intended to help you finish the novel you were working on?

Baldwin: It helped me finish the novel, it kept me *alive.* The novel didn't work, but I started doing book reviews for the *New Leader* at ten and twenty dollars a shot. I had to read everything and had to write all the time, and that's a great apprenticeship. The people I worked with were left-of-center Trotskyites, Socialist Trotskyites. I was a young Socialist. That was a very nice atmosphere for me; in a sense it saved me from despair. But most of the books I reviewed were Be Kind to Niggers, Be Kind to Jews, while America was going through one of its liberal convulsions. People suddenly discovered they had a Jewish problem, with books like *Gentleman's Agreement, Earth and High Heaven,* or they discovered they had niggers, with books like *King's Blood Royal* and *Pinky.*

Thousands of such tracts were published during those years and it seems to me I had to read every single one of them; the color of my skin made me an expert. And so, when I got to Paris, I had to discharge all that, which was really the reason for my essay, "Everybody's Protest Novel." I was convinced then — and I still am — that those sort of books do nothing but bolster up an image. All of this had quite a bit to do with the direction I took as a writer, because it seemed to me that if I took the role of a victim then I was simply reassuring the defenders of the status quo; as long as I was a victim they could pity me and add a few more pennies to my home relief check. Nothing would change in that way, I felt, and that essay was a beginning of my finding a new vocabulary and another point of view.

Interviewer: If you felt that it was a white man's world, what made you think that there was any point in writing? And why is writing a white man's world?

Baldwin: Because they own the business. Well, in retrospect, what it came down to was that I would not allow myself to be defined by other people, white or black. It was beneath me to blame anybody for what happened to me. What happened to me was *my* responsibility. I didn't want any pity. "Leave me alone, I'll figure it out." I was very wounded and I was very dangerous because you become what you hate. It's what happened to my father and I didn't want it to happen to me. His hatred was suppressed and turned against himself. He couldn't let it out — he could only let it out in the house with rage, and I found it happening to myself as well. And after my best friend jumped off the bridge, I knew that I was next. So — Paris. With forty dollars and a one-way ticket.

Interviewer: Once in Paris, you spent a lot of time upstairs at the Café de Flore. Is that where *Go Tell It on the Mountain* and *Giovanni's Room* were written?

Baldwin: A lot of *Go Tell It on the Mountain* had to be written there, between there and the Hotel Verneuil, where I stayed for a lot of the time I was in Paris. After ten years of carrying that book around, I finally finished it in Switzerland in three months. I remember playing Bessie Smith all the time while I was in the mountains, and playing her till I fell asleep. The book was very hard to write because I was too young when I started, seventeen; it was really about me and my father. There were things I couldn't deal with technically at first. Most of all, I couldn't deal with *me*. This is where reading Henry James helped me, with his whole idea about the center of consciousness and using a single intelligence to tell the story. He gave me the idea to make the novel happen on John's birthday.

Interviewer: Do you agree with Alberto Moravia, who said that one ought only to write in the first person, because the third projects a bourgeois point of view?

Baldwin: I don't know about that. The first person is the most terrifying view of all. I tend to be in accord with James, who hated the first person perspective, which the reader has no reason to trust — why should you need this *I*? How is this person real by dint of that bar blaring across the page?

Interviewer: Is there a big shifting of gears between writing fiction and writing non-fiction?

Baldwin: Shifting gears, you ask. Every form is difficult, no one is easier than another. They all kick your ass. None of it comes easy.

Interviewer: How many pages do you write in a day?

Baldwin: I write at night. After the day is over, and supper is over, I begin, and work until about three or four A.M.

Interviewer: That's quite rare, isn't it, because most people write when they're fresh, in the morning.

Baldwin: I start working when everyone has gone to bed. I've had to do that ever since I was young — I had to wait until the kids were asleep. And then I was working at various jobs during the day. I've always had to write at night. But now that I'm established I do it because I'm alone at night.

Interviewer: When do you know something is the way you want it?

Baldwin: I do a lot of rewriting. It's very painful. You know it's finished when you can't do anything more to it, though it's never exactly the way you want it. In fact, the hardest thing I ever wrote was that suicide scene in *Another Country*. I always knew that Rufus had to commit suicide very early on, because that was the key to the book. But I kept putting it off. It had to do, of course, with reliving the suicide of my friend who jumped off the bridge. Also, it was very dangerous to do from the technical point of view because this central character dies in the first hundred pages, with a couple of hundred pages to go. The point up to the suicide is like a long prologue, and it is the only light on Ida. You never go into her mind, but I had to make you see what is happening to this girl by making you feel the blow of her brother's death — the key to her relationship with everybody. She tries to make everybody pay for it. You cannot do that, life is not like that, you only destroy yourself.

Interviewer: Is that the way a book starts for you, though? Something like that?

Baldwin: Probably that way for everybody: something that irritates you and won't let you go. That's the anguish of it. Do this book, or die. You have to go through that.

Interviewer: Does it purge you in any way?

Baldwin: I'm not so sure about *that.* For me it's like a journey, and the only thing you know is that if when the book is over, you are prepared to continue — you haven't cheated.

Interviewer: What would cheating be?

Baldwin: Avoiding. Lying.

Interviewer: So there is a compulsion to get it out?

Baldwin: Oh yes, to get it out and get it right. The word I'm using is compulsion. And it is true of the essay as well.

Interviewer: But the essay is a little bit simpler, isn't it, because you're angry about something which you can put your finger on . . .

Baldwin: An essay is not simpler, though it may seem so. An essay is essentially an argument. The writer's point of view in an essay is always absolutely clear. The writer is trying to make the readers see something, trying to convince them of something. In a novel or a play you're trying to *show* them something. The risks, in any case, are exactly the same.

Interviewer: What are your first drafts like?

Baldwin: They are overwritten. Most of the rewrite, then, is cleaning. Don't describe it, show it. That's what I try to teach all young writers — take it out! Don't describe a purple sunset, make me see that it is purple.

Interviewer: As your experience about writing accrues, what would you say increases with knowledge?

Baldwin: You learn how little you know. It becomes much more difficult because the hardest thing in the world is simplicity. And the most fearful thing, too. It becomes more difficult because you have to strip yourself of all your disguises, some of which you didn't know you had. You want to write a sentence as clean as a bone. That is the goal.

Interviewer: Do you mind what people say about your writing?

Baldwin: Ultimately not. I minded it when I was younger. You care about the people you care about, what they say. You care about the reviews so that somebody will read the book. So, those things are important, but not of ultimate importance.

Interviewer: As a writer, are there any particular battles you feel you've won?

Baldwin: The battle of becoming a writer at all! "I'm going to be a great writer when I grow up," I used to tell my mother when I was a little boy. And I'm still going to be a great writer when I grow up.

Interviewer: What do you tell younger writers who come to you with the usual desperate question: How do I become a writer?

Baldwin: Write. Find a way to keep alive and write. There is nothing else to say. If you are going to be a writer there is nothing I can say to stop you; if you're not going to be a writer nothing I can say will help you. What you really need at the beginning is somebody to let you know that the effort is real.

Interviewer: Can you discern talent in someone?

Baldwin: Talent is insignificant. I know a lot of talented ruins. Beyond talent lie all the usual words: discipline, love, luck, but, most of all, endurance.

Interviewer: Would you suggest that a young writer from a minority consecrate himself to that minority, or is his first obligation his own self-realization as a writer?

Baldwin: Your self and your people are indistinguishable from each other, really, in spite of the quarrels you may have, and your people are all people.

JAMES BALDWIN

Autobiographical Notes   (1955)

I was born in Harlem thirty-one years ago. I began plotting novels at about the time I learned to read. The story of my childhood is the usual bleak fantasy, and we can dismiss it with the unrestrained observation that I certainly would not consider living it again. In those days my mother was given to the exasperating and mysterious habit of having babies. As they were born, I took them over with one hand and held a book with the other. The children probably suffered, though they have since been kind enough to deny it, and in this way I read *Uncle Tom's Cabin* and *A Tale of Two Cities* over and over and over again; in this way, in fact, I read just about everything I could get my hands on — except the Bible, probably because it was the only book I was encouraged to read. I must also confess that I wrote — a great deal — and my first professional triumph, in any case, the first effort of mine to be seen in print, occurred at the age of twelve or thereabouts, when a short story I had written about the Spanish revolution won some sort of prize in an extremely short-lived church newspaper. I remember the story was censored by the lady editor, though I don't remember why, and I was outraged.

Also wrote plays, and songs, for one of which I received a letter of congratulations from Mayor La Guardia, and poetry, about which the less said, the better. My mother was delighted by all these goings-on, but my father wasn't; he wanted me to be a preacher. When I was fourteen I became a preacher, and when I was seventeen I stopped. Very shortly thereafter I left home. For God knows how long I struggled with the world of commerce and industry — I guess they would say they struggled with *me* — and when I was about twenty-one I had enough done of a novel to get a Saxton Fellowship. When I was twenty-two the fellowship was over, the novel turned out to be unsalable, and I started waiting on tables in a Village[1] restaurant and writing book reviews—mostly, as it turned out, about the Negro problem, concerning which the color of my skin made me automatically an expert. Did another book, in company with photographer Theodore Pelatowski, about the storefront churches in Harlem. This book met exactly the same fate as my first—fellowship, but no sale. (It was a Rosenwald Fellowship.) By the time I was twenty-four I had decided to stop reviewing books about the Negro problem — which, by this time, was only slightly less horrible in print than it was in life—and I packed my bags and went to France, where I finished, God knows how, *Go Tell It on the Mountain.*

Any writer, I suppose, feels that the world into which he was born is nothing less than a conspiracy against the cultivation of his talent—which attitude certainly has a great deal to support it. On the other hand, it is only because the world looks on his talent with such a frightening indifference that the artist is compelled to make his talent important. So that any writer, looking back over even so short a span of time as I am here forced to assess, finds that the things which hurt him and the things which helped him cannot be divorced from each other; he could be helped in a certain way only because he was hurt in a certain way; and his help is simply to be enabled to move from one conundrum to the next—one is tempted to say that he moves from one disaster to the next. When one begins looking for influences one finds them by the score. I haven't thought much about my own, not enough anyway; I hazard that the King James Bible, the rhetoric of the store-front church, something ironic and violent and perpetually understated in Negro speech—and something of Dickens' love for bravura—have something to do with me today; but I wouldn't stake my life on it. Likewise, innumerable people have helped me in many ways; but finally, I suppose, the most difficult (and most rewarding) thing in my life has been the fact that I was born a Negro and was forced, therefore, to effect some kind of truce with this reality. (Truce, by the way, is the best one can hope for.)

One of the difficulties about being a Negro writer (and this is not special pleading, since I don't mean to suggest that he has it worse than anybody else) is that the Negro problem is written about so widely. The bookshelves groan under the weight of information, and everyone therefore considers himself informed. And this information, furthermore, operates usually (generally, popularly) to reinforce traditional attitudes. Of traditional attitudes there are only two—For or Against—and I, personally, find it difficult to say which attitude has caused me the most pain. I am perfectly aware that the change from ill-will to good-will, however motivated, however imperfect, however expressed, is better than no change at all.

---

[1] Greenwich Village in New York City. — Eds.

But it is part of the business of the writer — as I see it — to examine attitudes, to go beneath the surface, to tap the source. From this point of view the Negro problem is nearly inaccessible. It is not only written about so widely; it is written about so badly. It is quite possible to say that the price a Negro pays for becoming articulate is to find himself, at length, with nothing to be articulate about. ("You taught me the language," says Caliban to Prospero,[2] "and my profit on't is I know how to curse.") Consider: The tremendous social activity that this problem generates imposes on whites and Negroes alike the necessity of looking forward, of working to bring about a better day. This is fine, it keeps the waters troubled; it is all, indeed, that has made possible the Negro's progress. Nevertheless, social affairs are not generally speaking the writer's prime concern, whether they ought to be or not; it is absolutely necessary that he establish between himself and these affairs a distance that will allow, at least, for clarity, so that before he can look forward in any meaningful sense, he must first be allowed to take a long look back. In the context of the Negro problem neither whites nor blacks, for excellent reasons of their own, have the faintest desire to look back; but I think that the past is all that makes the present coherent, and further, that the past will remain horrible for exactly as long as we refuse to assess it honestly.

I know, in any case, that the most crucial time in my own development came when I was forced to recognize that I was a kind of bastard of the West; when I followed the line of my past I did not find myself in Europe but in Africa. And this meant that in some subtle way, in a really profound way, I brought to Shakespeare, Bach, Rembrandt, to the stones of Paris, to the cathedral at Chartres, and to the Empire State Building, a special attitude. These were not really my creations, they did not contain my history; I might search in them in vain forever for any reflection of myself. I was an interloper; this was not my heritage. At the same time I had no other heritage which I could possibly hope to use — I had certainly been unfitted for the jungle or the tribe. I would have to appropriate these white centuries, I would have to make them mine — I would have to accept my special attitude, my special place in this scheme — otherwise I would have no place in *any* scheme. What was the most difficult was the fact that I was forced to admit something I had always hidden from myself, which the American Negro has had to hide from himself as the price of his public progress; that I hated and feared white people. This did not mean that I loved black people; on the contrary, I despised them, possibly because they failed to produce Rembrandt. In effect, I hated and feared the world. And this meant, not only that I thus gave the world an altogether murderous power over me, but also that in such a self-destroying limbo I could never hope to write.

---

[2] In Shakespeare's *The Tempest,* Caliban, a slave to Prospero, is usually portrayed as a monster, a freak of nature. — Eds.

One writes out of one thing only — one's own experience. Everything depends on how relentlessly one forces from this experience the last drop, sweet or bitter, it can possibly give. This is the only real concern of the artist, to recreate out of the disorder of life that order which is art. The difficulty then, for me, of being a Negro writer was the fact that I was, in effect, prohibited from examining my own experience too closely by the tremendous demands and the very real dangers of my social situation.

I don't think the dilemma outlined above is uncommon. I do think, since writers work in the disastrously explicit medium of language, that it goes a little way towards explaining why, out of the enormous resources of Negro speech and life, and despite the example of Negro music, prose written by Negroes has been generally speaking so pallid and so harsh. I have not written about being a Negro at such length because I expect that to be my only subject, but only because it was the gate I had to unlock before I could hope to write about anything else. I don't think that the Negro problem in America can be even discussed coherently without bearing in mind its context; its context being the history, traditions, customs, the moral assumptions and preoccupations of the country; in short, the general social fabric. Appearances to the contrary, no one in America escapes its effects and everyone in America bears some responsibility for it. I believe this the more firmly because it is the overwhelming tendency to speak of this problem as though it were a thing apart. But in the work of Faulkner, in the general attitude and certain specific passages in Robert Penn Warren, and, most significantly, in the advent of Ralph Ellison, one sees the beginnings — at least — of a more genuinely penetrating search. Mr. Ellison, by the way, is the first Negro novelist I have ever read to utilize in language, and brilliantly, some of the ambiguity and irony of Negro life.

About my interests: I don't know if I have any, unless the morbid desire to own a sixteen-millimeter camera and make experimental movies can be so classified. Otherwise, I love to eat and drink — it's my melancholy conviction that I've scarcely ever had enough to eat (this is because it's *impossible* to eat enough if you're worried about the next meal) — and I love to argue with people who do not disagree with me too profoundly, and I love to laugh. I do *not* like bohemia, or bohemians, I do not like people whose principal aim is pleasure, and I do not like people who are *earnest* about anything. I don't like people who like me because I'm a Negro; neither do I like people who find in the same accident grounds for contempt. I love America more than any other country in the world, and, exactly for this reason, I insist on the right to criticize her perpetually. I think all theories are suspect, that the finest principles may have to be modified, or may even be pulverized by the demands of life, and that one must find, therefore, one's own moral center and move through the world hoping that this center will guide one aright. I consider that I have many responsibilities, but none greater than this: to last, as Hemingway says, and get my work done.

I want to be an honest man and a good writer.

JAMES BALDWIN

The Creative Process   (1962)

Perhaps the primary distinction of the artist is that he must actively cultivate that state which most men, necessarily, must avoid: the state of being alone. That all men *are,* when the chips are down, alone, is a banality — a banality because it is very frequently stated, but very rarely, on the evidence, believed. Most of us are not compelled to linger with the knowledge of our aloneness, for it is a knowledge that can paralyze all action in this world. There are, forever, swamps to be drained, cities to be created, mines to be exploited, children to be fed. None of these things can be done alone. But the conquest of the physical world is not man's only duty. He is also enjoined to conquer the great wilderness of himself. The precise role of the artist, then, is to illuminate that darkness, blaze roads through that vast forest, so that we will not, in all our doing, lose sight of its purpose, which is, after all, to make the world a more human dwelling place.

The state of being alone is not meant to bring to mind merely a rustic musing beside some silver lake. The aloneness of which I speak is much more like the aloneness of birth or death. It is like the fearful aloneness that one sees in the eyes of someone who is suffering, whom we cannot help. Or it is like the aloneness of love, the force and mystery that so many have extolled and so many have cursed, but which no one has ever understood or ever really been able to control. I put the matter this way, not out of any desire to create pity for the artist — God forbid! — but to suggest how nearly, after all, is his state the state of everyone, and in an attempt to make vivid his endeavor. The states of birth, suffering, love, and death are extreme states — extreme, universal, and inescapable. We all know this, but we would rather not know it. The artist is present to correct the delusions to which we fall prey in our attempts to avoid this knowledge.

It is for this reason that all societies have battled with that incorrigible disturber of the peace — the artist. I doubt that future societies will get on with him any better. The entire purpose of society is to create a bulwark against the inner and the outer chaos, in order to make life bearable and to keep the human race alive. And it is absolutely inevitable that when a tradition has been evolved, whatever the tradition is, the people, in general, will suppose it to have existed from before the beginning of time and will be most unwilling and indeed unable to conceive of any changes in it. They do not know how they will live without those traditions that have given them their identity. Their reaction, when it is suggested that they can or that they must, is panic. And we see this panic, I think, everywhere in the world today, from the streets of New Orleans to the grisly battleground of Algeria. And a higher level of consciousness among the people is the only hope we have, now or in the future, of minimizing human damage.

The artist is distinguished from all other responsible actors in society — the politicians, legislators, educators, and scientists — by the fact that he is his own test tube, his own laboratory, working according to very rigorous rules, however unstated these may be, and cannot allow any consideration to supersede his responsibility to reveal all that he can possibly discover concerning the mystery of the human being. Society must accept some things as real; but he must always know that visible reality hides a deeper one, and that all our action and achievement rest on things unseen. A society must assume that it is stable, but the artist must know, and he must let us know, that there is nothing stable under heaven. One cannot possibly build a school, teach a child, or drive a car without taking some things for granted. The artist cannot and must not take anything for granted, but must drive to the heart of every answer and expose the question the answer hides.

I seem to be making extremely grandiloquent claims for a breed of men and women historically despised while living and acclaimed when safely dead. But, in a way, the belated honor that all societies tender their artists proves the reality of the point I am trying to make. I am really trying to make clear the nature of the artist's responsibility to his society. The peculiar nature of this responsibility is that he must never cease warring with it, for its sake and for his own. For the truth, in spite of appearances and all our hopes, is that everything is always changing and the measure of our maturity as nations and as men is how well prepared we are to meet these changes and, further, to use them for our health.

Now, anyone who has ever been compelled to think about it — anyone, for example, who has ever been in love — knows that the one face that one can never see is one's own face. One's lover — or one's brother, or one's enemy — sees the face you wear, and this face can elicit the most extraordinary reactions. We do the things we do and feel what we feel essentially because we must — we are responsible for our actions, but we rarely understand them. It goes without saying, I believe, that if we understood ourselves better, we would damage ourselves less. But the barrier between oneself and one's knowledge of oneself is high indeed. There are so many things one would rather not know! We become social creatures because we cannot live any other way. But in order to become social, there are a great many other things that we must not become, and we are frightened, all of us, of these forces within us that perpetually menace our precarious security. Yet the forces are there: we cannot will them away. All we can do is learn to live with them. And we cannot learn this unless we are willing to tell the truth about ourselves, and the truth about us is always at variance with what we wish to be. The human effort is to bring these two realities into a relationship resembling reconciliation. The human beings whom we respect the most, after all — and sometimes fear the most — are those who are most deeply involved in this delicate and strenuous effort, for they have the unshakable authority that comes only from having looked on and endured and survived the worst. That nation is healthiest which has the least necessity to distrust or ostracize or victimize these people

—whom, as I say, we honor, once they are gone, because somewhere in our hearts we know that we cannot live without them.

The dangers of being an American artist are not greater than those of being an artist anywhere else in the world, but they are very particular. These dangers are produced by our history. They rest on the fact that in order to conquer this continent, the particular aloneness of which I speak — the aloneness in which one discovers that life is tragic, and therefore unutterably beautiful — could not be permitted. And that this prohibition is typical of all emergent nations will be proved, I have no doubt, in many ways during the next fifty years. This continent now is conquered, but our habits and our fears remain. And, in the same way that to become a social human being one modifies and suppresses and, ultimately, without great courage, lies to oneself about all one's interior, uncharted chaos, so have we, as a nation, modified and suppressed and lied about all the darker forces in our history. We know, in the case of the person, that whoever cannot tell himself the truth about his past is trapped in it, is immobilized in the prison of his undiscovered self. This is also true of nations. We know how a person, in such a paralysis, is unable to assess either his weaknesses or his strengths, and how frequently indeed he mistakes the one for the other. And this, I think, we do. We are the strongest nation in the Western world, but this is not for the reasons that we think. It is because we have an opportunity that no other nation has of moving beyond the Old World concepts of race and class and caste, to create, finally, what we must have had in mind when we first began speaking of the New World. But the price of this is a long look backward whence we came and an unflinching assessment of the record. For an artist, the record of that journey is most clearly revealed in the personalities of the people the journey produced. Societies never know it, but the war of an artist with his society is a lover's war, and he does, at his best, what lovers do, which is to reveal the beloved to himself and, with that revelation, to make freedom real.

JOHN M. REILLY

FROM *"Sonny's Blues": James Baldwin's Image of Black Community*   (1970)

The insight into suffering that Sonny displays establishes his priority in knowledge. Thus, he reverses the original relationship between the brothers, assumes the role of the elder, and proceeds to lead his brother, by means of the Blues, to a discovery of self in community.

As the brothers enter the jazz club where Sonny is to play, he becomes special. Everyone has been waiting for him, and each greets him familiarly. Equally special is the setting — dark except for a spotlight which the musicians approach as if it were a circle of flame. This is a sanctified spot where Sonny is to testify to the power of souls to commune in the Blues.

Baldwin explicates the formula of the Blues by tracing the narrator's thoughts while Sonny plays. Many people, he thinks, don't really hear music being played except so far as they invest it with "personal, private, vanishing evocations." He might be thinking of himself, referring to his having come to think of Sonny through the suffering of his own personal loss. The man who makes the music engages in a spiritual creation, and when he succeeds, the creation belongs to all present, "his triumph, when he triumphs, is ours."

In the first set Sonny doesn't triumph, but in the second, appropriately begun by "Am I Blue," he takes the lead and begins to form a musical creation. He becomes, in the narrator's words, "part of the family again." What family? First of all that of his fellow musicians. Then, of course, the narrator means to say that their fraternal relationship is at last fulfilled as their mother hoped it to be. But there is yet a broader meaning too. Like the sisters at the Seventh Avenue revival meeting Sonny and the band are not saying anything new. Still they are keeping the Blues alive by expanding it beyond the personal lyric into a statement of the glorious capacity of human beings to take the worst and give it a form of their own choosing.

At this point the narrator synthesizes feelings and perception into a conception of the Blues. He realizes Sonny's Blues can help everyone who listens be free, in his own case free of the conventions that had alienated him from Sonny and that dimension of Black culture represented in Sonny's style of living. Yet at the same time he knows the world outside of the Blues moment remains hostile.

The implicit statement of the esthetics of the Blues in this story throws light upon much of Baldwin's writing. The first proposition of the esthetics that we can infer from "Sonny's Blues" is that suffering is the prior necessity. Integrity of expression comes from "paying your dues." This is a point Baldwin previously made in *Giovanni's Room* (1956) and which he elaborated in the novel *Another Country* (1962).

The second implicit proposition of the Blues esthetics is that while the form is what it's all about, the form is transitory. The Blues is an art in process and in that respect alien from any conception of fixed and ideal forms. This will not justify weaknesses in an artist's work, but insofar as Baldwin identifies his writing with the art of the singers of Blues it suggests why he is devoted to representation, in whatever genre, of successive moments of expressive feeling and comparatively less concerned with achieving a consistent overall structure.

The final proposition of the esthetic in the story "Sonny's Blues" is that the Blues functions as an art of communion. It is popular rather than elite, worldly rather than otherwise. The Blues is expression in which one uses the skill he has achieved by practice and experience in order to reach toward others. It is this proposition that gives the Blues its metaphoric significance. The fraternal reconciliation brought about through Sonny's music is emblematic of a group's coming together, because the narrator learns to love his brother freely while he discovers the value of a characteristically Afro-American assertion of life-force. Taking Sonny on his own terms he must also abandon the ways of thought identified with middle-class position which historically has signified for Black people the adoption of "white" ways.

An outstanding quality of the Black literary tradition in America is its attention to the interdependence of personal and social experience. Obviously necessity has fostered this virtue. Black authors cannot luxuriate in the assumption that there is such a thing as a purely private life. James Baldwin significantly adds to this aspect of the tradition in "Sonny's Blues" by showing that artful expression of personal yet typical experience is one way to freedom.

KEITH E. BYERMAN
Words and Music: Narrative Ambiguity in "Sonny's Blues" (1982)

"Sonny's Blues" has generally been accorded status as the best of James Baldwin's short stories. It tells of the developing relationship between Sonny, a musician and drug addict, and the narrator, his brother, who feels a conflict between the security of his middle-class life and the emotional risks of brotherhood with Sonny. The critics, who differ on whether the story is primarily Sonny's or the narrator's, generally agree that it resolves its central conflict.[1] If, however, resolution is not assumed but taken as problematical, then new thematic and structural possibilities are revealed. The story becomes a study of the nature and relationship of art and language. The commentary on the story has centered on the moral issue; the purpose of this essay is to focus on the underlying aesthetic question.

According to Jonathan Culler, resolution can be accomplished in a story when a message is received or a code deciphered.[2] In most cases the message

---

[1] See Stanley Macebuh, *James Baldwin: A Critical Study* (New York: Third World Press, 1973); Sherley Anne Williams, *Give Birth to Brightness* (New York: Dial, 1972), pp. 145–166; Harry L. Jones, "Style, Form and Content in the Short Fiction of James Baldwin," in *James Baldwin: A Critical Evaluation,* ed. Therman O'Daniel (Washington, D.C.: Howard University Press, 1977), pp. 143–150; Suzy Bernstein Goldman, "James Baldwin's 'Sonny's Blues': A Message in Music," *Negro American Literature Forum,* 8 (1974), 231–233; John Reilly, "'Sonny's Blues': James Baldwin's Image of Black Community," *Negro American Literature Forum,* 4 (1970), 56–60; and Donald C. Murray, "James Baldwin's 'Sonny's Blues': Complicated and Simple," *Studies in Short Fiction,* 14 (1977), 353–357.

[2] *Structuralist Poetics: Structuralism, Linguistics, and the Study of Literature* (Ithaca: Cornell University Press, 1975), pp. 202–238.

is withheld in some manner — through deception, innocence, or ignorance — until a key moment in the narrative. In the case of "Sonny's Blues," however, the message is apparent from the beginning and is repeatedly made available to the narrator. The story, in part, is about his misreadings; more importantly, it is about his inability to read properly. The source of this inability is his reliance on a language that is at once rationalistic and metaphoric. His sentences are always complete and balanced, and his figurative language puts on display his literary intelligence. Even in the description of his own emotional states, the verbal pattern overshadows the experience. Whenever the message is delivered, he evades it through language; he creates and then reads substitute texts, such as the messenger, or distorts the sense of the message by changing it to fit his preconceived ideas.

The message is first presented in the simplest, most straightforward manner, as a newspaper story: "I read about it in the paper, in the subway, on my way to work. I read it, and I couldn't believe it, and I read it again. Then perhaps I just stared at it, at the newsprint spelling out his name, spelling out the story."[3] The information is clearly there, "spelled out," a text that cannot be ignored. But the narrator's immediate action is to refract his emotions through metaphor: "I stared at it in the swinging lights of the subway car, and in the faces and bodies of the people, and in my own face, trapped in the darkness which roared outside" (p. 86). This oblique allusion to the underground man is followed in the next paragraph by a reference to the ice at the center of his emotional Inferno. What is noteworthy is that these images call attention to themselves as images and not simply as natural expressions of emotional intensity. His response has built into it a strong sense of the need for proper verbal expression. This deflection from emotion to art is accompanied by repeated statements on the impossibility of believing the message.

The second scene dramatizes and verifies the information presented by the newspaper story. The narrator encounters an addict who had been a friend of Sonny's. In fact, "I saw this boy standing in the shadow of a doorway, looking just like Sonny" (p. 88). Again there is a darkness and an explicit identification with Sonny. Again there is distancing through figurative language: "But now, abruptly, I hated him. I couldn't stand the way he looked at me, partly like a dog, partly like a cunning child" (p. 88). Such language prepares us for, while guaranteeing, the failed communication of this episode. The narrator is offered knowledge, but he chooses to interpret the messenger rather than the message. He expresses a desire to know, and remorse when he does not listen, but he also repeats his unwillingness to understand.

A further complication occurs when, in the midst of this encounter, the

---

[3] "Sonny's Blues," in *Going to Meet the Man* (1965; rpt. New York: Dell, 1976), p. 86. All further references to this work appear in the text.

narrator turns his attention from the addict to the music being played in a bar. The mark of his refusal to know is in his act of interpreting those associated with the music. "The juke box was blasting away with something black and bouncy and I half watched the barmaid as she danced her way from the juke box to her place behind the bar. And I watched her face as she laughingly responded to something someone said to her, still keeping time to the music. When she smiled one saw the little girl, one sensed the doomed, still-struggling woman beneath the face of the semi-whore" (p. 90). Rather than listen to the conversation he is directly involved in, the narrator observes one he cannot possibly hear. In the process, he can distance himself by labeling the woman he sees. He is thereby at once protected from and superior to the situation. The music, a motif repeated in subsequent scenes, here is part of what the narrator refuses to know; he substitutes his words for the non-verbal communication that music offers. In telling the incident, he suggests that he is listening to the music to avoid the addict-messenger; in fact, their messages are identical, and he avoids both by imposing his verbal pattern.

A similar evasion occurs in the next major scene, which is a flashback within a flashback. The narrator's mother, after hearing her son reassure her that nothing will happen to Sonny, tells him the story of his father and uncle, a story that parallels the one occurring in the present time of the narration. Her story, of the uncle's death and the father's inability to prevent it, is a parable of proper brotherly relationships. After telling the tale, she indicates its relevance: "'I ain't telling you all this,' she said, 'to make you scared or bitter or to make you hate nobody. I'm telling you this because you got a brother. And the world ain't changed.'" (p 101). The narrator immediately offers his interpretation: "'Don't you worry, I won't forget. I won't let nothing happen to Sonny'" (p. 101). His mother corrects his impression: "'You may not he able to stop nothing from happening. But you got to let him know you's *there*'" (p. 101).

No ambiguity can be found here. The message is clearly delivered, in transparent, non-metaphoric language. What prevents it from being received can only be the substitutions in the pattern. The musically-talented uncle is Sonny's double and the helpless father is the narrator's. This parallel structure makes the point obvious to the reader, but the fact that it is *only* parallel justifies the continuation of the narrative. In his positivistic way, the narrator will not believe what does not occur to his immediate experience or what cannot be contained within his linguistic net. His mother's fatalistic message cannot be so contained. Thus, the story must continue until he has both evidence and the means of controlling it.

The final scene of the story, instead of validating the meaning, only deepens the ambiguity. The bar where Sonny plays and the people in it are presented as alien to the narrator's experience. The room is dark and narrow, suggestive not only of a birth passage, but also of the subway where the narrator first felt troubled by Sonny. The musicians tend to fit stereotypes of blacks; Creole, the band leader is "an enormous black man" and the drummer, "a coal-black, cheerful-looking man, built close to the ground . . . his teeth gleaming like a lighthouse and his laugh coming up out of him like the beginning of an earthquake" (p. 118). The language grows more serious when the music itself begins: "All I know about music is that not many people ever really hear it. And even then, on the rare occasions when something opens within, and the music enters, what we mainly hear, or hear corroborated, are personal, private, vanishing evocations. But the man who creates the music is hearing something else, is dealing with the roar rising from the void and imposing order on it as it hits the air. What is evoked in him, then, is of another order, more terrible because it has no words, and triumphant, too, for that same reason" (p. 119). Little preparation has been made for such a reaction to the music. The act of the musician seems a creative response to the impinging chaos described in the opening subway scene. But this perception springs full-bodied from the brow of a man who has repeatedly indicated his antagonism to such music. One resolution of this apparent contradiction might be found in his comment about the terrible wordlessness of what he is hearing. A man committed to language, he finds himself confronted with a form whose power seems precisely its ability to create order without language.

In this context, it is highly significant that he immediately undertakes to explain the music through the metaphor of conversation. "The dry, low, black man said something awful on the drums, Creole answered, and the drums talked back. Then the horn insisted, sweet and high, slightly detached perhaps, and Creole listened, commenting now and then, dry, and driving, beautiful and calm and old" (p. 121). If the terror of the music is its lack of words, then to explain it as language is to neutralize its power. By creating the metaphor, the narrator can control his experience and limit its effect. He can make the music fit the patterns that he chooses.

This is not readily apparent in what he calls the "tale" of Sonny's music. "For, while the tale of how we suffer, and how we are delighted, and how we may triumph is never new, it always must be heard. There isn't any other tale to tell, it's the only light we've got in all this darkness" (p. 121). While music is changed to language, with the attendant change in meaning, and while the obsession is still with bringing light and thus reason, the narrator is opening up the meaning with reference to "we" and to the emotional condition of suffering and delight. His language seems less logical and self-consciously artistic than before.

The specifics of the tale strengthen its emotional impact. The music frees the narrator and perhaps Sonny: "Freedom lurked around us and I understood, at last, that he could help us to be free if we would listen, that he would never be free until we did" (p. 122). The narrator's freedom comes through his recapturing and acceptance of the past; the music conjures up his mother's face, his uncle's death, Grace's death accompanied by Isabel's tears "and I felt my own tears begin to rise" (p. 122). Yet for all the emotional content, the form remains very logically, artistically structured. Sentences are very carefully balanced and arranged, the emotion is carried on such verbs as "saw" and "felt," and finally "we," after a series of generalizations, quickly becomes "I" again. This scene only has to be compared to the prologue of *Invisible Man* to demonstrate the extent of control. Both scenes deal with the emotional impact of the blues, but whereas Ellison's is surrealistic and high paradoxical, with its narrator barely living, through the history of the vision, Baldwin's narrator remains firmly planted in the bar and firmly in control of the emotion he describes.

The story's underlying ambiguity has its richest expression in the final metaphor, a cocktail that the narrator sends to Sonny. As a symbolic representation of the message of the narrative, the scotch and milk transformed into the cup of trembling suggests the relief from suffering that Yaweh promised the children of Israel. Thus, Sonny's suffering will be made easier by the narrator's willingness to be involved in his life. But, as in earlier cases, this is not the only possible reading. First, the drink itself, scotch and milk, is an emblem of simultaneous destruction and nurture to the system; it cannot be reduced to one or the other. Sonny's acceptance of it indicates that his life will continue on the edge between the poison of his addiction and the nourishment of his music.

The narrator's reading of the drink as the cup of trembling offers a second ambiguity, which is not consistent with the first, for it implies clear alternatives. The cup of trembling was taken from Israel when Yaweh chose to forgive the people for their transgressions. But it was Yaweh who had given the cup of suffering to them in the first place.[4] Thus, it becomes important to the meaning of the story which verse is being alluded to in the metaphor. If the cup is given, then Sonny will continue to suffer and feel guilt; if the cup is taken away, then Sonny returns to a state of grace. There is no Biblical reference to the cup merely remaining.

The choice of image indicates the continuation of the narrator's practice of reading events through the vehicle of his own language. But the very limits of language itself raise problems as to the meaning of the narrative. The need to turn an act into a metaphor and thereby "enrich" the meaning depends upon limitation in the use of language. The words, though, carry traces of meaning not intended. The result, as in this case, can be that the meaning can carry with it its very opposite. In such a situation, intended meaning is lost in the very richness of meaning.

"Sonny's Blues," then, is a story of a narrator caught in the "prison-house of language."[5] Both in describing experiences and explaining them, he is locked into a linguistic pattern that restricts his understanding. With the presentation of such a character, Baldwin offers an insight into the limits of language and the narrative art. In the very act of telling his story, the narrator

---

[4] See Isaiah 51:17–23.
[5] The phrase comes from Frederic Jameson, *The Prison-House of Language: A Critical Account of Structuralism and Russian Formalism* (Princeton: University Press, 1972).

falsifies (as do all storytellers) because he must use words to express what is beyond words. The irony is that much of Baldwin's own writing—essays, novels, stories—is premised on the transparency and sufficiency of language rather than on its duplicity.

Clearly a dialectic is at work. "Sonny's Blues" moves within the tension between its openly stated message of order and a community of understanding and its covert questioning, through form, allusion, and ambiguity, of the relationship between life and art. With the latter, the story suggests that literary art contributes to deceit and perhaps anarchy rather than understanding and order. What makes this tension dialectical is that the artifice of narration is necessary for the existence of the story and its overt message. The measure of Baldwin's success is his ability to keep this tension so well hidden, not his ability to resolve the conflict. What finally makes "Sonny's Blues" such a good story is its author's skill at concealing the fact that he must lie in order to tell the truth.

PANCHO SAVERY

FROM *Baldwin, Bebop, and "Sonny's Blues"*   (1990)

Ortiz Walton describes the musical revolution as "a major challenge to European standards of musical excellence and the beginning of a conscious black aesthetic in music" (1972, 104) because of Bebop's challenge to the European aesthetic emphasis on vibrato. This emphasis produced music that was easily imitable, and thus open to commercialization and co-optation. By revolting against this direction the music had taken and reclaiming it, "Afro-American musicians gained a measure of control over their product, a situation that had not existed since the expansion of the music industry in the Twenties" (106).

Another aspect of this Bop reclamation was a renewed emphasis on the blues. Although some people seem to think there is a dispute over this issue, it is clear from listening to Parker's first session as a leader that "Billie's Bounce" and "Now's the Time" are blues pieces. In his autobiography, Dizzy Gillespie asserts:

> Beboppers couldn't destroy the blues without seriously injuring themselves. The modern jazz musicians always remained very close to the blues musician. That was a characteristic of the bopper. (1979, 294)

To this we could add the following from Baraka:

> Bebop also re-established blues as the most important Afro-American form in Negro music by its astonishingly contemporary restatement of the basic blues impulse. The boppers returned to this basic form,

reacting against the all but stifling advance artificial melody had made into jazz during the swing era. (1963, 194)

We could also look at Bebop in terms of the movement from the diatonic to the chromatic, from a more closed to an open form, a movement in the direction of a greater concern with structure, the beginning of jazz postmodernism that would reach its zenith in the work of Ornette Coleman. In "The Poetics of Jazz," Ajay Heble concludes, "Whereas diatonic jazz attempts to posit musical language as a way of thinking about things in the real world, chromaticism begins to foreground *form* rather than *substance*" (1988, 62).

What becomes clear in most of the above is that Bebop must be viewed from two perspectives, the sociopolitical as well as the musical. In Gary Giddins's words, "The Second World War severely altered the texture and tempo of American life, and jazz reflected those changes with greater acuteness by far than the other arts" (1987, 77). When Bebop began in the 1940s, America was in a similar position to what it had been in the 1920s. A war had been fought to free the world (again) for democracy; and once again, African Americans had participated and had assumed that this "loyal" participation would result in new rights and new levels of respect. When, once again, this did not appear to be happening, a new militancy developed in the African American community. Bebop was part of this new attitude. The militancy in the African American community that manifested itself in the 1941 strike of black Ford workers and the 1943 Harlem riot also manifested itself in Bebop. As Eric Lott notes:

> Brilliantly outside, bebop was intimately if indirectly related to the militancy of its moment. Militancy and music were undergirded by the same social facts; the music attempted to resolve at the level of style what the militancy combatted in the streets. (1988, 599)

Of course, this made Bebop dangerous and threatening to some, who saw it as (or potentially as) "too militant," and perhaps even un-American. And in response to this, Dizzy Gillespie retorts:

> Damn right! We refused to accept racism, poverty, or economic exploitation, nor would we live out uncreative humdrum lives merely for the sake of survival. But there was nothing unpatriotic about it. If America wouldn't honor its Constitution and respect us as men, we couldn't give a shit about the American way. And they made it damn near un-American to appreciate our music. (1979, 287)

The threat represented by Bebop was not only felt by the white world, but by the assimilationist black middle class as well. Baraka offers these perspectives:

> When the moderns, the beboppers, showed up to restore jazz, in some sense, to its original separateness, to drag it outside the mainstream of American culture again, most middle-class Negroes (as most Americans) were stuck; they had passed, for the most part, completely into the Platonic

citizenship. The willfully harsh, *anti-assimilationist* sound of bebop fell on deaf or horrified ears, just as it did in white America. (1963, 181–82)

Bebop rebelled against the absorption into garbage, monopoly music; it also signified a rebellion by the people who played the music, because it was not just the music that rebelled, as if the music had fallen out of the sky! But even more, dig it, it signified a rebellion rising out of the masses themselves, since that is the source of social movement — the people themselves! (1979, 236)

What made bop strong is that no matter its pretensions, it was hooked up solidly and directly to the Afro-American blues tradition, and therefore was largely based in the experience and struggle of the black sector of the working class. (1979, 241)

In light of this historical context, Sonny's brother's never having heard of Bird is not just a rejection of the music of Bebop; it is also a rejection of the new political direction Bebop was representative of in the African American community.

When the story picks up several years later, some things have changed. Sonny has dropped out of high school, illegally enlisted in the navy and been shipped to Greece, returned to America, and moved to Greenwich Village. Other things have not changed: his brother has become an algebra teacher and a respected member of the black bourgeoisie. After Sonny has been released from prison, he invites his brother to watch him sit in "in a joint in the Village" (1966, 113).

What is usually discussed concerning this final scene is that the brother enters Sonny's world, recognizes that he is only a visitor to that world tolerated because of Sonny, that here Sonny is respected and taken care of, and that here is Sonny's true family:

I was introduced to all of them and they were all very polite to me. Yet, it was clear that, for them, I was only Sonny's brother. Here, I was in Sonny's world. Or, rather: his kingdom. Here, it was not even a question that his veins bore royal blood. (118)

When the music Sonny plays is discussed, it is usually done either abstractly, music as the bridge that allows Sonny and his brother to become reunited and Sonny to find his identity, or simply in terms of the blues. It is, of course, totally legitimate to discuss the music in either of these ways. After all, music does function as a bridge between Sonny and his brother; and twice we are reminded in the same page that "what they were playing was the blues," and "Now these are Sonny's blues" (121).

At the climactic moment of the story, when Sonny finally feels so comfortable that his "fingers filled the air with life" (122), he is playing "Am I

Blue." It is the first song of the second set, after a tentative performance by Sonny in the first set. Baldwin presents the moment of transition between sets by simply noting, "Then they finished, there was scattered applause, and then, without an instant's warning, Creole started into something else, it was almost sardonic, it was *Am I Blue*" (121). The word "sardonic," it seems to me, is key here. One of the characteristics of Bebop is taking an old standard and making it new. As Leonard Feather explains:

> In recent years it has been an increasingly common practice to take some definite chord sequence of a well-known song (usually a standard old favorite) and build a new melody around it. Since there is no copyright on a chord sequence, the musician is entitled to use this method to create an original composition and copyright it in his own name, regardless of who wrote the first composition that used the same chord pattern. (1977, 55–56)

This practice results in a song with a completely different title. Thus, "Back Home Again in Indiana" becomes Parker's "Donna Lee"; "Honeysuckle Rose" becomes "Scrapple from the Apple"; "I Got Rhythm" becomes "Dexterity," "Confirmation," and "Thriving on a Riff"; "How High the Moon" becomes "Bird Lore"; "Lover Come Back to Me" becomes "Bird Gets the Worm"; and "Cherokee" becomes "Warming Up a Riff" and "Ko-Ko." But it is also characteristic of Bebop to take the entire song, not simply a chord sequence, and play it in an entirely different way. Thus, for example, Bird's catalogue is filled with versions of tunes like "White Christmas," "Slow Boat to China," "East of the Sun and West of the Moon," "April in Paris," and "Embraceable You." As Baraka notes:

> Bebop was a much more open rebellion in the sense that the musicians openly talked of the square, hopeless, corny rubbish put forth by the bourgeoisie. They made fun of it, refused to play it except in a mocking fashion. (1979, 237)

Baldwin's use of the word "sardonic," therefore, is clearly intended to tell us that something more is going on than simply playing a standard tune or playing the blues. "Am I Blue" is exactly the type of song that by itself wouldn't do much for anyone, but which could become rich and meaningful after being heated in the crucible of Bebop.

The point of all this is that, through his playing, Sonny becomes "part of the family again" (121), his family with the other musicians; likewise, Sonny's brother also becomes part of the family again, his family with Sonny. But in both cases, Baldwin wants us to view the idea of family through the musical and social revolution of Bebop. Note the brother's language as Sonny plays:

> Then he began to make it his. It was very beautiful because it wasn't hurried and it was no longer a lament. I seemed to hear with what burning we had yet to make it ours, how we could cease lamenting. Freedom

lurked around us and I understood, at last, that he could help us to be free if we would listen, that he would never be free until we did. (122)

In the mid to late 1950s, the word "freedom" is obviously a highly charged one. Not only does it speak to the politics of the Civil Rights Movement, but it also points forward to the "Free Jazz" movement of the late 1950s and 1960s, the music of Ornette Coleman, Cecil Taylor, Albert Ayler, and Eric Dolphy. Baldwin's concept of family is, therefore, a highly political one, and one that has cultural implications.

In *Black Talk,* Ben Sidran concludes about Bebop:

> The importance of the bop musician was that he had achieved this confrontation — in terms of aesthetics and value structures as well as social action — well before organized legal or political action. Further, unlike the arguments of the NAACP, his music and his hip ethic were not subject to the kind of rationalization and verbal qualification that had all too often compromised out of existence all middle-class Negro gains. (1971, 115)

In "Sonny's Blues," Baldwin makes clear that contrary to many opinions, he is in fact a major fiction writer; and that, Larry Neal notwithstanding, he *has* used to its fullest extent "traditional aspects of Afro-American culture." The implications are clear. Not only does Baldwin's fiction need to be looked at again, but when we are looking at it, writing about it, and teaching it, we need to be conversant with the specific cultural context he is writing in and from. And when we are, new things are there to be seen and heard.

WORKS CITED

Baldwin, James. 1965. "Sonny's Blues." In *Going to Meet the Man,* 86–122. New York: Dial Press.

Baraka, Amiri. 1963. *Blues People: Negro Music in White America.* New York: Morrow.

———. 1979. "War/Philly Blues/Deeper Bop." In *Selected Plays and Prose of Amiri Baraka/LeRoi Jones,* 228–41. New York: Morrow.

Feather, Leonard. 1977 [1949]. *Inside Jazz (Inside Be-bop).* New York: Da Capo.

Giddins, Gary. 1987. *Celebrating Bird: The Triumph of Charlie Parker.* New York: Beech Tree Books/Morrow.

Gillespie, Dizzy, with Al Fraser. 1979. *To Be Or Not . . . To BOP: Memoirs.* Garden City: Doubleday.

Heble, Ajay. 1988. "The Poetics of Jazz: From Symbolic to Semiotic." *Textual Practice* 2: 51–68.

Lott, Eric. 1988. "Double V, Double-Time: Bebop's Politics of Style." *Callaloo* 11: 597–605.

Sidran, Ben. 1971. *Black Talk.* New York: Holt, Rinehart, and Winston.

Walton, Ortiz M. 1972. *Music: Black, White & Blue: A Sociological Survey of the Use and Misuse of Afro-American Music.* New York: Morrow.

STUDENT ESSAY

Listening to Sonny's Blues
by Zachary Roberts

I was six when I first picked up the recorder. The sounds I made might not have been recognizable music, but I pushed air through that instrument for three years before switching to the French horn, which I played for the next eight years. For the last three years I have been playing the guitar, and I know that I've finally found an instrument which allows me to articulate my creative and emotional energies, one which has also had the incredible effect of freeing me from an archaic conceptual framework of what music is "for."

As a musician and music worshiper, to me "Sonny's Blues" is more than just the story of the struggle for healing and understanding between Sonny, a jazz musician and former heroin addict, and his middle-class brother. Sonny's brother, the unnamed narrator, recognizes that music is Sonny's constructive outlet for releasing the tension of his philosophical and metaphysical questioning (as opposed to his destructive drug abuse), but still feels a strong ambivalence about the effectiveness of this approach: "Sonny's fingers filled the air with life, his life. . . . And I was yet aware that this was only a moment, that the world waited outside, as hungry as a tiger, and that trouble stretched above us, longer than the sky."

But what if we did have some sort of direct access into Sonny's mind, where we could feel what he felt and see what he saw without the intermediary narrator? The story's title is "Sonny's Blues," and on a fundamental level, this is Sonny's story. So how are we to listen to Sonny's blues? By going beyond the narrator. He is not a musician, and as Sonny states, "You're just hung up on the *way* some people try--it's not your way!" The narrator has neither an intense relationship with music nor finds it a particularly valid form of self-fulfilling work.

But I do, and so does Sonny. This is not to suggest that I can speak for Sonny, because there are major differences between how Sonny and I approach music. Whereas Sonny attempts to give meaning to his life and expression to his cultural heritage as an African American through his interaction with music, I see a universal reality in the music itself, in its form and structure and emotion, and in the projection of the self it embodies. Like friendship and tragedy, music is a tool that helps me comprehend what would otherwise remain hidden from me in this existence, and perhaps this understanding of myself will allow a broader understanding of Sonny's relationship to his music.

The Earth's flora is engaged in an extraordinary relationship with the sun. Plants and trees do not just grow "up" but actually dance in step with, stretching toward the sun, using photosynthesis to turn that star's energy into their own life force. The parallels I see between the relationship of plants and the sun on one hand, and people and music on the other, are strikingly vivid; I recognize that there is something outside of myself that I consider vital to my continued peace and existence, without which I am not complete. Just as plants thrive in the sun's presence and decay in its absence, so do I (along with many other musicians and music lovers) react to music's warmth and energy.

It would be pretty difficult for me not to feel this way, considering that I believe all people are utterly surrounded by music, actually fully immersed in the music of our existences and the existences of everything around us. People listen in different ways and hear different things; what I hear every day is the first thing I ever heard, my heartbeat thumping like a sacred bass drum. My reality pulsates with that rhythm, just as everything within my reality moves with its own esoteric secret, musics that weave into the fabric of the geometric space-time existence I am trapped within. Enveloped as I am by so much music, I must feel the impact of it on me in several different aspects of my self: my personality, my conceptions of self, my relationships with others, and my understanding of this world, all of which exist at different levels in my consciousness.

Listening to and playing music is a process that affects the core of my being, the quintessential center of my reality. When I listen to music I make it mine, through analysis and deconstruction of the elements of the music itself. Lyrics often make me re-evaluate how I feel about an important personal or social issue, while rhythm and melody trigger different responses. But my internalization of music also includes a reconstruction and judgment based on the power of the thrall whatever it is I am listening to casts on my unconsciousness, and on how it makes me feel. For example, when I listen to jazz I often hear the upbeat, self-confident voice of the musicians who are saying "Hey, here I am, look at me, dig me and my music and my reality," and the funk finds a chord in me that makes me begin to feel and think and carry myself with that much more confidence, with a piece of that new attitude.

What I find most incredible about music is that a particular piece can express an emotion or situation so perfectly that my need for a unique personal articulation is satisfied. The strength of my internalization of those songs is connected to my ability to reproduce them, because then the song is as much mine as I need it to be; I am not the author, but the author has freely given to me his or her creation, and so it becomes mine to use. Music and writing are the same in this regard; the audience is allowed full access to the creation, and to the emotions and the value judgments involved in the creation. As both audience and musician, I am an interpreter and a re-creator of the articulations that I lack (which, once gained, become my creation and my articulation).

It occurs to me now that I actually need to be a musician, both receptacle and dispenser of the sounds of my milieu. And I think Baldwin's character Sonny is the same way, for a similar reason, for being a musician helps him deal with himself: "That storm inside. You can't talk it and you can't make love with it, and when you finally try to get it out and play it, you realize nobody's listening. So you've got to listen. You got to find a way to listen."

I agree with Sonny that music can help alleviate the pain of this existence. To deny this release is self-punishment, but to embrace it is to open oneself up to knowledge about yourself and your individual reality. As Baldwin used one story, that of Sonny and his brother, to tell different stories on different levels--the different stories of African-American families, culture, and heritage--so can we all use music to express, to communicate, and to understand reality at levels otherwise unreachable.

KŌBŌ ABE   (1924–1994)

Blending realism with surrealism, Kōbō Abe often wrote in such popular forms as science fiction, fantasy, and mystery, using these forms to critique contemporary Japanese society.

Abe was born in Tokyo but spent his early years in Musden, Manchuria, which was occupied by the Japanese during World War II. Although the son of a Japanese physician, Abe sided with the Manchurians in the conflict. Returning to Japan after the war, Abe attended Tokyo University, where he received a medical degree. He never practiced medicine, however, turning instead to writing. Abe was a major influence on the younger generation of Japanese writers, and many of his novels have been translated into English: *The Woman in the Dunes* (1964), *The Ruined Map* (1969), *Inter Ice Age Four* (1970), *The Box Man* (1975), and *The Ark Sakura* (1988). He also wrote plays and one collection of stories, published in English as *Beyond the Curve* (1991), from which "The Magic Chalk" is taken.

Many of Abe's stories, novels, and plays emphasize the absurdity and the alienation of modern urban life; often, as in "The Magic Chalk," Abe's alienation takes the form of a smaller, secret world existing within the larger society.

The Magic Chalk   (1950)

Translated by Alison Kibrick

Next door to the toilet of an apartment building on the edge of the city, in a room soggy with roof leaks and cooking vapors, lived a poor artist named Argon.

The small room, nine feet square, appeared to be larger than it was because it contained nothing but a single chair set against the wall. His desk, shelves, paint box, even his easel had been sold for bread. Now only the chair and Argon were left. But how long would these two remain?

Dinnertime drew near. "How sensitive my nose has become!" Argon thought. He was able to distinguish the colors and proximity of the complex aromas entering his room. Frying pork at the butcher's along the streetcar line: yellow ocher. A southerly wind drifting by the front of the fruit stand: emerald green. Wafting from the bakery: stimulating chrome yellow. And the fish the housewife below was broiling, probably mackerel: sad cerulean blue.

The fact is, Argon hadn't eaten anything all day. With a pale face, a wrinkled brow, an Adam's apple that rose and fell, a hunched back, a sunken abdomen, and trembling knees, Argon thrust both hands into his pockets and yawned three times in succession.

His fingers found a stick in his pocket.

"Hey, what's this? Red chalk. Don't remember it being there."

Playing with the chalk between his fingers, he produced another large yawn.

"Aah, I need something to eat."

Without realizing it, Argon began scribbling on the wall with the chalk. First, an apple. One that looked big enough to be a meal in itself. He drew a paring knife beside it so that he could eat it right away. Next, swallowing hard as baking smells curled through the hallway and window to permeate his room, he drew bread. Jam-filled bread the size of a baseball glove. Butter-filled rolls. A loaf as large as a person's head. He envisioned glossy browned spots on the bread. Delicious-looking cracks, dough bursting through the surface, the intoxicating aroma of yeast. Beside the bread, then, a stick of butter as large as a brick. He thought of drawing some coffee. Freshly brewed, steaming coffee. In a large, jug-like cup. On a saucer, three matchbox-size sugar cubes.

"Damn it!" He ground his teeth and buried his face in his hands. "I've got to eat!"

Gradually his consciousness sank into darkness. Beyond the windowpane was a bread and pastry jungle, a mountain of canned goods, a sea of milk, a beach of sugar, a beef and cheese orchard—he scampered about until, fatigued, he fell asleep.

A heavy thud on the floor and the sound of smashing crockery woke him up. The sun had already set. Pitch black. Bewildered, he glanced toward the noise and gasped. A broken cup. The spilled liquid, still steaming, was definitely coffee, and near it were the apple, bread, butter, sugar, spoon, knife, and (luckily unbroken) the saucer. The pictures he had chalked on the wall had vanished.

"How could it . . . ?"

Suddenly every vein in his body was wide awake and pounding. Argon stealthily crept closer.

"No, no, it can't be. But look, it's real. Nothing fake about the smothering aroma of this coffee. And here, the bread is smooth to the touch. Be bold, taste it. Argon, don't you believe it's real even now? Yes, it's real. I believe it. But frightening. To believe it is frightening. And yet, it's real. It's edible!"

The apple tasted like an apple (a "snow" apple). The bread tasted like bread (American flour). The butter tasted like butter (same contents as the label on the wrapper—not margarine). The sugar tasted like sugar (sweet). Ah, they all tasted like the real thing. The knife gleamed, reflecting his face.

By the time he came to his senses, Argon had somehow finished eating and heaved a sigh of relief. But when he recalled why he had sighed like this, he immediately became confused again. He took the chalk in his fingers and stared at it intently. No matter how much he scrutinized it, he couldn't understand what he didn't understand. He decided to make sure by trying it once more. If he succeeded a second time, then he would have to concede that it had actually happened. He thought he would try to draw something different, but in his haste just drew another familiar-looking apple. As soon as he finished drawing, it fell easily from the wall. So this is real after all. A repeatable fact.

Joy suddenly turned his body rigid. The tips of his nerves broke through his skin and stretched out toward the universe, rustling like fallen leaves. Then, abruptly, the tension eased, and, sitting down on the floor, he burst out laughing like a panting goldfish.

"The laws of the universe have changed. My fate has changed, misfortune has taken its leave. Ah, the age of fulfillment, a world of desires realized . . . God, I'm sleepy. Well, then, I'll draw a bed. This chalk has become as precious as life itself, but a bed is something you always need after eating your fill, and it never really wears out, so no need to be miserly about it. Ah, for the first time in my life I'll sleep like a lamb."

One eye soon fell asleep, but the other lay awake. After today's contentment he was uneasy about what tomorrow might bring. However, the other eye, too, finally closed in sleep. With eyes working out of sync he dreamed mottled dreams throughout the night.

Well, this worrisome tomorrow dawned in the following manner.

He dreamed that he was being chased by a ferocious beast and fell off a bridge. He had fallen off the bed . . . No. When he awoke, there was no bed anywhere. As usual, there was nothing but that one chair. Then what had happened last night? Argon timidly looked around the wall, tilting his head.

There, in red chalk, were drawings of a cup (it was broken!), a spoon, a knife, apple peel, and a butter wrapper. Below these was a bed — a picture of the bed off which he was supposed to have fallen.

Among all of last night's drawings, only those he could not eat had once again become pictures and returned to the wall. Suddenly he felt pain in his hip and shoulder. Pain in precisely the place he should feel it if he had indeed fallen out of bed. He gingerly touched the sketch of the bed where the sheets had been rumpled by sleep and felt a slight warmth, clearly distinguishable from the coldness of the rest of the drawing.

He brushed his finger along the blade of the knife picture. It was certainly nothing more than chalk; there was no resistance, and it disappeared leaving only a smear. As a test he decided to draw a new apple. It neither turned into a real apple and fell nor even peeled off like a piece of unglued paper, but rather vanished beneath his chafed palm into the surface of the wall.

His happiness had been merely a single night's dream. It was all over, back to what it was before anything had happened. Or was it really? No, his misery had returned fivefold. His hunger pangs attacked him fivefold. It seemed that all he had eaten had been restored in his stomach to the original substances of wall and chalk powder.

When he had gulped from his cupped hands a pint or so of water from the communal sink, he set out toward the lonely city, still enveloped in the mist of early dawn. Leaning over an open drain that ran from the kitchen of a restaurant about a hundred yards ahead, he thrust his hands into the viscous, tarlike sewage and pulled something out. It was a basket made of wire netting. He washed it in a small brook nearby. What was left in it seemed edible, and he was particularly heartened that half of it looked like rice. An old man in his apartment building had told him recently that by placing the basket in the drain one could obtain enough food for a meal a day. Just about a month ago the man had found the means to afford bean curd lees, so he had ceded the restaurant drain to the artist.

Recalling last night's feast, this was indeed muddy, unsavory fare. But it wasn't magic. What actually helped fill his stomach was precious and so could not be rejected. Even if its nastiness made him aware of every swallow, he must eat it. Shit. This was the real thing.

Just before noon he entered the city and dropped in on a friend who was employed at a bank. The friend smiled wryly and asked, "My turn today?"

Stiff and expressionless, Argon nodded. As always, he received half of his friend's lunch, bowed deeply and left.

For the rest of the day, Argon thought.

He held the chalk lightly in his hand, leaned back in the chair, and as he sat absorbed in his daydreams about magic, anticipation began to crystallize around that urgent longing. Finally, evening once again drew near. His hope that at sunset the magic might take effect had changed into near confidence.

Somewhere a noisy radio announced that it was five o'clock. He stood up and on the wall drew bread and butter, a can of sardines, and coffee, not forgetting to add a table underneath so as to prevent anything from falling and breaking as had occurred the previous night. Then he waited.

Before long darkness began to crawl quietly up the wall from the corners of the room. In order to verify the course of the magic, he turned on the light. He had already confirmed last night that electric light did it no harm.

The sun had set. The drawings on the wall began to fade, as if his vision had blurred. It seemed as if a mist was caught between the wall and his eyes. The pictures grew increasingly faint, and the mist grew dense. And soon, just as he had anticipated, the mist had settled into solid shapes — success! The contents of the pictures suddenly appeared as real objects.

The steamy coffee was tempting, the bread freshly baked and still warm.

"Oh! Forgot a can opener."

He held his left hand underneath to catch it before it fell, and, as he drew, the outlines took on material form. His drawing had literally come to life.

All of a sudden, he stumbled over something. Last night's bed "existed" again. Moreover, the knife handle (he had erased the blade with his finger), the butter wrapper, and the broken cup lay fallen on the floor.

After filling his empty stomach, Argon lay down on the bed.

"Well, what shall it be next? It's clear now that the magic doesn't work in daylight. Tomorrow I'll have to suffer all over again. There must be a simple way out of this. Ah, yes! a brilliant plan — I'll cover up the window and shut myself in darkness."

He would need some money to carry out the project. To keep out the sun required some objects that would not lose their substance when exposed to sunlight. But drawing money is a bit difficult. He racked his brains, then drew a purse full of money . . . The idea was a success, for when he opened up the purse he found more than enough bills stuffed inside.

This money, like the counterfeit coins that badgers made from tree leaves in the fairy tale, would disappear in the light of day, but it would leave no trace behind, and that was a great relief. He was cautious nonetheless and deliberately proceeded toward a distant town. Two heavy blankets, five sheets of black woolen cloth, a piece of felt, a box of nails, and four pieces of squared lumber. In addition, one volume of a cookbook collection that caught his eye in a secondhand bookstore along the way. With the remaining money he bought a cup of coffee, not in the least superior to the coffee he had drawn on the wall. He was (why?) proud of himself. Lastly, he bought a newspaper.

He nailed the door shut, then attached two layers of cloth and a blanket. With the rest of the material, he covered the window, and he blocked the edges with the wood. A feeling of security, and at the same time a sense of being attacked by eternity, weighed upon him. Argon's mind grew distant, and, lying down on the bed, he soon fell asleep.

Sleep neither diminished nor neutralized his happiness in the slightest. When he awoke, the steel springs throughout his body were coiled and ready to leap, full of life. A new day, a new time . . . tomorrow wrapped in a mist of glittering gold dust, and the day after tomorrow, and more and more over-flowing armfuls of tomorrows were waiting expectantly. Argon smiled, overcome with joy. Now, at this very moment, everything, without any hindrance whatsoever, was waiting eagerly among myriad possibilities to be created by his own hand. It was a brilliant moment. But what, in the depths of his heart, was this faintly aching sorrow? It might have been the sorrow that God had felt just before Creation. Beside the muscles of his smile, smaller muscles twitched slightly.

Argon drew a large wall clock. With a trembling hand he set the clock precisely at twelve, determining at that moment the start of a new destiny.

He thought the room was a bit stuffy, so he drew a window on the wall facing the hallway. Hm, what's wrong? The window didn't materialize. Perplexed for a moment, he then realized that the window could not acquire any substance because it did not have an outside; it was not equipped with all the conditions necessary to make it a window.

"Well, then, shall I draw an outside? What kind of view would be nice? Shall it be the Alps or the Bay of Naples? A quiet pastoral scene wouldn't be bad. Then again, a primeval Siberian forest might be interesting." All the beautiful landscapes he had seen on postcards and in travel guides flickered before him. But he had to choose one from among them all, and he couldn't make up his mind. "Well, let's attend to pleasure first," he decided. He drew some whiskey and cheese and, as he nibbled, slowly thought about it.

The more he thought, the less he understood.

"This isn't going to be easy. It could involve work on a larger scale than anything I — or anyone — has ever tried to design. In fact, now that I think about it, it wouldn't do simply to draw a few streams and orchards, mountains and seas, and other things pleasing to the eye. Suppose I drew a mountain; it would no longer be just a mountain. What would be beyond it? A city? A sea? A desert? What kind of people would be living there? What kind of animals? Unconsciously I would be deciding those things. No, making this window a window is serious business. It involves the creation of a world. Defining a world with just a few lines. Would it be right to leave that to chance? No, the scene outside can't be casually drawn. I must produce the kind of picture that no human hand has yet achieved."

Argon sank into deep contemplation.

The first week passed in discontent as he pondered a design for a world of infinitude. Canvases once again lined his room, and the smell of turpentine hung in the air. Dozens of rough sketches accumulated in a pile. The more he thought, however, the more extensive the problem became, until finally he felt it was all too much for him. He thought he might boldly leave it up to chance, but in that case his efforts to create a new world would come to nothing. And if he merely captured accurately the inevitability of partial reality, the contradictions inherent in that reality would pull him back into the past, perhaps trapping him again in starvation. Besides, the chalk had a limited life-span. He had to capture the world.

The second week flew by in inebriation and gluttony.

The third week passed in a despair resembling insanity. Once again his canvases lay covered with dust, and the smell of oils had faded.

In the fourth week Argon finally made up his mind, a result of nearly total desperation. He just couldn't wait any longer. In order to evade the responsibility of creating with his own hand an outside for the window, he decided to take a great risk that would leave everything to chance.

"I'll draw a door on the wall. The outside will be decided by whatever is beyond the door. Even if it ends in failure, even if it turns out to be the same apartment scene as before, it'll be far better than being tormented by this responsibility. I don't care what happens, better to escape."

Argon put on a jacket for the first time in a long while. It was a ceremony in honor of the establishment of the world, so one couldn't say he was being extravagant. With a stiff hand he lowered the chalk of destiny. A picture of the door. He was breathing hard. No wonder. Wasn't the sight beyond the door the greatest mystery a man could contemplate? Perhaps death was awaiting him as his reward.

He grasped the knob. He took a step back and opened the door.

Dynamite pierced his eyes, exploding. After a while he opened them fearfully to an awesome wasteland glaring in the noonday sun. As far as he could see, with the exception of the horizon, there was not a single shadow. To the extent that he could peer into the dark sky, not a single cloud. A hot dry wind blew past, stirring up a dust storm.

"Aah . . . It's just as though the horizon line in one of my designs had become the landscape itself. Aah . . ."

The chalk hadn't resolved anything after all. He still had to create it all from the beginning. He had to fill this desolate land with mountains, water, clouds, trees, plants, birds, beasts, fish. He had to draw the world all over again. Discouraged, Argon collapsed onto the bed. One after another, tears fell unceasingly.

Something rustled in his pocket. It was the newspaper he had bought on that first day and forgotten about. The headline on the first page read, "Invasion Across 38th Parallel!" On the second page, an even larger space devoted to a photograph of Miss Nippon. Underneath, in small print, "Riot at N Ward Employment Security Office," and "Large-scale Dismissals at U Factory."

Argon stared at the half-naked Miss Nippon. What intense longing. What a body. Flesh of glass.

"This is what I forgot. Nothing else matters. It's time to begin everything from Adam and Eve. That's it — Eve! I'll draw Eve!"

Half an hour later Eve was standing before him, stark naked. Startled, she looked around her.

"Oh! Who are you? What's happened? Golly, I'm naked!"

"I am Adam. You are Eve." Argon blushed bashfully.

"I'm Eve, you say? Ah, no wonder I'm naked. But why are you wearing clothes? Adam, in Western dress — now that's weird."

Suddenly her tone changed.

"You're lying! I'm not Eve. I'm Miss Nippon."

"You're Eve. You really are Eve."

"You expect me to believe this is Adam — in those clothes — in a dump like this? Come on, give me back *my* clothes. What am I doing here anyway? I'm due to make a special modeling appearance at a photo contest."

"Oh, no. You don't understand. You're Eve, I mean it."

"Give me a break, will you? Okay, where's the apple? And I suppose this is the Garden of Eden? Ha, don't make me laugh. Now give me my clothes."

"Well, at least listen to what I have to say. Sit down over there. Then I'll explain everything. By the way, can I offer you something to eat?"

"Yes, go ahead. But hurry up and give me my clothes, okay? My body's valuable."

"What would you like? Choose anything you want from this cookbook."

"Oh, great! Really? The place is filthy, but you must be pretty well fixed. I've changed my mind. Maybe you really are Adam after all. What do you do for a living? Burglar?"

"No, I'm Adam. Also an artist, and a world planner."

"I don't understand."

"Neither do I. That's why I'm depressed."

Watching Argon draw the food with swift strokes as he spoke, Eve shouted, "Hey, great, that's great. This *is* Eden, isn't it? Wow. Yeah, okay, I'll be Eve. I don't mind being Eve. We're going to get rich — right?"

"Eve, please listen to me."

In a sad voice, Argon told her his whole story, adding finally, "So you see, with your cooperation we must design this world. Money's irrelevant. We have to start everything from scratch."

Miss Nippon was dumbfounded.

"Money's irrelevant, you say? I don't understand. I don't get it. I absolutely do not understand."

"If you're going to talk like that, well, why don't you open this door and take a look outside."

She glanced through the door Argon had left half open.

"My God! How awful!"

She slammed the door shut and glared at him.

"But how about *this* door," she said, pointing to his real, blanketed door. "Different, I'll bet."

"No, don't. That one's no good. It will just wipe out this world, the food, desk, bed, and even you. *You* are the new Eve. And we must become the father and mother of our world."

"Oh no. No babies. I'm all for birth control. I mean, they're such a bother. And besides, I won't disappear."

"You will disappear."

"I won't. I know myself best. I'm me. All this talk about disappearing — you're really weird."

"My dear Eve, you don't know. If we don't re-create the world, then sooner or later we're faced with starvation."

"What? Calling me 'dear' now, are you? You've got a nerve. And you say I'm going to starve. Don't be ridiculous. My body's valuable."

"No, your body's the same as my chalk. If we don't acquire a world of our own, your existence will just be a fiction. The same as nothing at all."

"Okay, that's enough of this junk. Come on, give me back my clothes. I'm leaving. No two ways about it, my being here is weird. I shouldn't be here. You're a magician or something. Well, hurry up. My manager's probably fed up with waiting. If you want me to drop in and be your Eve every now and then, I don't mind. As long as you use your chalk to give me what I want."

"Don't be a fool! You can't do that."

The abrupt, violent tone of Argon's voice startled her, and she looked into his face. They both stared at each other for a moment in silence. Whatever was in her thoughts, she then said calmly, "All right, I'll stay. But, in exchange, will you grant me one wish?"

"What is it? If you stay with me, I'll listen to anything you have to say."

"I want half of your chalk."

"That's unreasonable. After all, dear, you don't know how to draw. What good would it do you?"

"I do know how to draw. I may not look like it, but I used to be a designer. I insist on equal rights."

He tilted his head for an instant, then straightening up again, said decisively, "All right, I believe you."

He carefully broke the chalk in half and gave one piece to Eve. As soon as she received it, she turned to the wall and began drawing.

It was a pistol.

"Stop it! What are you going to do with that thing?"

"Death, I'm going to make death. We need some divisions. They're very important in making a world."

"No, that'll be the end. Stop it. It's the most unnecessary thing of all."

But it was too late. Eve was clutching a small pistol in her hand. She raised it and aimed directly at his chest.

"Move and I'll shoot. Hands up. You're stupid, Adam. Don't you know that a promise is the beginning of a lie? It's you who made me lie."

"What? *Now* what are you drawing?"

"A hammer. To smash the door down."

"You can't!"

"Move and I'll shoot!"

The moment he leaped the pistol rang out. Argon held his chest as his knees buckled and he collapsed to the floor. Oddly, there was no blood.

"Stupid Adam."

Eve laughed. Then, raising the hammer, she struck the door. The light streamed in. It wasn't very bright, but it was real. Light from the sun. Eve was suddenly absorbed, like mist. The desk, the bed, the French meal, all disappeared. All but Argon, the cookbook which had landed on the floor, and the chair were transformed back into pictures on the wall.

Argon stood up unsteadily. His chest wound had healed. But something stronger than death was summoning him, compelling him — the wall. The wall was calling him. His body, which had eaten drawings from the wall continuously for four weeks, had been almost entirely transformed by them. Resistance was impossible now. Argon staggered toward the wall and was drawn in on top of Eve.

The sound of the gunshot and the door being smashed were heard by others in the building. By the time they ran in, Argon had been completely absorbed into the wall and had become a picture. The people saw nothing but the chair, the cookbook, and the scribblings on the wall. Staring at Argon lying on top of Eve, someone remarked, "Starved for a woman, wasn't he."

"Doesn't it look just like him, though?" said another.

"What was he doing, destroying the door like that? And look at this, the wall's covered with scribbles. Huh. He won't get away with it. Where in the world did he disappear to? Calls himself a painter!"

The man grumbling to himself was the apartment manager.

After everyone left, there came a murmuring from the wall.

"It isn't chalk that will remake the world . . ."

A single drop welled out of the wall. It fell from just below the eye of the pictorial Argon.

Questions for Discussion

1. How do the economic level of the neighborhood and the economic status of the artist, Argon, affect the climax and resolution of the story?

2. Why is Argon obsessed with colors? How does his obsession help to explain why the stick he finds becomes transformed into a piece of chalk?

3. How does Abe use descriptive detail to make Argon's drawings seem real?

4. Why is Argon unable to create a complete alternative reality in his room, so that his drawings fade during the day? What do his attempt and failure signify? Interpret the meaning of the line "It isn't chalk that will remake the world."

5. This story parallels the book of Genesis and the story of Adam and Eve. Why do both Argon and his Eve wind up as only "scribblings on the wall"?

Ideas for Writing

1. Write an essay in which you interpret the way Abe integrates dreams, art, and reality to comment on the nature of the artistic experience as well as on the relationships between dreams and reality.

2. Write a story about a painting or another artwork that is transformed into "reality."

FLANNERY O'CONNOR   (1925–1964)

The stories of Flannery O'Connor are unique in American fiction; they are marked by a sharply realized southern milieu, bitingly humorous characterizations, sudden violence, and a focus on Christian grace.

Born in Savannah, Georgia, O'Connor was the only child of Roman Catholic parents. Her father died in 1941 of lupus, a disease that also weakened the writer's system, limited her activities, and led to her death at age thirty-nine. O'Connor graduated from Georgia State College for Women in 1945 and received a fellowship to the University of Iowa's Writers' Workshop, where she completed her M.F.A. in 1947. She moved to New York in 1949 to work as a professional writer, but when she learned only a year later that she had the same rare blood disease as her father, she returned to Georgia. For the last fourteen years of her life, O'Connor lived with her mother on the family's dairy farm. She published two novels, *Wise Blood* (1952) and *The Violent Bear It Away* (1960); a collection of essays and lectures, *Mystery and Manners* (1969); and two anthologies of short fiction, *A Good Man Is Hard to Find* (1955) and *Everything That Rises Must Converge* (1965), which includes "Revelation". Her posthumous *Complete Stories* (1970) won the National Book Award.

Although O'Connor's stories can be read as grotesque comedies of southern rural life, they are, in fact, intense and individual explorations of Catholic mysticism, stark indictments of a world without God.

Revelation   (1964)

The doctor's waiting room, which was very small, was almost full when the Turpins entered and Mrs. Turpin, who was very large, made it look even smaller by her presence. She stood looming at the head of the magazine table set in the center of it, a living demonstration that the room was inadequate and ridiculous. Her little bright black eyes took in all the patients as she sized up the seating situation. There was one vacant chair and a place on the sofa occupied by a blond child in a dirty blue romper who should have been told to move over and make room for the lady. He was five or six, but Mrs. Turpin saw at once that no one was going to tell him to move over. He was slumped down in the seat, his arms idle at his sides and his eye idle in his head; his nose ran unchecked.

Mrs. Turpin put a firm hand on Claud's shoulder and said in a voice that included anyone who wanted to listen, "Claud, you sit in that chair there," and gave him a push down into the vacant one. Claud was florid and bald and sturdy, somewhat shorter than Mrs. Turpin, but he sat down as if he were accustomed to doing what she told him to.

Mrs. Turpin remained standing. The only man in the room besides Claud was a lean stringy old fellow with a rusty hand spread out on each knee, whose eyes were closed as if he were asleep or dead or pretending to be so as not to get up and offer her his seat. Her gaze settled agreeably on a well-dressed gray-haired lady whose eyes met hers and whose expression said: if that child belonged to me, he would have some manners and move over — there's plenty of room there for you and him too.

Claud looked up with a sigh and made as if to rise.

"Sit down," Mrs. Turpin said. "You know you're not supposed to stand on that leg. He has an ulcer on his leg," she explained.

Claud lifted his foot onto the magazine table and rolled his trouser leg up to reveal a purple swelling on a plump marble-white calf.

"My!" the pleasant lady said. "How did you do that?"

"A cow kicked him," Mrs. Turpin said.

"Goodness!" said the lady.

Claud rolled his trouser leg down.

"Maybe the little boy would move over," the lady suggested, but the child did not stir.

"Somebody will be leaving in a minute," Mrs. Turpin said. She could not understand why a doctor — with as much money as they made charging five dollars a day to just stick their head in the hospital door and look at you — couldn't afford a decent-sized waiting room. This one was hardly bigger than a garage. The table was cluttered with limp-looking magazines and at one end of it there was a big green glass ash tray full of cigarette butts and cotton wads with little blood spots on them. If she had had anything to do with the running of the place, that would have been emptied every so often. There were no chairs against the wall at the head of the room. It had a rectangular-shaped panel in it that permitted a view of the office where the nurse came and went and the secretary listened to the radio. A plastic fern in a gold pot sat in the opening and trailed its fronds down almost to the floor. The radio was softly playing gospel music.

Just then the inner door opened and a nurse with the highest stack: of yellow hair Mrs. Turpin had ever seen put her face in the crack and called for the next patient. The woman sitting beside Claud grasped the two arms of her chair and hoisted herself up; she pulled her dress free from her legs and lumbered through the door where the nurse had disappeared.

Mrs. Turpin eased into the vacant chair, which held her tight as a corset. "I wish I could reduce," she said, and rolled her eyes and gave a comic sigh.

"Oh, *you* aren't fat," the stylish lady said.

"Ooooo I am too," Mrs. Turpin said. "Claud he eats all he wants to and never weighs over one hundred and seventy-five pounds, but me I just look at something good to eat and I gain some weight," and her stomach and shoulders shook with laughter. "You can eat all you want to, can't you, Claud?" she asked, turning to him.

Claud only grinned.

"Well, as long as you have such a good disposition," the stylish lady said, "I don't think it makes a bit of difference what size you are. You just can't beat a good disposition."

Next to her was a fat girl of eighteen or nineteen, scowling into a thick blue book which Mrs. Turpin saw was entitled *Human Development*. The girl raised her head and directed her scowl at Mrs. Turpin as if she did not like her looks. She appeared annoyed that anyone should speak while she tried to read. The poor girl's face was blue with acne and Mrs. Turpin thought how pitiful it was to have a face like that at that age. She gave the girl a friendly smile but the girl only scowled the harder. Mrs. Turpin herself was fat but she had always had good skin, and, though she was forty-seven years old, there was not a wrinkle in her face except around her eyes from laughing too much.

Next to the ugly girl was the child, still in exactly the same position, and next to him was a thin leathery old woman in a cotton print dress. She and Claud had three sacks of chicken feed in their pump house that was in the same print. She had seen from the first that the child belonged with the old woman. She could tell by the way they sat — kind of vacant and white-trashy, as if they would sit there until Doomsday if nobody called and told them to get up. And at right angles but next to the well-dressed pleasant lady was a lank-faced woman who was certainly the child's mother. She had on a yellow sweat shirt and wine-colored slacks, both gritty-looking, and the rims of her lips were stained with snuff. Her dirty yellow hair was tied behind with a little piece of red paper ribbon. Worse than riggers any day, Mrs. Turpin thought.

The gospel hymn playing was, "When I looked up and He looked down," and Mrs. Turpin, who knew it, supplied the last line mentally, "And wona these days I know I'll we-ara crown."

Without appearing to, Mrs. Turpin always noticed people's feet. The well-dressed lady had on red and gray suede shoes to match her dress. Mrs. Turpin had on her good black patent leather pumps. The ugly girl had on Girl Scout shoes and heavy socks. The old woman had on tennis shoes and the white-trashy mother had on what appeared to be bedroom slippers, black straw with gold braid threaded through them — exactly what you would have expected her to have on.

Sometimes at night when she couldn't go to sleep, Mrs. Turpin would occupy herself with the question of who she would have chosen to be if she couldn't have been herself. If Jesus had said to her before he made her, "There's only two places available for you. You can either be a nigger or white-trash," what would she have said? "Please, Jesus, please," she would have said, "just let me wait until there's another place available," and he would have said, "No, you have to go right now and I have only those two places so make up your mind." She would have wiggled and squirmed and begged and pleaded but it would have been no use and finally she would have said, "All right, make me a nigger then — but that don't mean a trashy one." And he would have made her a neat clean respectable Negro woman, herself but black.

Next to the child's mother was a red-headed youngish woman, reading one of the magazines and working a piece of chewing gum, hell for leather, as Claud would say. Mrs. Turpin could not see the woman's feet. She was not white-trash, just common. Sometimes Mrs. Turpin occupied herself at night naming the classes of people. On the bottom of the heap were most colored people, not the kind she would have been if she had been one, but most of them; then next to them — not above, just away from — were the white-trash; then above them were the home-owners, and above them the home-and-land owners, to which she and Claud belonged. Above she and Claud were people with a lot of money and much bigger houses and much more land. But here the complexity of it would begin to bear in on her, for some of the people with a lot of money were common and ought to be below she and Claud and some of the people who had good blood had lost their money and had to rent and then there were colored people who owned their homes and land as well. There was a colored dentist in town who had two red Lincolns and a swimming pool and a farm with registered white-face cattle on it. Usually by the time she had fallen asleep all the classes of people were moiling and roiling around in her head, and she would dream they were all crammed in together in a box car, being ridden off to be put in a gas oven.

"That's a beautiful clock," she said and nodded to her right. It was a big wall clock, the face encased in a brass sunburst.

"Yes, it's very pretty," the stylish lady said agreeably. "And right on the dot too," she added, glancing at her watch.

The ugly girl beside her cast an eye upward at the clock, smirked, then looked directly at Mrs. Turpin and smirked again. Then she returned her eyes to her book. She was obviously the lady's daughter because, although they didn't look anything alike as to disposition, they both had the same shape of face and the same blue eyes. On the lady they sparkled pleasantly but in the girl's seared face they appeared alternately to smolder and to blaze.

What if Jesus had said, "All right, you can be white-trash or a nigger or ugly"!

Mrs. Turpin felt an awful pity for the girl, though she thought it was one thing to be ugly and another to act ugly.

The woman with the snuff-stained lips turned around in her chair and looked up at the clock. Then she turned back and appeared to look a little to the side of Mrs. Turpin. There was a cast in one of her eyes. "You want to know wher you can get you one of themther clocks?" she asked in a loud voice.

"No, I already have a nice clock," Mrs. Turpin said. Once somebody like her got a leg in the conversation, she would be all over it.

"You can get you one with green stamps," the woman said. "That's most likely wher he got hisn. Save you up enough, you can get you most anythang. I got me some joo'ry."

Ought to have got you a wash rag and some soap, Mrs. Turpin thought.

"I get contour sheets with mine," the pleasant lady said.

The daughter slammed her book shut. She looked straight in front of her, directly through Mrs. Turpin and on through the yellow curtain and the plate glass window which made the wall behind her. The girl's eyes seemed lit all of a sudden with a peculiar light, an unnatural light like night road signs give. Mrs. Turpin turned her head to see if there was anything going on outside that she should see, but she could not see anything. Figures passing cast only a pale shadow through the curtain. There was no reason the girl should single her out for her ugly looks.

"Miss Finley," the nurse said, cracking the door. The gum-chewing woman got up and passed in front of her and Claud and went into the office. She had on red high-heeled shoes.

Directly across the table, the ugly girl's eyes were fixed on Mrs. Turpin as if she had some very special reason for disliking her.

"This is wonderful weather, isn't it?" the girl's mother said.

"It's good weather for cotton if you can get the niggers to pick it," Mrs. Turpin said, "but niggers don't want to pick cotton any more. You can't get the white folks to pick it and now you can't get the niggers — because they got to be right up there with the white folks."

"They gonna *try* anyways," the white-trash woman said, leaning forward.

"Do you have one of the cotton-picking machines?" the pleasant lady asked.

"No," Mrs. Turpin said, "they leave half the cotton in the field. We don't have much cotton anyway. If you want to make it farming now, you have to have a little of everything. We got a couple of acres of cotton and a few hogs and chickens and just enough white-face that Claud can look after them himself."

"One thang I don't want," the white-trash woman said, wiping her mouth with the back of her hand. "Hogs. Nasty stinking things, a-gruntin and a-rootin all over the place."

Mrs. Turpin gave her the merest edge of her attention. "Our hogs are not dirty and they don't stink," she said. "They're cleaner than some children I've seen. Their feet never touch the ground. We have a pig-parlor — that's where you raise them on concrete," she explained to the pleasant lady, "and Claud scoots them down with the hose every afternoon and washes off the floor." Cleaner by far than that child right there, she thought. Poor nasty little thing. He had not moved except to put the thumb of his dirty hand into his mouth.

The woman turned her face away from Mrs. Turpin. "I know I wouldn't scoot down no hog with no hose," she said to the wall.

You wouldn't have no hog to scoot down, Mrs. Turpin said to herself.

"A-gruntin and a-rootin and a-groanin," the woman muttered.

"We got a little of everything," Mrs. Turpin said to the pleasant lady. "It's no use in having more than you can handle yourself with help like it is. We found enough niggers to pick our cotton this year but Claud he has to go after them and take them home again in the evening. They can't walk that half a mile. No they can't. I tell you," she said and laughed merrily, "I sure am tired of buttering up niggers, but you got to love em if you want em to work for you. When they come in the morning, I run out and I say, 'Hi yawl this morning?' and when Claud drives them off to the field I just wave to beat the band and they just wave back." And she waved her hand rapidly to illustrate.

"Like you read out of the same book," the lady said, showing she understood perfectly.

"Child, yes," Mrs. Turpin said. "And when they come in from the field, I run out with a bucket of icewater. That's the way it's going to be from now on," she said. "You may as well face it."

"One thang I know," the white-trash woman said. "Two thangs I ain't going to do: love no niggers or scoot down no hog with no hose." And she let out a bark of contempt.

The look that Mrs. Turpin and the pleasant lady exchanged indicated they both understood that you had to *have* certain things before you could *know* certain things. But every time Mrs. Turpin exchanged a look with the lady, she was aware that the ugly girl's peculiar eyes were still on her, and she had trouble bringing her attention back to the conversation.

"When you got something," she said, "you got to look after it." And when you ain't got a thing but breath and britches, she added to herself, you can afford to come to town every morning and just sit on the Court House coping and spit.

A grotesque revolving shadow passed across the curtain behind her and was thrown palely on the opposite wall. Then a bicycle clattered down against the outside of the building. The door opened and a colored boy glided in with a tray from the drugstore. It had two large red and white paper cups on it with tops on them. He was a tall, very black boy in discolored white pants and a green nylon shirt. He was chewing gum slowly, as if to music. He set the tray down in the office opening next to the fern and stuck his head through to look for the secretary. She was not in there. He rested his arms on the ledge and waited, his narrow bottom stuck out, swaying to the left and right. He raised a hand over his head and scratched the base of his skull.

"You see that button there, boy?" Mrs. Turpin said. "You can punch that and she'll come. She's probably in the back somewhere."

"Is thas right?" the boy said agreeably, as if he had never seen the button before. He leaned to the right and put his finger on it. "She sometime out," he said and twisted around to face his audience, his elbows behind him on the counter. The nurse appeared and he twisted back again. She handed him a dollar and he rooted in his pocket and made the change and counted it out to her. She gave him fifteen cents for a tip and he went out with the empty tray. The heavy door swung to slowly and closed at length with the sound of suction. For a moment no one spoke.

"They ought to send all them niggers back to Africa," the white-trash woman said. "That's wher they come from in the first place."

"Oh, I couldn't do without my good colored friends," the pleasant lady said.

"There's a heap of things worse than a nigger," Mrs. Turpin agreed. "It's all kinds of them just like it's all kinds of us."

"Yes, and it takes all kinds to make the world go round," the lady said in her musical voice.

As she said it, the raw-complexioned girl snapped her teeth together. Her lower lip turned downwards and inside out, revealing the pale pink inside of her mouth. After a second it rolled back up. It was the ugliest face Mrs. Turpin had ever seen anyone make and for a moment she was certain that the girl had made it at her. She was looking at her as if she had known and disliked her all her life — all of Mrs. Turpin's life, it seemed too, not just all the girl's life. Why, girl, I don't even know you, Mrs. Turpin said silently.

She forced her attention back to the discussion. "It wouldn't be practical to send them back to Africa," she said. "They wouldn't want to go. They got it too good here."

"Wouldn't be what they wanted — if I had anythang to do with it," the woman said.

"It wouldn't be a way in the world you could get all the niggers back over there," Mrs. Turpin said. "They'd be hiding out and lying down and turning sick on you and wailing and hollering and raring and pitching. It wouldn't be a way in the world to get them over there."

"They got over here," the trashy woman said. "Get back like they got over."

"It wasn't so many of them then," Mrs. Turpin explained.

The woman looked at Mrs. Turpin as if here was an idiot indeed but Mrs. Turpin was not bothered by the look, considering where it came from.

"Nooo," she said, "they're going to stay here where they can go to New York and marry white folks and improve their color. That's what they all want to do, every one of them, improve their color."

"You know what comes of that, don't you?" Claud asked.

"No, Claud, what?" Mrs. Turpin said.

Claud's eyes twinkled. "White-faced niggers," he said with never a smile.

Everybody in the office laughed except the white-trash and the ugly girl. The girl gripped the book in her lap with white fingers. The trashy woman looked around her from face to face as if she thought they were all idiots. The old woman in the feed sack dress continued to gaze expressionless across the floor at the high-top shoes of the man opposite her, the one who had been pretending to be asleep when the Turpins came in. He was laughing heartily, his hands still spread out on his knees. The child had fallen to the side and was lying now almost face down in the old woman's lap.

While they recovered from their laughter, the nasal chorus on the radio kept the room from silence.

> *"You go to blank blank*
> *And I'll go to mine*
> *But we'll all blank along;*
> *To-geth-ther,*
> *And all along the blank*
> *We'll hep eachother out*
> *Smile-ling in any kind of*
> *Weath-ther!"*

Mrs. Turpin didn't catch every word but she caught enough to agree with the spirit of the song and it turned her thoughts sober. To help anybody out that needed it was her philosophy of life. She never spared herself when she found somebody in need, whether they were white or black, trash or decent. And of all she had to be thankful for, she was most thankful that this was so. If Jesus had said, "You can be high society and have all the money you want and be thin and svelte-like, but you can't be a good woman with it," she would have had to say, "Well don't make me that then. Make me a good woman and it don't matter what else, how fat or how ugly or how poor!" Her heart rose. He had not made her a nigger or white-trash or ugly! He had made her herself and given her a little of everything. Jesus, thank you! she said. Thank you thank you thank you! Whenever she counted her blessings she felt as buoyant as if she weighed one hundred and twenty-five pounds instead of one hundred and eighty.

"What's wrong with your little boy?" the pleasant lady asked the white-trashy woman.

"He has a ulcer," the woman said proudly. "He ain't give me a minute's peace since he was born. Him and her are just alike," she said, nodding at the old woman, who was running leathery fingers through the child's pale hair. "Look like I can't get nothing down them two but Co' Cola and candy."

That's all you try to get down em, Mrs. Turpin said to herself. Too lazy to light the fire. There was nothing you could tell her about people like them that she didn't know already. And it was not just that they didn't have anything. Because if you gave them everything, in two weeks it would all be broken or filthy or they would have chopped it up for lightwood. She knew all this from her own experience. Help them you must, but help them you couldn't.

All at once the ugly girl turned her lips inside out again. Her eyes fixed like two drills on Mrs. Turpin. This time there was no mistaking that there was something urgent behind them.

Girl, Mrs. Turpin exclaimed silently, I haven't done a thing to you! The girl might be confusing her with somebody else. There was no need to sit by and let herself be intimidated. "You must be in college," she said boldly, looking directly at the girl. "I see you reading a book there."

The girl continued to stare and pointedly did not answer.

Her mother blushed at this rudeness. "The lady asked you a question, Mary Grace," she said under her breath.

"I have ears," Mary Grace said.

The poor mother blushed again. "Mary Grace goes to Wellesley College," she explained. She twisted one of the buttons on her dress. "In Massachusetts," she added with a grimace. "And in the summer she just keeps right on studying. Just reads all the time, a real book worm. She's done real well at Wellesley; she's taking English and Math and History and Psychology and Social Studies," she rattled on, "and I think it's too much. I think she ought to get out and have fun."

The girl looked as if she would like to hurl them all through the plate glass window.

"Way up north," Mrs. Turpin murmured and thought, well, it hasn't done much for her manners.

"I'd almost rather to have him sick," the white-trash woman said, wrenching the attention back to herself. "He's so mean when he ain't. Look like some children just take natural to meanness. It's some gets bad when they get sick but he was the opposite. Took sick and turned good. He don't give me no trouble now. It's me waitin to see the doctor," she said.

If I was going to send anybody back to Africa, Mrs. Turpin thought, it would be your kind, woman. "Yes, indeed," she said aloud, but looking up at the ceiling, "it's a heap of things worse than a nigger." And dirtier than a hog, she added to herself.

"I think people with bad dispositions are more to be pitied than anyone on earth," the pleasant lady said in a voice that was decidedly thin.

"I thank the Lord he has blessed me with a good one," Mrs. Turpin said. "The day has never dawned that I couldn't find some thing to laugh at."

"Not since she married me anyways," Claud said with a comical straight face.

Everybody laughed except the girl and the white-trash.

Mrs. Turpin's stomach shook. "He's such a caution," she said, "that I can't help but laugh at him."

The girl made a loud ugly noise through her teeth.

Her mother's mouth grew thin and tight. "I think the worst thing in the world," she said, "is an ungrateful person. To have everything and not appreciate it. I know a girl," she said, "who has parents who would give her anything, a little brother who loves her dearly, who is getting a good education, who wears the best clothes, but who can never say a kind word to anyone, who never smiles, who just criticizes and complains all day long."

"Is she too old to paddle?" Claud asked.

The girl's face was almost purple.

"Yes," the lady said, "I'm afraid there's nothing to do but leave her to her folly. Some day she'll wake up and it'll be too late."

"It never hurt anyone to smile," Mrs. Turpin said. "It just makes you feel better all over."

"Of course," the lady said sadly, "but there are just some people you can't tell anything to. They can't take criticism."

"If it's one thing I am," Mrs. Turpin said with feeling, "it's grateful. When I think who all I could have been besides myself and what all I got, a little of everything, and a good disposition besides, I just feel like shouting, 'Thank you, Jesus, for making everything the way it is!' It could have been different!" For one thing, somebody else could have got Claud. At the thought of this, she was flooded with gratitude and a terrible pang of joy ran through her. "Oh thank you, Jesus, Jesus, thank you!" she cried aloud.

The book struck her directly over her left eye. It struck almost at the same instant that she realized the girl was about to hurl it. Before she could utter a sound, the raw face came crashing across the table toward her, howling. The girl's fingers sank like clamps into the soft flesh of her neck. She heard the mother cry out and Claud shout, "Whoa!" There was an instant when she was certain that she was about to be in an earthquake.

All at once her vision narrowed and she saw everything as if it were happening in a small room far away, or as if she were looking at it through the wrong end of a telescope. Claud's face crumpled and fell out of sight. The nurse ran in, then out, then in again. Then the gangling figure of the doctor rushed out of the inner door. Magazines flew this way and that as the table turned over. The girl fell with a thud and Mrs. Turpin's vision suddenly reversed itself and she saw everything large instead of small. The eyes of the white-trashy woman were staring hugely at the floor. There the girl, held down on one side by the nurse and on the other by her mother, was wrenching and turning in their grasp. The doctor was kneeling astride her, trying to hold her arm down. He managed after a second to sink a long needle into it.

Mrs. Turpin felt entirely hollow except for her heart which swung from side to side as if it were agitated in a great empty drum of flesh.

"Somebody that's not busy call for the ambulance," the doctor said in the off-hand voice young doctors adopt for terrible occasions.

Mrs. Turpin could not have moved a finger. The old man who had been sitting next to her skipped nimbly into the office and made the call, for the secretary still seemed to be gone.

"Claud!" Mrs. Turpin called.

He was not in his chair. She knew she must jump up and find him but she felt like some one trying to catch a train in a dream, when everything moves in slow motion and the faster you try to run the slower you go.

"Here I am," a suffocated voice, very unlike Claud's, said.

He was doubled up in the corner on the floor, pale as paper, holding his leg. She wanted to get up and go to him but she could not move. Instead, her gaze was drawn slowly downward to the churning face on the floor, which she could see over the doctor's shoulder.

The girl's eyes stopped rolling and focused on her. They seemed a much lighter blue than before, as if a door that had been tightly closed behind them was now open to admit light and air.

Mrs. Turpin's head cleared and her power of motion returned. She leaned forward until she was looking directly into the fierce brilliant eyes. There was no doubt in her mind that the girl did know her, knew her in some intense and personal way, beyond time and place and condition. "What you got to say to me?" she asked hoarsely and held her breath, waiting, as for a revelation.

The girl raised her head. Her gaze locked with Mrs. Turpin's. "Go back to hell where you came from, you old wart hog," she whispered. Her voice was low but clear. Her eyes burned for a moment as if she saw with pleasure that her message had struck its target.

Mrs. Turpin sank back in her chair.

After a moment the girl's eyes closed and she turned her head wearily to the side.

The doctor rose and handed the nurse the empty syringe. He leaned over and put both hands for a moment on the mother's shoulders, which were shaking. She was sitting on the floor, her lips pressed together, holding Mary Grace's hand in her lap. The girl's fingers were gripped like a baby's around her thumb. "Go on to the hospital," he said. "I'll call and make the arrangements."

"Now let's see that neck," he said in a jovial voice to Mrs. Turpin. He began to inspect her neck with his first two fingers. Two little moon-shaped lines like pink fish bones were indented over her windpipe. There was the beginning of an angry red swelling above her eye. His fingers passed over this also.

"Lea' me be," she said thickly and shook him off. "See about Claud. She kicked him."

"I'll see about him in a minute," he said and felt her pulse. He was a thin gray-haired man, given to pleasantries. "Go home and have yourself a vacation the rest of the day," he said and patted her on the shoulder.

Quit your pattin me, Mrs. Turpin growled to herself.

"And put an ice pack over that eye," he said. Then he went and squatted down beside Claud and looked at his leg. After a moment he pulled him up and Claud limped after him into the office.

Until the ambulance came, the only sounds in the room were the tremulous moans of the girl's mother, who continued to sit on the floor. The white-trash woman did not take her eyes off the girl. Mrs. Turpin looked straight ahead at nothing. Presently the ambulance drew up, a long dark shadow, behind the curtain. The attendants came in and set the stretcher down beside the girl and lifted her expertly onto it and carried her out. The nurse helped the mother gather up her things. The shadow of the ambulance moved silently away and the nurse came back in the office.

"That ther girl is going to be a lunatic, ain't she?" the white-trash woman asked the nurse, but the nurse kept on to the back and never answered her.

"Yes, she's going to be a lunatic," the white-trash woman said to the rest of them.

"Po' critter," the old woman murmured. The child's face was still in her lap. His eyes looked idly out over her knees. He had not moved during the disturbance except to draw one leg up under him.

"I thank Gawd," the white-trash woman said fervently, "I ain't a lunatic."

Claud came limping out and the Turpins went home.

As their pick-up truck turned into their own dirt road and made the crest of the hill, Mrs. Turpin gripped the window ledge and looked out suspiciously. The land sloped gracefully down through a field dotted with lavender weeds and at the start of the rise their small yellow frame house, with its little flower beds spread out around it like a fancy apron, sat primly in its accustomed place between two giant hickory trees. She would not have been startled to see a burnt wound between two blackened chimneys.

Neither of them felt like eating so they put on their house clothes and lowered the shade in the bedroom and lay down, Claud with his leg on a pillow and herself with a damp washcloth over her eye. The instant she was flat on her back, the image of a razor-backed hog with warts on its face and horns coming out behind its ears snorted into her head. She moaned, a low quiet moan.

"I am not," she said tearfully, "a wart hog. From hell." But the denial had no force. The girl's eyes and her words, even the tone of her voice, low but clear, directed only to her, brooked no repudiation. She had been singled out for the message, though there was trash in the room to whom it might justly have been applied. The full force of this fact struck her only now. There was a woman there who was neglecting her own child but she had been overlooked. The message had been given to Ruby Turpin, a respectable, hard-working, church-going woman. The tears dried. Her eyes began to burn instead with wrath.

She rose on her elbow and the washcloth fell into her hand. Claud was lying on his back, snoring. She wanted to tell him what the girl had said. At the same time, she did not wish to put the image of herself as a wart hog from hell into his mind.

"Hey, Claud," she muttered and pushed his shoulder.

Claud opened one pale baby blue eye.

She looked into it warily. He did not think about anything. He just went his way.

"Wha, whasit?" he said and closed the eye again.

"Nothing," she said. "Does your leg pain you?"

"Hurts like hell," Claud said.

"It'll quit terreckly," she said and lay back down. In a moment Claud was snoring again. For the rest of the afternoon they lay there. Claud slept. She scowled at the ceiling. Occasionally she raised her fist and made a small stabbing motion over her chest as if she was defending her innocence to invisible guests who were like the comforters of Job, reasonable-seeming but wrong.

About five-thirty Claud stirred. "Got to go after those niggers," he sighed, not moving.

She was looking straight up as if there were unintelligible handwriting on the ceiling. The protuberance over her eye had turned a greenish-blue. "Listen here," she said.

"What ? "

"Kiss me."

Claud leaned over and kissed her loudly on the mouth. He pinched her side and their hands interlocked. Her expression of ferocious concentration did not change. Claud got up, groaning and growling, and limped off. She continued to study the ceiling.

She did not get up until she heard the pick-up truck coming back with the Negroes. Then she rose and thrust her feet in her brown oxfords, which she did not bother to lace, and stumped out onto the back porch and got her red plastic bucket. She emptied a tray of ice cubes into it and filled it half full of water and went out into the back yard. Every afternoon after Claud brought the hands in, one of the boys helped him put out hay and the rest waited in the back of the truck until he was ready to take them home. The truck was parked in the shade under one of the hickory trees.

"Hi yawl this evening?" Mrs. Turpin asked grimly, appearing with the bucket and the dipper. There were three women and a boy in the truck.

"Us coin nicely," the oldest woman said. "Hi you doin?" and her gaze stuck immediately on the dark lump on Mrs. Turpin's forehead. "You done fell down, ain't you?" she asked in a solicitous voice. The old woman was dark and almost toothless. She had on an old felt hat of Claud's set back on her head. The other two women were younger and lighter and they both had new bright green sunhats. One of them had hers on her head; the other had taken hers off and the boy was grinning beneath it.

Mrs. Turpin set the bucket down on the floor of the truck. "Yawl hep yourselves," she said. She looked around to make sure Claud had gone. "No, I didn't fall down," she said, folding her arms. "It was something worse than that."

"Ain't nothing bad happen to you!" the old woman said. She said it as if they all knew that Mrs. Turpin was protected in some special way by Divine Providence. "You just had you a little fall."

"We were in town at the doctor's office for where the cow kicked Mr. Turpin," Mrs. Turpin said in a flat tone that indicated they could leave off their foolishness. "And there was this girl there. A big fat girl with her face all broke out. I could look at that girl and tell she was peculiar but I couldn't tell how. And me and her mama was just talking and going along and all of a sudden WHAM! She throws this big book she was reading at me and . . ."

"Naw!" the old woman cried out.

"And then she jumps over the table and commences to choke me."

"Naw!" they all exclaimed, "naw!"

"Hi come she do that?" the old woman asked. "What ail her?"

Mrs. Turpin only glared in front of her.

"Somethin ail her," the old woman said.

"They carried her off in an ambulance," Mrs. Turpin continued, "but before she went she was rolling on the floor and they were trying to hold her down to give her a shot and she said something to me." She paused. "You know what she said to me?"

"What she say?" they asked.

"She said," Mrs. Turpin began, and stopped, her face very dark and heavy. The sun was getting whiter and whiter, blanching the sky overhead so that the leaves of the hickory tree were black in the face of it. She could not bring forth the words. "Something real ugly," she muttered.

"She sho shouldn't said nothin ugly to you," the old woman said. "You so sweet. You the sweetest lady I know."

"She pretty too," the one with the hat on said.

"And stout," the other one said. "I never knowed no sweeter white lady."

"That's the truth befo' Jesus," the old woman said. "Amen! You des as sweet and pretty as you can be."

Mrs. Turpin knew exactly how much Negro flattery was worth and it added to her rage. "She said," she began again and finished this time with a fierce rush of breath, "that I was an old wart hog from hell."

There was an astounded silence.

"Where she at?" the youngest woman cried in a piercing voice.

"Lemme see her. I'll kill her!"

"I'll kill her with you!" the other one cried.

"She b'long in the sylum," the old woman said emphatically. "You the sweetest white lady I know."

"She pretty too," the other two said. "Stout as she can be and sweet. Jesus satisfied with her!"

"Deed he is," the old woman declared.

Idiots! Mrs. Turpin growled to herself. You could never say anything intelligent to a nigger. You could talk at them but not with them. "Yawl ain't drunk your water," she said shortly. "Leave the bucket in the truck when you're finished with it. I got more to do than just stand around and pass the time of day," and she moved off and into the house.

She stood for a moment in the middle of the kitchen. The dark protuberance over her eye looked like a miniature tornado cloud which might any moment sweep across the horizon of her brow. Her lower lip protruded dangerously. She squared her massive shoulders. Then she marched into the front of the house and out the side door and started down the road to the pig parlor. She had the look of a woman going single-handed, weaponless, into battle.

The sun was a deep yellow now like a harvest moon and was riding westward very fast over the far tree line as if it meant to reach the hogs before she did. The road was rutted and she kicked several good-sized stones out of her path as she strode along. The pig parlor was on a little knoll at the end of a lane that ran off from the side of the barn. It was a square of concrete as large as a small room, with a board fence about four feet high around it. The concrete floor sloped slightly so that the hog wash could drain off into a trench where it was carried to the field for fertilizer. Claud was standing on the outside, on the edge of the concrete, hanging onto the top board, hosing down the floor inside. The hose was connected to the faucet of a water trough nearby.

Mrs. Turpin climbed up beside him and glowered down at the hogs inside. There were seven long-snouted bristly shoats in it — tan with liver-colored spots — and an old sow a few weeks off from farrowing. She was lying on her side grunting. The shoats were running about shaking themselves like idiot children, their little slit pig eyes searching the floor for anything left. She had read that pigs were the most intelligent animal. She doubted it. They were supposed to be smarter than dogs. There had even been a pig astronaut. He had performed his assignment perfectly but died of a heart attack afterwards because they left him in his electric suit, sitting upright throughout his examination when naturally a hog should be on all fours.

A-gruntin and a-rootin and a-groanin.

"Gimme that hose," she said, yanking it away from Claud. "Go on and carry them niggers home and then get off that leg."

"You look like you might have swallowed a mad dog," Claud observed, but he got down and limped off. He paid no attention to her humors.

Until he was out of earshot, Mrs. Turpin stood on the side of the pen, holding the hose and pointing the stream of water at the hind quarters of any shoat that looked as if it might try to lie down. When he had had time to get over the hill, she turned her head slightly and her wrathful eyes scanned the path. He was nowhere in sight. She turned back again and seemed to gather herself up. Her shoulders rose and she drew in her breath.

"What do you send me a message like that for?" she said in a low fierce voice, barely above a whisper but with the force of a shout in its concentrated fury. "How am I a hog and me both? How am I saved and from hell too?" Her free fist was knotted and with the other she gripped the hose, blindly pointing the stream of water in and out of the eye of the old sow whose outraged squeal she did not hear.

The pig parlor commanded a view of the back pasture where their twenty beef cows were gathered around the hay-bales Claud and the boy had put out. The freshly cut pasture sloped down to the highway. Across it was their cotton field and beyond that a dark green dusty wood which they owned as well. The sun was behind the wood, very red, looking over the paling of trees like a farmer inspecting his own hogs.

"Why me?" she rumbled. "It's no trash around here, black or white, that I haven't given to. And break my back to the bone every day working. And do for the church."

She appeared to be the right size woman to command the arena before her. "How am I a hog?" she demanded. "Exactly how am I like them?" and she jabbed the stream of water at the shoats. "There was plenty of trash there. It didn't have to be me.

"If you like trash better, go get yourself some trash then," she railed. "You could have made me trash. Or a nigger. If trash is what you wanted why didn't you make me trash?" She shook her fist with the hose in it and a watery snake appeared momentarily in the air. "I could quit working and take it easy and be filthy," she growled. "Lounge about the sidewalks all day drinking root beer. Dip snuff and spit in every puddle and have it all over my face. I could be nasty.

"Or you could have made me a nigger. It's too late for me to be a nigger," she said with deep sarcasm, "but I could act like one. Lay down in the middle of the road and stop traffic. Roll on the ground."

In the deepening light everything was taking on a mysterious hue. The pasture was growing a peculiar glassy green and the streak of highway had turned lavender. She braced herself for a final assault and this time her voice rolled out over the pasture. "Go on," she yelled, "call me a hog! Call me a hog again. From hell. Call me a wart hog from hell. Put that bottom rail on top. There'll still be a top and bottom!"

A garbled echo returned to her.

A final surge of fury shook her and she roared, "Who do you think you are?"

The color of everything, field and crimson sky, burned for a moment with a transparent intensity. The question carried over the pasture and across the highway and the cotton field and returned to her clearly like an answer from beyond the wood.

She opened her mouth but no sound came out of it.

A tiny truck, Claud's, appeared on the highway, heading rapidly out of sight. Its gears scraped thinly. It looked like a child's toy. At any moment a bigger truck might smash into it and scatter Claud's and the niggers' brains all over the road.

Mrs. Turpin stood there, her gaze fixed on the highway, all her muscles rigid, until in five or six minutes the truck reappeared, returning. She waited until it had had time to turn into their own road. Then like a monumental statue coming to life, she bent her head slowly and gazed, as if through the very heart of mystery, down into the pig parlor at the hogs. They had settled all in one corner around the old sow who was grunting softly. A red glow suffused them. They appeared to pant with a secret life.

Until the sun slipped finally behind the tree line, Mrs. Turpin remained there with her gaze bent to them as if she were absorbing some abysmal life-giving knowledge. At last she lifted her head. There was only a purple streak in the sky, cutting through a field of crimson and leading, like an extension of the highway, into the descending dusk. She raised her hands from the side of the pen in a gesture hieratic and profound. A visionary light settled in her eyes. She saw the streak as a vast swinging bridge extending upward from the earth through a field of living fire. Upon it a vast horde of souls were rumbling toward heaven. There were whole companies of white-trash, clean for the first time in their lives, and bands of black riggers in white robes, and battalions of freaks and lunatics shouting and clapping and leaping like frogs. And bringing up the end of the procession was a tribe of people whom she recognized at once as those who, like herself and Claud, had always had a little of everything and the God-given wit to use it right. She leaned forward to observe them closer. They were marching behind the others with great dignity, accountable as they had always been for good order and common sense and respectable behavior. They alone were on key. Yet she could see by their shocked and altered faces that even their virtues were being burned away. She lowered her hands and gripped the rail of the hog pen, her eyes small but fixed unblinkingly on what lay ahead. In a moment the vision faded but she remained where she was, immobile.

At length she got down and turned off the faucet and made her slow way on the darkening path to the house. In the woods around her the invisible cricket choruses had struck up, but what she heard were the voices of the souls climbing upward into the starry field and shouting hallelujah.

Questions for Discussion

1. How does the opening scene — the doctor's crowded waiting room — along with Mrs. Turpin's responses to the other patients help to clarify her character and the story's central concerns?

2. What does Mrs. Turpin's dream of all the social classes "crammed in together in a box car, being ridden off to be put in a gas oven" reveal about her values?

3. Why does Mary Grace throw her psychology text at Mrs. Turpin, shouting, "Go back to hell where you come from, you old wart hog"? What is the significance of Mrs. Turpin's response to the assault?

4. Who is Mrs. Turpin addressing when she is speaking at sunset to her pigs in the field?

5. What is the meaning of Mrs. Turpin's final vision? How does it contrast with her original vision of social hierarchy in the doctor's waiting room? Why are the tribe of people like herself following behind the blacks and the "white-trash?"

Ideas for Writing

1. Write an essay that interprets Mary Grace's motivations and character. What is the significance of her name? Do you see her as a "lunatic" who has lost control? Does the story imply that Mary Grace is heroic or perhaps divinely inspired in revealing the truth to Mrs. Turpin?

2. Write a sequel to the story in which you imagine Mrs. Turpin's life after the day of the assault by Mary Grace. Do you think the incident helped her to see herself more accurately? Will she change her attitudes toward others?

YUKIO MISHIMA   (1925–1970)

Writing in the years following the World War II, Yukio Mishima explored Japan's difficult transition from a feudal society with clear hierarchies and traditions to a more democratic society increasingly influenced by Western values and materialism.

Mishima was the pen name of Kimitake Hiraoka, the son of a Tokyo public official. He studied law at Tokyo University and worked for the Japanese finance ministry while developing a varied career as an actor, motion picture and play director, essayist, playwright, novelist, and story writer. A devoted student of Zen Buddhism and traditional Japanese culture, Mishima created his own army, the Shield Society, which was committed to bringing Japan back to its prewar power and cultural heritage. After an attempt to take over the Japanese defense forces failed, Mishima committed a public Samurai-style suicide. He is best remembered for his novels, including *Confessions of a Mask* (1949), a passionate, semiautobiographical account of homosexuality, and *The Temple of the Gold Pavilion* (1957), about an obsessed young Buddhist monk who burns to the ground the beautiful temple where he worships.

Mishima's short stories have been translated in *Death in Midsummer and Other Stories* (1967), which includes "Swaddling Clothes." These stories are rich in tradition Japanese imagery, symbolism, and ritualized plots that are designed to emphasize the importance of a stable order that is lacking in the confusion and shifting values of contemporary Japanese society.

Swaddling Clothes   (1966)

Translated by Edward G. Seidensticker

He was always busy, Toshiko's husband. Even tonight he had to dash off to an appointment, leaving her to go home alone by taxi. But what else could a woman expect when she married an actor — an attractive one? No doubt she had been foolish to hope that he would spend the evening with her. And yet he must have known how she dreaded going back to their house, unhomely with its Western-style furniture and with the bloodstains still showing on the floor.

Toshiko had been oversensitive since girlhood: that was her nature. As the result of constant worrying she never put on weight, and now, an adult woman, she looked more like a transparent picture than a creature of flesh and blood. Her delicacy of spirit was evident to her most casual acquaintance.

Earlier that evening, when she had joined her husband at a night club she had been shocked to find him entertaining friends with an account of "the incident." Sitting there in his American-style suit, puffing at a cigarette, he had seemed to her almost a stranger.

"It's a fantastic story," he was saying, gesturing flamboyantly as if in an attempt to outweigh the attractions of the dance band. "Here this new nurse for our baby arrives from the employment agency, and the very first thing I notice about her is her stomach. It's enormous — as if she had a pillow stuck under her kimono! No wonder, I thought, for soon saw that she could eat more than the rest of us put together. She polished off the contents of our rice bin like that. . . ." He snapped his fingers. "'Gastric dilation' — that's how she explained her girth and her appetite. Well, the day before yesterday we heard groans and moans coming from the nursery. We rushed in and found her squatting on the floor, holding her stomach in her two hands, and moaning like a cow. Next to her our baby lay in his cot, scared out of his wits and crying at the top of his lungs. A pretty scene, I can tell you!"

"So the cat was out of the bag?" suggested one of their friends, a film actor like Toshiko's husband.

"Indeed it was! And it gave me the shock of my life. You see, I'd completely swallowed that story about 'gastric dilation.' Well, I didn't waste any time. I rescued our good rug from the floor and spread a blanket for her to lie on. The whole time the girl was yelling like a stuck pig. By the time the doctor from the maternity clinic arrived, the baby had already been born. But our sitting room was a pretty shambles!"

"Oh, that I'm sure of!" said another of their friends, and the whole company burst into laughter.

Toshiko was dumbfounded to hear her husband discussing the horrifying happening as though it were no more than an amusing incident which they chanced to have witnessed. She shut her eyes for a moment and all at once she saw the newborn baby lying before her: on the parquet floor the infant lay, and his frail body was wrapped in bloodstained newspapers.

Toshiko was sure that the doctor had done the whole thing out of spite. As if to emphasize his scorn for this mother who had given birth to a bastard under such sordid conditions, he had told his assistant to wrap the baby in some loose newspapers, rather than proper swaddling. This callous treatment of the newborn child had offended Toshiko. Overcoming her disgust at the entire scene, she had fetched a brand-new piece of flannel from her cupboard and, having swaddled the baby in it, had lain him carefully in an armchair.

This all had taken place in the evening after her husband had left the house. Toshiko had told him nothing of it, fearing that he would think her oversoft, oversentimental; yet the scene had engraved itself deeply in her mind. Tonight she sat silently thinking back on it, while the jazz orchestra brayed and her husband chatted cheerfully with his friends. She knew that she would never forget the sight of the baby, wrapped in stained newspapers and lying on the floor — it was a scene fit for a butchershop. Toshiko, whose own life had been spent in solid comfort, poignantly felt the wretchedness of the illegitimate baby.

I am the only person to have witnessed its shame, the thought occurred to her. The mother never saw her child lying there in its newspaper wrappings, and the baby itself of course didn't know. I alone shall have to preserve that terrible scene in my memory. When the baby grows up and wants to find out about his birth, there will be no one to tell him, so long as I preserve silence. How strange that I should have this feeling of guilt!

After all, it was I who took him up from the floor, swathed him properly in flannel, and laid him down to sleep in the armchair.

They left the night club and Toshiko stepped into the taxi that her husband had called for her. "Take this lady to Ushigome," he told the driver and shut the door from the outside. Toshiko gazed through the window at her husband's smiling face and noticed his strong, white teeth. Then she leaned back in the seat, oppressed by the knowledge that their life together was in some way too easy, too painless. It would have been difficult for her to put her thoughts into words. Through the rear window of the taxi she took a last look at her husband. He was striding along the street toward his Nash car, and soon the back of his rather garish tweed coat had blended with the figures of the passers-by.

The taxi drove off, passed down a street dotted with bars and then by a theatre, in front of which the throngs of people jostled each other on the pavement. Although the performance had only just ended, the lights had already been turned out and in the half dark outside it was depressingly obvious that the cherry blossoms decorating the front of the theatre were merely scraps of white paper.

Even if that baby should grow up in ignorance of the secret of his birth, he can never become a respectable citizen, reflected Toshiko, pursuing the same train of thoughts. Those soiled newspaper swaddling clothes will be the symbol of his entire life. But why should I keep worrying about him so much? Is it because I feel uneasy about the future of my own child? Say twenty years from now, when our boy will have grown up into a fine, carefully educated young man, one day by a quirk of fate he meets that other boy, who then will also have turned twenty. And say that the other boy, who has been sinned against, savagely stabs him with a knife. . . .

It was a warm, overcast April night, but thoughts of the future made Toshiko feel cold and miserable. She shivered on the back seat of the car.

No, when the time comes I shall take my son's place, she told herself suddenly. Twenty years from now I shall be forty-three. I shall go to that young man and tell him straight out about everything — about his newspaper swaddling clothes, and about how I went and wrapped him in flannel.

The taxi ran along the dark wide road that was bordered by the park and by the Imperial Palace moat. In the distance Toshiko noticed the pinpricks of light which came from the blocks of tall office buildings.

Twenty years from now that wretched child will be in utter misery. He will be living a desolate, hopeless, poverty-stricken existence — a lonely rat. What else could happen to a baby who has had such a birth? He'll be wandering through the streets by himself, cursing his father, loathing his mother.

No doubt Toshiko derived a certain satisfaction from her somber thoughts: she tortured herself with them without cease. The taxi approached Hanzomon and drove past the compound of the British Embassy. At that point the famous rows of cherry trees were spread out before Toshiko in all their purity. On the spur of the moment she decided to go and view the blossoms by herself in the dark night. It was a strange decision for a timid and unadventurous young woman, but then she was in a strange state of mind and she dreaded the return home. That evening all sorts of unsettling fancies had burst open in her mind.

She crossed the wide street — a slim, solitary figure in the darkness. As a rule when she walked in the traffic Toshiko used to cling fearfully to her companion, but tonight she darted alone between the cars and a moment later had reached the long narrow park that borders the Palace moat. Chidorigafuchi, it is called — the Abyss of the Thousand Birds.

Tonight the whole park had become a grove of blossoming cherry trees. Under the calm cloudy sky the blossoms formed a mass of solid whiteness. The paper lanterns that hung from wires between the trees had been put out; in their place electric light bulbs, red, yellow, and green, shone dully beneath the blossoms. It was well past ten o'clock and most of the flower-viewers had gone home. As the occasional passers-by strolled through the park, they would automatically kick aside the empty bottles or crush the waste paper beneath their feet.

Newspapers, thought Toshiko, her mind going back once again to those happenings. Bloodstained newspapers. If a man were ever to hear of that piteous birth and know that it was he who had lain there, it would ruin his entire life. To think that I, a perfect stranger, should from now on have to keep such a secret — the secret of a man's whole existence. . . .

Lost in these thoughts, Toshiko walked on through the park. Most of the people still remaining there were quiet couples; no one paid her any attention. She noticed two people sitting on a stone bench beside the moat, not looking at the blossoms, but gazing silently at the water. Pitch black it was, and swathed in heavy shadows. Beyond the moat the somber forest of the Imperial Palace blocked her view. The trees reached up, to form a solid dark mass against the night sky. Toshiko walked slowly along the path beneath the blossoms hanging heavily overhead.

On a stone bench, slightly apart from the others, she noticed a pale object — not, as she had at first imagined, a pile of cherry blossoms, nor a garment forgotten by one of the visitors to the park. Only when she came closer did she see that it was a human form lying on the bench. Was it, she wondered, one of those miserable drunks often to be seen sleeping in public places? Obviously not, for the body had been systematically covered with newspapers, and it was the whiteness of those papers that had attracted Toshiko's attention. Standing by the bench, she gazed down at the sleeping figure.

It was a man in a brown jersey who lay there, curled up on layers of news-papers, other newspapers covering him. No doubt this had become his normal night residence now that spring had arrived. Toshiko gazed down at the man's dirty, unkempt hair, which in places had become hopelessly matted. As she observed the sleeping figure wrapped in its newspapers, she was inevitably reminded of the baby who had lain on the floor in its wretched swaddling clothes. The shoulder of the man's jersey rose and fell in the darkness in time with his heavy breathing.

It seemed to Toshiko that all her fears and premonitions had suddenly taken concrete form. In the darkness the man's pale forehead stood out, and it was a young forehead, though carved with the wrinkles of long poverty and hardship. His khaki trousers had been slightly pulled up; on his sockless feet he wore a pair of battered gym shoes. She could not see his face and suddenly had an overmastering desire to get one glimpse of it.

She walked to the head of the bench and looked down. The man's head was half buried in his arms, but Toshiko could see that he was surprisingly young. She noticed the thick eyebrows and the fine bridge of his nose. His slightly open mouth was alive with youth.

But Toshiko had approached too close. In the silent night the newspaper bedding rustled, and abruptly the man opened his eyes. Seeing the young woman standing directly beside him, he raised himself with a jerk, and his eyes lit up. A second later a powerful hand reached out and seized Toshiko by her slender wrist.

She did not feel in the least afraid and made no effort to free herself. In a flash the thought had struck her. Ah, so the twenty years have already gone by! The forest of the Imperial Palace was pitch dark and utterly silent.

Questions for Discussion

1. What is implied through the use of a Western-style nightclub as the initial setting for the story?
2. Characterize Toshiko. Why does she feel guilty? How is she contrasted with her husband? Why is he so insensitive to her feelings of guilt and humiliation?
3. What is implied by Toshiko 's implied gesture of getting out of the cab at the park?
4. Discuss the symbolism of newspapers and cherry blossoms in the story. How are the two images related?
5. Why is the story called "Swaddling Clothes"? How is the title ironic?

Ideas for Writing

1. In an essay, interpret the story's ending. Why does Toshiko allow the homeless man to grab her without resistance? In what sense and for what reason is she sac-rificing herself?
2. Write a story about a character who makes an impulsive or self-destructive deci-sion out of guilt.

CLARICE LISPECTOR   (1925–1977)

An immigrant from the Ukraine, Clarice Lispector grew up in Rio de Janeiro, where she read widely, particularly such writers as Fyodor Dostoyevski, Hermann Hesse, and Katherine Mansfield. Her writing is distinguished by its intense, inward-looking style, which allows for striking revelations of the unusual mental states of her central viewpoint characters.

Lispector's first novel, *Near to the Wild Heart,* was published in Brazil in 1944 while she was working as a journalist. She continued to write regularly for the rest of her life; her twenty-two books include novels, story collections, and reflections drawn from her newspaper columns. Her novels available in English translation include *The Passion According to G. H.* (1988), *An Apprenticeship, or the Book of Delights* (1986), and *The Stream of Life* (1989). Many critics think that her stories are more powerful than her novels. Three collections are available in English: *Family Ties* (1985), *Soulstorm* (1989), and *The Foreign Legion* (1986), which includes "The Evolution of Myopia."

Lispector's fiction made important contributions to the international feminist movement, and she was an innovator in the use of fiction to search for the underlying nature of language and human consciousness. For Lispector, writing was a way of finding meaning in a confusing, changing world; she stated that she wrote "because of my inability to understand except through the process of writing."

The Evolution of Myopia   (1964)

Translated by Giovanni Pontiero

She did not know if he was intelligent. To be or not to be intelligent depended upon the instability of the others. At times, the things he said suddenly provoked a satisfied and sly look in the adults. Satisfied, because they concealed the fact that they found him intelligent and did not pamper him: sly, because they gained more than he himself did from the things he said. And so when he was considered intelligent, he had at the same time the uneasy sensation of unconsciousness; something had escaped him. For at times, in trying to imitate himself, he said things that were certain to provoke anew the rapid movement on the chessboard, for this was the impression of automatic mechanism which he associated with the members of his family: the moment he said something intelligent, the adults would rapidly exchange glances, with a smile clearly suppressed on their lips, a smile barely indicated with their eyes, "just as we should be smiling now were we not such good educators" —

and, just as in a square-dance in some western film, everybody would some-how change their partner and place. In short, the members of the family understood each other; and they understood each other at his expense. Be-sides understanding each other at his expense, they misunderstood each other permanently, as if it were a new form of square-dancing: even when they mis-understood each other, he felt that they were obeying the rules of a game, as if they had agreed to misunderstand each other.

At times, then, he tried to reproduce those phrases which had succeeded in provoking movement on the chessboard. Not exactly to reproduce past suc-cesses, nor exactly to provoke the silent movement from his family. But to try to gain possession of the key to his "intelligence." His efforts, however, to establish laws and causes met with failure. Whenever he tried to repeat one of his successful phrases, it brought no reaction whatsoever from the others. His eyes blinking with curiosity, the first symptoms of myopia, he pondered why he had once succeeded in setting his family in motion, while failing the sec-ond time. Was his intelligence judged by the lack of discipline in others?

Much later, when he substituted the instability of others with his own, he entered into a state of conscious instability. Grown to manhood, he maintained this habit of suddenly blinking at his own thoughts, and twitching his nose at the same time, which caused his spectacles to slip sideways—expressing with this nervous tic an attempt to substitute the judgement of others with his own, in his efforts to probe his own bewilderment. But he was a child with a capacity for balancing forces: he had always been capable of maintaining bewilderment as bewilderment, without it becoming transformed into some other feeling.

That he was not in possession of his own key was something which he had got used to knowing, even as a child, when his eyes would blink and his nose twitch, causing his spectacles to slip sideways. That no one held the key was something which he had gradually perceived without any disillusionment, his tranquil myopia demanding lenses that were ever more powerful.

Strange though it might seem, it was precisely because of this state of per-manent uncertainty and because of this premature acceptance that no one held the key—it was because of all this that he started growing normally, and liv-ing in a state of tranquil curiosity. Patient and curious. A trifle nervous, they said, referring to the tic which caused his spectacles to slip sideways. But "ner-vous" was the name which the family gave to their own unstable judgement.

Other names which these inconstant adults conferred on him were "well-behaved" and "docile." Thus giving a name not to what he was, but to the varying requirements of the moment.

Now and then, in the extraordinary calm of his spectacles, there occurred inside him something brilliant and almost spasmodic, akin to inspiration.

As, for example, when they told him that in a week's time he would spend the whole day at the home of a cousin. This married cousin was childless yet she adored children. "The whole day" included lunch, tea and dinner, before returning home almost asleep. As for his cousin, his cousin meant a surfeit of love with the unexpected advantages and an incalculable eagerness — and all this would open the way for special requests to be heeded. At his cousin's house, everything that he was would have its value guaranteed for a whole day. There love, so much more likely to be constant if merely for a day, would provide an opportunity for unstable judgements: for one whole day he would be judged the same boy.

During the week that preceded 'the whole day' he began by trying to decide if he would behave naturally or otherwise with his cousin. He tried to decide if he should say something intelligent upon arrival — which would result in his being judged intelligent for the whole day. Or if he should do something upon arrival that she would judge "well-behaved," which would mean that for the whole day he would be the well-behaved boy. To have the possibility of choosing what it should be and for the very first time, for one whole day, caused him to adjust his spectacles every other minute.

During the preceding week, the range of possibilities had gradually widened. And, with his capacity for tolerating confusion — he was precise and calm when confronted with confusion — he ended up by discovering that he could even capriciously decide to be a clown, for example, for a whole day. Or, if he so wished, he could spend that day being utterly miserable. What consoled him was to know that his cousin with her love of children and, above all, with her lack of experience in dealing with children, would accept the way in which he decided he wanted to be judged. It also reassured him to know that nothing he might be during that day would really change him. For prematurely — being a precocious child — he was superior to the instability of others and to his own instability. He somehow hovered over his own myopia and that of others. And this gave him considerable freedom. At times, it was simply the freedom of tranquil scepticism. Even when he grew up, and used the thickest of lenses, he never became conscious of this kind of superiority that he had over himself.

The week preceding the visit to his cousin was one of continuous anticipation. At times his stomach became cramped with anxiety: for in that house without children he would be totally at the mercy of the undiscriminating love of a woman. "Undiscriminating love" represented a threatening stability: it would be permanent, and would almost certainly result in a unique way of judging, and that was stability. For him, stability now meant danger: if the others should err in the first stages of stability, the error would become permanent, without the advantage of instability, which is a possible means of correction.

Another thing which worried him beforehand, was what he would do for a whole day in his cousin's house apart from eating and being loved. Well, there was always the solution of being able to go to the bathroom from time to time, and that would make the time pass more quickly. But, with the experience of being loved, he was already feeling apprehensive that his cousin, who was a stranger to him, would regard his trips to the bathroom with infinite affection. Generally speaking, the mechanism of his life had become a motive for tenderness. Well, it was also true that, as for going to the bathroom, the solution might be not to go to the bathroom even once. But not only would that be impossible to achieve for a whole day, but — but he did not wish to be judged as "a boy who does not go to the bathroom" — this, too, did not offer any advantage. His cousin, stabilized by her permanent desire to have children, would find herself, were he to go to the bathroom, with a false trail of immense love.

During the week that preceded "the whole day," he did not suffer on account of these evasions. For he had already taken the step that so many never get round to taking: he had accepted uncertainty, and was struggling with its components as intently as someone peering through the lens of a microscope.

During that week, as ideas came to him somewhat spasmodically, they gradually changed in substance. He abandoned the problem of deciding what elements he would give to his cousin so that she in turn might give him temporarily some certainty of "who he was." He abandoned these meditations and tried to establish beforehand the smell of his cousin's house, the size of the small backyard where he would play, the cupboards he would open when she was not looking. And finally, he came to the question of his cousin herself. In what way should he confront his cousin's love?

Meantime, he had overlooked one detail: his cousin had a gold tooth on the left side. And it was this detail — upon finally entering his cousin's house — it was this detail which upset in a flash the entire scene he had anticipated.

The rest of the day could be described as horrible, were the boy inclined to see things in terms of being horrible or not horrible. Or it could be described as wonderful, were he one of those people who hope that things either are or are not.

There was the gold tooth, with which he had not reckoned. But, with the reassurance that he derived from the idea of a permanent unpredictability, so much so that he wore spectacles, he did not become insecure upon encountering at the outset something with which he had not reckoned.

Afterwards, the surprise of his cousin's love. His cousin's love was not obvious at once, contrary to what he had imagined. She received him in a natural manner, which he found offensive to begin with, but soon afterwards it offended him no longer. She explained at once that she must tidy up the house and that he could play in the meantime. This gave the boy, quite unexpectedly, a whole sunny day to himself.

Some hours later, wiping his spectacles, he tried, with an air of indifference, to impress her with his intelligence and made an observation about the plants in the yard. For when he made an observation aloud, he was always thought to be very observant. But his cold observation about the plants received in reply a simple "of course," amidst rapid strokes with a broom. So he went to the bathroom, where he decided that, since everything had failed miserably, he would play at "not being judged": for a whole day he would be nothing, he simply would not exist. And he yanked the door open in a gesture of freedom.

As the sun rose higher, the gentle pressure of his cousin's love started making itself felt. And when he became aware of it, he was someone who was loved. At lunch, the food became pure love, errant and stable: beneath his cousin's tender gaze, he adapted himself with curiosity to the strange taste of that food, perhaps due to the type of oil, he adapted himself to a woman's love, a new love which was quite unlike the love of other adults: it was a love seeking fulfillment, for his cousin was not pregnant, which is already in itself a maternal love fulfilled. But it was a love without any pregnancy beforehand. It was a love seeking conception *a posteriori*. In short, impossible love.

The whole day long, love demanded a past that might redeem the present and the future. The whole day long, without saying a word, his cousin demanded from him that he might have been born from her womb. His cousin wanted nothing from him other than that. She demanded from the boy with spectacles that she should not be a woman without children. On that day, therefore, he knew one of the rare forms of stability: the stability of an impossible desire. The stability of an unattainable desire. For the first time, he, who was a creature given to moderation, for the first time, he felt himself attracted to the immoderate: an attraction for the impossible extreme. In a word, for the impossible. And for the first time he experienced passion.

And it was as if his myopia had vanished and he could see the world clearly. The deepest and most simple glimpse he had ever had of the kind of universe in which he lived and where he would continue to live. Not a mental glimpse. It was as if he had removed his spectacles, and myopia itself was helping him to see. Perhaps it was from that moment that he formed the habit which he would have for the rest of his life: whenever he was overcome by confusion and he could barely see anything, he would remove his spectacles on the pretext of cleaning them, and, without spectacles, he would stare at the person who was addressing him with the reverberating intensity of a blind man.

Questions for Discussion

1. Why does "he" lack a name or any more specific description of his appearance and physical surroundings?
2. Is "he" particularly intelligent? Why is "he" confused about the nature of his own intelligence? What might be the cause of his "instability"?
3. How do the metaphors of the chessboard and the square dance help us to understand "he" and his family life?
4. What are the origins and symbolic significance of the character's "tranquil" and increasing myopia?
5. How does "he" feel about his visit to the home of his childless, married cousin? How and why does she treat him differently from the way his parents treat him?

Ideas for Writing

1. Analyze in an essay the final scene of the story, the visit of "he" to the cousin's house. What does "he" learn through this long-anticipated visit? Why does his visit have a lasting effect on his myopia?

2. Write an essay about a character whose physical disability reflects an inner struggle or psychological dilemma.

GABRIEL GARCÍA MÁRQUEZ   (b. 1928)

Balancing careful attention to realistic detail with fantastical incidents that often reflect the mysticism of both Roman Catholic miracles and peasant fables, the works of Gabriel García Márquez have helped to define the Latin American style of fiction termed "magical realism."

García Márquez was born in a small town near the Caribbean coast of Colombia; he was the eldest of twelve children in a poor family. In 1947 he entered the National University in Bogotá and studied there until the school closed because of civil war. He continued his studies at the University of Cartagena and began to write a daily newspaper column. His first book of stories, *Leaf Storm and Other Stories* (1955), which includes "The Handsomest Drowned Man in the World," confirmed his commitment to politics and social change. From 1959 to 1961 he traveled to Rome, Paris, the Soviet Union, London, and Caracas while working for a Cuban news agency. After the Cuban revolution, García Márquez returned to Central America to encourage other revolutionary causes. With the publication of his novel *One Hundred Years of Solitude* (1967), he was recognized as one of the most talented writers of Latin America. Among his other widely read novels are *The Autumn of the Patriarch* (1975) and *Love in the Time of Cholera* (1988), and his short-story collections include *Collected Stories* (1984) and *Strange Pilgrims* (1993).

Because of his support of socialist causes in his native Colombia, García Márquez now lives in exile. He received the Nobel Prize for Literature in 1982 for "his novels and short stories, in which the fantastic and the realistic are combined in a richly composed world of imagination, reflecting a continent's life and conflicts."

The Handsomest Drowned Man in the World   (1955)
A Tale for Children

Translated by Gregory Rabassa

The first children who saw the dark and slinky bulge approaching through the sea let themselves think it was an empty ship. Then they saw it had no flags or masts and they thought it was a whale. But when it washed up on the beach, they removed the clumps of seaweed, the jellyfish tentacles, and the remains of fish and flotsam, and only then did they see that it was a drowned man.

They had been playing with him all afternoon, burying him in the sand and digging him up again, when someone chanced to see them and spread the alarm in the village. The men who carried him to the nearest house noticed that he weighed more than any dead man they had ever known, almost as much as a horse, and they said to each other that maybe he'd been floating too long and the water had got into his bones. When they laid him on the floor they said he'd been taller than all other men because there was barely enough room for him in the house, but they thought that maybe the ability to keep on growing after death was part of the nature of certain drowned men. He had the smell of the sea about him and only his shape gave one to suppose that it was the corpse of a human being, because the skin was covered with a crust of mud and scales.

They did not even have to clean off his face to know that the dead man was a stranger. The village was made up of only twenty-odd wooden houses that had stone courtyards with no flowers and which were spread about on the end of a desertlike cape. There was so little land that mothers always went about with the fear that the wind would carry off their children and the few dead that the years had caused among them had to be thrown off the cliffs. But the sea was calm and bountiful and all the men fit into seven boats. So when they found the drowned man they simply had to look at one another to see that they were all there.

That night they did not go out to work at sea. While the men went to find out if anyone was missing in neighboring villages, the women stayed behind to care for the drowned man. They took the mud off with grass swabs, they removed the underwater stones entangled in his hair, and they scraped the crust off with tools used for scaling fish. As they were doing that they noticed that the vegetation on him came from faraway oceans and deep water and that his clothes were in tatters, as if he had sailed through labyrinths of coral. They noticed too that he bore his death with pride, for he did not have the lonely look of other drowned men who came out of the sea or that haggard, needy look of men who drowned in rivers. But only when they finished cleaning him off did they become aware of the kind of man he was and it left them breathless. Not only was he the tallest, strongest, most virile, and best built man they had ever seen, but even though they were looking at him there was no room for him in their imagination.

They could not find a bed in the village large enough to lay him on nor was there a table solid enough to use for his wake. The tallest men's holiday pants would not fit him, nor the fattest ones' Sunday shirts, nor the shoes of the one with the biggest feet. Fascinated by his huge size and his beauty, the women then decided to make him some pants from a large piece of sail and a shirt from some bridal Brabant linen so that he could continue through his death with dignity. As they sewed, sitting in a circle and gazing at the corpse between stitches, it seemed to them that the wind had never been so steady nor the sea so restless as on that night and they supposed that the change had something to do with the dead man. They thought that if that magnificent man had lived in the village, his house would have had the widest doors, and highest ceiling, and the strongest floor; his bedstead would have been made from a midship frame held together by iron bolts, and his wife would have been the happiest woman. They thought that he would have had so much authority that he could have drawn fish out of the sea simply by calling their names and that he would have put so much work into his land that springs would have burst forth from among the rocks so that he would have been able to plant flowers on the cliffs. They secretly compared him to their own men, thinking that for all their lives theirs were incapable of doing what he could do in one night, and they ended up dismissing them deep in their hearts as the weakest, meanest, and most useless creatures on earth. They were wandering through that maze of fantasy when the oldest woman, who as the oldest had looked upon the drowned man with more compassion than passion, sighed:

"He has the face of someone called Esteban."

It was true. Most of them had only to take another look at him to see that he could not have any other name. The more stubborn among them, who were the youngest, still lived for a few hours with the illusion that when they put his clothes on and he lay among the flowers in patent leather shoes his name might be Lautaro. But it was a vain illusion. There had not been enough canvas, the poorly cut and worse sewn pants were too tight, and the hidden strength of his heart popped the buttons on his shirt. After midnight the whistling of the wind died down and the sea fell into its Wednesday drowsiness. The silence put an end to any last doubts: he was Esteban. The women who had dressed him, who had combed his hair, had cut his nails and shaved him were unable to hold back a shudder of pity when they had to resign themselves to his being dragged along the ground. It was then that they understood how unhappy he must have been with that huge body since it bothered him even after death. They could see him in life, condemned to going through doors sideways cracking his head on crossbeams, remaining on his feet during visits, not knowing what to do with his soft pink, sealion hands while the lady of the house looked for her most resistant chair and begged him, frightened to death, sit here, Esteban, please, and he, leaning against the wall, smiling, don't bother, ma'am, I'm fine where I am, his heels raw and his back roasted from having done the same thing so many times whenever he paid a visit, don't bother, ma'am, I'm fine where I am to avoid the embarrassment of breaking up the chair, and never knowing perhaps that the one who said don't go, Esteban, at least wait till the coffee's ready, were the ones who later on would whisper the big boob finally left, how nice, the handsome fool has gone. That was what the women were thinking beside the body a little before dawn. Later, when they covered his face with a handkerchief so that the light would not bother him, he looked so forever dead, so defenseless, so much like their men that the first furrows of tears opened in their hearts. It was one of the younger ones who began the weeping. The others, coming to, went from sighs to wails, and the more they sobbed the more they felt like weeping, because the drowned man was becoming all the more Esteban for them, and so they wept so much, for he was the most destitute, most peaceful, and most obliging man on earth, poor Esteban. So when the men returned with the news that the drowned man was not from the neighboring villages either, the women felt an opening of jubilation in the midst of their tears.

"Praise the Lord," they sighed, "he's ours!"

The men thought the fuss was only womanish frivolity. Fatigued because of the difficult nighttime inquiries, all they wanted was to get rid of the bother of the newcomer once and for all before the sun grew strong on that arid, windless day. They improvised a litter with the remains of foremasts and gaffs, tying it together with rigging so that it would bear the weight of the body until they reached the cliffs. They wanted to tie the anchor from a cargo ship to him so that he would sink easily into the deepest waves, where the fish are blind and divers die of nostalgia, and bad currents would not bring him back to shore, as had happened with other bodies. But the more they hurried, the more the women thought of ways to waste time. They walked about like startled hens, pecking with the sea charms on their breasts, some interfering on one side to put a scapular of the good wind on the drowned man, some on the other side to put a wrist compass on him, and after a great deal of *get away from there woman, stay out of the way, look, you almost made me fall on top of the dead man,* the men began to feel mistrust in their livers and started grumbling about why so many main-altar decorations for a stranger, because no matter how many nails and holywater jars he had on him, the sharks would chew him all the same, but the women kept on piling on their junk relics, running back and forth, stumbling, while they released in sighs what they did not in tears, so that the men finally exploded with *since when has there ever been such a fuss over a drifting corpse, a drowned nobody, a piece of cold Wednesday meat.* One of the women, mortified by so much lack of care, then removed the handkerchief from the dead man's face and the men were left breathless too.

He was Esteban. It was not necessary to repeat it for them to recognize him. If they had been told Sir Walter Raleigh, even they might have been impressed with his gringo accent, the macaw on his shoulder, his cannibal-killing blunderbuss, but there could be only one Esteban in the world and there he was, stretched out like a sperm whale, shoeless, wearing the pants of an undersized child, and with those stony nails that had to be cut with a knife. They had only to take the handkerchief off his face to see that he was ashamed, that it was not his fault that he was so big or so heavy or so handsome, and if he had known that this was going to happen, he would have looked for a more discreet place to drown in; seriously, I even would have tied the anchor off a galleon around my neck and staggered off a cliff like someone who doesn't like things in order not to be upsetting people now with this Wednesday dead body, as you people say, in order not to be bothering anyone with this filthy piece of cold meat that doesn't have anything to do with me. There was so much truth in his manner that even the most mistrustful men, the ones who felt the bitterness of endless nights at sea fearing that their women would tire of dreaming about them and begin to dream of drowned men, even they and others who were harder still shuddered in the marrow of their bones at Esteban's sincerity.

That was how they came to hold the most splendid funeral they could conceive of for an abandoned drowned man. Some women who had gone to get flowers in the neighboring villages returned with other women who could not believe what they had been told, and those women went back for more flowers when they saw the dead man, and they brought more and more until there were so many flowers and so many people that it was hard to walk about. At the final moment it pained them to return him to the waters as an orphan and they chose a father and mother from among the best people, and aunts and uncles and cousins, so that through him all the inhabitants of the village became kinsmen. Some sailors who heard the weeping from a distance went off course, and people heard of one who had himself tied to the mainmast, remembering ancient fables about sirens. While they fought for the privilege of carrying him on their shoulders along the steep escarpment by the cliffs, men and women became aware for the first time of the desolation of their streets, the dryness of their courtyards, the narrowness of their dreams as they faced the splendor and beauty of their drowned man. They let him go without an anchor so that he could come back if he wished and whenever he wished, and they all held their breath for the fraction of centuries the body took to fall into the abyss. They did not need to look to one another to realize that they were no longer all present, that they would never be. But they also knew that everything would be different from then on, that their houses would have wider doors, higher ceilings, and stronger floors so that Esteban's memory could go everywhere without bumping into beams and so that no one in the future would dare whisper the big boob finally died, too bad, the handsome fool has finally died, because they were going to paint their house fronts gay colors to make Esteban's memory eternal and they were going to break their backs digging for springs among the stones and planting flowers on the cliffs so that in future years at dawn the passengers on great liners would awaken, suffocated by the smell of gardens on the high seas, and the captain would have to come down from the bridge in his dress uniform, with his astrolabe, his pole star, and his row of war medals and, pointing to the promontory of roses on the horizon, he would say in fourteen languages, look there, where the wind is so peaceful now that it's gone to sleep beneath the beds, over there, where the sun's so bright that the sunflowers don't know which way to turn, yes, over there, that's Esteban's village.

Questions for Discussion

1. What is revealed through the initial description of the drowned man? Why was "there was no room for him in their [the villagers'] imagination"?

2. Why and how does the drowned man make the women happy and the sea peaceful?

3. Why does the community of women finally agree that this man must be Esteban? How did the women feel about Esteban when he was alive? How do they feel about him now that he is dead? Do the men of the village change their attitude toward the drowned man once they realize he is Esteban?

4. What is the significance of the villagers' making their island into a beautiful shrine dedicated to Esteban's size and beauty?

5. Why is the story subtitled "A Tale for Children"? What warning and what hope does the story offer?

Ideas for Writing

1. Write an essay that discusses the story's use of "magic realism." What is the effect of the mixing of the possible and the impossible? How does the story resemble a myth or a dream, and how does this mixture of reality and unreality help to emphasize the story's theme and meaning?

2. Write a fable about a magical or supernatural event that reveals a truth about society.

Born in eastern Nigeria, Chinua Achebe was raised as a Christian yet always felt at home with his community's Ibo religion and customs; Ibo was his first language. Writing in English, he captures the oral storytelling style of traditional Nigeria. Achebe attended one of the finest high schools in West Africa and went on to University College, Ibadan, which is associated with the University of London. In 1948 he began to work with the Nigerian Broadcasting Service and also decided to become a writer. His first and most highly acclaimed novel, *Things Fall Apart* (1958), explores the personal and social crises brought on by the European colonization of Africa. Achebe's other novels — *No Longer at Ease* (1960), *Arrow of God* (1964), *A Man of the People* (1966), and *Anthills of the Savannah* (1970) — are considered classics of African literature as well. He has also written essays, poetry, and short fiction, the best-known collection of which is *Girls at War and Other Stories* (1973), which includes "The Madman."

Achebe believes that "art is, and always was, at the service of man. Our ancestors created their myths and legends and told their stories for a human purpose. . . . [A]ny good story . . . should have a message, should have a purpose."

The Madman   (1973)

He was drawn to markets and straight roads. Not any tiny neighbourhood market where a handful of garrulous women might gather at sunset to gossip and buy ogili for the evening's soup, but a huge, engulfing bazaar beckoning people familiar and strange from far and near. And not any dusty, old footpath beginning in this village, and ending in that stream, but broad, black, mysterious highways without beginning or end. After much wandering he had discovered two such markets linked together by such a highway; and so ended his wandering. One market was Af<u>o</u>, the other Eke. The two days between them suited him very well: before setting out for Eke he had ample time to wind up his business properly at Af<u>o</u>. He passed the night there putting right again his hut after a day of defilement by two fat-bottomed market women who said it was their market stall. At first he had put up a fight but the women had gone and brought their menfolk — four hefty beasts of the bush — to whip him out of the hut. After that he always avoided them, moving out on the morning of the market and back in at dusk to pass the night. Then in the morning he rounded off his affairs swiftly and set out on that long, beautiful boa-constrictor of a road to Eke in the distant town of Ogbu. He held his staff and cudgel at the ready in his right hand, and with the left he steadied the basket of his belongings on his head. He had got himself this cudgel lately to deal with little beasts on the way who threw stones at him and made fun of their mothers' nakedness, not his own.

He used to walk in the middle of the road, holding it in conversation. But one day the driver of a mammy-wagon and his mate came down on him shouting, pushing and slapping his face. They said their lorry very nearly ran over their mother, not him. After that he avoided those noisy lorries too, with the vagabonds inside them.

Having walked one day and one night he was now close to the Eke market-place. From every little side-road, crowds of market people poured into the big highway to join the enormous flow to Eke. Then he saw some young ladies with water-pots on their heads coming towards him, unlike all the rest, away from the market. This surprised him. Then he saw two more water-pots rise out of a sloping footpath leading off his side of the highway. He felt thirsty then and stopped to think it over. Then he set down his basket on the roadside and turned into the sloping footpath. But first he begged his highway not to be offended or continue the journey without him. "I'll get some for you too," he said coaxingly with a tender backward glance. "I know you are thirsty."

Nwibe was a man of high standing in Ogbu and was rising higher; a man of wealth and integrity. He had just given notice to all the ozo men of the town that he proposed to seek admission into their honoured hierarchy in the coming initiation season.

"Your proposal is excellent," said the men of title. "When we see we shall believe." Which was their dignified way of telling you to think it over once again and make sure you have the means to go through with it. For ozo is not a child's naming ceremony; and where is the man to hide his face who begins the ozo dance and then is foot-stuck to the arena? But in this instance the caution of the elders was no more than a formality for Nwibe was such a sensible man that no one could think of him beginning something he was not sure to finish.

On that Eke day Nwibe had risen early so as to visit his farm beyond the stream and do some light work before going to the market at midday to drink a horn or two of palm-wine with his peers and perhaps buy that bundle of roofing thatch for the repair of his wives' huts. As for his own hut he had a couple of years back settled it finally by changing his thatch-roof to zinc. Sooner or later he would do the same for his wives. He could have done Mgboye's hut right away but decided to wait until he could do the two together, or else Udenkwo would set the entire compound on fire. Udenkwo was the junior wife, by three years, but she never let that worry her. Happily Mgboye was a woman of peace who rarely demanded the respect due to her from the other. She would suffer Udenkwo's provoking tongue sometimes for a whole day without offering a word in reply. And when she did reply at all her words were always few and her voice very low.

That very morning Udenkwo had accused her of spite and all kinds of wickedness on account of a little dog.

"What has a little dog done to you?" she screamed loud enough for half the village to hear. "I ask you, Mgboye, what is the offense of a puppy this early in the day?"

"What your puppy did this early in the day," replied Mgboye, "is that he put his shit-mouth into my soup-pot."

"And then?"

"And then I smacked him."

"You smacked him! Why don't you cover your soup-pot? Is it easier to hit a dog than cover a pot? Is a small puppy to have more sense than a woman who leaves her soup-pot about . . . ?"

"Enough from you, Udenkwo."

"It is not enough, Mgboye, it is not enough. If that dog owes you any debt I want to know. Everything I have, even a little dog I bought to eat my infant's excrement keeps you awake at nights. You are a bad woman, Mgboye, you are a very bad woman!"

Nwibe had listened to all of this in silence in his hut. He knew from the vigour in Udenkwo's voice that she could go on like this till market-time. So he intervened, in his characteristic manner by calling out to his senior wife.

"Mgboye! Let me have peace this early morning!"

"Don't you hear all the abuses Udenkwo . . ."

"I hear nothing at all from Udenkwo and I want peace in my compound. If Udenkwo is crazy must everybody else go crazy with her? Is one crazy woman not enough in my compound so early in the day?"

"The great judge has spoken," sang Udenkwo in a sneering sing-song. "Thank you, great judge. Udenkwo is mad. Udenkwo is always mad, but those of you who are sane let . . ."

"Shut your mouth, shameless woman, or a wild beast will lick your eyes for you this morning. When will you learn to keep your badness within this compound instead of shouting it to all Ogbu to hear? I say shut your mouth!"

There was silence then except for Udenkwo's infant whose yelling had up till then been swallowed up by the larger noise of the adults.

"Don't cry, my father," said Udenkwo to him. "They want to kill your dog, but our people say the man who decides to chase after a chicken, for him is the fall . . ."

By the middle of the morning Nwibe had done all the work he had to do on his farm and was on his way again to prepare for market. At the little stream he decided as he always did to wash off the sweat of work. So he put his cloth on a huge boulder by the men's bathing section and waded in. There was nobody else around because of the time of day and because it was market day. But from instinctive modesty he turned to face the forest away from the approaches.

The madman watched him for quite a while. Each time he bent down to carry water in cupped hands from the shallow stream to his head and body the madman smiled at his parted behind. And then remembered. This was the same hefty man who brought three others like him and whipped me out of my hut in the Af<u>o</u> market. He nodded to himself. And he remembered again: this was the same vagabond who descended on me from the lorry in the middle of my highway. He nodded once more. And then he remembered yet again: this was the same fellow who set his children to throw stones at me and make remarks about their mothers' buttocks, not mine. Then he laughed.

Nwibe turned sharply round and saw the naked man laughing, the deep grove of the stream amplifying his laughter. Then he stopped as suddenly as he had begun; the merriment vanished from his face.

"I have caught you naked," he said.

Nwibe ran a hand swiftly down his face to clear his eyes of water.

"I say I have caught you naked, with your thing dangling about."

"I can see you are hungry for a whipping," said Nwibe with quiet menace in his voice, for a madman is said to be easily scared away by the very mention of a whip. "Wait till I get up there. . . . What are you doing? Drop it at once . . . I say drop it!"

The madman had picked up Nwibe's cloth and wrapped it round his own waist. He looked down at himself and began to laugh again.

"I will kill you," screamed Nwibe as he splashed towards the bank, maddened by anger. "I will whip that madness out of you today!"

They ran all the way up the steep and rocky footpath hedged in by the shadowy green forest. A mist gathered and hung over Nwibe's vision as he ran, stumbled, fell, pulled himself up again and stumbled on, shouting and cursing. The other, despite his unaccustomed encumbrance steadily increased his lead, for he was spare and wiry, a thing made for speed. Furthermore, he did not waste his breath shouting and cursing; he just ran. Two girls going down to the stream saw a man running up the slope towards them pursued by a stark-naked madman. They threw down their pots and fled, screaming.

When Nwibe emerged into the full glare of the highway he could not see his cloth clearly any more and his chest was on the point of exploding from the fire and torment within. But he kept running. He was only vaguely aware of crowds of people on all sides and he appealed to them tearfully without stopping: "Hold the madman, he's got my cloth!" By this time the man with the cloth was practically lost among the much denser crowds far in front so that the link between him and the naked man was no longer clear.

Now Nwibe continually bumped against people's backs and then laid flat a frail old man struggling with a stubborn goat on a leash. "Stop the madman," he shouted hoarsely, his heart tearing to shreds, "he's got my cloth!" Everyone looked at him first in surprise and then less surprise because strange sights are common in a great market. Some of them even laughed.

"They've got his cloth he says."

"That's a new one I'm sure. He hardly looks mad yet. Doesn't he have people, I wonder."

"People are so careless these days. Why can't they keep proper watch over their sick relation, especially on the day of the market?"

Farther up the road on the very brink of the marketplace two men from Nwibe's village recognized him and, throwing down the one his long basket of yams, the other his calabash of palm-wine held on a loop, gave desperate chase, to stop him setting foot irrevocably within the occult territory of the powers of the market. But it was in vain. When finally they caught him it was well inside the crowded square. Udenkwo in tears tore off her top-cloth which they draped on him and led him home by the hand. He spoke just once about a madman who took his cloth in the stream.

"It is all right," said one of the men in the tone of a father to a crying child. They led and he followed blindly, his heavy chest heaving up and down in silent weeping. Many more people from his village, a few of his in-laws and one or two others from his mother's place had joined the grief-stricken party. One man whispered to another that it was the worst kind of madness, deep and tongue-tied.

"May it end ill for him who did this," prayed the other.

The first medicine-man his relatives consulted refused to take him on, out of some kind of integrity.

"I could say yes to you and take your money," he said. "But that is not my way. My powers of cure are known throughout Olu and Igbo but never have I professed to bring back to life a man who has sipped the spirit-waters of animmọ. It is the same with a madman who of his own accord delivers himself to the divinities of the market-place. You should have kept better watch over him."

"Don't blame us too much," said Nwibe's relative. "When he left home that morning his senses were as complete as yours and mine now. Don't blame us too much."

"Yes, I know. It happens that way sometimes. And they are the ones that medicine will not reach. I know."

"Can you do nothing at all then, not even to untie his tongue?"

"Nothing can be done. They have already embraced him. It is like a man who runs away from the oppression of his fellows to the grove of an alusi and says to him: Take me, oh spirit, I am your osu. No man can touch him thereafter. He is free and yet no power can break his bondage. He is free of men but bonded to a god."

The second doctor was not as famous as the first and not so strict. He said the case was bad, very bad indeed, but no one folds his arms because the condition of his child is beyond hope. He must still grope around and do his best. His hearers nodded in eager agreement. And then he muttered into his own inward ear: If doctors were to send away every patient whose cure they were uncertain of, how many of them would eat one meal in a whole week from their practice?

Nwibe was cured of his madness. That humble practitioner who did the miracle became overnight the most celebrated mad-doctor of his generation. They called him Sojourner to the Land of the Spirits. Even so it remains true that madness may indeed sometimes depart but never with all his clamorous train. Some of these always remain — the trailers of madness you might call them — to haunt the doorway of the eyes. For how could a man be the same again of whom witnesses from all the lands of Olu and Igbo have once reported that they saw today a fine, hefty man in his prime, stark naked, tearing through the crowds to answer the call of the market-place? Such a man is marked for ever.

Nwibe became a quiet, withdrawn man avoiding whenever he could the boisterous side of the life of his people. Two years later, before another initiation season, he made a new inquiry about joining the community of titled men in his town. Had they received him perhaps he might have become at least partially restored, but those o_zo_ men, dignified and polite as ever, deftly steered the conversation away to other matters.

Questions for Discussion

1. Why is the first traveler identified as a "madman"? Were you surprised by this label? Does it seem appropriate?
2. In what way might the madman's claims about what Nwibe has done to him be true? What does the madman's theft of Nwibe's cloth symbolize?
3. Why do the villagers think that Nwibe is mad? When the second doctor is able to help Nwibe, what does this "cure" imply about the nature of psychiatric medicine in the society where the story is set?
4. Why doesn't Nwibe get to join the o_zo_ men? What is the significance of their rejection of him?
5. What special powers does the marketplace seem to have? What does the marketplace represent?

Ideas for Writing

1. Write an essay in which you discuss the agreed-on definition of madness within the society portrayed in the story. Is this a definition that would be acceptable within your culture? Is the story's definition of madness accurate?
2. Write a story about an ordinary person in modern American society who is mistakenly seen as mad.

JOHN BARTH   (b. 1930)

Influenced by Jorge Luis Borges, Samuel Beckett, and other modernists, John Barth's writing is distinguished by the use of parody, social satire, and self-conscious narrators who invite the reader into the process of writing and telling the story. Growing up in Cambridge, Maryland, Barth was originally interested in music. After high school, he studied at the Juilliard School of Music in New York City but later majored in journalism at Johns Hopkins University, where he earned his M.A. in 1952. Barth published the first of his experimental fictions, *The Floating Opera*, in 1956; he has written seven other novels, the best known of which are *The Sot-Weed Factor* (1960), *Giles Goatboy* (1966), and *The Last Voyage of Somebody the Sailor* (1991). Barth's stories and novellas are collected in *Lost in the Funhouse* (1968); *Chimera* (1972), for which he received the National Book Award; and *On with the Story* (1996).

Like Borges, Barth loves reading and mental play, enjoying what he calls "improvising like a jazzman" in a wide range of literary forms. Of his story "Autobiography: A Self-Recorded Fiction," Barth notes in the introduction to *Lost in the Funhouse* that it was originally written for performance on "monophonic tape and visible but silent author." Barth interprets the title "Autobiography" as meaning "self-composition" rather than autobiography in the traditional sense, emphasizing that the story should be seen as "speaking of itself" and that "I [Barth] am its father; its mother is the recording machine."

Autobiography: A Self-Recorded Fiction   (1968)

You who   listen   give me life   in a manner of speaking.

I won't hold you responsible.

My first words weren't my first words. I wish I'd begun differently.

Among other things I haven't a proper name. The one I bear's misleading, if not false. I didn't choose it either.

I don't recall asking to be conceived! Neither did my parents come to think of it. Even so. Score to be settled. Children are vengeance.

I seem to've known myself from the beginning without knowing I knew; no news is good news; perhaps I'm mistaken.

Now that I reflect I'm not enjoying this life: my link with the world.

My situation appears to me as follows: I speak in a curious, detached manner, and don't necessarily hear myself. I'm grateful for small mercies. Whether anyone follows me I can't tell.

Are you there? If so I'm blind and deaf to you, or you are me, or both're both. One may be imaginary; I've had stranger ideas. I hope I'm a fiction without real hope. Where there's a voice there's a speaker.

I see I see myself as a halt narrative: first person, tiresome. Pronoun sans ante or precedent, warrant or respite. Surrogate for the substantive; contentless form, interestless principle; blind eye blinking at nothing. Who am I. A little *crise d'identité* for you.

I must compose myself.

Look, I'm writing. No, listen, I'm nothing but talk; I won't last long. The odds against my conception were splendid; against my birth excellent; against my continuance favorable. Are yet. On the other hand, if my sort are permitted a certain age and growth, God help us, our life expectancy's been known to increase at an obscene rate instead of petering out. Let me squeak on long enough, I just might live forever: a word to the wise.

My beginning was comparatively interesting, believe it or not. Exposition. I was spawned not long since in an American state and born in no better. Grew in no worse. Persist in a representative. Prohibition, Depression, Radicalism, Decadence, and what have you. An eye sir for an eye. It's alleged, now, that Mother was a mere passing fancy who didn't pass quickly enough; there's evidence also that she was a mere novel device, just in style, soon to become a commonplace, to which Dad resorted one day when he found himself by himself with pointless pen. In either case she was mere, Mom; at any event Dad dallied. He has me to explain. Bear in mind, I suppose he told her. A child is not its parents, but sum of their conjoinèd shames. A figure of speech. Their manner of speaking. No wonder I'm heterodoxical.

Nothing lasts longer than a mood. Dad's infatuation passed; I remained. He understood, about time, that anything conceived in so unnatural and fugitive a fashion was apt to be freakish, even monstrous—and an advertisement of his folly. His second thought therefore was to destroy me before I spoke a word. He knew how these things work; he went by the book. To expose ourselves publicly is frowned upon; therefore we do it to one another in private. He me, I him: one was bound to be the case. What fathers can't forgive is that their offspring receive and so broadcast their shortcomings. From my conception to the present moment Dad's tried to turn me off; not ardently, not consistently, not successfully so far; but persistently, persistently, with at least half a heart. How do I know. I'm his bloody mirror!

Which is to say, upon reflection I reverse and distort him. For I suspect that my true father's sentiments are the contrary of murderous. That one only imagines he begot me; mightn't he be deceived and deadly jealous? In his heart of hearts he wonders whether I mayn't after all be the get of a nobler spirit, taken by beauty past his grasp. Or else, what comes to the same thing, to me, I've a pair of dads, to match my pair of moms. How account for my contradictions except as the vices of their versus? Beneath self-contempt, I particularly scorn my fondness for paradox. I despise pessimism, narcissism, solipsism, truculence, word-play, and pusillanimity, my chiefer inclinations; loathe self-loathers *ergo me;* have no pity for self-pity and so am free of that sweet baseness. I doubt I am. Being me's no joke.

I continue the tale of my forebears. Thus my exposure; thus my escape. This cursed me, turned me out; that, curse him, saved me; right hand slipped me through left's fingers. Unless on a third hand I somehow preserved myself. Unless unless: the mercy-killing was successful. Buzzards let us say made brunch of me betimes but couldn't stomach my voice, which persists like the Nauseous Danaid. We . . . monstrosities are easilier achieved than got rid of.

In sum I'm not what either parent or I had in mind. One hoped I'd be astonishing, forceful, triumphant—heroical in other words. One dead. I myself conventional. I turn out I. Not every kid thrown to the wolves ends a hero: for each survivor, a mountain of beast-baits; for every Oedipus, a city of feebs.

So much for my dramatic exposition: seems not to've worked. Here I am, Dad: Your creature! Your caricature!

Unhappily, things get clearer as we go along. I perceive that I have no body. What's less, I've been speaking of myself without delight or alternative as self-consciousness pure and sour; I declare now that even that isn't true. I'm not aware of myself at all, as far as I know. I don't think . . . I know what I'm talking about.

Well, well, being well into my life as it's been called I see well how it'll end, unless in some meaningless surprise. If anything dramatic were going to happen to make me successfuller . . . agreeabler . . . endurabler . . . it should've happened by now, we will agree. A change for the better still isn't unthinkable; miracles can be cited. But the odds against a wireless *deus ex machina* aren't encouraging.

Here, a confession: Early on I too aspired to immortality. Assumed I'd be beautiful, powerful, loving, loved. At least commonplace. Anyhow human. Even the revelation of my several defects—absence of presence to name one—didn't fetch me right to despair: crippledness affords its own heroisms, does it not; heroes are typically gimpish, are they not. But your crippled hero's one thing, a bloody hero after all; your heroic cripple another, etcetcetcetcet. Being an ideal's warpèd image, my fancy's own twist figure, is what undoes me.

I wonder if I repeat myself. One-track minds may lead to their origins. Perhaps I'm still in utero, hung up in my delivery; my exposition and the rest merely foreshadow what's to come, the argument for an interrupted pregnancy.

Womb, coffin, can—in any case, from my viewless viewpoint I see no point in going further. Since Dad among his other failings failed to end me when he should've, I'll turn myself off if I can this instant.

Can't. *Then if anyone hears me, speaking from here inside like a sunk sub-mariner, and has the means to my end, I pray him do us both a kindness.*

Didn't. Very well, my ace in the hole: *Father, have mercy, I dare you! Wretched old fabricator, where's your shame? Put an end to this, for pity's sake! Now! Now!*

So. My last trump, and I blew it. Not much in the way of a climax; more a climacteric. I'm not the dramatic sort. May the end come quietly, then, without my knowing it. In the course of my breath. In the heart of any word. This one. This one.

Perhaps I'll have a posthumous cautionary value, like gibbeted corpses, pickled freaks. Self-preservation, it seems, may smell of formaldehyde.

A proper ending wouldn't spin out so.

I suppose I might have managed things to better effect, in spite of the old boy. Too late now.

Basket case. Waste.

Shark up some memorable last words at least. There seems to be time.

Nonsense, I'll mutter to the end, one word after another, string the rascals out, mad or not, heard or not, my last words will be my last words

Questions for Discussion

1. Who is the "self" that is doing the recording? Why is it significant that the auto-biography is a "fiction"?

2. If "you who listen" (presumably readers) give the speaker/character in the story "life," why doesn't the speaker/character hold the reader "responsible"? According to the story, who or what is ultimately responsible for the meaning and moral significance of a fictional text?

3. The speaker contemplates his/her immortality: "Let me squeak on long enough, I just might live forever." What does this line imply about the life span of written texts?

4. Because so much of the "life" of the speaker exists solely in words, it is not surprising that there is a special emphasis on such "depth" techniques as puns and ambiguities. Give examples of puns and ambiguous language in the text and then relate these to the observations they make about the origins and "life" of written texts.

5. Why does the speaker's father want to destroy the speaker "before [the speaker] spoke a word"? What distinction is made between the speaker's "true father" and his "murderous" father?

Ideas for Writing

1. In an essay, evaluate the story as a literary experiment. Is the speaker's self-evaluation at the story's conclusion accurate? What impact does this evaluation have on the reader's interpretation of the story? Is this a successful story? a failed literary experiment?

2. Write a story narrated by a character in a story who is aware of himself or herself as a fictional character and of you as his or her creator.

DONALD BARTHELME   (1931–1989)

One of the most innovative American writers of the 1960s and 1970s, Donald Barthelme used irony, parody, and unusual forms that drastically extended the range of the short story. Originally from Philadelphia, Barthelme grew up in Houston and attended the University of Houston. After college he moved to New York City, where he pursued a varied career, editing literary magazines, directing museums, teaching creative writing, and writing for the *New Yorker*. His novels include *Snow White* (1967) and *The Dead Father* (1975); his many short-story collections include *Come Back, Dr. Caligari* (1964); *In Sadness* (1973), from which "The Sandman" is taken; and *Amateurs* (1976). His later works include *Liquid City* (1987) and *Forty Stories* (1989).

Barthelme often used self-conscious narrators and played with the styles of European authors such as Fyodor Dostoyevski and Franz Kafka, creating dreamlike and often discontinuous story lines while poking fun at modern institutions and lifestyles.

The Sandman   (1971)

Dear Dr. Hodder, I realize that it is probably wrong to write a letter to one's girl friend's shrink but there are several things going on here that I think ought to be pointed out to you. I thought of making a personal visit but the situation then, as I'm sure you understand, would be completely untenable — I would be *visiting a psychiatrist*. I also understand that in writing to you I am in some sense interfering with the process but you don't have to discuss with Susan what I have said. Please consider this an "eyes only" letter. Please think of it as personal and confidential.

You must be aware, first, that because Susan is my girl friend pretty much everything she discusses with you she also discusses with me. She tells me what she said and what you said. We have been seeing each other for about six months now and I am pretty familiar with her story, or stories. Similarly, with your responses, or at least the general pattern. I know, for example, that my habit of referring to you as "the sandman" annoys you but let me assure you that I mean nothing unpleasant by it. It is simply a nickname. The reference is to the old rhyme: "Sea-sand does the sandman bring / Sleep to end the day / He dusts the children's eyes with sand / And steals their dreams away." (This is a variant; there are other versions, but this is the one I prefer.) I also understand that you are a little bit shaky because the prestige of analysis is now, as I'm sure you know far better than I, at a nadir. This must tend to make you nervous and who can blame you? One always tends to get a little bit shook when one's methodology is in question. Of course! (By the bye, let me say that I am very pleased that you are one of the ones that talk, instead of just sitting there. I think that's a good thing, an excellent thing, I congratulate you.)

To the point, I fully understand that Susan's wish to terminate with you and buy a piano instead has disturbed you. You have every right to be disturbed and to say that she is not electing the proper course, that what she says conceals something else, that she is evading reality, etc., etc. Go ahead. But there is one possibility here that you might be, just might be, missing. Which is that she means it.

Susan says: "I want to buy a piano."

You think: she wishes to terminate the analysis and escape into the piano.

Or: Yes, it is true that her father wanted her to be a concert pianist and that she studied for twelve years with Goetzmann. But she does not really want to reopen that can of maggots. She wants me to disapprove.

Or: Having failed to achieve a career as a concert pianist, she wishes to fail again. She is now too old to achieve the original objective. The spontaneous organization of defeat!

Or: She is flirting again.

Or:

Or:

Or:

Or:

The one thing you cannot consider, by the nature of your training and of the discipline itself, is that she really might want to terminate the analysis and buy a piano. That the piano might be more necessary and valuable to her than the analysis.[1]

What we really have to consider here is the locus of hope. Does hope reside in the analysis or rather in the piano? As a shrink rather than a piano salesman you would naturally tend to opt for the analysis. But there are differences. The piano salesman can stand behind his product; you, unfortunately, cannot. A Steinway is a known quantity, whereas an analysis can succeed or fail. I don't reproach you for this, I simply note it. (An interesting question: Why do laymen feel such a desire to, in plain language, fuck over shrinks? As I am doing here, in a sense? I don't mean hostility in the psychoanalytic encounter, I mean in general. This is an interesting phenomenon and should be investigated by somebody.)

It might be useful if I gave you a little taste of my own experience of analysis. I only went five or six times. Dr. Behring was a tall thin man who never said anything much. If you could get a "What comes to mind?" out of him you were doing splendidly. There was a little incident that is, perhaps, illustrative. I went for my hour one day and told him about something I was

---

[1] For an admirable discussion of this sort of communication failure and many other matters of interest see Percy, "Toward a Triadic Theory of Meaning." *Psychiatry*, Vol. 35 (February 1972), pp. 6–14 *et seq.*

worried about. (I was then working for a newspaper down in Texas.) There was a story that four black teenagers had come across a little white boy, about ten, in a vacant lot, sodomized him repeatedly and then put him inside a refrigerator and closed the door (this was before they had that requirement that abandoned refrigerators had to have their doors removed) and he suffocated. I don't know to this day what actually happened, but the cops had picked up *some* black kids and were reportedly beating the shit out of them in an effort to make them confess. I was not on the police run at that time but one of the police reporters told me about it and I told Dr. Behring. A good liberal, he grew white with anger and said what was I doing about it? It was the first time he had talked. So I was shaken — it hadn't occurred to me that I was required to do something about it, he was right — and after I left I called my then sister-in-law, who was at that time secretary to a City Councilman. As you can imagine, such a position is a very powerful one — the councilmen are mostly off making business deals and the executive secretaries run the office — and she got on to the chief of police with an inquiry as to what was going on and if there was any police brutality involved and if so, how much. The case was a very sensational one, you see; *Ebony* had a writer down there trying to cover it but he couldn't get in to see the boys and the cops had roughed him up some, they couldn't understand at that time that there could be such a thing as a black reporter. They understood that they had to be a little careful with the white reporters, but a black reporter was beyond them. But my sister-in-law threw her weight (her Councilman's weight) around a bit and suggested to the chief that if there was a serious amount of brutality going on the cops had better stop it, because there was too much outside interest in the case and it would be extremely bad PR if the brutality stuff got out. I also called a guy I knew pretty high up in the sheriff's department and suggested that *he* suggest to his colleagues that they cool it. I hinted at unspeakable political urgencies and he picked it up. The sheriff's department was separate from the police department, but they both operated out of the Courthouse Building and they interacted quite a bit, in the normal course. So the long and short of it was that the cops decided to show the four black kids at a press conference to demonstrate that they weren't really beat all to rags, and that took place at four in the afternoon. I went and the kids looked O.K., except for one whose teeth were out and who the cops said had fallen down the stairs. Well, we all know the falling-down-the-stairs story but the point was the *degree* of mishandling and it was clear that the kids had not been half-killed by the cops, as the rumor stated. They were walking and talking naturally, although scared to death, as who would not be? There weren't any TV pictures because the newspaper people always pulled out the plugs of the TV people, at important moments, in those days — it was a standard thing. Now while I admit it sounds callous to be talking about the degree of brutality being minimal, let me tell you that it was no small matter, in that time and place, to force the cops to show the kids to the press at all. It was an achievement, of sorts. So about eight o'clock I called Dr. Behring at home, I hope interrupting his supper, and told him that the kids were O.K., relatively, and he said that was fine, he was glad to hear it. They were later no-billed and I stopped seeing him. That was my experience of analysis and that it may have left me a little sour, I freely grant. Allow for this bias.

To continue. I take exception to your remark that Susan's "openness" is a form of voyeurism. This remark interested me for a while, until I thought about it. Voyeurism I take to be an eroticized expression of curiosity whose chief phenomenological characteristic is the distance maintained between the voyeur and the object. The tension between the desire to draw near the object and the necessity to maintain the distance becomes a libidinous energy nondischarge, which is what the voyeur seeks.[2] The tension. But your remark indicates, in my opinion, a radical misreading of the problem. Susan's "openness" — a willingness of the heart, if you will allow such a term — is not at all comparable to the activities of the voyeur. Susan draws near. Distance is not her thing — not by a long chalk. Frequently, as you know, she gets burned, but she always tries again. What is operating here, I suggest, is an attempt on your part to "stabilize" Susan's behavior in reference to a state-of-affairs that you feel should obtain. Susan gets married and lives happily ever after. Or: There is within Susan a certain amount of creativity which should be liberated and actualized. Susan becomes an artist and lives happily ever after.

But your norms are, I suggest, skewing your view of the problem, and very badly.

Let us take the first case. You reason: If Susan is happy or at least functioning in the present state of affairs (that is, moving from man to man as a silver dollar moves from hand to hand), then why is she seeing a shrink? Something is wrong. New behavior is indicated. Susan is to get married and live happily ever after. May I offer another view? That is, that "seeing a shrink" might be precisely a maneuver in a situation in which Susan *does not want* to get married and live happily ever after? That getting married and living happily ever after might be, for Susan, the worst of fates, and that in order to validate her non-acceptance of this norm she defines herself to herself as shrink-needing? That you are actually certifying the behavior which you seek to change? (When she says to you that she's not shrinkable, you should listen.)

Perhaps, Dr. Hodder, my logic is feeble, perhaps my intuitions are frail. It is, God knows, a complex and difficult question. Your perception that Susan is an artist of some kind *in potentia* is, I think, an acute one. But the proposition "Susan becomes an artist and lives happily ever after" is ridiculous. (I realize that I am couching the proposition in such terms — "happily ever after" — that it is ridiculous on the face of it, but there is ridiculousness piled

[2] See, for example, Straus, "Shame As a Historiological Problem," in *Phenomenological Psychology* (New York: Basic Books, 1966), p. 219.

upon ridiculousness.) Let me point out, if it has escaped your notice, that what an artist does, is fail. Any reading of the literature[3] (I mean the theory of artistic creation), however summary, will persuade you instantly that the paradigmatic artistic experience is that of failure. The actualization fails to meet, equal, the intuition. There is something "out there" which cannot be brought "here." This is standard. I don't mean bad artists, I mean good artists. There is no such thing as a "successful artist" (except, of course, in worldly terms). The proposition should read, "Susan becomes an artist and lives unhappily ever after." This is the case. Don't be deceived.

What I am saying is, that the therapy of choice is not clear. I deeply sympathize. You have a dilemma.

I ask you to note, by the way, that Susan's is not a seeking after instant gratification as dealt out by so-called encounter or sensitivity groups, nude marathons, or dope. None of this is what is going down. "Joy" is not Susan's bag. I praise her for seeking out you rather than getting involved with any of this other idiocy. Her forte, I would suggest, is mind, and if there are games being played they are being conducted with taste, decorum, and some amount of intellectual rigor. Not-bad games. When I take Susan out to dinner she does not order chocolate-covered ants, even if they are on the menu. (Have you, by the way, tried Alfredo's, at the corner of Bank and Hudson streets? It's wonderful.) (Parenthetically, the problem of analysts sleeping with their patients is well known and I understand that Susan has been routinely seducing you—a reflex, she can't help it—throughout the analysis. I understand that there is a new splinter group of therapists, behaviorists of some kind, who take this to be some kind of ethic? Is this true? Does this mean that they do it only when they want to, or whether they want to or not? At a dinner party the other evening a lady analyst was saying that three cases of this kind had recently come to her attention and she seemed to think that this was rather a lot. The problem of maintaining mentorship is, as we know, not easy. I think you have done very well in this regard, and God knows it must have been difficult, given those skirts Susan wears that unbutton up to the crotch and which she routinely leaves unbuttoned to the third button.)

Am I wandering too much for you? Bear with me. The world is waiting for the sunrise.

We are left, I submit, with the problem of her depressions. They are, I agree, terrible. Your idea that I am not "supportive" enough is, I think, wrong. I have found, as a practical matter, that the best thing to do is to just do ordinary things, read the newspaper for example, or watch basketball, or wash the dishes. That seems to allow her to come out of it better than any amount of so-called "support." (About the *chasmus hystericus* or hysterical yawning I

---

[3] Especially, perhaps, Ehrenzweig, *The Hidden Order of Art* (University of California Press, 1966), pp. 234–9.

don't worry any more. It is masking behavior, of course, but after all, you must allow us our tics. The world is waiting for the sunrise.) What do you do with a patient who finds the world unsatisfactory? The world *is* unsatisfactory; only a fool would deny it. I know that your own ongoing psychic structuralization is still going on—you are thirty-seven and I am forty-one—but you must be old enough by now to realize that shit is shit. Susan's perception that America has somehow got hold of the greed ethic and that the greed ethic has turned America into a tidy little hell is not, I think, wrong. What do you do with such a perception? Apply Band-Aids, I suppose. About her depressions, I wouldn't do anything. I'd leave them alone. Put on a record.[4]

Let me tell you a story.

One night we were at her place, about three A.M., and this man called, another lover, quite a well-known musician who is very good, very fast—a good man. He asked Susan "Is he there?," meaning me, and she said "Yes," and he said "What are you doing?," and she said, "What do you think?," and he said, "When will you be finished?," and she said, "Never." Are you, Doctor dear, in a position to appreciate the beauty of this reply, in this context?

What I am saying is that Susan is wonderful. *As is.* There are not so many things around to which that word can be accurately applied. Therefore I must view your efforts to improve her with, let us say, a certain amount of ambivalence. If this makes me a negative factor in the analysis, so be it. I will be a negative factor until the cows come home, and cheerfully. I can't help it, Doctor, I am voting for the piano.

With best wishes,

Questions for Discussion

1. Why does the narrator write a letter to his girlfriend's psychiatrist? Why does he call him "the sandman"?

2. What arguments does the boyfriend present to convince the psychiatrist that Susan needs no further analysis and can function independently? How convincing are they? What responses might the psychiatrist make to them?

3. The boyfriend uses the device of the story-within-a-story to share some of his own experiences in psychoanalysis with his girlfriend's doctor. What is the point of the story he tells about Dr. Behring, the liberal therapist from Texas? What impact would such a story have, if any, on Susan's psychiatrist?

4. The narrator uses footnotes to lend authority to his arguments. How effective and appropriate are they? Do they represent a parody of scholarly writing? Do they reflect the boyfriend's effort to impress the psychiatrist?

5. How does the narrator critique psychoanalysis? Does the critique seem valid? Does the narrator's bias undermine the validity of his arguments?

---

[4] For example, Harrison, "Wah Wah," Apple Records STCH 639, Side One, Track 3.

Ideas for Writing

1. Write an essay in which you discuss the way that the story satirizes contemporary single urban lifestyles.

2. Write a story in which a character writes a letter to someone with whom he or she would never ordinarily communicate, a letter not necessarily intended to be mailed.

ALICE MUNRO   (b. 1931)

Known for their psychological realism and gentle humor, Alice Munro's stories often explore the difficulties of establishing permanent and honest relationships in a world without consistent values and moral standards, where people often feel alienated, confused, trapped, and frustrated. Her stories are set in the rural area of Wingham, Ontario, where Munro was born and raised. Munro knew by the time she was fifteen that she wanted to be a writer, and after attending the University of Western Ontario for two years she moved to British Columbia with her husband and began her writing career. Her sole novel, *Lives of Girls and Women* (1971), won the Canadian Booksellers' Award, and her first collection of short stories, *Dance of the Happy Shades* (1968), won the Governor General's Literary Award (1968), the highest literary award in Canada, an honor she has received for two of her subsequent collections. These include *Something I've Been Meaning to Tell You* (1974), *The Beggar Maid* (1979), and *The Progress of Love* (1986), which contains "Circle of Prayer." Her most recent collection, *Selected Stories,* was published in 1996.

Fellow writer Joyce Carol Oates has praised Munro's "effortless, almost conversational tone" and her "evocation of emotions, ranging from bitter hatred to love, from bewilderment and resentment to awe."

Circle of Prayer   (1986)

Trudy threw a jug across the room. It didn't reach the opposite wall; it didn't hurt anybody, it didn't even break.

This was the jug without a handle — cement-colored with brown streaks on it, rough as sandpaper to the touch — that Dan made the winter he took pottery classes. He made six little handleless cups to go with it. The jug and the cups were supposed to be for sake, but the local liquor store doesn't carry sake. Once, they brought some home from a trip, but they didn't really like it. So the jug Dan made sits on the highest open shelf in the kitchen, and a few odd items of value are kept in it. Trudy's wedding ring and her engagement ring, the medal Robin won for all-round excellence in Grade 8, a long, two-strand necklace of jet beads that belonged to Dan's mother and was willed to Robin. Trudy won't let her wear it yet.

Trudy came home from work a little after midnight; she entered the house in the dark. Just the little stove light was on — she and Robin always left that on for each other. Trudy didn't need any other light. She climbed up on a chair without even letting go of her bag, got down the jug, and fished around inside it.

It was gone. Of course. She had known it would be gone.

She went through the dark house to Robin's room, still with her bag over her arm, the jug in her hand. She turned on the overhead light. Robin groaned and turned over, pulled the pillow over her head. Shamming.

"Your grandmother's necklace," Trudy said. "Why did you do that? Are you insane?"

Robin shammed a sleepy groan. All the clothes she owned, it seemed, old and new and clean and dirty, were scattered on the floor, on the chair, the desk, the dresser, even on the bed itself. On the wall was a huge poster showing a hippopotamus, with the words underneath "Why Was I Born So Beautiful?" And another poster showing Terry Fox running along a rainy highway, with a whole cavalcade of cars behind him. Dirty glasses, empty yogurt containers, school notes, a Tampax still in its wrapper, the stuffed snake and tiger Robin had had since before she went to school, a collage of pictures of her cat Sausage, who had been run over two years ago. Red and blue ribbons that she had won for jumping, or running, or throwing basketballs.

"You answer me!" said Trudy. "You tell me why you did it!"

She threw the jug. But it was heavier than she'd thought, or else at the very moment of throwing it she lost conviction, because it didn't hit the wall; it fell on the rug beside the dresser and rolled on the floor, undamaged.

You threw a jug at me that time. You could have killed me.

Not at you. I didn't throw it at you.

You could have killed me.

Proof that Robin was shamming: She started up in a fright, but it wasn't the blank fright of somebody who'd been asleep. She looked scared, but underneath that childish, scared look was another look — stubborn, calculating, disdainful.

"It was so beautiful. And it was valuable. It belonged to your grandmother."

"I thought it belonged to me," said Robin.

"That girl wasn't even your friend. Christ, you didn't have a good word to say for her this morning."

"You don't know who is my friend!" Robin's face flushed a bright pink and her eyes filled with tears, but her scornful, stubborn expression didn't change. "I knew her. I talked to her. So get out!"

Trudy works at the Home for Mentally Handicapped Adults. Few people call it that. Older people in town still say "the Misses Weir's house," and a number of others, including Robin — and, presumably, most of those her age — call it the Half-Wit House.

The house has a ramp now for wheelchairs, because some of the mentally handicapped may be physically handicapped as well, and it has a swimming pool in the back yard, which caused a certain amount of discussion when it was installed at taxpayers' expense. Otherwise the house looks pretty much the way it always did — the white wooden walls, the dark-green curlicues on the gables, the steep roof and dark screened side porch, and the deep lawn in front shaded by soft maple trees.

This month, Trudy works the four-to-midnight shift. Yesterday afternoon, she parked her car in front and walked up the drive thinking how nice the house looked, peaceful as in the days of the Misses Weir, who must have served iced tea and read library books, or played croquet, whatever people did then.

Always some piece of news, some wrangle or excitement, once you get inside. The men came to fix the pool but they didn't fix it. They went away again. It isn't fixed yet.

"We don't get no use of it, soon summer be over," Josephine said.

"It's not even the middle of June, you're saying summer'll be over," Kelvin said. "You think before you talk. Did you hear about the young girl that was killed out in the country?" he said to Trudy.

Trudy had started to mix two batches of frozen lemonade, one pink and one plain. When he said that, she smashed the spoon down on the frozen chunk so hard that some of the liquid spilled over.

"How, Kelvin?"

She was afraid she would hear that a girl was dragged off a country road, raped in the woods, strangled, beaten, left there. Robin goes running along the country roads in her white shorts and T-shirt, a headband on her flying hair. Robin's hair is golden; her legs and arms are golden. Her cheeks and limbs are downy, not shiny — you wouldn't be surprised to see a cloud of pollen delicately floating and settling behind her when she runs. Cars hoot at her and she isn't bothered. Foul threats are yelled at her, and she yells foul threats back.

"Driving a truck," Kelvin said.

Trudy's heart eased. Robin doesn't know how to drive yet.

"Fourteen years old, she didn't know how to drive," Kelvin said. "She got in the truck, and the first thing you know, she ran it into a tree. Where was her parents? That's what I'd like to know. They weren't watching out for her. She got in the truck when she didn't know how to drive and ran it into a tree. Fourteen. That's too young."

Kelvin goes uptown by himself; he hears all the news. He is fifty-two years old, still slim and boyish-looking, well-shaved, with soft, short, clean dark hair. He goes to the barbershop every day, because he can't quite manage to shave himself. Epilepsy, then surgery, an infected bone-flap, many more operations, a permanent mild difficulty with feet and fingers, a gentle head fog. The fog doesn't obscure facts, just motives. Perhaps he shouldn't be in the Home at all, but where else? Anyway, he likes it. He says he likes it. He tells the others they shouldn't complain; they should be more careful, they should behave themselves. He picks up the soft-drink cans and beer bottles that people have thrown into the front yard — though of course it isn't his job to do that.

When Janet came in just before midnight to relieve Trudy, she had the same story to tell.

"I guess you heard about that fifteen-year-old girl?"

When Janet starts telling you something like this, she always starts off with "I guess you heard." *I guess you heard Wilma and Ted are breaking up,* she says. *I guess you heard Alvin Stead had a heart attack.*

"Kelvin told me," Trudy said. "Only he said she was fourteen."

"Fifteen," Janet said. "She must've been in Robin's class at school. She didn't know how to drive. She didn't even get out of the lane."

"Was she drunk?" said Trudy. Robin won't go near alcohol, or dope, or cigarettes, or even coffee, she's so fanatical about what she puts into her body.

"I don't think so. Stoned, maybe. It was early in the evening. She was home with her sister. Their parents were out. Her sister's boyfriend came over — it was his truck, and he either gave her the keys to the truck or she took them. You hear different versions. You hear that they sent her out for something, they wanted to get rid of her, and you hear she just took the keys and went. Anyway, she ran it right into a tree in the lane."

"Jesus," said Trudy.

"I know. It's so idiotic. It's getting so you hate to think about your kids growing up. Did everybody take their medication okay? What's Kelvin watching?"

Kelvin was still up, sitting in the living room watching TV.

"It's somebody being interviewed. He wrote a book about schizophrenics," Trudy told Janet.

Anything he comes across about mental problems, Kelvin has to watch, or try to read.

"I think it depresses him, the more he watches that kind of thing," Janet said. "Do you know I found out today I have to make five hundred roses out of pink Kleenex for my niece Laurel's wedding? For the car. She said I promised I'd make the roses for the car. Well, I didn't. I don't remember promising a thing. Are you going to come over and help me?"

"Sure," said Trudy.

"I guess the real reason I want him to get off the schizophrenics is I want to watch the old *Dallas,*" said Janet. She and Trudy disagree about this. Trudy can't stand to watch those old reruns of *Dallas,* to see the characters, with their younger, plumper faces, going through tribulations and bound up in romantic complications they and the audience have now forgotten all about. That's what's so hilarious, Janet says; it's so unbelievable it's wonderful. All that happens and they just forget about it and go on. But to Trudy it doesn't seem so unbelievable that the characters would go from one thing to the next thing—forgetful, hopeful, photogenic, forever changing their clothes. That it's not so unbelievable is the thing she really can't stand.

Robin, the next morning, said, "Oh, probably. All those people she hung around with drink. They party all the time. They're self-destructive. It's her own fault. Even if her sister told her to go, she didn't have to go. She didn't have to be so stupid."

"What was her name?" Trudy said.

"Tracy Lee," said Robin with distaste. She stepped on the pedal of the garbage tin, lifted rather than lowered the container of yogurt she had just emptied, and dropped it in. She was wearing bikini underpants and a T-shirt that said "If I Want to Listen to an Asshole, I'll Fart."

"That shirt still bothers me," Trudy said. "Some things are disgusting but funny, and some things are more disgusting than funny."

"What's the problem?" said Robin. "I sleep alone."

Trudy sat outside, in her wrapper, drinking coffee while the day got hot. There is a little brick-paved space by the side door that she and Dan always called the patio. She sat there. This is a solar-heated house, with big panels of glass in the south-sloping roof—the oddest-looking house in town. It's odd inside, too, with the open shelves in the kitchen instead of cupboards, and the living room up some stairs, looking out over the fields at the back. She and Dan, for a joke, gave parts of it the most conventional, suburban-sounding names—the patio, the powder room, the master bedroom. Dan always had to joke about the way he was living. He built the house himself—Trudy did a lot of the painting and staining—and it was a success. Rain didn't leak in around the panels, and part of the house's heat really did come from the sun. Most people who have the ideas, or ideals, that Dan has aren't very practical. They can't fix things or make things; they don't understand wiring or carpentry, or whatever it is they need to understand. Dan is good at everything—at gardening, cutting wood, building a house. He is especially good at repairing motors. He used to travel around getting jobs as an auto mechanic, a small-engines repairman. That's how he ended up here. He came here to visit Marlene, got a job as a mechanic, became a working partner in an auto-repair business, and before he knew it—married to Trudy, not Marlene—he was a small-town businessman, a member of the Kinsmen. All without shaving off his nineteen-sixties beard or trimming his hair any more than he wanted to. The town was too small and Dan was too smart for that to be necessary.

Now Dan lives in a townhouse in Richmond Hill with a girl named Genevieve. She is studying law. She was married when she was very young, and has three little children. Dan met her three years ago when her camper broke down a few miles outside of town. He told Trudy about her that night. The rented camper, the three little children hardly more than babies, the lively little divorced mother with her hair in pigtails. Her bravery, her poverty, her plans to enter law school. If the camper hadn't been easily fixed, he was going to invite her and her children to spend the night. She was on her way to her parents' summer place at Pointe au Baril.

"Then she can't be all that poor," Trudy said.

"You can be poor and have rich parents," Dan said.

"No, you can't."

Last summer, Robin went to Richmond Hill for a month's visit. She came home early. She said it was a madhouse. The oldest child has to go to a special reading clinic, the middle one wets the bed. Genevieve spends all her time in the law library, studying. No wonder. Dan shops for bargains, cooks, looks after the children, grows vegetables, drives a taxi on Saturdays and Sundays. He wants to set up a motorcycle-repair business in the garage, but he can't get a permit; the neighbors are against it.

He told Robin he was happy. Never happier, he said. Robin came home firmly grownup — severe, sarcastic, determined. She had some slight, steady grudge she hadn't had before. Trudy couldn't worm it out of her, couldn't tease it out of her; the time when she could do that was over.

Robin came home at noon and changed her clothes. She put on a light, flowered cotton blouse and ironed a pale-blue cotton skirt. She said that some of the girls from the class might be going around to the funeral home after school.

"I forgot you had that skirt," said Trudy. If she thought that was going to start a conversation, she was mistaken.

The first time Trudy met Dan, she was drunk. She was nineteen years old, tall and skinny (she still is), with a wild head of curly black hair (it is cropped short now and showing the gray as black hair does). She was very tanned, wearing jeans and a tie-dyed T-shirt. No brassière and no need. This was in Muskoka in August, at a hotel bar where they had a band. She was camping with girlfriends. He was there with his fiancée, Marlene. He had taken Marlene home to meet his mother, who lived in Muskoka on an island in an empty hotel. When Trudy was nineteen, he was twenty-eight. She danced around by herself, giddy and drunk, in front of the table where he sat with Marlene, a meek-looking blonde with a big pink shelf of bosom all embroidered in little fake pearls. Trudy just danced in front of him until he got up and joined her. At the end of the dance, he asked her name, and took her back and introduced her to Marlene.

"This is Judy," he said. Trudy collapsed, laughing, into the chair beside Marlene's. Dan took Marlene up to dance. Trudy finished off Marlene's beer and went looking for her friends.

"How do you do?" she said to them. "I'm Judy!"

He caught up with her at the door of the bar. He had ditched Marlene when he saw Trudy leaving. A man who could change course quickly, see the possibilities, flare up with new enthusiasm. He told people later that he was in love with Trudy before he even knew her real name. But he told Trudy that he cried when he and Marlene were parting.

"I have feelings," he said. "I'm not ashamed to show them."

Trudy had no feelings for Marlene at all. Marlene was over thirty — what could she expect? Marlene still lives in town, works at the Hydro office, is not married. When Trudy and Dan were having one of their conversations about Genevieve, Trudy said, "Marlene must be thinking I got what's coming to me."

Dan said he had heard that Marlene had joined the Fellowship of Bible Christians. The women weren't allowed makeup and had to wear a kind of bonnet to church on Sundays.

"She won't be able to have a thought in her head but forgiving," Dan said. Trudy said, "I bet."

This is what happened at the funeral home, as Trudy got the story from both Kelvin and Janet.

The girls from Tracy Lee's class all showed up together after school. This was during what was called the visitation, when the family waited beside Tracy Lee's open casket to receive friends. Her parents were there, her married brother and his wife, her sister, and even her sister's boyfriend who owned the truck. They stood in a row and people lined up to say a few words to them. A lot of people came. They always do, in a case like this. Tracy Lee's grandmother was at the end of the row in a brocade-covered chair. She wasn't able to stand up for very long.

All the chairs at the funeral home are upholstered in this white-and-gold brocade. The curtains are the same, the wallpaper almost matches. There are little wall-bracket lights behind heavy pink glass. Trudy has been there several times and knows what it's like. But Robin and most of these girls had never been inside the place before. They didn't know what to expect. Some of them began to cry as soon as they got inside the door.

The curtains were closed. Soft music was playing — not exactly church music but it sounded like it. Tracy Lee's coffin was white with gold trim, matching all the brocade and the wallpaper. It had a lining of pleated pink satin. A pink satin pillow. Tracy Lee had not a mark on her face. She was not made up quite as usual, because the undertaker had done it. But she was wearing her favorite earrings, turquoise-colored triangles and yellow crescents, two to each ear. (Some people thought that was in bad taste.) On the part of the coffin that covered her from the waist down, there was a big heart-shaped pillow of pink roses.

The girls lined up to speak to the family. They shook hands, they said sorry-for-your-loss, just the way everybody else did. When they got through that, when all of them had let the grandmother squash their cool hands between her warm, swollen, freckled ones, they lined up again, in a straggling sort of way, and began to go past the coffin. Many were crying now, shivering. What could you expect? Young girls.

But they began to sing as they went past. With difficulty at first, shyly, but with growing confidence in their sad, sweet voices, they sang:

"Now, while the blossom still clings to the vine,
I'll taste your strawberries, I'll drink your sweet wine—"

They had planned the whole thing, of course, beforehand; they had got that song off a record. They believed that it was an old hymn.

So they filed past, singing, looking down at Tracy Lee, and it was noticed that they were dropping things into the coffin. They were slipping the rings off their fingers and the bracelets from their arms, and taking the earrings out of their ears. They were undoing necklaces, and bowing to pull chains and long strands of beads over their heads. Everybody gave something. All this jewellery went flashing and sparkling down on the dead girl, to lie beside her in her coffin. One girl pulled the bright combs out of her hair, let those go.

And nobody made a move to stop it. How could anyone interrupt? It was like a religious ceremony. The girls behaved as if they'd been told what to do, as if this was what was always done on such occasions. They sang, they wept, they dropped their jewellery. The sense of ritual made every one of them graceful.

The family wouldn't stop it. They thought it was beautiful.

"It was like church," Tracy Lee's mother said, and her grandmother said, "All those lovely young girls loved Tracy Lee. If they wanted to give their jewellery to show how they loved her, that's their business. It's not anybody else's business. I thought it was beautiful."

Tracy Lee's sister broke down and cried. It was the first time she had done so.

Dan said, "This is a test of love."

Of Trudy's love, he meant. Trudy started singing, "Please release me, let me go—"

She clapped a hand to her chest, danced in swoops around the room, singing. Dan was near laughing, near crying. He couldn't help it; he came and hugged her and they danced together, staggering. They were fairly drunk. All that June (it was two years ago), they were drinking gin, in between and during their scenes. They were drinking, weeping, arguing, explaining, and Trudy had to keep running to the liquor store. Yet she can't remember ever feeling really drunk or having a hangover. Except that she felt so tired all the time, as if she had logs chained to her ankles.

She kept joking. She called Genevieve "Jenny the Feeb."

"This is just like wanting to give up the business and become a potter," she said. "Maybe you should have done that. I wasn't really against it. You gave up on it. And when you wanted to go to Peru. We could still do that."

"All those things were just straws in the wind," Dan said.

"I should have known when you started watching the Ombudsman on TV," Trudy said. "It was the legal angle, wasn't it? You were never so interested in that kind of thing before."

"This will open life up for you, too," Dan said. "You can be more than just my wife."

"Sure. I think I'll be a brain surgeon."

"You're very smart. You're a wonderful woman. You're brave."

"Sure you're not talking about Jenny the Feeb?"

"No, you. You, Trudy. I still love you. You can't understand that I still love you."

Not for years had he had so much to say about how he loved her. He loved her skinny bones, her curly hair, her roughening skin, her way of coming into a room with a stride that shook the windows, her jokes, her clowning, her tough talk. He loved her mind and her soul. He always would. But the part of his life that had been bound up with hers was over.

"That is just talk. That is talking like an idiot!" Trudy said. "Robin, go back to bed!" For Robin in her skimpy nightgown was standing at the top of the steps.

"I can hear you yelling and screaming," Robin said.

"We weren't yelling and screaming," Trudy said. "We're trying to talk about something private."

"What?"

"I told you, it's something private."

When Robin sulked off to bed, Dan said, "I think we should tell her. It's better for kids to know. Genevieve doesn't have any secrets from her kids. Josie's only five, and she came into the bedroom one afternoon —"

Then Trudy did start yelling and screaming. She clawed through a cushion cover. "You stop telling me about your sweet fucking Genevieve and her sweet fucking bedroom and her asshole kids — you shut up, don't tell me anymore! You're just a big dribbling mouth without any brains. I don't care what you do, just shut up!"

Dan left. He packed a suitcase; he went off to Richmond Hill. He was back in five days. Just outside of town, he had stopped the car to pick Trudy a bouquet of wildflowers. He told her he was back for good, it was over.

"You don't say?" said Trudy.

But she put the flowers in water. Dusty pink milkweed flowers that smelled like face powder, black-eyed Susans, wild sweet peas, and orange lilies that must have got loose from old disappeared gardens.

"So you couldn't stand the pace?" she said.

"I knew you wouldn't fall all over me," Dan said. "You wouldn't be you if you did. And what I came back to is you."

She went to the liquor store, and this time bought champagne. For a month — it was still summer — they were back together being happy. She never really found out what had happened at Genevieve's house. Dan said he'd been having a middle-aged fit, that was all. He'd come to his senses. His life was here, with her and Robin.

"You're talking like a marriage-advice column," Trudy said.

"Okay. Forget the whole thing."

"We better," she said. She could imagine the kids, the confusion, the friends—old boyfriends, maybe—that he hadn't been prepared for. Jokes and opinions that he couldn't understand. That was possible. The music he liked, the way he talked—even his hair and his beard—might be out of style.

They went on family drives, picnics. They lay out in the grass behind the house at night, looking at the stars. The stars were a new interest of Dan's; he got a map. They hugged and kissed each other frequently and tried out some new things—or things they hadn't done for a long time—when they made love.

At this time, the road in front of the house was being paved. They'd built their house on a hillside at the edge of town, past the other houses, but trucks were using this street quite a bit now, avoiding the main streets, so the town was paving it. Trudy got so used to the noise and constant vibration she said she could feel herself jiggling all night, even when everything was quiet. Work started at seven in the morning. They woke up at the bottom of a river of noise. Dan dragged himself out of bed then, losing the hour of sleep that he loved best. There was a smell of diesel fuel in the air.

She woke up one night to find him not in bed. She listened to hear noises in the kitchen or the bathroom, but she couldn't. She got up and walked through the house. There were no lights on. She found him sitting outside, just outside the door, not having a drink or a glass of milk or a coffee, sitting with his back to the street.

Trudy looked out at the torn-up earth and the huge stalled machinery. "Isn't the quiet lovely?" she said.

He didn't say anything.

Oh. Oh.

She realized what she'd been thinking when she found his side of the bed empty and couldn't hear him anywhere in the house. Not that he'd left her, but that he'd done worse. Done away with himself. With all their happiness and hugging and kissing and stars and picnics, she could think that.

"You can't forget her," she said. "You love her."

"I don't know what to do."

She was glad just to hear him speak. She said, "You'll have to go and try again."

"There's no guarantee I can stay," he said. "I can't ask you to stand by."

"No," said Trudy. "If you go, that's it."

"If I go, that's it."

He seemed paralyzed. She felt that he might just sit there, repeating what she said, never be able to move or speak for himself again.

"If you feel like this, that's all there is to it," she said. "You don't have to choose. You're already gone."

That worked. He stood up stiffly, came over, and put his arms around her. He stroked her back.

"Come back to bed," he said. "We can rest for a little while yet."

"No. You've got to be gone when Robin wakes up. If we go back to bed, it'll just start all over again."

She made him a thermos of coffee. He packed the bag he had taken with him before. All Trudy's movements seemed skillful and perfect, as they never were, usually. She felt serene. She felt as if they were an old couple, moving in harmony, in wordless love, past injury, past forgiving. Their goodbye was hardly a ripple. She went outside with him. It was between four-thirty and five o'clock; the sky was beginning to lighten and the birds to wake, everything was drenched in dew. There stood the big harmless machinery, stranded in the ruts of the road.

"Good thing it isn't last night—you couldn't have got out," she said. She meant that the road hadn't been navigable. It was just yesterday that they had graded a narrow track for local traffic.

"Good thing," he said.

Goodbye.

"All I want is to know why you did it. Did you just do it for show? Like your father—for show? It's not the necklace so much. But it was a beautiful thing—I love jet beads. It was the only thing we had of your grandmother's. It was your right, but you have no right to take me by surprise like that. I deserve an explanation. I always loved jet beads. Why?"

"I blame the family," Janet says. "It was up to them to stop it. Some of the stuff was just plastic—those junk earrings and bracelets—but what Robin threw in, that was a crime. And she wasn't the only one. There were birthstone rings and gold chains. Somebody said a diamond cluster ring, but I don't know if I believe that. They said the girl inherited it, like Robin. You didn't ever have it evaluated, did you?"

"I don't know if jet is worth anything," Trudy says.

They are sitting in Janet's front room, making roses out of pink Kleenex.

"It's just stupid," Trudy says.

"Well. There is one thing you could do," says Janet. "I don't hardly know how to mention it."

"What?"

"Pray."

Trudy'd had the feeling, from Janet's tone, that she was going to tell her something serious and unpleasant, something about herself — Trudy — that was affecting her life and that everybody knew except her. Now she wants to laugh, after bracing herself. She doesn't know what to say.

"You don't pray, do you?" Janet says.

"I haven't got anything against it," Trudy says. "I wasn't brought up to be religious."

"It's not strictly speaking religious," Janet says. "I mean, it's not connected with any church. This is just some of us that pray. I can't tell you the names of anybody in it, but most of them you know. It's supposed to be secret. It's called the Circle of Prayer."

"Like at high school," Trudy says. "At high school there were secret societies, and you weren't supposed to tell who was in them. Only I wasn't."

"I was in everything going." Janet sighs. "This is actually more on the serious side. Though some people in it don't take it seriously enough, I don't think. Some people, they'll pray that they'll find a parking spot, or they'll pray they get good weather for their holidays. That isn't what it's for. But that's just individual praying. What the Circle is really about is, you phone up somebody that is in it and tell them what it is you're worried about, or upset about, and ask them to pray for you. And they do. And they phone one other person that's in the Circle, and they phone another and it goes all around, and we pray for one person, all together."

Trudy throws a rose away. "That's botched. Is it all women?"

"There isn't any rule it has to be. But it is, yes. Men would be too embarrassed. I was embarrassed at first. Only the first person you phone knows your name, who it is that's being prayed for, but in a town like this nearly everybody can guess. But if we started gossiping and ratting on each other it wouldn't work, and everybody knows that. So we don't. And it does work."

"Like how?" Trudy says.

"Well, one girl banged up her car. She did eight hundred dollars' damage, and it was kind of a tricky situation, where she wasn't sure her insurance would cover it, and neither was her husband — he was raging mad — but we all prayed, and the insurance came through without a hitch. That's only one example."

"There wouldn't be much point in praying to get the necklace back when it's in the coffin and the funeral's this morning," Trudy says.

"It's not up to you to say that. You don't say what's possible or impossible. You just ask for what you want. Because it says in the Bible, 'Ask and it shall be given.' How can you be helped if you won't ask? You can't, that's for sure. What about when Dan left — what if you'd prayed then? I wasn't in the Circle then, or I would have said something to you. Even if I knew you'd resist it, I would have said something. A lot of people resist. Now, even — it doesn't sound too great with that girl, but how do you know, maybe even now it might work? It might not be too late."

"All right," says Trudy, in a hard, cheerful voice. "All right." She pushes all the floppy flowers off her lap. "I'll just get down on my knees right now and pray that I get Dan back. I'll pray that I get the necklace back and I get Dan back, and why do I have to stop there? I can pray that Tracy Lee never died. I can pray that she comes back to life. Why didn't her mother ever think of that?"

Good news. The swimming pool is fixed. They'll be able to fill it tomorrow. But Kelvin is depressed. Early this afternoon — partly to keep them from bothering the men who were working on the pool — he took Marie and Josephine uptown. He let them get ice-cream cones. He told them to pay attention and eat the ice cream up quickly, because the sun was hot and it would melt. They licked at their cones now and then, as if they had all day. Ice cream was soon dribbling down their chins and down their arms. Kelvin had grabbed a handful of paper napkins, but he couldn't wipe it up fast enough. They were a mess. A spectacle. They didn't care. Kelvin told them they weren't so pretty that they could afford to look like that.

"Some people don't like the look of us anyway," he said. "Some people don't even think we should be allowed uptown. People just get used to seeing us and not staring at us like freaks and you make a mess and spoil it."

They laughed at him. He could have cowed Marie if he had her alone, but not when she was with Josephine. Josephine was one who needed some old-fashioned discipline, in Kelvin's opinion. Kelvin had been in places where people didn't get away with anything like they got away with here. He didn't agree with hitting. He had seen plenty of it done, but he didn't agree with it, even on the hand. But a person like Josephine could be shut up in her room. She could be made to sit in a corner, she could be put on bread and water, and it would do a lot of good. All Marie needed was a talking-to — she had a weak personality. But Josephine was a devil.

"I'll talk to both of them," Trudy says. "I'll tell them to say they're sorry."

"I want for them to *be* sorry," Kelvin says. "I don't care if they say they are. I'm not taking them ever again."

Later, when all the others are in bed, Trudy gets him to sit down to play cards with her on the screened veranda. They play Crazy Eights. Kelvin says that's all he can manage tonight; his head is sore.

Uptown, a man said to him, "Hey, which one of them two is your girlfriend?"

"Stupid," Trudy says. "He was a stupid jerk."

The man talking to the first man said, "Which one you going to marry?"

"They don't know you, Kelvin. They're just stupid."

But they did know him. One was Reg Hooper, one was Bud DeLisle. Bud DeLisle that sold real estate. They knew him. They had talked to him in the barbershop; they called him Kelvin. "Hey, Kelvin, which one you going to marry?"

"Nerds," says Trudy. "That's what Robin would say."

"You think they're your friend, but they're not," says Kelvin. "How many times I see that happen."

Trudy goes to the kitchen to put on coffee. She wants to have fresh coffee to offer Janet when she comes in. She apologized this morning, and Janet said all right, I know you're upset. It really is all right. Sometimes you think they're your friend, and they are.

She looks at all the mugs hanging on their hooks. She and Janet shopped all over to find them. A mug with each one's name. Marie, Josephine, Arthur, Kelvin, Shirley, George, Dorinda. You'd think Dorinda would be the hardest name to find, but actually the hardest was Shirley. Even the people who can't read have learned to recognize their own mugs, by color and pattern.

One day, two new mugs appeared, bought by Kelvin. One said Trudy, the other Janet.

"I'm not going to be too overjoyed seeing my name in that lineup," Janet said. "But I wouldn't hurt his feelings for a million dollars."

For a honeymoon, Dan took Trudy to the island on the lake where his mother's hotel was. The hotel was closed down, but his mother still lived there. Dan's father was dead, and she lived there alone. She took a boat with an outboard motor across the water to get her groceries. She sometimes made a mistake and called Trudy Marlene.

The hotel wasn't much. It was a white wooden box in a clearing by the shore. Some little boxes of cabins were stuck behind it. Dan and Trudy stayed in one of the cabins. Every cabin had a wood stove. Dan built a fire at night to take off the chill. But the blankets were damp and heavy when he and Trudy woke up in the morning.

Dan caught fish and cooked them. He and Trudy climbed the big rock behind the cabins and picked blueberries. He asked her if she knew how to make a piecrust, and she didn't. So he showed her, rolling out the dough with a whiskey bottle.

In the morning there was a mist over the lake, just as you see in the movies or in a painting.

One afternoon, Dan stayed out longer than usual, fishing. Trudy kept busy for a while in the kitchen, rubbing the dust off things, washing some jars. It was the oldest, darkest kitchen she had ever seen, with wooden racks for the dinner plates to dry in. She went outside and climbed the rock by herself, thinking she would pick some blueberries. But it was already dark under the trees; the evergreens made it dark, and she didn't like the idea of wild animals. She sat on the rock looking down on the roof of the hotel, the old dead leaves and broken shingles. She heard a piano being played. She scrambled down the rock and followed the music around to the front of the building. She walked along the front veranda and stopped at a window, looking into the room that used to be the lounge. The room with the blackened stone fireplace, the lumpy leather chairs, the horrible mounted fish.

Dan's mother was there, playing the piano. A tall, straight-backed old woman, with her gray-black hair twisted into such a tiny knot. She sat and played the piano, without any lights on, in the half-dark, half-bare room.

Dan had said that his mother came from a rich family. She had taken piano lessons, dancing lessons; she had gone around the world when she was a young girl. There was a picture of her on a camel. But she wasn't playing a classical piece, the sort of thing you'd expect her to have learned. She was playing "It's Three O'Clock in the Morning." When she got to the end, she started in again. Maybe it was a special favorite of hers, something she had danced to in the old days. Or maybe she wasn't satisfied yet that she had got it right.

Why does Trudy now remember this moment? She sees her young self looking in the window at the old woman playing the piano. The dim room, with its oversize beams and fireplace and the lonely leather chairs. The clattering, faltering, persistent piano music. Trudy remembers that so clearly and it seems she stood outside her own body, which ached then from the punishing pleasures of love. She stood outside her own happiness in a tide of sadness. And the opposite thing happened the morning Dan left. Then she stood outside her own unhappiness in a tide of what seemed unreasonably like love. But it was the same thing, really, when you got outside. What are those times that stand out, clear patches in your life — what do they have to do with it? They aren't exactly promises. Breathing spaces. Is that all?

She goes into the front hall and listens for any noise from upstairs.
All quiet there, all medicated.

The phone rings right beside her head.
"Are you still there?" Robin says. "You're not gone?"
"I'm still here."
"Can I run over and ride back with you? I didn't do my run earlier because it was so hot."

You threw the jug. You could have killed me.
Yes.

Kelvin, waiting at the card table, under the light, looks bleached and old. There's a pool of light whitening his brown hair. His face sags, waiting. He looks old, sunk into himself, wrapped in a thick bewilderment, nearly lost to her.

"Kelvin, do you pray?" says Trudy. She didn't know she was going to ask him that. "I mean, it's none of my business. But, like for anything specific?"

He's got an answer for her, which is rather surprising. He pulls his face up, as if he might have felt the tug he needed to bring him to the surface.

"If I was smart enough to know what to pray for," he says, "then I wouldn't have to."

He smiles at her, with some oblique notion of conspiracy, offering his halfway joke. It's not meant as comfort, particularly. Yet it radiates — what he said, the way he said it, just the fact that he's there again, radiates, expands the way some silliness can, when you're very tired. In this way, when she was young, and high, a person or a moment could become a lily floating on the cloudy river water, perfect and familiar.

Questions for Discussion
1. How does the throwing of the jug at the beginning of the story introduce Trudy and the inner conflicts she is experiencing?

2. What does the ritual at the funeral symbolize for Robin and her friends, for their parents, and for the reader?

3. Why does Trudy see a similarity between Robin giving her grandmother's beads to Tracy Lee at the funeral and Dan leaving her? What do the beads represent in the story?

4. How is prayer significant in the story even though none of the characters seems to have strong traditional religious beliefs?

5. What is important about Trudy's memory of Dan's mother playing the piano during the week of their honeymoon? Why does she feel that this moment was similar to the moment when Dan left her for Genevieve?

Ideas for Writing

1. Write an essay in which you discuss how the structure and meaning of the story are clarified through the "Circle of Prayer," its title.

2. Write an essay in which you discuss what the story implies about modern marriage and divorce, parenthood, and romantic relationships. Refer to the story and to your own experiences to support your conclusions.

JOHN UPDIKE   (b. 1932)

John Updike is known for his fictional explorations of suburban marriage, divorce, and family life. Born in Shillington, Pennsylvania, where his father taught at the local high school and his mother was a writer, Updike earned a full scholarship to Harvard University, where he completed his B.A. He was awarded a fellowship to study art at the Ruskin School in Oxford, England; when he returned to New York City, he joined the staff of the *New Yorker*. In 1959 he published his first collection of short fiction, *The Same Door*, and his first novel, *The Poorhouse Fair*. At this time he moved with his family to Ipswich, Massachusetts, and began writing full time. He is best known for his sequence of four novels about Harry "Rabbit" Angstrom, a former high school star athlete coping with the disaffections of middle-class suburban life; these include *Rabbit Run* (1960) and *Rabbit at Rest* (1990), which won the Pulitzer prize in 1991. Updike's most recent novel is *In the Beauty of the Lilies* (1996). His short-story collections include *Pigeon Feathers* (1962), *The Music School* (1966), *Trust Me* (1987), and *The Afterlife and Other Stories* (1994), which contains "The Brown Chest." Above all, Updike is known as a sophisticated stylist who uses language in inventive ways — ways that raise the most mundane characters and situations to a higher, lyrical level.

The Brown Chest   (1994)

In the first house he lived in, it sat up on the second floor, a big wooden chest, out of the way and yet not. For in this house, the house that he inhabited as if he would never live in any other, there were popular cheerful places, where the radio played and the legs of grown-ups went back and forth, and there were haunted bad places, like the coal bin behind the furnace, and the attic with its spiders and smell of old carpet, where he would never go without a grown-up close with him, and there were places in between, that were out of the main current but were not menacing, either, just neutral, and neglected. The entire front of the house had this neglected quality, with its guest bedroom where guests hardly ever stayed; it held a gray-painted bed with silver moons on the headboard and corner posts shaped at the top like mushrooms, and a little desk by the window where his mother sometimes, but not often, wrote letters and confided sentences to her diary in her tiny backslanting hand. If she had never done this, the room would have become haunted, even though it looked out on the busy street with its telephone wires and daytime swish of cars; but the occasional scratch of her pen exerted just enough pressure to keep away the frightening shadows, the sad spirits from long ago, locked into events that couldn't change.

Outside the guest-bedroom door, the upstairs hall, having narrowly sneaked past his grandparents' bedroom's door, broadened to be almost a room, with a window all its own, and a geranium on the sill shedding brown leaves when the women of the house forgot to water it, and curtains of dotted swiss he could see the telephone wires through, and a rug of braided rags shaped like the oval tracks his Lionel train went around and around the Christmas tree on, and, to one side, its front feet planted on the rag rug, with just enough space left for the attic door to swing open, the chest.

It was big enough for him to lie in, but he had never dared try. It was painted brown, but in such a way that the wood grain showed through, as if paint very thinned with turpentine had been used. On the side, wavy stripes of paint had been allowed to run, making dribbles like the teeth of a big wobbly comb. The lid on its brown had patches of yellow freckles. The hinges were small and black, and there was a keyhole that had no key. All this made the chest, simple in shape as it was, strange, and ancient, and almost frightening. And when he, or the grown-up with him, lifted the lid of the chest, an amazing smell rushed out — deeply sweet and musty, of mothballs and cedar, but that wasn't all of it. The smell seemed also to belong to the contents — lace tablecloths and wool blankets on top, but much more underneath. The full contents of the chest never came quite clear, perhaps because he didn't want to know. His parents' college diplomas seemed to be under the blankets, and other documents going back still farther, having to do with his grandparents, their marriage, or the marriage of someone beyond even them. There was a folded old piece of paper with drawn-on hearts and designs and words in German. His mother had once tried to explain the paper to him, but he hadn't wanted to listen. A thing so old disgusted him. And there were giant Bibles, and squat books with plush covers and a little square mottled mirror buried in the plush of one. These books had fat pages edged in gold, thick enough to hold, on both sides, stiff brown pictures, often oval, of dead people. He didn't like looking into these albums, even when his mother was explaining them to him. The chest went down and down, into the past, and he hated the feeling of that well of time, with its sweet deep smell of things unstirring, waiting, taking on the moldy flavor of time, not moving unless somebody touched them.

Then everything moved: the moving men came one day and everything in the house that had always been in a certain place was swiftly and casually uplifted and carried out the door. In the general upheaval the week before, he had been shocked to discover, glancing in, that at some point the chest had come to contain drawings he had done as a child, and his elementary-school report cards, and photographs — studio photographs lovingly mounted in folders of dove-gray cardboard with deckle edges — of him when he was five. He was now thirteen.

The new house was smaller, with more outdoors around it. He liked it less on both accounts. Country space frightened him, much as the coal bin and the dark triangles under the attic eaves had — spaces that didn't have enough to do with people. Fields that were plowed one day in the spring and harvested one day in the fall, woods where dead trees were allowed to topple and slowly rot without anyone noticing, brambled-around spaces where he felt nobody had ever been before he himself came upon them. Heaps and rows of overgrown stones and dumps of rusty cans and tinted bottles indicated that other people in fact had been here, people like those who had posed in their Sunday clothes in the gilded albums, but the traces they left weren't usable, the way city side-walks and trolley-car tracks were usable. His instinct was to stay in the little thick-walled country house, and read, and eat sandwiches he made for himself of raisins and peanut butter, and wait for this phase of his life to pass. Moving from the first house, leaving it behind, had taught him that a life had phases.

The chest, on that day of moving, had been set in the new attic, which was smaller than the other, and less frightening, perhaps because gaps in the cedar-shingled roof let dabs of daylight in. When the roof was being repaired, the whole space was thrown open to the weather, and it rained in, on all the furni-ture there was no longer room for, except up here or in the barn. The chest was too important for the barn; it perched on the edge of the attic steps, so an unpainted back he had never seen before, of two very wide pale boards, became visible. At the ends of each board were careless splashes of the thin brown paint — stain, really — left by the chestmaker when he had covered the sides.

The chest's contents, unseen, darkened in his mind. Once in a great while his mother had to search in there for something, or to confide a treasure to its depths, and in those moments, peeking in, he was surprised at how full the chest seemed, fuller than he remembered, of dotted-swiss curtains and cro-cheted lap rugs and photographs in folders of soft cardboard, all smelling of camphor and cedar. There the chest perched, an inch from the attic stairwell, and there it stayed, for over forty years.

Then it moved again. His children, adults all, came from afar and joined him in the house, where their grandmother had at last died, and divided up the furniture — some for them to carry away, some for the local auctioneer to sell, and some for him, the only survivor of that first house, with its long halls and haunted places, to keep and to assimilate to his own house, hundreds of miles away.

Two of the three children, the two that were married, had many responsi-bilities and soon left; he and his younger son, without a wife and without a job, remained to empty the house and pack the U-Haul van they rented. For days they lived together, eating takeout food, poisoning mice and trapping cats, moving from crowded cellar to jammed attic like sick men changing posi-tion in bed, overwhelmed by decisions, by accumulated possessions, now and then fleeing the house to escape the oppression of the past. He found the iron scales, quite rusted by the cellar damp, whereon his grandmother used to weigh out bundles of asparagus against a set of cylindrical weights. The weights were still heavy in his hand, and left rust stains on his palm. He studied a tin basin, painted in a white-on-gray spatter-pattern that had puzzled him as a child with its apparent sloppiness, and he could see again his grandfather's paper-white feet soaking in suds that rustled as the bubbles popped one by one.

The chest, up there in the attic along with old rolled carpets and rocking chairs with broken cane seats, stacked hatboxes from the Thirties and paperback mysteries from the Forties, was too heavy to lift, loaded as it was. He and his younger son took out layers of blankets and plush-covered albums, lace tablecloths and linen napkins; they uncovered a long cardboard box labelled in his mother's handwriting "Wedding Dress 1925," and, underneath that, rumpled silk dresses that a small girl might have worn when the century was young, and patent-leather baby shoes, and a gold-plated horseshoe, and faithful notations of the last century's weather kept by his grandfather's father in limp diaries bound in red leather, and a buggy-whip. A little box labelled in his mother's handwriting "Haircut July 1919" held, wrapped in tissue paper, coils of auburn hair startlingly silky to the touch. There were stiff brown photographs of his father's college football team, his father crouching at right tackle in an unpadded helmet, and of a stageful of posing young people among whom he finally found his mother, wearing a flimsy fairy dress and looking as if she had been crying. And so on and on, until he couldn't bear it and asked his son to help him carry the chest, half unemptied, down the narrow attic stairs whose bare wooden treads had been troughed by generations of use, and then down the slightly broader stairs carpeted decades ago, and out the back door to the van. It didn't fit; they had to go back to the city ten miles away to rent a bigger van. Even so, packing everything in was a struggle. At one point, exasperated and anxious to be gone, his broad-backed son, hunched in the body of the U-Haul van, picked up the chest single-handed, and inverted it, lid open, over some smaller items to save space. The old thin-painted wood gave off a sharp *crack*, a piercing quick cry of injury.

The chest came to rest in his barn. He now owned a barn, not a Pennsylvania barn with stone sides and pegged oak beams but a skimpier, New England barn, with a flat tarred roof and a long-abandoned horse stall. He found the place in the chest lid, near one of the little dark hinges, where a split had occurred, and with a few carefully driven nails repaired the damage well enough. He could not blame the boy, who was named Gordon, after his paternal grandfather, the one-time football player crouching for his picture in some sunny autumn when Harding was President. On the drive north in a downpour, Gordon had driven the truck, and his father tried to read the map, and in the dim light of the cab failed, and headed him the wrong way out of Westchester County, so they wound up across the Hudson River, amid blinding headlights, on an unfathomable, exitless highway. After that egregious piece of guidance, he could not blame the boy for anything, even for failing to get a job while concentrating instead on perfecting his dart game in the fake pubs of Boston. In a way not then immediately realized, the map-reading blunder righted the balance between them, himself and his son, as when under his grandmother's gnarled hands another stalk of asparagus would cause the tray holding the rusty cylindrical weights to rise with a soft *clunk*.

They arrived an hour late, after midnight. The unloading, including the reloading of the righted chest, all took place by flashlight, hurriedly, under the drumming sound of rain on the flat roof.

Now his barn felt haunted. He could scarcely bear to examine his inherited treasure, the chairs and cabinets and chinaware and faded best-sellers and old-fashioned bridge lamps clustered in a corner beyond the leaf-mulcher and the snow-blower and the rack of motorcycle tires left by the youngest son of the previous owner of the barn. He was the present owner. He had never imagined, as a child, owning so much. His wife saw no place in their house for even the curly-maple kitchen table and the walnut corner cupboard, his mother's pride. This section of the barn became, if not as frightening as the old coal bin, a place he avoided. These pieces that his infant eyes had grazed, and that had framed his parents' lives, seemed sadly shabby now, cheap in their time, most of them, and yet devoid of antique value: useless used furniture he had lacked the courage to discard.

So he was pleased, one winter day, two years after their wayward drive north, to have Gordon call and ask if he could come look at the furniture in the barn. He had a job, he said, or almost, and was moving into a bigger place, out from the city. He would be bringing a friend, he vaguely added. A male friend, presumably, to help him lift and load what he chose to take away.

But the friend was a female, small and exquisite, with fascinating large eyes, the whites white as china, and a way of darting back and forth like a hummingbird, her wings invisible. "Oh," she exclaimed, over this and that, explaining to Gordon in a breathy small voice how this would be useful, and that would fit right in. "Lamps!" she said. "I love lamps."

"You see, Dad," the boy explained, the words pronounced softly yet in a manner so momentous that it seemed to take all the air in the barn to give them utterance, "Morna and I are planning to get married."

"Morna" — a Celtic name, fittingly elfin. The girl was magical, there in the cold barn, emitting puffs of visible breath, moving through the clutter with quick twists of her denim-clad hips and graceful stabs of her narrow white hands. She spoke only to Gordon, as if a pane of shyness protected her from his hoary father — at this late phase of his life a kind of ogre, an ancestral, proprietorial figure full of potency and ugliness. "Gordon, what's this?" she asked.

The boy was embarrassed, perhaps by her innocent avidity. "Tell her, Dad."

"Our old guest bed." Which he used to lie diagonally across, listening to his mother's pen scratch as her diary tried to hold fast her days. Even then he knew it couldn't be done.

"We could strip off the ghastly gray, I guess," the boy conceded, frowning in the attempt to envision it and the work involved. "We *have* a bed," he reminded her.

"And this?" she went on, leaving the bed hanging in a realm of future possibility. Her headscarf had slipped back, exposing auburn hair glinting above the vapor of her breath, in evanescent present time.

She had paused at the chest. Her glance darted at Gordon, and then, receiving no response, at the present owner, looking him in the eyes for the first time. The ogre smiled. "Open it."

"What's in it?" she asked.

He said, "I forget, actually."

Delicately but fearlessly, she lifted the lid, and out swooped, with the same vividness that had astonished and alarmed his nostrils as a child, the sweetish deep cedar smell, undiminished, cedar and camphor and paper and cloth, the smell of family, family without end.

Questions for Discussion

1. What do the contents of the brown chest represent for the viewpoint character? Why is he "disgusted" as a child with the age of its contents? At what point does he begin to feel connected to the chest's contents?

2. The plot involves a series of moves of the chest throughout the main character's life. How does each of these moves underscore the narrator's evolving attitudes toward family and memory? How is the viewpoint character's relationship with his son emphasized through the moves made of the chest?

3. Does Gordon become closer to his father as the story progresses? Why or why not?

4. What values does Morna represent? How are her values seen through her response to the chest?

5. Updike is a master of descriptive detail. In what sense do the descriptions of the chest and its contents, as well as related descriptions, parallel the changing artistic and philosophical awareness of the viewpoint character as he matures and ages?

Ideas for Writing

1. Write an essay in which you discuss the symbolism of the brown chest in terms of family traditions and heritage.

2. Write a story focused on a central symbol that reveals a family's heritage and values.

ELENA PONIATOWSKA   (b. 1933)

Elena Poniatowska often uses humor and satire in her stories to mock the double standard of traditional gender roles as well as the conventional approaches to law and religion. Born in Paris, the daughter of a Polish father and a Mexican mother, she moved with her mother to Mexico City after the German invasion of France. She attended school in Mexico City for several years before moving to the United States to complete high school and college in New York City. Returning to Mexico City, she began a career as a journalist and interviewer, and she is a regular contributor to a number of Mexican periodicals. Her novels include *Flor de lis* (1988), about an upper-class young woman who seeks to explore the world beyond the conventions of her class and gender; her creative journalism includes an impressionistic account of the 1968 student riots in Mexico City, *Fuerte es el silencio* (1980), translated as *Massacre in Mexico*. Only two of her novels have been translated into English: *Dear Diego* (1986), a fictionalized series of letters between Mexican artist Diego Rivera and his lover, the painter Angela Beloff, and *Tinisima* (1996). "Park Cinema" was translated for inclusion in the collection *Short Stories by Latin American Women* (1990), edited by Celia Correas de Zappata.

Park Cinema   (1967)

Translated by Teres Mendeth-Faith and Elisabeth Heinicke

Señorita:

As of today, you will have to strike my name from the list of your admirers. Perhaps I ought not to inform you of this decision, but to do so would be to betray a personal integrity that has never shied away from the exigencies of the Truth. By thus divorcing myself from you, I am acting in accordance with a profound change in spirit, which leads me to the decision never again to number myself among the viewers of your films.

This afternoon — or rather, this evening — you have destroyed me. I do not know whether this matters to you, but I am a man shattered to pieces. Do you understand what I am saying? A devotee who has followed your image on the screens of first-run houses and neighborhood theaters, a loving critic who would justify the very worst of your moral behavior, I now swear on my knees to renounce you forever, though a mere poster from *Forbidden Fruit* is enough to shake my resolve. As you may see, I am yet a man seduced by appearances.

Comfortably ensconced in my seat I was one in a multitude, a creature lost in an anonymous darkness, who suddenly felt himself caught up in a personal sadness, bitter and inescapable. It was then that I was truly myself, the loner who suffers and now addresses you. For no brotherly hand reached to touch mine. While you were calmly destroying my heart on the screen, all those around me stayed passionately true. Yes, there was even one scoundrel who laughed shamelessly while I watched you swoon in the arms of that abominable suitor who dragged you to the final extremes of human degradation.

And let me ask you this, señorita: Is he worthless whose every ideal is suddenly lost?

You will say I am a dreamer, an eccentric, one of those meteorites that fall to earth against all calculated odds. You may dispense with your hypotheses: it is I who is judging you, and do me the favour of taking greater responsibilities for your actions, and before you sign a contract or accept a co-star, do consider that a man such as I might be among your future audience and might receive a fatal blow. It is not jealousy that makes me speak this way, but, believe me: in *Slaves of Desire,* you were kissed, caressed and assaulted to excess.

I do not know whether my memory makes me exaggerate, but in the cabaret scene there was no reason for you to half-open your lips in that way, to let your hair down over your shoulders, and to tolerate the impudent manners of that sailor who yawns as he leaves you, who abandons you like a sinking ship after he has drowned your honor on the bed.

I know that actors owe a debt to their audience; that they, in a sense, relinquish their free will and give themselves up to the capricious desires of a perverse director; moreover, I know that they are obliged to follow point by point all the deficiencies and inconsistencies of the script they must bring to life, but let me state that everyone, even in the worst of contingencies, retains a minimum of initiative, a fragment of freedom — and you could not or chose not to exercise it.

If you were to take the trouble, you might say in your defense that the very things I am accusing you of today you have done ever since your screen debut. True, and I am ashamed to admit that I cannot justify my feelings. I undertook to love you just as you are. Pardon — as I imagined you to be. Like anyone who has ever been disillusioned, I curse the day that linked my life with your cinematographic destiny. And I want to make clear that I accepted you when you were an obscure newcomer, when no one had ever heard of you, when they gave you the part of that streetwalker with crooked stockings and worn-down heels, a part no decent woman could have accepted. Nonetheless I forgave you, and in that dirty and indifferent theater I hailed the birth of a star. It was I who discovered you, I was the only one who could perceive your soul, immaculate as it was despite your torn handbag and your sheepish manner. By what is dearest to you in the world? Forgive the bluntness of my outburst.

Your mask has slipped, señorita. I have come to see the vileness of your deceit. You are not that creature of delights, that tender, fragile dove I had grown used to, that swallow innocent in flight, your face in my dreams hidden by a lacy veil — no, you are a tramp through and through, the dregs of the earth, a passing fancy in the worst sense of the word. From this moment on, my dear señorita, you must go your way and I mine. Go on, go, keep walking the streets, I have already drowned in your sewer like a rat. But I must stress that I continue to address you as "señorita" solely because, in spite of the blows you have dealt me, I am still a gentleman. My saintly old mother had instilled in my innermost being the importance of always keeping up appearances. Images linger, my life as well. Hence . . . señorita. Take it, if you will, as a sort of desperate irony.

I have seen you lavish kisses and receive caresses in hundreds of films, but never before did you receive your fortunate partner into your spirit. You kissed with simplicity like any good actress: as one would kiss a cardboard cutout. For — and I wish to make this clear once and for all — the only worthwhile sensuality is that which involves the soul, for the soul surrounds our body as the skin of the grape its pulp, as the peel contains the juice within. Before now, your love scenes did not upset me, for you always preserved a shred of dignity albeit profaned; I was always aware of an intimate rejection, a last-minute withdrawal that redeemed my anguish and consoled my lament. But in *Rapture in the Body,* your eyes moist with love, you showed me your true face, the one I never wish to see again. Go on, confess it: you really are in love with the scoundrel, that second-rate flash-in-the-pan comedian, aren't you? What avails an impudent denial? At least every word of mine, every promise I made, was true: and every one of your movements was the expression of a spirit that had surrendered itself. Why did you toy with me the way they all do? Why did you deceive me like all women deceive, wearing one different mask after another? Why would you not reveal all at once, in the beginning, the detestable face that now torments me?

This drama of mine is practically metaphysical, and I can find no possible solution. I am alone in the nighttime of my delirium. Well, all right, my wife does understand me completely, and at times she even shares in my distress. We were still revelling in the sweet delights appropriate to newlyweds when, our defenses down, we saw the first of your films. Do you still remember it? The one about the dumb athletic diver who ended up at the bottom of the sea because of you, wetsuit and all. I left the theater completely deranged and it would have been futile effort to try to keep it from my wife. But at least she was completely on my side, and had to admit that your deshabilles were truly splendid. Nor did she find it inconvenient to accompany me to the cinema six more times, believing in good faith that the enchantment would be broken by routine. But, alas, things grew worse with every new film of yours that opened. Our family budget underwent serious modifications in order to permit cinema attendance on the order of three times a week. And it goes without saying that after each cinematographic session we spent the rest of the night arguing. All the same, my mate did not get ruffled. For after all, you were but a defenseless shadow, a two-dimensional silhouette, subject to the deficiencies of light. And my wife good-naturedly accepted as her rival a phantom whose appearance could be controlled at will, although she wasted no opportunity to have a good laugh at our expense. I remember her pleasure on the fatal night when, due to technical difficulties, you spoke for a good ten minutes with an inhuman voice, almost that of a robot, going from a falsetto to deepest bass. And while we're on the subject of your voice, I would have you know that I set myself to studying French because I could not resign myself to the abridged subtitles in Spanish, colourless and misleading. I learned to decipher the melodious sound of your voice, and with that accomplishment came the intolerable scourge of hearing atrocious words directed at your person or issuing from your very lips. I longed for the time when these words had reached me by way of a priggish translation; now, they were slaps in the face.

The most serious aspect to this whole thing is that my wife is showing disquieting signs of ill-humor. Allusions to you and to your on-screen conduct are more and more frequent and ferocious. Lately she has concentrated on your intimate apparel and tells me that I am talking in vain to a woman of no substance. And sincerely now, just between ourselves, why this profusion of infamous transparency, this wasteful display of intimate bits of filmy acetate? When the only thing I want to find in you is that little sparkle, sad and bitter, that you once had in your eyes . . . But let's get back to my wife. She makes faces and mimics you. She makes fun of me too. Mockingly, she echoes some of my most heart-rending sighs. "Those kisses that pained me in *Unforgettable You* still burn me like fire." Wherever we may be, she is wont to speak of you; she says we must confront this problem from a purely rational angle, from a scientific point of view, and she comes up with absurd but potent arguments. She does no less than claim you are not real and that she herself is an actual woman. And by dint of proving it to me, she is demolishing my illusions one by one. I do not know what will happen to me if what is so far only a rumor should turn out to be the truth: that you will come here to make a film, that you will honor our country with a visit. For the love of God, by the holiest of holies — stay where you are, señorita!

No, I do not want to go see you again, for every time the music dies away and the action fades from the screen, I am overwhelmed. I'm speaking of that fatal barrier represented by the three cruel letters that put an end to the modest measure of happiness of my nights of love, at two pesos apiece. Bit by bit I have relinquished the desire to stay and live with you on film, and I no longer die of pain as I am towed away from the cinema by my wife, who has the bad habit of getting up as soon as the last frame has passed. Señorita, I leave you here. I do not even ask you for an autograph, for should you ever send me one I would be capable of forgetting your unpardonable treason. Please accept this letter as the final act of homage of a devastated soul, and forgive me for including you in my dreams. Yes, more than one night I dreamt about you, and there is nothing that I have to envy those fly-by-night lovers who collect a salary to hold you in their arms and ply you with borrowed eloquence.

Your humble servant

P.S.

I had neglected to tell you that I am writing from behind bars. This letter would never have reached your hands, had I not feared that the world would give you an erroneous account of me. For the newspapers (which always twist things around) are taking advantage of this ridiculous event: "Last night, an unknown man, either drunk or mentally deranged, interrupted a showing of *Slaves of Desire* at its most stirring point, when he ripped the screen of the Park Cinema by plunging a knife in the breast of Françoise Arnoul. In spite of the darkness, three members of the audience saw the maniac rush towards the actress brandishing a knife, and they got out of their seats to get a better look at him so they could identify him at the time of arraignment. This was easily done, as the individual collapsed once the crime had been committed."

I know that it's impossible, but I would give anything for you to remember always that sharp stab in your breast.

Questions for Discussion

1. Why does the narrator write a letter to the "señorita"? Why does he wish to strike his name "from the list of [her] admirers"?

2. What does the narrator mean when he says that he "was the only one who could perceive your soul"? What other comments does he make about the soul and its importance? What do these statements suggest about his judgment?

3. Trace the narrator's progressive infatuation and obsession with the film star. What has he sacrificed because of his obsession with her?

4. Discuss the "P.S." section of the letter. Why is this vital information reserved for a postscript?

5. What does the narrator's act of violence against the *image* of the film star reveal about his feelings for her? What events have led him to commit such a desperate act?

Ideas for Writing

1. Discuss the story's perspective on relationships between mass-media figures and their fans. How is the story critical of such fantasy relationships?

2. Write a first-person narrative from the point of view of a fan who is angry with or feels betrayed by a celebrity.

GERALD VIZENOR   (b. 1934)

A mixed-blood member of the Minnesota Chippewa tribe, Gerald Vizenor writes stories exploring the world of the modern Chippewa people both on and off the reservation. Born in Minneapolis, Vizenor attended New York University, completed his B.A. at the University of Minnesota, and continued his graduate study at the University of Minnesota and at Harvard University. He worked as a correction agent at the Minnesota State Reformatory and as a reporter for the *Minneapolis Tribune* before beginning a teaching career. He has taught at a number of colleges, including the University of Minnesota and Tianjin University in China, and he currently teaches Native American literature at the University of California at Berkeley.

Vizenor has published numerous books, including essay collections, an autobiography, poetry collections, and five novels. His second novel, *Griever: An American Monkey King in China* (1990), won the Fiction Collective Prize and the American Book Award. *Dead Voices: Natural Agonies in the New World* (1992) is his most recent novel. His story collections include *Landfill Meditation: Crossblood Stories* (1991), which contains "Almost Browne," and *Shadow Distance: A Gerald Vizenor Reader* (1994). As "Almost Browne" suggests, Vizenor's stories often mix earthy realism, fantasy, and dark humor while drawing on Native American imagery and tradition.

Almost Browne   (1991)

Almost Browne was born on the White Earth Indian Reservation in Minnesota. Well, he was *almost* born there; that much is the absolute truth about his birth. Almost, you see, is a crossblood and he was born on the road; his father is tribal and his mother is blonde.

Marthie Jean Peterson and Hare Browne met on the dock at Sugar Bush Lake. He worked for the conservation department on the reservation, and she was there on vacation with her parents. Marthie Jean trusted her heart and proposed in the back of an aluminum boat. Hare was silent, but they were married that year at the end of the wild rice season.

Hare and Marthie had been in the cities over the weekend with her relatives. The men told stories about fish farms, construction, the weather, and automobiles, and the women prepared five meals that were eaten in front of the television set in the amusement room.

Marthie loved fish sticks and baloney, but most of all she loved to eat orange Jell-O with mayonnaise. She had just finished a second bowl when she felt the first birth pain.

"Hare, your son is almost here," she whispered in his ear. Marthie did not want her parents to know about the pain; naturally, they never would have allowed her to return to the reservation in labor.

Marthie never forgot anything; even as a child she could recite the state capitals. She remembered birthdates and presidents, but that afternoon she packed two baloney sandwiches and forgot her purse. She was on the road in labor with no checkbook, no money, no proof of identity. She was in love and trusted her heart.

The leaves had turned earlier than usual that autumn, and the silent crows bounced on the cold black road a few miles this side of the reservation border. Ahead, the red sumac burned on the curve.

Hare was worried that the crows would not move in time, so he slowed down and honked the horn. The crows circled a dead squirrel. He honked again, but the crows were too wise to be threatened. The engine wheezed, lurched three times, and then died on the curve in the light of the sumac.

Almost earned his nickname in the back seat of that seventeen-year-old hatchback; he was born on the road, almost on the reservation. His father pushed the car around the curve, past the crows and red sumac, about a half a mile to a small town. There, closer to the reservation border, he borrowed two gallons of gas from the station manager and hurried to the hospital on the White Earth Reservation.

The hatchback thundered over the unpaved government road; a wild bloom of brown dust covered the birch on the shoulders. The dust shrouded the red arrow to the resort at Sugar Bush Lake. The hospital was located at the end of the road near the federal water tower.

Wolfie Wight, the reservation medical doctor, opened the hatchback and reached into the dust. Her enormous head, wide grin, and hard pink hands frightened the crossblood infant in the back seat.

Almost was covered with dust, darker at birth than he has ever been since then. Wolfie laughed when the child turned white in his first bath. He was weighed and measured, and a tribal nurse listened to his heartbeat. Later, the doctor raised her enormous black fountain pen over the birth certificate and asked the parents, "Where was your child born?"

"White Earth," shouted the father.

"Hatchback?" The doctor smiled.

"White Earth," he answered, uncertain of his rights.

"Hatchback near the reservation?"

"White Earth," said the father a third time.

"Almost White Earth," said the doctor.

"White Earth," he repeated, determined that the birth of his son would be recorded on the reservation. He was born so close to the border, and he never touched the earth outside the reservation.

"Indeed, Almost Browne," said the doctor, and printed that name on the birth certificate. Wolfie recorded the place of birth as "Hatchback at White

Earth" and signed the certificate with a flourish. "One more trail born half-breed with a new name," she told the nurse. The nurse was silent; she resisted medical humor about tribal people.

Almost was born to be a tribal trickster. He learned to walk and talk in the wild brush; he listened to birds, water, lightning, the crack of thunder and ice, the turn of seasons; and he moved with animals in dreams. But he was more at home on cracked polyvinyl chloride in the back seats of cars, a natural outcome of his birth in a used hatchback.

Almost told a blonde anthropologist one summer that he was born in the bottom of a boat and learned how to read in limousines; she was amused and recorded his stories in narrow blue notebooks. They sat in the back seat of an abandoned car.

"I grew up with mongrels," he told the anthropologist. "We lived in seven cars, dead ones, behind the house. One car, the brown one, that was my observatory. That's where I made the summer star charts."

"Indian constellations?" asked the anthropologist.

"Yes, the stars that moved in the sunroof," he explained. "I marked the stars on cards, the bright ones that came into the sunroof got names."

"What were the names?" asked the anthropologist.

"The sunroof stars."

"The names of the constellations?"

"We had nicknames," he answered.

"What were the names?"

"The sunroof charts were like cartoon pictures."

"What names?"

"Moths are on one chart."

"What are the other names?"

"Mosquitoes, white lies, pure gumption, private jones."

"Those are constellations?"

"The sunroof charts are named after my dogs," he said and called the mongrels into the back seat. White Lies licked the blonde hair on the arms of the anthropologist.

Almost learned how to read from books that had been burned in a fire at the reservation library. The books were burned on the sides. He read the centers of the pages and imagined the stories from the words that were burned.

Almost had one close friend; his nickname was Drain. They were so close that some people thought they must be brothers. The two were born on the same day near the same town on the reservation border. Drain lived on a farm, the fifth son of white immigrants.

Drain was a reservation consumer, because he believed the stories he heard about the tribe. He became what he heard, and when the old men told him to shout, he shouted; he learned to shout at shadows and thunderstorms.

Almost told stories that made the tribe seem more real; he imagined a trickster world of chance and transformation. Drain listened and consumed the adventures. The two were inseparable; one the crossblood trickster, the other a white consumer. Together, the reservation became their paradise in stories.

Almost never attended school; well, he almost never attended. He lived on the border between two school districts, one white and the other tribal. When he wanted to use the machines in school, the microscopes, lathes, and laboratories, he would attend classes, but not more than two or three times a month. Each school thought he attended the other, and besides, no one cared that much where he lived or what he learned.

Almost learned four natural deals about life from his grandmother; he learned to see the wild world as deals between memories and tribal stories. The first deal, she told him, was chance, where things just happen and that becomes the deal with animals and their languages; words were pictures in the second natural deal; the third deal, she said, was to eat from the real world, not from the pictures on menus; and the last deal, she told him, was to liberate his mind with trickster stories.

"In natural deals," he explained to his best friend, "we act, bargain, agree, deliver, and remember that birds never eat monarchs in our stories."

"What monarchs?" asked Drain.

"The milkweed butterflies."

"So, what's the deal?"

"We're the deal in our stories."

"Some deal," moaned Drain.

"The deal is that whites are fleas and the tribes are the best dealers," said Almost. "Indians are the tricksters, we are the rabbits, and when we get excited, our ears heat up and the white fleas breed."

Almost converted a reservation station wagon into a bookmobile; he sold books from a rack that unfolded out of the back. The books, however, were not what most people expected, not even in trickster stories, and he needed a loan to expand his business.

"We're almost a bookstore," said Almost.

"Blank books?" shouted Wolfie. "You can't sell books on a reservation, people don't read here, not even blank ones."

"Some of them are burned," said Almost.

"You're crazy, blank and burned books," said the doctor, "but you do have gumption, that much is worth a loan." She polished her black pen on the sleeve of her white coat and signed a check to the crossblood.

Almost the whole truth:

Almost is my name, my real name, believe that or not, because my father ran out of money and then out of gas on the way back. I was born in the back seat of a beatup reservation car, almost white, almost on the reservation, and almost a real person.

White Jaws, the government doctor who got her cold hands on my birth certificate, gave me my name. Imagine, if we had run out of gas ten miles earlier, near a white hospital, my name might be Robert, or how about Truman? Instead, White Jaws made me Almost.

Listen, there must be something to learn in public schools, but not by me. My imagination stopped at the double doors; being inside a school was like a drain on my brain. So, my chance to learn came in bad nature and white books. Not picture nature in a dozen bird names, but road kills, white pine in eagle nests, fleas in rabbit ears, the last green flies in late autumn, and moths that whisper, whisper at the mirror. Nature voices, crows in the poplars, not plastic bird mobiles over a baby crib. So, nature was my big book, imagination was my teacher.

Classrooms were nothing more than parking lots to me, places to park a mind rather than drive a mind wild in the glorious woods, through the dangerous present in the winter when the whole real world struggles to survive. For me, double doors and desks are the end of imagination, the end of animals, the end of nature, and the end of the tribes. I might never have entered the book business if I had been forced to attend a white school.

The truth is, I almost got into the book business before my time. A blonde anthropology student started a library on the reservation and she put me in charge of finding and sorting books. I found hundreds of books that summer, what a great time, books were like chance meetings, but the whole thing burned down before I learned how to read. The anthropologist told me not to use my finger on the page but we never practiced in any real books. She talked and talked and then when the building burned down she drove back home to the city. People always come here with some other place in mind.

Drain, he's my best friend, said it was a good thing the library burned because most of the stuff in there was worthless digest books that nobody wanted to read in the first place. Drain is a white farm kid who lives on the other side of the road, on the white side of the road, outside the reservation. He learned how to read in another language before he went to school.

I actually taught myself how to read with almost whole books, and that's the truth. I'd read with my finger first, word for word out loud right down to the burned parts and then I'd picture the rest, or imagine the rest of the words on the page. The words became more real in my imagination. From the words in pictures I turned back to the words on the center of the page. Finally, I could imagine the words and read the whole page, printed or burned.

Listen, there are words almost everywhere. I realized that in a chance moment. Words are in the air, in our blood, words were always there, way before my burned book collection in the back seat of a car. Words are in snow, trees, leaves, wind, birds, beaver, the sound of ice cracking; words are in fish and mongrels, where they've been since we came to this place with the animals. My winter breath is a word, we are words, real words, and the mongrels are their own words. Words are crossbloods too, almost whole right down to the cold printed page burned on the sides.

Drain never thought about real words because he found them in books, nowhere else. He taught me how to read better, and I showed him how to see real words where we lived, and the words that were burned on the pages of my books. Words burned but never dead. It was my idea to open a bookstore with blank books, a mobile bookstore.

Doctor Wolfie gave us a loan, so we packed up and drove to the city, where we started our blank book business near the university. Drain somehow knew the city like the back of his hand. I told him that was the same as finding words in animals. Everything was almost perfect; we were making good money on the street and going to parties with college students, but then the university police arrested us for false advertising, fraud, and trading on the campus without a permit. The car wasn't registered, and we didn't have a license. I think that was the real problem.

Drain played Indian because the judge said he would drop the charges if we went straight back to the reservation where we belonged and learned a useful trade.

"Almost Browne, that's my real name," I told the judge. "I was almost born in the city." The judge never even smiled. These men who rule words from behind double doors and polished benches miss the best words in the language, they miss the real words. They never hear the real words in court, not even the burned words. No one would ever bring real words to court.

Drain was bold and determined in the city. He drove right onto campus, opened the back of the station wagon, unfolded our book rack, and we were in business. That's how it happened, but the judge was not even listening. Wait, we played a shaman drum tape on a small recorder perched on the top of the car. The tape was old; the sound crackled like a pine fire, we told the judge.

Professor Monte Franzgomery was always there, every day. He would dance a little to the music, and he helped us sell blank books to college students. "Listen to that music," he shouted at the students. "That's real music, ethnic authenticity at the very threshold of civilization." That old professor shouted that we were real too, but we were never sure about him because he talked too much. We knew we were on the threshold of something big when we sold out our whole stock in a week, more than a hundred blank books in a week.

Monte said our blank books made more sense to him than anything he had ever read. This guy was really cracked. Our books were blank except on one page there was an original tribal pictomyth painted by me in green ink, a different pictomyth on a different page in every blank book. Yes, pictomyths, stories that are imagined about a picture, about memories. So, even our blank books had a story. I think those college students were tired of books filled with words behind double doors that never pictured anything. Our blank books said everything, whatever you could imagine in a picture. One pictomyth was almost worth a good story in those days.

Well, we were almost on our way to a fortune at the university when the police burned our blank books. Not really, but a ban on the sale of blank books is almost as bad as burning a book with print.

So, now we're back on the reservation in the mail-order business, a sovereign tribal blank book business in an abandoned car. Our business has been brisk, almost as good as it was at the university; better yet, there's no overhead in the back seat of a station wagon on the reservation. Listen, last week the best edition of our blank books was adopted in a cinema class at the University of California in Santa Cruz. Blank books are real popular on the coast.

Monte promised that he would use our blank books in his seminar on romantic literature. He told a newspaper reporter, when we were arrested, that the pictomyths were a "spontaneous overflow of powerful feelings."

Drain said we should autograph our blank books, a different signature on each book. I told him the pictomyths were enough. No, he said, the consumer wants something new, something different from time to time. The stories in the pictomyths are what's new, I told him. He was right, and we agreed. I made pictures and he signed the books. He even signed the names of tribal leaders, presidents, and famous authors.

Later, we published oversized blank books, and a miniature edition of blank books. Drain bought a new car, we did almost everything with blank books. We even started a blank book library on the reservation, but that's another story for another time.

Questions for Discussion
1. In what ways is Almost Browne's name symbolic of his origins and fate?
2. In what ways are the personalities of Drain and Browne complementary, like two sides of a coin? How do they make the tribe and reservation into a myth?
3. What does Browne learn from school, from the books he reads, from his grandmother? What is the significance of these diverse sources of his knowledge?
4. What distinction does Browne make between real words and words in books? Why does he believe that no one would bring real words into court? Do you agree with him?
5. What do the blank books that Drain and Browne sell represent? Why do these books have pictomyths? What is suggested by Drain and Browne's success at selling these books to college students?

Ideas for Writing
1. Write an essay about Vizenor's use of humor. What makes this story humorous? What is the purpose of Vizenor's humor, other than simply to tell a "tall tale"?
2. This story is a modern variation on the Native American "trickster myth," a kind of tall tale in which a tricky, clownlike character outwits more serious and powerful people. Create your own trickster story, using a devious but likable central character who uses his wits to triumph over his adversaries.

CHEN RONG   (b. 1935)

Chen Rong focuses her fiction on realistic, often humorous depictions of life in contemporary China. She was born in Hankow, where her father was a judge. After the revolution of 1949, she left school and took a job as a sales clerk and in 1952 went to work for the *Southwest Worker's Daily*. Two years later she began her study of Russian in Beijing, soon getting a job as a translator for a radio station. She later moved to the country to stay with a peasant family to recuperate from an illness. In 1964 she returned to Beijing and began her career as a playwright and novelist, joining the Chinese Writers Association. Her novella *Middle Age* — about a Chinese woman who experiences a conflict between her stressful duties as a doctor, wife, and mother living with her family in cramped urban quarters — was made into a successful film that won the Best Film Award in China for 1983. Chen Rong's stories and novellas have been published in English in *Seven Contemporary Chinese Women Writers* (1982) and *The Rose-Colored Dinner* (1988), which contains "Regarding the Problem of Newborn Piglets in Winter." This story uses precise irony and sharp humor to criticize the bureaucratic system of Communist China in its quest for "modernization."

Regarding the Problem of Newborn Piglets in Winter   (1988)

Translated by Chun-Ye Shih

1. "H'mm, have you considered . . . ?"

"Silent is the night over the military harbor . . ." On the color television screen gleamed the graceful white figure of Su Xiaoming singing in her low soft voice.

"Grandma, turn it louder," the six-year-old Babe issued a command from the large soft couch she was sprawled on.

"Loud enough!" Grandma nevertheless walked over to turn the volume up slightly.

Babe suddenly jumped up and knelt on the couch. "Grandpa, can you hear?" she cried over the back of the couch.

"Don't yell, Grandpa's resting."

"Let our sailors sleep in peace . . ." the song went on.

So Grandpa slept on.

Zhang Dingfan was resting; his eyes closed, his gray hair pillowed against the sofa back and his arm limp on the armrest. After a day's hard work his wrecked nerves found repose in the lull of his own snoring.

Suddenly, a wind blew up outside and the door and the window rattled. The green velveteen curtain gave a stir.

Zhang Dingfan turned his head and uttered a sound barely audible, "H'mm."

Madam Zhang, wife of the Secretary, rose to her feet and walked over to the door and the window for a quick inspection. Both were tightly shut. Then she touched the heater; it was toasty warm. Everything seemed to be in order so she fetched a light wool blanket from the bedroom and walked toward the Secretary. Just as she was about to cover him with the blanket, Zhang Dingfan sat up with a jerk and stopped her. He turned his face toward the door and called, "Little You."

Madam Zhang, startled for a second, piped up in unison, "Mr. You, Mr. You."

In reply, a young man in his thirties came in from the anteroom.

"Get me Chief Jiao of Agriculture and Forestry."

Mr. You stepped lightly toward the table in the corner. He turned the lamp on and dialed the telephone. After he was connected to the right party, he raised the receiver, turned round and said, "Comrade Dingfan."

Zhang Dingfan rose slowly and walked toward the telephone. He seated himself in a chair before he took the receiver in his hand.

"It's me," he coughed. "Looks like it's getting colder. H'mm . . ."

Quickly, Madam Zhang turned the volume of the television set to the lowest. Poor Su Xiaoming suddenly became mute, her red lips gaping and closing soundlessly.

"Grandma; I can't hear, I can't hear," Babe protested.

"Don't fuss, Grandpa is working."

Work is sacred; Babe stopped shouting.

"H'mm, have you considered — this sudden change in temperature and the problem of piglets in the winter — h'mm, we'd better do something. No, no, not by memorandum. First, notify every district in the county by telephone. Proceed level by level this very night. Don't let any piglet die from the cold. Then you may follow up by memorandum. Work on the draft right away."

He hung up the telephone, "These people, just like counters on an abacus — they only move when you give them a push. How can we ever achieve the Four Modernizations?"

"All right — it's all right now that you've alerted them," Madam Zhang comforted him.

"Grandma," Babe couldn't wait any longer.

The volume was once again adjusted. The singer had disappeared. With the tinkling of electronic music and sudden pop, eight modernized angels in their white tight-fitting costumes emerged on the color screen, dancing and twisting their slender waists.

"No, no, I want Su Xiaoming," Babe demanded, rolling in the sofa and kicking her feet in the air.

Zhang Dingfan bent down to pat his granddaughter's head and said cheerfully, "Why not this? The melody of youth. Very nice."

2. *"We'll have* wonton *tonight."*

Every light was burning in Chief Jiao's office, the Municipal Department of Agriculture and Forestry.

The young cadre had just finished a memorandum: "Regarding the Problem of Newborn Piglets in Winter" which he had been working on all evening. Now he was presenting it to the Chief for approval.

"No good, don't write this way." Chief Jiao quickly looked over the document and threw it on the desk. "Now, in writing a memorandum, you must avoid empty, boastful and irrelevant expressions."

He picked up the manuscript again and pointed at it, "Look here, 'After the winter solstice comes the Prelude of Cold,' who doesn't know that? And here, 'The development of a pig farm is a matter of great importance in promoting food production, supplies of meat to urban people, and reserve funds for the Four Modernizations of our country.' This is empty talk. Needless to say, more pigs means more money and more food. You have to use your brains to draft a memorandum."

The young cadre was totally lost — staring, wordless.

"Come here, sit down. Let's discuss this. A few concrete suggestions should make this memo more practical."

Burning the midnight oil was Chief Jiao's forté. He arose from his seat vigorously, while the young cadre sat down and opened his notebook.

"Regarding newborn piglets in winter — the first problem is to protect them from the cold. Isn't that right? The condition of winterization, in general, is not sufficient. Some pig farms are equipped with straw mats and curtains etc., but most are without even this minimum protection. Such conditions are contradictory to the objective of protecting newborn piglets. So the first and most important issue here is adequate winterization, and toward that end we must adopt every feasible and effective means." Chief Jiao rambled on, pacing the floor to and fro. He rolled his eyes and thought of more to say.

"The problem of piglets in the winter is mainly that of cold and hunger. Cold is an external cause, whereas hunger, an internal one — insufficient feeding will cause decline in body temperature, which in turn will cause decrease in resistance. Therefore, the second point is to keep the little piglets well fed. That's right. Be sure to include this point — increase the proportion of dietary nutrition in pigs' feed."

Chief Jiao made sure that the young cadre had jotted down what he had just said before he came to the third point:

"Furthermore, include the disease prevention. By the way, what is the most common disease that threatens pigs in the winter? As I remember we issued a special memo to that effect last time. You may repeat it here: how to prevent the premature death of newborn piglets."

Chief Jiao walked over to the file bureau, opened the door and gleefully produced a document, "Here is a good paragraph you may copy from: 'Report promptly any case of illness to the local Veterinary Disease Prevention Division. Meantime, take proper measures in treating the infected pig; in accordance with the rules and regulations currently in effect. In case of failure to report, a severe measure of action will be taken and the rule of accountability applies to all.' Add something to the effect that it is important to carry out the objective of prevention."

With an ache in his writing hand and a sense of relief in his heart, the young cadre peered at the Chief's thick babbling lips and could not help admiring him.

"The fourth point, emphasize the importance of political enlightenment. I need not provide you with the exact wording here. Also mention the material reward. You know that helps. Now, how many points do we have now? Four? H'mm . . ."

Chief Jiao stopped pacing the floor. The young cadre closed his notebook.

"Wait a minute. Last but not least: each level of the Party Committee should take the initiative by establishing the NEWBORN-PIGLETS-IN-THE-WINTER LEADERSHIP GROUP. Designate an assistant secretary to be in charge. Each related department should share the work responsibility. United we fight the problem. Report and follow up at regular intervals, and so on."

The young cadre bent down his head and wrote swiftly. One could hear the sound of his ball-point pen scratching the paper.

Chief Jiao stretched himself and heaved a deep breath. He cracked open his thick lips in a self-satisfied smile, "That's fine, now just add a little effort on your part — a bit of polishing up will do."

He looked at his watch. Eleven o'clock. "Let's go," he said while locking the desk drawer. "Time for our midnight snack. We'll have wonton tonight."

3. *"There'll be words aplenty at a memorial service."*

The cigarette butts piled up like a mound inside the ashtray. A ring of ashes scattered around it. The smoke, rising steadily from the tray, swirled around the room like a fog, dense and gray.

Ma Mingpeng, the Secretary of the County Committee, was leaning against the desk, holding a cigarette with his smoke-stained fingers. His small wearied eyes blinked in his dark and sullen face. Two little pouches hung under his eyes.

Since coming to the office early this morning, he had not stepped away except twice to go to the dining hall. The Committee meeting took up the whole morning, and the Study Group the afternoon. The evening was first occupied by the conference of Leadership Groups from the Security Promotion Committee, followed by the report of "No-Office Project" on the issues of disputes between a county chemical factory and a Production Group. Now sitting in front of him was an old cadre looking for a job. Every word the cadre uttered smashed like a nail on his numb and fatigued nerves.

"Secretary Ma, many years have gone by since the collapse of the Gang of Four. I am still wandering about like a desolate ghost, not a sign of work. Others have got their positions back. Why is it so hard in my case?"

"You're an old comrade, I'll be candid with you. We're having problems inside the Committee: more people than work. Every department is already staffed with seven or eight chiefs. People are talking: too many cooks but no broth. Where can I place you?"

"I need to work, even a doorman's job will do."

"That's what you think. Well, I know old comrades like you are dedicated to the Revolution, not your own interests. But what could I do? You were already a cadre before the Cultural Revolution. The authorities will have to place you in a proper position. Comrade, don't worry . . ."

"How can I help it? I'm reaching sixty."

The telephone rang. Ma Mingpeng picked up the receiver.

"What? Emergency notice from the City Committee — piglets in the winter. Erh . . . erh . . . well, very well. Ma Mingpeng rolled his eyes; procedures one after another turned up in his mind which he issued over the telephone as rapidly as an electronic computer, "First, telephone all the communes tonight and relate the message of the City Committee. Urge them to comply and adopt appropriate means. Second, as soon as you receive the memorandum from the City Committee, pass it on to the Regular Committee. Third, notify the Regular Committee to add one more agenda on Thursday's meeting — the problem of piglets in the winter. Fourth, request the people from the Cattle Office to draft a supplementary notice based on the ideas of the City Committee and present it for further discussion at the regular meeting. Fifth, ask the Cattle Office to send someone over to inspect and collect material for a further report. A report to the City Committee should be scheduled in a few days."

Putting the receiver down, Ma Mingpeng touched his temple with his smoke-stained fingers and closed his puffy eyelids.

"All these years, what am I? How could I justify myself to the people? Secretary Ma, just think one day I might drop dead and not even a memorial service in my honor . . ."

Ma Mingpeng opened his eyes and said with a half-smile, "Rest assured Comrade, there'll be words aplenty in a memorial service."

4. *"The peasants, they can't live without a son."*

"It's getting late. I say, let's call it a day. I've made up my mind today not to waste any more electricity. Go to bed early."

In the Commune Conference Room the fire in the fireplace had been out for a long time. Light from the smoking pipes and hand-rolled cigarettes flickered now and then and made the room cozy and seemingly warmer. Shen Guigeng, the Secretary of the Commune, was conferring with the cadres from the Production Group and Political Group.

"How many working units did you say have joined the System of Contract and Accountability? The Production Group reported fifty-seven units, which I think is a blown-up figure. Nowadays the emphasis is on truthful reports. We don't need to pad the figure."

No one said anything. The Production Group Leader made a mark on his papers.

"The Safety Training Class for truck drivers will begin day after tomorrow. But the majority of units have not yet handed in the enrollment list. This calls for our immediate attention. Three people died from accidents in one month. It's a matter of life and death, not to be overlooked. Will you, Chief Yu, take charge of this matter? Send someone to check tomorrow. Those drivers know nothing about safety regulations and some don't even have a driver's license. They race down the street like madmen. If we don't do something, our commune will soon become notorious."

Secretary Shen rubbed his bloodshot eyes and changed the subject to a few "trivial matters" such as forthcoming visitors to the commune. He then turned to ask the committee members, "Is there anything you wish to say?"

The plump Big Sister Gu, a member from Planned Parenthood, asked, "What are we to do when we report to the County Committee about the enforced birthrate? The goal is set for an increase of eight out of one thousand, but ours is way over eighteen."

"That's no good. Planned parenthood should be enforced. One more is too much."

"I know, but we can't make them do it. Our people from Planned Parenthood and doctors from the Public Health, they all dread going to the country. People point at their backs and curse them for doing such wicked things. Young wives scamper at the very sight of our white uniforms. The other day some woman hid in the closet for half a day, nearly died of suffocation."

"You should enlighten the masses."

"Enlighten them! How do you enlighten them? You just go and try. The peasants will tell you — without a son who would paint the house for me in the spring, harvest the grain for me in the autumn? These days, with the new bonus system, more labor means more money. Where would you be without manpower? They don't care if you restrict their rations, they want their son."

Secretary Shen sighed, "Ai, quite so. The peasants, they can't live without a son."

"What do you suggest we should do?"

"What to do, that's up to you. Why should we have Planned Parenthood if you ask me?"

Secretary Shen stood up, which meant the meeting was over. The roomful of people stretched and yawned and shuffled their respective chairs and stools. One after another they got up. At this moment Little Wang, the cadre of the Commune Office, entered the room.

"Secretary Shen, emergency telephone call from the County."

"Wait. Don't leave yet." Secretary Shen took the message from the cadre and looked at it. Then he said to Little Wang, "Telephone every group right away. Make sure they don't let any piglets die. Notify all of them tonight. If there is no answer by phone, you'll have to run over there. Every notice must be sent out before dawn."

Little Wang left. The roomful of people looked at one another and wondered why on earth the problem of piglets should become such a crisis.

"The County Committee telephoned to convey the message from the City Committee that we must deal with this issue of piglets in winter," Secretary Shen said as he seated himself again in his chair. "We'll have to discuss this problem and consume more electricity tonight. Let's see, all of you from the Production Group stay behind."

5. "Those city girls . . ."

The television program had already finished some time ago but a few youngsters still remained in the office. They were talking, eating watermelon seeds and teasing Grandpa Cao.

"Hi, you, lift your feet, stop throwing seeds on the floor, don't you see I'm sweeping behind you as fast as I can?"

Grandpa Cao, holding a big broom, was sweeping the floor which was strewn with cigarette butts, watermelon seeds and dust. Panting hard, he looked fierce, as though he was about to chase them out.

"Ya. This is our Group, not your home," a youngster answered back.

"What? As long as I'm paid for doing the job, I'm in charge here. Hey, move your butt over to the fireplace, will you?"

The youngster swaggered over to the fireplace and spat out a few more watermelon seeds, "What do you know? Grandpa Cao is in charge here. Looking after a fourteen-inch black and white television set so he can just sit and watch it all day long."

"I watch television!" Grandpa Cao scoffed and glared. "Pooh, what a disgrace. Nowadays, good-looking girls strip themselves half naked. That's the kind of fashion for you. I bet those city girls wear no pants. If I had a daughter who exposes herself like that, I'd break her neck."

The youngsters cracked up so hard that they almost fell over.

"What's so funny? None of you has a streak of decency left. You all want to follow the ways of those city slickers."

"You're right. If I get a job in the city, what I'll do first is buy myself a pair of bell-bottomed jeans and a pair of sandals. Then I'll wear my hair long and put on a pair of toad-like dark glasses. When I come to see you, Grandpa Cao, you won't even recognize me."

"You, I could recognize you even if you were burned to ashes! You good-for-nothing."

"Ah, you're as good as treasures from an excavation."

"What?" Grandpa Cao was shuffling the chairs around after the sweeping. The phrase "treasures from an excavation" sounded alien to his ears.

"He said you ought to keep company with the Emperors from the Ming Tombs," another youth explained, winking.

"I'm not that fortunate."

The roar of laughter nearly drowned out the ring of the telephone. Only the youth standing near the phone heard it. He picked up the receiver, "Yes, you want Old Cao? What do you have to say? Just tell me."

The other party refused.

"Tell you! You'd better step aside quick," Grandpa Cao smiled proudly. He rubbed his hands on his pants before he solemnly took the receiver, "Hello, the Commune, it's me. Are you Comrade Wang, still up? Ah, about piglets. Nothing wrong. We're expecting two litters — so I heard from the Guos. Any time now — what? Don't let any die from the cold. If there's any trouble, just ask for me — fine, good-bye."

Grandpa Cao replaced the telephone and looked at the young men in the room, "I say, who'll send a message to the Village Cadre?"

The young men grimaced and shrugged.

"Not me, I wouldn't dare. This is important business from the Commune Office. I can't be responsible."

"Whoever is paid should do the job."

"Then I'd better step aside."

Grandpa Cao glared at them, put on his old lamb wool tunic and left for the trip to the Village Cadre.

6. *"For the sake of the extra five dollars . . ."*

The wife of Xu Quan, the Village Cadre, was awakened by the pounding on the door. "What on earth is the matter? Scaring people like this in the middle of the night," she muttered.

Xu Quan was sitting in the chair with his quilted coat over his shoulders. He fished out his tobacco box from his pocket and rolled a cigarette. He slowly answered his wife. "A notice from the Commune: don't let any piglets die from the cold . . ."

"That's worrying for nothing. The pigs are contracted to the Guo family who are capable and clever people. Why should they let any pig die? You just come back to bed and get some sleep."

"No, I'll have to check the pigs," Xu Quan stretched an arm into the coat sleeve, "I heard this evening they're expecting piglets tonight. If anything should happen, I'll be the first one to blame."

"Look at yourself—so 'positive,' all for the sake of the extra five dollars a month. You think of it as something special, but not me," she suddenly sat up, pulling the quilt over her and becoming very agitated, "If you're really so 'positive,' try and earn more for your family. Look at our neighbor Old Du. After a couple of long trips and some secret deals, he's earned at least several thousand already and they're building a five-room brick house now."

"I won't do anything illegal."

"Is it illegal to contract the work of the rice field? Good for those who did. The price of rice is going up, plus the price for good production; one family can easily earn up to seven or eight hundred dollars. Only you, fool, hooked by the official title, have stuck with poverty. You can burn your eyes out with envy."

"It's a good thing for people to earn more. The policy nowadays is to let people prosper. What are you griping about?"

"I'm not unscrupulous. I'm only talking about you. If you were clever, you'd have put our name in at the time of signing the contract."

"Put my name in? How do I find the time? Half of my days are taken up by meetings. I'm only busy and concerned with the good of the public."

"Tut, tut, not that nonsense again. As a cadre for more than ten years, what have you done for your family? We're all in for misery with you. The good of the public indeed! You've got the whole village against you."

"You're envious. Why don't you work in the rice field yourself? Nobody's stopping you. You want to get rich by doing nothing but staying in bed. No such luck."

He pushed open the door and stepped over the threshold.

"Put on your dog-skin hat. If you get a cold, I've no money to buy medicine." A black furry object flew toward him and landed on the crook of his elbow.

He put the hat on his head and turned around, "Just leave me alone."

7. *"I'll make up words to suit
    Whatever tune the authority picks."*

In the pig farm lights were shining brightly. Xu Quan called once before he lifted the cotton curtain. A rush of warm air greeted him.

He held his hands together and looked around. Mammy Guo's second daughter was squatting in front of the fireplace, making a fire. Mammy Guo, in a blue apron and with sleeves rolled up high, was lifting the lid of a pot in which the rice broth was cooking.

"Newborn piglets?"

"Yes, a litter of twelve, every one alive." Mammy Guo wiped off the perspiration from her forehead with her elbow. She was all smiles. She replaced the lid and wiped her hands on the apron. She then led the cadre inside.

On the warm kang, twelve tiny piglets huddled together in a bundle of round, plump and quavering bodies. A little humming noise came out from the bundle.

"Our pig farm is doing well this time," Xu Quan complimented her cheerfully.

"The group trusts us to do the job and lets us contract the pig farm. Of course, we want to do our very best. We need all the help we can get so I sent for my father from the next village."

Xu Quan saw an old man in the far corner of the room, squatting in front of a broken table and drinking wine by himself.

"Come on, have a cup," Mammy Guo brought out a wine cup.

"Ha, have you moved here with the pigs?" Xu Quan, laughing, squatted down.

"I'm worried if I'm away. It's really more convenient staying right here with the pigs, especially early mornings and late at night."

"Let's drink. What a day." The old man lifted his cup.

With a lightened heart and prompted by the warm hospitality, Xu Quan lifted his cup and finished the wine in a few gulps. A current of heat came over him. Just think, twelve piglets — Mammy Guo really knows what she's doing. He asked her about her past farm experience and her suggestions for the future.

"I just feed them — that's all. I can't read a single word; don't ask me about my experience," Mammy Guo said, quite pleased with herself.

Yes, what could she say? I have to make up my own report. H'mm — "To carry out the System of Accountability — if every member in the Commune shares the responsibility, the cadre can be assured of success," — pretty good — but one sentence is not enough — this wine is not bad, must be at least sixty-five per cent alcohol, better than the one I bought last time — Mammy Guo is quite a capable woman, how she mobilizes everybody, old and young, the eighty-year-old father and the school-aged daughter — isn't this an "experience"? "Enlist all help, regardless of age or sex, in our care for the piglets" — sounds nice, but wait, how stupid can I get? This jingle is from the late fifties, no longer popular now. "Mass mobilization means massive achievement" — no good, you don't see such slogans on newspapers anymore. I have to use new expressions, such as "United in heart and spirit, we strive for the Four Modernizations" — that's better — one hears it broadcast eight times a day — but what category of modernization does Mammy Guo's work fit in? — I'd better stop drinking. Tomorrow I have to report to my superior — but what shall I say about "experience"? Pooh — never mind, when the time comes, I'll make up words to suit whatever tune the authority picks.

Questions for Discussion

1. How does the story's structure work to suggest the hierarchical nature of contemporary Chinese society? How do the first scene and the last stand in contrast?
2. How do Chief Jiao's stylistic revisions regarding the memo of the newborn piglets satirize bureaucratic jargon and propaganda?
3. How is Ma Mingpeng's encounter with the Old Cadre contrasted with his handling of the memo on the piglets? What is ironic about Ma Mingpeng's final words to the Old Cadre, "There'll be words aplenty in a memorial service"?
4. How is the meeting of the Production Group and the Political Group used to critique China's policy on birth control? How is the attitude toward human reproduction in this section contrasted ironically with the handling of the "issue of piglets"?
5. In what ways does the scene between Grandpa Cao and the young men satirize the breakdown of traditional Chinese attitudes toward the elderly and tradition? How does Mammy Guo's care of the newborn piglets reinforce the story's theme?

Ideas for Writing

1. In an essay, analyze the story's final section, which focuses on the Village Cadre and the Guo family who take care of the newborn piglets. What is significant about the story's conclusion, in which the piglets sleep in the Guos' bed while Xu Quan squats down and drunkenly plans his propaganda report on the piglet issue?
2. Write a satirical story about bureaucratic attitudes and attempts to solve non-pressing or imaginary problems in an environment with which you are familiar — for instance, school, the workplace, or the military.

BESSIE HEAD   (1937–1986)

Bessie Emory Head was one of the African continent's most vivid recorders of the convergence of modern and tribal ways. She was born in a psychiatric hospital in Pietermaritzburg, South Africa, where her mother, a wealthy white South African, had been committed because Head's father was a black stable hand. She was taken from her mother, who left money for her daughter's upbringing and education, and raised by black foster parents until she was thirteen; then she was educated in a mission orphanage where she earned a high school diploma and a teaching certificate. She went on to teach elementary school and began her writing career. Limited by the restrictions of apartheid, Head left South Africa in 1964 and lived as a refugee on a farm in Botswana — she was granted citizenship in 1979 — until her death at forty-nine from hepatitis. Her novels, which contain strong elements of autobiography, include *When Rain Clouds Gather* (1986), *Maru* (1971), and *A Question of Power* (1973). She published one collection of short stories, *The Collector of Treasures and Other Botswana Village Tales* (1977), which includes "Snapshots of a Wedding." She also published an oral history of nineteenth-century southern Africa as well as two volumes of essays.

While Head explores racism and alienation, she also argues for the importance of preserving one's culture and heritage, which she sees as essential components of human dignity.

Snapshots of a Wedding   (1977)

Wedding days always started at the haunting, magical hour of early dawn when there was only a pale crack of light on the horizon. For those who were awake, it took the earth hours to adjust to daylight. The cool and damp of the night slowly arose in shimmering waves like water and even the forms of the people who bestirred themselves at this unearthly hour were distorted in the haze; they appeared to be dancers in slow motion, with fluid, watery forms. In the dim light, four men, the relatives of the bridegroom, Kegoletile, slowly herded an ox before them towards the yard of MmaKhudu, where the bride, Neo, lived. People were already astir in MmaKhudu's yard, yet for a while they all came and peered closely at the distorted fluid forms that approached, to ascertain if it were indeed the relatives of the bridegroom. Then the ox, who was a rather stupid fellow and unaware of his sudden and impending end as meat for the wedding feast, bellowed casually his early morning yawn. At this the beautiful ululating of the women rose and swelled over the air like water bubbling rapidly and melodiously over the stones of a clear, sparkling stream.

In between ululating all the while, the women began to weave about the yard in the wedding dance; now and then they bent over and shook their buttocks in the air. As they handed over the ox, one of the bridegroom's relatives joked:

"This is going to be a modern wedding." He meant that a lot of the traditional courtesies had been left out of the planning for the wedding day; no one had been awake all night preparing diphiri or the traditional wedding breakfast of pounded meat and samp; the bridegroom said he had no church and did not care about such things; the bride was six months pregnant and showing it, so there was just going to be a quick marriage ceremony at the police camp.

"Oh, we all have our own ways," one of the bride's relatives joked back. "If the times are changing, we keep up with them." And she weaved away ululating joyously.

Whenever there was a wedding the talk and gossip that preceded it were appalling, except that this time the relatives of the bride, Neo, kept their talk a strict secret among themselves. They were anxious to be rid of her; she was an impossible girl with haughty, arrogant ways. Of all her family and relatives, she was the only one who had completed her "O" levels and she never failed to rub in this fact. She walked around with her nose in the air; illiterate relatives were beneath her greeting — it was done in a clever way, she just turned her head to one side and smiled to herself or when she greeted it was like an insult; she stretched her hand out, palm outspread, swung it down laughing with a gesture that plainly said: "Oh, that's you!" Only her mother seemed bemused by her education. At her own home Neo was waited on hand and foot. Outside her home nasty remarks were passed. People bitterly disliked conceit and pride.

"That girl has no manners!" the relatives would remark. "What's the good of education if it goes to someone's head so badly they have no respect for the people? Oh, she is not a person."

Then they would nod their heads in that fatal way, with predictions that one day life would bring her down. Actually, life had treated Neo rather nicely. Two months after completing her "O" levels she became pregnant by Kegoletile with their first child. It soon became known that another girl, Mathata, was also pregnant by Kegoletile. The difference between the two girls was that Mathata was completely uneducated; the only work she would ever do was that of a housemaid, while Neo had endless opportunities before her — typist, bookkeeper, or secretary. So Neo merely smiled; Mathata was no rival. It was as though the decision had been worked out by circumstance because when the families converged on Kegoletile at the birth of the children — he was rich in cattle and they wanted to see what they could get — he of course immediately proposed marriage to Neo; and for Mathata, he agreed to a court order to pay a maintenance of R10.00 a month until the child was twenty years old. Mathata merely smiled too. Girls like her offered no resistance to the approaches of men; when they lost them, they just let things ride.

"He is of course just running after the education and not the manners," Neo's relatives commented, to show they were not fooled by human nature. "He thinks that since she is as educated as he is they will both get good jobs and be rich in no time . . ."

Educated as he was, Kegoletile seemed to go through a secret conflict during the year he prepared a yard for his future married life with Neo. He spent most of his free time in the yard of Mathata. His behaviour there wasn't too alarming but he showered Mathata with gifts of all kinds — food, fancy dresses, shoes and underwear. Each time he came, he brought a gift and each time Mathata would burst out laughing and comment: "Ow, Kegoletile, how can I wear all these dresses? It's just a waste of money! Besides, I manage quite well with the R10.00 you give every month for the child . . ."

She was a very pretty girl with black eyes like stars; she was always smiling and happy; immediately and always her own natural self. He knew what he was marrying — something quite the opposite, a new kind of girl with false postures and acquired, grand-madame ways. And yet, it didn't pay a man these days to look too closely into his heart. They all wanted as wives, women who were big money-earners and they were so ruthless about it! And yet it was as though the society itself stamped each of its individuals with its own particular brand of wealth and Kegoletile had not yet escaped it; he had about him an engaging humility and eagerness to help and please that made him loved and respected by all who knew him. During those times he sat in Mathata's yard, he communicated nothing of the conflict he felt but he would sit on a chair with his arms spread out across its back, turn his head sideways and stare at what seemed to be an empty space beside him. Then he would smile, stand up and walk away. Nothing dramatic. During the year he prepared the huts in his new yard, he frequently slept at the home of Neo.

Relatives on both sides watched this division of interest between the two yards and one day when Neo walked patronisingly into the yard of an aunt, the aunt decided to frighten her a little.

"Well aunt," she said, with the familiar careless disrespect which went with her so called, educated, status. "Will you make me some tea? And how's things?"

The aunt spoke very quietly.

"You may not know it, my girl, but you are hated by everyone around here. The debate we have going is whether a nice young man like Kegoletile should marry bad-mannered rubbish like you. He would be far better off if he married a girl like Mathata, who though uneducated, still treats people with respect."

The shock the silly girl received made her stare for a terrified moment at her aunt. Then she stood up and ran out of the house. It wiped the superior smile off her face and brought her down a little. She developed an anxiety to greet people and also an anxiety about securing Kegoletile as a husband — that was why she became pregnant six months before the marriage could take place. In spite of this, her own relatives still disliked her and right up to the day of the wedding they were still debating whether Neo was a suitable wife for any man. No one would have guessed it though with all the dancing, ululating and happiness expressed in the yard and streams of guests gaily ululated themselves along the pathways with wedding gifts precariously balanced on their heads. Neo's maternal aunts, all sedately decked up in shawls, sat in a select group by themselves in a corner of the yard. They sat on the bare ground with their legs stretched out before them but they were served like queens the whole day long. Trays of tea, dry white bread, plates of meat, rice, and salad were constantly placed before them. Their important task was to formally hand over the bride to Kegoletile's maternal aunts when they approached the yard at sunset. So they sat the whole day with still, expressionless faces, waiting to fulfil this ancient rite.

Equally still and expressionless were the faces of the long column of women, Kegoletile's maternal aunts, who appeared outside the yard just as the sun sank low. They walked slowly into the yard indifferent to the ululating that greeted them and seated themselves in a group opposite Neo's maternal aunts. The yard became very silent while each group made its report. Kegoletile had provided all the food for the wedding feast and a maternal aunt from his side first asked:

"Is there any complaint? Has all gone well?"

"We have no complaint," the opposite party replied.

"We have come to ask for water," Kegoletile's side said, meaning that from times past the bride was supposed to carry water in her in-law's home.

"It is agreed to," the opposite party replied.

Neo's maternal aunts then turned to the bridegroom and counselled him: "Son, you must plough and supply us with corn each year."

Then Kegoletile's maternal aunts turned to the bride and counselled her: "Daughter, you must carry water for your husband. Beware, that at all times, he is the owner of the house and must be obeyed. Do not mind if he stops now and then and talks to other ladies. Let him feel free to come and go as he likes . . ."

The formalities over, it was now time for Kegoletile's maternal aunts to get up, ululate and weave and dance about the yard. Then, still dancing and ululating, accompanied by the bride and groom they slowly wound their way to the yard of Kegoletile where another feast had been prepared. As they approached his yard, an old woman suddenly dashed out and chopped at the ground with a hoe. It was all only a formality. Neo would never be the kind of wife who went to the lands to plough. She already had a well-paid job in an office as a secretary. Following on this another old woman took the bride by the hand and led her to a smeared and decorated courtyard wherein had been placed a traditional animal-skin Tswana mat. She was made to sit on the mat and a shawl and kerchief were placed before her. The shawl was ceremonially wrapped around her shoulders; the kerchief tied around her head — the symbols that she was now a married woman.

Guests quietly moved forward to greet the bride. Then two girls started to ululate and dance in front of the bride. As they both turned and bent over to shake their buttocks in the air, they bumped into each other and toppled over. The wedding guests roared with laughter. Neo, who had all this time been stiff, immobile, and rigid, bent forward and her shoulders shook with laughter.

The hoe, the mat, the shawl, the kerchief, the beautiful flute-like ululating of the women seemed in itself a blessing on the marriage but all the guests were deeply moved when out of the crowd, a woman of majestic, regal bearing slowly approached the bride. It was the aunt who had scolded Neo for her bad manners and modern ways. She dropped to her knees before the bride, clenched her fists together and pounded the ground hard with each clenched fist on either side of the bride's legs. As she pounded her fists she said loudly: "Be a good wife! Be a good wife!"

Questions for Discussion

1. How are the rhythms of the natural world incorporated into the wedding ritual?
2. One of the bridegroom's relatives jokes, "This is going to be a modern wedding." In what ways is the wedding modern? In what ways is the wedding traditional?
3. What does Kegoletile's decision to marry Neo, despite her general unpopularity and the fact that he has also gotten another woman pregnant, reveal about his personal values and the values of his class?
4. What comment does the story make about the values and liabilities of education and marriage for an African woman?
5. Contrast Neo and Mathata. How do you imagine that they feel about each other?

Ideas for Writing

1. Write a story about a wedding that is focused on the conflicting values evident between bride and groom, as well as between their families.
2. Write an essay in which you contrast the conflicting roles and expectations of African women as revealed in "Snapshots of a Wedding."

JOYCE CAROL OATES   (b. 1938)

A writer of great versatility, Joyce Carol Oates often explores in her fiction the psychological and sociological motivations of her characters, using settings that appear realistic on the surface yet often contain elements of gothic, nightmarish distortion. Born into a Roman Catholic family in Lockport, New York, Oates developed an interest in writing stories while still a child — an interest her parents encouraged. Oates completed her B.A. at Syracuse University and her M.A. at the University of Wisconsin. In 1959, while an undergraduate, she won the *Mademoiselle* college fiction award. She published her first story collection, *By the North Gate*, in 1963, and every year since then she has come out with a new collection of stories, a novel, a play, or a collection of literary essays. Oates has continued to win awards for her writing, including three O. Henry Prize awards and the National Book Award (1970). Her novels include *Them* (1969), *Black Water* (1992), *Foxfire: The Story of a Girl Gang* (1993), and *What I Lived For* (1994). Oates has published many story collections, including *The Wheel of Love and Other Stories* (1970), *Marriages and Infidelities* (1972), *Last Days: Stories* (1984), *Where Is Here?* (1992), and *"Will You Always Love Me?" and Other Stories* (1996).

Oates's stories are often drawn from her own past, though generally in a highly fictionalized form. "My writing is full of the lives I might have led," she has said. "A writer imagines what could have happened, not what really happened."

Why Don't You Come Live with Me It's Time   (1990)

The other day, it was a sunswept windy March morning, I saw my grandmother staring at me, those deep-socketed eyes, that translucent skin, a youngish woman with very dark hair as I hadn't quite remembered her who had died while I was in college, years ago, in 1966. Then I saw, of course it was virtually in the same instant I saw the face was my own, my own eyes in that face floating there not in a mirror but in a metallic mirrored surface, teeth bared in a startled smile and seeing my face that was not my face I laughed, I think that was the sound.

You're an insomniac, you tell yourself: there are profound truths revealed only to the insomniac by night like those phosphorescent minerals veined and glimmering in the dark but coarse and ordinary otherwise, you have to examine such minerals in the absence of light to discover their beauty: you tell yourself.

Maybe because I was having so much trouble sleeping at the time, twelve or thirteen years old, no one would have called the problem insomnia, that sounds too clinical, too adult and anyway they'd said "You can sleep if you try" and I'd overheard "She just wants attention — you know what she's like" and I was hurt and angry but hopeful too wanting to ask, But what am I like, are you the ones to tell me?

In fact, Grandmother had insomnia too — "suffered from insomnia" was the somber expression — but no one made the connection between her and me. Our family was that way: worrying that one weakness might find justification in another and things would slip out of containment and control.

In fact, I'd had trouble sleeping since early childhood but I had not understood that anything was wrong. Not secrecy nor even a desire to please my parents made me pretend to sleep, I thought it was what you do, I thought when Mother put me to bed I had to shut my eyes so she could leave and that was the way of releasing her though immediately afterward when I was alone my eyes opened wide and sleepless. Sometimes it was day, sometimes night. Often by night I could see, I could discern the murky shapes of objects, familiar objects that had lost their names by night as by night lying motionless with no one to observe me it seemed I had no name and my body was shapeless and undefined. The crucial thing was to lie motionless, scarcely breathing, until at last — it might be minutes or it might be hours, if there were noises in the house or out on the street (we lived on a busy street for most of my childhood in Hammond) it would be hours — a dark pool of warm water would begin to lap gently over my feet, eventually it would cover my legs, my chest, my face . . . what adults called "sleep" this most elusive and strange and mysterious of experiences, a cloudy transparency of ever-shifting hues and textures surrounding tense islands of wakefulness so during the course of a night I would sleep, and wake, and sleep, and wake, a dozen times, as the water lapped over my face and retreated from it, this seemed altogether natural it was altogether desirable, for when I slept another kind of sleep, heavily, deeply, plunged into a substance not water and not a transparency but an oozy lightless muck, when I plunged down into that sleep and managed to wake from it shivering and sweating with a pounding heart and a pounding head as if my brain trapped inside my skull (but "brain" and "skull" were not concepts I would have known, at that time) had been racing feverishly like a small machine gone berserk it was to a sense of total helplessness and an exhaustion so profound it felt like death: sheer nonexistence, oblivion: and I did not know, nor do I know now, decades later, which sleep is preferable, which sleep is normal, how is one defined by sleep, from where in fact does "sleep" arise.

When I was older, a teenager, with a room at a little distance from my parents' bedroom, I would often, those sleepless nights, simply turn on my bedside lamp and read, I'd read until dawn and day and the resumption of daytime routine in a state of complete concentration, or sometimes I'd switch on the radio close beside my bed, I was cautious of course to keep the volume low,

low and secret and I'd listen fascinated to stations as far away as Pittsburgh, Toronto, Cleveland, there was a hillbilly station broadcasting out of Cleveland, country-and-western music I would never have listened to by day. One by one I got to know intimately the announcers' voices along the continuum of the glowing dial, hard to believe those strangers didn't know *me*. But sometimes my room left me short of breath, it was fresh air I craved, hurriedly I'd dress pulling on clothes over my pajamas, and even in rainy or cold weather I went outside leaving the house by the kitchen door so quietly in such stealth no one ever heard, not once did one of them hear *I will do it: because I want to do it* sleeping their heavy sleep that was like the sleep of molluscs, eyeless. And outside: in the night: the surprise of the street transformed by the lateness of the hour, the emptiness, the silence: I'd walk to the end of our driveway staring, listening, my heart beating hard. *So this is — what it is!* The ordinary sights were made strange, the sidewalks, the street lights, the neighboring houses. Yet the fact had no consciousness of itself except through *me*.

For that has been one of the principles of my life.

And if here and there along the block a window glowed from within (another insomniac?), or if a lone car passed in the street casting its headlights before it, or a train sounded in the distance, or, high overhead, an airplane passed winking and glittering with lights, what happiness swelled my lungs, what gratitude, what conviction, I was utterly alone for the moment, and invisible, which is identical with being alone.

Come by anytime dear, no need to call first my grandmother said often, *Come by after school, anytime, please!* I tried not to hear the pleading in her voice, tried not to see the soft hurt in her eyes, and the hope.

Grandmother was a "widow": her husband, my step-grandfather had died of cancer of the liver when I was five years old.

Grandmother had beautiful eyes. Deep-set, dark, intelligent, alert. And her hair was a lovely silvery-gray, not coarse like others' hair but fine-spun, silky.

Mother said, "In your grandmother's eyes you can do no wrong." She spoke as if amused but I understood the accusation.

Because Grandmother loved me best of the grandchildren, yes and she loved me best of all the family, I basked in her love as in the warmth of a private sun. Grandmother loved me without qualification and without criticism which angered my parents since they understood that so fierce a love made me impervious to their more modulated love, not only impervious but indifferent to the threat of its being withdrawn . . . which is the only true power parents have over their children. Isn't it?

We visited Grandmother often, especially now she was alone. She visited us. Sundays, holidays, birthdays. And I would bicycle across the river to her house once or twice a week, or drop in after school, Grandmother encouraged me to bring my friends but I was too shy, I never stayed long, her happiness in my presence made me uneasy. Always she would prepare one of my favorite dishes, hot oatmeal with cream and brown sugar, apple cobbler, brownies, fudge, lemon custard tarts . . . and I sat and ate as she watched, and, eating, I felt hunger, the hunger was in my mouth. To remember those foods brings the hunger back now, the sudden rush of it, the pain. In my mouth.

At home Mother would ask, "Did you spoil your appetite again?"

The river that separated us was the Cassadaga, flowing from east to west, to Lake Ontario, through the small city of Hammond, New York.

After I left, aged eighteen, I only returned to Hammond as a visitor. Now everyone is dead, I never go back.

The bridge that connected us was the Ferry Street bridge, the bridge we crossed hundreds of times. Grandmother lived south of the river (six blocks south, two blocks west), we lived north of the river (three blocks north, one and a half blocks east), we were about three miles apart. The Ferry Street bridge, built in 1919, was one of those long narrow spiky nightmare bridges, my childhood was filled with such bridges, this one thirty feet above the Cassadaga, with high arches, steep ramps on both sides, six concrete supports, rusted iron grillwork, and neoclassical ornamentation of the kind associated with Chicago Commercial architecture, which was the architectural style of Hammond generally.

The Ferry Street bridge. Sometimes in high winds you could feel the bridge sway, I lowered my eyes when my father drove us over, he'd joke as the plank floor rattled and beneath the rattling sound there came something deeper and more sinister, the vibrating hum of the river itself, a murmur, a secret caress against the soles of our feet, our buttocks, and between our legs so it was an enormous relief when the car had passed safely over the bridge and descended the ramp to land. The Ferry Street bridge was almost too narrow for two ordinary-sized automobiles to pass but only once was my father forced to stop about a quarter of the way out, a gravel truck was bearing down upon us and the driver gave no sign of slowing down so my father braked the car, threw it hurriedly into reverse and backed up red-faced the way we'd come and after that the Ferry Street bridge was no joke to him, any more than it was to his passengers.

The other day, that sunny gusty day when I saw Grandmother's face in the mirror, I mean the metallic mirrored surface downtown, I mean the face that had seemed to be Grandmother's face but was not, I began to think of the Ferry Street bridge and since then I haven't slept well seeing the bridge in my mind's eye the way you do when you're insomniac, the images that should be in dreams are loosed and set careening through the day like lethal bubbles in the blood. I had not known how I'd memorized that bridge, and I'd forgotten why.

The time I am thinking of, I was twelve or thirteen years old, I know I was that age because the Ferry Street bridge was closed for repairs then and it was

over the Ferry Street bridge I went, to see Grandmother. I don't remember if it
was a conscious decision or if I'd just started walking, not knowing where I
was going, or why. It was three o'clock in the morning. No one knew where
I was. Beyond the barricade and the DETOUR — BRIDGE OUT signs, the moon
so bright it lit my way like a manic face.

A number of times I'd watched with trepidation certain of the neighborhood boys inch their way out across the steel beams of the skeletal bridge,
walking with arms extended for balance, so I knew it could be done without
mishap, I knew I could do it if only I had the courage, and it seemed to me I
had sufficient courage, now was the time to prove it. Below the river rushed
past slightly higher than usual, it was October, there had been a good deal of
rain, but tonight the sky was clear, stars like icy pinpricks, and that bright
glaring moon illuminating my way for me so I thought *I will do it* already
climbing up onto what would be the new floor of the bridge when at last it
was completed: not planks but a more modern sort of iron mesh, not yet laid
into place. But the steel beams were about ten inches wide and there was a grid
of them, four beams spanning the river and (I would count them as I crossed,
I would never forget that count) fourteen narrower beams at perpendicular
angles with the others, and about three feet below these beams there was a
complex crisscrossing of cables you might define as a net of sorts if you
wanted to think in such terms, a safety net, there was no danger really *I will
do it because I want to do it, because there is no one to stop me.*

And on the other side, Grandmother's house. And even if its windows
were darkened, even if I did no more than stand looking quietly at it, and then
come back home, never telling anyone what I'd done, even so I would have
proved something *Because there is no one to stop me* which has been one of the
principles of my life. To regret that principle is to regret my entire life.

I climbed up onto one of the beams, trembling with excitement. But how
cold it was! — I'd come out without my gloves.

And how loud the river below, the roaring like a kind of jeering applause;
and it smelled too, of something brackish and metallic. I knew not to glance
down at it, steadying myself as a quick wind picked up, teasing tears into my
eyes, I was thinking *There is no turning back: never* but instructing myself too
that the beam was perfectly safe if I was careful for had I not seen boys walking across without slipping? didn't the workmen walk across too, many times
a day? I decided not to stand, though — I was afraid to stand — I remained
squatting on my haunches, gripping the edge of the beam with both hands,
inching forward in this awkward way, hunched over, right foot, and then left
foot, and then right foot, and then left foot: passing the first of the perpendicular beams, and the second, and the third, and the fourth: and so in this
clumsy and painful fashion forcing myself to continue until my thigh muscles
ached so badly I had to stop and I made the mistake which even in that instant

I knew was a mistake of glancing down: seeing the river thirty feet below: the way it was flowing so swiftly and with such power, and seeming rage, ropy sinuous coils of churning water, foam-flecked, terrible, and its flow exactly perpendicular to the direction in which I was moving.

"Oh no. Oh no. Oh no."

A wave of sharp cold terror shot up into me as if into my very bowels, piercing me between the legs rising from the river itself and I could not move, I squatted there on the beam unable to move, all the strength drained out of my muscles and I was paralyzed knowing *You're going to die: of course, die* even as with another part of my mind (there is always this other part of my mind) I was thinking with an almost teacherly logic that the beam *was* safe, it was wide enough, and flat enough, and not damp or icy or greasy yes certainly it *was* safe: if this were land, for instance in our backyard, if for instance my father had set down a plank flat in the grass, a plank no more than half the width of the beam couldn't I, Claire, have walked that plank without the slightest tremor of fear? boldly? even gracefully? even blindfolded? without a moment's hesitation? not the flicker of an eyelid, not the most minute leap of a pulse? — *You know you aren't going to die: don't be silly* but it must have been five minutes before I could force myself to move again, my numbed right leg easing forward, my aching foot, I forced my eyes upward too and fixed them resolutely on the opposite shore, or what I took on faith to be the opposite shore, a confusion of sawhorses and barrels and equipment now only fitfully illuminated by the moon.

But I got there, I got to where I meant to go without for a moment exactly remembering why.

Now the worst of it's done: for now.

Grandmother's house, what's called a bungalow, plain stucco, one-story, built close to the curb, seemed closer to the river than I'd expected, maybe I was running, desperate to get there, hearing the sound of the angry rushing water that was like many hundreds of murmurous voices, and the streets surprised me with their emptiness — so many vacant lots, murky transparencies of space where buildings had once stood — and a city bus passed silently, lit gaily from within, yet nearly empty too, only the driver and a single (male) passenger sitting erect and motionless as mannequins, and I shrank panicked into the shadows so they would not see me: maybe I would be arrested: a girl of my age on the street at such an hour, alone, with deep-set frightened eyes, a pale face, guilty mouth, zip-up corduroy jacket and jeans over her pajamas, disheveled as a runaway. But the bus passed, turned a corner, and vanished. And there was Grandmother's house, not darkened as I'd expected but lighted, and from the sidewalk staring I could see Grandmother inside, or a figure I took to be Grandmother, but why was she awake at such an hour, how remarkable that she should be awake as if awaiting me, and I remembered then — how instantaneously these thoughts came to me, eerie as tiny bubbles that, bursting, yielded riches of a sort that would require a considerable expenditure of time to relate though their duration was in fact hardly more than an instant! — I remembered having heard the family speak of Grandmother's sometimes strange behavior, worrisome behavior in a woman of her age, or of any age, the problem was her insomnia unless insomnia was not cause but consequence of a malady of the soul, so it would be reported to my father, her son, that she'd been seen walking at night in neighborhoods unsafe for solitary women, she'd been seen at a midnight showing of a film in downtown Hammond, and even when my step-grandfather was alive (he worked on a lake freighter, he was often gone) she might spend time in local taverns, not drinking heavily, but drinking, and this was behavior that might lead to trouble, or so the family worried, though there was never any specific trouble so far as anyone knew, and Grandmother smoked too, smoked on the street which "looks cheap," my mother said, my mother too smoked but never on the street, the family liked to tell and retell the story of a cousin of my father's coming to Hammond on a Greyhound bus, arriving at the station at about six in the morning, and there in the waiting room was my grandmother in her old fox-fur coat sitting there with a book in her lap, a cigarette in one hand, just sitting there placidly and with no mind for the two or three others, distinctly odd near-derelict men, in the room with her, just sitting there reading her book (Grandmother was always reading, poetry, biographies of great men like Lincoln, Mozart, Julius Caesar, Jesus of Nazareth) and my father's cousin came in, saw her, said, "Aunt Tina, what on earth are you doing here?" and Grandmother had looked up calmly, and said, "Why not? — it's for waiting isn't it?"

Another strange thing Grandmother had done, it had nothing to do with her insomnia that I could see unless all our strangenesses, as they are judged in others' eyes, are morbidly related, was arranging for her husband's body to be cremated: not buried in a cemetery plot, but cremated: which means burnt to mere ash: which means annihilation: and though cremation had evidently been my step-grandfather's wish it had seemed to the family that Grandmother had complied with it too readily, and so immediately following her husband's death that no one had a chance to dissuade her. "What a thing," my mother said, shivering, "to do to your own husband!"

I was thinking of this now seeing through one of the windows a man's figure, a man talking with Grandmother in her kitchen, it seemed to me that perhaps my step-grandfather had not yet died, thus was not yet cremated, and some of the disagreement might be resolved, but I must have already knocked at the door since Grandmother was there opening it, at first she stared at me as if scarcely recognizing me then she laughed, she said, "What are *you* doing here?" and I tried to explain but could not: the words failed to come: my teeth were chattering with cold and fright and the words failed to come but Grandmother led me inside, she was taller than I remembered, and younger, her hair dark, wavy, falling to her shoulders, and her mouth red with lipstick, she laughed leading me into the kitchen where a man, a stranger, was waiting, "Harry this is my granddaughter Claire," Grandmother said, and the man stepped forward regarding me with interest, yet speaking of me as if I were somehow not present, "She's your granddaughter?" "She is." "I didn't know you had a granddaughter." "You don't know lots of things."

And Grandmother laughed at us both, who gazed in perplexity and doubt at each other. Laughing, she threw her head back like a young girl or a man, and bared her strong white teeth.

I was then led to sit at the kitchen table, in my usual place, Grandmother went to the stove to prepare something for me and I sat quietly, not frightened now, yet not quite at ease though I understood I was safe now, Grandmother would take care of me now and nothing could happen, I saw that the familiar kitchen had been altered, it was very brightly lit, almost blindingly lit, yet deeply shadowed in the corners, the rear wall where the sink should have been dissolved into what would have been the backyard but I had a quick flash of the backyard where there were flower and vegetable beds, Grandmother loved to work in the yard, she brought flowers and vegetables in the summer wherever she visited, the most beautiful of her flowers were peonies, big gorgeous crimson peonies, and the thought of the peonies was confused with the smell of the oatmeal Grandmother was stirring on the stove for me to eat, oatmeal was the first food of my childhood: the first food I can remember: but Grandmother made it her own way, her special way stirring in brown sugar, cream, a spoonful of dark honey, so just thinking of it I felt my mouth water violently, almost it hurt, the saliva flooded so and I was embarrassed that a trickle ran down my chin and I couldn't seem to wipe it off and Grandmother's friend Harry was watching me: but finally I managed to wipe it off on my fingers: and Harry smiled.

The thought came to me, not a new thought but one I'd had for years, but now it came with unusual force, like the saliva flooding my mouth, that when my parents died I would come live with Grandmother — of course: I would come live with Grandmother: and Grandmother at the stove stirring my oatmeal in a pan must have heard my thoughts for she said, "— Claire why don't you come live with me it's time isn't it?" and I said, "Oh yes," and Grandmother didn't seem to have heard for she repeated her question, turning now to look at me, to smile, her eyes shining and her mouth so amazingly red, two delicate spots of rouge on her cheeks so my heart caught seeing how beautiful she was, as young as my mother, or younger, and she laughed saying, " — Claire why don't you come live with me it's time isn't it?" and again I said, "Oh yes Grandmother," nodding and blinking tears from my eyes, they were tears of infinite happiness, and relief, " — oh Grandmother, *yes.*"

Grandmother's friend Harry was a navy radio operator, he said, or had been, he wore no uniform and he was no age I could have guessed, with silvery-glinting hair in a crewcut, muscular shoulders and arms, but maybe his voice was familiar? maybe I'd heard him over the radio? Grandmother was urging him to tell me about the universe, distinctly she said those odd words "Why don't you tell Claire about the universe," and Harry stared at me frowning and said, "Tell Claire what about the universe?" and Grandmother laughed and said, "Oh — anything!" and Harry said, shrugging, "Hell — I don't know," then raising his voice, regarding me with a look of compassion, " — the universe goes back a long way, I guess. Ten billion years? Twenty billion? Is there a difference? They say it got started with an explosion and in a second, well really a fraction of a second a tiny bit of tightness got flung out, it's flying out right now, expanding" — he drew his hands, broad stubby hands, dramatically apart — "and most of it is emptiness I guess, whatever 'emptiness' is. It's still expanding, all the pieces flying out, there's a billion galaxies like ours, or maybe a billion billion galaxies like ours, but don't worry it goes on forever even when we die —" but at this Grandmother turned sharply, sensing my reaction, she said, "Oh dear don't tell the child *that,* don't frighten poor little Claire with *that.*"

"You told me to tell her about the — "

"Oh just *stop.*"

Quickly Grandmother came to hug me, settled me into my chair as if I were a much smaller child sitting there at the kitchen table, my feet not touching the floor; and there was my special bowl, the bowl Grandmother kept for me, sparkling yellow with lambs running around the rim, yes and my special spoon too, a beautiful silver spoon with the initial *C* engraved on it which Grandmother kept polished so I understood I was safe, nothing could harm me, Grandmother would not let anything happen to me so long as I was there. She poured my oatmeal into my dish, she was saying, " — It's true we must all die one day, darling, but not just yet, you know, not tonight, you've just come to visit haven't you dear? and maybe you'll stay? maybe you won't ever leave? *now it's time?*"

The words *it's time* rang with a faint echo.

I can hear them now: *it's time: time.*

Grandmother's arms were shapely and attractive, her skin pale and smooth and delicately translucent as a candled egg, and I saw that she was wearing several rings, the wedding band that I knew but others, sparkling with light, and there so thin were my arms beside hers, my hands that seemed so small, sparrow-sized, and my wrists so bony, and it came over me, the horror of it, that meat and bone should define my presence in the universe: the point of entry in the universe that was *me* that was *me* that was *me:* and no other: yet of a fragile materiality that any fire could consume. "Oh Grandmother — I'm so afraid!" I whimpered, seeing how I would be burned to ash, and Grandmother comforted me, and settled me more securely into the chair, pressed my pretty little spoon between my fingers and said, "Darling don't think of such things, just *eat.* Grandmother made this for *you.*"

I was eating the hot oatmeal which was a little too hot, but creamy as I loved it, I was terribly hungry eating like an infant at the breast so blindly my head bowed and eyes nearly shut brimming with tears and Grandmother asked *is it good? is it good?* she'd spooned in some dark honey too *is it good?* and I nodded mutely, I could taste grains of brown sugar that hadn't melted into the oatmeal, stark as bits of glass, and I realized they were in fact bits of glass, some of them large as grape pits, and I didn't want to hurt Grandmother's feelings but I was fearful of swallowing the glass so as I ate I managed to sift the bits through the chewed oatmeal until I could maneuver it into the side of my mouth into a little space between my lower right gum and the inside of my cheek and Grandmother was watching asking *is it good?* and I said, "Oh yes," half choking and swallowing " — oh *yes.*"

A while later when neither Grandmother nor Harry was watching I spat out the glass fragments into my hand but I never knew absolutely, I don't know even now: if they were glass and not for instance grains of sand or fragments of eggshell or even bits of brown sugar crystallized into such a form not even boiling oatmeal could dissolve it.

I was leaving Grandmother's house, it was later, time to leave, Grandmother said, "But aren't you going to stay?" and I said, "No Grandmother I can't," and Grandmother said, "I thought you were going to stay dear," and I said, "No Grandmother I can't," and Grandmother said, "But why?" and I said, "I just can't," and Grandmother said, laughing so her laughter was edged with annoyance, "Yes but *why?*" Grandmother's friend Harry had disappeared from the kitchen, there was no one in the kitchen but Grandmother and me, but we were in the street too, and the roaring of the river was close by, so Grandmother hugged me a final time and gave me a little push saying, "Well — goodnight Claire," and I said apologetically, "Goodnight, Grandmother," wondering if I should ask her not to say anything to my parents about this visit in the middle of the night, and she was backing away, her dark somber gaze fixed upon me half in reproach, "Next time you visit Grandmother you'll stay — won't you? Forever?" and I said, "Yes Grandmother," though I was very frightened and as soon as I was out of Grandmother's sight I began to run.

At first I had a hard time finding the Ferry Street bridge. Though I could hear the river close by — I can always hear the river close by.

Eventually, I found the bridge again. I know I found the bridge, otherwise how did I get home? That night?

Questions for Discussion

1. Why is the narrator an insomniac? What two types of sleep does she experience?
2. Interpret the opening paragraphs in which the adult narrator sees her image in her grandmother's. Why does the narrator identify with her grandmother?

3. What is implied by the narrator's dangerous crossing of the Ferry Street bridge at three o'clock in the morning on a night when the bridge is closed for repairs? In crossing the bridge, what fears is the narrator confronting?
4. Does the story imply that Claire actually crossed the Ferry Street bridge in the middle of the night? Is the story the narrative of a dream?
5. What does the oatmeal the grandmother feeds Claire represent? What do the bits of glass in the oatmeal suggest? Why does Claire feel compelled to return home?

Ideas for Writing

1. Examine in an essay the possible reasons that the narrator is recalling this time of her childhood and what the incident reveals about her fears, needs, and aspirations.
2. Write a story in which a character has a vivid dream that reveals some of his or her deepest fears and desires.

RAYMOND CARVER   (1938–1988)

With a direct, unadorned style strongly influenced by Anton Chekhov and Ernest Hemingway, Raymond Carver is credited with bringing realism back into the esteem of younger writers and the reading public. A solid crafts-man, he revised his stories as many as thirty times before he was satisfied with them. Born in Clatskanie, Oregon, Carver was the son of a sawmill laborer. Like his father, Carver worked at a number of low-paying jobs: log-ger, deliveryman, janitor, and gas station attendant. While attending Chico State College in California, he met the novelist John Gardner, who had a great influence on Carver's understanding of the craft of the story. At Humboldt State University in California, he earned a B.A. in 1963 and subsequently studied at the University of Iowa and at Stanford University, where he received a Wallace Stegner Fellowship in 1972. By the late 1960s Carver had begun to publish his stories and poems regularly in *Esquire*, the *New Yorker,* and other national magazines. He published five volumes of poetry, and his stories were collected in *Will You Please Be Quiet, Please?* (1976); *What We Talk about When We Talk about Love* (1981); *Cathedral* (1983), which includes "Intimacy" and "Cathedral"; *Where I'm Calling From* (1988); and the posthu-mous *Short Cuts: Selected Stories* (1993). Carver's characters often live on the edge of bankruptcy, drinking heavily and surviving in menial jobs, while struggling to hold on to dignity and love.

Intimacy   (1983)

I have some business out west anyway, so I stop off in this little town where my former wife lives. We haven't seen each other in four years. But from time to time, when something of mine appeared, or was written about me in the magazines or papers — a profile or an interview — I sent her these things. I don't know what I had in mind except I thought she might be interested. In any case, she never responded.

It is nine in the morning, I haven't called, and it's true I don't know what I am going to find.

But she lets me in. She doesn't seem surprised. We don't shake hands, much less kiss each other. She takes me into the living room. As soon as I sit down she brings me some coffee. Then she comes out with what's on her mind. She says I've caused her anguish, made her feel exposed and humiliated.

Make no mistake, I feel I'm home.

She says, But then you were into betrayal early. You always felt comfort-able with betrayal. No, she says, that's not true. Not in the beginning, at any rate. You were different then. But I guess I was different too. Everything was different, she says. No, it was after you turned thirty-five, or thirty-six, whenever it was, around in there anyway, your mid-thirties somewhere, then you started in. You really started in. You turned on me. You did it up pretty then. You must be proud of yourself.

She says, Sometimes I could scream.

She says she wishes I'd forget about the hard times, the bad times, when I talk about back then. Spend some time on the good times, she says. Weren't there some good times? She wishes I'd get off that other subject. She's bored with it. Sick of hearing about it. Your private hobby horse, she says. What's done is done and water under the bridge, she says. A tragedy, yes. God knows it was a tragedy and then sôme. But why keep it going? Don't you ever get tired of dredging up that old business?

She says, Let go of the past, for Christ's sake. Those old hurts. You must have some other arrows in your quiver, she says.

She says, You know something? I think you're sick. I think you're crazy as a bedbug. Hey, you don't believe the things they're saying about you, do you? Don't believe them for a minute, she says. Listen, I could tell them a thing or two. Let them talk to me about it, if they want to hear a story.

She says, Are you listening to me?

I'm listening, I say. I'm all ears, I say.

She says, I've really had a bellyful of it, buster! Who asked you here today anyway? I sure as hell didn't. You just show up and walk in. What the hell do you want from me? Blood? You want more blood? I thought you had your fill by now.

She says, Think of me as dead. I want to be left in peace now. That's all I want anymore is to be left in peace and forgotten about. Hey, I'm forty-five years old, she says. Forty-five going on fifty-five, or sixty-five. Lay off, will you.

She says, Why don't you wipe the blackboard clean and see what you have left after that? Why don't you start with a clean slate? See how far that gets you, she says.

She has to laugh at this. I laugh too, but it's nerves.

She says, You know something? I had my chance once, but I let it go. I just let it go. I don't guess I ever told you. But now look at me. Look! Take a good look while you're at it. You threw me away, you son of a bitch.

She says, I was younger then and a better person. Maybe you were too, she says. A better person, I mean. You had to be. You were better then or I wouldn't have had anything to do with you.

She says, I loved you so much once. I loved you to the point of distraction. I did. More than anything in the whole wide world. Imagine that. What a laugh that is now. Can you imagine it? We were so *intimate* once upon a time I can't believe it now. I think that's the strangest thing of all now. The memory of being that intimate with somebody. We were so intimate I could puke. I can't imagine ever being that intimate with somebody else. I haven't been.

She says, Frankly, and I mean this, I want to be kept out of it from here on out. Who do you think you are anyway? You think you're God or somebody? You're not fit to lick God's boot, or anybody else's for that matter. Mister, you've been hanging out with the wrong people. But what do I know? I don't even know what I know any longer. I know I don't like what you've been dishing out. I know that much. You know what I'm talking about, don't you? Am I right?

Right, I say. Right as rain.

She says, You'll agree to anything, won't you? You give in too easy. You always did. You don't have any principles, not one. Anything to avoid a fuss. But that's neither here nor there.

She says, You remember that time I pulled the knife on you?

She says this as if in passing, as if it's not important.

Vaguely, I say. I must have deserved it, but I don't remember much about it. Go ahead, why don't you, and tell me about it.

She says, I'm beginning to understand something now. I think I know why you're here. Yes. I know why you're here, even if you don't. But you're a sly-boots. You know why you're here. You're on a fishing expedition. You're hunting for *material*. Am I getting warm? Am I right?

Tell me about the knife, I say.

She says, If you want to know, I'm real sorry I didn't use that knife. I am. I really and truly am. I've thought and thought about it, and I'm sorry I didn't use it. I had the chance. But I hesitated. I hesitated and was lost, as somebody or other said. But I should have used it, the hell with everything and everybody. I should have nicked your arm with it at least. At least that.

Well, you didn't, I say. I thought you were going to cut me with it, but you didn't. I took it away from you.

She says, You were always lucky. You took it away and then you slapped me. Still, I regret I didn't use that knife just a little bit. Even a little would have been something to remember me by.

I remember a lot, I say. I say that, then wish I hadn't.

She says, Amen, brother. That's the bone of contention here, if you hadn't noticed. That's the whole problem. But like I said, in my opinion you remember the wrong things. You remember the low, shameful things. That's why you got interested when I brought up the knife.

She says, I wonder if you ever have any regret. For whatever that's worth on the market these days. Not much, I guess. But you ought to be a specialist in it by now.

Regret, I say. It doesn't interest me much, to tell the truth. Regret is not a word I use very often. I guess I mainly don't have it. I admit I hold to the dark view of things. Sometimes, anyway. But regret? I don't think so.

She says, You're a real son of a bitch, did you know that? A ruthless, cold-hearted son of a bitch. Did anybody ever tell you that?

You did, I say. Plenty of times.

She says, I always speak the truth. Even when it hurts. You'll never catch me in a lie.

She says, My eyes were opened a long time ago, but by then it was too late. I had my chance but I let it slide through my fingers. I even thought for a while you'd come back. Why'd I think that anyway? I must have been out of my mind. I could cry my eyes out now, but I wouldn't give you that satisfaction.

She says, You know what? I think if you were on fire right now, if you suddenly burst into flame this minute, I wouldn't throw a bucket of water on you.

She laughs at this. Then her face closes down again.

She says, Why in hell *are* you here? You want to hear some more? I could go on for days. I think I know why you turned up, but I want to hear it from you.

When I don't answer, when I just keep sitting there, she goes on.

She says, After that time, when you went away, nothing much mattered after that. Not the kids, not God, not anything. It was like I didn't know what hit me. It was like I had *stopped living*. My life had been going along, going along, and then it just stopped. It didn't just come to a stop, it screeched to a stop. I thought, If I'm not worth anything to him, well, I'm not worth anything to myself or anybody else either. That was the worst thing I felt. I thought my heart would break. What am I saying? It did break. Of course it broke. It broke, just like that. It's still broke, if you want to know. And so there you have it in a nutshell. My eggs in one basket, she says. A tisket, a tasket. All my rotten eggs in one basket.

She says, You found somebody else for yourself, didn't you? It didn't take long. And you're happy now. That's what they say about you anyway: "He's happy now." Hey, I read everything you send! You think I don't? Listen, I know your heart, mister. I always did. I knew it back then, and I know it now. I know your heart inside and out, and don't you ever forget it. Your heart is a jungle, a dark forest, it's a garbage pail, if you want to know. Let them talk to me if they want to ask sombody something. I know how you operate. Just let them come around here, and I'll give them an earful. I was there. I served, buddy boy. Then you held me up for display and ridicule in your so-called work. For any Tom or Harry to pity or pass judgment on. Ask me if I cared. Ask me if it embarrassed me. Go ahead, ask.

No, I say, I won't ask that. I don't want to get into that, I say.

Damn straight you don't! she says. And you know *why*, too!

She says, Honey, no offense, but sometimes I think I could shoot you and watch you kick.

She says, You can't look me in the eyes, can you?

She says, and this is exactly what she says, You can't even look me in the eyes when I'm talking to you.

So, okay, I look her in the eyes.

She says, Right. Okay, she says. Now we're getting someplace, maybe. That's better. You can tell a lot about the person you're talking to from his eyes. Everybody knows that. But you know something else? There's nobody in this whole world who would tell you this, but I can tell you. I have the right. I *earned* that right, sonny. You have yourself confused with somebody else. And that's the pure truth of it. But what do I know? they'll say in a hundred years. They'll say, Who was she anyway?

She says, In any case, you sure as hell have *me* confused with somebody else. Hey, I don't even have the same name anymore! Not the name I was born with, not the name I lived with you with, not even the name I had two years ago. What is this? What is this in hell all about anyway? Let me say something. I want to be left alone now. Please. That's not a crime.

She says, Don't you have someplace else you should be? Some plane to catch? Shouldn't you be somewhere far from here at this very minute?

No, I say. I say it again: No. No place, I say. I don't have anyplace I have to be.

And then I do something. I reach over and take the sleeve of her blouse between my thumb and forefinger. That's all. I just touch it that way, and then I just bring my hand back. She doesn't draw away. She doesn't move.

Then here's the thing I do next. I get down on my knees, a big guy like me, and I take the hem of her dress. What am I doing on the floor? I wish I could say. But I know it's where I ought to be, and I'm there on my knees holding on to the hem of her dress.

She is still for a minute. But in a minute she says, Hey, it's all right, stupid. You're so dumb, sometimes. Get up now. I'm telling you to get up. Listen, it's okay. I'm over it now. It took me a while to get over it. What do you think? Did you think it wouldn't? Then you walk in here and suddenly the whole cruddy business is back. I felt a need to ventilate. But you know, and I know, it's over and done with now.

She says, For the longest while, honey, I was inconsolable. *Inconsolable,* she says. Put that word in your little notebook. I can tell you from experience that's the saddest word in the English language. Anyway, I got over it finally. Time is a gentleman, a wise man said. Or else maybe a worn-out old woman, one or the other anyway.

She says, I have a life now. It's a different kind of life than yours, but I guess we don't need to compare. It's my life, and that's the important thing I have to realize as I get older. Don't feel *too* bad, anyway, she says. I mean, it's all right to feel a *little* bad, maybe. That won't hurt you, that's only to be expected after all. Even if you can't move yourself to regret.

She says, Now you have to get up and get out of here. My husband will be along pretty soon for his lunch. How would I explain this kind of thing?

It's crazy, but I'm still on my knees holding the hem of her dress. I won't let it go. I'm like a terrier, and it's like I'm stuck to the floor. It's like I can't move.

She says, Get up now. What is it? You still want something from me. What do you want? Want me to forgive you? Is that why you're doing this? That's it, isn't it? That's the reason you came all this way. The knife thing kind of perked you up, too. I think you'd forgotten about that. But you needed me to remind you. Okay, I'll say something if you'll just go.

She says, I forgive you.

She says, Are you satisfied now? Is that better? Are you happy? He's happy now, she says.

But I'm still there, knees to the floor.

She says, Did you hear what I said? You have to go now. Hey, stupid. Honey, I said I forgive you. And I even reminded you about the knife thing. I can't think what else I can do now. You got it made in the shade, baby. Come *on* now, you have to get out of here. Get up. That's right. You're still a big guy, aren't you. Here's your hat, don't forget your hat.

You never used to wear a hat. I never in my life saw you in a hat before.

She says, Listen to me now. Look at me. Listen carefully to what I'm going to tell you.

She moves closer. She's about three inches from my face. We haven't been this close in a long time. I take these little breaths that she can't hear and I wait. I think my heart slows way down, I think.

She says, You just tell it like you have to, I guess, and forget the rest. Like always. You been doing that for so long now anyway it shouldn't be hard for you.

She says, There, I've done it. You're free, aren't you? At least you think you are anyway. Free at last. That's a joke, but don't laugh. Anyway, you feel better, don't you?

She walks with me down the hall.

She says, I can't imagine how I'd explain this if my husband was to walk in this very minute. But who really cares anymore, right? In the final analysis, nobody gives a damn anymore. Besides which, I think everything that can happen that way has already happened. His name is Fred, by the way. He's a decent guy and works hard for his living. He cares for me.

So she walks me to the front door, which has been standing open all this while. The door that was letting in light and fresh air this morning, and sounds off the street, all of which we had ignored. I looked outside and, Jesus, there's this white moon hanging in the morning sky. I can't think when I've ever seen anything so remarkable. But I'm afraid to comment on it. I am. I don't know what might happen. I might break into tears even. I might not understand a word I'd say.

She says, Maybe you'll be back sometime, and maybe you won't. This'll wear off, you know. Pretty soon you'll start feeling bad again. Maybe it'll make a good story, she says. But I don't want to know about it if it does.

I say good-bye. She doesn't say anything more. She looks at her hands, and then she puts them into the pockets of her dress. She shakes her head. She goes back inside, and this time she closes the door.

I move off down the sidewalk. Some kids are tossing a football at the end of the street. But they aren't my kids, and they aren't her kids either. There are these leaves everywhere, even in the gutters. Piles of leaves wherever I look. They're falling off the limbs as I walk. I can't take a step without putting my shoe into leaves. Somebody ought to make an effort here. Somebody ought to get a rake and take care of this.

Questions for Discussion

1. What do we learn about the narrator in the first three paragraphs of the story? Why has he come to see his ex-wife?
2. What accusations about the narrator does his ex-wife make? Can the reader tell whether she is justified in her criticism of him? In what sense might he have "caused her anguish, made her feel exposed"?
3. Does the wife's advice to her ex-husband, "Let go of the past, for Christ's sake," seem like good advice for a writer? Why doesn't the narrator respond or defend himself?
4. What definition of intimacy emerges in the story? Does it seem that this couple was ever really "intimate"? What is the significance of the ex-wife's comment about the couple's closeness, "so intimate I could puke"? Is it possible to be *too* intimate?
5. Does the ex-wife's accusation that the ex-husband is simply "hunting for *material*" seem justified, considering his profession and his behavior in the story? How do you interpret the narrator's dramatic gesture of getting down on his knees and taking the hem of his ex-wife's dress?

Ideas for Writing

1. Write an essay in which you discuss the complex tone of this story. For example, many of the ex-wife's comments seem intended to hurt the narrator and to underscore her sense of rage and tragic loss, yet in places her remarks seem comic, almost a parody of marital fighting.
2. In an essay, discuss the commentary the story makes on the "freedom" that divorced people experience. In what sense does the narrator still feel married? If the narrator is really free, why does the story end with him noting of the piles of leaves, "Somebody ought to get a rake and take care of this"?

Cathedral   (1983)

This blind man, an old friend of my wife's, he was on his way to spend the night. His wife had died. So he was visiting the dead wife's relatives in Connecticut. He called my wife from his in-laws'. Arrangements were made. He would come by train, a five-hour trip, and my wife would meet him at the station. She hadn't seen him since she worked for him one summer in Seattle ten years ago. But she and the blind man had kept in touch. They made tapes and mailed them back and forth. I wasn't enthusiastic about his visit. He was no one I knew. And his being blind bothered me. My idea of blindness came from the movies. In the movies, the blind moved slowly and never laughed. Sometimes they were led by seeing-eye dogs. A blind man in my house was not something I looked forward to.

That summer in Seattle she had needed a job. She didn't have any money. The man she was going to marry at the end of the summer was in officers' training school. He didn't have any money, either. But she was in love with the guy, and he was in love with her, etc. She'd seen something in the paper: HELP WANTED — *Reading to Blind Man,* and a telephone number. She phoned and went over, was hired on the spot. She'd worked with this blind man all summer. She read stuff to him, case studies, reports, that sort of thing. She helped him organize his little office in the county social-service department. They'd become good friends, my wife and the blind man. How do I know these things? She told me. And she told me something else. On her last day in the office, the blind man asked if he could touch her face. She agreed to this. She told me he touched his fingers to every part of her face, her nose — even her neck! She never forgot it. She even tried to write a poem about it. She was always trying to write a poem. She wrote a poem or two every year, usually after something really important had happened to her.

When we first started going out together, she showed me the poem. In the poem, she recalled his fingers and the way they had moved around over her face. In the poem, she talked about what she had felt at the time, about what went through her mind when the blind man touched her nose and lips. I can remember I didn't think much of the poem. Of course, I didn't tell her that. Maybe I just don't understand poetry. I admit it's not the first thing I reach for when I pick up something to read.

Anyway, this man who'd first enjoyed her favors, the officer-to-be, he'd been her childhood sweetheart. So okay. I'm saying that at the end of the summer she let the blind man run his hands over her face, said goodbye to him, married her childhood etc., who was now a commissioned officer, and she moved away from Seattle. But they'd kept in touch, she and the blind man. She made the first contact after a year or so. She called him up one night from an Air Force base in Alabama. She wanted to talk. They talked. He asked her to send him a tape and tell him about her life. She did this. She sent the tape. On the tape, she told the blind man about her husband and about their life together in the military. She told the blind man she loved her husband but she didn't like it where they lived and she didn't like it that he was a part of the military-industrial thing. She told the blind man she'd written a poem and he was in it. She told him that she was writing a poem about what it was like to be an Air Force officer's wife. The poem wasn't finished yet. She was still writing it. The blind man made a tape. He sent her the tape. She made a tape. This went on for years. My wife's officer was posted to one base and then another. She sent tapes from Moody AFB, McGuire, McConnell, and finally Travis, near

Sacramento, where one night she got to feeling lonely and cut off from people she kept losing in that moving-around life. She got to feeling she couldn't go it another step. She went in and swallowed all the pills and capsules in the medicine chest and washed them down with a bottle of gin. Then she got into a hot bath and passed out.

But instead of dying, she got sick. She threw up. Her officer — why should he have a name? he was the childhood sweetheart, and what more does he want? — came home from somewhere, found her, and called the ambulance. In time, she put it all on a tape and sent the tape to the blind man. Over the years, she put all kinds of stuff on tapes and sent the tapes off lickety-split. Next to writing a poem every year, I think it was her chief means of recreation. On one tape, she told the blind man she'd decided to live away from her offi-cer for a time. On another tape, she told him about her divorce. She and I began going out, and of course she told her blind man about it. She told him everything, or so it seemed to me. Once she asked me if I'd like to hear the lat-est tape from the blind man. This was a year ago. I was on the tape, she said. So I said okay, I'd listen to it. I got us drinks and we settled down in the liv-ing room. We made ready to listen. First she inserted the tape into the player and adjusted a couple of dials. Then she pushed a lever. The tape squeaked and someone began to talk in this loud voice. She lowered the volume. After a few minutes of harmless chitchat, I heard my own name in the mouth of this stranger, this blind man I didn't even know! And then this: "From all you've said about him, I can only conclude —" But we were interrupted, a knock at the door, something, and we didn't ever get back to the tape. Maybe it was just as well. I'd heard all I wanted to.

Now this same blind man was coming to sleep in my house.

"Maybe I could take him bowling," I said to my wife. She was at the drain-ing board doing scalloped potatoes. She put down the knife she was using and turned around.

"If you love me," she said, "you can do this for me. If you don't love me, okay. But if you had a friend, any friend, and the friend came to visit, I'd make him feel comfortable." She wiped her hands with the dish towel.

"I don't have any blind friends," I said.

"You don't have *any* friends," she said. "Period. Besides," she said, "god-damn it, his wife's just died! Don't you understand that? The man's lost his wife!"

I didn't answer. She'd told me a little about the blind man's wife. Her name was Beulah. Beulah! That's a name for a colored woman.

"Was his wife Negro?" I asked.

"Are you crazy?" my wife said. "Have you just flipped or something?" She picked up a potato. I saw it hit the floor, then roll under the stove. "What's wrong with you?" she said. "Are you drunk?"

"I'm just asking," I said.

Right then my wife filled me in with more detail than I cared to know. I made a drink and sat at the kitchen table to listen. Pieces of the story began to fall into place.

Beulah had gone to work for the blind man the summer after my wife had stopped working for him. Pretty soon Beulah and the blind man had themselves a church wedding. It was a little wedding—who'd want to go to such a wedding in the first place?—just the two of them, plus the minister and the minister's wife. But it was a church wedding just the same. It was what Beulah had wanted, he'd said. But even then Beulah must have been carrying the cancer in her glands. After they had been inseparable for eight years—my wife's word, *inseparable*—Beulah's health went into a rapid decline. She died in a Seattle hospital room, the blind man sitting beside the bed and holding on to her hand. They'd married, lived and worked together, slept together—had sex, sure—and then the blind man had to bury her. All this without his having ever seen what the goddamned woman looked like. It was beyond my understanding. Hearing this, I felt sorry for the blind man for a little bit. And then I found myself thinking what a pitiful life this woman must have led. Imagine a woman who could never see herself as she was seen in the eyes of her loved one. A woman who could go on day after day and never receive the smallest compliment from her beloved. A woman whose husband could never read the expression on her face, be it misery or something better. Someone who could wear makeup or not—what difference to him? She could, if she wanted, wear green eye-shadow around one eye, a straight pin in her nostril, yellow slacks and purple shoes, no matter. And then to slip off into death, the blind man's hand on her hand, his blind eyes streaming tears—I'm imagining now—her last thought maybe this: that he never even knew what she looked like, and she on an express to the grave. Robert was left with a small insurance policy and half of a twenty-peso Mexican coin. The other half of the coin went into the box with her. Pathetic.

So when the time rolled around, my wife went to the depot to pick him up. With nothing to do but wait—sure, I blamed him for that—I was having a drink and watching the TV when I heard the car pull into the drive. I got up from the sofa with my drink and went to the window to have a look.

I saw my wife laughing as she parked the car. I saw her get out of the car and shut the door. She was still wearing a smile. Just amazing. She went around to the other side of the car to where the blind man was already starting to get out. This blind man, feature this, he was wearing a full beard! A beard on a blind man! Too much, I say. The blind man reached into the back seat and dragged out a suitcase. My wife took his arm, shut the car door, and, talking all the way, moved him down the drive and then up the steps to the front porch. I turned off the TV. I finished my drink, rinsed the glass, dried my hands. Then I went to the door.

My wife said, "I want you to meet Robert. Robert, this is my husband. I've told you all about him." She was beaming. She had this blind man by his coat sleeve.

The blind man let go of his suitcase and up came his hand.

I took it. He squeezed hard, held my hand, and then he let it go.

"I feel like we've already met," he boomed.

"Likewise," I said. I didn't know what else to say Then I said, "Welcome. I've heard a lot about you." We began to move then, a little group, from the porch into the living room, my wife guiding him by the arm. The blind man was carrying his suitcase in his other hand. My wife said things like, "To your left here, Robert. That's right. Now watch it, there's a chair. That's it. Sit down right here. This is the sofa. We just bought this sofa two weeks ago."

I started to say something about the old sofa. I'd liked that old sofa. But I didn't say anything. Then I wanted to say something else, small-talk, about the scenic ride along the Hudson. How going *to* New York, you should sit on the right-hand side of the train, and coming *from* New York, the left-hand side.

"Did you have a good train ride?" I said. "Which side of the train did you sit on, by the way?"

"What a question, which side!" my wife said. "What's it matter which side?" she said.

"I just asked," I said.

"Right side," the blind man said. "I hadn't been on a train in nearly forty years. Not since I was a kid. With my folks. That's been a long time. I'd nearly forgotten the sensation. I have winter in my beard now," he said. "So I've been told, anyway. Do I look distinguished, my dear?" the blind man said to my wife.

"You look distinguished, Robert," she said. "Robert," she said. "Robert, it's just so good to see you."

My wife finally took her eyes off the blind man and looked at me. I had the feeling she didn't like what she saw. I shrugged.

I've never met, or personally known, anyone who was blind. This blind man was late forties, a heavy-set, balding man with stooped shoulders, as if he carried a great weight there. He wore brown slacks, brown shoes, a light-brown shirt, a tie, a sports coat. Spiffy. He also had this full beard. But he didn't use a cane and he didn't wear dark glasses. I'd always thought dark glasses were a must for the blind. Fact was, I wished he had a pair. At first glance, his eyes looked like anyone else's eyes. But if you looked close, there was something different about them. Too much white in the iris, for one thing, and the pupils seemed to move around in the sockets without his knowing it or being able to stop it. Creepy. As I stared at his face, I saw the left pupil turn in toward his nose while the other made an effort to keep in one place. But it was only an effort, for that eye was on the roam without his knowing it or wanting it to be.

I said, "Let me get you a drink. What's your pleasure? We have a little of everything. It's one of our pastimes."

"Bub, I'm a Scotch man myself," he said fast enough in this big voice.

"Right," I said. Bub! "Sure you are, I knew it."

He let his fingers touch his suitcase, which was sitting alongside the sofa. He was taking his bearings. I didn't blame him for that.

"I'll move that up to your room," my wife said.

"No, that's fine," the blind man said loudly. "It can go up when I go up."

"A little water with the Scotch?" I said.

"Very little," he said.

"I knew it," I said.

He said, "Just a tad. The Irish actor, Barry Fitzgerald? I'm like that fellow. When I drink water, Fitzgerald said, I drink water. When I drink whiskey, I drink whiskey." My wife laughed. The blind man brought his hand up under his beard. He lifted his beard slowly and let it drop.

I did the drinks, three big glasses of Scotch with a splash of water in each. Then we made ourselves comfortable and talked about Robert's travels. First the long flight from the West Coast to Connecticut, we covered that. Then from Connecticut up here by train. We had another drink concerning that leg of the trip.

I remembered having read somewhere that the blind didn't smoke because, as speculation had it, they couldn't see the smoke they exhaled. I thought I knew that much and that much only about blind people. But this blind man smoked his cigarette down to the nubbin and then lit another one. This blind man filled his ashtray and my wife emptied it.

When we sat down at the table for dinner, we had another drink. My wife heaped Robert's plate with cube steak, scalloped potatoes, green beans. I buttered him up two slices of bread. I said, "Here's bread and butter for you." I swallowed some of my drink. "Now let us pray," I said, and the blind man lowered his head. My wife looked at me, her mouth agape. "Pray the phone won't ring and the food doesn't get cold," I said.

We dug in. We ate everything there was to eat on the table. We ate like there was no tomorrow. We didn't talk. We ate. We scarfed. We grazed that table. We were into serious eating. The blind man had right away located his foods, he knew just where everything was on his plate. I watched with admiration as he used his knife and fork on the meat. He'd cut two pieces of meat, fork the meat into his mouth, and then go all out for the scalloped potatoes, the beans next, and then he'd tear off a hunk of buttered bread and eat that. He'd follow this up with a big drink of milk. It didn't seem to bother him to use his fingers once in a while, either.

We finished everything, including half a strawberry pie. For a few moments, we sat as if stunned. Sweat beaded on our faces. Finally, we got up from the table and left the dirty plates. We didn't look back. We took ourselves into the living room and sank into our places again. Robert and my wife sat on the sofa. I took the big chair. We had us two or three more drinks while they talked about the major things that had come to pass for them in the past ten years. For the most part, I just listened. Now and then I joined in. I didn't want him to think I'd left the room, and I didn't want her to think I was feeling left out. They talked of things that had happened to them — to them! — these past ten years. I waited in vain to hear my name on my wife's sweet lips:

"And then my dear husband came into my life" — something like that. But I heard nothing of the sort. More talk of Robert. Robert had done a little of everything, it seemed, a regular blind jack-of-all-trades. But most recently he and his wife had had an Amway distributorship, from which, I gathered, they'd earned their living, such as it was. The blind man was also a ham radio operator. He talked in his loud voice about conversations he'd had with fellow operators in Guam, in the Philippines, in Alaska, and even in Tahiti. He said he'd have a lot of friends there if he ever wanted to go visit those places. From time to time, he'd turn his blind face toward me, put his hand under his beard, ask me something. How long had I been in my present position? (Three years.) Did I like my work? (I didn't.) Was I going to stay with it? (What were the options?) Finally, when I thought he was beginning to run down, I got up and turned on the TV.

My wife looked at me with irritation. She was heading toward a boil. Then she looked at the blind man and said, "Robert, do you have a TV?"

The blind man said, "My dear, I have two TVs. I have a color set and a black-and-white thing, an old relic. It's funny, but if I turn the TV on, and I'm always turning it on, I turn on the color set. It's funny, don't you think?"

I didn't know what to say to that. I had absolutely nothing to say to that. No opinions. So I watched the news program and tried to listen to what the announcer was saying.

"This is a color TV," the blind man said. "Don't ask me how, but I can tell."

"We traded up a while ago," I said.

The blind man had another taste of his drink. He lifted his beard, sniffed it and let it fall. He leaned forward on the sofa. He positioned his ashtray on the coffee table, then put the lighter to his cigarette. He leaned back on the sofa and crossed his legs at the ankles.

My wife covered her mouth, and then she yawned. She stretched. She said, "I think I'll go upstairs and put on my robe. I think I'll change into some-thing else. Robert, you make yourself comfortable," she said.

"I'm comfortable," the blind man said.

"I want you to feel comfortable in this house," she said.

"I am comfortable," the blind man said.

After she'd left the room, he and I listened to the weather report and then to the sports roundup. By that time, she'd been gone so long I didn't know if she was going to come back. I thought she might have gone to bed. I wished she'd come back downstairs. I didn't want to be left alone with a blind man. I asked him if he wanted another drink, and he said sure. Then I asked if he wanted to smoke some dope with me. I said I'd just rolled a number. I hadn't, but I planned to do so in about two shakes.

"I'll try some with you," he said.

"Damn right," I said. "That's the stuff."

I got our drinks and sat down on the sofa with him. Then I rolled us two fat numbers. I lit one and passed it. I brought it to his fingers. He took it and inhaled.

"Hold it as long as you can," I said. I could tell he didn't know the first thing.

My wife came back downstairs wearing her pink robe and her pink slippers.

"What do I smell?" she said.

"We thought we'd have us some cannabis," I said.

My wife gave me a savage look. Then she looked at the blind man and said, "Robert, I didn't know you smoked."

He said, "I do now, my dear. There's a first time for everything. But I don't feel anything yet."

"This stuff is pretty mellow," I said. "This stuff is mild. It's dope you can reason with," I said. "It doesn't mess you up."

"Not much it doesn't, bub," he said, and laughed.

My wife sat on the sofa between the blind man and me. I passed her the number. She took it and toked and then passed it back to me. "Which way is this going?" she said. Then she said, "I shouldn't be smoking this. I can hardly keep my eyes open as it is. That dinner did me in. I shouldn't have eaten so much."

"It was the strawberry pie," the blind man said. "That's what did it," he said, and he laughed his big laugh. Then he shook his head.

"There's more strawberry pie," I said.

"Do you want some more, Robert?" my wife said.

"Maybe in a little while," he said.

We gave our attention to the TV. My wife yawned again. She said, "Your bed is made up when you feel like going to bed, Robert. I know you must have had a long day. When you're ready to go to bed, say so." She pulled his arm. "Robert?"

He came to and said, "I've had a real nice time. This beats tapes, doesn't it?"

I said. "Coming at you," and I put the number between his fingers. He inhaled, held the smoke, and then let it go. It was like he'd been doing it since he was nine years old.

"Thanks, bub," he said. "But I think this is all for me. I think I'm beginning to feel it," he said. He held the burning roach out for my wife.

"Same here," she said. "Ditto. Me, too." She took the roach and passed it to me. "I may just sit here for a while between you two guys with my eyes closed. But don't let me bother you, okay? Either one of you. If it bothers you, say so. Otherwise, I may just sit here with my eyes closed until you're ready to go to bed," she said. "Your bed's made up, Robert, when you're ready. It's right next to our room at the top of the stairs. We'll show you up when you're ready. You wake me up now, you guys, if I fall asleep." She said that and then she closed her eyes and went to sleep.

The news program ended. I got up and changed the channel. I sat back down on the sofa. I wished my wife hadn't pooped out. Her head lay across the back of the sofa, her mouth open. She'd turned so that her robe had slipped away from her legs, exposing a juicy thigh. I reached to draw her robe back over her, and it was then that I glanced at the blind man. What the hell! I flipped the robe open again.

"You say when you want some strawberry pie," I said.

"I will," he said.

I said, "Are you tired? Do you want me to take you up to your bed? Are you ready to hit the hay?"

"Not yet," he said. "No, I'll stay up with you, bub. If that's all right. I'll stay up until you're ready to turn in. We haven't had a chance to talk. Know what I mean? I feel like me and her monopolized the evening." He lifted his beard and he let it fall. He picked up his cigarettes and his lighter.

"That's all right," I said. Then I said, "I'm glad for the company."

And I guess I was. Every night I smoked dope and stayed up as long as I could before I fell asleep. My wife and I hardly ever went to bed at the same time. When I did go to sleep, I had these dreams. Sometimes I'd wake up from one of them, my heart going crazy.

Something about the church and the Middle Ages was on the TV. Not your run-of-the-mill TV fare. I wanted to watch something else. I turned to the other channels. But there was nothing on them, either. So I turned back to the first channel and apologized.

"Bub, its all right," the blind man said. "It's fine with me. Whatever you want to watch is okay. I'm always learning something. Learning never ends. It won't hurt me to learn something tonight. I got ears," he said.

We didn't say anything for a time. He was leaning forward with his head turned at me, his right ear aimed in the direction of the set. Very disconcerting. Now and then his eyelids drooped and then they snapped open again. Now and then he put his fingers into his beard and tugged, like he was thinking about something he was hearing on the television.

On the screen, a group of men wearing cowls was being set upon and tormented by men dressed in skeleton costumes and men dressed as devils. The men dressed as devils wore devil masks, horns, and long tails. This pageant was part of a procession. The Englishman who was narrating the thing said it took place in Spain once a year. I tried to explain to the blind man what was happening.

"Skeletons," he said. "I know about skeletons," he said, and he nodded.

The TV showed this one cathedral. Then there was a long, slow look at another one. Finally, the picture switched to the famous one in Paris, with its flying buttresses and its spires reaching up to the clouds. The camera pulled away to show the whole of the cathedral rising above the skyline.

There were times when the Englishman who was telling the thing would shut up, would simply let the camera move around over the cathedrals. Or else the camera would tour the countryside, men in fields walking behind oxen. I waited as long as I could. Then I felt I had to say something. I said, "They're showing the outside of this cathedral now. Gargoyles. Little statues carved to look like monsters. Now I guess they're in Italy. Yeah, they're in Italy. There's paintings on the walls of this one church."

"Are those fresco paintings, bub?" he asked, and he sipped from his drink.

I reached for my glass. But it was empty. I tried to remember what I could remember. "You're asking me are those frescoes?" I said. "That's a good question. I don't know."

The camera moved to a cathedral outside Lisbon. The differences in the Portuguese cathedral compared with the French and Italian were not that great. But they were there. Mostly the interior stuff. Then something occurred to me, and I said, "Something has occurred to me. Do you have any idea what a cathedral is? What they look like, that is? Do you follow me? If somebody says cathedral to you, do you have any notion what they're talking about? Do you know the difference between that and a Baptist church, say?"

He let the smoke dribble from his mouth. "I know they took hundreds of workers fifty or a hundred years to build," he said. "I just heard the man say that, of course. I know generations of the same families worked on a cathedral. I heard him say that too. The men who began their life's work on them, they never lived to see the completion of their work. In that wise, bub, they're no different from the rest of us, right?" He laughed. Then his eyelids drooped again. His head nodded. He seemed to be snoozing. Maybe he was imagining himself in Portugal. The TV was showing another cathedral now. This one was in Germany. The Englishman's voice droned on. "Cathedrals," the blind man said. He sat up and rolled his head back and forth. "If you want the truth, bub, that's about all I know. What I just said. What I heard him say. But maybe you could describe one to me? I wish you'd do it. I'd like that. If you want to know, I really don't have a good idea."

I stared hard at the shot of the cathedral on the TV. How could I even begin to describe it? But say my life depended on it. Say my life was being threatened by an insane guy who said I had to do it or else.

I stared some more at the cathedral before the picture flipped off into the countryside. There was no use. I turned to the blind man and said, "To begin with, they're very tall." I was looking around the room for clues. "They reach way up. Up and up. Toward the sky. They're so big, some of them, they have to have these supports. To help hold them up, so to speak. These supports are called buttresses. They remind me of viaducts, for some reason. But maybe you don't know viaducts, either? Sometimes the cathedrals have devils and such carved into the front. Sometimes lords and ladies. Don't ask me why this is," I said.

He was nodding. The whole upper part of his body seemed to be moving back and forth.

"I'm not doing so good, am I?" I said.

He stopped nodding and leaned forward on the edge of the sofa. As he listened to me, he was running his fingers through his beard. I wasn't getting through to him, I could see that. But he waited for me to go on just the same. He nodded, like he was trying to encourage me. I tried to think what else to say. "They're really big," I said. "They're massive. They're built of stone. Marble, too, sometimes. In those olden days, when they built cathedrals, men wanted to be close to God. In those olden days, God was an important part of everyone's life. You could tell this from their cathedral-building. I'm sorry," I said, "but it looks like that's the best I can do for you. I'm just no good at it."

"That's all right, bub," the blind man said. "Hey, listen. I hope you don't mind my asking you. Can I ask you something? Let me ask you a simple question, yes or no. I'm just curious and there's no offense. You're my host. But let me ask if you are in any way religious? You don't mind my asking?"

I shook my head. He couldn't see that, though. A wink is the same as a nod to a blind man. "I guess I don't believe in it. In anything. Sometimes it's hard. You know what I'm saying?"

"Sure I do," he said.

"Right," I said.

The Englishman was still holding forth. My wife sighed in her sleep. She drew a long breath and went on with her sleeping.

"You'll have to forgive me," I said. "But I can't tell you what a cathedral looks like. It just isn't in me to do it. I can't do any more than I've done."

The blind man sat very still, his head down, as he listened to me.

I said, "The truth is, cathedrals don't mean anything special to me. Nothing. Cathedrals. They're something to look at on late-night TV. That's all they are."

It was then that the blind man cleared his throat. He brought something up. He took a handkerchief from his back pocket. Then he said, "I get it, bub. It's okay. It happens. Don't worry about it," he said. "Hey, listen to me. Will you do me a favor? I got an idea. Why don't you find us some heavy paper? And a pen. We'll do something. We'll draw one together. Get us a pen and some heavy paper. Go on, bub, get the stuff," he said.

So I went upstairs. My legs felt like they didn't have any strength in them. They felt like they did after I'd done some running. In my wife's room, I looked around. I found some ballpoints in a little basket on her table. And then I tried to think where to look for the kind of paper he was talking about.

Downstairs, in the kitchen, I found a shopping bag with onion skins in the bottom of the bag. I emptied the bag and shook it. I brought it into the living room and sat down with it near his legs. I moved some things, smoothed the wrinkles from the bag, spread it out on the coffee table.

The blind man got down from the sofa and sat next to me on the carpet.

He ran his fingers over the paper. He went up and down the sides of the paper. The edges, even the edges. He fingered the corners.

"All right," he said. "All right, let's do her."

He found my hand, the hand with the pen. He closed his hand over my hand. "Go ahead, bub, draw," he said. "Draw. You'll see. I'll follow along with you. It'll be okay. Just begin now like I'm telling you. You'll see. Draw," the blind man said.

So I began. First I drew a box that looked like a house. It could have been the house I lived in. Then I put a roof on it. At either end of the roof, I drew spires. Crazy.

"Swell," he said. "Terrific. You're doing fine," he said.

"Never thought anything like this could happen in your lifetime, did you, bub? Well, it's a strange life, we all know that. Go on now. Keep it up."

I put in windows with arches. I drew flying buttresses. I hung great doors. I couldn't stop. The TV station went off the air. I put down the pen and closed and opened my fingers. The blind man felt round over the paper. He moved the tips of his fingers over the paper, all over what I had drawn, and he nodded.

"Doing fine," the blind man said.

I took up the pen again, and he found my hand. I kept at it. I'm no artist. But I kept drawing just the same.

My wife opened up her eyes and gazed at us. She sat up on the sofa, her robe hanging open. She said, "What are you doing? Tell me, I want to know."

I didn't answer her.

The blind man said, "We're drawing a cathedral. Me and him are working on it. Press hard," he said to me. "That's right. That's good," he said. "Sure. You got it, bub. I can tell. You didn't think you could. But you can, can't you? You're cooking with gas now. You know what I'm saying? We're going to really have us something here in a minute. How's the old arm?" he said. "Put some people in there now. What's a cathedral without people?"

My wife said, "What's going on? Robert, what are you doing? What's going on?"

"It's all right," he said to her. "Close your eyes now," the blind man said to me.

I did it. I closed them just like he said.

"Are they closed?" he said. "Don't fudge."

"They're closed," I said.

"Keep them that way," he said. He said, "Don't stop now. Draw."

So we kept on with it. His fingers rode my fingers as my hand went over the paper. It was like nothing else in my life up to now.

Then he said, "I think that's it. I think you got it," he said. "Take a look. What do you think?"

But I had my eyes closed. I thought I'd keep them that way for a little longer. I thought it was something I ought to do.

"Well?" he said. "Are you looking?"

My eyes were still closed. I was in my house. I knew that. But I didn't feel like I was inside anything.

"It's really something," I said.

Questions for Discussion

1. How does the narrator feel about the relationship between his wife and the blind man? What stereotypes does the narrator have of the blind, and how are these stereotypes broken down in the course of the story?
2. What is the significance of the poem the narrator's wife has written about the blind man? How have the two kept in touch over the years?
3. Why does the narrator believe Beulah's life was "pitiful"? Do you think it was?
4. What impression does the blind man, Robert, make on the narrator when they first meet? How do Robert's appearance and behavior change the narrator's expectations?
5. What does the narrator learn through his attempt to draw a cathedral with the blind man? What does the narrator mean by his final response to the blind man, "It's really something"? What is "it"?

Ideas for Writing

1. Explore in an essay the theme of loneliness in the story. The narrator says he is "glad for the company," as he makes a decision to stay up and watch television with the blind man. Why is the narrator lonely? Is the blind man lonely, too? How about the narrator's wife?
2. Write a story about a person who meets a "handicapped" individual who changes preconceptions or stereotypes that the person has held.

MARGARET ATWOOD (b. 1939)

One of Canada's most highly regarded writers, Margaret Atwood emphasizes in her fiction political issues, social satire, and the inner worlds of women. Born in Ottawa, Atwood spent her childhood in rural areas of Canada and received her B.A. at the University of Toronto and her M.A. at Radcliffe College. She started her literary career as a poet with the publication of *Double Persephone* in 1961. Since then she has published numerous collections of poems, stories, and essays and popular novels such as *Surfacing* (1972), *The Handmaid's Tale* (1986), *Cat's Eye* (1989), *The Robber Bride* (1994), and *Alias Grace* (1996). Atwood's analysis of the literature of her homeland, *Survival: A Thematic Guide to Canadian Literature* (1972), is also highly regarded. Her story collections include *Dancing Girls* (1982), *Bluebeard's Egg* (1986), *Wilderness Tips* (1991), and *Murder in the Dark* (1983), which contains "Simmering."

Atwood has been a strong advocate for Canadian independence from American influences, political and cultural, as well as a champion of women's rights. While her style is generally realistic, with clear narration and sharply revealing dialogue, she also experiments with utopian fiction and psychologically oriented, stream-of-consciousness writing.

Simmering (1983)

It started in the backyards. At first the men concentrated on heat and smoke, and on dangerous thrusts with long forks. Their wives gave them aprons in railroad stripes, with slogans on the front — Hot Stuff, The Boss — to spur them on. Then it began to get all mixed up with who should do the dishes, and you can't fall back on paper plates forever, and around that time the wives got tired of making butterscotch brownies and jello salads with grated carrots and baby marshmallows in them and wanted to make money instead, and one thing led to another. The wives said that there were only twenty-four hours in a day; and the men, who in that century were still priding themselves on their rationality, had to agree that this was so.

For a while they worked it out that the men were in charge of the more masculine kinds of food: roasts, chops, steaks, dead chickens and ducks, gizzards, hearts, anything that had obviously been killed, that had visibly bled. The wives did the other things, the glazed parsnips and the prune whip, anything that flowered or fruited or was soft and gooey in the middle. That was all right for about a decade. Everyone praised the men to keep them going, and the wives, sneaking out of the houses in the mornings with their squeaky new briefcases, clutching their bus tickets because the men needed the station wagons to bring home the carcasses, felt they had got away with something.

But time is not static, and the men refused to stay put. They could not be kept isolated in their individual kitchens, kitchens into which the wives were allowed less and less frequently because, the men said, they did not sharpen the knives properly, if at all. The men began to acquire kitchen machines, which they would spend the weekends taking apart and oiling. There were a few accidents at first, a few lost fingers and ends of noses, but the men soon got the hang of it and branched out into other areas: automatic nutmeg graters, electric gadgets for taking the lids off jars. At cocktail parties they would gather in groups at one end of the room, exchanging private recipes and cooking yarns, tales of soufflés daringly saved at the last minute, pears flambées which had gone out of control and had to be fought to a standstill. Some of these stories had risqué phrases in them, such as *chicken breasts*. Indeed, sexual metaphor was changing: bowls and forks became prominent, and *eggbeater, pressure cooker* and *turkey baster* became words which only the most daring young women, the kind who thought it was a kick to butter their own toast, would venture to pronounce in mixed company. Men who could not cook very well hung about the edges of these groups, afraid to say much, admiring the older and more experienced ones, wishing they could be like them.

Soon after that, the men resigned from their jobs in large numbers so they could spend more time in the kitchen. The magazines said it was a modern trend. The wives were all driven off to work, whether they wanted to or not: someone had to make the money, and of course they did not want their husbands' masculinity to be threatened. A man's status in the community was now displayed by the length of his carving knives, by how many of them he had and how sharp he kept them, and by whether they were plain or ornamented with gold and precious jewels.

Exclusive clubs and secret societies sprang up. Men meeting for the first time would now exchange special handshakes — the Béchamel twist, the chocolate mousse double grip — to show that they had been initiated. It was pointed out to the women, who by this time did not go into the kitchens at all on pain of being thought unfeminine, that *chef* after all means *chief* and that Mixmasters were common but no one had ever heard of a Mixmistress. Psychological articles began to appear in the magazines on the origin of women's kitchen envy and how it could be cured. Amputation of the tip of the tongue was recommended, and, as you know, became a widespread practice in the more advanced nations. If Nature had meant women to cook, it was said, God would have made carving knives round and with holes in them.

This is history. But it is not a history familiar to many people. It exists only in the few archival collections that have not yet been destroyed, and in manuscripts like this one, passed from woman to woman, usually at night, copied out by hand or memorized. It is subversive of me even to write these words. I am doing so, at the risk of my own personal freedom, because now, after so many centuries of stagnation, there are signs that hope and therefore change have once more become possible.

The women in their pinstripe suits, exiled to the living rooms where they dutifully sip the glasses of port brought out to them by the men, used to sit uneasily, silently, listening to the loud bursts of male and somehow derisive laughter from behind the closed kitchen doors. But they have begun whispering to each other. When they are with those they trust, they tell of a time long ago, lost in the fogs of legend, hinted at in packets of letters found in attic trunks and in the cryptic frescoes on abandoned temple walls, when women too were allowed to participate in the ritual which now embodies the deepest religious convictions of our society: the transformation of the consecrated flour into the holy bread. At night they dream, long clandestine dreams, confused and obscured by shadows. They dream of plunging their hands into the earth, which is red as blood and soft, which is milky and warm. They dream that the earth gathers itself under their hands, swells, changes its form, flowers into a thousand shapes, for them too, for them once more. They dream of apples; they dream of the creation of the world; they dream of freedom.

Questions for Discussion

1. What history does the narrator relate in the story's opening paragraph? What is significant about the comment that men "in that century were still priding themselves on their rationality"?
2. How does the balance of power between men as cooks and women as breadwinners and commuters gradually shift? In what ways does the men's command of technology play a role in the shift of power?
3. As sex roles change and evolve in the story, how does the use of language by men and women also gradually change? In what ways is the shift in meaning of key words and expressions significant?
4. Why do "exclusive clubs and secret societies" grow up among the men? What function do they serve? How are these clubs similar to ones that men and women have formed in our own society?
5. Why have women lost their freedom under the new regime of male cooks? What else have they lost that is part of the traditional power and identity of women? Is what they have gained valued?

Ideas for Writing

1. Write an essay about the significance of dreams in the story. Of what do the narrator — and other women — dream? How do these dreams present a critique of women's status both within the world of the story and in our own society?
2. Write a story set in a future society in which gender roles are significantly different from those of our current culture.

TONI CADE BAMBARA   (1939–1995)

Toni Cade Bambara's stories are noted for their humor and their vividly realized voices that explore the web of relationships in African-American communities and the fabric of urban neighborhoods. Born and raised in New York City, Bambara earned her B.A. at Queens College in 1959, attended the University of Florence, and then returned to New York, where she completed her M.A. at City College in 1964. She also studied filmmaking and dance at a number of schools. Bambara worked for the New York State Department of Welfare from 1959 to 1961, as an instructor at the City University of New York from 1965 to 1969, and as the director of the Pamoja Writers Collective (which she founded) from 1976 to 1985. Her novel *The Salt Eaters* won the American Book Award in 1981. Her story collections include *Gorilla, My Love* (1972), which contains "Raymond's Run"; *The Sea Birds Are Still Alive* (1977); and *Collected Stories* (1977). Bambara also wrote numerous screenplays.

The writer John Edgar Wideman has said, "Bambara emphasizes the necessity for black people to maintain their best traditions, to remain healthy and whole as they struggle for political power."

Raymond's Run   (1972)

I don't have much work to do around the house like some girls. My mother does that. And I don't have to earn my pocket money by hustling; George runs errands for the big boys and sells Christmas cards. And anything else that's got to get done, my father does. All I have to do in life is mind my brother Raymond, which is enough.

Sometimes I slip and say my little brother Raymond. But as any fool can see he's much bigger and he's older too. But a lot of people call him my little brother cause he needs looking after cause he's not quite right. And a lot of smart mouths got lots to say about that too, especially when George was minding him. But now, if anybody has anything to say to Raymond, anything to say about his big head, they have to come by me. And I don't play the dozens or believe in standing around with somebody in my face doing a lot of talking. I much rather just knock you down and take my chances even if I am a little girl with skinny arms and a squeaky voice, which is how I got the name Squeaky. And if things get too rough, I run. And as anybody can tell you, I'm the fastest thing on two feet.

There is no track meet that I don't win the first place medal. I use to win the twenty-yard dash when I was a little kid in kindergarten. Nowadays it's the fifty-yard dash. And tomorrow I'm subject to run the quarter-meter relay all by myself and come in first, second, and third. The big kids call me Mercury cause I'm the swiftest thing in the neighborhood. Everybody knows that — except two people who know better, my father and me.

He can beat me to Amsterdam Avenue with me having a two fire-hydrant headstart and him running with his hands in his pockets and whistling. But that's private information. Cause can you imagine some thirty-five-year-old man stuffing himself into PAL shorts to race little kids? So as far as everyone's concerned, I'm the fastest and that goes for Gretchen, too, who has put out the tale that she is going to win the first place medal this year. Ridiculous. In the second place, she's got short legs. In the third place, she's got freckles. In the first place, no one can beat me and that's all there is to it.

I'm standing on the corner admiring the weather and about to take a stroll down Broadway so I can practice my breathing exercises, and I've got Raymond walking on the inside close to the buildings cause he's subject to fits of fantasy and starts thinking he's a circus performer and that the curb is a tightrope strung high in the air. And sometimes after a rain, he likes to step down off his tightrope right into the gutter and slosh around getting his shoes and cuffs wet. Then I get hit when I get home. Or sometimes if you don't watch him, he'll dash across traffic to the island in the middle of Broadway and give the pigeons a fit. Then I have to go behind him apologizing to all the old people sitting around trying to get some sun and getting all upset with the pigeons fluttering around them, scattering their newspapers and upsetting the waxpaper lunches in their laps. So I keep Raymond on the inside of me, and he plays like he's driving a stage coach which is O.K. by me so long as he doesn't run me over or interrupt my breathing exercises, which I have to do on account of I'm serious about my running and don't care who knows it.

Now some people like to act like things come easy to them, won't let on that they practice. Not me. I'll high prance down 134th Street like a rodeo pony to keep my knees strong even if it does get my mother uptight so that she walks ahead like she's not with me, don't know me, is all by herself on a shopping trip, and I am somebody else's crazy child.

Now you take Cynthia Procter for instance. She's just the opposite. If there's a test tomorrow, she'll say something like, "Oh I guess I'll play handball this afternoon and watch television tonight," just to let you know she ain't thinking about the test. Or like last week when she won the spelling bee for the millionth time, "A good thing you got 'receive,' Squeaky, cause I would have got it wrong. I completely forgot about the spelling bee." And she'll clutch the lace on her blouse like it was a narrow escape. Oh, brother.

But of course when I pass her house on my early morning trots around the block, she is practicing the scales on the piano over and over and over and over. Then in music class, she always lets herself get bumped around so she falls accidently on purpose onto the piano stool and is so surprised to find herself sitting there, and so decides just for fun to try out the ole keys and what do you know — Chopin's waltzes just spring out of her fingertips and she's the most surprised thing in the world. A regular prodigy. I could kill people like that.

I stay up all night studying the words for the spelling bee. And you can see me anytime of day practicing running. I never walk if I can trot and shame on Raymond if he can't keep up. But of course he does, cause if he hangs back someone's liable to walk up to him and get smart, or take his allowance from him, or ask him where he got that great big pumpkin head. People are so stupid sometimes.

So I'm strolling down Broadway breathing out and breathing in on counts of seven, which is my lucky number, and here comes Gretchen and her side-kicks — Mary Louise who used to be a friend of mine when she first moved to Harlem from Baltimore and got beat up by everybody till I took up for her on account of her mother and my mother used to sing in the same choir when they were young girls, but people ain't grateful, so now she hangs out with the new girl Gretchen and talks about me like a dog; and Rosie who is as fat as I am skinny and has a big mouth where Raymond is concerned and is too stupid to know that there is not a big deal of difference between herself and Raymond and that she can't afford to throw stones. So they are steady coming up Broadway and I see right away that it's going to be one of those Dodge City scenes cause the street ain't that big and they're close to the building just as we are. First I think I'll step into the candy store and look over the new comics and let them pass. But that's chicken and I've got a reputation to consider. So then I think I'll just walk straight on through them or over them if necessary. But as they get to me, they slow down. I'm ready to fight, cause like I said I don't feature a whole lot of chitchat, I much prefer to just knock you down right from the jump and save everybody a lotta precious time.

"You signing up for the May Day races?" smiles Mary Louise, only it's not a smile at all.

A dumb question like that doesn't deserve an answer. Besides, there's just me and Gretchen standing there really, so no use wasting my breath talking to shadows.

"I don't think you're going to win this time," says Rosie, trying to signify with her hands on her hips all salty, completely forgetting that I have whupped her behind many times for less salt than that.

"I always win cause I'm the best," I say straight at Gretchen who is, as far as I'm concerned, the only one talking in this ventriloquist-dummy routine.

Gretchen smiles but it's not a smile and I'm thinking that girls never really smile at each other because they don't know how and don't want to know how and there's probably no one to teach us how cause grown-up girls don't know either. Then they all look at Raymond who has just brought his mule team to a standstill. And they're about to see what trouble they can get into through him.

"What grade you in now, Raymond?"

"You got anything to say to my brother, you say it to me, Mary Louise Williams of Raggedy Town, Baltimore."

"What are you, his mother?" sasses Rosie.

"That's right, Fatso. And the next word out of anybody and I'll be their mother too." So they just stand there and Gretchen shifts from one leg to the other and so do they. Then Gretchen puts her hands on her hips and is about to say something with her freckle-face self but doesn't. Then she walks around me looking me up and down but keeps walking up Broadway, and her sidekicks follow her. So me and Raymond smile at each other and he says "Gidyap" to his team and I continue with my breathing exercises, strolling down Broadway toward the icey man on 145th with not a care in the world cause I am Miss Quicksilver herself.

I take my time getting to the park on May Day because the track meet is the last thing on the program. The biggest thing on the program is the May Pole dancing which I can do without, thank you, even if my mother thinks it's a shame I don't take part and act like a girl for a change. You'd think my mother'd be grateful not to have to make me a white organdy dress with a big satin sash and buy me new white baby-doll shoes that can't be taken out of the box till the big day. You'd think she'd be glad her daughter ain't out there prancing around a May Pole getting the new clothes all dirty and sweaty and trying to act like a fairy or a flower or whatever you're supposed to be when you should be trying to be yourself, whatever that is, which is, as far as I am concerned, a poor Black girl who really can't afford to buy shoes and a new dress you only wear once a lifetime cause it won't fit next year.

I was once a strawberry in a Hansel and Gretel pageant when I was in nursery school and didn't have no better sense than to dance on tiptoe with my arms in a circle over my head doing umbrella steps and being a perfect fool just so my mother and father could come dressed up and clap. You'd think they'd know better than to encourage that kind of nonsense. I am not a strawberry. I do not dance on my toes. I run. That is what I am all about. So I always come late to the May Day program, just in time to get my number pinned on and lay in the grass till they announce the fifty-yard dash.

I put Raymond in the little swings, which is a tight squeeze this year and will be impossible next year. Then I look around for Mr. Pearson who pins the numbers on. I'm really looking for Gretchen if you want to know the truth, but she's not around. The park is jam-packed. Parents in hats and corsages and breast-pocket handkerchiefs peeking up. Kids in white dresses and light blue suits. The parkees unfolding chairs and chasing the rowdy kids from Lenox as if they had no right to be there. The big guys with their caps on backwards, leaning against the fence swirling the basketballs on the tips of their fingers waiting for all these crazy people to clear out the park so they can play. Most of the kids in my class are carrying bass drums and glockenspiels and flutes. You'd think they'd put in a few bongos or something for real like that.

Then here comes Mr. Pearson with his clipboard and his cards and pencils and whistles and safety pins and fifty million other things he's always dropping all over the place with his clumsy self. He sticks out in a crowd cause he's on stilts. We used to call him Jack and the Beanstalk to get him mad. But I'm the only one that can outrun him and get away, and I'm too grown for that silliness now.

"Well, Squeaky," he says checking my name off the list and handing me number seven and two pins. And I'm thinking he's got no right to call me Squeaky, if I can't call him Beanstalk.

"Hazel Elizabeth Deborah Parker," I correct him and tell him to write it down on his board.

"Well, Hazel Elizabeth Deborah Parker, going to give someone else a break this year?" I squint at him real hard to see if he is seriously thinking I should lose the race on purpose just to give someone else a break.

"Only six girls running this time," he continues, shaking his head sadly like it's my fault all of New York didn't turn out in sneakers. "That new girl should give you a run for your money." He looks around the park for Gretchen like a periscope in a submarine movie. "Wouldn't it be a nice gesture if you were . . . to ahhh . . ."

I give him such a look he couldn't finish putting that idea into words. Grownups got a lot of nerve sometimes. I pin number seven to myself and stomp away — I'm so burnt. And I go straight for the track and stretch out on the grass while the band winds up with "Oh the Monkey Wrapped His Tail Around the Flag Pole," which my teacher calls by some other name. The man on the loudspeaker is calling everyone over to the track and I'm on my back looking at the sky trying to pretend I'm in the country, but I can't, because even grass in the city feels hard as sidewalk and there's just no pretending you are anywhere but in a "concrete jungle" as my grandfather says.

The twenty-yard dash takes all of the two minutes cause most of the little kids don't know no better than to run off the track or run the wrong way or run smack into the fence and fall down and cry. One little kid though has got the good sense to run straight for the white ribbon up ahead so he wins. Then the second graders line up for the thirty-yard dash and I don't even bother to turn my head to watch cause Raphael Perez always wins. He wins before he even begins by psyching the runners, telling them they're going to trip on their shoelaces and fall on their faces or lose their shorts or something, which he doesn't really have to do since he is very fast, almost as fast as I am. After that is the forty-yard dash which I use to run when I was in first grade. Raymond is hollering from the swings cause he knows I'm about to do my thing cause the man on the loudspeaker has just announced the fifty-yard dash, although he might just as well be giving a recipe for Angel Food cake cause you can hardly make out what he's saying for the static. I get up and slip off my sweat pants and then I see Gretchen standing at the starting line kicking her legs out like a pro. Then as I get into place I see that ole Raymond is in line on the other side of the fence, bending down with his fingers on the ground just like he knew what he was doing. I was going to yell at him but then I didn't. It burns up your energy to holler.

Every time, just before I take off in a race, I always feel like I'm in a dream, the kind of dream you have when you're sick with fever and feel all hot and weightless. I dream I'm flying over a sandy beach in the early morning sun, kissing the leaves of the trees as I fly by. And there's always the smell of apples, just like in the country when I was little and use to think I was a choo-choo train, running through the fields of corn and chugging up the hill to the orchard. And all the time I'm dreaming this, I get lighter and lighter until I'm flying over the beach again, getting blown through the sky like a feather that weighs nothing at all. But once I spread my fingers in the dirt and crouch over for the Get on Your Mark, the dream goes and I am solid again and am telling myself, Squeaky you must win, you must win, you are the fastest thing in the world, you can even beat your father up Amsterdam if you really try. And then I feel my weight coming back just behind my knees then down to my feet then into the earth and the pistol shot explodes in my blood and I am off and weightless again, flying past the other runners, my arms pumping up and down and the whole world is quiet except for the crunch as I zoom over the gravel in the track. I glance to my left and there is no one. To the right a blurred Gretchen who's got her chin jutting out as if it would win the race all by itself. And on the other side of the fence is Raymond with his arms down to his side and the palms tucked up behind him, running, in his very own style and the first time I ever saw that and I almost stop to watch my brother Raymond on his first run. But the white ribbon is bouncing toward me and I tear past it racing into the distance till my feet with a mind of their own start digging up footfuls of dirt and brake me short. Then all the kids standing on the side pile on me, banging me on the back and slapping my head with their May Day programs, for I have won again and everybody on 151st Street can walk tall for another year.

"In first place . . ." the man on the loudspeaker is clear as a bell now. But then he pauses and the loudspeaker starts to whine. Then static. And I lean down to catch my breath and here comes Gretchen walking back for she's overshot the finish line too, huffing and puffing with her hands on her hips taking it slow, breathing in steady time like a real pro and I sort of like her a little for the first time. "In first place . . ." and then three or four voices get all mixed up on the loudspeaker and I dig my sneaker into the grass and stare at Gretchen who's staring back, we both wondering just who did win. I can hear old Beanstalk arguing with the man on the loudspeaker and then a few others running their mouths about what the stop watches say.

Then I hear Raymond yanking at the fence to call me and I wave to shush him, but he keeps rattling the fence like a gorilla in a cage like in them gorilla movies, but then like a dancer or something he starts climbing up nice and easy but very fast. And it occurs to me, watching how smoothly he climbs hand over hand and remembering how he looked running with his arms down to his side and with the wind pulling his mouth back and his teeth showing and all, it occurred to me that Raymond would make a very fine runner. Doesn't he always keep up with me on my trots? And he surely knows how to breathe in counts of seven cause he's always doing it at the dinner table, which drives my brother George up the wall. And I'm smiling to beat the band cause if I've lost this race, or if me and Gretchen tied, or even if I've won, I can always retire as a runner and begin a whole new career as a coach with Raymond as my champion. After all, with a little more study I can beat Cynthia and her phony self at the spelling bee. And if I bugged my mother, I could get piano lessons and become a star. And I have a big rep as the baddest thing around. And I've got a roomful of ribbons and medals and awards. But what has Raymond got to call his own?

So I stand there with my new plan, laughing out loud by this time as Raymond jumps down from the fence and runs over with his teeth showing and his arms down to the side which no one before him has quite mastered as a running style. And by the time he comes over I'm jumping up and down so glad to see him — my brother Raymond, a great runner in the family tradition. But of course everyone thinks I'm jumping up and down because the men on the loudspeaker have finally gotten themselves together and compared notes and are announcing "In first place — Miss Hazel Elizabeth Deborah Parker." (Dig that.) "In second place — Miss Gretchen P. Lewis." And I look over at Gretchen wondering what the P stands for. And I smile. Cause she's good, no doubt about it. Maybe she'd like to help me coach Raymond; she obviously is serious about running, as any fool can see. And she nods to congratulate me and then she smiles. And I smile. We stand there with this big smile of respect between us. It's about as real a smile as girls can do for each other, considering we don't practice real smiling every day you know, cause maybe we too busy being flowers or fairies or strawberries instead of something honest and worthy of respect . . . you know . . . like being people.

Questions for Writing

1. Characterize the narrator's voice. How do her language, her sentence rhythms, and the details she provides about her life help you to understand how she feels about her brother, her friends, and herself?

2. What motivates the narrator to want to run and win? What is the significance of her nickname, Squeaky?

3. Analyze the narrator's memory of the pageant before the race. What contrasting images does this sequence reveal? What do her attitudes suggest about her confusion and the complexity of her inner world?

4. What does the smile exchanged between the narrator and Gretchen after the race suggest about what they have learned and how they have changed through competing in the race?

5. What does the narrator discover about and learn from Raymond at the end of the story? Why is the story entitled "Raymond's Run"?

Ideas for Writing

1. Write an essay in which you discuss "Raymond's Run" as a story of initiation. How do Squeaky's inner monologue and observations reveal her growth and self-realization?

2. Using the present tense, write an initiation story in a young person's voice; focus on a moment of self-awareness and understanding.

AMOS OZ   (b. 1939)

Israeli writer Amos Oz is concerned in all his work with the spiritual and ethical values of present-day Israel; seeing a conflict between the idealism of the original Zionist settlers and Israeli life today, Oz is particularly critical of the treatment of Arab and Palestinian residents. Born into a scholarly, middle-class Jerusalem family, Oz began to live on a kibbutz (farming collective) at the age of fifteen as an act of rebellion. He received his B.A. at the Hebrew University of Jerusalem and his M.A. at Oxford. After his education, Oz fought in the Israeli army, then returned to live on the kibbutz and work. The author of novels and journalistic essays, Oz draws extensively on his day-to-day experience on the kibbutz for his characters and plots. His translated works include the novels *Elsewhere, Perhaps* (1973); *Touch the Water, Touch the Wind* (1974); *A Perfect Peace* (1985); and *Don't Call It Night* (1995). The story collection *Where the Jackals Howl and Other Stories* (1981) contains "Nomad and Viper." The world Oz creates is often a nighttime, hallucinatory place of intense idealism, religious fanaticism, guilty conscience, and rebellion against authority. As Oz said in an interview in the *Partisan Review,* "Nocturnal Israel is a refugee camp with more nightmares per square mile than I guess any other place in the world. Almost everyone has seen the devil."

Nomad and Viper   (1965)

1

The famine brought them.

They fled north from the horrors of famine, together with their dusty flocks. From September to April the desert had not known a moment's relief from drought. The loess was pounded to dust. Famine had spread through the nomads' encampments and wrought havoc among their flocks.

The military authorities gave the situation their urgent attention. Despite certain hesitations, they decided to open the roads leading north to the Bedouins. A whole population—men, women, and children—could not simply be abandoned to the horrors of starvation.

Dark, sinuous, and wiry, the desert tribesmen trickled along the dirt paths, and with them came their emaciated flocks. They meandered along gullies hidden from town dwellers' eyes. A persistent stream pressed northward, circling the scattered settlements, staring wide-eyed at the sights of the settled land. The dark flocks spread into the fields of golden stubble, tearing and chewing with strong, vengeful teeth. The nomads' bearing was stealthy and subdued; they shrank from watchful eyes. They took pains to avoid encounters. Tried to conceal their presence.

If you passed them on a noisy tractor and set billows of dust loose on them, they would courteously gather their scattered flocks and give you a wide passage, wider by far than was necessary. They stared at you from a distance, frozen like statues. The scorching atmosphere blurred their appearance and gave a uniform look to their features: a shepherd with his staff, a woman with her babes, an old man with his eyes sunk deep in their sockets. Some were half-blind, or perhaps feigned half-blindness from some vague alms-gathering motive. Inscrutable to the likes of you.

How unlike our well-tended sheep were their miserable specimens: knots of small, skinny beasts huddling into a dark, seething mass, silent and subdued, humble as their dumb keepers.

The camels alone spurn meekness. From atop tall necks they fix you with tired eyes brimming with scornful sorrow. The wisdom of age seems to lurk in their eyes, and a nameless tremor runs often through their skin.

Sometimes you manage to catch them unawares. Crossing a field on foot, you may suddenly happen on an indolent flock standing motionless, noon-struck, their feet apparently rooted in the parched soil. Among them lies the shepherd, fast asleep, dark as a block of basalt. You approach and cover him with a harsh shadow. You are startled to find his eyes wide open. He bares most of his teeth in a placatory smile. Some of them are gleaming, others decayed. His smell hits you. You grimace. Your grimace hits him like a punch in the face. Daintily he picks himself up, trunk erect, shoulders hunched. You fix him with a cold blue eye. He broadens his smile and utters a guttural syllable. His garb is a compromise: a short, patched European jacket over a white desert robe. He cocks his head to one side. An appeased gleam crosses his face. If you do not upbraid him, he suddenly extends his left hand and asks for a cigarette in rapid Hebrew. His voice has a silken quality, like that of a shy woman. If your mood is generous, you put a cigarette to your lips and toss another into his wrinkled palm. To your surprise, he snatches a gilt lighter from the recesses of his robe and offers a furtive flame. The smile never leaves his lips. His smile lasts too long, is unconvincing. A flash of sunlight darts off the thick gold ring adorning his finger and pierces your squinting eyes.

Eventually you turn your back on the nomad and continue on your way. After a hundred, two hundred paces, you may turn your head and see him standing just as he was, his gaze stabbing your back. You could swear that he is still smiling, that he will go on smiling for a long while to come.

And then, their singing in the night. A long-drawn-out, dolorous wail drifts on the night air from sunset until the early hours. The voices penetrate to the gardens and pathways of the kibbutz and charge our nights with an uneasy heaviness. No sooner have you settled down to sleep than a distant drumbeat sets the rhythm of your slumber like the pounding of an obdurate heart. Hot are the nights, and vapor-laden. Stray clouds caress the moon like a train of gentle camels, camels without any bells.

The nomads' tents are made up of dark drapes. Stray women drift around at night, barefoot and noiseless. Lean, vicious nomad hounds dart out of the camp to challenge the moon all night long. Their barking drives our kibbutz dogs insane. Our finest dog went mad one night, broke into the henhouse, and massacred the young chicks. It was not out of savagery that the watchmen shot him. There was no alternative. Any reasonable man would justify their action.

2

You might imagine that the nomad incursion enriched our heat-prostrated nights with a dimension of poetry. This may have been the case for some of our unattached girls. But we cannot refrain from mentioning a whole string of prosaic, indeed unaesthetic disturbances, such as foot-and-mouth disease, crop damage, and an epidemic of petty thefts.

The foot-and-mouth disease came out of the desert, carried by their live-stock, which had never been subjected to any proper medical inspection. Although we took various early precautions, the virus infected our sheep and cattle, severely reducing the milk yield and killing off a number of animals.

As for the damage to the crops, we had to admit that we had never managed to catch one of the nomads in the act. All we ever found were the tracks of men and animals among the rows of vegetables, in the hayfields, and deep inside the carefully fenced orchards. And wrecked irrigation pipes, plot markers, farming implements left out in the fields, and other objects.

We are not the kind to take such things lying down. We are no believers in forbearance or vegetarianism. This is especially true of our younger men. Among the veteran founders there are a few adherents of Tolstoyan ideas and such like. Decency constrains me not to dwell in detail on certain isolated and exceptional acts of reprisal conducted by some of the youngsters whose patience had expired, such as cattle rustling, stoning a nomad boy, or beating one of the shepherds senseless. In defense of the perpetrators of the last-mentioned act of retaliation I must state clearly that the shepherd in question had an infuriatingly sly face. He was blind in one eye, broken-nosed, drooling; and his mouth — on this the men responsible were unanimous — was set with long, curved fangs like a fox's. A man with such an appearance was capable of anything. And the Bedouins would certainly not forget this lesson.

The pilfering was the most worrisome aspect of all. They laid hands on the unripe fruit in our orchards, pocketed the faucets, whittled away piles of empty sacks in the fields, stole into the henhouses, and even made away with the modest valuables from our little houses.

The very darkness was their accomplice. Elusive as the wind, they passed through the settlement, evading both the guards we had posted and the extra guards we had added. Sometimes you would set out on a tractor or a battered jeep toward midnight to turn off the irrigation faucets in an outlying field and your headlights would trap fleeting shadows, a man or a night beast. An irritable guard decided one night to open fire, and in the dark he managed to kill a stray jackal.

Needless to say, the kibbutz secretariat did not remain silent. Several times Etkin, the secretary, called in the police, but their tracking dogs betrayed or failed them. Having led their handlers a few paces outside the kibbutz fence, they raised their black noses, uttered a savage howl, and stared foolishly ahead.

Spot raids on the tattered tents revealed nothing. It was as if the very earth had decided to cover up the plunder and brazenly outstare the victims. Eventually the elder of the tribe was brought to the kibbutz office, flanked by a pair of inscrutable nomads. The short-tempered policemen pushed them forward with repeated cries of "Yallah, yallah."

We, the members of the secretariat, received the elder and his men politely and respectfully. We invited them to sit down on the bench, smiled at them, and offered them steaming coffee prepared by Geula at Etkin's special request. The old man responded with elaborate courtesies, favoring us with a smile which he kept up from the beginning of the interview till its conclusion. He phrased his remarks in careful, formal Hebrew.

It was true that some of the youngsters of his tribe had laid hands on our property. Why should he deny it. Boys would be boys, and the world was getting steadily worse. He had the honor of begging our pardon and restoring the stolen property. Stolen property fastens its teeth in the flesh of the thief, as the proverb says. That was the way of it. What could one do about the hotheadedness of youth? He deeply regretted the trouble and distress we had been caused.

So saying, he put his hand into the folds of his robe and drew out a few screws, some gleaming, some rusty, a pair of pruning hooks, a stray knife-blade, a pocket flashlight, a broken hammer, and three grubby bank notes, as a recompense for our loss and worry.

Etkin spread his hands in embarrassment. For reasons best known to himself, he chose to ignore our guest's Hebrew and to reply in broken Arabic, the residue of his studies during the time of the riots and the siege. He opened his remarks with a frank and clear statement about the brotherhood of nations — the cornerstone of our ideology — and about the quality of neighborliness of which the peoples of the East had long been justly proud, and never more so than in these days of bloodshed and groundless hatred.

To Etkin's credit, let it be said that he did not shrink in the slightest from reciting a full and detailed list of the acts of theft, damage, and sabotage that our guest — as the result of oversight, no doubt — had refrained from mentioning in his apology. If all the stolen property were returned and the vandalism stopped once and for all, we would be wholeheartedly willing to open a new page in the relations of our two neighboring communities. Our children would doubtless enjoy and profit from an educational courtesy visit to the Bedouin encampment, the kind of visit that broadens horizons. And it went without saying that the tribe's children would pay a return visit to our kibbutz home, in the interest of deepening mutual understanding.

The old man neither relaxed nor broadened his smile, but kept it sternly at its former level as he remarked with an abundance of polite phrases that the gentlemen of the kibbutz would be able to prove no further thefts beyond those he had already admitted and for which he had sought our forgiveness.

He concluded with elaborate benedictions, wished us health and long life, posterity and plenty, then took his leave and departed, accompanied by his two barefooted companions wrapped in their dark robes. They were soon swallowed up by the wadi that lay outside the kibbutz fence.

Since the police had proved ineffectual — and had indeed abandoned the investigation — some of our young men suggested making an excursion one night to teach the savages a lesson in a language they would really understand.

Etkin rejected their suggestion with disgust and with reasonable arguments. The young men, in turn, applied to Etkin a number of epithets that decency obliges me to pass over in silence. Strangely enough, Etkin ignored their insults and reluctantly agreed to put their suggestion before the kibbutz secretariat. Perhaps he was afraid that they might take matters into their own hands.

Toward evening, Etkin went around from room to room and invited the committee to an urgent meeting at eight-thirty. When he came to Geula, he told her about the young men's ideas and the undemocratic pressure to which he was being subjected, and asked her to bring along to the meeting a pot of black coffee and a lot of good will. Geula responded with an acid smile. Her eyes were bleary because Etkin had awakened her from a troubled sleep. As she changed her clothes, the night fell, damp and hot and close.

3

Damp and close and hot the night fell on the kibbutz, tangled in the dust-laden cypresses, oppressed the lawns and ornamental shrubs. Sprinklers scattered water onto the thirsty lawn, but it was swallowed up at once: perhaps it evaporated even before it touched the grass. An irritable phone rang vainly in the locked office. The walls of the houses gave out a damp vapor. From the kitchen chimney a stiff column of smoke rose like an arrow into the heart of the sky, because there was no breeze. From the greasy sinks came a shout. A dish had been broken and somebody was bleeding. A fat house-cat had killed a lizard or a snake and dragged its prey onto the baking concrete path to toy with it lazily in the dense evening sunlight. An ancient tractor started to rumble in one of the sheds, choked, belched a stench of oil, roared, spluttered, and finally managed to set out to deliver an evening meal to the second shift, who were toiling in an outlying field. Near the Persian lilac Geula saw a bottle dirty with the remnants of a greasy liquid. She kicked at it repeatedly, but instead of shattering, the bottle rolled heavily among the rosebushes. She picked up a big stone. She tried to hit the bottle. She longed to smash it. The stone missed. The girl began to whistle a vague tune.

Geula was a short, energetic girl of twenty-nine or so. Although she had not yet found a husband, none of us would deny her good qualities, such as the dedication she lavished on local social and cultural activities. Her face was pale and thin. No one could rival her in brewing strong coffee — coffee to raise the dead, we called it. A pair of bitter lines were etched at the corners of her mouth.

On summer evenings, when the rest of us would lounge in a group on a rug spread on one of the lawns and launch jokes and bursts of cheerful song heavenward, accompanied by clouds of cigarette smoke, Geula would shut herself up in her room and not join us until she had prepared the pot of scalding, strong coffee. She it was, too, who always took pains to ensure that there was no shortage of biscuits.

What had passed between Geula and me is not relevant here, and I shall make do with a hint or two. Long ago we used to stroll together to the orchards in the evening and talk. It was all a long time ago, and it is a long time since it ended. We would exchange unconventional political ideas or argue about the latest books. Geula was a stern and sometimes merciless critic: I was covered in confusion. She did not like my stories, because of the extreme polarity of situations, scenery, and characters, with no intermediate shades between black and white. I would utter an apology or a denial, but Geula always had ready proofs and she was a very methodical thinker. Sometimes I would dare to rest a conciliatory hand on her neck, and wait for her to calm down. But she never relaxed completely. If once or twice she leaned against me, she always blamed her broken sandal or her aching head. And so we drifted apart. To this day she still cuts my stories out of the periodicals, and arranges them in a cardboard box kept in a special drawer devoted to them alone.

I always buy her a new book of poems for her birthday. I creep into her room when she is out and leave the book on her table, without any inscription or dedication. Sometimes we happen to sit together in the dining hall. I avoid her glance, so as not to have to face her mocking sadness. On hot days, when faces are covered in sweat, the acne on her cheeks reddens and she seems to have no hope. When the cool of autumn comes, I sometimes find her pretty and attractive from a distance. On such days Geula likes to walk to the orchards in the early evening. She goes alone and comes back alone. Some of the youngsters come and ask me what she is looking for there, and they have a malicious snicker on their faces. I tell them that I don't know. And I really don't.

4

Viciously Geula picked up another stone to hurl at the bottle. This time she did not miss, but she still failed to hear the shattering sound she craved. The stone grazed the bottle, which tinkled faintly and disappeared under one of the bushes. A third stone, bigger and heavier than the other two, was launched from ridiculously close range: the girl trampled on the loose soil of the flower bed and stood right over the bottle. This time there was a harsh, dry explosion, which brought no relief. Must get out.

Damp and close and hot the night fell, its heat prickling the skin like broken glass. Geula retraced her steps, passed the balcony of her room, tossed her sandals inside, and walked down barefoot onto the dirt path.

The clods of earth tickled the soles of her feet. There was a rough friction, and her nerve endings quivered with flickers of vague excitement. Beyond the rocky hill the shadows were waiting for her: the orchard in the last of the light. With determined hands she widened the gap in the fence and slipped through. At that moment a slight evening breeze began to stir. It was a warmish summer breeze with no definite direction. An old sun rolled westward, trying to be sucked up by the dusty horizon. A last tractor climbed back to the depot, panting along the dirt road from the outlying plots. No doubt it was the tractor that had taken the second-shift workers their supper. It seemed shrouded in smoke or summer haze.

Geula bent down and picked some pebbles out of the dust. Absently she began to throw them back again, one by one. There were lines of poetry on her lips, some by the young poets she was fond of, others her own. By the irrigation pipe she paused, bent down, and drank as though kissing the faucet. But the faucet was rusty, the pipe was still hot, and the water was tepid and foul. Nevertheless she bent her head and let the water pour over her face and neck and into her shirt. A sharp taste of rust and wet dust filled her throat. She closed her eyes and stood in silence. No relief. Perhaps a cup of coffee. But only after the orchard. Must go now.

5

The orchards were heavily laden and fragrant. The branches intertwined, converging above the rows of trunks to form a shadowy dome. Underfoot the irrigated soil retained a hidden dampness. Shadows upon shadows at the foot of those gnarled trunks. Geula picked a plum, sniffed and crushed it. Sticky juice dripped from it. The sight made her feel dizzy. And the smell. She crushed a second plum. She picked another and rubbed it on her cheek till she was spattered with juice. Then, on her knees, she picked up a dry stick and scratched shapes in the dust. Aimless lines and curves. Sharp angles. Domes. A distant bleating invaded the orchard. Dimly she became aware of a sound of bells. She was far away. The nomad stopped behind Geula's back, as silent as a phantom. He dug at the dust with his big toe, and his shadow fell in front of him. But the girl was blinded by a flood of sounds. She saw and heard nothing. For a long time she continued to kneel on the ground and draw shapes in the dust with her twig. The nomad waited patiently in total silence. From time to time he closed his good eye and stared ahead of him with the other, the blind one. Finally he reached out and bestowed a long caress on the air. His obedient shadow moved in the dust. Geula stared, leapt to her feet, and leaned against the nearest tree, letting out a low sound. The nomad let his shoulders drop and put on a faint smile. Geula raised her arm and stabbed the air with her twig. The nomad continued to smile. His gaze dropped to her bare feet. His voice was hushed, and the Hebrew he spoke exuded a rare gentleness:

"What time is it?"

Geula inhaled to her lungs' full capacity. Her features grew sharp, her glance cold. Clearly and dryly she replied:

"It is half past six. Precisely."

The Arab broadened his smile and bowed slightly, as if to acknowledge a great kindness.

"Thank you very much, miss."

His bare toe had dug deep into the damp soil, and the clods of earth crawled at his feet as if there were a startled mole burrowing underneath them.

Geula fastened the top button of her blouse. There were large perspiration stains on her shirt, drawing attention to her armpits. She could smell the sweat on her body, and her nostrils widened. The nomad closed his blind eye and looked up. His good eye blinked. His skin was very dark; it was alive and warm. Creases were etched in his cheeks. He was unlike any man Geula had ever known, and his smell and color and breathing were also strange. His nose was long and narrow, and a shadow of a mustache showed beneath it. His cheeks seemed to be sunk into his mouth cavity. His lips were thin and fine, much finer than her own. But the chin was strong, almost expressing contempt or rebellion.

The man was repulsively handsome, Geula decided to herself. Unconsciously she responded with a mocking half-smile to the nomad's persistent grin. The Bedouin drew two crumpled cigarettes from a hidden pocket in his belt, laid them on his dark, outstretched palm, and held them out to her as though proffering crumbs to a sparrow. Geula dropped her smile, nodded twice, and accepted one. She ran the cigarette through her fingers, slowly, dreamily, ironing out the creases, straightening it, and only then did she put it to her lips. Quick as lightning, before she realized the purpose of the man's sudden movement, a tiny flame was dancing in front of her. Geula shielded the lighter with her hand even though there was no breeze in the orchard, sucked in the flame, closed her eyes. The nomad lit his own cigarette and bowed politely.

"Thank you very much," he said in his velvety voice.

"Thanks," Geula replied. "Thank you."

"You from the kibbutz?"

Geula nodded.

"Goo-d." An elongated syllable escaped from between his gleaming teeth. "That's goo-d."

The girl eyed his desert robe.

"Aren't you hot in that thing?"

The man gave an embarrassed, guilty smile, as if he had been caught red-handed. He took a slight step backward.

"Heaven forbid, it's not hot. Really not. Why? There's air, there's water. . . ." And he fell silent.

The treetops were already growing darker. A first jackal sniffed the oncoming night and let out a tired howl. The orchard filled with a scurry of small, busy feet. All of a sudden Geula became aware of the throngs of black goats intruding in search of their master. They swirled silently in and out of the fruit trees. Geula pursed her lips and let out a short whistle of surprise.

"What are you doing here, anyway? Stealing?"

The nomad cowered as though a stone had been thrown at him. His hand beat a hollow tattoo on his chest.

"No, not stealing, heaven forbid, really not." He added a lengthy oath in his own language and resumed his silent smile. His blind eye winked nervously. Meanwhile an emaciated goat darted forward and rubbed against his leg. He kicked it away and continued to swear with passion:

"Not steal, truly, by Allah not steal. Forbidden to steal."

"Forbidden in the Bible," Geula replied with a dry, cruel smile. "Forbidden to steal, forbidden to kill, forbidden to covet, and forbidden to commit adultery. The righteous are above suspicion."

The Arab cowered before the onslaught of words and looked down at the ground. Shamefaced. Guilty. His foot continued to kick restlessly at the loose earth. He was trying to ingratiate himself. His blind eye narrowed. Geula was momentarily alarmed: surely it was a wink. The smile left his lips. He spoke in a soft, drawn-out whisper, as though uttering a prayer.

"Beautiful girl, truly very beautiful girl. Me, I got no girl yet. Me still young. No girl yet. Yaaa," he concluded with a guttural yell directed at an impudent goat that had rested its forelegs against a tree trunk and was munching hungrily at the foliage. The animal cast a pensive, skeptical glance at its master, shook its beard, and solemnly resumed its munching.

Without warning, and with amazing agility, the shepherd leapt through the air and seized the beast by the hindquarters, lifted it above his head, let out a terrifying, savage screech, and flung it ruthlessly to the ground. Then he spat and turned to the girl.

"Beast," he apologized. "Beast. What to do. No brains. No manners."

The girl let go of the tree trunk against which she had been resting and leaned toward the nomad. A sweet shudder ran down her back. Her voice was still firm and cool.

"Another cigarette?" she asked. "Have you got another cigarette?"

The Bedouin replied with a look of anguish, almost of despair. He apologized. He explained at length that he had no more cigarettes, not even one, not even a little one. No more. All gone. What a pity. He would gladly, very gladly, have given her one. None left. All gone.

The beaten goat was getting shakily to its feet. Treading circumspectly, it returned to the tree trunk, disingenuously observing its master out of the corner of its eye. The shepherd watched it without moving. The goat reached up, rested its front hoofs on the tree, and calmly continued munching. The Arab picked up a heavy stone and swung his arm wildly. Geula seized his arm and restrained him.

"Leave it. Why. Let it be. It doesn't understand. It's only a beast. No brains, no manners."

The nomad obeyed. In total submission he let the stone drop. Then Geula let go of his arm. Once again the man drew the lighter out of his belt. With thin, pensive fingers he toyed with it. He accidentally lit a small flame, and hastily blew at it. The flame widened slightly, slanted, and died. Nearby a jackal broke into a loud, piercing wail. The rest of the goats, meanwhile, had followed the example of the first and were absorbed in rapid, almost angry munching.

A vague wail came from the nomad encampment away to the south, the dim drum beating time to its languorous call. The dusky men were sitting around their campfires, sending skyward their single-noted song. The night took up the strain and answered with dismal cricket-chirp. Last glimmers of light were dying away in the far west. The orchard stood in darkness. Sounds gathered all around, the wind's whispering, the goats' sniffing, the rustle of ravished leaves. Geula pursed her lips and whistled an old tune. The nomad listened to her with rapt attention, his head cocked to one side in surprise, his mouth hanging slightly open. She glanced at her watch. The hands winked back at her with a malign, phosphorescent glint, but said nothing. Night.

The Arab turned his back on Geula, dropped to his knees, touched his forehead on the ground, and began mumbling fervently.

"You've got no girl yet," Geula broke into his prayer. "You're still too young." Her voice was loud and strange. Her hands were on her hips, her breathing still even. The man stopped praying, turned his dark face toward her, and muttered a phrase in Arabic. He was still crouched on all fours, but his pose suggested a certain suppressed joy.

"You're still young," Geula repeated, "very young. Perhaps twenty. Perhaps thirty. Young. No girl for you. Too young."

The man replied with a very long and solemn remark in his own language. She laughed nervously, her hands embracing her hips.

"What's the matter with you?" she inquired, laughing still. "Why are you talking to me in Arabic all of a sudden? What do you think I am? What do you want here, anyway?"

Again the nomad replied in his own language. Now a note of terror filled his voice. With soft, silent steps he recoiled and withdrew as though from a dying creature. She was breathing heavily now, panting, trembling. A single wild syllable escaped from the shepherd's mouth: a sign between him and his goats. The goats responded and thronged around him, their feet pattering on the carpet of dead leaves like cloth ripping. The crickets fell silent. The goats huddled in the dark, a terrified, quivering mass, and disappeared into the darkness, the shepherd vanishing in their midst.

Afterward, alone and trembling, she watched an airplane passing in the dark sky above the treetops, rumbling dully, its lights blinking alternately with a rhythm as precise as that of the drums: red, green, red, green, red. The night covered over the traces. There was a smell of bonfires on the air and a smell of dust borne on the breeze. Only a slight breeze among the fruit trees. Then panic struck her and her blood froze. Her mouth opened to scream but she did not scream, she started to run and she ran barefoot with all her strength for home and stumbled and rose and ran as though pursued, but only the sawing of the crickets chased after her.

6

She returned to her room and made coffee for all the members of the secretariat, because she remembered her promise to Etkin. Outside the cool of evening had set in, but inside her room the walls were hot and her body was also on fire. Her clothes stuck to her body because she had been running, and her armpits disgusted her. The spots on her face were glowing. She stood and counted the number of times the coffee boiled — seven successive boilings, as she had learned to do it from her brother Ehud before he was killed in a reprisal raid in the desert. With pursed lips she counted as the black liquid rose and subsided, rose and subsided, bubbling fiercely as it reached its climax.

That's enough, now. Take clean clothes for the evening. Go to the showers.

What can that Etkin understand about savages. A great socialist. What does he know about Bedouins. A nomad sniffs out weakness from a distance. Give him a kind word, or a smile, and he pounces on you like a wild beast and tries to rape you. It was just as well I ran away from him.

In the showers the drain was clogged and the bench was greasy. Geula put her clean clothes on the stone ledge. I'm not shivering because the water's cold. I'm shivering with disgust. Those black fingers, and how he went straight for my throat. And his teeth. And the goats. Small and skinny like a child, but so strong. It was only by biting and kicking that I managed to escape. Soap my belly and everything, soap it again and again. Yes, let the boys go right away tonight to their camp and smash their black bones because of what they did to me. Now I must get outside.

7

She left the shower and started back toward her room, to pick up the coffee and take it to the secretariat. But on the way she heard crickets and laughter, and she remembered him bent down on all fours, and she was alarmed and stood still in the dark. Suddenly she vomited among the flowering shrubs. And she began to cry. Then her knees gave way. She sat down to rest on the dark earth. She stopped crying. But her teeth continued to chatter, from the cold or from pity. Suddenly she was not in a hurry any more, even the coffee no longer seemed important, and she thought to herself: There's still time. There's still time.

Those planes sweeping the sky tonight were probably on a night-bombing exercise. Repeatedly they roared among the stars, keeping up a constant flashing, red, green, red, green, red. In counterpoint came the singing of the nomads and their drums, a persistent heartbeat in the distance: One, one, two. One, one, two. And silence.

8

From eight-thirty until nearly nine o'clock we waited for Geula. At five to nine Etkin said that he could not imagine what had happened; he could not recall her ever having missed a meeting or been late before; at all events, we must now begin the meeting and turn to the business on the agenda.

He began with a summary of the facts. He gave details of the damage that had apparently been caused by the Bedouins, although there was no formal proof, and enumerated the steps that had been taken on the committee's initiative. The appeal to good will. Calling in the police. Strengthening the guard around the settlement. Tracking dogs. The meeting with the elder of the tribe. He had to admit, Etkin said, that we had now reached an impasse. Nevertheless, he believed that we had to maintain a sense of balance and not give way to extremism, because hatred always gave rise to further hatred. It was essential to break the vicious circle of hostility. He therefore opposed with all the moral force at his disposal the approach — and particularly the intentions — of certain of the younger members. He wished to remind us, by way of conclusion, that the conflict between herdsmen and tillers of the soil was as old as human civilization, as seemed to be evidenced by the story of Cain, who rose up against Abel, his brother. It was fitting, in view of the social gospel we had adopted, that we should put an end to this ancient feud, too, just as we had put an end to other ugly phenomena. It was up to us, and everything depended on our moral strength.

The room was full of tension, even unpleasantness. Rami twice interrupted Etkin and on one occasion went so far as to the use the ugly word "rubbish." Etkin took offense, accused the younger members of planning terrorist activities, and said in conclusion, "We're not going to have that sort of thing here."

Geula had not arrived, and that was why there was no one to cool down the temper of the meeting. And no coffee. A heated exchange broke out between me and Rami. Although in age I belonged with the younger men, I did not agree with their proposals. Like Etkin, I was absolutely opposed to answering the nomads with violence — for two reasons, and when I was given permission to speak I mentioned them both. In the first place, nothing really serious had happened so far. A little stealing perhaps, but even that was not certain: every faucet or pair of pliers that a tractor driver left in a field or lost in the garage or took home with him was immediately blamed on the Bedouins. Secondly, there had been no rape or murder. Hereupon Rami broke in excitedly and asked what I was waiting for. Was I perhaps waiting for some small incident of rape that Geula could write poems about and I could make into a short story? I flushed and cast around in my mind for a telling retort.

But Etkin, upset by our rudeness, immediately deprived us both of the right to speak and began to explain his position all over again. He asked us how it would look if the papers reported that a kibbutz had sent out a lynch mob to settle scores with its Arab neighbors. As Etkin uttered the phrase "lynch mob," Rami made a gesture to his young friends that is commonly used by basketball players. At this signal they rose in a body and walked out in disgust, leaving Etkin to lecture to his heart's content to three elderly women and a long-retired member of Parliament.

After a moment's hesitation I rose and followed them. True, I did not share their views, but I, too, had been deprived of the right to speak in an arbitrary and insulting manner.

If only Geula had come to the meeting and brought her famous coffee with her, it is possible that tempers might have been soothed. Perhaps, too, her understanding might have achieved some sort of compromise between the conflicting points of view. But the coffee was standing, cold by now, on the table in her room. And Geula herself was lying among the bushes behind the Memorial Hall, watching the lights of the planes and listening to the sounds of the night. How she longed to make her peace and to forgive. Not to hate him and wish him dead. Perhaps to get up and go to him, to find him among the wadis and forgive him and never come back. Even to sing to him. The sharp slivers piercing her skin and drawing blood were the fragment of the bottle she had smashed here with a big stone at the beginning of the evening. And the living thing slithering among the slivers of glass among the clods of earth was a snake, perhaps a venomous snake, perhaps a viper. It stuck out a forked tongue, and its triangular head was cold and erect. Its eyes were dark glass. It could never close them, because it had no eyelids. A thorn in her flesh, perhaps a sliver of glass. She was very tired. And the pain was vague, almost pleasant. A distant ringing in her ears. To sleep now. Wearily, through the thickening film, she watched the gang of youngsters crossing the lawn on their way to the fields and the wadi to even the score with the nomads. We were carrying short, thick sticks. Excitement was dilating our pupils. And the blood was drumming in our temples.

Far away in the darkened orchards stood somber, crust-laden cypresses, swaying to and fro with a gentle, religious fervor. She felt tired, and that was why she did not come to see us off. But her fingers caressed the dust and her face was very calm and almost beautiful.

Questions for Discussion

1. Why does the physical bearing of the nomads arouse suspicion among the residents of the kibbutz? What is implied by the description "The scorching atmosphere blurred their appearance and gave a uniform look to their features"?

2. Of what crimes are the nomads suspected? What are the grounds for suspicion?

3. What is the attitude of the narrator, a resident of the kibbutz, toward both Geula and the nomads? What does his attitude reveal about his values and conflicting ideals? How does his attitude about the nomads evolve during the course of the story?

4. How does Geula's attitude change during her encounter with the Bedouin and immediately thereafter? How is her attitude toward the nomad related to her feelings about both the death of her brother and her own sexuality? Why does the nomad run from her?

5. What motivates Geula to describe a rape scenario when she has had no sexual contact with the nomad? What is the significance of her lying in the grass as the young men set out to attack the nomad camp?

Ideas for Writing

1. In an essay, discuss the significance of the viper that appears at the end of the story. Why is the story titled "Nomad and Viper"?

2. Write a story about a community that unites against an outsider group such as homeless people or minority youth, scapegoating the group for the community's problems.

BHARATI MUKHERJEE   (b. 1940)

Indian-born writer Bharati Mukherjee has used her fiction to document the immigrant experience in Canada and the United States, illuminating "the basic confrontation," in one critic's view, "between the Third World and the First." A native of Calcutta, Mukherjee was raised in London and educated at the University of Calcutta. She immigrated to the United States in 1961, completed her M.F.A. and Ph.D. in English at the University of Iowa. In 1966 she married and moved to Canada, not returning to live in the United States until 1980. She became an American citizen in 1988. Currently Mukherjee is a professor of English at the University of California at Berkeley.

Mukherjee has written short stories, nonfiction, and several novels, including *The Tiger's Daughter* (1972), *Wife* (1975), *Jasmine* (1989), and *Holder of the World* (1993). *The Middleman and Other Stories* (1988), which includes "A Wife's Story," established her reputation in the United States. She has collaborated with her husband, Clark Blaise, on the journal *Days and Nights in Calcutta* (1977), which shares their impressions of India. Speaking both of her own life and the tension that she explores in much of her writing, Mukherjee has said, "While changing citizenship is easy, swapping cultures is not."

A Wife's Story   (1988)

Imre says forget it, but I'm going to write David Mamet. So Patels are hard to sell real estate to. You buy them a beer, whisper Glengarry Glen Ross, and they smell swamp instead of sun and surf.[1] They work hard, eat cheap, live ten to a room, stash their savings under futons in Queens, and before you know it they own half of Hoboken. You say, where's the sweet gullibility that made this nation great?

Polish jokes, Patel jokes: that's not why I want to write Mamet.

Seen their women?

Everybody laughs. Imre laughs. The dozing fat man with the Barnes & Noble sack between his legs, the woman next to him, the usher, everybody. The theater isn't so dark that they can't see me. In my red silk sari I'm conspicuous. Plump, gold paisleys sparkle on my chest.

The actor is just warming up. *Seen their women?* He plays a salesman, he's had a bad day and now he's in a Chinese restaurant trying to loosen up. His

---

[1] *Glengarry Glen Ross*, a Broadway play by David Mamet, is about unscrupulous real estate salesmen. *Patel* refers to an Indian immigrant. — Eds.

face is pink. His wool-blend slacks are creased at the crotch. We bought our tickets at half-price, we're sitting in the front row, but at the edge, and we see things we shouldn't be seeing. At least I do, or think I do. Spittle, actors goosing each other, little winks, streaks of makeup.

Maybe they're improvising dialogue too. Maybe Mamet's provided them with insult kits, Thursdays for Chinese, Wednesdays for Hispanics, today for Indians. Maybe they get together before curtain time, see an Indian woman settling in the front row off to the side, and say to each other: "Hey, forget Friday. Let's get *her* today. See if she cries. See if she walks out." Maybe, like the salesmen they play, they have a little bet on.

Maybe I shouldn't feel betrayed.

Their women, he goes again. *They look like they've just been fucked by a dead cat.*

The fat man hoots so hard he nudges my elbow off our shared armrest.

"Imre. I'm going home." But Imre's hunched so far forward he doesn't hear. English isn't his best language. A refugee from Budapest, he has to listen hard. "I didn't pay eighteen dollars to be insulted."

I don't hate Mamet. It's the tyranny of the American dream that scares me. First, you don't exist. Then you're invisible. Then you're funny. Then you're disgusting. Insult, my American friends will tell me, is a kind of acceptance. No instant dignity here. A play like this, back home, would cause riots. Communal, racist, and antisocial. The actors wouldn't make it off stage. This play, and all these awful feelings, would be safely locked up.

I long, at times, for clear-cut answers. Offer me instant dignity, today, and I'll take it.

"What?" Imre moves toward me without taking his eyes off the actor. "Come again?"

Tears come. I want to stand, scream, make an awful scene. I long for ugly, nasty rage.

The actor is ranting, flinging spittle. *Give me a chance. I'm not finished. I can get back on the board. I tell that asshole, give me a real lead. And what does that asshole give me? Patels. Nothing but Patels.*

This time Imre works an arm around my shoulders. "Panna, what is Patel? Why are you taking it all so personally?"

I shrink from his touch, but I don't walk out. Expensive girls' schools in Lausanne and Bombay have trained me to behave well. My manners are exquisite, my feelings are delicate, my gestures refined, my moods undetectable. They have seen me through riots, uprootings, separation, my son's death.

"I'm not taking it personally."

The fat man looks at us. The woman looks too, and shushes.

I stare back at the two of them. Then I stare, mean and cool, at the man's elbow. Under the bright blue polyester Hawaiian shirt sleeve, the elbow looks soft and runny. "Excuse me," I say. My voice has the effortless meanness of well-bred displaced Third World women, though my rhetoric has been learned elsewhere. "You're exploiting my space."

Startled, the man snatches his arm away from me. He cradles it against his breast. By the time he's ready with comebacks, I've turned my back on him. I've probably ruined the first act for him. I know I've ruined it for Imre.

It's not my fault; it's the *situation*. Old colonies wear down. Patels—the new pioneers—have to be suspicious. Idi Amin's lesson is permanent. AT&T wires move good advice from continent to continent. Keep all assets liquid. Get into 7-11s, get out of condos and motels. I know how both sides feel, that's the trouble. The Patel sniffing out scams, the sad salesmen on the stage: postcolonialism has made me their referee. It's hate I long for; simple, brutish, partisan hate.

After the show Imre and I make our way toward Broadway. Sometimes he holds my hand; it doesn't mean anything more than that crazies and drunks are crouched in doorways. Imre's been here over two years, but he's stayed very old-world, very courtly, openly protective of women. I met him in a seminar on special ed. last semester. His wife is a nurse somewhere in the Hungarian countryside. There are two sons, and miles of petitions for their emigration. My husband manages a mill two hundred miles north of Bombay. There are no children.

"You make things tough on yourself," Imre says. He assumed Patel was a Jewish name or maybe Hispanic; everything makes equal sense to him. He found the play tasteless, he worried about the effect of vulgar language on my sensitive ears. "You have to let go a bit." And as though to show me how to let go, he breaks away from me, bounds ahead with his head ducked tight, then dances on amazingly jerky legs. He's a Magyar, he often tells me, and deep down, he's an Asian too. I catch glimpses of it, knife-blade Attila cheekbones, despite the blondish hair. In his faded jeans and leather jacket, he's a rock video star. I watch MTV for hours in the apartment when Charity's working the evening shift at Macy's. I listen to WPLJ on Charity's earphones. Why should I be ashamed? Television in India is so uplifting.

Imre stops as suddenly as he'd started. People walk around us. The summer sidewalk is full of theatergoers in seersucker suits; Imre's year-round jacket is out of place. European. Cops in twos and threes huddle, lightly tap their thighs with night sticks and smile at me with benevolence. I want to wink at them, get us all in trouble, tell them the crazy dancing man is from the Warsaw Pact. I'm too shy to break into dance on Broadway. So I hug Imre instead.

The hug takes him by surprise. He wants me to let go, but he doesn't really expect me to let go. He staggers, though I weigh no more than 104 pounds, and with him, I pitch forward slightly. Then he catches me, and we walk arm in arm to the bus stop. My husband would never dance or hug a woman on Broadway. Nor would my brothers. They aren't stuffy people, but they went to Anglican boarding schools and they have a well-developed sense of what's silly.

"Imre." I squeeze his big, rough hand. "I'm sorry I ruined the evening for you."

"You did nothing of the kind." He sounds tired. "Let's not wait for the bus. Let's splurge and take a cab instead."

Imre always has unexpected funds. The Network, he calls it, Class of '56.

In the back of the cab, without even trying, I feel light, almost free. Memories of Indian destitutes mix with the hordes of New York street people, and they float free, like astronauts, inside my head. I've made it. I'm making something of my life. I've left home, my husband, to get a Ph.D. in special ed. I have a multiple-entry visa and a small scholarship for two years. After that, we'll see. My mother was beaten by her mother-in-law, my grandmother, when she'd registered for French lessons at the Alliance Française. My grandmother, the eldest daughter of a rich zamindar, was illiterate.

Imre and the cabdriver talk away in Russian. I keep my eyes closed. That way I can feel the floaters better. I'll write Mamet tonight. I feel strong, reckless. Maybe I'll write Steven Spielberg too; tell him that Indians don't eat monkey brains.

We've made it. Patels must have made it. Mamet, Spielberg: they're not condescending to us. Maybe they're a little bit afraid.

Charity Chin, my roommate, is sitting on the floor drinking Chablis out of a plastic wineglass. She is five foot six, three inches taller than me, but weighs a kilo and a half less than I do. She is a "hands" model. Orientals are supposed to have a monopoly in the hands-modelling business, she says. She had her eyes fixed eight or nine months ago and out of gratitude sleeps with her plastic surgeon every third Wednesday.

"Oh, good," Charity says. "I'm glad you're back early. I need to talk."

She's been writing checks, MCI, Con Ed, Bonwit Teller. Envelopes, already stamped and sealed, form a pyramid between her shapely, knee-socked legs. The checkbook's cover is brown plastic, grained to look like cowhide. Each time Charity flips back the cover, white geese fly over sky-colored checks. She makes good money, but she's extravagant. The difference adds up to this shared, rent-controlled Chelsea one-bedroom.

"All right. Talk."

When I first moved in, she was seeing an analyst. Now she sees a nutritionist.

"Eric called. From Oregon."

"What did he want?"

"He wants me to pay half the rent on his loft for last spring. He asked me to move back, remember? He *begged* me."

Eric is Charity's estranged husband.

"What does your nutritionist say?" Eric now wears a red jumpsuit and tills the soil in Rajneeshpuram.

"You think Phil's a creep too, don't you? What else can he be when creeps are all I attract?"

Phil is a flutist with thinning hair. He's very touchy on the subject of *flautists* versus *flutists*. He's touchy on every subject, from music to books to foods to clothes. He teaches at a small college upstate, and Charity bought a used blue Datsun ("Nissan," Phil insists) last month so she could spend weekends with him. She returns every Sunday night, exhausted and exasperated.

Phil and I don't have much to say to each other—he's the only musician I know; the men in my family are lawyers, engineers, or in business—but I like him. Around me, he loosens up. When he visits, he bakes us loaves of pumpernickel bread. He waxes our kitchen floor. Like many men in this country, he seems to me a displaced child, or even a woman, looking for something that passed him by, or for something that he can never have. If he thinks I'm not looking, he sneaks his hands under Charity's sweater, but there isn't too much there. Here, she's a model with high ambitions. In India, she'd be a flat-chested old maid.

I'm shy in front of the lovers. A darkness comes over me when I see them horsing around.

"It isn't the money," Charity says. Oh? I think. "He says he still loves me. Then he turns around and asks me for five hundred."

What's so strange about that, I want to ask. She still loves Eric, and Eric, red jumpsuit and all, is smart enough to know it. Love is a commodity, hoarded like any other. Mamet knows. But I say, "I'm not the person to ask about love." Charity knows that mine was a traditional Hindu marriage. My parents, with the help of a marriage broker, who was my mother's cousin, picked out a groom. All I had to do was get to know his taste in food.

It'll be a long evening, I'm afraid. Charity likes to confess. I unpleat my silk sari—it no longer looks too showy—wrap it in muslin cloth and put it away in a dresser drawer. Saris are hard to have laundered in Manhattan, though there's a good man in Jackson Heights. My next step will be to brew us a pot of chrysanthemum tea. It's a very special tea from the mainland. Charity's uncle gave it to us. I like him. He's a humpbacked, awkward, terrified man. He runs a gift store on Mott Street, and though he doesn't speak much English, he seems to have done well. Once upon a time he worked for the railways in Chengdu, Szechwan Province, and during the Wuchang Uprising, he was shot at. When I'm down, when I'm lonely for my husband, when I think of our son, or when I need to be held, I think of Charity's uncle. If I hadn't left home, I'd never have heard of the Wuchang Uprising. I've broadened my horizons.

Very late that night my husband calls me from Ahmadabad, a town of textile mills north of Bombay. My husband is a vice president at Lakshmi Cotton Mills. Lakshmi is the goddess of wealth, but LCM (Priv.), Ltd., is doing poorly. Lock-outs, strikes, rock-throwings. My husband lives on digitalis, which he calls the food for our *yuga* of discontent.

"We had a bad mishap at the mill today." Then he says nothing for seconds.

The operator comes on. "Do you have the right party, sir? We're trying to reach Mrs. Butt."

"Bhatt." I insist. "*B* for Bombay, *H* for Haryana, *A* for Ahmadabad, double *T* for Tamil Nadu." It's a litany. "This is she."

"One of our lorries was firebombed today. Resulting in three deaths. The driver, old Karamchand, and his two children."

I know how my husband's eyes look this minute, how the eye rims sag and the yellow corneas shine and bulge with pain. He is not an emotional man—the Ahmadabad Institute of Management has trained him to cut losses, to look on the bright side of economic catastrophes—but tonight he's feeling low. I try to remember a driver named Karamchand, but can't. That part of my life is over, the way *trucks* have replaced *lorries* in my vocabulary, the way Charity Chin and her lurid love life have replaced inherited notions of marital duty. To-morrow he'll come out of it. Soon he'll be eating again. He'll sleep like a baby. He's been trained to believe in turnovers. Every morning he rubs his scalp with cantharidine oil so his hair will grow back again.

"It could be your car next." Affection, love. Who can tell the difference in a traditional marriage in which a wife still doesn't call her husband by his first name?

"No. They know I'm a flunky, just like them. Well paid, maybe. No need for undue anxiety, please."

Then his voice breaks. He says he needs me, he misses me, he wants me to come to him damp from my evening shower, smelling of sandalwood soap, my braid decorated with jasmines.

"I need you too."

"Not to worry, please," he says. "I am coming in a fortnight's time. I have already made arrangements."

Outside my window, fire trucks whine, up Eighth Avenue. I wonder if he can hear them, what he thinks of a life like mine, led amid disorder.

"I am thinking it'll be like a honeymoon. More or less."

When I was in college, waiting to be married, I imagined honeymoons were only for the more fashionable girls, the girls who came from slightly racy families, smoked Sobranies in the dorm lavatories and put up posters of Kabir Bedi, who was supposed to have made it as a big star in the West. My husband wants us to go to Niagara. I'm not to worry about foreign exchange. He's arranged for extra dollars through the Gujarati Network, with a cousin in San Jose. And he's bought four hundred more on the black market. "Tell me you need me. Panna, please tell me again."

I change out of the cotton pants and shirt I've been wearing all day and put on a sari to meet my husband at JFK. I don't forget the jewelry; the mar-riage necklace of *mangalsutra,* gold drop earrings, heavy gold bangles. I don't wear them every day. In this borough of vice and greed, who knows when, or whom, desire will overwhelm.

My husband spots me in the crowd and waves. He has lost weight, and changed his glasses. The arm, uplifted in a cheery wave, is bony, frail, almost opalescent.

In the Carey Coach, we hold hands. He strokes my fingers one by one. "How come you aren't wearing my mother's ring?"

"Because muggers know about Indian women," I say. They know with us it's 24-karat. His mother's ring is showy, in ghastly taste anywhere but India: a blood-red Burma ruby set in a gold frame of floral sprays. My mother-in-law got her guru to bless the ring before I left for the States.

He looks disconcerted. He's used to a different role. He's the knowing, suspicious one in the family. He seems to be sulking, and finally he comes out with it. "You've said nothing about my new glasses." I compliment him on the glasses, how chic and Western-executive they make him look. But I can't help the other things, necessities until he learns the ropes. I handle the money, buy the tickets. I don't know if this makes me unhappy.

Charity drives her Nissan upstate, so for two weeks we are to have the apartment to ourselves. This is more privacy than we ever had in India. No parents, no servants, to keep us modest. We play at housekeeping. Imre has lent us a hibachi, and I grill saffron chicken breasts. My husband marvels at the size of the Perdue hens. "They're big like peacocks, no? These Americans, they're really something!" He tries out pizzas, burgers, McNuggets. He chews. He explores. He judges. He loves it all, fears nothing, feels at home in the summer odors, the clutter of Manhattan streets. Since he thinks that the American palate is bland, he carries a bottle of red peppers in his pocket. I wheel a shopping cart down the aisles of the neighborhood Grand Union, and he follows, swiftly, greedily. He picks up hair rinses and high-protein diet powders. There's so much I already take for granted.

One night, Imre stops by. He wants us to go with him to a movie. In his work shirt and red leather tie, he looks arty or strung out. It's only been a week, but I feel as though I am really seeing him for the first time. The yellow hair worn very short at the sides, the wide, narrow lips. He's a good-looking man, but self-conscious, almost arrogant. He's picked the movie we should see. He always tells me what to see, what to read. He buys the *Voice*. He's a natural avant-gardist. For tonight he's chosen *Numéro Deux*.[2]

"Is it a musical?" my husband asks. The Radio City Music Hall is on his list of sights to see. He's read up on the history of the Rockettes. He doesn't catch Imre's sympathetic wink.

Guilt, shame, loyalty. I long to be ungracious, not ingratiate myself with both men.

That night my husband calculates in rupees the money we've wasted on

---

[2] A French "art-house" film directed by Jean-Luc Godard. — Eds.

Godard. "That refugee fellow, Nagy, must have a screw loose in his head. I paid very steep prices for dollars on the black market."

Some afternoons we go shopping. Back home we hated shopping, but now it is a lovers' project. My husband's shopping list startles me. I feel I am just getting to know him. Maybe, like Imre, freed from the dignities of old-world culture, he too could get drunk and squirt Cheez Whiz on a guest. I watch him dart into stores in his gleaming leather shoes. Jockey shorts on sale in outdoor bins on Broadway entrance him. White tube socks with different bands of color delight him. He looks for microcassettes, for anything small and electronic and smuggleable. He needs a garment bag. He calls it a "wardrobe," and I have to translate.

"All of New York is having sales, no?"

My heart speeds watching him this happy. It's the third week in August, almost the end of summer, and the city smells ripe, it cannot bear more heat, more money, more energy.

"This is so smashing! The prices are so excellent!" Recklessly, my prudent husband signs away traveler's checks. How he intends to smuggle it all back I don't dare ask. With a microwave, he calculates, we could get rid of our cook.

This has to be love, I think. Charity, Eric, Phil: they may be experts on sex. My husband doesn't chase me around the sofa, but he pushes me down on Charity's battered cushions, and the man who has never entered the kitchen of our Ahmadabad house now comes toward me with a dish tub of steamy water to massage away the pavement heat.

Ten days into his vacation my husband checks out brochures for sight-seeing tours. Shortline, Grayline, Crossroads: his new vinyl briefcase is full of schedules and pamphlets. While I make pancakes out of a mix, he comparison-shops. Tour number one costs $10.95 and will give us the World Trade Center, Chinatown, and the United Nations. Tour number three would take us both uptown *and* downtown for $14.95, but my husband is absolutely sure he doesn't want to see Harlem. We settle for tour number four: Downtown and the Dame. It's offered by a new tour company with a small, dirty office at Eighth and Forty-eighth.

The sidewalk outside the office is colorful with tourists. My husband sends me in to buy the tickets because he has come to feel Americans don't understand his accent.

The dark man, Lebanese probably, behind the counter comes on too friendly. "Come on, doll, make my day!" He won't say which tour is his. "Number four? Honey, no! Look, you've wrecked me! Say you'll change your mind." He takes two twenties and gives back change. He holds the tickets, forcing me to pull. He leans closer. "I'm off after lunch."

My husband must have been watching me from the sidewalk. "What was the chap saying?" he demands. "I told you not to wear pants. He thinks you are Puerto Rican. He thinks he can treat you with disrespect."

The bus is crowded and we have to sit across the aisle from each other. The tour guide begins his patter on Forty-sixth. He looks like an actor, his hair bleached and blow-dried. Up close he must look middle-aged, but from where I sit his skin is smooth and his cheeks faintly red.

"Welcome to the Big Apple, folks." The guide uses a microphone. "Big Apple. That's what we native Manhattan degenerates call our city. Today we have guests from fifteen foreign countries and six states from this U. S. of A. That makes the Tourist Bureau real happy. And let me assure you that while we may be the richest city in the richest country in the world, it's okay to tip your charming and talented attendant." He laughs. Then he swings his hip out into the aisle and sings a song.

"And it's mighty fancy on old Delancey Street, you know. . . ."

My husband looks irritable. The guide is, as expected, a good singer. "The bloody man should be giving us histories of buildings we are passing, no?" I pat his hand, the mood passes. He cranes his neck. Our window seats have both gone to Japanese. It's the tour of his life. Next to this, the quick business trips to Manchester and Glasgow pale.

"And tell me what street compares to Mott Street, in July. . . ."

The guide wants applause. He manages a derisive laugh from the Americans up front. He's working the aisles now. "I coulda been somebody, right? I coulda been a star!" Two or three of us smile, those of us who recognize the parody. He catches my smile. The sun is on his harsh, bleached hair. "Right, your highness? Look, we gotta maharani with us! Couldn't I have been a star?"

"Right!" I say, my voice coming out a squeal. I've been trained to adapt; what else can I say?

We drive through traffic past landmark office buildings and churches. The guide flips his hands. "Art Deco," he keeps saying. I hear him confide to one of the Americans: "Beats me. I went to a cheap guide's school." My husband wants to know more about this Art Deco, but the guide sings another song.

"We made a foolish choice," my husband grumbles. "We are sitting in the bus only. We're not going into famous buildings." He scrutinizes the pamphlets in his jacket pocket. I think, at least it's air-conditioned in here. I could sit here in the cool shadows of the city forever.

Only five of us appear to have opted for the "Downtown and the Dame" tour. The others will ride back uptown past the United Nations after we've been dropped off at the pier for the ferry to the Statue of Liberty.

An elderly European pulls a camera out of his wife's designer tote bag. He takes pictures of the boats in the harbor, the Japanese in kimonos eating popcorn, scavenging pigeons, me. Then, pushing his wife ahead of him, he climbs back on the bus and waves to us. For a second I feel terribly lost. I wish we were on the bus going back to the apartment. I know I'll not be able to describe any of this to Charity, or to Imre. I'm too proud to admit I went on a guided tour.

The view of the city from the Circle Line ferry is seductive, unreal. The sky-line wavers out of reach, but never quite vanishes. The summer sun pushes through fluffy clouds and dapples the glass of office towers. My husband looks thrilled, even more than he had on the shopping trips down Broadway. Tourists and dreamers, we have spent our life's savings to see this skyline, this statue.

"Quick, take a picture of me!" my husband yells as he moves toward a gap of railings. A Japanese matron has given up her position in order to change film. "Before the Twin Towers disappear!"

I focus, I wait for a large Oriental family to walk out of my range. My hus-band holds his pose tight against the railing. He wants to look relaxed, an international businessman at home in all the financial markets.

A bearded man slides across the bench toward me. "Like this," he says and helps me get my husband in focus. "You want me to take the photo for you?" His name, he says, is Goran. He is Goran from Yugoslavia, as though that were enough for tracking him down. Imre from Hungary. Panna from India. He pulls the old Leica out of my hand, signaling the Orientals to beat it, and clicks away. "I'm a photographer," he says. He could have been a camera thief. That's what my husband would have assumed. Somehow, I trusted. "Get you a beer?" he asks.

"I don't. Drink, I mean. Thank you very much." I say those last words very loud, for everyone's benefit. The odd bottles of Soave with Imre don't count.

"Too bad." Goran gives back the camera.

"Take one more!" my husband shouts from the railing. "Just to be sure!" The island itself disappoints. The Lady has brutal scaffolding holding her in. The museum is closed. The snack bar is dirty and expensive. My husband reads out the prices to me. He orders two french fries and two Cokes. We sit at picnic tables and wait for the ferry to take us back.

"What was that hippie chap saying?"

As if I could say. A day-care center has brought its kids, at least forty of them, to the island for the day. The kids, all wearing name tags, run around us. I can't help noticing how many are Indian. Even a Patel, probably a Bhatt if I looked hard enough. They toss hamburger bits at pigeons. They kick sty-rofoam cups. The pigeons are slow, greedy, persistent. I have to shoo one off the table top. I don't think my husband thinks about our son.

"What hippie?"

"The one on the boat. With the beard and the hair."

My husband doesn't look at me. He shakes out his paper napkin and tries to protect his french fries from pigeon feathers.

"Oh, him. He said he was from Dubrovnik." It isn't true, but I don't want trouble.

"What did he say about Dubrovnik?"

I know enough about Dubrovnik to get by. Imre's told me about it. And about Mostar and Zagreb. In Mostar white Muslims sing the call to prayer. I would like to see that before I die: white Muslims. Whole peoples have moved before me; they've adapted. The night Imre told me about Mostar was also the night I saw my first snow in Manhattan. We'd walked down to Chelsea from Columbia. We'd walked and talked and I hadn't felt tired at all.

"You're too innocent," my husband says. He reaches for my hand. "Panna," he cries with pain in his voice, and I am brought back from perfect, floating memories of snow, "I've come to take you back. I have seen how men watch you."

"What?"

"Come back, now. I have tickets. We have all the things we will ever need. I can't live without you."

A little girl with wiry braids kicks a bottle cap at his shoes. The pigeons wheel and scuttle around us. My husband covers his fries with spread-out fingers. "No kicking," he tells the girl. Her name, Beulah, is printed in green ink on a heart-shaped name tag. He forces a smile, and Beulah smiles back. Then she starts to flap her arms. She flaps, she hops. The pigeons go crazy for fries and scraps.

"Special ed. course is two years," I remind him. "I can't go back."

My husband picks up our trays and throws them into the garbage before I can stop him. He's carried disposability a little too far. "We've been taken," he says, moving toward the dock, though the ferry will not arrive for another twenty minutes. "The ferry costs only two dollars round-trip per person. We should have chosen tour number one for $10.95 instead of tour number four for $14.95."

With my Lebanese friend, I think. "But this way we don't have to worry about cabs. The bus will pick us up at the pier and take us back to midtown. Then we can walk home."

"New York is full of cheats and whatnot. Just like Bombay." He is not accusing me of infidelity. I feel dread all the same.

That night, after we've gone to bed, the phone rings. My husband listens, then hands the phone to me. "What is this woman saying?" He turns on the pink Macy's lamp by the bed. "I am not understanding these Negro people's accents."

The operator repeats the message. It's a cable from one of the directors of Lakshmi Cotton Mills. "Massive violent labor confrontation anticipated. Stop. Return posthaste. Stop. Cable flight details. Signed Kantilal Shah."

"It's not your factory," I say. "You're supposed to be on vacation."

"So, you are worrying about me? Yes? You reject my heartfelt wishes but you worry about me?" He pulls me close, slips the straps of my nightdress off my shoulder. "Wait a minute."

I wait, unclothed, for my husband to come back to me. The water is running in the bathroom. In the ten days he has been here he has learned American rites: deodorants, fragrances. Tomorrow morning he'll call Air India; tomorrow evening he'll be on his way back to Bombay. Tonight I should make up to him for my years away, the gutted trucks, the degree I'll never use in India. I want to pretend with him that nothing has changed.

In the mirror that hangs on the bathroom door, I watch my naked body turn, the breasts, the thighs glow. The body's beauty amazes. I stand here shameless, in ways he has never seen me. I am free, afloat, watching somebody else.

Questions for Discussion

1. How does Panna feel about the portrayal of Indians in the David Mamet play? What does her response to the play reveal about her feelings about her heritage?

2. Contrast Panna's reaction to the play with Imre's. How has their adjustment to life in New York City been similar and different? Why does Panna long to feel hate?

3. Contrast Imre with Panna's husband. Does Panna love either of them? Contrast Charity Chin's relationships with men to Panna's. What conclusions can you draw from the differences?

4. In what ways is Panna's lifestyle both nontraditional and also reflective of her traditional Indian values learned at home and at boarding school? How do you think Panna feels about herself?

5. Discuss the significance of Panna's thought that "love is a commodity, hoarded like any other." In what ways does the story exemplify this statement through Panna's interactions with her husband?

Ideas for Writing

1. Explore in an essay the story's commentary on the way that the marriage and values of people from traditional cultures may change through immigration to the United States.

2. Write a sequel to the story, set a few years later. Will Panna and her husband still be together? Will they be able to redefine their marriage so that it satisfies both of them? Will Panna decide to start a new life for herself in the United States without her husband?

BOBBIE ANN MASON   (b. 1940)

Much of Bobbie Ann Mason's writing depicts the working-class people of western Kentucky where she grew up and reflects her interest in the influences of war, divorce, chain-store merchandising, and the mass media on the lifestyles of small-town people.

Mason was born in Mayfield, Kentucky, where her parents ran a dairy farm. She received her Ph.D. from the University of Connecticut in 1972 after working for several years as a writer for newspapers and such popular magazines as *Movie Life* and *TV Star Parade*. Mason taught at Mansfield State College in Pennsylvania from 1972 until 1979. In 1982 she won the Hemingway Foundation award for her first story collection, *Shiloh and Other Stories*. Her first novel, *In Country* (1985), was made into a film; this was followed by *Spence & Lila* in 1988 and the story collection *Love Life* (1989), which includes "Airwaves." In 1993 Mason published her third novel, *Feather Crowns*. She continues to contribute to the *New Yorker*, the first magazine to publish her stories.

Mason's fiction is noted for her close observation of rural and suburban settings, her use of authentic dialogue, and her ability to evoke the inner worlds of confused, inarticulate characters whose lives are in a state of transition. She finds inspiration for her characters in the varied and unpredictable choices people make to find meaning and purpose: "Some people will stay at home and be content. Others are born to run. It's that conflict that fascinates me."

Airwaves   (1989)

When Jane lived with Coy Wilson, he couldn't listen to rock music before noon or after supper. In the morning, it was too jarring; at night, the vibrations lingered in his head and interfered with his sleep. But now that they are apart, Jane listens to Rock-95 all the time. Rock-95 is a college station — "your station for kick-ass rock and roll." She sets the radio alarm every night for 8 A.M., and when it goes off she dozes and dreams while the music blasts in her ears for an hour or more. Women rock singers snarl and scream their independence. The sounds are numbing. Jane figures if she can listen to hard rock in her sleep, she won't care that Coy has gone.

Jane stands in the window in pink shortie pajamas, watching her landlady, Mrs. Bush, hang out her wash. Today is white things: sheets, socks, underwear, towels. Jane's mother used to say, "Always separate your colored things from your white things!" as though there were something morally significant about the way you do laundry. Jane never follows the rules. All her sheets have flowers on them, and her underwear is bright colors. Anything white is outnumbered. The men's shorts on Mrs. Bush's wash line flap in the breeze like flags of surrender.

The coffee is bitter. She bought the store brand, because Mrs. Bush gave her a fifty-cent coupon and the store paid double coupons. Mrs. Bush, who is a waitress at the Villa Romano, keeps asking Jane when she is going to get a job. When Coy lived there, Mrs. Bush was always asking him when he was going to marry Jane. Six weeks ago, not long after she split up with Coy, Jane was laid off from the Holiday Clothing Company. First she was a folder, then a presser. Folding was more satisfying than pressing — the heat from the presser took the curl out of her hair — but when she was switched to the pressing room, she got a fifty-cents-an-hour raise. She was hoping to go to the Villa Romano that night with Coy and have a spaghetti supper to celebrate, but he chose that day to move back home with his mother. His unemployment had run out two weeks before, and he had been at loose ends. He thought he was getting an ulcer. When Jane got home, he had lined up their joint possessions on the floor — the toaster, the blender, the records, the TV tables, a whatnot, even the kitchen utensils.

"The TV's mine," he said apologetically. "I had it when we started out."

"I told you I'd pay the rent," she said, as he punched his jeans into a duffel bag. When he wouldn't answer, she set the coffeepot in the cabinet and shut the door. "I got the coffeepot with Green Stamps," she said.

"I'm going to cut out coffee anyway."

"Good. It makes you irritable."

Coy set the toaster in a grocery box with some shaving cream and socks — all his mateless socks from what Jane called his Lonely Sock Drawer. Jane tried to keep from crying as she pleaded with him to stay.

"I can't let you go on supporting me," he said. "I wasn't raised that way."

"What's the difference? Your mother will support you. You could even watch her TV."

He divided the record albums as though he were dealing out cards. "One for you and one for me." He left his favorite Willie Nelson record in her pile.

When he left, she said, "You just let me know when you get yourself straightened out, and we'll take it from there."

"That's my whole point," said Coy. "I have to work things out."

Jane knew she should have been more understanding. He was appreciative of delicate, fine things most men wouldn't notice, such as flowers and pretty dishes. Coy was tender in his lovemaking, with more sensitivity than men were usually given credit for. On Phil Donahue's show, when the topic was sex, the women in the audience always said they wanted men who were gentle and considerate and involved in a lot of touching during the day instead of "wham-bam-thank-you-ma'am" at the end of the day. Coy was the answer to those women's prayers, but he went too far. He was so fragile, with his nervous stomach. He couldn't watch meat being cut up. Jane still finds broken rolls of Tums stashed around the apartment.

Unemployed, Jane is adrift. She watches a lot of TV. She managed to buy a TV on sale before she lost her job. She has had to stop smoking (not a serious problem) and eating out so that she can keep up her car and TV payments. She canceled her subscription to a cosmetics club. She has accumulated a lot of bizarre eye shadows and creams that she doesn't use. When she goes out to a job interview, she paints her face and feels silly. Job-hunting is like going to church — a pointless ritual of dressing up. At the factory, she had to wear a blue smock over a dark skirt. Pants weren't allowed. "I wish I could get on at the Villa Romano," she tells Mrs. Bush. "The uniform is nice, and I could wear pants."

Coy used to go to Kentucky Lake alone sometimes, for the whole week-end, to meditate and restore himself. She once thought his desire to be alone was peculiar, but now she appreciates it. Being alone is incredibly easy. Her mind sails off into unexpected trances. Sometimes she pretends she is an invalid recovering from a coma, and she rediscovers everything around her — simple things, like the noise the rotary antenna makes, a sound she never heard when the TV volume was loud. Or she pretends she is in a wheelchair, viewing the world from one certain level. She likes to see things suddenly, from new angles. Once when Coy lived there, she stepped up on a crate to dust the top of a shelf, and Coy suddenly appeared and caught her in an embrace. On the crate, she was exactly his height. The dusty shelf was at eye level. For a day or two, she went around noticing the spaces that would be in his line of vision — the top of the refrigerator, the top of an old cardboard wardrobe her father had given her, curtain rods, moldings.

Today, when Jane leaves the apartment to pick up her unemployment check, Mrs. Bush is outside, watering her petunias. She pulls a letter from her pocket and waves it at Jane.

"My boy's in California," she says. "They're going to let him have a fur-lough, but he likes it so much out there he won't come home."

"I don't blame him," says Jane. "It's too far, and California must be a lot more fun than here."

"They started him out on heavy-duty equipment, but that didn't suit him and they've switched him to electronics. They take a hundred dollars out of his pay every month, and then when he gets out they'll double it and give him a bonus so he can go to school."

Mrs. Bush fires water at a border of hollyhocks. Jane steps over the coiled hose and casually thinks of evil serpents. She says, "My brother couldn't get in the Army because he had high arches, so he became a Holy Roller preacher instead. He used to cuss like the devil, but now he's preaching up a storm." Jane looks Mrs. Bush straight in the eyes. She's not old but looks old. If she died, maybe Jane could get her job.

"My cousin was a Holy Roller," says Mrs. Bush. "He got sanctified and then got hit by a truck the next day."

Nervously, Mrs. Bush tears off the edging of paper where she has ripped open the letter from her son. She balls the bit of paper and drops it into a pot of hen and chickens.

Jane's mother died when she was fifteen, and her father, Vernon Motherall, has never learned to cook for himself. "What's in this?" he asks suspiciously that weekend, when she takes him a tuna casserole.

"Macaroni. Tuna fish. Mushroom soup."

"I don't like mushrooms. Mushrooms is poison."

"This isn't poison. It's Campbell's." Jane has brought him this same kind of casserole dozens of times, and he always argues against mushrooms. He's convinced that someday a mushroom is going to get him.

Vernon rents the bottom half of a dilapidated clapboard house. He has two dump trucks in the backyard. He hauls rock and sand and asphalt — "whatever needs hauling," his ad in the yellow pages says. His dingy office is filled with greasy papers on spikes and piles of *Field and Stream* magazines. In a ray of sunlight, the dust whirls and sparkles. Jane sweeps her hand through it.

"I wish I had some money," she says. "I'd buy you one of those things that takes the negative ions out of the air."

"What good's that do?" Vernon is swigging a Pabst, though it's still morning.

"It knocks the dust out of the air."

"What for?" The way Jane's father speaks is more like an extended grunt than conversation. He sits in a large stuffed chair that seems to be part of his own big lumpy body.

"I don't know. I think the dust just falls down instead of circulating. If you had one of those, your sinuses wouldn't be so bad."

"They ain't been bothering me none lately."

"Those ionizers make you feel good, too. They do something to your mood."

"I've got all I need for my mood," he says, lifting his bottle of beer.

"You drink too much."

"Don't look at my beer belly."

"I will if I want to," Jane says, playfully thumping his belt buckle. "You get loaded and go out and have wrecks. You're going to get yourself killed."

Vernon grins at her mockingly. They always have this conversation, and he never takes her seriously.

"Here, eat this," Jane says, plopping a scoop of casserole on a melamine plate that has discolorations on it.

Vernon plucks another beer from the refrigerator and sits down at the card table in his dirty kitchen. He eats without comment, then mops his plate with a bread heel. When he finishes, he says, "I went to hear Joe preach at his new church the other Sunday. How did I turn out a boy like that? He's bound and determined to make a fool out of himself. His wife runs out on him, and he turns around and starts preaching Holy Roller. Did you know he talks in tongues now? What will he think of next?"

"Well, Joe goes at anything like killing snakes," says Jane. "It's all or nothing."

Vernon laughs. "His text for the day was the Twenty-third Psalm, and he comes to the part where the Lord maketh me lie down in green pastures and restoreth my soul? And he reads it 'he *storeth* my soul,' and starts preaching on the Lord's storehouses." Vernon doubles over laughing. "He thinks the Lord stores souls — like corn in a grain elevator!"

"I wonder what ever happened to all those grain-elevator explosions we used to hear about," Jane says, giggling.

"If the Lord stores some of those pitiful souls Joe's dragged in, his storehouse is liable to explode!" Vernon laughs, and beer sprays out of his mouth.

"Have some more tuna casserole," Jane says affectionately. When it comes to her brother, who was always in trouble, she and her father are in cahoots.

"You should have a good man to cook for. Not Coy Wilson. He's too prissy, and he took advantage of you, living with you with no intention of marrying."

"You're still feeling guilty 'cause you ran out on me and Joe and Mother that time," says Jane, shifting the subject.

"The trouble is, too many women are working and the men can't get jobs," her father says. "Women should stay home."

"Don't start in," Jane says in a warning voice. "I've got enough trouble."

"You could move back home with me," Vernon says plaintively. "Parents always used to take care of their kids till they married."

"I guess that's why Coy ran home to his mama."

"You can come home to your old daddy anytime," Vernon says, moving back to his easy chair. The vinyl upholstery makes obscene noises when he lands.

"It would never work," Jane says. "We don't like the same TV shows anymore."

Waiting in the unemployment line the next afternoon is tedious, and all the faces have deadpan expressions, but Jane is feeling elated, almost euphoric, though for no substantial reason. In the car, driving past a local radio transmitter, she suddenly realized that she had no idea how sound got from the transmitter to the radio. She felt so ignorant. The idea of sound waves seemed farfetched. She went to the library and asked for a book about radio. The librarian showed her a pamphlet about Nathan Stubblefield.

"He invented radio," the woman said. "They say it was Marconi, but Stubblefield was really the first, and he was from right around here. He lived five miles from my house."

"I always heard radio was invented in Kentucky," Jane said.

"He just never got credit for it." The woman reminded Jane of a bouncy game-show contestant. "Kentucky never gets enough credit, if you ask me. We've got so much here to be proud of. Kentucky even has a Golden Pond, like in the movie."

Reading the pamphlet in the unemployment line, Jane feels strangely connected to something historically important. It is a miracle that sound can travel long distances through the air and then appear instantaneously, like a genie from a bottle, and that a man from Kentucky was the first to make it happen. Who can she tell? Who would care? This is the sort of thing that wouldn't register on her father, and Coy would think she was crazy. Her brother, though, would recognize the feeling. It occurs to Jane that he probably hears voices from heaven every day, just as though he were tuned in to heaven's airways. She wonders if he can really talk in tongues. Her brother is a radio! Jane feels like dancing. In her mind, the unemployment line suddenly turns into a chorus line, a movie scene. For a moment, she's afraid she's going nuts. The line inches forward.

After collecting her check, she cashes it at the bank's drive-in window, talking to the teller through a speaker, then goes to Jerry's Drive-In and orders a Coke through another speaker. A voice confirms her order, and in the background behind the voice, Jane hears a radio playing — Rock-95, the same station she is hearing on her car radio.

Coy calls up during a "Mary Tyler Moore" rerun that week, one Jane hasn't seen before. Jane is eating canned ravioli. The clarity of his voice startles her. He could be in the same room.

"I got a job! Floorwalking at Wal-Mart."

"Oh, I'm glad." Jane spears a pillow of ravioli and listens while Coy describes his hours and his duties and the amount of take-home pay he gets — less than he made at the plant before his layoff, but with more security. The job sounds incredibly boring.

"When I get on my feet, maybe we can reconsider some things," he says.

"If you're floorwalking, you're already on your feet," she says. "That's a joke," she says, when he doesn't respond. "I don't want to get back together if money's the issue."

"I thought we went through all that."

"I've been thinking, and I can't let you support me."

"Well, I've got a job now, and you don't."

"You wouldn't let *me* support *you*," Jane says. "Why should I let you support me?"

"If we got back together, you could go to school part-time."

"I have to find a job first. I'd go to school now if I could go and still draw unemployment, but they won't let you draw and go to school too. Let's change the subject. How's your stomach?"

Coy tells Jane that on the news he saw pictures of starving children in Africa, and managed to watch without getting queasy. Jane always told him he was too sensitive to misfortunes that had nothing to do with him.

An awkward silence follows. Finally, Jane says, "My brother's got a Holy Roller church. He's preaching."

"That sounds about like him," Coy says, without surprise.

"I think I'll go Sunday. I need some religion. Do you want to go?"

"Hell, no. I don't want to invite a migraine."

"I thought your nerves were getting better."

"They are, but they're not that good yet."

After Coy hangs up, Jane feels lonely, wishing Coy were there, touching her lightly with promising caresses, like the women on "Donahue" always wanted. Once, Rita Jenrette, whose husband was involved in a political scandal, was on Donahue's show, and during the program her husband called up. Coy's job sounds so depressing. Jane wishes he were the host of a radio call-in show. She could call him up and talk to him, pretending there was nothing personal between them. She would ask him about love. She'd ask whether he thought the magic of love worked anything like radio waves. Her ravioli grows cold.

Joe's church is called the Foremost Evangelical Assembly. The church is a converted house trailer, with a perpendicular extension. There is a Coke machine in the corridor. People sit around drinking Cokes and 7-Ups. No one is dressed up.

"Can you believe it!" cries Joe, clasping both of Jane's hands and jerking her forward as though about to swing her around in a game children play.

"Can you pray for me to find a job?" Jane says, grinning. "Daddy said you could talk in tongues, and I thought that might help."

"Was Daddy drinking when you saw him last?" Joe asks anxiously.

"Of course. Is the Pope Catholic?"

"I told him I could stop him from that if he'd just get his tail down here every Sunday." Joe has on a pin-striped double-knit suit with an artificial daisy in the lapel. He looks the part.

"Are you going to talk in tongues today?" Jane asks. "I want to see how you do it."

"Watch close," he says with a wink. "But I'm not allowed to give away the secret."

"Is it like being a magician?"

Her brother only grins mysteriously.

Jane sits cross-legged on the floor behind the folding chairs. People turn around and stare at her, probably wondering if she is Joe's girlfriend. The congregation loves Joe. He is a large man, and his size makes him seem powerful and authoritative, like an Army general. He has always been a goof-off, calling attention to himself, staging some kind of show. If Alexander Haig[1] became a stand-up comedian, he would be just like Joe. He stands behind a card table with two overturned plastic milk crates stacked on it. On his right, a TV set stares at the congregation.

The service is long and peculiar and filled with individual testimonials that seem to come randomly, interrupting Joe's talk. It's not really a sermon. It's just Joe telling stories about how bad he used to be before he found Christ. He always had the gift of the gab, Vernon used to say. Joe tells a long anecdote about how his wife's infidelity made him turn to the Lord. He exaggerates parts of the story that Jane recognizes. (He *never* gave his wife a beautiful house with a custom-built kitchen and a two-car garage. It was a dumpy old house that they rented.) She almost giggles aloud when he opens the Bible and reads from "the Philippines," and she makes a mental note to tell her father. A woman takes a crying baby into the corridor and tries to make it drink some Coke. Jane wishes she had a cigarette. In this crazy setting, if Joe talked in tongues, nobody would notice it as anything odd.

When a young couple brings forth a walleyed child to be healed, Joe cries out in astonishment, "Who, me? I can't heal nobody!" He paces around in front of the TV set. "But I can guarantee that if you just let the spirit in, miracles have been known to happen." He rambles along on this point, and the little girl's head droops indifferently. "Just open up your heart and let him in!" Joe shouts. "Let the spirit in, and the Lord will shake up the alignment of them eyes." A song from *Hair,* "Let the Sunshine In," starts going through Jane's head. The child's eye shoots out across the room. While Joe is ranting, Jane gets a Coke and stands in the doorway.

"Icky-bick-eye-bo!" Joe cries suddenly. He looks embarrassed and bows his head. "Freema-di-kibbi-fidra," he says softly.

Jane has been thinking of talking in tongues as an involuntary expression —a kind of gibberish that pours forth when people are possessed by the spirit of God. But now, in amazement, she watches her brother, his hands folded and eyes closed, as though bowing his head for a moment of prayer, chanting strange words slowly and carefully, as methodically as Mrs. Bush hangs out her wash. He is speaking a singsong language made of hard, disturbing sounds. "Shecky-beck-be-floyt-I-shecky-tibby-libby. Dab-cree-la-croo-la-crow." He seems to be trying hard not to say "abracadabra" or any other familiar words. Jane, disappointed, doubts that these words are messages from heaven. Joe seems afraid that some repressed obscenity might rush out. He used to cuss freely. Now he probably really believes he is tuned in to heaven.

"Where's Coy?" he asks her after the service. He has failed to correct the child's eyes but won't admit it.

"We don't get along so good. After he lost his job, he couldn't handle it."

---

[1] U.S. general and secretary of state under President Reagan (1981–82). — Eds.

"Well, get him on down here! We'll help him."

He tries to talk Jane into bringing Coy for Wednesday-night prayer meeting. "There's two kinds of men," Joe says. "Them that goes to church and them that don't. You should never get mixed up with some boy who won't take you to church."

"I know."

Joe says goodbye, with his arms around her like a lover's. Jane can smell the Tic Tacs on his breath.

"Do you want one hamburger patty or two?" Jane asks her father.

"One. No, two." Vernon looks confused. "No, make it one."

They are at the lake, in a trailer belonging to Jane's former boss, who had promised to let her use it some weekend. Jane, wanting a change of scene for her father, brought a cooler of supplies, and Vernon brought his dog, Buford. He grumbled because Jane wouldn't let him bring any beer, but he sneaked along a quart of Heaven Hill, and he is already drunk. Jane is furious.

"How can you watch 'Hogan's Heroes' on that cruddy TV?" she asks. "The reception's awful."

"I've seen this one so many times I know what's going on. See that machine gun? Watch that guy in the tower. He's going to shoot."

"That's a tower? I thought it was a giraffe."

When they sit down to eat at the picnic table outside, Buford tries to get in Jane's lap. He has the broad shoulders of a bulldog and the fine facial features of a chihuahua. He goes around in a little cloud of gnats.

"I can't eat with a dog in my lap," Jane says, pushing the dog away. "Coy wants to come back to me," she tells her father. "He's got his pride again."

"Don't let him."

"He's more of a man than you think." Jane laughs. "Joe says he can help us work things out. He wants us to come to Wednesday-night prayer meetings."

"How did I go wrong?" Vernon asks helplessly, addressing a tree. "One kid starts preaching just to stay out of jail, and the other one wants to live in sin and ruin her reputation." Vernon turns to the dog and says, "It's all my fault. Children always hurt you."

"And what about you?" Jane shouts at him. "You worry us half to death with your drinking and then expect us to be little angels."

She takes her plate indoors and turns on "M*A*S*H." The reception is so poor without a cable that the figures undulate on the screen. Hawkeye and B.J. turn into wavy lines, staggering drunks.

That night, Vernon's drunken sleep on the couch is loud and unrestrained. Jane thinks of his sleep as slumber. She always thought of Coy's sleep as catnapping. She misses Coy, but wonders if she can ever get along with any man. In all her relationships with people, she has to deal with one or another intolerable habit. Jane is not sure the hard-rock music has hardened her to pain and distraction. Her father is hopeless. He used to get drunk and throw her mother's good dishes against the wall. He lined them up on the table and broke them one by one until her mother relented and gave him the keys to the car. He had accidents. He was always apologetic afterward, and he made it up to them in lavish ways, bringing home absurd presents, such as a bushel of peaches or a pint of oysters in a little white fold-together cardboard container like the ones goldfish come in. Once, he brought goldfish, but Jane's mother had expected oysters. Her disappointment hurt him, and he went back and bought oysters. One year, he ran away to Detroit. When he came back, months later, Jane's mother forgave him. By then, she was dying of cancer, and Jane suspects that he never really forgave himself for being there too late to make it up to her.

Buford paces around the trailer fretfully. Jane can't sleep. The bed is musty and lumpy. She recalls a story her mother once told her about a woman who was trapped in a lion cage by a lion who tried to mate with her. From outside the cage, the lion's trainer yelled instructions to her — how she had to stroke the lion until he was satisfied. Pinned under the lion, the woman saved her life by obeying the man's instructions. That was more or less how her mother always told her she had to be with a husband, or a rapist. She thinks of her mother as the woman in the cage, listening to the lion tamer shouting instructions — do anything to keep from being murdered. As Jane recalls her mother telling it, the lion's eyes went all dreamy, and he rolled over on his back and went to sleep.

Jane suspects that what she really wants is a man something like the lion. She loves Coy's gentleness, but she wants him to be aggressive at times. The women on "Donahue" said they wanted that, too. Someone in the audience said women can't have it both ways.

During the weekend, Jane tries to get Vernon to go fishing, but he hasn't renewed his fishing license since the price went up. He complains about the snack cakes she brought, and he sits around drinking. Jane listens to the radio and reads a book called *Working*, about people's jobs. "It takes all kinds," she tells her father when he asks about the book. She has given up trying to entertain him, but by Sunday evening he seems mellow and talkative.

At the picnic table, Jane watches the sun setting behind the oak trees. "Look how pretty it is. The light on the water looks like a melted orange Popsicle."

Vernon grunts, acknowledging the sunset.

"I want you to enjoy yourself," Jane says calmly.

"I'm an old fool," he says, sloshing his drink. "I never amounted to anything. This country is taking away every chance the little man ever had. If it weren't for the Republicans and the Democrats, we'd be better off."

"Don't we have to have one or the other?"

"Throw 'em all out. They cancel each other out anyway." Vernon snatches at a mosquito. "The minorities rule this country. They've meddled with the Constitution till it's all out of shape."

The sun disappears, and the mosquitoes come out. Jane slaps her arms. Her toes are under the dog, warming like buns in a toaster oven. She nudges him away, and he pads across the porch, taking his gnat cloud with him.

"Tell me something," Jane asks later, as they are eating. "What did you do in Detroit that time when you ran off and left Mom with Joe and me?"

Vernon shrugs and drinks from a fresh drink. "Worked at Chrysler."

"Why did you leave us?"

"Your mother couldn't put up with me."

Jane can't see her father's face in the growing dark, so she feels bolder. Taking a deep breath, she says, "I guess for a long time I felt guilty after you left — not because you left but because I wanted you to leave. Mom and Joe and me got along just fine without you. I liked moving into that restaurant, living upstairs with Mom, and her going downstairs to cook hamburgers for people. I think I liked it so much not just because I could have all the hamburgers and milk shakes I wanted but because *she* loved it. She loved waiting on people and cooking for the public. But we were glad when you came back and we moved back home."

Vernon nods and nods, about to say something. Jane gets up and turns on the bug light on the porch. She says, "That's how I've been feeling, living by myself. If I found something I liked as much as Mom liked cooking for the public, I'd be happy."

Vernon pours some more bourbon into his Yosemite Sam jelly glass and nods thoughtfully. He sips his drink and looks out onto the darkening lake for so long that Jane thinks he must be working up to a spectacular confession or apology. Finally, he says, "The Constitution is damaged all to hell." He sets his plate on the ground for the dog to lick.

The next morning is work-pants day. On Mrs. Bush's line is a row of dark-green work pants and matching shirts. The pants are heavy and wrinkled. The sun comes out, and by afternoon, when Jane returns from shopping, the wrinkles are gone and the pants look fluffy. Jane reaches into the back seat of her car for her sack of groceries — soup, milk, cereal, and a Sara Lee cheesecake, marked down.

"Faired up nice, didn't it?" cries Mrs. Bush, appearing with her laundry basket. "They say another front's coming through and we'll have a storm."

"I hope so," says Jane, wishing it would be a tornado.

"I've got some news for you," Mrs. Bush says, as she drops clothespins into a plastic bucket. "A girl I work with is pregnant, and she's quitting next week."

"I thought I wanted to work at the Villa Romano more than anything, but now I'm not sure," Jane says. What would it be like, waiting tables with Mrs. Bush?

"It's a good job, and they feed you all you can eat. They've got the *best* ambrosia!"

She drops a clothespin and Jane picks it up. Jane says, "I think I'll join the Army."

Mrs. Bush laughs. "Jimmy's still in California. They would have flown him here and back, but he wouldn't come home. Is that any way for a boy to do his mama?" She tests a pant leg for dampness, and frowns. "I've got to go. Could you bring in these britches for me later?" she asks. "If I'm late to work, my boss will shoot me."

When Jane puts her groceries away, the cereal tumbles to the floor. The milk carton is leaking. She turns on Rock-95 full blast, then rips the cover off the cheesecake and starts eating from the middle. Jane feels strange, quivery. One simple idea could suddenly change everything, the same way a tornado could. Everything in her life is converging, narrowing, like a multitude of tiny lines trying to get through one pinhole. She imagines straightening out a rainbow and rolling it up in a tube. The sound waves travel on rainbows. She can't explain these notions to Coy. They don't even make sense to her. Today, he looked worried about her when she stopped in at Wal-Mart. It has been a crazy day, a stupid weekend. After picking up her unemployment check, she applied for a job at Betty's Boutique, but the opening had been filled five minutes earlier. At Wal-Mart, Coy was patrolling the pet department. In his brown plaid pants, blue shirt, and yellow tie, he looked stylish and comfortable, as though he had finally found a place where he belonged. He seemed like a man whose ambition was to get a service award so he could have his picture in the paper, shaking hands with his boss.

"I hope you're warming a place in the bed for me," he whispered to her, within earshot of customers. He touched her elbow, and his thumb poked surreptitiously at her waist. "I have to work tonight," he went on. "We're doing inventory. But we've got to talk."

"O.K.," she said, her eyes fixing on a fish tank in which some remarkably blue fish were darting around like darning-needle flies.

On her way out of the store, without thinking, she stopped and bought a travel kit for her cosmetics, with plastic cases inside for her toothbrush, lotion, and soap. She wasn't sure where she was going. Driving out of the parking lot, she thought how proudly Coy had said, "We're taking inventory," as though he were in thick with Wal-Mart executives. It didn't seem like him. She had deluded herself, expecting more of him just because he was such a sweet lover. She had thought he was an ideal man, like the new contemporary man described in the women's magazines, but he was just a floorwalker. There was no future in that. Women had been walking the floors for years. She remembered her mother walking the floor with worry, when her father was out late, drinking.

At the Army recruiting station, Jane stuffed the literature into her purse. She took one of everything. On a bulletin board, she read down a list of career-management fields, strange-sounding phrases like Air Defense Artillery, Missile Maintenance, Ballistic Missile Maintenance, Combat Engineering, Intercept

Systems Maintenance, Cryptologic Operations, Topographic Engineering. The words stirred her, filled her with awe.

"Here's what I want," she said to the recruiter. "Communications and Electronics Operations."

"That's our top field," said the man, who was wearing a beautiful uniform trimmed with bright ribbons. "You join that and you'll get somewhere."

Later, in her kitchen, her mouth full of cheesecake, Jane reads the electronics brochure, pausing over the phrases "field radio," "teletype," and "radio relay equipment." Special security clearance is required for some electronics operations. She pictures herself someplace remote, in a control booth, sending signals for war, like an engineer in charge of a sports special on TV. She doesn't want to go to war, but if there is one, women should go. She imagines herself in a war, crouching in the jungle, sweating, on the lookout for something to happen. The sounds of warfare, would be like the sounds of rock and roll, hard-driving and satisfying.

She sleeps so soundly that when Coy calls the next morning, the telephone rings several times. Rock-95 is already blasting away, and she wonders groggily if it is loud enough over the telephone to upset his equilibrium.

"I'm trying to remember what you used to say about waking up," she says sleepily.

"You know I could never talk till I had my coffee."

"I thought you were giving up coffee. Does your mama make you coffee?"

"Yeah."

"I knew she would." Jane sits up and turns down the radio. "Oh, now I remember what you said. You said it was like being born."

Coy had said that the relaxation of sleep left him defenseless and shattered, so that the daytime was spent restructuring himself, rebuilding defenses. Sleep was a forgetting, and in the daylight he had to gather his strength, remember who he was. For him, the music was an intrusion on a fragile life, and now it makes Jane sad that she hasn't been fair to him.

"Can I come for breakfast?" he asks.

"You took the toaster, and I can't make toast the way you like it."

"Let's go to the Dairy Barn and have some country ham and biscuits."

Jane's sheets are dirty. She was going to wash them at the laundromat and bring them home to dry — to save money and to score a point with her landlady. She says, "I'll meet you as soon as I drop off my laundry at the Washeteria. I've got something to tell you."

"I hope it's good."

"It's not what you think." On the radio, Rod Stewart is bouncing blithely away on "Young Turks." Jane feels older, too old for her and Coy to be young hearts together, free tonight, as the song directs. Jane says, "Red-eye gravy. That's what I want. Do you think they'll have red-eye gravy?"

"Of course they'll have red-eye gravy. Who ever heard of country ham without red-eye gravy?"

After hanging up, Jane lays the sheets on the living-room rug, and in the center she tosses her underwear and blouses and slacks. The colors dash. A tornado in a flower garden. After throwing in her jeans, she ties the corners of the sheets and sets the bundle by the door. As she puts on her makeup, she rehearses what she has to tell Coy. She has imagined his stunned silence. She imagines gathering everyone she knows in the same room, so she can make her announcement as if she were holding a press conference. It would be so much more official.

With her bundle of laundry, she goes bumping down the stairs. A stalk of light from a window on the landing shoots down the stairway. Jane floats through the light, with the dust motes shining all around her, penetrating silently, and then she remembers a dirty T-shirt in the bathroom. Letting the bundle slide to the bottom of the stairs, she turns back to her apartment. She has left the radio on, and for a moment on the landing she thinks that someone must be home.

Questions for Discussion

1. What does Jane's breakup with Coy reveal about her values?
2. What impact do language and images from the electronic media have on the way that Jane and the other characters see their world and express themselves?
3. What is the significance of Jane's refusal to separate her wash into white and colored loads?
4. What is Jane's initial attitude toward the jobs of the people she knows and her own unemployment? How does her attitude toward meaningful employment change as the story develops?
5. What does Jane learn from her visit to her brother's church? What is revealed through her confusion about whether Joe is sincere in his sermons and his "talking in tongues"?

Ideas for Writing

1. In an essay, evaluate both the causes and the appropriateness of the decision Jane makes at the end of the story. Why does she imagine herself "calling a press conference" to tell her friends and family? Does the story imply that she will stick with her decision?
2. Write a story in which a character makes a final decision to break with his or her old ways and start a new, more meaningful life.

JOHN EDGAR WIDEMAN   (b. 1941)

Raised in Homewood, a poor Pittsburgh neighborhood of African Americans who had come from the South in search of a better life, John Edgar Wideman writes of poverty and strength of spirit, oppression and cultural heritage in the black community. Wideman attended the University of Pennsylvania on a basketball scholarship and studied psychology and English. He attended Oxford University in England on a Rhodes scholarship, then returned to the United States to study at the University of Iowa Writer's Workshop and to teach at the University of Pennsylvania, the University of Wyoming, and the University of Massachusetts at Amherst. Although Wideman escaped the despair that crippled many who grew up in Homewood, he has never forgotten his old neighborhood and sets many of his stories and novels there. His novels include *Hurry Home* (1969), *Sent for You Yesterday* (1983), *Philadelphia Fire* (1990), and *The Cattle Killing* (1996). He has also published a memoir, *Brothers and Keepers* (1984), in which he reflects on his brother's criminal life and imprisonment. "Doc's Story" is from the collection *Fever* (1989); his collected stories appeared in 1992. Wideman is an experimentalist in form and style, and he uses many of the devices of modernist fiction, yet his themes and concerns are constant and fundamental.

Doc's Story   (1989)

He thinks of her small, white hands, blue veined, gaunt, awkwardly knuckled. He'd teased her about the smallness of her hands, hers lost in the shadow of his when they pressed them together palm to palm to measure. The heavy drops of color on her nails barely reached the middle joints of his fingers. He'd teased her about her dwarf's hands but he'd also said to her one night when the wind was rattling the windows of the apartment on Cedar and they lay listening and shivering though it was summer on the brass bed she'd found in a junk store on Haverford Avenue, near the Woolworth's five-and-dime they'd picketed for two years, that God made little things closer to perfect than he ever made big things. Small, compact women like her could be perfectly formed, proportioned, and he'd smiled out loud running his hand up and down the just-right fine lines of her body, celebrating how good she felt to him.

She'd left him in May, when the shadows and green of the park had started to deepen. Hanging out, becoming a regular at the basketball court across the street in Regent Park was how he'd coped. No questions asked. Just the circle of stories. If you didn't want to miss anything good you came early and stayed late. He learned to wait, be patient. Long hours waiting were not time lost but time doing nothing because there was nothing better to do. Basking in sunshine on a stone bench, too beat to play any longer, nowhere to go but an empty apartment, he'd watch the afternoon traffic in Regent Park, dog strollers, baby carriages, winos, kids, gays, students with blankets they'd spread out on the grassy banks of the hollow and books they'd pretend to read, the black men from the neighborhood who'd search the park for braless young mothers and white girls on blankets who didn't care or didn't know any better than to sit with their crotches exposed. When he'd sit for hours like that, cooking like that, he'd feel himself empty out, see himself seep away and hover in the air, a fine mist, a little, flattened-out gray cloud of something wavering in the heat, a presence as visible as the steam on the window as he stares for hours at winter.

He's waiting for summer. For the guys to begin gathering on the court again. They'll sit in the shade with their backs against the Cyclone fencing or lean on cars parked at the roller-coaster curb or lounge in the sun on low, stone benches catty-corner from the basketball court. Some older ones still drink wine, but most everybody cools out on reefer, when there's reefer passed along, while they bullshit and wait for winners. He collects the stories they tell. He needs a story now. The right one now to get him through this long winter because she's gone and won't leave him alone.

In summer fine grit hangs in the air. Five minutes on the court and you're coughing. City dirt and park dust blowing off bald patches from which green is long gone, and deadly ash blowing over from New Jersey. You can taste it some days, bitter in your spit. Chunks pepper your skin, burn your eyes. Early fall while it's still warm enough to run outdoors the worst time of all. Leaves pile up against the fence, higher and higher, piles that explode and jitterbug across the court in the middle of a game, then sweep up again, slamming back where they blew from. After a while the leaves are ground into coarse, choking powder. You eat leaf trying to get in a little hoop before the weather turns, before those days when nobody's home from work yet but it's dark already and too cold to run again till spring. Fall's the only time sweet syrupy wine beats reefer. Ripple, Manischewitz, Taylor's Tawny Port coat your throat. He takes a hit when the jug comes round. He licks the sweetness from his lips, listens for his favorite stories one more time before everybody gives it up till next season.

His favorite stories made him giggle and laugh and hug the others, like they hugged him when a story got so good nobody's legs could hold them up. Some stories got under his skin in peculiar ways. Some he liked to hear because they made the one performing them do crazy stuff with his voice and body. He learned to be patient, learned his favorites would be repeated, get a turn just like he got a turn on the joints and wine bottles circulating the edges of the court.

Of all the stories, the one about Doc had bothered him most. Its orbit was unpredictable. Twice in one week, then only once more last summer. He'd only heard Doc's story three times, but that was enough to establish Doc behind and between the words of all the other stories. In a strange way Doc presided over the court. You didn't need to mention him. He was just there. Regent Park stories began with Doc and ended with Doc and everything in between was preparation, proof the circle was unbroken.

They say Doc lived on Regent Square, one of the streets like Cedar, dead-ending at the park. On the hottest afternoons the guys from the court would head for Doc's stoop. Jars of ice water, the good feeling and good talk they'd share in the shade of Doc's little front yard was what drew them. Sometimes they'd spray Doc's hose on one another. Get drenched like when they were kids and the city used to turn on fire hydrants in the summer. Some of Doc's neighbors would give them dirty looks. Didn't like a whole bunch of loud, sweaty, half-naked niggers backed up in their nice street where Doc was the only colored on the block. They say Doc didn't care. He was just out there like everybody else having a good time.

Doc had played at the University. Same one where Doc taught for a while. They say Doc used to laugh when white people asked him if he was in the Athletic Department. No reason for niggers to be at the University if they weren't playing ball or coaching ball. At least that's what white people thought, and since they thought that way, that's the way it was. Never more than a sprinkle of black faces in the white sea of the University. Doc used to laugh till the joke got old. People freedom-marching and freedom-dying, Doc said, but some dumb stuff never changed.

He first heard Doc's story late one day, after the yellow streetlights had popped on. Pooner was finishing the one about gang warring in North Philly: Yeah. They sure nuff lynched this dude they caught on their turf. Hung him up on the goddamn poles behind the backboard. Little kids found the sucker in the morning with his tongue all black and shit down his legs, and the cops had to come cut him down. Worst part is them little kids finding a dead body swinging up there. Kids don't be needing to find nothing like that. But those North Philly gangs don't play. They don't even let the dead rest in peace. Run in a funeral parlor and fuck up the funeral. Dumping over the casket and tearing up the flowers. Scaring people and turning the joint out. It's some mean shit. But them gangs don't play. They kill you they ain't finished yet. Mess with your people, your house, your sorry-ass dead body to get even. Pooner finished telling it and he looked round at the fellows and people were shaking their heads and then there was a chorus of You got that right, man. It's a bitch out there, man. Them niggers crazy, boy, and Pooner holds out his hand and somebody passes the joint. Pooner pinches it in two fingers and takes a deep drag. Everybody knows he's finished, it's somebody else's turn.

One of the fellows says, I wonder what happened to old Doc. I always be thinking about Doc, wondering where the cat is, what he be doing now . . .

Don't nobody know why Doc's eyes start to going bad. It just happen. Doc never even wore glasses. Eyes good as anybody's far as anybody knew till one day he come round he got goggles on. Like Kareem. And people kinda joking, you know. Doc got him some goggles. Watch out, youall. Doc be skyhooking youall to death today. Funning, you know. Cause Doc like to joke and play. Doc one the fellas like I said, so when he come round in goggles he subject to some teasing and one another thing like that cause nobody thought nothing serious wrong. Doc's eyes just as good as yours or mine, far as anybody knew.

Doc been playing all his life. That's why you could stand him on the foul line and point him at the hoop and more times than not, Doc could sink it. See he be remembering. His muscles know just what to do. You get his feet aimed right, line him up so he's on target, and Doc would swish one for you. Was a game kinda. Sometimes you get a sucker and Doc win you some money. Swish. Then the cat lost the dough start crying. He ain't blind. Can't no blind man shoot no pill. Is you really blind, brother? You niggers trying to steal my money, trying to play me for a fool. When a dude start crying the blues like that Doc wouldn't like it. He'd walk away. Wouldn't answer.

Leave the man lone. You lost fair and square. Doc made the basket so shut up and pay up, chump.

Doc practiced. Remember how you'd hear him out here at night when people sleeping. It's dark but what dark mean to Doc? Blacker than the rent-man's heart but don't make no nevermind to Doc, he be steady shooting fouls. Always be somebody out there to chase the ball and throw it back. But shit, man. When Doc into his rhythm, didn't need nobody chase the ball. Ball be swishing with that good backspin, that good arch bring it back blip, blip, blip, three bounces and it's coming right back to Doc's hands like he got a string on the pill. Spooky if you didn't know Doc or know about foul shooting and understand when you got your shit together don't matter if you blindfolded. You put the motherfucker up and you know it's spozed to come running back just like a dog with a stick in his mouth.

Doc always be hanging at the court. Blind as wood but you couldn't fool Doc. Eyes in his ears. Know you by your walk. He could tell if you wearing new sneaks, tell you if your old ones is laced or not. Know you by your breath. The holes you make in the air when you jump. Doc was hip to who fucking who and who was getting fucked. Who could play ball and who was jiving. Doc use to be out here every weekend, steady rapping with the fellows and doing his foul-shot thing between games. Every once in a while somebody tease him, Hey, Doc. You want to run winners next go? Doc laugh and say, No, Dupree . . . I'm tired today, Dupree. Besides which you ain't been on a winning team in a week have you, Du? And everybody laugh. You know, just funning cause Doc one the fellas.

But one Sunday the shit got stone serious. Sunday I'm telling youall about, the action was real nice. If you wasn't ready, get back cause the brothers was cooking. Sixteen points, rise and fly. Next. Who got next? . . . Come on out here and take your ass kicking. One them good days when it's hot and every-body's juices is high and you feel you could play till next week. One them kind of days and a run's just over. Doc gets up and he goes with Billy Moon to the foul line. Fellas hanging under the basket for the rebound. Ain't hardly gon be a rebound Doc get hisself lined up right. But see, when the ball drop through the net you want to be the one grab it and throw it back to Billy. You want to be out there part of Doc shooting fouls just like you want to run when the running's good.

Doc bounce the ball, one, two, three times like he does. Then he raise it. Sift it in his fingers. You know he's a ballplayer, a shooter already way the ball spin in them long fingers way he raises it and cocks his wrist. You know Doc can't see a damn thing through his sunglasses but swear to God you'd think he was looking at the hoop way he study and measure. Then he shoots and ain't a sound in whole Johnson. Seems like everybody's heart stops. Everybody's breath behind that ball pushing it and steadying it so it drops through clean as new money.

But that Sunday something went wrong. Couldna been wind cause wasn't no wind. I was there. I know. Maybe Doc had playing on his mind. Couldn't help have playing on his mind cause it was one those days wasn't nothing better to do in the world than play. Whatever it was, soon as the ball left his hands, you could see Doc was missing, missing real bad. Way short and way off to the left. Might hit the backboard if everybody blew on it real hard.

A young boy, one them skinny, jumping-jack young boys got pogo sticks for legs, one them kids go up and don't come back down till they ready, he was standing on the left side the lane and leap up all the sudden catch the pill out the air and jams it through. Blam. A monster dunk and everybody break out in Goddamn. Do it, Sky, and Did you see that nigger get up? People slapping five and all that mess. Then Sky, the young boy they call Sky, grinning like a Chessy cat and strutting out with the ball squeezed in one hand to give it to Doc. In his glory. Grinning and strutting.

Gave you a little help, Doc.

Didn't ask for no help, Sky. Why'd you fuck with my shot, Sky?

Well, up jumped the Devil. The joint gets real quiet again real quick. Doc ain't cracked smile the first. He ain't playing.

Sorry, Doc. Didn't mean no harm, Doc.

You must think I'm some kind of chump fucking with my shot that way.

People start to feeling bad. Doc is steady getting on Sky's case. Sky just a young, light-in-the-ass kid. Jump to the moon but he's just a silly kid. Don't mean no harm. He just out there like everybody else trying to do his thing. No harm in Sky but Doc ain't playing and nobody else says shit. It's quiet like when Doc's shooting. Quiet as death and Sky don't know what to do. Can't wipe that lame look off his face and can't back off and can't hand the pill to Doc neither. He just stands there with his arm stretched out and his rusty fingers wrapped round the ball. Can't hold it much longer, can't let it go.

Seems like I coulda strolled over to Doc's stoop for a drinka water and strolled back and those two still be standing there. Doc and Sky. Billy Moon off to one side so it's just Doc and Sky.

Everybody holding they breath. Everybody want it over with and finally Doc says, Forget it, Sky. Just don't play with my shots anymore. And then Doc say, Who has next winners?

If Doc was joking nobody took it for no joke. His voice still hard. Doc ain't kidding around.

Who's next? I want to run.

Now Doc knows who's next. Leroy got next winners and Doc knows Leroy always saves a spot so he can pick up a big man from the losers. Leroy tell you to your face, I got my five, man, but everybody know Leroy saving a place so he can build him a winner and stay on the court. Leroy's a cold dude that way, been that way since he first started coming round and ain't never gon change and Doc knows that, everybody knows that but even Leroy ain't cold enough to say no to Doc.

I got it, Doc.

You got your five yet?

You know you got a spot with me, Doc. Always did.

Then I'ma run.

Say to myself, Shit . . . Good God Almighty. Great Googa-Mooga. What is happening here? Doc can't see shit. Doc blind as this bench I'm sitting on. What Doc gon do out there?

Well, it ain't my game. If it was, I'd a lied and said I had five. Or maybe not. Don't know what I'da done, to tell the truth. But Leroy didn't have no choice. Doc caught him good. Course Doc knew all that before he asked.

Did Doc play? What kinda question is that? What you think I been talking about all this time, man? Course he played. Why the fuck he be asking for winners less he was gon play? Helluva run as I remember. Overtime and shit. Don't remember who won. Somebody did, sure nuff. Leroy had him a strong unit. You know how he is. And Doc? Doc ain't been out on the court for a while but Doc is Doc, you know. Held his own . . .

If he had tried to tell her about Doc, would it have made a difference? Would the idea of a blind man playing basketball get her attention or would she have listened the way she listened when he told her stories he'd read about slavery days when Africans could fly, change themselves to cats and hummingbirds, when black hoodoo priests and conjure queens were feared by powerful whites even though ordinary black lives weren't worth a penny. To her it was folklore, superstition. Interesting because it revealed the psychology, the pathology of the oppressed. She listened intently, not because she thought she'd hear truth. For her, belief in magic was like belief in God. Nice work if you could get it. Her skepticism, her hardheaded practicality, like the smallness of her hands, appealed to him. Opposites attracting. But more and more as the years went by, he'd wanted her with him, wanted them to be together . . .

They were walking in Regent Park. It was clear to both of them that things weren't going to work out. He'd never seen her so beautiful, perfect.

There should have been stars. Stars at least, and perhaps a sickle moon. Instead the edge of the world was on fire. They were walking in Regent Park and dusk had turned the tree trunks black. Beyond them in the distance, below the fading blue of sky, the colors of sunset were pinched into a narrow, radiant band. Perhaps he had listened too long. Perhaps he had listened too intently for his own voice to fill the emptiness. When he turned back to her, his eyes were glazed, stinging. Grit, chemicals, whatever it was coloring, poisoning the sky, blurred his vision. Before he could blink her into focus, before he could speak, she was gone.

If he'd known Doc's story he would have said: *There's still a chance. There's always a chance. I mean this guy, Doc. Christ. He was stone blind. But he got out on the court and played. Over there. Right over there. On that very court across the hollow from us. It happened. I've talked to people about it many times. If Doc could do that, then anything's possible. We're possible . . .*

If a blind man could play basketball, surely we . . . If he had known Doc's story, would it have saved them? He hears himself saying the words. The ball arches from Doc's fingertips, the miracle of it sinking. Would she have believed any of it?

Questions for Discussion

1. In the opening paragraph, the viewpoint character recalls the hands of his former girl-friend. What is revealed here about this character's relationships and motivations?

2. How are stories important to the central character? Why does he need to collect them at this stage of his life? What is the relationship between his need to listen to the stories and his partaking of wine and "reefer"?

3. What is it about Doc's story that bothers the viewpoint character? What is the significance of Doc's game with Leroy?

4. How does Pooner's story about the North Philly gangs that refuse to play and that lynch other gang members who invade their turf contrast and compare to Doc's story?

5. What is Doc's relationship to the university? to the white and black communities? Is he really "one [of] the fellas"? What does his blindness represent?

Ideas for Writing

1. It is clear from the story's conclusion that the viewpoint character identifies strongly with Doc, the blind player. Write an essay in which you examine the similarities and differences between the main character and Doc. Who is more heroic? Why does the viewpoint character believe in Doc's struggle?

2. Write an essay in which you discuss the failed relationship between the main character and his girlfriend. What impression might Doc's story have made on the girl-friend and on the relationship between her and the main character?

ISABEL ALLENDE   (b. 1942)

Influenced by Gabriel García Márquez and magic realism, Isabel Allende's stories explore, from a feminist perspective, the changing relationships between the sexes in Latin America as well as the impact of political matters on private and erotic life.

Born in Lima, Peru, the daughter of a Chilean diplomat, Allende was raised by her maternal grandparents after her parents divorced. During her adolescence she lived in Bolivia, the Middle East, and Europe and later worked as a journalist in Chile. As the niece of Chilean President Salvador Allende, her life changed dramatically when he was assassinated in 1973. She was forced into exile, first to Venezuela and later to California. After the death of her grandparents in 1981, Allende began to write her first novel, which was inspired by a letter from her grandfather: "My grandfather thought that people died only when you forgot them. I wanted to prove to him that I had forgotten nothing, that his spirit was going to live with us forever." That work, *The House of the Spirits* (1982), was an international success. All of her subsequent novels have been widely read; they include *Of Love and Shadows* (1987), *Eva Luna* (1988), and *Infinite Plan* (1993). Her stories are collected in *The Stories of Eva Luna* (1991), which includes "Phantom Palace." In that collection the character Eva Luna, created originally for Allende's 1988 novel, spins a series of tales of love and politics in Latin American life.

Phantom Palace   (1991)

Translated by Margaret Sayers Peden

When five centuries earlier the bold renegades from Spain with their bone-weary horses and armor candescent beneath an American sun stepped upon the shores of Quinaroa, Indians had been living and dying in that same place for several thousand years. The conquistadors announced with heralds and banners the "discovery" of a new land, declared it a possession of a remote emperor, set in place the first cross, and named the place San Jerónimo, a name unpronounceable to the natives. The Indians observed these arrogant ceremonies with some amazement, but the news had already reached them of the bearded warriors who advanced across the world with their thunder of iron and powder; they had heard that wherever these men went they sowed sorrow and that no known people had been capable of opposing them: all armies had succumbed before that handful of centaurs. These Indians were an ancient tribe, so poor that not even the most befeathered chieftain had bothered to exact taxes from them, and so meek that they had never been recruited for war. They had lived in peace since the dawn of time and were not eager to change their habits because of some crude strangers. Soon, nevertheless, they comprehended the magnitude of the enemy and they understood the futility of attempting to ignore them; their presence was overpowering, like a heavy stone bound to every back. In the years that followed, the Indians who had not died in slavery or as a result of the different tortures improvised to entrench the new gods, or as victims of unknown illnesses, scattered deep into the jungle and gradually lost even the name of their people. Always in hiding, like shadows among the foliage, they survived for centuries, speaking in whispers and mobilizing by night. They came to be so skillful in the art of dissimulation that history did not record them, and today there is no evidence of their passage through time. Books do not mention them, but the *campesinos* who live in the region say they have heard them in the forest, and every time the belly of a young unmarried woman begins to grow round and they cannot point to the seducer, they attribute the baby to the spirit of a lustful Indian. People of that place are proud of carrying a few drops of the blood of those invisible beings mingled with the torrential flow from English pirates, Spanish soldiers, African slaves, adventurers in search of El Dorado, and, later, whatever immigrant stumbled onto these shores with his pack on his back and his head filled with dreams.

Europe consumed more coffee, cocoa, and bananas than we as a nation could produce, but all that demand was no bonanza for us; we continued to be as poor as ever. Events took a sudden turn when a black man digging a well along the coast drove his pick deep into the ground and a stream of petroleum spurted over his face. Toward the end of the Great War there was a widely held notion that ours was a prosperous country, when in truth most of the inhabitants still squished mud between their toes. The fact was that gold flowed only into the coffers of El Benefactor and his retinue, but there was hope that someday a little would spill over for the people. Two decades passed under this democratic totalitarianism, as the President for Life called his government, during which any hint of subversion would have been crushed in the name of his greater glory. In the capital there were signs of progress; motorcars, movie houses, ice cream parlors, a hippodrome, and a theater that presented spectaculars from New York and Paris. Every day dozens of ships moored in the port, some carrying away petroleum and others bringing in new products, but the rest of the country drowsed in a centuries-long stupor.

One day the people of San Jerónimo awakened from their siesta to the deafening pounding that presaged the arrival of the steam engine. The railroad tracks would unite the capital with this small settlement chosen by El Benefactor as the site for his Summer Palace, which was to be constructed in the style of European royalty — no matter that no one knew how to distinguish summer from winter, since both were lived under nature's hot, humid breath. The sole reason for erecting such a monumental work on this precise spot was that a certain Belgian naturalist had affirmed that if there was any truth to the myth of the Earthly Paradise, this landscape of incomparable beauty would have been the location. According to his observations the forest harbored more than a thousand varieties of brightly colored birds and numerous species of wild orchids, from the *Brassia,* which is as large as a hat, to the tiny *Pleurothallis,* visible only under a magnifying glass.

The idea of the Palace had originated with some Italian builders who had called on His Excellency bearing plans for a hodgepodge of a villa, a labyrinth of countless columns, wide colonnades, curving staircases, arches, domes and capitals, salons, kitchens, bedchambers, and more than thirty baths decorated with gold and silver faucets. The railroad was the first stage in the enterprise, indispensable for transporting tons of materials and hundreds of workmen to this remote corner of the world, in addition to the supervisors and craftsmen brought from Italy. The task of putting together that jigsaw puzzle lasted four years: flora and fauna were transmuted in the process, and the cost was equivalent to that of all the warships of the nation's fleet, but it was paid for punctually with the dark mineral that flowed from the earth, and on the anniversary of the Glorious Ascent to Power the ribbon was cut to inaugurate the Summer Palace. For the occasion the locomotive of the train was draped in the colors of the flag, and the freight cars were replaced by parlor cars upholstered in plush and English leather; the formally attired guests included members of the oldest aristocracy who, although they detested the cold-blooded Andean who had usurped the government, did not dare refuse his invitation.

El Benefactor was a crude man with the comportment of a peon; he bathed in cold water and slept on a mat on the floor with his boots on and his pistol within arm's reach; he lived on roast meat and maize, and drank nothing but water and coffee. His black cigars were his one luxury; he considered anything else a vice befitting degenerates or homosexuals — including alcohol, which he disapproved of and rarely offered at his table. With time, nevertheless, he was forced to accept a few refinements, because he understood the need to impress diplomats and other eminent visitors if they were not to carry the report abroad that he was a barbarian. He did not have a wife to mend his Spartan ways. He believed that love was a dangerous weakness. He was convinced that all women, except his own mother, were potentially perverse and that the most prudent way to treat them was to keep them at arm's length. He had always said that a man asleep in an amorous embrace was as vulnerable as a premature baby; he demanded, therefore, that his generals sleep in the barracks and limit their family life to sporadic visits. No woman had ever spent the night in his bed or could boast of anything more than a hasty encounter. No woman, in fact, had ever made a lasting impression until Marcia Lieberman entered his life.

The celebration for the inauguration of the Summer Palace was a stellar event in the annals of El Benefactor's government. For two days and two nights alternating orchestras played the most current dance tunes and an army of chefs prepared an unending banquet. The most beautiful mulatto women in the Caribbean, dressed in sumptuous gowns created for the occasion, whirled through salons with officers who had never fought in a battle but whose chests were covered with medals. There was every sort of diversion: singers imported from Havana and New Orleans, flamenco dancers, magicians, jugglers and trapeze artists, card games and dominoes, and even a rabbit hunt. Servants released the rabbits from their cages, and the guests pursued the scampering pack with finely bred greyhounds; the chase came to an end when one wit blasted all the black-necked swans gliding across the lake. Some guests passed out in their chairs, drunk with dancing and liquor, while others jumped fully clothed into the swimming pool or drifted off in pairs to the bedchambers. El Benefactor did not want to know the details. After greeting his guests with a brief speech, and beginning the dancing with the most aristocratic lady present, he had returned to the capital without a farewell. Parties put him in a bad humor. On the third day the train made the return journey, carrying home the enervated *bons vivants*. The Summer Palace was left in a calamitous state: the baths were dunghills, the curtains were dripping with urine, the furniture was gutted, and the plants drooped in their flowerpots. It took the servants a week to clean up the ravages of that hurricane.

The Palace was never again the scene of a bacchanal. Occasionally El Benefactor went there to get away from the pressures of his duties, but his repose lasted no more than three or four days, for fear that a conspiracy might be hatched in his absence. The government required eternal vigilance if power was not to slip through his fingers. The only people left in all that enormous edifice were the personnel entrusted with its maintenance. When the clatter of the construction equipment and the train had stilled, and the echoes of the inaugural festivities died down, the region was once again calm, and the orchids flowered and birds rebuilt their nests. The inhabitants of San Jerónimo returned to their habitual occupations and almost succeeded in forgetting the presence of the Summer Palace. That was when the invisible Indians slowly returned to occupy their territory.

The first signs were so subtle that no one paid attention to them; footsteps and whispers, fleeting silhouettes among the columns, the print of a hand on the clean surface of a table. Gradually food began to disappear from the kitchens, and bottles from the wine cellars; in the morning, some beds seemed to have been slept in. The servants blamed one another but never raised their voices because no one wanted the officer of the guard to take the matter into his hands. It was impossible to watch the entire expanse of that house, and while they were searching one room they would hear sighs in the adjoining one; but when they opened that door they would find only a curtain fluttering, as if someone had just stepped through it. The rumor spread that the Palace was under a spell, and soon the fear spread even to the soldiers, who stopped walking their night rounds and limited themselves to standing motionless at their post, eyes on the surrounding landscape, weapons at the ready. The frightened servants stopped going down to the cellars and, as a precaution, locked many of the rooms. They confined their activities to the kitchen and slept in one wing of the building.

The remainder of the mansion was left unguarded, in the possession of the incorporeal Indians who had divided the rooms with invisible lines and taken up residence there like mischievous spirits. They had survived the passage of history, adapting to changes when they were inevitable, and when necessary taking refuge in a dimension of their own. In the rooms of the Palace they at last found refuge; there they noiselessly made love, gave birth without celebration, and died without tears. They learned so thoroughly all the twists and turns of that marble maze that they were able to exist comfortably in the same space with the guards and servants, never so much as brushing against them, as if they existed in a different time.

Ambassador Lieberman debarked in the port with his wife and a full cargo of personal belongings. He had traveled with his dogs, all his furniture, his library, his collection of opera recordings, and every imaginable variety of sports equipment, including a sailboat. From the moment his new destination had been announced, he had detested that country. He had left his post as Vice Consul in Vienna motivated by the ambition to obtain an ambassadorship, even if it meant South America, a bizarre continent for which he had not an ounce of sympathy. Marcia, his wife, took the appointment with better humor. She was prepared to follow her husband throughout his diplomatic pilgrimage — even though each day she felt more remote from him and had little interest in his mundane affairs — because she was allowed a great deal of freedom. She had only to fulfill certain minimal wifely requirements, and the remainder of her time was her own. In fact, her husband was so immersed in his work and his sports that he was scarcely aware of her existence; he noticed her only when she was not there. Lieberman's wife was an indispensable complement to his career; she lent brilliance to his social life and efficiently managed his complicated domestic staff. He thought of her as a loyal partner, but he had never been even slightly curious about her feelings. Marcia consulted maps and an encyclopedia to learn the particulars of that distant nation, and began studying Spanish. During the two weeks of the Atlantic crossing she read books by the famous Belgian naturalist and, even before arriving, was enamored of that heat-bathed geography. As she was a rather withdrawn woman, she was happier in her garden than in the salons where she had to accompany her husband, and she concluded that in the new post she would have fewer social demands and could devote herself to reading, painting, and exploring nature.

Lieberman's first act was to install fans in every room of his residence. Immediately thereafter he presented his credentials to the government authorities. When El Benefactor received him in his office, the couple had been in the city only a few days, but the gossip that the Ambassador's wife was a beautiful woman had already reached the caudillo's ears. For reasons of protocol he invited them to dinner, although he found the diplomat's arrogance and garrulity insufferable. On the appointed night Marcia Lieberman entered the

Reception Hall on her husband's arm and, for the first time in a long lifetime, a woman caused El Benefactor to gasp for breath. He had seen more lithe figures, and faces more beautiful, but never such grace. She awakened memories of past conquests, fueling a heat in his blood that he had not felt in many years. He kept his distance that evening, observing the Ambassador's wife surreptitiously, seduced by the curve of her throat, the shadow in her eyes, the movement of her hands, the solemnity of her bearing. Perhaps it crossed his mind that he was more than forty years older than she and that any scandal would have repercussions far beyond the national boundaries, but that did not discourage him; on the contrary, it added an irresistible ingredient to his nascent passion.

Marcia Lieberman felt the man's eyes fastened on her like an indecent caress, and she was aware of the danger, but she did not have the strength to escape. At one moment she thought of telling her husband they should leave, but instead remained seated, hoping the old man would approach her and at the same time ready to flee if he did. She could not imagine why she was trembling. She had no illusions about her host; the signs of age were obvious from where she was sitting: the wrinkled and blemished skin, the dried-up body, the hesitant walk. She could imagine his stale odor and knew intuitively that his hands were claws beneath the white kid gloves. But the dictator's eyes, clouded by age and the exercise of so much cruelty, still held a gleam of power that held her frozen in her chair.

El Benefactor did not know how to pay court to a woman; until that moment he had never had need to do so. That fact acted in his favor, for had he harassed Marcia with a Lothario's gallantries she would have found him repulsive and would have retreated with scorn. Instead she could not refuse him when a few days later he knocked at her door, dressed in civilian clothes and without his guards, looking like a dreary great-grandfather, to tell her that he had not touched a woman for ten years and that he was past temptations of that sort but, with all respect, he was asking her to accompany him that afternoon to a private place where he could rest his head in her queenly lap and tell her how the world had been when he was still a fine figure of a macho and she had not yet been born.

"And my husband?" Marcia managed to ask in a whisper-thin voice.

"Your husband does not exist, my child. Now only you and I exist," the President for Life replied as he led her to his black Packard.

Marcia did not return home, and before the month was out Ambassador Lieberman returned to his country. He had left no stone unturned in searching for his wife, refusing at first to accept what was no secret, but when the evidence of the abduction became impossible to ignore, Lieberman had asked for an audience with the Chief of State and demanded the return of his wife. The interpreter tried to soften his words in translation, but the President captured the tone and seized the excuse to rid himself once and for all of that imprudent husband. He declared that Lieberman had stained the honor of the nation with his absurd and unfounded accusations and gave him three days to leave the country. He offered him the option of withdrawing without a scandal, to protect the dignity of the country he represented, since it was to no one's interest to break diplomatic ties and obstruct the free movement of the oil tankers. At the end of the interview, with the expression of an injured father, he added that he could understand the Ambassador's dilemma and told him not to worry, because in his absence, he, El Benefactor, would continue the search for his wife. As proof of his good intents he called the Chief of Police and issued instructions in the Ambassador's presence. If at any moment Lieberman had thought of refusing to leave without Marcia, a second thought must have made clear to him that he was risking a bullet in the brain, so he packed his belongings and left the country before the three days were up.

Love had taken El Benefactor by surprise at an age when he no longer remembered the heart's impatience. This cataclysm rocked his senses and thrust him back into adolescence, but not sufficiently to dull his vulpine cunning. He realized that his was a passion of sensuality, and he could not imagine that Marcia returned his emotions. He did not know why she had followed him that afternoon, but his reason indicated that it was not for love, and, as he knew nothing about women, he supposed that she had allowed herself to be seduced out of a taste for adventure, or greed for power. In fact, she had fallen prey to compassion. When the old man embraced her, anxiously, his eyes watering with humiliation because his manhood did not respond as it once had, she undertook, patiently and with good will, to restore his pride. And thus after several attempts the poor man succeeded in passing through the gates and lingering a few brief instants in the proffered warm gardens, collapsing immediately thereafter with his heart filled with foam.

"Stay with me," El Benefactor begged, as soon as he had recovered from fear of succumbing upon her.

And Marcia had stayed, because she was moved by the aged caudillo's loneliness, and because the alternative of returning to her husband seemed less interesting than the challenge of slipping past the iron fence this man had lived behind for eighty years.

El Benefactor kept Marcia hidden on one of his estates, where he visited her daily. He never stayed the night with her. Their time together was spent in leisurely caresses and conversation. In her halting Spanish she told him about her travels and the books she had read; he listened, not understanding much, content simply with the cadence of her voice. In turn he told her stories of his childhood in the arid lands of the Andes, and of his life as a soldier; but if she formulated some question he immediately threw up his defenses, observing her from the corner of his eyes as if she were the enemy. Marcia could not fail to note this implacable stoniness and realized that his habit of distrust was much stronger than his need to yield to tenderness, and so, after a few weeks, she resigned herself to defeat. Once she had renounced any hope of winning him over with love, she lost interest in him and longed to escape the walls that sequestered her. But it was too late. El Benefactor needed her by his side because she was the closest thing to a companion he had known; her husband had returned to Europe and she had nowhere to turn in this land; and even her name was fading from memory. The dictator perceived the change in her and his mistrust intensified, but that did not cause him to stop loving her. To console her for the confinement to which she was now condemned — her appearance outside would have confirmed Lieberman's accusations and shot international relations to hell — he provided her with all the things she loved: music, books, animals. Marcia passed the hours in a world of her own, every day more detached from reality. When she stopped encouraging him, El Benefactor found it impossible to embrace her, and their meetings resolved into peaceful evenings of cookies and hot chocolate. In his desire to please her, El Benefactor invited her one day to go with him to the Summer Palace, so she could see the paradise of the Belgian naturalist she had read so much about.

The train had not been used since the inaugural celebration ten years before and was so rusted that they had to make the trip by automobile, escorted by a caravan of guards; a crew of servants had left a week before, taking everything needed to restore the Palace to its original luxury. The road was no more than a trail defended by chain gangs against encroaching vegetation. In some stretches they had to use machetes to clear the ferns, and oxen to haul the cars from the mud, but none of that diminished Marcia's enthusiasm. She was dazzled by the landscape. She endured the humid heat and the mosquitoes as if she did not feel them, absorbed by a nature that seemed to welcome her in its embrace. She had the impression that she had been there before, perhaps in dreams or in another life, that she belonged there, that until that moment she had been a stranger in the world, and that her instinct had dictated every step she had taken, including that of leaving her husband's house to follow a trembling old man, for the sole purpose of leading her here. Even before she saw the Summer Palace, she knew that it would be her last home. When the edifice finally rose out of the foliage, encircled by palm trees and shimmering in the sun, Marcia breathed a deep sigh of relief, like a shipwrecked sailor when he sees home port.

Despite the frantic preparations that had been made to receive them, the mansion still seemed to be under a spell. The Roman-style structure, conceived as the center of a geometric park and grand avenues, was sunk in the riot of a gluttonous jungle growth. The torrid climate had changed the color of the building materials, covering them with a premature patina; nothing was visible of the swimming pool and gardens. The greyhounds had long ago broken their leashes and were running loose, a ferocious, starving pack that greeted the newcomers with a chorus of barking. Birds had nested in the capitals of the columns and covered the reliefs with droppings. On every side were signs of disorder. The Summer Palace had been transformed into a living creature defenseless against the green invasion that had surrounded and overrun it. Marcia leapt from the automobile and ran to the enormous doors where the servants awaited, oppressed by the heat of the dog days. One by one she explored all the rooms, the great salons decorated with crystal chandeliers that hung from the ceilings like constellations and French furniture whose tapestry upholstery was now home to lizards, bedchambers where bed canopies were blanched by intense sunlight, baths where moss had grown in the seams of the marble. Marcia never stopped smiling; she had the face of a woman recovering what was rightfully hers.

When El Benefactor saw Marcia so happy, a touch of the old vigor returned to warm his creaking bones, and he could embrace her as he had in their first meetings. Distractedly, she acceded. The week they had planned to spend there lengthened into two, because El Benefactor had seldom enjoyed himself so much. The fatigue accumulated in his years as tyrant disappeared, and several of his old man's ailments abated. He strolled with Marcia around the grounds, pointing out the many species of orchids climbing the treetrunks or hanging like grapes from the highest branches, the clouds of white butterflies that covered the ground, and the birds with iridescent feathers that filled the air with their song. He frolicked with her like a young lover, he fed her bits of the delicious flesh of wild mangoes, with his own hands he bathed her in herbal infusions, and he made her laugh by serenading her beneath her window. It had been years since he had been away from the capital, except for brief flights to provinces where his presence was required to put down some insurrection and to renew the people's belief that his authority was not to be questioned. This unexpected vacation had put him in a fine frame of mind; life suddenly seemed more fun, and he had the fantasy that with this beautiful woman beside him he could govern forever. One night he unintentionally fell asleep in her arms. He awoke in the early morning, terrified, with the clear sensation of having betrayed himself. He sprang out of bed, sweating, his heart galloping, and observed Marcia lying there, a white odalisque in repose, her copper hair spilling across her face. He informed his guards that he was returning to the city. He was not surprised when Marcia gave no sign of going with him. Perhaps in his heart he preferred it that way, since he understood that she represented his most dangerous weakness, that she was the only person who could make him forget his power.

El Benefactor returned to the capital without Marcia. He left behind a half-dozen soldiers to guard the property and a few employees to serve her, and he promised he would maintain the road so that she could receive his gifts, provisions, mail, and newspapers and magazines. He assured her that he would visit her often, as often as his duties as Chief of State permitted, but when he said goodbye they both knew they would never meet again. El Benefactor's caravan disappeared into the ferns and for a moment silence fell over the Summer Palace. Marcia felt truly free for the first time in her life. She removed the hairpins holding her hair in a bun, and shook out her long hair. The guards unbuttoned their jackets and put aside their weapons, while the servants went off to hang their hammocks in the coolest corners they could find.

For two weeks the Indians had observed the visitors from the shadows. Undeceived by Marcia Lieberman's fair skin and marvelous curly hair, they recognized her as one of their own but they had not dared materialize in her presence because of the habit of centuries of clandestinity. After the departure of the old man and his retinue, they returned stealthily to occupy the space where they had lived for generations. Marcia knew intuitively that she was never alone, that wherever she went a thousand eyes followed her, that she moved in a ferment of constant murmuring, warm breathing, and rhythmic pulsing, but she was not afraid; just the opposite, she felt protected by friendly spirits. She became used to petty annoyances: one of her dresses disappeared for several days, then one morning was back in a basket at the foot of her bed; someone devoured her dinner before she entered the dining room; her water-colors and books were stolen, but also she found freshly cut orchids on her table, and some evenings her bath waited with mint leaves floating in the cool water; she heard ghostly notes from pianos in the empty salons, the panting of lovers in the armoires, the voices of children in the attics. The servants had no explanation for those disturbances and she stopped asking, because she imag-ined they themselves were part of the benevolent conspiracy. One night she crouched among the curtains with a flashlight, and when she felt the thudding of feet on the marble, switched on the beam. She thought she saw shadowy, naked forms that for an instant gazed at her mildly and then vanished. She called in Spanish, but no one answered. She realized she would need enor-mous patience to uncover those mysteries, but it did not matter because she had the rest of her life before her.

A few years later the nation was jolted by the news that the dictatorship had come to an end for a most surprising reason: El Benefactor had died. He was a man in his dotage, a sack of skin and bones that for months had been decaying in life, and yet very few people imagined that he was mortal. No one remembered a time before him; he had been in power so many decades that people had become accustomed to thinking of him as an inescapable evil, like the climate. The echoes of the funeral were slow to reach the Summer Palace. By then most of the guards and servants, bored with waiting for replacements that never came, had deserted their posts. Marcia listened to the news without emotion. In fact, she had to make an effort to remember her past, what had happened beyond the jungle, and the hawk-eyed old man who had changed the course of her destiny. She realized that with the death of the tyrant the rea-sons for her remaining hidden had evaporated; she could return to civiliza-tion, where now, surely, no one was concerned with the scandal of her kid-napping. She quickly discarded that idea, however, because there was nothing outside the snarl of the surrounding jungle that interested her. Her life passed peacefully among the Indians; she was absorbed in the greenness, clothed only in a tunic, her hair cut short, her body adorned with tattoos and feathers. She was utterly happy.

A generation later, when democracy had been established in the nation and nothing remained of the long history of dictators but a few pages in scholarly books, someone remembered the marble villa and proposed that they restore it and found an Academy of Art. The Congress of the Republic sent a commission to draft a report, but their automobiles were not up to the grueling trip, and when finally they reached San Jerónimo no one could tell them where the Summer Palace was. They tried to follow the railroad tracks, but the rails had been ripped from the ties and the jungle had erased all traces. Then the Congress sent a detachment of explorers and a pair of military engineers who flew over the area in a helicopter; the vegetation was so thick that not even they could find the site. Details about the Palace were misplaced in people's memories and the municipal archives; the notion of its existence became gossip for old women; reports were swallowed up in the bureaucracy and, since the nation had more urgent problems, the project of the Academy of Art was tabled.

Now a highway has been constructed that links San Jerónimo to the rest of the country. Travelers say that sometimes after a storm, when the air is damp and charged with electricity, a white marble palace suddenly rises up beside the road, hovers for a few brief moments in the air, like a mirage, and then noiselessly disappears.

Questions for Discussion
1. Describe the Indians of San Jerónimo. What values do they represent?
2. Characterize El Benefactor. Why is his regime able to survive for so many years? What are his values? What qualities of political power in the New World does he symbolize?
3. What critique is the story making about "civilized" relationships through the portrayal of the Lieberman marriage?
4. Why does El Benefactor want to possess Marcia? What advantages does the relationship have for her?
5. How does Marcia change as the story develops? How have her relationships with El Benefactor and the Indians changed? What implications do these changes make about the cultures portrayed in the story? How does the "phantom palace" contribute to these meanings?

Ideas for Writing
1. Write an essay in which you interpret the story's central symbol and setting, the phantom palace. How does it change physically? What does each of the transformations of the palace symbolize? What is the significance of its loss and rebirth as a ghost or legend?
2. Write a story about a person who gives up his or her "civilized" culture and adopts the ways of a repressed or colonized culture.

SERGIO RAMÍREZ   (b. 1942)

Sergio Ramírez, Nicaragua's most renowned fiction writer, portrays in his work Nicaraguan cultural history and sensibilities, emphasizing the unlikely juxtapositions and conflicting loyalties experienced by a people long under the control of American military power and conditioned to be consumers of American mass culture and values.

Ramírez was born and raised in Masatepe, later studying law and living abroad for a number of years, first in Costa Rica, where he was an official of the Council of Central American Universities, and later in Europe, as a political exile during the years of the Sandinista uprising. Ramírez was a member of the Sandinista Liberation Front, and after the fall of the Somoza regime he returned from exile to take the position of vice president of Nicaragua under the Sandinista government of Daniel Ortega. His personal commentaries on the Sandinista revolt have been collected in *Sandino: The Testimony of a Nicaraguan Patriot* (1990). In the novel *To Bury Our Fathers* (1984), he created an epic account of Nicaraguan life under Anastasio Somoza; his short fiction has been translated into English in the collection *Stories* (1986), which includes "Charles Atlas Also Dies." Ramírez's writing is characterized by humor, grotesque characters, symbolism based on myths and popular culture, as well as both realistic and dreamlike description.

Charles Atlas Also Dies   (1976)

Translated by Nick Caistor

Charles Atlas swears that sand story is true.
— *Edwin Pope, Sports Editor,*
The Miami Herald

How well I remember Captain Hatfield USMC on the day he came down to the quayside at Bluefields to see me off on the boat to New York. He gave me his parting words of advice, and lent me his English cashmere coat: it must be cold up there, he said. He came with me to the gangway and then, after I had clambered into the launch, gave me a long handshake. As I rode out to the steamer, which stood well off the coast, I saw him for the last time, a lean, bent figure in army boots and fatigues, waving me good-bye with his cap. I say for the last time because three days later he was killed in a Sandinista attack on Puerto Cabezas, where he was garrison commander.

Captain Hatfield USMC was a good friend. He taught me to speak English with his Cortina method records, played for me every night in the barracks at

San Fernando on the wind-up gramophone. It was he who introduced me to American cigarettes. But above all, I remember him for one thing: he enrolled me in the Charles Atlas correspondence course, and later helped me get to New York to see the great man in person.

It was in San Fernando, a small town up in the Segovias Mountains, that I first met Captain Hatfield USMC. That was back in 1926: I was a telegraph operator, and he arrived in command of the first column of Marines, with the task of forcing General Sandino and his followers down from Mount Chipote, where they had holed up. It was me who transmitted his messages to Sandino and received the replies. Our close friendship, though, started from the day he gave me a list of the inhabitants of San Fernando and asked me to mark all those I thought might be involved with the rebels or had relatives among them. The next day they were all marched off, tied up, to Ocotal, where the Americans had their regional headquarters. That night, to show his gratitude, he gave me a packet of Camels (which were completely unknown in Nicaragua in those days) and a magazine with pin-up photos. It was there I read the ad that changed my whole life, transforming me from a weakling into a new man:

THE 97-POUND WEAKLING
WHO MADE HIMSELF THE WORLD'S
MOST PERFECTLY DEVELOPED MAN

Ever since I was a child, I had suffered from being puny. I can remember how once when I was strolling around the square in San Fernando after Mass with my girlfriend Ethel — I was 15 at the time — two big hefty guys walked past us, laughing at me. One of them turned back and kicked sand in my face. When Ethel asked me, "Why did you let them do that?" all I could find to reply was: "First of all, he was a big bastard; and second, I couldn't see a thing for the sand in my eyes."

I asked Captain Hatfield USMC for help in applying for the course advertised in the magazine, and he wrote on my behalf to Charles Atlas in New York, at 115 East 23rd Street, to ask for the illustrated brochure. Almost a year later — San Fernando is in the midst of the mountains, where the heaviest fighting was going on — I received the manila envelope containing several colored folders and a letter signed by Charles Atlas himself. "The Complete Dynamic Tension Course, the summit in body-building. Simply tell me where on your body you'd like muscles of steel. Are you fat and flabby? Limp and listless? Do you tire easily and lack energy? Do you stay in your shell and let others walk off with the prettiest girls, the best jobs, etc? Give me just seven days and I'll prove that I can turn you too into a real man, full of health, of confidence in yourself and your own strength."

Mr. Atlas also said in his letter that this course would cost a total of thirty dollars. That kind of money was far beyond my means, so again I turned to Captain Hatfield USMC, who presented me with another list of local people, almost all of whom I marked for him. The money was soon sent off, and within the year I had received the complete course of 14 lessons with their 42 exercises. Captain Hatfield took personal charge of me. The exercises took only 15 minutes a day. "Dynamic Tension is a completely natural system. It requires no mechanical apparatus that might strain the heart or other vital organs. You need no pills, special diet, or other tricks. All you need are a few minutes of your spare time each day—and you'll really enjoy it!"

But since I had more spare time than I knew what to do with, I could dedicate myself wholeheartedly to the exercises for three hours rather than fifteen minutes every day. At night I was studying English with Captain Hatfield. After only a month, my progress was astonishing. My shoulders had broadened, my waist had slimmed down, and my legs had firmed up. Scarcely four years after that big bully had kicked sand in my eyes, I was a different man. One day, Ethel showed me a photo of the mythological god Atlas in a magazine. "Look," she said, "he's just like you." Then I knew I was on the right track and would one day fulfill my dreams.

Four months later, my English was good enough for me to be able to write and thank Mr. Atlas myself: "Everything is OK." I was a new man with biceps of steel, and capable of a feat like the one I performed in the capital, Managua, the day that Captain Hatfield USMC took me there to give a public demonstration of my strength. Dressed in a tiger-skin leotard, I pulled a Pacific Railway car full of chorus girls for a distance of two hundred yards. President Moncada himself, together with the special American envoy Mr. Hanna and Colonel Friedmann, the commander of the Marines in Nicaragua, all came to see me.

Doubtless it was this achievement, which was reported in all the newspapers, that made it easier for Captain Hatfield to forward the application I had made when the two of us left San Fernando: a trip to the United States to meet Charles Atlas in person. Captain Hatfield's superiors in Managua made a formal request to Washington, and just over a year later this was approved. The news appeared in the papers at the time; more precisely, in *La Noticia* for September 18, 1931, I was photographed standing next to the US cultural attaché, a certain Mr. Fox, this being almost certainly the first cultural exchange between our two countries, although they became so common afterwards. The caption read: "Leaving for a tour of physical culture centers in the United States, where he will also meet outstanding personalities from the world of athletics."

So it was that, following a peaceful crossing with a short call at the port of Veracruz, we arrived in New York on November 23, 1931. I must confess that, as the ship berthed, a feeling of great desolation overwhelmed me, despite all the warnings Captain Hatfield USMC had given me. From books, photographs, and maps, I had formed a precise image of New York City—but it was a static one. This was torn to shreds by the frenetic movement of animate and inanimate objects around me, and I was plunged into a terrifying fantasy full of invisible trains, a sky blackened by countless chimneys, a stench of soot and sewage, the scream of distant sirens, and a constant rumbling from the earth beneath my feet.

I was met by someone from the State Department, who took care of immigration and drove me to my hotel — the Hotel Lexington to be exact — a huge brick building on 48th Street. He told me everything had been arranged for me to see Mr. Atlas the following morning. I was to be picked up at my hotel and taken to the offices of Charles Atlas, Inc., where everything would be explained to me. With that we said good-bye, as he had to return to Washington the same evening.

It was cold in New York, so I went to bed early, full of an understandable excitement now that I was reaching my journey's end and seeing my greatest ambition fulfilled. I looked out at the infinity of lights from skyscraper windows that sparkled through the fog. Somewhere out there, I thought, behind one of those windows, is Charles Atlas. He's reading, having dinner, sleeping, or talking to someone. Or perhaps he's doing the nightly exercises — numbers 23 and 24 in the handbook (flexing the neck and wrists). Maybe he has a smile on his fresh, cheerful face beneath hair greying at the temples. Or perhaps he is still busy replying to the thousands of letters he receives every day, and sending off the packages with the handbooks. One thing suddenly occurred to me: I couldn't imagine Charles Atlas with clothes on. I always thought of him in his swimming trunks, with his muscles flexed, but found it impossible to picture him in a suit or hat. I rummaged in my suitcase till I found the signed photograph he had sent me on completion of the course. There he stood, hands cupped behind his head, body slightly arched and his pectoral muscles effortlessly tensed, his legs together, and one shoulder tilted higher than the other. It was beyond me to try and imagine such a body clothed, and the idea was still turning in my mind as I fell asleep.

By five in the morning I was already awake. I carried out exercises 1 and 2 (how thrilling to be doing them in New York for the very first time) and imagined that Charles Atlas was probably performing the same ones right at that moment. I took my shower and dressed as slowly as possible, killing time, but by seven o'clock I was downstairs in the hotel lobby waiting to be picked up as instructed. Although Charles Atlas did not exactly specify it, I never ate breakfast anyway.

At nine o'clock sharp the man from Charles Atlas, Inc., arrived. Waiting for us outside was a black limousine with gold trim on its windows and grey velvet curtains. The escort did not open his mouth once during the whole trip, nor did the chauffeur so much as glance around. We drove for half an hour along streets lined with the same brick buildings, row upon row of windows, and always the dull daylight between the skyscrapers as though it was about to rain. The black car finally pulled up in front of the eagerly awaited number 115 on East 23rd Street. It was a depressing street full of warehouses and wholesale depositories. I remember that across from Charles Atlas, Inc., was an umbrella factory and a small park of dusty, withered trees. All the buildings seemed to have their windows boarded up.

To reach the front entrance of Charles Atlas, Inc., we climbed some stone steps up to a small terrace, where a life-sized statue of the mythological god Atlas was carrying the world on his shoulders. The inscription read: *Mens sana in corpore sano*.[1] We went in through a squeaky revolving door of polished glass set in black enamelled frames. The walls of the lobby were covered with huge blow-ups of all the photographs of Charles Atlas I knew so well. What a thrill to recognize each of them in turn: particularly the one in the center, which showed him, a harness around his neck, pulling ten automobiles while a shower of ticker-tape fell about him. Magnificent!

I was shown into the office of Mr. William Rideout, Jr., the general manager of Charles Atlas, Inc. Within a few moments I was joined by a middle-aged man with a gaunt face and eyes sunk deep into dark sockets. He held out a pale hand, on which a mass of blue veins stood out, then sat down behind a small, square desk. He switched on a lamp behind him, though to me this hardly seemed necessary, as the window let in enough light already.

The offices were rather shabby. The desk was littered with piles of letters identical to the one I had received at the start of the course. The wall in front of me was dominated by an enormous photograph (one I had never seen before) of Charles Atlas proudly showing off his pectoral muscles. Mr. Rideout asked me to take a seat, then began to speak without so much as looking up at me. He kept staring at a paperweight on the desk, and had his hands crossed in front of him. It was plain from his expression that he found it a great effort to talk. I was trying so hard to follow his dull monotonous voice that it wasn't until he paused to wipe the corners of his mouth that I noticed something my nervousness had prevented me from seeing before: his clenched hands and lowered head could only mean exercise 18 of the Dynamic Tension System. I must admit I was so moved I came close to tears.

"I welcome you most cordially," Mr. Rideout Jr. had begun, "and I hope you have an enjoyable stay in New York. I'm sorry not to be able to talk proper Spanish with you as I should have wished, but I only speak *un poquito*." As he said this, he measured out a tiny gap between the thumb and first finger of his right hand, then burst out laughing for the first and only time, as though he had said something tremendously funny.

Mr. Rideout Jr. then beamed at me condescendingly while he straightened his tie. "I am the general manager of Charles Atlas, Inc., and it is a great pleasure for my company to receive you as an official guest of the US State Department. We will do all we can to make your stay here with us a pleasant one." He again dabbed at his lips with the handkerchief, then launched into a

---

[1] Sound mind in a sound body. — Eds.

longer speech, which gave me the opportunity to observe his aged secretary as
she turned down the Venetian blind on the street window, throwing the room
into semi-darkness. Its whole appearance changed in an instant, and new
objects came to the fore, as if Charles Atlas had suddenly shifted his pose in
the many photographs displayed on the walls.

"I'm delighted that you should have come from so far away to meet
Charles Atlas, and must confess that this is the first time anything of the kind
has happened in the entire history of the company," Mr. Rideout Jr. was saying. "As in any commercial enterprise, we keep to ourselves certain matters
which, should they become public knowledge, would only harm our interests.
For that reason I must ask you to swear a solemn oath of silence concerning
what I am about to tell you."

He repeated the same warning several times, speaking calmly and evenly
now. I swallowed and nodded my agreement.

"Swear out loud," he said.

"I swear," I managed to get out.

Although by now we were completely alone in the room, and the only
sound was the hum of the radiator, Mr. Rideout Jr. looked all around him
before he spoke.

"Charles Atlas doesn't exist," he whispered, leaning over towards me.
Then he dropped back into his seat, and stared at me with a grave expression
on his face. "I know this must come as a great shock to you, but it's the truth.
We invented our product in the last century, and Charles Atlas is a trademark
like any other, like the cod fisherman on the Scott's emulsion box or the clean-
shaven face on Gillette razor-blades. It's simply what we sell."

During our long talks after the English classes back in San Fernando,
Captain Hatfield USMC had often warned me about this kind of situation:
never drop your guard. Be like a boxer—don't be taken by surprise. Stand up
for yourself. Don't let them fool you.

"Very well," I said, rising to my feet, "I shall have to inform Washington
of this."

"What's that?" Mr. Rideout Jr. exclaimed, also getting to his feet.

"Yes, that's right, I'll have to tell Washington about this setback."
(Washington is a magic word, Captain Hatfield USMC had taught me. Use it
when you're in a tight spot, and if by any chance that doesn't work, hit them
with the other, the State Department: that's a knockout.)

"I beg you to believe me. I'm telling you the truth," Mr. Rideout said, but
with a faltering voice.

"I'd like to cable the State Department."

"I swear I'm not lying to you . . ." were his parting words as he backed his
way out of the room, closing a narrow door behind him. I was left all on my
own in the gloom. If I were to believe Captain Hatfield, the trembling in my
legs must be caused by passing underground trains.

It was late afternoon before Mr. Rideout Jr. appeared again. Hammer away, keep hammering at them, I could hear Captain Hatfield USMC advising me.

"I will never believe that Charles Atlas doesn't exist," I said before he had a chance to speak. He crumpled into his chair.

"All right, you win," he conceded, with a wave of his hand. "The firm has agreed for you to meet Mr. Atlas."

I smiled and thanked him with a satisfied nod. Be kind and polite once you know you've won, another of Captain Hatfield USMC's recommendations.

"But you must promise to adhere strictly to the following conditions. The State Department has been consulted, and they have approved the document that you are to sign. You must undertake to leave the country after seeing Mr. Atlas. A passage has been booked for you on the *Vermont,* which sails at midnight. You must also refrain from making any public or private comment on your meeting, and from relating anything that may happen, or your personal impressions, to anyone at all. It is only on these conditions that the board has given its approval."

The aging secretary came in again and handed Mr. Rideout a sheet of paper. He pushed it over to me. "Sign here," he said peremptorily.

Without another word, I signed where he was pointing. Once you've got what you want, sign any damn thing apart from your death sentence: Captain Hatfield USMC.

Mr. Rideout Jr. took the document, folded it carefully, and put it in the middle drawer of the desk. Even as he was doing so, I felt myself being lifted from the chair. I looked round and saw two huge muscle-bound men dressed in black, with identical shaven heads and scowls. No doubt their bodies too had been developed thanks to the rigors of the Dynamic Tension System.

"These gentlemen will go with you. Follow their instructions to the letter." At that, Mr. Rideout Jr. disappeared once more through the narrow door, without so much as a farewell handshake.

The two men, without ever loosening their grip, led me out into a long corridor, which eventually brought us to a wooden staircase. They barked at me to go down first: by the bottom, I was in complete darkness. One of them pushed past me and knocked on a door. It was opened from the far side by a third man who was the mirror image of my two. We stepped out onto a small concrete landing-stage. I couldn't say for certain where we were, because the fog had come swirling down again, but I'm pretty certain it was the river front, for they led me over to a tugboat, which set off at a snail's pace into the mist. The stench from the refuse barges it was pulling reached us even up in the prow.

Night had fallen by the time we disembarked and continued our way on foot along an alley lined with stacks of empty bottle crates. We pushed our way through circles of black children playing marbles by the light of gas lamps and finally emerged into a square where tufts of withered grass alternated with dirty strips of trampled ice left from a snowfall. In front of us were the backs of four or five dark buildings with their tangled web of fire escapes. The hum of distant traffic and the wail of trains miles away came and went on the smoke-filled air.

Renewed pressure on my arms directed me to one side of the square, and we entered the courtyard of a grim edifice that turned out to be a church, whose dank, acrid-smelling walls were covered in bas-reliefs of angels, flowers and saints. By the light of a match that one of my companions struck to find the door knocker, I managed to read the name on a bronze plaque: Abyssinian Baptist Church. As the booming echoes of the knocker faded in the icy night, the door was opened by another guard, also huge, muscle-bound and tough-looking.

We walked up the main nave to the high altar, then I was pushed towards a door on the left. I was filled with sadness and exhaustion. I felt so unsure of what might happen next that I almost regretted having provoked the situation I now found myself in. Again though, Captain Hatfield USMC's voice raised my spirits: once you're on your way, my boy, never look back.

An old woman in a starched white uniform stood waiting for me. My two friends finally let go of me, and positioned themselves on either side of the door. "You've got precisely half an hour," one of them growled. The aged nurse led the way along a dazzlingly white corridor. Ceiling, walls, all the doors we passed, even the floor tiles were white, while the fluorescent strips only added to this pure, empty light.

The old woman hobbled slowly to a double door at the end of the corridor. One side was open, but the view inside was blocked by a folding screen. With a trembling hand she gestured for me to go in, then vanished. I knocked gently three times, but nobody seemed to have heard the timid rap of my knuckles on the blistered layers of paint that had been daubed repeatedly on the door.

My heart was in my mouth as I knocked once more, determined that if there was no answer this time I would turn back. But suddenly a tall, ungainly nurse with thinning, bleached hair who was also dressed in dazzling white appeared from behind the screen. She gave me a broad, relaxed smile that revealed her perfect horse teeth.

"Come in," she said. "Mr. Atlas is expecting you."

The room was bathed in the same artificial whiteness, the same empty light in which millions of tiny dust particles floated. All the objects in the room were white too: the chairs and a medical trolley piled with cotton wool, gauze, bottles and surgical instruments. The walls were bare, apart from a painting that showed the white naked body of a beautiful young woman stretched out on a table while an ancient surgeon held up the heart he had just cut from her. There were bed pans on the floor, and the windows were covered with blinds that during the day must filter out nearly all the light.

At the back of the room on a raised platform was a high, jointed bed with a complicated system of levers and springs. I tiptoed slowly towards it, then stopped halfway, almost overcome by the smell of disinfectant. I looked around for one of the white chairs to sit on, but the nurse, who was already beside the bed, beckoned me, smiling, to come forward.

On the bed lay the unmoving apparition of a giant, muscular body, its head buried somewhere among the pillows. When the nurse leaned over to whisper something, the body stirred with difficulty and came upright. Two of the pillows fell to the floor, but as I started to pick them up, she stopped me with her hand.

"Welcome," said a voice that echoed strangely as though through an antiquated megaphone. It brought a lump to my throat — I wished with all my heart I hadn't started this.

"Thank you, thank you so much for your visit," the voice was now saying. "Believe me, I really appreciate it," the words came bubbling out, as though the voice were drowning in a sea of thick saliva. Then there was silence, and the huge body fell back onto the pillows.

I cannot describe my grief. I would have preferred a thousand times to have believed that Charles Atlas was an invention, that he had never existed, than to have to confront the reality that *this* was he. He spoke from behind a gauze mask, but I glimpsed that a metal plate had been screwed in to replace his lower jaw.

"Cancer of the jaw," he gasped, "spreading now to the vital organs. Until I was 95, I had an iron constitution. Now that I'm over a hundred, I can't complain. I've never smoked, and never drunk more than an occasional glass of champagne at Christmas or New Year. I never had any illness worse than a common cold, and the doctor was always telling me, until just recently, that I could have children if I wanted to. When in 1843 I won the title of the world's most perfectly developed man . . . in Chicago . . . remember . . ." but at this point his voice trailed off in a series of pitiful wheezes, and he remained silent for some time.

"It was 1843 when I discovered the Dynamic Tension System and set up the correspondence courses, on the advice of a sculptress, Miss Ethel Whitney, who I used to pose for as a model."

Then Charles Atlas lifted his enormous arms from under the sheets. He flexed his biceps and cupped his hands behind his head. In doing so he dislodged the bed covers so that I caught sight of his torso, still identical to the photos, apart from the white fuzz on his chest. It must have cost him a great effort, because he began to moan, and the nurse rushed to his side. She pulled the sheets back up, and adjusted the plate on his jaw.

"I was 14 years old when I left Italy with my mother," he went on. "I had no idea then that I was going to make a fortune with my courses. I was born in Calabria in 1827. My real name is Angelo Siciliano; my father had come to New York a year earlier and we followed him. One day when I was at Coney Island with my girl friend, a big bully kicked sand in my face, so I . . ."

"Exactly the same happened to me, that's why . . ." I tried to explain, but he kept on as though he were completely oblivious to my presence.

". . . began to do exercises. My body developed tremendously. One day my girlfriend pointed to a statue of the mythological god Atlas on a hotel roof and said to me: Look, you are just like that statue."

"Listen," I put in, "that statue . . ." It was no use. His voice swept on like a muddy river, brushing aside everything in its path.

"I stared up at the statue and thought to myself: you're not going to get ahead with a name like yours, people here are too prejudiced. Why not call yourself Atlas? And I also changed Angelino for Charles. Then came my days of glory. I can remember when I pulled a railcar full of chorus girls for two hundred yards . . ."

"Good God," I cried out, "exactly the same as . . ." but his voice, precise and eternal, ploughed on.

"Have you seen the statue of Alexander Hamilton outside the Treasury building in Washington? Well, that's me." He again raised his arms and made as though he were hauling a heavy weight, a railcar full of chorus girls perhaps. This time the pain must have been even more intense, because he groaned at length and fell prone on the bed. After a long while, he started to speak again, but by now all I wanted to do was leave.

"I remember Calabria," he said, squirming in the bed. The nurse tried to calm him, then went over to the trolley to make up some drops for him. ". . . Calabria, and my mother singing, her face ruddy from the flames of the oven." He gurgled something I couldn't follow, the sound of his voice echoing through the room in a series of agonised croaks. "A song . . ."

I had lost all notion of what was going on, when suddenly the insistent buzzing of a bell brought me back to myself. It resounded all down the corridors before bouncing back to its point of departure in the room, and I finally realized it came from the nurse tugging at a bell cord above the bed, while Charles Atlas lay sprawled naked on his back on the floor spattered with blood, the metal plate dangling from his jaw.

All at once the room was filled with footsteps, voices, and shadows. I felt myself being lifted bodily from the chair by the same strong arms that had guided me there. In the jumble of images and sounds as I was being dragged from the room I heard the nurse cry out: "My God, the strain was too much for him; he couldn't resist that last pose!" and saw several men lifting the body onto a stretcher and hurrying it out.

Now, in old age as I write these lines, I still find it hard to believe that Charles Atlas isn't alive. I wouldn't have the heart to disillusion all the youngsters who write to him every day asking about his course, still under the spell of his colossal figure, his smiling, confident face, as he holds a trophy or hauls a railcar full of chorus girls, a hundred laughing, crushed girls waving their flowery bonnets through the windows, and in the incredulous crowds thronging the pavements to watch, a hand raises a hat to the sky.

I left New York the same night. I was weighed down with sorrow and remorse, convinced I was guilty in some way, if only of having witnessed such a tragedy. Back in Nicaragua, with Captain Hatfield USMC dead and the war over, I tried my hand at various things: working in a circus, as a weightlifter, then as a bodyguard. My physique isn't what it once was. Thanks to the Dynamic Tension System, though, I could still have children. If I wanted to.

Questions for Discussion

1. In what sense is Captain Hatfield a symbol? Why is he described as "a lean, bent figure"? Why is it significant that he is killed by the Sandinistas just after seeing the narrator off to America?

2. Give examples of how the "wisdom" of Hatfield influences the narrator's choices and behavior. At what point, if at all, does the narrator become disillusioned with Hatfield's beliefs and values?

3. What does the character of Charles Atlas represent in the story? How are Atlas, his values, and his demise paralleled with Captain Hatfield and with the narrator's life story? How does Atlas's Italian immigrant background reflect on the cultural assimilation of the immigrant and on the American dream?

4. Why is Charles Atlas's existence denied by his company? What does the narrator discover about Charles Atlas in his encounter in the hospital room? Discuss the symbolism of the "artificial whiteness, the . . . empty light" of his room, the painting on the wall of a young woman with her heart cut out, and Atlas's illness (cancer of the jaw).

5. Why is it significant that neither Atlas nor the narrator takes advantage of the opportunity to have children provided them by the "dynamic tension system," even though they are both capable?

Ideas for Writing

1. Write an essay in which you examine the story as a contrast between the power, history, and opportunities available in the United States and Nicaragua. How can the story be seen as a critique of American policy in Nicaragua and in Latin America?

2. Charles Atlas is a mythical figure created by the media of advertising and comics. Write an essay in which you analyze the meaning of Charles Atlas, Superman, or another comic book, cartoon, or media-created fictional "myth" figure. What is the source of the character's power? What weaknesses or adversaries does he/she have, and who does the myth figure suppress or defeat in typical episodes?

JAMES ALAN McPHERSON   (b. 1943)

James Alan McPherson, who was raised in Savannah, Georgia, has said that his stable family and diverse cultural experiences as a youth helped him to overcome the racial barriers he faced in his later life. With humor and compassion, McPherson's stories realistically capture the hardships, failures, and occasional successes of his black and white working-class characters. McPherson earned a law degree at Harvard University and later an M.F.A. at the University of Iowa, where since 1981 he has been a professor of creative writing. McPherson's first collection of short stories, *Hue and Cry* (1969), explores characters whose desperate lives are filled with rage. *Elbow-Room* (1977), which includes "A Loaf of Bread," was awarded the Pulitzer prize. McPherson was also awarded a Guggenheim fellowship in 1972 and a MacArthur fellowship in 1981.

Ralph Ellison praised McPherson as an accomplished writer, a full master of "the crafts and forms of fiction." Discussing his writing goals, McPherson has said that he prefers not simply protesting injustice through his stories but rather "defining, affirming the values and cultural institutions of our people."

A Loaf of Bread   (1977)

It was one of those obscene situations, pedestrian to most people, but invested with meaning for a few poor folk whose lives are usually spent outside the imaginations of their fellow citizens. A grocer named Harold Green was caught red-handed selling to one group of people the very same goods he sold at lower prices at similar outlets in better neighborhoods. He had been doing this for many years, and at first he could not understand the outrage heaped upon him. He acted only from habit, he insisted, and had nothing personal against the people whom he served. They were his neighbors. Many of them he had carried on the cuff during hard times. Yet, through some mysterious access to a television station, the poor folk were now empowered to make grand denunciations of the grocer. Green's children now saw their father's business being picketed on the Monday evening news.

No one could question the fact that the grocer had been overcharging the people. On the news even the reporter grimaced distastefully while reading the statistics. His expression said, "It is my job to report the news, but sometimes even I must disassociate myself from it to protect my honor." This, at least, was the impression the grocer's children seemed to bring away from the television. Their father's name had not been mentioned, but there was a close-up of his store with angry black people and a few outraged whites marching in groups of three in front of it. There was also a close-up of his name. After seeing this, they were in no mood to watch cartoons. At the dinner table, disturbed by his children's silence, Harold Green felt compelled to say, "I am not a dishonest man." Then he felt ashamed. The children, a boy and his older sister, immediately left the table, leaving Green alone with his wife. "Ruth, I am not dishonest," he repeated to her.

Ruth Green did not say anything. She knew, and her husband did not, that the outraged people had also picketed the school attended by their children. They had threatened to return each day until Green lowered his prices. When they called her at home to report this, she had promised she would talk with him. Since she could not tell him this, she waited for an opening. She looked at her husband across the table.

"I did not make the world," Green began, recognizing at once the seriousness in her stare. "My father came to this country with nothing but his shirt. He was exploited for as long as he couldn't help himself. He did not protest or picket. He put himself in a position to play by the rules he had learned." He waited for his wife to answer, and when she did not, he tried again. "I did not make this world," he repeated. "I only make my way in it. Such people as these, they do not know enough to not be exploited. If not me, there would be a Greek, a Chinaman, maybe an Arab or a smart one of their own kind. Believe me, I deal with them. There is something in their style that lacks the patience to run a concern such as mine. If I closed down, take my word on it, someone else would do what has to be done."

But Ruth Green was not thinking of his leaving. Her mind was on other matters. Her children had cried when they came home early from school. She had no special feeling for the people who picketed, but she did not like to see her children cry. She had kissed them generously, then sworn them to silence. "One day this week," she told her husband, "you will give free, for eight hours, anything your customers come in to buy. There will be no publicity, except what they spread by word of mouth. No matter what they say to you, no matter what they take, you will remain silent." She stared deeply into him for what she knew was there. "If you refuse, you have seen the last of your children and myself."

Her husband grunted. Then he leaned toward her. "I will not knuckle under," he said. "I will *not* give!"

"We shall see," his wife told him.

The black pickets, for the most part, had at first been frightened by the audacity of their undertaking. They were peasants whose minds had long before become resigned to their fate as victims. None of them, before now, had thought to challenge this. But now, when they watched themselves on television, they hardly recognized the faces they saw beneath the hoisted banners and placards. Instead of reflecting the meekness they all felt, the faces looked angry. The close-ups looked especially intimidating. Several of the first pickets, maids who worked in the suburbs, reported that their employers, seeing the activity on the afternoon news, had begun treating them with new respect. One woman, midway through the weather report, called around the neighborhood to disclose that her employer had that very day given her a new china plate for her meals. The paper plates, on which all previous meals had been served, had been thrown into the wastebasket. One recipient of this call, a middle-aged woman known for her bashfulness and humility, rejoined that her husband, a sheet-metal worker, had only a few hours before been called "Mister" by his supervisor, a white man with a passionate hatred of color. She added the tale of a neighbor down the street, a widow woman named Murphy, who had at first been reluctant to join the picket; this woman now was insisting it should be made a daily event. Such talk as this circulated among the people who had been instrumental in raising the issue. As news of their victory leaked into the ears of others who had not participated, they received all through the night calls from strangers requesting verification, offering advice, and vowing support. Such strangers listened and then volunteered stories about indignities inflicted on them by city officials, policemen, other grocers. In this way, over a period of hours, the community became even more incensed and restless than it had been at the time of the initial picket.

Soon the man who had set events in motion found himself a hero. His name was Nelson Reed, and all his adult life he had been employed as an assembly-line worker. He was a steady husband, the father of three children, and a deacon in the Baptist church. All his life he had trusted in God and gotten along. But now something in him capitulated to the reality that came suddenly into focus. "I was wrong," he told people who called him. "The onliest thing that matters in this world is *money*. And when was the last time you seen a picture of Jesus on a dollar bill?" This line, which he repeated over and over, caused a few callers to laugh nervously, but not without some affirmation that this was indeed the way things were. Many said they had known it all along. Others argued that although it was certainly true, it was one thing to live without money and quite another to live without faith. But still most callers laughed and said, "You right. You *know* I know you right. Ain't it the truth, though?" Only a few people, among them Nelson Reed's wife, said nothing and looked very sad.

Why they looked sad, however, they would not communicate. And anyone observing their troubled faces would have to trust his own intuition. It is known that Reed's wife, Betty, measured all events against the fullness of her own experience. She was skeptical of everything. Brought to the church after a number of years of living openly with a jazz musician, she had embraced religion when she married Nelson Reed. But though she no longer believed completely in the world, she nonetheless had not fully embraced God. There was something in the nature of Christ's swift rise that had always bothered her, and something in the blood and vengeance of the Old Testament that was mellowing and refreshing. But she had never communicated these thoughts to anyone, especially her husband. Instead, she smiled vacantly while others professed leaps of faith, remained silent when friends spoke fiercely of their convictions. The presence of this vacuum in her contributed to her personal mystery; people said she was beautiful, although she was not outwardly so. Perhaps it was because she wished to protect this inner beauty that she did not smile now, and looked extremely sad, listening to her husband on the telephone.

Nelson Reed had no reason to be sad. He seemed to grow more energized and talkative as the days passed. He was invited by an alderman, on the Tuesday after the initial picket, to tell his story on a local television talk show. He sweated heavily under the hot white lights and attempted to be philosophical. "I notice," the host said to him, "that you are not angry at this exploitative treatment. What, Mr. Reed, is the source of your calm?" The assembly-line worker looked unabashedly into the camera and said, "I have always believed in *Justice* with a capital *J*. I was raised up from a baby believin' that God ain't gonna let nobody go *too* far. See, in *my* mind God is in charge of *all* the capital letters in the alphabet of this world. It say in the Scripture He is Alpha and Omega, the first and the last. He is just about the *onliest* capitalizer they is." Both Reed and the alderman laughed. "Now, when *men* start to capitalize, they gets *greedy*. They put a little *j* in *joy* and a littler one in *justice*. They raise up a big *G* in *Greed* and a big *E* in *Evil*. Well, soon as they commence to put a little *g* in *god*, you can expect some kind of reaction. The Savior will just raise up the *H* in *Hell* and go on from there. And that's just what I'm doin', giving these sharpies *HELL* with a big *H*." The talk show host laughed along with Nelson Reed and the alderman. After the taping they drank coffee in the back room of the studio and talked about the sad shape of the world.

Three days before he was to comply with his wife's request, Green, the grocer, saw this talk show on television while at home. The words of Nelson Reed sent a chill through him. Though Reed had attempted to be philosophical, Green did not perceive the statement in this light. Instead, he saw a vindictive-looking black man seated between an ambitious alderman and a smug talk show host. He saw them chatting comfortably about the nature of evil. The cameraman had shot mostly close-ups, and Green could see the set in Nelson Reed's jaw. The color of Reed's face was maddening. When his children came into the den, the grocer was in a sweat. Before he could think, he had shouted at them and struck the button turning off the set. The two children rushed from the room screaming. Ruth Green ran in from the kitchen. She knew why he was upset because she had received a call about the show, but she said nothing and pretended ignorance. Her children's school had been picketed that day, as it had the day before. But both children were still forbidden to speak of this to their father.

"Where do they get so much power?" Green said to his wife. "Two days ago nobody would have cared. Now everywhere, even in my home, I am condemned as a rascal. And what do I own? An airline? A multinational? Half of South America? *No!* I own three stores, one of which happens to be in a certain neighborhood inhabited by people who cost me money to run it." He sighed and sat upright on the sofa, his chubby legs spread wide. "A cabdriver has a meter that clicks as he goes along. I pay extra for insurance, iron bars, pilfering by customers and employees. Nothing clicks. But when I add a little overhead to my prices, suddenly everything clicks. But for someone else. When was there last such a world?" He pressed the palms of both hands to his temples, suggesting a bombardment of brain-stinging sounds.

This gesture evoked no response from Ruth Green. She remained standing by the door, looking steadily at him. She said, "To protect yourself, I would not stock any more fresh cuts of meat in the store until after the giveaway on Saturday. Also, I would not tell it to the employees until after the first customer of the day has begun to check out. But I would urge you to hire several security guards to close the door promptly at seven-thirty, as is usual." She wanted to say much more than this, but did not. Instead she watched him. He was looking at the blank gray television screen, his palms still pressed against his ears. "In case you need to hear again," she continued in a weighty tone of voice, "I said two days ago, and I say again now, that if you fail to do this you will not see your children again for many years."

He twisted his head and looked up at her. "What is the color of these people?" he asked.

"Black," his wife said.

"And what is the name of my children?"

"Green."

The grocer smiled. "There is your answer," he told his wife. "Green is the only color I am interested in."

His wife did not smile. "Insufficient," she said.

"The world is mad!" he moaned. "But it is a point of sanity with me to not bend. I will not bend." He crossed his legs and pressed one hand firmly atop his knee. *"I will not bend,"* he said.

"We will see," his wife said.

Nelson Reed, after the television interview, became the acknowledged leader of the disgruntled neighbors. At first a number of them met in the kitchen at his house; then, as space was lacking for curious newcomers, a mass meeting was held on Thursday in an abandoned theater. His wife and three children sat in the front row. Behind them sat the widow Murphy, Lloyd Dukes, Tyrone Brown, Les Jones — those who had joined him on the first picket line. Behind these sat people who bought occasionally at the store, people who lived on the fringes of the neighborhood, people from other neighborhoods come to investigate the problem, and the merely curious. The middle rows were occupied by a few people from the suburbs, those who had seen the talk show and whose outrage at the grocer proved much more powerful than their fear of black people. In the rear of the theater crowded aging, old-style leftists, somber students, cynical young black men with angry grudges to explain with inarticulate gestures. Leaning against the walls, huddled near the doors at the rear, tape-recorder-bearing social scientists looked as detached and serene as bookies at the track. Here and there, in this diverse crowd, a politician stationed himself, pumping hands vigorously and pressing his palms gently against the shoulders of elderly people. Other visitors passed out leaflets, buttons, glossy color prints of men who promoted causes, the familiar and obscure. There was a hubbub of voices, a blend of the strident and the playful, the outraged and the reverent, lending an undercurrent of ominous energy to the assembly.

Nelson Reed spoke from a platform on the stage, standing before a yellowed, shredded screen that had once reflected the images of matinee idols. "I don't mind sayin' that I have always been a sucker," he told the crowd. "All my life I have been a sucker for the words of Jesus. Being a natural-born fool, I just ain't never had the *sense* to learn no better. Even right today, while the whole world is sayin' wrong is right and up is down, I'm so dumb I'm *still* steady believin' what is wrote in the Good Book. . . ."

From the audience, especially the front rows, came a chorus singing, "Preach!"

"I have no doubt," he continued in a low baritone, "that it's true what is writ in the Good Book: 'The last shall be first and the first shall be last.' I don't know about y'all, but I have *always* been the last. I never wanted to be the first, but sometimes it look like the world get so bad that them that's holdin' onto the tree of life is the onliest ones left when God commence to blowin' dead leafs off the branches."

"Now you preaching," someone called.

In the rear of the theater a white student shouted an awkward "Amen."

Nelson Reed began walking across the stage to occupy the major part of his nervous energy. But to those in the audience, who now hung on his every word, it looked as though he strutted. "All my life," he said, "I have claimed to be a man without earnin' the right to call myself that. You know, the *average* man ain't really a man. The average man is a *bootlicker.* In fact, the *average* man would *run away* if he found hisself standing alone facin' down a adversary. I have done that *too many a time* in my life! But *not no more.* Better to be *once* was than *never* was a man. I will tell you tonight, there is somethin' *wrong* in being average. *I intend to stand up!* Now, if your average man that ain't really a man stand up, two things gonna happen: *one,* he gon bust through all the weights that been place on his head, and, *two,* he gon feel a lot of pain. But that same hurt is what make things fall in place. That, and gettin' your hands on one of these slick four-flushers tight enough so's you can squeeze him and say, *'No more!'* You do that, you g'on hurt some, but *you won't be average no more.* . . ."

"No *more!*" a few people in the front rows repeated.

"I say *no more!*" Nelson Reed shouted.

"No more! No more! No more!" The chant rustled through the crowd like the rhythm of an autumn wind against a shedding tree.

Then people laughed and chattered in celebration.

As for the grocer, from the evening of the television interview he had begun to make plans. Unknown to his wife, he cloistered himself several times with his brother-in-law, an insurance salesman, and plotted a course. He had no intention of tossing steaks to the crowd. "And why should I, Tommy?" he asked his wife's brother, a lean, bald-headed man named Thomas. "I don't cheat anyone. I have never cheated anyone. The businesses I run are always on the up-and-up. So why should I pay?"

"Quite so," the brother-in-law said, chewing an unlit cigarillo. "The world has gone crazy. Next they will say that people in my business are responsible for prolonging life. I have found that people who refuse to believe in death refuse also to believe in the harshness of life. I sell well by saying that death is a long happiness. I show people the realities of life and compare this to a funeral with dignity, *and* the promise of a bundle for every loved one salted away. When they look around hard at life, they usually buy."

"So?" asked Green. Thomas was a college graduate with a penchant for philosophy.

"So," Thomas answered. "You must fight to show these people the reality of both your situation and theirs. How would it be if you visited one of their meetings and chalked out, on a blackboard, the dollars and cents of your operation? Explain your overhead, your security fees, all the additional expenses. If you treat them with respect, they might understand."

Green frowned. "That I would never do," he said. "It would be admission of a certain guilt."

The brother-in-law smiled, but only with one corner of his mouth. "Then you have something to feel guilty about?" he asked.

The grocer frowned at him. *"Nothing!"* he said with great emphasis.

"So?" Thomas said.

This first meeting between the grocer and his brother-in-law took place on Thursday, in a crowded barroom.

At the second meeting, in a luncheonette, it was agreed that the grocer should speak privately with the leader of the group, Nelson Reed. The meeting at which this was agreed took place on Friday afternoon. After accepting this advice from Thomas, the grocer resigned himself to explain to Reed, in as finite detail as possible, the economic structure of his operation. He vowed to suppress no information. He would explain everything: inventories, markups, sale items, inflation, balance sheets, specialty items, overhead, and that mysterious item called profit. This last item, promising to be the most difficult to explain, Green and his brother-in-law debated over for several hours. They agreed first of all that a man should not work for free, then they agreed that it was unethical to ruthlessly exploit. From these parameters, they staked out an area between fifteen and forty percent, and agreed that someplace between these two borders lay an amount of return that could be called fair. This was easy, but then Thomas introduced the factor of circumstance. He questioned whether the fact that one serviced a risky area justified the earning of profits, closer to the forty-percent edge of the scale. Green was unsure. Thomas smiled. "Here is a case that will point out an analogy," he said, licking a cigarillo. "I read in the papers that a family wants to sell an electric stove. I call the home and the man says fifty dollars. I ask to come out and inspect the merchandise. When I arrive I see they are poor, have already bought a new stove that is connected, and are selling the old one for fifty dollars because they want it out of the place. The electric stove is in good condition, worth much more than fifty. But because I see what I see I offer forty-five."

Green, for some reason, wrote down this figure on the back of the sales slip for the coffee they were drinking.

The brother-in-law smiled. He chewed his cigarillo. "The man agrees to take forty-five dollars, saying he has had no other calls. I look at the stove again and see a spot of rust. I say I will give him forty dollars. He agrees to this, on condition that I myself haul it away. I say I will haul it away if he comes down to thirty. You, of course, see where I am going."

The grocer nodded. "The circumstances of his situation, his need to get rid of the stove quickly, placed him in a position where he has little room to bargain?"

"Yes," Thomas answered. "So? Is it ethical, Harry?"

Harold Green frowned. He had never liked his brother-in-law, and now he thought the insurance agent was being crafty. "But," he answered, "this man does not *have* to sell! It is his choice whether to wait for other calls. It is not the fault of the buyer that the seller is in a hurry. It is the right of the buyer to get what he wants at the lowest price possible. That is the rule. That has *always* been the rule. And the reverse of it applies to the seller as well."

"Yes," Thomas said, sipping coffee from the Styrofoam cup. "But suppose that in addition to his hurry to sell, the owner was also of a weak soul. There are, after all, many such people." He smiled. "Suppose he placed no value on the money?"

"Then," Green answered, "your example is academic. Here we are not talking about real life. One man lives by the code, one man does not. Who is there free enough to make a judgment?" He laughed. "Now you see," he told his brother-in-law. "Much more than a few dollars are at stake. If this one buyer is to be condemned, then so are most people in the history of the world. An examination of history provides the only answer to your question. This code will be here tomorrow, long after the ones who do not honor it are not."

They argued fiercely late into the afternoon, the brother-in-law leaning heavily on his readings. When they parted, a little before five o'clock, nothing had been resolved.

Neither was much resolved during the meeting between Green and Nelson Reed. Reached at home by the grocer in the early evening, the leader of the group spoke coldly at first, but consented finally to meet his adversary at a nearby drugstore for coffee and a talk. They met at the lunch counter, shook hands awkwardly, and sat for a few minutes discussing the weather. Then the grocer pulled two gray ledgers from his briefcase. "You have for years come into my place," he told the man. "In my memory I have always treated you well. Now our relationship has come to this." He slid the books along the counter until they touched Nelson Reed's arm.

Reed opened the top book and flipped the thick green pages with his thumb. He did not examine the figures. "All I know," he said, "is over at your place a can of soup cost me fifty-five cents, and two miles away at your other store for white folks you chargin' thirty-nine cents." He said this with the calm authority of an outraged soul. A quality of condescension tinged with pity crept into his gaze.

The grocer drummed his fingers on the counter top. He twisted his head and looked away, toward shelves containing cosmetics, laxatives, toothpaste. His eyes lingered on a poster of a woman's apple-red lips and milk-white teeth. The rest of the face was missing.

"Ain't no use to hide," Nelson Reed said, as to a child. "I know you wrong, you know you wrong, and before I finish, *everybody in this city* g'on know you wrong. God don't *like* ugly." He closed his eyes and gripped the cup of coffee. Then he swung his head suddenly and faced the grocer again. "Man, why you want to *do* people that way?" he asked. "We human, same as you."

"Before *God!*" Green exclaimed, looking squarely into the face of Nelson Reed. "Before God!" he said again. "*I am not an evil man!*" These last words sounded more like a moan as he tightened the muscles in his throat to lower the sound of his voice. He tossed his left shoulder as if adjusting the sleeve of his coat, or as if throwing off some unwanted weight. Then he peered along the counter top. No one was watching. At the end of the counter the waitress was scrubbing the coffee urn. "Look at these figures, please," he said to Reed.

The man did not drop his gaze. His eyes remained fixed on the grocer's face.

"All right," Green said. "Don't look. I'll tell you what is in these books, believe me if you want. I work twelve hours a day, one day off per week, running my business in three stores. I am not a wealthy person. In one place, in the area you call white, I get by barely by smiling lustily at old ladies, stocking gourmet stuff on the chance I will build a reputation as a quality store. The two clerks there cheat me; there is nothing I can do. In this business you must be friendly with everybody. The second place is on the other side of town, in a neighborhood as poor as this one. I get out there seldom. The profits are not worth the gas. I use the loss there as a write-off against some other properties," he paused. "Do you understand write-off?" he asked Nelson Reed.

"Naw," the man said.

Harold Green laughed. "What does it matter?" he said in a tone of voice intended for himself alone. "In this area I will admit I make a profit, but it is not so much as you think. But I do not make a profit here because the people are black. I make a profit because a profit is here to be made. I invest more here in window bars, theft losses, insurance, spoilage; I deserve to make more here than at the other places." He looked, almost imploringly, at the man seated next to him. "You don't accept this as the right of a man in business?"

Reed grunted. "Did the bear shit in the woods?" he said.

Again Green laughed. He gulped his coffee awkwardly, as if eager to go. Yet his motions slowed once he had set his coffee cup down on the blue plastic saucer. "Place yourself in *my* situation," he said, his voice high and tentative. "If *you* were running my store in this neighborhood, what would be *your* position? Say on a profit scale of fifteen to forty percent, at what point in between would you draw the line?"

Nelson Reed thought. He sipped his coffee and seemed to chew the liquid. "Fifteen to forty?" he repeated.

"Yes."

"I'm a churchgoin' man," he said. "Closer to fifteen than to forty."

"How close?"

Nelson Reed thought. "In church you tithe ten percent."

"In restaurants you tip fifteen," the grocer said quickly.

"All right," Reed said. "Over fifteen."

"How much over?"

Nelson Reed thought.

"Twenty, thirty, thirty-five?" Green chanted, leaning closer to Reed.

Still the man thought.

"Forty? Maybe even forty-five or fifty?" the grocer breathed in Reed's ear. "In the supermarkets, you know, they have more subtle ways of accomplishing such feats."

Reed slapped his coffee cup with the back of his right hand. The brown liquid swirled across the counter top, wetting the books. *"Damn this!"* he shouted.

Startled, Green rose from his stool.

Nelson Reed was trembling. "I ain't *you*," he said in a deep baritone. "I ain't the *supermarket* neither. All I is is a poor man that works *too* hard to see his pay slip through his fingers like rainwater. All I know is you done *cheat* me, you done *cheat* everybody in the neighborhood, and we organized now to get some of it *back!*" Then he stood and faced the grocer. "My daddy sharecropped down in Mississippi and bought in the company store. He owed them twenty-three years when he died. I paid off five of them years and then run away to up here. Now, I'm a deacon in the Baptist church. I raised my kids the way my daddy raise me and don't bother nobody. Now come to find out, after all my runnin', they done lift that *same company store* up out of Mississippi and slip it down on us here! Well, my daddy was a *fighter,* and if he hadn't owed all them years he would of raise him some hell. Me, I'm steady my daddy's child, plus I got seniority in my union. I'm a free man. Buddy, don't you know *I'm gonna raise me some hell!*"

Harold Green reached for a paper napkin to sop the coffee soaking into his books.

Nelson Reed threw a dollar on top of the books and walked away.

"I *will not* do it!" Harold Green said to his wife that same evening. They were in the bathroom of their home. Bending over the face bowl, she was washing her hair with a towel draped around her neck. The grocer stood by the door, looking in at her. "I will not bankrupt myself tomorrow," he said.

"I've been thinking about it, too," Ruth Green said, shaking her wet hair. "You'll do it, Harry."

"Why should I?" he asked. "You won't leave. You know it was a bluff. I've waited this long for you to calm down. Tomorrow is Saturday. This week has been a hard one. Tonight let's be realistic."

"Of course you'll do it," Ruth Green said. She said it the way she would say "Have some toast." She said, "You'll do it because you want to see your children grow up."

"And for what other reason?" he asked.

She pulled the towel tighter around her neck. "Because you are at heart a moral man."

He grinned painfully. "If I am, why should I have to prove it to *them?*"

"Not them," Ruth Green said, freezing her movements and looking in the mirror. "Certainly not them. By no means them. They have absolutely nothing to do with this."

"Who, then?" he asked, moving from the door into the room. "Who else should I prove something to?"

His wife was crying. But her entire face was wet. The tears moved secretly down her face.

"Who else?" Harold Green asked.

It was almost eleven P.M. and the children were in bed. They had also cried when they came home from school. Ruth Green said, "For yourself, Harry. For the love that lives inside your heart."

All night the grocer thought about this.

Nelson Reed also slept little that Friday night. When he returned home from the drugstore, he reported to his wife as much of the conversation as he could remember. At first he had joked about the exchange between himself and the grocer, but as more details returned to his conscious mind he grew solemn and then bitter. "He ask me to put myself in *his* place," Reed told his wife. "Can you imagine that kind of gumption? I never cheated nobody in my life. All my life I have lived on Bible principles. I am a deacon in the church. I have work all my life for other folks and I don't even own the house I live in." He paced up and down the kitchen, his big arms flapping loosely at his sides. Betty Reed sat at the table, watching. "This here's a low-down, ass-kicking world," he said. "I swear to God it is! All my life I have lived on principle and I ain't got a dime in the bank. Betty," he turned suddenly toward her, "don't you think I'm a fool?"

"Mr. Reed," she said. "Let's go on to bed."

But he would not go to bed. Instead, he took the fifth of bourbon from the cabinet under the sink and poured himself a shot. His wife refused to join him. Reed drained the glass of whiskey, and then another, while he resumed pacing the kitchen floor. He slapped his hands against his sides. "I think I'm a fool," he said. "Ain't got a dime in the bank, ain't got a pot to *pee* in or a wall to pitch it over, and that there *cheat* ask me to put myself inside *his* shoes. Hell, I can't even *afford* the kind of shoes he wears." He stopped pacing and looked at his wife.

"Mr. Reed," she whispered, "tomorrow ain't a work day. Let's go to bed."

Nelson Reed laughed, the bitterness in his voice rattling his wife. "The *hell* I will!" he said.

He strode to the yellow telephone on the wall beside the sink and began to dial. The first call was to Lloyd Dukes, a neighbor two blocks away and a lieutenant in the organization. Dukes was not at home. The second call was to McElroy's Bar on the corner of Sixty-fifth and Carroll, where Stanley Harper, another of the lieutenants, worked as a bartender. It was Harper who spread the word, among those men at the bar, that the organization would picket the grocer's store the following morning. And all through the night, in the bedroom of their house, Betty Reed was awakened by telephone calls coming from Lester Jones, Nat Lucas, Mrs. Tyrone Brown, the widow-woman named Murphy, all coordinating the time when they would march in a group against the store owned by Harold Green. Betty Reed's heart beat loudly beneath the covers as she listened to the bitterness and rage in her husband's voice. On several occasions, hearing him declare himself a fool, she pressed the pillow against her eyes and cried.

The grocer opened later than usual this Saturday morning, but still it was early enough to make him one of the first walkers in the neighborhood. He parked his car one block from the store and strolled to work. There were no birds singing. The sky in this area was not blue. It was smog-smutted and gray, seeming on the verge of a light rain. The street, as always, was littered with cans, papers, bits of broken glass. As always the garbage cans overflowed. The morning breeze plastered a sheet of newspaper playfully around the sides of a rusted garbage can. For some reason, using his right foot, he loosened the paper and stood watching it slide into the street and down the block. The movement made him feel good. He whistled while unlocking the bars shielding the windows and door of his store. When he had unlocked the main door he stepped in quickly and threw a switch to the right of the jamb, before the shrill sound of the alarm could shatter his mood. Then he switched on the lights. Everything was as it had been the night before. He had already tele-phoned his two employees and given them the day off. He busied himself doing the usual things—hauling milk and vegetables from the cooler, putting cash in the till—not thinking about the silence of his wife, or the look in her eyes, only an hour before when he left home. He had determined, at some point while driving through the city, that today it would be business as usual. But he expected very few customers.

The first customer of the day was Mrs. Nelson Reed. She came in around nine-thirty A.M. and wandered about the store. He watched her from the checkout counter. She seemed uncertain of what she wanted to buy. She kept glancing at him down the center aisle. His suspicions aroused, he said finally, "Yes, may I help you, Mrs. Reed?" His words caused her to jerk, as if some devious thought had been perceived going through her mind. She reached over quickly and lifted a loaf of whole wheat bread from the rack and walked with it to the counter. She looked at him and smiled. The smile was a broad, shy one, that rare kind of smile one sees on virgin girls when they first con-fess love to themselves. Betty Reed was a woman of about forty-five. For some reason he could not comprehend, this gesture touched him. When she pulled a dollar from her purse and laid it on the counter, an impulse, from no place he could locate with his mind, seized control of his tongue. "Free," he told Betty Reed. She paused, then pushed the dollar toward him with a firm and determined thrust of her arm. "Free," he heard himself saying strongly, his right palm spread and meeting her thrust with absolute force. She clutched the loaf of bread and walked out of his store.

The next customer, a little girl, arriving well after ten-thirty A.M., selected a candy bar from the rack beside the counter. "Free," Green said cheerfully. The little girl left the candy on the counter and ran out of the store.

At eleven-fifteen A.M. a wino came in looking desperate enough to sell his soul. The grocer watched him only for an instant. Then he went to the wine counter and selected a half-gallon of medium-grade red wine. He shoved the jug into the belly of the wino, the man's sour breath bathing his face. "Free," the grocer said. "But you must not drink it in here."

He felt good about the entire world, watching the wino through the win-dow gulping the wine and looking guiltily around.

At eleven twenty-five A.M. the pickets arrived.

Two dozen people, men and women, young and old, crowded the pave-ment in front of his store. Their signs, placards, and voices denounced him as a parasite. The grocer laughed inside himself. He felt lighthearted and wild, like a man drugged. He rushed to the meat counter and pulled a long roll of brown wrapping paper from the rack, tearing it neatly with a quick shift of his body resembling a dance step practiced fervently in his youth. He laid the paper on the chopping block and with the black-inked, felt-tipped marker scrawled, in giant letters, the word FREE. This he took to the window and pasted in place with many strands of Scotch tape. He was laughing wildly.

"Free!" he shouted from behind the brown paper. "Free! Free! Free! Free! Free! Free!" He rushed to the door, pushed his head out, and screamed to the confused crowd, *"Free!"* Then he ran back to the counter and stood behind it, like a soldier at attention.

They came in slowly.

Nelson Reed entered first, working his right foot across the dirty tile as if tracking a squiggling worm. The others followed: Lloyd Dukes dragging a placard, Mr. and Mrs. Tyrone Brown, Stanley Harper walking with his fists clenched, Lester Jones with three of his children, Nat Lucas looking sheepish and detached, a clutch of winos, several bashful nuns, ironic-smiling teenagers and a few students. Bringing up the rear was a bearded social scientist holding a tape recorder to his chest. "Free!" the grocer screamed. He threw up his arms in a gesture that embraced, or dismissed, the entire store. *"All free!"* he shouted. He was grinning with the grace of a madman.

The winos began grabbing first. They stripped the shelf of wine in a matter of seconds. Then they fled, dropping bottles on the tile in their wake. The others, stepping quickly through this liquid, soon congealed it into a sticky, bloodlike consistency. The young men went for the cigarettes and luncheon meat and beer. One of them had the prescience to grab a sack from the counter, while the others loaded their arms swiftly, hugging cartons and packages of cold cuts like long-lost friends. The students joined them, less for greed than for the thrill of the experience. The two nuns backed toward the door. As for the older people, men and women, they stood at first as if stuck to the wine-smeared floor. Then Stanley Harper, the bartender, shouted, "The man said *free,* y'all heard him." He paused. "Didn't you say *free* now?" he called to the grocer.

"I said free," Harold Green answered, his temples pounding.

A cheer went up. The older people began grabbing, as if the secret lusts of a lifetime had suddenly seized command of their arms and eyes. They grabbed toilet tissue, cold cuts, pickles, sardines, boxes of raisins, boxes of starch, cans of soup, tins of tuna fish and salmon, bottles of spices, cans of boned chicken, slippery cans of olive oil. Here a man, Lester Jones, burdened himself with several heads of lettuce, while his wife, in another aisle, shouted for him to drop those small items and concentrate on the gourmet section. She herself took imported sardines, wheat crackers, bottles of candied pickles, herring, anchovies, imported olives, French wafers, an ancient, half-rusted can of paté, stocked, by mistake, from the inventory of another store. Others packed their arms with detergents, hams, chocolate-coated cereal, whole chickens with hanging asses, wedges of bologna and salami like squashed footballs, chunks of cheeses, yellow and white, shriveled onions, and green peppers. Mrs. Tyrone Brown hung a curve of pepperoni around her neck and seemed to take on instant dignity, much like a person of noble birth in possession now of a long sought-after gem. Another woman, the widow Murphy, stuffed tomatoes into her bosom, holding a half-chewed lemon in her mouth. The more enterprising fought desperately over the three rusted shopping carts, and the victors wheeled these along the narrow aisles, sweeping into them bulk items — beer in six-packs, sacks of sugar, flour, glass bottles of syrup, toilet cleanser, sugar cookies, prune, apple and tomato juices — while others endeavored to snatch the carts from them. There were several fistfights and much cursing. The grocer, standing behind the counter, hummed and rang his cash register like a madman.

Nelson Reed, the first into the store, followed the nuns out, empty-handed.

In less than half an hour the others had stripped the store and vanished in many directions up and down the block. But still more people came, those late in hearing the news. And when they saw the shelves were bare, they cursed soberly and chased those few stragglers still bearing away goods. Soon only the grocer and the social scientist remained, the latter stationed at the door with his tape recorder sucking in leftover sounds. Then he, too, slipped away up the block.

By twelve-ten P.M. the grocer was leaning against the counter, trying to make his mind slow down. Not a man given to drink during work hours, he nonetheless took a swallow from a bottle of wine, a dusty bottle from beneath the wine shelf, somehow overlooked by the winos. Somewhat recovered, he was preparing to remember what he should do next when he glanced toward a figure at the door. Nelson Reed was standing there, watching him.

"All gone," Harold Green said. "My friend, Mr. Reed, there is no more." Still the man stood in the doorway, peering into the store.

The grocer waved his arms about the empty room. Not a display case had a single item standing. "All gone," he said again, as if addressing a stupid child. "There is nothing left to get. You, my friend, have come back too late for a second load. I am cleaned out."

Nelson Reed stepped into the store and strode toward the counter. He moved through wine-stained flour, lettuce leaves, red, green, and blue labels, bits and pieces of broken glass. He walked toward the counter.

"All day," the grocer laughed, not quite hysterically now, "all day long I have not made a single cent of profit. The entire day was a loss. This store, like the others, is *bleeding* me." He waved his arms about the room in a magnificent gesture of uncaring loss. "Now do you understand?" he said. "Now will you put yourself in my shoes? I have nothing here. Come, now, Mr. Reed would it not be so bad a thing to walk in my shoes?"

"Mr. Green," Nelson Reed said coldly. "My wife bought a loaf of bread in here this mornin'. She forgot to pay you. I, myself, have come here to pay you your money."

"Oh," the grocer said.

"I think it was brown bread. Don't that cost more than white?"

The two men looked away from each other, but not at anything in the store.

"In my store, yes," Harold Green said. He rang the register with the most casual movement of his finger. The register read fifty-five cents.

Nelson Reed held out a dollar.

"And two cents tax," the grocer said.

The man held out the dollar.

"After all," Harold Green said. "We are all, after all, Mr. Reed, in debt to the government."

He rang the register again. It read fifty-seven cents.

Nelson Reed held out a dollar.

Questions for Discussion

1. How does Green defend the unequal prices he charges at his stores in different communities? Do his ideas on pricing seem fair and reasonable?

2. Compare and contrast Betty Reed and Ruth Green. What critical attitude does each have about her husband's role in the economic struggle over Green's prices?

3. Analyze the scene between Green and his brother-in-law. Why doesn't the brother-in-law's advice and the examples he provides help Green to solve his problem? Why does Reed reject Green's economic philosophy?

4. Why does Ruth Green insist that her husband give away free food? Are her motivations any more altruistic than his? Do you think he really understands why it is important to create the "give-away"?

5. With whose point of view are you more sympathetic? Does the story present a realistic solution to the problem?

Ideas for Writing

1. Write an essay that explores what the story implies about the possibility for change and understanding across classes and races. Have Green and Reed been changed as they have worked to solve the problems caused by Green's prices? Do they understand each other better at the end of the story?

2. Write a sequel to the story in which you imagine what will happen to Green's business and community relations in a year or so. How has his give-away helped or harmed the community and his position within it?

ALICE WALKER   (b. 1944)

Most widely known as the author of the Pulitzer prize–winning novel *The Color Purple* (1982), Alice Walker was born in Eatonton, Georgia, the eighth child in a family of sharecroppers dominated by her older brothers. Walker earned a B.A. from Sarah Lawrence College in 1965, then became involved in the civil rights movement in Mississippi and taught at a number of colleges, including Wellesley College, Yale University, and the University of California at Berkeley. Her other novels include *Meridian* (1976) and *The Temple of My Familiar* (1989); her essay collections include *In Search of Our Mothers' Gardens* (1983) and *Warrior Masks* (1993). Her stories are collected in *In Love and Trouble* (1973), which includes "Roselily"; *You Can't Keep a Good Woman Down* (1981); and *The Complete Stories of Alice Walker* (1994). She has also written several volumes of poetry and edited an anthology of the writings of Zora Neale Hurston.

Walker's writings often cast a critical eye on oppressive institutions of race, class, and gender and on contemporary lack of respect for the natural environment. All the while, however, Walker affirms the creative spirit and kinship of women of color around the world. She believes that writing is a healing act: "I think if you write long enough, you will become a healthy person."

Roselily   (1973)

Dearly Beloved

She dreams; dragging herself across the world. A small girl in her mother's white robe and veil, knee raised waist high through a bowl of quicksand soup. The man who stands beside her is against this standing on the front porch of her house, being married to the sound of cars whizzing by on highway 61.

we are gathered here

Like cotton to be weighed. Her fingers at the last minute busily removing dry leaves and twigs. Aware it is a superficial sweep. She knows he blames Mississippi for the respectful way the men turn their heads up in the yard, the women stand waiting and knowledgeable, their children held from mischief by teachings from the wrong God. He glares beyond them to the occupants of the cars, white faces glued to promises beyond a country wedding, noses thrust forward like dogs on a track. For him they usurp the wedding.

in the sight of God

Yes, open house. That is what country black folks like. She dreams she does not already have three children. A squeeze around the flowers in her hands chokes off three and four and five years of breath. Instantly she is ashamed and frightened in her superstition. She looks for the first time at the preacher, forces humility into her eyes, as if she believes he is, in fact, a man of God. She can imagine God, a small black boy, timidly pulling the preacher's coattail.

to join this man and this woman

She thinks of ropes, chains, handcuffs, his religion. His place of worship. Where she will be required to sit apart with covered head. In Chicago, a word she hears when thinking of smoke, from his description of what a cinder was, which they never had in Panther Burn. She sees hovering over the heads of the clean neighbors in her front yard black specks falling, clinging, from the sky. But in Chicago. Respect, a chance to build. Her children at last from underneath the detrimental wheel. A chance to be on top. What a relief, she thinks. What a vision, a view, from up so high.

in holy matrimony.

Her fourth child she gave away to the child's father who had some money. Certainly a good job. Had gone to Harvard. Was a good man but weak because good language meant so much to him he could not live with Roselily. Could not abide TV in the living room, five beds in three rooms, no Bach except from four to six on Sunday afternoons. No chess at all. She does not forget to worry about her son among his father's people. She wonders if the New England climate will agree with him. If he will ever come down to Mississippi, as his father did, to try to right the country's wrongs. She wonders if he will be stronger than his father. His father cried off and on throughout her pregnancy. Went to skin and bones. Suffered nightmares, retching and falling out of bed. Tried to kill himself. Later told his wife he found the right baby through friends. Vouched for, the sterling qualities that would make up his character.

It is not her nature to blame. Still, she is not entirely thankful. She supposes New England, the North, to be quite different from what she knows. It seems right somehow to her that people who move there to live return home completely changed. She thinks of the air, the smoke, the cinders. Imagines cinders big as hailstones; heavy, weighing on the people. Wonders how this pressure finds it way into the veins, roping the springs of laughter.

If there's anybody here that knows a reason why

But of course they know no reason why beyond what they daily have come to know. She thinks of the man who will be her husband, feels shut away from him because of the stiff severity of his plain black suit. His religion. A lifetime of black and white. Of veils. Covered head. It is as if her children are already gone from her. Not dead, but exalted on a pedestal, a stalk that has no roots. She wonders how to make new roots. It is beyond her. She wonders what one does with memories in a brand-new life. This had seemed easy, until she thought of it. "The reasons why . . . the people who" . . . she thinks, and does not wonder where the thought is from.

these two should not be joined

She thinks of her mother, who is dead. Dead, but still her mother. Joined. This is confusing. Of her father. A gray old man who sold wild mink, rabbit, fox skins to Sears, Roebuck. He stands in the yard, like a man waiting for a train. Her young sisters stand behind her in smooth green dresses, with flowers in their hands and hair. They giggle, she feels, at the absurdity of the wedding. They are ready for something new. She thinks the man beside her should marry one of them. She feels old. Yoked. An arm seems to reach out from behind her and snatch her backward. She thinks of cemeteries and the long sleep of grandparents mingling in the dirt. She believes that she believes in ghosts. In the soil giving back what it takes.

together

In the city. He sees her in a new way. This she knows, and is grateful. But is it new enough? She cannot always be a bride and virgin, wearing robes and veil. Even now her body itches to be free of satin and voile, organdy and lily of the valley. Memories crash against her. Memories of being bare to the sun. She wonders what it will be like. Not to have to go to a job. Not to work in a sewing plant. Not to worry about learning to sew straight seams in working-men's overalls, jeans, and dress pants. Her place will be in the home, he has said, repeatedly, promising her rest she had prayed for. But now she wonders. When she is rested, what will she do? They will make babies — she thinks practically about her fine brown body, his strong black one. They will be inevitable. Her hands will be full. Full of what? Babies. She is not comforted.

let him speak

She wishes she had asked him to explain more of what he meant. But she was impatient. Impatient to be done with sewing. With doing everything for three children, alone. Impatient to leave the girls she had known since childhood, their children growing up, their husbands hanging around her, already old, seedy. Nothing about them that she wanted, or needed. The fathers of her children driving by, waving, not waving; reminders of times she would just as soon forget. Impatient to see the South Side, where they would live and build and be respectable and respected and free. Her husband would free her. A romantic hush. Proposal. Promises. A new life! Respectable, reclaimed, renewed. Free! In robe and veil.

or forever hold

She does not even know if she loves him. She loves his sobriety. His refusal to sing just because he knows the tune. She loves his pride. His blackness and his gray car. She loves his understanding of her *condition*. She thinks she loves the effort he will make to redo her into what he truly wants. His love of her makes her completely conscious of how unloved she was before. This is something; though it makes her unbearably sad. Melancholy. She blinks her eyes. Remembers she is finally being married, like other girls. Like other girls, women? Something strains upward behind her eyes. She thinks of the something as a rat trapped, concerned, scurrying to and fro in her head, peering through the windows of her eyes. She wants to live for once. But doesn't know quite what that means. Wonders if she has ever done it. If she ever will. The preacher is odious to her. She wants to strike him out of the way, out of her light, with the back of her hand. It seems to her he has always been standing in front of her, barring her way.

his peace.

The rest she does not hear. She feels a kiss, passionate, rousing, within the general pandemonium. Cars drive up blowing their horns. Firecrackers go off. Dogs come from under the house and begin to yelp and bark. Her husband's hand is like the clasp of an iron gate. People congratulate. Her children press against her. They look with awe and distaste mixed with hope at their new father. He stands curiously apart, in spite of the people crowding about to grasp his free hand. He smiles at them all but his eyes are as if turned inward. He knows they cannot understand that he is not a Christian. He will not explain himself. He feels different, he looks it. The old women thought he was like one of their sons except that he had somehow got away from them. Still a son, not a son. Changed.

She thinks how it will be later in the night in the silvery gray car. How they will spin through the darkness of Mississippi and in the morning be in Chicago, Illinois. She thinks of Lincoln, the president. That is all she knows about the place. She feels ignorant, *wrong*, backward. She presses her worried fingers into his palm. He is standing in front of her. In the crush of well-wishing people, he does not look back.

Questions for Discussion

1. What differences between the couple about to be married are suggested in the first part of the story? Why do the white people driving by "usurp the wedding" for the groom? What does this response reveal about his racial attitudes?

2. What hopes does Roselily have for her future in Chicago? What fears does she have? What do her hopes and fears reveal about her values?

3. Roselily is marrying for the second time. How was her first husband different from her new husband? What is revealed about her values and self-concept by her choice of a second husband?

4. How does Roselily feel about traditional, organized religion such as that practiced by the preacher? How does she feel about ghosts and other elements of folk belief or "superstition"? What is her new husband's religion ("he is not a Christian")?

5. How does the story's stream-of-consciousness interior monologue contribute to our understanding of Roselily and her personality? What is the significance of Roselily's interior monologue being interrupted by the preacher's recitation of the traditional marriage vows?

Ideas for Writing

1. Write a story that explores Roselily's married life in her new home in the North. Will her marriage be a happy one? You might consider the story's final sentence: "In the crush of well-meaning people, he does not look back."

2. Write an essay in which you discuss how the social problems implied in this story affect contemporary marriages.

ROBERT OLEN BUTLER   (b. 1944)

The formative experience in Robert Olen Butler's life was his service in Vietnam, where he was a translator for the U.S. Army and became deeply involved with the Vietnamese people and their culture. His stories embody the many voices inside him: those of the Vietnamese, of mainstream Americans, and of veterans who are troubled by the Vietnam War and are trying to create a code of values and a view of history that makes sense within a multicultural society.

Born in Illinois, Butler attended Northwestern University and the University of Iowa. He currently teaches creative writing in Lake Charles, Louisiana, at McNeese State University. He has won many awards for his fiction, including a Guggenheim fellowship, a National Endowment for the Arts fellowship, and, in 1993, a Pulitzer prize for his stories collected in *A Good Scent from a Strange Mountain,* which are about Vietnamese who have immigrated to America after the war. "Letters from My Father" is from this collection. Butler has published seven novels, including *Sun Dogs* (1982), *Wabash* (1987), and *They Whisper* (1994). His most recent story collection is *Tabloid Dreams* (1996). Story writer and literary critic Madison Smart Bell has said that Butler's achievement is "not only to reveal the inner lives of the Vietnamese, but to show, through their eyes, how the rest of us appear from an outside perspective."

Letters from My Father   (1992)

I look through the letters my father sent to me in Saigon and I find this: "Dear Fran. How are you? I wish you and your mother were here with me. The weather here is pretty cold this time of year. I bet you would like the cold weather." At the time, I wondered how he would know such a thing. Cold weather sounded very bad. It was freezing, he said, so I touched the tip of my finger to a piece of ice and I held it there for as long as I could. It hurt very bad and that was after only about a minute. I thought, How could you spend hours and days in weather like that?

It makes no difference that I had misunderstood the cold weather. By the time he finally got me and my mother out of Vietnam, he had moved to a place where it almost never got very cold. The point is that in his letters to me he often said this and that about the weather. It is cold today. It is hot today. Today there are clouds in the sky. Today there are no clouds. What did that have to do with me?

He said "Dear Fran" because my name is Fran. That's short for Francine and the sound of Fran is something like a Vietnamese name, but it isn't, really.

So I told my friends in Saigon that my name was Trán, which was short for Hôn Trán, which means "a kiss on the forehead." My American father lived in America but my Vietnamese mother and me lived in Saigon, so I was still a Saigon girl. My mother called me Francine, too. She was happy for me to have this name. She said it was not just American, it was also French. But I wanted a name for Saigon and Trán was it.

I was a child of dust. When the American fathers all went home, including my father, and the communists took over, that's what we were called, those of us who had faces like those drawings you see in some of the bookstalls on Nguyễn Huệ Street. You look once and you see a beautiful woman sitting at her mirror, but then you look again and you see the skull of a dead person, no skin on the face, just the wide eyes of the skull and the bared teeth. We were like that, the children of dust in Saigon. At one look we were Vietnamese and at another look we were American and after that you couldn't get your eyes to stay still when they turned to us, they kept seeing first one thing and then another.

Last night I found a package of letters in a footlocker that belongs to my father. It is in the storage shack at the back of our house here in America. I am living now in Lake Charles, Louisiana, and I found this package of letters outside — many packages, hundreds of letters — and I opened one, and these are all copies he kept of letters he sent trying to get us out of Vietnam. I look through these letters my father wrote and I find this: "What is this crap that you're trying to give me now? It has been nine years, seven months, and fifteen days since I last saw my daughter, my own flesh-and-blood daughter."

This is an angry voice, a voice with feeling. I have been in this place now for a year. I am seventeen and it took even longer than nine years, seven months, fifteen days to get me out of Vietnam. I wish I could say something about that, because I know anyone who listens to my story would expect me right now to say how I felt. My mother and me were left behind in Saigon. My father went on ahead to America and he thought he could get some paperwork done and prepare a place for us, then my mother and me would be leaving for America very soon. But things happened. A different footlocker was lost and some important papers with it, like their marriage license and my birth certificate. Then the country of South Vietnam fell to the communists, and even those who thought it might happen thought it happened pretty fast, really. Who knew? My father didn't.

I look at a letter he sent me in Saigon after it fell and the letter says: "You can imagine how I feel. The whole world is let down by what happened." But I could not imagine that, if you want to know the truth, how my father felt. And I knew nothing of the world except Saigon, and even that wasn't the way the world was, because when I was very little they gave it a different name, calling it Hồ Chí Minh City. Now, those words are a man's name, you know, but the same words have several other meanings, too, and I took the name like everyone took the face of a child of dust: I looked at it one way and it meant one thing and then I looked at it a different way and it meant something else. Hồ Chí Minh also can mean "very intelligent starch-paste," and that's what we thought of the new name, me and some friends of mine who also had American fathers. We would meet at the French cemetery on Phan Thanh Giản Street and talk about our city — Hồ, for short; starch-paste. We would talk about our lives in Starch-Paste City and we had this game where we'd hide in the cemetery, each in a separate place, and then we'd keep low and move slowly and see how many of our friends we would find. If you saw the other person first, you would get a point. And if nobody ever saw you, if it was like you were invisible, you'd win.

The cemetery made me sad, but it felt very comfortable there somehow. We all thought that, me and my friends. It was a ragged place and many of the names were like Couchet, Picard, Vernet, Believeau, and these graves never had any flowers on them. Everybody who loved these dead people had gone home to France long ago. Then there was a part of the cemetery that had Vietnamese dead. There were some flowers over there, but not very many. The grave markers had photos, little oval frames built into the stone, and these were faces of the dead, mostly old people, men and women, the wealthy Vietnamese, but there were some young people, too, many of them dead in 1968 when there was much killing in Saigon. I would always hide over in this section and there was one boy, very cute, in sunglasses, leaning on a motorcycle, his hand on his hip. He died in February of 1968, and I probably wouldn't have liked him anyway. He looked cute but very conceited. And there was a girl nearby. The marker said she was fifteen. I found her when I was about ten or so and she was very beautiful, with long black hair and dark eyes and a round face. I would always go to her grave and I wanted to be just like her, though I knew my face was different from hers. Then I went one day — I was almost her age at last — and the rain had gotten into the little picture frame and her face was nearly gone. I could see her hair, but the features of her face had faded until you could not see them, there were only dark streaks of water and the picture was curling at the edges, and I cried over that. It was like she had died.

Sometimes my father sent me pictures with his letters. "Dear Fran," he would say. "Here is a picture of me. Please send me a picture of you." A friend of mine, when she was about seven years old, got a pen pal in Russia. They wrote to each other very simple letters in French. Her pen pal said, "Please send me a picture of you and I will send you one of me." My friend put on her white áo dài and went downtown and had her picture taken before the big banyan tree in the park on Lê Thánh Tôn. She sent it off and in return she got a picture of a fat girl who hadn't combed her hair, standing by a cow on a collective farm.

My mother's father was some government man, I think. And the communists said my mother was an agitator or collaborator. Something like that. It was all mostly before I was born or when I was just a little girl, and whenever my mother tried to explain what all this was about, this father across the sea and us not seeming to ever go there, I just didn't like to listen very much and my mother realized that, and after a while she didn't say any more. I put his picture up on my mirror and he was smiling, I guess. He was outside somewhere and there was a lake or something in the background and he had a T-shirt on and I guess he was really more squinting than smiling. There were several of these photographs of him on my mirror. They were always outdoors and he was always squinting in the sun. He said in one of his letters to me: "Dear Fran, I got your photo. You are very pretty, like your mother. I have not forgotten you." And I thought: I am not like my mother. I am a child of dust. Has he forgotten that?

One of the girls I used to hang around with at the cemetery told me a story that she knew was true because it happened to her sister's best friend. The best friend was just a very little girl when it began. Her father was a soldier in the South Vietnam Army and he was away fighting somewhere secret, Cambodia or somewhere. It was very secret, so her mother never heard from him and the little girl was so small when he went away that she didn't even remember him, what he looked like or anything. But she knew she was supposed to have a daddy, so every evening, when the mother would put her daughter to bed, the little girl would ask where her father was. She asked with such a sad heart that one night the mother made something up.

There was a terrible storm and the electricity went out in Saigon. So the mother went to the table with the little girl clinging in fright to her, and she lit an oil lamp. When she did, her shadow suddenly was thrown upon the wall and it was very big, and she said, "Don't cry, my baby, see there?" She pointed to the shadow. "There's your daddy. He'll protect you." This made the little girl very happy. She stopped shaking from fright immediately and the mother sang the girl to sleep.

The next evening before going to bed, the little girl asked to see her father. When the mother tried to say no, the little girl was so upset that the mother gave in and lit the oil lamp and cast her shadow on the wall. The little girl went to the wall and held her hands before her with the palms together and she bowed low to the shadow. "Good night, Daddy," she said, and she went to sleep. This happened the next evening and the next and it went on for more than a year.

Then one evening, just before bedtime, the father finally came home. The mother, of course, was very happy. She wept and she kissed him and she said to him, "We will prepare a thanksgiving feast to honor our ancestors. You go in to our daughter. She is almost ready for bed. I will go out to the market and get some food for our celebration."

So the father went in to the little girl and he said to her, "My pretty girl, I am home. I am your father and I have not forgotten you."

But the little girl said, "You're not my daddy. I know my daddy. He'll be here soon. He comes every night to say good night before I go to bed."

The man was shocked at his wife's faithlessness, but he was very proud, and he did not say anything to her about it when she got home. He did not say anything at all, but prayed briefly before the shrine of their ancestors and picked up his bag and left. The weeks passed and the mother grieved so badly that one day she threw herself into the Saigon River and drowned.

The father heard news of this and thought that she had killed herself from shame. He returned home to be a father to his daughter, but on the first night, there was a storm and the lights went out and the man lit the oil lamp, throwing his shadow on the wall. His little girl laughed in delight and went and bowed low to the shadow and said, "Good night, Daddy." When the man saw this, he took his little girl to his own mother's house, left her, and threw himself into the Saigon River to join his wife in death.

My friend says this story is true. Everyone in the neighborhood of her sister's friend knows about it. But I don't think it's true. I never did say that to my friend, but for me, it doesn't make sense. I can't believe that the little girl would be satisfied with the shadow father. There was this darkness on the wall, just a flatness, and she loved it. I can see how she wouldn't take up with this man who suddenly walks in one night and says, "I'm your father, let me tell you good night." But the other guy, the shadow — he was no father either.

When my father met my mother and me at the airport, there were people with cameras and microphones and my father grabbed my mother with this enormous hug and this sound like a shout and he kissed her hard and all the people with microphones and cameras smiled and nodded. Then he let go of my mother and he looked at me and suddenly he was making this little choking sound, a kind of gacking in the back of his throat like a rabbit makes when you pick him up and he doesn't like it. And my father's hands just fluttered before him and he got stiff-legged coming over to me and the hug he gave me was like I was soaking wet and he had on his Sunday clothes, though he was just wearing some silly T-shirt.

All the letters from my father, the ones I got in Saigon, and the photos, they're in a box in the back of the closet of my room. My closet smells of my perfume, is full of nice clothes so that I can fit in at school. Not everyone can say what they feel in words, especially words on paper. Not everyone can look at a camera and make their face do what it has to do to show a feeling. But years of flat words, grimaces at the sun, these are hard things to forget. So I've been sitting all morning today in the shack behind our house, out here with the tree roaches and the carpenter ants and the smell of mildew and rotting wood and I am sweating so hard that it's dripping off my nose and chin. There are many letters in my lap. In one of them to the U.S. government my father says: "If this was a goddamn white woman, a Russian ballet dancer and her daughter, you people would have them on a plane in twenty-four hours. This is my wife and my daughter. My daughter is so beautiful you can put her face on your dime and quarters and no one could ever make change again in your goddamn country without stopping and saying, Oh my God, what a beautiful face."

I read this now while I'm hidden in the storage shack, invisible, soaked with sweat like it's that time in Saigon between the dry season and the rainy season, and I know my father will be here soon. The lawn mower is over there in the corner and this morning he got up and said that it was going to be hot today, that there were no clouds in the sky and he was going to have to mow the lawn. When he opens the door, I will let him see me here, and I will ask him to talk to me like in these letters, like when he was so angry with some stranger that he knew what to say.

Questions for Discussion

1. What is implied by Fran's misunderstanding about the importance of weather conditions in the letters she receives from her father?

2. Fran devotes several sentences to explaining her name. What are its connotations? Why does she provide a "Vietnamese" version of her name for her friends in Saigon?

3. What is a "child of dust"? How does Fran explain her feelings as a child of dust through her description of the drawings in the Saigon bookstalls?

4. What is the significance of the information that Fran learns about her father and his feelings for her by reading the old letters in the footlocker? What does she learn from the grave markers at the cemetery?

5. What is revealed in the story that Fran hears from the girl at the cemetery? How is this story of a "shadow father" similar to her own relationship with her father? How is it different?

Ideas for Writing

1. Write an essay in which you examine the future possibility of a strong relationship between Fran and her father. How does Fran hope to break through to him at the end of the story? Will she be successful?

2. Write a story about an adolescent who is united with a parent whom he or she has never known. What would the reunion scene be like? What tensions and joys would exist between them?

TOBIAS WOLFF (b. 1945)

One critic has described Tobias Wolff's stories as scrutinizing "the disorders of daily living to find significant order . . . [informing] us not only of
what happened but why it had to happen as it did . . . [depicting] lives
crowded with the results of previous choices."

Born in Birmingham, Alabama, Wolff lived in many places as he grew
up. Raised by his mother in the Pacific Northwest after his parents divorced,
he kept in contact with his father and his older brother, Geoffrey, who also
became a writer. Wolff served as a lieutenant during the war in Vietnam and
then went on to earn a B.A. from Oxford University and an M.A. from
Stanford University. He currently teaches in the creative writing program
at Syracuse University. His novel *The Barracks Thief* (1982) won the
PEN/Faulkner award, and he has published several volumes of short stories,
including *In the Garden of the North American Martyrs* (1982), *Back in the
World* (1985), and *The Night in Question* (1996), which includes "Lady's
Dream." He has also written two memoirs: *This Boy's Life* (1991), about his
childhood, and *In Pharaoh's Army* (1994), about his service in Vietnam.

Wolff's work is distinguished by his use of offbeat details to create half-
comic, half-tragic heroes, central characters who stand a little apart from the
world around them. He believes that storytelling is "one of the most intimate
things that people do together. . . . [T]he very act of being a writer seems to me
to be an optimistic act."

Lady's Dream (1992)

Lady's suffocating. Robert can't stand to have the windows down because
the air blowing into the car bothers his eyes. The fan is on but only at the lowest speed, as the sound distracts him from driving. Lady's head is getting
heavy, and when she blinks she has to raise her eyelids by an effort of will. The
heat and dampness of her skin give her the sensation of a fever. She's beginning to see things in the lengthening moments when her eyes are closed,
things more distinct and familiar than the dipping wires and blur of trees and
the silent staring man she sees when they're open.

"Lady?" Robert's voice calls her back, but she keeps her eyes closed.

That's him to the life. Can't stand her sleeping when he's not. But he'd
have some good reason to wake her. Never a mean motive. Never. When he's
going to ask somebody for a favor he always calls first and just passes the time,
then calls back the next day and says how great it was to talk to them, he
enjoyed it so much he forgot to ask if they would mind doing something for

997

him. Has no idea he does this. She's never heard him tell a lie, not even to make a story better. Tells the most boring stories. Just lethal. Considers every word. Considers everything. Early January he buys twelve vacuum cleaner bags and writes a different month on each one so she'll remember to change them. Of course she goes as long as she can on every bag and throws away the extras at the end of the year, otherwise he'd find them and know. Not say anything—just know. Once she threw away seven. Sneaked them outside through the snow and stuffed them in the garbage can.

Considerate. Everything a matter of principle. Justice for all, yellow brown black or white they are precious in his sight. Can't say no to any charity but forgets to send the money. Asks her questions about his own self. *Who's that actress I like so much? What's my favorite fish?* Is calm in every circumstance. Polishes his glasses all the time. They gleam so you can hardly see his eyes. Has to sleep on the right side of the bed. The sheets have to be white. Any other color gives him nightmares, forget about patterns. Patterns would kill him. Wears a hard hat when he works around the house. Says her name a hundred times a day. Always has. Any excuse.

He loves her name. Lady. Married her name. Shut her up in her name. Shut her up.

"Lady?"

Sorry, sir. Lady's gone.

She knows where she is. She's back home. Her father's away but her mother's home and her sister Jo. Lady hears their voices. She's in the kitchen running water into a glass, letting it overflow and pour down her fingers until it's good and cold. She lifts the glass and drinks her fill and sets the glass down, then walks slow as a cat across the kitchen and down the hall to the bright doorway that opens onto the porch where her mother and sister are sitting. Her mother straightens up and settles back again as Lady goes to the railing and leans on her elbows and looks down the street and then out to the fields beyond.

Lordalmighty it's hot.

Isn't it hot, though.

Jo is slouched in her chair, rolling a bottle of Coke on her forehead. I could just die.

Late again, Lady?

He'll be here.

Must have missed his bus again.

I suppose.

I bet those stupid corn-pones were messing with him like they do. I wouldn't be a soldier.

He'll be here. Else he'd call.

I wouldn't be a soldier.

Nobody asked you.

Now, girls.

I'd like to see you a soldier anyway, sleeping all day and laying in bed eating candy. Mooning around. Oh, general, don't make me march, that just wears me out. Oh, do I have to wear that old green thing, green just makes me look sick, haven't you got one of those in red? Why, I can't eat lima beans, don't you know about me and lima beans?

Now, Lady . . .

But her mother is laughing and so is Jo in spite of herself. Oh the goodness of that sound. And of her own voice. Just like singing. General, honey, you know I can't shoot that nasty thing, how about you ask one of those old boys to shoot it for me, they just love to shoot off their guns for Jo Kay.

Lady!

The three of them on the porch, waiting but not waiting. Sufficient unto themselves. Nobody has to come.

But Robert is on his way. He's leaning his head against the window of the bus and trying to catch his breath. He missed the first bus and had to run to catch this one because his sergeant found fault with him during inspection and stuck him on a cleanup detail. The sergeant hates his guts. He's ignorant trash and Robert is an educated man from Vermont, an engineer just out of college, quit Shell Oil in Louisiana to enlist the day North Korea crossed the parallel. The only Yankee in his company. Robert says when they get overseas there won't be any more Yankees and Southerners, just Americans. Lady likes him for believing that, but she gives him the needle because she knows it isn't true.

He changed uniforms in a hurry and didn't check the mirror before he left the barracks. There's a smudge on his right cheek. Shoe polish. His face is flushed and sweaty, his blouse soaked through. He's watching out the window and reciting a poem to himself. He's a great one for poems, this Robert. He has poems for running and poems for drill and poems for going to sleep, and poems for when the corn-pones start getting him down.

> Out of the night that covers me
> Black as the Pit from Pole to Pole
> I thank whatever Gods may be
> For my unconquerable Soul.

That's the poem he uses to fortify himself. He thinks it over and over even when they're yelling in his face. It keeps him strong. Lady laughs when he tells her things like this, and he always looks at her a little surprised and then he laughs, too, to show he likes her sass, though he doesn't. He thinks it's just her being young and spoiled and that it'll go away if he can get her out of that house and away from her family and among sensible people who don't think everything's a joke. In time it'll wear off and leave her quiet and dignified and respectful of life's seriousness — leave her pure Lady.

That's what he thinks some days. Most days he sees no hope at all. He thinks of taking her home, into the house of his father, and when he imagines what she might say to his father he starts hearing his own excuses and apologies. Then he knows that it's impossible. Robert has picked up some psychology here and there, and he believes he understands how he got himself into this mess. It's rebellion. Subconscious, of course. A subconscious rebellion against his father, falling in love with a girl like Lady. Because you don't fall in love. No. Life isn't a song. You choose to fall in love. And there is a reason for that choice, as there is a reason for every choice, if you can get to the bottom of it. It's as simple as that.

Robert is looking out the window but he's not really seeing anything.

It's impossible. Lady is just a kid, she doesn't know anything about life. There's a rawness to her that will take years to correct. She's spoiled and will-ful and half-wild, except for her tongue, which is all wild. And she's Southern, not that there's anything wrong with that per se, but a particular kind of Southern. Not trash, as she would put it, but too proud of not being trash. Irrational. Superstitious. Clannish.

And what a clan it is, clan Cobb. Mr. Cobb a suspender-snapping paint salesman always on the road, full of drummer's banter and jokes about Nigras and watermelon. Mrs. Cobb a morning-to-night gossip, weepily religious, con-tent to live on her daughters' terms rather than raise them to woman's estate with discipline and right example. And the sister. Jo Kay. You can write that sad story before it happens.

All in all, Robert can't imagine a better family than the Cobbs to beat his father over the head with. That must be why he's chosen them, and why he has to undo that choice. He's made up his mind. He meant to tell her last time, but there was no chance. Today. No matter what. She won't understand. She'll cry. He will be gentle about it. He'll say she's a fine girl but too young. He'll say that it isn't fair to ask her to wait for him when who knows what might happen, and then to follow him to a place she's never been, far from family and friends.

He'll tell Lady anything but the truth, which is that he's ashamed to have picked her to use against his father. That's his own fight. He's been running from it for as long as he can remember, and he knows he has to stop. He has to face the man.

He will, too. He will, after he gets home from the Army, from this war. His father will have to listen to him then. Robert will make him listen. He will tell him, he will face his father and tell him . . .

Robert's throat tightens and he sits up straight. He hears himself breath-ing in quick shallow gasps and wonders if anyone else has noticed. His heart is kicking. His mouth is dry. He closes his eyes and forces himself to breathe more slowly and deeply, imitating calm until it becomes almost real.

They pass the power company and the Greyhound station. Red-faced sol-diers in shiny shoes stand around out front smoking. The bus stops on a street lined with bars and the other men get off, hooting and pushing one another. There's just Robert and four women left on board. They turn off Jackson and bump across the railroad tracks and head east past the lumberyard. Black men are throwing planks into a truck, their shirts off, skin gleaming in the hazy light. Then they're gone behind a fence. Robert pulls the cord for his stop, waits behind a wide woman in a flowered dress. The flesh swings like hammocks under her arms. She takes forever going down the steps.

The sun dazzles his eyes. He pulls down the visor of his cap and walks to the corner and turns right. This is Arsenal Street. Lady lives two blocks down, where the street gives out into fields. There's no plan to the way it ends — it just gives out. From here on there's nothing but farms for miles. At night Lady and Jo Kay steal strawberries from the field behind their house, dish them up with thick fresh cream and grated chocolate. The strawberries have been stewing in the heat all day and burst open at the first pressure of the teeth. Robert disapproves of reaping another man's labor, but he eats his share and then some. The season's about over. He'll be lucky if he gets any tonight.

He's thinking about strawberries when he sees Lady on the porch, and just then the sweetness of that taste fills his mouth. It surprises him. He stops as if he's remembered something, then comes toward her again. Her lips are moving but he can't hear her, he's aware of nothing but the taste in his mouth, and the closer he comes the stronger it gets. His pace quickens, his hand goes out for the railing. He takes the steps as if he means to devour her.

No, she's saying, no. She's talking to him and to the girl whose life he seeks. She knows what will befall her if she lets him have it. Stay here on this porch with your mother and your sister, they will soon have need of you. Gladden your father's eye yet awhile. This man is not for you. He will patiently school you half to death. He will kindly take you among unbending strangers to watch him fail to be brave. To suffer his carefulness, and to see your children writhe under it and fight it off with every kind of self-hurting recklessness. To be changed. To hear yourself and not know who is speaking. Wait, young Lady. Bide your time.

"Lady?"

It's no good. She won't hear. Even now she's bending toward him as he comes up the steps. She reaches for his cheek, to brush away the smudge he doesn't know is there. He thinks it's something else that makes her do it, and his fine lean face confesses everything, asks everything. There's no turning back from this touch. But she can't be stopped. She has a mind of her own, and she knows something Lady doesn't. She knows how to love him.

Lady hears her name again.

Wait, sir.

She blesses the girl. She turns to the far-rolling fields she used to dream an ocean, this house the ship that ruled it. She takes a last good look and opens her eyes.

Questions for Discussion

1. The story begins with the sentence "Lady's suffocating." How does this sentence establish the mood of the story? In what ways is Lady suffocating, both literally and figuratively?

2. The story is structured around a dream-flashback to Lady's youth, as she waits for a visit from her husband-to-be, Robert. What triggers the dream? How does it end? What is the "meaning" of the dream sequence?
3. Although the story is called "Lady's Dream," much of the story concerns the thoughts and feelings of Robert, Lady's husband. How does Wolff manage the shifts in viewpoint between Lady's sensations and inner world and those of Robert? What is the effect and significance of the movement back and forth between their minds?
4. Contrast the personalities and cultural backgrounds of Robert and Lady. What do you think brought them together? What keeps them from having a satisfactory relationship?
5. What is the significance of the story's last paragraphs, particularly the lines "She knows how to love him. . . . Wait, sir. She blesses the girl"?

Ideas for Writing

1. Does the story's conclusion imply that the couple will have a happy future? Write an essay or story in which you predict the course of their relationship.
2. Write an essay in which you discuss the nature of Lady and Robert's relationship. Would it be accurate to call this an abusive relationship? Does Robert still seem to love Lady? Does he only desire to control her? What does Lady want from the relationship?

TIM O'BRIEN   (b. 1946)

Influenced by its author's two years in the infantry during the Vietnam War, much of Tim O'Brien's work focuses on violence, paranoia, and despair, but it also offers depictions of courage and personal honor.

Born in Austin, Minnesota, O'Brien received his B.A. from Macalester College in St. Paul in 1968. After his service in Vietnam, for which he received a Purple Heart, he did graduate work in government at Harvard University. He was working as a national affairs reporter for the *Washington Post* when he published his first book, the memoir *If I Die in a Combat Zone* (1973), which explores his Vietnam experiences. O'Brien's novels include *Going after Cacciato* (1978), considered one of the finest novels about combat in Vietnam, and *The Nuclear Age* (1985), which tells the story of a Vietnam-era radical and draft evader who builds a bomb shelter in his backyard many years after the war. O'Brien's most highly praised work is the collection of related war stories, *The Things They Carried* (1990), which includes "The Man I Killed." His most recent book is a novel of political intrigue and deception, *The Lake in the Woods* (1994).

O'Brien's style has been described by reviewer Michiko Kakutani as one "that combines the sharp, unsentimental rhythms of Hemingway with gentler, more lyric descriptions." O'Brien has said that he writes in order "to use stories to alert readers to the complexity and ambiguity of a set of moral issues — but without preaching a moral lesson."

The Man I Killed   (1990)

His jaw was in his throat, his upper lip and teeth were gone, his one eye was shut, his other eye was a star-shaped hole, his eyebrows were thin and arched like a woman's, his nose was undamaged, there was a slight tear at the lobe of one ear, his clean black hair was swept upward into a cowlick at the rear of the skull, his forehead was lightly freckled, his fingernails were clean, the skin at his left cheek was peeled back in three ragged strips, his right cheek was smooth and hairless, there was a butterfly on his chin, his neck was open to the spinal cord and the blood there was thick and shiny and it was this wound that had killed him. He lay face-up in the center of the trail, a slim, dead, almost dainty young man. He had bony legs, a narrow waist, long shapely fingers. His chest was sunken and poorly muscled — a scholar, maybe. His wrists were the wrists of a child. He wore a black shirt, black pajama pants, a gray ammunition belt, a gold ring on the third finger of his right hand. His rubber sandals had been blown off. One lay beside him, the other a few meters up the trail. He had been born, maybe, in 1946 in the village of My Khe near the central coastline of Quang Ngai Province, where his parents farmed, and where his family had lived for several centuries, and where, during the time of the French, his father and two uncles and many neighbors had joined in the struggle for independence. He was not a Communist. He was a citizen and a soldier. In the village of My Khe, as in all of Quang Ngai, patriotic resistance had the force of tradition, which was partly the force of legend, and from his earliest boyhood the man I killed would have listened to stories about the heroic Trung sisters and Tran Hung Dao's famous rout of the Mongols and Le Loi's final victory against the Chinese at Tot Dong. He would have been taught that to defend the land was a man's highest duty and highest privilege. He had accepted this. It was never open to question. Secretly, though, it also frightened him. He was not a fighter. His health was poor, his body small and frail. He liked books. He wanted someday to be a teacher of mathematics. At night, lying on his mat, he could not picture himself doing the brave things his father had done, or his uncles, or the heroes of the stories. He hoped in his heart that he would never be tested. He hoped the Americans would go away. Soon, he hoped. He kept hoping and hoping, always, even when he was asleep.

"Oh, man, you fuckin' trashed the fucker," Azar said. "You scrambled his sorry self, look at that, you *did,* you laid him out like Shredded fuckin' Wheat."

"Go away," Kiowa said.

"I'm just saying the truth. Like oatmeal."

"Go," Kiowa said.

"Okay, then, I take it back," Azar said. He started to move away, then stopped and said, "Rice Krispies, you know? On the dead test, this particular individual gets A-plus."

Smiling at this, he shrugged and walked up the trail toward the village behind the trees.

Kiowa kneeled down.

"Just forget that crud," he said. He opened up his canteen and held it out for a while and then sighed and pulled it away. "No sweat, man. What else could you do?"

Later, Kiowa said, "I'm serious. Nothing *anybody* could do. Come on, stop staring."

The trail junction was shaded by a row of trees and tall brush. The slim young man lay with his legs in the shade. His jaw was in his throat. His one eye was shut and the other was a star-shaped hole.

Kiowa glanced at the body.

"All right, let me ask a question," he said. "You want to trade places with him? Turn it all upside down — you *want* that? I mean, be honest."

The star-shaped hole was red and yellow. The yellow part seemed to be getting wider, spreading out at the center of the star. The upper lip and gum and teeth were gone. The man's head was cocked at a wrong angle, as if loose at the neck, and the neck was wet with blood.

"Think it over," Kiowa said.

Then later he said, "Tim, it's a *war.* The guy wasn't Heidi — he had a weapon, right? It's a tough thing, for sure, but you got to cut out that staring."

Then he said, "Maybe you better lie down a minute."

Then after a long empty time he said, "Take it slow. Just go wherever the spirit takes you."

The butterfly was making its way along the young man's forehead, which was spotted with small dark freckles. The nose was undamaged. The skin on the right cheek was smooth and fine-grained and hairless. Frail-looking, delicately boned, the young man would not have wanted to be a soldier and in his heart would have feared performing badly in battle. Even as a boy growing up in the village of My Khe, he had often worried about this. He imagined covering his head and lying in a deep hole and closing his eyes and not moving until the war was over. He had no stomach for violence. He loved mathematics. His eyebrows were thin and arched like a woman's, and at school the boys sometimes teased him about how pretty he was, the arched eyebrows and long shapely fingers, and on the playground they mimicked a woman's walk and made fun of his smooth skin and his love for mathematics. The young man could not make himself fight them. He often wanted to, but he was afraid, and this increased his shame. If he could not fight little boys, he thought, how could he ever become a soldier and fight the Americans with their airplanes and helicopters and bombs? It did not seem possible. In the presence of his father and uncles, he pretended to look forward to doing his patriotic duty, which was also a privilege, but at night he prayed with his mother that the war might end soon. Beyond anything else, he was afraid of disgracing himself, and therefore his family and village. But all he could do, he thought, was wait and pray and try not to grow up too fast.

"Listen to me," Kiowa said. "You feel terrible, I know that."

Then he said, "Okay, maybe I *don't* know."

Along the trail there were small blue flowers shaped like bells. The young man's head was wrenched sideways, not quite facing the flowers, and even in the shade a single blade of sunlight sparkled against the buckle of his ammunition belt. The left cheek was peeled back in three ragged strips. The wounds at his neck had not yet clotted, which made him seem animate even in death, the blood still spreading out across his shirt.

Kiowa shook his head.

There was some silence before he said, "Stop *staring.*"

The young man's fingernails were clean. There was a slight tear at the lobe of one ear, a sprinkling of blood on the forearm. He wore a gold ring on the third finger of his right hand. His chest was sunken and poorly muscled — a scholar, maybe. His life was now a constellation of possibilities. So, yes, maybe a scholar. And for years, despite his family's poverty, the man I killed would have been determined to continue his education in mathematics. The means for this were arranged, perhaps, through the village liberation cadres, and in 1964 the young man began attending classes at the university in Saigon, where he avoided politics and paid attention to the problems of calculus. He devoted himself to his studies. He spent his nights alone, wrote romantic poems in his journal, took pleasure in the grace and beauty of differential equations. The war, he knew, would finally take him, but for the time being he would not let himself think about it. He had stopped praying; instead, now, he waited. And as he waited, in his final year at the university, he fell in love with a classmate, a girl of seventeen, who one day told him that his wrists were like the wrists of a child, so small and delicate, and who admired his narrow waist and the cowlick that rose up like a bird's tail at the back of his head. She liked his quiet manner; she laughed at his freckles and bony legs. One evening, perhaps, they exchanged gold rings.

Now one eye was a star.

"You okay?" Kiowa said.

The body lay almost entirely in shade. There were gnats at the mouth, little flecks of pollen drifting above the nose. The butterfly was gone. The bleeding had stopped except for the neck wounds.

Kiowa picked up the rubber sandals, clapping off the dirt, then bent down to search the body. He found a pouch of rice, a comb, a fingernail clipper, a few soiled piasters, a snapshot of a young woman standing in front of a parked motorcycle. Kiowa placed these items in his rucksack along with the gray ammunition belt and rubber sandals.

Then he squatted down.

"I'll tell you the straight truth," he said. "The guy was dead the second he stepped on the trail. Understand me? We all had him zeroed. A good kill — weapon, ammunition, everything." Tiny beads of sweat glistened at Kiowa's forehead. His eyes moved from the sky to the dead man's body to the knuckles of his own hands. "So listen, you best pull your shit together. Can't just sit here all day."

Later he said, "Understand?"

Then he said, "Five minutes, Tim. Five more minutes and we're moving out."

The one eye did a funny twinkling trick, red to yellow. His head was wrenched sideways, as if loose at the neck, and the dead young man seemed to be staring at some distant object beyond the bell-shaped flowers along the trail. The blood at the neck had gone to a deep purplish black. Clean fingernails, clean hair — he had been a soldier for only a single day. After his years at the university, the man I killed returned with his new wife to the village of My Khe, where he enlisted as a common rifleman with the 48th Vietcong Battalion. He knew he would die quickly. He knew he would see a flash of light. He knew he would fall dead and wake up in the stories of his village and people.

Kiowa covered the body with a poncho.

"Hey, you're looking better," he said. "No doubt about it. All you needed was time — some mental R&R."

Then he said, "Man, I'm sorry."

Then later he said, "Why not talk about it?"

Then he said, "Come on, man, talk."

He was a slim, dead, almost dainty young man of about twenty. He lay with one leg bent beneath him, his jaw in his throat, his face neither expressive nor inexpressive. One eye was shut. The other was a star-shaped hole.

"Talk," Kiowa said.

Questions for Discussion

1. How does the narrator describe the man he killed? Why does the narrator repeat these details throughout the story? Why does he contrast the details of his features with their mutilation from the grenade?

2. What is the significance of the butterfly that moves along the dead man's face and finally flies away?

3. What fantasy biography does the narrator provide for the dead man? Why is it woven throughout the story, rather than being presented in a single section? What impact does the biography have?

4. What are the different responses of the other soldiers to the killing? Why are all their attempts to reconcile the narrator with the killing unsuccessful?

5. What is implied by Kiowa's final word of advice to the narrator, "Talk"? Do you think the narrator follows his advice? Why or why not?

Ideas for Writing

1. Write an essay about "The Man I Killed" as an antiwar story. How does it reveal the long-term effects of soldiers' experiences under war conditions?

2. Write a story about the narrator's experiences prior to killing a man in war. What might have drawn him into the war? What experiences might he have had that could be related to the "fantasy biography" he creates for the young soldier?

ANN BEATTIE   (b. 1947)

Ann Beattie's style is often compared with Raymond Carver's: her descriptions are straightforward and realistic, and she writes about people whose lives are unsettled, in transition. Her themes and settings, however, are more reminiscent of John Cheever's and John Updike's, with many stories focusing on well-educated, comfortably positioned suburbanites.

Beattie was born and raised in Washington, D.C., and earned her B.A. from American University and her M.A. from the University of Connecticut. She left a position at Harvard University to write full time when she was awarded a Guggenheim fellowship in 1978. Currently she is a visiting writer and lecturer at the University of Virginia in Charlottesville. Although she has written several popular novels, such as *Picturing Will* (1989) and *Another You* (1995), Beattie is best known for her story collections, which include *Distortions* (1976), *The Burning House* (1982), and *What Was Mine and Other Stories* (1991). "Janus" is included in the collection *Where You'll Find Me* (1986).

Beattie has said about her fiction, "My stories are a lot about chaos . . . and many of the simple flat statements that I bring together are usually non sequiturs or bordering on being non sequiturs — which reinforces the chaos. I write in those flat simple sentences because that's the way I think. I don't mean to do it as a technique."

Janus   (1986)

The bowl was perfect. Perhaps it was not what you'd select if you faced a shelf of bowls, and not the sort of thing that would inevitably attract a lot of attention at a crafts fair, yet it had real presence. It was as predictably admired as a mutt who has no reason to suspect he might be funny. Just such a dog, in fact, was often brought out (and in) along with the bowl.

Andrea was a real-estate agent, and when she thought that some prospective buyers might be dog-lovers, she would drop off her dog at the same time she placed the bowl in the house that was up for sale. She would put a dish of water in the kitchen for Mondo, take his squeaking plastic frog out of her purse and drop it on the floor. He would pounce delightedly, just as he did every day at home, batting around his favorite toy. The bowl usually sat on a coffee table, though recently she had displayed it on top of a pine blanket chest and on a lacquered table. It was once placed on a cherry table beneath a Bonnard still-life, where it held its own.

Everyone who has purchased a house or who has wanted to sell a house must be familiar with some of the tricks used to convince a buyer that the house is quite special: a fire in the fireplace in early evening; jonquils in a pitcher on the kitchen counter, where no one ordinarily has space to put flowers; perhaps the slight aroma of spring, made by a single drop of scent vaporizing from a lamp bulb.

The wonderful thing about the bowl, Andrea thought, was that it was both subtle and noticeable — a paradox of a bowl. Its glaze was the color of cream and seemed to glow no matter what light it was placed in. There were a few bits of color in it — tiny geometric flashes — and some of these were tinged with flecks of silver. They were as mysterious as cells seen under a microscope; it was difficult not to study them, because they shimmered, flashing for a split second, and then resumed their shape. Something about the colors and their random placement suggested motion. People who liked country furniture always commented on the bowl, but then it turned out that people who felt comfortable with Biedermeier loved it just as much. But the bowl was not at all ostentatious, or even so noticeable that anyone would suspect that it had been put in place deliberately. They might notice the height of the ceiling on first entering a room, and only when their eye moved down from that, or away from the refraction of sunlight on a pale wall, would they see the bowl. Then they would go immediately to it and comment. Yet they always faltered when they tried to say something. Perhaps it was because they were in the house for a serious reason, not to notice some object.

Once, Andrea got a call from a woman who had not put in an offer on a house she had shown her. That bowl, she said — would it be possible to find out where the owners had bought that beautiful bowl? Andrea pretended that she did not know what the woman was referring to. A bowl, somewhere in the house? Oh, on a table under the window. Yes, she would ask, of course. She let a couple of days pass, then called back to say that the bowl had been a present and the people did not know where it had been purchased.

When the bowl was not being taken from house to house, it sat on Andrea's coffee table at home. She didn't keep it carefully wrapped (although she transported it that way, in a box); she kept it on the table, because she liked to see it. It was large enough so that it didn't seem fragile, or particularly vulnerable if anyone sideswiped the table or Mondo blundered into it at play. She had asked her husband to please not drop his house key in it. It was meant to be empty.

When her husband first noticed the bowl, he had peered into it and smiled briefly. He always urged her to buy things she liked. In recent years, both of them had acquired many things to make up for all the lean years when they were graduate students, but now that they had been comfortable for quite a while, the pleasure of new possessions dwindled. Her husband had pronounced the bowl "pretty," and he had turned away without picking it up to examine it. He had no more interest in the bowl than she had in his new Leica.

She was sure that the bowl brought her luck. Bids were often put in on houses where she had displayed the bowl. Sometimes the owners, who were always asked to be away or to step outside when the house was being shown, didn't even know that the bowl had been in their house. Once — she could not imagine how — she left it behind, and then she was so afraid that something might have happened to it that she rushed back to the house and sighed with relief when the woman owner opened the door. The bowl, Andrea explained — she had purchased a bowl and set it on the chest for safekeeping while she toured the house with the prospective buyers, and she . . . She felt like rushing past the frowning woman and seizing her bowl. The owner stepped aside, and it was only when Andrea ran to the chest that the lady glanced at her a little strangely. In the few seconds before Andrea picked up the bowl, she realized that the owner must have just seen that it had been perfectly placed, that the sunlight struck the bluer part of it. Her pitcher had been moved to the far side of the chest, and the bowl predominated. All the way home, Andrea wondered how she could have left the bowl behind. It was like leaving a friend at an outing — just walking off. Sometimes there were stories in the paper about families forgetting a child somewhere and driving to the next city. Andrea had only gone a mile down the road before she remembered.

In time, she dreamed of the bowl. Twice, in a waking dream — early in the morning, between sleep and a last nap before rising — she had a clear vision of it. It came into sharp focus and startled her for a moment — the same bowl she looked at every day.

She had a very profitable year selling real estate. Word spread, and she had more clients than she felt comfortable with. She had the foolish thought that if only the bowl were an animate object she could thank it. There were times when she wanted to talk to her husband about the bowl. He was a stockbroker, and sometimes told people that he was fortunate to be married to a woman who had such a fine aesthetic sense and yet could also function in the real world. They were a lot alike, really — they had agreed on that. They were both quiet people — reflective, slow to make value judgments, but almost intractable once they had come to a conclusion. They both liked details, but while ironies attracted her, he was more impatient and dismissive when matters became many-sided or unclear. But they both knew this; it was the kind of thing they could talk about when they were alone in the car together, coming home from a party or after a weekend with friends. But she never talked to him about the bowl. When they were at dinner, exchanging their news of the day, or while they lay in bed at night listening to the stereo and murmuring sleepy disconnections, she was often tempted to come right out and say that she thought that the bowl in the living room, the cream-colored bowl, was responsible for her success. But she didn't say it. She couldn't begin to explain it. Sometimes in the morning, she would look at him and feel guilty that she had such a constant secret.

Could it be that she had some deeper connection with the bowl — a relationship of some kind? She corrected her thinking: how could she imagine such a thing, when she was a human being and it was a bowl? It was ridiculous. Just think of how people lived together and loved each other . . . But was that always so clear, always a relationship? She was confused by these thoughts, but they remained in her mind. There was something within her now, something real, that she never talked about.

The bowl was a mystery, even to her. It was frustrating, because her involvement with the bowl contained a steady sense of unrequited good fortune; it would have been easier to respond if some sort of demand were made in return. But that only happened in fairy tales. The bowl was just a bowl. She did not believe that for one second. What she believed was that it was something she loved.

In the past, she had sometimes talked to her husband about a new property she was about to buy or sell — confiding some clever strategy she had devised to persuade owners who seemed ready to sell. Now she stopped doing that, for all her strategies involved the bowl. She became more deliberate with the bowl, and more possessive. She put it in houses only when no one was there, and removed it when she left the house. Instead of just moving a pitcher or a dish, she would remove all the other objects from a table. She had to force herself to handle them carefully, because she didn't really care about them. She just wanted them out of sight.

She wondered how the situation would end. As with a lover, there was no exact scenario of how matters would come to a close. Anxiety became the operative force. It would be irrelevant if the lover rushed into someone else's arms, or wrote her a note and departed to another city. The horror was the possibility of the disappearance. That was what mattered.

She would get up at night and look at the bowl. It never occurred to her that she might break it. She washed and dried it without anxiety, and she moved it often, from coffee table to mahogany corner table or wherever, without fearing an accident. It was clear that she would not be the one who would do anything to the bowl. The bowl was only handled by her, set safely on one surface or another; it was not very likely that anyone would break it. A bowl was a poor conductor of electricity: it would not be hit by lightning. Yet the idea of damage persisted. She did not think beyond that — to what her life would be without the bowl. She only continued to fear that some accident would happen. Why not, in a world where people set plants where they did not belong, so that visitors touring a house would be fooled into thinking that dark corners got sunlight — a world full of tricks?

She had first seen the bowl several years earlier, at a crafts fair she had visited half in secret, with her lover. He had urged her to buy the bowl. She didn't *need* any more things, she told him. But she had been drawn to the bowl, and they had lingered near it. Then she went on to the next booth, and he came up behind her, tapping the rim against her shoulder as she ran her fingers over a wood carving. "You're still insisting that I buy that?" she said. "No" he said. "I bought it for you." He had bought her other things before this — things she liked more, at first — the child's ebony-and-turquoise ring that fitted her little finger;

the wooden box, long and thin, beautifully dovetailed, that she used to hold paper clips; the soft gray sweater with a pouch pocket. It was his idea that when he could not be there to hold her hand she could hold her own — clasp her hands inside the lone pocket that stretched across the front. But in time she became more attached to the bowl than to any of his other presents. She tried to talk herself out of it. She owned other things that were more striking or valuable. It wasn't an object whose beauty jumped out at you; a lot of people must have passed it by before the two of them saw it that day.

Her lover had said that she was always too slow to know what she really loved. Why continue with her life the way it was? Why be two-faced, he asked her. He had made the first move toward her. When she would not decide in his favor, would not change her life and come to him, he asked her what made her think she could have it both ways. And then he made the last move and left. It was a decision meant to break her will, to shatter her intransigent ideas about honoring previous commitments.

Time passed. Alone in the living room at night, she often looked at the bowl sitting on the table, still and safe, unilluminated. In its way, it was perfect: the world cut in half, deep and smoothly empty. Near the rim, even in dim light, the eye moved toward one small flash of blue, a vanishing point on the horizon.

Questions for Discussion

1. The bowl is "predictably admired as a mutt who has no reason to suspect he might be funny." What does this quality suggest about the bowl's charm and Andrea's relation to it?

2. How does the knowledge that the bowl is a gift from a former lover — who feels Andrea is "too slow to know what she really loved" — affect your sense of its symbolic meaning?

3. Why does Andrea believe that the bowl was meant to be empty? What does her affection for the empty bowl imply about her marriage and her future?

4. Why does Andrea believe that the bowl brings her luck? Does her perception of the bowl as "lucky" seem accurate? Does she have luck because she believes in herself and her own talent?

5. Janus is a two-faced god, the Roman god of doorways, and the Janus image has been used as a theatrical icon — the coupled masks of comedy and tragedy. Why is the title "Janus" appropriate for the story?

Ideas for Writing

1. Retell this story from another perspective: that of the husband, the lover, a client, or even the bowl itself.

2. Interpret the story by focusing on the bowl as the central organizing symbol. How does its meaning change as the story develops? What does the bowl reveal about Andrea, her profession, her lover, and her future prospects?

LESLIE MARMON SILKO   (b. 1948)

Of Laguna Native American, Mexican, and Anglo-American ancestry, Leslie Marmon Silko often blends Western forms with native storytelling traditions and approaches to nature and spirituality. Born in Albuquerque, New Mexico, and raised on the Laguna Pueblo Reservation, Silko completed her B.A. at the University of New Mexico. She studied law and taught for two years at Navajo Community College in Arizona. Then she spent two years traveling in Alaska, where she studied Eskimo-Aleut culture and wrote *Ceremony* (1977), her first novel. She has completed two books of poetry, *Laguna Woman: Poems* (1974) and *Sacred Water* (1994), and a collection of short stories, *Storyteller* (1981), from which "Yellow Woman" is taken. *Almanac of the Dead* (1991) is her most recent novel. Her essays are collected in *Yellow Woman and a Beauty of the Spirit* (1996). She has also taught at the University of Arizona and the University of New Mexico.

Silko's writing explores social issues within Pueblo reservation life as well as Native American folklore, philosophy, and religious concerns. She has described the "yellow woman" of Navajo folklore as "one who shatters the cultural paradigm or steps through or steps out. She does that because there's a real overpowering sexual power that's felt . . . that is actually the animal and human world, those two being drawn together."

Yellow Woman   (1981)

I

My thigh clung to his with dampness, and I watched the sun rising up through the tamaracks and willows. The small brown water birds came to the river and hopped across the mud, leaving brown scratches in the alkali-white crust. They bathed in the river silently. I could hear the water, almost at our feet where the narrow fast channel bubbled and washed green ragged moss and fern leaves. I looked at him beside me, rolled in the red blanket on the white river sand. I cleaned the sand out of the cracks between my toes, squinting because the sun was above the willow trees. I looked at him for the last time, sleeping on the white river sand.

I felt hungry and followed the river south the way we had come the afternoon before, following our footprints that were already blurred by the lizard tracks and bug trails. The horses were still lying down, and the black one whinnied when he saw me but he did not get up — maybe it was because the corral was made out of thick cedar branches and the horses had not yet felt the sun like I had. I tried to look beyond the pale red mesas to the pueblo. I knew it was there, even if I could not see it, on the sand rock hill above the river, the same river that moved past me now and had reflected the moon last night.

The horse felt warm underneath me. He shook his head and pawed the sand. The bay whinnied and leaned against the gate trying to follow, and I remembered him asleep in the red blanket beside the river. I slid off the horse and tied him close to the other horse. I walked north with the river again, and the white sand broke loose in footprints over footprints.

"Wake up."

He moved in the blanket and turned his face to me with his eyes still closed. I knelt down to touch him.

"I'm leaving."

He smiled now, eyes still closed. "You are coming with me, remember?" He sat up now with his bare dark chest and belly in the sun.

"Where?"

"To my place."

"And will I come back?"

He pulled his pants on. I walked away from him, feeling him behind me and smelling the willows.

"Yellow Woman," he said.

I turned to face him. "Who are you?" I asked.

He laughed and knelt on the low, sandy bank, washing his face in the river. "Last night you guessed my name, and you knew why I had come."

I stared past him at the shallow moving water and tried to remember the night, but I could only see the moon in the water and remember his warmth around me.

"But I only said that you were him and that I was Yellow Woman — I'm not really her — I have my own name and I come from the pueblo on the other side of the mesa. Your name is Silva and you are a stranger I met by the river yesterday afternoon."

He laughed softly. "What happened yesterday has nothing to do with what you will do today, Yellow Woman."

"I know — that's what I'm saying — the old stories about the ka'tsina spirit[1] and Yellow Woman can't mean us."

My old grandpa liked to tell those stories best. There is one about Badger and Coyote who went hunting and were gone all day, and when the sun was going down they found a house. There was a girl living there alone, and she had light hair and eyes and she told them that they could sleep with her. Coyote wanted to be with her all night so he sent Badger into a prairie-dog hole, telling him he thought he saw something in it. As soon as Badger crawled in, Coyote blocked up the entrance with rocks and hurried back to Yellow Woman.

---

[1] Spirit associated with the mountains in Pueblo folklore. — Eds.

"Come here," he said gently.

He touched my neck and I moved close to him to feel his breathing and to hear his heart. I was wondering if Yellow Woman had known who she was — if she knew that she would become part of the stories. Maybe she'd had another name that her husband and relatives called her so that only the ka'tsina from the north and the storytellers would know her as Yellow Woman. But I didn't go on; I felt him all around me, pushing me down into the white river sand.

Yellow Woman went away with the spirit from the north and lived with him and his relatives. She was gone for a long time, but then one day she came back and she brought twin boys.

"Do you know the story?"

"What story?" He smiled and pulled me close to him as he said this. I was afraid lying there on the red blanket. All I could know was the way he felt, warm, damp, his body beside me. This is the way it happens in the stories, I was thinking, with no thought beyond the moment she meets the ka'tsina spirit and they go.

"I don't have to go. What they tell in stories was real only then, back in time immemorial, like they say."

He stood up and pointed at my clothes tangled in the blanket. "Let's go," he said.

I walked beside him, breathing hard because he walked fast, his hand around my wrist. I had stopped trying to pull away from him, because his hand felt cool and the sun was high, drying the river bed into alkali. I will see someone, eventually I will see someone, and then I will be certain that he is only a man — some man from nearby — and I will be sure that I am not Yellow Woman. Because she is from out of time past and I live now and I've been to school and there are highways and pickup trucks that Yellow Woman never saw.

It was an easy ride north on horseback. I watched the change from the cottonwood trees along the river to the junipers that brushed past us in the foothills, and finally there were only piñons, and when I looked up at the rim of the mountain plateau I could see pine trees growing on the edge. Once I stopped to look down, but the pale sandstone had disappeared and the river was gone and the dark lava hills were all around. He touched my hand, not speaking, but always singing softly a mountain song and looking into my eyes.

I felt hungry and wondered what they were doing at home now — my mother, my grandmother, my husband, and the baby. Cooking breakfast, saying, "Where did she go? — maybe kidnapped," and Al going to the tribal police with the details: "She went walking along the river."

The house was made with black lava rock and red mud. It was high above the spreading miles of arroyos and long mesas. I smelled a mountain smell of pitch and buck brush. I stood there beside the black horse, looking down on the small, dim country we had passed, and I shivered.

"Yellow Woman, come inside where it's warm."

II

He lit a fire in the stove. It was an old stove with a round belly and an enamel coffeepot on top. There was only the stove, some faded Navajo blankets, and a bedroll and cardboard box. The floor was made of smooth adobe plaster, and there was one small window facing east. He pointed at the box.

"There's some potatoes and the frying pan." He sat on the floor with his arms around his knees pulling them close to his chest and he watched me fry the potatoes. I didn't mind him watching me because he was always watching me — he had been watching me since I came upon him sitting on the river bank trimming leaves from a willow twig with his knife. We ate from the pan and he wiped the grease from his fingers on his Levis.

"Have you brought women here before?" He smiled and kept chewing, so I said, "Do you always use the same tricks?"

"What tricks?" He looked at me like he didn't understand.

"The story about being a ka'tsina from the mountains. The story about Yellow Woman."

Silva was silent; his face was calm.

"I don't believe it. Those stories couldn't happen now," I said.

He shook his head and said softly, "But someday they will talk about us, and they will say, 'Those two lived long ago when things like that happened.'"

He stood up and went out. I ate the rest of the potatoes and thought about things — about the noise the stove was making and the sound of the mountain wind outside. I remembered yesterday and the day before, and then I went outside.

I walked past the corral to the edge where the narrow trail cut through the black rim rock. I was standing in the sky with nothing around me but the wind that came down from the blue mountain peak behind me. I could see faint mountain images in the distance miles across the vast spread of mesas and valleys and plains. I wondered who was over there to feel the mountain wind on those sheer blue edges — who walks on the pine needles in those blue mountains.

"Can you see the pueblo?" Silva was standing behind me.

I shook my head. "We're too far away."

"From here I can see the world." He stepped out on the edge. "The Navajo reservation begins over there." He pointed to the east. "The Pueblo boundaries are over here." He looked below us to the south, where the narrow trail seemed to come from. "The Texans have their ranches over there, starting with that valley, the Concho Valley. The Mexicans run some cattle over there too."

"Do you ever work for them?"

"I steal from them," Silva answered. The sun was dropping behind us and shadows were filling the land below. I turned away from the edge that dropped forever into the valleys below.

"I'm cold," I said; "I'm going inside." I started wondering about this man who could speak the Pueblo language so well but who lived on a mountain and rustled cattle. I decided that this man Silva must be Navajo, because Pueblo men didn't do things like that.

"You must be a Navajo."

Silva shook his head gently. "Little Yellow Woman," he said, "you never give up, do you? I have told you who I am. The Navajo people know me, too." He knelt down and unrolled the bedroll and spread the extra blankets out on a piece of canvas. The sun was down, and the only light in the house came from outside — the dim orange light from sundown.

I stood there and waited for him to crawl under the blankets.

"What are you waiting for?" he said, and I lay down beside him. He undressed me slowly like the night before beside the river — kissing my face gently and running his hands up and down my belly and legs. He took off my pants and then he laughed.

"Why are you laughing?"

"You are breathing so hard."

I pulled away from him and turned my back to him.

He pulled me around and pinned me down with his arms and chest. "You don't understand, do you, little Yellow Woman? You will do what I want."

And again he was all around me with his skin slippery against mine, and I was afraid because I understood that his strength could hurt me. I lay underneath him and I knew that he could destroy me. But later, while he slept beside me, I touched his face and I had a feeling — the kind of feeling for him that overcame me that morning along the river. I kissed him on the forehead and he reached out for me.

When I woke up in the morning he was gone. It gave me a strange feeling because for a long time I sat there on the blankets and looked around the little house for some object of his — some proof that he had been there or maybe that he was coming back. Only the blankets and the cardboard box remained. The .30-30 that had been leaning in the corner was gone, and so was the knife I had used the night before. He was gone, and I had my chance to go now. But first I had to eat, because I knew it would be a long walk home.

I found some dried apricots in the cardboard box, and I sat down on a rock at the edge of the plateau rim. There was no wind and the sun warmed me. I was surrounded by silence. I drowsed with apricots in my mouth, and I didn't believe that there were highways or railroads or cattle to steal.

When I woke up, I stared down at my feet in the black mountain dirt. Little black ants were swarming over the pine needles around my foot. They must have smelled the apricots. I thought about my family far below me. They would be wondering about me, because this had never happened to me before. The tribal police would file a report. But if old Grandpa weren't dead he would tell them what happened — he would laugh and say, "Stolen by a ka'tsina, a mountain spirit. She'll come home — they usually do." There are enough of them to handle things. My mother and grandmother will raise the baby like they raised me. Al will find someone else, and they will go on like before, except that there will be a story about the day I disappeared while I was walking along the river. Silva had come for me; he said he had. I did not decide to go. I just went. Moonflowers blossom in the sand hills before dawn, just as I followed him. That's what I was thinking as I wandered along the trail through the pine trees.

It was noon when I got back. When I saw the stone house I remembered that I had meant to go home. But that didn't seem important any more, maybe because there were little blue flowers growing in the meadow behind the stone house and the gray squirrels were playing in the pines next to the house. The horses were standing in the corral, and there was a beef carcass hanging on the shady side of a big pine in front of the house. Flies buzzed around the clotted blood that hung from the carcass. Silva was washing his hands in a bucket full of water. He must have heard me coming because he spoke to me without turning to face me.

"I've been waiting for you."

"I went walking in the big pine trees."

I looked into the bucket full of bloody water with brown-and-white animal hairs floating in it. Silva stood there letting his hand drip, examining me intently.

"Are you coming with me?"

"Where?" I asked him.

"To sell the meat in Marquez."

"If you're sure it's O.K."

"I wouldn't ask you if it wasn't," he answered.

He sloshed the water around in the bucket before he dumped it out and set the bucket upside down near the door. I followed him to the corral and watched him saddle the horses. Even beside the horses he looked tall, and I asked him again if he wasn't Navajo. He didn't say anything; he just shook his head and kept cinching up the saddle.

"But Navajos are tall."

"Get on the horse," he said, "and let's go."

The last thing he did before we started down the steep trail was to grab the .30-30 from the corner. He slid the rifle into the scabbard that hung from his saddle.

"Do they ever try to catch you?" I asked.

"They don't know who I am."

"Then why did you bring the rifle?"

"Because we are going to Marquez where the Mexicans live."

III

The trail leveled out on a narrow ridge that was steep on both sides like an animal spine. On one side I could see where the trail went around the rocky gray hills and disappeared into the southeast where the pale sandrock mesas stood in the distance near my home. On the other side was a trail that went west, and as I looked far into the distance I thought I saw the little town. But Silva said no, that I was looking in the wrong place, that I just thought I saw houses. After that I quit looking off into the distance; it was hot and the wild-flowers were closing up their deep-yellow petals. Only the waxy cactus flow-ers bloomed in the bright sun, and I saw every color that a cactus blossom can be; the white ones and the red ones were still buds, but the purple and the yel-low were blossoms, open full and the most beautiful of all.

Silva saw him before I did. The white man was riding a big gray horse, coming up the trail toward us. He was traveling fast and the gray horse's feet sent rocks rolling off the trail into the dry tumbleweeds. Silva motioned for me to stop and we watched the white man. He didn't see us right away, but finally his horse whinnied at our horses and he stopped. He looked at us briefly before he loped the gray horse across the three hundred yards that separated us. He stopped his horse in front of Silva, and his young fat face was shadowed by the brim of his hat. He didn't look mad, but his small, pale eyes moved from the blood-soaked gunny sacks hanging from my saddle to Silva's face and then back to my face.

"Where did you get the fresh meat?" the white man asked.

"I've been hunting," Silva said, and when he shifted his weight in the sad-dle the leather creaked.

"The hell you have, Indian. You've been rustling cattle. We've been look-ing for the thief for a long time."

The rancher was fat, and sweat began to soak through his white cowboy shirt and the wet cloth stuck to the thick rolls of belly fat. He almost seemed to be panting from the exertion of talking, and he smelled rancid, maybe be-cause Silva scared him.

Silva turned to me and smiled. "Go back up the mountain, Yellow Woman."

The white man got angry when he heard Silva speak in a language he couldn't understand. "Don't try anything, Indian. Just keep riding to Marquez. We'll call the state police from there."

The rancher must have been unarmed because he was very frightened and if he had a gun he would have pulled it out then. I turned my horse around and the rancher yelled, "Stop!" I looked at Silva for an instant and there was something ancient and dark — something I could feel in my stomach — in his eyes, and when I glanced at his hand I saw his finger on the trigger of the .30-30 that was still in the saddle scabbard. I slapped my horse across the flank and the sacks of raw meat swung against my knees as the horse leaped up the trail. It was hard to keep my balance, and once I thought I felt the saddle slip-ping backward; it was because of this that I could not look back.

I didn't stop until I reached the ridge where the trail forked. The horse was breathing deep gasps and there was a dark film of sweat on its neck. I looked down in the direction I had come from, but I couldn't see the place. I waited.

The wind came up and pushed warm air past me. I looked up at the sky, pale blue and full of thin clouds and fading vapor trails left by jets.

I think four shots were fired — I remember hearing four hollow explosions that reminded me of deer hunting. There could have been more shots after that, but I couldn't have heard them because my horse was running again and the loose rocks were making too much noise as they scattered around his feet.

Horses have a hard time running downhill, but I went that way instead of uphill to the mountain because I thought it was safer. I felt better with the horse running southeast past the round gray hills that were covered with cedar trees and black lava rock. When I got to the plain in the distance I could see the dark green patches of tamaracks that grew along the river; and beyond the river I could see the beginning of the pale sandrock mesas. I stopped the horse and looked back to see if anyone was coming; then I got off the horse and turned the horse around, wondering if it would go back to its corral under the pines on the mountain. It looked back at me for a moment and then plucked a mouthful of green tumbleweeds before it trotted back up the trail with its ears pointed forward, carrying its head daintily to one side to avoid stepping on the dragging reins. When the horse disappeared over the last hill, the gunny sacks full of meat were still swinging and bouncing.

IV

I walked toward the river on a wood-hauler's road that I knew would eventually lead to the paved road. I was thinking about waiting beside the road for someone to drive by, but by the time I got to the pavement I had decided it wasn't very far to walk if I followed the river back the way Silva and I had come.

The river water tasted good, and I sat in the shade under a cluster of silvery willows. I thought about Silva, and I felt sad at leaving him; still, there was something strange about him, and I tried to figure it out all the way back home.

I came back to the place on the river bank where he had been sitting the first time I saw him. The green willow leaves that he had trimmed from the branch were still lying there, wilted in the sand. I saw the leaves and I wanted to go back to him — to kiss him and to touch him — but the mountains were too far away now. And I told myself, because I believe it, he will come back sometime and be waiting again by the river.

I followed the path up from the river into the village. The sun was getting low, and I could smell supper cooking when I got to the screen door of my house. I could hear their voices inside — my mother was telling my grandmother how to fix the Jell-O and my husband, Al, was playing with the baby. I decided to tell them that some Navajo had kidnapped me, but I was sorry that old Grandpa wasn't alive to hear my story because it was the Yellow Woman stories he liked to tell best.

Questions for Discussion

1. Why are stories important to the narrator of this story?
2. What do you know about the Yellow Woman who is telling this story? What are her values and concerns? How does her point of view shape the telling and meaning of the story?
3. Why does the narrator stay with Silva when she knows she could escape?
4. What strategies does Silko use to make the story seem dreamlike? How does the story's dreamlike mood affect your interpretation of the events that occur?
5. Why does the narrator return home? What has she learned from her adventure, and what is the significance of her experience with Silva?

Ideas for Writing

1. Write an essay in which you interpret the narrator's encounter with Silva. What forces does he represent? What does the story imply about relationships between men, women, and the spirit world in Pueblo society?
2. The Yellow Woman returns home at the end of the story. Write a sequel to the story that examines how her life is changed through her meeting with Silva.

JAMAICA KINCAID   (b. 1949)

Born in Antigua, West Indies, Jamaica Kincaid left the islands when she was seventeen, but she still has strong feelings about her country of origin and writes about Antigua with fond remembrance: "America [has] given me a place to be myself — but . . . I was formed somewhere else." An only child, Kincaid was the center of attention in her family until she moved to the United States. She attended college in New Hampshire but was soon disillusioned with her courses and decided to educate herself. In 1974 she began publishing stories in magazines such as *Rolling Stone*, the *Paris Review*, and the *New Yorker*, whose staff she joined in 1978. Her first collection of short stories, *At the Bottom of the River* (1983), won the Morton Dauwen Zabel Award from the American Academy and Institute of Arts and Letters. *Annie John* (1985) interweaves related short stories about a girl coming of age in the West Indies. Life in the West Indies continues to be the subject of *A Small Place* (1988); *Lucy* (1989), which includes "Poor Visitor"; and her latest novel, *The Autobiography of My Mother* (1995). Much of Kincaid's fiction is highly autobiographical; like the narrator of "Poor Visitor," for example, she initially came to the United States to work as an au pair in New York City.

Poor Visitor   (1989)

It was my first day. I had come the night before, a gray-black and cold night before — as it was expected to be in the middle of January, though I didn't know that at the time — and I could not see anything clearly on the way in from the airport, even though there were lights everywhere. As we drove along, someone would single out to me a famous building, an important street, a park, a bridge that when built was thought to be a spectacle. In a daydream I used to have, all these places were points of happiness to me; all these places were lifeboats to my small drowning soul, for I would imagine myself entering and leaving them, and just that — entering and leaving over and over again — would see me through a bad feeling I did not have a name for. I only knew it felt a little like sadness. Now that I saw these places, they looked ordinary, dirty, worn down by so many people entering and leaving them in real life, and it occurred to me that I could not be the only person in the world for whom they were a fixture of fantasy. It was not my first bout with the disappointment of reality and it would not be my last. The undergarments that I wore were all new, bought for my journey, and as I sat in the car, twisting this way and that to get a good view of the sights before me, I was reminded of how uncomfortable the new can make you feel.

I got into an elevator, something I had never done before, and then I was in an apartment and seated at a table, eating food just taken from a refrigerator. In Antigua, where I came from, I had always lived in a house, and my house did not have a refrigerator in it. Everything I was experiencing — the ride in the elevator, being in an apartment, eating day-old food that had been stored in a refrigerator — was such a good idea that I could imagine I would grow used to it and like it very much, but at first it was all so new that I had to smile with my mouth turned down at the corners. I slept soundly that night, but it wasn't because I was happy and comfortable — quite the opposite; it was because I didn't want to take in anything else.

That morning, the morning of my first day, the morning that followed my first night, was a sunny morning. It was not the sort of bright sun-yellow making everything curl at the edges, almost in fright, that I was used to, but a pale-yellow sun, as if the sun had grown weak from trying too hard to shine; but still it was sunny, and that was nice and made me miss my home less. And so, seeing the sun, I got up and put on a dress, a gay dress made out of madras cloth — the same sort of dress that I would wear if I were at home and setting out for a day in the country. It was all wrong. The sun was shining but the air was cold. It was the middle of January, after all. But I did not know that the sun could shine and the air remain cold; no one had ever told me. What a feeling that was! How can I explain? Something I had always known — the way I knew my skin was the color brown of a nut rubbed repeatedly with a soft cloth, or the way I knew my own name — something I took completely for granted, "the sun is shining, the air is warm," was not so. I was no longer in a tropical zone, and this realization now entered my life like a flow of water dividing formerly dry and solid ground, creating two banks, one of which was my past — so familiar and predictable that even my unhappiness then made me happy now just to think of it — the other my future, a gray blank, an overcast seascape on which rain was falling and no boats were in sight. I was no longer in a tropical zone and I felt cold inside and out, the first time such a sensation had come over me.

In books I had read — from time to time, when the plot called for it — someone would suffer from homesickness. A person would leave a not very nice situation and go somewhere else, somewhere a lot better, and then long to go back where it was not very nice. How impatient I would become with such a person, for I would feel that I was in a not very nice situation myself, and how I wanted to go somewhere else. But now I, too, felt that I wanted to be back where I came from. I understood it, I knew where I stood there. If I had had to draw a picture of my future then, it would have been a large gray patch surrounded by black, blacker, blackest.

What a surprise this was to me, that I longed to be back in the place that I came from, that I longed to sleep in a bed I had outgrown, that I longed to be with people whose smallest, most natural gesture would call up in me such a rage that I longed to see them all dead at my feet. Oh, I had imagined that with my one swift act — leaving home and coming to this new place — I could leave behind me, as if it were an old garment never to be worn again, my sad thoughts, my sad feelings, and my discontent with life in general as it presented itself to me. In the past, the thought of being in my present situation had been a comfort, but now I did not even have this to look forward to, and so I lay down on my bed and dreamt that I was eating a bowl of pink mullet and green figs cooked in coconut milk, and it had been cooked by my grandmother, which was why the taste of it pleased me so, for she was the person I liked best in all the world and those were the things I liked best to eat also.

The room in which I lay was a small room just off the kitchen — the maid's room. I was used to a small room, but this was a different sort of small room. The ceiling was very high and the walls went all the way up to the ceiling, enclosing the room like a box — a box in which cargo travelling a long way should be shipped. But I was not cargo. I was only an unhappy young woman living in a maid's room, and I was not even the maid. I was the young girl who watches over the children and goes to school at night. How nice everyone was to me, though, saying that I should regard them as my family and make myself at home. I believed them to be sincere, for I knew that such a thing would not be said to a member of their real family. After all, aren't family the people who become the millstone around your life's neck? On the last day I spent at home, my cousin — a girl I had known all my life, an unpleasant person even before her parents forced her to become a Seventh-Day Adventist — made a farewell present to me of her own Bible, and with it she made a little speech about God and goodness and blessings. Now it sat before me on a dresser, and I remembered how when we were children we would sit under my house and terrify and torment each other by reading out loud passages from the Book of Revelations, and I wondered if ever in my whole life a day would go by when these people I had left behind, my own family, would not appear before me in one way or another.

There was also a small radio on this dresser, and I had turned it on. At that moment, almost as if to sum up how I was feeling, a song came on some of the words of which were "Put yourself in my place, if only for a day; see if you can stand the awful emptiness inside." I sang these words to myself over and over, as if they were a lullaby, and I fell asleep again. This time I dreamt that I was holding in my hands one of my old cotton-flannel nightgowns, and it was printed with beautiful scenes of children playing with Christmas-tree decorations. The scenes printed on my nightgown were so real that I could actually hear the children laughing. I felt compelled to know where this nightgown came from, and I started to examine it furiously, looking for the label. I found it just where a label usually is, in the back, and it read "Made in Australia." I was awakened from this dream by the actual maid, a woman who had let me know right away, on meeting me, that she did not like me, and gave as her reason the way I talked. I thought it was because of something else, but I did not know what. As I opened my eyes, the word "Australia" stood between our faces, and I remembered then that Australia was settled as a prison for bad people, people so bad that they couldn't be put in a prison in their own country.

My waking hours soon took on a routine. I walked four small girls to their school, and when they returned at midday I gave them a lunch of soup from a tin, and sandwiches. In the afternoon, I read to them and played with them. When they were away, I studied my books, and at night I went to school. I was unhappy. I looked at a map. The Atlantic Ocean stood between me and the place I came from, but would it have made a difference if it had been a teacup of water? I could not go back.

Outside, always it was cold, and everyone said it was the coldest winter they had ever experienced; but the way they said it made me think they said this every time winter came around. And I couldn't blame them for not really remembering each year how unpleasant, how unfriendly winter weather could be. The trees with their bare, still limbs looked dead, and as if someone had just placed them there and planned to come back and get them later; all the windows of the houses were shut tight, the way windows are shut up when a house will be empty for a long time; when people walked on the streets they did it quickly, as if they were doing something behind someone's back, as if they didn't want to draw attention to themselves, as if being out in the cold too long would cause them to dissolve. How I longed to see someone lingering on a corner, trying to draw my attention to him, trying to engage me in conversation, someone complaining to himself in a voice I could overhear about a god whose love and mercy fell on the just and the unjust.

I wrote home to say how lovely everything was, and I used flourishing words and phrases, as if I were living life in a greeting card—the kind that has a satin ribbon on it, and quilted hearts and roses, and is expected to be so precious to the person receiving it that the manufacturer has placed a leaf of plastic on the front to protect it. Everyone I wrote to said how nice it was to hear from me, how nice it was to know that I was doing well, that I was very much missed, and that they couldn't wait until the day came when I returned.

One day the maid who said she did not like me because of the way I talked told me that she was sure I could not dance. She said that I spoke like a nun, I walked like one also, and that everything about me was so pious it made her feel at once sick to her stomach and sick with pity just to look at me. And so, perhaps giving way to the latter feeling, she said that we should dance, even though she was quite sure I didn't know how. There was a little portable record-player in my room, the kind that when closed up looked like a ladies' vanity case, and she put on a record she had bought earlier that day. It was a song that was very popular at the time—three girls, not older than I was, singing in harmony and in a very insincere and artificial way about love and so on. It was very beautiful all the same, and it was beautiful because it was so insincere and artificial. She enjoyed this song, singing at the top of her voice, and she was a wonderful dancer — it amazed me to see the way in which she moved. I could not join her and I told her why: melodies of her song were so shallow, and the words, to me, were meaningless. From her face, I could see she had only one feeling about me: how sick to her stomach I made her. And so I said that I knew songs, too, and I burst into a calypso about a girl who ran away to Port-au-Spain, Trinidad, and had a good time, with no regrets.

The household in which I lived was made up of a husband, a wife, and the four girl children. The husband and wife looked alike and their four children looked just like them. In photographs of themselves, which they placed all over the house, their six yellow-haired heads of various sizes were bunched as if they were a bouquet of flowers tied together by an unseen string. In the pictures, they smiled out at the world, giving the impression that they found everything in it unbearably wonderful. And it was not a farce, their smiles. From wherever they had gone, and they seemed to have been all over the world, they brought back some tiny memento, and they could each recite its history from its very beginning. Even when a little rain fell, they would admire the way it streaked through the blank air.

At dinner, when we sat down at the table — and did not have to say grace (such a relief; as if they believed in a God that did not have to be thanked every time you turned around) — they said such nice things to each other, and the children were so happy. They would spill their food, or not eat any of it at all, or make up rhymes about it that would end with the words "smelt bad." How they made me laugh, and I wondered what sort of parents I must have had, for even to think of such words in their presence I would have been scolded severely, and I vowed that if I ever had children I would make sure that the first words out of their mouths were bad ones.

It was at dinner one night not long after I began to live with them that they began to call me the Visitor. They said I seemed not to be a part of things, as if I didn't live in their house with them, as if they weren't like a family to me, as if I were just passing through, just saying one long Hallo!, and soon would be saying a quick Goodbye! So long! It was very nice! For look at the way I looked at them eating, Lewis said. Had I never seen anyone put a forkful of French-cut green beans in his mouth before? This made Mariah laugh, but almost everything Lewis said made Mariah happy, and so she would laugh. When I didn't laugh also, Lewis said, Poor Visitor, poor Visitor, over and over, a sympathetic tone to his voice, and then he told me a story about an uncle he had who had gone to Canada and raised monkeys, and of how after a while the uncle loved monkeys so much and was so used to being around them that he found actual human beings hard to take. He had told me this story about his uncle before, and while he was telling it to me this time I was remembering a dream I had

had about them: Lewis was chasing me around the house. I wasn't wearing any clothes. The ground on which I was running was yellow, as if it had been paved with cornmeal. Lewis was chasing me around and around the house, and though he came close he could never catch up with me. Mariah stood at the open windows saying, Catch her, Lewis, catch her. Eventually I fell down a hole, at the bottom of which were some silver and blue snakes.

When Lewis finished telling his story, I told them my dream. When I finished, they both fell silent. Then they looked at me and Mariah cleared her throat, but it was obvious from the way she did it that her throat did not need clearing at all. Their two yellow heads swam toward each other and, in unison, bobbed up and down. Lewis made a clucking noise, then said, Poor, poor Visitor. And Mariah said, Dr. Freud for Visitor. Then they laughed in a soft, kind way. I had meant by telling them my dream that I had taken them in, because only people who were very important to me had ever shown up in my dreams, and I could see that they already understood that.

Questions for Discussion

1. What is revealed by the narrator's unhappiness in her new position and her surprise at her feelings of homesickness?
2. Contrast the narrator's feelings about her own family and the details she remembers from her life in Antigua with the feelings and details she uses to describe the family with whom she has come to live.
3. Why is the maid's perspective on the narrator useful to the reader in evaluating the narrator's character and difficulties in adjusting to her new position?
4. Why do Mariah and Lewis call the narrator "Poor Visitor"? Do they seem genuinely concerned about her? How do the children's feeling about her help the reader to understand the problems she faces?
5. Interpret the narrator's two dreams. How do Mariah and Lewis interpret her second dream? How is their understanding of the dream's implications different from the narrator's understanding of it?

Ideas for Writing

1. Write a story in which you imagine the narrator's future. Will she adjust to her new life? remain an isolated and unhappy individual? return to her native land? find a new and hopeful sense of identity in her new community?
2. In an essay, evaluate the narrator's adjustment as an immigrant. In what ways is the narrator's experience as an immigrant representative, normal? In what ways does it seem exceptional or even neurotic?

HARUKI MURAKAMI (b. 1949)

An active translator of the works of American writers such as F. Scott Fitzgerald, John Irving, and Raymond Carver into Japanese, Haruki Murakami is an international writer who has taught in the United States at Princeton University and currently lives in Rome. Born in Kyoto, Japan, Murakami was raised in Kobe in a bilingual household; his father taught American literature. While studying Greek classical theater at Waseda University, Murakami ran a jazz bar in Tokyo to make extra money, in addition to translating documents into English. His first novel, *A Wild Sheep Chase* (1982), won Japan's Noma Literary Award. Since then he has published the novels *Norwegian Wood* (1987), which sold four million copies in Japan; *Hardboiled Wonderland and the End of the World* (1993), which won the Tanizaki Prize; and *Dance, Dance, Dance*, which was published in the United States in 1994. "A Window" appears in Murakami's recent short-story collection, *The Elephant Vanishes* (1993).

Murakami has been strongly influenced by American culture and makes frequent references in his writings to the detective novel, American films, popular music, and commercial products. His writings often have strong elements of fantasy and science fiction, yet they are whimsical in tone and often satirical of an international consumer society in which rapid change, hedonism, hypercommercialism, interpersonal alienation, and an accelerated pace of life are increasingly the norm.

A Window (1989)

Translated by Jay Rubin

Greetings.

The winter cold diminishes with each passing day, and now the sunlight hints at the subtle scent of springtime. I trust that you are well.

Your recent letter was a pleasure to read. The passage on the relationship between hamburger steak and nutmeg was especially well written, I felt: so rich with the genuine sense of daily living. How vividly it conveyed the warm aromas of the kitchen, the lively tapping of the knife against the cutting board as it sliced through the onion!

In the course of my reading, your letter filled me with such an irrepressible desire for hamburger steak that I had to go to a nearby restaurant and have one that very night. In fact, the particular neighborhood establishment in question offers eight different varieties of hamburger steak; Texas-style,

Hawaiian-style, Japanese-style, and the like. Texas-style is big. Period. It would no doubt come as a shock to any Texans who might find their way to this part of Tokyo. Hawaiian-style is garnished with a slice of pineapple. California-style . . . I don't remember. Japanese-style is smothered with grated daikon. The place is smartly decorated, and the waitresses are all pretty, with extremely short skirts.

Not that I had made my way there for the express purpose of studying the restaurant's interior décor or the waitresses' legs. I was there for one reason only, and that was to eat hamburger steak — not Texas-style or California-style or any other style, but plain, simple hamburger steak.

Which is what I told the waitress. "I'm sorry," she replies, "but such-and-such-style hamburger steak is the only kind we have here."

I couldn't blame the waitress, of course. *She* hadn't set the menu. *She* hadn't chosen to wear this uniform that revealed so much thigh each time she cleared a dish from a table. I smiled at her and ordered a Hawaiian-style hamburger steak. As she pointed out, I merely had to set the pineapple aside when I ate the steak.

What a strange world we live in! All I want is a perfectly ordinary hamburger steak, and the only way I can have it at this particular point in time is Hawaiian-style without pineapple.

Your own hamburger steak, I gather, is the normal kind. Thanks to your letter, what I wanted most of all was an utterly normal hamburger steak made by you.

By contrast, the passage on the National Railways' automatic ticket machines struck me as a bit superficial. Your angle on the problem is a good one, to be sure, but the reader can't vividly grasp the scene. Don't try so hard to be the penetrating observer. Writing is, after all, a makeshift thing.

Your overall score on this newest letter is 70. Your style is improving slowly but surely. Don't be impatient. Just keep working as hard as you have been all along. I look forward to your next letter. Won't it be nice when spring really comes?

P.S. Thank you for the box of assorted cookies. They are delicious. The Society's rules, however, strictly forbid personal contact beyond the exchange of letters. I must ask you to restrain your kindness in the future.

Nevertheless, thank you once again.

I kept this part-time job going for a year. I was twenty-two at the time.

I ground out thirty or more letters like this every month at two thousand yen per letter for a strange little company in the Iidabashi district that called itself "The Pen Society."

"You, too, can learn to write captivating letters," boasted the company's advertisements. New "members" paid an initiation fee and monthly dues, in return for which they could write four letters a month to The Pen Society. We

"Pen Masters" would answer their letters with letters of our own, such as the one quoted above, containing corrections, comments, and guidance for future improvement. I had gone for a job interview after seeing an ad posted in the student office of the literature department. At the time, certain events had led me to delay my graduation for a year, and my parents had informed me that they would consequently be decreasing my monthly support. For the first time in my life, I was faced with having to make a living. In addition to the interview, I was asked to write several compositions, and a week later I was hired. Then came a week of training in how to make corrections, offer guidance, and other tricks of the trade, none of which was very difficult.

All Society members are assigned to Pen Masters of the opposite sex. I had a total of twenty-four members, ranging in age from fourteen to fifty-three, the majority in the twenty-five-to-thirty-five range. Which is to say, most of them were older than I was. The first month, I panicked: The women were far better writers than I was, and they had a lot more experience as correspondents. I had hardly written a serious letter in my life, after all. I'm not quite sure how I made it through that first month. I was in a constant cold sweat, convinced that most of the members in my charge would demand a new Pen Master — a privilege touted in the Society's rules.

The month went by, and not one member raised a complaint about my writing. Far from it. The owner said I was very popular. Two more months went by, and it even began to seem that my charges were improving thanks to my "guidance." It was weird. These women looked up to me as their teacher with complete trust. When I realized this, it enabled me to dash off my critiques to them with far less effort and anxiety.

I didn't realize it at the time, but these women were lonely (as were the male members of the Society). They wanted to write but they had no one to write to. They weren't the type to send fan letters to a deejay. They wanted something more personal — even if it had to come in the form of corrections and critiques.

And so it happened that I spent a part of my early twenties like a crippled walrus in a warmish harem of letters.

And what amazingly varied letters they were! Boring letters, funny letters, sad letters. Unfortunately, I couldn't keep any of them (the rules required us to return all letters to the company), and this happened so long ago that I can't recall them in detail, but I do remember them as filled to overflowing with life in all its aspects, from the largest of questions to the tiniest of trivia. And the messages they were sending seemed to me — to me, a twenty-two-year-old college student — strangely divorced from reality, seemed at times to be utterly meaningless. Nor was this due solely to my own lack of life experience. I realize now that the reality of things is not something you convey to people but something you make. It is this that gives birth to meaning. I didn't know it then, of course, and neither did the women. This was surely one of the reasons that everything in their letters struck me as oddly two-dimensional.

When it came time for me to leave the job, all the members in my care expressed their regret. And though, quite frankly, I was beginning to feel that I had had enough of this endless job of letter writing, I felt sorry, too, in a way. I knew that I would never again have so many people opening themselves to me with such simple honesty.

Hamburger steak. I did actually have the opportunity to eat a hamburger steak made by the woman to whom the earlier-quoted letter was addressed.

She was thirty-two, no children, husband worked for a company that was generally considered the fifth-best-known in the country. When I informed her in my last letter that I would have to be leaving the job at the end of the month, she invited me to lunch. "I'll fix you a perfectly normal hamburger steak," she wrote. In spite of the Society's rules, I decided to take her up on it. The curiosity of a young man of twenty-two was not to be denied.

Her apartment faced the tracks of the Odakyu Line. The rooms had an orderliness befitting a childless couple. Neither the furniture nor the lighting fixtures nor the woman's sweater was of an especially costly sort, but they were nice enough. We began with mutual surprise — mine at her youthful appearance, hers at my actual age. She had imagined me as older than herself. The Society did not reveal the ages of its Pen Masters.

Once we had finished surprising each other, the usual tension of a first meeting was gone. We ate our hamburger steak and drank coffee, feeling much like two would-be passengers who had missed the same train. And speaking of trains, from the window of her third-floor apartment one could see the electric train line below. The weather was lovely that day, and over the railings of the building's verandas hung a colorful assortment of sheets and futons drying in the sun. Every now and then came the slap of a bamboo whisk fluffing out a futon. I can bring the sound back even now. It was strangely devoid of any sense of distance.

The hamburger steak was perfect — the flavor exactly right, the outer surface grilled to a crisp dark brown, the inside full of juice, the sauce ideal. Although I could not honestly claim that I had never eaten such a delicious hamburger in my life, it was certainly the best I had had in a very long time. I told her so, and she was pleased.

After the coffee, we told each other our life stories while a Burt Bacharach record played. Since I didn't really have a life story as yet, she did most of the talking. In college she had wanted to be a writer, she said. She talked about Françoise Sagan, one of her favorites. She especially liked *Aimez-vous Brahms?* I myself did not dislike Sagan. At least, I didn't find her as cheap as everyone said. There's no law requiring everybody to write novels like Henry Miller or Jean Genet.

"I can't write, though," she said.

"It's never too late to start," I said.

"No, I know I can't write. You were the one who informed me of that." She smiled. "Writing letters to you, I finally realized it. I just don't have the talent."

I turned bright red. It's something I almost never do now, but when I was twenty-two I blushed all the time. "Really, though, your writing had something honest about it."

Instead of answering, she smiled — a tiny smile.

"At least one letter made me go out for a hamburger steak."

"You must have been hungry at the time."

And indeed, maybe I had been.

A train passed below the window with a dry clatter.

When the clock struck five, I said I would be leaving. "I'm sure you have to make dinner for your husband."

"He comes home very late," she said, her cheek against her hand. "He won't be back before midnight."

"He must be a very busy man."

"I suppose so," she said, pausing momentarily. "I think I once wrote to you about my problem. There are certain things I can't really talk with him about. My feelings don't get through to him. A lot of the time, I feel we're speaking two different languages."

I didn't know what to say to her. I couldn't understand how one could go on living with someone to whom it was impossible to convey one's feelings.

"But it's all right," she said softly, and she made it sound as if it really were all right. "Thanks for writing letters to me all these months. I enjoyed them. Truly. And writing back to you was my salvation."

"I enjoyed your letters, too," I said, though in fact I could hardly remember anything she had written.

For a while, without speaking, she looked at the clock on the wall. She seemed almost to be examining the flow of time.

"What are you going to do after graduation?" she asked.

I hadn't decided, I told her. I had no idea what to do. When I said this, she smiled again. "Maybe you ought to do some kind of work that involves writing," she said. "Your critiques were beautifully written. I used to look forward to them. I really did. No flattery intended. For all I know, you were just writing them to fulfill a quota, but they had real feeling. I've kept them all. I take them out every once in a while and reread them."

"Thank you," I said. "And thanks for the hamburger."

Ten years have gone by, but whenever I pass her neighborhood on the Odakyu Line I think of her and of her crisply grilled hamburger steak. I look out at the buildings ranged along the tracks and ask myself which window could be hers. I think about the view from that window and try to figure out where it could have been. But I can never remember.

Perhaps she doesn't live there anymore. But if she does, she is probably still listening to that same Burt Bacharach record on the other side of her window.

Should I have slept with her?

That's the central question of this piece.

The answer is beyond me. Even now, I have no idea. There are lots of things we never understand, no matter how many years we put on, no matter how much experience we accumulate. All I can do is look up from the train at the windows in the buildings that might be hers. Every one of them could be her window, it sometimes seems to me, and at other times I think that none of them could be hers. There are simply too many of them.

Questions for Discussion

1. The story begins with what is traditionally the initial greeting in a Japanese letter — a poetic comment on the weather: "now the sunlight hints at the subtle scent of springtime." Why is this opening ironic? How does this greeting contrast with the letter's content?

2. What positive and critical comments does the narrator make in his letter to the woman who has written about cooking hamburger steak? Are his comments appropriate? Is he being self-indulgent? Is the letter effective?

3. What is the real service provided by the Pen Society? Why is the narrator sorry to leave his job? What does he mean when he says that he now realizes that "the reality of things is not something you convey to people but something you make"?

4. What does the narrator learn from his encounter with the correspondent? How does he feel about her when he passes her neighborhood on the train? Why is the question he asks himself important?

5. Why is the story titled "A Window"? Why not "The Window"?

Ideas for Writing

1. Write an essay that examines the story's portrayal of alienation in modern society. Does the narrator become more or less alienated and isolated as the story progresses? How is the Pen Society a symbol of alienation?

2. Write a story from the point of view of a protagonist who only contacts other human beings through letters or e-mail.

GLORIA NAYLOR   (b. 1950)

One of Gloria Naylor's motives as a writer has been to reflect the diversity of the African-American experience; she has said that she grew up "totally ignorant . . . of literature that reflected my experience as a black American." Naylor was born and raised in New York City; her parents were originally from Mississippi. After high school she spent seven years as a missionary for the Jehovah's Witnesses, after which she turned from religion to a strong belief in feminism. Naylor then attended Brooklyn College of the City University of New York, earning her B.A. in 1981. She went on to study at Yale University and completed her M.A. in African-American studies in 1983. She has taught at a number of colleges, including Princeton University, New York University, Boston University, Brandeis University, and the University of Pennsylvania. Her first novel, *The Women of Brewster Place: A Novel in Seven Stories* (1982), which includes "The Two," won the American Book Award and was later made into a television miniseries. She won a National Endowment for the Arts fellowship in 1985 and a Guggenheim fellowship in 1988. Her subsequent novels — *Linden Hills* (1985), *Mama Day* (1988), and *Bailey's Cafe* (1992) — reflect Naylor's continuing belief in the importance of courage, community, and cultural identity.

The Two   (1983)

At first they seemed like such nice girls. No one could remember exactly when they had moved into Brewster. It was earlier in the year before Ben was killed — of course, it had to be before Ben's death. But no one remembered if it was in the winter or spring of that year that the two had come. People often came and went on Brewster Place like a restless night's dream, moving in and out in the dark to avoid eviction notices or neighborhood bulletins about the dilapidated condition of their furnishings. So it wasn't until the two were clocked leaving in the mornings and returning in the evenings at regular intervals that it was quietly absorbed that they now claimed Brewster as home. And Brewster waited, cautiously prepared to claim them, because you never knew about young women, and obviously single at that. But when no wild music or drunken friends careened out of the corner building on weekends, and especially, when no slightly eager husbands were encouraged to linger around that first-floor apartment and run errands for them, a suspended sigh of relief floated around the two when they dumped their garbage, did their shopping, and headed for the morning bus.

The women of Brewster had readily accepted the lighter, skinny one. There wasn't much threat in her timid mincing walk and the slightly protruding teeth she seemed so eager to show everyone in her bell-like good mornings and evenings. Breaths were held a little longer in the direction of the short dark one — too pretty, and too much behind. And she insisted on wearing those thin Qiana dresses that the summer breeze molded against the maddening rhythm of the twenty pounds of rounded flesh that she swung steadily down the street. Through slitted eyes, the women watched their men watching her pass, knowing the bastards were praying for a wind. But since she seemed oblivious to whether these supplications went answered, their sighs settled around her shoulders too. Nice girls.

And so no one even cared to remember exactly when they had moved into Brewster Place, until the rumor started. It had first spread through the block like a sour odor that's only faintly perceptible and easily ignored until it starts growing in strength from the dozen mouths it had been lying in, among clammy gums and scum-coated teeth. And then it was everywhere — lining the mouths and whitening the lips of everyone as they wrinkled up their noses at its pervading smell, unable to pinpoint the source or time of its initial arrival. Sophie could — she had been there.

It wasn't that the rumor had actually begun with Sophie. A rumor needs no true parent. It only needs a willing carrier, and it found one in Sophie. She had been there — on one of those August evenings when the sun's absence is a mockery because the heat leaves the air so heavy it presses the naked skin down on your body, to the point that a sheet becomes unbearable and sleep impossible. So most of Brewster was outside that night when the two had come in together, probably from one of those air-conditioned movies downtown, and had greeted the ones who were loitering around their building. And they had started up the steps when the skinny one tripped over a child's ball and the darker one had grabbed her by the arm and around the waist to break her fall. "Careful, don't wanna lose you now." And the two of them had laughed into each other's eyes and went into the building.

The smell had begun there. It outlined the image of the stumbling woman and the one who had broken her fall. Sophie and a few other women sniffed at the spot and then, perplexed, silently looked at each other. Where had they seen that before? They had often laughed and touched each other — held each other in joy or its dark twin — but where had they seen *that* before? It came to them as the scent drifted down the steps and entered their nostrils on the way to their inner mouths. They had seen that — done that — with their men. That shared moment of invisible communion reserved for two and hidden from the rest of the world behind laughter or tears or a touch. In the days before babies, miscarriages, and other broken dreams, after stolen caresses in barn stalls and cotton houses, after intimate walks from church and secret kisses with boys who were now long forgotten or permanently fixed in their lives — that was where. They could almost feel the odor moving about in their mouths, and they slowly knitted themselves together and let it out into the air like a yellow mist that began to cling to the bricks on Brewster.

So it got around that the two in 312 were *that* way. And they had seemed like such nice girls. Their regular exits and entrances to the block were viewed with a jaundiced eye. The quiet that rested around their door on the weekends hinted of all sorts of secret rituals, and their friendly indifference to the men on the street was an insult to the women as a brazen flaunting of unnatural ways.

Since Sophie's apartment windows faced theirs from across the air shaft, she became the official watchman for the block, and her opinions were deferred to whenever the two came up in conversation. Sophie took her position seriously and was constantly alert for any telltale signs that might creep out around their drawn shades, across from which she kept a religious vigil. An entire week of drawn shades was evidence enough to send her flying around with reports that as soon as it got dark they pulled their shades down and put on the lights. Heads nodded in knowing unison — a definite sign. If doubt was voiced with a "But I pull my shades down at night too," a whispered "Yeah, but you're not *that* way" was argument enough to win them over.

Sophie watched the lighter one dumping their garbage, and she went outside and opened the lid. Her eyes darted over the crushed tin cans, vegetable peelings, and empty chocolate chip cookie boxes. What do they do with all them chocolate chip cookies? It was surely a sign, but it would take some time to figure that one out. She saw Ben go into their apartment, and she waited and blocked his path as he came out, carrying his toolbox.

"What ya see?" She grabbed his arm and whispered wetly in his face.

Ben stared at her squinted eyes and drooping lips and shook his head slowly. "Uh, uh, uh, it was terrible."

"Yeah?" She moved in a little closer.

"Worst busted faucet I seen in my whole life." He shook her hand off his arm and left her standing in the middle of the block.

"You old sop bucket," she muttered, as she went back up on her stoop. A broken faucet, huh? Why did they need to use so much water?

Sophie had plenty to report that day. Ben had said it was terrible in there. No, she didn't know exactly what he had seen, but you can imagine — and they did. Confronted with the difference that had been thrust into their predictable world, they reached into their imaginations and, using an ancient pattern, weaved themselves a reason for its existence. Out of necessity they stitched all of their secret fears and lingering childhood nightmares into this existence, because even though it was deceptive enough to try and look as they looked, talk as they talked, and do as they did, it had to have some hidden stain to invalidate it — it was impossible for them both to be right. So they leaned back, supported by the sheer weight of their numbers and comforted by the woven barrier that kept them protected from the yellow mist that enshrouded the two as they came and went on Brewster Place.

Lorraine was the first to notice the change in the people on Brewster Place. She was a shy but naturally friendly woman who got up early, and had read the morning paper and done fifty sit-ups before it was time to leave for work. She came out of her apartment eager to start her day by greeting any of her neighbors who were outside. But she noticed that some of the people who had spoken to her before made a point of having something else to do with their eyes when she passed, although she could almost feel them staring at her back as she moved on. The ones who still spoke only did so after an uncomfortable pause, in which they seemed to be peering through her before they begrudged her a good morning or evening. She wondered if it was all in her mind and she thought about mentioning it to Theresa, but she didn't want to be accused of being too sensitive again. And how would Tee even notice anything like that anyway? She had a lousy attitude and hardly ever spoke to people. She stayed in that bed until the last moment and rushed out of the house fogged-up and grumpy, and she was used to being stared at — by men at least — because of her body.

Lorraine thought about these things as she came up the block from work, carrying a large paper bag. The group of women on her stoop parted silently and let her pass.

"Good evening," she said, as she climbed the steps.

Sophie was standing on the top step and tried to peek into the bag. "You been shopping, huh? What ya buy?" It was almost an accusation.

"Groceries." Lorraine shielded the top of the bag from view and squeezed past her with a confused frown. She saw Sophie throw a knowing glance to the others at the bottom of the stoop. What was wrong with this old woman? Was she crazy or something?

Lorraine went into her apartment. Theresa was sitting by the window, reading a copy of *Mademoiselle*. She glanced up from her magazine. "Did you get my chocolate chip cookies?"

"Why good evening to you, too, Tee. And how was my day? Just wonderful." She sat the bag down on the couch. "The little Baxter boy brought in a puppy for show-and-tell, and the damn thing pissed all over the floor and then proceeded to chew the heel off my shoe, but, yes, I managed to hobble to the store and bring you your chocolate chip cookies."

Oh, Jesus, Theresa thought, she's got a bug up her ass tonight.

"Well, you should speak to Mrs. Baxter. She ought to train her kid better than that." She didn't wait for Lorraine to stop laughing before she tried to stretch her good mood. "Here, I'll put those things away. Want me to make dinner so you can rest? I only worked half a day, and the most tragic thing that went down was a broken fingernail and that got caught in my typewriter."

Lorraine followed Theresa into the kitchen. "No, I'm not really tired, and fair's fair, you cooked last night. I didn't mean to tick off like that; it's just that . . . well, Tee, have you noticed that people aren't as nice as they used to be?"

Theresa stiffened. Oh, God, here she goes again. "What people, Lorraine? Nice in what way?"

"Well, the people in this building and on the street. No one hardly speaks anymore. I mean, I'll come in and say good evening—and just silence. It wasn't like that when we first moved in. I don't know, it just makes you wonder; that's all. What are they thinking?"

"I personally don't give a shit what they're thinking. And their good evenings don't put any bread on my table."

"Yeah, but you didn't see the way that woman looked at me out there. They must feel something or know something. They probably—"

"They, they, they!" Theresa exploded. "You know, I'm not starting up with this again, Lorraine. Who in the hell are they? And where in the hell are we? Living in some dump of a building in this God-forsaken part of town around a bunch of ignorant niggers with the cotton still under their fingernails because of you and your theys. They knew something in Linden Hills, so I gave up an apartment for you that I'd been in for the last four years. And then they knew in Park Heights, and you made me so miserable there we had to leave. Now these mysterious theys are on Brewster Place. Well, look out the window, kid. There's a big wall down that block, and this is the end of the line for me. I'm not moving anymore, so if that's what you're working yourself up to—save it!"

When Theresa became angry she was like a lump of smoldering coal, and her fierce bursts of temper always unsettled Lorraine.

"You see, that's why I didn't want to mention it." Lorraine began to pull at her fingers nervously. "You're always flying up and jumping to conclusions—no one said anything about moving. And I didn't know your life has been so miserable since you met me. I'm sorry about that," she finished tearfully.

Theresa looked at Lorraine, standing in the kitchen door like a wilted leaf, and she wanted to throw something at her. Why didn't she ever fight back? The very softness that had first attracted her to Lorraine was now a frequent cause for irritation. Smoked honey. That's what Lorraine had reminded her of, sitting in her office clutching that application. Dry autumn days in Georgia woods, thick bloated smoke under a beehive, and the first glimpse of amber honey just faintly darkened about the edges by the burning twigs. She had flowed just that heavily into Theresa's mind and had stuck there with a persistent sweetness.

But Theresa hadn't known then that this softness filled Lorraine up to the very middle and that she would bend at the slightest pressure, would be constantly seeking to surround herself with the comfort of everyone's goodwill, and would shrivel up at the least touch of disapproval. It was becoming a drain to be continually called upon for this nurturing and support that she just didn't understand. She had supplied it at first out of love for Lorraine, hoping that she would harden eventually, even as honey does when exposed to the cold. Theresa was growing tired of being clung to — of being the one who was leaned on. She didn't want a child — she wanted someone who could stand toe to toe with her and be willing to slug it out at times. If they practiced that way with each other, then they could turn back to back and beat the hell out of the world for trying to invade their territory. But she had found no such sparring partner in Lorraine, and the strain of fighting alone was beginning to show on her.

"Well, if it was that miserable, I would have been gone a long time ago," she said, watching her words refresh Lorraine like a gentle shower.

"I guess you think I'm some sort of a sick paranoid, but I can't afford to have people calling my job or writing letters to my principal. You know I've already lost a position like that in Detroit. And teaching is my whole life, Tee."

"I know," she sighed, not really knowing at all. There was no danger of that ever happening on Brewster Place. Lorraine taught too far from this neighborhood for anyone here to recognize her in that school. No, it wasn't her job she feared losing this time, but their approval. She wanted to stand out there and chat and trade makeup secrets and cake recipes. She wanted to be secretary of their block association and be asked to mind their kids while they ran to the store. And none of that was going to happen if they couldn't even bring themselves to accept her good evenings.

Theresa silently finished unpacking the groceries. "Why did you buy cottage cheese? Who eats that stuff?"

"Well, I thought we should go on a diet."

"If *we* go on a diet, then you'll disappear. You've got nothing to lose but your hair."

"Oh, I don't know. I thought that we might want to try and reduce our hips or something." Lorraine shrugged playfully.

"No, thank you. We are very happy with our hips the way they are," Theresa said, as she shoved the cottage cheese to the back of the refrigerator. "And even when I lose weight, it never comes off there. My chest and arms just get smaller, and I start looking like a bottle of salad dressing."

The two women laughed, and Theresa sat down to watch Lorraine fix dinner. "You know, this behind has always been my downfall. When I was coming up in Georgia with my grandmother, the boys used to promise me penny candy if I would let them pat my behind. And I used to love those jawbreakers — you know, the kind that lasted all day and kept changing colors in your mouth. So I was glad to oblige them, because in one afternoon I could collect a whole week's worth of jawbreakers."

"Really. That's funny to you? Having some boy feeling all over you."

Theresa sucked her teeth. "We were only kids, Lorraine. You know, you remind me of my grandmother. That was one straight-laced old lady. She had a fit when my brother told her what I was doing. She called me into the smokehouse and told me in this real scary whisper that I could get pregnant from letting little boys pat my butt and that I'd end up like my cousin Willa.

But Willa and I had been thick as fleas, and she had already given me a step-by-step summary of how she'd gotten into her predicament. But I sneaked around to her house that night just to double-check her story, since that old lady had seemed so earnest. 'Willa, are you sure?' I whispered through her bedroom window. 'I'm tellin' ye, Tee,' she said. 'Just keep both feet on the ground and you home free.' Much later I learned that advice wasn't too biologically sound, but it worked in Georgia because those country boys didn't have much imagination."

Theresa's laughter bounced off of Lorraine's silent, rigid back and died in her throat. She angrily tore open a pack of the chocolate chip cookies. "Yeah," she said, staring at Lorraine's back and biting down hard into the cookie, "it wasn't until I came up north to college that I found out there's a whole lot of things that a dude with a little imagination can do to you even with both feet on the ground. You see, Willa forgot to tell me not to bend over or squat or—"

"Must you!" Lorraine turned around from the stove with her teeth clenched tightly together.

"Must I what, Lorraine? Must I talk about things that are as much a part of life as eating or breathing or growing old? Why are you always so uptight about sex or men?"

"I'm not uptight about anything. I just think it's disgusting when you go on and on about—"

"There's nothing disgusting about it, Lorraine. You've never been with a man, but I've been with quite a few—some better than others. There were a couple who I still hope to this day will die a slow, painful death, but then there were some who were good to me—in and out of bed."

"If they were so great, then why are you with me?" Lorraine's lips were trembling.

"Because—" Theresa looked steadily into her eyes and then down at the cookie she was twirling on the table. "Because," she continued slowly, "you can take a chocolate chip cookie and put holes in it and attach it to your ears and call it an earring, or hang it around your neck on a silver chain and pretend it's a necklace—but it's still a cookie. See—you can toss it in the air and call it a Frisbee or even a flying saucer, if the mood hits you, and it's still just a cookie. Send it spinning on a table—like this—until it's a wonderful blur of amber and brown light that you can imagine to be a topaz or rusted gold or old crystal, but the law of gravity has got to come into play, sometime, and it's got to come to rest—sometime. Then all the spinning and pretending and hoopla is over with. And you know what you got?"

"A chocolate chip cookie," Lorraine said.

"Uh-huh." Theresa put the cookie in her mouth and winked. "A lesbian." She got up from the table. "Call me when dinner's ready, I'm going back to read." She stopped at the kitchen door. "Now, why are you putting gravy on that chicken, Lorraine? You know it's fattening."

Questions for Discussion

1. How does the sentence "they seemed like such nice girls" set the tone for the direction of the story? How often is this phrase repeated? At what point does it become ironic?

2. Describe Brewster Place and the people who live there. Why are they such gossips and rumor spreaders? What is their first impression of Lorraine and Theresa? Why does their attitude toward the women change?

3. What is the connection between the story's theme and the shift in point of view midway through? Why did the author wait to present the two women's perspective and names?

4. Contrast Lorraine and Theresa's attitudes about their neighbors. How do their different attitudes reflect deeper differences in their personalities and within their relationship?

5. In what ways does the chocolate chip cookie symbolize and clarify Theresa's point about her sexual orientation? Does Lorraine see the cookie in the same way as Theresa does?

Ideas for Writing

1. In an essay, compare the two sections of the story — the first part that reflects the perspective of the neighbors and the second part that involves a dialogue between Lorraine and Theresa. How does this contrasting structure help to emphasize the values reflected in the story?

2. Write a sequel to the story in which you narrate the next event in the conflict between Lorraine and Theresa and their suspicious, homophobic neighbors.

ALBERTO ALVARO RÍOS   (b. 1952)

A poet as well as a fiction writer, Alberto Ríos often creates stories influenced by the magic realist movement in Latin American fiction — stories that exist on a border between poetry and narrative.

Born on the border of Mexico to an English mother and a Mexican father in Nogales, Arizona, Ríos went to schools where he was allowed to speak only English. He made up for this loss of Spanish by inventing a personal language, neither Spanish nor English, that formed the basis for his early poetry. He continued to write rebellious and at times abstract poems throughout high school, later attending the University of Arizona, where he earned a B.A. in English and creative writing, as well as a B.A. in psychology. In 1979 he completed his M.F.A. in creative writing at the University of Arizona. Currently he is a professor of English and director of the Creative Writing Program at Arizona State University. His books of poetry include *Sleeping on Fists* (1981), *Whispering to Fool the Wind* (1982), and *Five Indiscretions* (1985). Because Ríos's poetry uses a strong narrative line combined with elements of magic realism, the transition to writing short stories was a natural one for him. His first story collection, *The Iguana Killer* (1984), won the Western States Book Award and portrays the lives of young people growing up in the border culture of Arizona. His most recent collection, *Pig Cookies and Other Stories* (1995), which includes "Not like Us," continues to explore language, family, identity, magic, and the culture of the southwestern borderlands.

Not like Us   (1995)

His laugh was like rabbit droppings, each separate gatling sound small, high-pitched, not much of anything. But added up together into his version of a laugh, these spitted sounds were suddenly a gang, menacing by virtue of their numbers. These noises connected like pearls on a string but without their shine, or Chinese firecrackers, too close. Too ready to explode. When one burst out, the rest could only follow.

His was a laugh, but only if he said so.

The desk clerk was clear on this point, and waited for instruction obediently.

The visitor stood there waiting, for information on his room, but not for long. When the clerk did not respond, the man reached over and took a key from the shelf.

Well, he said, *I can see if a man wants to get any sleep around here, he's got to do it himself.*

The journals of Columbus recount mermaids in the New World, said Mr.

Lee. The sailors called them *Sirenas,* and implicit in that notation was the existence of the *Tritones,* their husbands, though not one of them was ever actually spotted. They were more of a Saturday evening guess.

Perhaps, the townspeople said, the *Tritones* were simply too lazy to show themselves, or so terrible that nobody who saw one ever survived. No good either way.

The journals recount the mermaids singing as God's own daughters at night. Of course, we think now, common sense, said Mr. Lee, this singing at night. Who sings their best songs in daylight, without a dark stage from which to emerge, without artificial, and therefore special, footlights? Who hands over a tip in the daytime, where everyone can see? The *Sirenas* sing their songs only at night. They sing when the world is halfway toward the show of dream, when reaching into the pocket for a coin is a reach down into sleep and what resides there by way of desire.

At sea, anyway, no one sings in the daytime. Not for show. There is work to be done in the daylight, whatever work it is that sailors do, trim the sails, avast the hearties.

But when the sun sets, the accordions come out. The tattooed sailors smile their fish-like grins, full of sea meat and eel tongue and North wind. They start the push and pull of their musical boxes. They dance in their striped shirts and, slyly so that the other sailors do not see, retie their bandannas against the air, which has begun to cool. We imagine them half reasonable men who get cold, half something from the old movies.

At night the sailors drink their rum and sing out too loud every song the sea has ever heard. They do their singing at night because they cannot see what is out there. They cannot aim their sails very well, or swab the decks. They cannot use their eyes, which in this darkness try to be hands. Squinting in the dark, the sailors try to make their eyes feel ahead. Everyone does it.

The ocean at night is a whale-like cavern, but with the mouth of a tarantula, something unthinkable. One imagines the blackness and the movement to be many things. The night is beyond even the strength of the muscle a father makes for his son to see.

One will do anything to keep the teeth away, to keep the stars from coming down and the juice waters from coming up. Anything, any type of song, any kind of prayer. Because of this the sailor practices tying knots just to keep a rope near. Because of this a sailor practices knife-throwing just to keep a knife handy. Anything to use on himself, should the teeth of the night come together.

Sometimes the *Sirenas* answered the sailors back in song or in conversation. Sometimes their angry husbands all wet and foul-mouthed and careless drunk did the answering back to the sailors, and sometimes the sounds out there in the night were nothing at all.

This man who had come to town was a Triton. The townspeople were certain. Good or bad, one way or the other, no one could yet say. This was the story: he arrived in town from out of the dark, at night under a new moon, and no one had seen who or what had brought him.

He simply came to be at the front register of the two-room hotel, and laughed his laugh. No one knew how long he had waited before letting go of that singular noise, which sounded as if the stars themselves had come down from the night, so many little sparks, but without the light, so many little pin-pricks in a row. No one knew how long he had waited, but the wait must have been long since so many sounds made themselves inside that laugh, so many sounds the laugh could not stop properly once it got started.

Armida, the hotel maid, led him away to one of the two rooms along the rollers of that laugh. Even when he closed the door, Armida said, she could still hear something of it. The laugh was full of small saws and bees, strong enough to cut through the walls and with enough wings to fly into the garden and along the street. Armida could not tell with any precision when it ended, or if it ever did. Some noises in that room in later years were simply unexplainable except for this.

When the man woke the next morning, Armida, the maid and the room service as well, said he ordered a *coctel de abulón* brought over to his room. I don't want it so much for the abalone, he said to her, as for the tomato juice and lemon. Armida nodded to him as if she understood, but she did not.

What he felt in his head was very big.

That is what the man said, she told everyone, as he had continued to talk. The townspeople who gathered nodded their own heads now. Something was inside the words he had spoken, but no one could yet say what. They nodded their heads, understanding only that if the man said something in his head was very big, then they had better get out of the way in case he let it out.

No one knew for certain how to interpret the man's words. Nor did they know their role as townspeople. Should they stay out of his way because they feared him, or stay out of his way because they had little interest in a visitor to town? That they should stay away was the only point needing no discussion.

The townspeople immediately called the visitor Triton because, before he retired, he said something more to the clerk of the two rooms. He said either he was looking for his wife, or that he was looking for *a* wife.

The man moaned, and held his head. Then he laughed. Perhaps it was not a laugh at all, someone said. Perhaps they had mistaken the sound, and it was the moan he began with that had not stopped. A moan and not a laugh at all.

This made no one feel better, and no one wanted it as an explanation for anything.

This man had no drink at the bar, but that did not mean he had not been drinking. For that matter, he did not seem to have a gun, but that did not mean he was not hiding one. No one had seen horns on him either, but as they began to understand, that did not mean much.

Perhaps, they said at first, this man was only a bear, not something more. Things like this, a bear or a wolf passing through, things like this had happened before. Maybe he was just passing through, which would not be too bad. Or better, he was simply a vendor, with brushes or medicines under his greatcoat. A traveling vendor was something they had seen before as well.

The remark about his wife, however, or *a* wife, gave everyone second thoughts. Did this visitor know about their daughters? Should they hide them? The town had hidden people before. But no one knew what to do now.

Did he say anything about his wife singing, they asked both Armida and the clerk.

Had some one of their daughters sung too loudly, dreamed too much, or too hard? Had this Triton come to take one of them, who had called him without knowing? Had the tide of the ocean come up this far, so many hundreds of miles? In their Saturday evening talks they had often worried about the ocean. They worried about it coming up as far as the town some evening, not quite enough to swallow them all, but leaving one of its own lost to them. People knew for a fact stranger stories than this. And, as if by coincidence, many of them had to do with the ocean. So this story was possible.

Neither the clerk nor Armida could remember for certain whether the stranger mentioned any singing or any water. Perhaps he had said nothing, or perhaps he had.

After his breakfast of abalone the visitor fell back asleep, snoring in much the same manner as he had laughed.

Mr. Lee was consulted.

The town had once saved Mr. Lee by hiding him from the soldiers who took all the Chinese and put them on trains. In return, he himself had saved the town, more than once. Though he said he knew nothing about strange occurrences, he always seemed willing to lend his ear to the moment.

Mr. Lee was brought over to the bar next to the two-room hotel where the Triton was asleep. Someone told Mr. Lee of the comparison between the visitor's laugh and a string of firecrackers.

He too nodded his head, but the townspeople felt sure that when Mr. Lee nodded his head *ahhh* it meant something different from when they themselves nodded.

Mr. Lee worked as a translator in this town. Every important document was taken to him for copying into Chinese, which had been a service to the community when there had been more Chinese in town. But since the trains took most of the Chinese away, the townspeople used his services differently.

The town hall had burned down two years previous, and Mr. Lee's job now was to translate various documents back from Chinese. He had kept his own library and at this point had the only town records left. When a question arose about some civic detail or other, Mr. Lee was consulted. He would go into his library and emerge with the appropriate document, which he would then bring back to life in a manner and language familiar to the townspeople.

On occasion, Mr. Lee's laws seemed different from what people could remember, but who could argue with the written word, regardless of its curvature.

From time to time, Mr. Lee himself would volunteer some arcane bit of law or other, some decision of the grandfathers for the good of the town. In this way, he showed them several new holidays, and with them he had the town order by special messenger a variety of foods that, somewhere in the business of everyday life, he said, people had forgotten — several roots for spice, some thin black sauces.

If anyone could discern something from the presence of this stranger, it was Mr. Lee. After all, the story of the Triton as mate to the mermaid had first come from a particular tapestry Mr. Lee owned, a tapestry with threads that shone.

The mermaids themselves came from the journals of Columbus. The further story of the *Tritones,* however, came with a little help from the dark inside of Mr. Lee's outer room. While he had not given Triton as the sea-creature's name in Chinese, that is what he called the thing for these townspeople. This was a name they would understand.

He had a mouth, this Triton, said Mr. Lee, which could blow hard enough to make a boat capsize. It was a simple example, but they each knew from experience what a boat capsizing meant. They supplied their own details. No one forgets this kind of story.

Suddenly this man appears, if he was a man, asleep next door, and with a laugh made from who knew what. It was cause for another beer, at the very least. A beer and a deep breath.

Mr. Lee nodded his head *ahhh* and listened to everything. By now each of the townspeople had something to say about the visitor. Each gave a new detail concerning the laugh, or said something about what seemed to take shape beneath that black greatcoat.

Who even wore a greatcoat around here anyway, they said to Mr. Lee in turn. Each had a different detail, but each had the same question. What was to be done?

By now it was time for the *botana,* the requisite social gathering of the townspeople in weekly celebration of Saturday afternoons. A little beer, a little food, some fried bits of one common thing and another, with tortillas, some *chicharrones,* then whole cucumbers with red chili powder and lemon and salt. A few prickly pear *tunas,* some purple ones and some green. A baseball game on the radio.

A hundred small pieces of conversation, an argument, which on these afternoons seemed like a large French bread, or better, a chair. Something there every time, but finally ignored. Someone in love, who wanted to be left alone. Some kids, who would eat quickly, not wipe their mouths, then run around drinking lemon-lime sodas, or shaking them and wetting the walls, seeing who could reach highest. Smoke, which was itself a second ceiling in this room. Some days it was a light cloud cover, some days a full cumulonimbus assemblage with a life of its own and animal shapes for the little kids.

Young people did not come to the *botana*. They were left to do chores at home. All of them, all alone, at home on Saturday afternoons. In truth, not much got done. Invariably the next Sunday a particular boy smiled at a certain girl a little differently. By some mysterious manner, some postal system not known to the grown-ups, they now knew each other better.

Who could say about these things. As everyone knew, however, and though they pretended coincidence, all the people who came for *botana* now had themselves met each other as youngsters on Saturday afternoons. They had met, and met often, when their own parents were off with their younger brothers and sisters to the great *botanas* of the earlier years in the century.

Mr. Lee had not a little to do with this, as he had clarified for the town that, indeed, these Saturday leisures were *de facto* the law. The law was a good one, the townspeople thought, after a while, whispering around their beers about things. It was their civic duty and good for business, talking things over and eating the small leftovers of the day. Progress worked this way. Who would not want to move forward like the new locomotives?

Mr. Lee nodded his head, ate a few of the shrimps and *tripas* from this *botana,* and listened to everyone. He summoned Armida and the clerk each in turn, and Armida would come back periodically with reports of what she heard at the stranger's door.

Mr. Lee sent a youngster to fetch his tapestry, which he then held up.

Did the visitor look like this? he asked.

The hour was dark, they said, and so late. Their eyes had been only half open, ready for sleep. As things turned out, only a few people had actually seen the man, and even then they had seen only his back. It was a large back, they agreed.

Armida and the clerk had seen him, however, from the front. They knew.

No, the two of them said, he did not precisely look like this picture in the tapestry. Not in the face, though he did have a beard. They could not look into his greatcoat, which he had kept well buttoned. This was at odds with the night, which was not so cold, said Armida. She was the maid and the room service, but her job was also to carry out the trash sometimes, or take one object or another outside at night. She spoke with the authority of many offices, and always with particular eloquence about the weather. Last night, I was out there, she said, and nodded her head from side to side — not so cold.

Not so cold, see, said the clerk. Armida says so. But this man, he kept that coat buttoned to the top.

Now, they said to Mr. Lee, look how long this Triton-man is sleeping, and in the daylight. Perhaps he is a creature of the night after all. Wasn't it possible?

Mr. Lee used his old explanation about these things, the one he used to explain everything that seemed curious at first. Without him saying so, it was an explanation from his own life. In putting on a belt in the morning, Mr. Lee said, a person should understand why another person somewhere else might be putting on a small dress of feathers, or how two artful sticks might be the equal of a fork.

At times like this, Mr. Lee always wanted to say a person is a person, but saying as much would have sounded too easy, too regular, not big enough. So he invariably took the long way around to explain this to everybody. We are all living out our days, he began. We do what is in need of doing.

Perhaps, if you will listen, our man's visit is not unlike *dim sum*. That is what others might call the *botana*, said Mr. Lee. Another people at another time of day, in another place, but these are the same thing. Different foods, different words, but the same thing. Perhaps, then, our visitor is just another man. Not like us, to be sure, but enough like us.

Mr. Lee shrugged his shoulders and nodded his head yes, once, firmly, which was also another way of telling them not to worry. Sometimes this kind of language worked better, letting people see an answer with their eyes.

Mr. Lee always came for the *botana,* he told them. He knew a good thing when he saw one. What they called it didn't matter to him — *botana, dim sum.* They could call it a purple people's picnic for all he cared. As long as they stacked up food on the tables.

Did they understand? he asked. This visitor had provided them with so many details, each so tasty, Mr. Lee said. Perhaps this was even a good man. Had he not been an entertainment, after all?

They nodded their heads in agreement. This was not the usual Saturday afternoon fare. This was true.

Firecrackers and pearls, stars and cowboy guns, unfolded serpents from the sea — Mr. Lee himself had paid good money to see these things at a theater in Nogales.

Mr. Lee looked around and took a moment for his story. This was also the law, to tell one's story when there was one.

At the theater in Nogales, he said, as they all knew, Mr. Martínez played the piano. Mr. Martínez played the best he could, perhaps more with emotion than with a delicacy of hand. Mr. Lee said this with a wink, which they all understood. He played the piano to make the action seem stronger. You know — a fast piano for a fast horse. Sometimes Mr. Martínez fell off his chair, and was better to watch than the movie. At the very least, he was half the movie himself.

Just like an opera, Mr. Lee said. They had all heard Don Lázaro's records. A word said in an opera becomes a word spoken by someone who has swallowed a piano — a word with force, with music. Sometimes it was the movie talking, sometimes Mr. Martínez. Was he not in this way heroic, an equal to those on the screen?

Well, then, did they recall Señora Piñeda? She used to live here until her new husband moved the family to Guadalajara, then somewhere after that? The first several times she went to the movies, she yelled at the people on the screen to be careful! and not to trust the other one up there, not even for a moment. With Mr. Martínez up there, whom she had known all her life, and with all the action, shouting a warning seemed like the responsible thing to do.

Everyone nodded that they remembered her. More important, as seen in the quick tenor of their nods, they appreciated Mr. Lee's speaking only about her. It could have been any one of them. They had all yelped out at the screen also their first times. With the cowboys and the soldiers and the kings and queens up there, one could not help shouting, as a reflex, and as a friend.

And this man Mr. Martínez, said Mr. Lee, he did not even charge them anything at all for so many pleasurable hours. But to give away so much of himself was almost a crime. Of course, little did Mr. Martínez realize the entertainment was not in the piano. Still, no one could dare tell him, at least not anyone with upbringing.

They nodded their heads like Mr. Lee, *ahhh.*

Perhaps in homage to Mr. Martínez, to pay off their debt to him, the townspeople should offer this stranger something. Did Mr. Lee think so? Perhaps this was the way to make the world right. They could start off on the right foot again by paying this stranger for the entertainment he had provided, rather than letting the thing be unsaid, as was now irrevocably the case with Mr. Martínez.

Perhaps, said Mr. Lee. In homage to Mr. Martínez. As they were all friends of the Martínez family in those days, it was true they could not have insulted Mr. Martínez with the offering of money there on stage. They could not have made him bend down for something that was not a handshake, not in front of everyone else at the theater.

Leaving some gift now would be the thing to do, said Mr. Lee, a good way to remember. We should offer something to this stranger in appreciation of the lesson taught by Mr. Martínez. Did they not think so?

Heads were nodded, a bowl was passed, and a few beers went undrunk. After all, as Mr. Lee had said, paying for the services of an entertainment was the honest thing to do.

The clerk of the hotel thought the owner would go along with no charge for the room. After all, said Mr. Lee.

After all, they said.

Being scared had been good, Mr. Lee said, but not too good. Just right.

They nodded their heads in a slow *yes*. Nobody said aloud that the being scared had not quite gone away, or that they would leave early to check if their daughters were, at least, somewhere still in town. This Triton had done a good job of scaring them, and shaking it off would take a while. But they tried laughing, with Mr. Lee, and they felt better.

Armida was put in charge of leaving the bowl of money outside the door. The clerk would leave a note neatly stamped with the red PAID IN FULL on top of the bowl.

The plan was a good one, they all said.

This town, Mr. Lee said, while shaking his head. Here there was no need of wind, not with so many whispers, no sir. Were they not lucky living so close to nature?

At first they nodded their heads, but then they laughed. They returned to the strategies of the *botana,* declaring what should be eaten in turn, what was most medicinal, what was in need of salt. They remarked again on the striking aspect offered by the shiny threads on Mr. Lee's tapestry, which was still in the room, oversized with its full head of the Triton.

This brought on, again, the very first parts of the Saturday's conversation, Columbus, and his sighting of the mermaids. The *Sirenas,* they have done it to us again, everyone agreed. This was a music they had all heard, a fast melodic scale coming as if from the mouth of each of them, all about the stranger. These were melodies and harmonies perfectly meshed, coming as if they themselves were the half-fish and lived inside the sea, crying out to anyone who would listen for help. What a surprise their cries had been, and to have them come out like songs, so that everyone listened.

This is the way the conversation went, but it was not after all real conversation. The townspeople simply could not go away. Each waited to see if the man would leave, if the money and the hotel would be enough.

Underneath it all, the *botana,* the friendships, the stories, the beers and the *norteño* music, the afternoon air, and no matter what Mr. Lee said — underneath everything, and not to be rude, but *hijo de la chingada,* son of a bitch, they knew a Triton when they saw one. A laugh like that, so many pearls but without light, something from underneath the water, very far.

Real pearls leave a roughness in the mouth, not in the ear. Mr. Lee could make them feel better about the visit. But this man could not fool them.

Questions for Discussion

1. What is the significance of the story's title? What happens when people are "not like us"? How do the characters in the story handle the "difference" in their community?

2. Why do the villagers single out the "visitor" and label him as different, menacing? Does he seem that unusual or threatening?

3. What are the origins of the legends of the *Tritones* and the *Sirenas?* To what extent has Mr. Lee elaborated on earlier legends, giving them a unique flavor?

4. What is Mr. Lee's role in the community? In what sense is he, like the visitor, "not like us"? What is important about his job of copying and translating the town's history from Chinese into Spanish? How is the original meaning of the history changed in his translation?

5. What is the function of the *botana* in the community? Why has Mr. Lee modified this traditional leisuretime activity and made attendance mandatory?

Ideas for Writing

1. Although at the *botana* Mr. Lee attempts to convince the community members of the harmlessness of the visitor and to demonstrate that the man is not a creature of myth and legend, he is not entirely successful in his efforts. Write an essay in which you discuss what the story suggests about the nature of legend and its function in a community.
2. Write a story or essay about a myth or legend that a group of people believe even though it has no basis in fact; discuss people's reasons for clinging to the legend.

GARY SOTO   (b. 1952)

Gary Soto is known for both the intense sensory language of his stories and the humor with which he explores issues of poverty and Mexican-American identity, along with more universal experiences of childhood adventure and adolescent mischief, adult love and domesticity.

Soto was born in Fresno, California, and raised in the San Joaquin Valley in a large Spanish-speaking family of factory and field workers. At Fresno City College, reading modern poetry convinced him to try to understand more about the power of language to capture universal feelings and personal experiences. He transferred to California State University at Fresno, where he studied poetry with Pulitzer prize–winning poet Philip Levine. He completed his M.F.A. at the University of California at Irvine in 1976 and has been teaching in the English and Chicano studies departments at the University of California at Berkeley since 1977. His first book of poetry, *The Elements of San Joaquin* (1977), established his reputation; since then, he has won many awards for his poetry. He won the American Book Award in 1985 for his autobiographical vignettes in *Living up the Street: Narrative Recollections*. His recent works also include novels for children and the story collection *Local News* (1993), in which "El Radio" appears. Of his narrative writing, Soto has said that he strives toward a style that is "plain, direct, unadorned."

El Radio   (1993)

At seven-fifteen in the evening, Patricia Ruiz's mother dabbed lipstick on her small, shapely mouth. Her father worked a red tie around his neck, swallowing twice so that his Adam's apple rode up and down like an elevator. At seven twenty-two, both were standing at the mirror in the bathroom, her mother rubbing Passion-scented lotion on her wrists and her father spraying Obsession in the cove of his neck.

They were in a rush to go to the opera, a recent interest Patricia couldn't understand. Only a year ago they were listening every Friday night to "The Slow-Low Show" of oldies-but-goodies, hosted by *El Tigre*. Now it was opera on Friday nights, and a new Lexus in the driveway, a sleek machine that replaced their '74 Monte Carlo.

"Lock all the doors, *mi'ja*," Patricia's mother said, swishing in her chiffon dress. To Patricia, her mother looked like a talking flower, for she was slim as a flower and a bouquet of wonderful smells rose up from her.

Her father came into the living room plucking lint from the sleeve of his jacket. Patricia thought her father was handsome: his trim mustache, the silver at his temples, his romantically sad looking eyes. Her girlfriends said he resembled Richard Gere, especially when he was in a stylish suit, as he was now.

"Pat, I rented you a movie," her father said, pointing vaguely at the cassette on the coffee table. "We'll be home by ten-thirty, eleven at the latest."

From the couch, a *Seventeen* in her lap, Patricia watched her parents get ready for the evening. She thought they were cute, like a boyfriend and girlfriend brimming with puppy love.

"I'll be okay," she said. She got up from the couch and kissed them. Their delicious smells were pleasantly overwhelming.

As her parents hurried out the front door, Patricia hurried to the telephone in the kitchen. Her best friend, Melinda, who lived two blocks away, was waiting for her call.

"They're gone," she announced. "Come on over."

Patricia hung up and took down a can of frozen orange juice from the freezer. While she was mixing the juice, spanking the clods of frozen orange pulp with a paddlelike spoon until they broke apart, she snapped her fingers and said, "It's party time!" She remembered that "The Slow-Low Show" of oldies-but-goodies was on the air. She turned on the small radio on the windowsill and the stereo in the living room. *El Tigre,* the host of the program, was sending out the message, "Now this one goes out to Slinky from Mystery Girl in Tulare. And this goes to Johnny Y in Corcoran from *La Baby Tears,* who says, 'I'll be waiting for you.' And we got special love coming from Yolanda to her old man, Raul, who says, 'Baby, I'm the real thing.' Yes, *gente,* the world turns with plenty of slow-low romance."

While *El Tigre* put on the record, "Let's Get It On," Patricia went to the kitchen to make popcorn. She got a bottle of vegetable oil from the cupboard and a pot from the oven. The oven's squeaky door grated on her nerves when it was opened or closed. She was pouring in a handful of kernels when Melinda pounded on the back door.

"Hey, *Ruca,*" Melinda greeted her when Patricia unlatched the door. Melinda was a chubby classmate in eighth grade at Kings Canyon Junior High. She was wearing a short black dress and her lipstick was brownish red against a pale, pancaked face. Her eyelashes were dark and sticky with mascara.

"*Ruca,* yourself, *esa,*" Patricia greeted, shaking the pot over the burner and its flower of bluish flames. The kernels were exploding into white popcorn.

Melinda turned up the radio and screamed, "Ay, my favorite." "Ninety-Six" was playing, and Melinda, standing at the counter, was pretending to play the keyboard. She lip-synched the words and bobbed her head to the beat. When the song ended, Melinda poured herself a glass of orange juice and asked her friend, "Patty, you ever count how many tears you cried?"

Patricia shook her head and started giggling.

"One time, when my mom wouldn't let me go to the Valentine's dance — the one last year when the homeboys from Sanger showed up — I cried exactly ninety-six tears. Just like the song."

"Get serious," Patricia said, her eyes glinting in disbelief. She poured the popcorn into a bowl, with just a pinch of salt because she heard a spoonful of salt was worse for your complexion than nine Milky Way candy bars devoured in an hour. "How can you count your tears?"

"I used my fingers."

"No way."

"*De veras,*" Melinda argued. She clicked her fingernails against the counter, and the sound resembled the *click-click* of a poodle's nails on a linoleum floor.

The two of them took the popcorn and orange juice into the living room and cuddled up on the couch, careful not to spill. On the radio, *El Tigre* was whispering, "This one goes out from Marta to *El Güero*. And we got a late bulletin from Enrique to Patricia. Message is — "

"Hey, Patty, some guy's got eyes for you," Melinda said. Her eyes were shiny with excitement. She jumped up and boosted the volume of the stereo. "The message is," *El Tigre* continued, "'don't get fooled by plastic love.'"

"I like that," Melinda said.

"*Chale.* No way," Patricia said, trying to laugh it off. She got up and turned down the volume. "I don't know no Enrique."

"Enrique de la Madrid!" Melinda screamed. "Danny's brother."

"That little squirt? The *vato* just lost his baby teeth last week." The girls laughed and started dancing separately to Mary Wells's song, "My Guy." They continued dancing, fingers snapping and bodies waving in slow motion when the song ended and was followed by Aretha Franklin's "I Heard It Through the Grapevine."

When that song faded to a thumping bass followed by a scratchy silence, they sat down on the couch, legs folded underneath them. There was a glow of happiness about them, a shine in their eyes. Patricia took a single popcorn and threw it in Melinda's mouth. Melinda threw a single popcorn at Patricia's mouth. It hit her in the eye, and they laughed and threw handfuls of popcorn at each other. They liked hanging out together. They liked that they could dance wildly and lip-synch nonsense without feeling stupid.

They became quiet when *El Tigre* cleared his voice and whispered, "From Fowler, we celebrate the first but not last anniversary of Susie and Manny. From us, *su familia,* steady love for that eternal couple. And check it out, real serious commotion from Softy, who says to his Lorena in Dinuba, 'Let's get back together.'"

When "Angel Baby" came on, the girls eased into the couch and nursed their orange juice and slowly chewed their popcorn. Their feelings were smoky. They synched the words, certain that the singer must have had a deep relationship. Patricia figured that the singer's boyfriend must have found another girl, and then lost that girl and joined the Army.

Melinda looked at Patricia, who looked at Melinda. Melinda asked, "Anyone ever call you Angel Baby?"

Patricia sat up and, giggling, said, "*Cállate,* Melinda, you're ruinin' the song." She thought for a second about Melinda's question. "No, no one's ever called me Angel Baby. But my dad calls me Sweetie."

"My dad calls me *La* Pumpkin."

"*Órale.* Your *papi's* got it right," Patricia laughed. She bounced off the couch and, heading to the kitchen, asked, "You want more orange juice?"

"*Simón, esa,*" Melinda said.

While Patricia was in the kitchen, Melinda spent her time at the mirror on the far wall, where Patricia's baby pictures hung, wrapped in the dust of years. She dabbed her lips with lipstick and picked up a picture. She looked at her friend and had to admit that she was a cute little thing.

When Jr. Walker and the All-Stars' "Shotgun" began its soulful blare, Melinda put down the picture and started chugging to the song, elbows churning at her side, singing, "You're a lousy, no-good, stinkin' Shot-gunnnnnnnn."

"Go, brown girl, go!" Patricia yelled when she came into the living room. She put down the glasses of orange juice and chugged along with Melinda, elbows flapping at her side like the wings of a wet chicken. They laughed and felt happy, and couldn't think of a better time. When the song ended, Patricia felt her cheek with the back of her hand. She was hot but feeling great. She took a drink of orange juice.

"Yeah, we're gonna have to come up with a name for you, *ruca,*" Melinda said. She sized Patricia up, and, stroking her chin, said, "How 'bout *La Flaca?*"

"*Y tu, La* Pumpkin!" Patricia chided. She ran her hands down her hips. Yeah, I am skinny, she told herself, but at least I'm not a fat *mamacita!*

"*La Flaca!*"

"*La* Pumpkin!"

"*La Flaca!*"

"*La* Pumpkin!"

The girls laughed at their nicknames and threw popcorn at each other. Melinda then suggested that they call *El Tigre* and dedicate a song.

"*A quién?*" Patricia asked.

"Enrique de la Madrid," teased Melinda as she jumped over the couch and headed for the telephone in the hallway.

"*Chale!*" Patricia screamed, her heart pounding from the fear and delight. "I don't like that squirt."

"But he got eyes for you."

"You mean *you.*"

"*Pues no.* You mean, *you!*"

Patricia pulled on Melinda's arm and Melinda pushed Patricia. Suddenly they were on the floor wrestling, both laughing and calling the other by her nickname. In the background, *El Tigre* was whispering, "Now stay cool, *y* stay in school."

When Melinda reached for the telephone, the receiver fell off the hook and corkscrewed on its cord. Even though her mouth was inches away and she had yet to dial the radio station, she was yelling, "*Esta ruca, se llama la Flaca de* Kings Canyon Junior High, wants to dedicate a song to her sleepy boyfriend. She wants —"

Patricia put her hand over Melinda's mouth and felt the smear of lipstick working into her palm. Melinda pulled Patricia's hair, lightly, and Patricia pulled on Melinda, not so lightly. They struggled and laughed, and finally Melinda said, "Okay, okay, you win."

They both sat up, breathing hard but feeling good. After catching her breath, Patricia said, "I'll call *El Tigre* and have him do a *dedica* to my parents."

"*Que idea!*"

Patricia dialed "El Radio," and immediately she got *El Tigre,* who said in a low, low-riding voice, "*Qué pasa? Cómo te llamas, esa?*"

Without thinking, Patricia said, "*La Flaca y mi carnala La* Pumpkin *del barrio de* South Fresno."

"*Y tu escuela?*"

"Roosevelt High," Patricia lied. She didn't want *El Tigre* to know that he was rapping with a junior high kid.

"And what oldie-but-goodie do you want me to spin for you? *Y tu dedica?*"

"I wanna hear 'Oh, Donna,' by Ritchie Valens." Patricia moved the telephone to her other ear, giving her time to think about the dedication. "And I . . . I want to dedicate the song to my parents, Jerry and Sylvia, I do love you, from your only but eternal daughter, Patricia."

"*Pues,* I'll get it on in a sec. Stay cool, *ruca,* and keep up the grades."

Patricia hung up, heart pounding. She had never been so nervous. She put the telephone back on the table.

"You did good. 'Oh, Donna' is my next favorite," Melinda said. Melinda got up slowly from the floor and went to the mirror to tease her hair back into shape. She looked down at her hand and made a face. "*Ay,* Patty, you broke one of my fingernails."

Patricia felt her cheek. She was hot from wrestling and talking with *El Tigre.* The only other famous personality she had spoken to was Ronald McDonald when he came down in a helicopter at the McDonald's on Kings Canyon Boulevard. And Ronald was nothing like *El Tigre;* he only gave away french fries, not oldies-but-goodies.

"You ever been on TV?" Patricia asked. She was high about her voice carrying over all of Fresno on "The Slow-Low Show."

"Nah," Melinda said. She had her compact out and was retouching her face. "I was in the newspaper once."

"You were?"

"Yeah, it was when they reopened the pool at Roosevelt. I was first in line." She closed the compact and brought out her mascara. "The paper was hard up."

On the radio, the Supremes' "I Hear a Symphony" was playing, a song which prompted Melinda to ask, "So your dad and mom are at the symphony?"

"Opera," Patricia corrected.

"They like that stuff?"

"*Quién sabe?* I think they want to try something they don't know about."

"Shoot, if I had their car, I'd be cruisin' Blackstone," Melinda said. She began to fumble in her purse for her lipstick.

"But you don't have a license," Patricia said.

"*Pues,* I'll just put on some more makeup, and who can tell?"

"But you don't know how to drive."

"It's easy. Just put the stick on 'D,' and press the *cosita.*"

"Yeah, but what happened when your brother took out your mom's car?"

"You comparin' me to my brother? The guy *es un tonto.*" Melinda took a fingernail file from her purse and began to whittle down her broken fingernail. "Yeah, your dad's Lexus is sharp, but so was his Monte Carlo."

"Yeah, I don't know why he traded it in," Patricia reflected.

At that moment there was the jingling of keys at the front door. Melinda gave Patricia a frightened look. Patricia's eyes flashed to the spilled popcorn and the blaring stereo, then to the clock on the end table. It was only 9:35.

"It's either the cops or my parents," Patricia said.

"Same thing," Melinda said, as she started to rush to the kitchen in hopes of making it to the back door.

But it was too late. The door opened with a sigh and the two girls were staring at Patricia's shocked parents. Her father took the key from the door, and her mother looked around the room trying to assess the damage.

"What's been going on?" her mother snapped as she walked toward Patricia. For a moment, Patricia thought she was going to pinch her but she only stomped into the kitchen. "Are there any boys here?" she asked. Her voice was edged with anger.

"No, just me and Melinda."

Her mother sniffed the air for boys and cigarettes. She saw the popcorn spewed over the rug.

"I spilled the bowl, Mrs. Ruiz," Melinda volunteered as she and Patricia scrambled to pick up the popcorn. "I tripped."

"I can't leave you alone! Can't I trust you?"

"Mom, we were just listening to *El Tigre.*"

Patricia's father was quiet and withdrawn. He undid his tie and turned down the stereo. He threw himself into his easy chair, feet up on the hassock.

"What's wrong?" Patricia asked her father. He seemed unusually quiet.

He turned his sad eyes to his daughter. "The car broke down. It's brand-new."

"Broke down!" Patricia shouted.

"Yes, *broke down,*" her mother repeated. Turning to Melinda, she asked, "Does your mother know where you are?"

"Ah, sort of," Melinda lied, her face turned away from Patricia's mother. She hated lying to grown-ups, especially parents with bad tempers.

Patricia's mother gave Melinda a doubtful glare and muttered, "*mentirosas,* both of you." She wiped away a few loose kernels of popcorn from the couch and sat down, her high heels dropping off her feet like heavy petals from a branch.

"You mean you didn't get to the opera?" Patricia asked. Before her mother or father could answer, a quick-thinking Melinda raced to the stereo and turned up the volume. *El Tigre,* in his Slow-Low low-riding voice, was whispering, "I'm coming at you at nine thirty-nine, and I hope you're kicking back in the heart of *Aztlán.*"

"Yes, and I might be kicking these low-class *cholas* in the behind," her mother spoke to the radio. Patricia could see that her mother was softening and that she and Melinda were out of danger.

"We got *una dedica,*" *El Tigre* continued, "from Larry M. to Shy Girl in West Fresno, who says, 'I lost a good thing.' To Gina of Los Banos, 'Happy Birthday,' from her father and mother. And from *La Flaca* to her parents Jerry and Sylvia, I do love you, from your only but eternal daughter. *La Flaca* has asked for "Oh, Donna," *y pues,* why not?"

"That's me, Mom. *La Flaca!*" Patricia yelled.

"You?" her mother asked, giving her daughter a questioning look.

"Yeah. I'm *La Flaca* and Melinda's *La* Pumpkin."

"My dad calls me *La* Pumpkin." Melinda grinned.

Patricia's father laughed. He laughed long and hard until a single tear rolled from one of his eyes. "Did you hear these *cholas? La Flaca y La* Pumpkin." He got up and boosted the volume of the radio, which was playing "Oh, Donna." He asked his daughter playfully, "How'd you know my first girlfriend was named Donna?"

Patricia's mother slapped his arm and said, "*Ay, hombre.* Now look at you with a broken-down Lexus."

"Dad, you should have kept the Monte Carlo," Patricia said, feeling truly out of danger.

"Yeah, you're right." He smiled wearily.

"Come on, Dad, let's dance," Patricia suggested.

"Let's party down!" Melinda yelled. She chugged off to the kitchen, lip-synching the words to "Oh, Donna."

"The heck with the opera," he said after a moment of hesitation. "It's better with *El Tigre.*" He took his daughter's hands in his and they danced, one-two, one-two, while her mother snapped her fingers to the beat. In the kitchen Melinda stood at the stove making a new batch of popcorn.

Questions for Discussion

1. What do Patricia's feelings about her parents and their evening at the opera reveal about her relationship with them?

2. Interpret Melinda and Patricia's party ritual: the food they prepare, their outfits, the radio station they play. How do their cultural values contrast with those of their parents?

3. Does the story suggest that the songs the girls listen to are preparing them for the adult world and for real romantic relationships?

4. Why do the girls finally call *El Tigre?* What does *El Tigre* represent? Which of the girls' remarks reflect their awareness that they are not yet adults and are practicing to grow up?

5. When their parents return home, how does the song the girls have dedicated help to ease the disappointments of the parents' evening?

Ideas for Writing

1. Write an essay that discusses the relationship between Patricia and her parents. In what ways has Patricia been influenced by them? In what ways is she rebelling against them? In what ways is her behavior typical of a modern teenager?

2. Write a story about one or more teenage characters who shape their values according to the music they hear on the radio and the things they are told by popular DJs.

AMY TAN   (b. 1952)

Drawing on her own family experiences and on the earlier experiences of her Chinese immigrant parents, Amy Tan has created a series of works of great nuance set both in the United States and China. Tan was born two years after her parents immigrated to Oakland, California, but she has said that as a child she felt like an American girl trapped in a Chinese body and often chose to follow American traditions. After her father's death when she was fifteen, Tan went to live in Switzerland with her mother, which put her Chinese-American identity in a clearer perspective. Her understanding of her dual heritage was completed after she visited relatives in China with her mother, realizing that "I belonged to my family and my family belonged to China." Although her mother had wanted her to become a doctor or a concert pianist, Tan earned an M.A. in English and linguistics at San Jose State University. While working as a freelance technical writer, she started writing fiction to develop more self-understanding. Her books include *The Joy Luck Club* (1989), *The Kitchen God's Wife* (1991), and *The One Hundred Secret Senses* (1995). Originally written as a series of short stories about the tensions between American-born Chinese daughters and their mothers, her first novel, *The Joy Luck Club,* was an immediate best-seller that was nominated for a National Book Award and subsequently made into a popular film. "Best Quality" is a story from this novel.

Best Quality   (1989)

Five months ago, after a crab dinner celebrating Chinese New Year, my mother gave me my "life's importance," a jade pendant on a gold chain. The pendant was not a piece of jewelry I would have chosen for myself. It was almost the size of my little finger, a mottled green and white color, intricately carved. To me, the whole effect looked wrong: too large, too green, too garishly ornate. I stuffed the necklace in my lacquer box and forgot about it.

But these days, I think about my life's importance. I wonder what it means, because my mother died three months ago, six days before my thirty-sixth birthday. And she's the only person I could have asked, to tell me about life's importance, to help me understand my grief.

I now wear that pendant every day. I think the carvings mean something, because shapes and details, which I never seem to notice until after they're pointed out to me, always mean something to Chinese people. I know I could ask Auntie Lindo, Auntie An-mei, or other Chinese friends, but I also know they would tell me a meaning that is different from what my mother intended.

What if they tell me this curving line branching into three oval shapes is a pomegranate and that my mother was wishing me fertility and posterity? What if my mother really meant the carvings were a branch of pears to give me purity and honesty? Or ten-thousand-year droplets from the magic mountain, giving me my life's direction and a thousand years of fame and immortality?

And because I think about this all the time, I always notice other people wearing these same jade pendants — not the flat rectangular medallions or the round white ones with holes in the middle but ones like mine, a two-inch oblong of bright apple green. It's as though we were all sworn to the same secret covenant, so secret we don't even know what we belong to. Last weekend, for example, I saw a bartender wearing one. As I fingered mine, I asked him, "Where'd you get yours?"

"My mother gave it to me," he said.

I asked him why, which is a nosy question that only one Chinese person can ask another; in a crowd of Caucasians, two Chinese people are already like family.

"She gave it to me after I got divorced. I guess my mother's telling me I'm still worth something."

And I knew by the wonder in his voice that he had no idea what the pendant really meant.

At last year's Chinese New Year dinner, my mother had cooked eleven crabs, one crab for each person, plus an extra. She and I had bought them on Stockton Street in Chinatown. We had walked down the steep hill from my parents' flat, which was actually the first floor of a six-unit building they owned on Leavenworth near California. Their place was only six blocks from where I worked as a copywriter for a small ad agency, so two or three times a week I would drop by after work. My mother always had enough food to insist that I stay for dinner.

That year, Chinese New Year fell on a Thursday, so I got off work early to help my mother shop. My mother was seventy-one, but she still walked briskly along, her small body straight and purposeful, carrying a colorful flowery plastic bag. I dragged the metal shopping cart behind.

Every time I went with her to Chinatown, she pointed out other Chinese women her age. "Hong Kong ladies," she said, eyeing two finely dressed women in long, dark mink coats and perfect black hairdos. "Cantonese, village people," she whispered as we passed women in knitted caps, bent over in layers of padded tops and men's vests. And my mother — wearing light-blue polyester pants, a red sweater, and a child's green down jacket — she didn't look like anybody else. She had come here in 1949, at the end of a long journey that started in Kweilin in 1944; she had gone north to Chungking, where she met my father, and then they went southeast to Shanghai and fled farther south to Hong Kong, where the boat departed for San Francisco. My mother came from many different directions.

And now she was huffing complaints in rhythm to her walk downhill. "Even you don't want them, you stuck," she said. She was fuming again about the tenants who lived on the second floor. Two years ago, she had tried to evict them on the pretext that relatives from China were coming to live there. But the couple saw through her ruse to get around rent control. They said they wouldn't budge until she produced the relatives. And after that I had to listen to her recount every new injustice this couple inflicted on her.

My mother said the gray-haired man put too many bags in the garbage cans: "Cost me extra."

And the woman, a very elegant artist type with blond hair, had supposedly painted the apartment in terrible red and green colors. "Awful," moaned my mother. "And they take bath, two three times every day. Running the water, running, running, running, never stop!"

"Last week," she said, growing angrier at each step, "the *waigoren* accuse me." She referred to all Caucasians as *waigoren,* foreigners. "They say I put poison in a fish, kill that cat."

"What cat?" I asked, even though I knew exactly which one she was talking about. I had seen that cat many times. It was a big one-eared tom with gray stripes who had learned to jump on the outside sill of my mother's kitchen window. My mother would stand on her tiptoes and bang the kitchen window to scare the cat away. And the cat would stand his ground, hissing back in response to her shouts.

"That cat always raising his tail to put a stink on my door," complained my mother.

I once saw her chase him from her stairwell with a pot of boiling water. I was tempted to ask if she really had put poison in a fish, but I had learned never to take sides against my mother.

"So what happened to that cat?" I asked.

"That cat gone! Disappear!" She threw her hands in the air and smiled, looking pleased for a moment before the scowl came back. "And that man, he raise his hand like this, show me his ugly fist and call me worst Fukien landlady. I not from Fukien. Hunh! He know nothing!" she said, satisfied she had put him in his place.

On Stockton Street, we wandered from one fish store to another, looking for the liveliest crabs.

"Don't get a dead one," warned my mother in Chinese. "Even a beggar won't eat a dead one."

I poked the crabs with a pencil to see how feisty they were. If a crab grabbed on, I lifted it out and into a plastic sack. I lifted one crab this way, only to find one of its legs had been clamped onto by another crab. In the brief tug-of-war, my crab lost a limb.

"Put it back," whispered my mother. "A missing leg is a bad sign on a Chinese New Year."

But a man in a white smock came up to us. He started talking loudly to my mother in Cantonese, and my mother, who spoke Cantonese so poorly it sounded just like her Mandarin, was talking loudly back, pointing to the crab and its missing leg. And after more sharp words, that crab and its leg were put into our sack.

"Doesn't matter," said my mother. "This number eleven, extra one."

Back home, my mother unwrapped the crabs from their newspaper liners and then dumped them into a sinkful of cold water. She brought out her old wooden board and cleaver, then chopped the ginger and scallions, and poured soy sauce and sesame oil into a shallow dish. The kitchen smelled of wet newspapers and Chinese fragrances.

Then, one by one, she grabbed the crabs by their backs, hoisted them out of the sink and shook them dry and awake. The crabs flexed their legs in midair between sink and stove. She stacked the crabs in a multileveled steamer that sat over two burners on the stove, put a lid on top, and lit the burners. I couldn't bear to watch so I went into the dining room.

When I was eight, I had played with a crab my mother had brought home for my birthday dinner. I had poked it, and jumped back every time its claws reached out. And I determined that the crab and I had come to a great understanding when it finally heaved itself up and walked clear across the counter. But before I could even decide what to name my new pet, my mother had dropped it into a pot of cold water and placed it on the tall stove. I had watched with growing dread, as the water heated up and the pot began to clatter with this crab trying to tap his way out of his own hot soup. To this day, I remember that crab screaming as he thrust one bright red claw out over the side of the bubbling pot. It must have been my own voice, because now I know, of course, that crabs have no vocal cords. And I also try to convince myself that they don't have enough brains to know the difference between a hot bath and a slow death.

For our New Year celebration, my mother had invited her longtime friends Lindo and Tin Jong. Without even asking, my mother knew that meant including the Jongs' children: their son Vincent, who was thirty-eight years old and still living at home, and their daughter, Waverly, who was around my age. Vincent called to see if he could also bring his girlfriend, Lisa Lum. Waverly said she would bring her new fiancé, Rich Schields, who, like Waverly, was a tax attorney at Price Waterhouse. And she added that Shoshana, her four-year-old daughter from a previous marriage, wanted to know if my parents had a VCR so she could watch *Pinocchio,* just in case she got bored. My mother also reminded me to invite Mr. Chong, my old piano teacher, who still lived three blocks away at our old apartment.

Including my mother, father, and me, that made eleven people. But my mother had counted only ten, because to her way of thinking Shoshana was just a child and didn't count, at least not as far as crabs were concerned. She hadn't considered that Waverly might not think the same way.

When the platter of steaming crabs was passed around, Waverly was first and she picked the best crab, the brightest, the plumpest, and put it on her daughter's plate. And then she picked the next best for Rich and another good one for herself. And because she had learned this skill, of choosing the best, from her mother, it was only natural that her mother knew how to pick the next-best ones for her husband, her son, his girlfriend, and herself. And my mother, of course, considered the four remaining crabs and gave the one that looked the best to Old Chong, because he was nearly ninety and deserved that kind of respect, and then she picked another good one for my father. That left two on the platter: a large crab with a faded orange color, and number eleven, which had the torn-off leg.

My mother shook the platter in front of me. "Take it, already cold," said my mother.

I was not too fond of crab, ever since I saw my birthday crab boiled alive, but I knew I could not refuse. That's the way Chinese mothers show they love their children, not through hugs and kisses but with stern offerings of steamed dumplings, duck's gizzards, and crab.

I thought I was doing the right thing, taking the crab with the missing leg. But my mother cried, "No! No! Big one, you eat it. I cannot finish."

I remember the hungry sounds everybody else was making—cracking the shells, sucking the crab meat out, scraping out tidbits with the ends of chop-sticks—and my mother's quiet plate. I was the only one who noticed her prying open the shell, sniffing the crab's body and then getting up to go to the kitchen, plate in hand. She returned, without the crab, but with more bowls of soy sauce, ginger, and scallions.

And then as stomachs filled, everybody started talking at once.

"Suyuan!" called Auntie Lindo to my mother. "Why you wear that color?" Auntie Lindo gestured with a crab leg to my mother's red sweater.

"How can you wear this color anymore? Too young!" she scolded.

My mother acted as though this were a compliment. "Emporium Cap-well," she said. "Nineteen dollar. Cheaper than knit it myself."

Auntie Lindo nodded her head, as if the color were worth this price. And then she pointed her crab leg toward her future son-in-law, Rich, and said, "See how this one doesn't know how to eat Chinese food."

"Crab isn't Chinese," said Waverly in her complaining voice. It was amaz-ing how Waverly still sounded the way she did twenty-five years ago, when we were ten and she had announced to me in that same voice, "You aren't a genius like me."

Auntie Lindo looked at her daughter with exasperation. "How do you know what is Chinese, what is not Chinese?" And then she turned to Rich and said with much authority, "Why you are not eating the best part?"

And I saw Rich smiling back, with amusement, and not humility, showing in his face. He had the same coloring as the crab on his plate: reddish hair, pale cream skin, and large dots of orange freckles. While he smirked, Auntie Lindo demonstrated the proper technique, poking her chopstick into the orange spongy part: "You have to dig in here, get this out. The brain is most tastiest, you try."

Waverly and Rich grimaced at each other, united in disgust. I heard Vincent and Lisa whisper to each other, "Gross," and then they snickered too.

Uncle Tin started laughing to himself, to let us know he also had a private joke. Judging by his preamble of snorts and leg slaps, I figured he must have practiced this joke many times: "I tell my daughter, Hey, why be poor? Marry rich!" He laughed loudly and then nudged Lisa, who was sitting next to him, "Hey, don't you get it? Look what happen. She gonna marry this guy here. Rich. 'Cause I tell her to, *marry Rich*."

"When *are* you guys getting married?" asked Vincent.

"I should ask you the same thing," said Waverly. Lisa looked embarrassed when Vincent ignored the question.

"Mom, I don't *like* crab!" whined Shoshana.

"Nice haircut," Waverly said to me from across the table.

"Thanks, David always does a great job."

"You mean you still go to that guy on Howard Street?" Waverly asked, arching one eyebrow. "Aren't you afraid?"

I could sense the danger, but I said it anyway: "What do you mean, afraid? He's always very good."

"I mean, he *is* gay," Waverly said. "He could have AIDS. And he is cutting your hair, which is like cutting a living tissue. Maybe I'm being paranoid, being a mother, but you just can't be too safe these days. . . ."

And I sat there feeling as if my hair were coated with disease.

"You should go see my guy," said Waverly. "Mr. Rory. He does fabulous work, although he probably charges more than you're used to."

I felt like screaming. She could be so sneaky with her insults. Every time I asked her the simplest of tax questions, for example, she could turn the conversation around and make it seem as if I were too cheap to pay for her legal advice.

She'd say things like, "I really don't like to talk about important tax matters except in my office. I mean, what if you say something casual over lunch and I give you some casual advice. And then you follow it, and it's wrong because you didn't give me the full information. I'd feel terrible. And you would too, wouldn't you?"

At that crab dinner, I was so mad about what she said about my hair that I wanted to embarrass her, to reveal in front of everybody how petty she was. So I decided to confront her about the free-lance work I'd done for her firm, eight pages of brochure copy on its tax services. The firm was now more than thirty days late in paying my invoice.

"Maybe I could afford Mr. Rory's prices if someone's firm paid me on time," I said with a teasing grin. And I was pleased to see Waverly's reaction. She was genuinely flustered, speechless.

I couldn't resist rubbing it in: "I think it's pretty ironic that a big accounting firm can't even pay its own bills on time. I mean, really, Waverly, what kind of place are you working for?"

Her face was dark and quiet.

"Hey, hey, you girls, no more fighting!" said my father, as if Waverly and I were still children arguing over tricycles and crayon colors.

"That's right, we don't want to talk about this now," said Waverly quietly.

"So how do you think the Giants are going to do?" said Vincent, trying to be funny. Nobody laughed.

I wasn't about to let her slip away this time. "Well, every time I call you on the phone, you can't talk about it then either," I said.

Waverly looked at Rich, who shrugged his shoulders. She turned back to me and sighed.

"Listen, June, I don't know how to tell you this. That stuff you wrote, well, the firm decided it was unacceptable."

"You're lying. You said it was great."

Waverly sighed again. "I know I did. I didn't want to hurt your feelings. I was trying to see if we could fix it somehow. But it won't work."

And just like that, I was starting to flail, tossed without warning into deep water, drowning and desperate. "Most copy needs fine-tuning," I said. "It's . . . normal not to be perfect the first time. I should have explained the process better."

"June, I really don't think . . ."

"Rewrites are free. I'm just as concerned about making it perfect as you are."

Waverly acted as if she didn't even hear me. "I'm trying to convince them to at least pay you for some of your time. I know you put a lot of work into it. . . . I owe you at least that for even suggesting you do it."

"Just tell me what they want changed. I'll call you next week so we can go over it, line by line."

"June — I can't," Waverly said with cool finality. "It's just not . . . sophisticated. I'm sure what you write for your other clients is *wonderful*. But we're a big firm. We need somebody who understands that . . . our style." She said this touching her hand to her chest, as if she were referring to *her* style.

Then she laughed in a lighthearted way. "I mean, really, June." And then she started speaking in a deep television-announcer voice: "*Three* benefits, *three* needs, *three* reasons to buy . . . Satisfaction *guaranteed* . . . for today's and tomorrow's tax needs . . ."

She said this in such a funny way that everybody thought it was a good joke and laughed. And then, to make matters worse, I heard my mother saying to Waverly: "True, cannot teach style. June not sophisticate like you. Must be born this way."

I was surprised at myself, how humiliated I felt. I had been outsmarted by Waverly once again, and now betrayed by my own mother. I was smiling so hard my lower lip was twitching from the strain. I tried to find something else to concentrate on, and I remember picking up my plate, and then Mr. Chong's, as if I were clearing the table, and seeing so sharply through my tears the chips on the edges of these old plates, wondering why my mother didn't use the new set I had bought her five years ago.

The table was littered with crab carcasses. Waverly and Rich lit cigarettes and put a crab shell between them for an ashtray. Shoshana had wandered over to the piano and was banging notes out with a crab claw in each hand. Mr. Chong, who had grown totally deaf over the years, watched Shoshana and applauded: "Bravo! Bravo!" And except for his strange shouts, nobody said a word. My mother went to the kitchen and returned with a plate of oranges sliced into wedges. My father poked at the remnants of his crab. Vincent cleared his throat, twice, and then patted Lisa's hand.

It was Auntie Lindo who finally spoke: "Waverly, you let her try again. You make her do too fast first time. Of course she cannot get it right."

I could hear my mother eating an orange slice. She was the only person I knew who crunched oranges, making it sound as if she were eating crisp apples instead. The sound of it was worse than gnashing teeth.

"Good one take time," continued Auntie Lindo, nodding her head in agreement with herself.

"Put in lotta action," advised Uncle Tin. "Lotta action, boy, that's what I like. Hey, that's all you need, make it right."

"Probably not," I said, and smiled before carrying the plates to the sink.

That was the night, in the kitchen, that I realized I was no better than who I was. I was a copywriter. I worked for a small ad agency. I promised every new client, "We can provide the sizzle for the meat." The sizzle always boiled down to "Three Benefits, Three Needs, Three Reasons to buy." The meat was always coaxial cable, T-1 multiplexers, protocol converters, and the like. I was very good at what I did, succeeding at something small like that.

I turned on the water to wash the dishes. And I no longer felt angry at Waverly. I felt tired and foolish, as if I had been running to escape someone chasing me, only to look behind and discover there was no one there.

I picked up my mother's plate, the one she had carried into the kitchen at the start of the dinner. The crab was untouched. I lifted the shell and smelled the crab. Maybe it was because I didn't like crab in the first place. I couldn't tell what was wrong with it.

After everybody left, my mother joined me in the kitchen. I was putting dishes away. She put water on for more tea and sat down at the small kitchen table. I waited for her to chastise me.

"Good dinner, Ma," I said politely.

"Not so good," she said, jabbing at her mouth with a toothpick.

"What happened to your crab? Why'd you throw it away?"

"Not so good," she said again. "That crab die. Even a beggar don't want it."

"How could you tell? I didn't smell anything wrong."

"Can tell even before cook!" She was standing now, looking out the kitchen window into the night. "I shake that crab before cook. His legs — droopy. His mouth — wide open, already like a dead person."

"Why'd you cook it if you knew it was already dead?"

"I thought . . . maybe only just die. Maybe taste not too bad. But I can smell, dead taste, not firm."

"What if someone else had picked that crab?"

My mother looked at me and smiled. "Only *you* pick that crab. Nobody else take it. I already know this. Everybody else want best quality. You thinking different."

She said it in a way as if this were proof — proof of something good. She always said things that didn't make any sense, that sounded both good and bad at the same time.

I was putting away the last of the chipped plates and then I remembered something else. "Ma, why don't you ever use those new dishes I bought you? If you didn't like them, you should have told me. I could have changed the pattern."

"Of course, I like," she said, irritated. "Sometimes I think something is so good, I want to save it. Then I forget I save it."

And then, as if she had just now remembered, she unhooked the clasp of her gold necklace and took it off, wadding the chain and the jade pendant in her palm. She grabbed my hand and put the necklace in my palm, then shut my fingers around it.

"No, Ma," I protested. "I can't take this."

"Nala, nala" — Take it, take it — she said, as if she were scolding me. And then she continued in Chinese. "For a long time, I wanted to give you this necklace. See, I wore this on my skin, so when you put it on your skin, then you know my meaning. This is your life's importance."

I looked at the necklace, the pendant with the light green jade. I wanted to give it back. I didn't want to accept it. And yet I also felt as if I had already swallowed it.

"You're giving this to me only because of what happened tonight," I finally said.

"What happen?"

"What Waverly said. What everybody said."

"Tss! Why you listen to her? Why you want to follow behind her, chasing her words? She is like this crab." My mother poked a shell in the garbage can. "Always walking sideways, moving crooked. You can make your legs go the other way."

I put the necklace on. It felt cool.

"Not so good, this jade," she said matter-of-factly, touching the pendant, and then she added in Chinese: "This is young jade. It is a very light color now, but if you wear it every day it will become more green."

My father hasn't eaten well since my mother died. So I am here, in the kitchen, to cook him dinner. I'm slicing tofu. I've decided to make him a spicy bean-curd dish. My mother used to tell me how hot things restore the spirit and health. But I'm making this mostly because I know my father loves this dish and I know how to cook it. I like the smell of it: ginger, scallions, and a red chili sauce that tickles my nose the minute I open the jar.

Above me, I hear the old pipes shake into action with a *thunk!* and then the water running in my sink dwindles to a trickle. One of the tenants upstairs must be taking a shower. I remember my mother complaining: "Even you don't want them, you stuck." And now I know what she meant.

As I rinse the tofu in the sink, I am startled by a dark mass that appears suddenly at the window. It's the one-eared tomcat from upstairs. He's balancing on the sill, rubbing his flank against the window.

My mother didn't kill that damn cat after all, and I'm relieved. And then I see this cat rubbing more vigorously on the window and he starts to raise his tail.

"Get away from there!" I shout, and slap my hand on the window three times. But the cat just narrows his eyes, flattens his one ear, and hisses back at me.

Questions for Discussion

1. Why does the narrator's mother give her the jade pendant? Since her mother's death, what has the narrator learned about the importance and meaning of the pendant?
2. How does the way in which each guest at the Chinese New Year dinner selects a crab become symbolic of his or her personality?
3. Who wins the argument between the narrator and Waverly? What does the narrator come to understand about herself and her relationship with her mother after this conflict?
4. Why is the story titled "Best Quality"? How does the meaning of the concept of "best quality" change for the narrator as the story develops and concludes?
5. Why is the narrator relieved to see the tomcat at the end of the story? How does this scene reflect her changing judgments and feeling about her mother?

Ideas for Writing

1. Write an essay in which you discuss the story's sources of humor. How does the humor emphasize the story's themes and values?
2. Write an essay in which you compare and contrast the narrator and her mother. How are their values and outlooks on life similar and yet different? How does the narrator become more conscious of her similarity to her mother as the story develops?

(b. 1954)

Sandra Cisneros's stories focus on the experiences of young women growing up in Latin American and Mexican-American cultures. Cisneros has noted that there typically are only two models of female behavior available to such women: "La Molinchi y la Virgen de Guadalupe" — the prostitute and the virgin. These polarities make it difficult for Hispanic women to discover authentic identities.

The only girl among seven children, Cisneros grew up in a struggling family that traveled back and forth between Chicago and Mexico. When she was twelve her family settled in a Puerto Rican neighborhood of Chicago. Cisneros, an introverted child who loved to read, attended Loyola University, graduating in 1976 with a B.A. in English. She earned an M.F.A. from the University of Iowa's Writing Workshop in 1978. While Cisneros has taught at all levels, she now works full time on her writing. Her first collection, *The House on Mango Street* (1983), from which the story "The Monkey Garden" is taken, captures the experiences of a maturing adolescent girl discovering life around her in an impoverished urban neighborhood similar to the one in which Cisneros grew up. Of her second collection, *Woman Hollering Creek and Other Stories* (1991), Bebe Moore Campell wrote, "These stories about women struggling to take control of their lives traverse geographical, historical, and emotional borders and invite us into the souls of characters as unforgettable as a first kiss." Cisneros has also published two collections of poetry, *My Wicked Wicked Ways* (1987) and *Loose Women* (1996). She is now working on a novel entitled *Caramelo*.

The Monkey Garden (1983)

The monkey doesn't live there anymore. The monkey moved—to Kentucky—and took his people with him. And I was glad because I couldn't listen anymore to his wild screaming at night, the twangy yakkety-yak of the people who owned him. The green metal cage, the porcelain table top, the family that spoke like guitars. Monkey, family, table. All gone.

And it was then we took over the garden we had been afraid to go into when the monkey screamed and showed its yellow teeth.

There were sunflowers big as flowers on Mars and thick cockscombs bleeding the deep red fringe of theater curtains. There were dizzy bees and bow-tied fruit flies turning somersaults and humming in the air. Sweet sweet peach trees. Thorn roses and thistle and pears. Weeds like so many squinty-eyed stars and brush that made your ankles itch and itch until you washed with soap and water. There were big green apples hard as knees. And every-where the sleepy smell of rotting wood, damp earth and dusty hollyhocks thick and perfumy like the blue-blond hair of the dead.

Yellow spiders ran when we turned rocks over and pale worms blind and afraid of light rolled over in their sleep. Poke a stick in the sandy soil and a few blue-skinned beetles would appear, an avenue of ants, so many crusty lady bugs. This was a garden, a wonderful thing to look at in the spring. But bit by bit, after the monkey left, the garden began to take over itself. Flowers stopped obeying the little bricks that kept them from growing beyond their paths. Weeds mixed in. Dead cars appeared overnight like mushrooms. First one and then another and then a pale blue pickup with the front windshield missing. Before you knew it, the monkey garden became filled with sleepy cars.

Things had a way of disappearing in the garden, as if the garden itself ate them, or, as if with its old-man memory, it put them away and forgot them. Nenny found a dollar and a dead mouse between two rocks in the stone wall where the morning glories climbed, and once when we were playing hide and seek, Eddie Vargas laid his head beneath a hibiscus tree and fell asleep there like a Rip Van Winkle until somebody remembered he was in the game and went back to look for him.

This, I suppose, was the reason why we went there. Far away from where our mothers could find us. We and a few old dogs who lived inside the empty cars. We made a club-house once on the back of that old blue pickup. And besides, we liked to jump from the roof of one car to another and pretend they were giant mushrooms.

Somebody started the lie that the monkey garden had been there before anything. We liked to think the garden could hide things for a thousand years. There beneath the roots of soggy flowers were the bones of murdered pirates and dinosaurs, the eye of a unicorn turned to coal.

This is where I wanted to die and where I tried one day but not even the monkey garden would have me. It was the last day I would go there.

Who was it that said I was getting too old to play the games? Who was it I didn't listen to? I only remember that when the others ran, I wanted to run too, up and down and through the monkey garden, fast as the boys, not like Sally who screamed if she got her stockings muddy.

I said, Sally, come on, but she wouldn't. She stayed by the curb talking to Tito and his friends. Play with the kids if you want, she said, I'm staying here. She could be stuck-up like that if she wanted to, so I just left.

It was her own fault too. When I got back Sally was pretending to be mad . . . something about the boys having stolen her keys. Please give them back to me, she said punching the nearest one with a soft fist. They were laughing. She was too. It was a joke I didn't get.

I wanted to go back with the other kids who were still jumping on cars, still chasing each other through the garden, but Sally had her own game.

One of the boys invented the rules. One of Tito's friends said you can't get the keys back unless you kiss us and Sally pretended to be mad at first but she said yes. It was that simple.

I don't know why, but something inside me wanted to throw a stick. Something wanted to say no when I watched Sally going into the garden with Tito's buddies all grinning. It was just a kiss, that's all. A kiss for each one. So what, she said.

Only how come I felt angry inside. Like something wasn't right. Sally went behind that old blue pickup to kiss the boys and get her keys back, and I ran up three flights of stairs to where Tito lived. His mother was ironing shirts. She was sprinkling water on them from an empty pop bottle and smoking a cigarette.

Your son and his friends stole Sally's keys and now they won't give them back unless she kisses them and right now they're making her kiss them, I said all out of breath from the three flights of stairs.

Those kids, she said, not looking up from her ironing.

That's all?

What do you want me to do, she said, call the cops? And kept on ironing.

I looked at her a long time, but couldn't think of anything to say, and ran back down the three flights to the garden where Sally needed to be saved. I took three big sticks and a brick and figured this was enough.

But when I got there Sally said go home. Those boys said, leave us alone. I felt stupid with my brick. They all looked at me as if *I* was the one that was crazy and made me feel ashamed.

And then I don't know why but I had to run away. I had to hide myself at the other end of the garden, in the jungle part, under a tree that wouldn't mind if I lay down and cried a long time. I closed my eyes like tight stars so that I wouldn't, but I did. My face felt hot. Everything inside hiccupped.

I read somewhere in India there are priests who can will their heart to stop beating. I wanted to will my blood to stop, my heart to quit its pumping. I wanted to be dead, to turn into the rain, my eyes melt into the ground like two black snails. I wished and wished. I closed my eyes and willed it, but when I got up my dress was green and I had a headache.

I looked at my feet in their white socks and ugly round shoes. They seemed far away. They didn't seem to be my feet anymore. And the garden that had been such a good place to play didn't seem mine either.

Questions for Discussion

1. Why were the narrator and her friends previously afraid to enter the monkey garden? What is the garden's appeal to them?

2. Read the description of the garden, both before and after it "began to take over itself." What do the screaming monkey, the exuberance of natural growth and decay, and the "sleepy cars" signify?

3. What kind of game do Tito and his friends play with Sally, and what does the game represent? Why does the narrator feel Sally needs to be "saved"?

4. Why does the narrator want "to be dead . . . to . . . melt into the ground"? What role do death and loss play in the story?

5. In the final paragraph, the narrator experiences an epiphany as she looks at her body and the garden in a new way. What final realization does she come to? How has she changed in the course of the story?

Ideas for Writing

1. Write an essay comparing the adolescent epiphany portrayed in "The Monkey Garden" with the epiphanies of the adolescent characters in Joyce's "Araby" and Mansfield's "The Garden-Party."

2. Using the point of view of the narrator in "The Monkey Garden," write a sequel set some time after the events portrayed in the original story. How has the narrator's view of the garden, of her childhood friends, and of herself changed?

LOUISE ERDRICH (b. 1954)

Louise Erdrich often writes of "mixed-blood" people, some of whom continue to live on Chippewa reservations but most of whom have become part of mainstream American culture, while still maintaining some awareness of Native American values and traditions. Erdrich herself is from a mixed German-Chippewa heritage, although she was raised in North Dakota as a member of the Turtle Mountain Chippewa tribe. Her parents encouraged her to write, and her Native American culture valued storytelling. "When you grow up constantly hearing the stories rise, break and fall, it gets into you somehow." Erdrich earned her B.A. from Dartmouth College in 1976 and her M.F.A. in creative writing from Johns Hopkins University several years later. Before beginning her career as a writer, Erdrich taught poetry in prisons and edited the *Circle,* a Boston Indian Council newspaper. *Jacklight* (1984), a collection of Erdrich's poetry, was followed by the novel *Love Medicine* (1984; expanded edition 1993), which won the National Book Critics' Circle Award. *Love Medicine* introduces many of the characters and clan histories that are developed in Erdrich's later novels: *The Beet Queen* (1986); *Tracks* (1988), which introduces as a young woman the Chippewa sorceress Fleur; *The Bingo Palace* (1994), which deals with the growth of gambling on reservation lands; and, most recently, *Tales of Burning Love* (1996), from which the story "Eleanor's Tale: The Leap" is taken.

Erdrich has noted that she was inspired to write through contacts she made working with prisoners and the urban poor: "There were lots of people with mixed blood, lots of people who had their own confusions. I realized that this was part of my life — it wasn't something that I was making up — and that it was something I *wanted* to write about."

Fleur (1986)

The first time she drowned in the cold and glassy waters of Lake Turcot, Fleur Pillager was only a girl. Two men saw the boat tip, saw her struggle in the waves. They rowed over to the place she went down, and jumped in. When they dragged her over the gunwales, she was cold to the touch and stiff, so they slapped her face, shook her by the heels, worked her arms back and forth, and pounded her back until she coughed up lake water. She shivered all over like a dog, then took a breath. But it wasn't long afterward that those two men disappeared. The first wandered off, and the other, Jean Hat, got himself run over by a cart.

It went to show, my grandma said. It figured to her, all right. By saving Fleur Pillager, those two men had lost themselves.

The next time she fell in the lake, Fleur Pillager was twenty years old and no one touched her. She washed onshore, her skin a dull dead gray, but when George Many Women bent to look closer, he saw her chest move. Then her eyes spun open, sharp black riprock, and she looked at him. "You'll take my place," she hissed. Everybody scattered and left her there, so no one knows how she dragged herself home. Soon after that we noticed Many Women changed, grew afraid, wouldn't leave his house, and would not be forced to go near water. For his caution, he lived until the day that his sons brought him a new tin bathtub. Then the first time he used the tub he slipped, got knocked out, and breathed water while his wife stood in the other room frying breakfast.

Men stayed clear of Fleur Pillager after the second drowning. Even though she was good-looking, nobody dared to court her because it was clear that Misshepeshu, the waterman, the monster, wanted her for himself. He's a devil, that one, love-hungry with desire and maddened for the touch of young girls, the strong and daring especially, the ones like Fleur.

Our mothers warn us that we'll think he's handsome, for he appears with green eyes, copper skin, a mouth tender as a child's. But if you fall into his arms, he sprouts horns, fangs, claws, fins. His feet are joined as one and his skin, brass scales, rings to the touch. You're fascinated, cannot move. He casts a shell necklace at your feet, weeps gleaming chips that harden into mica on your breasts. He holds you under. Then he takes the body of a lion or a fat brown worm. He's made of gold. He's made of beach moss. He's a thing of dry foam, a thing of death by drowning, the death a Chippewa cannot survive.

Unless you are Fleur Pillager. We all knew she couldn't swim. After the first time, we thought she'd never go back to Lake Turcot. We thought she'd keep to herself, live quiet, stop killing men off by drowning in the lake. After the first time, we thought she'd keep the good ways. But then, after the second drowning, we knew that we were dealing with something much more serious. She was haywire, out of control. She messed with evil, laughed at the old women's advice, and dressed like a man. She got herself into some half-forgotten medicine, studied ways we shouldn't talk about. Some say she kept the finger of a child in her pocket and a powder of unborn rabbits in a leather thong around her neck. She laid the heart of an owl on her tongue so she could see at night, and went out, hunting, not even in her own body. We know for sure because the next morning, in the snow or dust, we followed the tracks of her bare feet and saw where they changed, where the claws sprang out, the pad broadened and pressed into the dirt. By night we heard her chuffing cough, the bear cough. By day her silence and the wide grin she threw to bring down our guard made us frightened. Some thought that Fleur Pillager should be driven off the reservation, but not a single person who spoke like this had the nerve. And finally, when people were just about to get together and throw her out, she left on her own and didn't come back all summer. That's what this story is about.

During that summer, when she lived a few miles south in Argus, things happened. She almost destroyed that town.

When she got down to Argus in the year of 1920, it was just a small grid of six streets on either side of the railroad depot. There were two elevators, one central, the other a few miles west. Two stores competed for the trade of the three hundred citizens, and three churches quarreled with one another for their souls. There was a frame building for Lutherans, a heavy brick one for Episcopalians, and a long narrow shingled Catholic church. This last had a tall slender steeple, twice as high as any building or tree.

No doubt, across the low, flat wheat, watching from the road as she came near Argus on foot, Fleur saw that steeple rise, a shadow thin as a needle. Maybe in that raw space it drew her the way a lone tree draws lightning. Maybe, in the end, the Catholics are to blame. For if she hadn't seen that sign of pride, that slim prayer, that marker, maybe she would have kept walking.

But Fleur Pillager turned, and the first place she went once she came into town was to the back door of the priest's residence attached to the landmark church. She didn't go there for a handout, although she got that, but to ask for work. She got that too, or the town got her. It's hard to tell which came out worse, her or the men or the town, although the upshot of it all was that Fleur lived.

The four men who worked at the butcher's had carved up about a thousand carcasses between them, maybe half of that steers and the other half pigs, sheep, and game animals like deer, elk, and bear. That's not even mentioning the chickens, which were beyond counting. Pete Kozka owned the place, and employed Lily Veddar, Tor Grunewald, and my stepfather, Dutch James, who had brought my mother down from the reservation the year before she disappointed him by dying. Dutch took me out of school to take her place. I kept house half the time and worked the other in the butcher shop, sweeping floors, putting sawdust down, running a hambone across the street to a customer's bean pot or a package of sausage to the corner. I was a good one to have around because until they needed me, I was invisible. I blended into the stained brown walls, a skinny, big-nosed girl with staring eyes. Because I could fade into a corner or squeeze beneath a shelf, I knew everything, what the men said when no one was around, and what they did to Fleur.

Kozka's Meats served farmers for a fifty-mile area, both to slaughter, for it had a stock pen and chute, and to cure the meat by smoking it or spicing it in sausage. The storage locker was a marvel, made of many thicknesses of brick, earth insulation, and Minnesota timber, lined inside with sawdust and vast blocks of ice cut from Lake Turcot, hauled down from home each winter by horse and sledge.

A ramshackle board building, part slaughterhouse, part store, was fixed to the low, thick square of the lockers. That's where Fleur worked. Kozka hired her for her strength. She could lift a haunch or carry a pole of sausages without stumbling, and she soon learned cutting from Pete's wife, a string-thin blonde who chain-smoked and handled the razor-sharp knives with nerveless precision, slicing close to her stained fingers. Fleur and Fritzie Kozka worked afternoons, wrapping their cuts in paper, and Fleur hauled the packages to the lockers. The meat was left outside the heavy oak doors that were only opened at 5:00 each afternoon, before the men ate supper.

Sometimes Dutch, Tor, and Lily ate at the lockers, and when they did I stayed too, cleaned floors, restoked the fires in the front smokehouses, while the men sat around the squat cast-iron stove spearing slats of herring onto hardtack bread. They played long games of poker or cribbage on a board made from the planed end of a salt crate. They talked and I listened, although there wasn't much to hear since almost nothing ever happened in Argus. Tor was married, Dutch had lost my mother, and Lily read circulars. They mainly discussed about the auctions to come, equipment, or women.

Every so often, Pete Kozka came out front to make a whist, leaving Fritzie to smoke cigarettes and fry raised doughnuts in the back room. He sat and played a few rounds but kept his thoughts to himself. Fritzie did not tolerate him talking behind her back, and the one book he read was the New Testament. If he said something, it concerned weather or a surplus of sheep stomachs, a ham that smoked green or the markets for corn and wheat. He had a good-luck talisman, the opal-white lens of a cow's eye. Playing cards, he rubbed it between his fingers. That soft sound and the slap of cards was about the only conversation.

Fleur finally gave them a subject.

Her cheeks were wide and flat, her hands large, chapped, muscular. Fleur's shoulders were broad as beams, her hips fishlike, slippery, narrow. An old green dress clung to her waist, worn thin where she sat. Her braids were thick like the tails of animals, and swung against her when she moved, deliberately, slowly in her work, held in and half-tamed, but only half. I could tell, but the others never saw. They never looked into her sly brown eyes or noticed her teeth, strong and curved and very white. Her legs were bare, and since she padded around in beadwork moccasins they never saw that her fifth toes were missing. They never knew she'd drowned. They were blinded, they were stupid, they only saw her in the flesh.

And yet it wasn't just that she was a Chippewa, or even that she was a woman, it wasn't that she was good-looking or even that she was alone that made their brains hum. It was how she played cards.

Women didn't usually play with men, so the evening that Fleur drew a chair up to the men's table without being so much as asked, there was a shock of surprise.

"What's this," said Lily. He was fat, with a snake's cold pale eyes and precious skin, smooth and lily-white, which is how he got his name. Lily had a dog, a stumpy mean little bull of a thing with a belly drum-tight from eating pork rinds. The dog liked to play cards just like Lily, and straddled his barrel thighs through games of stud, rum poker, vingt-un.[1] The dog snapped at Fleur's arm that first night, but cringed back, its snarl frozen, when she took her place.

"I thought," she said, her voice soft and stroking, "you might deal me in."

There was a space between the heavy bin of spiced flour and the wall where I just fit. I hunkered down there, kept my eyes open, saw her black hair swing over the chair, her feet solid on the wood floor. I couldn't see up on the table where the cards slapped down, so after they were deep in their game I raised myself up in the shadows, and crouched on a sill of wood.

I watched Fleur's hands stack and ruffle, divide the cards, spill them to each player in a blur, rake them up and shuffle again. Tor, short and scrappy, shut one eye and squinted the other at Fleur. Dutch screwed his lips around a wet cigar.

"Gotta see a man," he mumbled, getting up to go out back to the privy. The others broke, put their cards down, and Fleur sat alone in the lamplight that glowed in a sheen across the push of her breasts. I watched her closely, then she paid me a beam of notice for the first time. She turned, looked straight at me, and grinned the white wolf grin a Pillager turns on its victims, except that she wasn't after me.

"Pauline there," she said, "how much money you got?"

We'd all been paid for the week that day. Eight cents was in my pocket.

"Stake me," she said, holding out her long fingers. I put the coins in her palm and then I melted back to nothing, part of the walls and tables. It was a long time before I understood that the men would not have seen me no matter what I did, how I moved. I wasn't anything like Fleur. My dress hung loose and my back was already curved, an old woman's. Work had roughened me, reading made my eyes sore, caring for my mother before she died had hardened my face. I was not much to look at, so they never saw me.

When the men came back and sat around the table, they had drawn together. They shot each other small glances, stuck their tongues in their cheeks, burst out laughing at odd moments, to rattle Fleur. But she never minded. They played their vingt-un, staying even as Fleur slowly gained. Those pennies I had given her drew nickels and attracted dimes until there was a small pile in front of her.

Then she hooked them with five-card draw, nothing wild. She dealt, discarded, drew, and then she sighed and her cards gave a little shiver. Tor's eye gleamed, and Dutch straightened in his seat.

"I'll pay to see that hand," said Lily Veddar.

Fleur showed, and she had nothing there, nothing at all.

Tor's thin smile cracked open, and he threw his hand in too.

---

[1] A card game. — Eds.

"Well, we know one thing," he said, leaning back in his chair, "the squaw can't bluff."

With that I lowered myself into a mound of swept sawdust and slept. I woke up during the night, but none of them had moved yet, so I couldn't either. Still later, the men must have gone out again, or Fritzie come out to break the game, because I was lifted, soothed, cradled in a woman's arms and rocked so quiet that I kept my eyes shut while Fleur rolled me into a closet of grimy ledgers, oiled paper, balls of string, and thick files that fit beneath me like a mattress.

The game went on after work the next evening. I got my eight cents back five times over, and Fleur kept the rest of the dollar she'd won for a stake. This time they didn't play so late, but they played regular, and then kept going at it night after night. They played poker now, or variations, for one week straight, and each time Fleur won exactly one dollar, no more and no less, too consistent for luck.

By this time, Lily and the other men were so lit with suspense that they got Pete to join the game with them. They concentrated, the fat dog sitting tense in Lily Veddar's lap, Tor suspicious, Dutch stroking his huge square brow, Pete steady. It wasn't that Fleur won that hooked them in so, because she lost hands too. It was rather that she never had a freak hand or even anything above a straight. She only took on her low cards, which didn't sit right. By chance, Fleur should have gotten a full or flush by now. The irritating thing was she beat with pairs and never bluffed, because she couldn't, and still she ended up each night with exactly one dollar. Lily couldn't believe, first of all, that a woman could be smart enough to play cards, but even if she was, that she would then be stupid enough to cheat for a dollar a night. By day I watched him turn the problem over, his hard white face dull, small fingers probing at his knuckles, until he finally thought he had Fleur figured out as a bit-time player, caution her game. Raising the stakes would throw her.

More than anything now, he wanted Fleur to come away with something but a dollar. Two bits less or ten more, the sum didn't matter, just so he broke her streak.

Night after night she played, won her dollar, and left to stay in a place that just Fritzie and I knew about. Fleur bathed in the slaughtering tub, then slept in the unused brick smokehouse behind the lockers, a windowless place tarred on the inside with scorched fats. When I brushed against her skin I noticed that she smelled of the walls, rich and woody, slightly burnt. Since that night she put me in the closet I was no longer afraid of her, but followed her close, stayed with her, became her moving shadow that the men never noticed, the shadow that could have saved her.

August, the month that bears fruit, closed around the shop, and Pete and Fritzie left for Minnesota to escape the heat. Night by night, running, Fleur had won thirty dollars, and only Pete's presence had kept Lily at bay. But Pete was gone now, and one payday, with the heat so bad no one could move but Fleur, the men sat and played and waited while she finished work. The cards sweat, limp in their fingers, the table was slick with grease, and even the walls were warm to the touch. The air was motionless. Fleur was in the next room boiling heads.

Her green dress, drenched, wrapped her like a transparent sheet. A skin of lakeweed. Black snarls of veining clung to her arms. Her braids were loose, half-unraveled, tied behind her neck in a thick loop. She stood in steam, turning skulls through a vat with a wooden paddle. When scraps boiled to the surface, she bent with a round tin sieve and scooped them out. She'd filled two dishpans.

"Ain't that enough now?" called Lily. "We're waiting." The stump of a dog trembled in his lap, alive with rage. It never smelled me or noticed me above Fleur's smoky skin. The air was heavy in my corner, and pressed me down. Fleur sat with them.

"Now what do you say?" Lily asked the dog. It barked. That was the signal for the real game to start.

"Let's up the ante," said Lily, who had been stalking this night all month. He had a roll of money in his pocket. Fleur had five bills in her dress. The men had each saved their full pay.

"Ante a dollar then," said Fleur, and pitched hers in. She lost, but they let her scrape along, cent by cent. And then she won some. She played unevenly, as if chance was all she had. She reeled them in. The game went on. The dog was stiff now, poised on Lily's knees, a ball of vicious muscle with its yellow eyes slit in concentration. It gave advice, seemed to sniff the lay of Fleur's cards, twitched and nudged. Fleur was up, then down, saved by a scratch. Tor dealt seven cards, three down. The pot grew, round by round, until it held all the money. Nobody folded. Then it all rode on one last card and they went silent. Fleur picked hers up and blew a long breath. The heat lowered like a bell. Her card shook, but she stayed in.

Lily smiled and took the dog's head tenderly between his palms.

"Say, Fatso," he said, crooning the words, "you reckon that girl's bluffing?"

The dog whined and Lily laughed. "Me too," he said, "let's show." He swept his bills and coins into the pot and then they turned their cards over.

Lily looked once, looked again, then he squeezed the dog up like a fist of dough and slammed it on the table.

Fleur threw her arms out and drew the money over, grinning that same wolf grin that she'd used on me, the grin that had them. She jammed the bills in her dress, scooped the coins up in waxed white paper that she tied with string.

"Let's go another round," said Lily, his voice choked with burrs. But Fleur opened her mouth and yawned, then walked out back to gather slops for the one big hog that was waiting in the stock pen to be killed.

The men sat still as rocks, their hands spread on the oiled wood table.

Dutch had chewed his cigar to damp shreds, Tor's eye was dull. Lily's gaze was the only one to follow Fleur. I didn't move. I felt them gathering, saw my stepfather's veins, the ones in his forehead that stood out in anger. The dog had rolled off the table and curled in a knot below the counter, where none of the men could touch it.

Lily rose and stepped out back to the closet of ledgers where Pete kept his private stock. He brought back a bottle, uncorked and tipped it between his fingers. The lump in his throat moved, then he passed it on. They drank, quickly felt the whiskey's fire, and planned with their eyes things they couldn't say out loud.

When they left, I followed. I hid out back in the clutter of broken boards and chicken crates beside the stock pen, where they waited. Fleur could not be seen at first, and then the moon broke and showed her, slipping cautiously along the rough board chute with a bucket in her hand. Her hair fell, wild and coarse, to her waist, and her dress was a floating patch in the dark. She made a pig-calling sound, rang the tin pail lightly against the wood, froze suspiciously. But too late. In the sound of the ring Lily moved, fat and nimble, stepped right behind Fleur and put out his creamy hands. At his first touch, she whirled and doused him with the bucket of sour slops. He pushed her against the big fence and the package of coins split, went clinking and jumping, winked against the wood. Fleur rolled over once and vanished in the yard.

The moon fell behind a curtain of ragged clouds, and Lily followed into the dark muck. But he tripped, pitched over the huge flank of the pig, who lay mired to the snout, heavily snoring. I sprang out of the weeds and climbed the side of the pen, stuck like glue. I saw the sow rise to her neat, knobby knees, gain her balance, and sway, curious, as Lily stumbled forward. Fleur had backed into the angle of rough wood just beyond, and when Lily tried to jostle past, the sow tipped up on her hind legs and struck, quick and hard as a snake. She plunged her head into Lily's thick side and snatched a mouthful of his shirt. She lunged again, caught him lower, so that he grunted in pained surprise. He seemed to ponder, breathing deep. Then he launched his huge body in a swimmer's dive.

The sow screamed as his body smacked over hers. She rolled, striking out with her knife-sharp hooves, and Lily gathered himself upon her, took her foot-long face by the ears and scraped her snout and cheeks against the trestles of the pen. He hurled the sow's tight skull against an iron post, but instead of knocking her dead, he merely woke her from her dream.

She reared, shrieked, drew him with her so that they posed standing upright. They bowed jerkily to each other, as if to begin. Then his arms swung and flailed. She sank her black fangs into his shoulder, clasping him, dancing him forward and backward through the pen. Their steps picked up pace, went wild. The two dipped as one, box-stepped, tripped each other. She ran her split foot through his hair. He grabbed her kinked tail. They went down and came up, the same shape and then the same color, until the men couldn't tell one from the other in that light and Fleur was able to launch herself over the gates, swing down, hit gravel.

The men saw, yelled, and chased her at a dead run to the smokehouse. And Lily too, once the sow gave up in disgust and freed him. That is where I should have gone to Fleur, saved her, thrown myself on Dutch. But I went stiff with fear and couldn't unlatch myself from the trestles or move at all. I closed my eyes and put my head in my arms, tried to hide, so there is nothing to describe but what I couldn't block out, Fleur's hoarse breath, so loud it filled me, her cry in the old language, and my name repeated over and over among the words.

The heat was still dense the next morning when I came back to work. Fleur was gone but the men were there, slack-faced, hung over. Lily was paler and softer than ever, as if his flesh had steamed on his bones. They smoked, took pulls off a bottle. It wasn't noon yet. I worked awhile, waiting shop and sharpening steel. But I was sick, I was smothered, I was sweating so hard that my hands slipped on the knives, and I wiped my fingers clean of the greasy touch of the customers' coins. Lily opened his mouth and roared once, not in anger. There was no meaning to the sound. His boxer dog, sprawled limp beside his foot, never lifted its head. Nor did the other men.

They didn't notice when I stepped outside, hoping for a clear breath. And then I forgot them because I knew that we were all balanced, ready to tip, to fly, to be crushed as soon as the weather broke. The sky was so low that I felt the weight of it like a yoke. Clouds hung down, witch teats, a tornado's green-brown cones, and as I watched one flicked out and became a delicate probing thumb. Even as I picked up my heels and ran back inside, the wind blew suddenly, cold, and then came rain.

Inside, the men had disappeared already and the whole place was trembling as if a huge hand was pinched at the rafters, shaking it. I ran straight through, screaming for Dutch or for any of them, and then I stopped at the heavy doors of the lockers, where they had surely taken shelter. I stood there a moment. Everything went still. Then I heard a cry building in the wind, faint at first, a whistle and then a shrill scream that tore through the walls and gathered around me, spoke plain so I understood that I should move, put my arms out, and slam down the great iron bar that fit across the hasp and lock.

Outside, the wind was stronger, like a hand held against me. I struggled forward. The bushes tossed, the awnings flapped off storefronts, the rails of porches rattled. The odd cloud became a fat snout that nosed along the earth and sniffled, jabbed, picked at things, sucked them up, blew them apart, rooted around as if it was following a certain scent, then stopped behind me at the butcher shop and bored down like a drill.

I went flying, landed somewhere in a ball. When I opened my eyes and looked, stranger things were happening.

A herd of cattle flew through the air like giant birds, dropping dung, their mouths opened in stunned bellows. A candle, still lighted, blew past, and tables, napkins, garden tools, a whole school of drifting eyeglasses, jackets on hangers, hams, a checkerboard, a lampshade, and at last the sow from behind the lockers, on the run, her hooves a blur, set free, swooping, diving, screaming as everything in Argus fell apart and got turned upside down, smashed, and thoroughly wrecked.

Days passed before the town went looking for the men. They were bachelors, after all, except for Tor, whose wife had suffered a blow to the head that made her forgetful. Everyone was occupied with digging out, in high relief because even though the Catholic steeple had been torn off like a peaked cap and sent across five fields, those huddled in the cellar were unhurt. Walls had fallen, windows were demolished, but the stores were intact and so were the bankers and shop owners who had taken refuge in their safes or beneath their cash registers. It was a fair-minded disaster, no one could be said to have suffered much more than the next, at least not until Fritzie and Pete came home.

Of all the businesses in Argus, Kozka's Meats had suffered worst. The boards of the front building had been split to kindling, piled in a huge pyramid, and the shop equipment was blasted far and wide. Pete paced off the distance the iron bathtub had been flung — a hundred feet. The glass candy case went fifty, and landed without so much as a cracked pane. There were other surprises as well, for the back rooms where Fritzie and Pete lived were undisturbed. Fritzie said the dust still coated her china figures, and upon her kitchen table, in the ashtray, perched the last cigarette she'd put out in haste. She lit it up and finished it, looking through the window. From there, she could see that the old smokehouse Fleur had slept in was crushed to a reddish sand and the stockpens were completely torn apart, the rails stacked helter-skelter. Fritzie asked for Fleur. People shrugged. Then she asked about the others and, suddenly, the town understood that three men were missing.

There was a rally of help, a gathering of shovels and volunteers. We passed boards from hand to hand, stacked them, uncovered what lay beneath the pile of jagged splinters. The lockers, full of the meat that was Pete and Fritzie's investment, slowly came into sight, still intact. When enough room was made for a man to stand on the roof, there were calls, a general urge to hack through and see what lay below. But Fritzie shouted that she wouldn't allow it because the meat would spoil. And so the work continued, board by board, until at last the heavy oak doors of the freezer were revealed and people pressed to the entry. Everyone wanted to be the first, but since it was my stepfather lost, I was let go in when Pete and Fritzie wedged through into the sudden icy air.

Pete scraped a match on his boot, lit the lamp Fritzie held, and then the three of us stood still in its circle. Light glared off the skinned and hanging carcasses, the crates of wrapped sausages, the bright and cloudy blocks of lake ice, pure as winter. The cold bit into us, pleasant at first, then numbing. We must have stood there a couple of minutes before we saw the men, or more rightly, the humps of fur, the iced and shaggy hides they wore, the bearskins they had taken down and wrapped around themselves. We stepped closer and tilted the lantern beneath the flaps of fur into their faces. The dog was there, perched among them, heavy as a doorstop. The three had hunched around a barrel where the game was still laid out, and a dead lantern and an empty bottle, too. But they had thrown down their last hands and hunkered tight, clutching one another, knuckles raw from beating at the door they had also attacked with hooks. Frost stars gleamed off their eyelashes and the stubble of their beards. Their faces were set in concentration, mouths open as if to speak some careful thought, some agreement they'd come to in each other's arms.

Power travels in the bloodlines, handed out before birth. It comes down through the hands, which in the Pillagers were strong and knotted, big, spidery, and rough, with sensitive fingertips good at dealing cards. It comes through the eyes, too, belligerent, darkest brown, the eyes of those in the bear clan, impolite as they gaze directly at a person.

In my dreams, I look straight back at Fleur, at the men. I am no longer the watcher on the dark sill, the skinny girl.

The blood draws us back, as if it runs through a vein of earth. I've come home and, except for talking to my cousins, live a quiet life. Fleur lives quiet too, down on Lake Turcot with her boat. Some say she's married to the waterman, Misshepeshu, or that she's living in shame with white men or windigos, or that she's killed them all. I'm about the only one here who ever goes to visit her. Last winter, I went to help out in her cabin when she bore the child, whose green eyes and skin the color of an old penny made more talk, as no one could decide if the child was mixed blood or what, fathered in a smokehouse, or by a man with brass scales, or by the lake. The girl is bold, smiling in her sleep, as if she knows what people wonder, as if she hears the old men talk, turning the story over. It comes up different every time and has no ending, no beginning. They get the middle wrong too. They only know that they don't know anything.

Questions for Discussion

1. How does the description of Misshepeshu reveal both his legendary desires and his powers?

2. What role does the narrator, Pauline, play in the story's action? What is her perspective on the way that the men treat Fleur? What mixed feelings does she have about Fleur? How is she changed by what she has seen and learned?

3. Why are the men in Argus attracted to Fleur? Why are they both frustrated and impressed by her card-playing strategies? Why does she beat them?

4. Who avenges Fleur's rape? Is it clear whose baby she gives birth to?

5. Why does the story about Fleur's powers and the incident in Argus end with the cryptic statement "They only know that they don't know anything"? What does this statement imply about the possible "supernatural" elements in the story?

Ideas for Writing

1. Write an essay in which you interpret the significance of the character of Fleur. What values does she represent? Consider why she drowns twice and her relationship to Misshepeshu. Why are men fearful of Fleur? Do they have reason to be? Does she seem to have supernatural powers?

2. Retell the story from Fleur's point of view. How would she perceive the men and Pauline? What secrets might Fleur reveal?

Eleanor's Tale: The Leap (1996)

All of our love stories begin with our mothers. For although it is our fathers, we are told, whose love we seek, it is our mother whom we imitate. If she was a huntress then we beat him through the woods, out into the open. If she was a temptress we are standing in the clearing as he emerges, slowly removing our clothes. A whiner? We draw him toward us through quick tears. Strong. We dominate. If she was equal, if she was one of those souls who stood beside him, naked to the core and unafraid, more is the luck.

Anna Schlick is all of the above.

My mother is the surviving half of a blindfold trapeze act. You saw her at the funeral moving easily through the room. She never falters, in spite of her big, square feet. Her arms are soft now, but she never makes an unnecessary gesture. Perhaps she looks a bit clumsy, overblown, her thighs so bold, her clothing tight. But she never upsets an object or so much as brushes a cobweb onto the floor. I have never seen her lose her balance or bump into a closet door left carelessly open. And even though I owe my life to her agility and courage, there are times I can't help resent her irritating sense of balance.

Her poise still tempts me. As a child I once tied string on a dark stairway to catch her feet — I could have killed her! She neatly stepped over, sensing it in the dim light. The catlike precision of her movements is instinct now — the result of her early training in the family of Flying Kuklenskis. She was a Montana barrel rider who ran off young with a circus. An ancient family of third-rate Polish trapeze artists adopted her. Artists? The old master had dropped a daughter and his son a former wife. My mother knew this, but had her name added to the stage posters anyway.

My father doesn't like to see the photographs or advertisements from that part of her youth. He let me play with her brilliant costumes until I wore them to shreds. There was very little left at home to remind us of her life in the air.

I would have tended to think that all memory of double somersaults and heart-stopping catches had left her arms and legs, were it not that sometimes, when she and I sit sewing and talking in the same little room that I slept in as a child, I hear the crackle, catch a whiff of smoke from the stove downstairs. Suddenly the room goes dark, the stitches burn beneath our fingers, and we are sewing with needles of hot silver, threads of fire.

I owe her my existence three times. The first was when she saved herself. South of Fargo, there stands the replica of a cracked and splintered tent pole, cast in concrete. It commemorates the disaster that put the town on the front page of the tabloids of that day. It is from those old newspapers, now historical records, that you can find information, not from Anna of the Flying Kuklenskis, nor from any of her Montana relatives, or certainly from the other half of her particular act. In the news accounts, it said, "the day was mildly overcast but nothing in the air or temperature gave any hint of the sudden force with which the deadly gale would strike."

I have lived beyond the trees, where you can see the weather coming for miles, and it is true that in town we are at something of a disadvantage. When extremes of temperatures collide, a hot and cold front, winds are generated instantaneously and crash upon you without warning. That, I think, was the likely situation on that day in August. People probably commented on the pleasant breeze, grateful that no hot sun beat upon the striped tent that stretched over them. They bought their tickets and surrendered them in anticipation. They sat. They ate caramelized popcorn and roasted peanuts. There was time, before the storm, for three acts. The White Arabians of Ali-Khazar rose on their hind legs and waltzed. The Mysterious Bernie folded himself into a painted cracker tin, and the Lady of the Mists made herself appear and disappear in surprising places. As the clouds gathered outside, unnoticed, the ringmaster cracked his whip, shouted his introduction, and pointed to the ceiling of the tent, where the Flying Kuklenskis were perched.

They tried to drop gracefully from nowhere, like two sparkling birds. Sometimes they rode down on a gleaming, painted moon that jerked and rocked. Blowing kisses, they doffed their glittering helmets and high-collared capes. They skipped to all sides of the ring to accept applause, and flirted openly as the moon hauled them up again on the trapeze bars. In the final vignette of their act, they were supposed to kiss in midair, pausing, almost hovering as they swooped past each other. On the ground, between bows, Harry Kuklenski lithely bounded to the front rows and pointed out the smear of Anna's lipstick, just off the edge of his mouth. There was a small rouge pot hidden on the pole of the trapeze landing, but who was to know? They made a romantic pair all right, especially in the blindfold sequence.

That afternoon, as the anticipation increased, as Harry and Anna Kuklenski tied sparkling masks onto each other's faces and as they puckered their lips in mock kisses, lips destined "never again to meet" as one long breathless article put it, the wind rose, only miles off, wrapped itself into a cone, and howled.

There came a rumble of electrical energy, drowned out by the sudden roll of drums. One detail, not mentioned by the press, perhaps unknown—Anna was pregnant at the time, seven months and hardly showing, her stomach muscles were that strong. It seems incredible that she would work high above the ground, when any fall could be so dangerous, but the explanation, I know from watching her, is that she always lived comfortably in extreme elements. Perhaps too comfortably. It astounds me to see how she is becoming one with the failings of her age, her sick heart, just as the air had been her home, familiar to her, safe, before the storm that afternoon.

From opposite ends of the tent they waved, blind and smiling, to the crowd below. Then the ringmaster removed his hat and called for silence, so that the two above could concentrate. They rubbed their hands in chalky powder, then Harry launched himself and swung, once, twice, in huge calibrated beats across space. He hung from his knees and on the third swing stretched wide his arms, held out his hands to receive his pregnant wife as she dove from her shining bar.

It was while the two were in midair, their hands about to meet, that lightning struck the main pole and sizzled down the guy wires, filling the air with blue heat and light that Harry must certainly have seen, even through the silk of his blindfold. The tent buckled, the edifice toppled him forward. The swing continued and did not return in its sweep. Harry went down, down unkissed into the crowd with his last thought, perhaps, just a prickle of surprise at his empty hands.

My mother once told me that I'd be amazed at how many things a person can do in the act of falling. Perhaps at the time she was teaching me not to fear the inevitable grounding of my designs, or my own emotional plunges, for I associate the idea with the drift of reason. But I also think she meant that even in that awful doomed second one could think. She certainly did. When her hands did not meet her husband's, Anna tore away her blindfold. As he swept past her on the wrong side she could have grasped his ankle, the toe-end of his tights, and gone down clutching him. Instead, she changed direction. She chose herself and in so choosing, me. Her body twisted toward a heavy wire and she managed to hang on to the braided metal, still hot from the lightning strike. Her palms were burned so terribly that once healed they bore no lines, only the blank scar tissue of a quieter future. She was lowered, gently, to the sawdust ring just underneath the dome of the canvas roof, which did not entirely settle but was held up on one end and jabbed through, torn, and even on fire in places from the giant spark, though rain and men's jackets soon put that out.

Three people died including Harry, but except for her hands my mother was not seriously harmed until an overeager rescuer broke her arm in extricating her and also, in the process, collapsed a portion of the tent bearing a huge buckle that knocked her unconscious. She was taken to the hospital, run by Franciscans, where she must have hemorrhaged, for they kept her confined to her bed a month and a half before her baby was born without life.

Harry Kuklenski had always wanted to be buried in the circus cemetery next to the original Kuklenski, his uncle, and so she sent him back to
Milwaukee with his brothers. The stillborn child, however, is buried at the
edge of town. I used to walk across the unpaved field there, just to sit. The
child was a girl, but I never thought of her as a sister, or even as a separate
person, really. It is egotistical, an odd defense, but I always considered her a
less finished version of myself.

When the snow fell, throwing shadows among the cemetery stones, I could
always pick her out easily from the road as I passed on my way to school. Her
marker was bigger than the others and it was the shape of an actual lamb at
rest, its legs curled beneath. The carved lamb looms larger in my thoughts as
the years pass, though it is probably just my eyes, the vision slowly changing
— the way it has for my mother — as what is close to us sifts away and distances sharpen. In odd moments, I think it is the edge drawing near, the edge
of everything, the horizon I did not have to confront in my parents' closed yard.
And it also seems to me, although this is probably an idle fantasy, that somewhere my sister's statue is also growing more sharply etched as if, instead of
weathering itself into a porous mass, it is hardening on the flat field with each
snowfall, perfecting itself.

Early during her confinement in the hospital my mother met Lawrence
Schlick, then known as Fargo Businessman of the Year, personally delivering
flowers to the circus victims as a goodwill gesture. He stayed, sitting at her
bedside, then came back week after week, at first telling himself that it was
because he was something of an armchair traveler, and had spent meditative
hours reading of the places Anna had visited in fact — Kansas City, Chicago,
St. Paul, New York, Omaha. The Kuklenskis had toured the big cities before
the war, then gradually based themselves farther and farther into the boon-
docks as bigger acts including elephants and raging tigers drove them into
small-town territory.

It was in the hospital that Anna began to read passionately, a way of overcoming the boredom and depression of those months. It was Lawrence Schlick
who insisted on bringing her books. Between them, they read aloud, speaking
into each other's eyes. Falling. I sometimes wonder whether as he fell in love
my father had time to think. For he went down fast. He plunged. He would
never be the same.

I owe my existence, the second time then, to the two of them and the hospital that brought them together. That is the debt I do not ever take for
granted. None of us asks for life in the first place. It is only once we have it,
of course, that we hang on so dearly.

I was only six years old the year that our house caught fire, probably from
standing ash. It can rekindle, and my mother, forgetful around the house,
probably shoveled what she thought were dead coals into wooden or cardboard containers. The fire could have started from a flaming box. Or perhaps

a buildup of creosote inside the chimney ignited. The blaze started in our living room, and the heart of the house was gutted. I woke to find the stairway to my upstairs bedroom cut off by flames.

There was only one staircase and that was gone. My parents were out and the baby-sitter, panicked, had run out the door to the neighbor's house. As soon as I awakened, I smelled the smoke. I did things by the letter then, was good at memorizing instructions, and also I was happy. Never to be underestimated, the pleasure I took in existence probably helped to keep me calm. For I knew, completely trusted, that I would be saved. So I conducted myself exactly as I was taught in the first-grade fire drill. I got up. I touched the back of my door before opening it. Finding it hot, I left it closed and stuffed my rolled-up rug beneath the crack. I did not hide beneath my bed or crawl into my closet. I put on my flannel robe, and then I sat down to wait.

My mother and father, returning in their formal coats and thin shoes, stood below my dark window and saw clearly that there was no rescue. A fire truck arrived, but flames had pierced one sidewall and the glare of the fire lighted the mammoth limbs and trunk of the vigorous old oak that had probably planted itself a hundred years, at least, before the house was built. No branch touched the wall, and just one thin limb scraped the roof. From below, it looked as though even a squirrel would have had trouble jumping from the tree onto the house, for the growth of that small branch was no bigger than my wrist.

Standing there, Anna asked my father to unzip her dress.

When he treated her too gently, as though she'd lost her reason, she made him understand her intentions. She stripped off her stockings, stood barefoot in bra and half-slip and pearls. Then she directed one of the firemen to lean the superannuated extension ladder up against the trunk of the tree. In surprise, he complied. She ascended. She vanished. Then she could be seen moving easily among the leafless branches. She made her way up and up. Along her stomach, she inched the length of a bough that curved above the branch that knocked on the roof of the house.

Once there, swaying, she stood and balanced. There were plenty of people in the crowd and many who still remember, or think they do, my mother's leap through the ice-dark air toward that thinnest extension, and how she broke that branch in falling so that it cracked in her hands, cracked louder than the flames but gave her the necessary purchase as she vaulted with it toward the edge of the roof, and how it hurtled down end over end without her, and their eyes went up, again, to see where she had flown.

I didn't see her stretch through air, only heard the sudden thump and looked out my window. She was hanging by her toes and feet from the new gutter we had put in that year, and she was smiling. I was not surprised to see her, she was so matter-of-fact. She tapped on the window. I remember how she did it, too; it was the friendliest tap, a bit tentative, as if she were afraid she had arrived too early at a friend's party. Then she gestured at the latch, and when I opened the window she told me to raise it wider, and prop it up with the stick so it wouldn't crush her fingers. She swung down, caught the ledge, and crawled through the opening. Once she was in my room, I realized she wore only underclothing, a tight bra of the heavy circular-stitched cotton women used to wear, an abrasive scapular, and silky half-slip. I remember feeling light-headed, of course, terribly relieved and then embarrassed for her, to be seen by the crowd undressed.

I was still embarrassed as we flew out the window, toward earth, me in her lap, her toes pointed as we rushed toward the striped target of the firefighters' tarp held below.

I know that she's right. I knew it even then. As you fall there is time to think. Curled as I was, against her stomach, I was not startled by the cries of the crowd or the looming faces. The wind roared and beat its hot breath at our back, the flames whistled. I slowly wondered what would happen if we missed the blanket, or bounced out of it. Then I forgot fear. I wrapped my hands around my mother's hands. I felt the brush of her lips, and I heard the beat of her heart in my ears — loud as thunder, long as the roll of drums.

Questions for Discussion

1. The original version of this story (published in 1990 as "The Leap") began with the third paragraph of the present text: "My mother is the surviving half of a blindfold trapeze act." What is accomplished by the addition of the two paragraphs that begin the current version?
2. Describe Eleanor's mother, Anna Schlick. How does her previous life as a trapeze artist help to define her character?
3. Analyze the language and details of the description of the storm, the lightning strike, and the fall of Harry. How would you characterize Erdrich's style based on this description?
4. Compare Anna's second husband, Lawrence, with Harry: How and why is the imagery of falling used to characterize both men?
5. Contrast the description of Eleanor's salvation by her mother from the fire and the leap out the window with the description in the passage about the storm and Harry's fall. Which passage seems more realistic? Why is the language different in the two passages?

Ideas for Writing

1. Write a story or descriptive passage about a relationship between two characters in which you compare that relationship to a trapeze act.
2. This story focuses on images of leaping, trusting, falling, and being saved: "As you fall there is time to think." Write an essay about the comment the story seems to be making about issues of risk and trust in relationships.

Louise Erdrich

Critical writing on Louise Erdrich generally focuses on her novels, a number of which contain segments that were originally published as short stories in magazines such as *Harper's*. Erdrich often revises and works her stories into the larger fabric of her multivoiced novels, which are themselves interlinked through recurring characters and family groups. In a 1993 interview with Nancy and Allan Chavkin, Erdrich discusses a number of issues central to her fiction: her use of childhood memories, her interest in magic realism, her writing process, her feelings about being labeled a "Native American" writer, and her response to the political and social issues critics sometimes see in her writing. In the essay that follows, "Where I Ought to Be: A Writer's Sense of Place" (1985), Erdrich discusses the tribal worldview in which "the landscape becomes enlivened by a sense of group and family history."

Kathleen M. Sands's comments on Erdrich's *Love Medicine* emphasize the importance of the oral tradition in Erdrich's fiction as well as the tradition of the gossip narrative. Sands goes on to describe the structure of Erdrich's novel as a "flashback–pivotal year–progressive chronology" — which is complex but not confusing owing to the novel's underlying structure and carefully worked "overlap of characters." On a more political note, Native American writer Leslie Marmon Silko in her 1986 review of *The Beet Queen* criticizes Erdrich's "post-modern, self-referential writing" that reflects only "isolation and alienation," obscuring the realities of race and economic want in Native American life. Silko's review aroused considerable response; Susan Meisenhelder's "Race and Gender in Louise Erdrich's *The Beet Queen*" (1994) offers a supportive view of the novel. Meisenhelder argues that Erdrich shows the price that those who fail to fit into narrowly accepted boundaries of race and gender must pay for their difference; she sees Erdrich focusing particularly on the "profound mistake" people of different races and genders make "in seeing one another as the enemy."

In her 1992 review of Erdrich's *Tracks*, Jennifer Sergi explores the oral storytelling tradition present in Erdrich's novel, emphasizing in particular the dominant voice in the narrative, that of Nanapush, a "story-backed old man," the voice of tribal history. Sergi also examines Erdrich's use of Chippewa myth in her fiction. In our final review, Michael Lee, a literature professor at the University of New Hampshire, writes of Erdrich's most recent book, *Tales of Burning Love* (1996), seeing it as part of a unified cycle. In Lee's view the novel continues Erdrich's ongoing meditation on the nature of modern love as a dangerous and unpredictable force framed within "darker and colder realities of life in the culturally determined nexus of Louise Erdrich's North Dakota." Our final selection, a student research paper by Sage Van Wing ("A Cultural Heritage: Louise Erdrich's Fiction"), examines several Native American cultural themes in Erdrich's novels — family, mythology, and the "homing" ritual of loyalty to place — and points out how Erdrich's novels reveal both the breakdown and the persistence of such traditions.

NANCY FEYL CHAVKIN AND ALLAN CHAVKIN

FROM *An Interview with Louise Erdrich* (1993)

Chavkin: Can you give us some examples of how ideas for some of your stories came to you?

Erdrich: Getting a first line is immensely satisfying. The first line of "Scales" is written on the back of a Travelhost napkin. The first line of "Saint Marie" came to me in the bathtub where I was sulking after Michael[1] told me that the Nth draft of the story wasn't quite right. My grandmother once got irritated with a yapping dog and excused herself to "go pound the dog." It became a line in a story. She didn't end up pounding the dog, by the way. She loved animals. My father told me about his first ride in a barnstormer's airplane. My sisters and brothers and aunts and uncles like to talk. Stories came from just about anywhere, unpredictability, and I try to stay open. Try to leave the door open.

Chavkin: One of the things we like so much about your writing is the feeling of unpredictability, that anything is possible — it's a feeling one often has when reading "magical realism." Joyce Carol Oates calls you a "magical realist." Do you see yourself as one? Do you think that's a useful term to describe your work?

Erdrich: That must have been a while ago, and it was very good of her, a great compliment, but I think now that the rage to imitate Márquez has declined. Probably your word unpredictable is more accurate. It is certainly the reaction I'd like. The thing is, the events people pick out as magical don't seem unreal to me. Unusual, yes, but I was raised believing in miracles and hearing of true events that may seem unbelievable. I think the term is one applied to writers from cultures more closely aligned to religious oddities and the natural and strange world. . . .

Chavkin: Why does Pauline hate Fleur?

Erdrich: She is afraid of Fleur, as many women who allow themselves to be controlled are threatened by women who do as they please.

---

[1] Michael Dorris, Erdrich's former husband and collaborator. — Eds.

Chavkin: What were you trying to suggest by interweaving "real" and imaginary events in *Tracks?*

Erdrich: There is no quantifiable reality. Points of view change the reality of a situation and there is a reality to madness, imagined events, and perhaps something beyond that.

Chavkin: Why did you have Pauline tell Fleur's story? Is "Fleur" as much about Pauline as it is about Fleur? Did you ever consider having Fleur tell her own story?

Erdrich: I don't have omnipotent control over the characters and voices, and the answer to these questions is that this is the only way I could write the story. Pauline's was the voice that presented itself, that I "heard." . . .

Chavkin: One of the qualities we especially like about your work is a sympathy, a real compassion, for your characters — a quality one finds so often in Chekhov's short stories but often lacking in many contemporary writers, where there's a cold-heartedness disguised as ironic detachment. Is that sympathy something you consciously attempt to inject into your work?

Erdrich: I'm glad that you find it there, and no, I'm not conscious of putting it in the work. I don't think that compassion is a quality that can be injected or added as an afterthought. Either it is there, or it is not, and certainly the reader brings hidden shades of that sympathy into existence during the act of reading. . . .

Chavkin: At what point in the writing do you know how the story will end?

Erdrich: Sometimes I don't and write past the end and then Michael notices I could drop off two paragraphs — it is common for writers to do this, he does the same. We always try to make the reader "get it" when so much more can be said enigmatically. . . .

Chavkin: Are you concerned that being labelled a "Native American writer" or a "woman writer" might result in your being marginalized? Do you object to those labels?

Erdrich: I think they originate in course descriptions and that there is some use in them. If the work survives, perhaps they'll fall away. If not, there isn't much I can do about it. After all, I don't think we read George Eliot, Jane Austen, Virginia Woolf, or Flannery O'Connor as "women writers" anymore, but as vital voices of their time. I know that, for instance, Toni Morrison will be read in this fashion. She is already. The point we're striving for is one at which the criteria for the work is its worth to readers, its excellence, the qualities that shine out and endure. . . .

Chavkin: In an article published in *American Literature* in September 1990, Catherine Rainwater argues that you include in your work structural features that "frustrate narrativity" in order to produce in the reader an "experience of marginality." What do you think of this argument?

Erdrich: I think it is true although of course I don't do it with such an object directly in mind. I am on the edge, have always been on the edge, flourish on the edge, and I don't think I belong anywhere else.

Chavkin: In your work is a Native American's knowledge of Roman Catholic beliefs and Native American religious beliefs an advantage, or is he/she torn between two systems of belief?

Erdrich: Torn, I believe, honestly torn. Religion is a deep force, and a people magnetize around the core of a belief system. It is very difficult for one individual to remain loyal to both although my own grandfather managed the trick quite well, by not fully participating in either traditional or Roman Catholic Church, and also by refusing to see distinctions between the embodiments of spirit. He prayed in the woods, he prayed in the mission, to him it was all connected, and all politics.

Chavkin: In his essay "Opening the Text: *Love Medicine* and the Return of the Native American Woman" published in *Narrative Chance,* edited by Gerald Vizenor (Albuquerque: University of New Mexico Press 1989), Robert Silberman suggests that in Native American literature the book is accepted as a necessary evil — the story and story-telling are the ideals. How important is the oral tradition in your work?

Erdrich: It is the reason so many stories are written in the first person — I hear the story told. At the same time I believe in and deeply cherish books and believe the library is a magical and sacred storehouse. A refuge. I'm a poorly-educated person in some ways. Not even Dartmouth could catch me up in having missed an intellectual life in high school. The town library was my teacher every bit as much as sitting in the kitchen or out under the trees swapping stories or listening to older relatives. So the two are not incompatible to me. I love the voice and I love the texture of writing, the feel of the words on the page, the construction.

Chavkin: Do you think that it's useful to view contemporary Native American writers such as James Welch, Simon Ortiz, N. Scott Momaday, Leslie Silko, and you and Michael as forming a literary movement, "Native American Literature"?

Erdrich: I think that literary movements often issue a manifesto. I'm stumped by the very idea.

Chavkin: Is one of your goals to undermine not only racist ideas but also romantic notions many people have about Native Americans?

Erdrich: This is not a specific conscious goal, but one which I hope would occur as a result of a reader following a story in which Native people were portrayed as complex and unpredictable.

Chavkin: Why are romantic notions (Native Americans as the first ecologists, as stoical) harmful?

Erdrich: Any notions that categorize a people limit a people, even such perfectly romantic notions.

Chavkin: Yeats, Henry James, Gore Vidal, and other writers have substantially revised previously published work. You have revised previously published work — how substantial are those revisions?

Erdrich: I have not revised previously published work, but I do add to it, as stories or additional scenes occur. There is no reason to think of publication as a final process. I think of it as temporary storage.

Chavkin: Yes, "temporary storage" is a good way of looking at it. The story "Destiny," published in *The Atlantic Monthly,* is told again but in a different form in Chapter 11 of *The Beet Queen.* Does the retelling of this story become more complex in the second published version?

Erdrich: Perhaps short pieces become more connected, more resonant, within the context of a novel, and then again, I miss how as short stories these pieces once stood alone. I'm not so thrifty about the work that I do this on purpose, it is just that the novels consume the short pieces while at the same time the pieces suggest additions to the novel. . . .

Chavkin: When did you decide you wanted to be a writer?

Erdrich: By the time I was twenty it was clear to me that I was good for, and good at, nothing else. I hated every job I had because I couldn't tolerate authority and found any sort of repetition painfully tedious. I hadn't the abstract mind of a philosopher or academic, or the physical patience of an artist. I knew that if I were to have any chance at all for happiness in work I had better throw myself at the writing life.

Chavkin: What were these jobs? Were you writing much while working at them?

Erdrich: Picking cucumbers, hoeing beets, selling popcorn, life-guarding, waitressing, selling Kentucky Fried Chicken, short order cooking breakfast shift (I can crack two, sometimes four, eggs at once, one-handed), construction crew, and later, North Dakota Poet in the Schools, ad-manager, psychiatric aide, candy-striper at an elderly care center, newspaper deliveries, and others I can't remember. . . .

Chavkin: Is part of your intention in some of your work to instruct and to reform?

Erdrich: God, no!

Chavkin: One of the remarkable aspects of your writing is that it "instructs" in subtle ways without seeming to instruct. That is, it enables the reader to see the world through the eyes of people from different cultures, different classes, and different historical periods. Sensitive readers come to understand that people from different cultures with different values and beliefs are human and similar to themselves in the most basic ways. Was this your conscious intention?

Erdrich: Thank you, that is very kind, but none of this is conscious intention. My one intention is to tell stories, or maybe just tell one long convoluted story. I don't think I can do much else. . . .

Chavkin: In a review entitled "Here's an Odd Artifact for the Fairy-Tale Shelf" published in *Impact/Albuquerque Journal* (October 8, 1986), Leslie Silko attacks your work for its supposed postmodern literary aesthetic. For example, she sees *The Beet Queen* as an autoreferential text and therefore as outside the Native American oral tradition. She characterizes your writing as the product of "academic, post-modern, so-called experimental influences" which de-emphasizes the referential dimension of words. Usually, professors and critics of your work have said the exact opposite of what Silko says. Who is closer to the truth — Silko or the other critics?

Erdrich: The other critics. . . .

Chavkin: Silko suggests you are ambivalent about your Native American origins. How would you respond to this charge?

Erdrich: Of course, I'm ambivalent, I'm human. There are times I wish that I were one thing or the other, but I am a mixed-blood. *Psychically doomed,* another mixed-blood friend once joked. The truth is that my background is such a rich mixed bag I'd be crazy to want to be anything else. Nor would Silko, probably, or any Native writer who understands that through the difficulty of embracing our own contradictions we gain sympathy for the range of ordinary failures and marvels.

Chavkin: Silko suggests your work lacks political commitment. Has she misunderstood your work or is this criticism accurate?

Erdrich: Any human story is a political story.

Chavkin: How many drafts of a story do you usually write? How many for a novel?

Erdrich: I have never counted and don't think I'll ever start. It would make me worry, and, perhaps imagine there was a magic number.

Chavkin: Your style no matter how lyrical is always precise. Do you do a lot of "polishing" of your language?

Erdrich: Yes, I polish, and Michael does extensive and demanding work on the draft as we go along: He's very particular about word repetitions and awkwardness. In addition to all else, he is a fine editor. . . .

Chavkin: Where is your greatest effort made — in the first draft or in subsequent revisions?

Erdrich: My greatest effort is made in living in such a way that the writing is possible in the first place. Writing is an escape from my own sins and failures, so although there is a great deal of work involved, I don't think of it as effort.

Chavkin: At what point do you begin revising? Do you write a whole draft and then rewrite it, revise as you go along, or follow some other procedure?

Erdrich: I revise all of the time, as the work demands. The procedure changes all of the time. Some pieces are so old that they've gone through a hundred drafts. One piece included in the expanded *Love Medicine* was written well before *Love Medicine*. Once in a great grand while I get "a piece" as though it is dictated to me from the character. This usually follows an intense solitary experience, or a long frank talk with Michael, or after a long drive through open country, alone, no radio just wind, or a walk in the woods, or a run. Often, words drop into my head while I slog pathetically along the side of the road with our dog. . . .

Chavkin: How elaborate are your outlines before you begin writing? Do you depart much from your original plans?

Erdrich: I have no rules about writing. Sometimes a book has an outline and other times I feel my way along, piecing it together bit by bit until the book answers itself.

Chavkin: Jerzy Kosinski has stated that he begins a novel by writing the opening and the end of the novel. When you are writing a novel, do you write chronologically from beginning to end or do you skip around, or do you have some other procedure?

Erdrich: I skip around everywhere, writing the pieces that I can't wait to write. It's like always eating your favorite part of the meal first. It's a greedy habit. But, why not?

Chavkin: Your ability to capture the voices of your first-person narrators is quite impressive. Do you ever use a tape recorder to capture these voices or act out parts of a story?

Erdrich: Absolutely not!

Chavkin: You have been quite prolific, publishing much in a relatively short period of time. Do you write quickly? Are you disciplined in your work habits?

Erdrich: Thank you, but I don't see it that way and am not satisfied with the work and the time it has taken. I am driven and become depressed without the writing. I'm not disciplined, I just like being happy. Writing is a pleasure for me even when I fail.

Chavkin: Do you write for the sheer joy of writing?

Erdrich: Yes, I do, I find solace in work. . . . I'm always trying to write, to get to the writing, to play around with it, and so I do try to write seven days a week. . . .

Chavkin: How many pages can you write on an average day?

Erdrich: I really don't know because I've never had an average day. Either they are good days or dismal ones, impossible days or delicious ones when I don't worry about the writing at all. I never count up pages in any case.

Chavkin: Why do you prefer to write early drafts in longhand?

Erdrich: I can write anywhere and need no equipment. Longhand feels more personal, as though I'm physically touching the subject. If I get a good idea in a bar I can walk back to Women, Females, Damsels, Does, etc., shut and lock the stall, then jot.

Lately I've been writing nonfiction directly onto the computer. It all seems magical and goes so quickly, but most of the pieces started as journal entries.

Chavkin: How important is your writing in your journal? How does it "feed into" your fiction and nonfiction?

Erdrich: I keep several notebooks going all at once besides daily diaries and letters and I go back to notebooks I kept many years ago for emotional context or to get a sense of character, or to turn up ideas. I keep scraps, keep drafts, it all collects. That's what I mean by compost.

Chavkin: Do you ever write up biographical sketches of your characters when you are writing a novel?

Erdrich: Sometimes I try to do a page or two of character sketching, but I usually don't end up using a thing I've written. The characters seem to appear via their reaction to story events, in the first instance, and then once they are written down they seem somehow called into being and I can't get rid of them.

Chavkin: Too much planning and outlining for a work of fiction are not useful, then? They hamper your creativity?

Erdrich: I don't know, maybe I could really get something perfect if I plotted, but I don't think I'd have such a good time uncovering the plot day to day. Of course, around ³/₄ through I do get a plot and write down what I know — and then there are frequent conversations with Michael. I'm not a completely instinctive writer, but I do have a high level of tolerance for chaos and disorder. . . .

Chavkin: When you were growing up in North Dakota, did you ever feel as if you were an outsider because of your background? Did you feel as if you were an outsider at Dartmouth?

Erdrich: Sure, always an outsider, but that's a gift for a writer because one is schooled early on in observation, in reading others for survival. People who belong don't become writers, they're immersed and have no edge, or so I tell myself, anyway, when I need reassurance. . . .

Chavkin: Do you ever fear that your work might be regarded as too bleak and that readers will miss the humor in it?

Erdrich: I don't write to please readers, but out of a sense of necessity, which is not to say I don't *want* to please readers. I like to, and especially love that people find the work comic in certain episodes. If you're really living, life encompasses extremes.

LOUISE ERDRICH

Where I Ought to Be: A Writer's Sense of Place   (1985)

In a tribal view of the world, where one place has been inhabited for generations, the landscape becomes enlivened by a sense of group and family history. Unlike most contemporary writers, a traditional storyteller fixes listeners in an unchanging landscape combined of myth and reality. People and place are inseparable. The Tewa Pueblo, for example, begin their story under ground, in complete darkness. When a mole comes to visit, they learn there is another world above and decide to go there. In this new place the light is so intense that they put their hands over their eyes to shield them. Grandmother Spider suggests that they adjust their vision to the light by gradually removing their hands and she points them to Sandia Mountain, the place where they will live. A great deal of wandering, bickering, lessons learned and even bloodshed occur, but once there, they stay for good.

This is the plot but not the story. For its full meaning, it should be heard in the Tewa language and understood within that culture's world view. Each place would then have personal and communal connotations. At the telling of it we would be lifetime friends. Our children would be sleeping or playing nearby. Old people would nod when parts were told the right way. It would be a new story and an old story, a personal story and a collective story, to each of us listening.

What then of those authors nonindigenous to this land? In renaming and historicizing our landscapes, towns and neighborhoods, writers from Hawthorne to Cather to Faulkner have attempted to weld themselves and their readers closer to the New World. As Alfred Kazin notes in "On Native Grounds," "the greatest single fact about our American writing" is "our writers' absorption in every last detail of this American world, together with their deep and subtle alienation from it." Perhaps this alienation is the result of one difficult fact about Western culture — its mutability. Unlike the Tewa and other Native American groups who inhabited a place until it became deeply and particularly known in each detail, Western culture is based on progressive movement. Nothing, not even the land, can be counted on to stay the same. And for the writers I've mentioned, and others, it is therefore as if, in the very act of naming and describing what they love, they lose it.

Faulkner's story "The Bear" is set in "that doomed wilderness whose edges were being constantly and punily gnawed at by men with plows and axes who feared it because it was wilderness." That shrinking area is haunted by a spirit, the bear, which is "shaggy, tremendous, red-eyed, not malevolent but just big, too big for the dogs which tried to bay it, for the horses which tried to ride it down, for the men and the bullets they fired into it; too big for the very country which was its constricting scope."

To Europeans the American continent was so vast that only a hundred years ago it seemed that nothing and no one could ever truly affect it. Yet William Faulkner wrote nostalgically of a wilderness that had already vanished. What is invented, and lamented, is the bigness and vastness that was lost piecemeal to agriculture. The great bear, which is the brooding and immense spirit of the land, had all but disappeared from settled areas before Faulkner was born and exists today largely by virtue of human efforts on his behalf. The wilderness that once claimed us is now named and consumed by us. Carefully designated scraps of it are kept increasingly less pristine to remind us of what was.

Just as Faulkner laments the passing of the Southern forest into farmland, so Willa Cather's novels about Nebraska homesteaders are elegies to vanishing virtues, which she links with an unmechanized and pastoral version of agriculture. That view has given way ever since as developments in chemical fertilizers, hybrid seed, animal steroids and farm equipment become part of a more technological treatment of the land.

Douglas Unger's recent novel, "Leaving the Land," tells of the rise and fall of a small town in South Dakota that bases its economy on large-scale turkey farming. When prices fall and the farmers can't afford to ship their stock, they slaughter the turkey themselves, pile them in a trench and burn them. Mr. Unger writes of the unlikely, apocalyptic scene, "The prairie filled with black smoke whirling up day after day, rolling, tumbling, dark scarves of smoke blown for an instant to the shapes of godheads, vague monuments, black smoke tornadoes that scarred the summer skies with waste and violence."

Instead of viewing a stable world, as in pre-invasion Native American culture, instead of establishing a historical background for the landscape, American writers seem bound into the process of chronicling change and forecasting destruction, of recording a world before that world's very physical being shifts. As we know, neighborhoods are leveled in a day, the Army Corps of Engineers may change the course of a river. In the ultimate kitsch gesture of a culture's desperation to engrave itself upon an alien landscape, a limestone mountain may be blasted into likenesses of important men.

Our suburbs and suburban life may be more sustaining and representative monuments than Mount Rushmore. There is a boring grandeur to the acres on acres of uniform cul-de-sacs and wide treeless streets, each green yard adorned with a swimming pool that sparkles like a blue opal. The large malls are awe-inspiring Xanadus of artificial opulence. Although created as escapes, as places halfway between country and city life, but without the isolation of the one or the crime of the other, suburbs and the small-town way of life that they imitate are often, in our literature, places to escape from. One departs either back to the evil thrills, pace and pollution of the city, or to the country, where life is supposedly more deeply felt, where the people are supposedly more genuine, where place is idiosyncratic and not uniform.

Writers such as John Cheever and Joy Williams admirably show that suburbs can be as strange as the next place in fiction. Any completely imagined description, from neighborhood to small town, creates a locus that the reader mentally inhabits. . . .

Of course not every writer feels compelled to make specific his or her setting. Samuel Beckett, Alain Robbe-Grillet, Nathalie Sarraute and Donald Barthelme are among those whose fiction could take place anywhere, or nowhere. Besides, in our society mobility is characteristic of our experience.

Most of us don't grow up in a single community anymore, and even if we do we usually leave it. How many of us live around the corner from parents, grandparents, even brothers and sisters? How many of us come to know a place intimately over generations? How many places even exist that long? We are part of a societal ebb and flow, a people washing in and out of suburbs and cities. We move with unparalleled ease, assisted by Mayflower Van Lines and superhighways. We are nomadic, both by choice, relocating in surroundings that please us, and more often by necessity. Like hunter-gatherers, we must go where we will be fed, where the jobs are listed.

But if for many readers and writers place is not all-important, there still remains the problem of identity and reference. An author needs his or her characters to have something in common with the reader. If not the land, which changes, if not a shared sense of place, what is it then that currently provides a cultural identity? What is it that writers may call on now for communal references in the way that a Tewa could mention Sandia Mountain?

Whether we like it or not, we are bound together by that which may be cheapest and ugliest in our culture, but which may also have an austere and resonant beauty in its economy of meaning. We are united by mass culture to the brand names of objects, to symbols like the golden arches, to stories of folk heroes like Ted Turner and Colonel Sanders, to entrepreneurs of comforts that cater to our mobility, like Conrad Hilton and Leona Helmsley. These symbols and heroes may annoy us, or comfort us, but when we encounter them in literature, at the very least, they give us context.

Brand names and objects in fiction connote economic status, upbringing, aspirations, even regional background. It is one thing for a character to order an imported Heineken, another for that person to order a Schlitz. There is a difference in what we perceive in that character's class and sensibility. It means a third thing for that person to order a Hamm's beer, a brew said to be made of Minnesota's sky-blue waters and which is not widely available outside the Middle West. Very few North Dakotans drive Volvos even though quite a few North Dakotans are of Swedish descent. The Trans-Am is not the car of choice for most professors of English in Eastern colleges.

In Bobbie Ann Mason's short stories, characters drink bourbon and Coke out of coffee cups, while the people in Robb Forman Dew's novels use pitchers for milk instead of pouring it from cartons, and transfer jam from jars to crystal dishes. Raymond Carver's characters drink Teachers, nameless gins or cheap pink champagne. Few of Eudora Welty's characters imbibe that sort of thing, while some of William Kennedy's characters would be happy to get it.

Though generalized, these examples show the intricacies of our cultural shorthand. And if it seems trivial or vulgar to cling to and even celebrate the stuff that inundates us, consider America without football, television, or the home computer, a prospect that would only be possible in the event of some vast and terrible catastrophe.

We live with the threat of nuclear obliteration, and perhaps this is a sub-liminal reason that as writers we catalogue streets, describe landmarks, create even our most imaginary landscapes as thoroughly as we can. No matter how monotonous our suburbs, no matter how noxious our unzoned Miracle Miles and shopping centers, every inch would seem infinitely precious were it to disappear.

In her essay "Place in Fiction," Eudora Welty speculates that the loss of place might also mean the loss of our ability to respond humanly to anything. She writes: "It is only too easy to conceive that a bomb that could destroy all traces of places as we know them, in life and through books, could also destroy all feelings as we know them, so irretrievably and so happily are recognition, memory, history, valor, love, all the instincts of poetry and praise, worship and endeavor, bound up in place."

I don't know whether this is true. I hope that it is not, and that humanity springs from us and not only from our surroundings. I hope that even in the unimaginable absence of all familiar place, something of our better human qualities would survive.

But the danger that they wouldn't, *we* wouldn't, that nothing else would either, is real and present. Leonard Lutwack urges, in his book "The Role of Place in Literature," that this very fear should inform the work of contempo-rary writers and act as a tool to further the preservation of the earth. "An increased sensitivity to place seems to be required," he says, "a sensitivity inspired by aesthetic as well as ecological values, imaginative as well as func-tional needs. . . . Literature must now be seen in terms of the contemporary concern for survival."

In our worst nightmares, all of us have conceived what the world might be like *afterward* and have feared that even our most extreme versions of a dev-astated planet are not extreme enough. Consider, then, that to American Indians it is as if the unthinkable has already happened, and relatively recently. Many Native American cultures were annihilated more thoroughly than even a nuclear disaster might destroy ours, and others live on with the fallout of that destruction, effects as persistent as radiation — poverty, fetal alcohol syn-drome, chronic despair.

Through diseases such as measles and smallpox, and through a systematic policy of cultural extermination, the population of Native North Americans shrank from an estimated 15 million in the mid-15th century to just over 200,000 by 1910. That is proportionately as if the population of the United States were to decrease from its present level to the population of Cleveland. Entire pre-Columbian cities were wiped out, whole linguistic and ethnic groups decimated. Since these Old World diseases penetrated to the very heart of the continent even faster than the earliest foreign observers, the full mag-nificence and variety of Native American cultures were never chronicled, per-ceived, or known by Europeans.

Contemporary Native American writers have therefore a task quite differ-ent from that of other writers I've mentioned. In the light of enormous loss, they must tell the stories of contemporary survivors while protecting and cel-ebrating the cores of cultures left in the wake of the catastrophe.

And in this, there always remains the land. The approximate three percent of the United States that is still held by Native American nations is cherished in each detail, still informed with old understandings, still known and used, in some cases, changelessly.

All of this brings me, at last, to describe what a sense of place means from my own perspective. I grew up in a small North Dakota town, on land that once belonged to the Wahpeton-Sisseton Sioux but had long since been leased out and sold to non-Indian farmers. Our family of nine lived on the very edge of town in a house that belonged to the Government and was rented to employees of the Bureau of Indian Affairs boarding school, where both my parents worked, and where my grandfather, a Turtle Mountain Chippewa named Pat Gourneau, had been educated. The campus consisted of an immense central playground, classrooms, two dormitories and numer-ous outbuildings. All of these places were made of a kind of crumbly dark red local brick. When cracked, smashed, or chipped back to clay this brick gave off a peculiar, dry, choking dust that I can almost still taste.

On its northern and western sides, the campus ran, with no interference from trees or fence lines, into fields of corn, wheat, soybeans, or flax. I could walk for miles and still find nothing but fields, more fields, and the same per-fectly straight dirt township road. I often see this edge of town — the sky and its towering and shifting formations of clouds, that beautifully lighted empti-ness — when I am writing. But I've never been able to describe it as well as Isak Dinesen, even though she was not writing of the American Great Plains but about the high country of Kenya.

"Looking back," she says in her reminiscence, "Out of Africa," "you are struck by your feeling of having lived for a time up in the air. The sky was rarely more than pale blue or violet, with a profusion of mighty, weightless, everchanging clouds towering up and sailing on it, but it had a blue vigour in it, and at a short distance it painted the ranges of hills and woods a fresh deep blue. In the middle of the day the air was alive over the land, like a flame burn-ing; it scintillated, waved and shone like running water, mirrored and doubled all objects. . . . Up in this high air you breathed easily, drawing in a vital assur-ance and lightness of heart. In the highlands you woke up in the morning and thought: Here I am, where I ought to be."

Here I am, where I ought to be.

A writer must have a place where he or she feels this, a place to love and be irritated with. One must experience the local blights, hear the proverbs, endure the radio commercials. Through the close study of a place, its people and character, its crops, products, paranoias, dialects and failures, we come closer to our own reality. It is difficult to impose a story and a plot on a place.

But truly knowing a place provides the link between details and meaning. Location, whether it is to abandon it or draw it sharply, is where we start.

In our own beginnings, we are formed out of the body's interior landscape. For a short while, our mothers' bodies are the boundaries and personal geography which are all that we know of the world. Once we emerge we have no natural limit, no assurance, no grandmotherly guidance like the Tewa, for technology allows us to reach even beyond the layers of air that blanket earth. We can escape gravity itself, and every semblance of geography, by moving into sheer space, and yet we cannot abandon our need for reference, identity or our pull to landscapes that mirror our most intense feelings.

The Macondo of Gabriel García Márquez, Faulkner's Yoknapatawpha County, the island house of Jean Rhys in "Wide Sargasso Sea" are as real to me as any place I've actually been. And although fiction alone may lack the power to head us off the course of destruction, it affects us as individuals and can spur us to treat the earth, in which we abide and which harbors us, as we would treat our own mothers and fathers. For, once we no longer live beneath our mother's heart, it is the earth with which we form the same dependent relationship, relying completely on its cycles and elements, helpless without its protective embrace.

KATHLEEN M. SANDS

Comments on <u>Love Medicine</u> (1985)

Love Medicine by Louise Erdrich is a novel of hard edges, multiple voices, disjointed episodes, erratic tone shifts, bleak landscapes, eccentric characters, unresolved antagonisms, incomplete memories. It is a narrative collage that seems to splice random margins of experience into a patchwork structure. Yet ultimately it is a novel, a solid, nailed down, compassionate and coherent narrative that uses sophisticated techniques toward traditional ends. It is a novel that focuses on spare essentials, those events and moments of understanding that change the course of life forever.

Like many contemporary novels, *Love Medicine* is metafiction, ironically self-conscious in its mode of telling, concerned as much with exploring the process of storytelling as with the story itself. As marginal and edges, episodic and juxtaposed as this narrative is, it is not the characters or events of the novel that are dislocated and peripheral. Each is central to an element of the narrative. It is the reader who is placed at a distance, who is the observer on the fringes of the story, forced to shift position, turn, ponder, and finally integrate the story into a coherent whole by recognizing the indestructible connections between the characters and events of the narrative(s). Hence the novel places the reader in a paradoxically dual stance, simultaneously on the fringe of the story yet at the very center of the process—distant and intimate, passive yet very actively involved in the narrative process.

The fact that this is a novel written by an Indian about Indians may not be the reason for Erdrich's particular choice of narrative technique and reader control, but it does provide a point for speculation and perhaps a clue to the novel as not just incidentally Indian but compellingly tribal in character.

We have come to expect certain things from American Indian contemporary fiction. Novels from the Southwest have been overwhelmingly concerned with story, traditional stories reenacted in a ceremonial structure at once timeless and timely. Novels like N. Scott Momaday's *House Made of Dawn* and Leslie Marmon Silko's *Ceremony* are rich in oral tradition and ritual and demand intense involvement of the reader in the texture and event of tribal life and curing processes. James Welch's novels, *Winter in the Blood* and *The Death of Jim Loney*, are less obviously immersed in oral tradition but draw on tribal history, landscape, and psychology to develop stories and characters that are plausible within Northern Plains tribal ways. Gerald Vizenor's *St. Louis Bearheart* draws on various Plains oral traditions and manipulates them in a satirically comic indictment of a blasted American landscape and culture. In each case, these major American Indian novelists have drawn heavily on the storytelling traditions of their peoples and created new visions of the role of oral tradition in both the events of narrative and narrative process.

In these novels it is the responsibility of both the major characters and the reader to make the story come out right. The authors consciously involve readers in the process of narration, demanding activity that is both intellectual and emotional, remote and intimate. Louise Erdrich's novel works in much the same way, but the materials are different and the storytelling process she draws upon is not the traditional ceremonial process of the reenactment of sacred myth, nor is it strictly the tradition of telling tales on winter nights, though there is some reliance on that process. The source of her storytelling technique is the secular anecdotal narrative process of community gossip, the storytelling sanction toward proper behavior that works so effectively in Indian communities to identify membership in the group and insure survival of group values and its valued individuals. Erdrich's characters are aware of the importance of this tradition in their lives. At one point the lusty Lulu Lamartine matter of factly says, "I always was a hot topic" (233). And the final narrator of the novel, searching for the right ingredients for his love potion, comments, "After a while I started to remember things I'd heard gossiped over" (199). Later, on the run from the law with his father, he says, "We talked a good long time about the reservation then. I caught him up on all the little blacklistings and scandals that had happened. He wanted to know everything . . ." (268). Gossip affirms identity, provides information, and binds the absent to the family and the community.

The inclination toward this anecdotal form of storytelling may well derive from the episodic nature of traditional tales that are brief and elliptical because the audience is already familiar with the characters, their cultural context, and the values they adhere to. The spare, elliptical nature of Erdrich's novel can be loosely related to this narrative process in which the order of the telling is up to the narrator, and the audience members are intimately involved in the fleshing out of the narrative and the supplying of the connections between related stories. The gossip tradition within Indian communities is even more elliptical, relying on each member's knowledge of every individual in the group and the doings of each family (there are no strangers). Moreover, such anecdotal narration is notoriously biased and fragmented, no individual privy to the whole story. The same incidents are told and retold, accumulating tidbits of information. There is, after all, no identifiable right version, right tone, right interpretation. The very nature of gossip is instability, each teller limited by his or her own experience and circumstances. It is only from all the episodes, told by many individuals in random order that the whole may be known — probably not to some community member, but, ironically, to some outsider patient enough to listen and frame the episodes into a coherent whole. In forming that integrated whole, the collector has many choices but a single intention, to present a complete story in a stable form.

Perhaps the novelist, in this case, then, is that investigator (of her own imagination and experience) who manipulates the fleeting fragments of gossip into a stable narrative form, the novel, and because of her artistic distance from the events and characters, supplies the opportunity for irony that the voices in the episodes of the novel are incapable of. Secrets are revealed and the truth emerges from the threads of information. Like the everyday life it emerges from, gossip is not inherently coherent, but the investigator can use both its unreliable substance and ambiguous form to create a story that preserves the multiplicity of individual voices and the tensions that generate gossip. The novelist can create a sense of the ambiguity of the anecdotal community tradition yet allow the reader to comprehend. Gossip then is neither "idle" nor "vicious"; it is a way of revealing secrets and generating action.

So it is with *Love Medicine*. There is no single version of this story, no single tone, no consistent narrative style, no predictable pattern of development, because there is no single narrator who knows all the events and secrets. The dialogue is terse and sharp, as tense as the relationships between the characters. Narrators are introduced abruptly to turn the action, jar the reader's expectation, give words to their tangled lives. This is a novel of voices, the voices of two families whose members interpret and misinterpret, and approve or disapprove (mostly the latter) of one another's activities.

The novel begins with a story that suggests a very conventional linear narrative. June Kashpaw, the erratic and once vivacious beauty of the family, is down and out, heading for the bus that will take her back to her North Dakota reservation. But she is easily seduced by a mud engineer and ends up on a lonely back road on a subfreezing night, wheezing under the drunken weight of her ineffective lover. She walks — not just away, but across the plains into the freezing night and death from exposure. In one chapter she is gone — but memory of her vitality and the mystery of her death will endure. She is the catalyst for the narrations which follow, stories that trace the intricate and often antagonistic relationships in the two families from which she came. One life — not a very special life at that — just a life of a woman on the fringes of her tribe and community, a woman living on the margins of society, living on the hard edge of survival and failing, but a woman whose death brings the family together briefly, violently, and generates a multitude of memories and stories that slowly develop into a coherent whole. It is June (and the persistent desire of the family members who survive her to understand her, and consequently, themselves) who allows us to penetrate the chaotic and often contradictory world of the Kashpaw and Lamartine families and bring a sense of history and order to the story, to bring art out of anecdote and gossip.

The structure of the narrative is not as chaotic and episodic as it first may appear. Time is carefully controlled, with 1981, the year of June's death, the central date in the novel. Subsequent to her death, the family gathers, and even those not present, but central to the narration, are introduced by kinship descriptions. The family genealogies are laid out, and as confusing as they are in that first chapter, they become easy and familiar as the episodes unfold and family secrets are revealed. Chapters 2 through 6 of the novel leap back in time — 1934, 1948, 1957, 1980 — until the pivotal date, 1981, is reached again at the center of the novel. As one of the characters puts it, "Events loop around and tangle again" (95). From this year, the novel progresses to 1984 and begins to weave together the separate stories into an intricately patterned fabric that ironically, even in the end, no single character fully understands — one secret is never told. This flashback-pivotal year-progressive chronology, however, is by no means straightforward. Within chapters, time is convoluted by injection of memory, and each chapter is controlled by the narration of a different character whose voice (style) is markedly different from all the other voices and whose recollection of dialogue complicates the narrative process even further. The system of discourse in the novel is thus dazzlingly complex, demanding very close attention from the reader. But the overlap of characters allows for comprehension. The novel is built layer upon layer. Characters are not lost. Even June, vitally alive at least in memory, stays until the end. In fact, it is she who connects the last voice and the final events of the novel to all the others. It is through June that each character either develops or learns identity within the community, but also, since this is metafiction, in the novel itself.

LESLIE MARMON SILKO

Here's an Odd Artifact for the Fairy-Tale Shelf   (1986)

Review of The Beet Queen

The Beet Queen is Louise Erdrich's second novel. (Her first novel, *Love Medicine*, won the National Book Critics Circle Award for fiction in 1984.) Erdrich's prose is dazzling and sleek. Each sentence has been carefully wrought, pared lean and then polished. I call this "poet's prose," and many of Erdrich's descriptions in *The Beet Queen* are right on target. Mary, as the newly arrived waif, describes her aunt Fritzie's butcher shop and residence:

> I smelled the air, pepper and warm from the sausagemakers. I heard the rhythmical whine of meat saws, slicers, the rippling beat of fans. Aunt Fritzie was smoking her sharp Viceroys in the bathroom. Uncle Pete was outside feeding the big white German Shepherd that was kept in the shop at night to guard the canvas bags of money.

Erdrich's prose is an outgrowth of academic, post-modern, so-called experimental influences. The idea is to "set language free," to allow words to interact like magic chemicals in a word sorcerer's pristine laboratory, where a word and its possible relationships with other words may be seen "as they really are, in and of themselves" without the tiresome interference of any historical, political or cultural connections the words may have had in the past. Any characters or plot are imagined within a world that answers only to "itself," the inner created world of the novel or poem itself. Self-referential writing has an ethereal clarity and shimmering beauty because no history or politics intrudes to muddy the well of pure necessity contained within the language itself.

Post-modern, self-referential writing reflects the isolation and alienation of the individual who shares nothing in common with other human beings but language and its hygienic grammatical mechanisms. Self-referential writing is light-years away from shared or communal experience that underlies oral narrative and modern fiction. Thus it is interesting to see how effectively the post-modern style of fiction functions in a family saga, rife with complexities of the heart, a saga that races back and forth from 1932 to 1972, from city to small white town to Indian reservation. Can this stylish post-modern prose refer itself to any world beyond?

The Beet Queen works best when Erdrich is exploring the depths of the subconscious, where her characters dream, hallucinate, fantasize and turn ever inward on themselves. Occasionally there is a confusing similarity in the imagery used to evoke the subconscious of characters who are supposed to be drastically different from one another. But for the most part, this is the level on which Erdrich's prose works best. So long as Erdrich writes about her characters' tenacious involvement with one another, their huge strange passions that coalesce into bisexuality, incest and love triangles, *The Beet Queen* is quite effective.

But then Erdrich leaves her element and tries to place her characters and action in places and points in history that are loaded with "referential" significance. Good fiction need not be factual, but it doesn't obscure basic truth. In Erdrich's hands, the rural North Dakota of Indian-hating, queer-baiting white farmers, of the Depression, becomes magically transformed. Or maybe "transported." Rural New Hampshire seems a far more probable location for *The Beet Queen* and its characters, white and Indian, straight and gay.

What Erdrich, who is half-Indian and grew up in North Dakota, attempts to pass off as North Dakota may be the only North Dakota she knows. But hers is an oddly rarified place in which the individual's own psyche, not racism or poverty, accounts for all conflict and tension. In this pristine world all misery, suffering, and loss are self-generated, just as conservative Republicans have been telling us for years.

Although I read the novel three times, I am still not sure which characters are of Indian ancestry except for Celestine, who is half-Indian, and her half-brother, Russell, who is full-blood. Apparently Mary is part Indian, but I never figured out whether her glamorous irresponsible mother, Adelaide, was part Indian or whether it was Mary's father (who Adelaide claims is responsible for Mary's "stringy black hair"). Mary's brother Karl might be part Indian, too, but Adelaide claims the dead banker who kept them is Karl's father. In which case, does Karl get his possibly Indian looks from Adelaide?

You'd think that as the novel unfolded, who's who would become clear. After all, in 1932 in a small North Dakota town near an Indian reservation, whether one was white, Indian or part Indian mattered a hell of a lot. The fact is, it *still* matters.

In Erdrich's North Dakota, the deepest levels of the human consciousness appear untouched by racism or bigotry. Though Mary, Karl and their infant brother are abandoned in a devastating way, never once do they wonder if being part Indian might have contributed to their abandonment. The rivalry and jealousy between Mary and her slender blond cousin, Sita, are portrayed as fierce, and Sita appears envious and shallow. But even when Mary "steals" Celestine from Sita, Sita's expressions of bitterness and hurt are curiously free of racial slurs we might expect from a high school–age girl obsessed with appearance, acceptance and status. The Sita that Erdrich shows seems unlikely to have had anything to do with someone as different as Celestine, let alone be best friends with her. Certainly not in 1932 in a small North Dakota town. After all, the Wounded Knee Massacre is only 42 years and 400 miles south of Sita and the others in Erdrich's novel.

Erdrich delves into the psyche of Celestine and Mary, and while they are not ordinary young women, still they have no consciousness (neither does Erdrich) of how their Indian ancestry in a white town may be related to their feeling of separateness and difference from the others.

The issue of Indian ancestry might recede except Erdrich makes much of juxtaposing Mary's stolid dark looks and Celestine's towering half-breed stature with the blond, willowy "beauty" of Sita. Erdrich swallows white sexist standards of beauty rather than challenging them. Slender and blond, Sita is the beauty, but Erdrich trots out the old cliché in which the dark, ugly girls are nicer, smarter and work harder. Mary buys and wears hideously ugly clothing in loud colors, and Erdrich implies this propensity to violate fashion codes belies Mary's Indian ancestry.

The Beet Queen [sic] is Wallacette or Dot, as she is called, the result of one night of passion between Celestine and Karl, Mary's bisexual, wandering brother. Erdrich emphasizes the incongruity of Dot's stocky dark figure in a floor-length formal and high heels as Dot competes with the other contestants, "all and tanned orange from laying on their garage roofs smeared with iodined baby oil." The implications and the humor are clear: Dot doesn't fit in. Dot is as incongruous as the Beet Queen as Mary, Celestine and Wallace, a white homosexual, are as citizens in this small North Dakota town.

Erdrich never ventures near the reservation. The reservation is where, for most of the novel, Erdrich keeps Russell, Celestine's half-brother, a full-blooded Chippewa. What Russell does, who Russell visits and how Russell feels about moving back and forth between the white town and the Indian reservation are a mystery. The one time Erdrich shows us Russell's interior, his thoughts and feelings are flat and literal, focused only on the moment at hand.

Compared to the lush, sensuous chaotic inner worlds of characters like Karl and Mary and Celestine, Russell might be the stereotype of "primitive" man mercifully focused on what is concrete, here and now [sic], not like the other characters whose white blood pulses with abstract mental activity — fantasy, desire and willfulness. Because Erdrich can't find much to put inside Russell, she forces him to spend much of the novel on the reservation. Strangely, Celestine never visits the reservation or ever even thinks about her elder Chippewa half-sisters who raised her. But most strange of all, after Mary and Celestine take over Aunt Fritzie's business, not one person from the reservation, not even one Indian cousin, ever steps through the door of the butcher shop.

Erdrich makes much of Russell's war wounds, which give him hero status. But we don't have a clue to what Russell feels about all the blood and bone he's lost defending a government and people who will always exclude him. We never know what reasons or feelings made Russell volunteer for two foreign wars. In the entire 338 pages, only once is any bitterness over racism ever expressed: On page 70, Mary relates that war hero Russell was offered a bank-clerk Job in Argus "even though he was an Indian."

The Beet Queen is a strange artifact, an eloquent example of the political climate in America in 1986. It belongs on the shelf next to the latest report from the United States Civil Rights Commission, which says black men have made tremendous gains in employment and salary. This is the same shelf that holds the *Collected Thoughts of Edwin Meese on First Amendment Rights* and Grimm's *Fairy Tales*.

SUSAN MEISENHELDER

Race and Gender in Louise Erdrich's
The Beet Queen   (1994)

To a number of reviewers and critics, Louise Erdrich's novel *The Beet Queen* is unusual in Native American literature because of its apparent silence on the issue of race. As Louis Owens has argued, the "excruciating quest for an Indian identity in late twentieth century America that haunts other fiction and poetry by Indian writers is simply not here" ("Acts" 55).[1] Certainly the most strident expression of this idea has been a review of the novel written by another Native American writer, Leslie Marmon Silko. Although she praises Erdrich's style, Silko attacks the novel for its failure to treat the social and political dimension of Native American concerns; the book, she argues, reduces society's problems to individual ones: "In this pristine world all misery, suffering, and loss are self-generated, just as conservative Republicans have been telling us for years" (10).[2] My purpose in this paper is to show that *The Beet Queen* does in fact speak to questions of Native American identity in important ways. Far from being silent on sociopolitical concerns, Erdrich sustains an examination of the relationship between two crucial issues, race and gender, throughout the novel.

At first glance, gender seems the more sharply foregrounded theme in *The Beet Queen,* for Erdrich details through a number of characters the price both women and men pay for defying society's gender expectations. Mary, for instance, with her "blunt ways" (66) and her smell "like white pepper from the sausage table" (66) where she works as town butcher, throughout the novel remains loveless and childless, without a consort to match her fantasies (79). A woman of almost mythic spiritual proportions, she finds in modern American society no

---

[1] Owens repeats this sentiment in *Other Destinies: Understanding the American Indian Novel:* "Indian identity is not . . . at the heart of the novel, and cultural conflict here is never explicit; there is no overt racism, no jagged sense of lost Indian culture or identity" (206). It is also a view expressed about other of Erdrich's novels. Matchie, for instance, has suggested that *Love Medicine* is "different from so much of Native American literature in that it is not polemic — there is no ax to grind, no major indictment of white society" (478).

[2] In a thoughtful response to Silko, Perez Castillo argues that Silko's attack involves "a restrictive view of ethnicity and an essentialist, logocentric concept of textual representation" (285). She concludes that "the cultural ambivalence reflected in *The Beet Queen* may be mimetic in character, mirroring the fragmented ontological landscape in which many Native Americans exist today, shuttling between radically diverse realities" (288–89). Another insightful treatment of the issue of identity in the novel is that offered by Ann Rayson. She describes *The Beet Queen* as "a novel of the interior life of 'the other' — the orphan, the homosexual, the bisexual, the Indian, the mixed-blood, the disfigured, the crippled, the mentally ill, the unattractive. . . . The central core of the novel concerns the psychological and sociological consequences of having a mixed or indeterminate identity" (Rayson 33).

channel for her supernatural powers other than tarot cards and yarrow sticks. Similarly, Wallace (in many ways, the most maternal character in the book), comfortable in the traditional female role of midwife and host *extraordinaire* of children's birthday parties, must as a gay man in an intolerant society submerge his sexuality by masquerading as the grief-stricken lover of an unknown woman whose picture he displays.

While Erdrich chronicles the toll that defiance of gender norms takes on these characters, she reserves the direst fate for two characters in the book who come closest to fulfilling social definitions of ideal male and female. In her treatment of the white woman, Sita, who bases her identity on physical beauty and marriage, and Russell, the Native American male who strives for success through football and military exploits, Erdrich both critiques white America's ideals of masculinity and femininity and suggests underlying similarities between racial and gender oppression in American society. By juxtaposing chapters focusing on Sita and Russell and thus highlighting symbolic parallels between their situations, she shows that, despite the racial gulf that separates the two, they are similarly dehumanized, reduced to objects serving the interests of a society dominated by white males.

With marriage as her "dream" (76), Sita, as a young woman, plans to move to Fargo and become a model in a department store:

> She imagined that she would also work behind the men's hat counter. There she would meet a young rising professional. They would marry. He would buy her a house near the county courthouse, on the street of railroad mansions not far from Island Park. Every winter she would walk down the hill to skate. She would wear powder blue tights and a short dress with puffs of rabbit fur at the sleeves, collar, and all around a flared hem that would lift as she twirled. (76)

Unable to imagine an independent identity for herself and wary of the "determination" (84) it takes to keep her twenty-two and a half-inch waist as she approaches thirty, she is convinced that the "only thing that would save [her], now, was to find the ideal husband" (84). However, marriage and the traditional conception of femaleness she brings to it, in fact, destroy her. The threat to selfhood that marriage poses for Sita is foreshadowed even before her first wedding: although she is irritated that Jimmy calls her the names of his favourite desserts, she fails to see his increasing weight as evidence that she is being consumed.[3] As the skating image of herself in her fantasy foreshadows, she remains a child (she likes to be called "girl" [208] even as an older woman) in her relationship with both her husbands.

---

[3] Unable to interpret her own situation, Sita mistakes other women as the danger to her. She sees Mary and Celestine as enemies and the old woman in the mental ward as the vampire in her life (208–12).

While Sita's story in isolation highlights gender oppression, Erdrich goes further to draw parallels between her fate and Russell's.[4] Similarities between white treatment of women and Native Americans are starkly drawn in the description of Sita's first marriage. In Erdrich's telling revision of a theme from white folklore — the white woman's kidnapping and ravishment by "savage Indians," Sita is "kidnap[ped]" (97) by the groom's male relatives as a joke. As this fact and Sita's stricken look of "surrender" (97) imply, marriage represents, for Sita, not self-fulfilment but loss of autonomy. Erdrich further illustrates how marriage echoes the treatment of Native Americans when the men, uncertain where to leave her, finally, with a stroke of "genius" (99), decide to dump her on the reservation, a grimly appropriate place to symbolize her fate. Like Russell, who is present in the bar where Sita takes refuge, and who later returns to the reservation after his usefulness as football star and war hero is exhausted, Sita is, as a woman, as imprisoned in the institution of marriage as he is, because of his race, on the reservation. Sita's degradation is unmistakable beneath the humour in the kidnapping scene — when wind turns her dress inside out and blows her through the door, she enters the bar not as a human being but as "a sudden explosion of white net, a rolling ball of it" (100). As happens often, she loses her voice (98, 99, 100), reduced to "muffled and inhuman croaking" (100).

For Russell, too, the success society offers involves self-destruction. Although with his picture in the papers as football star and his war medals in the state museum, he achieves masculine "success" beyond what he could expect as an Indian, Celestine, early in the novel, grimly forecasts the emptiness of that apparent achievement: "People say he is one Indian who won't go downhill in life but have success, and he does, later, depending on how you look at it" (44). Ironically, for both Sita and Russell, the symbols of their status as ideal male and female — Sita's garnet necklace and Russell's war medals, which both wear with pride throughout the novel — are, in fact, stark emblems of their enslavement.

For both characters, the attempt to emulate the gender ideals of white culture results in profound dehumanization; in different ways (Sita as sex object and Russell as cannon fodder), both have social value only as bodies and receive approval only through physical sacrifice. The scene of Sita as a young girl bearing her new breasts in hopes of receiving affection and affirmation (35) is reenacted throughout her life, first as she works as a model and later as she struggles to preserve her fragile physical beauty. This pivotal scene in Sita's life (she remembers it years later as she prepares to commit suicide [288]) takes

---

[4] Erdrich reinforces the gender dimension of Sita's story by alluding to Charlotte Perkins Gilman's classic story of female oppression, "The Yellow Wallpaper." Like the female protagonist in that story, Sita is imprisoned in a yellow room when she becomes ill, one that makes her "sick to her stomach" and prevents her from sleeping (207). Both rooms symbolize the imprisonment of the female characters in confining female roles.

place, significantly, in a cemetery. Dancing on the graves after Celestine rejects her, Sita simultaneously enters the world of female sexuality and spiritual death. Russell's physical sacrifice is even more graphic: "getting shot apart is what [Russell] live[s] for all his life" (111). Behind the accolade accorded him as "North Dakota's most-decorated hero" is, as his sister recognizes, a drama of objectification: "Now he must wait until some statehouse official scores the other veterans, counting up their wounds on a paper tablet, and figures out who gave away the most flesh" (111).

Physical mutilation mirrors the psychic and emotional fragmentation both characters experience. After fighting in war after war, Russell becomes covered with "scars and stripes" (112), Erdrich's satirical comment on his misplaced patriotism. "Mapp[ed]" (70) like the land of his ancestors, he is exploited as a natural resource, his wounds "ridged like a gullied field," his body "plowed like a tractor gone haywire" (71–75). Despite "heroic" efforts, like Russell, Sita becomes a physical wreck in seeking the perfect body (300); she "ends up looking stuffed and preserved" (112). Both ultimately appear scarcely human. Just as Russell's face, which looks "all sewn together" (118), seems freakish with its "claw marks, angry and long, even running past his temples and parting his hair crooked" (70), Sita's face becomes "cavernous" and "wrinkled" (245), distorted "into a Halloween mask, witchlike and gruesome" (120).

The physical destruction and dehumanization both characters suffer is also paralleled in mental deterioration. The debilitating "nervous" disorders both endure — Sita's drug dependency and mental breakdown, Russell's alcoholism and stroke — reflect the spiritual deaths preceding their literal ones at the end of the novel (both are, in fact, described as "stiffs" [71, 293] and associated with death imagery throughout the novel). Further, both become paralyzed (Sita first emotionally [207] and then later when injured [283]). As both characters become increasingly debilitated, they lose their powers of self-expression: when they break out of the silence that often characterizes them (98, 203, 205), no one understands Sita's "jammed-up sentences" (207) or Russell's "shattered vowels" (196). Voiceless "puppets" (121) and "robots" (121), both characters remain dependent for their identities on external sources. Not surprisingly, Erdrich describes both as rootless — Sita is like a blossom on a tree, "the same frail kind of beauty that could be broken off a tree by any passing boy and discarded, cast away when the fragrance died" (21) and Russell "like a tree half uprooted in a wind" (203).

As creations of American society, both Sita and Russell symbolically inhabit a white male world with little space for females and Native Americans. Just as Russell winds up on the reservation created by whites, Sita spends her last days in the basement recreation room of her house, a distinctly male preserve filled with memorabilia signifying the personalities of her husbands — Jimmy's stereo equipment and beer lamps (one "a silhouette of a stagecoach pulled by horses that flee silently around and around a lit screen of mountains and desert cacti," another "of a canoe endlessly revolving in a blue lake" [283]) and Louis's short wave radio sets. In this room, a "monument to both of [her husbands] and to neither one" (281), Sita sleeps on the pool table, a kind of centrepiece in this masculine world. As always, Sita misunderstands her position as a female in a male-dominated world. Having moved her possessions in, she has the illusion of ownership — "It is mine now" (281) — and power, imagining "all that [she] could do by remote control" (282):

> From here, I can turn on the television if I want. The face of the Morning Hostess might be flipping in a blur, but I can stabilize her with one twist. Headphones are at my elbow. I can push on the stereo power, the radio. I can listen to 8-track tapes, or, in silence, watch the brightly lit dials and barometers slide and flicker. I can operate the light control to dim or illuminate the imitation Tiffany overhead. I can turn on all of the beer lamps and watch them. (282–83)

Sita, is, despite her fantasies, merely another object in this world, more like a ruined piece of electronics equipment, with the "nerve connections" in her brain "short[ed] out" (283), than an empowered human being. Just as she has mistaken marriage as the route to identity, she here confuses residence in a male world with meaningful power in it. Rather than becoming more alive in the home of her dreams, Sita resides in a house of death, a home with a lawn of grass like that in cemeteries (148) in a town built on Indian burial grounds (278). Sita is spiritually buried there, "swathed in covers that have absorbed an earthen smell from the basement air" (282). In more ways than one, Sita's death follows the shape of her life. Celestine and Mary find her dead outside her house, her body snagged on a broken branch and held up by her garnet necklace. She dies as frustrated as she has lived, her lips "set in exasperation, as if she had just been about to say something and found out her voice was snatched in death" (291).

Parallels between Russell and Sita culminate in the parade, the piece of Americana that concludes the novel. Through a bizarre set of circumstances (Sita mistakenly enters the parade as a corpse), both Russell and she, icons of American masculinity and femininity, ride in the parade with the Beet Queen and her court. Significantly, both appear in the symbols of their gender aspirations — Sita in a white dress and her garnet necklace, with a "white leatherette purse in her lap" (294); Russell in his uniform with medals pinned in a "bright pattern over his heart" (298) and a rifle in his lap. Both parade before the crowd as mindless, passive bodies, the dead Sita propped in Mary's truck (emblazoned with its name, House of Meats), and the paraplegic Russell propped up and strapped into a wheelchair. Just as Sita is buried in a male world, Russell ends up in a symbolically white one. Seemingly the centrepiece in this tribute to American military exploits, he is (as his physical condition starkly betrays) actually one of its victims.[5] Like Sita, he is also buried on foreign turf, set on the float amidst a "field of graves . . . plastic grass and red poppies[,] [a] plain white cross . . . planted at his feet" (299).

Although they are the ostensible objects of the town's admiration, it is bitterly ironic that no one notices Sita's death or Russell's near-deadly stroke during the procession. In fact, both characters—mute and completely immobilized—receive unqualified approval. The townspeople, for instance, assume Sita was "someone important, an alderwoman or the governor's wife" (296), and her long-lost cousin thinks she looks better than ever (321). While Russell is amused that "the town he'd lived in and the members of the American Legion were solemnly saluting a dead Indian" (300), Erdrich's message is much more serious. Just as Nector's experience with the movies in *Love Medicine* proves to him the white man's belief that "The only good Indian is a dead Indian" (91), Russell's presence in the parade starkly demonstrates the dependency and spiritual death American society offers as success to Native Americans. In this episode, Erdrich develops this idea about racial oppression further to suggest that in white American culture, the only "good woman" is also lifeless.

At a time when the interrelations between race and gender concern many American women writers of colour, Erdrich, as a Native American herself, offers an interesting perspective on racial and gender oppression in *The Beet Queen* by uncovering similarities between the fates of white women and men of colour. Even though Sita consistently makes "fun of [Russell] for being an Indian, and he is always glad to see her taken down a notch" (44), Erdrich suggests not only their unacknowledged affinities, but also their profound mistake in seeing one another as the enemy.

WORKS CITED

Allen, Paula Gunn. *The Sacred Hoop: Recovering the Feminine in American Indian Traditions.* Boston: Beacon P, 1986.

Barry, Nora and Mary Prescott. "The Triumph of the Brave: *Love Medicine*'s Holistic Vision." *Critique* 30:2 (1989): 123–38.

Erdrich, Louise. *The Beet Queen.* New York: Bantam Books, 1986.

———. *Love Medicine.* New York: Bantam Books, 1984.

Flavin, Louise. "Louise Erdrich's *Love Medicine:* Loving Over Time and Distance." *Critique* 31:1 (1989): 55–64.

Matchie, Thomas. "*Love Medicine.* A Female *Moby-Dick.*" *The Midwest Quarterly* 30:4 (1989): 478–91.

---

[5] Henry Lamartine, Jr., who kills himself in *Love Medicine,* suffers a similar fate: "He is less a victim of reservation life than of a war that is not of his own making. The Indian brave no longer fights for his own land and good but in a foreign war in which he has no stake" (Flavin 60).

Owens, Louis. "Acts of Recovery: The American Indian Novel in the '80's." *Western American Literature* 22:1 (1987): 53–57.

————. *Other Destinies: Understanding the American Indian Novel.* Norman: U of Oklahoma P, 1992.

Perez Castillo, Susan. "Postmodernism, Native American Literature and the Real: The Silko-Erdrich Controversy." *Massachusetts Review* 32:2 (1991): 285–94.

Rayson, Ann. "Shifting Identity in the Work of Louise Erdrich and Michael Dorris." *Studies in American Indian Literature* 3:4 (1991): 27–36.

Silko, Leslie. "Here's an Odd Artifact for the Fairy-Tale Shelf," *Studies in American Indian Literature* 10 (1986): 177–84. Orig. pub. in *Impact/Albuquerque Journal* 8 October 1986: 10–11.

JENNIFER SERGI

Storytelling: Tradition and Preservation in Louise Erdrich's Tracks (1992)

Without stories there is no articulation of experience: people would be unable to understand and celebrate the experiences of self, community, and world. And so cultures value the tellers of stories. The storyteller takes what he or she tells from experience — his or her own or that reported by others — and in turn makes it the experience of those who are listening to the tale (WB, 87). The storyteller relies on memory (his or hers and his or her listener's) and creates a chain of tradition that passes on a happening from generation to generation.

Louise Erdrich is just such a storyteller. In her third novel, *Tracks* (1988), she not only chronicles the story of the Chippewas' struggle to preserve their land and culture; she also gives us the story of these stories and their tellers as well. She is telling this novel "the Indian way." The "artistry of the Indian 'word sender' characterizes reality: peoples, landscapes, seasons, tonalizes, lightens, spiritualizes, brightens, and darkens human experience, all the while working with the reality that is" (KL, 223). This reality is shown to readers by two storytellers who alternate chapters, in separate, very distinct voices: Pauline, a young mixed-blood who is confused and psychologically damaged by her unbalanced commitment to Catholic martyrdom and Chippewa tradition; and Nanapush, a wise old tribal leader gifted in the ancient art of storytelling. It is through Nanapush that Erdrich captures the act of Indian storytelling. It is written down, but Erdrich wishes to record and preserve not just the memories, intertwined closely with personal history and a sense of loss, but a cultural tradition, one that is oral, performed, formulaic, and perpetuated by the storyteller, who learns the rhythms and melodies — the craft — and expands, ornaments, and varies the tradition his or her own way. Thus Erdrich's Native American, and more specifically Chippewa, "tracks" are evident in her narratives, if not as those of the one who experienced it, then as those of the one who reports it.

How this oral tradition and history is being recorded is important, therefore, and "tracing the connective threads between the cultural past and its expression in the present" become a primary focus of scholars as well as novelists (KL, 2). How are translators and Native American artists, like Erdrich, bringing the oral and mythic traditions of their ancestors into print for native and non-native readers? Erdrich does this in a number of ways in *Tracks*: 1) she captures the form and purpose of oral storytelling; 2) she includes the contents of Chippewa myth and legend; and 3) she preserves these cultural traditions in a voice that harks back to the old as it creates anew.

Kenneth Lincoln, a Native American literature scholar, is also exploring the nature of the transition from orality to writing, and within his definition of Indian storytelling he describes the "story-backed old man giv[ing] the child eyes and voices, narratives that touch and are carried for life: words incarnate, flesh-and-blood ties, an embodied imagination. And the tribal backbone extends through ancestors who carry history in their bodies" (KL, 222). The fictional prototype of this "story-backed old man" is Erdrich's narrator, Nanapush. Nanapush is telling the story to his adopted granddaughter Lulu: "My girl, I saw the passing of times you will never know." He knows the old ways: "I guided the last buffalo hunt. I saw the last bear shot. I trapped the last beaver with a pelt of more than two years' growth. I spoke aloud the words of the government treaty, and refused to sign the settlement papers that would take away our woods and lake" (2). He also tells Lulu how she fits into this history: "You were born on the day we shot the last bear" (58).

Moreover, much as in Indian storytelling, it is not only what Nanapush has to say and to whom, but also the way in which he says it that is important. Nanapush's narrative style points to the novel's roots in Chippewa oral tradition. Erdrich is sensitive to the immediate difference between the printed word and the spoken, and she effects an accommodation between her printed text and her narrator's delivery. The stylistic devices of repetition and parallelism, employed as early as page 2 of the novel, work to create tension, balance, and symmetry in the words of Nanapush. His words suggest the rhythms of speech: at key moments in the narrative, readers sense a whispered statement, an abrupt phrase, a long pause. Before he tells the story of how Margaret loses her braids, for instance, he leads in with: "I can only tell it step by step" (109). Erdrich also continually and skillfully reminds *us* of *his* audience and the intimacy attached to their relationship: "This is where you come in, my girl, so listen" (57). Lulu sometimes grows tired of the long story, and in his own style Nanapush manages to reprimand the youngster and, in the process, remind her of her roots and her role in this storytelling tradition: "I made her sit down and listen, just the way you are sitting now. Your mother always showed the proper respect to me. Even when I bored her, she made a good effort at pretending some interest" (178).

Erdrich's narrator not only serves to remind us of the importance of the ancient art of storytelling to a tribe, but his name also recalls the novel's debt to Chippewa mythic tradition. In Chippewa woodland myth Nanapush is the trickster-transformer who "wanders in mythic time and space between tribal experiences and dreams" (GV, 3). He is a teacher and healer and upholder of ancient and living traditions; but he is also human. He is sometimes prone to violence and overactive appetites. This paradoxical character is part of Chippewa creation and ceremonial stories. In my research of Chippewa tradition, myth, and legend the stories about the trickster vary, as does the spelling of his name (most likely because of phonetic transcription from oral tradition), but there are several similarities in all of them to Erdrich's Nanapush. (I must pause here to make a distinction. *Chippewa* is a comparatively modern and English term for the tribe; an older term is *Ojibway*. The name for these people in the language itself is *Anishinaabe*. Erdrich uses both *Chippewa* and *Anishinaabe* in the novel; all three were found in my research.) In most of the translations he possesses magic and wit. He plays tricks and is the victim of tricks. He is fond of and is good at hunting. He travels in a birchbark canoe, and the Anishinaabe honor and respect him. In chapter 3 of *Tracks* Nanapush tells us part of the origin of his name: "My father said, 'Nanapush. That's what you'll be called. Because it's got to do with trickery and living in the bush. Because it's got to do with something a girl can't resist. The first Nanapush stole fire. You will steal hearts'" (33). Erdrich's Old Nanapush, then, serves a triple purpose in reminding readers of *Tracks* of the importance of tribal tradition, mythic condition, and storytelling.

Along with this trickster figure, there is other evidence in the novel that Erdrich is interested in preserving and presenting Chippewa cultural tradition to her audience. I cannot know for sure if Erdrich heard these stories as a child, read the accounts and research of Chippewa myth, tradition, legend, and religion, or discussed them as a member of an academic community. However, I do know they are incorporated, integrated, and an important part of her novel. So, like the creation figure Nanabush and her storyteller Nanapush, Erdrich imagines and desires her own variation of the mythic stories for the enjoyment and knowledge of her modern reading audience.

The setting of her novel is the fictional Matchimanito Lake. It may not be a real geographic location, but Matchimanito is an evil manito in modern Ojibwa myth (CV, 82). The name of the lake is not the only reminder of Chippewa myth in *Tracks*. There is talk of windigos and manitous, burying the dead in trees, dreamcatchers, Jeesekeewinini (medicine man), and "Anishinabe characters, the old gods," as Nanapush refers to them (110). In chapter 6 Pauline gives us a description of "the heaven of the Chippewa," where Fleur goes to gamble for the life of her child. The gambling crowd "play for drunkenness, or sorrow, or loss of mind. They play for ease, they play for penitence, and sometimes for living souls" (160).

Gerald Vizenor, a mixed-blood member of the Minnesota Chippewa tribe as well as a teacher and scholar, records a number of the oral creation stories in his book *The People Named the Chippewas: Narrative Histories*. In his prologue Vizenor recounts a story told by Odinigun, an elder from the White Earth Reservation, telling of Naanabozho's gambling in "the land of darkness." In this story Naanabozho must play the great gambler for "the destinies of the trickster and tribal people of the woodland." The tone and, of course, the setting of these two stories are similar; the stakes and energies are high. The outcomes are very different, however: Fleur's baby dies, while Naanabozho succeeds in not losing his tribes' spirit to the land of darkness.

One of the most prevalent and important "signs" of Chippewa myth in *Tracks* is Misshepeshu, the water monster. In the novel Misshepeshu's origin is tied to the arrival of the Pillager clan on Matchimanito Lake. The monster was thought to be responsible for Fleur's powers and the demise of her enemies. Pauline describes him in chapter 2:

> He's a devil, that one, love hungry with desire and maddened for the touch of young girls, the strong and daring especially, the ones like Fleur.
>
> Our mothers warn us that we'll think he's handsome, for he appears with green eyes, copper skin, a mouth tender as a child's. But if you fall into his arms, he sprouts horns, fangs, claws, fins. His feet are joined as one and his skin, brass scales, rings to the touch. . . . He holds you under. Then he takes the body of a lion, a fat brown worm, or a familiar man. . . . He's a thing of dry foam, a thing of death by drowning, the death a Chippewa cannot survive. (11)

Erdrich's description of the lake monster is very similar to that given by Christopher Vecsey, another scholar interested in recording Chippewa oral myth. According to his account of this Chippewa myth, the Underwater Manito is "associated with both the lion and the serpent" (CV, 74). It inspired both awe and terror, as well as reverence, and was thought to be responsible for both malicious and good deeds: "It could cause rapids and stormy waters; it often sank canoes and drowned Indians." In some tales, however, it "fed and sheltered those who fell through the ice."

Erdrich uses this dialectical being throughout *Tracks*. When Fleur returns to Matchimanito from Argus, the townspeople attribute good fishing and no lost boats to Fleur's ability to "keep the lake thing controlled" (35). Her special connection to Misshepeshu is even thought to be sexual, and the paternity of Lulu is questioned: "Lulu's eyes blazed bright as his, . . . eyes hollow and gold" (70). Just before Pauline takes her vows and becomes Sister Leopolda, she tells the story (in chapter 8) of her entanglement with the lake monster.

For Pauline, who has just recovered from self inflicted burns, the lake monster represents the devil. She is delusional and very confused about her religious faith and her Chippewa traditional beliefs: "Christ had hidden out of frailty, overcome by the glitter of copper scales, appalled at the creature's unwinding length and luxury. New devils require new gods" (195). She makes a last visit to Matchimanito Lake, "determined to wait for my tempter, the one who enslaved the ignorant, who damned them with belief" (200). She tells her story of a sexual, violent encounter with the monster in which she strangles him with her rosary, but the thing "grew a human shape . . . the physical form of Napoleon Morrissey" (202–3). She feels no guilt for murdering the father of her child, because "he had appeared . . . as the water thing, glass breastplate and burning iron rings" (203). Pauline believed she "tamed the monster that night, sent [him] to the bottom of the lake and chained [him] there by [her] deed. . . . [She] was a poor and noble creature now, dressed in earth like Christ, in furs like Moses Pillager [the medicine man and Fleur's brother], draped in snow or simple air" (203–4). This description symbolizes the utter confusion some Chippewa could feel because of the crisis in their belief system brought on by Christian influences. Of course Pauline is an extreme example of the pull between Catholic teachings and Chippewa traditions, but Erdrich uses the lake monster, the underwater manito Misshepeshu, in this case as a symbol of the crisis of identity for Pauline.

Misshepeshu serves several symbolic purposes for Erdrich: he is an example of native tradition and lore; he brings the crisis between Chippewa myth and Catholic teachings to a state of rupture in the novel; and the language used to describe him becomes symbolic of the storytelling itself. According to Nanapush:

> Talk is an old man's last vice. I opened my mouth and wore out the boy's ears, but that is not my fault. I shouldn't have been caused to live so long, shown so much of death, had to squeeze so many stories in the corners of my crain. They're all attached, and once I start there is no end to telling because they're hooked from one side to the other, mouth to tail. (46)

The stories are circular and continuous and serpentlike. By telling tribal stories, singing old songs, Nanapush gives his culture a chance for continuation: "During the year of my sickness, when I was the last one left, I saved myself by starting a story. . . . I got well by talking. Death could not get a word in edgewise, grew discouraged, and traveled on" (46). He not only discouraged death, but he encouraged life and continued his name with his storytelling. When a priest comes to baptize Fleur's illegitimate child, Nanapush tells him the baby is his: "There were so many tales, so many possibilities, so many lies. The waters were so muddy I thought I'd give them another stir" (61). He later saves this child with his talking. Nanapush knew "certain cure songs, words that throw the sick one into a dream . . . holding you motionless with talking."

Lulu was "lulled with the sound of [his] voice" and cured of frostbite with Nanapush's ancient gift (167).

For Nanapush, being a talker was a form of survival; he used his words and his "brain as a weapon" (118). This gave him his identity as a trickster and a leader (32). He learned to ask questions and tell stories "without limit or end" (145). As much power as the spoken word has for Nanapush, he has learned to fear the printed words the white man brings to his land: "Nanapush is a name that loses power every time that it is written and stored in a government file" (32). Still, when he is about to lose his land, he admits to Father Damien that he should have tried to "wield influence with this [new] method of leading others with a pen and piece of paper" (209).

As Nanapush is exploring the dichotomous nature of the transition from orality to writing, so is Erdrich. Readers are learning of the Chippewas' oral tradition through a printed text. Erdrich shows this duality through Nanapush. Although he expresses his disgust with the "barbed pens" of the bureaucrats encroaching on his people, making them "a tribe of file cabinets and triplicates, a tribe of single-space documents, directives, policy. A tribe of pressed trees. A tribe of chicken-scratch that can be scattered by a wind, diminished to ashes by one struck match" (225). Nanapush tells us that he saves his granddaughter and brings her to his home with papers and records from the church: "I became a bureaucrat myself . . . to draw you home" (225). It is interesting that Erdrich chooses the word *draw* in this case, evoking an image of the pen rather than of the voice. She realizes the conflict, to which she in part contributes: the Indian "oral tradition of medicine, religion, history, and tribal ceremony bridged from living ritual performance into the marketplace of print" (KL, 82). Nevertheless, for Nanapush and the Native Americans, the last word must be survival. His stories preserve and pass along, tracing and trying to make sense of living history. Erdrich gives us these stories in print; through her language she gives poetic voice and historical witness to human events, which is what all cultures expect from their storytellers.

University of Rhode Island

WORKS CITED

Victor Barnouw. *Wisconsin Chippewa Myths and Their Relation to Chippewa Life.* Madison. University of Wisconsin Press. 1977.

Walter Benjamin. *Illuminations.* New York. Harcourt, Brace & World. 1955 (References use the abbreviation WB.)

Louise Erdrich. *Tracks.* New York. Henry Holt. 1988.

Basil Johnston. *Ojibway Heritage.* New York. Columbia University Press. 1976.

Ruth Landes. *Ojibwa Religion and the Midewiwin.* Madison. University of Wisconsin Press. 1968.

Kenneth Lincoln. *Native American Renaissance*. Berkeley. University of California Press. 1983. (References use the abbreviation KL.)

Christopher Vecsey. *Traditional Ojibwa Religion and Its Historical Changes*. Philadelphia. American Philosophical Society. 1983. (References use the abbreviation CV.)

Gerald Vizenor. *The People Named the Chippewa: Narrative Histories*. Minneapolis. University of Minnesota Press. 1984. (References use the abbreviation GV.)

MICHAEL LEE

Erdrich's Dakota as Metaphor for American Culture (1996)

Review of Tales of Burning Love

Each of Louise Erdrich's novels offers new evidence that by the time her writing career has ended, her fictional world will prove to be larger than the sum of its novelistic parts.

In this ever-widening world, history and geography give way to mythic time and space, characters become more interesting than the merely plausible versions of the people they represent and events are capable of becoming imbued with magic and mystery even as they depict the mores and manners of a particular place and time.

As characters from one novel reemerge in another and as events once told are retold with a new twist or from a different point of view, Erdrich's narrative voices reveal heretofore hidden facts or facets of character and her plots offer illuminations that sometimes dispel points of prior confusion, but just as often add to a growing sense that life is better embraced as mystery than partially understood via mere surface knowledge and factual information.

To put it another way, Erdrich subordinates her narratives to a larger Narrative. Her stories, each compelling in its own right, take on added dimension as installments in an ongoing saga of her own fictional equivalent of William Faulkner's mythical Yoknapatawpha — her vision of a North Dakota whose unique cultural blend of Ojibwa and Euro-American peoples, reservation politics and gaming interests, agribusiness and real-estate development, alcoholism and Catholicism, racism and tribal pride, promiscuity and asceticism, tribal memory and official story, make it both microcosm and metaphor for a larger postmodern American culture born of fusions and confusions, tensions between and affirmations of cultural identities, all undergirded by fundamental questionings of both culture and identity.

Tales of Burning Love, Erdrich's fifth venture into the myth-history of her region, opens with the same event that opened her first novel, *Love Medicine*

(1984). On Holy Saturday, 1981, June Morrisey, a Chippewa woman who has become something of a prostitute, begins a journey from the oil fields near Williston, N.D., to her actual and spiritual homeland on the Turtle Mountain Reservation, more than 200 miles to the east.

Her journey is interrupted by an encounter with a man in a bar, a bout of drinking and a botched attempt at sex in the man's truck, following which June climbs out of the truck and attempts to continue on foot her quest for home. In the early hours of Easter morning she is found dead in a freak blizzard. While *Love Medicine* goes on to explore ways in which June's search for a home is played out by a host of others and ultimately completed by her son who never knew her except in tribal legend, *Tales of Burning Love* charts the subsequent life and marriages of the man whose sexual failing contributed to June's death.

Jack Mauser, himself a half-Chippewa who has consciously suppressed what the novel calls "the Ojibwa part" of his core identity, finds himself 13 years later haunted by the memory of the woman he failed to save, facing in each of the four women he has since married the ghost of June Morrisey.

Erdrich makes full use of comic novelistic license in recasting the Easter 1981 incident as the foundation for her creation of Jack as a man who, we now discover, tasted true love and actually married June Morrisey during their brief, alcohol-fueled encounter, and has been seeking to recapture that love in four subsequent marriages, even as he seeks to assuage the guilt he feels for having abandoned June to her death in the snow.

The narrative present finds him the owner of a financially shaky Fargo construction company, recently married to Dot Adare Nanapush, his fifth wife, while, still obsessed with thoughts of Eleanor, wife No. 2, herself torn between an obsession with sex and a fascination with the saintly asceticism of a nun whose biography she is writing. This nun is the ancient Sr. Leopolda, parts of whose tormented past are recounted in *Love Medicine* and in *Tracks*.

Dot, meanwhile, is still legally married to Gerry Nanapush, the irrepressible Chippewa trickster-hero whose escape from a plane crash en route to a federal prison (recounted in detail in *The Bingo Palace*) paves the way for a symbolic crossing of the paths of one character who politicizes his Indian identity and another who hides his.

Complicating matters for Jack and the others is the fact that wives three and four, Candice and Marlis, are now living together as lovers and parenting partners to Jack's infant son, John, to whom Marlis gave birth just prior to her divorce from Jack.

Erdrich has clearly enjoyed herself in exploiting to the full the comic potential of this multiple-wife plot. Readers as well will relish her depiction of Jack's often absurdly misdirected search for love and forgiveness, compounded as it is of male ego gratification, narcissistic sexual impulse, foggy romanticism, financial greed, lots of alcohol and the occasional urge to do the right thing in spite of himself.

In several scenes, the comic potential ripens into pure fun as Jack Mauser becomes a kind of postmodern Tom Jones, his sexual exploits forcing him into situations and guises—twice he finds himself "cross-dressed" by former wives, once as the Virgin Mary—that subvert the very sexual prowess that seems to be his primary attraction.

Embedded in this delightful chaos of accidental twists and coincidences, surprises and contrivances, the book's central events become plausible only for the reader willing to suspend disbelief within the comic framework of Erdrich's magical brand of realism.

When the house Jack built for Dot burns down on New Year's Eve, Jack's four surviving wives get together at a memorial service for the man everyone thinks has been killed in the fire. After the service, they find themselves stranded in a blizzard and spend the night of Jan. 5 staying alive by telling the stories of their lives and their affairs with Jack.

As the night turns into the early hours of the feast of the Epiphany, the tales of love that are told burn bright to illuminate, if not always to make rational sense of, the impulses and strategies that made each of these women a medium for Jack Mauser's attempt to resurrect the love he failed to save in another blizzard 13 years ago.

The coincidences are many as Jack himself (not dead!) and Gerry Nanapush (not dead!) arrive in the vicinity of the stranded car. Jack and Eleanor both have epiphanies in the snow, starting them down the path of redemption through recognition of their burning love for each other.

While the idea of four ex-wives sitting out a snowstorm in their former husband's car, sharing intimate details of their sexual lives, borders on soap-opera absurdity, the tales they tell force even the most skeptical reader to ignore the contrived structure and relish the rich stories and the fully individualized voices of their tellers. After Eleanor urges them to "pretend this car is a confessional," Dot imposes some rules: "Tell a true story. The story has to be about you. Something that you've never told another person, a story that would scorch paper, heat up the air." And, for the most part, this is exactly what they do.

The ensuing tales of burning love underscore a point about love relationships hinted at in a remark Eleanor makes early in their discourse: "Jack probably showed a separate facet of himself to each one of us. Or we brought it out in him. Made him as different as we are different from one another. In fact, it isn't entirely farfetched to say that we each married a different man."

Framed by this remark, the tales call into question courtly and romantic ideals of altruistic love, suggesting that to some extent human love is an exercise in reciprocal narcissism. This narcissism is rendered comically as Jack imagines his wives at his funeral: "He returned to the fantasy—what would they do with his supposed remains? Who would cry and who would pray? He saw it all—wives and wives and wives approaching—waves of women marching like the sea toward his casket!"

But it is conveyed more darkly in the character of Eleanor's father, whose obsessive and possessive love for his wife leads him to an ultimate desperate act of burning love in a crematorium where his remains and hers are comingled in death.

Providing a coda to the tales told by the wives are the words of Sr. Leopolda, who appears before Eleanor during the blizzard: "You have spoken of love, I have heard it all. You and your sisters are blind women touching the vast body of the elephant, each describing the oddness beneath the surface of her hands." Eleanor suspends her rational skepticism long enough to allow Leopolda's image to signify to her that "she herself was frozen dead" and to guide her safely back to life. At this very moment Jack, too, is having visions, first of his mother in "the other world of the Ojibwa dead," and then of June Morrisey "wearing a wedding dress, a real one this time." As he follows June, he realizes that "she was bringing him home."

For both Jack and Eleanor, "home" finally means revisiting their love for each other. After their near-death experiences, Erdrich leaves open the question of the kind of love that will define their "resurrected" lives together. While the novel's end finds them united in an intensely erotic, passionately charged reversal of the sexual failure Jack had known with June so long ago, the narrative voice is tentative: "Maybe through the years they had grown strong enough to wrestle love, to hold on and not let go. Perhaps it was true that they were bound together in a thief's trust. Perhaps such deep love is always stolen, as there is not enough to go around."

But despite the ambiguity suggested by words like *maybe* and *perhaps,* Erdrich surrounds the passage with imagery meant to affirm natural life forces in classical comic fashion. Jack and Eleanor's renewal of love occurs "one night, in a moon drift, the late August air billowing and succulent, in the lush scents of turned dirt and growing plants and ancient skunk musk and the sweet pink rugosa roses."

In a note of Whitmanesque affirmation, we are told that "outside, the spears of grass rustled in their sheaths."

The symbolic implication of all this is that Jack and Eleanor, in their dance of love, will become part of a natural continuum that the novel has already identified as specifically Indian. With Eleanor, and through their love, Jack will embrace the Ojibwa part of himself that had once been inaccessible, "an inner life still hidden to him," a part of him "that was so buried it didn't know what it saw looking at the dirt or sky or into a human face."

The novel's natural imagery of rebirth is unconvincing, though, for even as Jack is shedding the tears that express the depth of what he feels for Eleanor, we have reason to doubt his sincerity, knowing that he is part of a scheme with the mercenary Chippewa Lyman Lamartine, to expand the gambling casino on Turtle Mountain Reservation. Hardly the most life-affirming means of getting in touch with the Ojibwa within!

Given the author's penchant for revisiting characters in books to come, maybe the question we should ask is not whether Jack returned home to discover his Ojibwa core self, but rather will he do so? Those of us who have enjoyed watching this fictional world evolve anticipate hearing more about Jack Mauser and Eleanor to see if their burning natural love survives the often darker and colder realities of life in the culturally determined human nexus of Louise Erdrich's North Dakota.

STUDENT ESSAY

A Cultural Heritage: Louise Erdrich's Fiction
by Sage Van Wing

Authors usually write about what they know. Thus an author's upbringing and culture will affect not only her subjects, but also her general themes and writing styles. This effect can be seen in the fiction of Native American author Louise Erdrich, who writes about both the history of her people and their current struggles. She does this not in traditional narrative form, but rather through stories told by many different characters, imitating the oral tradition of her culture. Using many traditional Native American themes, she is able to further the connection between her writing and her culture. Also, the complex interconnections among her characters span more than five volumes of work, closely mirroring the continuity of Native American culture. While showing the fragmentation of modern Indian traditions, Erdrich's novels celebrate Native American survival and credit the spiritual values of her culture with that survival.

Leslie Silko, another well-known Native American author, is critical of Louise Erdrich in her article entitled "Here's an Odd Artifact for the Fairy-Tale Shelf." In this negative review of Erdrich's novel *The Beet Queen* (1986), Silko argues that Erdrich's text has "an ethereal clarity and shimmering beauty because no history or politics intrudes to muddy "the well of pure necessity contained within the language itself" (179). Silko claims that while Erdrich's writing style is "dazzling and sleek" (178), her novels give preference to "the interaction of words and de-emphasize their referential dimension" (Castillo 286). Silko claims that this style does well to explore the "depths of the subconscious of characters" (180), but in doing so Erdrich leaves out the larger political, historic, and cultural world of Native Americans.

Most of Silko's argument rests upon the fact that Erdrich is a gifted and sophisticated writer, deeply aware of currents in modern literature. In her mind this means that Erdrich's fragmented contemporary style cannot reflect the oral tradition and instead presents Native American existence as it would be seen by a modernist, mainstream novelist, thus seemingly implying that Erdrich is ambivalent or somehow disloyal to her Indian origins.

I find this argument severely flawed and can only hope that Silko would react differently now after reading Erdrich's more recent novels such as *Tracks* (1988) and *The Bingo Game* (1994), both of which focus in depth on Native American characters and themes. Because Erdrich has an excellent *writing* style does not mean that she cannot incorporate her culture's *oral* tradition and certainly does not mean that she has an ambivalent attitude toward her origins. Of course there is an inherent contradiction and a risk of inauthenticity in preserving an oral tradition when literature is by definition written and crafted, becoming through this process a part of the world of high art rather than remaining exclusively within the folk tradition, but Erdrich manages to overcome this problem.

Erdrich's success lies in her ability to write in such a way that we are reminded of an oral telling, while at the same time feeling that we are also reading literature that is sophisticated and controlled in its style and form. The novel *Love Medicine* has six different first-person narrators and five other partly omniscient characters. In *Tracks,* the narrative of the Native American tribal elder Nanapush is told entirely in the form of a story to his step-granddaughter Lulu. One Native American reviewer has remarked that "this device is particularly striking to me, because it reminds me of my grandmother talking incessantly at me when I was very young" (Larson 8). However, to make the narrative richer and more complex, in the same novel the nun Pauline is allowed to reveal her own storytelling abilities in a parallel, entwined narrative of the story of her arch-enemy, Fleur, Lulu's mother.

One of the results of this multitude of narrators is that each chapter feels like a story within itself. In fact, many of Erdrich's chapters were actually published as short stories prior to their release as part of a complete book. Consequently, an Erdrich novel does not form a whole unit without the intertwining of the relationships of the characters in the individual stories told by all of the different narrators. This leaves Erdrich's books feeling more like a "collection of folklore, stories, anecdotes, and jokes . . . [and] brings a sense of immediacy to her fiction that is like oral storytelling" (Towery 109). This preservation of oral storytelling, because it was so intrinsic in the transmission of culture in the past, helps to preserve and to carry on the Native American culture in modern society.

The intertwining of characters' lives bound together through the individual story-chapters is in itself a tie to Native American culture, reflecting the continuity and connectedness of traditional life. While the connections between the characters are only revealed by the many differing and sometimes unreliable narrators, these connections are nonetheless impossible to ignore: "In fact, within the structure of the novels and stories, the narrators' memories, true or false, form the basis of 'the story'" (Towery 100). As Marvin Magalaner notes, "In *Love Medicine* the Chippewa family line, as well as the lines of the Kashpaws and the Lamartines, is filtered to the reader through the memory flow of family members: a quick-running stream of remembrance here, a slow and deliberately muddy flow of recollection there" (107).

Erdrich's focus on individual characters reveals yet another tie to Native American culture. Instead of implying an ambivalence toward her Indian heritage as

Silko suggested, Erdrich's approach reveals the personal side of Native American politics and history. That Erdrich does not tell a traditional historical story of the Indian does not mean that she is ignoring her culture, but rather that she is telling the story of real people, and of modern Indian life.

The political and social problems in modern Indian life, such as alcoholism, poverty, education, and the loss of land, are explored in all of Erdrich's novels. *Tracks* focuses for a large part on the issue of land allotment and "how it affects innocent bystanders" (Larson 4). Other Erdrich novels look at the issue of mixed-bloods and the breakdown of the traditional tribal structure. Also, all of the books, but particularly *Love Medicine,* deal with the effects of Catholicism as it has been imposed upon the Native Americans. These themes expose clearly the breakdown of traditional culture and the trauma facing modern Native Americans in the search for a cultural identity.

Such a search often leads back to traditional stories and myths, many of which are included in Erdrich's novels. The result of this is that while there are often problems of maintaining traditional culture in current society, it is the culture itself which helps Erdrich's characters overcome those problems. For example, as Nora Barry and Mary Prescott observe in their essay "The Triumph of the Brave," "Erdrich re-enacts folklore tradition through Gerry and Lipsha, particularly the figures of Trickster and the unpromising hero" (Barry and Prescott 126). According to traditional myths, the unpromising hero is an orphan who is raised by an old woman and who demonstrates no supernatural powers in the beginning but is later revealed to be the son of a powerful spirit (Barry and Prescott 134).

Erdrich's character Lipsha Morrissey follows this pattern exactly. Lipsha is raised by Marie, who becomes like a grandmother to him. Also, he himself admits that he was often called "the biggest waste on the reservation" (qtd. in Barry and Prescott 134). Originally he knows nothing of his powerful grandfather, Old Man Pillager, and his magical father, Gerry Nanapush. Although Lipsha does show some initial promise with the power to heal, he later misuses, and loses, this power, only to gain it back after a series of trials and hardships through which he finds his place on the reservation (Barry and Prescott 134).

A similar type of connection to traditional patterns is evident in the character of Lipsha's father, Gerry. Gerry is "Erdrich's modern equivalent of the ancient Trickster" (Barry and Prescott 132). He is "defiant against authority, mischievous, capable of appearing and disappearing almost at will, living beyond the norm, yet tolerated and even revered on the reservation" (132). Lipsha describes him in *The Bingo Game* as a complex, wily outsider:

> Gerry Nanapush, famous politicking hero, dangerous armed criminal, judo expert, escape artist, charismatic member of the American Indian Movement, and smoker of many pipes of kinnikinnik in the most radical groups. That was . . . Dad. (qtd. in Barry and Prescott 133)

These words could easily describe the Trickster character in many traditional Native American stories. The same is true for Lipsha and the character of the unpromising hero. Also, the character of Fleur in *Tracks* can be interpreted as a traditional witch, exploring the Native American aspects of magic and witchcraft. Not only does this tie Erdrich's texts to Native American culture, but it also helps to provide a framework for the survival of these characters in the fragmented world of a modern reservation: "By calling on ancient types, Erdrich injects vitality into a situation where her Chippewas appear to be doomed" (Barry and Prescott 134).

Another traditional activity Erdrich uses in her novels is the "homing" ritual. While most American novels are about an individual leaving his or her original home and setting out into the world at large to find success and fulfillment, critic William Bevis points out that "in Native American novels, coming home, staying put, contracting, even what we call 'regressing' to a place, a past where one has been before, is not only the primary story, it is a primary mode of knowledge and a primary good" (qtd. in Towery 109). According to Bevis, "Indian 'homing' is presented as the opposite of competitive individualism, which is white success" (109).

Fulfillment in the Native American sense means unification with native family (including the extended families of clan, community, and nature) and cultural past. In order for such a unification to occur in Erdrich's novels, the hero/heroine must confront the problems of modern Indian life. Today, in search of jobs, more and more Indians are leaving their primarily rural reservations where close ties to the land and nature as well as family and clan links are preserved. However, as Louise Flavin observes, "When the American Indian moves off the reservation and begins life in a culture essentially different from his own, the results can be disastrous" (55).

Erdrich clearly emphasizes the importance of connections to family and nature in her books. This is particularly evident in *Tracks,* the first of her novels in historical chronological order, which covers the most with traditional Native American society as it had still been preserved in the lifestyles of several of the characters, particularly Fleur and Nanapush. The struggle of these two characters is to continue living in the traditional way off the land even when their land is being divided up and taken away from them. Most of the main characters are living off the land in the traditional way; Fleur, at least, manages to keep her strong connection to the land in the end.

However, Erdrich's "story is not one of continuity, relatedness, and harmony with the land and nature, with culture and tradition" (Flavin 58). Instead, she presents a bleak picture of modern-day reservation life where a returning Indian would find that the tribe has disintegrated, the past has been forgotten, and the land no longer supports a livelihood. In *Love Medicine* "Eli Kashpaw is the last man on the reservation who could snare a deer, who knew how to skin a skunk and knew the ways of the woods. His twin, Nector, educated in the schools, loses his mind and cannot remember the history of his tribal battles" (Flavin 64).

Erdrich's novels portray a culture in which not only has much of the traditional knowledge been lost, but most of the land has also been sold off to whites. As a result, much of the younger generation cannot make a living off the land and is forced to find work off the reservation. Outward migration of the young does not become the central focus of Erdrich's books, however. In her novels, most of those who have left return shortly afterward and find connectedness to the land and their culture despite the hardships. As the tribal elder, Nanapush, concludes in *Tracks:*

> Land is the only thing that lasts life to life. Money burns like tinder, flows off like water. And as for government promises, the wind is steadier. I am a hold-out, like the Pillagers, although I told the Captain and the Agent what I thought of their papers in good English. I could have written my name, and much more too, in script. I had a Jesuit education in the halls of Saint John before I ran back to the woods and forgot all my prayers. (Erdrich, *Tracks* 33)

Because her fiction is replete with characters struggling to maintain their cultural identity, Erdrich asserts the enduring nature of Native American culture even in a modern society not at all supportive of its traditional way of life. While she does focus on the fragmented existence of contemporary reservation life, the style and content of her writing highlights the continuity and collectiveness intrinsic to her culture, which has survived even to today (Towery 113). As Erdrich herself says, "Native American writers must tell the stories of contemporary survivors while protecting and celebrating the cores of cultures left in the wake of the catastrophe" (qtd. in Towery 99).

Works Cited

Barry, Nora, and Mary Prescott. "The Triumph of the Brave: *Love Medicine*'s Holistic Vision." *Critique* 30.2 (1989): 123–37.

Castillo, Susan Pérez. "Postmodernism, Native American Literature and the Real: The Silko-Erdrich Controversy." *Massachusetts Review* 32.2 (1991): 285–96.

Erdrich, Louise. *The Beet Queen.* New York: Holt, 1986.

---. *The Bingo Game.* New York: Harper, 1994.

---. *Love Medicine.* New York: Holt, 1984.

---. *Tracks.* New York: Holt, 1988.

Flavin, Louise. "Louise Erdrich's *Love Medicine:* Loving Over Time and Distance." *Critique* 31.1 (1990): 55–64.

Larson, Sidner. "The Fragmentation of a Tribal People in Louise Erdrich's *Tracks.*" *American Indian Culture and Research Journal* 17.2 (1993): 1–15.

Magalaner, Marvin. "Of Cars, Time, and the River." *American Women Writing Fiction: Memory, Identity, Family, Space.* Ed. Mickey Pearlman. Lexington: U of Kentucky P, 1989. 95–108.

Silko, Leslie. "Here's an Odd Artifact for the Fairy-Tale Shelf." Rev. of *The Beet Queen* by Louise Erdrich. *Studies in American Indian Literature* 10.4 (1986): 178–84.

Towery, Margie. "Continuity and Connection: Characters in Louise Erdrich's Fiction." *American Indian Culture and Research Journal* 16.4 (1992): 99–122.

ELIZABETH TALLENT   (b. 1954)

Critic Andrea Barnet has noted that Elizabeth Tallent's stories are "shaped less by plot than by immediately precise imagery." Tallent is concerned with the nuances of character and feeling.

Born in Washington D.C., Tallent lived in the Midwest during her adolescence. She earned a B.A. in anthropology from Illinois State University in 1975 and then moved to Santa Fe, where she began to write stories and novels. She has been a visiting writer at a number of colleges, including the University of Iowa; before becoming the director of the Creative Writing Program at Stanford University, she was a professor of English at the University of California at Davis. In 1982 and 1986 she was awarded National Endowment for the Arts fellowships. She won the O. Henry Prize in 1980, and her stories have been included in *The Best American Short Stories* for 1980 and 1992. She has written one novel, *Museum Pieces* (1985); her story collections include *In Constant Flight* (1983), *Time with Children* (1987), and *Honey* (1993), which contains "Ciudad Juárez."

Tallent's writing reflects her interest in relationships between men and women and between children and their parents.

Ciudad Juárez   (1993)

The Subaru's air-conditioning purrs arduously, pitted against the one-hundred-and-one-degree radiance of Texas, turning the dust on its dash to platinum lint and burning twin suns into the big black lenses hiding Tom's wife's eyes. Tatters of orange peel, a Styrofoam cup whose crescent indentations are the repeated nickings of Tom's wife's thumbnail, a foxed map folded to the Rio Grande, a tiny quartz arrowhead — bird point — from the desert beyond the last rest stop: the litter, cumulatively somehow depressing, of five hours' conversationless travel. Her silence isn't aimed at him, Tom knows. They're not a couple to nurse mutual incomprehension in silence; they're more likely to expect too much of each other, and so, after a little oblique study, he decided to leave Nina alone.

Ten miles back, she'd caught his wrist and slanted it toward herself to read his watch, and then, he'd thought, she would say something; she'd say, "It's two o'clock," or "It's getting late," in the faintly marveling tone she reserves for that observation, but she'd said nothing after all. In essence, despite touching him, she had not felt compelled to acknowledge his existence. She'd simply taken possession of his wrist. For years they had done such things back and forth without their meaning anything. She had straightened his tie, or he had brushed strands of hair from the corner of her smile. He can remember using a fingertip to rub lipstick from one of her front teeth, the left, which minutely, endearingly, overlaps the other, his favorite imperfection in her body. Just now her clasp was too light to alter the peacefulness with which his hand lay on the wheel. Her touch was utterly familiar, light, practical, dismissive, quick. It made him nervous. Yet they can't make each other nervous; it's a possibility that vanished from their marriage long ago. They're so deeply unselfconscious with each other, in fact, that it's not even clear that she "borrowed" his wrist, or "took temporary possession" of it. It's as if she read her own watch, really, moving her own arm slightly to do so, thinking nothing of it. Her touch couldn't have been more neutral, so why did he experience it as so suddenly, exquisitely sexual? If a stranger, someone he'd never seen before, touched him unexpectedly, wanting only to learn the time, he would feel this intruded on, this moved. How can Nina's touch be as disturbing as a stranger's?

A generous interpretation: sex, sensing a vacuum, nimbly presents itself as a way of making contact.

Here, on the map, the Rio Grande's blue hairline intersects the black dashes of the Mexican border, but if the river's down there, it's lost in the glare of sunstruck sand. The American traffic slows for the bridge. On its far side the sentry boxes that should house Mexican Customs are boarded shut, spray-painted in slashes and scrawls naming couples and sexual acts. Nina asks, "Nobody stops us?"

"Hey, they want us," Tom says, relieved. Garbo talks. She goes further, twisting in her seat belt to report, of the baby behind them in his car seat, "Still out. Thumb in his mouth."

"Is he getting enough air-conditioning?"

She leans over the seat back to not-quite-touch the baby's forehead. "I think so."

The books say parents should spend time alone with each twin, but this is almost the first occasion Wills and Griffin have been separated. Griffin has been left in Santa Fe with the boys' sitter, Carmelita Diáz, who was hardly in the door before she cocked a confident hip for Griffin to straddle and told Nina to leave now, please, before the *hijito* knew what was happening. If Nina had only trusted her with Wills, too, this weekend would surely be easier.

Juárez is, first, a small park of dead grass edged with dying palms and an asphalt spur where drivers lean against their cabs, surveying the crush of tourist traffic. Tom could park the Subaru, safe in its shiny, uninsured Americanness, and bargain for a cab. Too late. Traffic carries him past the turnoff. His sunglasses are so clouded with baby fingerprints that he hands them to Nina to burnish on her skirt, hoping that her gesture will clear his mind as well.

What he wants wiped away is a scene: himself, growling like an airplane, aiming a spoon at Griffin's mouth, while in his high chair Wills yelled, "Da! Da-da!" Nina came up behind, putting an arm around Tom's neck, weighing against him until he knew from the tightening helplessness of her hold that something was wrong and asked, "O.K., what?" She said, "I am," and he had to look from the brilliant blue slip of litmus paper into her eyes, also brilliant, reading there that until he too saw this proof, she had not believed it. "Oh, Nina, no," he said. "It can't be right."

"It is right. I knew anyway. I feel like before."

Griffin threw his bowl to the floor, and oatmeal splattered Nina's bare feet. She bent to wipe them clean with the sleeve of her sweatshirt, and he couldn't see her face for the fall of her hair when she said, "I can't have another baby."

"I know."

He was agreeing, but she went on as if he hadn't, her voice as furious as when they quarreled. "These two take everything. I'd be gone. I'd disappear. My life would be gone."

He turns his head briefly for Nina to slide his glasses back on. Her touch smarts on his nose, burned from the few desert minutes in which, walking away from the rest stop into an arroyo whose air had the sick shimmer of gasoline-tainted heat, past the inevitable charred tires and shattered glass, he'd found the quartz point. It had a fresh whiteness like salt's, and was weightless as a contact lens, ancient, intact, still pristinely sharp. He'd wished he could walk farther — an archaeologist's constant impulse — but Nina was waiting, and he hadn't worn his baseball cap. Usually he's pretty self-protective. The sun at his dig in Chaco Canyon has an X-ray intensity. He's in the sun a lot. Gone a lot. Nina's needed him, and he just hasn't been home. The sleepless intensity of the twins' first ten months fell almost entirely on her. This time there's anguish in the commonplace recognition that he could have been more careful.

"This traffic," Nina says vaguely.

"Want to stop?"

"Where? And it would wake Wills."

"How's he doing?"

Absurd to ask for the second time in five minutes, but again Nina reassures him, "He's really out. He's fine," the tenderness in her tone referring backward, as she assumes his anxiety does, to ten months ago, to a relief so pure that time has scarcely diluted it. His brother was fine, but Wills, too small, spent his first week in neonatal care, heels periodically pricked for blood, fists small as violin scrolls, chapped skin distressingly red against sterile cotton; even his mewing sounded raw, fetal, exposed. Nina would not touch him. The nurses said this was not an uncommon response. It wasn't unusual, even, that Nina didn't want to name him. Attachment, at this point, seemed too dangerous, but a touch or a name would be good signs. Under the heat lamp's mild aura the newborn waited, silver disks taped to his chest, wires flexing minutely with his breathing, illumined dials presiding, until one night Nina, stepping cautiously across the trailing wires, stroked his cheek. His head jerked, his eyes opened to her gaze. In a corner, there was a rocking chair. The nurses whispered back and forth. Wills gained two ounces — three — to weigh four and a half pounds. Rocking, Nina looked up at Tom as if she didn't remember him. The baby that might not make it was always crying,

Nina's head bent until her lips grazed his hair, repeating the name she'd given him: Will, to add, with each repetition, a feather's weight to the side opposite death. Tom was stunned, when once a vial of the baby's blood was carried past him, by the wish to cry out.

Ten days, then two weeks. Their neighbor Carmelita Díaz had moved into their house, taking over Griffin. Though he needed a way to pass the time, there were only so many phone calls Tom could stand to make, so many quarters he could stand to send *chinging* into the pay phone in the corridor. Once as he waited there, about to dial his home number again, a night-gowned girl in labor approached, wheeling her IV stand, stopping to brace herself against a wall when a contraction hit. Tom found himself wanting to ask, as her breathing eased, if he could do something, get her something, but his T-shirt was sweated through under the arms; he probably smelled of his own sick tension. He hung up the phone. He went to the window: outside was a July evening, birds skimming past, cumulonimbus clouds boiling up over the Sangre de Cristos. Tom leaned his forehead and forearm against glass alive with the permanent, mute, scarcely perceptible tremor of air-conditioning, while the girl, with small moans, rode out another contraction.

In the end, they were lucky: Wills weighing five pounds, they went home, but the emotional constellation formed in neonatal care subversively persists. It's Wills whose hold on his parents is the more potent and infatuated, Griffin who chose to wean himself abruptly, biting Nina whenever she unbuttoned for him. Letting himself in one evening, wondering at the silence, Tom padded in stocking feet through the house to find Nina asleep in a pile of dirty laundry, the naked twins crawling around her. As Tom caught Wills, Griffin peed, crowing, on Tom's favorite shirt. It was an hour before Tom got both boys bathed and in bed, and still Nina lay dreaming in a welter of sheets and shirts and small overalls.

"Did we lose a dirty diaper in here?" Tom asks. "No," Nina says shortly. A lick of red hair, loosed from her chignon, clings to Nina's nape, and her freckles are out in force. Six lanes of idling American cars are the Avenida de la Revolución. Neon ice in cones: their vendor, a pretty girl ducking to Tom's window, smiles brightly to show missing front teeth. Nina shakes her head, and the girl is gone. Glacierlike, the glittering cars grind forward in concerted, decisive inches. Nina bites her thumbnail in rapid, critical clicks. What her ob-gyn in Santa Fe gently told Nina was that abortions are not considered safe before six weeks. She was — the sonogram proved — only four weeks along. The wait is now almost behind them. The abortion is scheduled for Monday, the day after tomorrow, in Santa Fe, but they couldn't have stood waiting at home.

When a street opens to their right, Tom tries it. "How hot do you think it is?" Nina says. "Do you know where we're going?"

"*Is* there a dirty diaper lost in here?" Tom demands, with such miserable rudeness that she scrabbles underfoot even as he chooses street after street for their increasing emptiness, and the buildings on either side grow smaller, meeker, older, and more foreign, their plaster no longer pink or turquoise but dusty ocher, no neon advertising *cerveza,* no iron flourishes. When Nina sits up, having found nothing, the world is poor and shut against them.

"I hate this," she says.

"Well, we're lost." Desperately, he's trying to reconstruct the turns he made, each on the spur of the moment, no logic linking them, when Nina says, "Look," and a bicycle whisks alongside agilely as a trotting dog. The bicycle's crouching child, a wing of black hair falling just shy of his eyes, asks Tom, "Where to?" This phrase exhausts the boy's English and he can only, pitched forward optimistically over the handlebars, wait on Tom's answer; he does this by gracefully, agreeably coasting, adding not a pedal's stroke of pressure to his sweet selling job.

Nina leans across Tom, her hand on his leg, and asks in Spanish to be led to the big shopping *mercado, por favor.* The bicycle flicks away, down an even narrower street, and Tom asks, "Did we have a deal?"

"He's showing off," Nina says, "but yes."

"What are you getting us into?" Tom wrenches the Subaru into the turn, but it's tight, and he's glancing back to check the fender when Nina cries "No!" in time for Tom to brake, the Subaru jolting to a stop, the boy inches before them, holding up his arms to show no harm was done. Nina calls, *"¡Oye, chico, demasiado cerca!"*

"Can you get him back? I'm going to get out and scream at him. That was fucking dangerous."

"In what language?"

"He'd get it."

"He thought he'd lost his rich customers," Nina says, "plus he's a little macho."

"Now where are we?" Tom asks, because this street is wider, opening into another, where spandex-legged girls balance on high heels and iron arabesques guard shop windows. Here it is again, the blazing Avenida, traffic locked tight, and Tom hammers the wheel with a fist.

"It's O.K., it's O.K.," Nina says.

"How is this O.K.?"

"So he made a mistake. He can't be more than ten."

"I should never have followed him," Tom says, and then, "Did you notice his hand?"

"His hand?"

"He's got it bandaged in something filthy."

"All I saw was his face. His face is beautiful."

"I haven't given him a dime," Tom says, "and he's sitting out there for us in that sun."

Tremors of movement run toward them through the traffic. The boy waits for an opening to the right, taking it so fast that Tom pops his turn signal and

begs over his shoulder for a way in. Granted, by an Isuzu pickup; Nina waves
thanks, and the boy shoots away again, another lane over, behind a refrigerator truck.

"I'm going to lose him again if he's not careful."

"Pay attention."

"This is his fault," Tom insists, because it's infuriating, the adroit bicycle,
the blocked traffic unpredictably spurting ahead, the glare he's squinting into
when Nina cries out. Something thumps into them and spills with a raggedly
rolling momentum across the hood and down. He has automatically slowed
and stopped, he has even assured himself from the rearview that he won't get
hit from behind, because while his fear is great, it has endowed Tom with the
lucidity of adrenaline, plowing him through a single vast thought at a time as
everything around him shudders, slows, and stalls, and the beautiful life he
has lived until this moment breaks off and floats away.

Nina pleads, "Don't go," in a tone so passionate and clear that he listens
to her; he stops, thinking she knows something he's missed, but of course she
doesn't, and though he hates leaving her now he answers in a voice as clear as
her own, "I killed him," and climbs from the car to crouch at what should be
the body of the boy and is, instead, *instead,* a khaki duffel from which, by lifting and violently shaking, he spills five pairs of boots, their leather superheat-
edly slick in the sun, unreal, real. From nearby cars, he is called a whore's son,
an idiot, a *chingal,* but he feels an exquisite high, setting each miraculous boot
onto its sharp-toed shadow. Nina is squatting, asking, "Are you all right?"

"I'm wonderful."

"Please don't lose it. Not now."

They stand up together. He takes her sunglasses off for the first time that
day to tell her eyes "I love you."

"I know."

"How are you? Are you O.K.?"

"I'm fine," she says, but the bearded guy who's climbing out of the
Mercedes in front of them, having heard Tom's question, feels obscurely bound
to repeat it, and when Nina doesn't answer, he tries Tom. "How are you? How
is she?" He's wearing a Dodgers cap, and mirror shades; little of his expression
shows. "I'm a doctor," he adds.

"What's with the boots?" Tom asks, over the symphony of horns and
insults.

"I bring my boots down here to get them reheeled. A Mexican guy does it
for me. Hospital floors wear them right down. We're having one hell of a fight,
and she says she can't stand it, and chucks these boots out the window before
I can stop her. Throws the back door right open. She's always throwing things
of mine away. Sometimes I come home after a long day to find two dozen shirts
on the lawn, flung all over, getting rained on by the sprinklers. Next time we
come down to Juárez it's for a divorce." He shakes his head heavily. "My insurance is taking care of this." He flicks through a satiny black wallet for a card.

"Good," Tom says.

Nina says, "We're leaving. I'm driving," hooking her sunglasses; Tom had forgotten he had them. She tells the bearded doctor, "We never want to hear from you. Never, got it?"

The guy appeals to Tom — "You should take this" — but Nina drops the card into the street. Nina drives, and either Juárez does not confuse her or the accident has, oddly, cleared her mind. A small street with one pretty restaurant in its middle appears for her. They park under palms. Inside, the restaurant is wonderfully cold and dark. Nina deciphers the handwritten menu while Wills peels cellophane from a saltine. The waitress stops to admire Wills's corn-silk blondness before liberating him from his high chair and waltzing him away.

"I should trust this, but I don't," Nina says, and follows. From the kitchen comes high, ecstatic Spanish — a baby party. The fuss is even worse when both twins are together. Tom agrees with himself that he's light-headed and should eat. The waitress reappears, alone but bearing huge plates. Tom tarts up his Tecate with salt and lime. In the poster above him, the bull's head is lowered, the cape soars out, and the matador's golden backside is beautiful as a girl's.

"It's nice you didn't go crazy back there with that guy," Nina says, returning to buckle Wills into his chair.

"I was so scared it was that kid I hit."

"You told me, 'I killed him.'"

"I remember."

"'I killed him.'"

"Well, didn't you think that?"

"I didn't think it was him you hit, no. You weren't being rational."

"So I'm the one who panics," he marvels, meaning he very slightly doubts her word. He doubts he went through those frantic emotions alone.

"Do you know that story Paula tells?" Paula is a friend of theirs, an anthropologist working in Cuzco; he nods, and she goes on. "The earthquake wakes her in the middle of the night, and she grabs her husband, and they're flat in the bed with fear, and it's this long, long time for them before they think of the baby in his crib across the room."

"And?"

"Don't be like that. Don't expect me to be like that."

"I still don't understand."

"I mean" — she sets her fork down — "Paula fears for herself. That's natural. You feared for that boy. That's natural. All I think of is Wills right behind us in his car seat, strapped in, safe, quiet, O.K., and my fear stops right there, and that's natural. I'm not going to judge the way any of us responds to things. In what people feel, they're alone."

"But that's so lonely," Tom says. "I couldn't stand to believe that."

"You want to know the first time I even remembered that boy? When we got back into the car and traffic had carried him away, I thought, 'He's not going to get paid.' Then I felt sorry for him."

Tom says, "His instinct would be not to hang around trouble. The cops could come."

Wills oils a piece of avocado with saliva and skates it around his tray. Nina says, "Eat it, Wills. Eat it. Eat it." Wills says, "Da fix," and sweeps it to the floor. He trades stares with his mother, angelic sweetness on his side, maternal inscrutability on hers. Nina says, "I want to go home *now*."

Under a half-moon, the border has backed up into a vast plain of taillights in which the only moving things are beggars. Tom hangs his hand out the window, but when a crippled girl lifts twenty dollars from his fingers and seesaws away on her crutches, he feels nothing, no more than if the wind had blown it away. U.S. Customs is the distant waist of the hourglass, letting a red grit of taillights tick through. In the seat behind him, Nina nurses Wills, being discreet because now and then a beggar leans right into the window, having observed that the driver is vulnerable, is guilty, will give. Though Tom empties his wallet, Nina says nothing. She doesn't say, "Save at least something." Nursing, Wills fools around, cooing to the breast. "I wish I was you," Tom tells Nina.

"Why?"

"Because all you do is sit there, and he gets what he needs."

Tom keeps the Subaru nuzzled up against the rear of an old Ford pickup. Four men are sleeping there, dirty straw hats slanted down. When the truck reaches Customs, the inspector lowers his clipboard and lets his flashlight wake the men. He orders them out. They clamber down, standing ashamed in the concentrated light of waiting cars.

"These guys could take forever," Tom tells Nina. "They're Mexican, crossing on a big night. I'd be suspicious."

"Of what?"

"Don't you worry that Carmelita's husband comes and goes this way?"

Carmelita's husband periodically disappears back to his Oaxacan hometown. "Sure," Nina says. "But he's paid somebody here. He knows how to get away with it. I'm not even sure she'd mind if he went to jail."

"The last time he was home, I could hear them making love," Tom says.

"What do you mean, you could hear them?"

She's not going to like this part. "It was when you had the flu and she stayed over. They were on the floor of the babies' room."

"My God," Nina says. "She's fired."

"They weren't loud. It was just their voices, talking."

"Were they happy?"

He thinks. "Yes, they were happy. I think so." He waits a moment. "Nina, we'll be happy again. We'll be fine."

"You don't wish you were me," she says.

She's still behind him, so he can't see her. "Why don't I?"

"You couldn't stand to feel what I'm feeling."

The four men swing themselves in, the pickup rolls forward, and Nina and Tom are asked what country they're citizens of. The flashlight splashes the backseat bright as daylight and starts Wills crying, and he cries as they're waved through, he cries all the way through an El Paso abandoned for Saturday night, he cries at the desk under the disapproving gaze of the clerk and up the elevator of the hotel, the first hotel Tom noticed, Nina holding Wills and humming against his head. Somebody, some drunk, has punched all the buttons, and Wills cries in gusting wails until finally, as the elevator doors break apart on a last genteelly lit and carpeted corridor, he quiets.

Tom lugs bags around and settles them in while Nina bathes Wills. When Tom looks in on them, the mother leaning into the tub, the baby standing up sucking a washcloth, Nina yawns. "I can't stay awake," she says. "Please stay awake," he says, "we have to talk," but once she's put Wills down, singing him through his resistance to yet another strange place, she drags her T-shirt off, her shoulder blades set tight with fatigue, her bare back brilliant in the moment before the bathroom door closes. Fresh water is run into the baby's leftover bath, a hairbrush clicks down against the sink, and then Tom hears her gratefulness as she enters the water, the skid of her bottom against porcelain, her chin tilted up, he imagines, so that her head can rest against the rim. While still distantly conscious of needing to stay awake, he's asleep. He's almost asleep. Wills whimpers and is shushed. Nina's in bed, then, and to his surprise she wants to make love. When they're done, she's still lying across him, breathing past his ear into the pillow; she says, "Sadness. Just such sadness" — answer to a question he can't remember asking. She kisses him before he can say "What?" His tongue finds the imprecision in her front teeth, that minute edge of overlap, and maybe because he's so tired he thinks something strange: if they were buried just like this, then someone unearthing Nina's skull could see that same flaw a hundred, a thousand, years from now, could even touch it, could be that far from now and not know what to feel.

Questions for Discussion

1. Why are Nina and Tom going to Ciudad Juárez? What does this trip represent for them? How is Juárez and the drive through it used as a backdrop for Nina and Tom's problems?

2. Characterize the relationship between Tom and Nina. Why does Tom wish he were Nina? Why does Nina feel he would be unhappy if he were her? Which character has a more realistic outlook?

3. In what ways are social status and economic need presented as issues in the story?

4. Why are the parents bonded differently to each twin? Why did Nina name the twin who had to be in neonatal care Will? How have the twins affected the couple's decision to have the abortion?

5. What is the significance of the image of time and geology at the end of the story? How have Tom and Nina been affected by their experiences on the trip?

Ideas for Writing
1. Write an essay that discusses the story's perspective on abortion. Would you consider the story critical of abortion as a choice, or does it seem neutral in its presentation of the characters' decisions on the issue?
2. Write a story based on a dialogue between a male character and a female character about a controversial social issue that relates to gender.

REGINALD McKNIGHT   (b. 1958)

Born in Germany, Reginald McKnight served in the U.S. Marine Corps before attending Colorado College, where he received his B.A. in 1981. McKnight then left the United States again, this time to teach English in Senegal, an experience that provided material for his first collection of stories, *Montaha's Eclipse* (1988), which won the Foundation Award. After receiving his M.A. from the University of Denver in 1987, he devoted himself to teaching and writing, first at Metropolitan State University in Denver and, since 1989, at the University of Pittsburgh. McKnight has written a hallucinatory novel set in Senegal, *On the Bus* (1990), and a second collection of stories, *The Kind of Light That Shines on Texas* (1992), which contains the following story.

McKnight's fiction focuses on characters he describes as "deracinated African Americans who came of age after the civil rights struggle. . . . They lose their culture sometimes, but not their color that calls up fear, rage, and derision. . . . And often in these rootless blacks a self-hatred takes hold, or a pathological passiveness, an emptiness, and this is what I've written about."

The Kind of Light That Shines on Texas   (1992)

I never liked Marvin Pruitt. Never liked him, never knew him, even though there were only three of us in the class. Three black kids. In our school there were fourteen classrooms of thirty-odd white kids (in '66, they considered Chicanos provisionally white) and three or four black kids. Primary school in primary colors. Neat division. Alphabetized. They didn't stick us in the back, or arrange us by degrees of hue, apartheidlike. This was real integration, a ten-to-one ratio as tidy as upper-class landscaping. If it all worked, you could have ten white kids all to yourself. They could talk to you, get the feel of you, scrutinize you bone deep if they wanted to. They seldom wanted to, and that was fine with me for two reasons. The first was that their scrutiny was irritating. How do you comb your hair—why do you comb your hair—may I please touch your hair — were the kinds of questions they asked. This is no way to feel at home. The second reason was Marvin. He embarrassed me. He smelled bad, was at least two grades behind, was hostile, dark skinned, homely, close-mouthed. I feared him for his size, pitied him for his dress, watched him all the time. Marveled at him, mystified, astonished, uneasy.

He had the habit of spitting on his right arm, juicing it down till it would glisten. He would start in immediately after taking his seat when we'd finished with the Pledge of Allegiance, "The Yellow Rose of Texas," "The Eyes of Texas Are upon You," and "Mistress Shady." Marvin would rub his spit-flecked arm with his left hand, rub and roll as if polishing an ebony pool cue. Then he would rest his head in the crook of his arm, sniffing, huffing deep like black-jacket boys huff bagsful of acrylics. After ten minutes or so, his eyes would close, heavy. He would sleep till recess. Mrs. Wickham would let him.

There was one other black kid in our class, a girl they called Ah-so. I never learned what she did to earn this name. There was nothing Asian about this big-shouldered girl. She was the tallest, heaviest kid in school. She was quiet, but I don't think any one of us was subtle or sophisticated enough to nickname our classmates according to any but physical attributes. Fat kids were called Porky or Butterball; skinny ones were called Stick or Ichabod. Ah-so was big, thick, and African. She would impassively sit, sullen, silent as Marvin. She wore the same dark blue pleated skirt every day, the same ruffled white blouse every day. Her skin always shone as if worked by Marvin's palms and fingers. I never spoke one word to her, nor she to me.

Of the three of us, Mrs. Wickham called only on Ah-so and me. Ah-so never answered one question, correctly or incorrectly, so far as I can recall. She wasn't stupid. When asked to read aloud she read well, seldom stumbling over long words, reading with humor and expression. But when Wickham asked her about Farmer Brown and how many cows, or the capital of Vermont, or the date of this war or that, Ah-so never spoke. Not one word. But you always felt she could have answered those questions if she'd wanted to. I sensed no tension, embarrassment, or anger in Ah-so's reticence. She simply refused to speak. There was something unshakable about her, some core so impenetrably solid, you got the feeling that if you stood too close to her she could eat your thoughts like a black star eats light. I didn't despise Ah-so as I despised Marvin. There was nothing malevolent about her. She sat like a great icon in the back of the classroom, tranquil, guarded, sealed up, watchful. She was close to sixteen, and it was my guess she'd given up on school. Perhaps she was just obliging the wishes of her family, sticking it out till the law could no longer reach her.

There were at least half a dozen older kids in our class. Besides Marvin and Ah-so there was Oakley, who sat behind me, whispering threats into my ear; Varna Willard with the large breasts; Eddie Limon, who played bass for a high school rock band; and Lawrence Ridderbeck, whom everyone said had a kid and a wife. You couldn't expect me to know anything about Texan educational practices of the 1960s, so I never knew why there were so many older kids in my sixth grade class. After all, I was just a boy and had transferred into the school around midyear. My father, an air force sergeant, had been sent to Viet Nam. The air force sent my mother, my sister Claire, and me to Connolly Air Force Base, which during the war housed "unaccompanied wives." I'd been to so many different schools in my short life that I ceased wondering about their differences. All I knew about the Texas schools is that they weren't afraid to flunk you.

Yet though I was only twelve then, I had a good idea why Wickham never once called on Marvin, why she let him snooze in the crook of his polished arm. I knew why she would press her lips together, and narrow her eyes at me whenever I correctly answered a question, rare as that was. I knew why she badgered Ah-so with questions everyone knew Ah-so would never even consider answering. Wickham didn't like us. She wasn't gross about it, but it was clear she didn't want us around. She would prove her dislike day after day with little stories and jokes. "I just want to share with you all," she would say, "a little riddle my daughter told me at the supper table th'other day. Now, where do you go when you injure your knee?" Then one, two, or all three of her pets would say for the rest of us, "We don't know, Miz Wickham," in that skin-chilling way suckasses speak, "where?" "Why, to Africa," Wickham would say, "where the knee grows."

The thirty-odd white kids would laugh, and I would look across the room at Marvin. He'd be asleep. I would glance back at Ah-so. She'd be sitting still as a projected image, staring down at her desk. I, myself, would smile at Wickham's stupid jokes, sometimes fake a laugh. I tried to show her that at least one of us was alive and alert, even though her jokes hurt. I sucked ass, too, I suppose. But I wanted her to understand more than anything that I was not like her other nigra children, that I was worthy of more than the non-attention and the negative attention she paid Marvin and Ah-so. I hated her, but never showed it. No one could safely contradict that woman. She knew all kinds of tricks to demean, control, and punish you. And she could swing her two-foot paddle as fluidly as a big league slugger swings a bat. You didn't speak in Wickham's class unless she spoke to you first. You didn't chew gum, or wear "hood" hair. You didn't drag your feet, curse, pass notes, hold hands with the opposite sex. Most especially, you didn't say anything bad about the Aggies, Governor Connolly, LBJ, Sam Houston, or Waco. You did the forbidden and she would get you. It was that simple.

She never got me, though. Never gave her reason to. But she could have invented reasons. She did a lot of that. I can't be sure, but I used to think she pitied me because my father was in Viet Nam and my uncle A.J. had recently died there. Whenever she would tell one of her racist jokes, she would always glance at me, preface the joke with, "Now don't you nigra children take offense. This is all in fun, you know. I just want to share with you all something Coach Gilchrest told me th'other day." She would tell her joke, and glance at me again. I'd giggle, feeling a little queasy. "I'm half Irish," she would chuckle, "and you should hear some of those Irish jokes." She never told any, and I never really expected her to. I just did my Tom-thing. I kept my shoes shined, my desk neat, answered her questions as best I could, never brought gum to school, never cursed, never slept in class. I wanted to show her we were not all the same.

I tried to show them all, all thirty-odd, that I was different. It worked to some degree, but not very well. When some article was stolen from someone's locker or desk, Marvin, not I, was the first accused. I'd be second. Neither Marvin, nor Ah-so nor I were ever chosen for certain classroom honors —

"Pledge leader," "flag holder," "noise monitor," "paper passer outer," but Mrs. Wickham once let me be "eraser duster." I was proud. I didn't even care about the cracks my fellow students made about my finally having turned the right color. I had done something that Marvin, in the deeps of his never-ending sleep, couldn't even dream of doing. Jack Preston, a kid who sat in front of me, asked me one day at recess whether I was embarrassed about Marvin. "Can you believe that guy?" I said. "He's like a pig or something. Makes me sick."

"Does it make you ashamed to be colored?"

"No," I said, but I meant yes. Yes, if you insist on thinking us all the same. Yes, if his faults are mine, his weaknesses inherent in me.

"I'd be," said Jack.

I made no reply. I was ashamed. Ashamed for not defending Marvin and ashamed that Marvin even existed. But if it had occurred to me, I would have asked Jack whether he was ashamed of being white because of Oakley. Oakley, "Oak Tree," Kelvin "Oak Tree" Oakley. He was sixteen and proud of it. He made it clear to everyone, including Wickham, that his life's ambition was to stay in school one more year, till he'd be old enough to enlist in the army. "Them slopes got my brother," he would say. "I'mna sign up and git me a few slopes. Gonna kill them bastards deader'n shit." Oakley, so far as anyone knew, was and always had been the oldest kid in his family. But no one contradicted him. He would, as anyone would tell you, "snap yer neck jest as soon as look at you." Not a boy in class, excepting Marvin and myself, had been able to avoid Oakley's pink bellies, Texas titty twisters, moon pie punches, or worse. He didn't bother Marvin, I suppose, because Marvin was closer to his size and age, and because Marvin spent five-sixths of the school day asleep. Marvin probably never crossed Oakley's mind. And to say that Oakley hadn't bothered me is not to say he had no intention of ever doing so. In fact, this haphazard sketch of hairy fingers, slash of eyebrow, explosion of acne, elbows, and crooked teeth, swore almost daily that he'd like to kill me.

Naturally, I feared him. Though we were about the same height, he out-weighed me by no less than forty pounds. He talked, stood, smoked, and swore like a man. No one, except for Mrs. Wickham, the principal, and the coach, ever laid a finger on him. And even Wickham knew that the hot lines she laid on him merely amused him. He would smile out at the classroom, goofy and bashful, as she laid down the two, five or maximum ten strokes on him. Often he would wink, or surreptitiously flash us the thumb as Wickham worked on him. When she was finished, Oakley would walk so cool back to his seat you'd think he was on wheels. He'd slide into his chair, sniff the air, and say, "Somethin's burnin. Do y'all smell smoke? I swanee, I smell smoke and fahr back here." If he made these cracks and never threatened me, I might have grown to admire Oakley, even liked him a little. But he hated me, and took every opportunity during the six-hour school day to make me aware of this. "Some Sambo's gittin his ass broke open one of these days," he'd mumble. "I wanna fight somebody. Need to keep in shape till I git to Nam."

I never said anything to him for the longest time. I pretended not to hear him, pretended not to notice his sour breath on my neck and ear. "Yep," he'd whisper. "Coonies keep ya in good shape for slope killin." Day in, day out, that's the kind of thing I'd pretend not to hear. But one day when the rain dropped down like lead balls, and the cold air made your skin look plucked, Oakley whispered to me, "My brother tells me it rains like this in Nam. Maybe I oughta go out at recess and break your ass open today. Nice and cool so you don't sweat. Nice and wet to clean up the blood." I said nothing for at least half a minute, then I turned half right and said, "Thought you said your brother was dead." Oakley, silent himself, for a time, poked me in the back with his pencil and hissed, "*Yer* dead." Wickham cut her eyes our way, and it was over.

It was hardest avoiding him in gym class. Especially when we played murderball. Oakley always aimed his throws at me. He threw with unblinking intensity, his teeth gritting, his neck veining, his face flushing, his black hair sweeping over one eye. He could throw hard, but the balls were squishy and harmless. In fact, I found his misses more intimidating than his hits. The balls would whizz by, thunder against the folded bleachers. They rattled as though a locomotive were passing through them. I would duck, dodge, leap as if he were throwing grenades. But he always hit me, sooner or later. And after a while I noticed that the other boys would avoid throwing at me, as if I belonged to Oakley.

One day, however, I was surprised to see that Oakley was throwing at everyone else but me. He was uncommonly accurate, too; kids were falling like tin cans. Since no one was throwing at me, I spent most of the game watching Oakley cut this one and that one down. Finally, he and I were the only ones left on the court. Try as he would, he couldn't hit me, nor I him. Coach Gilchrest blew his whistle and told Oakley and me to bring the red rubber balls to the equipment locker. I was relieved I'd escaped Oakley's stinging throws for once. I was feeling triumphant, full of myself. As Oakley and I approached Gilchrest, I thought about saying something friendly to Oakley: Good game, Oak Tree, I would say. Before I could speak, though, Gilchrest said, "All right boys, there's five minutes left in the period. Y'all are so good, looks like, you're gonna have to play like men. No boundaries, no catch outs, and you gotta hit your opponent three times in order to win. Got me?"

We nodded.

"And you're gonna use these," said Gilchrest, pointing to three volleyballs at his feet. "And you better believe they're pumped full. Oates, you start at that end of the court. Oak Tree, you're at th'other end. Just like usual, I'll set the balls at mid-court, and when I blow my whistle I want y'all to haul your cheeks to the middle and th'ow for all you're worth. Got me?" Gilchrest nodded at our nods, then added, "Remember, no boundaries, right?"

I at my end, Oakley at his, Gilchrest blew his whistle. I was faster than Oakley and scooped up a ball before he'd covered three quarters of his side. I aimed, threw, and popped him right on the knee. "One-zip!" I heard Gilchrest shout. The ball bounced off his knee and shot right back into my hands. I hurried my throw and missed. Oakley bent down, clutched the two remaining balls. I remember being amazed that he could palm each ball, run full out, and throw left-handed or right-handed without a shade of awkwardness. I spun, ran, but one of Oakley's throws glanced off the back of my head. "One-one!" hollered Gilchrest. I fell and spun on my ass as the other ball came sailing at me. I caught it. "He's out!" I yelled. Gilchrest's voice boomed, "No catch outs. Three hits. Three hits." I leapt to my feet as Oakley scrambled across the floor for another ball. I chased him down, leapt, and heaved the ball hard as he drew himself erect. The ball hit him dead in the face, and he went down flat. He rolled around, cupping his hands over his nose. Gilchrest sped to his side, helped him to his feet, asked him whether he was OK. Blood flowed from Oakley's nose, dripped in startlingly bright spots on the floor, his shoes, Gilchrest's shirt. The coach removed Oakley's T-shirt and pressed it against the big kid's nose to stanch the bleeding. As they walked past me toward the office I mumbled an apology to Oakley, but couldn't catch his reply. "You watch your filthy mouth, boy," said Gilchrest to Oakley.

The locker room was unnaturally quiet as I stepped into its steamy atmosphere. Eyes clicked in my direction, looked away. After I was out of my shorts, had my towel wrapped around me, my shower kit in hand, Jack Preston and Brian Nailor approached me. Preston's hair was combed slick and plastic looking. Nailor's stood up like frozen flames. Nailor smiled at me with his big teeth and pale eyes. He poked my arm with a finger. "You fucked up," he said.

"I tried to apologize."

"Won't do you no good," said Preston.

"I swanee," said Nailor.

"It's part of the game," I said. "It was an accident. Wasn't my idea to use volleyballs."

"Don't matter," Preston said. "He's jest lookin for an excuse to fight you."

"I never done nothing to him."

"Don't matter," said Nailor. "He don't like you."

"Brian's right, Clint. He'd jest as soon kill you as look at you."

"I never done nothing to him."

"Look," said Preston, "I know him pretty good. And jest between you and me, it's cause you're a city boy —"

"Whadda you mean? I've never —"

"He don't like your clothes —"

"And he don't like the fancy way you talk in class."

"What fancy —"

"I'm tellin him, if you don't mind, Brian."

"Tell him then."

"He don't like the way you say 'tennis shoes' instead of sneakers. He don't like coloreds. A whole bunch of things, really."

"I never done nothing to him. He's got no reason — "

"*And*," said Nailor, grinning, "*and*, he says you're a stuck-up rich kid." Nailor's eyes had crow's-feet, bags beneath them. They were a man's eyes.

"My dad's a sergeant," I said.

"You chicken to fight him?" said Nailor.

"Yeah, Clint, don't be chicken. Jest go on and git it over with. He's whupped pert near ever'body else in the class. It ain't so bad."

"Might as well, Oates."

"Yeah, yer pretty skinny, but yer jest about his height. Jest git im in a head-lock and don't let go."

"Goddamn," I said, "he's got no reason to — "

Their eyes shot right and I looked over my shoulder. Oakley stood at his locker, turning its tumblers. From where I stood I could see that a piece of cotton was wedged up one of his nostrils, and he already had the makings of a good shiner. His acne burned red like a fresh abrasion. He snapped the locker open and kicked his shoes off without sitting. Then he pulled off his shorts, revealing two paddle stripes on his ass. They were fresh red bars speckled with white, the white speckles being the reverse impression of the paddle's suction holes. He must not have watched his filthy mouth while in Gilchrest's presence. Behind me, I heard Preston and Nailor pad to their lockers.

Oakley spoke without turning around. "Somebody's gonna git his skinny black ass kicked, right today, right after school." He said it softly. He slipped his jock off, fumed around. I looked away. Out of the corner of my eye I saw him stride off, his hairy nakedness a weapon clearing the younger boys from his path. Just before he rounded the corner of the shower stalls, I threw my toilet kit to the floor and stammered, "I — I never did nothing to you, Oakley." He stopped, turned, stepped closer to me, wrapping his towel around himself. Sweat streamed down my rib cage. It felt like ice water. "You wanna go at it right now, boy?"

"I never did nothing to you." I felt tears in my eyes. I couldn't stop them even though I was blinking like mad. "Never."

He laughed. "You busted my nose, asshole."

"What about before? What'd I ever do to you?"

"See you after school, Coonie." Then he turned away, flashing his acne-spotted back like a semaphore. "Why?" I shouted. "Why you wanna fight me?" Oakley stopped and turned, folded his arms, leaned against a toilet stall. "Why you wanna fight *me*, Oakley?" I stepped over the bench. "What'd I do? Why me?" And then unconsciously, as if scratching, as if breathing, I walked toward Marvin, who stood a few feet from Oakley, combing his hair at the mirror. "Why not him?" I said. "How come you're after *me* and not *him*?" The room froze. Froze for a moment that was both evanescent and eternal, somewhere between an eye blink and a week in hell. No one moved, nothing happened; there was no sound at all. And then it was as if all of us at the same moment looked at Marvin. He just stood there, combing away, the only body in motion, I think. He combed his hair and combed it, as if seeing only his image, hearing only his comb scraping his scalp. I knew he'd heard me. There's no way he could not have heard me. But all he did was slide the comb into his pocket and walk out the door.

"I got no quarrel with Marvin," I heard Oakley say. I turned toward his voice, but he was already in the shower.

I was able to avoid Oakley at the end of the school day. I made my escape by asking Mrs. Wickham if I could go to the restroom.

"'Restroom,'" Oakley mumbled. "It's a damn toilet, sissy."

"Clinton," said Mrs. Wickham. "Can you *not* wait till the bell rings? It's almost three o'clock."

"No ma'am," I said. "I won't make it."

"Well, I should make you wait just to teach you to be more mindful about . . . hygiene . . . uh things." She sucked in her cheeks, squinted. "But I'm feeling charitable today. You may go." I immediately left the building, and got on the bus. "Ain't you a little early?" said the bus driver, swinging the door shut. "Just left the office," I said. The driver nodded, apparently not giving me a second thought. I had no idea why I'd told her I'd come from the office, or why she found it a satisfactory answer. Two minutes later the bus filled, rolled and shook its way to Connolly Air Base.

When I got home, my mother was sitting in the living room, smoking her Slims, watching her soap opera. She absently asked me how my day had gone and I told her fine. "Hear from Dad?" I said.

"No, but I'm sure he's fine." She always said that when we hadn't heard from him in a while. I suppose she thought I was worried about him, or that I felt vulnerable without him. It was neither. I just wanted to discuss something with my mother that we both cared about. If I spoke with her about things that happened at school, or on my weekends, she'd listen with half an ear, say something like, "Is that so?" or "You don't say?" I couldn't stand that sort of thing. But when I mentioned my father, she treated me a bit more like an adult, or at least someone who was worth listening to. I didn't want to feel like a boy that afternoon. As I turned from my mother and walked down the hall I thought about the day my father left for Viet Nam. Sharp in his uniform, sure behind his aviator specs, he slipped a cigar from his pocket and stuck it in mine. "Not till I get back," he said. "We'll have us one when we go fishing. Just you and me, out on the lake all day, smoking and casting and sitting. Don't let Mamma see it. Put it in y'back pocket." He hugged me, shook my hand, and told me I was the man of the house now. He told me he was depending on me to take good care of my mother and sister. "Don't you let me down, now, hear?" And he tapped his thick finger on my chest. "You almost as big as me. Boy, you something else." I believed him when he told me those things. My heart swelled big enough to swallow my father, my mother, Claire. I loved, feared, and respected myself, my manhood. That day I could have put all of Waco, Texas, in my heart. And it wasn't till about three months later that I discovered I really wasn't the man of the house, that my mother and sister, as they always had, were taking care of me.

For a brief moment I considered telling my mother about what had happened at school that day, but for one thing, she was deep down in the halls of "General Hospital," and never paid you much mind till it was over. For another thing, I just wasn't the kind of person — I'm still not, really — to discuss my problems with anyone. Like my father I kept things to myself, talked about my problems only in retrospect. Since my father wasn't around, I consciously wanted to be like him, doubly like him, I could say. I wanted to be the man of the house in some respect, even if it had to be in an inward way. I went to my room, changed my clothes, and laid out my homework. I couldn't focus on it. I thought about Marvin, what I'd said about him or done to him — I couldn't tell which. I'd done something to him, said something about him; said something about and done something to myself. *How come you're after me and not him?* I kept trying to tell myself I hadn't meant it that way. *That* way. I thought about approaching Marvin, telling him what I really meant was that he was more Oakley's age and weight than I. I would tell him I meant I was no match for Oakley. *See, Marvin, what I meant was that he wants to fight a colored guy, but is afraid to fight you cause you could beat him.* But try as I did, I couldn't for a moment convince myself that Marvin would believe me. I meant it *that* way and no other. Everybody heard. Everybody knew. That afternoon I forced myself to confront the notion that tomorrow I would probably have to fight both Oakley and Marvin. I'd have to be two men.

I rose from my desk and walked to the window. The light made my skin look orange, and I started thinking about what Wickham had told us once about light. She said that oranges and apples, leaves and flowers, the whole multi-colored world, was not what it appeared to be. The colors we see, she said, look like they do only because of the light or ray that shines on them. "The color of the thing isn't what you see, but the light that's reflected off it." Then she shut out the lights and shone a white light lamp on a prism. We watched the pale splay of colors on the projector screen; some people ooohed and aaahed. Suddenly, she switched on a black light and the color of everything changed. The prism colors vanished, Wickham's arms were purple, the buttons of her dress were as orange as hot coals, rather than the blue they had been only seconds before. We were all very quiet. "Nothing," she said after a while, "is really what it appears to be." I didn't really understand then. But as I stood at the window, gazing at my orange skin, I wondered what kind of light I could shine on Marvin, Oakley, and me that would reveal us as the same.

I sat down and stared at my arms. They were dark brown again. I worked up a bit of saliva under my tongue and spat on my left arm. I spat again, then rubbed the spittle into it, polishing, working till my arm grew warm. As I spat, and rubbed, I wondered why Marvin did this weird, nasty thing to himself, day after day. Was he trying to rub away the black, or deepen it, doll it up? And if he did this weird nasty thing for a hundred years, would he spit-shine himself invisible, rolling away the eggplant skin, revealing the scarlet muscle, blue vein, pink and yellow tendon, white bone? Then disappear? Seen through, all colors, no colors. Spitting and rubbing. Is this the way you do it? I leaned forward, sniffed the arm. It smelled vaguely of mayonnaise. After an hour or so, I fell asleep.

I saw Oakley the second I stepped off the bus the next morning. He stood outside the gym in his usual black penny loafers, white socks, high water jeans, T-shirt, and black jacket. Nailor stood with him, his big teeth spread across his bottom lip like playing cards. If there was anyone I felt like fighting, that day, it was Nailor. But I wanted to put off fighting for as long as I could. I stepped toward the gymnasium, thinking that I shouldn't run, but if I hurried I could beat Oakley to the door and secure myself near Gilchrest's office. But the moment I stepped into the gym, I felt Oakley's broad palm clap down on my shoulder. "Might as well stay out here, Coonie," he said. "I need me a little target practice." I turned to face him and he slapped me, one-two, with the back, then the palm of his hand, as I'd seen Bogart do to Peter Lorre in "The Maltese Falcon." My heart went wild. I could scarcely breathe. I couldn't swallow.

"Call me a nigger," I said. I have no idea what made me say this. All I know is that it kept me from crying. "Call me a nigger, Oakley."

"Fuck you, ya black ass slope." He slapped me again, scratching my eye. "I don't do what coonies tell me."

"Call me a nigger."

"Outside, Coonie."

"Call me one. Go ahead."

He lifted his hand to slap me again, but before his arm could swing my way, Marvin Pruitt came from behind me and calmly pushed me aside. "Git out my way, boy," he said. And he slugged Oakley on the side of his head. Oakley stumbled back, stiff-legged. His eyes were big. Marvin hit him twice more, once again to the side of the head, once to the nose. Oakley went down and stayed down. Though blood was drawn, whistles blowing, fingers pointing, kids hollering, Marvin just stood there, staring at me with cool eyes. He spat on the ground, licked his lips, and just stared at me, till Coach Gilchrest and Mr. Calderon tackled him and violently carried him away. He never struggled, never took his eyes off me.

Nailor and Mrs. Wickham helped Oakley to his feet. His already fattened nose bled and swelled so that I had to look away. He looked around, bemused, wall-eyed, maybe scared. It was apparent he had no idea how bad he was hurt. He didn't even touch his nose. He didn't look like he knew much of anything. He looked at me, looked me dead in the eye in fact, but didn't seem to recognize me.

That morning, like all other mornings, we said the Pledge of Allegiance, sang "The Yellow Rose of Texas," "The Eyes of Texas Are upon You," and "Mistress Shady." The room stood strangely empty without Oakley, and without

Marvin, but at the same time you could feel their presence more intensely somehow. I felt like I did when I'd walk into my mother's room and could smell my father's cigars, or cologne. He was more palpable, in certain respects, than when there in actual flesh. For some reason, I turned to look at Ah-so, and just this once I let my eyes linger on her face. She had a very gentle-looking face, really. That surprised me. She must have felt my eyes on her because she glanced up at me for a second and smiled, white teeth, downcast eyes. Such a pretty smile. That surprised me too. She held it for a few seconds, then let it fade. She looked down at her desk, and sat still as a photograph.

Questions for Discussion

1. How does the narrator feel about his fellow African-American classmates, Marvin and Ah-so? What does his attitude toward them reveal about his self-concept and values?

2. What does the attitude of Miss Wickham and her white students toward the African-American students in her class imply about the failure of integration in the Texas schools of the 1960s?

3. What is Miss Wickham's attitude toward the use of physical violence to keep control in the classroom? How do the teachers' attitudes toward violence influence their students?

4. The narrator repeatedly states that his father is fighting in the Vietnam conflict, leaving him as "the man of the house," with extra burdens and responsibilities. How does this extra responsibility influence his behavior at school?

5. What is the significance of the narrator's request to Oakley, "Call me a nigger"? In what ways is this remark directed at three different audiences: Oakley, Marvin, and the narrator himself?

Ideas for Writing

1. Write an essay in which you examine both the short- and long-term effects of the narrator's triumph over Oakley. In what ways is the narrator's "triumph" an ironic one?

2. Write an essay in which you relate the significance of the story's title to the key images and meaning of the story as a whole. At what point in the story is the significance of the title made clear?

DAVID LEAVITT   (b. 1961)

David Leavitt was born in Pittsburgh and grew up in Palo Alto, California; his father was a professor at Stanford University. While studying English at Yale University, Leavitt wrote the short story "Territory," which won the O. Henry Prize. About his early success, Leavitt has said, "I think possibly one thing that was very beneficial to me was the fact that, while I was writing, I was rigorously discussing the history of literature. . . . I know people who are basically uneducated or self-educated who have become wonderful writers. But I think my particular abilities were developed through the process of very formal education."

After his graduation in 1983, Leavitt worked in New York as an assistant editor for a short time before devoting himself full time to writing. He has published two collections of stories, *Family Dancing* (1984) and *A Place I've Never Been* (1990), which includes "Gravity," and two novels, *The Lost Language of Cranes* (1986) and *While England Sleeps* (1993; reissued in a revised edition, 1995). Although Leavitt's stories sometimes explore the tensions between gay men and their families, he sees himself primarily as a writer interested in human relationships that bring comfort and stability to a world with an uncertain future rather than as a spokesperson for a cause. Leavitt is committed to the careful crafting of his fiction: "There's a constant revision going on, and constant rewriting, and constant new writing. At least that's what I try for."

Gravity   (1990)

Theo had a choice between a drug that would save his sight and a drug that would keep him alive, so he chose not to go blind. He stopped the pills and started the injections — these required the implantation of an unpleasant and painful catheter just above his heart — and within a few days the clouds in his eyes started to clear up; he could see again. He remembered going into New York City to a show with his mother, when he was twelve and didn't want to admit he needed glasses. "Can you read that?" she'd shouted, pointing to a Broadway marquee, and when he'd squinted, making out only one or two letters, she'd taken off her own glasses — harlequins with tiny rhinestones in the corners — and shoved them onto his face. The world came into focus, and he gasped, astonished at the precision around the edges of things, the legibility, the hard, sharp, colorful landscape. Sylvia had to squint through *Fiddler on the Roof* that day, but for Theo, his face masked by his mother's huge glasses, everything was as bright and vivid as a comic book. Even though people stared at him, and muttered things, Sylvia didn't care; he could *see*.

Because he was dying again, Theo moved back to his mother's house in New Jersey. The DHPG injections she took in stride — she'd seen her own mother through *her* dying, after all. Four times a day, with the equanimity of a nurse, she cleaned out the plastic tube implanted in his chest, inserted a sterilized hypodermic and slowly dripped the bag of sight-giving liquid into his veins. They endured this procedure silently, Sylvia sitting on the side of the hospital bed she'd rented for the duration of Theo's stay — his life, he sometimes thought — watching reruns of *I Love Lucy* or the news, while he tried not to think about the hard piece of pipe stuck into him, even though it was a constant reminder of how wide and unswimmable the gulf was becoming between him and the ever-receding shoreline of the well. And Sylvia was intricately cheerful. Each day she urged him to go out with her somewhere — to the library, or the little museum with the dinosaur replicas he'd been fond of as a child — and when his thinness and the cane drew stares, she'd maneuver him around the people who were staring, determined to shield him from whatever they might say or do. It had been the same that afternoon so many years ago, when she'd pushed him through a lobbyful of curious and laughing faces, determined that nothing should interfere with the spectacle of his seeing. What a pair they must have made, a boy in ugly glasses and a mother daring the world to say a word about it!

This warm, breezy afternoon in May they were shopping for revenge. "Your cousin Howard's engagement party is next month," Sylvia explained in the car. "A very nice girl from Livingston. I met her a few weeks ago, and really, she's a superior person."

"I'm glad," Theo said. "Congratulate Howie for me."

"Do you think you'll be up to going to the party?"

"I'm not sure. Would it be okay for me just to give him a gift?"

"You already have. A lovely silver tray, if I say so myself. The thank-you note's in the living room."

"Mom," Theo said, "why do you always have to —"

Sylvia honked her horn at a truck making an illegal left turn. "Better they should get something than no present at all, is what I say," she said. "But now, the problem is, *I* have to give Howie something, to be from me, and it better be good. It better be very, very good."

"Why?"

"Don't you remember that cheap little nothing Bibi gave you for your graduation? It was disgusting."

"I can't remember what she gave me."

"Of course you can't. It was a tacky pen-and-pencil set. Not even a real leather box. So naturally, it stands to reason that I have to get something truly spectacular for Howard's engagement. Something that will make Bibi blanch. Anyway, I think I've found just the thing, but I need your advice."

"Advice? Well, when my old roommate Nick got married, I gave him a garlic press. It cost five dollars and reflected exactly how much I felt, at that moment, our friendship was worth."

Sylvia laughed. "Clever. But my idea is much more brilliant, because it makes it possible for me to get back at Bibi *and* give Howard the nice gift he and his girl deserve." She smiled, clearly pleased with herself. "Ah, you live and learn."

"You live," Theo said.

Sylvia blinked. "Well, look, here we are." She pulled the car into a handicapped-parking place on Morris Avenue and got out to help Theo, but he was already hoisting himself up out of his seat, using the door handle for leverage. "I can manage myself," he said with some irritation. Sylvia stepped back.

"Clearly one advantage to all this for you," Theo said, balancing on his cane, "is that it's suddenly so much easier to get a parking place."

"Oh Theo, please," Sylvia said. "Look, here's where we're going."

She leaned him into a gift shop filled with porcelain statuettes of Snow White and all seven of the dwarves, music boxes which, when you opened them, played "The Shadow of Your Smile," complicated-smelling potpourris in purple wallpapered boxes, and stuffed snakes you were supposed to push up against drafty windows and doors.

"Mrs. Greenman," said an expansive, gray-haired man in a cream-colored cardigan sweater. "Look who's here, Archie, it's Mrs. Greenman."

Another man, this one thinner and balding, but dressed in an identical cardigan, peered out from the back of the shop. "Hello there!" he said, smiling. He looked at Theo, and his expression changed.

"Mr. Sherman, Mr. Baker. This is my son, Theo."

"Hello," Mr. Sherman and Mr. Baker said. They didn't offer to shake hands.

"Are you here for that item we discussed last week?" Mr. Sherman asked.

"Yes," Sylvia said. "I want advice from my son here." She walked over to a large ridged crystal bowl, a very fifties sort of bowl, stalwart and square-jawed. "What do you think? Beautiful, isn't it?"

"Mom, to tell the truth, I think it's kind of ugly."

"Four hundred and twenty-five dollars," Sylvia said admiringly. "You have to feel it."

Then she picked up the big bowl and tossed it to Theo, like a football.

The gentlemen in the cardigan sweaters gasped and did not exhale. When Theo caught it, it sank his hands. His cane rattled as it hit the floor.

"That's heavy," Sylvia said, observing with satisfaction how the bowl had weighted Theo's arms down. "And where crystal is concerned, heavy is impressive."

She took the bowl back from him and carried it to the counter. Mr. Sherman was mopping his brow. Theo looked at the floor, still surprised not to see shards of glass around his feet.

Since no one else seemed to be volunteering, he bent over and picked up the cane.

"Four hundred and fifty-nine, with tax," Mr. Sherman said, his voice still a bit shaky, and a look of relish came over Sylvia's face as she pulled out her checkbook to pay. Behind the counter, Theo could see Mr. Baker put his hand on his forehead and cast his eyes to the ceiling.

It seemed Sylvia had been looking a long time for something like this, something heavy enough to leave an impression, yet so fragile it could make you sorry.

They headed back out to the car.

"Where can we go now?" Sylvia asked, as she got in. "There must be someplace else to go."

"Home," Theo said. "It's almost time for my medicine."

"Really? Oh. All right." She pulled on her seat belt, inserted the car key in the ignition and sat there.

For just a moment, but perceptibly, her face broke. She squeezed her eyes shut so tight the blue shadow on the lids cracked.

Almost as quickly she was back to normal again, and they were driving. "It's getting hotter," Sylvia said. "Shall I put on the air?"

"Sure," Theo said. He was thinking about the bowl, or more specifically, about how surprising its weight had been, pulling his hands down. For a while now he'd been worried about his mother, worried about what damage his illness might secretly be doing to her that of course she would never admit. On the surface things seemed all right. She still broiled herself a skinned chicken breast for dinner every night, still swam a mile and a half a day, still kept used teabags wrapped in foil in the refrigerator. Yet she had also, at about three o'clock one morning, woken him up to tell him she was going to the twenty-four-hour supermarket, and was there anything he wanted. Then there was the gift shop: She had literally pitched that bowl toward him, pitched it like a ball, and as that great gleam of flight and potential regret came sailing his direction, it had occurred to him that she was trusting his two feeble hands, out of the whole world, to keep it from shattering. What was she trying to test? Was it his newly regained vision? Was it the assurance that he was there, alive, that he hadn't yet slipped past all her caring, a little lost boy in rhinestone-studded glasses? There are certain things you've already done before you even think how to do them — a child pulled from in front of a car, for instance, or the bowl, which Theo was holding before he could even begin to calculate its brief trajectory. It had pulled his arms down, and from that apish posture he'd looked at his mother, who smiled broadly, as if, in the war between heaviness and shattering, he'd just helped her win some small but sustaining victory.

Questions for Discussion

1. Discuss Theo's mother's recollections of helping her son to see as a boy and helping him as a sick adult to survive. In what double sense is Theo "learning to see" again at this stage in his life?

2. What is the irony of the shopping expedition Theo and his mother go on to buy an engagement present for Theo's cousin Howie?

3. Point out some of the details that give us the impression that Theo is a gay man dying of AIDS. How does the reality of AIDS underscore the relationships and situations portrayed in the story?

4. Interpret the mother's unusual decision to toss Theo the heavy and expensive bowl: What is she trying to accomplish by this gesture? What does the bowl symbolize?

5. Comment on the shift in point of view in the story's final paragraph, from that of Theo's mother to Theo. What do we learn about his attitude toward his illness and his relationship with his mother through this shift?

Ideas for Writing

1. Write a brief narrative in the third person; in the final paragraph shift from one major character's perspective to that of another.

2. In an essay discuss the ways in which the title "Gravity" reflects and focuses the main themes of the story. Consider all the possible meanings and the etymology of the word *gravity*.

APPENDIXES

APPENDIXES

A Brief History
of the Story

The historical sense involves a perception, not only of the pastness
of the past, but of its presence.
　　　— T. S. Eliot, "Tradition and the Individual Talent" (1919)

Tradition is a guide and not a jailer.
　　　— W. Somerset Maugham, "The Summing Up" (1938)

History isn't just a record of the dead past; it is alive around us today in
the form of architecture, political and philosophical positions, and contemporary art and literature, which continue to be influenced by the cultural debates
of the past. Thus when we read a particular story, that story contains a number
of earlier stories and many historical influences, each contained within the
story we are reading in the present, like a set of nesting Russian dolls. Knowing
something about the history of the story form, its gradual emergence as a literary genre, and the literary movements that contributed to its traditions can help
you to understand some of these influences, and thus to appreciate individual
stories in a fuller way.

In a literal sense, history itself can be thought of as an infinite collection
of stories that are told and retold from many vantage points in order to help
make sense of the forces at play in the world. In fact, among the first stories
were oral narratives designed to pass on creation myths, family stories, and
legends. It is not surprising that the earliest collections of written stories were
histories of creation in the form of religious texts such as the Bible and the Rig
Veda. Mythical histories of the affairs of the gods and larger-than-life legendary
heroes were collected in epics such as the *Iliad* and the *Odyssey* (ca. the eighth
century B.C.) of Homer.

Eventually the recording of human events and the relating of great
deeds by human leaders became more important than chronicling divine and
legendary accomplishments. Thus stories of princes and kings, such as those
collected by the Greek historian Herodotus (480–425 B.C.) in his *History*,
became popular, along with the historical narratives of Hebrew leaders and

kings contained in the Old Testament. Thucydides (460–?404 B.C.), considered the greatest historian of ancient Greece, is famous for his long personal narrative covering over twenty years of Athenian life, the *History of the Peloponnesian War*. These early historical narratives, like the legendary epics before them, relied on literary techniques such as invented speeches, heightened dramatic conflicts, and characterizations to make points while holding readers' attention.

Just as every literate culture has collected stories to preserve the heroic accomplishments of humans and gods, people also have a universal need to create imaginative tales intended to entertain while teaching lessons and conveying values; such stories help a culture to maintain its sense of cohesion and purpose. Aesop's *Fables* (from the second century A.D.) provided a series of short, moralistic animal stories that were translated and retold repeatedly. In India, the *Panchatantra* (from the third century A.D.), a collection of related animal and human fables with morals, has remained one of the world's most popular and influential books, its tales translated into every major language of the ancient and modern world. Based on medieval and Roman legends, the *Gesta Romanorum* (ca. 1300), widely available throughout Europe until the eighteenth century, is a collection of fables and tales designed to instruct and amuse. From the Middle East came the *Thousand and One Nights*, based on Persian fairy tales that began to be collected in about A.D. 1000 and eventually evolved into the timeless tales of Scheherazade.

Along with portraits of heroes, fanciful tales, and fables, people have long enjoyed more down-to-earth stories presenting humorous, satirical, and frequently bawdy portraits of daily life. Among the earliest of these, the Latin *Satiricon* of Petronius (from the first century A.D.), is a satirical novel in the form of a series of tales told at the banquet of a wealthy noble. The stories in the *Satiricon* depict the world during the age of the Roman emperor Nero realistically, using a number of distinct fictional characters. In the late medieval and early Renaissance periods, the realistic mode in storytelling was revived in the form of collections of often bawdy tales, such as Giovanni Boccaccio's *Decameron* (composed between 1348 and 1368), a series of stories told by a group of travelers who take refuge in the country during the plague. In the *Decameron* as well as in Geoffrey Chaucer's *Canterbury Tales* (1478), there is an emphasis on vernacular speech and joyous secular love. *The Canterbury Tales*, although written in verse, provided realistic, enduring portraits of contemporary characters on a pilgrimage, including individuals from common backgrounds such as the Miller and the Wife of Bath.

The Influence of Print and the Rise of the Essay

Although it had its origins in China, the printing press was not developed as a method of book production until about 1455, when Johannes Gutenberg of Germany used his metal-type press to produce the first major printed book, the Forty-two-Line Bible, named after the number of lines per printed column. The printing press influenced literature in many ways. It helped to spread literacy, made it possible for works such as *The Canterbury Tales* to reach a larger audience, and helped to standardize authoritative versions of texts. The printing press also gave rise to new types of writing such as the journalistic mass periodical, the personal essay, and the novel,—forms of writing that were not reliant on the traditional oral storytelling traditions.

In France, informal, meditative essays Michaelde Montaigne published (collected in his book *Essais* of 1580) explore the inner world of a reflective author in a way that sometimes suggests the voice of a first, person narrative story. British writers such as Francis Bacon were attracted to the new form and soon began to publish their own essay collections. The satirical descriptive essay gained popularity in Britain in the early eighteenth century as the essays of Joseph Addison and Sir Richard Steele were published in widely read coffeehouse journals such as the *Tatler* and the *Spectator* . Some of these essays— many of them satires of contemporary life—were designed to illustrate points of social etiquette by depicting fictional clubs and characters, as well as creating voices for invented correspondents. Often these essays approached the kind of setting, plot, and characterization found in short stories.

The Rise of the Modern Novel

The novel, a longer literary form whose name literally means "new" (suggesting its links to currents of, change in writing, society, and technology), arose in Europe in the seventeenth century, owning in large part to the ease of printed book production. The form evolved from earlier collections of loosely related tales into longer, more unified narratives organized into chapters focusing on continuous character development and social satire. One of the most popular early novels was the Spanish picaresque work by Miguel de Cenantes, *Don Quixote* (1605; translated into English 1612). In this work the elderly knight Don Quixote de La Mancha, confused by reading historical romances, wanders through Spain in a series of misadventures designed to satirize the gap between the medieval ideal and the realities of contemporary life. Near the end of the seventeenth century the realistic novel of society and manners became popular in Europe with the publication in 1678 of Madame de La Fayette's *La Princesse de Clèves*. In the early eighteenth century the new form of the novel also gained enormous popularity in England. Many consider journalist Daniel Defoe's *Robinson Crusoe* (1719) to be the earliest novel in English; though fictional, it was published as an authentic memoir. Samuel Richardson's *Pamela* (1740) and Henry Fielding's *Joseph Andrews* (1742) are "epistolary" novel—works composed as a series of letters and presenting a number of "voices" in short, linked pieces designed to represent a fictional correspondence. This form has survived in modern novel such a Alice Walker's *The Color Purple* (1982) and in stories that use the letter form (usually revealing the correspondence of one character only) as a type of dramatic monologue.

The popularity of the novel temporarily eclipsed the development of the story as a printed form; this is suggested by the course that Daniel Defoe's work took. Before he began to write novels, Defoe created one of the earliest examples of a carefully plotted ghost story, "A True Relation of the Apparition of Mrs. Veal" (1706). This story was realistic, journalistic in style, and based on current events; however, Defoe wrote only a few more stories and made no real impact on the development of the form.

Romanticism and the Tale

Romanticism helped to revive the popularity of short fiction and to lay the foundation for the modern story. A movement that spanned the first third of the nineteenth century, from the late 1700s until the 1830s, Romanticism was not merely a literary trend but a revolution in thought, feeling, and behavior that was international in scope. Its rise coincided with a wave of national revolt against traditional monarchy that had swept over Europe in the latter years of the eighteenth century. The Romantics rejected traditional moral and political beliefs, emphasized individualism and democracy, criticized technology, and strongly identified with nature and the primitive. In literature, Romanticism emphasized the freedom of the artist to live and create according to individual feelings and personal vision. At the same time, the Romantics were drawn to folk culture and a sympathetic (if idealized) identification with peasant life. Romantic writers often went back into the "primitive" past of myth and legend in order to discover what they believed to be more authentic, deeper ways of

Fairy tales and folk stories, which were very popular during the Romantic period, were important influences on the development of the modern story. The fairy tale is an artistically reworked version of earlier, oral folk tales. Many collections of fairy tales had been published before the romantic period, including Charles Perrault's *Histoires ou contes du temps passè* (1697), the French version of the *Thousand and One Nights* (1714, translated by Antoine Galland), and Charles Mayer's forty-one-volume Cabinet des fées (1785°–89). The clever and somewhat artificial French fairy tales of the eighteenth century were designed to delight both children and adults, instructing children with suitable morals while helping them to solve problems through wit and resourcefulness. The Romantic writers, on the other hand, focused on the irrational, magical, and often violent nature of folk culture. In Germany the Brothers Grimm brought together a collection of traditional German folkstories, Household Tale (1912–15), which in turn influenced the story writers of the German Romantic movement, such as poet and dramatist Henrich von Kleist and E. T. A. Hoffmann, one of the most influential European story writers of the Romantic period. Intensely imaginative and psychologically perceptive, Hoffman wrote several collections. including *Strange Stories* (published in German in 1817 as *Nachstuche*), that were widely translated and influenced the development of fantasy and horror stories in the literatures of Europe, Russia, Latin America, Great Britain, and the United States.

The world of the peasant provided important subject matter and popular settings for Romantic fiction, which favored rural settings and extended descriptions of nature. Sir Walter Scott created novels and stories that explored the medieval past of his native Scotland; his story "Two Drovers" examines a conflict between two Scottish Highlands cattle herders, giving heroic dimension to a peasant lifestyle. In France, Prosper Mérimée also wrote stories that focused on the theme of honor and dignity among peasants, such as "Mateo Falcone" (1833),

America and the Story Form

European Romanticism came to America through British and continental journals as well as through educated, sophisticated Americans who traveled abroad. There had been a tradition of stories of moralistic instruction and "tall tales" in the popular periodicals that had flourished since the mid-1700s in the New World. In the early 1820s the widely traveled Washington Irving brought German Romantic tales such as those by Hoffmann to the American public. In European-influenced horror stories like "The Adventure of the German Student," as well as in tales that drew upon America's native tradition of history, legend, and folklore, such as "The Legend of Sleepy Hollow" and "Rip Van Winkle," Irving continued and elaborated on the Romantic tradition of the tale. His collections, such as the famous *Sketchbook* (1820), were published in England and were well, reviewed abroad, which helped to legitimize the story as an authentically American form of writing for readers used to perceiving foreign authors as superior to writers from the United States.

The success of Irving's tales in turn made it easier for the early-nineteenth-century American creators of short fiction, Nathaniel Hawthorne and Edgar Allen Poe, to gain acceptance. Like Irving, Hawthorne was influenced by local folklore and American history, and the somber New England allegories of *Twice-Told Tales* (1837) helped readers to understand the religious conflicts that helped to mold American character and culture. Poe, who was one of America's earliest literary critics and theorists of the story, admired Hawthorne's artistic control but preferred the atmosphere of the Gothic horror story popular in Europe during the Romantic period. Poe's critical writings on the form, particularly his 1842 review of Hawthorne's *Twice-Told Tales*, argued that the story should be a true work of art, like a painting or a lyric poem, with a single unity of effect rather than existing for the traditional purposes of instruction, entertainment, or character development. Poe created tightly patterned horror stories, such as those collected in his *Tales of the Grotesque and Arabesque* (1839), in which plot and image are elevated to the level of artistic design. Yet Poe also was able to insert realism and logic into his writing; in fact, his interest in rationality and the psychological motivation of the criminal led him to write several classic tales that defined the method of the modern detective story, including "The Murders in the Rue Morgue" (1841) and "The Purloined Letter" (1845).

Although Poe's view of the story was limited and artificial, his emphasis on conscious creation, unity, careful plotting, tend the dominant mood or impression was to have an enormous impact on writers throughout the world, both in the later nineteenth century's "art-for-art's-sake" and symbolist movements and into the modernist movement of the early twentieth century. The translation of Poe's work into French by the poet Charles Baudelaire in the mid-1800s helped to spread ideas about the need for the compression and artistic purity of short fiction among writers around the world.

The Rise of Realism

By the latter part of the nineteenth century, authors began to reject the Romantic emphasis on individual rebellion and the world of dream and fantasy as they grew aware of the increasingly technological and class-oriented nature of both warfare and work in modern society. The Romantic's admiration for nature was replaced by a more scientific concern for the relationship between human beings and the natural world. Influenced by a disillusionment with the brutality of war (as reflected in many of the stories of Guy de Maupassant and the Civil War stories of his American counterparts Ambrose Bierce and Stephen Crane); an increasing awareness of the degrading conditions of urban life and the unhealthy, dangerous, and exploitive working conditions in factories; as well and the plethora of scientific and sociological ideas that emphasized determinism by natural forces and the social order, writers of the later part of the century began to formulate a literary movement known loosely as realism or naturalism. Realist authors included Emile Zola, Gustave Flaubert, and Guy de Maupassant in France; Thomas Hardy in England; and Ambrose Bierce, Stephen Crane, and Kate Chopin in the United States. These writers looked at the working class and peasants with a less idealized perspective than did the Romantics, focusing instead on the overwhelming power of nature, class, and economics. Sexuality was often treated frankly and directly, particularly in the stories of Maupassant and his American disciple, Chopin, while nature was often perceived as an overpowering adversary, indifferent to human desires, as in Crane's "Open Boat" (1898).

Authors of the end of the nineteenth century and the early twentieth century continued to refine the structure and language of their stories and to use symbolism drawn from ordinary life rather than the traditional world of myth and allegory. Influenced by the emerging pictorial forms of photography and the impressionist style in painting, realist writers began to concentrate on brief moments of experience, so that the plot contained fewer events and less action. This "snapshot of reality" approach is seen in the highly descriptive, imagistic stories of Crane and Maupassant and was developed even further by the Russian writer Anton Chekhov, who preferred brief stories with little exposition and focus on the present moment, sharply observed descriptive detail, and vernacular dialogue, with the traditional narrator either dropped or drastically reduced in presence. The writers of this era moved far away from the conception of the tale as an oral form involving a "teller"; instead they attempted to create a sense of the real world within the story—that was so intensely conveyed that the reader could directly experience the feelings and perceptions of the characters. Yet realist writers did not see themselves as simple recorders of reality but as artists of the real. As Maupassant put it, "To make things real on the page consists in giving the complete *illusion* of reality, following the logical order of facts, and not servilely transcribing the pell-mell succession of chronological events in life."

Psychological and Reflective Realism: Henry James and Edith Wharton

Henry James and Edith Wharton were turn-of-the-century American writers who began a movement away from external physical realism and toward a deeper exploration of the inner worlds of sophisticated, well-educated characters. Both read widely and were more influenced by European writers such as Maupassant than by their American contemporaries. James and Wharton came from wealthy backgrounds; both traveled and lived abroad for extended periods. In their stories James and Wharton attempted to achieve unity of vision and control through the use of a third-person-limited—or "central intelligence"—point of view rather than a first—person narrative voice. Perfectionists of style, James and Wharton worked hard to capture the exact nuances of subtle, often intellectual and emotionally oblique conversation. Joseph Conrad referred to James as the "historian of fine consciences"; the same could be said for Wharton. Although concerned with issues of manners and social class, the work of James and Wharton also explored the subtlety of unconscious motivation and the complexity of human psychology and choice. Their settings and characters today seem more artificial than those of the realistic writers (largely because of the restrained, codified social environment in which James and Wharton lived and wrote), but they were realists in their emphasis on a close inspection and recording of actual life, on the in-depth examination of mental and emotional processes and social struggles.

The Modernists

The seeds of the modernist movement are contained within the realist and naturalist stories of the late 1800s, as well as in the psychologically oriented stories of Henry James. The shift to the modernist style was marked by a reduction

of plot and external character development. Influenced by movements in painting that focused more on the artist's subjective perception of reality than on the
object itself, the new focus in the modernist story was the subjective world of
feeling and perception. Modernist stories such as those of experimental writers
of the period after the First World War—James Joyce, Virginia Woolf, D. H.
Lawrence, and Katherine Mansfield—often use only a few main scenes. These
stories often focus on a crucial moment, lasting perhaps only a few minutes, in
which a character experiences a flash of insight or revelation, not fully articu-
lated in philosophical terms but understood primarily through the senses in a
vision that is often described in colorful, imagistic language. Such moments of
insight were called "epiphanies" by the Irish expatriate writer James Joyce, and
the term can be applied to the turning point or climactic moment of many modernist stories. Originating in the "art-for-art's sake" movement, the modernist
story lacked a strong political perspective, but social criticism is nonetheless
implicit in the stories of James Joyce's *Dubliners* (1914), all of which focus on
moments in which the author's lower-middle-class Dublin characters acquire a
heightened realization of the limits and contradictions in Dublin society and values. New Zealand-born Katherine Mansfield also used modernist techniques to
explore themes of class and gender relationships.

Modernist Writers in America

American writers of the 1920s, 1930s, and 1940s—among them
Sherwood Anderson, Ernest Hemingway, Scott Fitzgerald, Katherine Anne
Porter, William Faulkner, and Eudora Welty—studied the European modernist story and applied it in varying degrees applied its methods to their own
work. Anderson in the character sketches and stories contained in his
Winesburg Ohio (1919) and Welty in stories like "Death of a Traveling
Salesman," and "A Worn Path" (1941) tended to use the modernist approach
of following the perceptions and moments of realization of characters who are
essentially isolated and at extreme points of crisis in their lives. Porter adapted
the flowing stream-of-consciousness narrative style developed by Virgina
Woolf and James Joyce in her story "The Jilting of Granny Weatherall, (1930)
Faulkner, although he had a strong historical sensibility, sometimes made use
of a modernist stream-of-consciousness narrative style in which normal sentence boundaries disappear and the reader is propelled directly and unremit-
tingly into the inner universe of a central character—or, as in stories like "A
Rose for Emily" (1930), into the collective perceptions of a small community.
Although he was influenced by the traditions of realism and naturalism,
Hemingway is approached fiction by emphasizing the single scene, the heightened moment of insight, and the disappearance of the narrator—all characteristics of modernist. Yet in stories such as "Hills like White Elephants"
(1927) and in his famous novels, Hemingway was a minimalist writer who
avoided description of feeling and environment; he preferred to strip the story

down, avoiding direct insight into his characters' interior worlds, and focusing instead on seemingly flat, rootless, emotionally numb people seen from without, as in a film.

A Return to Realism

Although modernism explored the possibilities of the story as an art form in tune with the rhythms of twentieth-century life, it failed to satisfy the traditional needs of readers for suspense, development and resolution of conflict, and coherent social perspectives. The late Depression era and World War II and its aftermath brought a need for stories that explored and helped people to make immediate sense of a rapidly changing and materialistic society. Following the Marxist-influenced social realism and protest novels of the late 1930s, many of the British and American stories of the 1940s and 1950s fall back on traditional narrative forms and focus on exploring relationships in families, realistically rendered urban and suburban environments, and tensions in the workplace and the community. Authors such as John Steinbeck, Saul Bellow, and John Cheever use devices of traditional realism combined with selected elements of modernism, such as an adaptation of the epiphany technique, to create stories that examine the changing class structure in America. In Steinbeck's novels and story collections, such as *The Long Valley* (1937), the dispossessed and homeless agricultural workers of the Depression are presented sympathetically, while in Cheever's stories such as "The Five-Forty-Eight" (1958), readers found a group with which many of them could more readily identify—the newly emerging suburban class of commuters. Meanwhile, African-American writers such as Richard Wright, Ralph Ellison, and James Baldwin drew primarily on realism, but they also reveal a sophisticated awareness of symbolism, the use of the inner voice, and the heightened moments of awareness typical of American and European modernism to create a literature that spoke to an emerging audience of educated, socially conscious African-Americans as well as to mainstream readers who were beginning to recognize the racial diversity of American culture.

The Decline of Magazine Fiction

Although some of the American realist writers of the 1940s and 1950s were able to publish their stories in popular periodicals such as the *Saturday Evening Post* and *Collier's*, as had the writers of the pre-war years, the popular periodical was in decline by the mid 1950s, a victim of competition from film and television. Many authors who wished to write realistic stories for middle-class audiences turned either to the lucrative best-selling novel or to film and television scriptwriting.

By the 1960s, except for a handful of urban magazines such as the *New Yorker*, *Harper's*, and the *Atlantic Monthly*, the only outlets for short fiction

were academic journals and nonprofit "small-press" periodicals that were usually supported by grant money. Most authors of short fiction from the 1960s
to the present have made their primary living through teaching literature and
creative writing, although some, such as John Updike, make their living primarily as writers, succeeding through writing best-selling novels. Instead of
killing the short story, these changes have heightened the intellectual level and
the willingness of authors to take risks with experimental writing.

The Postmodern Story

American authors of the 1960s—for instance, Donald Barthelme, Robert
Coover, and John Barth—were influenced by international experimental writers such as James Joyce and Gertrude Stein, Jorge Luis Borges, and Samuel
Beckett, as well as by literary and philosophical movements such as surrealism
and semiotics. Postmodernist writers rejected both the continuous plot as well
as coherent "realistic" characters and settings popular among the writers of the
1940s and 1950s. Unlike modernist stories that aimed for a high literary polish, the postmodern story may seem like a work-in-progress, its story line frequently broken into short fragments of text that rely on juxtaposition, as in
film montage, rather than on linear time lines. As in the experimental writing
of Gertrude Stein and James Joyce, language itself might become the subject
of a postmodernist story, and authors might operate at the level of the sentence
or even of the phrase or word, using repetition and variation of key sentences
and phrases or explorations of varied meanings of a particular word. Narrators
might be character who glide in and out of consciousness, as in the older
stream-of-consciousness style, but their identity is less coherent than in the
modernist story, which, although a subjective distortion of reality, still seem
written with a confidence that there is a fundamental, if at times subjective,
reality to explore. The postmodernist story might at times resemble a dream,
a fantasy, a playful philosophical reflection, or, as in "metafictions" such as
those contained in John Barth's *Lost in the Funhouse* (1968), a meditation on
the creative process itself.

Magic Realism

Despite the sophisticated academic environment that nourished postmodernism lacked a strong subject matter and coherence that would give vitality
and a sense of the magic of fiction to its experiments in style and cognition.
In the 1980s and 1990s short fiction has shifted again back and forth between
fantasy and a kind of realism tempered and expanded by the enormous growth
and discovery of the past hundred years, using a style referred to loosely as
"magic realism." Magic realism owes a significant debt to the dream explorations of surrealism and to the socially critical and fantasy-oriented stories
and parables of the Czech writer Franz Kafka, such as "A Report to an

Academy" (1917). As Kafka did earlier in the century, writers today frequently turn to legend, myth, fairy tale, and fantasy for the forms and material of their stories, updating old myths and tales according to the needs and values of the current era, often combining myth and fantasy with contemporary social satire. Stories written in this new/old form are popular in many parts of the world where folklore, legend, and the oral tradition in storytelling remain popular: Latin America, the Middle East, Pakistan, and India, as well as in the United States in many recent stories by Native American writers as well as those of more "mainstream" Americans. Gabriel García Márquez of Colombia, Clarice Lispector of Mexico, Isabel Allende of Chile, Kobo Abe and Haruki Murakami of Japan, Italo Calvino of Italy, and Naguib Mahfouz of Egypt have all written many stories using elements of magic realism. Recent practitioners of the form in the United States include Louise Erdrich, Leslie Marmon Silko, and Alberto Ríos.

Other contemporary writers use realistic detail to explore heightened or distorted states of awareness, often relying on a firstperson point of view. Stories such as those by Gerald Vizenor, Sandra Cisneros, Louise Erdrich, John Edgar Wideman, Kate Braverman, and Thom Jones often blur the lines between dream, fantasy, and reality with often unreliable or erratic narrators, relating events that may seem cruel and: bizarre but that are perceived by the narrators as normal. Stories of today frequently emphasize characters from impoverished or socially marginalized backgrounds and push the boundaries of familiar and acceptable subject matter; however the techniques used may resemble those of the earlier twentieth century. For instance, the minimalist realist stories of Raymond Carver, were inspired by the writings of Hemingway and Chekhov but who wrote primarily about socially marginal families ravaged by alcoholism, while the stories of David Leavitt combine modernist epiphany story with contemporary subject matter, as in "Gravity" (1990) about a young man in the last stages of AIDS.

The Short Story of Today and Tomorrow: An International Form

Just as the medieval and Renaissance European story tradition was influenced by tales that had their origins in India and the Middle East, key works of the major American and European story writers spread rapidly to Latin American, African, and Asian cultures in the nineteenth century and twentieth centuries through translation, helping to form new, mixed-cultural storytelling traditions. Although the story was from its origins an international form of literature, in the past few decades the form has experienced ever more complex influences. With the increase of travel and immigration to and from developing countries, readers and writers of the United States and Europe have turned increasingly to non-Western writers for knowledge and inspiration. Novelists and story writers in Japan, India, Latin America, Africa, and the Caribbean have been translated into many different languages, frequently attending writer's conferences, teaching, and lecturing in Europe and the United States so that their influence is experienced widely. Stories are now being posted on the World Wide Web for commentary from all parts of the globe, and some innovative writers are using hypertext, the common form of the web itself, to communicate fictional situations, images, and themes in a new, nonlinear fashion. These international influences have opened up the form of the story, as never before; its future potential is truly as large as the planet and just as diverse. It may be that in time a kind of universal story form and voice will emerge from the present rich mixture of styles and forms. Whatever happens, the story of the future remains a bright and vibrant possibility, a possibility constantly nourished and enriched by its tradition and history, yet always open to experiment and innovation.

Suggested Reading

Argulo, Maria-Elena. *Magic Realism: Social Context and Discourse.* New York: Garland, 1995.

Beachcroft, Thomas Owen. *The Modest Art: A Survey of the Short Story in English.* London: Oxford UP, 1968.

Bone, Robert. *Down Home: A History of Afro-American Short Fiction from Its Beginnings to the End of the Harlem Renaissance.* New York: Capricorn, 1975.

Bonheim, Helmut. *The Narrative Modes: Techniques of the Short Story.* Cambridge: D. S. Brewer, 1982.

Current-García, Eugene. *The American Short Story before 1850.* Boston: Twayne, 1985.

Fusco, Richard. *Maupassant and the American Short Story.* University Park: Pennsylvania State UP, 1994.

Hanson, Clare. *Short Stories and Short Fictions. 1880-1980.* London: Macmillan, 1985.

Mann, Susan Garland. *The Short Story Cycle.* New York: Greenwood, 1989.

Peden, Margaret Sayers, ed. *The Latin American Short Story: A Critical History.* Boston: Twayne 1983.

Moser, Charles A., ed. *The Russian Short Story: A Critical History.* Boston: Twayne, 1986.

Stevick, Philip, ed. *The American Short Story. 1900–1945.* Boston: Twayne, 1984.

Tallack, Douglas. *The Nineteenth-Century American Short Story.* London: Routledge, 1993.

Finding and Documenting
Source Materials
for Research Papers

This appendix is divided into two parts. In the first, we offer suggestions about useful source material on short-story writers and the short-story form. In the second, you will find guidelines for documenting sources in your paper and for preparing a list of works cited according to the format recommended by the Modern Language Association.

Useful Source Material on
the Short Story and Its Writers

BOOKS

Check your library's catalog of holdings for books about an author: collections of critical essays, studies by a single critic, biographies, and other works by the author that may shed light on his or her stories (letters, journals, autobiographies, and works or collections of criticism or theory).

The following general works and collections of theory and criticism on the form and other aspects of the story may also be among your library's holdings. See Appendix A for a list of books on story history and the development of the genre.

Bonheim, Helmut. *The Narrative Modes: Techniques of the Short Story.* Cambridge: D. S. Brewer, 1982.

Bruck, Peter. *The Black American Short Story in the Twentieth Century: A Collection of Critical Essays.* Amsterdam: Gruner, 1977.

Hanson, Clare, ed. *Re-reading the Short Story.* New York: St. Martin's, 1989.

Lohafer, Susan. *Coming to Terms with the Short Story.* Baton Rouge: Louisiana State UP, 1983.

Lohafer, Susan, and Jo Aellyn Clarey, eds. *Short Story Theory at a Crossroads.* Baton Rouge: Louisiana State UP, 1989.

May, Charles E. *The New Short Story Theories.* Athens: Ohio UP, 1994.
————. *Short Story Theories.* Athens: Ohio UP, 1976.
O'Connor, Frank. *The Lonely Voice: A Study of the Short Story.* Cleveland: World, 1963.
Trask, Georgianne, and Charles Burkhart, eds. *Storytellers and Their Art.* New York: Doubleday Anchor, 1963.

PERIODICALS

Here are some periodicals that publish short-story criticism.

American Short Fiction
Critique: Studies in Contemporary Fiction
Explicator
Fiction: A Magazine for the Art of Storytelling
Fiction International
International Fiction Review
Journal of the Short Story in English
Modern Fiction Studies
Publications of the Modern Language Association (PMLA)
Review of Contemporary Fiction
Studies in American Fiction
Studies in Short Fiction
University of Texas Studies in Contemporary Spanish-American Fiction

BIOGRAPHICAL AND CRITICAL REFERENCES

Your library's reference section may include multivolume series of literary biography and criticism published annually by Gale Research. For these, check the cumulative index to find out whether the author is included and, if so, in what volume or volumes. Here are some of the more commonly available series.

Contemporary Authors
Contemporary Literary Criticism
Dictionary of Literary Biography
Nineteenth-Century Literary Criticism
Short Story Criticism
Twentieth-Century Literary Criticism

Other helpful encyclopedias include the following.

American Writers
British Writers
Critical Survey of Short Fiction

Reference Guide to Short Fiction
Twentieth-Century Authors
World Authors

BIBLIOGRAPHIES, INDEXES, AND DIGESTS

Use the following to help you find critical articles, reviews, and interviews in periodicals and essay collections. Some are available on-line and on CD-ROM; your reference librarian can help you access these.

American Ethnic Literatures: An Annotated Bibliography
American Short Fiction Criticism and Scholarship, 1959–1977:
    A Checklist
Book Review Digest
Essay and General Literature Index
Fiction Catalog
MLA International Bibliography
Readers' Guide to Periodical Literature

DOCUMENTING SOURCES USING THE MLA FORMAT

The Modern Language Association (MLA) is an international organization devoted to the scholarly study of literature. The format for documenting sources recommended by the MLA is generally used for literary papers in college courses. For an example of a complete student research paper using the MLA format and works-cited page, see the essay by Sage Van Wing in the Louise Erdrich Casebook.

The current MLA format was designed to simplify the process of documenting sources and also to be a check on the tendency of writers to provide an impressive-looking bibliography full of works that they did not consult. In MLA format, every work used in a paper must appear on the works-cited list, which replaces the traditional bibliography for the essay. Likewise, no work may be listed on the works-cited page that is not mentioned or "cited" in the body of the paper. Instead of using footnotes or endnotes, MLA format uses parenthetical citations that must appear after every quotation, paraphrased idea, or summary of an author's ideas in the research paper.

The following text provides a brief explanation and some examples of the most common parenthetical citations and works-cited entries. For more extensive advice on how to write and document a research paper using the MLA style, refer to Joseph Gibaldi's *MLA Handbook*, 4th edition (New York: Modern Language Association, 1995). This edition also presents updated information on working with electronic databases and documenting electronic sources of all kinds.

PARENTHETICAL CITATIONS

Parenthetical citations must be used whenever you quote directly from any source, or paraphrase, summarize, or express an idea that may be traced back to a source. You don't have to use citations when you are expressing your own ideas, interpretations, or conclusions, or commonly known facts about authors or works.

The parenthetical citation—so termed because it is enclosed within parentheses—usually consists of the last name of the author of a source followed directly by the appropriate page number (or numbers), with no comma in between. Commonly a citation comes at the end of a sentence, in which case the final parenthesis is followed by a period.

> Some critics believe that Eudora Welty's work is strongly influenced by the tradition of the modernist story (Smith 101).

When the author's name is mentioned in the sentence or several references are made in the same paragraph to a work by an author whose name has been mentioned, then only the page number goes within the parentheses.

> Julius Lester writes in his introduction to an interview with the writer that "[t]he intensity and passion that characterize [Baldwin's] writing are evident in conversation" (1)

Here are some variations on this basic citation style. Keep in mind that your objective is always to proved enough information in your text so that readers can easily find the full citation in your works-cited list.

Works with two or three authors
(Smith, Jones, and Barrett 25).

Unsigned. titled article or review
("Authors Come to Town" 5).

Unsigned untitled review
(Rev. of *The Bingo Palace* 95).

More than one work by the same author on the works-cited list
You can use a shortened version of the title in this case.

> For James Baldwin, the black American blues may have seemed a "natural vehicle to structure his ideas" (Mosher, "James Baldwin's Blues" 112).

Quotation contained within another work: indirect source
When an interviewer asked Eudora Welty to list her favorite authors, she stated that as a child she "read lots of fairy tales and all the childhood books" (qtd. in Freeman 174).

Citing more than one work in a sentence

Steinbeck's "The Chrysanthemums" begins with an image of "high gray-flannel fog" (492), while Mansfield's "The Garden-Party" begins with the image of "a perfect day . . . Windless, warm, the sky without a cloud" (418).

Citing quotations of four or more lines

Quotations of four or more lines are indented ten spaces and the parenthetical citation follows the final period.

In her essay "Is Phoenix Jackson's Grandson Really Dead?" Eudora Welty talks about ambiguity in fiction:

> It's *all right*, I want to say to the students who write to me, for things to be what they appear to be, and for words to mean what they say. It's all right, too, for words and appearances to mean more than one thing--ambiguity is a fact of life. . . . But it is not all right, not in good faith, for things *not* to mean what they say. (536)

THE WORKS-CITED PAGE

MLA format works-cited pages can be found at the end of several of the student essays included in the six casebooks in *A Web of Stories*. The works-cited page is an alphabetical list of all works mentioned in your text. If the work has one or more authors, alphabetize by the first author's last name (the last name goes first); if there is no author, alphabetize by the first word of the title, excluding the articles "a," "an," or "the." The normal sequence of information in a works-cited entry is (1) author name, (2) title of work, (3) city and publisher (if a book), and (4) date. For stories and articles in collections, as well as for those in periodicals, page numbers of the article or story appear at the end of the entry. Each entry ends with a period, and periods separate the main parts of each entry. The first line of each entry is flush with the left margin; subsequent lines are indented five spaces, as in this example:

Mansfield, Katherine. *The Garden-Party and Other Stories*. Middlesex, England: Penguin, 1951.

If you have more than one work by the same author, subsequent entries by the author do not have to give the author's name; instead, simply provide the rest of the bibliographical information following an initial three hyphens and a period; alphabetize by first main word of title.

Erdrich, Louise. *The Beet Queen*. New York: Holt, 1986.
---. *The Bingo Game*. New York: Harper, 1994.

Here are some of the more common works-cited entries found in literary research; if the type of source you are looking for is not found below, check the *MLA Handbook* or a good college English handbook.

Book by one author
Mann, Susan Garland. *The Short Story Cycle.* New York: Greenwood, 1989.

Book by two or three authors
Chavkin, Allan, and Nancy Feyl Chavkin, eds. *Conversations with Louise Erdrich and Michael Dorris.* Jackson: UP of Mississippi, 1994.

Edited collection or anthology
Hanson, Clare, ed. *Re-reading the Short Story.* New York: St. Martin's, 1989.

Work in an edited collection
Ferguson, Suzanne C. "The Rise of the Short Story and the Hierarchy of Genres." *Short Story Theory at a Crossroads.* Ed. Susan Lohafer and Jo Aellyn Clarey. Baton Rouge: Louisiana State UP, 1989. 176–92.

Article in daily or weekly periodical
Erdrich, Louise. "Where I Ought to Be: A Writer's Sense of Place." *New York Times Review of Books* 28 July 1985: 1+.

Note that the plus sign is used to indicate page numbers that are not consecutive.

Article in a monthly periodical
Wolff, Tobias. "Raymond Carver Had His Cake and Ate It Too." *Esquire* Sept. 1989: 240+.

Article in a scholarly journal: issue number only
Pauly, Thomas H. "'Hop-Frog'--Is the Last Laugh Best?" *Studies in Short Fiction* 11 (1974): 307–09.

Article in a scholarly journal: issues paged separately;
issue and volume numbers
Roth, Martin. "Inside 'The Masque of the Red Death.'" *Substance: A Review of Theory and Literary Criticism* 13.2 (1984): 50–53.

Review
Messud, Claire. Rev. of *The Bingo Palace,* by Louise Erdrich. *Times Literary Supplement* 17 June 1994: 23.

Interview

Plimpton, George. "Eudora Welty: Two Encounters." Interview with Eudora Welty. *Paris Review* 35 (Spring 1995): 258–62.

Translated work

Kawabata, Yasunari. *Palm of the Hand Stories*. Trans. Lane Dunlap and J. Martin Holman. San Francisco: North Point, 1988.

Article in a reference work (dictionary, encyclopedia, etc.)

"Faulkner, William." *The Encyclopedia Americana*. 1993 ed.

Introduction, preface, or afterword

Porter, Katherine Anne. Introduction. *A Curtain of Green and Other Stories*. By Eudora Welty. New York: Harcourt, 1941. xi–xxiii.

Film or video

Hills like White Elephants. Dir. Tony Richardson. Perf. Melanie Griffith and James Wood. Videocassette. HBO Video, 1990.

On-line electronic text

Conrad, Joseph. *Youth and Two Other Stories*. New York: McClure, Phillips, 1903. On-line. U of Virginia Lib. Internet. 2 Oct. 1996.

CONTENT NOTES

The MLA format does permit occasional footnotes in cases where further information needs to be indicated, as in the following example. (The full data on the source would be included in your works-cited list.)

[1]For a more affirmative critical view of Louise Erdrich's *Tracks*, see Robert D. Narveson's review in *Prairie Schooner* (Fall 1990).

Acknowledgments

SELECTIONS

Kōbō Abe, "The Magic Chalk," translated by Alison Kibrick. Originally titled "Maho no Chalk" from *Ningren* (December 1950). Copyright 1950, © 1982, 1985 by Kōbō Abe. Reprinted with the permission of International Creative Management.

Chinua Achebe, "The Madman" from *Girls at War and Other Stories*. Copyright © 1972, 1973 by Chinua Achebe. Reprinted with the permission of Doubleday, a division of Bantam Doubleday Dell Publishing Group, Inc. and Harold Ober Associates, Incorporated.

Isabel Allende, "Phantom Palace," translated from the Spanish by Margaret Sayers Peden, from *The Stories of Eva Luna*. Copyright © 1989 by Isabel Allende. English translation copyright © 1991 by Macmillan Publishing Company. Reprinted with the permission of Scribner, a division of Simon & Schuster, Inc. and Key Porter Books.

Margaret Atwood, "Simmering" from *Murder in the Dark,* published in the United States as *Good Bones and Simple Murders*. Copyright © 1983 by Margaret Atwood. Reprinted with the permission of Doubleday, a division of Bantam Doubleday Dell Publishing Group, Inc. and the author.

Isaac Babel, "Guy de Maupassant," translated by Walter Morison, from *The Collected Stories of Isaac Babel*. Copyright © 1955 by S. G. Philips, Inc. Reprinted with the permission of the publishers.

James Baldwin, "The Rockpile" and "Sonny's Blues" from *Going to Meet the Man* (New York: Vintage Books). "Sonny's Blues" originally appeared in *The Partisan Review.* Copyright © 1957, 1965 and renewed 1985 by James Baldwin. Reprinted with the permission of The James Baldwin Estate.

Toni Cade Bambara, "Raymond's Run" from *Gorilla, My Love*. Copyright © 1972 by Toni Cade Bambara. Reprinted with the permission of Random House, Inc.

John Barth, "Autobiography: A Self-Recorded Fiction" from *Lost in the Funhouse*. Copyright © 1968 by John Barth. Reprinted with the permission of Doubleday, a division of Bantam Doubleday Dell Publishing Group, Inc. and the author.

Donald Barthelme, "The Sandman." Copyright © 1972 by Donald Barthelme. Reprinted with the permission of The Wylie Agency, Inc.

Ann Beattie, "Janus" from *Where You'll Find Me*. Copyright © 1985, 1986 by Irony & Pity, Inc. Reprinted with the permission of Scribner, a division of Simon & Schuster, Inc.

Jorge Luis Borges, "The Book of Sand," translated by Norman Thomas Di Giovanni, from *The Book of Sand*. Copyright © 1971, 1975, 1976, 1977 by Emecee Editores, S.A. Reprinted with the permission of Dutton Signet, a division of Penguin Books USA Inc.

Robert Olen Butler, "Letters from My Father" from *A Good Scent From a Strange Mountain*. Copyright © 1992 by Robert Olen Butler. Reprinted with the permission of Henry Holt and Company, Inc.

Italo Calvino, "The Adventure of a Reader," translated by William Weaver, Archibald Colquhoun and Peggy Wright, from *Difficult Loves*. Copyright 1949, 8 1958 by Guilo Einaudi Editore, Torino. English translation copyright © 1984 by Harcourt Brace & Company. Reprinted with the permission of Harcourt Brace & Company and The Wylie Agency, Inc.

Raymond Carver, "Cathedral" from *Cathedral*. Copyright © 1983 by Raymond Carver. Reprinted with the permission of Alfred A. Knopf, Inc. "Intimacy" from Esquire (1986). Copyright © 1986 by Tess Gallagher. Reprinted with the permission of International Creative Management.

John Cheever, "Clancy in the Tower of Babel" and "The Five-Forty-Eight" from *The Stories of John Cheever.* Copyright © 1951, 1954 by John Cheever. Reprinted with the permission of Alfred A. Knopf, Inc.

Chen Rong, "Regarding the Problem of Newborn Piglets in Winter," translated by Chun-Yun Shih, from Nienling Liu, ed., *The Rose Colored Dinner: New Works by Contemporary Chinese Women Writers.* Copyright © 1988 by Reprinted with the permission of Nienling Liu on behalf of the translator.

Sandra Cisneros, "The Monkey Garden" from *Woman Hollering Creek and Other Stories* (New York: Random House, 1991). Copyright © 1991 by Sandra Cisneros. Reprinted with the permission of Susan Bergholz Literary Services, New York.

Ralph Ellison, "King of the Bingo Game" from *Flying Home and Other Stories.* Originally appeared in *Tomorrow* 4 (1944). Copyright 1944 by Ralph Ellison. Copyright © 1996 by Fanny Ellison. Reprinted with the permission of Random House, Inc.

Louise Erdrich, "Fleur" from *Tracks* (New York: HarperCollins Publishers, 1991). Copyright © 1991 by Louise Erdrich. Reprinted with the permission of the author, c/o Rembar & Curtis, New York. "Eleanor's Tale: The Leap" from *Tales of Burning Love.* Originally appeared in *Harper's* (March 1990). Copyright © 1990 by Louise Erdrich. Reprinted with the permission of HarperCollins Publishers, Inc.

William Faulkner, "A Rose for Emily" and "Barn Burning" from *Collected Stories of William Faulkner.* Copyright 1930, 1950 and renewed © 1958 by William Faulkner, © 1977 by Jill Faulkner Summers. Reprinted with the permission of Random House, Inc.

F. Scott Fitzgerald, "The Baby Party" from Malcolm Cowley, ed., *The Stories of F. Scott Fitzgerald.* Copyright 1925 by Hearst's International Magazines, Inc., renewed 1953 by Frances Scott Fitzgerald Lanahan. Reprinted with the permission of Scribner, a division of Simon & Schuster, Inc.

E. M. Forster, "The Other Side of the Hedge" from *The Collected Tales of E. M. Forster* (New York: Alfred A. Knopf, 1947). Originally published 1903. Reprinted with the permission of Kings College, Cambridge, and The Society of Authors as the literary representatives of the E. M. Forster Estate.

Gabriel García Márquez, "The Handsomest Drowned Man in the World," translated by Gregory Rabassa, from *Leaf Storm and Other Stories.* Copyright © 1971 by Gabriel García Márquez. Reprinted with the permission of HarperCollins Publishers, Inc.

Gail Godwin, "The Watcher at the Gate" (excerpt) from the *New York Times* (January 9, 1977). Copyright © 1977 by the New York Times Company. Reprinted with the permission of the *New York Times.*

Nadine Gordimer, "Crimes of Conscience" from *Something Out There.* Copyright © 1982 by Nadine Gordimer. Reprinted with the permission of Viking Penguin, a division of Penguin Books USA Inc. and Penguin Books Canada Limited.

Bessie Head, "Snapshots from a Wedding" from *The Collector of Treasures and Other Botswana Village Tales.* Copyright © 1977 by the Estate of Bessie Head. Reprinted with the permission of John Johnson, Authors' Agent, Ltd. and William Heinemann, Ltd.

Ernest Hemingway, "Hills like White Elephants" from *Men Without Women.* Copyright 1927 by Charles Scribner's Sons, renewed © 1955 by Ernest Hemingway. Reprinted with the permission of Scribner, a division of Simon & Schuster, Inc.

Franz Kafka, "A Report to an Academy," translated by Willa and Edwin Muir, from *Franz Kafka: The Complete Stories,* edited by Nahum N. Glatzer. Copyright 1948 by Schocken Books, Inc. Reprinted with the permission of Schocken Books, distributed by Pantheon Books, a division of Random House, Inc.

Jamaica Kincaid, "Poor Visitor" from *Lucy.* Copyright © 1989, 1990 by Jamaica Kincaid. Reprinted with the permission of Farrar, Straus & Giroux, Inc.

D. H. Lawrence, "The Rocking-Horse Winner" and "Wintry Peacock" from *Complete Short Stories of D. H. Lawrence.* Copyright 1933 by The Estate of D. H. Lawrence, renewed © 1961 by Angelo Ravagli and C. M. Weekley, Executors of the Estate of Frieda Lawrence.

Reprinted with the permission of Viking Penguin, a division of Penguin Books USA Inc.

David Leavitt, "Gravity" from *A Place I've Never Seen*. Copyright © 1990 by David Leavitt. Originally appeared in the *East Hampton Star*. Reprinted with the permission of Viking Penguin, a division of Penguin Books USA Inc.

Doris Lessing, "How I Finally Lost My Heart" from *Stories*. Copyright © 1978 by Doris Lessing. Reprinted with the permission of Alfred A. Knopf, Inc. "The Mother of the Child in Question" from *The Real Thing*. Copyright © 1987, 1988, 1989, 1990, 1991, 1992 by Doris Lessing. Reprinted with the permission of HarperCollins Publishers, Inc.

Clarice Lispector, "The Evolution of Myopia," translated by Giovanni Pontiero, from *The Foreign Legion: Stories and Chronicles*. English translation copyright © 1986 by Giovanni Pontiero. Reprinted with the permission of Carcanet Press, Ltd.

Naguib Mahfouz, "The Norwegian Rat," translated by Denys Johnson-Davies, from *The Time and the Place and Other Stories*. Copyright © 1991 by the American University in Cairo Press. Reprinted with the permission of Doubleday, a division of Bantam Doubleday Dell Publishing Group, Inc.

Bernard Malamud, "Angel Levine" from *The Magic Barrel and Other Stories*. Copyright © 1958 and renewed 1986 by Bernard Malamud. Reprinted with the permission of Farrar, Straus & Giroux, Inc.

Bobbie Ann Mason, "Airwaves" from *Love Life*. Originally appeared in *The Atlantic Monthly*. Copyright © 1990 by Bobbie Ann Mason. Reprinted with the permission of HarperCollins Publishers, Inc.

Guy de Maupassant, "The Necklace," translated by Marjorie Laurie, from *Short Stories of Guy de Maupassant* (New York: E. P. Dutton, 1934). Reprinted with the permission of Everyman's Library/David Campbell Publishers. Maupassant, "Confessing," translated by Artine Artinian, from *The Complete Short Stories of Guy de Maupassant*. Copyright 1924 and renewed 1952 by Alfred A. Knopf, Inc. Reprinted with the permission of the publishers.

Reginald McKnight, "The Kind of Light That Shines on Texas" from *The Kind of Light That Shines on Texas* (Boston: Little, Brown and Company, 1992). Originally appeared in *The Kenyon Review*. Copyright © 1992 by Reginald McKnight. Reprinted with the permission of the author.

James Alan McPherson, "A Loaf of Bread" from *Elbow Room*. Copyright © 1972 by James Alan McPherson. Reprinted with the permission of Little, Brown and Company.

Yukio Mishima, "Swaddling Clothes," translated by Ivan Morris, from *Death in Midsummer*. Copyright © 1966 by New Directions Publishing Corporation. Reprinted with the permission of the publishers.

Bharati Mukherjee, "A Wife's Story" from *The Middleman and Other Stories*. Copyright © 1988 by Bharati Mukherjee. Reprinted with the permission of Grove/Atlantic, Inc. and Penguin Books Canada Limited.

Alice Munro, "Circle of Prayer" from *The Progress of Love*. Copyright © 1986 by Alice Munro. Reprinted with the permission of the Alfred A. Knopf, Inc. and the Virginia Barber Literary Agency.

Haruki Murakami, "A Window," translated by Jay Rubin, from *The Elephant Vanishes and Other Stories*, translated by Alfred Birnbaum and Jay Rubin. Copyright © 1993 by Haruki Murakami. Reprinted with the permission of Alfred A. Knopf, Inc.

R. K. Narayan, "An Astrologer's Day" from *Malgudi*. Copyright © 1982 by R. K. Narayan. Reprinted with the permission of Viking Penguin, a division of Penguin Books USA Inc.

Gloria Naylor, "The Two" from *The Women of Brewster Place*. Copyright © 1982 by Gloria Naylor. Reprinted with the permission of Viking Penguin, a division of Penguin Books USA Inc.

Joyce Carol Oates, "Why Don't You Come Live with Me It's Time" from *Tikkun: A Bimonthly Jewish Critique of Politics, Culture and Society* (1990). Copyright © 1990 by Ontario Review Press. Reprinted with the permission of John Hawkins & Associates, Inc.

Alice Walker, "Roselily" from *In Love and Trouble: Stories of Black Women.* Copyright © 1972 by Alice Walker. Reprinted with the permission of Harcourt Brace & Company.

Eudora Welty, "A Visit of Charity" and "A Worn Path" from *A Curtain of Green and Other Stories.* Copyright 1939, 1941 and renewed © 1967, 1969 by Eudora Welty. Reprinted with the permission of Harcourt Brace & Company.

John Edgar Wideman, "Doc's Story" from *Fever.* Originally appeared in *Esquire* (August 1986). Copyright © 1986 by John Edgar Wideman. Reprinted with the permission of Henry Holt and Company, Inc.

Tobias Wolff, "Lady's Dream" from *Harper's* (December 1992). Copyright © 1992 by Tobias Wolff. Reprinted with the permission of International Creative Management.

Virginia Woolf, "The Symbol" from Susan Dick, ed., *The Complete Shorter Fiction of Virginia Woolf.* Copyright © 1985 by Quentin Bell and Angelica Garnett. Reprinted with the permission of Harcourt Brace & Company.

CASEBOOKS

Conrad Aiken, "Anton Chekhov" from *Collected Criticism.* (New York: Oxford University Press, 1968). Copyright © 1968 by Conrad Aiken. Reprinted with the permission of Brandt and Brandt Literary Agents, Inc.

Alfred Appel, Jr., excerpts from *A Season of Dreams: The Fiction of Eudora Welty.* Copyright © 1965 by Louisiana State University Press. Reprinted with the permission of the publishers.

James Baldwin, "Autobiographical Notes" from *Notes of a Native Son.* Copyright © 1955 and renewed 1983 by James Baldwin. Reprinted with the permission of Beacon Press. "The Creative Process" *Creative America* (Ridge Press, 1962), later collected in *The Price of the Ticket: Collected Nonfiction* (New York: St. Martin's Press, 1985). Copyright © 1962 by James Baldwin. Reprinted with the permission of The James Baldwin Estate.

Elizabeth Bowen, "A Living Writer: Katherine Mansfield" (excerpt) from *Seven Winters: Memories of a Dublin Childhood and Afterthoughts, Pieces on Writing* (New York: Alfred A. Knopf, 1962). Copyright © 1962 by Elizabeth Bowen. Reprinted with the permission of Curtis Brown, Ltd., Literary Executors of the Estate of Elizabeth Bowen.

Jo Brans, "Struggling against the Plaid: An Interview with Eudora Welty" (excerpt) from *Listen to the Voices: Conversations with Contemporary Writers* (Dallas: Southern Methodist University Press, 1988): 57-76. Originally appeared in Southwest Review 66 (Summer 1981). Copyright © 1981 by Jo Brans. Reprinted with the permission of the author.

Mason J. Brewer, "The Barn Is Burning" from *Worse Days and Better Times.* Copyright © 1965 by Mason J. Brewer. Reprinted with the permission of Times Books, a division of Random House, Inc.

Mary Burgan, excerpt from *Illness, Gender, and Writing: The Case of Katherine Mansfield.* Copyright © 1994 by The Johns Hopkins University Press. Reprinted with the permission of the publishers.

Keith E. Byerman, "Words and Music: Narrative Ambiguity in 'Sonny's Blues'" from *Studies in Short Fiction* 19 (1982): 367–372. Copyright © 1982 by Newberry College. Reprinted with the permission of Studies in Short Fiction.

"A Dispute in Sign Language" from Dov Noy, *Folktales of Israel.* Copyright © 1963 by The University of Chicago. Reprinted with the permission of The University of Chicago Press.

Jordan Elgrably and George Plimpton, "The Art of Fiction: Interview with James Baldwin" (excerpt) from *The Paris Review* 26 (Spring 1984). Copyright © 1984. Reprinted with the permission of *The Paris Review.*

Louise Erdrich, "Where I Ought to Be: A Writer's Sense of Place" from the *New York Times Book Review* (July 28, 1985): 1. Copyright © 1985 by Louise Erdrich. Reprinted with the permission of the author, c/o Rembar & Curtis, New York.

Nancy Feyl and Allan Chavkin, "An Interview with Louise Erdrich" (excerpts) from *Conversations with Louise Erdrich and Michael Dorris.* Copyright © 1994. Reprinted with the permission of University Press of Mississippi.

Maxim Gorky, "Fragments from Reminiscences" (excerpt), translated by Leslie Jackson and Robert Louis Jackson, from Robert Louis Jackson, ed., *Chekhov: A Collection of Critical Essays.* Copyright © 1967 by Prentice-Hall, Inc. Reprinted with the permission of Simon & Schuster, Inc.

Michael Henry Heim and Simon Karlinsky, trans., *Letters of Anton Chekhov.* Copyright © 1973 by Harper & Row, Publishers, Inc. Reprinted with the permission of HarperCollins Publishers, Inc.

"Helping to Lie" from Kurt Ranke, *Folktales of Germany.* Copyright © 1966 by The University of Chicago. Reprinted with the permission of The University of Chicago Press.

Joseph Hsieh, "Inner and Outer Worlds: A Comparison of Chekhov's 'The Schoolmistress' and 'The Darling.'" Reprinted with the permission of the author.

S. S. Koteliansky and Philip Tomlinson, eds. and trans., *The Life and Letters of Anton Tchekov* (New York: George H. Doran, 1925), reprinted New York: Benjamin Blom, 1965.

Michael Lee, "Erdrich's Dakota as Metaphor for American Culture: A Review of *Tales of Burning Love*" from *National Catholic Reporter* (May 29, 1996): 21, 30. Copyright © 1996 by Michael Lee. Reprinted with the permission of the author and the National Catholic Reporter Publishing Company.

Marvin Magalaner, "Analysis of 'A Dill Pickle' and 'The Garden-Party'" (editors' title), excerpted from "The Legacy of Fiction" from *The Fiction of Katherine Mansfield.* Copyright © 1971 by Southern Illinois University Press. Reprinted with the permission of the publishers.

Charles May, "Chekhov and the Modern Short Story" (excerpt) from Toby W. Clyman, ed., *A Chekhov Companion.* Copyright © 1985. Reprinted with the permission of The Greenwood Publishing Group, Inc.

Susan Meisenhelder, "Race and Gender in Louise Erdrich's *The Beet Queen,*" *ARIEL: A Review of International English Literature* 25, no. 1 (January 1994). Copyright © 1994. Reprinted with the permission of *ARIEL,* Department of English, The University of Calgary.

Amanda Morgan, "The Shadow Child: A Sequel to 'A Worn Path.'" Reprinted with the permission of the author.

John Middleton Murry, ed., excerpts from *The Journal of Katherine Mansfield.* Copyright 1927 by Alfred A. Knopf, Inc., renewed © 1955 by J. Middleton Murry. Reprinted with the permission of Alfred A. Knopf, Inc. and The Society of Authors as the Literary Representatives of the Estate of Katherine Mansfield.

John Middleton Murry, ed., excerpts from *Letters of Katherine Mansfield.* Copyright 1929 by Alfred A. Knopf, Inc., renewed © 1957 by John Middleton Murry. Reprinted with the permission of The Society of Authors as the Literary Representatives of the Estate of Katherine Mansfield.

John Middleton Murry, excerpt from *Katherine Mansfield and Other Literary Studies.* Reprinted with the permission of Constable Publishers, Ltd.

Vladimir Nabokov, "Chekhov's Prose" from *Lectures on Russian Literature.* Copyright © 1981 by The Estate of Vladimir Nabokov. Reprinted with the permission of Harcourt Brace & Company.

Renato Poggioli, "Storytelling in a Double Key" (excerpt) from *The Phoenix and the Spider.* Copyright © 1957 by the President and Fellows of Harvard College. Reprinted with the permission of Harvard University Press.

John M. Reilly, "'Sonny's Blues': James Baldwin's Image of Black Community" (excerpt) from *Negro-American Literature Forum* 4, no. 2 (1970): 56-60. Copyright © 1970 by Indiana State University. Reprinted with the permission of the publishers.

Index of Authors and Titles